The Cambridge Handbook of Play

Play takes up much of the time budget of young children, and many animals, but its importance in development remains contested. This comprehensive collection brings together multidisciplinary and developmental perspectives on the forms and functions of play in animals, in children in different societies, and through the lifespan.

The Cambridge Handbook of Play covers the evolution of play in animals, especially mammals; the development of play from infancy through childhood and into adulthood; historical and anthropological perspectives on play; theories and methodologies; the role of play in children's learning; play in special groups such as children with impairments or those suffering political violence; and the practical applications of playwork and play therapy. Written by an international team of scholars from diverse disciplines such as psychology, education, neuroscience, sociology, evolutionary biology, and anthropology, this essential reference presents the current state of the field in play research.

PETER K. SMITH is Emeritus Professor of Psychology at the Unit for School and Family Studies, Department of Psychology at Goldsmiths, University of London. He has published thirty books, and more than 200 refereed journal articles. He is author of *Understanding School Bullying* (2014), co-author of *Understanding Children's Development* (sixth edition, 2015) and co-editor of the *Handbook of Childhood Social Development* (second edition, 2010).

JAIPAUL L. ROOPNARINE is the Pearl S. Falk Professor of Human Development at Syracuse University, New York, and Professor of Developmental Psychology at Anton de Kom University of Suriname. He has co-edited several notable volumes on culture and development and is the editor of the *Caribbean Journal of Psychology.*

The Cambridge Handbook of Play

Developmental and Disciplinary Perspectives

Edited by

Peter K. Smith
Goldsmiths College, University of London

Jaipaul L. Roopnarine
Syracuse University

CAMBRIDGE
UNIVERSITY PRESS

CAMBRIDGE
UNIVERSITY PRESS

University Printing House, Cambridge CB2 8BS, United Kingdom

One Liberty Plaza, 20th Floor, New York, NY 10006, USA

477 Williamstown Road, Port Melbourne, VIC 3207, Australia

314–321, 3rd Floor, Plot 3, Splendor Forum, Jasola District Centre,
New Delhi – 110025, India

79 Anson Road, #06–04/06, Singapore 079906

Cambridge University Press is part of the University of Cambridge.

It furthers the University's mission by disseminating knowledge in the pursuit of
education, learning, and research at the highest international levels of excellence.

www.cambridge.org
Information on this title: www.cambridge.org/9781107192515
DOI: 10.1017/9781108131384

© Cambridge University Press 2019

First published 2019

Printed and bound in Great Britain by Clays Ltd, Elcograf S.p.A.

A catalogue record for this publication is available from the British Library.

Library of Congress Cataloging-in-Publication Data
Names: Smith, Peter K., editor.
Title: The Cambridge handbook of play : developmental and disciplinary perspectives /
    edited by Peter K. Smith, Goldsmiths College, University of London, Jaipaul L.
    Roopnarine, Syracuse University, New York.
Description: Cambridge, United Kingdom ; New York, NY : Cambridge University
    Press, 2019. | Includes bibliographical references and index.
Identifiers: LCCN 2018024260 | ISBN 9781107192515 (hardback : alk. paper) |
    ISBN 9781316640906 (paperback : alk. paper)
Subjects: LCSH: Play. | Child development.
Classification: LCC GV1200 .C365 2019 | DDC 649/.5–dc23
LC record available at https://lccn.loc.gov/2018024260

ISBN 978-1-107-19251-5 Hardback
ISBN 978-1-316-64090-6 Paperback

Contents

Figures

Tables

Contributors

E. J. MARIJKE ACHTERBERG, Department of Animals in Science and Society, Faculty of Veterinary Medicine, Utrecht University, the Netherlands

COLLEEN BAISH CAMERON, Department of Human Development and Family Science, Syracuse University, Syracuse, NY, USA

DORIS BERGEN, Educational Psychology, University of Miami, Oxford, OH, USA

CAROL BERMAN, Department of Anthropology, The State University of New York, NY, USA

ANNA BERESIN, University of the Arts, Philadelphia, PA, USA

ELENA BODROVA, Tools of the Mind, Lakewood, CO, USA

ANNA BORTOLI, RMIT University, Melbourne, Australia

ADAM HOWELL BOYETTE, Writing Program, Duke University, Durham, NC, USA

MILDA BREDIKYTE, Vilnius, Lithuania

FRASER BROWN, Childhood Development and Playwork Team, Leeds Beckett University, Leeds, UK

P. MARGARET BROWN, Melbourne Graduate School of Education, University of Melbourne, Parkville, Australia

GORDON M. BURGHARDT, Department of Psychology, University of Tennessee, Knoxville, TN, USA

ANA M. A. CARVALHO, Institute of Psychology, University of Sao Paulo, Sao Paulo, Brazil

ESTHER COHEN, Baruch Ivcher School of Psychology Interdisciplinary Center (IDC), Hebrew University of Jerusalem, Herzliya, Israel

CYNTHIA J. CRESS, Department of Special Education and Communication Disorders, University of Nebraska-Lincoln, Lincoln, NE, USA

ELISE CUSCHIERI, Arts and Play Therapies, Department of Psychology, University of Roehampton, Surrey, UK

KIMBERLY L. DAVIDSON, Human Development and Family Studies, Central Michigan University, Mount Pleasant, MI, USA

CRYSTAL DAY-HESS, Marsico Institute for Early Learning, University of Denver, Denver, CO, USA

ELIF DEDE YILDIRIM, Department of Human Development and Family Studies, Auburn University, Auburn, AL, USA

POOL IP DONG, Department of Curriculum and Instruction, College of Education, Pennsylvania State University, State College, PA, USA

SUSAN ENGEL, Williams College, Williamstown, MA, USA

BETH FERHOLT, Early Childhood Education, Brooklyn College, Brooklyn, NY, USA

MARILYN FLEER, Foundation Chair of Early Childhood Education and Development, Monash University, Frankston Victoria, Australia

CARRIE GERMEROTH, Marzano Research, Centennial, CO, USA

ARTIN GÖNCÜ, Educational Psychology, University of Illinois at Chicago, Chicago, IL, USA

YUMI GOSSO, Institute of Psychology, University of Sao Paulo, Sao Paulo, Brazil

PETER GRAY, Department of Psychology, Boston College, Chestnut Hill, MA, USA

PENTTI HAKKARAINEN, Vilnius, Lithuania

SOPHIA HAN, College of Education, University of South Florida, Tampa, FL, USA

MARITTA HÄNNIKÄINEN, Department of Education, University of Jyväskylä, Jyväskylä, Finland

JENNIFER L. HART, School of Education, University of the Sunshine Coast, Queensland, Australia

THOMAS S. HENRICKS, Department of Sociology, Elon University, Elon, NC, USA

JAMES E. JOHNSON, Department of Curriculum and Instruction, College of Education, Pennsylvania State University, State College, PA, USA

EUNJOO JUNG, Department of Human Development and Family Science, Syracuse University, Syracuse, NY, USA

LILA KOSSYVAKI, Department of Disability Inclusion and Special Needs, School of Education, University of Birmingham, Birmingham, UK

ANNE KULTTI, Department of Education, Communication and Learning, University of Gothenburg, Göteborg, Sweden

ROBERT LECUSAY, School of Education and Communication, Jönköping University, Jönköping, Sweden

DEBORAH J. LEONG, Tools of the Mind, Golden, CO , USA

ALEXANDRA LONG, Childhood Development and Playwork Team, Leeds Beckett University, Leeds, UK

LAUREN MCNAMARA, Department of Child and Youth Studies, Brock University, St. Catharines, Canada

GAIL F. MELSON, Department of Human Development and Family Studies, Purdue University, West Lafayette, IN, USA

HILKKA MUNTER, Kajaani, Finland

AGELIKI NICOLOPOULOU, Psychology Department, Lehigh University, Bethlehem, PA, USA

MONICA NILSSON, Stockholm, Sweden

DESPINA PAPOUDI, Department of Disability Inclusion and Special Needs, School of Education, University of Birmingham, Birmingham, UK

MICHAEL M. PATTE, Department of Elementary Education, Bloomsburg University, Bloomsburg, PA, USA

ANTHONY D. PELLEGRINI, Bloomington, MN, USA

SERGIO M. PELLIS, Department of Neuroscience, University of Lethbridge, Canada

LACEY E. PETERS, School of Education, Hunter College, CUNY, New York, NY, USA

LINDA POLLOCK, Department of History, Tulane University, New Orleans, LA, USA

NIKLAS PRAMLING, Department of Education, Communication and Learning, University of Gothenburg, Göteborg, Sweden

BRISEIDA D. RESENDE, Institute of Psychology, University of Sao Paulo, Sao Paulo, Brazil

JAIPAUL L. ROOPNARINE, Department of Human Development and Family Science, Syracuse University, Syracuse, NY, USA, and Department of

Psychology and IGSR, Anton de Kom University of Suriname, Paramaribo, Suriname

KATHLEEN ROSKOS, Department of Education and School Psychology, John Carrol University, University Heights, OH, USA

INGRID PRAMLING SAMUELSSON, Department of Education, Communication and Learning, University of Gothenburg, Göteborg, Sweden

FIONA SCOTT, School of Education, University of Sheffield, Sheffield, UK

LYNDA L. SHARPE, Research School of Biology, Australian National University, Canberra, Australia

PETER K. SMITH, Department of Psychology, Goldsmiths, University of London, UK

JOHN A. SUTTERBY, College of Education and Human Development, University of Texas-San Antonio, San Antonio TX, USA

BETH BLUE SWADENER, School of Social Transformation, Arizona State University, Tempe, AZ, USA

MICHELLE T. TANNOCK, Child, Family and Community Studies, Douglas College, Vancouver, Canada

VIVIANA TREZZA, Department of Science, Roma Tre University, Rome, Italy

JENNIFER A. VADEBONCOEUR, Educational Psychology, University of Illinois at Chicago, Chicago, IL, USA

LOUK J. M. J. VANDERSCHUREN, Department of Animals in Science and Society, Faculty of Veterinary Medicine, Utrecht University, the Netherlands

DITTE WINTHER-LINDQVIST, Aarhus University, Tuborgvej, Denmark

MIKE WRAGG, Childhood Development and Playwork Team, Leeds Beckett University, Leeds, UK

AKIE YANAGI, Department of Anthropology, The State University of New York, NY USA

1 Editorial Introduction

Peter K. Smith and Jaipaul L. Roopnarine

Play remains a topic of continuing interest and fascination, for parents, teachers, researchers, and anyone interested in human nature. Play takes up much of the time budget of young children and many animals. Yet its nature and function remain contested. This book brings together a comprehensive collection of disciplinary and developmental perspectives on the topic. Different sections cover the evolution of play in animals, especially mammals including monkeys and apes; the development of play from infancy through childhood and into the lifespan; historical and anthropological perspectives on play; theories of play and methods of studying its different dimensions; the role of play in children's learning and development; play in special groups such as children with impairments; and play spaces and the rights of children.

There are of course classical theories of play (see Chapter 20), and for children's play the work of Lev Vygotsky from the 1930s remains influential, as is apparent in many chapters in Part V on play and learning. However, the modern study of play, in both animals and humans, became active again in the 1970s and 1980s. After a quieter period in the 1990s and early 2000s, recent years have seen a resurgence of interest in theorizing and research on play. With international contributors from thirteen countries and a range of disciplinary perspectives from evolutionary biology, neuroscience, developmental psychology, early childhood education, special education, anthropology, sociology, cultural and media studies, and history, we have aimed to provide a comprehensive collection of chapters on play, so that readers will get a clear picture of state-of-the-art thinking on the topic.

Part I of this Handbook focuses on the evolution of play. Gordon Burghardt and Sergio Pellis (Chapter 2) discuss five criteria for recognising and defining play, and consider the evolution of play in animal species, distinguishing primary, secondary, and tertiary process play in terms of function. This chapter emphasises the heterogeneity of play and indicates the use of computer simulations for modelling the costs and benefits of play. Neuroscience and particularly neurochemistry has also taken great strides in the study of play, as reviewed by Viviana Trezza, Marijke Achterberg, and Louk Vanderschuren (Chapter 3). Focusing on the proverbial laboratory rat, they make clear how sophisticated experimental techniques have given much insight into the neural underpinnings of social play in this species. Drawing on more naturalistic observations and experimental studies in a range of mammalian species, Lynda Sharpe (Chapter 4) takes a critical look at a range of hypotheses advanced to explain the functions of play, and the evidence for costs and benefits in various domains. It is clear that the evidence for benefits is mixed at best, and this chapter concludes with a plea for more focused hypothesis-testing experiments. Akie Yanagi and Carol Berman (Chapter 5) consider social play in non-human primates (monkeys and apes) and document the costs of such play (mostly play fighting, which can be risky); they argue that there are likely social skills benefits to balance such costs. They discuss how such costs can be reduced by use of play signals and appropriate choice of play partners. In considering human play, Peter Gray (Chapter 6) also opens with considerations of definition. He mentions five characteristics of human play (these may be compared with the five criteria in Chapter 2; there is some overlap but also some differences). Reviewing the pioneering work of Groos, as well as more recent work on animal play, Gray moves on to consider play in hunter-gatherer groups (as best representing the kind of societal structure that humans evolved in). He considers hypotheses such as the role of play in learning and innovation and in promoting cooperation and egalitarianism. Humans also play with animals; indeed, the domestication of dogs from wolf-like ancestors, as well as later partial domestication of many other species, probably played a crucial role in human evolution. In Chapter 7, Gail Melson describes human-animal play, particularly focusing on the contemporary phenomenon of play with pets, raising interesting issues around the role of play in attachment, and the scaffolding of play (also picked up in discussions in the next section on parent-infant/child play).

Part II examines various types of human play from a developmental perspective. Building on the work of Piaget, Bruner, Gibson, and Thelen, as well as what we know from more recent work on brain development, Doris Bergen (Chapter 8) discusses infant sensorimotor play. She describes this as a dynamic systems process, ending by considering how such sensorimotor play is affected by recent technological developments (see also Chapter 14). In Chapter 9, Jaipaul Roopnarine, Elif Dede Yildirim, and Kimberly Davidson summarize a considerable amount of research on mother-child and father-child play in the early years. They pay particular attention to cultural and gender differences, and what may explain these. Possible links to developmental outcomes are considered. Much parent-child play is social, but Anthony Pellegrini (Chapter 10) discusses the development of play with objects. He carefully considers how play with objects can be distinguished from exploration, construction, and tool use and tool making. Much object play can be solitary, but Pellegrini also considers the role of object play in social learning and innovation. In Chapter 11, Ageliki Nicolopoulou examines pretend and social pretend play – the most distinctive kind of childhood play. She considers its development and possible cultural universality and discusses how Lillard and colleagues have critiqued the evidence on the functional significance of pretend play, in part countering this with ideas from Vygotsky and Harris. Play fighting shows much more continuity with social play in mammals, and Jennifer Hart and Michelle Tannock (Chapter 12) survey the research on what they call rough play. They distinguish parent-child and peer-peer rough play, describing it as mainly a male phenomenon and emphasizing positive aspects of such play for learning and skill development. They end with important comments on how educators may sometimes misperceive such kinds of play, and how they can best support it. These different forms of play (object, pretend, rough) overlap, but also by middle childhood tend to mutate into rule-governed, game-like activities. Ditte Winther-Lindqvist (Chapter 13) contrasts the positions of Piaget and Vygotsky in the development of games with rules, and illustrates the developmental origins of this with extensive field notes based on his own observations. Once beyond early childhood, however (and increasingly even in early childhood, Chapter 8), modern digital technologies are an increasingly salient aspect of the sociocultural environment, with important ramifications on children's play. Fiona Scott (Chapter 14) describes the developmental course of this, drawing especially on research in the cultural and media studies tradition. In Chapter 15, Jennifer Vadeboncoeur and Artin Göncü discuss playing and imagining in a lifespan perspective. They draw specially on Vygotsky and the sociocultural perspective and discuss how playing and imagining can contribute to, for example, abstract thinking and self-direction.

Most research on human play is on contemporary children in Western societies, but in Part III several chapters foreground historical and anthropological perspectives. In Chapter 16, Linda Pollock looks at the historical evidence on play in early modern Europe. She documents how play was often seen as a distraction from learning, but how attitudes to play also changed over the centuries, partly influenced by philosophical and educational writings. In Chapter 17, Adam Boyette considers play in foraging societies; although the evidence is from contemporary societies, they may provide insight into the kind of selection pressures affecting play through much of human evolution. He reviews different kinds of play and points out how play and work contexts may intermingle. Boyette also critiques Gray's view (Chapter 6) that play in forager societies promotes egalitarianism but does consider what lessons may be learnt from the characteristics of forager play. Yumi Gosso, Briseida Resende, and Ana Carvalho (Chapter 18) document studies of play in various South American indigenous communities, who also live by hunting and foraging but also small-scale agriculture. They too comment on how work activities for children (such as washing dishes or looking after younger siblings) can be used as play opportunities. Eunjoo Jung and Sophia Han (Chapter 19) examine play in societies, such as China, Japan, and Korea, influenced by Confucian values. They summarise six main aspects of Confucian values and how these may impact adult-child relationships and play, including ritual-based play and gendered play. They also consider the impact of Western influences and culture change in these societies on engagement in play.

Three chapters in Part IV are on theories of play and on research methodology. Some contemporary theories of play are considered in many other chapters, but Thomas Henricks (Chapter 20) overviews the classic theories of play, from Schiller, Spencer, and Groos onward through the nineteenth and twentieth centuries. His chapter provides a roll-call of important theorists, many very well known but some less so. Among contemporary theorists, especially of human play, Brian Sutton-Smith has had a preeminent position. In Chapter 21, Anna Beresin, Fraser Brown, and Michael Patte provide an account of Sutton-Smith's early children's books, his critique of Piaget, and his work on children's folklore, ending with his theorising on play generally, including his posthumous book on play as emotional survival. Turning to methods of studying play, James Johnson and Pool Ip Dong (Chapter 22) start with conceptual issues, and then review a range of quantitative and qualitative methodologies. They conclude with examples of innovative methods being used in some contemporary play research.

An enduring topic of discussion and debate has been the role of play in young children's learning. Part V provides an extensive examination of this topic. Throughout, the influence of Vygotsky's thinking, even more than 80 years after his death in 1934, remains a key inspiration for many researchers in this area. Marilyn Fleer (Chapter 23) considers play and learning in family contexts. She provides an in-depth discussion of this, drawing on observations of various forms of play, and how they are structured, in an Australian family. In Chapter 24, Elena Bodrova, Deborah Leong, Carrie Germeroth, and Crystal Day-Hess draw very specifically on Vygotsky's ideas, describing levels of pretend or make-believe play. They discuss how such play can be scaffolded in *Tools of the Mind*, an early childhood curriculum based on these ideas. In Chapter 25, Pentti Hakkarainen and Milda Bredikyte similarly draw on Vygotsky's levels of play, but especially emphasise his concept of the zone of proximal development (ZPD). They use this concept to consider in detail the role of the adult as a mediator of development in children's play, for example, in structuring imaginative storytelling. Such themes are developed further by Niklas Pramling, Anne Kultti and Ingrid Pramling Samuelsson (Chapter 26). In particular, they discuss what is meant by concepts such as learning, and teaching, in the early child curriculum, how play relates to these, and how skilful adults can enhance this through socially responsive actions. In Chapter 27, Maritta Hännikäinen and Hilkka Munter develop similar themes, referring not only to the ZPD but to Vygotsky's notion of the social situation of development – the changing relations between a child and his or her social reality. The ways in which teachers can enhance, but also sometimes hinder, children's play are considered in detail. In Chapter 28, Beth Ferholt, Robert Lecusay, and Monica Nilsson describe the concept of playworlds, in which creative play is developed between adults and children, based on Vygotsky's theories. Besides picking up familiar themes around children's play and learning, these authors highlight how adults too are learning and developing, illustrating this with a case study of a discussion among three preschool teachers. Pretend play, especially in its narrative or sociodramatic forms, is often linked to literacy development, and in Chapter 29, Kathleen Roskos (echoing Donald Rumsfeld) discusses the known knowns, the known unknowns, and the unknown unknowns in what is a considerable area of research. She covers many aspects of this, including recent digital developments such as use of apps and robotic puppets. In Chapter 30, Susan Engel discusses how gathering information, inquiry, and invention contributes to play, and how play in turn contributes to developing ideas. This is illustrated by four examples of play observed in 3- to 7-year-olds.

While much research on children's play has described its educational implications in mainstream settings, there has also been interest in how play may be relevant for special groups of children and/or have more therapeutic implications. The chapters in Part VI consider such issues. One such special group comprises children with autism or autism spectrum disorders (ASD). It is known that these children have some delay or lack of interest in the full range of pretend play behaviours. Despina Papoudi and Lila Kossyvaki (Chapter 31) discuss the research on this and the educational implications, including how such play can be scaffolded by various kinds of social interaction and technological support. In Chapter 32, Margaret Brown and Anna Bortoli consider play in children with sensory impairments, in particular visual and hearing impairments. Depending on context, there can be delays in social pretend play with peers, for example, and the authors discuss the role of adults and the risks and benefits of inclusive education in this respect. Another category of disability, physical impairments, covers primary conditions such as cerebral palsy and traumatic brain injury, and secondary outcomes of conditions such as Down syndrome or premature birth. In Chapter 33, Cynthia Cress describes how such conditions can affect object play and coordination, and interactions with parents and peers. She discusses how accurate assessment of difficulties, direct treatment, and specific skill training or coaching for parents can be helpful interventions. Play can also have diagnostic and therapeutic benefits for those with a range of medical conditions. Colleen Baish Cameron and Michael Patte (Chapter 34) review the provision of play facilities and opportunities for children in hospital, and how in the United States, for example, this can be facilitated by trained child life specialists. They end with a range of practical suggestions for improving play practices in health care settings. The psychoanalytic tradition has contributed to the development of play therapy for emotionally disturbed children, and in Chapter 35 Elise Cuschieri describes how ideas of play therapy have developed. She discusses the space, materials, therapeutic relationship, and the research evidence for effectiveness, drawing on a detailed case study of therapy with one child to illustrate the processes involved. Political violence and terrorism can be sources of trauma for any child unfortunate enough to witness these, and in Chapter 36, Esther Cohen describes the impact of this on children's development and mental health. She enumerates four ways in which play can function to help children cope with these situations. She considers the phenomenon of post-traumatic play, often serious and morbid, and draws practical implications for ways of helping children in these circumstances.

Part VII concludes this Handbook by bringing together four chapters on play spaces and the rights of children. In Chapter 37, John Sutterby gives a comprehensive overview of play spaces, both indoors and outdoors. He first considers space and materials in indoor classrooms, and then the design of outdoor play spaces. These raise considerations of accessibility and safety. He considers community and adventure playgrounds, and the concepts of democratic, commercial, and virtual play spaces. For school-aged children, recess provides an opportunity for play, and this is the topic of Chapter 38 by Lauren McNamara. She provides a historical account of how attitudes and practice regarding recess breaks have changed, and the arguments for and against it in an educational context. She discusses the available research and gives a thorough account of the various aspects to be considered in optimising the social and play potential of recess. For older children, outdoor and adventure playgrounds provide opportunities for play, and the discipline of playwork has evolved in connection with the supervision of playgrounds and the facilitation of such play opportunities. This is described in Chapter 39, by Fraser Brown, Alexandra Long, and Mike Wragg, as a unique way of working with children. They enunciate the principles of playwork, and it is clear that while adult supervision and facilitation is important, the playwork movement generally places great emphasis on children's freedom and the right to play as they wish (within broad constraints of safety and respect for others). In this context they cite the UN Convention on the Rights of the Child (CRC). This theme of children's rights and the implications of the CRC are elaborated in Chapter 40 by Lacey Peters and Beth Swadener. They discuss how theories of play and attitudes to play can impact on the kinds of play opportunities provided for children. Giving examples from several countries, they strongly emphasise the rights of children, not only to be consulted but to be active participants in research and decision making.

As researchers in the field for more than several decades, we have enjoyed bringing together a wide range of scholars to contribute to this Handbook. Some have been in the field a long time; others are earlier in their careers and bringing fresh perspectives on the topic. However, on a sadder note, while this Handbook was in preparation, several notable play scholars died. These include Brian Sutton-Smith, whose seminal work starting in folklore and moving into diverse areas of play is reviewed in Chapter 21. Another loss in the folklore area was Iona Opie, who with her husband Peter pioneered publications on observations of children's games. Jaak Panksepp pioneered work in the neuroscience of emotions and was originally scheduled to write

Chapter 3; the present authors of this chapter dedicate it to him. Panksepp is also a dedicatee of Chapter 2, as is Stan Kuczaj, one of the first psychologists to write on language play. Another sad loss is Jim Christie, who wrote extensively on play and literacy. The work in this Handbook is in part a tribute to these recent scholars, and to those of earlier generations, who have helped take forward our understanding of an activity that is both enjoyable and valuable, that of play behaviour.

PART I

Evolution of Play

2 New Directions in Studying the Evolution of Play

Gordon M. Burghardt and Sergio M. Pellis

Historically, theories and findings on the evolution of play have focused on identifying possible positive consequences or adaptive functions of play behaviour. This approach concentrated on play in the most playful species, primarily mammals, with special emphasis on non-human primates and humans. Today, we have a much greater comparative database on play and have more descriptive details on play in many species, not only within mammals but also in all other vertebrate classes as well as some invertebrates, and experimental support for some functions of play is accumulating. We now have some theories, such as surplus resource theory, that help to characterize the settings that facilitate play and its evolution. However, play is also a heterogeneous category and specific examples are better evaluated with narrower 'micro' theories that utilize more focused ethological, developmental, and life history data. In other words, global overarching theories for play are no longer viable in terms of prediction, even in humans, and thus evolutionary studies must take a more comparative and phylogenetic approach. By themselves, studies of selected species such as laboratory rodents, rhesus monkeys, dogs, horses, chimpanzees, and children are not useful in addressing the evolution of play. This chapter will review new comparative research on diverse types of play in a wide range of species, computer simulation and modelling studies, neurophysiological substrates of play, and other areas to identify possible scenarios for play evolution, their implications for play researchers generally, and, most importantly, how they can be tested.

Our understanding of the evolution of play has had a controversial history. In this chapter, we characterize play in animals and briefly discuss its diversity. We then give a brief overview of this history, citing sources reviewing these views in more depth than is possible here. We then present a few recent

* We dedicate this chapter to two recently deceased colleagues, Jaak Panksepp and Stan Kuczaj, who contributed so much to the study of play. We thank the many students and colleagues who have enriched our research and thinking about play over several decades, numerous granting agencies, and the participants in the Play, Evolution, and Sociality Working Group at the National Institute for Mathematical and Biological Synthesis at the University of Tennessee sponsored by the National Science Foundation, the US Department of Homeland Security, and the US Department of Agriculture through NSF Awards EF-0832858 and DBI-1300426, with additional support from the University of Tennessee, Knoxville. We also thank Vivien Pellis for her comments.

theories that revisit the origin and evolution issue, giving most attention to current empirical and theoretical treatments on the phylogeny of play and some implications for studies of play in humans. Some of this material overlaps another recent chapter we wrote (Pellis & Burghardt, 2017) and we cite other sources for more details on the topics we introduce. We hope to whet the reader's appetite for exploring this fascinating topic in more detail, as progress is coming fast after decades of relative stasis, especially since the publication of Fagen's major review (Fagen, 1981) and the edited volume by Smith (1984).

Questions of origins and evolution address different, though related, processes. Recall that in *On the Origin of Species* Darwin (1859) never actually discussed the origin of species (or life from non-life), instead devoting his efforts to the transmutation process of one (or groups of) species to a different one. Here he famously championed natural selection as a primary, but not sole, underlying process, or mechanism, for such changes. Similarly, but even more pertinently, we address the origin of play from non-playful behaviour, as well as the course of play evolution among species once play has evolved. Our task is complicated by the fact that we now know that play is a heterogeneous category and that while all play shares some basic properties, or criteria by which we recognize instances of play, the evolutionary, developmental, functional, causal, and experiential aspects may differ considerably (Burghardt, 2005; Pellis & Pellis, 2009). Here we will only discuss other aspects of play insofar as they help explicate issues of origins and evolution. Just as issues of origin and evolution need to be differentiated, so too the function of play has often been conflated with its origins and evolution (e.g., Müller-Schwarze, 1978), also leading to confusion that has bedevilled research and that we address elsewhere (Pellis et al., 2015).

What Is Play?

We recognize as play any behaviour in any animal that satisfies all five play criteria set forth by Burghardt (2005, 2011), which have been used by many authors to identify play in species and contexts where it has not formally been recognized, as well as accommodating all generally accepted traditional examples of play (Burghardt, 2014). These criteria are also helpful in focusing research on species for which preliminary descriptive observations or natural history reports suggest that at least some of the criteria are met, but the jury is out on others due to insufficient data. These problematic examples are called "play at the margins" in Burghardt's survey of play throughout the animal kingdom and are particularly seen in invertebrates (Burghardt, 2005).

The five play criteria, all of which need to be satisfied in at least one respect, can be summarized as behaviour that

1. appears incompletely functional in the context expressed
2. is voluntary, rewarding, pleasurable, or done for its own sake
3. is in some ways modified structurally or developmentally as compared with its functional counterpart
4. is repeated in recognizable but not necessarily invariant form
5. is initiated when the animal is not under more than mild stress due to poor health, bad environmental conditions, social upheaval, or intense conflicting motivational states such as hunger, thirst, wariness of enemies or predators, and so on.

These criteria have allowed identification of behaviour meeting the play criteria in some members of all vertebrate classes as well as in octopus, insects, spiders, and crustaceans (Burghardt, 2005, 2014; Graham & Burghardt, 2010; Pellis & Burghardt, 2017; also see the special issue of *Current Biology*, *25*(1), 2015, on the Biology of Fun).

Play, of course, as in humans, can take many forms in diverse species. Traditionally, animal play has been divided into three types: locomotor/rotational, object/predatory, and social, with the latter including play fighting, chasing, and sexual/courtship play. In humans, many other types of play are recognized such as circular reactions (infants shaking a rattle), babbling, joking/teasing, sociodramatic, pretence, construction, games, and imaginary/mental play. As many instances, albeit rudimentary, of virtually all types of human play occur in non-humans, it is reasonable to assume that they derived from the more basic forms of play observed in other species (Burghardt, 2005). The task for students of play evolution is not only to trace the phylogeny of different types of play in extant, and perhaps ancestral, species but also to formulate and test hypotheses as to how the various types of play both originated and evolved from one another. Does the behaviour, for example, of animals pretending that a rubber mouse is prey or a Cuban crocodile blowing courtship bubbles at a red ball contain precursors to the elaborate pretend or make-believe play found in young children (Russ, 2015; Russ et al., 1999)? As physically vigorous social play fighting is most commonly studied in animals, our examples focus on this type of social play. Note that such rough-and-tumble play is often neglected in humans, especially children (Pellegrini & Smith, 1998). Social play fighting in animals is, in fact, highly complex and involves many features usually shown in social play such as play signals, metacommunication, role reversals, and self-handicapping (Bekoff, 1972, 1975, 1995; Fagen, 1981; Pellis & Pellis, 2017).

The diverse signals used in mammalian play involving facial expressions, vocalizations, and body postures (such as the play bow in dogs) have been recently reviewed (Palagi et al., 2016). Controversy exists, however, on the communicatory function of many of these putative signals, as many of them involve movements and postures that occur during play fighting. Consequently, it is often indeterminate whether a particular action is performed for a combat function rather than a communicatory one (Pellis & Pellis, 2015). For example, although rolling over to supine during play in dogs has been subsumed as part of the behavioural measures thought to signify dominance asymmetries (Bauer & Smuts, 2007), detailed analysis of the correlated actions by both participants suggests that rolling over is mostly used as a defensive tactic. However, rolling over on the back can also be used as an invitation to play in dogs (Norman et al., 2015) and a number of other species, such as in black bear cubs (Burghardt & Burghardt, 1972) and juvenile vervet monkeys (Pellis et al., 2014b). In this way, such an action can have multiple functions during play (Smuts et al., 2015), suggesting that commonly recognized 'signals', such as the play bow in dogs, need to be evaluated empirically (Byosiere et al., 2016) to ensure that the different functional uses can be discerned.

The main lesson from these controversies regarding overt behavioural actions during play is that the communicatory functions of presumed play signals need to be empirically assessed rather than uncritically accepted (Pellis & Pellis, 2015). Signals that are not essential to combat, such as adding facial gestures beyond the opening of the mouth, which is necessary to bite the partner during play fighting in some primates (e.g., Pellis & Pellis, 2011; Scopa & Palagi, 2016), or vocal signals that are independent of combat actions (e.g., Kipper & Todt, 2002; Kisko et al., 2017), may be useful for understanding the contexts in which communication is critical.

Thus, even with a common type of play in a species that virtually everyone, of all ages and cultures, has observed, the nature of some essential elements has only recently been scrutinized. What we conclude about the mechanisms and function of specific play types and components does impact our analysis of their origin and evolution. Play indeed comprises a complicated set of phenomena. We will focus on the general origins of play and then selected phylogenetic approaches to the diversity of play observed in closely related species dealing primarily with changes within play of a given type.

Origins

The play bow in dogs is a specific component of play, as is play fighting generally, be it in dogs, monkeys, or rats. How did such play originate? Of course, we were not there when the first animals played, but can we gain some plausible ideas? Today we recognize that given the heterogeneous nature of play, the diverse types of play, and the observation that play seems to have evolved multiple times, no encompassing hypothesis or theory can adequately specify the origins, function, or causal mechanisms underlying all kinds of play. Historically, however, there are several views that have tried to do so. Three of these views, originating in the nineteenth century, are particularly associated with animal play and have been described in detail elsewhere (e.g., Burghardt, 2005; Henricks, 2015a; Müller-Schwarze, 1978) and briefly highlighted here. We will not, in this chapter, discuss the many subsequent views, theories, and viewpoints on play largely limited to human play by scholars such as Freud, Piaget, Huizinga, Vygotsky, Bakhtin, Turner, Caillois, Fein, Geertz, Sutton-Smith, Henricks, Smith, Pellegrini, and others that are covered in other chapters in this handbook and other sources (e.g., Henricks, 2015b; Johnson et al., 2015; Pellegrini, 2011). All theories of play, of course, ultimately depend on evolutionary support: biological, cultural, or both (Boyd & Richerson, 1985; Richerson & Boyd, 2005).

The earliest of these three classic views is by Herbert Spencer (1872), who, building on Schiller, provided a causal theory for play by positing that only 'advanced' animals such as mammals with extended parental care would have the surplus metabolic energetic reserves enabling them to be able to blow off, as it were, excess energy through apparently useless behaviour that resembled their serious instinctive repertoire. This became known as surplus energy theory. Groos (1898) also focused on the importance of parental care by claiming that relatively carefree youth allowed animals to perfect the skills they would later need for survival in a relatively safe context. This became known as the instinct practice theory. Hall (1904) argued that play, especially in humans, could be explained as recapitulation of behaviour from ancestral stages, building on Haeckel's views of species evolution. For example, adults often engage in hunting and fishing even when not needed for survival and find these activities enjoyable and rewarding for their own sake. Similarly, most active competitive games involve activities formerly essential in warfare or other fighting contexts involving hitting, tackling, throwing, chasing, etc., and this was no accident. Developmentally, recapitulation was seen in children playing with objects prior to engaging with them seriously, for example, girls with dolls and boys with toy weapons, and so on.

All these theories have been amended, critiqued, dismissed, and ridiculed, but all capture some truths about play. In an ecumenical approach to the work of these thoughtful pioneers and other early scholars, Burghardt (1984, 1988, 2005) combined their insights into a broad-scale theoretical approach, surplus resource theory to target the physiological, behavioural, ecological, social, and developmental factors that seem to underlie, in diverse ways, the appearance of play in many groups of animals. Surplus resource theory posits that surpluses of time and energy, along with a diverse behavioural repertoire and parental care that buffers animals from the necessity of protecting them-selves and acquiring all their resources on their own, accompany and facilitate play. This helps explain, for example, why play is much more common in endothermic (warm-blooded) animals born in an altricial state or necessitating extended parental care (Figure 2.1).

Furthermore, play can differ in its functional evolution. Some play may have no function, as play, at all (*primary process play*). *Secondary process play* serves to maintain functions, such as physical fitness or sensory and motor abilities. *Tertiary process play* truly increases an animal's competence in

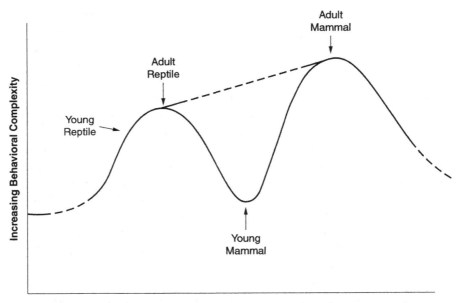

Figure 2.1 *Topographic landscape illustrating how the more complex behavioural and cognitive repertoire in endothermic vertebrates, especially mammals, may have resulted from a reorganization of the ontogeny of some response systems. Changes in neonatal behaviour and its experiential basis derive from a more effective metabolism, extended parental care, and the consequent deterioration of precocial response systems that allowed play to evolve in response to the motivational and stimulus needs of the young animals and to provide an avenue for secondary and tertiary play processes. Reprinted from Burghardt, 1988.*

various domains (foraging, defensive, social among others) and may even produce evolutionarily and culturally important novel and innovative behaviour. These processes have been summarized in a figure available in Burghardt (2005), Pellis et al. (2015), Pellis et al. (2014a), and Pellis and Burghardt (2017).

What is very helpful in looking at the origins of play, unlike seeking ancestral conditions for the origins of life or key morphological and physiological innovations, is that all three processes of play can be observed in many species, including humans. Incipient play – play that appears prior to any functional consequences and thus is termed primary process play, may result from many factors including the need or drive to be active (boredom), developmental precursors of adult-like behaviour (precocious behaviour), motivational conflicts, lowered thresholds to stimuli, and intention movements. Such primary process play is not done for any specific adaptive function but may, through individual experiences and both genetic and cultural evolutionary processes, gain both secondary and tertiary functions. Indeed, the social play in rats (Pellis et al., 2014a), ground squirrels (Marks et al., 2017), and several species of primates (Palagi, 2011) has been shown to have tertiary properties. Tertiary process play may also undergird creativity and innovation (Bateson & Martin, 2013; Burghardt, 2015; Kuczaj, 2017), the transition from behavioural to mental imagination and planning, and the pace of evolution itself. But play can also evolve into apparently non-playful behaviour such as rituals (Burghardt, 2017).

Besides comparative observations on extant species, hypotheses on play origins can also be tested by mathematical and computer modelling. Auerbach et al. (2015) used a very simple model to show that play could originate from non-play in animals and become established in a population, albeit at low rates, even though it was costly and non-functional ("frivolous"). When play was made functional by aiding foraging success, the play genes increased, but eventually collapsed if the animals were living with finite resources. If the play allowed new resources to become available, then play might continue to expand, though not in an unlimited fashion. The irony of the model's findings is that costly play behaviour may result in greater costs to the nonplayers. A recent study on male macaque monkeys (*Macaca assamensis*) showed that while vigorous play facilitated rapid acquisition of motor skills, the cost was somewhat slower growth (Berghänel et al., 2015). A life history dynamic state-dependent model based on social play enhancing foraging success also has appeared (Grunloh & Mangel, 2015) but did not address nonfunctional play, yet was more realistic than the Auerbach model in that sexual reproduction was incorporated. Other types of mathematical models and simulations are also needed and now possible, especially individual agent-based ones (Schank, Burghardt, & Pellis, 2018) that can test both the role of various costs and benefits of play such as predation risk, energy depletion, skill acquisition, and so on, and how actions used during play are constructed (Bell et al., 2015).

Social play models necessitate more complex modelling. For example, Durand and Schank (2015) published an intriguing agent-based model in which juvenile play facilitated cooperation, and individuals with social play experiences were more successful in the stag hunt game. In this game, both cooperating and not cooperating produces a beneficial payoff, but the payoff associated with cooperating is larger. The model found that if cooperators and non-cooperators selectively congregated together into small groups, the players would be more successful. The authors view this as a way in which cooperation could have evolved through learning indirectly via playful inter-actions early in life. The model has similarities to the finding that learning facilitates the evolution of communication (MacLennan & Burghardt, 1993).

Evolutionary Transformations of Play

The diversity of social play in rodents provides a detailed example of how evolutionary transformation in play may occur and offers insights on the mechanisms involved and the novel functions that may arise (Pellis & Pellis,

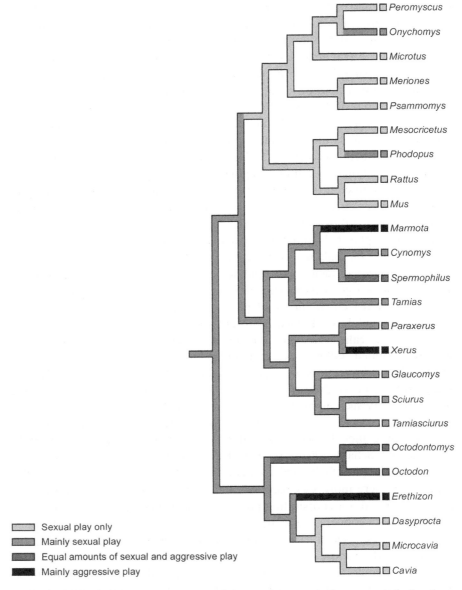

Sexual play only
Mainly sexual play
Equal amounts of sexual and aggressive play
Mainly aggressive play

Figure 2.2 *A cladogram, a tree diagram that reveals the pattern of relatedness across a group of species, for rodents, spanning the three major divisions of the order. The clade that includes the rat (*Rattus*), the domestic mouse (*Mus*), the deer mouse (*Peromyscus*), the grasshopper mouse (*Onychomys*), the fat sand rat (*Psammomys*), the Syrian golden hamster (*Mesocricetus*), the Djungarian hamster (*Phodopus*), voles (montane vole, *Microtus montanus; prairie vole, *M. ochrogaster; and European vole, *M. agrestis*) represents murid (mouse-like) rodents. The clade that includes the North American ground squirrels (*Spermophilus*) and the grey tree squirrel*

2009; Pellis et al., 2014a). There are two major dimensions along which the organization of play fighting in this order can vary. First, play fighting can involve competition for body targets that are derived from several different functional contexts. Play fighting can involve competition for access to body targets otherwise competed over during aggressive encounters, sexual encounters, greeting and grooming encounters, or, in some cases for obligate carnivores, such as the grasshopper mouse, predatory encounters (Pellis & Pellis, 2017). Comparison of the distribution of sex-derived playful competition with aggression-derived playful competition across the order shows that some lineages predominantly engage in the sexual version, others the aggressive version, and others combine both to varying degrees, with the ancestral condition being a state in which the two co-occur (Figure 2.2).

Why different lineages engage in one type of play fighting more than another remains unresolved, but some clues are suggestive. In ground squirrels, there is a marked variation even among closely related species, with some mostly competing for sexual targets and some mostly for aggressive targets. Those mostly engaging in the sexual version live in social systems in which males live separately from females, whereas those that predominantly engage in the aggressive version tend to live in relatively stable mixed sex groups. It is possible that in the former, the primary pathway to reproductive success for males is to access receptive females as quickly as possible, whereas in the latter, reproductive success may depend more on the ability of males within a group to gain dominance (Pellis & Iwaniuk, 2004). In this regard, it is interesting that in some social marmots it has been shown that juvenile play fighting influences dominance status in adulthood (Blumstein et al., 2013). That is, the social or mating systems of different species may influence which traits are more salient and so which are more likely to be engaged in as play, and this, in turn, may have differential selective advantages. Larger datasets, not only for rodents but also for other taxa, such as primates, are needed, to test these possibilities using modern comparative statistical methods (O'Meara et al., 2015).

Second, within a more limited clade of rodents – the murid (mouse-like rodents) – which predominantly engage in the same form of play fighting, competing for targets otherwise contacted during precopulatory behaviour, there is a marked variation in the complexity involved (Pellis et al., 2014a).

Figure 2.2 (*cont.*) (*Sciurus*) *represents squirrel-like rodents. The third clade that includes the guinea pig (*Cavia*) and the degu (*Octodon*) represents the guinea pig–like rodents. Whether the play fighting is mostly aggressive, mostly sexual, or some combination of both is mapped onto the cladogram. The degree of complexity in the form of play performed is not indicated, which will be discussed for murid rodents below. Legend: dotted, sexual play only; dashed, mostly sexual play; grey, about equal amounts of sexual and aggressive play; black, mostly aggressive play. Reprinted from Pellis & Iwaniuk (2004), with permission of the authors.*

For example, while renowned for their acrobatic locomotor/rotational play, house mice do occasionally launch attacks toward the nape of the neck. This is like the targeting of the nape present during adult sexual encounters but is unlike the biting attacks directed at the lower flanks and dorsum during serious fighting, so akin to other murid rodents with regard to social play, mimicking sex not aggression (see Figure 2.2). Moreover, when one mouse jumps or runs toward the neck of another, the recipient evades contact by jumping and fleeing away.

Thus, the play fighting evident in this species is rare and relatively simple, but it can be even simpler in some species (Pellis & Pellis, 2009). In some, such as the European vole, there is nape attack, but no attempt to defend the nape, and in others, such as some species of Australian hopping mice, there is neither attack nor defence. Complexity is added when the recipient of an attack actively defends against contact, which then leads to playful wrestling. As shown in a sequence in deer mice (Figure 2.3), play fighting involves one animal attacking another as it reaches to contact the play target (in this case, the nape of the neck) (panels a–c), which is then accompanied by the recipient defending itself and so blocking access to the target (b–e). Once the target is successfully defended, the defending animal may launch a counterattack (f–h), which can lead to a successful role reversal (i and j). As shown in deer mice, the defending animal rolls over onto its back (see panels c–e in Figure 2.3) and by doing so maximizes bodily contact. Different species, even closely related ones, use such tactics to varying degrees – for example, prairie voles do so much more than do montane voles. Of those species that engage in defence that leads to wrestling, some follow this up with counterattacks, as seen in Figure 2.3, that not only prolong further wrestling, but also lead to role reversals, and some do not.

Even among species that engage in all three subcomponents leading to the most complex forms of play fighting – attack, wrestling defence, and counter-attack – there are quantitative differences as well. In deer mice, for example, encounters that include counterattacks constitute less than 10% of inter-actions, whereas in rats, it is more than 40%. Importantly, in this subclade of rodents, the play fighting mostly involves competition for targets otherwise contacted during precopulatory behaviour, thus behaviour from the same functional system is being compared during play (Pellis & Pellis, 2009). Coalescing these different aspects of play fighting into an index of complexity and then mapping this onto a cladogram reveals several important features of how play may evolve (Figure 2.4). First, the base of the tree shows that the ancestral condition involves species that have moderate degrees of complexity in their play; second, the most complex forms can emerge independently in different branches of the clade; third, some terminal branches show that play can be reduced in complexity over evolution. As will be detailed below, the most complex forms of play fighting constitute tertiary process play, and the tree shows that it is built on by transformations from secondary process (i.e., intermediate levels of complexity). That play can regress to primary process play, or even to no play, suggests that complex forms of play are sustained by

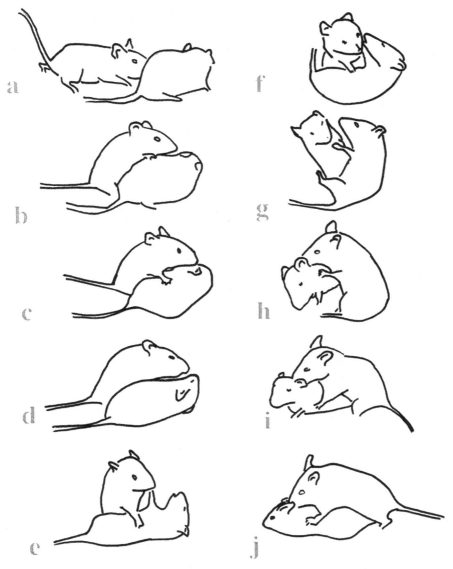

Figure 2.3 *A sequence of play fighting for a pair of juvenile deer mice.*
As detailed in the text, the sequence includes attack, defence, and
counterattack. Reprinted from Pellis et al. (1989), with permission from Wiley.

adaptive functions, so that in the absence of such functions, play is eliminated (i.e., the costs exceed the benefits).

In studying the subcomponents of play fighting in a diverse range of rodents, it becomes evident that changes in the frequency of attack and in the likelihood of defence, or in the type of defence tactics most often used, vary across species independently of one another. Moreover, developmental studies

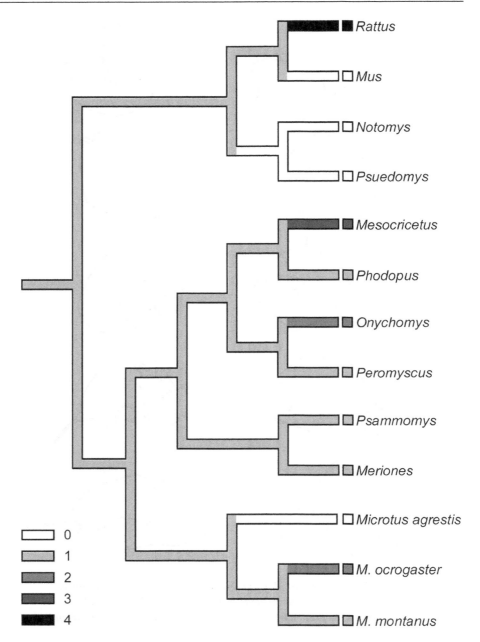

Figure 2.4 *A cladogram for murid rodents (see Figure 2.2), on which is mapped the degree of complexity of play fighting. Legend: white or light stippling for absent or simple play; dark stippling for moderately complex play; grey or black for complex play. Note that the position of some species has been altered in this cladogram to that shown in Figure 2.2. Especially evident is the changed clustering of the hamsters (*Mesocricetus *and* Phodopus*), which arose from the use of more recent consensus about*

within some of these species similarly reveal that the frequency of attack, likelihood of defence, and differential use of different defensive tactics wax and wane independently of one another. Rats, with one of the most complex patterns of play fighting in murid rodents (see *Rattus* in Figure 2.4), having been domesticated for well over 100 years and selectively bred to produce diverse strains, provide further insights into how play may evolve.

Domesticated laboratory rats are all derived from wild Norwegian brown rats, with different strains having different selection histories. There are many different strains, but for current purposes we will focus on strains that have been used extensively for research on play. For example, one of the first strains selected from wild rats is the pure albino Wistar strain; then with a backcross with a wild rat, a hooded line (pigmented eyes, black head, and hood extending down the shoulders) was developed, the Long–Evans hooded strain. Further selective breeding of Wistar rats led to the Sprague Dawley strain. As an independent lineage to consider, the domesticated brown rat was derived more recently, directly from wild congeners. A systematic comparison of the play of wild rats with that of Wistar, Long–Evans, Sprague Dawley, and brown rats revealed that all domesticated strains initiate more playful attacks – consistent with the view that domestication leads to increased playfulness (Burghardt, 1984). However, with regard to defence tactics, all differed from the wild type in some ways, although differently across strains (see Himmler et al., 2016, for a summary of this comparative work). That is, playful attack and playful defence can be selected for change in different ways. This conclusion is supported by comparisons involving specially selected lines of rats derived from these and other strains (for primary sources, see references in Himmler et al., 2016; Pellis & Pellis, 2009).

Comparisons across closely related species of murid rodents and across strains of domesticated rats show that play fighting is comprised of independent subcomponents, suggesting that evolutionary change in play fighting may be mosaic in form. Identifying the genetic and neural substrates of these different subcomponents and how they are transformed during evolution would be a major step forward in understanding the phylogeny of play. Again, a clue into such mechanisms is afforded by focusing on the tertiary process play of rats.

Starting with the pioneering work by Jaak Panksepp (1998), a network of neural structures from the hindbrain, midbrain, and forebrain has been shown to be engaged in the play fighting of rats (Siviy, 2016; Vanderschuren et al.,

Figure 2.4 (*cont.*) *phylogenetic relationships. These changes do not affect the main take-home messages from both figures – the relative simulation of sex and aggression varies markedly across lineages (Figure 2.2) and changes in complexity occur independently across lineages (Figure 2.3). Reprinted from Whishaw et al. (2001), with permission by Wiley.*

2016; and see Chapter 3). This network includes the prefrontal cortex, which regulates executive functions (e.g., attention, short-term memory, emotional regulation, decision-making) (Pellis et al., 2014a). Play fighting experience in the juvenile period modifies development of the prefrontal cortex, and this, in part, is responsible for play-induced improvements in executive function skills and associated social competence (primary sources reviewed in Pellis & Pellis, 2016). Even though play fighting in rats, like many other murid rodents, is derived from the simulation of precopulatory behaviour, the finding that experiencing such play affects not only adult sexual performance but also a variety of social and non-social cognitive skills strongly supports the view that, in this species, play has been transformed into tertiary process play.

Conclusions

Progress has been made in taking some of the mystery out of the origins and evolution of play in recent decades, but much more needs to be done. We see future research focusing on several questions.

First, comprehensive databases on play in diverse species need to be compiled and observations on little studied taxa collected and published. A start has been made by O'Meara and others (https://docs.google.com/a/utk.edu/forms/d/e/1FAIpQLSew9vTyGyuW9Sr4p1kDQAckYigkUkPqrbIDWr0TXnLjQbUK_A/viewform). This should also include intraspecific variation among different populations. For example, food resource availability seems to underlie the amount and nature of play in some species (Baldwin & Baldwin, 1974, 1976; other citations in Burghardt, 2005). Human play also various greatly across cultures, but this is rarely given the attention it deserves (Lancy, 2015).

Second, study of breed differences in play can aid both in understanding the process of domestication in often facilitating play and in understanding how selection for different behaviours may lead to different adult play variants and ontogenetic trajectories of play. While social play in rat breeds is the most studied, dogs also are prime targets for study of breed differences, since they have been selected for many features involving hunting, guarding, herding, and so on (e.g., Coppinger & Coppinger, 1998), and a comprehensive molecular phylogeny of breeds is available (Parker et al., 2017). Differences among breeds in the ontogeny of object play have been documented (Burghardt et al., 2016).

Third, the role of neural mechanisms underlying play and differences across taxa, especially in vertebrates, may be highly useful in determining convergent or homologous aspects of play. Consider, for example, the debate of whether fish feel pain even though they respond to noxious stimuli in ways behaviourally similar to the responses of mammals (Fry, 2016, and commentaries/response). Fry argues that the neural pathways are too dissimilar to claim that the experiential aspects are comparable. Although humans and other mammals clearly experience pain, the conclusion is that we have no reason to conclude that fish do as well. But this does not follow since play, as we have seen, is very heterogeneous in origins and mechanisms and yet shares traits across diverse taxonomic lineages.

Fourth, more modelling and computer simulations are needed to test the role of various putative life history and ecological factors in the evolution and retention of play in animals. O'Meara et al. (2015) reported the most comprehensive analysis to date, involving primates, but too much information is still lacking.

Last, the finding in rodents that at least some of the means by which transforming secondary process play into tertiary process play involves the most cognitively sophisticated portions of the cortex (Pellis & Pellis, 2016) suggests a mechanism that could be evaluated in other taxa. For example, the same neural circuit engaged in during social play in rats (Siviy, 2016) is similarly active in primates (Graham, 2018). Most critically, the work on primates shows that these areas are differentially enlarged in species that engage in more social play, but not in those that engage in more solitary forms of play, further supporting the notion that social play is a demanding emotional and cognitive activity (Palagi et al., 2016). Given that about 50% of primate species retain play fighting as adults and use it strategically for social assessment and manipulation, primates may be a particularly useful taxon to explore the transformations in juvenile play that promote social skill development (see primary sources cited in Pellis et al., 2014a), and the factors and mechanisms that facilitate the evolution of tertiary process play. Cultural transmission can subsequently serve as a ratchet effect in the evolution of play and may be particularly salient in humans (Nielsen et al., 2012).

With the revitalization of interest in play in animals of all kinds, more clarity in identifying play, empirical evidence of play benefits as well as their lack, advances in computer modelling, and neuroscience studies identifying neural systems underlying specific types and components of play, we envision that play, delightful to watch, may become less of an evolutionary mystery.

References

Auerbach, J. D., Kanarek, A., & Burghardt, G. M. (2015). To play or not to play? That's a resource abundance question. *Adaptive Behavior*, *23*, 354–361.

Baldwin, J. D., & Baldwin, J. I. (1974). Exploration and social play in squirrel monkeys (*Saimiri*). *American Zoologist*, *14*, 303–315.

Baldwin, J. D., & Baldwin, J. I. (1976). Effects of ecology on social play: A laboratory simulation. *Ethology*, *40*, 1–14.

Bateson, P., & Martin, P. (2013). *Play, playfulness, creativity, and innovation*. Cambridge: Cambridge University Press.

Bauer, E., & Smuts, B. B. (2007). Cooperation and competition during dyadic play in domestic dogs. *Animal Behaviour, 73*, 489–499.

Bekoff, M. (1972). The development of social interaction, play, and metacommunication in mammals: An ethological perspective. *Quarterly Review of Biology, 47*, 412–434.

Bekoff, M. (1975). The communication of play intention: Are play signals intentional? *Semiotica, 15*, 231–239.

Bekoff, M. (1995). Play signals as punctuation: The structure of social play in canids. *Behaviour, 132*, 419–429.

Bell, H. C., Bell, G. D., Schank, J. A., & Pellis, S. M. (2015). Attack and defense of body targets in play fighting: Insights from simulating the 'keep away game' in rats. *Adaptive Behaviour, 23*, 371–380.

Berghänel, A., Schülke, O., & Ostner, J. (2015). Locomotor play drives motor skill acquisition at the expense of growth: A life history trade-off. *Science Advances, 1*, e1500451.

Blumstein, D. T., Chung, L. K., & Smith, J. E. (2013). Early play may predict later dominance relationships in yellow-bellied marmots (*Marmota flaviventris*). *Proceedings of the Royal Society B: Biological Sciences, 280*, 20130485.

Boyd, R., & Richerson, P. J. (1985). *Culture and the evolutionary process.* Chicago, IL: University of Chicago Press.

Burghardt, G. M. (1984). On the origins of play. In P. K. Smith (Ed.), *Play in animals and humans* (pp. 5–41). Oxford: Basil Blackwell.

Burghardt, G. M. (1988). Precocity, play, and the ectotherm–endotherm transition: Profound reorganization or superficial adaptation. In E. M. Blass (Ed.), *Handbook of behavioral neurobiology, vol. 9: Developmental psychobiology and behavioral ecology* (pp. 107–148). New York: Plenum.

Burghardt, G. M. (2005). *The genesis of animal play: Testing the limits.* Cambridge, MA: MIT Press.

Burghardt, G. M. (2014). A brief glimpse at the long evolutionary history of play. *Animal Behavior and Cognition, 1*, 90–98.

Burghardt, G. M. (2015). Creativity, play, and the pace of evolution. In A. B. Kaufman & J. C. Kaufman (Eds.), *Animal creativity and innovation* (pp. 129–159). Philadelphia: Elsevier.

Burghardt, G. M. (2017). The origins, evolution, and interconnections of play and ritual: Setting the stage. In C. Renfrew, I. Morley, & M. Boyd (Eds.), *Play, ritual, and belief in animals and early human societies* (pp. 23–39). Cambridge: Cambridge University Press.

Burghardt, G. M., Albright, J. D., & Davis, K. M. (2016). Motivation, development, and object play: Comparative perspectives with lessons from dogs. *Behaviour, 153*, 767–793.

Burghardt, G. M., & Burghardt, L. S. (1972). Notes on the behavioral development of two female black bear cubs: The first eight months. In S. Herrero (Ed.), *Bears: Their biology and management* (vol. 23, pp. 255–273). Morges, Switzerland: International Union for the Conservation of Nature and Natural Resources.

Byosiere, S.-E., Espinosa, J., & Smuts, B. (2016). Investigating the function of play bows in adult pet dogs (*Canis lupus familiaris*). *Behavioural Processes, 125*, 106–113.

Coppinger, R., & Coppinger, L. (1998). Differences in the behavior of dog breeds. In J. Serpell (Ed.), *Genetics and the behavior of domestic animals* (pp. 167–202). New York: Academic Press.

Darwin, C. (1859). *On the origin of species*. London: Murray.

Durand, S., & Schank, J. C. (2015). The evolution of social play by learning to cooperate. *Adaptive Behavior*, *23*, 340–353.

Fagen, R. (1981). *Animal play behavior*. New York: Oxford University Press.

Graham, K. L. (2018). Social play and the brain: Examining the correlated evolutionary relationships in nonhuman primates. In M. Bezanson, K. C. MacKinnon & C. A. Schmitt (Eds.), *The emerging primate: Juvenile evolution, ecology, and behavior*. New York: Springer Press.

Graham, K. L., & Burghardt, G. M. (2010). Current perspectives on the biological study of play: Signs of progress. *Quarterly Review of Biology*, *85*, 393–418.

Groos, K. (1898). *The play of animals* (E. L. Baldwin, trans.). New York: D. Appleton.

Grunloh, N., & Mangel, M. (2015). State-dependent behaviorall theory and the evolution of play. *Adaptive Behavior*, *23*, 362–370.

Hall, G. S. (1904). *Adolescence: Its psychology and its relations to physiology, anthropology, sociology, sex, crime, religion and education*. New York: D. Appleton.

Henricks, T. S. (2015a). Classic theories of play. In J. E. Johnson, S. G. Eberle, T. S. Henricks, & D. Kuschner (Eds.), *The handbook of the study of play* (vol. 1, pp. 163–179). Lanham, MD: Rowman & Littlefield.

Henricks, T. S. (2015b). *Play and the human condition*. Urbana-Champaign: University of Illinois Press.

Henry, J. D. (1986). *Red fox: The catlike canine*. Washington, DC: Smithsonian Institution Press.

Himmler, S. M., Himmler, B. T., Pellis, V. C., & Pellis, S. M. (2016). Play, variation in play and the development of socially competent rats. *Behaviour*, *153*, 1103–1137.

Johnson, J. E., Eberle, S. G., Henricks, T. S., & Kuschner, D. (Eds.). (2015). *The handbook of the study of play*. Lanham, MD: Rowman & Littlefield.

Key, B. (2016). Why fish do not feel pain. *Animal Sentience*, *3*(1).

Kipper, S., & Todt, D. (2002). The use of vocal signals in the social play of Barbary macaques. *Primates*, *43*, 3–17.

Kisko, T. M., Wöhr, M., Pellis, V. C., & Pellis, S. M. (2017). From play to aggression: High-frequency 50kHz vocalizations as play and appeasement signals in rats. *Current Topics in Behavioral Neuroscience*, *30*, 91–108.

Kuczaj, S. A. (2017). Animal creativity and innovation. In J. Call, G. M. Burghardt, I. M. Pepperberg, C. T. Snowdon & T. Zentall (Eds.), *APA handbook of comparative psychology*, vol. 2: Perception, learning, and cognition (pp. 627–641). Washington, DC: American Psychological Association.

Lancy, D. F. (2015). *The anthropology of childhood: Cherubs, chattel, changelings* (2nd edn.). Cambridge: Cambridge University Press.

MacLennan, B. J., & Burghardt, G. M. (1993). Synthetic ethology and the evolution of cooperative communication. *Adaptive Behavior*, *2*, 161–187.

Marks, K. A., Vizconde, D. L., Gibson, E. S., Rodriguez, J. R., & Nunes, S. (2017). Play behavior and responses to novel situations in juvenile ground squirrels. *Journal of Mammalogy*, *98*, 1202–1210.

Müller-Schwarze, D. (Ed.) (1978). *Evolution of play behavior*. Stroudsburg, PA: Dowden, Hutchinson & Ross.

Nielsen, M., Cucchiaro, J., & Mohamedally, J. (2012). When the transmission of culture is child's play. *PLoS ONE, 7*(3), e34066.

Norman, K., Pellis, S. M., Barrett, L., & Henzi, S. P. (2015). Down but not out: Supine postures as facilitators of play in domestic dogs. *Behavioural Processes, 110,* 88–95.

O'Meara, B. C., Graham, K. L., Pellis, S. M., & Burghardt, G. M., (2015). Evolutionary models for the retention of adult–adult social play in primates: The roles of diet and other factors associated with resource acquisition. *Adaptive Behavior, 23*, 381–391.

Palagi, E. (2011). Playing at every age: Modalities and potential functions in non-human primates. In A. D. Pellegrini (Ed.), *Oxford handbook of the development of play* (pp. 70–82). Oxford: Oxford University Press.

Palagi, E., Burghardt, G. M., Smuts, B., Cordoni, G., Dall'Olio, S., Fouts, H. N., ... & Pellis, S. M. (2016). Rough-and-tumble play as a window on animal communication. *Biological Reviews, 91*, 111–127.

Panksepp, J. (1998). *Affective neuroscience*. Oxford: Oxford University Press.

Parker, H. G., Dreger, D. L., Rimbault, M., Davis, B. W., Mullen, A. B., Carpintero-Ramirez, G., & Ostrander, E. A. (2017). Genomic analyses reveal the influence of geographic origin, migration, and hybridization on modern dog breed development. *Cell Reports, 19*, 697–708.

Pellegrini, A. D. (Ed.) (2011). *The Oxford handbook of the development of play*. New York: Oxford University Press.

Pellegrini, A. D., & Smith, P. K. (1998). Physical activity play: The nature and function of a neglected aspect of play. *Child Development, 69*, 577–598.

Pellis, S. M., & Burghardt, G. M. (2017). Play and exploration. In J. Call, G. M. Burghardt, I. M. Pepperberg, C. T. Snowdon, & T. Zentall (Eds.), *APA handbook of comparative psychology*, vol. 1: *Basic concepts, methods, neural substrate, and behavior* (pp. 699–722). Washington, DC: American Psychological Association.

Pellis, S. M., Burghardt, G. M., Palagi, E., & Mangel, M. (2015). Modeling play: Distinguishing between origins and current functions. *Adaptive Behavior, 23*, 331–339.

Pellis, S. M., & Iwaniuk, A. N. (2004). Evolving a playful brain: A levels of control approach. *International Journal of Comparative Psychology, 17*, 90–116.

Pellis, S. M., & Pellis, V. C. (2009). *The playful brain: Venturing to the limits of neuroscience*. Oxford: Oneworld Press.

Pellis, S. M., & Pellis, V. C. (2011). To whom the play signal is directed: A study of head shaking in black-handed spider monkeys (*Ateles geoffroi*). *Journal of Comparative Psychology, 125*, 1–10.

Pellis, S. M., & Pellis, V. C. (2015). Are agonistic behavior patterns signals or combat tactics – Or does it matter? Targets as organizing principles of fighting. *Physiology & Behavior, 146*, 73–78.

Pellis, S. M., & Pellis, V. C. (2016). Play and cognition: The final frontier. In M. C. Olmstead (Ed.), *Animal cognition: Principles, evolution, and development* (pp. 201–230). Hauppauge, NY: Nova Science Publishers.

Pellis, S. M., & Pellis, V. C. (2017). What is play fighting and what is it good for? *Learning & Behavior, 45*, 355–366.

Pellis, S. M., Pellis, V. C., Barrett, L., & Henzi, S. P. (2014b). One good turn deserves another: Combat versus other functions of acrobatic maneuvers in the play fighting of vervet monkeys (*Chlorocebus aethiops*). *Animal Behavior & Cognition, 1*, 128–143.

Pellis, S. M., Pellis, V. C., & Dewsbury, D. A. (1989). Different levels of complexity in the playfighting of muroid rodents appear to result from different levels of intensity of attack and defense. *Aggressive Behavior, 15*, 297–310.

Pellis, S. M., Pellis, V. C., & Himmler, B. T. (2014a). How play makes for a more adaptable brain: A comparative and neural perspective. *American Journal of Play, 7*, 73–98.

Richerson, P. J., & Boyd, R. (2005). *Not by genes alone: How culture transformed human evolution.* Chicago, IL: University of Chicago Press.

Russ, S. W. (2015). Commentary on chapter 5: Play – A multipurpose vehicle. In A. B. Kaufman & J. C. Kaufman (Eds.), *Animal creativity and innovation* (pp. 159–161). Philadelphia: Elsevier.

Russ, S. W., Robins, A. L., & Christiano, B. A. (1999). Pretend play: Longitudinal prediction of creativity and affect in fantasy in children. *Creativity Research Journal, 12*, 129–139.

Schank, J. C., Burghardt, G. M., & Pellis, S. M. (2018) Toward a theory of the evolution of fair play. Frontiers in Psychology, 9, article 1167, pp 1–15, DOI: 10.3389/psyg.2018.01167 (July 24, 2018).

Scopa, C., & Palagi, E. (2016). Mimic me while playing! Social tolerance and rapid facial mimicry in macaques (*Macaca tonkeana* and *Macaca fuscata*). *Journal of Comparative Psychology, 130*, 153–161.

Siviy, S. M. (2016). A brain motivated to play: Insights into the neurobiology of playfulness. *Behaviour, 153*, 819–844.

Smith, P. K. (Ed.) (1984). *Play in animals and humans.* Oxford: Basil Blackwell.

Smuts, B., Bauer, E., & Ward, C. (2015). Rollovers during play: Complementary perspectives. *Behavioural Processes, 116*, 50–52.

Spencer, H. (1872). *Principles of psychology* (2nd edn., vol. 2). New York: D. Appleton.

Vanderschuren, L. J. M. J., Acterberg, E. J. M., & Trezza, V. (2016). The neurobiology of social play and its rewarding value in rats. *Neuroscience & Biobehavioral Reviews, 70*, 86–105.

Whishaw, I. Q., Metz, G., Kolb, B., & Pellis, S. M. (2001). Accelerated nervous system development contributes to behavioral efficiency in the laboratory mouse: A behavioral review and theoretical proposal. *Developmental Psychobiology, 39*, 151–170.

3 The Neurochemistry of Social Play Behaviour in Rats

Viviana Trezza, E. J. Marijke Achterberg,
and Louk J. M. J. Vanderschuren

Social play behaviour is a vigorous and highly rewarding social activity abundantly expressed by young mammals, including humans. Social play behaviour is important for the development of brain and behaviour, and it is disrupted in certain child and adolescent psychiatric disorders. Here, we summarize our knowledge of the neurotransmitter systems that modulate social play behaviour in rats, since most of the neurochemical studies on social play behaviour have been performed in this species. Opioids, endocannabinoids, dopamine, and noradrenaline are involved in several aspects of social play, i.e., its positive emotional, incentive motivational, and cognitive subcomponents. These neurotransmitter systems regulate social play through a distributed network of brain regions in the frontal cortex and the limbic system. Opioid neurotransmission plays an important role in the pleasurable properties of social play; cannabinoids affect both emotional and cognitive aspects of social play. Dopamine is implicated in the motivation for social play, whereas noradrenaline likely influences emotional and cognitive aspects of social play behaviour. Serotonin also modulates social play behaviour, although its precise role in this behaviour still needs to be determined. In sum, social play behaviour is the result of coordinated activity in a network of cortical and limbic brain structures, and its monoamine, opioid, and endocannabinoid innervation.

Social Play Behaviour in Rats

In between weaning and puberty, the young of many mammalian species, including humans, display a characteristic, energetic, and highly rewarding form of social behaviour, known as social play behaviour, play

* We would like to dedicate this chapter to the memory of Jaak Panksepp, who passed away in April 2017. Among his many contributions to behavioural neuroscience is his pioneering work on the neural underpinnings of social play behaviour, which has laid the groundwork for our present knowledge on the brain mechanisms of social play.

  Our work on social play behaviour in the last decade has been generously supported by the National Institute on Drug Abuse (R01 DA022628 to LJMJV), the Netherlands Organization for Scientific Research (NWO; Veni grant 91611052 to VT), the European Union (Marie Curie Career Reintegration Grant PCIG09-GA-2011-293589 to VT), and the Dutch Top Institute Pharma (project T5-107).

fighting, or rough-and-tumble play (Panksepp et al., 1984; Pellis & Pellis, 2009; Vanderschuren & Trezza, 2014; Vanderschuren et al., 1997). Social play behaviour contains elements of aggressive, predatory, and sexual behaviour, but it is generally accepted that social play behaviour is a separate category of behaviour, on the basis of two arguments. First, there are clear distinctions in the microstructure of social play behaviour, on the one hand, and sexual and aggressive behaviour, on the other. That is, the sexual and aggressive behavioural elements seen during social play are performed in a modified or exaggerated form (Blanchard & Blanchard, 1977; Panksepp et al., 1984; Pellis, 1988; Pellis & Pellis, 1987, 2009; Vanderschuren et al., 1997). Second, social play is accompanied or preceded by explicit physical, facial, or vocal signals indicating that the intention of the behaviour is playful in nature.

Although there likely are major differences between species, it is well accepted that social play behaviour has important benefits to the animals, both immediate and delayed (Pellis & Pellis, 2009; Spinka et al., 2001; Vanderschuren & Trezza, 2014). Given its rewarding properties, its most likely immediate benefits are the positive emotions evoked by play. In other words, animals play because it is a pleasurable activity. In the long run, this may facilitate the development of neural systems underlying emotions (Baarendse et al., 2014; Lesscher et al., 2015; Leussis et al., 2008; Lukkes et al., 2009; Vanderschuren & Trezza, 2014; Whitaker et al., 2013; Wright et al., 1991). In addition, its social aspects, i.e., seeking out company, engaging in interactions with conspecifics, and establishing and maintaining social bonds, also contribute to the immediate motivation to play, and in the long term facilitate the development of an adaptive social repertoire (Pellis & Pellis, 2009; Vanderschuren & Trezza, 2014). However, the benefits of social play behaviour likely stretch beyond the social domain. Thus, since play involves mixing up behavioural elements in a different, but relatively safe situation, it is thought that this comprises experimenting with one's own behaviours. Ultimately, this may stimulate the development of cognitive functions such as flexibility and creativity (Bateson, 2015; Spinka et al., 2001). Indeed, the notion that social play behaviour facilitates the development of social, cognitive, and emotional skills has been supported by laboratory experiments that show that deprivation of social play behaviour leads to long-lasting impairments in these domains (Vanderschuren & Trezza, 2014).

The importance of social play for the development of brain and behaviour is underscored by the fact that in humans, social play is impaired in pediatric mental disorders, such as autism, disruptive behaviour disorders, attention-deficit/hyperactivity disorder, and early-onset schizophrenia (Alessandri, 1992; Helgeland & Torgersen, 2005; Jones et al., 1994; Jordan, 2003; Møller & Husby, 2000). Conversely, dysfunctional social interactions during childhood and adolescence have a long-lasting negative impact on social abilities and cognitive function (Braun & Bock, 2011; Cacioppo & Hawkley, 2009).

Altogether, understanding the brain mechanisms of social play behaviour therefore increases our knowledge of how the brain processes social signals to generate expression of rewarding social behaviours. In addition, it may help us to grasp how social interactions in the young promote the development of brain and behaviour. Last, profound insight into the neural underpinnings of social play may ultimately contribute to improved treatments for child and adolescent mental disorders characterized by social aberrations. This chapter summarizes our knowledge of the neurotransmitter mechanisms that modulate social play behaviour in rats, since the great majority of the neurochemical studies on social play behaviour have been performed in this species.

Opioid Modulation of Social Play Behaviour

The endogenous opioid system has been widely implicated in reward mechanisms, i.e., the positive emotional properties of food, sex, drugs of abuse (Berridge & Kringelbach, 2015; Le Merrer et al., 2009; van Ree et al., 1999), as well as social play behaviour (Vanderschuren et al., 2016). Perhaps the most widely reported findings regarding the neurochemical modulation of social play are that treating rats with an opioid receptor agonist such as morphine increases social play behaviour and that treatment with opioid receptor antagonists, such as naloxone and naltrexone, reduces it (Siviy & Panksepp, 2011; Trezza et al., 2010). Further pharmacological and anatomical analysis of opioid influences on social play behaviour has revealed that beta-endorphin, an endogenous opioid peptide, positively modulates social play by acting on mu-opioid receptors within the nucleus accumbens, a brain area that is part of the basal ganglia and has a key role in reward processes (Niesink & Van Ree, 1989; Trezza et al., 2011b; Vanderschuren et al., 1995b).

Given the widely accepted role of opioid neurotransmission in reward processes, it is likely that opioid drugs modulate play through an influence on its pleasurable properties. In support of this notion, Normansell and Panksepp (1990) used a T-maze set-up, in which rats learned to enter one of two goal boxes to be rewarded with the opportunity to play. They showed that treatment with morphine enhanced, and naloxone reduced, the expression of play and that naloxone accelerated, and morphine retarded, extinction of T-maze performance. However, treatment with neither drug altered choice behaviour or latency to enter the goal box. In a more recent study (Trezza et al., 2011b), it was found that blocking mu-opioid receptors in the nucleus accumbens by administering a mu-opioid receptor antagonist directly into this brain area prevented the development of social play–induced conditioned place preference (CPP) in rats. Place conditioning is a paradigm widely used in preclinical research to study the positive and negative emotional properties of natural and drug rewards. In this paradigm, animals learn to associate a set of environmental cues with the positive or negative properties of food, sex, drugs, or social play, so that the animals come to prefer (or avoid, in the case of negative emotional events) the environment associated with the reward, over a control environment that has been associated with a neutral event (Trezza et al., 2011a). Further behavioural analysis of opioid effects on social play showed that morphine does not increase social play by stimulating feelings of safety or reduced anxiety, since its effect on social play was not different in a familiar versus an unfamiliar environment (Trezza & Vanderschuren, 2008b; Vanderschuren et al., 1995a). Moreover, morphine did not change the behavioural structure of social play. Rather, the internal coherence of social play appeared to be enhanced, so that playful interactions are prolonged (Vanderschuren et al., 1995c). Importantly, the initiation of social play was enhanced in a test in which only one animal in a test pair was treated with morphine (Trezza & Vanderschuren, 2008b), suggesting that certain motivational aspects of social play are under the influence of opioid neurotransmission.

In sum, opioid neurotransmission has an important role in the modulation of social play behaviour. Converging evidence suggests that opioids particularly influence the pleasurable properties of social play. This notion is based on the involvement of mu receptors in the nucleus accumbens, which are heavily implicated in the positive emotional effects of rewards (Berridge & Kringelbach, 2015; Le Merrer et al., 2009; van Ree et al., 1999), as well as behavioural evidence that opioids modulate social play reward in operant and classical conditioning experiments (Normansell & Panksepp, 1990; Trezza et al., 2011b).

Cannabinoid Modulation of Social Play Behaviour

The endocannabinoid system is a unique neuromodulatory system that consists of cannabinoid receptors (CB1 and CB2, mainly expressed in the brain and periphery, respectively), endogenous molecules that bind to these receptors (called endocannabinoids, including anandamide and 2-arachidonoylglycerol (2-AG)), and the enzymes for endocannabinoid synthesis and degradation. Cannabinoid receptors are highly expressed in brain areas that modulate cognitive processes and emotional states, where endocannabinoids regulate ion channel activity and neurotransmitter release (Kendall & Yudowski, 2016; Mechoulam et al., 2014).

Given the involvement of endocannabinoids in reward processes, including pleasure, motivation, and reinforcement (Fattore et al., 2010; Gardner, 2005; Viveros et al., 2007; Zanettini et al., 2011), it is not surprising that they are involved in the modulation of social play behaviour. Studies with systemic drug administration have shown that pharmacological interference with endocannabinoid neurotransmission has different effects on social play behaviour in rats, depending on the type of drug used. Thus, when rats were treated with direct cannabinoid receptor agonists, i.e., drugs that directly activate cannabinoid receptors, social play was markedly reduced (Siviy & Panksepp, 2011; Trezza et al., 2010). These results are consistent with findings showing that both acute (Genn et al., 2004; van Ree et al., 1984) and chronic (O'Shea et al., 2006; Schneider & Koch, 2005; Schneider et al., 2008) treatment with cannabinoid receptor agonists reduced social interaction in rats.

Opposite effects on social play behaviour are observed following administration of drugs that increase local endocannabinoid neurotransmission by interfering with endocannabinoid deactivation. Thus, systemic administration of drugs that inhibit either endocannabinoid hydrolysis or endocannabinoid reuptake increased social play behaviour in rats (Siviy & Panksepp, 2011; Trezza et al., 2010). These results suggest that, during social play, endocannabinoids are released in brain areas mediating this behaviour and that the increased endocannabinoid tone induced by drugs that interfere with endocannabinoid deactivation makes rats more playful. To support this possibility, it has been shown that, during social play, levels of the endocannabinoid anandamide increased in the rat nucleus accumbens, amygdala (Trezza et al., 2012), and dorsal striatum (Marco et al., 2011). An in-depth analysis of the brain regions involved in endocannabinoid modulation of social play revealed that the amygdala (Trezza et al., 2012) and nucleus accumbens core (Manduca et al., 2016a) have a crucial role in the modulation of social play by the endocannabinoids anandamide- and 2-AG, respectively. As outlined below, endocannabinoid, opioid, and dopaminergic neurotransmission interact in the regulation of social play (Manduca et al., 2016a, 2016b; Trezza & Vanderschuren, 2008a, 2009). Furthermore, endocannabinoids have been implicated in the play-enhancing effects of nicotine and ethanol in rats (Trezza et al., 2009), a finding in line with the role of the endocannabinoid system role in the reinforcing effects of these drugs (Economidou et al., 2006; Gamaleddin et al., 2015; Pava & Woodward, 2012).

Interestingly, endocannabinoids likely drive the expression of social play behaviour as a whole, without differentially affecting its motivational or pleasurable properties. Indeed, when an anandamide degradation inhibitor was administered at a dose known to increase the expression of social play behaviour, it did not affect operant responding for social play or social play-induced CPP in rats (Achterberg et al., 2016b). Pharmacological blockade of CB1 cannabinoid receptors reduced operant responding for play, although this effect may be secondary to concurrent drug-induced stereotypic behaviours (i.e., grooming and scratching) (Tallett et al., 2007).

To summarize, endocannabinoids modulate the performance of social play behaviour in rats acting in limbic brain areas, such as the nucleus accumbens and amygdala.

Dopaminergic Modulation of Social Play Behaviour

Dopamine neurotransmission has a well-established role in incentive motivational processes (Berridge, 2007; Floresco, 2015; Kelley, 2004; Robbins & Everitt, 2007; Salamone & Correa, 2012). Since social play behaviour is a rewarding activity, a modulatory role for dopamine in this behaviour is therefore highly likely. Treatment with non-selective as well as D1- and D2-receptor agonists has been reported to increase (Beatty et al., 1984; Vanderschuren et al., 2008) or decrease social play (Niesink & Van Ree, 1989; Siviy et al., 1996). Conversely, treatment with non-selective as well as selective dopamine D1- and D2-receptor antagonists inhibited social play behaviour (Siviy & Panksepp, 2011; Trezza et al., 2010). Psychostimulant drugs such as amphetamine, methylphenidate, and cocaine, which increase dopamine neurotransmission by inhibiting dopamine reuptake or enhancing its release, are very effective play-suppressors (Siviy & Panksepp, 2011; Trezza et al., 2010). Importantly, the effect of cocaine only partially depends on dopaminergic neurotransmission, whereas the effects of amphetamine and methylphenidate are mediated through another neurotransmitter, i.e., noradrenaline (Achterberg et al., 2014; Vanderschuren et al., 2008). Also, selectively increasing extracellular dopamine levels using the reuptake blocker GBR-12909 did not alter social play (Vanderschuren et al., 2008). Together, these data suggest that an optimal level of dopamine is required for the proper execution of social play behaviour, as both stimulating and reducing dopaminergic neurotransmission can disrupt it. In addition, systemic drug treatment may cause altered dopaminergic neurotransmission in several brain regions, potentially causing a dysbalance in dopamine signalling between different neural circuits (Cools & Robbins, 2004). With regard to the neural structures involved, the nucleus accumbens has recently been identified as an important site of action of dopamine to influence social play behaviour (Manduca et al., 2016b).

Given the involvement of dopamine in incentive motivational processes (Berridge, 2007; Floresco, 2015; Kelley, 2004; Robbins & Everitt, 2007; Salamone & Correa, 2012), we recently investigated whether dopamine also modulates the motivation for social play behaviour (Achterberg et al., 2016b). We found that treatment with drugs that increase dopamine neurotransmission, such as cocaine, methylphenidate, and GBR-12909, increased responding for social play under a progressive ratio schedule of reinforcement, which taxes the willingness of animals to work for rewards. These effects were blocked by pretreatment with a dopamine receptor antagonist. Intriguingly, cocaine and methylphenidate reduced the expression of social play during reinforced play periods, but these effects depended not on dopamine but on noradrenergic neurotransmission (see later; Achterberg et al., 2016b), supporting the notion that motivation for play and its performance are mediated through distinct neural mechanisms. We also tested the role of dopamine in social play reward in a place conditioning set-up. Intriguingly, we found only a minimal involvement of dopamine in social play–induced CPP. Treatment with cocaine or a dopamine receptor antagonist did not influence the development of social play–induced CPP, whereas treatment with GBR12909 disrupted social play–induced CPP (Vanderschuren et al., 2016). The underlying mechanisms of this latter effect are unclear. Perhaps, increased dopaminergic neurotransmission throughout the brain results in a dysbalance in dopamine activity between different brain regions (Cools & Robbins, 2004), causing the functions that underlie learning a place–reward association to become disrupted.

In sum, an important role for dopamine in social play behaviour has been identified. It modulates the motivation for social play (Achterberg et al., 2016b), whereby the nucleus accumbens is a critical site of action (Manduca et al., 2016b). However, consistent with the notion that pleasurable properties of rewards do not depend on dopamine function (Berridge, 2007; Salamone & Correa, 2012), this neurotransmitter does not affect the rewarding properties of social play as tested in a place-conditioning paradigm.

Opioid, Cannabinoid, and Dopamine Interactions in the Modulation of Social Play Behaviour

Close interactions between the endocannabinoid, dopaminergic, and endogenous opioid systems have been implicated in the positive emotional properties of natural and drug rewards (Gardner, 2005; van Ree et al., 1999). Indeed, a functional interplay between these neurotransmitter systems in affective responses and social behaviours has been described (Fattore et al., 2010; Loureiro et al., 2015). In line with this kind of functional interplay, studies with systemic drug administration have shown that endocannabinoid, opioid, and dopaminergic neurotransmission interact in the regulation of social play (Manduca et al., 2016a; Trezza & Vanderschuren, 2008a, 2009). More recently, we have shown that endocannabinoid–dopamine–opioid interactions in social play occur via the nucleus accumbens. Thus, blocking dopamine receptors in the nucleus accumbens counteracted the increase in social play behaviour induced by systemic administration of either an anandamide degradation inhibitor or an opioid receptor agonist (Manduca et al., 2016b). Furthermore, the increases in social play induced by systemic administration of either an opioid receptor agonist or a 2-AG degradation inhibitor were prevented when either cannabinoid or opioid receptors in the nucleus accumbens core were blocked by local infusion of cannabinoid or opioid receptor antagonists, respectively (Manduca et al., 2016a).

Noradrenergic Modulation of Social Play Behaviour

Noradrenergic neurotransmission has been implicated in a variety of cognitive processes, including learning, attention, and flexibility (Aston-Jones & Cohen, 2005; Berridge & Waterhouse, 2003; Robbins & Arnsten, 2009; Roozendaal & McGaugh, 2011). In addition, it plays a role in the generation and perception of emotions, and an emerging body of work suggests that noradrenaline is involved in reward processes as well (e.g., Bouret & Richmond, 2015; Ventura et al., 2005). Given that the expression of social play likely depends on a complex interplay between cognitive and emotional processes, an important role for noradrenaline in the proper performance of social play behaviour is well conceivable.

Indeed, systemic treatment with drugs that interfere with noradrenergic neurotransmission alters social play behaviour in rats. Atomoxetine, a drug that increases noradrenergic neurotransmission by inhibiting the reuptake of noradrenaline, inhibits social play. This effect depends on stimulation of α2-noradrenaline receptors (Vanderschuren et al., 2008). In addition, treatment with drugs that stimulate α2-noradrenaline receptors reduced social play, whereas treatment with drugs that block α2-noradrenaline receptors both enhanced and reduced social play, depending on the drug used (Beatty et al., 1984; Normansell & Panksepp, 1985a; Siviy & Baliko, 2000; Siviy et al., 1994; Vanderschuren et al., 2008). Moreover, treatment with a drug that blocks α1-noradrenaline receptors reduced social play behaviour, whereas a drug that activates this receptor did not alter social play (Siviy et al., 1994). Propranolol, a drug that blocks β-noradrenaline receptors, decreased social play behaviour as well (Beatty et al., 1984). Importantly, the widely reported suppressant effects on social play of psychostimulant drugs, such as methylphenidate and amphetamine (Siviy & Panksepp, 2011; Trezza et al., 2010), were found to depend on stimulation of α2-noradrenaline receptors. Thus, the inhibitory effects of methylphenidate and amphetamine on social play were counteracted by pretreatment with a drug that blocks α2-noradrenaline receptors, but not by drugs that block α1- or β-noradrenaline receptors or dopamine receptors (Achterberg et al., 2014; Vanderschuren et al., 2008). With regard to the brain regions through which noradrenaline influences social play, we recently reported that the social play–suppressant effects of methylphenidate and atomoxetine are mediated through a distributed network of prefrontal and limbic subcortical regions implicated in cognitive control and emotional processes, i.e., the anterior cingulate cortex, infralimbic cortex, basolateral amygdala, and habenula (Achterberg et al., 2015).

As described above, treatment with methylphenidate increased the motivation for social play behaviour under a progressive ratio schedule of reinforcement, but suppressed its performance during reinforced play periods. The former effect was blocked by pretreatment with a dopamine receptor antagonist, and the latter by pretreatment with an α2-noradrenaline receptor antagonist (Achterberg et al., 2016b). Moreover, treatment with atomoxetine decreased responding for social play as well as its performance. Together, these data indicate that the play-suppressant effects of methylphenidate (as well as atomoxetine) depend on noradrenergic neurotransmission, whereas dopaminergic neurotransmission mediates the psychostimulant-induced increase in the motivation for social play. With regard to a role for noradrenaline in social play reward, we found that treatment with atomoxetine did not affect social play–induced CPP (Vanderschuren et al., 2016). Using this same place-conditioning paradigm, we also showed that noradrenaline is involved in the reconsolidation of social play reward, a mechanism by which memories can be modified and restabilized after retrieval (Achterberg et al., 2012).

In sum, the available data indicate that noradrenergic neurotransmission though stimulation of α1-, α2-, and β-adrenoceptors modulates both the emotional and cognitive aspects of social play behaviour in rats, whereby a variety of prefrontal and subcortical limbic brain structures is involved.

Serotonergic Modulation of Social Play Behaviour

Studies in rodents have shown that serotonin has a modulatory role in social play (Kiser et al., 2012). Treatment with drugs that enhance serotonergic neurotransmission such as the selective serotonin reuptake inhibitor fluoxetine, the serotonin releaser drug 3,4-methylenedioxymethamphetamine (MDMA), and the serotonin releaser/reuptake inhibitor fenfluramine reduced social play (Homberg et al., 2007; Knutson et al., 1996). Similar effects were induced by treatment with the non-selective serotonin receptor agonist quipazine (Normansell & Panksepp, 1985b), whereas treatment with a serotonin 1A-receptor agonist reduced the asymmetry in playfulness between rats with a different motivation to play (Siviy et al., 2011). Moreover, social play behaviour was reduced in mutant rats that lack the serotonin transporter gene, and therefore show constitutively increases in extra-neuronal serotonin levels (Homberg et al., 2007). To further support the involvement of serotonin in social play, prenatal and postnatal administration of a drug that activates serotonin receptors has been found to disrupt social play behaviour in rats. This behavioural alteration was accompanied by changes in the expression of serotonin-1A and -2A receptors in the paraventricular nucleus of the hypothalamus (Madden & Zup, 2014). Similarly, prenatal fluoxetine exposure has been found to decrease social play behaviour in the rat offspring (Olivier et al., 2011). Collectively, these data suggest that there is an inverse relationship between serotonin neurotransmission and social play behaviour in rats.

Other Neurotransmitter Systems Involved in Social Play Behaviour

The stimulating effects of alcohol on social play behaviour have been well documented. Thus, treatment with low doses of alcohol increased social play, and this effect was not secondary to changes in locomotion (Trezza et al., 2009; Varlinskaya & Spear, 2002, 2006, 2009; Varlinskaya et al., 2001). Furthermore, the increase in social play induced by low doses of alcohol was not likely to be a result of its anti-anxiety properties. That is, the effects of alcohol on social play were largely comparable in familiar and unfamiliar test environments and not associated with an anti-anxiety effect on the elevated plus maze, a well-known test for anxiety in rodents (Trezza et al., 2009). Moreover, the facilitating effects of alcohol on social play were particularly apparent in early adolescent rats, suggesting that it is the playful aspects of social interaction, which are most abundant at this age, that are facilitated by alcohol. Older animals appeared to be more sensitive to the social disinhibition (i.e., relief of the reduction in social interaction in an unfamiliar environment) by alcohol (Varlinskaya & Spear, 2002, 2006). In terms of mechanism of action, dopamine and nicotine receptor stimulation is involved in the alcohol-induced increase in social play (Trezza et al., 2009), whereas mixed findings have been reported regarding the role of opioid neurotransmission (Trezza et al., 2009; Varlinskaya & Spear, 2009).

Cholinergic neurotransmission also has a modulatory influence on play. Treatment with low doses of nicotine, which stimulates the nicotinic subtype of acetylcholine receptors, has been reported to increase social play behaviour. This effect was independent of changes in locomotion and anxiety, and blocked by pretreatment with a nicotine, dopamine, or opioid receptor antagonist (Trezza et al., 2009). Interestingly, nicotine and social play interact synergistically in rats, resulting in a greater CPP than either reward given alone. Thus, when doses of nicotine (or cocaine) that are insufficient to induce CPP by themselves are combined with the opportunity for a playful interaction that is also insufficient for inducing CPP, then a robust place preference is observed (Thiel et al., 2009). As for the role of the muscarinic subtype of acetylcholine receptors in social play, treatment with pilocarpine and arecoline, drugs that activate these receptors, reduced social play (Wilson et al., 1986). Treatment with the muscarinic receptor antagonist scopolamine also reduced social play, while methylscopolamine, which poorly penetrates the blood–brain barrier, was ineffective (Wilson et al., 1986). The fact that both muscarinic receptor agonists and antagonists reduced social play favors the hypothesis that brain nicotinic rather than muscarinic receptors have a modulatory role in social play (Wilson et al., 1986).

Other substances with positive subjective properties that have been investigated in the context of play are a drug that blocks the NMDA subtype of glutamate receptors, which was reported to have biphasic effects on social play (i.e., facilitation at low doses and reduction at higher doses) (Siviy et al., 1995), and the benzodiazepine drug diazepam, which reduced social play and increased non-playful social exploratory behaviour at a dose that had anti-anxiety effects in the elevated plus maze (Trezza et al., 2009), providing additional evidence for a dissociation between social play behaviour and anxiety. Last, recent studies have started to investigate the role of vasopressin and oxytocin, neuropeptides implicated in a range of social behaviours (Donaldson & Young, 2008; Meyer-Lindenberg et al., 2011; Stoesz et al., 2013) in social play. These studies have indicated that these neuropeptides intricately influence social play in rats and hamsters, the directionality of the effects being dependent on sex, familiarity of the test environment, and brain region (Bredewold et al., 2015; Cheng & Delville, 2009; Veenema et al., 2013).

Discussion

This chapter aims to provide a concise summary of our current knowledge of the neurochemical modulation of social play behaviour in rats. The information available today implicates opioid, cannabinoid, dopamine, noradrenaline, and serotonin in several aspects of social play, i.e., its positive emotional, incentive motivational, and cognitive subcomponents. Opioid neurotransmission, most prominently within the nucleus accumbens, plays an important role in the pleasurable properties of social play; cannabinoids affect both emotional and cognitive aspects of social play, whereby the nucleus accumbens and basolateral amygdala are important sites of action. Dopamine, within the nucleus accumbens, is implicated in the motivation for social play, whereas noradrenaline, through a distributed network of prefrontal and subcortical brain structures, likely influences emotional and cognitive aspects of social play behaviour. Altogether, this shows that our understanding of how social play behaviour comes about in the brain has substantially increased in the last decades (Pellis & Pellis, 2009; Siviy, 2016; Siviy & Panksepp, 2011; Trezza et al., 2010; Vanderschuren et al., 1997; Vanderschuren et al., 2016).

Despite this remarkable progress, caveats and outstanding questions remain. For example, although we are beginning to understand the neural sites of action through which the different neuromodulator systems influence social play behaviour, much more detailed information will be necessary to fully comprehend the brain mechanisms of play. In addition, for the most part, and understandably, the different neurotransmitter systems have been studied separately with respect to their involvement in social play. However, these systems modulate behaviour not in isolation but in interaction with one another. We already have evidence for interactions between opioid, cannabinoid, and dopamine neurotransmission in the regulation of social play (see earlier; e.g., Manduca et al., 2016a, 2016b; Trezza & Vanderschuren, 2008a, 2009), but obviously, these interactions are likely much more widespread and complex. Last, more detailed information is necessary on the behavioural subcomponents of social play behaviour that are modulated by the different neural mechanisms, such as the pleasurable and motivational aspects of social play, as well as cognitive functions (attention, flexibility, impulse regulation, communication, cooperation) that subserve the appropriate execution of this behaviour.

To conclude, our understanding of the neural mechanisms of social play behaviour is increasing, but much remains to be revealed. Given the importance of social play for proper development of brain and behaviour, we are confident that increased insight into the neural underpinnings of social play in laboratory animals will contribute to a firmer grasp on the social, emotional, and cognitive development of animals and humans. Furthermore, since a lack of or altered patterns of social play behaviour are a hallmark of several developmental psychiatric disorders (Alessandri, 1992; Helgeland & Torgersen, 2005; Jones et al., 1994; Jordan, 2003; Møller & Husby, 2000), elucidating the neural substrates of social play may also aid in the development of innovative treatments for pediatric mental disorders with a social dimension.

References

Achterberg, E. J. M., Trezza, V., Siviy, S. M., Schrama, L., Schoffelmeer, A. N. M., & Vanderschuren, L. J. M. J. (2014). Amphetamine and cocaine suppress social play behavior in rats through distinct mechanisms. *Psychopharmacology*, *231*(8), 1503–1515.

Achterberg, E. J. M., Trezza, V., & Vanderschuren, L. J. M. J. (2012). Beta-adrenoreceptor stimulation mediates reconsolidation of social reward-related memories. *PLoS One*, *7*(6), e39639.

Achterberg, E. J. M., van Kerkhof, L. W. M., Damsteegt, R., Trezza, V., & Vanderschuren, L. J. M. J. (2015). Methylphenidate and atomoxetine inhibit social play behavior through prefrontal and subcortical limbic mechanisms in rats. *Journal of Neuroscience*, *35*(1), 161–169.

Achterberg, E. J., van Kerkhof, L. W., Servadio, M., van Swieten, M. M., Houwing, D. J., Aalderink, M., Driel, N. V., Trezza, V., & Vanderschuren, L. J. M. J. (2016a). Contrasting roles of dopamine and noradrenaline in the motivational properties of social play behavior in rats. *Neuropsychopharmacology*, *41*(3), 858–868.

Achterberg, E. J. M., van Swieten, M. M. H., Driel, N. V., Trezza, V., & Vanderschuren, L. J. M. J. (2016b). Dissociating the role of endocannabinoids in the pleasurable and motivational properties of social play behaviour in rats. *Pharmacologcial Research*, *110*, 151–158.

Alessandri, S. M. (1992). Attention, play, and social behavior in ADHD preschoolers. *Journal of Abnormal Child Psychology*, *20*(3), 289–302.

Aston-Jones, G., & Cohen, J. D. (2005). An integrative theory of locus coeruleus-norepinephrine function: Adaptive gain and optimal performance. *Annual Review of Neuroscience, 28*, 403–450.

Baarendse, P. J. J., Limpens, J. H. W., & Vanderschuren, L. J. M. J. (2014). Disrupted social development enhances the motivation for cocaine in rats. *Psychopharmacology, 231*(8), 1695–1704.

Bateson, P. (2015). Playfulness and creativity. *Current Biology, 25*(1), R12–R16.

Beatty, W. W., Costello, K. B., & Berry, S. L. (1984). Suppression of play fighting by amphetamine: Effects of catecholamine antagonists, agonists and synthesis inhibitors. *Pharmacology Biochemistry and Behavior, 20*(5), 747–755.

Berridge, C. W., & Waterhouse, B. D. (2003). The locus coeruleus-noradrenergic system: Modulation of behavioral state and state-dependent cognitive processes. *Brain Research Reviews, 42*(1), 33–84.

Berridge, K. C. (2007). The debate over dopamine's role in reward: The case for incentive salience. *Psychopharmacology, 191*(3), 391–431.

Berridge, K. C., & Kringelbach, M. L. (2015). Pleasure systems in the brain. *Neuron, 86*(3), 646–664.

Blanchard, R. J., & Blanchard, D. C. (1977). Aggressive behavior in the rat. *Behavioral Biology, 21*, 197–224.

Bouret, S., & Richmond, B. J. (2015). Sensitivity of locus ceruleus neurons to reward value for goal-directed actions. *Journal of Neuroscience, 35*(9), 4005–4014.

Braun, K., & Bock, J. (2011). The experience-dependent maturation of prefronto-limbic circuits and the origin of developmental psychopathology: Implications for the pathogenesis and therapy of behavioural disorders. *Developmental Medicine and Child Neurology, 53*(Suppl 4), 14–18.

Bredewold, R., Schiavo, J. K., van der Hart, M., Verreij, M., & Veenema, A. H. (2015). Dynamic changes in extracellular release of GABA and glutamate in the lateral septum during social play behavior in juvenile rats: Implications for sex-specific regulation of social play behavior. *Neuroscience, 307*, 117–127.

Cacioppo, J. T., & Hawkley, L. C. (2009). Perceived social isolation and cognition. *Trends in Cognitive Science, 13*(10), 447–454.

Cheng, S. Y., & Delville, Y. (2009). Vasopressin facilitates play fighting in juvenile golden hamsters. *Physiology and Behavior, 98*(1–2), 242–246.

Cools, R., & Robbins, T. W. (2004). Chemistry of the adaptive mind. *Philosophical Transactions of the Royal Society A: Mathematical Physical and Engineering Sciences, 362*(1825), 2871–2888.

Donaldson, Z. R., & Young, L. J. (2008). Oxytocin, vasopressin, and the neurogenetics of sociality. *Science, 322*(5903), 900–904.

Economidou, D., Mattioli, L., Cifani, C., Perfumi, M., Massi, M., Cuomo, V., Trabace, L., & Ciccocioppo, R. (2006). Effect of the cannabinoid CB1 receptor antagonist SR-141716A on ethanol self-administration and ethanol-seeking behaviour in rats. *Psychopharmacology (Berl), 183*(4), 394–403.

Fattore, L., Melis, M., Fadda, P., Pistis, M., & Fratta, W. (2010). The endocannabinoid system and nondrug rewarding behaviours. *Experimental Neurology, 224*(1), 23–36.

Floresco, S. B. (2015). The nucleus accumbens: An interface between cognition, emotion, and action. *Annual Review of Psychology, 66*, 25–52.

Gamaleddin, I. H., Trigo, J. M., Gueye, A. B., Zvonok, A., Makriyannis, A., Goldberg, S. R., & Le Foll, B. (2015). Role of the endogenous cannabinoid system in nicotine addiction: Novel insights. *Frontiers in Psychiatry, 6*, 41.

Gardner, E. L. (2005). Endocannabinoid signaling system and brain reward: Emphasis on dopamine. *Pharmacology Biochemistry and Behavior, 81*(2), 263–284.

Genn, R. F., Tucci, S., Marco, E. M., Viveros, M. P., & File, S. E. (2004). Unconditioned and conditioned anxiogenic effects of the cannabinoid receptor agonist CP 55,940 in the social interaction test. *Pharmacology Biochemistry and Behavior, 77*(3), 567–573.

Helgeland, M. I., & Torgersen, S. (2005). Stability and prediction of schizophrenia from adolescence to adulthood. *European Child and Adolescent Psychiatry, 14*(2), 83–94.

Homberg, J. R., Schiepers, O. J. G., Schoffelmeer, A. N. M., Cuppen, E., & Vanderschuren, L. J. M. J. (2007). Acute and constitutive increases in central serotonin levels reduce social play behaviour in peri-adolescent rats. *Psychopharmacology, 195*(2), 175–182.

Jones, P., Rodgers, B., Murray, R., & Marmot, M. (1994). Child development risk factors for adult schizophrenia in the British 1946 birth cohort. *Lancet, 344* (8934), 1398–1402.

Jordan, R. (2003). Social play and autistic spectrum disorders: A perspective on theory, implications and educational approaches. *Autism, 7*(4), 347–360.

Kelley, A. E. (2004). Ventral striatal control of appetitive motivation: Role in ingestive behavior and reward-related learning. *Neuroscience & Biobehavioral Reviews, 27*(8), 765–776.

Kendall, D. A., & Yudowski, G. A. (2016). Cannabinoid receptors in the central nervous system: Their signaling and roles in disease. *Frontiers in Cellular Neuroscience, 10*, 294.

Kiser, D., Steemers, B., Branchi, I., & Homberg, J. R. (2012). The reciprocal interaction between serotonin and social behaviour. *Neuroscience & Biobehavioral Reviews, 36*(2), 786–798.

Knutson, B., Panksepp, J., & Pruitt, D. (1996). Effects of fluoxetine on play dominance in juvenile rats. *Aggressive Behavior, 22*, 297–307.

Le Merrer, J., Becker, J. A., Befort, K., & Kieffer, B. L. (2009). Reward processing by the opioid system in the brain. *Physiological Reviews, 89*(4), 1379–1412.

Lesscher, H. M. B., Spoelder, M., Rotte, M. D., Janssen, M. J., Hesseling, P., Lozeman-van't Klooster, J. G., Baars, A.M., & Vanderschuren, L. J. M. J. (2015). Early social isolation augments alcohol consumption in rats. *Behavioral Pharmacology, 26*(7), 673–680.

Leussis, M. P., Lawson, K., Stone, K., & Andersen, S. L. (2008). The enduring effects of an adolescent social stressor on synaptic density, part II: Poststress reversal of synaptic loss in the cortex by adinazolam and MK-801. *Synapse, 62*(3), 185–192.

Loureiro, M., Renard, J., Zunder, J., & Laviolette, S. R. (2015). Hippocampal cannabinoid transmission modulates dopamine neuron activity: Impact on rewarding memory formation and social interaction. *Neuropsychopharmacology, 40*(6), 1436–1447.

Lukkes, J. L., Mokin, M. V., Scholl, J. L., & Forster, G. L. (2009). Adult rats exposed to early-life social isolation exhibit increased anxiety and conditioned fear behavior, and altered hormonal stress responses. *Hormonal Behavior*, *55*(1), 248–256.

Madden, A. M., & Zup, S. L. (2014). Effects of developmental hyperserotonemia on juvenile play behavior, oxytocin and serotonin receptor expression in the hypothalamus are age and sex dependent. *Physiology & Behavior*, *128*, 260–269.

Manduca, A., Lassalle, O., Sepers, M., Campolongo, P., Cuomo, V., Marsicano, G., Kieffer, B., Vanderschuren, L. J. M. J., Trezza, V., & Manzoni, O. J. J. (2016a). Interacting cannabinoid and opioid receptors in the nucleus accumbens core control adolescent social play. *Frontiers in Behavioral Neuroscience*, *10*, 211.

Manduca, A., Servadio, M., Damsteegt, R., Campolongo, P., Vanderschuren, L. J. M. J., & Trezza, V. (2016b). Dopaminergic neurotransmission in the nucleus accumbens modulates social play behavior in rats. *Neuropsychopharmacology*, *41*(9), 2215–2223.

Marco, E. M., Rapino, C., Caprioli, A., Borsini, F., Maccarrone, M., & Laviola, G. (2011). Social encounter with a novel partner in adolescent rats: Activation of the central endocannabinoid system. *Behavior and Brain Research*, *220*(1), 140–145.

Mechoulam, R., Hanus, L. O., Pertwee, R., & Howlett, A. C. (2014). Early phytocannabinoid chemistry to endocannabinoids and beyond. *Nature Reviews Neuroscience*, *15*(11), 757–764.

Meyer-Lindenberg, A., Domes, G., Kirsch, P., & Heinrichs, M. (2011). Oxytocin and vasopressin in the human brain: Social neuropeptides for translational medicine. *Nature Reviews Neuroscience*, *12*(9), 524–538.

Møller, P., & Husby, R. (2000). The initial prodrome in schizophrenia: Searching for naturalistic core dimensions of experience and behavior. *Schizophrenia Bulletin*, *26*(1), 217–232.

Niesink, R. J., & Van Ree, J. M. (1989). Involvement of opioid and dopaminergic systems in isolation-induced pinning and social grooming of young rats. *Neuropharmacology*, *28*(4), 411–418.

Normansell, L., & Panksepp, J. (1985a). Effects of clonidine and yohimbine on the social play of juvenile rats. *Pharmacology Biochemistry and Behavior*, *22*(5), 881–883.

Normansell, L., & ,Panksepp, J. (1985b). Effects of quipazine and methysergide on play in juvenile rats. *Pharmacology Biochemistry and Behavior*, *22*(5), 885–887.

Normansell, L., & Panksepp, J. (1990). Effects of morphine and naloxone on play-rewarded spatial discrimination in juvenile rats. *Developmental Psychobiology*, *23*(1), 75–83.

Olivier, J. D., Valles, A., van Heesch, F., Afrasiab-Middelman, A., Roelofs, J. J., Jonkers, M., … & Homberg, J. R. (2011). Fluoxetine administration to pregnant rats increases anxiety-related behavior in the offspring. *Psychopharmacology (Berl)*, *217*(3), 419–432.

O'Shea, M., McGregor, I. S., & Mallet, P. E. (2006). Repeated cannabinoid exposure during perinatal, adolescent or early adult ages produces similar longlasting deficits in object recognition and reduced social interaction in rats. *Journal of Psychopharmacology*, *20*(5), 611–621.

Panksepp, J., Siviy, S., & Normansell, L. (1984). The psychobiology of play: Theoretical and methodological perspectives. *Neuroscience & Biobehavioral Reviews*, *8*(4), 465–492.

Pava, M. J., & Woodward, J. J. (2012). A review of the interactions between alcohol and the endocannabinoid system: Implications for alcohol dependence and future directions for research. *Alcohol*, *46*(3), 185–204.

Pellis, S. M. (1988). Agonistic versus amicable targets of attack and defense: Consequences for the origin, function and descriptive classification of play-fighting. *Aggressive Behavior*, *14*, 85–104.

Pellis, S. M., & Pellis, V. (2009). *The playful brain: Venturing to the limits of neuroscience*. Oxford: Oneworld Publications.

Pellis, S. M., & Pellis, V. C. (1987). Play-fighting differs from serious fighting in both target of attack and tactics of fighting in the laboratory rat *Rattus norvegicus*. *Aggressive Behavior*, *13*, 227–242.

Robbins, T. W., & Arnsten, A. F. (2009). The neuropsychopharmacology of fronto-executive function: Monoaminergic modulation. *Annual Review of Neuroscience*, *32*, 267–287.

Robbins, T. W., & Everitt, B. J. (2007). A role for mesencephalic dopamine in activation: Commentary on Berridge (2006). *Psychopharmacology (Berlin)*, *191*(3), 433–437.

Roozendaal, B., & McGaugh, J. L. (2011). Memory modulation. *Behavioral Neuroscience*, *125*(6), 797–824.

Salamone, J. D., & Correa, M. (2012). The mysterious motivational functions of mesolimbic dopamine. *Neuron*, *76*(3), 470–485.

Schneider, M., & Koch, M. (2005). Deficient social and play behavior in juvenile and adult rats after neonatal cortical lesion: Effects of chronic pubertal cannabinoid treatment. *Neuropsychopharmacology*, *30*(5), 944–957.

Schneider, M., Schomig, E., & Leweke, F. M. (2008). Acute and chronic cannabinoid treatment differentially affects recognition memory and social behavior in pubertal and adult rats. *Addiction Biology*, *13*(3–4), 345–357.

Siviy, S. M. (2016). A brain motivated to play: Insights into the neurobiology of playfulness. *Behaviour*, *153*, 819–844.

Siviy, S. M., & Baliko, C. N. (2000). A further characterization of alpha-2 adrenoceptor involvement in the rough-and-tumble play of juvenile rats. *Developmental Psychobiology*, *37*(1), 25–34.

Siviy, S. M., Fleischhauer, A. E., Kerrigan, L. A., & Kuhlman, S. J. (1996). D2 dopamine receptor involvement in the rough-and-tumble play behavior of juvenile rats. *Behavioral Neuroscience*, *110*(5), 1168–1176.

Siviy, S. M., Fleischhauer, A. E., Kuhlman, S. J., & Atrens, D. M. (1994). Effects of alpha-2 adrenoceptor antagonists on rough-and-tumble play in juvenile rats: Evidence for a site of action independent of non-adrenoceptor imidazoline binding sites. *Psychopharmacology (Berl)*, *113*(3–4), 493–499.

Siviy, S. M., Line, B. S., & Darcy, E. A. (1995). Effects of MK-801 on rough-and-tumble play in juvenile rats. *Physiology and Behavior*, *57*(5), 843–847.

Siviy, S. M., & Panksepp, J. (2011). In search of the neurobiological substrates for social playfulness in mammalian brains. *Neuroscience & Biobehavioral Reviews, 35*(9), 1821–1830.

Spinka, M., Newberry, R. C., & Bekoff, M. (2001). Mammalian play: Training for the unexpected. *Quarterly Review of Biology, 76*(2), 141–168.

Stoesz, B. M., Hare, J. F., & Snow, W. M. (2013). Neurophysiological mechanisms underlying affiliative social behavior: Insights from comparative research. *Neuroscience & Biobehavioral Reviews, 37*(2), 123–132.

Tallett, A. J., Blundell, J. E., & Rodgers, R. J. (2007). Grooming, scratching and feeding: Role of response competition in acute anorectic response to rimonabant in male rats. *Psychopharmacology (Berlin), 195*(1), 27–39.

Thiel, K. J., Sanabria, F., & Neisewander, J. L. (2009). Synergistic interaction between nicotine and social rewards in adolescent male rats. *Psychopharmacology (Berlin), 204*(3), 391–402.

Trezza, V., Baarendse, P. J. J., & Vanderschuren, L. J. M. J. (2009). Prosocial effects of nicotine and ethanol in adolescent rats through partially dissociable neurobehavioral mechanisms. *Neuropsychopharmacology, 34*(12), 2560–2573.

Trezza, V., Baarendse, P. J. J., & Vanderschuren, L. J. M. J. (2010). The pleasures of play: Pharmacological insights into social reward mechanisms. *Trends in Pharmacological Science, 31*(10), 463–469.

Trezza, V., Campolongo, P., & Vanderschuren, L. J. M. J. (2011a). Evaluating the rewarding nature of social interactions in laboratory animals. *Developmental Cognitive Neuroscience, 1*(4), 444–458.

Trezza, V., Damsteegt, R., Achterberg, E. J. M., & Vanderschuren, L. J. M. J. (2011b). Nucleus accumbens mu-opioid receptors mediate social reward. *Journal of Neuroscience, 31*(17), 6362–6370.

Trezza, V., Damsteegt, R., Manduca, A., Petrosino, S., Van Kerkhof, L. W. M., Pasterkamp, R. J., Zhou, Y., Campolongo, P., Cuomo, V., Di Marzo, V., & Vanderschuren, L. J. M. J. (2012). Endocannabinoids in amygdala and nucleus accumbens mediate social play reward in adolescent rats. *Journal of Neuroscience, 32*(43), 14899–14908.

Trezza, V., & Vanderschuren, L. J. M. J. (2008a). Bidirectional cannabinoid modulation of social behavior in adolescent rats. *Psychopharmacology (Berlin), 197*(2), 217–227.

Trezza, V., & Vanderschuren, L. J. M. J. (2008b). Cannabinoid and opioid modulation of social play behavior in adolescent rats: Differential behavioral mechanisms. *European Neuropsychopharmacology, 18*(7), 519–530.

Trezza, V., & Vanderschuren, L. J. M. J. (2009). Divergent effects of anandamide transporter inhibitors with different target selectivity on social play behavior in adolescent rats. *Journal of Pharmacology and Experimental Therapeutics, 328*(1), 343–350.

van Ree, J. M., Gerrits, M. A. F. M., & Vanderschuren, L. J. M. J. (1999). Opioids, reward and addiction: An encounter of biology, psychology, and medicine. *Pharmacological Review, 51*(2), 341–396.

van Ree, J. M., Niesink, R. J. M., & Nir, I. (1984). Delta 1-tetrahydrocannabinol but not cannabidiol reduces contact and aggressive behavior of rats tested in dyadic encounters. *Psychopharmacology (Berlin), 84*(4), 561–565.

Vanderschuren, L. J. M. J., Achterberg, E. J. M., & Trezza, V. (2016). The neurobiology of social play and its rewarding value in rats. *Neuroscience & Biobehavioral Reviews, 70*, 86–105.

Vanderschuren, L. J. M. J., Niesink, R. J. M., Spruijt, B. M., & Van Ree, J. M. (1995a). Effects of morphine on different aspects of social play in juvenile rats. *Psychopharmacology, 117*(2), 225–231.

Vanderschuren, L. J. M. J., Niesink, R. J. M., Spruijt, B. M., & Van Ree, J. M. (1995b). Mu- and kappa-opioid receptor-mediated opioid effects on social play in juvenile rats. *European Journal of Pharmacology, 276*(3), 257–266.

Vanderschuren, L. J. M. J., Niesink, R. J. M., & Van Ree, J. M. (1997). The neurobiology of social play behavior in rats. *Neuroscience & Biobehavioral Reviews, 21*(3), 309–326.

Vanderschuren, L. J. M. J., Spruijt, B. M., Hol, T., Niesink, R. J. M., & Van Ree, J. M. (1995c). Sequential analysis of social play behavior in juvenile rats: Effects of morphine. *Behavioural Brain Research, 72*(1–2), 89–95.

Vanderschuren, L. J. M. J., & Trezza, V. (2014). What the laboratory rat has taught us about social play behavior: Role in behavioral development and neural mechanisms. *Current Topics in Behavioral Neuroscience, 16*, 189–212.

Vanderschuren, L. J. M. J., Trezza, V., Griffioen-Roose, S., Schiepers, O. J. G., Van Leeuwen, N., De Vries, T. J., & Schoffelmeer, A. N. M. (2008). Methylphenidate disrupts social play behavior in adolescent rats. *Neuropsychopharmacology, 33*(12), 2946–2956.

Varlinskaya, E. I., & Spear, L. P. (2002). Acute effects of ethanol on social behavior of adolescent and adult rats: Role of familiarity of the test situation. *Alcohol Clin Exp Res, 26*(10), 1502–1511.

Varlinskaya, E. I., & Spear, L. P. (2006). Differences in the social consequences of ethanol emerge during the course of adolescence in rats: Social facilitation, social inhibition, and anxiolysis. *Developmental Psychobiology, 48*(2), 146–161.

Varlinskaya, E. I., & Spear, L. P. (2009). Ethanol-induced social facilitation in adolescent rats: Role of endogenous activity at mu opioid receptors. *Alcoholism: Clinical and Experimental Research, 33*(6), 991–1000.

Varlinskaya, E. I., Spear, L. P., & Spear, N. E. (2001). Acute effects of ethanol on behavior of adolescent rats: Role of social context. *Alcoholism: Clinical and Experimental Research, 25*(3), 377–385.

Veenema, A. H., Bredewold, R., & De Vries, G. J. (2013). Sex-specific modulation of juvenile social play by vasopressin. *Psychoneuroendocrinology, 38*(11), 2554–2561.

Ventura, R., Alcaro, A., & Puglisi-Allegra, S. (2005). Prefrontal cortical norepinephrine release is critical for morphine-induced reward, reinstatement and dopamine release in the nucleus accumbens. *Cerebral Cortex, 15*(12), 1877–1886.

Viveros, M. P., Marco, E. M., Llorente, R., & Lopez-Gallardo, M. (2007). Endocannabinoid system and synaptic plasticity: Implications for emotional responses. *Neural Plasticity, 2007*, 52908.

Whitaker, L. R., Degoulet, M., & Morikawa, H. (2013). Social deprivation enhances VTA synaptic plasticity and drug-induced contextual learning. *Neuron, 77*(2), 335–345.

Wilson, L. I., Bierley, R. A., & Beatty, W. W. (1986). Cholinergic agonists suppress play fighting in juvenile rats. *Pharmacology Biochemistry and Behavior*, *24*(5), 1157–1159.

Wright, I. K., Upton, N., & Marsden, C. A. (1991). Resocialisation of isolation-reared rats does not alter their anxiogenic profile on the elevated X-maze model of anxiety. *Physiology and Behavior*, *50*(6), 1129–1132.

Zanettini, C., Panlilio, L. V., Alicki, M., Goldberg, S. R., Haller, J., & Yasar, S. (2011). Effects of endocannabinoid system modulation on cognitive and emotional behavior. *Frontiers in Behavioral Neuroscience*, *5*, 57.

4 Fun, Fur, and Future Fitness

The Evolution of Play in Mammals

Lynda L. Sharpe

Play behaviour is one of the greatest mysteries in the field of animal behaviour. Despite more than four decades of research, the reason why animals indulge in play remains unknown. No other behaviour has laboured under so much misinformation – churned out endlessly by the popular media – or has engendered so much scientific speculation. Yet, although we do not know why play evolved or what evolutionary benefits it confers, the play of young mammals remains one of the most appealing sights of nature.

Play is found in all mammalian orders and appears to be ubiquitous in carnivores, primates, pinnepeds (i.e., seals, sea lions), and ungulates (i.e., antelope, deer, sheep, cattle) (Fagen, 1981; Smith, 1982). Within some orders, such as rodents, the amount that individuals play varies greatly between species. For example, the laboratory rat (*Rattus norvegicus*) is one of the most playful species known, but social play has been regarded as virtually non-existent in the laboratory mouse (*Mus musculus*) (Poole & Fish, 1975; see also Chapter 2). Attempts to ascertain why some mammals play while others do not have met with limited success. Although relative brain size is positively correlated with playfulness when broad taxonomic groups are compared, this relationship disappears at the species level (Byers, 1999; Iwaniuk et al., 2001). Degree of sociality also does not appear to explain how much a species plays (Biben, 1983; Pellis & Iwaniuk, 1999b) and neither does phylogeny (sharing common ancestors) (Pellis & Iwaniuk, 1999b, 2000a). However, play does appear to be associated with a protracted juvenile period, during which parents or other group members shield youngsters from hunger, predators, and aggression (Fagen, 1993; Pellis & Iwaniuk, 2000b).

Why young mammals engage in the apparently purposeless activity of play is a question that has long intrigued scientists (e.g., Groos, 1898). An obvious answer is that play is fun. Rats will work for the opportunity to play-wrestle with their peers (Humphreys & Einon, 1981), and chimpanzees (*Pan troglodytes*) value play as much as their favourite foods (Mason et al., 1963). Recent research has revealed that play is associated with the release of opioids in the brain (Trezza et al., 2010; Vanderschuren, 2010; and Chapter 3), making it inherently rewarding and pleasurable. But pleasure – from an evolutionary perspective – is simply a means to an end (a proximate cause). Just as the body uses pain to prevent animals from pursuing harmful activities, so it uses pleasure to promote behaviours (like mating or eating) that help an animal survive and reproduce. What we do not know is how play improves a player's chances of passing on its genes (play's ultimate, evolutionary cause).

In wild populations, natural selection winnows out any behaviour that is more costly than beneficial. For example, a youngster who squanders energy on play instead of accruing fat to survive the winter will almost certainly leave fewer offspring than a non-player, and thus the genes for play will be whittled gradually from the population. For play to persist in so many mammal species, it must provide players with a tangible benefit, or else not actually be costly.

Although play takes up only a small proportion of a young mammal's waking time (1%–10%) and this translates into a modest energetic investment (1%–9% of daily energy expenditure) (Martin & Caro, 1985), such costs may not be trivial from a selective viewpoint (Bekoff & Byers, 1992; Miller & Byers, 1991). For instance, Assamese macaques (*Macaca assamensis*) appear to suffer a sizable developmental cost from undertaking locomotor play (running, climbing, jumping): during periods of moderate food scarcity, the rate at which infants grow is strongly negatively correlated with how much they play, and play is responsible for up to 50% of observed variation in growth (Berghanel et al., 2015). Similarly, pronghorn antelope fawns (*Antilocapra americana*) – although devoting only 2% of their energy budget to play – would be 7% bigger at weaning if they had used this energy for growth (Miller & Byers, 1991). Even small differences in growth can have serious consequences later in life. In wild meerkats (*Suricata suricatta*), large juveniles are more likely to breed as adults (Clutton-Brock et al., 2001), and so play – which is carefully tailored to nutritional state in this species (Sharpe et al., 2002) – must provide considerable adaptive advantages to offset these potential costs.

Energy expenditure is not the only cost of play. Playing individuals often suffer an increased risk of injury or death from mishaps, such as falls, becoming trapped in mud, impaled on cacti, washed out to sea, or separated from their mothers (Fagen, 1981). Research on wild chimpanzees has found that social play is largely responsible for spreading lethal respiratory infections between youngsters (Kuehl et al., 2008). Playing animals are also more prone to predation because they are less vigilant and more conspicuous to predators (Caro, 1988). For example, although South American fur seal pups (*Arctocephalus australis*) devote only 6% of their day to play, 85% of pups seen captured by sea lions were playing at the time (Harcourt, 1991). Play can also have indirect survivorship costs: play in cheetah cubs (*Acinonyx jubatus*) reduces the hunting success of their mother (by alerting prey), causing 9% of failed hunts (Caro, 1987).

So if play is costly, it must provide players with measurable benefits or it would cease to exist. Several studies have indeed found a link between play and an individual's ability to survive and reproduce (i.e., its fitness). In wild horses (*Equus caballus*), foals that devoted more time to play are more likely to survive beyond 12 months of age and are in better condition as yearlings (Cameron et al., 2008). A study of Belding's ground squirrels (*Urocitellus beldingi*) found that females that successfully reared a litter during their first breeding season played more during infancy than unsuccessful breeders (Nunes, 2014). The strongest evidence that play increases an individual's fitness comes from a study of wild American brown bears (*Ursus arctos*) that found a positive correlation between how much a cub played during its first summer and its subsequent likelihood of surviving to independence, even after the effects of body mass, mother's condition, litter size, and food availability were controlled (Fagen & Fagen, 2009).

However, it is still unclear *how* play helps young mammals. Play researchers have come up with more than two dozen possible benefits of play (Martin & Caro, 1985), but it is difficult to effectively test these hypotheses because preventing an animal from playing almost always interferes with other aspects of its life (thereby confounding the results). Additionally, play may serve different functions in different species. Given its widespread distribution, play probably originated in the earliest mammals, at least 70 million years ago (Byers, 1984). Since then, diverse selection pressures have been operating on different groups of mammals. Just as the mammalian forelimb has evolved to serve specialized functions in particular taxa (e.g., seals' flippers, bats' wings, moles' shovel-like paws, human's dextrous hands), so play is likely to have been coopted for unique purposes in some groups. There is growing evidence, for example, that social play in laboratory rats serves a developmental role, modifying neural connections within the brain's prefrontal cortex and thereby enhancing cognitive function (Pellis et al., 2014). Yet this benefit of play appears to be unique to rats and is not found in other rodent species (Pellis et al., 2014).

Even though play probably has specialized functions in certain taxa, the fundamental characteristics of mammalian play are so prevalent and widespread (i.e., most frequent in juveniles, comprised of balance-effecting movements and behaviours derived from high-arousal activities, most frequent between closely matched play-partners) that play is very likely to function in a similar way in most extant mammal species (Spinka et al., 2001). The remainder of this chapter examines some of the ways in which play may increase an individual's evolutionary fitness and evaluates the empirical evidence for and against each of these hypotheses of function.

Motor Skills

This hypothesis asserts that play helps young mammals acquire the basic motor skills (e.g., jumping, running, climbing, dodging) that they need to survive the hazards of the juvenile period. Only three studies have attempted to test the hypothesis. Chalmers and Locke-Haydon (1984) found little evidence that play influenced motor skills in common marmosets (*Callithrix jacchus*), although the amount of social play undertaken by infants aged 11–13 weeks was positively correlated with their ability to negotiate an obstacle at 14 weeks. In Belding's ground squirrels, juveniles that played with several partners (rather than few) were more efficient at balancing on an elevated rod, and those that played more frequently and with more male partners showed the greatest improvement over time (Nunes et al., 2004). The most convincing support for this hypothesis comes from a study of wild Assamese macaques (Berghänel et al., 2015). Infants that spent more time in vigorous rough-and-tumble play displayed certain climbing, running, and leaping skills (components of play) at a younger age than infants that played less. The researchers controlled for the confounding effect of body condition and showed that the early acquisition of skills was related to play undertaken *prior* to the skill's appearance but not to that after, suggesting that play was influencing the skill, not vice versa. Unfortunately, none of these studies can discount the possibility that a third variable (such as the individual's level of health) influenced both play and motor ability.

One of the ways in which play could enhance a youngster's motor ability is by altering those parts of the brain that influence movement, such as the cerebellum (Byers, 1998; Byers & Walker, 1995). Physical activity in infants is known to modify the interconnectedness of neurons (i.e., synapses) in the cerebellum and there is a rough correlation between the age at which play peaks – in domestic cats (*Felis catus*) and laboratory rats and mice – and the final stage of synapse formation (Byers & Walker, 1995). However, at least 80% of synapses in the cerebellum are fixed prior to the appearance of play (Byers & Walker, 1995) and play persists well beyond the 'sensitive period' in many mammals, suggesting that this is not a primary function of play. Play in infants could also help to ensure the development of appropriate muscle types (altering the ratio of slow to fast fibres within a muscle) (Byers, 1998; Byers & Walker, 1995). However, in vitro studies suggest that muscle fibre type is fixed prior to birth (Schafer et al., 1987) and – if postnatal changes are possible – they are determined by the muscle's nerves (Baldwin, 1984), which develop prior to the appearance of play.

Strength and Endurance

This hypothesis asserts that play increases a young mammal's chances of survival by providing exercise that increases its cardiovascular capacity, endurance, and skeletomuscular strength (Brownlee, 1954; Fagen, 1981; Gomendio, 1988; Hass & Jenni, 1993). For example, field-reared foals have stronger and more flexible tendons than stall-reared foals (Cherdchutham et al., 2001) and play is likely to contribute to this difference. Cameron et al.

(2008), studying wild horses, suggested that the increased survival enjoyed by foals that played more was a result of this improved motor function.

However, play is unlikely to be effective in this regard because the benefits of exercise training can be acquired only if a subject exercises until near-fatigue (Byers & Walker, 1995; Nieman, 1990). Such sustained bouts of exercise rarely, if ever, occur during play, with the average duration of play bouts being 5–20 seconds in numerous species (e.g., Symons 1978; Watson & Croft, 1993). Play bouts in laboratory rats, for example, generally last 5–8 seconds (Birke & Sadler, 1983), but exercise bouts of one hour are needed to produce an exercise training response in this species (Xia, 1990).

Another important characteristic of strength and endurance training is that its benefits are transitory, rapidly diminishing once exercise ceases (Byers & Walker, 1995; Nieman, 1990). It is possible that play occurs primarily in juvenile mammals because this age group is particularly prone to mortality and thus benefits most from maximizing their physical capacity. However, a study of wild meerkats found no evidence to support this. When meerkat pups first leave the natal burrow to begin accompanying their group, they often have to travel several kilometres a day, and getting left behind is a major source of mortality. Yet despite this strong selection pressure, the pups do not attempt to increase their endurance by undertaking more play (or favouring locomotor play) in the week prior to leaving the burrow; in fact, they play considerably less than older individuals that have no trouble in keeping up (Sharpe, 2005b).

Practice of Adult Skills

This very popular hypothesis (Caro, 1988; Fagen, 1981; Groos 1898; Smith, 1982) posits that play provides animals with an opportunity to safely practice and refine the motor skills they will need in adulthood, e.g., fighting (Byers, 1980; Watson & Croft, 1993), catching prey (Biben, 1982), avoiding predators (Gomendio, 1988; Hass & Jenni, 1993), or mating (Moore, 1985).

Although this hypothesis is espoused relentlessly by the popular media and was widely accepted in the 1980–1990s, it is one of the few that can be confidently rejected. Supportive evidence is limited solely to arguments regarding play's general characteristics. For example, in many mammal species, males engage in both more serious fighting and more play fighting (Meaney et al., 1985), and species differences in 'serious' adult behaviours are reflected in equivalent differences in their play (Caro, 1988). Additionally, the movements performed in play appear very similar to those used in real 'flight or fight' behaviours, suggesting that play is 'optimally designed' to practice these skills (Martin & Caro, 1985). However, detailed analyses of motor patterns have revealed that the resemblance between play and 'serious' behaviours is often only superficial. During play fighting in rats, for example, the targets of attack and defence differ from those used in real fighting (Pellis, 1988) and – since a motor skill can be practiced only if the *exact* same motor pattern is undertaken (Byers, 1998) – play fighting cannot assist in the refinement of fighting skills in this species.

Experimental studies have consistently demonstrated that play does not lead to an improvement in adult skills. Kittens reared without play (through social isolation, the wearing of goggles, or no access to toys) did not differ in their prey-catching ability from normal kittens or those reared in a toy-enriched environment (Caro, 1988). Davies and Kemble (1983) found no correlation between any measure of play and the subsequent predatory ability of northern grasshopper mice (*Onychomys leucogaster*), and neither did Vincent and Bekoff (1978), who undertook a similar study with young coyotes (*Canis latrans*). Chalmers and Locke-Haydon (1984) compared frequency of social play in common marmosets with their subsequent ability to perform many different skills. They concluded that "a major feature of our results is the absence of correlations". Sharpe (2005d) found that frequency of play fighting in wild meerkats was not related to their subsequent likelihood of winning play fights (or improvement in play fighting success) as would be expected if play improved fighting manoeuvres. Adult meerkats that won dominance by fighting had not played any more frequently, or been any better at winning play fights, than the littermates that they defeated in combat.

Reduction of Aggression

This hypothesis asserts that play serves to reduce aggression between play partners, thereby ameliorating social tension and promoting harmony between group members. For example, juvenile play in solitary predatory species could serve to lessen the antipathy that these animals feel for their own kind, allowing littermates to cohabit safely. Consistent with this, captive litters of polecats (*Mustela putorius*), domestic cats, and chuditch (western quoll of Australia, *Dasyurus geoffroii*) show a marked decline in play at the age at which litters normally disperse in the wild (Sharpe & Cherry, 2003).

There is, however, little sound evidence that play is able to reduce aggression. The frequency of play and agonism are unrelated in pairs of male red-necked wallabies (*Macropus rufogriseus*; Watson, 1993) and adult gray wolves (*Canis lupus*; Cordoni, 2009). Wild meerkats that play together frequently are just as aggressive toward one another as those that play rarely, regardless of whether they are pups squabbling over food (Sharpe & Cherry, 2003), subadults competing for status (Sharpe, 2005b), or dominant females evicting other group members (Sharpe, 2005c).

In contrast, in captive voles (*Microtus agrestis*), autumn-born males – which do not play – are aggressive toward one another at sexual maturity, while spring-born males – which play extensively – remain tolerant (Wilson, 1973).

In infant spotted hyenas (*Crocuta crocuta*) social play increases over time, concurrent with a fall in sibling aggression (Drea et al.,1996), and in both juvenile golden-mantled ground xsquirrels (*Spermophilus literalis*; Holmes, 1995) and adult ring-tailed lemurs (*Lemur catta*; Palagi, 2009), pairs that exhibit less agonism play together more frequently. In intensively farmed piglets (*Sus scrofa*), litters reared in larger pens tend to play more and – although just as aggressive as juveniles – show less food-related aggression later in life (Chaloupkova et al., 2007).

Unfortunately, even when a negative correlation between aggression and play is observed, it tells us little about the pacifying properties of play because aggression inhibits play in many species (e.g., Cordoni & Palagi, 2016; Symons, 1978; Thompson, 1998). In meerkat pups, for example, sharing a play bout has no effect on the subsequent likelihood of the pair fighting, but pups that have fought are 40% less likely to play together during the next 10 minutes than pups that met without aggression (Sharpe & Cherry, 2003).

One study of wild lemurs has found notable evidence to support the tenet that play reduces aggression. In Verreaux's sifaka (*Propithecus verreauxi*) encounters between groups are often aggressive, but adult males will engage in play with strange males that approach their group. Resident males play more frequently with the strangers than with one another, and rates of male aggression (between resident and stranger) are lower in the period after the first play bout than in the period before play was initiated (Antonacci et al., 2010). This suggests that play lessens enmity, but it is possible that the lemurs did not begin to play until initial hostilities had been overcome. It has been asserted that adult chimpanzees and bonobos (*Pan paniscus*) also use play to defray aggression during periods of social tension, but this is based only on the observation that a single captive group (of each species) played more frequently prior to feeding time (Palagi et al., 2004; Palagi et al., 2006). More convincingly, Pellis and Iwanuik (1999a) examined the prevalence of adult play in 35 species of primate and found that species in which the sexes rarely associated were more likely to indulge in play during courtship. They suggested that these adults were using play to defray hostility and/or to assess the quality of unfamiliar mates.

Social Bonding

There is no evidence to support the popular view that play strengthens social bonds, enhancing friendships, consolidating long-term alliances and coalitions, and promoting group cohesion and cooperation (Berman, 1982; Byers, 1984; Smith, 1982). Although social grooming does appear to enhance social ties (Schino, 2007), virtually all studies that have compared social grooming with social play (Antonacci et al., 2010; Palagi, 2009; Palagi et al., 2006; Sharpe, 2005c) have found no correspondence between the two behaviours, suggesting that they are functionally distinct. Adult wolves do not preferentially associate with their play partners or support them during conflict (Cordoni, 2009). Similarly, male red-necked wallabies do not favour play partners during affiliative interactions or spend more time resting in their company (Watson, 1993).

Although an individual's decision to remain within its group may be influenced by its involvement in non-agonistic social interactions (Blumstein et al., 2009), frequency of social play is unrelated to dispersal age in wild horses (Cameron et al., 2008) and meerkats (Sharpe, 2005c). Meerkats play no more frequently with their future dispersal partners than with age-matched individuals with whom they do not disperse (Sharpe, 2005a). Frequency of meerkat play, or number of partners, is not correlated with group size (as would be expected if meerkats in large groups need to bond with more individuals); preferred playmates are not favoured as grooming partners; and frequency of play is not related to a meerkat's cooperative contribution (Sharpe, 2005c).

Establishment or Reinforcement of Rank

This hypothesis posits that play allows individuals to establish or reinforce dominance relationships without aggression (Berman, 1982; Carpenter, 1934; Paquette, 1994), and it is lent some credence by the finding that the roles adopted during play fighting often reflect the players' dominance relationships (Bauer & Smuts, 2007; Biben, 1998; Cordoni, 2009; Essler et al., 2016; Humphreys & Smith, 1987; Myer & Weber, 1996; Pellis & Pellis, 1992; Sharpe, 2005d). A study of wild yellow-bellied marmots (*Marmota flaviventris*) found that the tendency for juvenile marmots to 'win' play interactions was correlated with their subsequent dominance rank as yearlings, even after controlling for body mass (Blumstein et al., 2013). This relationship did not persist into adulthood (when the marmots were no longer interacting with their previous play partners), suggesting that play helped them evaluate competitive ability, or contest rank, rather than enhanced their combat skills.

Although Paquette (1994) found some evidence that adolescent chimpanzees may use play to challenge dominance relationships, his study was restricted to four captive individuals whose play fights routinely escalated into real aggression. Symons (1978), by contrast, found that rank-reversals in free-ranging rhesus macaques (*Macaca mulatta*) did not derive from play, and only individuals not actively competing for status engaged in play. He argues convincingly that play fights could not be used to establish rank and still remain playful, because individuals would have to react to play initiations as they would to a threat or challenge (i.e., with either submission or escalation).

Although it is possible that some species exploit play to contest rank, in most mammals play and periods of dominance competition do not overlap across development, with species either curtailing play at the onset of agonism or establishing dominance rank prior to the appearance of play (Smith, 1982). A number of studies have found that increased agonism inhibits play (e.g., Cordoni & Palagi, 2016), and taxa with strict, despotic hierarchies play less than closely related species with more relaxed, egalitarian social relationships (canids: Biben, 1983; chimpanzees: Palagi, 2006; macaques: Ciani et al., 2012; Reinhart et al., 2010; social mongooses: personal observation). Similarly, juvenile play is just as prevalent in species in which an individual's dominance rank is fixed by its mother's status as in species in which rank is mutable by contest (Smith, 1982).

Training for the Unexpected

This hypothesis asserts that play helps animals learn to cope (both physically and psychologically) with unexpected events involving a sudden loss of control (Spinka et al., 2001). Play is posited to increase the versatility of movements that an individual can use to recover from shocks during 'flight and fight' activities (e.g., falling while fleeing a predator, becoming disadvantaged during a serious fight) and increase its ability to cope emotionally with these stressful situations (see section 'Coping with Stress' later).

Although there are clear survival benefits in being able to recover efficiently from mishaps and avoid 'blind panic' in life-threatening situations, there is currently no evidence that play can produce these outcomes. The only possible exception is the finding that wild, juvenile Belding's ground squirrels that undertake social play at high rates (as compared with low) show greater improvement in their ability to handle being placed on a thin, cylindrical rod held 40 centimetres above the ground (Nunes et al., 2004).

If play serves as training for the unexpected, individuals should strive to maximize loss of control during play (Spinka et al., 2001). This could be achieved by favoring play partners that can 'beat' them or movements that impair their performance (e.g., running backward, frolicking on slippery surfaces) or maximize disorientation (e.g., head tossing, rolling, somersaulting). Such disorientating movements – that stimulate the vestibular system and impair balance – are fundamental to mammalian play (Barber, 1991). A systematic study of play in ungulates, for example, found that head shakes, head jerks, or neck twists are the most widely occurring play behaviour, after running (Byers, 1984). Humans also favour this type of sensory stimulation, as exemplified by our playground equipment; from swings, slides, and see-saws to round-a-bouts and roller coasters. The tendency for unfamiliar objects and unusual substrates (loose straw, ice, mud, shallow water, etc.) to stimulate play in many species (Spinka et al., 2001; Wood-Gush & Vestergaard, 1991) is also consistent with players attempting to maximize loss of control.

However, the prevalence of self-handicapping in play remains unclear. A study of play movements in five monkey species found that handicapping manoeuvres (which impair physical performance) were common, but self-handicapping during play-fighting (i.e., allowing the other partner to win) was rare (Petru et al., 2009). Although such self-handicapping is known to occur (e.g., Biben, 1998; Pereira & Preisser, 1998), it is usually limited to adult/offspring play (Biben, 1998). In some species, players go to considerable lengths to *avoid* 'losing control' during social play, preferentially initiating play with partners they can defeat and avoiding those that are likely to win (e.g., Biben, 1998; Byers, 1980; Humphreys & Smith, 1987). In domestic dogs, self-handicapping gestures are relatively rare and are performed more frequently by the disadvantaged player (smaller, younger, or lower ranking than its partner) (Bauer & Smuts, 2007), which is inconsistent with strong players attempting to gain experience of losing. The very marked preference that almost all taxa show for play partners that are closely matched in size and ability (e.g., Berger, 1980; Byers, 1980; Nunes et al., 2004; Sharpe, 2005b; Thompson, 1996; Watson, 1993) suggests that individuals are trying to maximize their chances of winning rather than to lose control. In fact, it has been proposed that the psychological empowerment generated by winning is an important benefit of play (Biben, 1998), and a study of children found that repeated losing in play can have negative social and psychological consequences (Sutton-Smith & Kelly-Byrne, 1984).

Coping with Stress

This hypothesis asserts that play helps animals to cope more effectively with anxiety and stress. There are two ways in which this may occur. First, play may be used as a form of 'self-medication' during periods of stress, making the player more relaxed and thereby enhancing its overall health and well-being (Lewis, 1982; Pellis & Pellis 2009). The self-medication hypothesis has received little scientific attention, even though it is well established that unremitting stress severely curtails an individual's ability to fight off disease (Apanius, 1998) and impairs the cognitive and motor skills of laboratory rats (Pellis et al., 2010). Play is associated with the release of opioids in the brain, creating pleasure (Vanderschuren, 2010; and Chapter 3) and an experimental study of squirrel monkeys (*Saimiri sciureus*) found a linear negative relationship between frequency of play and the level of cortisol (stress hormone) in the blood, consistent with the assertion that play reduces stress (Biben & Champoux, 1999). Similarly, play is associated with lowered cortisol levels in older hospitalized children (Potasz et al., 2013). However, although mild levels of tension or excitement are known to stimulate play (e.g., Antonacci et al., 2010; Dudink et al., 2006; Palagi et al., 2004; Pellis, 1991), individuals suffering severe stress (and presumably in greatest need of 'medication') do not partake in play (Biben, 1998; Fagen, 1981).

The second way in which play may help a young animal cope with stress is by modifying the way its brain responds to stress, thereby allowing it to fine-tune its own stress response (Spinka et al., 2001). One of the ubiquitous features of mammalian play is that it is comprised of behavioural elements derived from a species' most critical, high-arousal 'flight or fight' activities (fleeing predators, fighting, hunting, or mating; Fagen, 1981). Behaviours derived from low-arousal activities are conspicuous by their absence. For example, although digging skills are critical to meerkat survival (for foraging and the excavation of sleeping burrows and hundreds of predator-escape 'bolt holes'), digging is never incorporated into meerkat play. The link between arousal and play is further underscored by the finding that mild excitement, such as that generated by novel objects, substrates, or partners, or the anticipation of food, increases play (Dudink et al., 2006; Palagi et al., 2004; Wood-Gush & Vestergaard,1991). A range of different neurochemical systems are activated during play, including the monoamines (dopamine, norepinephrine, and serotonin), which also serve to coordinate an animal's response to stress (Siviy, 1998; and Chapter 3). The global activation of this system during play will almost certainly alter the brain's sensitivity to these neurochemicals (e.g., Antelman et al., 1992), thereby potentially improving a young animal's ability to handle psychological stressors (Siviy, 1998) by 'damping down' its emotional reaction to future stressful events and/or allowing it to recover more quickly after a scare.

Consistent with these predictions is the finding that rats isolated during the period when play is most frequent are unable to deal appropriately with social stressors (Baarendse et al., 2013; Potegal & Einon, 1989), have higher levels of stress hormone than normal rats (von Frijtag et al., 2002), and show greater anxiety when placed in unfamiliar environments (Arakawa, 2003). However, these differences are eliminated when isolated rats are given one hour of play experience daily (Potegal & Einon, 1989). Nevertheless, a study of laboratory mice found the opposite effect: mice that played more as juveniles appeared to be more anxious than less playful juveniles when they were placed in stressful situations in adolescence and adulthood (Richter et al., 2016). Given that there appears to be a positive relationship between childhood play experience and the ability to cope with stressful life experiences in humans (Brown, 1998; Saunders et al., 1999), this hypothesis of play's function definitely warrants further study.

Future Research

There are a number of plausible hypotheses that have not been addressed in this overview (see Barber, 1991; Bateson, 2014; Biben, 1998; Pellis et al., 2014; Thompson, 1998), yet it is clear that we do not have compelling evidence to support any of the hypotheses advanced to explain play's function. This failure to identify an overarching adaptive benefit of play is often attributed to play's multifunctionality, but this cannot explain why we have not demonstrated unequivocally the function of play in any species (with the possible exception of the laboratory rat; Pellis & Pellis, 2009). There is a huge need for rigorous, hypothesis-testing studies of play. Although observational studies, which test for correlations between play and potential benefits, are of restricted value (because they cannot not establish causality), their usefulness can be greatly enhanced by quantifying potential confounding factors (such as food availability, body weight, indicators of health, group size, or composition) and controlling for them statistically. Research also needs to target hypotheses that offer individuals a very strong selective advantage (e.g., improved fighting skills in a species where reproduction is secured through combat) because then a lack of correlation provides strong evidence that play is incapable of providing such outcomes.

Unfortunately, conclusive evidence of play's adaptive benefits is obtainable only by manipulating how much individuals play. Yet, with ingenuity, such experiments can be conducted effectively both in captivity and in the wild. For example, play can be stimulated by the provision of supplementary food (Sharpe et al., 2002), toys, or novel substrates (e.g., shallow water, mud wallows) or by prolonging excited anticipation (Dudink et al., 2006). Alternatively, play can be curtailed by limiting the availability of preferred playmates, exacerbating within-group aggression during play periods (e.g., by promoting competition over food) or by introducing predator cues (a tuft of cat fur inhibits play in rats for several days; Bateson, 2014). A comprehensive list of possible methods is provided by Ahloy Dallaire (2015). Only through the use of rigorous, thoughtfully designed manipulation experiments can we hope to reveal the evolutionary benefits conferred by play.

References

Ahloy Dallaire, J. (2015). Investigating the functions of rough-and-tumble play in American mink, *Neovison vison*. PhD dissertation, University of Guelph.

Antelman, S. M., Kocan, D., Knopf, S., Edwards, D. J., & Caggiula, A. R. (1992). One brief exposure to a psychological stressor induces long-lasting time-dependent sensitization of both the cataleptic and neurochemical response to haloperidol. *Life Sciences, 51,* 261–266.

Antonacci, D., Norscia, I., & Palagi, E. (2010). Stranger to familiar: Wild strepsirhines manage xenophobia by playing. *PLoS ONE, 5,* e13218.

Apanius, V. (1998). Stress and immune defense. In A. P. Moller, M. Milinski, & P. J. B. Slater (Eds.), *Advances in the study of behavior*, vol. 27: *Stress and behavior* (pp. 133–153). San Diego, CA: Academic Press.

Arakawa, H. (2003). The effects of isolation rearing on open-field behavior in male rats depends on developmental stages. *Developmental Psychobiology*, *43*, 11–19.

Arnold, W., & Trillmich, F. (1985). Time budget in Galapagos fur seal pups: The influence of mother's presence and absence on pup activity and play. *Behaviour*, *92*, 302–321.

Baarendse, P. J., Counotte, D. S., O'Donnell, P., & Vanderschuren, L. J. (2013). Early social experience is critical for the development of cognitive control and dopamine modulation of prefrontal cortex function. *Neuropsychopharmacology*, *38*(8), 1485–1494.

Baldwin, K. M. (1984). Muscle development: Neonatal to adult. *Exercise Sports Science Review*, *12*, 1–20.

Barber, N. (1991). Play and energy regulation in mammals. *Quarterly Review of Biology*, *66*, 129–147.

Bateson, P. (2014). Play, playfulness, creativity and innovation. *Animal Behavior and Cognition*, *1*, 99–112.

Bauer, E. B., & Smuts, B. B. (2007). Cooperation and competition during dyadic play in domestic dogs, *Canis familiaris*. *Animal Behaviour*, *73*, 489–499.

Bekoff, M., & Byers, J. A. (1992). Time, energy and play. *Animal Behaviour*, *44*, 981–982.

Berger, J. (1980). The ecology, structure and function of social play in Bighorn sheep (*Ovis canadensis*). *Journal of Zoology*, *192*, 531–542.

Berghänel, A., Schülke, O., & Ostner, J. (2015). Locomotor play drives motor skill acquisition at the expense of growth: A life history trade-off. *Science Advances*, *1*(7), e1500451.

Berman, C. M. (1982). Functions of play: First steps toward evolutionary explanation. *Behavioral and Brain Sciences*, *5*, 157–158.

Biben, M. (1982). Object play and social treatment of prey in bush dogs and crab-eating foxes. *Behaviour*, *79*, 201–211.

Biben, M. (1983). Comparative ontogeny of social behaviour in three South American canids, the maned wolf, crab-eating fox and bush dog: Implications for sociality. *Animal Behaviour*, *31*, 814–826.

Biben, M. (1998). Squirrel monkey playfighting: Making the case for cognitive training function for play. In M. Bekoff & J. A. Byers (Eds.), *Animal play: Evolutionary, comparative, and ecological perspectives* (pp. 161–182). Cambridge: Cambridge University Press.

Biben, M., & Champoux, M. (1999). Play and stress: Cortisol as a negative correlate of play in *Saimiri*. In S. Reifel (Ed.), *Play and culture studies* (vol. 2, pp. 191–208). Stamford, CT: Ablex.

Birke, L. I. A., & Sadler, D. (1983). Progestin-induced changes in play behavior of the prepubertal rat. *Physiology and Behavior*, *33*, 217–219.

Blumstein, D. T., Chung, L. K., & Smith, J. E. (2013). Early play may predict later dominance relationships in yellow-bellied marmots (*Marmota flaviventris*). *Proceedings of Royal Society, B*, *280*, 20130485.

Blumstein, D. T., Wey, T. W., & Tang, K. (2009). A test of the social cohesion hypothesis: Interactive female marmots remain at home. *Proceedings of Royal Society, B*, *276*, 3007–3012.

Brown, S. (1998). Play as an organizing principle: Clinical evidence and personal observations. In M. Bekoff & J. A. Byers (Eds.), *Animal play: Evolutionary, comparative, and ecological perspectives* (pp. 243–259). Cambridge: Cambridge University Press.

Brownlee, A. (1954). Play in domestic cattle: An analysis of its nature. *British Veterinary Journal, 110*, 48–68.

Byers, J. A. (1980). Play partner preferences in Siberian ibex, *Capra ibex sibirica*. *Zeitschrift für Tierpsychologie, 53*, 23–40.

Byers, J. A. (1984). Play in ungulates. In P. K. Smith (Ed.), *Play in animals and humans* (pp. 43–65). Oxford: Basil Blackwell.

Byers, J. A. (1998). Biological effects of locomotor play: Getting into shape or something more specific? In M. Bekoff & J. A. Byers (Eds.), *Animal play: Evolutionary, comparative, and ecological perspectives* (pp. 161–182). Cambridge: Cambridge University Press.

Byers, J. A. (1999). The distribution of play behaviour among *Australian marsupials*. *Journal of Zoology, 247*, 349–356.

Byers, J. A., & Walker, C. (1995). Refining the motor training hypothesis for the evolution of play. *American Naturalist, 146*, 25–40.

Cameron, E. Z., Linklater, W. L., Stafford, K. J., & Minot, E. O. (2008). Maternal investment results in better foal condition through increased play behaviour in horses. *Animal Behaviour, 76*, 1511–1518.

Caro, T. M. (1987). Indirect costs of play: Cheetah cubs reduce maternal hunting success. *Animal Behaviour, 35*, 295–297.

Caro, T. M. (1988). Adaptive significance of play: Are we getting closer? *Trends in Ecology and Evolution, 3*, 50–54.

Carpenter, C. R. (1934). A field study of the behaviour and social relations of howling monkeys. *Comparative Psychology Monograph, 10*, 1–168.

Chalmers, N. R., & Locke-Haydon, J. (1984). Correlations among measures of playfulness and skillfulness in captive common marmosets (*Callithrix jacchus jacchus*). *Developmental Psychobiology, 17*, 191–208.

Chaloupkova, H., Illmann, G., Bartos, L., & Spinka, M. (2007). The effect of preweaning housing on the play and agonistic behaviour of domestic pigs. *Applied Animal Behaviour Science, 103*, 25–34.

Cherdchutham, W., Meershoek, L. S., van Weeren, P. R., & Barneveld, A. (2001). Effects of exercise on biomechanical properties of the superficial digital flexor tendon in foals. *American Journal of Veterinary Research, 62*, 1859–1864.

Ciani, F., Dall'Olio, S., Stanyon, R., & Palagi, E. (2012). Social tolerance and adult play in macaque societies: A comparison with different human cultures. *Animal Behaviour, 84*, 1313–1322.

Clutton-Brock, T. H., Russell, A. F., Sharpe, L. L., Brotherton, P. N. M., McIlrath, G.M., White, S., & Cameron, E. Z. (2001). Effects of helpers on juvenile development and survival in meerkats. *Science, 293*, 2446–2449.

Cordoni, G. (2009). Social play in captive wolves (*Canis lupus*): Not only an immature affair. *Behaviour, 146*, 1363–1385.

Cordoni, G., & Palagi, E. (2016). Aggression and hierarchical steepness inhibit social play in adult wolves. *Behaviour, 153*, 749–766.

Davies, V. A., & Kemble, E. D. (1983). Social play behaviours and insect predation in northern grasshopper mice (*Onychomys leucogaster*). *Behavioural Processes, 8*, 197–204.

Drea, C. M., Hawk, J. E., & Glickman, S. E. (1996). Aggression decreases as play emerges in infant spotted hyaenas: Preparation for joining the clan. *Animal Behaviour, 51*, 1323–1336.

Dudink, S., Simonse, H., Marks, I., de Jonge, F. H., & Spruijt, B. M. (2006). Announcing the arrival of enrichment increases play behaviour and reduces weaning-stress-induced behaviours of piglets directly after weaning. *Applied Animal Behaviour Science, 101*, 86–101.

Essler, J. L., Cafazzo, S., Marshall-Pescini, S., Virányi, Z., Kotrschal, K., & Range, F. (2016). Play behavior in wolves: Using the '50:50' rule to test for egalitarian play styles. *PLoS ONE, 11*(5): e0154150.

Fagen, R. M. (1981). *Animal play behavior*. New York: Oxford University Press.

Fagen, R. (1993). Primate juvenile and primate play. In M. E. Pereira & L. A. Fairbanks (Eds.), *Juvenile primates* (pp. 182–196). Oxford: Oxford University Press.

Fagen, R., & Fagen, J. (2009). Play behaviour and multi-year juvenile survival in free-ranging brown bears, *Ursus arctos. Evolutionary Ecology Research, 11*, 1–15.

Gomendio, M. (1988). The development of different types of play in gazelles: Implications for the nature and functions of play. *Animal Behaviour, 36*, 825–836.

Groos, K. (1898). *The play of animals* (E. L. Baldwin, trans.). London: D. Appleton & Co.

Harcourt, R. (1991). Survivorship costs of play in the South American fur seal. *Animal Behaviour, 42*, 509–511.

Hass, C. C., & Jenni, D.A. (1993). Social play among juvenile bighorn sheep: Structure, development and relationship to adult behavior. *Ethology, 93*, 105–116.

Holmes, W. G. (1995). The ontogeny of littermate preferences in juvenile golden-mantled ground squirrels: Effects of rearing and relatedness. *Animal Behaviour, 50*, 309–322.

Humphreys, A. P., & Einon, D. F. (1981). Play as a reinforcer for maze learning in juvenile rats. *Animal Behaviour, 29*, 259–270.

Humphreys, A., & Smith, P. K. (1987). Rough and tumble, friendship and dominance in school children: Evidence for continuity and change with age. *Child Development, 58*, 201–212.

Iwaniuk, A. N., Nelson, J. E., & Pellis, S. M. (2001). Do big-brained animals play more? Comparative analyses of play and relative brain size in mammals. *Journal of Comparative Psychology, 115*(1), 29–41.

Kuehl, H. S., Elzner, C., Moebius, Y., Boesch, C., & Walsh, P. D. (2008). The price of play: Self-organized infant mortality cycles in chimpanzees. *PLoS ONE, 3*, www.plosone.org/article/info/info%3Adoi%2F10.1371%2Fjournal.pone .0002440.

Lewis, M. (1982). Play as whimsy. *Behavioral and Brain Sciences, 5*, 166.

Martin, P., & Caro, T. M. (1985). On the functions of play and its role in behavioral development. *Advances in the Study of Behavior, 15*, 59–103.

Mason, W. A., Sharpe, L. G., & Saxon, S. V. (1963). Preferential responses of young chimpanzees to food and social rewards. *Psychological Record, 13*, 341–345.

Meaney, M. J., Stewart, J., & Beatty, W. W. (1985). Sex differences in social play: The socialization of sex roles. *Advances in the Study of Behavior, 15*, 1–58.

Myer, S., & Weber, J. M. (1996). Ontogeny of dominance in free-living red foxes. *Ethology*, *102*, 1008–1019.

Miller, M. N., & Byers, J. A. (1991). Energetic cost of locomotor play in pronghorn fawns. *Animal Behaviour*, *41*, 1007–1013.

Moore, C. L. (1985). Development of mammalian sexual behavior. In E. S. Gollin (Ed.), *The comparative development of adaptive skills: Evolutionary implications* (pp. 19–56). Hillsdale, NJ: Lawrence Erlbaum.

Nieman, D. C. (1990). *Fitness and sports medicine: An introduction*. Palo Alto, CA: Bull.

Nunes, S. (2014). Juvenile social play and yearling behavior and reproductive success in female Belding's ground squirrels. *Journal of Ethology*, *32*, 45–153.

Nunes, S., Muecke, E.-M., Sanchez, Z., Hoffmeier, R. R., & Lancaster, L. T. (2004). Play behavior and motor development in juvenile Belding's ground squirrels (*Spermophilus beldingi*). *Behavioral Ecology & Sociobiology*, *56*, 97–105.

Palagi, E. (2006). Social play in bonobos (*Pan paniscus*) and chimpanzees (*Pan troglodytes*): Implications for natural social systems and interindividual relationships. *American Journal of Physical Anthropology*, *129*, 418–426.

Palagi, E. (2009). Adult play fighting and potential role of tail signals in ringtailed lemurs (*Lemur catta*). *Journal of Comparative Psychology*, *123*, 1–9.

Palagi, E., Cordoni, G., & Borgognini Tarli, S. M. (2004). Immediate and delayed benefits of play behaviour: New evidence from chimpanzees (*Pan troglodytes*). *Ethology*, *110*, 949–962.

Palagi, E., Paoli, T., & Borgognini Tarli, S. M. (2006). Short-term benefits of play behavior and conflict prevention in *Pan paniscus*. *International Journal of Primatology*, *27*, 1257–1270.

Paquette, D. (1994). Fighting and playfighting in captive adolescent chimpanzees. *Aggressive Behavior*, *20*, 49–65.

Pellis, S. M. (1988). Agonistic versus amicable targets of attack and defence: Consequences for the origin, function and descriptive classification of play-fighting. *Aggressive Behavior*, *14*, 85–104.

Pellis, S. (1991). How motivationally distinct is play? A preliminary case study. *Animal Behaviour*, *42*, 851–853.

Pellis, S. M., & Iwaniuk, A. N. (1999a). The problem of adult play fighting: A comparative analysis of play and courtship in primates. *Ethology*, *105*, 783–806.

Pellis, S. M., & Iwaniuk, A. N. (1999b). The roles of phylogeny and sociality in the evolution of social play in muroid rodents. *Animal Behaviour*, *58*, 361–373.

Pellis, S. M., & Iwaniuk, A. N. (2000a). Adult–adult play in primates: Comparative analyses of its origin, distribution and evolution. *Ethology*, *106*, 1083–1104.

Pellis, S. M., & Iwaniuk, A. N. (2000b). Comparative analyses of the roles of postnatal development in the expression of play fighting in juveniles and adults. *Developmental Psychobiology*, *36*, 136–147.

Pellis, S. M., & Pellis, V. C. (1992). Juvenilized play fighting in subordinate male rats. *Aggressive Behavior*, *18*, 449–457.

Pellis, S., & Pellis, V. (2009). *The playful brain*. Oxford: Oneworld Publications.

Pellis, S. M., Pellis, V. C., & Bell, H. C. (2010). The function of play in the development of the social brain. *American Journal of Play*, *2*, 278–296.

Pellis, S. M., Pellis, V. C., & Himmler, B. T. (2014). How play makes for a more adaptable brain. *American Journal of Play*, *7*, 73–98.

Pereira, M. E., & Preisser, M. C. (1998). Do strong primate players self-handicap during competitive social play? *Folia Primatologica*, *69*, 177–180.

Petru, M., Spinka, M., Charvatova, V., & Lhota, S. (2009). Revisiting play elements and self-handicapping in play: A comparative ethogram of five Old World monkey species. *Journal of Comparative Psychology*, *123*(3), 250–263.

Poole, T. B., & Fish, J. (1975). An investigation of playful behaviour in *Rattus norvegicus* and *Mus musculus* (Mammalia). *Journal of Zoology*, *179*, 249–260.

Potasz, C., Varela, M. J. V. D., Carvalho, L. C. D., Prado, L. F. D., & Prado, G. F. D. (2013). Effect of play activities on hospitalized children's stress: A randomized clinical trial. *Scandinavian Journal of Occupational Therapy*, *20*, 71–79.

Potegal, M., & Einon, D. (1989). Aggressive behaviors in adult rats deprived of playfighting experience as juveniles. *Developmental Psychobiology*, *22*, 159–172.

Reinhart, C., Pellis, V. C., Thierry, B., Gauthier, C., VanderLaan, D. P., Vasey, P. L., & Pellis, S. M. (2010). Targets and tactics of play fighting: Competitive versus cooperative styles of play in Japanese and *Tonkean macaques*. *International Journal of Comparative Psychology*, *23*, 166–200.

Richter, S. H., Kastner, N., Kriwet, M., Kaiser, S., & Sachser, N. (2016). Play matters: The surprising relationship between juvenile playfulness and anxiety in later life. *Animal Behaviour*, *114*, 261–271.

Saunders, I., Sayer, M., & Goodale, A. (1999). The relationship between playfulness and coping in preschool children: A pilot study. *American Journal of Occupational Therapy*, *53*, 221–226.

Schafer, D. A., Miller, J. B., & Stockdale, F. E. (1987). Cell diversification within the myogenic lineage: In vitro generation of two types of myoblasts from a single progenitor cell. *Cell*, *48*, 659–670.

Schino, G. (2007). Grooming and agonistic support: A metaanalysis of primate reciprocal altruism. *Behavioral Ecology*, *18*, 115–120.

Sharpe, L. L. (2005a). Frequency of social play does not affect dispersal partnerships in wild meerkats. *Animal Behaviour*, *70*, 559–569.

Sharpe, L. L. (2005b). Play and social relationships in the meerkat, *Suricata suricatta*. PhD dissertation, Stellenbosch University.

Sharpe, L. L. (2005c). Play does not enhance social cohesion in a cooperative mammal. *Animal Behaviour*, *70*, 551–558.

Sharpe, L. L. (2005d). Play fighting does not affect subsequent fighting success in wild meerkats. *Animal Behaviour*, *69*, 1023–1029.

Sharpe, L. L., & Cherry, M. I. (2003). Social play does not reduce aggression in wild meerkats. *Animal Behaviour*, *66*, 989–997.

Sharpe, L. L., Clutton-Brock, T. H., Brotherton, P. N. M., Cameron, E. Z., & Cherry, M. I. (2002). Experimental provisioning increases play in free-ranging meerkats. *Animal Behaviour*, *64*, 113–121.

Siviy, S. M. (1998). Neurobiological substrates of play behavior: Glimpses into the structure and function of mammalian playfulness. In M. Bekoff & J. A. Byers

(Eds.), *Animal play: Evolutionary, comparative, and ecological perspectives* (pp. 221–242). Cambridge: Cambridge University Press.

Siviy, S. M., & Atrens, D. M. (1992). The energetic costs of rough-and-tumble play in the juvenile rat. *Developmental Psychobiology, 25,* 137–148.

Smith, P. K. (1982). Does play matter? Functional and evolutionary aspects of animal and human play. *Behavioral and Brain Sciences, 5,* 139–184.

Spinka, M., Newberry, R. C., & Bekoff, M. (2001). Mammalian play: Training for the unexpected. *Quarterly Review of Biology, 76,* 141–168.

Sutton-Smith, B., & Kelly-Byrne, D. (1984). The idealization of play. In P. K. Smith (Ed.), *Play in animals and humans* (pp. 305–321). Oxford: Blackwell.

Symons, D. (1978). *Play and aggression: A study of rhesus monkeys.* New York: Columbia University Press.

Thompson, K. V. (1996). Play-partner preferences and the function of social play in infant sable antelope, *Hippotragus niger. Animal Behaviour, 52,* 1143–1155.

Thompson, K. V. (1998). Self assessment in juvenile play. In M. Bekoff & J. A. Byers (Eds.), *Animal play: Evolutionary, comparative, and ecological perspectives* (pp. 161–182). Cambridge: Cambridge University Press.

Trezza, V., Baarendse, P. J. J., & Vanderschuren, L. J. M. J. (2010). The pleasures of play: Pharmacological insights into social reward mechanisms. *Trends in Pharmacological Sciences, 31,* 463–469.

Vanderschuren, L. J. M. J. (2010). How the brain makes play fun. *American Journal of Play, 2,* 315–337.

Vincent, L. E., & Bekoff, M. (1978). Quantitative analyses of the ontogeny of predatory behaviour in coyotes, *Canis latrans. Animal Behaviour, 26,* 225–231.

von Frijtag, J. C., Schot, M., van den Bos, R., & Spruijt, B. M. (2002). Individual housing during the play period results in changed responses to and consequences of a psychosocial stress situation in rats. *Developmental Psychobiology, 41,* 58–69.

Watson, D. M. (1993). The play associations of red-necked wallabies (*Macropus rufogiseus banksianus*) and relation to other social contexts. *Ethology, 94,* 1–20.

Watson, D. M., & Croft, D. B. (1993). Play-fighting in captive red-necked wallabies, *Macropus rufogiseus banksianus. Behaviour, 126,* 219–245.

Wilson, S. (1973). The development of social behaviour in the vole (*Microtus agrestis*). *Zoological Journal of the Linnaean Society, 52,* 45–62.

Wood-Gush, D. G. M., & Vestergaard, K. (1991). The seeking of novelty and its relation to play. *Animal Behaviour, 42,* 599–606.

Xia, Q. (1990). Morphological study of myocardial capillaries in endurance trained rats. *British Journal of Sports Medicine, 24,* 113–116.

5 Non-Human Primate Social Play

Coping with Costs

Akie Yanagi and Carol Berman

All primate species engage in social play, from prosimians (e.g., tarsiers, *Tarisus spectrum*: MacKinnon & MacKinnon, 1980), monkeys (e.g., geladas, *Theropithecus gelada*: Barale et al., 2015; *Macaca* spp.: Hayaki, 1983; Petit et al., 2008; Reinhart et al., 2010; Symons, 1978a), apes (e.g., chimpanzees, *Pan troglodytes*: Flack et al., 2004; gorillas, *Gorilla gorilla gorilla*: Brown, 1988; orangutans, *Pongo pygmaeus*: Poole, 1987) to humans, *Homo sapiens* (Smith, 2009). Although there is a near consensus that play behaviour is adaptive, the precise benefits and costs are not clearly understood. Nor are the ways in which individuals regulate play to access its benefits and minimize its costs understood. In this chapter, we provide a general overview of costs potentially involved in non-human primate social play, focusing on social costs, and behavioural strategies by which primates manage these costs: issues of partner choice, play with unmatched partners or protective third parties, and apparent strategic play via adjustments of play qualities and use of play signals.

In many primate species, play first appears soon after infants start to make short excursions away from their caregivers (Chalmers, 1984), while still in frequent contact with their mothers (Hinde & Simpson, 1975). Play opportunities increase as contact with the mother decreases and as infants begin to synchronize their activities with others (e.g., de Jonge et al., 1981). As play rates increase in developing primates (and in mammals in general), it also becomes more complex and interactive (Levy, 1979); in primates, locomotor play (e.g., running, chasing, and jumping) appears to precede rough-and-tumble play (play fighting) (Chalmers, 1984). As play becomes more complex, males and females begin to exhibit sex differences in the frequency, intensity, and preferred style of play. In various primate species, infant play groups are often composed of mixed sex players, but become more typically male biased as they mature into juveniles (e.g., Owens, 1975). This is likely because play becomes costly to females when males tend to play more roughly than them (e.g., Eaton et al., 1986), and females may prefer to avoid play fights with the intensity of male play (Meaney et al., 1985). As females mature, they engage in chasing play, solitary play, and play mothering more frequently than males (Levy, 1979; Meaney et al., 1985). With some exceptions (review in Pellis & Iwaniuk, 2000), play decreases after the juvenile period. Why this occurs is not thoroughly understood at either a proximate or functional level. It may be related to various costs involved in play at different ages and increased nutritional demands at older ages (Fagen, 1993). For instance, animals may start to avoid rough play and to decrease the speed and forcefulness during play as they become older and larger (Levy, 1979).

Costs Associated with Social Play

Today, most researchers agree that play is functional, although there is little empirical evidence to support or evaluate specific hypothetical functions (Power, 2000). This consensus is based on two observations: (1) play appears to have evolved independently in a number of vertebrate taxa (Burghardt, 1998; Fagen, 1981) and (2) play has costs (Auerback et al., 2015) in terms of energy (Miller & Byers, 1991) and time lost from productive activities such as foraging (Barber, 1991), as well as other more social costs. The facts that play is widespread across taxa and that individual players are typically highly motivated to play (both socially and individually) despite these potential costs also suggest that play serves important function(s) (see Chapter 4 for a detailed discussion of the evolution of play).

One hypothesized cost involves an increased risk of predation (Fagen, 1981). Young animals make themselves conspicuous to predators by moving vigorously or vocalizing loudly during play, raising the risk of detection (e.g., Biben et al., 1989). Exuberant play also carries physical costs such as injuries or deaths from falls (e.g., Clarke & Glander, 1984). On a more subtle level, social play may lead to aggression between the players (Biben, 1998; Thompson, 1998) especially when the form is difficult to distinguish from aggression, as is often the case when playing animals engage in chasing, wrestling (Chalmers, 1984; Hayaki, 1983), play-fighting (Fagen, 1981), or rough-and-tumble play (Smith, 1995). Although these play behaviours may differ in intensity and frequency, involve less body tension, or vary in sequence from those that are observed during non-playful contexts, vigorous play bouts can easily be misunderstood as actual aggression by potential partners or third parties. Moreover, play bouts sometimes become too rough for one partner and escalate into real aggression (Fedigan, 1972; Symons, 1978a).

Such negative outcomes are not surprising, given that the interests of any two social players may only rarely coincide, and as a result, their needs and requirements for play often differ. This sort of conflict is based on the premise that play is highly functional and that the nature of optimal play interactions from each individual's point of view depends on that individual's size, sex, temperament, developmental level, and past experience (Fagen, 1981). The need to overcome such conflicts makes play a challenging form of cooperation, requiring a number of behavioural adjustments between players related to initiation, maintenance, termination, intensity (Bekoff, 1974, 1995), and play type (Mendoz-Granados & Sommer, 1995). If two animals differ in preferred intensity of play, for example, they may compromise by playing at some intermediate intensity value or by playing at each individual's preferred intensity part of the time. However, they may not play at all with each other if the cost of resolving their conflict exceeds the benefit expected from play. The frequent occurrence of play refusals suggests that young animals frequently disagree about aspects of play and thus may be constrained in their efforts to gain potential benefits of play.

Another potential social cost of play involves third parties, i.e., mothers or close kin, who may have an interest in when and how youngsters play, as evidenced by their tendencies to become more vigilant or intervene during social play (Biben et al., 1989; De Oliveira et al., 2003; Flack et al., 2004; Hayaki, 1985; Hoff et al., 1981; Owens, 1975). A seemingly rough play session, in particular, may provoke aggression from third parties who are disturbed by play or who are motivated to protect one partner over the other (Flack et al., 2004; Yanagi & Berman, 2017). Mothers are most likely to intervene and even attack their offspring's partner when the play is intense or perceived as risky, e.g., when the partners are not matched for age or strength, when they are not close in rank or when they are non-kin and/or unfamiliar with one another (Fagen, 1981). Conversely, the presence of a protective third party may also encourage the disadvantaged player to play more roughly (Pereira & Preisser, 1998).

In rhesus macaques, it has been shown that mothers are sensitive to variations in the vocalizations of playing juveniles and that they respond by interrupting play (Gouzoules et al., 1984). In golden lion tamarins, *Leontopithecus rosalia*, adults also show more vigilance when youngsters play than when not (De Oliveira et al., 2003). Mothers and other non-players may also influence social play indirectly (Tartabini, 1991); in rhesus monkeys physical contact decreases more rapidly between mothers and male infants than female infants, providing more opportunities for male infants to play freely at an early age.

Behavioural Strategies to Reduce Costs of Social Play

Despite these costs, play somehow tends to remain playful much of the time. To understand how this is accomplished, it is important to see play as two opposite components: competition and cooperation (Bauer & Smuts, 2007). Social play, and particularly play fighting, is competitive in that each animal attempts to overpower the other by biting, pushing, grappling, and pinning its partner to the ground (Biben, 1998; Symons, 1978a). It is also cooperative because two animals must be able to maintain a playful manner for a bout to be successfully sustained; it must remain appealing for both parties and both must trust the other to continue interacting in a non-hostile manner (Bauer & Smuts, 2007). This may be especially difficult when play occurs between partners that are unmatched physically or socially (Biben, 1998). The fact that many play fights can maintain a playful manner suggests that animals have mechanisms to cooperate and cope with possibly ambiguous situations. Below we provide an overview of common behavioural mechanisms that non-human primates are hypothesized to employ to cope with the costs of play and to facilitate successful play interaction with potential partners.

Choosing the "Right" Partner

Multiple factors including sex, age, kin relatedness, and dominance rank influence play partner choice, and often these factors are intertwined. One way to reduce physical or social costs of social play is via the right partner choice. Play partners may select individuals with certain characteristics or avoid those with other characteristics (e.g., Biben, 1998; Hayaki, 1983, 1985).

Many studies report that if matched partners are available, play solicitations occur primarily among partners that are already familiar with each other or comparable in size and strength (Cleveland & Snowdon, 1984; Lee, 1983; Lewis, 2005; Palagi et al., 2007), age (e.g., Cheney, 1978; Govindarajulu et al., 1993; Mendoza-Granados & Sommer, 1995; Symons, 1978a), sex (e.g., Biben, 1986; Hayaki, 1983; Owens, 1975), and kinship (e.g., Box, 1975; Caine & Mitchell, 1979; Southwick et al., 1965). In fact, in some primates, players are disproportionately likely to refrain from playing with each other altogether if their social attributes are unmatched (e.g., rhesus macaques: Yanagi & Berman, 2017).

With a few exceptions (e.g., mantled howlers, *Alouatta palliata*: Zucker & Clarke, 1992), social play in many primate species reflects their (and their mothers') dominance relationships. For example, Tartabini and Dienske (1979) found that rhesus infants of higher-ranking mothers receive and initiate more play and are more likely to play with partners whose mothers rank near to their own (but see Symons, 1978a). Offspring of higher-ranking females appear to play more frequently than those of lower-ranking females in most of primate species (Breuggeman, 1978). Correlations between the ranks of mothers and their infants have been widely described (e.g., Cheney, 1977; Gard & Meier, 1977; Gouzoules, 1975), and both social inheritance and experience with others including social play may contribute to such correlations (e.g., Berman, 1980; Horrocks & Hunte, 1983; Prud'homme & Chapais, 1993). For example, when the mothers' ranks are far apart, mothers may prevent their infants from playing together. Baldwin (1986) hypothesizes that offspring of high-ranking mothers play more frequently partly because they are preferred partners and because their mothers are more permissive. Low-ranking individuals tend to play among themselves (e.g., pigtailed macaques, *Macaca nemestrina*: Kirkevold et al., 1982) and rest away at the periphery of their group, which may further reduce their opportunities to seek higher-ranking playmates (Sichuan snub-nosed monkeys, *Rhinopithecus roxellana*: Li et al., 2004). In so doing, maternal rank order may be reinforced and perpetuated through play at an early stage of development (Tartabini & Dienske, 1979).

It has been suggested that when animals choose partners of the same size and strength (i.e., matched partners), play is less likely to be refused or terminated prematurely (Altmann, 1962; Baldwin & Baldwin, 1972; Cheney, 1978), because both partners have similar opportunities to direct or dominate play interaction, allowing them to concur about preferred play types, durations, or intensities. Practice with well-matched partners is hypothesized to provide partners with safe contexts to test their abilities and competitive strategies (Dolhinow, 1999; Mendoza-Granados & Sommer, 1995; Owens, 1975).

Playing for Short Durations

Despite preferences for partners with similar attributes, much play involves unmatched partners, likely due to the lack of availability or accessibility of matched partners within a social group. When this occurs, one might expect to observe behavioural adjustments that serve as mechanisms to facilitate play interaction between mismatched pairs. For example, they may play for relatively short durations with unmatched partners or under unfavourable conditions (e.g., in front of the partner's mother), an adjustment that may serve to prevent play from escalating into actual fights or interventions by mothers (Hayaki, 1985). In some primate species, many play bouts last for only brief periods of time (< 10 seconds) with many pauses within bouts (e.g., Chalmers, 1984; Owens, 1975; Symons, 1978a). Further evidence that short durations may be means to reduce costs is that free-ranging male juvenile rhesus macaques play for shorter durations when partners' mothers are within an arm's reach than when they are at a distance or out of sight (Yanagi & Berman, 2017).

Self-Handicapping and Role Reversals

If there are great disparities between two players in their physical or social attributes, a play experience may not benefit either partner. For example, if two players differ greatly in dominance rank, the lower-ranking player may not play as roughly as the high-ranking one due to fear of an aggressive response, or the higher-ranking player may not find play with a fearful lower-ranking partner satisfying. In fact, Baldwin (1969) found that initiations of play by infant squirrel monkeys were often rejected by juveniles that showed little interest in playing with them. Conversely, younger partners may reject play invitations from older ones, possibly because younger partners fear rough play from them (e.g., Hakai, 1985). As such, individuals with similar attributes may provide the most pleasant and successful play experience for them, optimizing the benefits of social play.

Alternatively, where there are great age or size discrepancies between play partners, the older or larger partner may engage in self-handicapping (review in Špinka et al., 2001), in which they restrain themselves, allow their partners to freely attack them, or play less roughly. During social play, it is also hypothesized that normal social rules can be bent by restraint or role reversal (Aldis, 1975; Altmann, 1962). Usual dominant-subordinate rules can be altered by each player taking both roles during play (Biben 1998), regardless of their dominance rank relationships outside the play context (Bauer & Smuts, 2007), thereby allowing mismatched play to take place (review in Fagen, 1981). When hamadryas baboons self-handicap, an older (and larger) player exhibits more gentle play especially when he is in proximity to the powerful adult male allies of the younger (and smaller) playmate (Pereira & Preisser, 1998). Flack et al. (2004) also report intensity matching on the part of both partners, not only restraint on the part of the older partner. This suggests that play intensity is determined to some extent by the age and size differences between the partners and by the partners' responses to one another, and that the "right" intensity serves to maintain social play (Flack et al., 2004).

The Use of Play Signals

When play is unmatched, individuals may also adjust their use of metacommunicative play signals (Altmann, 1962, 1967; Bateson, 1972; Bekoff, 1974) in a manner that enhances communication of a playful intent, e.g., by varying their intensity and frequency of their signals (Burdhardt, 2005; Palagi et al., 2007). Play signals typically involve particular vocalizations (apes), movements, postures, or facial expressions (apes and monkeys) that function to solicit and maintain social play and to show playful intentions (Bekoff, 1974, 2001; Fagen, 1981; Palagi, 2006, 2008, 2009; Pellis & Pellis, 1996, 1997; Symons, 1974; Waller & Cherry, 2012; Yanagi & Berman, 2014a) and avoid escalation to real aggression (Waller & Dunbar, 2005). Evidence that play signals communicate playful rather than serious intent includes the fact that they typically precede and accompany play, particularly types of play that could be most easily misunderstood as aggression (e.g., boisterous play fighting and chasing: Loizos, 1967). As such, they are hypothesized to help regulate play initiation, termination, and intensity (Kipper & Todt, 2002). When used strategically, players can attempt to enhance the probability of successful play (Yanagi & Berman, 2017) or reduce the probability of maternal intervention, particularly when the partners are not well matched in age and the risk of maternal intervention is high (Flack et al., 2004).

The best-documented and well-established play signal is the play face or the relaxed open-mouth face (van Hooff, 1962, 1967) (e.g., Palagi, 2008; Palagi & Mancini, 2011; Pellis & Pellis, 1997; Preuschoft, 1992; van Hooff & Preuschoft, 2003; Waller & Dunbar, 2005), which is used almost exclusively in playful contexts (de Boer et al., 2013; Gervais & Wilson, 2005; Preuschoft & van Hooff, 1997; Waller & Cherry, 2012). Some species have been reported to use a repertoire of play signals involving particular body movements and postures (rhesus macaques: Levy, 1979; Symons, 1974, 1978a, 1978b; Yanagi & Berman, 2014a, 2014b; chimpanzees: Liebal et al., 2004; adult ring-tailed lemurs, *Lemur catta*: Palagi, 2009; black-handed spider monkeys, *Ateles geoffroyi*: Pellis & Pellis, 2011; but see langurs, *Semnopithecus entellus*: Petrů et al., 2008). For instance, in addition to play faces, gambolling play-gaits, arm extension, and looking between the legs are used to maintain play in primates (Tomasello & Call, 1997). Touching, slapping, pawing at, or pushing can also solicit play in many species. Play-hitting is an important part of the rough-and-tumble play of chimpanzees (*Pan troglodytes*), and many individuals use an arm-raise to initiate play (Liebal et al., 2004).

Some studies have reported play vocalizations much like the sound of human laughter, during play encounters that occur with or without a facial display (Preuschoft, 1992; Vettin & Todt, 2005). When these auditory signals occur with facial displays, they may improve the chance of the visual signal being detected between the playmates (Vettin & Todt, 2005). Kipper and Todt (2002) report that in Barbary macaques, vocal play signals are more frequent during high levels of body contact (e.g., wrestling) and sudden play movements than in other forms of play, supplementing or substituting visual signal effects of the play face.

Some researchers maintain that facial expressions and gestures observed in aggressive encounters are absent during the play fights and that those observed in playful contexts are in fact unique to play behaviour (e.g., Symons, 1974). At the same time, in some species, agonistic signals are indeed observed during play fights but are not used to terminate play or to escalate into a serious fight (Pellis & Pellis, 1998). Rather, they are used to keep the playful interaction going in the context of play. Chest beating, for example, which serves as a threat among gorillas, can also be observed during play fighting (Brown, 1988). Ear flattening is a common defensive threat movement that is also observed in play in mammal species, including primates (e.g., Andrew, 1963; Levy, 1979). In adult patas monkeys, the bouncing threat display is also observed during juvenile play fighting (Hall et al., 1965). Having said that, recent studies on play signals suggest that there needs to be a distinction between these multicontextual signals and those that are used exclusively in the context of play (e.g., Yanagi & Berman, 2014a). Furthermore, when these multicontextual "signals" are examined in detail, many of them have been shown to differ somewhat between contexts in form, intensity, or temporal patterning. For example, chest beating among captive gorillas in aggressive contexts uses cupped hands with louder sounds, whereas the same behaviour in playful contexts uses flat hands (Weigel & Berman, 2018).

Evidence suggests that intense social play is typically accompanied by higher frequencies of signalling in many organisms (e.g., Bekoff, 1974, 1995; Biben, 1998; De Oliveira et al., 2003; Flack et al., 2004; Hayaki, 1985; Watson & Croft, 1996). Intense social play, resembling actual fights, is potentially costlier than gentle play because (1) such play could result in injuries or even deaths and (2) it could be perceived as aggressive interaction rather than playful by the potential play partner or by third parties. This may particularly be the case for despotic primates (Burghardt, 2005; Palagi, 2006, 2009) with strict hierarchies and relatively low tolerance and conciliatory tendencies (Katsukake & Castles, 2001; Thierry, 2006).

Among captive primates, chimpanzees give more play signals and more intense signals when the potential for escalation to aggression is high, for example, when an older player solicits play with a younger partner or when the younger partner's mother is present (Flack et al., 2004; but see Cordoni & Palagi, 2011). Captive bonobos repeat their play signals more frequently during play fights, polyadic play, or aggressive play in nature (Palagi, 2008) or when space available for play is limited (Palagi et al., 2007; Tacconi & Palagi, 2009). When the form of play becomes riskier, i.e., contact play versus noncontact play or solitary play, both adult bonobos and chimpanzees increase their frequencies of play faces (Cordoni & Palagi, 2011; Palagi & Paoli, 2007). Male–male play in captive gorillas involves more frequent play signal use, compared with other sex combinations (Palagi et al., 2007), suggesting that their signal use is associated with the prevalence of aggressive elements during social play. Similarly, male ring-tailed lemurs direct tail-play to transmit playful mood, when playing with female partners who can be aggressive toward them (Palagi et al., 2016). Captive adult ringtail lemurs that groom each other at relatively low rates (and are relatively less familiar with each other) signal more frequently with each other during play (Palagi, 2009; see also Palagi, 2008 for similar findings in captive bonobos).

Evidence from wild or free-ranging primate populations is currently more limited. Nevertheless, semi-free-ranging Barbary macaques (Preuschoft, 1992) display more frequent use of the play face during contact play or "partner-directed behavior" versus during locomotor behaviour such as walking or running away (from the partner). Free-ranging rhesus male juveniles enhance their play signals, signalling at least once, signalling repeatedly, and signalling more intensely, when they play with partners that are unmatched in their dominance rank, kinship, or when partners' mothers are nearby during social play (Yanagi & Berman, 2017).

There are issues regarding the efficacy of current interpretations of play signalling. First, signals are not always present when individuals engage in play (LeResche, 1976; Pellis & Pellis, 1996). Even when present, they are not necessarily displayed during play fighting (Maple & Zucker, 1978), suggesting that the use of play signals is not always necessary to make a play bout successful. Finally, even when they are present in play fighting, the recipient may not successfully detect them (Aldis, 1975). Pellis and Pellis (1996) also point out that some play signals are observed in contexts in addition to play. Further, the presence of agonistic signals during play fights makes it difficult for the players to interpret the playmate's actions. Pellis and Pellis (1996, 1998) argue that individuals must use contextual (e.g., attributes such as age) and stylistic cues (e.g., differences in timing) to distinguish playful intent instead. These cues may not be sufficient at times, in which case amicable signals may be additionally required for play to continue (Pellis & Pellis, 1996).

Problems and Future Directions

In this chapter, we have presented a general overview of the costs of non-human primate social play and behavioural mechanisms to reduce these costs. Although we discussed physical and social costs that are likely to be unavoidable in social play, empirical evidence of the presence of these costs is still scarce. Understanding what primate youngsters consider "risky" during play is a complex question that encompasses both behavioural and cognitive capacities. Only with the evidence from a collaboration of observational and well-controlled experimental studies can we truly understand their perception of social costs and what types of behavioural mechanisms they may employ to avoid or decrease these costs.

Adults that play are likely to have mastered these coping skills since they learn the rules governing social parameters as they grow up. A more insightful question would be: how sensitive to and knowledgeable about social cues related to the costs of social play are primate youngsters, who still need to learn to thrive as adults? One of the primary activities of young primates is play, and it is very likely that they learn at least some social skills through this behaviour. Do they become more skilled at reducing costs as they become older from infancy to juvenility to pre-adulthood? If so, in what order are various strategies learned? For example, learning to refrain from play may come naturally as they are likely to learn this in other social contexts (e.g., from mother's differential responses to various group members). In contrast, appropriate use of play signals toward potential play partners and in various contexts may require trial and error. Hence this strategy may be learned later than other tactics, and older juveniles may be more adept at this than younger counterparts. In their study of signalling in rhesus juveniles, Yanagi and Berman (2017) found suggestive evidence that infants are not yet capable of perceiving or responding to play signals appropriately; both male and female juveniles were disproportionately unlikely to signal to infants compared with peers even though play invitations to infants appeared to involve more risk. Although ontogenetic studies of play signalling are currently rare, they have the potential to shed considerable light on our understanding of the development of play communication, social intelligence, and life histories.

Additionally, many studies that investigate the ways in which animals reduce play costs have looked at only one strategy at a time. Hence we have accumulated evidence on each behavioural strategy separately. However, as shown in this chapter, primate social play is a notoriously complex phenomenon. Young animals that are acquiring skills necessary to thrive as adults, in particular, have opportunities to experience or exhibit more than one strategy during a single play session. What needs to be accomplished as a next step then is to look at these mutually non-exclusive strategies simultaneously. How do players choose one strategy over another? Is one strategy more effective than others in decreasing social costs during play? Do all primate species use the same strategies? If not, are there any patterns observed based on phylogenetic or socioecological variation? Asking these questions will clarify many unresolved questions in current animal play research, including the origins of play signalling and of the cognitive abilities that underlie it. As discussed briefly above, it remains unclear why all primate species do not use play signals or why they do not necessarily use play signals in all play encounters, given evidence that play signalling functions to promote successful playful interaction. For example, is the distribution of play signalling versus other strategies related to social style or other aspects of social structure? Within species, it may be that each behavioural strategy is used for different purposes or in slightly different contexts, and only studies that look at all these strategies simultaneously can give insights into this question.

There are also definitional issues surrounding play signals. Some researchers contend that some "play signals" are observed in both playful and other functional contexts, while others are exclusive to play. Should those that are used in multiple contexts be considered as play signals as long as they function similarly in playful contexts, or should we consider only those that are exclusively used in playful contexts as so? Part of the difficulty stems from uncertainty over the proximate cause of these signals; some signals, especially those that are also observed in agonistic contexts (e.g., ear flaps or grunts), may be reflective of the individual's excited emotional state during play, rather than of its specific playful intent. As pointed out, social play can resemble aggressive interaction, and players can be easily aroused during a playful encounter, which could lead to expression of their emotional arousal especially during speedy, rough play bouts. Nevertheless, regardless of their underlying cause, such signals could convey information to receivers during play related to the signallers' playful intent and enthusiasm, which receivers can use to make the playful interaction more pleasant. An important question to be asked then is in what contexts these two types of communication are used. For instance, do the youngsters emit "agonistic play signals" only during rough or intense play bouts? Are they truly the same as those used in agonism, or do they differ subtly in form, sequence, or temporal patterning?

Although space prevents us from discussing other issues regarding play signalling in detail, we close by pointing out two final areas for future research. One is related to the question of why some animals display a repertoire of play signals if their function is simply to advertise playful intentions (Fagen, 1981). Yanagi and Berman (2014b) tackled this question with free-ranging rhesus juveniles and found that they use body-based signals more selectively than play faces in specific play contexts to emphasize aspects of play (e.g., play type to come), possibly reducing a potential play partner's uncertainty. However, we need further research to determine whether some are examples of functionally referential signalling. The second area concerns whether the flexible use of play signals to reduce potential costs involves forethought and/or high-level intentionality, since signalling may simply be the outcome of increased arousal of players caused by a perception of potential costs, fear, or subtle threats by third parties. In captive chimpanzee (Flack et al., 2004) and free-ranging rhesus macaque (Yanagi & Berman, 2017) juveniles, play signalling appears to be related to perceptions about the degree of potential social cost, but these studies do not point definitively to the use of foresight because they analyzed signals given before play bouts together with those given during play bouts. Studies of signals given only prior to play initiations are needed to understand the use of foresight. If evidence of foresight is found, further studies will need to examine whether it is based on simple associational learning or more sophisticated cognitive processes.

References

Aldis, O. (1975). *Play fighting*. New York: Academic Press.

Altmann, S. A. (1962). A field study of the sociobiology of rhesus monkeys, *Macaca mulatta*. *Annals New York Academy of Sciences, 102*, 338–435.

Altmann, S. A. (1967). The structure of primate social communication. In S. A. Altmann (Ed.), *Social communication among primates* (pp. 325–362). Chicago, IL: University of Chicago Press.

Andrew, R. J. (1963). The origin and evolution of the calls and facial expressions of the primates. *Behaviour, 20*, 1–109.

Auerbach, J., Kanarek, A. R., & Burghardt, G. M. (2015). To play or not to play? That's a resource abundance question. *Adaptive Behavior, 23*(6), 354–361.

Baldwin, J. D. (1969). The ontogeny of social behavior of squirrel monkeys (*Saimiri sciureus*) in a semi-natural environment. *Folia Primatologica, 11*, 35–79.

Baldwin, J. D. (1986). Behavior in infancy: Exploration and play. In G. Mitchell & J. Erwin (Eds.), *Comparative primate biology, vol. 2A: Behavior, conservation, and ecology* (pp. 295–326). New York: Alan R. Liss.

Baldwin, J. D., & Baldwin, J. J. (1972). The ecology and behavior of squirrel monkeys (*Saimiri oerstedi*) in a natural forest in western Panama. *Folia Primatologica, 18*, 161–184.

Barale, C. L., Rubenstein, D. I., & Beehner, J. C. (2015). Juvenile social relationships reflect adult patterns of behaviour in wild geladas. *American Journal of Primatology*, *77*, 1086–1096.

Barber, N. (1991). Play and energy regulation in mammals. *Quarterly Review of Biology*, *66*, 129–147.

Bateson, G. (1972). A theory of play and fantasy. In G. Bateson (Ed.), *Steps to an ecology of mind* (pp. 177–193). New York: Ballantine Books.

Bauer, E. B., & Smuts, B. B. (2007). Cooperation and competition during dyadic play in domestic dogs, *Canis familiaris*: *Animal Behaviour*, *73*, 489–499.

Bekoff, M. (1974). Social play and play soliciting by infant canids. *American Zoologist*, *14*, 323–340.

Bekoff, M. (1978). Social play: Structure, function, and the evolution of a cooperative social behavior. In G. Burghardt & M. Bekoff (Eds.), *The development of behavior: Comparative and evolutionary aspects* (pp. 367–383). New York: Garland Press.

Bekoff, M. (1995). Play signals as punctuation: The structure of social play in canids. *Behaviour*, *132*, 419–429.

Bekoff, M. (2001). Social play behavior: Cooperation, fairness, trust, and the evolution of morality. *Journal of Consciousness Studies*, *8*, 81–90.

Bekoff, M., & Byers, J. A. (1998). *Animal play: Evolutionary, comparative, and ecological perspectives*. Cambridge: Cambridge University Press.

Berman, C. M. (1980). Mother–infant relationships among free-ranging rhesus monkeys on Cayo Santiago: A comparison with captive pairs. *Animal Behaviour*, *28*, 860–873.

Biben, M. (1986). Individual and sex-related strategies of wrestling play in captive squirrel monkeys. *Ethology*, *71*, 229–241.

Biben, M. (1998). Squirrel monkey play fighting: Making the case for a cognitive training function for play. In M. Bekoff & J. A. Byers (Eds.), *Animal play: Evolutionary, comparative, and ecological perspectives* (pp. 161–182). Cambridge: Cambridge University Press.

Biben, M., Symmes, D., & Bernhards, D. (1989). Vigilance during play in squirrel monkeys. *American Journal of Primatology*, *17*, 41–49.

Box, H. O. (1975). Quantitative studies of behavior within captive groups of marmoset monkeys (*Callithrix jacchus*). *Primates*, *16*, 155–174.

Breuggeman, J. A. (1978). The function of adult play in free-ranging *Macaca mulatta*. In E. O. Smith (Ed.), *Social play in primates* (pp. 169–191). New York: Academic Press.

Brown, S. G. (1988). Play behaviour in lowland gorillas: Age differences, sex differences, and possible functions. *Primates*, *29*, 219–228.

Burghardt, G. M. (1998). The evolutionary origins of play revisited: Lessons from turtles. In M. Bekoff & J. A. Byers (Eds.), *Animal play: Evolutionary, comparative, and ecological perspectives* (pp. 1–26). Cambridge: Cambridge University Press.

Burghardt, G. M. (2005). *The genesis of animal play: Testing the limits*. Cambridge, MA: MIT Press.

Caine, N., & Mitchell, G. (1979). The relationship between maternal rank and companion choice in immature macaques (*Macaca mulatta* and *M. radiate*). *Primates*, *20*, 583–590.

Chalmers, N. R. (1984). Social play in monkeys: Theories and data. In P. K. Smith (Ed.), *Play in animals and humans* (pp. 119–141). Oxford: Basil Blackwell.

Cheney, D. L. (1977). The acquisition of rank and the development of reciprocal alliances among free-ranging immature baboons. *Behavioral Ecology and Sociobiology*, *2*, 303–318.

Cheney, D. L. (1978). The play partner of immature baboon. *Animal Behaviour*, *26*, 1038–1050.

Clarke, M. R., & Glander, K. E. (1984). Female reproductive success in a group of free-ranging group of howling monkeys (*Alouatta palliate*). *American Journal of Primatology*, *1*, 469–472.

Cleveland, J., & Snowdon, C. T. (1984). Social development during the first twenty weeks in the cotton top tamarin (*Saguinus oedipus*). *Animal Behaviour*, *32*, 432–444.

Cordoni, G., & Palagi, E. (2011) Ontogenetic trajectories of chimpanzee social play: Similarities with humans. *PLOS One*, *6*(11), e27344.

de Boer, R. A., Overduin-de Vries, A. M., Louwerse, A. L., & Sterck, E. H. M. (2013). The behavioral context of visual displays in common marmosets (*Callithrix jacchus*). *American Journal of Primatology*, *75*, 1084–1095.

de Jonge, G., Dienske, H., van Luxemburg, E. A., & Ribbins, L. (1981). How rhesus monkey infants budget their time between mothers and peers. *Animal Behaviour*, *29*, 598–609.

De Oliveira, C. R., Ruiz-Miranda, C. R., Kleiman, D. G., & Beck, B. B. (2003). Play behavior in juvenile golden lion tamarins (*Callitrichidae*: Primates): Organization in relation to costs. *Ethology*, *109*, 593–612.

Dolhinow, P. J. (1999). Play: A critical process in the developmental system. In P. Dolhinow & A. Fuentes (Eds.), *The nonhuman primates* (pp. 231–236). Mountain View, CA: Mayfield.

Drea, C. M., & Frank, L. G. (2003). The social complexity of spotted hyenas. In F. B. M. de Waal & P. L. Tyack (Eds.), *Animal social complexity* (pp. 260–287). Cambridge, MA: Harvard University Press.

Drea, C. M., Hawak, J. E., & Glickman, S. E. (1996). Aggression decreases as play emerges in infant spotted hyenas: Preparation for joining the clan. *Animal Behaviour*, *51*, 1323–1336.

Eaton, G. G., Johnson, D. F., Glick, B. B., & Worlein, J. M. (1986). Japanese macaque (*Macaca fuscata*) social development: Sex differences in juvenile behavior. *Primates*, *27*, 141–150.

Fagen, R. (1981). *Animal play behavior*. Oxford: Oxford University Press.

Fagen, R. (1993). Primate juveniles and primate play. In M. E. Pereira & L. A. Fairbanks (Eds.), *Juvenile primates: Life history, development, and behavior* (pp. 182–196). Oxford: Oxford University Press.

Fedigan, L. M. (1972). Social and solitary play in a colony of vervet monkeys (*Cercopithecus aethiops*). *Primates*, *13*, 347–364.

Flack, J. C., Jeannotte, L. A., & de Waal, F. B. M. (2004). Play signaling and the perception of social rules by juvenile chimpanzees (*Pan troglodytes*). *Journal of Comparative Psychology*, *118*(2), 149–159.

Gard, C. G., & Meier, G. W. (1977). Social and contextual factors of play behavior in sub-adult rhesus monkeys. *Primates*, *18*, 367–377.

Gervais, M., & Wilson, D. S. (2005). The evolution and function of laughter and humor: A synthetic approach. *Quarterly Review of Biology, 80*, 395–430.

Gouzoules, H. (1975). Maternal rank and early social interactions of infant stumptail macaques, *Macaca arctoides. Primates, 16*, 405–418.

Gouzoules, H., Gouzoules, S., & Marler, P. (1984). Rhesus monkey (*Macaca mulatta*) screams: Representational signalling in the recruitment of agonistic aid. *Animal Behaviour, 32*, 185–193.

Govindarajulu, P., Hunte, W., Vermeer, L. A., & Horrocks, J. A. (1993). The ontogeny of social play in a feral troop of vervet monkeys (*Cercopithecus aethiops sabaeus*): The function of early play. *International Journal of Primatology, 14*, 701–719.

Hall, K. R. L., Boelkins, R. C., & Goswell, M. J. (1965). Behaviour of patas monkeys in captivity. *Folia Primatologica, 3*, 22–49.

Hayaki, H. (1983). The social interactions of juvenile Japanese monkeys on Koshima islet. *Primates, 24*(2), 139–153.

Hayaki, H. (1985). Social play of juvenile and adolescent chimpanzees in the Mahale Mountains National Park, Tanzania. *Primates, 26*, 342–360.

Hinde, R. A., & Simpson, M. J. A. (1975). Qualities of mother–infant relationships in monkeys. In R. Porter & M. O'Connor (Eds.), *Parent–infant interaction, Ciba Foundation 33* (pp. 39–67). Amsterdam: Elsevier.

Hoff, M. P., Nadler, R. D., & Maple, T. L. (1981). The development of infant play in a captive group of lowland gorillas. *American Journal of Primatology, 1*, 65–72.

Horrocks, J., & Hunte, W. (1983). Maternal rank and offspring rank in vervet monkeys: An appraisal of the mechanisms of rank acquisition. *Animal Behaviour, 31*, 772–782.

Katsukake, N., & Castles, D. N. (2001). Reconciliation and variation in post-conflict stress in Japanese macaques (*Macaca fuscata fuscata*): Testing the integrated hypothesis. *Animal Cognition, 4*, 259–268.

Kipper, S., & Todt, D. (2002). The use of vocal signals in the social play of Barbary macaques. *Primates, 43*(1), 3–17.

Kirkevold, B. C., Lockard, J. S., & Heestand, J. E. (1982). Developmental comparisons of grimace and play mouth in infant pigtail macaques (*Macaca nemestrina*). *American Journal of Primatology, 3*, 277–283.

Lee, P. C. (1983). Play as a mean for developing relationships. In R. A. Hinde (Ed.), *Primate social relationships* (pp. 82–89). Oxford: Blackwell Scientific Publications.

LeResche, L. A. (1976). Dyadic play in hamadryas baboons. *Behaviour, 57*, 190–205.

Levy, J. (1979). Play behavior and its decline during development in rhesus monkeys (*Macaca mulatta*). Dissertation, University of Chicago.

Lewis, K. P. (2005). Social play in the great apes. In A. D. Pellegrini & P. K. Smith (Eds.) *The nature of play: Great apes and humans* (pp. 27–53). New York: Guilford.

Li, Y., Tan C. L., & Li, B. (2004). Social play in infant Sichuan snub-nosed monkeys (*Rhinopithecus roxellana*) in Qinling Mountains, China (Abstract). *Folia Primatologica, 75*(S1), 390.

Liebal, K., Call, J., & Tomasello, M. (2004). Use of gesture sequences in chimpanzees. *American Journal of Primatology, 64*, 377–396.

Loizos, C. (1967). Play behavior in higher primates: A review. In D. Morris (Ed.), *Primate ethology* (pp. 176–218). London: Weidenfeld and Nicolson.

MacKinnon, J., & MacKinnon, K. (1980). The behaviour of wild spectral tarsiers. *International Journal of Primatology, 1*, 361–379.

Maple, T., & Zacker, E. U. (1978). Ethological studies of play behavior in captive great apes. In E. O. Smith (Ed.), *Social play in primates* (pp. 113–142). New York: Academic Press.

Meaney, M. J., Stewart, J., & Beatty, W. W. (1985). Sex differences in social play: The socialization of sex roles. *Advances in the Study of Behavior, 15*, 1–58.

Mendoza-Granados, D., & Sommer, V. (1995). Play in chimpanzees of the Arnhem Zoo: Self-serving compromises. *Primates, 36*, 57–68.

Miller, M. N., & Byers, J. A. (1991). Energetic cost of locomotor play in pronghorn fawns. *Animal Behaviour, 41*, 1007–1013.

Owens, N. W. (1975). Social play behavior in free-living baboons, *Papio anubis*. *Animal Behaviour, 23*, 387–408.

Palagi, E. (2006). Social play in bonobos (*Pan paniscus*) and chimpanzees (*Pan troglodytes*): Implications for natural social systems and interindividual relationships. *American Journal of Physical Anthropology, 129*, 418–426.

Palagi, E. (2008). Sharing the motivation to play: The use of signals in adult bonobos. *Animal Behaviour, 75*, 887–896.

Palagi, E. (2009). Adult play fighting and potential role of tail signals in ringtailed lemurs (*Lemur catta*). *Journal of Comparative Psychology, 123*(1), 1–9.

Palagi, E., Antonacci, D., & Cordoni, G. (2007). Fine-tuning of social play by juvenile lowland gorillas (*Gorilla gorilla gorilla*). *Developmental Psychobiology, 49*, 433–445.

Palagi, E., Burghardt, G. M., Smuts, B., Cordoni, G., Dall'Olio, S., Fouts, H. N., Rehakova-Petru, M., Siviy, S. M., & Pellis, S. M. (2016). Rough-and-tumble play as a window on animal communication. *Biological Reviews, 91*(2), 311–327.

Palagi, E., & Mancini, G. (2011). Playing with the face: Playful facial "chattering" and signal modulation in a monkey species (*Theropithecus gelada*). *Journal of Comparative Psychology, 125*(1), 11–21.

Palagi, E., & Paoli, T. (2007). Play in adult bonobos (*Pan paniscus*): Modality and potential meaning. *American Journal of Physical Anthropology, 134*, 219–225.

Pellis, S. M., & Iwaniuk, A. N. (2000). Adult–adult play in primates: Comparative analyses of its origin, distribution, and evolution. *Ethology, 106*, 1083–1104.

Pellis, S. M., & Pellis, V. C. (1996). On knowing it's only play: The role of play signals in play fighting. *Aggression and Violent Behavior, 1*, 249–268.

Pellis, S. M., & Pellis, V. C. (1997). Targets, tactics, and the open mouth face during play fighting in three species of primates. *Aggressive Behavior, 23*, 41–57.

Pellis, S. M., & Pellis, V. C. (1998). The structure–function interface in the analysis of play fighting. In M. Bekoff & J. A. Byers (Eds.), *Animal play: Evolutionary, comparative, and ecological perspectives* (pp. 115–140). Cambridge: Cambridge University Press.

Pellis, S. M., & Pellis, V. C. (2011). To whom the play signal is directed: A study of headshaking in black-handed spider monkeys (*Ateles geoffroyi*). *Journal of Comparative Psychology, 125*(1), 1–10.

Pereira, M. E., & Preisser, M. C. (1998). Do strong primate players "self-handicap" during competitive social play? *Folia Primatologica*, *69*, 177–180.

Petit, O., Bertrand, F., & Thierry, B. (2008). Social play in crested and Japanese macaques: Testing the covariation hypothesis. *Developmental Psychobiology*, *50*, 399–407.

Petrů, M., Špinka, M., Lhota, S., & Šípek, P. (2008). Head rotations in the play of Hanuman langurs (*Semnopithecus entellus*): Description and analysis of function. *Journal of Comparative Psychology*, *122*(1), 9–18.

Poole, T. B. (1987). Social behavior of a group of orangutans (*Pongo pygmaeus*) on an artificial island in Singapore Zoological Gardens. *Zoo Biology*, *6*(4), 315–330.

Power, T. G. (2000). *Play and exploration in children and animals*. Mahwah, NJ: Lawrence Erlbaum.

Preuschoft, S. (1992). "Laughter" and "smile" in barbary macaques (*Macaca sylvanus*). *Ethology*, *91*, 220–236.

Preuschoft, S., & van Hooff, J. A. R. A. M. (1997). The social function of "smile" and "laughter": Variations across primate species and societies. In U. C. Segerstrále & P. Molnár (Eds), *Nonverbal communication: Where nature meets culture* (pp. 171–189) Mahwah, NJ: Lawrence Erlbaum.

Prud'homme, J., & Chapais, B. (1993). Rank relations among sisters in semi-free-ranging Barbary macaques (*Macaca sylvanus*). *International Journal of Primatology*, *14*, 1–16.

Reinhart, C. J., Pellis, V. C., Thierry, B., Gauthier, C., Vanderlaan, D. P., Vasey, P. L., & Pellis, S. M. (2010). Targets and tactics of play fighting: Competitive versus cooperative styles of play in Japanese and Tonkean macaques. *International Journal of Comparative Psychology*, *23*(2), 166–200.

Smith, E. O. (1978). A historical review on the study of play: Statement of the problem in social play. In E. O. Smith (Ed.), *Social play in primates* (pp. 1–32). New York: Academic Press.

Smith, P. K. (1995). Play, ethology, and education: A personal account. In A. D. Pellegrini (Ed.), *The future of play theory: A multidisciplinary inquiry into the contributions of brain* (pp. 3–21). Albany, NY: SUNY Press.

Smith, P. K. (2009). *Children and play: Understanding children's worlds*. London: Wiley-Blackwell.

Southwick, C. H., Beg, M. A., & Siddiqi, M. R. (1965). Rhesus monkeys in North India. In I. DeVore (Ed.), *Primate behavior: Field studies of monkeys and apes* (pp. 111–159). New York: Holt, Rinehart & Winston.

Špinka, M., Newberry, R. C., & Bekoff, M. (2001). Mammalian play: Training for the unexpected. *Quarterly Review of Biology*, *76*, 141–168.

Symons, D. (1974). Aggressive play and communication in rhesus monkeys (*Macaca mulatta*). *American Zoologist*, *14*, 317–322.

Symons, D. (1978a). *Play and aggression: A study of rhesus monkeys*. New York: Columbia University Press.

Symons, D. (1978b). The question of function: Dominance and play. In E. O. Smith (Ed.), *Social play in primates* (pp. 193–230). New York: Academic Press.

Tacconi, G., & Palagi, E. (2009). Play behavioural tactics under space reduction: Social challenges in bonobos, *Pan paniscus. Animal Behaviour*, *78*, 469–476.

Tartabini, A. (1991). Social play behaviour in young rhesus monkeys, *Macaca mulatta*, at three different ages: From the 3rd to the 6th month of life. *Behavioural Processes*, *24*(3), 185–192.

Tartabini, A., & Dienske, H. (1979). Social play and rank order in rhesus monkeys (*Macaca mulatta*). *Behavioural Processes*, *4*, 375–383.

Thierry, B. (2006). The macaques: A double-layered social organization. In C. J. Campbell, A. Fuentes, K. C. MacKinnon, M. Panger, & S. K. Bearder (Eds.), *Primates in perspective* (pp. 224–239). Oxford: Oxford University Press.

Thompson, K. V. (1998). Self assessment in juvenile play. In M. Bekoff & J. A. Byers (Eds.), *Animal play: Evolutionary, comparative, and ecological perspectives* (pp. 183–204). Cambridge: Cambridge University Press.

Tomasello, M., & Call, J. (1997). *Primate cognition*. New York: Oxford University Press.

van Hooff, J. A. R. A. M. (1962). Facial expressions in higher primates. *Symposium of the Zoological Society of London*, *8*, 97–125.

van Hooff, J. A. R. A. M. (1967). The facial displays of the catarrhine monkeys and apes. In D. Morris (Ed.), *Primate ethology* (pp. 7–68). Chicago, IL: Aldine de Gruyter.

van Hooff, J. A. R. A. M., & Preuschoft, S. (2003). Laughter and smiling: The intertwining of nature and culture. In F. B. M. de Waal & P. L. Tyack (Eds.), *Animal social complexity: Intelligence, culture, and individualized societies* (pp. 260–287). Cambridge, MA: Harvard University Press.

Vettin, J., & Todt, D. (2005). Human laughter, social play, and play vocalizations of non-human primates: An evolutionary approach. *Behaviour*, *142*, 217–240.

Waller, B. M., & Cherry, L. (2012). Facilitating play through communication: Significance of teeth exposure in the gorilla play face. *American Journal of Primatology*, *74*, 157–164.

Waller, B. M., & Dunbar, R. I. M. (2005). Differential behavioural effects of silent bared teeth displays and relaxed open mouth displays in chimpanzees (*Pan troglodytes*). *Ethology*, *111*, 129–142.

Watson, D. M., & Croft, D. B. (1996). Age-related differences in playfighting strategies of captive male red-necked wallabies (*Macropus rufogriseus banksianus*). *Ethology*, *102*, 336–346.

Weigel, E., & Berman, C. M. (2018). Body signals used during social play in captive immature western lowland gorillas (*Gorilla gorilla gorilla*). *Primates*, *59*(3), 253–265.

Yanagi, A., & Berman, C. M. (2014a). Body signals during social play in free-ranging rhesus macaques (*Macaca mulatta*): A systematic analysis. *American Journal of Primatology*, *76*, 168–179.

Yanagi, A., & Berman, C. M. (2014b). Functions of multiple play signals in free-ranging juvenile rhesus macaques (*Macaca mulatta*). *Behaviour*, *151*, 1983–2014.

Yanagi, A., & Berman, C. M. (2017). Does behavioural flexibility contribute to successful play among juvenile rhesus macaques? *Behavioral Ecology and Sociobiology*, *71*, 156.

Zucker, E. L., & Clarke, M. R. (1992). Developmental and comparative aspects of social play of mantled howling monkeys in Costa Rica. *Behaviour*, *123*(1–2), 145–171.

6 Evolutionary Functions of Play

Practice, Resilience, Innovation, and Cooperation

Peter Gray

Nobody has to teach young mammals to play. They come into the world biologically designed for it. Why? Why would natural selection have promoted a class of behavior that, almost by definition, looks purposeless? Play clearly has costs. It uses energy; it is sometimes noisy and attracts predators; and some common forms of it can produce injuries. From an evolutionary perspective, play is either an accident – a side effect of evolution that natural selection could not weed out – or it does, after all, serve adaptive functions that outweigh the costs. The assumption underlying this chapter, backed up by a great deal of research, is that play is no accident.

Play comes in many forms and probably serves a wide variety of life-promoting ends. Among the categories of functions supported by research and theory, four stand out. Play may be a means by which individuals (1) practice skills that are essential to their survival and reproduction; (2) learn to cope physically and emotionally with unexpected, potentially harmful events; (3) generate new, sometimes useful creations; and (4) reduce hostility and enable cooperation.

This chapter begins with a section on how play is identified and then proceeds through sections devoted to each of the four just-listed categories of putative functions. Although play may exist in in a wide variety of non-mammalian species as well as mammals (Burghardt, 2005), the focus here is solely on mammals, with special attention to humans.

Definitions of Play

Researchers who study play in humans commonly emphasize that play is defined not so much by the specific actions involved as by the attitudes and motives underlying those actions. Two people might be doing the same thing – maybe pounding nails with a hammer – and one might be playing while the other is not. In his classic book *Homo Ludens*, Johan Huizinga (1938/1955, p. 13) summed up an extended definition of play with these words: "Play is a free activity standing quite consciously outside 'ordinary' life as being 'not serious,' but at the same time absorbing the player intensely and utterly. It is an activity connected with no material interest, and no profit can be gained by it. It proceeds within its own proper boundaries of time and space according to fixed rules and in an orderly manner." In his influential essay, *The Role of Play in Development*, Lev Vygotsky (1978, pp. 93–94) characterized play as activity that is "desired" by the player, "involves an imaginary situation," and "always involves rules."

Drawing partly from these and other classic and contemporary definitions, I have elsewhere defined play, for humans, as activity that has the five characteristics listed in the following paragraphs (Gray, 2012a, 2013). As I list them, I will comment briefly on how each characteristic provides some clue concerning play's value in children's development. It is also worth noting that play can occur in matters of degree. An activity may be more or less playful depending on the degree to which each of the characteristics listed here is present.

1. *Play is self-chosen and self-directed.* Play, first and foremost, is what one wants to do, as opposed to what one feels obliged to do. An activity motivated by coercion or necessity, real or perceived, rather than by free choice is not play. Players choose not only to play, but also how to play. If there is a coach involved, telling the "players" what to do, it is not play, or at least not fully play. Thus, play may be a means by which children learn how to take control of their own lives, a means of practicing independence. In social play (play involving more than one player), the players must decide together what and how they will play. Thus, play may be a vehicle for learning to negotiate, compromise, and cooperate.

2. *Play is intrinsically motivated.* Play is activity that, from the conscious perspective of the player, is done for its own sake, not for some reward outside itself. Play may have goals, but those are experienced as part and parcel of the activity, not as the primary reason for the activity. For example, constructive play (the playful building of something) is always directed toward the goal of creating the object that the player has in mind; but the primary objective is the *creation* of the object, not the having of the object. Similarly, competitive play is directed toward scoring points and winning, but if the activity is truly play, then it is the process of scoring and winning that matters to the player, not some subsequent consequence of having scored and won. When people are *not* playing, they typically take the most direct, least effortful route that they know to achieve the goal. When they are playing, however, they may try a variety of routes, including novel ones that may be quite inefficient. Thus, play may be a means to try out new ways of behaving, some of which might prove useful later, in serious contexts.

3. *Play is guided by mental rules, but the rules leave room for creativity.* Play is freely chosen activity, but not free-form activity. Play always has structure, which derives from rules in the players' minds about what is permitted or not. Players may change rules as play progresses, but if rules are abandoned completely play dissolves. The rules provide boundaries within which the actions must occur, but they always leave room for creativity. Thus, play

may provide practice at being creative within the bounds of rules. In social play, the rules must be understood and agreed on by all the players. For example, in a play fight, the rules might include "no biting, scratching, kicking, or punching, and if you throw someone it must be upon something soft." You must go through the motions of fighting without actually hurting the other person. The rules might be implicit rather than explicit, but if a player violates one, the other players are likely to make it explicit. The rule-based nature of play is the characteristic that Vygotsky (1978) emphasized most strongly, as he contended that play is the primary means by which children learn to control their impulses and abide by socially agreed-on rules, a skill that is crucial for human social life.

4. *Play is imaginative.* Play always involves some degree of mental removal of oneself from the immediately present real world. This is the characteristic that Huizinga (1938/1955) emphasized most strongly as he built his argument that play provides the engine for cultural innovations. This is also the characteristic emphasized by researchers who focus on the role of play in the development of creativity and the ability to think in ways that go beyond the concrete here-and-now. Imagination underlies all higher-order human thinking. The ability to think hypothetically, or about anything that is not immediately present, involves imagination, and children continuously practice imagination in play.

5. *Play is conducted in an alert, active, but relatively non-stressed frame of mind.* This final characteristic follows naturally from the others. Because play involves conscious control of one's own behavior, with attention to means and rules, it requires an active, alert mind. Yet because play is not a response to external demands, because it takes place in a fantasy world, and because the ends do not have immediate real-world consequences, the person at play is relatively free from pressure or stress. Some degree of mental tension may arise, as players challenge themselves and strive to perform well; but, as play is always self-chosen, so is any tension that accompanies it. If the tension becomes too great, the player is free to quit or change the structure of the play at any time and thereby relieve the tension. This state of mind – of relaxed alertness and absorption in the activity – is the state of mind that Mihalyi Csikszentmihalyi (1990) has called *flow*. In fact, Csikszentmihalyi's first publications on flow were explicitly about the mental state accompanying play (Csikszentmihalyi, 1975a, 1975b). This state of mind has been shown, in many psychological research studies, to be ideal for creativity and the learning of new skills (Csikszentmihalyi, 1990; Gray, 2013).

Researchers who study play in non-human animals have no direct way to ask their subjects about attitudes or motives. They must rely entirely on non-verbal behavioural cues to decide whether an activity is play or not. Generally, the clues are indications that the actions are being conducted in such a way that they are not effective in achieving a serious, immediate, survival-promoting goal. Perhaps the most often-quoted definition of animal play is the one offered originally by Bekoff and Byers (1981): "Play is all activity performed postnatally that appears to have no obvious immediate benefits for the player, in which the motor patterns resembling those used in serious functional contexts may be used in modified forms. The motor acts constituting play have some or all of the following structural features: exaggeration of movements, repetition of motor acts, and fragmentation or disordering of sequences of motor acts."

One way to envision how this definition might apply is to imagine the difference between a cat that is seriously *preying* on a mouse and one that is *playing* at preying on a mouse. The former takes the quickest route for killing the mouse. The latter tries various ways of catching the mouse, not all very efficient, with perhaps some exaggerated pouncing on, scurrying after, and batting at the mouse rather than biting, and then lets the mouse go each time so it can catch it again. For the preying cat, the reward is the delicious mouse. For the playing cat, the reward is the act of catching or trying to catch the mouse.

Absent from most definitions of animal play is any reference to imagination or fantasy. There is no way at present to know if animal play is accompanied by imagination as human play is. For example, there is no way to know if rats engaging in a play fight understand it to be a pretend fight. It is entirely possible that the rats experience a play fight and a real one as entirely distinct, such that one is in no way symbolic of the other.

Play as Practice of Survival-Promoting Skills: Karl Groos's Theory

Without question, the leading pioneer in applying evolutionary theory to the study of play was the German philosopher and naturalist Karl Groos, whose work has not received the attention it deserves. Well before a scientific consensus had been reached on Darwin's theory of evolution by natural selection, Groos applied that theory in a remarkably insightful analysis of play in two books, published originally in German as *Die Spiele der Tiere* (1896) and *Die Spiele der Menschen* (1899) and subsequently in English as *The Play of Animals* (1898) and *The Play of Man* (1901).

According to Groos, "the higher animals," especially mammals, come into the world with incompletely formed neuromuscular systems and behavioural repertoires. In order to become competent adults, who can fend for themselves, they must exercise their bodies and practice behaviours that are essential to their survival. Play, he contended, is the means of such exercise and practice. In *The Play of Animals* (pp. 23–24), he wrote: "Without it [play in youth] the adult animal would be but poorly equipped for the tasks of life.

He would have far less than the requisite amount of practice in running and leaping, in springing on his prey, in seizing and strangling the victim, in fleeing from his enemies, in fighting his opponents, etc. The muscular system would not be sufficiently developed and trained for all these tasks. Moreover, much would be wanting in the structure of his skeleton, much that must be supplied by functional adaptation during the life of each individual, even in the period of growth."

Groos's theory explains some rather obvious facts about play. It explains why young animals play more than older ones: they play more because they have more to learn. It explains why those animal species that depend least on rigid instincts and most on learning, for survival, play the most. And it explains the different ways of playing that are seen in different species. To a considerable degree you can predict how an animal will play by knowing what skills it must develop to survive and reproduce. For example, young predatory animals play at chasing or stalking and pouncing on prey-like objects, including one another. In contrast, predatory animals play at fleeing and dodging, and in their chasing games they show more interest in being chased than in chasing (Groos, 1898).

At Groos's time, a prominent theory of play was the "surplus energy theory," which held that play is a by-product of the high level of energy and free time that young animals have. Groos argued that, from a Darwinian perspective, this theory was backward. He wrote (1898, p. 75): "Animals can not be said to play because they are young and frolicsome, *but rather they have a period of youth in order to play*; for only in so doing can they supplement the insufficient hereditary endowment with individual experience, in view of the coming tasks of life." In *The Play of Animals*, he categorized varieties of play into domains important for survival, including movement play (playful walking, running, leaping, etc.), predatory play, fighting play, nursing play (playful care of young), and love play (play associated with mating).

In *The Play of Man*, Groos extended his insights about animal play to humans. He noted that young humans practice the same categories of skills in play that other mammals practice, but also practice skills that are uniquely human. Concerning the latter, he wrote about language play and constructive play, and he devoted a rather large section to "playful use of the mental abilities," in which he described how children exercise their memory, imagination, attention, and reasoning in play. He also pointed out that humans, unlike the young of other animals, must learn not just the skills that are crucial to their species everywhere but also skills that are unique to the culture in which they are growing up. Therefore, he argued, natural selection led to a strong drive, in human children, to observe the activities of their elders and incorporate them into their play. He referred to this as "imitative play" but made it clear that the imitation is not blind. Children expand, in their play, on the kinds of behaviours that they see in adults and modify them creatively.

Subsequent Evidence Concerning Play as Practice in Animals

Since Groos's time, much research has been conducted that bears on his practice theory of animal play. Here is a small sample.

In line with Groos's theory, sex differences in play, like species differences, generally reflect differences in skills needed in adulthood. In species where adult males fight for mating opportunities, young males regularly engage in more play fighting than young females (Meaney et al., 1985). As another example, Kahlenberg and Wrangham (2010) observed that young female chimpanzees, much more often than young male chimpanzees, played with sticks as if they were infants. They would carry a stick in ways resembling a mother's carrying of an infant, tucked between their abdomen and thigh, and would often take the stick into their day nest and play with it in a manner resembling maternal play with an infant. Consistent with the idea that this is practice for motherhood, such play peaked in the late juvenile period (around 8 years) and was never observed to occur after a female had given birth to her first infant.

Gomendio (1988) studied the timing of various forms of play in Cuvier's gazelles. During their first three months of life, young gazelles are in what is called the "hiding" stage of their development. Their main defence against predation is to remain hidden, and when a predator is near they freeze rather than run. This is also the period in which they most frequently play in ways that resemble the ways that older gazelles escape from predators. Their locomotor play at this stage consists of quick starts and stops, sudden leaps, and much twisting and turning. Gomendio suggests that the timing of such play is consistent with the idea that it prepares the youngster to leave the hiding stage. Only after the movements have been well practiced in play does the fawn stop hiding and start fleeing to avoid predation.

Byers and Walker (1995; also Byers, 1998) proposed a "motor training hypothesis" of play that is a direct derivative of Groos's more general practice theory. According to this hypothesis, early play provides the experience needed for the nervous system to develop the connections required for subsequent effective motor activity. As support of this hypothesis, they presented data showing that peak periods of play in house mice, Norway rats, and domestic cats correspond, in each species, with a sensitive period of neural development, in which connections are formed that permanently influence the animal's capacities to move in rapid, well-coordinated ways. In particular, during this period neurons in the cerebellum that are involved in the rapid timing and sequencing of muscular movements, and muscle fibres and motor neurons innervating them, are undergoing a final phase of differentiation.

Another research approach has been to map in detail the behaviour patterns of play and compare them with the patterns of the adult behaviour for which the play may be preparation. This approach has led Pellis and his colleagues to suggest that play fighting, at least in some species, may not effectively prepare animals for serious fighting, but might serve other purposes instead (Pellis & Burghardt, 2017). In rats, mice, hamsters, and other muroid rodents, the seemingly most difficult movements of play fighting resemble adult precopulatory behaviour more than adult fighting (Pellis et al., 2014). Interestingly, Groos (1898) also speculated that play fighting might, in some species, be rehearsal for sex more than for fighting.

A number of field studies have addressed the question of whether frequent play in youth correlates reliably with a survival or reproductive advantage later in life. A study of free-living yellow-bellied marmots revealed that those who played most as juveniles were the most likely to gain high dominance status in adulthood (Blumstein et al., 2013). In another study, juvenile social play correlated positively with adult reproductive success in female Belding's ground squirrels (Nunes, 2014). In a rather heroic study of brown bears in Alaska, Fegan and Fegan (2009) assessed various measures of the behaviour and health of cubs and their mothers during the cubs' first summer. They found that the best predictor of which cubs would survive the winter and through the next summer was play. Those cubs that played the most were most likely to survive. It is not clear why, but the researchers suggest that play allowed the cubs to develop the physical and emotional resilience needed to confront any of a number of possible survival challenges.

The Role of Play in Children's Natural Ways of Educating Themselves

Groos is much more often referred to by researchers who study animal play than by those who study human play. In fact, Groos's *The Play of Man* was out of print for many years because there was no demand for it. Yet *The Play of Man* is in some ways the more profound book of the two and deserves the attention of anyone interested in child development and education. Groos described his theory as a theory of play, but, as I have argued elsewhere (Gray, 2013, 2016a), it is also a theory of education.

Education, broadly defined, is cultural transmission. It is the set of processes by which each new generation of humans acquires and builds on the skills, knowledge, lore, and values of the previous generation. We humans are the cultural animal and, as such, are, by nature, the educative animal. Beginning at least 2 million years ago, early humans began moving along an evolutionary track that made them ever more dependent on education. They developed means of hunting, gathering, processing foods, protecting themselves from predators, courtship, birthing, caring for infants, navigating their environment, and cooperating with one another that were culture specific and passed from generation to generation. In any cultural group, children who failed to acquire crucial aspects of their culture would be at a serious survival and reproductive disadvantage, so natural selection would strongly favour characteristics that promoted children's desires and abilities to acquire the culture. If Groos's theory is correct, the expansion of play was a big part of this evolutionary change. According to Groos, children come into the world designed by natural selection to attend to the skills, ideas, and values of their culture and practice and rehearse them in play.

In Groos's theory, children play at species-specific skills, like other young mammals, but their ways of playing even at these are influenced by the culture. They play at all sorts of natural locomotor activities – walking, running, jumping, climbing. But then, depending on culture, the locomotor play may move on to such culture-dependent forms as paddling dugout canoes, riding horses, or skiing. They play rough-and-tumble games, but the nature of these games can depend on culture. For example, Fry (1992) found that children growing up in a village where there was much physical fighting among adults played at fighting more than children growing up in an otherwise similar but more peaceful village.

Children in all cultures acquire language through play. Their earliest production of language-like sounds (cooing and babbling) and first words always are playful (Bloom & Lahey, 1978). Later, children playfully rehearse more complex linguistic constructions, sometimes in monologues when alone (e.g., Kuczaj, 1985). But, of course, their language play is influenced by culture. Infants gradually restrict their babbling to the phonemes of their native language and, later, play with the words and grammatical constructions of that language. Children everywhere also engage in constructive play, thereby exercising the crucial human skill of building things, but what they build depends on what they see in the world around them. And, as Groos pointed out, children everywhere play in ways that exercise the human mental capacities of imagination and reasoning, but the scenes they imagine and the ideas they rehearse in such play derive from the culture.

The most compelling evidence for the role of children's play in education comes from observations in hunter-gatherer cultures. During all but the last 10,000 years or so, all humans were hunter-gatherers. A few such cultures, in isolated parts of the world, survived into the mid- to late twentieth century and were studied by anthropologists. Several years ago, I reviewed the literature on children's lives in such cultures and supplemented that with a survey of ten anthropologists who, among them, had spent significant amounts of time in seven different hunter-gatherer cultures on three different continents (Gray, 2009, 2012b).

A message that came through in all of these reports is that children, including adolescents, in these cultures were free to play and explore essentially all day, every day, and they spent much of their time playing at activities that were essential to success in their culture. Digging up tubers, fishing, cooking, caring for infants, climbing trees, building vine ladders, building huts, using knives and other tools, making tools, building rafts, making fires, defending against make-believe predators, imitating animals (a means of identifying animals and learning their habits), making music, making musical instruments, and dancing were all mentioned by one or more respondents. The specific lists differed from culture to culture, in accordance with differences in the skills exemplified by adults in each culture. In all of these cultures the boys played endlessly at tracking and hunting, which are especially difficult skills to learn. Nobody had to require or even encourage children to play in these ways. They played at these activities because they saw them as important in the world in which they were growing up. They played mostly in age-mixed groups, away from adults, and younger children learned from older ones in the context of their play.

Boyette (2016) has systematically studied children among the Aka, of the Congo Basin in Africa, the largest group of people still living a hunter-gatherer way of life (see Chapter 17, this volume). He classified play into various types and found that about a third of all the play he observed was pretend play, in which children typically acted out activities they observed regularly among adults. As an example, he described a scene in which two boys, roughly 7 and 10 years old, assembled a miniature version of a *pendi*, the type of bark basket that adults use to collect honey, and then "tied a long forest cord to the *pendi* and ascended the tree to perform the conventional motions of chopping a hole in a limb to open the bees' nest, pulling up on the *pendi*, and filling the leaf-lined container with imaginary honey to be lowered down to those waiting below."

As another example, Bock (2002) found that young girls, among people in Botswana involved in farming as well as hunting and gathering, engaged frequently in "play pounding," mimicking the actions that older girls and women used in processing grain. They would use a stick to simulate a pestle and imagine a mortar. He found that such play began at about age 3, peaked at about age 6–8, and then declined rapidly. About age 8 is when girls in this culture began to process grain with mortar and pestle as part of their family work. Bock's observations, and his testing of young girls' efficiency in actual grain processing, suggested to him that their pretend play significantly improved their efficiency in actual grain pounding, a task that requires considerable skill as well as strength.

In a review of anthropological research on education worldwide, Lancy (2016) concluded that nowhere outside Western or Westernized cultures is verbal teaching common. Everywhere, children learn primarily by observing, listening, and then incorporating what they see and hear into their play with other children. Such findings provide strong support for Groos's theory. Elsewhere I have reviewed evidence, based partly on research at a radically alternative school in Massachusetts, that children in our modern culture who are provided with an appropriate learning environment, including a mixed-age group of playmates, learn such skills as reading, writing, and numerical calculations quite efficiently through observing and playing with children who have already acquired these skills (Gray, 2013, 2016a, 2016b).

Play as Training for the Unexpected and as Fear Management

Play often involves exaggerated, inefficient, sometimes awkward and unbalanced movements, quite different from what one might expect if it were practice for serious, skilled tasks. Miller (1973) has referred to this as the "galumphing" quality of play. Young mammals also often play in risky ways, which seem almost designed to produce a mishap. Such observations led Spinka et al. (2001) to propose that the original, most basic function of play is what they call "training for the unexpected." They wrote (p. 143): "We hypothesize that a major ancestral function of play is to rehearse behavioral sequences in which animals lose full control over their locomotion, position, or sensory/spatial input and need to regain these faculties quickly ... Besides the development of locomotor versatility in unanticipated situations, we hypothesize that animals in play learn how to deal with the emotional aspect of being surprised or temporarily disoriented or disabled."

Consistent with this theory, many observers have pointed out the apparently dangerous nature of much animal play. For example, Pellis and Pellis (2011) noted that, in play fighting, young animals of many species deliberately put themselves into vulnerable positions, and then struggle to get out of those positions. Others have observed that many young mammals appear to enjoy the thrill and danger of heights and rapid or unusual movements. Examples include goat kids frolicking along cliffs, young chimpanzees dropping from high branches and catching themselves on lower ones before hitting the ground, young macaques swinging on saplings and diving into water, and young polar bears sliding down icy slopes (Aldis, 1975).

Human children, when free to do so, also play in such ways. Groos himself gave examples of children's play that, he suggested, serve as practice in dealing with surprise and fear, including infants' enjoyment of "peak-a-boo" and somewhat older children's enjoyment of fantasy play at fearful themes, such as witches and devils (Groos, 1901, pp. 163–166). More recently, Sandseter (2011) described six categories of risky play that appear to be universal among children: play with great heights, rapid speeds, dangerous tools, dangerous elements (e.g., fire and deep water), rough and tumble, and disappearing/ getting lost. Sandseter contends that these are natural ways by which children learn to master fear, both physically and psychologically. One line of evidence supporting this contention derives from research showing that, as children's freedom to play in risky ways has been declining in recent decades, there has been a dramatic, well-documented increase in anxiety and decline in emotional resilience among children and young adults (Gray, 2011, 2013).

In research designed as a direct test of the training-for-the-unexpected theory, Marks, Vizconde, Gibson, Rodriguez, and Nunes (in press) found that young free-living Belding's ground squirrels that engaged in more social play showed greater improvement, over time, in their coping ability in novel, and therefore frightening, test arenas. They showed less fear, explored more, and were quicker to find a hidden escape route back to their natural environment. In another study, Mustoe et al. (2014) found that young marmosets that engaged in more rough-and-tumble play showed reduced cortisol responses (a sign of less distress), over time in repeated stress tests, relative to those that engaged in less such play.

The studies just described are correlational, so we cannot be certain that greater play caused the decline in fear, or decreased fear caused greater play (or both). A number of studies with laboratory-caged rats have tested the effects of play experimentally. In what seems to be the best-controlled such study, Einon et al. (1978) housed young rats in socially isolating cages under three conditions. One condition was total isolation – these were never exposed to other young rats. A second condition involved 1 hour of social contact per day with a normal, playful young rat, during which rough-and-tumble play occurred. A third condition involved 1 hour of social contact per day with a young rat that had been treated with a drug that knocked out rough-and-tumble play but not other social behaviours, such as sniffing and nuzzling. Later, when tested in a novel environment, the animals that had been permitted an hour a day of rough-and-tumble exhibited less fear and more exploration than did those in either of the other two groups.

Other studies have examined the brains of rats that had been allowed rough-and-tumble play compared with those of play-deprived rats (reviewed by Pellis et al., 2014). A repeated finding is that play appears to strengthen neural pathways connecting the prefrontal cortex with emotion-control areas lower in the brain. These brain changes may mediate the effect of play on animals' abilities to modulate their emotions in stressful situations.

Play as an Engine of Innovation

In *Homo Ludens*, Huizinga (1938/1955) argued that human culture arises and advances through play. He contended that the greatest developments in such realms as literature, art, philosophy, and even jurisprudence have occurred at those times and places where a significant number of adults had time and freedom to play. Huizinga stated explicitly in his introduction that his was a cultural theory, not a biological one. Yet it does not take much of a stretch to extend it to become a biological, evolutionary theory.

It seems quite plausible that one evolutionary function of play is to generate, just for fun, novel behaviours and creations, some of which turn out later on to be useful in survival-promoting ways. According to this theory, play, not necessity, is the mother of invention. Necessity generally leads one to try to apply behavioural repertoires or artefacts already available to solve a problem. It takes play, free from necessity, to develop entirely new repertoires and artefacts.

Much psychological research that is not usually described as play research is consistent with this theory. For example, in many experiments, Amabile (1996) showed that people who are asked to make a collage, paint a picture, or create a poem produce more creative and interesting products if they believe they are doing it anonymously, just for fun, than if they are doing it to win a prize or impress a judge. In another set of studies, Isen and her colleagues have shown that people who have been put in a "good mood" – through such means as watching a clip from a slapstick comedy – perform much better in solving insight problems, which require novel ways of thinking, than do people who are given the same problems without that sort of prior experience (e.g., Isen et al., 1987).

On the basis of such research, Fredrikson (2001, 2006) developed what she calls the *broaden-and-build theory of positive emotions*. According to this theory, positive emotions broaden a person's perception and range of thought, allowing the person to see and think in new ways, thereby building a new repertoire of ideas for possible future use. Concerning play, she wrote: "*Joy,* for instance, creates the urge to play, push the limits, and be creative, urges evident not only in social and physical behavior, but also in intellectual and artistic behavior." This association of play with creativity is also consistent with the point made earlier in this chapter, that human play is associated with the state of mind referred to as *flow*, a state conducive of creative thinking and innovation.

Although this theory of play's purpose seems most applicable to humans, it may also apply, at least to some degree, to some other species of primates (Bateson, 2014). In one classic, small-scale experiment, a chimpanzee that had previously had the opportunity to play with sticks figured out how to join sticks together in order to reach a banana that was otherwise out of reach, whereas chimpanzees that had not had such play experience failed to solve that problem (Birch, 1945).

More recent evidence for play's role in innovation derives from studies of stone play in free-ranging macaque monkeys. Huffman et al. (2008) report that such play consists of "manipulation of stones in various ways, including rubbing or clacking them together, pounding them onto other hard surfaces, picking up and rolling them together in the hands; and cuddling, carrying, pushing, or throwing them." Such behaviour is passed culturally from generation to generation within the troop, occurring in some troops and not others. In the troop of Japanese macaques that Huffman and his colleagues observed over many years, stone play was first exhibited by a single juvenile female, in 1979. Subsequently, other juveniles, but not adults, began to play in the same ways. As these monkeys grew up, however, many of them continued to play with stones, and then the behaviour was transferred from adults to offspring in subsequent generations.

In this and most other groups of macaques in which stone play has been observed, it appears to be pure play, serving no instrumental function.

However, Tan (2017) has described coastal-living long-tailed macaques that not only play with stones but also use them instrumentally to crack open shellfish. It seems quite plausible that this is a case where monkeys began banging with stones, just for play, but later discovered that they could use that banging to open up shellfish. Stones were initially toys, but then became tools. The same could be said of many human inventions.

Play as a Means of Reducing Hostility and Promoting Cooperation

Social play always requires the voluntary participation of all partners, so it is always an exercise in cooperation and restraint. Players must control their actions so as to avoid hurting or frightening one another. For example, in rough-and-tumble play, which is the most common form of mammalian social play, the larger, stronger, individual must continuously self-handicap, so as not to overwhelm the other.

Marc Bekoff (2001, 2004), who has long studied play in various species of canids, has suggested that animals at play exhibit what we humans consider to be core elements of morality. Play starts with signals that represent an "agreement" to play, not hurt or threaten the other. For dogs, wolves, and other canids, this is the *play bow*, in which each animal crouches down on its forelimbs, with rump and head up, so the back curves down and the neck is exposed – a vulnerable position. For primates, the signal is the *relaxed open mouth display*, also known as the *play face*, which is homologous to playful laughing and smiling in humans. Once play commences, if one animal accidently hurts the other, such as by nipping too hard, an "apology" is due. That comes through the offending animal's backing off and, again, manifesting the play signal. "Forgiveness" is manifested when the offended animal, too, reasserts the play signal and play resumes.

Such an analysis suggests that one function of play may be that of enabling animals to form social bonds, which allow them to coexist relatively peacefully and cooperate in life-promoting activities. This theory is supported by evidence that animals that must cooperate for their survival generally play more in adulthood than do other species. For example, adult play is more common among pack-hunting animals, such as wolves, which must cooperate in killing large game, than it is among animals that do not hunt cooperatively (Cordoni, 2009). It may also explain why, among primates, adult social play often involves individuals that know one another but have been separated for a period of time, or a male and female prior to mating (Pellis & Iwaniuk, 2000). In such cases, play may serve to establish or reestablish affiliation, so that subsequent cooperation can occur.

Further support for the cooperation theory comes from research comparing different species of macaque monkeys. All macaques live in colonies that include both males and females, but species differ from one another in colony organization (Matsumuru, 1999; Thierry, 2000). In some species, most notably Japanese macaques, colonies are steeply hierarchical, such that dominant individuals regularly subjugate and intimidate those who rank lower. At the other end of the spectrum are species – including Tonkean macaques and crested macaques – that live in relatively egalitarian colonies, where dominance hierarchies are muted, fighting is rare, and cooperation is common. Species differences in play may help create or maintain these different ways of living.

In a comparison of Tonkean and Japanese macaques, living in semi-natural conditions, Ciani et al. (2012) found much more play in the former than the latter, among adults as well as juveniles. For adults, however, that difference occurred only for females. Adult female Tonkean macaques played frequently with one another, while adult female Japanese macaques did not play at all, consistent with the idea that, for females, play helps to maintain the cooperative relationships characteristic of Tonkean colonies. Adult males, in contrast, played about equally frequently in the two species. The researchers suggest that, for male macaques, adult play may serve functions beyond that for females. Males, but not females, must leave their natal colony and join a new one when they reach adulthood, so play for them may be a way of establishing new relationships, which may be as crucial for entering a steeply hierarchical society as it is for entering an egalitarian one. For male Japanese macaques, play may be a safe way to test one another's strength and skill, in preparation for future dominance battles.

Other research has revealed different styles of juvenile social play in egalitarian macaque species contrasted with that in Japanese macaques. Young Tonkean and crested macaques commonly wrestle while lying on their sides or backs, in a way that does not resemble serious fighting, and often engage in play with multiple partners, in which they cluster into "writhing masses of bodies" (Reinhart et al., 2010). In contrast, young Japanese macaques almost always play in pairs, in which they adopt defensive postures and play-bite in ways that mimic serious fighting. Such observations suggest that young macaques in the more egalitarian species, in play, practice skills that will enable them to coexist peacefully in close contact, while young Japanese macaques are practicing skills that will facilitate subsequent fighting for dominance.

Other evidence for a relationship between social play and cooperation comes from studies of bonobos. Bonobos are closely related to chimpanzees, but are much more egalitarian and cooperative than are chimpanzees in their social organization, and they are much more playful in adulthood (Palagi, 2008). The most striking characteristic of bonobos, compared with chimpanzees or any other primates, is that the females are generally dominant over males (Parish & de Waal, 2000). This is true even though female bonobos are smaller and weaker than males. They achieve dominance by banding together and coming to one another's aid in aggressive encounters with males. Their capacity to cooperate in this way, and in many other ways, may be created at least partly through social play. In studies of captive colonies, Palagi (2006; Palagi & Paoli, 2007) found that adult female bonobos engaged in far more rough-and-tumble play with one another than did adult male bonobos. Palagi and her colleagues have also reported that adult bonobos of both sexes appear to use play to prevent conflict in stressful situations. In one study, play was most frequent during the pre-feeding period, when tension would be high in anticipation of competition for food (Palagi et al., 2006). In another study, play signals and non-contact forms of play increased when bonobos were temporarily restricted to crowded indoor quarters (Tacconi & Palagi, 2009).

Elsewhere, with what I have called *the play theory of hunter-gatherer egalitarianism*, I have extended the idea that adult play enables cooperation among humans (Gray, 2014). Anthropologists report regularly that band hunter-gatherer societies are the most egalitarian, non-hierarchical, and highly cooperative societies that have been found anywhere (e.g., Boehm, 1999; Ingold, 1999; Lee, 1988). My analysis of the anthropological literature indicates that they are also the most playful of all societies (Gray, 2009, 2014). Children and even teenagers in such societies are free to play essentially all day, every day. Moreover, and even more telling, all of adult social life in hunter-gather cultures appears to be suffused with play. Their religious practices are playful; their work is conducted in a playful manner; even their manner of settling disputes generally involves humour and play; and their games are playful and cooperative, not competitive. This seems to be true of all band hunter-gatherer societies that have been studied, regardless of which continent they are on and whether they live in rainforests or deserts, or in hot or cold climates.

The hunter-gatherer way of life, everywhere, requires an intense degree of cooperation and sharing, which is incompatible with struggles for dominance. To enable such cooperation, hunter-gatherers had to develop cultural practices that suppress the drive to dominate. Social play is the one category of activity, across mammals, that requires the suppression of dominance. Therefore, I suggest, hunter-gatherers developed ways of turning essentially all of social life into play, which allowed them to share and cooperate more fully than is true of any other primates.

Concluding Thoughts

Research such as that summarized here makes it clear that play, in its many manifestations, serves a wide variety of survival-promotion functions pertaining to learning, emotional regulation, innovation, and social cooperation. This understanding is especially important, in today's world, because of the ever-increasing restrictions our culture places on children's play, as children spend ever more time in school and at other adult-directed activities and are prevented, ostensibly for safety reasons, from playing in the free, self-directed, and sometimes risky ways that always characterized children's play in the past. There is good reason to believe that such restrictions are deleterious to children's emotional, social, and intellectual development (Gray, 2011, 2013).

References

Aldis, O. (1975). *Play-fighting*. New York: Academic Press.

Amabile, T. (1996). *Creativity in context: Update to the social psychology of creativity*, Boulder, CO: Westview Press.

Bateson, P. (2014). Play, playfulness, creativity and innovation. *Animal Behavior and Cognition, 1*, 99–112.

Bekoff, M. (2001). Social play behavior: Cooperation, fairness, trust, and the evolution of morality. *Journal of Consciousness Studies, 8*, 81–90.

Bekoff, M. (2004). Wild justice and fair play: Cooperation, forgiveness, and morality in animals. *Biology and Philosophy, 19*, 489–520.

Bekoff, M., & Byers, J. A. (1981). A critical reanalysis of the ontogeny of mammalian social and locomotor play: An ethological hornet's nest. In K. Immelmann, G. W. Barlow, L. Petrivoch, & M. Main (Eds.), *Behavioral development: The Bielefeld interdisciplinary project*, pp. 296–337. New York: Cambridge University Press.

Birch, H. G. (1945). The relation of previous experience to insightful problem-solving. *Journal of Comparative Psychology, 38*, 367–383.

Bloom, L. M., & Lahey, M. (1978). *Language development and language disorders*. New York: Wiley.

Blumstein, D. T., Chung, L. K., & Smith, J. E. (2013). Early play may predict later dominance relationships in yellow-bellied marmots (*Marmota flaviventris*). *Proceedings of the Royal Society, B. Biological Sciences, 280*, 20130485.

Bock, J. (2002). Learning, life history, and productivity: Children's lives in the Okavango Delta, Botswana. *Human Nature, 13*, 161–197.

Boehm, C. (1999). *Hierarchy in the forest: The evolution of egalitarian behavior*. Cambridge, MA: Harvard University Press.

Boyette, A. H. (2016). Children's play and the integration of social and individual learning: A cultural niche construction perspective. In B. S. Hewlett & H. Terashima (Eds.), *Social learning and innovation in contemporary hunter-gatherer cultures: Evolutionary and ethnographic perspectives*, pp. 159–169. Tokyo: Springer Japan.

Burghardt, C. (2005). *The genesis of animal play: Testing the limits*. Cambridge, MA: MIT Press.

Byers, J. A. (1998). Biological effects of locomotor play: : Getting into shape, or something more specific? In M. Bekoff & J. A. Byers (Eds.), *Animal play: Evolutionary, comparative, and ecological perspectives*, pp. 205–220. Cambridge: Cambridge University Press.

Byers, J. A., & Walker, C. (1995). Refining the motor training hypothesis for the evolution of play. *The American Naturalist, 146*, 25–40.

Ciani, F., Dall'Olio, S., Stanyon, R., & Palagi, E. (2012). Social tolerance and adult play in macaque societies: A comparison with different human cultures. *Animal Behaviour*, *84*, 1313–1322.

Cordoni, G. (2009). Social play in captive wolves (*Canis lupus*): Not only an immature affair. *Behaviour*, *146*, 1363–1385.

Csikszentmihalyi, M. (1975a). *Beyond boredom and anxiety: The experience of play in work and games*. San Francisco, CA: Jossey-Bass.

Csikszentmihalyi, M. (1975b). Play and intrinsic rewards. *Journal of Humanistic Psychology*, *15*, 41–63.

Csikszentmihalyi, M. (1990). *Flow: The psychology of optimal experience*. New York: Harper & Row.

Einon, D., Morgan, M. J., & Kibbler, C. C. (1978). Brief periods of socialization and later behavior in the rat. *Developmental Psychobiology*, *11*, 213–225.

Fagen, R. A., & Fagen, J. (2009). Play behavior and multi-year survival in free-ranging brown bears, *Ursus arctos*. *Evolutionary Ecology Research*, *11*, 1053–1067.

Fredrickson, B. L. (2001). The role of positive emotions in positive psychology: The broaden-and-build theory of positive emotions. *American Psychologist*, *56*, 218–226.

Fredrickson, B. L. (2006). The broaden-and-build theory of positive emotions. In M. Csikszentmihalyi & I. S. Csikszentmihalyi (Eds.), *A life worth living: Contributions to positive psychology* (pp. 85–103). Oxford: Oxford University Press.

Fry, D. P. (1992). "Respect for the rights of others is peace": Learning aggression versus nonaggression among the Zapotec. *American Anthropologist*, *94*, 621–639.

Gomendio, M. (1988). The development of different types of play in gazelles: Implications for the nature and functions of play. *Animal Behavior*, *36*, 825–836.

Gray, P. (2009). Play as the foundation for hunter-gatherer social existence. *American Journal of Play*, *1*, 476–522.

Gray, P. (2011). The decline of play and the rise of psychopathology in childhood and adolescence. *American Journal of Play*, *3*, 443–463.

Gray, P. (2012a). Peter Gray. Definition of play. In *Encyclopedia of play science*. Available at www.scholarpedia.org/article/Encyclopedia_of_Play_Science.

Gray, P. (2012b). The value of a play-filled childhood in development of the hunter-gatherer individual. In D. Narvaez, J. Panksepp, A. Schore, & T. Gleason (Eds.), *Evolution, early experience and human development: From research to practice and policy* (pp. 352–370). New York: Oxford University Press.

Gray, P. (2013). *Free to learn: Why unleashing the instinct to play will make our children happier, more self-reliant, and better students for life*. New York: Basic Books.

Gray, P. (2014). The play theory of hunter-gatherer egalitarianism. In D. Narvaez, K. Valentino, A. Fuentes, J. McKenna, & P. Gray (Eds.), *Ancestral landscapes in human evolution: Culture, childrearing and social wellbeing* (pp. 190–213). New York: Oxford University Press.

Gray, P. (2016a). Children's natural ways of learning still work – Even for the three Rs. In D. C. Geary & D. B. Berch (Eds.), *Evolutionary perspectives on child development and education* (pp. 63–93). New York: Springer.

Gray, P. (2016b). Mother Nature's pedagogy: How children educate themselves. In H. Lees & N. Noddings (Eds.), *Palgrave international handbook of alternative education* (pp. 49–62). London: Palgrave.

Groos, K. (1898). *The play of animals.* New York: Appleton.

Groos, K. (1901). *The play of man.* New York: Appleton.

Huffman, M. A., Nahallage, C. A. D., & Leca, J.-B. (2008). Cultured monkeys: Social learning cast in stones. *Current Directions in Psychological Science, 17,* 410–414.

Huizinga, J. (1938/1955). *Homo ludens: A study of the play-element in culture.* Boston: Beacon.

Ingold, T. (1999). On the social relations of the hunter-gatherer band. In R. B. Lee & R. H. Daly (Eds.), *The Cambridge encyclopedia of hunters and gatherers* (pp. 399–410). Cambridge: Cambridge University Press.

Isen, A. M., Daubman, K. A., & Nowicki, G. P. (1987). Positive affect facilitates creative problem solving. *Journal of Personality and Social Psychology, 52,* 1122–1131.

Kahlenberg, S. M., & Wrangham, R. W. (2010). Sex differences in chimpanzees' use of sticks as play objects resemble those of children. *Current Biology, 20,* R1067–R1068.

Kuczaj, S. A. (1985). Language play. *Early Child Development and Care, 19,* 53–67.

Lancy, D. F. (2016). Teaching: Natural or cultural? In D. C. Geary & D. B. Berch (Eds.), *Evolutionary perspectives on child development and education* (pp. 63–93). New York: Springer.

Lee, R. B. (1988). Reflections on primitive communism. In T. Ingold, D. Riches, & J. Woodburn (Eds.), *Hunters and gatherers 1.* Oxford: Berg.

Marks, K. A., Vizconde, D. L., Gibson, E. S., Rodriguez, J. R., & Nunes, S. (in press). Play behavior and responses to novel situations in juvenile ground squirrels. *Journal of Mammalogy.*

Matsumura, S. (1999). The evolution of "egalitarian" and "despotic" social systems among macaques. *Primates, 40,* 23–31.

Meaney, M. J., Stewart, J., & Beatty, W. W. (1985). Sex differences in social play: The socialization of sex roles. *Advances in the Study of Behavior, 15,* 1–58.

Miller, N. (1973). Ends, means, and galumphing: Some leitmotifs of play. *American Anthropologist, 75,* 87–98.

Mustoe, A. C., Taylor, J. H., Birnie, A. K., Huffman, M. C., & French, J. A. (2014). Gestational cortisol and social play shapes development of marmosets' HPA functioning and behavioral responses to stressors. *Developmental Psychobiology, 56,* 1229–1243.

Nunes, S. (2014). Juvenile social play and yearling behavior and reproductive success in female Belding's ground squirrels. *Journal of Ethology, 32,* 145–153.

Palagi, E. (2006). Social play in bonobos (*Pan paniscus*) and chimpanzees (*Pan troglodytes*): Implications for natural social systems and interindividual relationships. *American Journal of Physical Anthropology, 129,* 415–426.

Palagi, E. (2008). Sharing the motivation to play: The use of signals in adult bonobos. *Animal Behaviour, 75,* 887–896.

Palagi, E., & Paoli, T. (2007). Play in adult bonobos (*Pan paniscus*): Modality and potential meaning. *American Journal of Physical Anthropology 134,* 219–225.

Palagi, E., Paoli, T., & Tarli, S. B. (2006). Short-term benefits of play behavior and conflict prevention in *Pan paniscus*. *International Journal of Primatology*, *27*, 1257–1269.

Parish, A. R., & de Waal, F. B. (2000). The other "closest living relative": How bonobos (*Pan paniscus*) challenge traditional assumptions about females, dominance, intra- and intersexual interactions, and hominid evolution. *Annals of the New York Academy of Sciences*, *907*, 96–113.

Pellis, S. M., & Burghardt, G. M. (2017). Play and exploration. In J. Call (Ed.), *APA handbook of comparative psychology* (pp. 699–722). Washington, DC: American Psychological Association.

Pellis, S. M., & Iwaniuk, A. N. (2000). Adult–adult play in primates: Comparative analysis of its origin, distribution and evolution. *Ethology*, *106*, 1083–1104.

Pellis, S. M., & Pellis, V. C. (2011). Rough and tumble play: Training and using the social brain. In A. D. Pellegrini (Ed.), *The Oxford handbook of the development of play* (pp. 245–259). New York: Oxford University Press.

Pellis, S. M., Pellis, V. C., & Himmler, B. T. (2014). How play makes for a more adaptable brain: A comparative and neural perspective. *American Journal of Play*, *7*, 73–98.

Reinhart, C. J., Pellis, V. C., Thierry, B., Gauthier, C.-A., VanderLaan, D. P., Vasey, P. L., & Pellis, S. M. (2010). Targets and tactics of play fighting: Competitive versus cooperative styles of play in Japanese and Tonkean macaques. *International Journal of Comparative Psychology*, *23*, 166–200.

Sandseter, E. (2011). Children's risky play from an evolutionary perspective: The antiphobic effects of thrilling experiences. *Evolutionary Psychology*, *9*, 257–284.

Spinka, M., Newberry, R. C., & Bekoff, M. (2001). Mammalian play: Training for the unexpected. *Quarterly Review of Biology*, *76*, 141–168.

Tacconi, G., & Palagi, E. (2009) Play behavioural tactics under space reduction: Social challenges in bonobos, *Pan paniscus*. *Animal Behaviour*, *78*, 469–476.

Tan, A. W. Y. (2017). From play to proficiency: The ontogeny of stone-tool use in coastal-foraging long-tailed macaques (*Macaca fascicularis*) from a comparative perception-action perspective. *Journal of Comparative Psychology*. Advance online publication, http://dx.doi.org/10.1037/com0000068.

Thierry, B. (2000). Covariation and conflict management patterns across macaque species. In F. Aureli & F. B. M. de Waal (Eds.), *Natural conflict resolution*, pp. 106–128. Berkeley: University of California Press.

Vygotsky, L. S. (1978). The role of play in development. In M. Cole, V. John-Steiner, S. Scribner, & E. Souberman (Eds.), *Mind in society: The development of higher psychological processes*, pp. 92–104. Cambridge, MA: Harvard University Press.

7 Human–Animal Play

Play with Pets

Gail F. Melson

Children and adult pet owners play with their pets. This is the conclusion of both self-report and observational studies (Melson, 2010). But what does such "play" mean? In what way is play across species similar to and different from play among humans? Are theories of play and its significance robust enough to extend to play between a human and an animal? What is the significance of play with animals for humans of all ages?

This chapter examines the theoretical and empirical literature on play between humans of varying ages and pets or companion animals. I consider the nature of such play, its determinants, and its consequences, as well as individual differences, based on both human and animal characteristics and contextual factors. Because empirical studies are sparse, this chapter will focus on generating research questions, through application of theories of play, rather than hypothesis testing. I argue for the need for a theory-driven research agenda in this field, and suggest hypotheses and research designs.

A Note about Terminology: The term "pets" is generally used synonymously with that of "companion animals," although the latter is somewhat broader, encompassing horses and other large mammals. Some writers, from the perspective of animal rights, object to these terms as implying ownership and objectification of living creatures that should have autonomy and self-determination. Instead, these writers have advanced the term "companion animal guardian" rather than "pet owner" (Staats et al., 2008). In this chapter, I use the term "pet" and "pet owner" as well as "companion animal" to reflect common usage, without taking a position on the moral or ethical issues these terms may imply. In addition, although humans are obviously animals, it is common usage to use "humans" or "persons" to refer to human animals and to refer to non-human animals as "animals." I adopt this common usage throughout.

The Pervasiveness of Pets in Human Lives

Before addressing play with pets, one must establish how common relationships with pets are. Demographic data on pet ownership in North America and Europe show the pervasiveness of animals, most commonly dogs and cats, sharing human lives. Both the American Veterinary Medical Association (AVMA) and the Humane Society of the United States, in independent national surveys, estimate that 62% of all US households had pets in 2012, with 36.5% owning dogs and 30.4% owning cats. (Ownership of multiple pets is typical of pet-owning families.) A 2014 survey by the American Pet Products Association found 68% of American households had at least one pet. Similar high rates exist in Western Europe. In developing countries and in developed societies in Asia, such as Japan and South Korea, pet ownership rates are rapidly approaching those in the West. In fact, given Western demographic trends toward smaller family size and lower birth rate, increasingly households are more likely to have pets than children. For example, in Australia, 66% of all households have pets, while 64% have children under 18.

Although pet ownership is high across all household types, those with minor children are most likely also to have pets. In non-agricultural societies, pets or companion animals are the type of animal most likely to share the intimate environment, i.e., the home, of children and their families. Thus, the majority of children in the United States, Eurozone, and other industrialized nations are growing up alongside pets, with estimates ranging from two-thirds to 75%. However, one should note that estimates of pet ownership are imprecise, since census data in the United States and elsewhere do not include assessments of non-human household members. Nonetheless, the high rates of pet ownership found in existing surveys argue for the inclusion of non-human occupants in any study or census of the ecology of households.

Companion animals are also common in school settings, particularly in the elementary school years. For example, a survey of 30 California schools found that 59% of elementary school teachers had resident classroom pets (Zasloff et al., 1999). Similarly, a survey of Indiana elementary school teachers found that half either had classroom pets or wanted them, perceiving them as educationally beneficial (Rud & Beck, 2003). Children also encounter other people's pets in their neighbourhoods and communities. Thus, Bryant (1985) found that 10- and 14-year-olds in a Northern California neighbourhood identified "neighbourhood" pets, owned by others, as part of their social network.

The Significance of Pets for Adults and Children

Pets are not merely ubiquitous. They are socially and emotionally important for families and households. In surveys, most adult pet owners describe their resident animals as "members of the family" and often treat them in ways similar to human family members, such as buying gifts, displaying photographs, and celebrating birthdays (AVMA, 2012). For example, a Pew Research Center survey in 2006 found that 85% of adult dog owners consider their canines to be family members. Adults queried about "close relationships," without asking about pets, overwhelmingly volunteer their pets, with 94% mentioning their dogs and 84% their cats (for comparison, 87% mentioned mothers and 74% mentioned fathers; Taylor et al., 2006).

Emotional Closeness: As with adults, children consistently report emotionally close relationships with pets (Hall et al., 2016). When asked: "What makes you happy?" 8- to 18-year-olds most frequently talked about "people and pets" (Chaplin, 2009). (The relative frequency of "pets" was not reported.) Children reported pets as sources of their well-being more frequently than parents and teachers thought they would (Sixmith et al., 2007). In addition, children often feel a tie toward *other people's* pets as well. In a neighbourhood study of 10- and 14-year-olds, Brenda Bryant (1985) asked these children to name "special friends." Neighbourhood pets appeared on the list, on average, as two of the "ten most important ties."

Emotional Support: Emotionally close relationships have the potential to provide social support. In times of stress, both children and adults report turning to their pets for emotional support, talking to them, telling them secrets, and, as a result, feeling reassured and validated. When university students and community members (mean age = 50 years) were queried about their reasons for having pets, the most frequent response was to counteract loneliness (Staats et al., 2008). With respect to children, 72% of German fourth-graders in one interview study reported that, when they are sad, they turned to their pets for reassurance (Rost & Hartmann, 1994). In another study, 75% of Michigan 10- to 14-year-olds interviewed said that when upset, they turned to their pets (Covert et al., 1985). Melson (2001) interviewed 56 five-year-olds (with pets at home) about three months before each child was to begin kindergarten, an important and potentially stressful transition. Almost half the children (42%) spontaneously mentioned their pets when asked to whom they turned when feeling the emotions of anger, sadness, fear, happiness or the need to tell a secret. At the same time, these children (and even younger children in other studies) were aware that their dogs, cats, and other pets cannot literally understand what the children are saying. Yet the supportive function remained.

In studies that place attachment to pets in the context of ties to humans, pets continue to be important. Feelings of support from and attachment to pets interact in complex ways with human social bonds. For example, 6- to 10-year-olds were asked to rank relationships on multiple dimensions. Pets were ranked as "more important" than ties with friends or parents as a relationship "most likely to last no matter what" and "even if you get mad at each other" (Furman, 1989). In another interview study of 10-year-olds, children's attachment to their dogs was not strongly linked to attachment to parents, suggesting that each type of tie serves different functions (Hall et al., 2016). Among adults living alone, those with both strong emotional attachment to their pets and low human social support reported feeling less lonely and depressed than did their peers who either lacked pets or had low attachment to them

(Antonopoulos & Pychyl, 2010). Similarly, adults who report feeling anxious about human social relationships seek more social support from their pets (Paul et al., 2014). Thus, social ties to pets and to humans are distinct, but appear to interact with each other in predicting emotional health.

Drawing emotional support from pets, like emotional support from other humans, has been associated with better coping with stress. In surveys, most adult pet owners believe that their pets contribute to both their physical (e.g., by keeping them active) and mental (e.g., by cheering them up) health (Staats et al., 2008). This belief may function as a powerful placebo effect, even in the absence of a clear establishment of cause and effect. However, there are indications that close relationships with pets do, in fact, lower stress. In the Melson study noted earlier, after children had made the transition to kindergarten, their mothers and fathers, who were unaware of their children's responses, perceived less anxiety and better positive adjustment for those children who had previously reported emotional support coming from their pets (Melson, 2001).

Animal-assisted therapy (AAT) programs with traumatized children and adults are based on the premise that contact with a friendly animal is stress-reducing. While most AAT interventions involve dogs, others include such animals as rabbits, guinea pigs, gerbils, birds, and turtles (Fine, 2012). While AAT programs have proliferated, it remains unclear whether and, if so, how they reduce stress and promote adaptive functioning. It is noteworthy that the content of AAT interventions often involves structured or unstructured play with a therapy animal, in conjunction with a human therapist. Unfortunately, no empirical research is available concerning the quality and impact of play interactions within such therapeutic contexts.

Pets as Attachment Figures: This evidence of pets' providing emotional support, particularly in times of stress, suggests that pets serve as attachment figures, at least potentially. According to attachment theory, the hallmark of an attachment figure is its ability to reduce stress and provide reassurance when the "attachment system" is activated, that is, when the child senses insecurity and lack of safety. Hall et al. (2016) find that children who regularly spend time taking care of their dogs (feeding, walking, or grooming) are more strongly attached, their dogs are more responsive, and, in turn, the children derive more emotional support from the dog. In a comprehensive literature review, Jalongo (2015) documents how children often use pets, especially dogs, as a "secure base" and as attachment objects that reduce stress. In addition, there is considerable evidence that dogs reciprocally develop attachment bonds with their owners. Thus, as in human–human attachment relationships, there is a dynamic interplay between two mutually attached individuals. An important question (to which we will return) is the extent to which play with a pet is part of this attachment relationship.

This perceived emotional support in childhood also has been associated with more adaptive functioning later in adulthood. Retrospective accounts

(Girardi & Pozzulo, 2015) describe stronger childhood bonds with pets as associated with lower depression and anxiety in early adulthood. These findings are suggestive but need to be buttressed by prospective and experimental data.

Pets also may play a compensatory role for children or adults having difficulty with or lacking certain human relationships. Thus, adults who report being anxious about human social relationships are more likely to seek social support from pets and to anthropomorphize them, by projecting human emotions onto them (Paul et al., 2014). Pet-owning children without siblings report stronger attachment to pets and spend more time with them than do children who have siblings, particularly younger ones (Melson & Fogel, 1996). Young children from single-parent families express more attachment to their pets than do their counterparts in dual-parent families (Bodsworth & Coleman, 2001). Play and nurturing behaviours, often qualities of older-younger sibling relationships, may transfer to the child–pet relationship in the absence of younger sibs (Pelletier-Stiefel et al., 1986).

Negative Components of the Human–Pet Relationship: While positive components of human–pet relationships have been emphasized in research, the widespread presence of pets, and their dependence on human care, can make them vulnerable to negative relationships as well. Children report *both* positive and negative feelings about their pets. When queried about problems, many children admit feeling stressed and worried about their pets' safety and health, particularly when the children are away at school or on trips (Bryant, 1990). More serious problems can arise. Surveys of college students have found a correlation between bullying (as both perpetrator and victim) and animal abuse (Henry & Sanders, 2007). In general, animal abuse and family violence often co-occur (McPhedran, 2009). Thus, relationships with pets have the potential for strong positive attachment and feelings of emotional support as well as aggression and abuse.

This suggests that both positive and negative qualities might be observed in child–pet play. Children may play with pets in ways that are insensitive, aggressive, or neglectful, thereby endangering animal welfare. Research on animal abuse during childhood indicates that most maltreatment is unintentional, fuelled by curiosity and ignorance (Lockwood & Ascione, 1998). For the small minority of children who repeatedly and intentionally harm animals, and derive pleasure from their suffering, such abuse may be an early marker of serious psychopathology. Because fine-grained analyses of components of human–pet play are sparse, the role of play interactions in animal maltreatment and abuse is unclear.

Human Behaviour with Pets: Having established both the pervasiveness and the importance of the human–pet relationship, one must look into the "black box" of daily life with a pet. What exactly do pet owners do with their pets? In this way, we establish the frequency, quality, and significance of play with pets. Before doing this, however, a theoretical detour is necessary. Theories and definitions of social play have almost exclusively been applied to conspecifics, either social play among humans or social play among members of other species. One can derive from this work general characteristics of play behaviour and of play-friendly contexts. How do these general characteristics apply to human–pet play?

Characteristics of Play Behaviour and Contexts

Mark Twain put it most succinctly: "Play consists of whatever a body is not obliged to do" (1895, p. 33). Social scientists have unpacked and elaborated this statement. According to Rubin et al. (1983), Garvey (1990), Power (2000), and others, play can be distinguished from other behaviours by the following: (1) intrinsic rather than extrinsic motivation; (2) internal or self-directed control; (3) flexibility and creativity; (4) active engagement; (5) "playfulness," i.e., physical, social, and cognitive spontaneity; and (6) unpredictability, joy, and release. Within a social constructivist perspective, play behaviours might be more broadly defined as *any* behaviours that one or more participants signal or define as "play." For example, when two children "play grocery store," they enact many of the work behaviours characteristic of shopping for or selling items, but do so within an agreed "play frame," a mutual understanding that "we are now playing" (Goffman, 1959). While, in theory, any activity can be transformed into "play" by participant agreement, "play-friendly" contexts or "play spaces" (Chudacoff, 2007) have been identified as those most likely to give rise to "play frames" (Rubin et al., 1983). Such contexts are unstructured, participant directed, non-judgemental, and relaxed.

Play Behaviours between Humans and Their Pets

The general characteristics of play behaviours noted above map fairly well onto interspecies play, at least when one considers human–dog (*Canis familiaris*) interaction (Melson, 2010). First, such play generally arises from intrinsic rather than extrinsic motivation, with one or more partners (human or animal) signalling play or establishing a "play frame." Many pet owners are undoubtedly aware of the developmental needs of their pets, such as dog breeds that require a great deal of exercise. In that case, a pet owner might play games such as "fetch" or "chase" out of a sense of obligation to provide daily exercise for the dog's well-being. If so, one would characterize the dog in a "play frame," with the human in a "work frame." (However, there is little empirical information about pet owners' knowledge concerning the developmental and health needs of their animals and no research linking such information with play.) Second, play with pets is generally controlled by one or both partners, using play initiation, continuation, and termination signals. Because they co-evolved with humans, dogs, even more than non-human primates, are adept at interpreting human signals and maintaining joint attention (Hare & Tomasello, 1999; Miklosi et al., 2004). Flexibility, spontaneity, active engagement, and playfulness all characterize the observed play behaviours between owners and their dogs in unstructured interactions, for example, in dog parks (Horowitz & Bekoff, 2007).

Pets as a Play-Friendly Context

It is clear that both children and adults often experience pets as a play-friendly context. One reason stems from historical changes in the human–companion animal relationship. As Catherine Grier (2006) documents, as the United States became more industrialized, urbanized, and modernized in the nineteenth and twentieth centuries, the roles companion animals played became less utilitarian. Work horses, herding and hunting dogs, and rat-catching felines gradually were replaced by pets viewed solely as companions, loved ones, and play partners. As a result, many pet owners describe time with their pets in terms of amusement, fun, relaxation, and playfulness. (The many viral videos of funny pet tricks attest to this.) Not surprisingly, interactions of people with pets often have a playful, humorous quality. In observations of 46 dog–human play interactions, all were characterized by positive affect, and 61% included human laughter, usually occurring when the dog did something unexpected (Mitchell & Sinkhorn, 2014). This playful quality of human–pet play, together with the fact that pets are nonverbal and dependent, contribute to the perception of pets as non-judgemental, available, and sources of fun.

Most pet owners describe "play" as a frequent activity (Melson & Fogel, 1996). For example, in a study of 50 dog–adult human pairs, owners reported they had play sessions with their dogs for a median of seven times per week, with play sessions lasting a median 1.75 hours. Dogs usually initiated these play sessions, according to 29 of the 50 adult humans interviewed, while 21 adults reported that they initiated the play sessions. In no cases were play sessions initiated by non-participants (Rooney & Bradshaw, 2003). These play sessions with dogs also were unstructured or, more precisely, structured only by the signals, intent, and mutual agreement of the participants themselves. Specifically, owners and their dogs played games such as fetch, rough and tumble, tug of war, chase, and keep away (Rooney & Bradshaw, 2003). These games reflect both the play repertoire of the dogs and the mutual adaptation of humans and dogs. Thus, observations (Bradshaw et al., 2015) of dog–human tug of war games in comparison to such dog–dog games reveal that dogs play with humans differently. In a tug of war with other dogs, dogs compete over objects, while in tug-of-war with a human, dogs behave more cooperatively, signalling playfulness rather than dominance. In summary, with respect to the key features, interspecies play between humans and pets maps quite well onto definitions of intraspecies play.

Unique Features of Interspecies Play

While theories of play applied within species can be generalized to human play with pets, there are important differences, as yet poorly understood. Play behaviours evolved within species for conspecific interaction. Thus, interspecies play requires coordination of different species-dependent play repertoires. For example, observations of dogs playing with each other show that dogs use rolling over as part of a play bout (Norman et al., 2015). To what extent do they do so in play with humans? Observational research of dog–human play is just beginning to document how such play involves modifications by both play partners. As already noted, dogs modify tug of war games over objects when they play with humans rather than other dogs. What other behaviours are modified, and how?

Humans too have their challenges in adapting to interspecies play. In one observational study, dog owners were observed signalling to their dogs the intent to play. The adults did so by grabbing the dog, patting the floor, or lunging forward. Dogs responded appropriately mostly to the forward lunge, rather than to the other behaviours (Rooney et al., 2000). It appears that the pet owners were not aware that other attempts to engage their dogs in play were ineffective.

Other evidence suggests a frequent disconnect between human and dog perceptions and behaviours. Humans may misread dog behaviour and misattribute emotions, intentions, and personality. Such a 'misread' is more likely when humans evaluate unfamiliar dogs, rather than their own pets. For example, when adults were asked to rate unfamiliar dogs from short videos of a child and dog playing, most of the adults (68%) viewed the dogs as "relaxed" and "confident" and their behaviour as playful and friendly, even though the dogs previously had been rated by experts as fearful and anxious (Demirbas et al., 2016).

Second, humans must rely primarily on the nonverbal channel of communication, decoding behaviours and vocalizations of another species. Despite this, virtually all children and adults talk to their pets, although they clearly do not expect a verbal reply (Beck & Katcher, 1983). Human speech to pets often employs "motherese," a high-pitched, sing-song speech register originally identified in maternal speech to infants, hence the name. A recent study found that adults used motherese when asked to 'speak' to photographs of dogs of various ages. When these recordings were played to dogs, however, only puppies, not adult dogs, responded (Ben-Aderet et al., 2017). When dog owners were directly observed speaking to their pets, adult dogs responded primarily to the sound of their name and to eye contact with the owner, not to other speech or behavioural cues (Kaminski et al., 2012). In sum, both humans and their dogs have an imperfect understanding of each other's communication in play interactions. Each interactive partner responds selectively to communicative cues of the other, but neither partner may fully understand this. (Of course, humans' intraspecies play can suffer from similar limitations.)

Third, because companion animals are dependent on human care, interactions with pets often involve a mixture of caregiving – feeding, cleaning, exercising – affection, and play. (This is also the case within species with respect to human infants and children.) Thus, observations of children with a friendly dog show children stroking the dog's fur, petting the dog, and playing ball with the dog (Melson et al., 2009). When 7- to 13-year-olds were queried on the needs of pets, especially dogs and cats, the children identified love and attention as basic components of animal welfare, along with adequate nutrition, medical care, and exercise (Muldoon et al., 2016). Parental reports of child–pet relationships indicate both frequent play and caregiving activities (Melson & Fogel, 1996). In this way, interactions with pets contain both vertical (e.g., parent–child or older sib–younger sib) and horizontal (e.g., peer–peer) elements.

Scaffolding: These communication challenges, coupled with species-specific behavioural repertoires and pet dependence on humans, often result in scaffolding of play interactions with pets. "Scaffolding" is a concept derived from observational studies of early mother–infant interaction (Kaye & Charney, 1981). Because the human infant's interactional repertoire is limited, mothers (and other caregivers) tend to supply, verbally and nonverbally, both sides of the interaction, much as a wooden scaffold supports the skeleton of a building during its construction. Over time, as the infant acquires interactive competencies, the scaffold gradually falls away. Thus, a caregiver might prop up an infant to maximize face-to-face eye contact, take advantage of a momentary smile, and say, smiling as well: "Oh, so, are you happy?" At the next eye contact and smile, the caregiver might supply the infant's 'answer': "Yes, you *are* happy!" and so on, through several interactive rounds.

When humans create a "play frame" with pets, particularly with non-dog species, they may scaffold in a similar way. For example, if a child is playing "tea party" with a cat, the child may enlist the cat in the play frame by scaffolding: "Would you like a cup of tea?" "Oh, yes, you would, here" etc., at least until the cat walks away. While the structure of scaffolding may be similar to that occurring in caregiver–infant interaction, the goal is different. Pet owners do not expect that the cat, turtle, or guinea pig will gradually acquire the interactive skills that scaffolding temporarily supplies. Rather, in the case of pets, humans may scaffold in order to permit a "play frame" to proceed. Unfortunately, we lack observational data on the extent, quality, and meaning of scaffolding in human–pet interactions.

Anthropomorphism: The human tendency toward *anthropomorphism* (Guthrie, 1997), attributing human motivations, feelings, and thoughts to other species and even inanimate objects, means that humans often misinterpret intentions or behaviour when interacting with pets. This tendency is accentuated by heavy media use of anthropomorphic animals, particularly directed toward children (Geerdts, 2016), although anthropomorphic animals are ubiquitous in marketing to all ages (Brown, 2010). Anthropomorphism is readily observed in interactions of pets with people. For example, a parrot might tilt its head, and the human might respond: "Oh, so you're puzzled?" Or a dog licking a human's hand might be interpreted as always expressing affection. Anthropomorphism can lead pet owners to impose a "play frame" where there is none from the animal's point of view, or ignore a play invitation when it occurs.

This tendency toward anthropomorphism is accentuated by *neoteny*, or *paedomorphism*, the persistence of juvenile features and behaviours into adulthood. These features include relative largeness of head to size of body, widely spaced eyes, and foreshortened nose, among other features. Behaviourally, neoteny includes juvenile, often submissive behaviours. As an illustration, compare the visual appearance and behavioural repertoire of a wolf and a German Shepherd dog. In general, species most frequently kept as pets tend to exhibit neoteny.

Neoteny functions to increase proximity, positive emotion, and readiness to help and care. Human babies whose faces show more neoteny get more baby talk and caregiving from adults. Among adults, those whose faces retain more neoteny receive more social approval and helping. Neoteny functions in the same way between species. For example, adult humans express more liking for photos of dogs with facial expressions that enhance neoteny (Waller et al., 2013). Even non-mammalian species are perceived as "cuter" when they are seen as more dependent on parental care (Kruger, 2015).

Anthropomorphism, together with neoteny, may have complex effects when it comes to human–pet play. On the one hand, these features increase human attraction to pets, bring both species into close proximity, and contribute to creating a play-friendly context. On the other hand, anthropomorphism can distort an accurate understanding of the interactive repertoire of the pet as play partner and invite imposition of a play frame.

Nonetheless, scaffolding, anthropomorphism, and neoteny should not be construed as rendering pets as little more than props, indistinguishable from stuffed animal toys. Studies are consistent in showing that even young children perceive living animals as subjectivities, not objects, i.e., agents with intentions, feelings, and even claims to moral regard (Melson, 2009, 2013; Myers, 2007). Thus, children (and adults) see pets and other living animals as agents, not objects. This recognition of a pet as a social "other" tempers the arbitrary imposition of a play frame. Children who are ready to play with a pet are nonetheless attentive to the behavioural repertoire of a distinct species and modify their behaviour to adapt to those behaviours (Myers, 2007).

Influences on Human–Pet Play

Pet Variables: Though empirical evidence is sparse, there are good candidates for variables that influence interspecies play. First, pet species differences are likely to be important. Not surprisingly, observational studies of human–pet play have been exclusively of pet owners and their dogs (Horowitz & Bekoff, 2007). Because of their co-evolution with humans, dogs are uniquely able to engage with them in coordinated, mutually agreed-on play bouts. Play-relevant canine skills include (1) understanding human goal-directed behaviour (Marshall-Pescini et al., 2014), (2) interpreting eye contact and the sound of one's name (Kaminski et al., 2012), (3) joint attention and response to pointing, and (4) learning from observing human play with another dog (Rooney & Bradshaw, 2006).

Within-species individual differences also may be important. For example, dogs (as well as other species) differ in sociability and other temperamental characteristics. Rooney and Bradshaw (2003) assessed dog temperament in terms of dominance/submission and "confident interactivity" (i.e., tail wagging, playfulness, licking owner). In observations of adult–dog unstructured play, games like tug of war and fetch were played more frequently and longer with dogs who had higher "confident interactivity" and lower dominance. Pet owners whose dogs scored higher on dominance reported that their dogs more frequently initiated play interactions.

Because dogs bond with owners, the attachment relationship, from the dog's point of view, may also be important. When the dog's quality of attachment to its owner was assessed using a modification of the Strange Situation, a standard observational tool (Ainsworth et al., 1978), dogs who preferred their owner to an unfamiliar adult engaged in longer play sessions with their owners than did dogs who showed no preference (Rooney & Bradshaw, 2003).

Physiological changes accompanying emotional bonding are receiving greater attention but remain poorly understood. The neuropeptide oxytocin has been associated with human–dog play behaviours. Naturally occurring variations in oxytocin levels, related to the quality of the attachment bond, may mediate human–dog play. When dogs are given oxytocin intranasally, they show increased social behaviours toward humans with more frequent play signals (Romero et al., 2015). Similarly, doses of oxytocin improved dogs' skill at finding hidden food by attending to human social cues. This improvement lasted 5–15 days after oxytocin had left the dogs' bloodstream (Oliva et al., 2015). Such increased attentiveness to human signals could influence play interactions, although these were not directly observed.

In addition to individual variables such as temperament and personality, developmental age of the animal may play a role. Rooney and Bradshaw (2003) found that younger dogs showed less dominance and, hence, played differently with their owners than did older dogs. The neotenous features of the young of many species are likely to enhance humans' perceptions of friendliness, likeability, and readiness to play.

Human Variables: As with intraspecies play, human–pet play is undoubtedly influenced by variations in human characteristics and behaviours, although lack of empirical evidence leads us to hypothesis generation here as well. First, developmental differences are likely. Children spend more time in play than do adults, and there are well-documented changes in type and quality of play as children develop. Parental reports of time spent in play with pets indicate that children play on average daily with their pets, with levels unchanged from age 5 to 13. By contrast, the same parents reported that play with younger siblings decreases over that time period (Melson & Fogel, 1996).

Because humans become emotionally attached to their pets, as documented earlier, variations in that attachment relationship are likely to influence play. More attached pet owners are likely to perceive their pet, and even other people's pets, in more positive terms. For example, 7- to 15-year-old children who report higher attachment to their pets attribute more psychological characteristics and moral regard to an unfamiliar but friendly dog with whom they have a brief play session (Melson et al., 2009).

As with dogs, human oxytocin levels have been associated with pet interaction, at least with dogs. When oxytocin levels are measured in adult men and women who were all bonded with their dogs, women's (but not men's) oxytocin levels increase from before to after a play session (Miller et al., 2009). Adult female dog owners who are observed to show greater affection (by kissing their dogs) during a play session have higher oxytocin levels in their blood than do their less affectionate counterparts (Handling, 2012). Taken together, these results also suggest possible gender differences in human–dog relationships, including play behaviours, but empirical data are sparse here.

Individual differences in human temperament, personality, and empathy may also influence human–pet play. Although data are scarce, a small-scale ($n = 34$) study found that high-empathy adults responded more quickly and with greater intensity to images of threatening faces (both human and dog) than did their lower empathy peers (Kujala et al., 2017). In general, respondents tended to use similar patterns in evaluating the emotions of both humans and dogs. This would suggest that most people generalize from decoding human expressions and behaviour to other species, especially dogs. Such generalization might be accentuated by anthropomorphism. Indeed, lack of animal experience or information has been associated with greater tendency to anthropomorphize (Bahlig-Pieren & Turner, 1999).

In sum, one might generate several hypotheses concerning individual human variables and interspecies play. One hypothesis suggests a compensatory role for pets in countering low human social interaction and support. Sociability and empathy have been defined almost exclusively vis-à-vis other humans, not other species. Persons with low sociability may be more likely to seek out and benefit from interactions with pets, including play. A competing hypothesis suggests that sociability and empathy may be robust across species, such that highly sociable and empathic persons (toward other humans) are also that way toward pets. This would be consistent with Kujala et al.'s (2017) finding that adults employed generally similar patterns in evaluating the facial expressions of humans and of dogs.

Relational Characteristics: In addition to individual variables, human and pet, qualities of their relationship may affect play. For example, the mutual bonding of a human with a pet dog results in bidirectional influences. Thus, in a study (Handling, 2012) of 10 adult female dog owners and their dogs, oxytocin levels of both pair members were positively correlated. In addition, those owners who reported that the benefits of their pet were much higher than the costs (an indicator of attachment) had dogs with elevated levels of oxytocin.

Qualities of the human–pet relationship over time are likely to affect play. While we have little data, one might speculate about early versus mature phases of the relationship. Does human–dog play become more mutually responsive, synchronized, or routinized over time, as both partners build up expectations? How do events, such as separations, loss or addition of other family members, illness, etc. affect play? The lack of longitudinal data, including case studies with repeated measurements over time, preclude answers to these questions.

Situational Characteristics: It is plausible that the ecological context will influence human–pet play. Much of the observational data on human–dog play is derived from interactions observed in dog parks or laboratory settings. Much less is known about play within the home or outside, in non–dog park areas. When humans and their dogs are in a specifically designated play-friendly context, such as a dog park, interactions may well differ from those in other contexts. In particular, daily life within the home often combines caregiving (feeding, exercising, etc.) with physical proximity (for example, a dog rests at the feet of a human who is watching TV) and perhaps play (for example, a teenager dangles a string for a cat to catch while checking her messages on a smartphone). This results in complex interactions with elements of play mixed with other behaviours and goals.

Significance of Human–Pet Play

Perhaps the most important of unanswered questions are the consequences or sequelae of interspecies play. The lack of prospective, longitudinal studies makes this difficult to answer. In addition, most studies have focused, understandably, on human–canine play, given the interactive abilities of both play partners. This leaves us with little understanding of play with other pet species. Moreover, most studies fail to place human–pet interactions, including play, within the context of other social relationships, particularly those within species. The acontextual focus extends to cultural, historical, and developmental differences, all of which have received minimal attention.

Many questions await further research. For children, is such play developmentally significant? For adults, does human–pet play contribute to the quality of that relationship? If so, how? Is human–pet play related to adaptive outcomes, such as stress reduction? If so, which elements of such play are most significant? What is the interplay between human–pet play and human–human interactions? To guide a future research agenda, one might advance several areas of inquiry.

Rough and Tumble Play: Play with dogs provides opportunity for rough and tumble (R&T) play. The physical games of tug of war, chase, and parallel running frequently observed in human play with dogs are examples of R&T play. This type of play may not be readily available to children during peer play. Observations of young children in childcare settings find that teachers, especially females, often view R&T play negatively, confuse it with aggression, and seek to restrict it (Bosacki et al., 2015; Storli & Sandseter, 2015). At the same time, play experts such as Pellegrini (1987) argue that R&T play has many developmental benefits. In addition to aiding physical development through vigorous movement, R&T play may afford practice in social skills, especially in differentiating social signals from aggressive ones. Such play also may aid self-regulation of arousal and emotion, and provide touch and body contact stimulation (Melson, 2001).

Building Empathy: There are some data suggesting a link between attachment to one's pet and empathy, both human- and animal-directed (Daly, 2009; Melson et al., 1992). To understand this association further, one should investigate which aspects of the human–pet bond are linked to empathy. One might hypothesize that in play with pets, children and adults may attune to the different behavioural and emotional characteristics of a different species member, thereby taking the perspective of a very different "other." Myers (2007), in detailed observations of preschool children in interaction with a variety of animals, including a rabbit, turtle, tarantula, and monkey, showed that these children were aware of and attempted to adjust to the distinct behavioural repertoires of each animal. Such perspective-taking may mediate increased empathy.

Play as Relaxation and Stress Reduction: Another hypothesis is derived from previously discussed research showing that both adults and children find their pets to be sources of support and stress reduction, particularly when emotionally bonded to the pet. The specific behaviours that humans engage in with pets that contribute to this stress reduction are unclear. However, experimental studies show decreased heart rate, blood pressure, and cortisol, a stress hormone, when children or adults are engaged in a quiet interaction with a friendly dog. For example, in one study (Polheber & Matchock, 2014), undergraduates had a quiet play time with a novel but friendly dog, during which they could give treats, pet, and talk to the dog. As compared with a quiet time with a friend, or alone, those in the "dog condition" had lower cortisol and heart rate levels. The benefits of dog presence remained when the students underwent a social stress test (a mock high-pressure job interview). This physiological "pet effect" is even more pronounced when young adult participants have self-reported elevated anxiety (Wheeler & Faulkner, 2015).

Another component of stress reduction may be the general positive affect that often infuses human play with pets. As noted earlier, smiling and laughing often are observed in human play with pets. Pet owners themselves often describe their interactions with pets as sources of fun and amusement. In this way, human–pet play may serve as a distraction or even as a source of positive feeling for family members.

Conclusion

Most children and adults are living with household pets. In addition, pets are common in classrooms, in neighbourhood homes, and throughout communities. Cultural imagery is saturated with pets, primarily, but not exclusively, dogs and cats, who adorn clothing, serve as mascots for sports teams, 'sell' products, and play leads in major motion pictures and videos. Pet products are a multi-billion-dollar industry, reflecting the dominant view that pets are "family members." Supplanting the historic role of pets and domestic animals as economically beneficial workers, today's pets are portrayed as sources of love, companionship, fun, affection, and play.

Not surprisingly, then, both adults and children often express close emotional ties to their pets. Human pet owners derive feelings of emotional support from their companion animals, an effect that may be heightened when humans feel stress. (It should be noted that dogs who are positively attached to their owners often seek emotional support from them as well.) Some evidence suggests that a close bond with a pet may serve as an attachment figure, providing a sense of security and safety and serving as a "secure base." Other studies document a physiological relaxation effect from the presence of a friendly animal (usually a dog). By contrast, interactions with a human friend often involve physiological arousal.

When ties to pets are placed in the context of human social networks, it is presently unclear how pet and human social support are related. In some cases, pet support may compensate for the absence or weakness of human support. However, other evidence suggest that relationships with pets may offer distinct, non-substituting emotional benefits. Finally, some evidence suggests that both kinds of support may be positively correlated and indeed traced to antecedent variables, such as a human's general social skill.

Beyond providing emotional support, human bonds with pets often involve caregiving and nurturance, since companion animals are dependent on human care. Thus, relationships with pets are distinctive in that they often combine supporting and being supported, nurturing and being nurtured.

Studies of human–animal interaction reflect an emerging, interdisciplinary field. There are many gaps in research and more questions than answers. Extension of findings to non-canine species and particularly to 'pocket pets' such as hamsters, guinea pigs, rabbits, and turtles is important in establishing the robustness and generalizability of findings. Of particular interest to this chapter and volume is the nature of play across species. While theories of intraspecies play, both human–human and those within non-human species, map quite well onto human–pet play, there are differences. As noted, play with pets involves decoding and adapting to another species' play repertoire and signals, perhaps enlisting perspective-taking and empathic skills. Human propensity toward anthropomorphism and attraction to neoteny further complicate understanding of the pet as play partner. Play with pets tends to be asymmetrical and non-reciprocal (excepting play with dogs), inviting imposition of a 'play frame' and use of scaffolding to create the illusion of reciprocity. Many sources of variation – human, animal, and relational – affect interspecies play, but these variables are poorly understood. Importantly, we are just beginning to see fine-grained studies of the 'black box' of human play with a pet. Such studies, currently only of human–dog play, need to be married to interview and survey data concerning the qualities of human–pet relationships. For example, if children derive emotional support from a pet, which play behaviours, if any, contribute to that effect? If children see a pet as an attachment figure, what occurs during play to affect that attachment relationship? Would a dog who occasionally nips or growls at the child contribute to an insecure attachment?

More detailed studies of the components of human–pet play are needed in order to understand how such play might be connected to other dimensions of human functioning. If friendly dog presence is relaxing, causing lower heart rate, blood pressure, and cortisol levels, do any play behaviours predict these outcomes? Is play, on the other hand, more physiologically arousing than quiet presence? Are there adaptive consequences to such arousal?

The study of human play with pets expands our understanding of play from an intraspecies to interspecies phenomenon. Importantly, it sheds light on a significant but hitherto largely ignored aspect of human and other animal life. We live as one species among many; our lives are entwined in a web of diversity. Our understanding of play is incomplete unless we include how we play with other animals.

References

Ainsworth, M., Blehar, M. C., Waters, E., & Wall, S. (1978). *Patterns of attachment: A psychological study of the strange situation.* Hillsdale, NJ: Erlbaum.

American Veterinary Medical Association (AVMA) (2012). *U.S. pet ownership and demographic sourcebook.* Schaumburg, IL: AVMA.

Antonocopoulus, N. M. D., & Pychyl, T. A. (2010). An examination of the potential role of pet ownership, human social support, and pet attachment in the psychological health of individuals living alone. *Anthrozoos*, *23*, 37–54.

Bahlig-Pieren, Z., & Turner, D. T. (1999). Anthropomorphic interpretations and ethological descriptions of dog and cat behavior by lay people. *Anthrozoos*, *12*, 205–210.

Beck, A. M., & Katcher, A. M. (Eds.) (1983). *New perspectives on our lives with companion animals*. Philadelphia: University of Pennsylvania Press.

Bekoff, M., & Byers, J. (Eds.) (1998). *Animal play: Evolutionary, comparative, and ecological perspectives*. Cambridge: Cambridge University Press.

Ben-Aderet, T., Gallego-Abenza, M., Reby, D., & Mathevon, M. (2017). Dog-directed speech: Why do we use it and do dogs pay attention to it? *Proceedings of the Royal Society B: Biological Sciences 284*, 1–7.

Bodsworth, W., & Coleman, G. J. (2001). Children's companion animal attachment bonds in single and two parent families. *Anthrozoos*, *14*, 216–223.

Bosacki, S., Woods, H., & Coplan, R. (2015). Canadian female and male early childhood educators' perceptions of children's aggression and rough-and-tumble play. *Early Childhood Development and Care*, *185*, 1134–1147.

Bradshaw, J. W. S., Pullen, A. J., & Rooney, N. J. (2015). Why do adult dogs play? *Behavioral Processes*, *110*, 82–87.

Brown, S. (2010). Where the wild brands are: Some thoughts on anthropomorphic marketing. *The Marketing Review*, *10*, 204–224.

Bryant, B. (1985). The neighborhood walk: Sources of support in middle childhood. *Monographs of the Society for Research in Child Development*, *50*, 1–114.

Bryant, B. (1990). The richness of the child–pet relationship: A consideration of both benefits and costs of pets to children. *Anthrozoos*, *3*, 253–261.

Chaplin, L. N. (2009). Please may I have a bike? Better yet, may I have a hug? An examination of children's and adolescents' happiness. *Journal of Happiness Studies*, *10*, 541–562.

Chudacoff, H. P. (2007). *Children at play: An American history*. New York: NYU Press.

Covert, A. M., et al. (1985). Pets, early adolescents and families. *Marriage and Family Review*, *8*, 95–108.

Daly, B. (2009). Empathic differences in adults as a function of childhood and adult pet ownership and pet type. *Anthrozoos*, *22*, 371–382.

Demirbas, Y. S., Ozturk, H., Emre, B., Kockaya, M., Ozvardar, T., & Scott, A. (2016). Adults' ability to interpret canine body language during a dog–child interaction. *Anthrozoos*, *29*, 581–596.

Fine, A. H. (Ed.) (2012). *Handbook of animal-assisted therapy* (3rd edn.). New York: Elsevier.

Furman, W. (1989). The development of children's social networks. In D. Belle (Ed.), *Children's social networks and social supports* (pp. 151–172). New York: Wiley.

Garvey, C. (1990). *Play*. Cambridge, MA: Harvard University Press.

Geerdts, M. B. (2016). (Un)real animals: Anthropomorphism and early learning about animals. *Child Development Perspectives*, *10*, 10–14.

Girardi, A., & Pozzulo, J. D. (2015). Childhood experiences with family pets and internalizing symptoms in early adulthood. *Anthrozoos, 28*, 421–436.

Goffman, E. (1959). *The presentation of self in everyday life.* New York: Anchor Books.

Grier, C. (2006). *Pets in America: A history.* Chapel Hill: University of North Carolina Press.

Guthrie, S. E. (1997). Anthropomorphism: A definition and a theory. In R. W. Mitchell, N. S. Thompson, & H. L. Miles (Eds.), *Anthropomorphism, anecdotes and animals* (pp. 50–58). Albany: State University of New York Press.

Hall, N. J., Liu, J., Kertes, D. A., & Wynne, C. D. L. (2016). Behavioral and self-report measures influence children's reported attachment to their dog. *Anthrozoos, 29*, 137–150.

Handling, L. (2012). Association between the psychological characteristics of the human–dog relationship and oxytocin and cortisol levels. *Anthrozoos, 25*, 215–228.

Hare, B., & Tomasello, M. (1999). Domestic dogs (*Canis familiaris*) use human and conspecific social clues to locate hidden food. *Journal of Comparative Psychology, 113*, 173–177.

Henry, B. C., & Sanders, C. E. (2007). Bullying and animal abuse: Is there a connection? *Society & Animals, 15*, 107–126.

Horowitz, A. C., & Bekoff, M. (2007). Naturalizing anthropomorphism: Behavioral prompts to our humanizing of animals. *Anthrozoos, 20*, 23–35.

Humane Society of the United States. (2012). Pets by the numbers. www.humanesociety.org/issues/pet_overpopulation/facts/pet_ownership_statistics.html.

Jalongo, M. R. (2015). An attachment perspective on the child–dog bond: Interdisciplinary and international research findings. *Early Childhood Education Journal, 43*, 395–405.

Kaminski, J., Schultz, L., & Tomasello, M. (2012). How dogs know when communication is intended for them. *Developmental Science, 15*, 222–232.

Kaye, K., & Charney, R. (1981). Conversational asymmetry between mother and child. *Journal of Child Language, 8*, 35–50.

Kruger, D. J. (2015). Non-mammalian infants requiring parental care elicit more human caregiving reactions than superprecocial infants do. *Ethology, 121*, 769–774.

Kujala, M., Somppi, S., Jokela, M., Vainio, O., & Parkkonen, L. (2017). Human empathy, personality and experience affect the emotion ratings of dog and human facial expressions. *PlosOne.* https://doi.org/10.1371/journal.pone.0170730.

Lockwood, R., & Ascione, F. R. (Eds.) (1998). *Cruelty to animals and interpersonal violence: Readings in research and application.* West Lafayette, IN: Purdue University Press.

Marshall-Pescini, S., Ceretta, M., & Prato-Previde, E. (2014). Do domestic dogs understand human actions as goal-directed? *PlosOne, 9*, 1–8.

McPhedran, S. (2009). Animal abuse, family violence and child well-being: A review. *Journal of Family Violence, 24*, 41–52.

Melson, G. F. (2001). *Why the wild things are: Animals in the lives of children.* Cambridge, MA: Harvard University Press.

Melson, G. F. (2010). Play between children and domestic animals. In E. Enwokah (Ed.), *Play as engagement and communication* (pp. 23–39). New York: University Press of America.

Melson, G. F. (2013). Children's ideas about the moral standing and social welfare of non-human species. *Journal of Sociology and Social Welfare, 90,* 81–106.

Melson, G. F., & Fogel, A. (1996). Parental perceptions of their children's involvement with household pets: A test of a specificity model of nurturance. *Anthrozoos, 9,* 95–105.

Melson, G. F., Kahn, P. H. Jr., Beck, A., Friedman, B., Roberts, T., Garrett, E., & Gill, B. T. (2009). Children's behavior toward and understanding of robotic and living dogs. *Journal of Applied Developmental Psychology, 30,* 92–102.

Melson, G. F., Peet, S., & Sparks, C. (1992). Children's attachment to their pets: Links to socioemotional development. *Children's Environments Quarterly, 8,* 55–65.

Miklosi, A., Topal, J., & Csanyi, V. (2004). Comparative social cognition: What can dogs teach us? *Animal Behavior, 67,* 995–1004.

Miller, S. C., Kennedy, C. C., DeVoe, D. C., Hickey, M., Nelson, T., & Kogan, L. (2009). An examination of changes in oxytocin levels in men and women before and after interaction with a bonded dog. *Anthrozoos, 22,* 31–42.

Mitchell, R., & Sinkhorn, K. (2014). Why do people laugh during dog–human play interactions? *Anthrozoos, 27,* 235–250.

Muldoon, J. C., Williams, J. M., & Lawrence, A. (2016). Exploring children's perspectives on the welfare needs of pet animals. *Anthrozoos, 29*(3), 357–375.

Myers, G. (2007). *The significance of children and animals.* West Lafayette, IN: Purdue University Press.

Norman, K., Pellis, S., Barrett, L., & Henzi, S. P. (2015). Down but not out: Supine posture as facilitator of play in domestic dogs. *Behavioral Processes, 110,* 88–95.

Oliva, J., Rault, J. L., Appleton, B., & Lill, A. (2015). Oxytocin enhances the appropriate use of human social cues by the domestic dog (*Canis Familiaris*) in an object choice task. *Animal Cognition, 18,* 767–775.

Paul, E. S., Moore, A., McAinsh, P., Symonds, E., McCune, S., & Bradshaw, J. W. S. (2014). Sociality motivation and anthropomorphic thinking about pets. *Anthrozoos, 27,* 499–512.

Pellegrini, A. (1987). Rough-and-tumble play: Developmental and educational significance. *Educational Psychologist, 22,* 23–43.

Pelletier-Stiefel, J., Pepler, D., Crozier, K., Stanhope, L., Corter, C., & Abramovitch, R. (1986). Nurturance in the home: A longitudinal study of sibling interaction. In A. Fogel & G. F. Melson (Eds.), *Origins of nurturance: Developmental, biological and cultural perspectives on caregiving* (pp. 3–24). Hillsdale, NJ: Erlbaum.

Pew Research Center (2006). *Gauging family intimacy: Dogs edge cats (dads trail both).* Washington, DC. www.pewsocialtrends.org/2006/03/07/gauging-family-intimacy.

Polheber, J. P., & Matchock, R. L. (2014). The presence of a dog attenuates cortisol and heart rate in the Trier Social Stress Test compared to human friends. *Journal of Behavioral Medicine, 37,* 860–867.

Power, T. G. (2000). *Play and exploration in children and animals*. Mahwah, NJ: Erlbaum.

Romero, T., Nagasawa, M., Mogi, K., Hasegawa, T., & Kikusui, T. (2015). Intranasal administration of oxytocin promotes social play in domestic dogs. *Communicative and Integrative Biology*, *8*(3), e1017157.

Rooney, N. J., & Bradshaw, J. W. S. (2002). An experimental study of the effects of play on the dog–human relationship. *Applied Animal Behavior Science*, *75*, 161–176.

Rooney, N. J., & Bradshaw, J. W. S. (2003). Links between play and dominance and attachment dimensions of dog–human relationships. *Journal of Applied Animal Welfare Science*, *6*, 67–94.

Rooney, N. J., & Bradshaw, J. W. S. (2006). Social cognition in the domestic dog: Behavior of species toward participation in inter-specific games. *Animal Behavior*, *72*, 343–352.

Rooney, N. J., Bradshaw, J. W. S., & Robinson, I. H. (2000). A comparison of dog–dog and dog–human play behavior. *Applied Animal Behavior Science*, *66*, 235–248.

Rost, D. H., & Hartmann, A. (1994). Children and their pets. *Anthrozoos*, *7*, 242–252.

Rubin, K. H., Fein, G. G., & Vandenberg, B. (1983). Play. In P. Mussen & E. M. Hetherington (Eds.), *Handbook of child psychology* (vol. 4, pp. 693–774).

Rud, A. J., & Beck, A. (2003). Companion animals in Indiana elementary schools. *Anthrozoos*, *7*, 242–252.

Sixsmith, J., Gabhainn, S. N., Fleming, C., & O'Higgins, S. (2007). Children's, parents' and teachers' perceptions of well-being. *Health Education*, *107*, 511–513.

Staats, S., et al. (2008). Reasons for companion animal guardianship (pet ownership) from two populations. *Society & Animals*, *16*, 279–291.

Storli, R., & Sandseter, E. B. H. (2015). Preschool teachers' perceptions of children's rough-and-tumble (R&T) play in indoor and outdoor environments. *Early Childhood Development and Care*, *185*, 1995–2009.

Taylor, P., Funk, C., & Craighill, C. (2006.) Gauging family intimacy: Dog edge cats (dads trail both). Pew Research Center. Available at http://pewresearch.org/assets/social/pdf/Pets.pdf.

Twain, M. (1895). *The adventures of Huckleberry Finn*. New York: Harper & Bros.

Waller, B. M., Peirce, K., Caeiro, C. C., Scheider, L., Burrows, A. M., McCunbe, S., & Kaminski, J.(2013). Paedomorphic facial expressions give dogs a selective advantage. *PlosOne*, *8*, 1–6.

Wheeler, E. A., & Faulkner, M. (2015). The "pet effect." *Society and Animals*, *23*, 425–438.

Zasloff, R. L., Hart, L. A., & DeArmond, H. (1999). Animals in elementary school education in California. *Journal of Applied Animal Welfare Science*, *2*, 347–357.

PART II

Development of Play in Humans

8 Infant Sensorimotor Play

Development of Sociocultural Competence and Enactive Cognition

Doris Bergen

Because the visual, sensory, and motor areas of the brain are actively developing during the first year of life and making connections to the emotional brain centres, the early manifestations of infant play typically involve these areas. For example, infants exercise these brain areas when they visually examine various objects and actions of people, shake and roll objects and toys, press buttons or levers, move their bodies to music and rhythm, place toys into and out of containers, play peek-a-boo with other humans, touch faces and various materials, and show enjoyment when engaging in many other physically based interactions with the people and objects in their environments. While an observer might conclude that such behaviours have little sociocultural or cognitive involvement, theorists who have studied infant behaviour in depth have noted that this sensorimotor play is really the precursor to other levels of social and emotional, as well as cognitive development. Recent research on mirror neurons has suggested that infants are primed for noticing and imitating other human's behaviours, and this ability seems to be essential for their social-emotional as well as other areas of development. This chapter reviews early brain development and early play behaviours and discusses theoretical perspectives on the sensorimotor play/socioemotional/cognitive development dynamic systems. It concludes with a discussion of the implications of recent technological influences on early play that may be affecting this dynamic system and thus reducing opportunities for the development of sociocultural competence and enactive cognition.

Sensorimotor Behaviour

Anyone who has spent time caring for or just observing infants and toddlers will have noticed many sensorimotor-based manifestations of their behaviour, involving actions such as visually examining various objects and movements of people; touching faces, surfaces, and different materials; shaking and rolling objects and toys; pressing buttons or levers; moving their bodies to music and rhythm; placing toys into and out of containers; and playing peek-a-boo with other humans. This playful engagement in a wide range of sensory and physically active interactions with the people and objects in their environments is evident in the behaviour of all typically developing infants, and while an observer might conclude that such sensorimotor play behaviours have little long-term social, emotional, or cognitive meaning, those who have studied infant behaviour in depth have noted that this sensorimotor play is really the precursor to other levels of social and emotional, as well as cognitive development. In fact, researchers are beginning to conclude that later executive functioning and embodied cognition skills are based on these early sensorimotor behaviours (e.g., Diamond, 2006). While researchers are using new methodologies to investigate and discover more information about the relationships among infant sensorimotor behaviours and cognitive development, the view that there is a sensorimotor component affecting other areas of development is not a new idea, however.

For example, Arnold Gesell (1928; Gesell & Ilg, 1943) studied the longitudinal development of physical/motor, social, and cognitive abilities from infancy to adolescents, and he reported on the close connections among these areas of development. His statements about the principals of infant motor development included descriptions of concepts such as motor growth gradients (e.g., cephalocaudal, proximal-distal, and ulnar-radial) and functional asymmetry (e.g., initially hand symmetry and later hand asymmetry), and some of his physical/motor skill assessment methods are incorporated in infant developmental testing even today. Also, his preschool-age fine motor tests, such as ability to copy a circle, square, and triangle, and his gross motor tests, such as skipping ability, often are incorporated in kindergarten academic readiness tests.

Other important theorists, notably Piaget (1945), Bruner (1964), and Gibson (1969), also have hypothesized about the ways that sensorimotor experiences provide the basis for cognitive development, and each has described how such experiences provide a foundation for higher-order thinking. It is only now, however, as neuroscience begins to provide evidence of the early activation of the visual, sensory, and motor areas of the brain, that the vital importance of infant sensorimotor experiences, many of which can be defined as play, is being confirmed. Current empirical research is supporting the theoretical view that infant sensorimotor actions provide a foundation not only for physical development but also for social-cultural competence and higher cognition (e.g., Thelen & Smith, 1994). Koziol et al. (2012) have discussed the importance of the role of the sensorimotor brain areas in the development of executive functioning and embodied cognition, and they have asserted that brain evolution really has been focused on the control of action rather than on the development of cognition. They state that higher-level executive functioning skills are based on these early sensorimotor experiences and assert, "We were not born to think. We were born to move" (p. 515). Because much of infant movement involves sensorimotor types of play, the views of these various theorists and researchers support the important role that infant sensorimotor play has in fostering higher levels of brain development, social-emotional competence, and complex cognitive skills.

Early Brain Development

An infant comes into the world with a brain that already contains most of the neurons that the child will have throughout life. However, at birth the connecting neural network is not extensive in most brain areas. The infant arrives in the world with a set of basic reflexes that are involuntary, automatic, and complex but also stereotypical, and these are mediated through the brainstem and spinal cord (Bergen & Woodin, 2010). Because there is auditory learning in the womb, the newborn's auditory system already has the capability of being sensitive to rhythmic cycles (Winkler et al., 2009). One area of the brain that has rapid development during the premature period is the cerebellum (Koziol et al., 2012), and there is now mounting evidence that premature infants may have learning problems later if their cerebellum development has not matured before their birth (Volpe, 2009).

At birth, the neonate's brain has more synaptic connections in the sensorimotor areas of the cortex and the cerebellum, and thus, infant reflexive behaviours are most active initially. Infants also can express emotion at an early age, however, because the amygdala, part of the limbic system, is well formed at birth. By the time infants are 2 or 3 months old, brain activity has become greater in the cerebellar hemispheres, parietal and temporal lobes, primary visual cortex, and basal ganglia (Bergen & Woodin, 2010), resulting in the infant beginning to have intentional movements. Koziol and colleagues (2012) state that it is the cerebellum, the structure in the hindbrain specialized for motor coordination, that has an especially important role in the early development of both movement and cognitive processes. These authors suggest that the infant's continuous sensorimotor interaction with the environment lays the groundwork for later brain development, including the development of executive functioning. They indicate that activity of the cerebellum also provides instruction to the developing frontal cortex systems on anticipatory control functioning, suggesting that activities enjoyed by infants related to being touched; reaching for and touching people and objects; looking, tasting, and manipulating objects; and being bounced, swung, or lifted contribute not only to coordination of voluntary movement but also to the development of goal-directed behaviour.

At about 6 months the dorsal and medial frontal regions of the infant brain show greater activity, and by 8–9 months, other areas of the frontal lobe become more active. The limbic cortex, where emotions are recognized or "felt," matures during the 6- to 18-month period. A commonly observed behaviour in infants is their imitation of their observed actions of others, usually their parents or other children. This behaviour appears to be related to the activation of "mirror neurons" located in the parietal and frontal lobe (Coude et al., 2016; Rizzolatti & Craighero, 2004). As infants gain increased motor control, enabling them to crawl and walk, engage in more elaborated play with objects and people, understand language and express language sounds, and learn through imitating the actions of others, their initial executive functioning skills continue to be refined (Diamond, 2006). Many of these skills can often be observed during the varied and extensive types of sensorimotor play that infants demonstrate, particularly in the second half of their first year of life.

Also, starting at about age 1 and continuing during the second year of life, there is exponential growth of synaptic connections, and this expansion is demonstrated in infant behaviours that give evidence of initial representational thinking abilities, such as pretend play and early language (Epstein, 1978). The number of synaptic connections in the toddler brain reaches adult level by age 2 and these connections continue to increase, eventually reaching twice the density of brain synapses in adults (Shore, 1997). Toddler brains also have more neurotransmitters, which facilitate brain communication, and their brains show higher metabolic rates related to greater brain activity. During the later infant age period, myelination by glial cells increases the speed of message transmission, and the emotional centres in the lower limbic system gain stronger connections with the frontal lobe of the brain, promoting toddlers' ability to understand and regulate emotions (Bergen & Woodin, 2010).

Very young children have implicit memories stored in the lower and midbrain area, and new methods of research have indicated that even infants may have some types of longer-term memory (Bauer, 2002). Explicit memories, which depend on the maturation of the cerebral cortex, also become evident in the toddler year (Newcombe et al., 2014). Blood flow increases in the sensorimotor and parietotemporal regions, and this supports development of handedness (related to brain hemispheric growth), greater sensory and motor control (related to sensorimotor area maturation), and aspects of perceptual and language growth (related to parietotemporal area maturation). Synaptic increases in Broca's area and myelination increases in Wernike's area support greater language growth (Bergen & Woodin, 2010). It is now generally acknowledged that, because of the extensive brain development occurring during the first two years of life, infants' experiences, including their sensorimotor play experiences, are crucial for optimum brain development. For example, Bornstein and colleagues (2006) report a strong relationship between types and variations of play experiences of toddlers and their later cognitive performance.

Early Play Development

For young children play really provides a "learning medium" for enhancing other developmental areas (Bergen, 1998). The first signs of behaviours that could be characterized as play usually occur over the first few months of infant life and initially involve infant-initiated repetitive motor behaviours focused on their own bodies; that is, infants regard their fingers, arms, legs, and other parts of the body as objects of play, and they initiate repetitive behaviours over and over, often expressing pleasure in these manipulations. At about 4 months of age infants' sensorimotor play shifts from being primarily focused on their own bodies and begins to be focused on the objects and people in their immediate environment. They begin to engage with objects (e.g., toys) using many sensorimotor actions, such as mouthing, banging, and shaking, and at first in this play they perform similar actions on every object. According to Fischer and Hogan (1989, p. 298), in their play, "the body plays a fundamental role ... there is no such thing as a brain without a body." Thus, although infant sensorimotor brain areas are developing and motoric practice is a major type of sensorimotor play, this play also is engaging other areas of the developing brain.

When infants reach 5–7 months, they begin to discriminate and use different sensorimotor behaviours with objects that have different characteristics. Whereas initially they used similar actions on all objects, such as mouthing or shaking, by this age they begin to shake rattles, bang blocks, hold a soft doll close, and mouth food (Uzgiris & Hunt, 1975). As infants achieve more and more motor development milestones, they access a wider variety of environmental features that attract their interest. When they have learned to sit, they can use visual guidance to reach and grasp toys and other objects, and they can bring their hands to midline to hold them and to use visual and motor skills to explore them. Thus, as their physical and sensory control increases, their playful actions become more and more diverse and more highly related to the characteristics of the objects. When they begin walking, their increased mobility allows them to interact with many more environmental features.

As their sensorimotor skills continue to increase during the latter part of the first year, infants become able to use both hands independently for exploration, repeat actions that are most interesting, and engage in a wide range of actions appropriate for the characteristics of the objects. By about 16 months, infants can begin to make inferences about novel objects based on very brief exposures to an exemplar (Baldwin et al., 1993). That is, when they are given toys with similar appearance and properties, infants use similar sensorimotor play patterns, but if they are given dissimilar toys with other features they will use an expanded set of sensorimotor behaviours. Older infants also use visual qualities of an object to infer underlying functional properties. For example, if the toy has movable parts, the infant will focus on moving those parts. Through this object play infants learn basic concepts of causality and, depending on the object's features, such as stability or movability, they gain initial cause/effect knowledge.

As functional play, which involves goal-related object play, increases, young children combine sensorimotor action patterns, such as putting a spoon in a bowl, a comb on a doll's hair, or a lid on a pot. By 12 months, most infants have learned to dump items out of a container, and they usually learn to dump before they learn to fill up the container. If a toy has movable parts, infants will focus on moving those parts. Infants from 12 to 18 months prefer toys that react to their actions. For example, toys activated by pressing buttons, pulling strings, or touching pictures are especially interesting to them. Through this object play infants learn basic concepts of causality and, depending on the object's features, such as stability or movability, they gain cause/effect knowledge. By 19 months, infants treat symbolic objects, such as pictures, differently from three-dimensional objects. For example, they will look at pictures of objects and point to them rather than trying to use them as toys (DeLoache et al., 1998). This ability to make quick and correct inferences helps explain how infant's knowledge base expands so rapidly over this period. Because a wide variation in the objects infants can access in an environment has an impact on their cognitive development, the best environments for older infants are ones with a rich variety of objects available for sensorimotor play.

Gopnik and colleagues (2001) have stated that toddlers seem to act like scientists as they experiment with what objects can do and learn what the affordances of the objects enable them to do. By the end of the second year, they enjoy manipulative materials such as clay, water, paint; begin to use simple puzzles; and build with blocks. This play is functional; that is, it is in the service of a self-chosen play goal, rather than being simply exploration of object characteristics (Garner & Bergen, 2015). Children of age 2 are more physically active than at any other time of life, and the availability of safe climbing structures, toys that can be pushed and pulled, riding toys, and jumping platforms encourage many types of sensorimotor play. Most toddlers can run with ease and pleasure, imitate motor activities of other children, and participate in games of motor imitation with peers. They practice fine motor skills by poking fingers into holes, picking up small objects, and using toys activated by buttons or knobs. They also like objects that make marks, such as crayons, pencils, and chalk. However, they are primarily interested in manipulating and learning about the medium, rather than creating a product (Garner & Bergen, 2015). Today's children also are using these sensorimotor skills to activate electronic tablets and phone apps, and it is now common to see young children focused on fingering such electronic devices for long periods of time.

In addition to sensorimotor play with objects, infant social play involves exercising sensorimotor skills such as seeing, hearing, and movement. Family members, especially parents and older children, usually are infants' first play partners, and they often initiate sensorimotor play with vocalizations, physical movements, and presentation of objects (Tamis-Lemonda et al., 2002). Although these sensory-based social interactions are initially initiated by others, infants soon begin to initiate such actions themselves. By 12 months, sensorimotor games such as giving and taking objects and pointing and naming objects are pervasive, and infants seek frequent repetition of the actions. Older infants also enjoy physically active sensorimotor play such as roughhousing and run-and-chase games, often played with fathers or older siblings. Mothers typically initiate early pretence that has a high sensorimotor component. For example, early pretend involves activities such as "pouring milk" and "drinking milk" from empty cups, putting the dolls to bed, or driving the truck filled with animals to the "farm."

Play with peers also has a large sensorimotor component. Young infants stare intently at activity of other infants, and older infants interact in play with peers by joint looking at objects, offering and taking objects, and touching common objects (Garner & Bergen, 2015). Sensorimotor social play at toddler age involves running-and-chasing and hiding-and-finding, although toddlers often think they are hidden if their eyes are closed. Many toddler toys now have computer chips enabling the toys to produce words, songs, numbers, and alphabet letters, and some of these toys continue automated actions for extensive time periods, thus making adult or peer social interaction less necessary. Whether such toys promote as many sensorimotor-based initiated play actions or social experiences as non-automated toys do is unknown presently.

Researchers studying young children with disabilities have found both similarities and differences in their play trajectory, depending on the type of disability. For example, the earliest sensorimotor play of infants with diagnoses of autism appears to be similar to the play of typically developing infants, but higher types of sensorimotor play often may be delayed (Baranek et al., 2005). However, Williams (2003) suggests that qualitative and quantitative differences in such children's play need to be studied longitudinally because current knowledge is incomplete. DiCarlo and colleagues (2003) have reported that toddlers with disabilities need greater adult participation and encouragement to advance their sensorimotor and other types of play abilities.

Theoretical Perspectives on Sensorimotor Play and Its Relation to Other Developmental Domains

Many theorists and researchers have described various ways that sensorimotor play development seems to co-occur and interact with other areas of infant and toddler development. Four theorists who have been clear about the importance of this sensorimotor-focused age period on later development are Jean Piaget, Jerome Bruner, Eleanor Gibson, and Esther Thelen.

Piaget's Cognitive Theory

An especially influential voice for the importance of sensorimotor play was that of Jean Piaget (1945), who suggested that early sensorimotor play, which he called practice play, is instrumental in fostering both higher levels of play and higher levels of cognitive development. From his extensive observations of his own children, he described six stages of sensorimotor-initiated actions during the infant-toddler age period. Piaget observed that in the earliest intentional sensorimotor play behaviour (Period of Primary Circular Reactions, birth to 6 weeks) infants are intrinsically motivated to perform these sensorimotor actions on the objects in the environment. In the next phase (Secondary Circular Reactions, 1–4 months) infants have more varied action schema but they still use sensorimotor actions indiscriminately, and in the third stage (Tertiary Circular Reactions, 8–12 months) they will use different sensorimotor actions on objects to get a variety of responses. In the final stage (Inventions of New Means by Mental Combinations, 18–24 months) older infants expand the range of their sensorimotor behaviours and during their play they begin to use objects symbolically, accompany their play with language, and engage in pretence.

Although language, cognition, and play become much more extensive and elaborated during the later stages of cognitive development that Piaget described, there is still a play–cognition relationship. For example, in the Preoperational period pre-schoolers engage in extensive and elaborated pretence, and in the Concrete Operational period elementary-age children focus on games with rules. However, Piaget has clearly stated that these later cognitive stages are preceded by and built on this first period of Sensorimotor Operations. That is, he stressed that infant sensorimotor development, including sensorimotor play development, is an important precursor to and serves as a basis for later higher levels of cognitive development.

Piaget's theoretical ideas related to his later stages of cognitive development have been very influential in both psychological research and educational practice. However, his views of the importance of the sensorimotor stage as the basis for these later advanced cognitive stages has not always received as much attention. Based on recent brain development research information, Piaget's discussion of the importance of this earliest stage may be reexamined more deeply because new findings on brain sensorimotor development are confirming his observational conclusions.

Bruner's Representation Theory

Jerome Bruner (1964), building on the work of Piaget, hypothesized that humans develop their intellectual power by learning to use and understand objects through three "modes of representation" (p. 2), and these are sequenced in the process of cognitive development. The first of these is based on sensorimotor activity and is the basis of later cognitive reasoning and learning about the world. He labelled the three representation modes as *Enactive*, *Iconic*, and *Symbolic*. Enactive representation is the earliest type and involves sensorimotor interactions with "real" objects. For example, infants' touching, shaking, tasting, and manipulating of objects and young children's step climbing, water play, and block building all involve direct sensorimotor exploration and interactions with their physical and human environments. According to Bruner, these enactive representations serve to encode "body" knowledge in the muscles and sensorimotor areas of the brain. Infants often use the physical knowledge they have learned from interacting with one object on novel objects, exploring their features with their available sensorimotor actions. Through this process, infants gradually learn to match their sensorimotor actions to the novel characteristics of objects.

Bruner has stated that this first level of "enactive" knowledge provides the basis for all other types of knowledge. That is, he has asserted that the sensorimotor experiences of seeing, touching, moving, tasting, and manipulating real objects are essential for the human ability to move to higher levels of knowledge. After experiencing enactive knowledge, Bruner states that children of toddler age begin to understand *Iconic* representations, which are replica representations of real objects, such as pictures, video images, or models of real objects (e.g., cars, dolls). However, their prior experiences with real-world objects (i.e., enactive knowledge) are essential in order for young children to understand that such images (e.g., iconic knowledge) can "stand for" the real features of the environment. For example, having held and worn shoes, petted a kitten, and ridden in a car, they can now point to a picture of "shoe" or "kitten" or find the "car" in a storybook.

Bruner has asserted that experience with these two levels of objects – enactive and iconic – then becomes the essential basis for young children's ability to understand the third level of knowledge, which he called *Symbolic* representation. This level of representation requires being able to interpret arbitrary symbols, such as letters or numbers, that can encode meanings. For example, preschool children can learn that a written symbol, such as "Bill," can stand for their name, and they learn to point to the symbol "3" to show how old they are. They ultimately learn how to interpret much symbolic information.

Bruner argued that once all three of these modes of representation are understood, higher-order thinking is possible. Thus, although all three levels of representational knowledge are important, the first one, the "enactive," is the one on which the other two are built, and it is the way infants and young children initially come to understand their world. Bruner's view supporting the importance of infant sensorimotor experiences as the basis for higher levels of thought is related to the body of literature on "embodied cognition," which is presently being discussed as important throughout life. In a review of the recent theoretical and research literature on embodied cognition, Wilson has suggested that, "it is possible that mental concepts may be built up out of cognitive primitives that are themselves sensorimotor in nature" (Wilson, 2002, p. 634).

Gibson's Perceptual Theory

Eleanor Gibson (1969, 1997) provided another theoretical view of the importance of the sensorimotor experiences of infants with the research-based assertion that perceptual experiences (e.g., sensory, motoric, visual) can be directly understood even by very young children without mediation of cognitive processes. She stated that every environment affords opportunities for perception and action, and the properties of an object suggest even to young children how the object should be used (Gibson, 1969; McGrenere & Ho, 2000). That is, the stimulus features of the environment, labelled "affordances" by Gibson's husband, J. J. Gibson (1979), enable experiencing direct perceptual knowledge and thus action related to that knowledge. Eleanor Gibson posited that, in contrast to Piaget's view that perceptions were inferred by cognitive processes, infants could use the affordances of the environment to directly perceive information. She stated that infants perceive these affordances through their spontaneous exploratory activity and play. Gibson's perceptually based experiments with infants included the famous "visual cliff" experiment (Gibson & Walk, 1960), in which infants could perceive that a clear platform appeared to be unsafe and refuse to crawl across it, thus supporting her theoretical view. From the results of her experiments she concluded that there is always perception–action reciprocity and that the human ability to select an appropriate behaviour from a repertoire of behaviours can be observed even in infants shortly after their birth.

Of course, the infant repertoire of sensorimotor behaviours is more limited, but those behaviours that are available are used by the infant to gain direct knowledge from the environment. Gibson stated that perceptual development arises from infants' initial ability to perceive the affordances in the environment through their spontaneous sensorimotor exploratory activity, observations of the consequences of such activity, and selection of additional means of exploration. This process then contributes to higher-order thinking by providing behavioural flexibility, problem-solving ability, discrimination of objects and self, and perception of others as causal agents (i.e., human agency) (Bergen, 2008). Thus, the types of sensorimotor play experiences that young children have can directly affect their knowledge of the physical and social world. Drawing on Gibson's theoretical base, Carr (2000) has noted that affordances of objects have three characteristics relevant for understanding the types of playful actions young children use when they interact with toys and other objects: (1) transparency, i.e. the object signals which actions can be used; (2) challenge, i.e., different objects have many or few actions that can be used; and (3) accessibility, i.e., objects differ in how easily various actions can be used. These differing affordances of various play materials affect the quality of children's play, and observations of such play can provide information about young children's brain,perceptual, and cognitive development (Bergen, 2012).

Thelen's Dynamic Theory

Esther Thelen provided new insights into young children's sensorimotor and cognitive development by observing this development through the lens of dynamic systems theory. She stated that "dynamic systems theory presents a flexible, time-dependent, and emergent view of behavioral change" (2005, p. 255). Thelen and her colleagues (e.g., Thelen & Smith, 1994; Thelen & Spencer, 1998) have studied infant development through this theoretical perspective and have concluded that early human development involves continuous interactions of different systems at many developmental levels. They have stated that the development of mental functions is not a separate developmental process but rather is built on biological growth and physical functions. Thelen's theoretical view thus extends the Gibsonian perspective that cognition is based on perception and action. According to this perspective, human developmental processes are "modular, heterochronic, context-dependent, and multidimensional" (Thelen & Smith, 1994, p. 121). Developmental structures and functions are interactive and involve many individual parts and processes, although they result in "self-organization" (Thelen, 1989).

Thelen's ideas have been derived from research on the processes involved in the development of infant locomotion, reaching behaviour, and other sensorimotor developmental achievements. For example, her studies of infants' learning to crawl and walk have uncovered a causal web of dynamic interaction among perception, action, and cognition. Thelen's perspective makes explicit the view that human developmental processes do not follow a linear progression; rather, they involve a dynamic interplay among a wide variety of systemic variables. Thus, Thelen's theoretical view suggests that, because infant brain maturation, sensorimotor achievements, and early play development all exhibit qualities of dynamic systems, they must be investigated and understood as parts of a larger complex dynamic system.

Infant Brain Maturation and Sensorimotor Play Development as Dynamic Processes

According to Van Geert (2000), dynamic systems models are much better at explaining most human developmental processes than are linear theories. Because both play development and brain maturation are complex phenomena that have not been well explained by linear systems thinking, these phenomena may be better understood through the lens of non-linear dynamic systems theory (Bergen, 2012; Fromberg, 2010; Vanderven, 2006). Some of the concepts of dynamic system theory that are relevant for both brain maturation and play development are highlighted in the following sections.

Brain Maturation as a Dynamic Systems Process

Even in the prenatal period, the brain shows *self-organization*, with patterns that spontaneously emerge from chaotic appearances. For example, the cortex is formed by neurons systematically climbing "ladders" of glia cells to create the higher brain centres (Bergen & Woodin, 2017). *Sensitive dependence on initial conditions* is also evident, as there are harmful effects of drugs on prenatal brain development and harmful effects of abuse or neglect on infant brain development (Carlson & Earls, 1997). Early brain development shows both *openness* and the presence of *control parameters* that guide brain developmental patterns. There are also *phase shifts* in the timing of myelination of the limbic system and frontal lobe. Brain development also involves *soft assembly* as it is not initially "hard-wired." Throughout life, the brain demonstrates *plasticity*, and there are both *attractor* (i.e., stable) and *disequilibrium* periods. There are also *recursive* patterns and repeating (*fractal*) patterns as various areas of the brain develop. Because it exhibits these qualities of a non-linear dynamic system, brain development can be considered such a system.

Play Development as a Dynamic Systems Process

Play development also is a *self-organizing* system that may appear chaotic but that moves toward order, with emerging patterns of *attractor* states. Play development involves *phase shifts*, involving moves to higher levels of play, and periods of *disequilibrium* and *recursive* elements. Play shows *sensitive dependence on initial conditions* because small inputs into play situations may cause disparate results. Play also demonstrates *openness* because players receive energy from sources outside the "playframe" (Bateson, 1956). There are play *control parameters*, with different play patterns at various ages and skill levels. Play also shows *interdependence* because all levels of play are interrelated, and because of its *soft assembly*, play has both stable and dynamic alternating periods and thus it is not "hard-wired." Play epitomizes *plasticity* because capacity for change is always present. Thus, because play also exhibits these qualities, play development can be characterized as a non-linear dynamic system.

Brain Maturation and Play Development Dynamic Interactions

There are complementary non-linear systems qualities involving dynamic interactions among these two dynamic systems. For example, early infant brain synaptogenesis occurs in visual and other sensorimotor areas and early infant play involves practice of such sensorimotor systems. As the sensorimotor areas of the brain further develop, infants enjoy looking and reaching for objects, hearing and making interesting sounds, and engaging in exploratory play. When sensory and motor areas gain greater synaptic connections, practice play involving repeating and elaborating on actions becomes the most common play type. Similarly, by 9–12 months, when infant brain development involves active frontal lobe synaptogenesis and mirror neuron activity, infant sensorimotor-based social play such as peek-a-boo is common, and these actions become more complex during the toddler year. Also, during the toddler year, as brain maturation continues in areas where language and conceptual thought are located, play development is elaborated in pretence and language. Studies of the concept "theory of mind" (the ability to imagine what others are thinking) indicate that toddlers demonstrate that ability first in pretence. As brain maturation continues during the second year of life, sensorimotor-based (practice) play remains a major mode, with many dynamic combinations of construction and pretence. Thus, there is a synergy between these two dynamic systems: brain maturation and play development. These two dynamic systems have been in interaction throughout most of human history, but they also have interacted with another dynamic system: technology.

Brain Maturation, Play Development, and Technology Dynamic Interactions

In his discussion of the various forms of knowledge, Bruner (1964) also described the process by which human evolution has advanced through the human ability to use various technological artefacts. He described a number of technological artefacts that have increased human capacities; for example, those that amplified human motor capabilities (e.g., wheels), those that amplified human sensory capabilities (e.g., radios); and those that amplified human cognitive abilities (e.g., language, mathematical symbols). According to Bruner, technological artefacts and human actions on such artefacts have propelled subsequent advances in human thought and achievements. Within the theoretical perspective of dynamic systems, these technological artefacts also can be characterized as having qualities such as *openness, sensitive dependence on initial conditions, attractor states, fractal qualities,* and *phase transitions.* Of course, the technology dynamic system has the potential to affect other dynamic systems, such as those of brain maturation and play development.

Technology changes in the past (e.g., radio, television, baby carriages, toy trucks, dolls, tricycles) always have been in dynamic interaction with infant development, and thus, these have affected both brain and play developmental systems. However, there has been an increasingly rapid expansion of the technology dynamic system that may affect infant sensorimotor development. For example "talking" toys, electronic tablets and phones, and computer games have the potential to affect both infant brain maturation and infant sensorimotor play development in different ways from those of the past. That is, they do not always encourage traditional infant physical activity and typical sensorimotor experiences. Thus, as infants use their emerging skills to activate the new features of the technology dynamic system, these actions may interact differentially with the brain dynamic system, the play dynamic systems, and the play/brain dynamic system. A question of major interest is whether and how the presence of new features of this technology dynamic system, such as technology-augmented play materials, may differentially affect the typical dynamic interactions among the brain and play systems.

Recent Technological Influences on Infant Sensorimotor Play and Brain Development

Because of the substantial body of both theoretical and research work that suggests that typical sensorimotor play experiences are crucial for infant brain development and thus for both their social-emotional and enactive cognitive development, there is a question of whether and how technology-augmented toys, and electronic tablets and phones, might interact with brain maturation processes and sensorimotor play processes and thus affect these developmental phenomena in new ways. These technology-augmented play materials are becoming pervasive even for very young children, who are now exposed to types of play materials that did not exist in earlier times. Many of these devices primarily involve looking or pointing at or touching screens. For example, it is now the case that some infants watch virtual scenes on phones, tablets, and television screens for long periods of time, even though advice from paediatricians suggest that they should not do so (Vandwater et al., 2007).

Most of these technology-augmented devices do not require a wide variety of sensorimotor actions, other than perhaps "finger pointing and pressing." If the sensorimotor play experiences with these devices diminish the time infants spend in other types of sensorimotor active play, both indoors and out of doors, then there may be different developmental consequences on infant social, emotional, and cognitive development. Older infants and toddlers now have become experienced users of "talking" and "directing" toys, as well as virtual tablets and other play materials involving technological components. Typically, sensorimotor play requires the young child to act on various objects that have a wide variety of affordance qualities. These newer toys often take on the "actor" role and the child then becomes the "reactor" (Bergen, 2001). Thus, such play materials may involve a narrower set of physical, cognitive, and social-emotional experiences.

During this early sensorimotor play period, the infant brain's synaptic connections are very active and the brain is gaining much of its structural and functional capacity; thus, it is likely that the brains of infants of the future may differ in some ways from the brains of infants in the past. That is, this type of play material may differently affect brain development, sensorimotor play, and the types of social and cognitive schema that are strengthened in such play. At present, the long-term effects of such play on children's socio-cultural competence and enactive cognition is unknown. Research, preferably longitudinal research, derived from the theoretical perspectives of Piaget, Bruner, Gibson, and Thelen is greatly needed to investigate the effects of these new, technologically augmented play materials on sensorimotor play and on the brain/play dynamic system. If the assertion of Allievi and colleagues regarding brain development is correct – that "the final pattern of life-long connectivity is established during the first few post-natal years, through activity-dependent mechanisms" (2014, p. 1) – then the effect of these newer technological devices on infant sensorimotor play must be examined. Future theoretical and research directions will be needed to understand how infant sensorimotor play and brain development will differ or stay the same in this new, technologically augmented play world.

References

Allievi, A. G., Arichi, T., Gordon, A. L., Burdet, E. (2014). Technology-aided assessment of sensorimotor function in early infancy. *Frontiers in Neurology, 5*, 197.

Baldwin, D. A., Markman, E. M., & Melartin, R. L. (1993). Infants' ability to draw inferences about nonobvious object properties: Evidence from exploratory play. *Child Development, 64*, 711–728.

Baranek, G. T., Barnett, C. R., Adams, E. M., Wolcott, N. A., Watson, L. R., & Crais, E. R. (2005). Object play in infants with autism: Methodological issues in retrospective video analysis. *American Journal of Occupational Therapy, 59*(1), 20–30.

Bateson, G. (1956). The message "This is play." In B. Schaffner (Ed.), *Group processes: Transactions of the second conference* (pp. 145–241). New York: Josiah Macy Jr. Foundation.

Bauer, P. J. (2002). Long-term recall memory: Behavioral and neuro-developmental changes in the first 2 years of life. *Current Directions in Psychological Science, 11*(4), 137–141.

Bergen, D. (Ed.) (1998). *Readings from play as a medium for learning and development.* Olney, MD: Association for Childhood Education International.

Bergen, D. (2001). Technology in the classroom: Learning in the robotic world: Active or reactive? *Childhood Education, 78*(1), 249–250.

Bergen, D. (2008). *Human development: Traditional and contemporary theories.* Upper Saddle River, NJ: Pearson/Prentice-Hall.

Bergen, D. (2012). Play, technology toy affordances, and brain development: Considering research and policy issues. In S. Waite-Stupiansky & L. Cohen (Eds.), *Play: A polyphony of research, theories and issue* (vol. 12, pp. 163–174). Lanham, MD: Information Age.

Bergen, D., & Woodin, M. (2010). Neuropsychological development of newborns, infants, and toddlers (0–3). In A. Davis (Ed.), *Handbook of pediatric neuropsychology* (pp. 13–30). New York: Springer.

Bergen, D., & Woodin, M. (2017). *Brain research and childhood education: Implications for educators, parents, and society.* New York: Routledge.

Bornstein, M. H., Hahn, C., Bell, C, Haynes, O. M., Slater, A., Golding, J., et al. (2006). Stability in cognition across early childhood: A developmental cascade. *Psychological Science, 17*(2), 151–158.

Bruner, J. S. (1964). The course of cognitive growth. *American Psychologist, 19*(1), 1–15.

Budding, D. E., & Chidekel, D. (2012). From movement to thought: Executive function, embodied cognition, and the cerebellum. *Cerebellum, 11*(2), 505–525.

Carlson, M., & Earls, F. (1997). Psychological and neuroendocrinological sequelae of early social deprivation in institutionalized children in Romania. *Annals of the New York Academy of Sciences*, *807*(1), 419–428.

Carr, M. (2000). Technological affordances, social practice and learning narratives in an early childhood setting. *International Journal of Technology and Design Education*, *10*, 61–79.

Coude, G., Festante, F., Cilla, A., Lolacono, V., Bimbi, M., Fogassi, L., & Francesco Ferrari, P. (2016). Mirror neurons of ventral premotor cortex are modulated by social cues provided by others' gaze. *Journal of Neuroscience*, 36(11), 3145–3156.

DeLoache, J. S., Pierroutsakos, S. L., Uttal, D. H., Rosengren, K. S., & Gottlieb, A. (1998). Grasping the nature of pictures. *Psychological Science*, *9*(3), 205–210.

Diamond, A. (2006). The early development of executive functions. In C. Bjialystok & F. I. M. Craik (Eds.), *Lifespan cognition: Mechanisms of change* (pp. 70–95). Oxford: Oxford University Press.

DiCarlo, C. F., Reid, D. H., & Stricklin, S. B. (2003). Increasing toy play among toddlers with multiple disabilities in an inclusive classroom: A more-to less, child-directed intervention continuum. *Research in Developmental Disabilities*, *24*, 195–209.

Epstein, H. (1978). Growth spurts during brain development: Implications for educational policy and practice. In J. Chall & A. Mirsky (Eds.), *Education and the brain. The 77th National Society for the Study of Education Yearbook, Part II* (pp. 343–370). Chicago: University of Chicago Press.

Fischer, K. W., & Hogan, A. E. (1989). The big picture for infant development: Levels and variations. In J. J. Lockman & N. L. Hazen (Eds.), *Action in social context: Perspectives on early development* (pp. 275–300). New York: Plenum.

Fromberg, D. P. (2010). How nonlinear systems inform meaning and early education. *Nonlinear Dynamics, Psychology, and Life Sciences*, *14*(1), 47–68.

Garner, B. P., & Bergen, D. (2015). Play development from birth to age four. In D. P. Fromberg & D. Bergen (Eds.), *Play from birth to twelve: Contexts, perspectives, and meanings* (3rd edn.) (pp. 3–11). New York: Routledge.

Gesell, A. (1928). *Infancy and human growth.* New York: Macmillan.

Gesell, A., & Ilg, F. L. (1943). *Infant and child in the culture of today.* New York: Harper.

Gibson, E. J. (1969). *Principles of perceptual learning and development.* New York: Appleton-Century-Croft.

Gibson, E. J. (1997). An ecological psychologist's prolegomena for perceptual development: A functional approach. In C. Dent-Read & P. Zukkow-Goldring (Eds.), *Evolving explanations of development: Ecological approaches to organism–environment systems* (pp. 23–54). Washington, DC: American Psychological Association.

Gibson, E. J., & Walk, R. D. (1960) The "visual cliff." *Scientific American*, 202, 64–71.

Gibson, J. J. (1979). *The ecological approach to visual perception.* Boston: Houghton Mifflin.

Gopnik, A., Meltzoff, A., & Kuhl, P. (2001). *The scientist in the crib: What early learning tells us about the mind.* New York: HarperCollins.

Koziol, L. F., Budding, D. E., & Chidekel, D. (2012). From movement to thought: Executive function, embodied cognition, and the cerebellum. *Cerebellum, 11*(2), 505–525.

McGrenere, J., & Ho, W. (2000). Affordances: Clarifying and evolving a concept. In *Proceedings of Graphic Interface 2000*, May 15–17, Montreal, Canada, pp. 179–186.

Newcombe, N. S., Balcomb, F., Ferrara, K., Hansen, M., & Koski, J. (2014). Two rooms, two representations? Episodic-like memory in toddlers and preschoolers. *Developmental Science, 17*, 743–756.

Piaget, J. (1945). *Play, dreams and imitation in childhood.* London: Heinemann.

Rizzolatti, G., & Craighero, L. (2004). The mirror-neuron system. *Annual Review of Neuroscience, 27*, 169–192.

Shore, R. (1997). *Rethinking the brain: New insights into early development.* New York: Families and Work Institute.

Tamis-LeMonda, C. S., Užgiris, I. C., & Bornstein, M. H. (2002). Play in parent–child interactions. In *Handbook of Parenting, vol. 5: Practical Issues in Parenting* (pp. 221–241). Mahwah, NJ: Lawrence Erlbaum.

Thelen, E. (1989). Self-organization in developmental processes: Can systems approaches work? In M. Gunnar & E. Thelen (Eds.), *Systems in development: The Minnesota Symposia in Child Psychology* (vol. 22, pp. 77–117). Hillsdale, NJ: Erlbaum.

Thelen, E. (2005). Dynamic systems theory and the complexity of change. *Psychoanalytic Dialogues, 15*(2), 255–283.

Thelen, E., & Smith, L. B. (1994). *A dynamic systems approach to the development of cognition and action.* Cambridge, MA: MIT Press.

Thelen, E., & Spencer, J. P. (1998). Postural control during reaching in young infants: A dynamic systems approach. *Neuroscience & Biobehavioral Reviews, 22*(4), 507–514.

Uzgiris, I., & Hunt, J. M. (1975). *Assessment in infancy.* Urbana: University of Illinois Press.

Van Geert, P. (2000). The dynamics of general developmental mechanisms: From Piaget and Vygotsky to dynamic systems models. *Current Directions in Psychological Science, 9*, 64–88.

VanderVen, K. (2006). Attaining the protean self in a rapidly changing world. In D. Fromberg & D. Bergen (Eds.), *Play from birth to twelve: Contexts, perspectives, and meanings* (pp. 405–416). New York: Routledge.

Vandewater, E. A., Rideout, V. J., Wartella, E. A., Huang, X., Lee, J. H., & Shim, M. S. (2007). Digital childhood: Electronic media and technology use among infants, toddlers, and preschoolers. *Pediatrics, 119*(5), e1006–e1015.

Volpe, J. J. (2009). Brain injury in premature infants: A complex amalgam of destructive and developmental disturbances. *The Lancet Neurology, 8*(1), 110–124.

Williams, E. (2003). A comparative review of early forms of object-directed play and parent–infant play in typical infants and young children with autism. *Autism, 7*(4), 361–374.

Wilson, M. (2002). Six views of embodied cognition. *Psychonomic Bulletin & Review, 9*(4), 625–636.

Winkler, I., Háden, G. P., Ladinig, O., Sziller, I., & Honing, H. (2009). Newborn infants detect the beat in music. *Proceedings of the National Academy of Sciences, 106*(7), 2468–2471.

9 Mother–Child and Father–Child Play in Different Cultural Contexts

Jaipaul L. Roopnarine, Elif Dede Yildirim, and Kimberly L. Davidson

Neuroscience and child development research points to the beneficial role of parent–child activities in influencing childhood development during the early childhood years (Anda et al., 2006; Engle et al., 2007; Shonkoff et al., 2012). Accordingly, bio-developmental models (Shonkoff, 2010) and child development experts stress the importance of maternal and paternal engagement in early play and playful activities that involve language and object use as a way of boosting cognitive and social skills in children. Documenting parent–child play engagement and identifying pathways of associations between different dimensions of parent–child play and childhood development across cultural communities can do much to advance indigenous and cross-indigenous perspectives on the role and function of play in human societies (see Roopnarine et al., 2014). The overall goals of this chapter include providing an overview of maternal and paternal beliefs about the value of play for childhood development, outlining levels of mothers' and fathers' engagement in different play activities with young children, and exploring associations between mother–child and father–child play activities and children's cognitive and social skills in different cultural communities around the world.

Despite increasing interest in parent–child play (see Johnson et al., 2015; Pellegrini, 2011; Roopnarine et al., 2014; Smith, 2010) and the call for intervention programs to utilize early parent–child play stimulation activities as a remediation tool against the effects of harsh economic conditions and poor home environments in economically underdeveloped societies (Engle et al., 2007), much of the research on mother–child and father–child play is concentrated in developed societies (e.g., United States, Australia, and different parts of Europe). Because of the lack of data on adult–child play in diverse family constellations (e.g., lesbian and gay families; extended family systems), our focus is on mother–child and father–child play in mostly two-parent, heterosexual families. Following Sutton-Smith (1997), parent–child play is considered more broadly to include play and playful activities during the early childhood years.

Parental Ethnotheories about Play

Researchers within cultural developmental science and psychological anthropology (Bornstein, 2010; Super & Harkness, 1997, 2002) have urged greater consideration of parental beliefs or ethnotheories as major driving forces behind child-rearing practices. Belief systems about child-rearing and development guide how parents structure and calibrate cognitive, social, and cultural activities for children, which, in turn, exert direct and indirect influences on childhood development (Murphy, 1992; Roopnarine & Davidson, 2015). Across cultural communities, parents hold different beliefs about child-rearing practices, about when children acquire basic developmental skills (Goodnow & Collins, 1990; Roopnarine et al., 2015; Sigel & MiGillicuddy-Delisi, 2002), and about the benefits of engagement in particular activities (e.g., play, physical discipline, homework). For example, across the English-speaking Caribbean countries of Barbados, Dominica, Guyana, Jamaica, and Trinidad and Tobago, parents believe that children should be obedient and show unilateral respect to adults, and they use different methods of control during child-rearing to accomplish these expectations, independent of children's input (Leo-Rhynie & Brown, 2013; Roopnarine et al., 2013; Wilson et al., 2003). Parental beliefs about child-rearing and development are passed on from generation to generation. They are not static and are subject to modifications or revisions depending on socioeconomic conditions, intercultural contact, the changing ethos of parenting and childhood, and social pressures from the immediate ecological niche (Goodnow & Collins, 1990; Sigel & McGillicuddy-DeLisi, 2002).

Just as parents possess diverse beliefs about child-rearing, they vary in the degree to which they embrace play as an important activity for childhood development. It has been suggested that parental beliefs about the merit of play for fostering childhood development fall along a continuum: from play as something children engage in naturally without adult encouragement to play as important in providing opportunities for learning early social and cognitive skills (Roopnarine, 2011). At one end of the continuum are parents in developing societies who are less likely to endorse play as a vehicle for the acquisition of childhood skills. At the other end are parents in Europe, North America, and other developed societies who view play as an activity that contributes to childhood development and as undergirding developmentally appropriate early education practices (see National Education of Young Children guidelines in the United States). Then there are parents (e.g., Asian parents, Caribbean parents) who fall somewhere in the middle and view play as contributing to the development of social and physical skills, but stress the benefits of academic training for young children through didactic processes. This continuum notwithstanding, internal working models about child-rearing and development do change as parents become more aware of child-rearing practices that are more amenable to optimal childhood development (see Roopnarine & Jin, 2012).

Using the tenets of diverse theories and models within cultural, cross-cultural, and indigenous psychology (e.g., collectivism-individualism, developmental niche, autonomous-relational, adaptationist) (Greenfield et al., 2003; Kağitcibaşi, 2007; Super & Harkness, 2002), research studies confirm the wide range of beliefs about play and childhood development that exists across small- and large-scale societies. In some cases, the value of play is overshadowed by continued focus on work-related tasks. For example, the Baining of the Gazelle Peninsula of East New Britain (Papua, New Guinea) reported that children learn everyday skills through work, not play (Fajans, 1997). Parents in Thailand had more positive attitudes toward work-related activities (e.g., counting, learning the Thai alphabet) than play-related activities (make-believe, playing with blocks, putting puzzles together) (Bloch & Wichaidat, 1986), and parents in Taiwan emphasized hard work over play activities (Kim, 2007); play was viewed as a recreational activity.

Neutral, ambivalent, or mixed attitudes toward play have been expressed in some cultures. The pastoralist Turkana of Kenya believe that when children are around their mothers a lot, rather than playing independently or with peers, it is a sign of incompetence (Ng'asike, 2014). In an Indonesian sample, only about one-third of mothers saw value in children's play activities: 39% believed that play contributed to the development of intelligence and creativity, 32% believed that play kept children happy, occupied, and not fussy, and 29% thought that play contributed to the development of social skills (Farver & Wimbarti, 1995). Mothers in northern India considered play a natural, pleasurable activity of childhood but with vague implications for childhood development (Chaudhary & Shukla, 2014).

Yet other studies have shown more positive beliefs regarding play. In a cross-comparative analysis of play in 2,400 families in 16 countries across Asia, Africa, North America, South America, and Europe, Singer et al. (2009) found that 93% of mothers believed that play kept children healthy (only 33% viewed experiential learning as important); this view was echoed by Yucatec Mayan parents in Central America (Gaskins, 2014). The social benefits of play were recognized by mothers in Hong Kong (Holmes, 2001) and among a mixed ethnic sample of caregivers in Lana'i, Hawaii (Holmes, 2011). Among European and European American families, the value of play stimulation activities for childhood development is more clearly articulated. Dutch mothers believed that play interactions contribute to children's cognitive, social, personality, and socioemotional development, and to their creativity (van der Kooj & Slatts-van den Hurk, 1991). Other analyses have shown that Dutch, German, and Norwegian mothers had more positive views about child-rearing and play than Polish mothers (Van der Kooij & Neukater, 1989), Estonian mothers had less controlling attitudes toward play than non-Estonian mothers (Saar & Nigalis, 2001), and highly educated Turkish fathers had more positive views about play than less educated Turkish fathers (Ivrendi & Isikoglu, 2010). Along similar lines, Midwestern European American mothers and fathers reported that pretend play activities are important for children's creativity and cognitive development (Haight et al., 1997), and European American mothers in the northeastern United States reported that play was important for children's cognitive and individual development (Parmer et al., 2004).

However, with increasing diversity in the population of some developed societies (e.g., England, United States, Canada), differences exist in beliefs about play between ethnic groups within countries. As examples, Asian Americans, African Americans, and Latino Americans differ in their beliefs about play and childhood development from European Americans. Mexican-origin migrant workers in Florida (Mathur, 2014), Latina mothers in Boston (Holloway et al., 1995), and Asian American mothers in the northeastern United States (Parmar et al., 2004) all emphasized learning academic skills and hard work over play-based experiential learning, and African American mothers seem to value both activities (Fogle & Mendez, 2006). Simply put, some cultural groups who have experienced oppression see academic effort as a way of breaking out of the cycle of poverty or as part of the immigrant drive to succeed in a new cultural community. In this respect, play becomes secondary to the academic effort and its benefits are often aligned with social and physical (rather than cognitive and linguistic) development.

Within such broad patterns of parental beliefs about play and early development, it is likely that in cultural communities in which beliefs about the value of play for childhood development are not well defined, play interactions between parents and children may be less frequent (Gaskins, 2014; Gosso et al., 2014). Adults simply let children play (Chaudhary & Shukla, 2014). Under these circumstances, children may freely explore the object and social world away from adults, often replicating adult activities in their everyday play, or they combine play and work activities imposed by parents and kinship members (e.g., Turkana of Kenya, rural children in India). These children may not be monitored in a formal sense but parents are aware of their social activities. By contrast, in developed societies reciprocal, responsive parent–child engagement (e.g., playing, book reading, and storytelling) is seen as a hallmark of good parenting. Middle-income parents engage in the systematic practice of "concerted cultivation" (Lareau, 2003) wherein proto-conversations are common, play objects are furnished early in children's lives (e.g., mobiles, technological gadgets), and mothers and fathers engage in tactile and verbal games starting soon after the birth of the child. Thus, a high value is placed on learning cognitive skills for a post-modern world marked by rapid technological growth.

Parent–Child Play across Cultures

Different forms of parent–child play and playfulness have been observed in different cultures around the world. In some cases, documenting parent–child play was not the explicit purpose of some of these studies but rather a part of efforts to examine parent–child interactions, stimulation activities, or the health of young children. For instance, the UNICEF Micro Indicator Cluster Surveys (MICS) conducted on families across many developing societies focus primarily on health issues but include a global measure of whether mothers and fathers play with children (UNICEF MICS, 2014, 2015). In a similar vein, studies on parent–child attachment have coded physical play in the context of assessing the quality of parent–child emotional bonds (see Lamb, 2002). Both groups of studies that gathered data through observations (field and laboratory), self-reports, and interviews and employed quantitative and qualitative data reduction techniques are considered here. Because other chapters in this volume cover much of the play literature in North America and Europe, special attention is given to more recent work conducted in developing countries.

Levels of Parent–Child Play

Although by no means comprehensive, levels of parent–child play provide a general index of how much and how often mothers and fathers invest in the social and cognitive lives of children. Three large-scale studies (Bornstein & Putnick, 2012; Roopnarine & Yildirim, 2017; Yildirim & Roopnarine, 2017) used global measures to catalog the percentages of mothers and fathers who engaged in play with children irrespective of type or quality of play. Bornstein and Putnick (2012) found that among 127,000 families across 28 developing countries, 60% of mothers reported playing with their young children (under 5 years of age) and 64% reported taking them outdoors, whereas 25% reported singing, 35% told stories, 25% spent time reading, and 47% spent time in academic activities such as counting, naming, and drawing with their children in the past three days. These estimates on levels of play involvement are below those obtained for children in the United States (Civitas Initiative et al., 2000) and in an Australian sample (Baxter & Smart, 2010).

Two other analyses (Roopnarine & Yildirim, 2017; Yildirim & Roopnarine, 2017) of the UNICEF MICS data focused on parent–child play in 12 Caribbean and Latin American and 18 African countries. Figures 9.1 and 9.2 indicate the countries included in the analyses and the percentages of mothers and fathers who played with children during the past three days. The Caribbean and Latin American and African countries reflect a rich linguistic and ethnic diversity not seen in other parts of the world. Furthermore, these countries are at different levels of economic development as measured by Human Development Indices. Across all 12 Caribbean and Latin American countries, mothers were more likely to engage in play with children than were fathers. With the exception of Suriname, a majority of mothers engaged in play with children across countries (ranging from 85% in Uruguay to 47% in Suriname). Father–child play was low overall but seems particularly so in the Dominican Republic, Jamaica, Panama, and Suriname. On average, 34% of fathers engaged in play with children across countries.

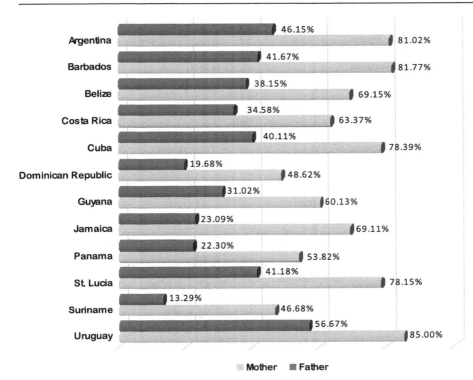

Figure 9.1 *Percentages of mothers and fathers who played with children in Caribbean and Latin American countries.*

A similar pattern of gender-differentiated involvement in play was determined for the 18 African countries (see Figure 9.2). However, the percentages of mothers and fathers who engaged in play with children were low compared with those of parents in the Caribbean and Latin American countries and in other parts of the world. To this end, less than 40% of mothers played with children. Mothers in Tunisia had the highest rates of participation in play, and those in Kenya and Guinea Bissau had the lowest rates of participation. Across countries, a meagre 14.6% of fathers played with children. In Chad, Kenya, and Guinea Bissau, play between fathers and children was almost non-existent.

What might account for the low rates of play in African countries and between fathers and children in particular? Admittedly, limited knowledge about early parent–child stimulation activities may be a major reason for the lack of commitment to engage in play and playful activities with children. But this alone cannot account for the low levels of play between parents and children because children seem to play freely on their own (Chaudhary & Shukla, 2014). Educational attainment and socioeconomic factors are also associated with maternal and paternal investment in play with children (Roopnarine & Yildirim, 2017). As far as fathers are concerned, we speculate that their traditional ideological beliefs about early caregiving

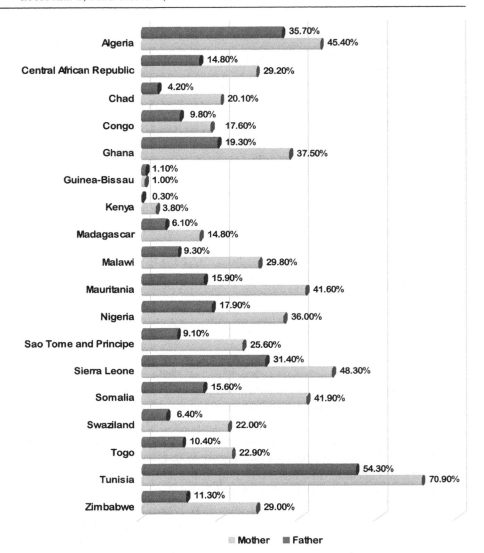

Figure 9.2 *Percentages of mothers and fathers who played with children in African countries.*

and their investment in economic activities stand in the way of their engagement in social and cognitive activities with children.

Time Investment in Play

Turning to time investment in play, mothers in the United States acted as playmates to children 47% of the time observed, compared with 7% of the time in Guatemala and 24% of the time in India (Rogoff et al., 1993).

Another comparison showed that children played with one adult 17% of the time in Massachusetts and 16% of the time in Utah, 4% of the time among Efe hunter-gatherer communities of the Democratic Republic of the Congo, and 3% of the time among the Mayans of Guatemala (Morelli et al., 2003). Perhaps because play is embedded in other parental responsibilities toward children, anthropologists have also calculated how much time parents invest in play compared with caregiving activities. In the Central African Republic, Aka fathers' relative time investment in play with infants was 23% compared with emotional caregiving such as displaying affection (27%), soothing (18%), and physical care (cleaning, 15%). Mothers' relative time investment in play was a bit lower: 13% compared with 4% of the time displaying affection, 12% of the time in physical care, and 5% of the time cleaning infants (Hewlett, 1987). Among other groups in central Africa, Lese fathers spent more time in play (18%) than Efe fathers (7%) (Fouts, 2013).

Using a slightly different approach, some studies have asked mothers and fathers to report on their time investment in play without distinguishing types of play. Evidence suggests that differences in time investment in play between mothers and fathers have narrowed quite a bit over the last two decades. In fact, in some cases mothers surpass fathers in amount of time invested in general levels of play. For instance, in dual-earner families, Jamaican mothers spent significantly more time playing with infants per day than fathers ($M_{mothers}$ = 3.53 hours, $M_{fathers}$ = 2.95 hours) (Roopnarine et al., 1995), as did mothers from different ethnic groups in Malaysia (rural Malay Muslim: $M_{mothers}$ = 4.92, $M_{fathers}$ = 2.77 hours; urban Kadazan: $M_{mothers}$ = 4.59, $M_{fathers}$ = 3.03 hours) (Hossain et al., 2005; Hossain et al., 2007). Smaller differences in maternal and paternal play involvement with children were reported in cultural communities in Portugal ($M_{mothers}$ = 53, $M_{fathers}$ = 51 minutes/day) and Brazil ($M_{mothers}$ = 2.97, $M_{fathers}$ = 2.33 hours/day) (Benetti & Roopnarine, 2006; Wall, 2015). A study conducted on Canadian (Quebecois) families with infants and another on families in the United States showed convergence in maternal and paternal interaction and play patterns (Laflamme et al., 2002; Yeung et al., 2001).

As per belief systems about early parent–child stimulation and taking into consideration economic and subsistence patterns, overall time investment in play varies noticeably across cultural communities. In the past, fathers were featured as "playmates" to children. Today, the changing role patterns within families and more emphasis on engaged parenting (e.g., moral socialization, teaching, nurturance, companions, economic providers) across cultural communities may be responsible for more equal involvement in play between mothers and fathers in developed and emerging economies. However, qualitative differences still exist in paternal and maternal play patterns across cultures, and these are discussed next.

Nature of Parent–Child Play Interactions

Theoretical frameworks and models on parenting (Baumrind, 1967; Rohner & Khaleque, 2005) stress the importance of the quality of parent–child interactions for maximizing childhood development. For example, based on extensive research conducted in 66 cultures across the world (see meta-analysis by Khaleque & Rohner, 2012), interpersonal acceptance–rejection theory (Rohner & Khaleque, 2005) highlights the underlying role of parental warmth and care in the development of social and cognitive competence in children. Baumrind's (1967) authoritative parenting style, tested in diverse cultures around the world, also demonstrates the benefits of warmth and appropriate control for the development of social competence in children. According to these frameworks and related research findings, parental sensitivity is a likely precursor to sustained play interactions with children. That is, knowledge about childhood development and the ability of mothers and fathers to interact with children in a responsive, reciprocal, developmentally appropriate manner are both important for meaningful parent–child play stimulation activities. Attention is allocated here to activities that have been more commonly assessed between parents and children across cultures: physical play, object play, and pretend play. An attempt is made to connect parental socialization goals with parent–child play activities.

For over four decades now, researchers have discussed the importance of physical play for the development of attachment bonds to parents. A persistent argument is that physically arousing play provides opportunities for children to develop close emotional ties to the father (Paquette, 2004; Paquette & Dumont, 2012). Among European Americans and in samples of families in Montreal, rough play (bouncing, tossing, tickling, rough-and-tumble) occurred with regularity during father–child interactions but to a lesser degree during mother–child interactions (Macdonald & Parke, 1986; Paquette & Bagras, 2010; Paquette & Dumont, 2013). In other developed societies, where individualistic child-rearing practices, egalitarian roles, and engaged fathering are valued, such as in Israel and Sweden, rough play between fathers and children occurred about once per hour (Lamb et al., 1982; Sagi et al., 1985).

Similarly, in societies driven by collectivistic tendencies (relatedness and autonomy are valued) such as India, Taiwan, and Thailand, father–infant physical play occurred on average less than once per hour of observation and only in very small percentages of families. Father–child physical play occurred at far lower frequencies than object-mediated play and the expression of affection toward children in all three societies (Roopnarine et al., 1990; Sun & Roopnarine, 1996; Tulananda & Roopnarine, 2001). Among mothers in India, Taiwan, and Thailand, physical play was exceedingly low. It has been argued that in these Asian cultural communities, child-rearing tendencies are more relaxed and socialization goals emphasize interpersonal connectedness. Bearing this in mind, vigorous play may be of little interest to parents.

The low level of physical play observed in Asian cultural communities is also evident in the foraging communities of central Africa. As mentioned earlier, Aka foragers of the Central African Republic exemplify gentle, relaxed parenting practices that can be deemed permissive by Western standards. Extensive ethnographic work conducted on the Aka and Baka foragers indicate that major physical play (e.g., rough-housing) and minor physical play (tickling, poking) was visibly absent in these cultural communities (Hewlett, 1987; Hirawasa, 2005). On those rare occasions when physical play did occur, siblings were the ones to engage in it, not adults and children. The low level of investment in physical play among parents in foraging and Asian cultural communities may speak to the cultural specificity of physical play and to its questionable role in the development of parent–child attachment relationships across cultural communities. As discussions about the value of parent–child physical play for the development of close emotional ties to fathers continue, its role in the development of mother–child and father–child relationships in the developing world remains vague.

Wide variations were also noted for parent–child object-mediated play and parent–child games across cultural communities. Although object-mediated play is quite common among families in North America and Europe (Roopnarine et al., 2005) where face-to-face and object play are encouraged through verbal and social exchanges, gestures, labelling, and pointing (Keller et al., 2010), Indian mothers and fathers in New Delhi tend to shun object play with children (Roopnarine et al., 1990). Object-mediated play also appears less appealing to Aka foragers and to Taiwanese families (Hewlett, 1987; Sun & Roopnarine, 1996). Face-to-face play was preferred to other modes of play among the Aka but is not common among the Marquesans or Kaluli (Martini & Kirkpatrick, 1992; Schieffelin, 1990). The inconsistency of object use during play and the limited use of face-to-face interactions in some cultural communities suggest that parents may rely on social interactions during playful encounters. Indeed, parent–child games in a number of cultural communities involve more touching, patting, hugging, singing, and dancing (Goncu et al., 2000; Rogoff et al., 1993). For example, parallel forms of the game of peek-a-boo are played differently in terms of approach and level of verbal input across South Africa, Japan, Malaysia, Iran, Brazil, Russia, India, Turkey, and Korea (Fernald & O'Neill, 1993).

Further examples of the contrasting modes of play engagement based on socialization values and goals are aptly captured in studies on parents in Asia, Europe, and the United States. In one study on Indian and German mother–infant play, New Delhi mothers engaged in more didactic than autonomous play and Berlin mothers engaged in more autonomous than didactic play. There was more didactic play among New Delhi mother–infant dyads than among Berlin mother–infant dyads, and there was more autonomous play among Berlin mother–infant dyads than among New Delhi mother–infant dyads. These play patterns are congruent with cultural emphasis on the socialization of interdependence in India and independence in Germany (Keller et al., 2010). Japanese and American parents present yet another variation on this theme. During play, Japanese mothers used visual attention and held and touched infants, whereas European American mothers used verbal interchanges during face-to-face interactions (Fogel et al., 1993).

Arguably one of the most important forms of play for learning early cognitive and social development, parent–child fantasy play in different cultural settings is not widely understood. It has been linked to cognitive and social development (see Smith, 2010) and to the transmission of cultural knowledge and the reproduction of culture (Hirschfeld, 2002). What we can gather from existing studies is that in developed societies, mothers assume an active role in initiating fantasy play with the use of objects and often entered play as an actor (Bornstein et al., 1999; Suizzo & Bornstein, 2006; Tamis-LeMonda et al., 1992). This is in contrast to what happens in some developing societies where relatives are playmates to young children and older siblings organize pretend play for children (Gaskins & Miller, 2009).

A comparative longitudinal study of child-initiated and adult-initiated pretend play in Taiwanese and Irish American families found that all children engaged in pretend play with their caregivers at 30, 36, and 48 months of age (Haight et al., 1999). Child-initiated pretend play was significantly greater and caregiver-initiated pretend play was more frequent and contained more themes in Irish American than in Taiwanese families. Caregiver–child pretend play in Irish American families was more likely to reflect caretaking themes, and in Taiwanese families pretend play was more likely to involve social interactions. There were no overall differences in symbolic play between French and European American mothers, but French mothers were less likely to solicit symbolic play from children than European American mothers (Suzzio & Bornstein, 2006). Other comparisons of involvement in symbolic play with children in the developed world have found significant differences between immigrant and non-immigrant groups (Bornstein et al., 1999).

The findings of two other observational studies from cultural communities with collectivistic child-rearing practices indicate that Thai mothers and fathers in Chiang Mai Province engaged in low levels of pretend play with preschool-aged children (Tulananda & Roopnarine, 2001). Thai families prefer to use other activities such as teasing, joking, and telling stories in a playful manner rather than pretense during social interactions with children, and this may have accounted for the low levels of pretend play in these families. In Javanese families, older siblings joined the play of younger children and made comments and suggestions for pretend play more frequently than mothers did. Sibling play interactions were more positively attuned than mother–child play interactions. Mother–child play contained more family role themes, and sibling play contained more danger in the environment themes (Farver & Wimbarti, 1995).

Gender of Child Differences in Parent–Child Play

Maternal and paternal roles are still demarcated along traditional lines in most of the developing world, and in some Asian societies (e.g., India, China) there is a strong son preference (Kakar & Kakar, 2007; Shwalb et al., 2004). On the basis of these practices, one might expect mothers and fathers to invest in play interactions with boys and girls differently. From the body of work we reviewed, besides the well-known differences in the different types of play (physical, putting puzzles together) mothers and fathers engaged in with boys and girls (e.g., Lamb, 2002), we did not find much in the way of gender-of-child differences during parent–child play interactions in the developing world. This surprised us, and what was most interesting was that in the son preference cultures (Indian, Chinese), fathers and mothers did not behave differently toward young boys and girls (e.g., Roopnarine et al., 1990). Of course, most studies examined global indices of play, and few showed any explicit interest in exploring this issue in depth during early childhood. As children age, cultural rituals and play patterns between mothers and fathers with boys and girls do become differentiated (Jankowiak et al., 2011).

Associations between Parent–Child Play and Childhood Outcomes

Although there is ample evidence on the associations between other aspects of parent–child relationships such as warmth and control (see meta-analysis by Gershoff & Grogan-Kaylor, 2016; Khaleque & Rohner, 2012), parent–child verbal interactions (Cabrera et al., 2011), parent–child book reading (see Isbell et al., 2004; Mol & Bus, 2011) and children's social and cognitive skills across cultural communities, there is far less on the links between parent–child play activities and childhood development. For the most part, the associations between play and childhood development are based on small-scale, correlational studies (see Smith, 2010). Adding to the correlational studies reviewed by Smith (2010), we discuss some of the newer findings on the associations between play and children's cognitive and social skills. It should be made clear that these findings are unidirectional from parents to children. There is a sizable body of work on bidirectional influences in diverse areas of parent–child relationships (e.g., Landry et al., 2012; Lugo-Gil & Tamis-LeMonda, 2008; Zhang, 2013).

Data from the United States indicate that fathers' interactions in semi-structured free-play situations were associated with mental development scores at 24 and 36 months and to higher receptive vocabulary scores (Tamis-LeMonda et al., 2004); nurturance during play was related to receptive vocabulary scores as well (Black et al., 1999). Japanese fathers' use of structure/limit setting, respect for the child's autonomy, and sensitivity during play interactions was related to pre-schoolers' emotional regulation during conflicts with peers (Kato & Kondo, 2007). Among Caribbean immigrants residing in the New York City area, maternal beliefs about play moderated the associations between mothers' time in play and children's number, letter, and word skills, expressive skills, and a composite score as measured by the Kaufman Scales (Roopnarine & Jin, 2012). In the developing world, father–child symbolic play was associated with pre-schoolers' social skills in Thai families (Tulunanda & Roopnarine, 2001).

How does parent–child play stack up against other forms of parental engagement such as book reading and storytelling that may contain playful activities? The two large-scale studies discussed earlier on families in the 12 Caribbean and Latin American and 18 African countries (Roopnarine & Yildirim, 2017; Yidirim & Roopnarine, 2017) begin to provide some insights into this question. In the first study, data from the UNICEF Multiple Indicator Cluster Survey 4 and 5 involving 10,976 preschool-aged children and their caregivers from Belize, the Dominican Republic, Guyana, Jamaica, and Suriname were used to determine the relative contributions of play, book reading, and storytelling to children's early literacy skills in the same model. Research findings (Isbell et al., 2004; Mol & Bus, 2011) suggest that these three parent engagement activities are central to early literacy skills development. Unlike the findings of studies in the developed world on parental involvement and language development (Isbell et al., 2004; Tamis-LeMonda et al., 2004), analyses showed that with one exception (mothers' play in the Dominican Republic), mothers' and fathers' play with children was not significantly related to children's literacy skills (identification of letters, recognizing symbols, reading words) across countries. However, mothers' and fathers' engagement in book reading (Dominican Republic) and mothers' engagement in storytelling (Dominican Republic and Jamaica) were associated with identifying letters. Mothers' engagement in book reading in the Dominican Republic and mothers' engagement in storytelling in Guyana and Jamaica were associated with reading words.

Again using the UNICEF Multiple Indicator Cluster Survey 4 and 5 (UNICEF, 2006, 2015) involving 50,005 preschool-aged children and their caregivers in Algeria, Central African Republic, Chad, Congo, Ghana, Guinea Bissau, Kenya, Malawi, Mauritania, Nigeria, Sao Tome, Sierra Leone, Somali, Swaziland, Togo, Tunisia, and Zimbabwe, an identical attempt was made to unravel the relative associations between parent–child play, book reading, and storytelling and children's literacy skills. In only a few countries was mother–child play related to children's letter skills (Chad, Ghana, Malawi, and Somalia), to children's ability to read words (Ghana and Somalia), and to children's recognition of symbols (Algeria, Ghana, and Malawi). Only in Nigeria was father–child play related to children's letter skills, ability to read words, and their recognition of symbols. The associations between storytelling and children's literacy skills were even less compelling. Book reading showed the most promise in contributing to children's literacy skills. In Algeria, Chad, Congo, Malawi, Mauritania, Sao Tome, Sierra Leone, and Somalia, mother–child book reading was linked to children's letter skills. It was associated with children's ability to read words in Algeria, Chad, Congo, Mauritania, Sao Tome, Sierra Leone, Somalia, and Zimbabwe and to children's recognition of symbols in Algeria, Central African Republic, Congo, Mauritania, Nigeria, Sao Tome, Somalia, and Swaziland. In nine countries, father–child book reading was associated with one of the three literacy skills outcomes.

While the absence of associations between paternal engagement in play and children's literacy skills may be due to the low rates of father involvement with children across countries, the lower than expected associations between mother–child play and children's literacy skills could be due to inadequate knowledge about sensitively attuned parenting and the value of play for childhood development in most Caribbean and African countries. Other factors such as economic conditions, educational attainment, parenting skills, and the number of books in the home have all been shown to be associated with children's early literacy skills (Morrison & Cooney, 2002). What is of concern are the low levels of paternal engagement in play in cultural communities with multiple risk factors that could exacerbate developmental difficulties in children (Engle & Black, 2007). A body of work across cultures indicates the important contributions of fathers to children's early development (Cabrera & Tamis-LeMonda, 2103; Roopnarine, 2015; Shwalb, Shwalb, & Lamb, 2013).

Two early intervention studies with roots in Jamaica offer more concrete evidence of the associations between parent–child play and children's social and cognitive development in developing societies: The Roving Caregivers Program (RCP) (Powell, 2004) and the Early Childhood Stimulation Program are instructive in this regard (Walker et al., 2005). Basically, the RCP program uses play enrichment activities in home settings during early infancy to assist low-income mothers to stimulate cognitive development in children in several Caribbean countries. The Early Childhood Stimulation Program offered children with stunted growth (9–24 months old) psychosocial stimulation that involved play as well as nutrition supplements during early childhood. After a year of play stimulation administered weekly in the RCP, Jamaican children in the treatment group had a higher developmental quotient score and performed better on the hand-and-eye coordination and performance subscales of the Griffiths compared with controls. A second study using a difference-in-differences approach found that St. Lucian children who received RCP services realized benefits in visual reception and motor skills (Spijk et al., 2008). With regard to the other program, a follow-up assessment when the children were 17–18 years of age indicated that there were superior intellectual outcomes for children who received stimulation compared with those who did not receive stimulation (Walker et al., 2005).

Concluding Remarks

This chapter provides a broad overview of some of the literature on mother–child and father–child play across cultural communities with a focus on the developing world. When compared with the developed world, data on parent–child play in the developing societies are still thin. From what exists, it appears that positive beliefs about the role of play for early learning are more firmly planted in the developed than developing societies. With respect to involvement in parent–child play, gender-differentiated patterns of involvement are quite evident in the Caribbean and Latin American region and across Africa. Mothers are the ones who play with children. Physical, object-mediated, and fantasy play are not that prevalent in parent–child play encounters, and the associations between mother–child and father–child play and childhood outcomes are not as clear-cut in developing cultural communities relative to those in the developed world.

Despite the fact that Article 31 of the United Nations Convention on the Rights of Children stipulates the right to play, oddly we have rarely catalogued children's opinions about the value of parent–child play or what types of play engagement they prefer. Data on older Brazilian children's conceptions of mothering and fathering indicate that play is the foremost function of fathers (Carvallho et al., 2010). On the research front, more sophisticated analyses (e.g., moderation, mediation, and multilevel modelling) are needed to determine the cultural pathways through which mother–child and father–child play influence social and cognitive development in developing societies, taking into consideration socioeconomic factors, neighbourhood quality, parenting styles and quality, and parental belief systems about play.

References

Anda, R. F., Felitti, V. J., Bremner, J. D., Walker, J. D., Whitfield, C., Perry, B. D., Dube, S. R., & Giles, W. H. (2006). The enduring effects of abuse and related adverse experiences in childhood: A convergence of evidence from neurobiology and epidemiology. *European Archives of Psychiatry and Clinical Neuroscience, 256*(3), 174–186.

Baumrind, D. (1967). Child care practices anteceding three patterns of preschool behavior. *Genetic Psychology Monographs, 75*, 43–88.

Baumrind, D. (1996). The discipline controversy revisited. *Family Relations, 45*, 405–414.

Baxter, J. A., & Smart, D. (2010). Fathering in Australia among couple families with young children. Occasional Paper No. 37. Canberra, Australia: Department of Families, Community Services and Indigenous Affairs.

Benetti, S. P., & Roopnarine, J. L. (2006). Paternal involvement with school-aged children in Brazilian families: Association with childhood competence. *Sex Roles, 55*, 669–678.

Black, M. M., Dubowitz, H., & Starr, R. H. Jr. (1999). African American fathers in low-income urban families: Development, behavior, and home environment of their three-year-old children. *Child Development, 70,* 967–978.

Bloch, M., & Wichaidat, W. (1986). Play and school work in the kindergarten curriculum: Attitudes of parents and teachers in Thailand. *Early Child Development and Care, 24*, 197–218.

Bornstein, M. (Ed.). (2010). *Handbook of cultural developmental science.* New York: Psychology Press.

Bornstein, M. H., Haynes, O. M., Pascual, L., Painter, K. M., & Galperín, C. (1999). Play in two societies: Pervasiveness of process, specificity of structure. *Child Development, 70*, 317–331.

Bornstein, M. H., & Putnick, D. L. (2012). Cognitive and socioemotional caregiving in developing countries. *Child Development, 83*(1), 46–61.

Cabrera, N., Fagan, J., Wight, V., & Schadler, C. (2011). The influence of mother, father, and child risk on parenting and children's cognitive and social behaviors. *Child Development, 82*(6), 1985–2005.

Cabrera, N., & Tamis-LeMonda, C. (Eds.) (2013). *Handbook of father involvement.* New York: Routledge Press.

Carvalho, A. M. A., Moreira, L. V. C., & Rabinovich, E. P. (2010). Olhares de crianças sobre a família: um enfoque quantitativo [Children's conceptions of family: a quantitative approach]. *Psicologia, Teoria e Pesquisa, 26*(3), 417–426.

Chaudhary, N., & Shukla, S. (2014). "Children's work is to play": Beliefs and practices related to childhood play among Indians. In J. L. Roopnarine, M. Patte, J. E. Johnson, & D. Kuschner (Eds.), *International perspectives on children's play* (pp. 146–158). London: Open University Press/McGraw Hill.

Civitas Initiative, Zero to Three, & Brio Corporation. (2000). *What grown-ups understand about child development.* Washington, DC: Zero to Three. Available at www.buildinitiative.org/files/grown-ups.pdf.

Cote, L. R., & Bornstein, M. H. (2005). Child and mother play in cultures of origin, acculturating cultures, and cultures of destination. *International Journal of Behavioral Development, 29*, 479–488.

Engle, P. L., Black, M. M., Behrman, J. R., Cabral de Mello, M., Gertler, P. J., Kapiriri, L., ... & Young, M. E. (2007). Strategies to avoid the loss of developmental potential in more than 200 million children in the developing world. *Lancet, 369*, 229–252.

Fajans, J. (1997). *They make themselves: Work and play among the Baining of Papua New Guinea.* Chicago, IL: University of Chicago Press.

Farver, J. M., & Wimbarti, S. (1995). Indonesian toddlers' social play with their mothers and older siblings. *Child Development, 66*, 1493–1513.

Fernald, A., & O'Neill, D. (1993). Peek-a-boo across cultures. In K. Macdonald (Ed.), *Parent–child play* (pp. 259–285). Albany: State University of New York Press.

Fogel, A., Nwokah, E., & Karns, J. (1993). Parent–infant games as dynamic social systems. In K. Macdonald (Ed.), *Parent–child play* (pp. 43–70). Albany: State University of New York Press.

Fogle, L. M., & Mendez, J. L. (2006). Assessing the play beliefs of African American mothers with preschool children. *Early Childhood Research Quarterly, 21,* 507–518.

Fouts, H. N. (2013). Fathering in Central and East Africa: Cultural and adaptationist perspectives in small-scale societies. In D. W. Shwalb, B. J. Shwalb, & M. E. Lamb (Eds.), *Fathers in cultural context* (pp. 151–172). New York: Routledge.

Gaskins, S. (2014). Yucatec Mayan children's play. In J. L. Roopnarine, M. Patte, J. E. Johnson, & D. Kuschner (Eds.), *International perspectives on children's play* (pp. 11–22). London: Open University Press/McGraw Hill.

Gaskins, S., & Miller, P. J. (2009). The cultural roles of emotions in pretend play. In C. D. Clark (Ed.), Play and culture studies, vol. 9: Transactions at play (pp. 5–21). Lanham, MD: University Press of America.

Gershoff, E. T., & Grogan-Kaylor, A. (2016). Spanking and child outcomes: Old controversies and new meta-analyses. *Journal of Family Psychology, 30,* 453–469.

Goncu, A., Mistry, J., & Mosier, C. (2000). Cultural variations in the play of toddlers. *International Journal of Behavioral Development, 24,* 321–329.

Goodnow, J. J., & Collins, W. A. (1990). *Development according to parents: The nature, sources, and consequences of parents' ideas.* Hillsdale, NJ: Lawrence Erlbaum.

Gosso, Y., Bichara, I. D., & Carvalho, A. M. A. (2014). Brazilian children at play: Reviewing relationships between play and culture. In J. L. Roopnarine, M. Patte, J. E. Johnson, & D. Kuschner (Eds.), *International perspectives on children's play* (pp. 23–33). London: Open University Press/McGraw Hill.

Greenfield, P. M., Keller, H., Fuligni, A., & Maynard, A. (2003). Cultural pathways through universal development. *Annual Review of Psychology, 54,* 461–490.

Haight, W., Parke, R., & Black, J. (1997). Mothers' and fathers' beliefs about and spontaneous participation in toddlers' play. *Merrill-Palmer Quarterly, 43,* 271–290.

Haight, W., Wang, X.-L., Fung, H. H., Williams, K., & Mintz, J. (1999). Universal, developmental, and variable aspects of young children's play: A cross-cultural comparison of pretending at home. *Child Development, 70,* 1477–1488.

Hart, B., & Risley, T. R. (1995). *Meaningful differences in the everyday experience of young American children.* Baltimore, MD: Brookes.

Hewlett, B. (1987). Patterns of parental holding among Aka pygmies. In M. Lamb (Ed.), *The father's role: Cross-cultural perspectives* (pp. 295–330). Hillsdale, NJ: Erlbaum.

Hirasawa, A. (2005). Infant care among the sedentarized Baka hunter-gatherers in southeastern Cameroon. In B. S. Hewlett & M. E. Lamb (Eds.), *Hunter-gatherer childhoods: Evolutionary, developmental, and cultural perspectives* (pp. 365–384). New Brunswick, NJ: Aldine/Transaction Publishers.

Hirschfeld, L. A. (2002). Why don't anthropologists like children? *American Anthropologist, 104*, 611–627.

Holloway, S., Rambaud, M. F., Fuller, B., & Eggers-Pierola, C. (1995). What is "appropriate practice" at home and in child care?: Low-income mothers' views on preparing their children for school. *Early Childhood Research Quarterly, 10*, 451–473.

Holmes, R. (2001). Parental notions about their children's playfulness and children's notions of play in the United States and Hong Kong. In S. Reifel (Ed.), *Play and culture studies,* vol. 3: *Theory in context and out* (pp. 291–314). Westport, CT: Ablex.

Holmes, R. M. (2011). Adult attitudes and beliefs regarding play on Lāna'i. *American Journal of Play, 3*(3), 356–384.

Hossain, Z., Roopnarine, J. L., Isamel, R., Menon, S., & Sombuling, A. (2007). Fathers' and mothers' reports of involvement in caring for infants in Kadazan families in Sabah, Malaysia. *Fathering, 5*, 58–72.

Hossain, Z., Roopnarine, J. L., Masud, J., Muhamed, A. A., Baharudin, R., Abdullah, R., & Jahur, R. (2005). Mothers' and fathers' childcare involvement with young children in rural families in Malaysia. *International Journal of Psychology, 40*, 385–394.

Isbell, R., Sobol, J., Lindauer, L., & Lowrence, A. (2004). The effects of storytelling and story reading on the oral language complexity and story comprehension on young children. *Early Childhood Education Journal, 32*, 157–163.

Ivrendi, A., & Isikoglu, N. (2010). A Turkish view on fathers' involvement in children's play. *Early Childhood Education Journal, 37*, 519–526.

Jankowiak, W., Joiner, A., & Khatib, C. (2011). What observation studies can tell us about single child play patterns, gender, and changes in Chinese society. *Cross-Cultural Research, 45*(2), 155–177.

Johnson, J. Eberle, S., Henricks, T., & Kuschner, D. (2015). *The handbook of the study of play* (2 vols.). Lanham, MD: Rowan & Littlefield.

Kağitcibaşi, C. (2007). *Family and human development across countries: A view from the other side* (2nd edn.). Hove, UK: Psychology Press.

Kakar, S., & Kakar, K. (2007). *The Indians: Portrait of a people*. New Delhi: Viking.

Kamei, N. (2005). Play among Baka children in Cameroon. In B. S. Hewlett & M. E. Lamb (Eds.), *Hunter-gatherer childhoods: Evolutionary, developmental, and cultural perspectives* (pp. 343–349). New Brunswick, NJ: Aldine/Transaction Publishers.

Kato, K., & Kondo, K. (2007). A comparison between fathers and mothers in a play situation with three-year-olds. *Japanese Journal of Developmental Psychology, 18*, 35–44.

Keller, H., Borke, J., Chaudhary, N., Lamm, B., & Kleis, A. (2010). Continuity in parenting strategies: A cross-cultural comparison. *Journal of Cross-Cultural Psychology, 41*(3), 391–409.

Khaleque, A., & Rohner, R. P. (2012). Pancultural associations between perceived parental acceptance-rejection and psychological adjustment of children and adults: A meta-analytic review of worldwide research. *Journal of Cross-Cultural Psychology*, *43*, 784–800.

Kim, K. H. (2007). Exploring the interaction between Asian culture (Confucianism) and creativity. *Journal of Creative Behavior*, *41*, 28–53.

Laflamme, D., Pomerleau, A., & Malcuit, G. (2002). A comparison of fathers' and mothers' involvement in childcare and stimulation behaviors during free-play with their infants at 9 and 15 months. *Sex Roles*, *47*, 507–518.

Lamb, M. E. (2002). Infant–father attachments and their impact on child development. In C. S. Tamis-LeMonda & N. Cabrera (Eds.), *Handbook on father involvement: Multidisciplinary perspectives* (pp. 93–117). Mahwah, NJ: Erlbaum.

Lamb, M. E., Frodi, A. M., Frodi, M., & Hwang, C. P. (1982). Characteristics of maternal and paternal behavior in traditional and nontraditional Swedish families. *International Journal of Behavioral Development*, *5*, 131–141.

Lancy, D. (2007). Accounting for variability in mother–child play. *American Anthropologist*, *109*, 273–284.

Landry, S. H., Smith, K. E., Swank, P. R., Zucker, T., Crawford, A. D., & Solari, E. F. (2012). The effects of a responsive parenting intervention on parent–child interactions during shared book reading. *Developmental Psychology*, *48*(4), 969–986.

Lareau, A. (2003). *Unequal childhoods: Class, race, and family life*. Berkeley: University of California Press.

Leo-Rhynie, E., & Brown, J. (2013). Child rearing practices in the Caribbean in the early childhood years. In C. Logie & J. L. Roopnarine (Eds.), *Issues and perspectives in early childhood education in the Caribbean* (pp. 30–62). La Romaine, Trinidad and Tobago: Caribbean Publishers.

Lugo-Gil, J., & Tamis-LeMonda, C. S. (2008). Family resources and parenting quality: Links to children's cognitive development across the first 3 years. *Child Development*, *79*(4), 1065–1085.

MacDonald, K., & Parke, R. D. (1986). Parent–child physical play: The effects of sex and age of children and parents. *Sex Roles*, *15*, 367–378.

Martini, M., & Kirkpatrick, J. (1992). Parenting in Polynesia: A view from the Marquesas. In J. L. Roopnarine & B. Carter (Eds.), *Parent–child socialization in diverse cultures* (pp. 199–222). Norwood, NJ: Ablex.

Mathur, S. (2014). The ecology of play among young children of Mexican origin seasonal farmworkers. In J. L. Roopnarine, M. Patte, J. E. Johnson, & D. Kuschner (Eds.), *International perspectives on children's play* (pp. 49–61). London: Open University Press/McGraw Hill.

Meunier, J. C., Roskam, I., & Browne, D. T. (2011). Relations between parenting and child behavior: Exploring the child's personality and parental self-efficacy as third variables. *International Journal of Behavioral Development*, *35*(3), 246–259.

Mol, S., & Bus, A. G. (2011). To read or not to read: A meta-analysis of print exposure from infancy to early adulthood. *Psychological Bulletin*, *137*, 267–296.

Morelli, G. A., Rogoff, B., & Angelillo, C. (2003). Cultural variation in young children's access to work or involvement in specialized child-focused activities. *International Journal of Behavioral Development*, *27*, 264–274.

Morrison, F. J., & Cooney, R. R. (2002). Parenting and academic achievement: Multiple paths to early literacy. In J. G. Borkowski, S. L. Ramey, & M. Bristol-Power (Eds.), *Parenting and the child's world: Influences on academic, intellectual, and social-emotional development* (pp. 141–160). Mahwah, NJ: Erlbaum.

Murphy, D. A. (1992). Constructing the child: Relations between parental beliefs and child outcomes. *Developmental Review, 12*, 199–232.

Ng'asike, J. T., (2014). Take me to the (dry) river: Children's play in the Turkana pastoralist communities in Kenya. In J. L. Roopnarine, M. Patte, J. E. Johnson, & D. Kuschner (Eds.), *International perspectives on children's play* (pp. 103–116). London: Open University Press/McGraw Hill.

Oyserman, D., Coon, H. M., & Kemmelmeiter, M. (2002). Rethinking individualism and collectivism: Evaluation of theoretical assumptions and meta-analysis. *Psychological Bulletin, 128*, 3–72.

Paquette, D. (2004). Dichotomizing paternal and maternal functions as a means to better understand their primary contributions. *Human Development, 47*, 237–238.

Paquette, D., & Bigras, M. (2010). The risky situation: A procedure for assessing the father–child activation relationship. *Early Child Development and Care, 180* (1–2), 33–50.

Paquette, D., & Dumont, C. (2012). Is father–child rough-and-tumble play associated with attachment or activation relationships? *Early Child Development and Care, 183*, 760–773.

Paquette, D., & Dumont, C. (2013). Is father–child rough-and-tumble play associated with attachment or activation relationships? *Early Child Development and Care, 183*(6), 760–773.

Parmar, P., Harkness, S., & Super, C. (2004). Asian and European American parents' ethnotheories of play and learning: Effects on preschool children's home routines and social behavior. *International Journal of Behavioral Development, 28*, 97–104.

Pellegrini, A. D. (Ed.). (2011). *The Oxford handbook of the development of play.* New York: Oxford University Press.

Powell, C. (2004). An evaluation of the Roving Caregiver Program. Unpublished manuscript, Tropical Medicine Unit, University of the West Indies, Mona, Jamaica.

Rogoff, B., Goncu, A., Mistry, J., & Mosier, C. (1993). Guided participation in cultural activity by toddlers and caregivers. *Monographs of the Society for Research in Child Development*, serial no. 236, vol. 58, no. 8.

Rohner, R. P., & Khaleque, A. (Eds.) (2005). *Handbook for the study of parental acceptance and rejection.* Storrs, CT: Rohner Research Publications.

Roopnarine, J. L. (2011). Cultural variations in beliefs about play, parent–child play, and children's play: Meaning for childhood development. In A. Pellegrini (Ed.), *Oxford encyclopedia on play* (pp. 19–37). Oxford: Oxford University Press.

Roopnarine, J. L. (2013). The Roving Caregivers Program: A home-based early childhood intervention program in Caribbean countries. In C. Logie & J. L. Roopnarine (Eds.), *Issues and perspectives in childhood development and early education in Caribbean countries* (pp. 213–241). La Romaine, Trinidad: Caribbean Publishers.

Roopnarine, J. L. (Ed.) (2015). *Fathers across cultures: The importance, roles, and diverse practices of dads.* New York: Praeger Press.

Roopnarine, J. L., Brown, J., Snell-White, P., Riegraf, N. B., Crossley, D., Hossain, Z., & Webb, W. (1995). Father involvement in child care and household work in common-law dual-earner and single-earner families. *Journal of Applied Developmental Psychology, 16,* 35–52.

Roopnarine, J. L., & Davidson, K. L. (2015). Parent–child play across cultures: Advancing play research. *American Journal of Play, 7,* 228–252.

Roopnarine, J. L., Fouts, H. N., Lamb, M. E., & Lewis-Elligan , T. E. L. (2005). Mothers' and fathers' behaviors toward their 3–4 month old infants in lower-, middle-, and upper-SES African American families. *Developmental Psychology, 41,* 723–732.

Roopnarine, J. L., & Jin, B. (2012). Indo Caribbean immigrant beliefs about play and its impact on early academic performance. *American Journal of Play, 4*(4), 441–463.

Roopnarine, J. L., Patte, M., Johnson, J. E., & Kuschner, D. (Eds.) (2014). *International perspectives on children's play.* London: Open University Press/ McGraw Hill.

Roopnarine, J. L., Talukder, E., Jain, D., Joshi, P., & Srivastav, P. (1990). Characteristics of holding, patterns of play and social behaviors between parents and infants in New Delhi, India. *Developmental Psychology, 26,* 667–673.

Roopnarine, J. L. Wang, Y., Krishnakumar, A., & Davidson, K. (2013). Parenting practices in Guyana and Trinidad and Tobago: Connections to preschoolers' social and cognitive skills. *Interamerican Journal of Psychology, 47*(2), 313–328.

Roopnarine, J. L., & Yildirim, E. D. (2018). Paternal and maternal engagement in play, story telling, and reading in five Caribbean countries: Associations with preschoolers' literacy skills. International Journal of Play, DOI: https://doi .org/10.1080/21594937.2018.149600010.1080/21594937.2018.1496000.

Saar, A., & Niglas, K. (2001) Estonian and Russian parental attitudes to childrearing and play. *Early Child Development and Care, 168,* 39–47.

Sagi, A., Lamb, M. E., Shoham, R., Dvir, R., & Lewkowicz, K. S. (1985). Parent–infant interaction on Israeli kibbutzim. *International Journal of Behavioral Development, 8,* 273–284.

Schieffelin, B. B. (1990). *The give and take of everyday life: Language acquisition of Kaluli children.* Cambridge: Cambridge University Press.

Shonkoff, J. P. (2010). Building a new biodevelopmental framework to guide the future of early childhood policy. *Child Development, 81*(1), 357–367.

Shonkoff, J. P., Garner, A. S., The Committee on Psychosocial Aspects of Child and Family Health, Committee on Early Childhood, Adoption, and Dependent Care, & Section on Developmental and Behavioral Pediatrics. (2012). The lifelong effect of early childhood adversity and chronic stress. *Pediatrics, 129,* 232–246.

Shwalb, D. W., Nakazawa, J., Yamamoto, T., & Hyun, J.-H. (2004). Fathering in Japanese, Chinese, and Korean cultures. In M. E. Lamb (Ed.), *The role of the father in child development* (pp. 146–181). New York: Wiley & Sons.

Shwalb, D., Shwalb, B., & Lamb, M. E. (Eds.). *Fathers in cultural context*. New York: Routledge.

Sigel, I., & McGillicuddy-De Lisi, A. (2002). *Parental beliefs as cognitions: The dynamic belief systems mode*. In M. Bornstein (Ed.), *Handbook of parenting* (vol. 3, 2nd edn.). Mahwah, NJ: Erlbaum.

Singer, D. G., Singer, J. L., D'Agostino, H., & DeLong, R. (2009). Children's pastimes and play in sixteen nations: Is free-play declining? *American Journal of Play*, *1*(3), 283–312.

Smith, P. K. (2010). *Children and play*. Sussex, UK: Wiley-Blackwell.

Spijk, J. V., Rosmberg, C., & Janssens, W. (2008). RCP impact evaluation in St. Lucia. Amsterdam Institute for International Development, Amsterdam, Netherlands.

Suizzo, M.-A., & Bornstein, M. H. (2006). French and European American child–mother play: Culture and gender considerations. *International Journal of Behavioral Development*, *30*, 498–508.

Sun, L., & Roopnarine, J. L. (1996). Mother–infant and father–infant interaction and involvement in childcare and household labor among Taiwanese families. *Infant Behavior and Development*, *19*, 121–129.

Super, C., & Harkness, S. (1997). The cultural structuring of child development. In J. Berry, P. Dasen, & T. S. Saraswathi (Eds.), *Handbook of cross-cultural psychology: Basic processes and human development* (pp. 1–39). Needham, MA: Allyn & Bacon.

Super, C., & Harkness, S. (2002). Culture structures the environment for development. *Human Development*, *45*, 270–274.

Sutton-Smith, B. (1997). *The ambiguity of play*. Cambridge, MA: Harvard University Press.

Tamis-Lemonda, C. S., Bornstein, M. H., Cyphers, L., Toda, S., & Ogino, M. (1992). Language and play at one year: A comparison of toddlers and mothers in the United States and Japan. *International Journal of Behavioral Development*, *15*, 19–42.

Tamis-LeMonda, C. S., Shannon, J. D., Cabrera, N., & Lamb, M. E. (2004). Fathers and mothers at play with their 2- and 3-year-olds: Contributions to language and cognitive development. *Child Development*, *75*, 1806–1820.

Tulananda, O., & Roopnarine, J. L. (2001). Mothers' and fathers' interactions with preschoolers in the home in northern Thailand: Relationships to teachers' assessments of children's social skills. *Journal of Family Psychology*, *14*, 676–687.

United Nations Children's Fund (UNICEF) (2006). *Multiple indicator cluster survey manual 2005: monitoring the situation of women and children*. New York: UNICEF.

United Nations Children Fund (2015). *Monitoring the situation of children and women for 20 years: the multiple indicator cluster surveys (MICS) 1995–2015*. New York: UNICEF. Available at http://mics.unicef.org/publications/reports-and-methodological-papers.

Van der Kooij, R., & Neukater, H. (1989) Elterliches Erzieherverhalten und Spiel im internationalen Vergleich. *Zeitschrift für Pädagogische Psychologie*, *3*, 259–263.

Van der Kooij, R., & Slaats-van den Hurk, W. (1991). Relations between parental opinions and attitudes about play and childrearing. *Play and Culture, 4*, 108–123.

Walker, S. P., Chang, S. M., Powell, C. A., & Grant-McGregor, S. M. (2005). Effects of early childhood psychosocial stimulation and nutritional supplementation on cognition and education in growth-stunted Jamaican children: Prospective cohort study. *Lancet, 366*, 1804–1807.

Wall, K. (2015). Fathers in Portugal: From old to new masculinities. In J. L. Roopnarine (Ed.), *Fathers across cultures: The importance, roles, and diverse practices of dads* (pp. 132–154). New York: Praeger Press.

Wilson, L. C., Wilson, C. M., & Berkeley-Caines, L. (2003). Age, gender and socio-economic differences in parental socialization preferences in Guyana. *Journal of Comparative Family Studies, 34*, 213–227.

Yeung, W. J., Sandberg, J. F., Davis-Kean, P. E., & Hofferth, S. L. (2001). Children's time with fathers in intact families. *Journal of Marriage and Family, 63*, 136–154.

Yildirim, E. D., & Roopnarine, J. L. (2017). Paternal and maternal engagement in play in African countries: Associations with children's literacy skills. In preparation.

Zhang, X. (2013). Bidirectional longitudinal relations between father–child relationships and Chinese children's social competence during early childhood. *Early Childhood Research Quarterly, 28*, 83–93.

10 Object Use in Childhood

Development and Possible Functions

Anthony D. Pellegrini

The various ways that objects are used by children has been subjected to a considerable amount of theoretical and empirical attention across a number of different disciplines, from anthropology (e.g., Bock, 2005) to developmental psychology (e.g., Piaget, 1952) and zoology (Beck, 1980). Perhaps most centrally, Piaget's (1952) theory suggests that children's cognitive development is rooted in their sensorimotor interactions with objects. In this theory, individuals construct representations for those objects and their associated actions through repeated interactions. Piaget's sensorimotor theory has also been applied to the use of objects in non-human primates (Hallock & Worobey, 1984). Furthermore and by extension, one school of thought holds that human cognition evolved in the context of apes' manipulation and use of objects and tools (Tomasello & Call, 1997). However, much of what developmental psychologists know about children's object use, especially during infancy and early childhood, is often subsumed under the labels 'object play' and 'construction'. These labels have been used so loosely that it is very difficult to chart ontogenetic or functional courses for the diverse ways in which children use objects. A basic premise of ethology (Tinbergen, 1963), and this chapter, is that behavior categories should be induced through empirical observation and hypotheses tested subsequent to this.

Further, the importance of social interaction around object uses in early cognitive development, especially in Piaget's theory, has been ignored. This view persisted even though there were numerous observations, especially involving young children, that interactions with objects take place in a social contexts and that children spend considerable time observing others using objects (e.g., Tomasello & Call, 1997). Unfortunately, however, the extant child developmental literature on object uses pays only limited attention to the ways that different types of object are used in a variety of social as well nonsocial contexts (though see Flynn & Whiten, 2008, and Pellegrini & Hou, 2011).

In this chapter I will first describe the different forms of object use (i.e., exploration, construction, play, tool use, and tool making) in childhood. This is an important exercise given the variety of labels used to describe the different ways that children interact with objects. Correspondingly, I will establish time budgets for each type of object uses and make functional inferences about each and the social context in which each is embedded.

Object Uses in Childhood

Given the centrality of object use in child developmental theory, it is surprising how little descriptive information there is about the varied ways in which children use objects. Where efforts have been made to address the different types of object use and play exhibited by children, researchers have often conflated object play with different forms of object use. Specifically, much of the study of children's interactions with objects during childhood has been influenced by Smilansky's (1968) adaptation of Piaget's (1951) theory of play and the ways that she categorized behaviors directed at objects as 'constructive play', an ends-oriented activity with objects where something was built. Piaget, in contrast, did not consider construction to be play because of its ends, not means, orientation (Smith et al., 1986). I will discuss each form of object use, in the order in which they occur in ontogeny.

Exploration

Exploration is the behavior exhibited when individuals first encounter unfamiliar objects; they manipulate, or explore, their properties and attributes (Hutt, 1966; West, 1977). Through exploration, children find out that objects, for example, are flat or rounded, long or short. While often conflated with play with objects, they differ behaviorally. Specifically, exploration, relative to play, is characterized by elevated heart rate, low distractibility, and negative/flat affect. By contrast, children playing with objects have lower heart rates, are highly distractible, and display positive affect (Hutt, 1966).

Further, exploration precedes other forms of object use, including play in human ontogeny (Belsky & Most, 1981; McCall, 1974), as well in other animals (e.g., West, 1977). In a study of children from 7.5 to 21 months, Belsky and Most found that exploration of toys was the predominant activity of the youngest children (7.5–10.5 months), with no instances of pretend play with objects. From around 9–10.5 months, children named objects as they manipulated them. At 12 months, pretend play with objects appeared, co-occurring with exploration and naming of the objects, and then pretend displaced exploration. And, like Hutt (1966), Belsky and Most (1981) noted that exploration of an object precedes play with that object. These trends are consistent with a view that the processes involved in exploring are precursors to play with objects.

By the time children are of preschool age, exploration accounts for a relatively small portion of their object time budgets, between 2% and 15% of children's total observed behaviour (Pellegrini & Gustafson, 2005; Pellegrini & Hou, 2011). In the case of the high end of the range, exploration spikes when children are exposed to novel objects, such as when they return to their preschool classrooms after their winter holidays. Given the relative infrequency of exploration during the preschool years, there are few documented age differences for directly observed exploration (Pellegrini & Gustafson, 2005), though differences do appear when the construct is widened to include such behaviours as asking questions and other elicited behaviours (Henderson & Moore, 1979).

There are reported sex differences in exploration, where boys exhibit more than girls (Pellegrini & Hou, 2011), though experimental study of infants' and pre-schoolers' exploration do not consistently test for sex differences (e.g., Ross et al., 1972).

Exploration of objects occurs in both social and solitary contexts. Piaget (1967) described how solitary infants, especially, as well as young children explored objects, yet children's exploration can be facilitated by adults, such as parental presence (Rheingold & Eckerman, 1970). Adult facilitation continues through early childhood (~ 5.5 years of age), where adult encouragement significantly increases exploration (Henderson, 1984). However, we find that when children explore objects in preschool classrooms, they tend to do so in solitary contexts (Pellegrini, unpublished data). Correspondingly, preschool children's exploration does not attract their peers' attention (Pellegrini & Hou, 2011).

Play with Objects

Play, following Burghardt (2005), should be defined categorically, not continuously, and must meet all of the following criteria: voluntary, observed in a "relaxed field," not completely functional in the immediately observed context, and have elements that are exaggerated, segmented, and nonsequential in relation to the functional behavior. A relaxed field is one in which the individual, typically a juvenile, is well provisioned, safe, and healthy. Further, the child voluntarily chooses to engage in an activity that is not completely functional. The nature and sequence of these behaviors should not resemble those in a functional context. For example, a child could approach a peer, take an exaggerated swipe at his peer, fall to the ground, and then switch roles, so his peers can hit at him. Distilling Burghardt's definition, I suggest that the most important criteria are the emphases on means over ends and incompletely functional behavior in the immediate context because they are probably antecedents, and sufficient conditions, for children generating novel behaviors. That is, by not being concerned with the usefulness of behavior, individuals are free to experiment with its form and place in behavioral sequences (e.g., Bateson, 2005; Fagen, 1981). The resulting behavioral and cognitive flexibility characteristic of different forms of play, such as exaggerated, non-sequential, and segmented behavioral routines, is crucial to the development of what Bruner (1972) and West-Eberhard (2003) labeled behavioral 'modules'.

From this definition, object play typically involves pretending with an object. Using objects in pretend initially entails that children are simulating someone else's use of those objects. With experience, children learn to have more abstract objects represent other objects. Correspondingly, children's play with objects is typified by them using objects in novel and varied ways (Pellegrini & Hou, 2011). This begins in the context of parent–child interactions (and then to interaction with peers; Lillard, 2006). Indeed, of all the ways in which children use objects, play with objects is most highly related to creative uses of objects (Pellegrini & Hou, 2011).

Play with objects, like other forms of play, follows an inverted-U function; it first appears at around 12 months of age, increases through the preschool years, and then declines (Fein, 1981). Establishing an accurate time budget for play with objects during childhood is difficult because object play has typically been conflated with other forms of object use. In those cases where object play was clearly differentiated from other forms of object use, it begins at around one year (Belsky & Most, 1981) and increases among 3- to 5-year-olds in US and UK preschool settings to 18%–30% of children's time budgets (McGrew, 1972; Pellegrini & Gustafson, 2005; Pellegrini & Hou, 2011).

Given the clear differences in antecedents, ontogeny, and function between play and exploration, it is confusing when the terms are used interchangeably and in combination (i.e., 'exploratory play'), even within the same research articles (e.g., Baldwin et al., 1993), to describe exploration as defined in this chapter. Such loose word usage has confused, and will continue to confuse, the meaning of each construct and further muddy the play and object use literatures. Correspondingly, it is nearly impossible for researchers to document time budgets of different types of behaviour during childhood, when terms are not used accurately and consistently. Perhaps most basically, when behavioural categories are not based on empirical observation, as exists between play and exploration, our theories and subsequent hypotheses will remain on the borders of science; from my view, science should involve both induction (to empirically form categories) and deduction (to test hypotheses) (Russell, 1931/1959; Smith, 2011; Tinbergen, 1963).

Sex differences in object play are equivocal and not consistent with the more general literature on pretend play where girls, relative to boys, exhibit more and more sophisticated pretend (Pellegrini, 2009). In an observational study of pre-schoolers' object use (i.e., exploration, construction, object play, and tool use) across one year, object play was not influenced by sex (Pellegrini & Hou, 2011). It may be that in this study girls' general facility with pretence was diluted by their interactions across a wider variety of objects (beyond replicate toys), while boys' play with some forms of objects (such as using a rake for a pretend gun) increased, thus attenuating sex differences.

Object play becomes increasingly social with age (Rubin et al., 1983). For example, less than 2% of preschool and kindergarten children's play is solitary, while 12% and 28% of pre-schoolers' and kindergarteners', respectively, is social (Rubin et al., 1978). Thus, not only does object play increase across childhood, but it also becomes increasingly social.

Construction

Much of what we know about construction is subsumed under the Smilansky-inspired label of 'constructive play,' which, according to Smilansky, has the child learning the "various uses of play materials" and the "building" of something (1968, p. 6). However, construction, according to Piaget (1951) and others (e.g., Smith et al., 1986), is not considered to be play. For Piaget, on whom Smilansky based her work, construction is more accommodative and concerned with the end product of activity – the construction per se – while play is more assimilative and concerned with the activity, or means, than with the end and consequently is not play per se (Piaget, 1951). In further support of the claim that construction is not a form of play, it does not follow the typical inverted-U age-related trajectory (Smith et al., 1986)

Smilansky's categories of 'play' were expanded into a heuristic for describing the social and cognitive dimensions of play by Rubin and colleagues (1983) and considered 'constructive play' as the manipulation of objects to create something. This scheme has been used to generate massive and valuable amounts of descriptive data on the ways that young children use objects (summarized in Rubin et al., 1983). Rubin and colleagues rightfully questioned the validity of 'constructive play' as a form of play because of its incongruity with Piagetian theory. Despite these qualifications, little effort has been made to differentiate construction from play with objects and other forms of object use.

The above definition given by Smilansky, and subsequently revised by Rubin et al. (1983), includes a diverse constellation of goal-directed and non-goal-directed uses of objects. For example, using blocks to build steps might be considered constructive or pretend play. The same act, however, might also actually be considered 'tool use' if a child uses the steps to enhance his or her reach (Amant & Horton, 2008). Thus, the descriptive data generated by the Smilansky model provide very general descriptions of children's object use. However, to the extent that the category 'constructive play' is too general it limits our knowledge of the role of 'object play' and construction in children's development

'Constructive play', as defined by Rubin and colleagues, has been found to account for between 40% (Rubin et al., 1976) and 51% (Rubin et al., 1976, 1978) of all observed behaviour subsumed under the Smilansky–Parten play matrix. When construction is defined more consistent with Piaget (1951), Pellegrini and colleagues found that construction accounted for between 15% (Pellegrini & Gustafson, 2005) and 17% (Pellegrini & Hou, 2011) of behaviour. The very different figures derived from the Rubin and Pellegrini studies may reflect the fact that what Rubin and colleagues coded as constructive play probably included other forms of object use, such as tool use and perhaps solitary object play.

In terms of sex differences for 'constructive play', defined according to Smilansky, it is reported that females engage in more than males (Rubin et al., 1976; Rubin et al., 1978). However, boys' constructions tend to be more complex than girls' (Rubin et al., 1983). Data from two naturalistic studies of pre-schoolers' object use using the differentiated categories proffered here help to clarify this confusion. Beginning with an observational study with a limited sample, girls, relative to boys, spend more time in construction, but boys spend more time than girls in object play (Pellegrini & Gustafson, 2005). In the other, larger observational study, there were no moderating effects of sex on construction (Pellegrini & Hou, 2011).

Tool Use and Tool Making

Tool use has individuals using objects not attached to the environment or being part of individuals' bodies, in the service of a goal, such as getting food, and includes both using and making tools (Hansell & Ruxton, 2008). For example, using a fingernail to twist a screw would not be an example of tool use but using a screwdriver would; shaping the tip of a stick to do so would be an example of tool making. Thus, tool use is a convergent activity, involving children learning to use a tool according to cultural conventions, such as using a fork, while making tools is a more divergent and creative act such that individuals use an object to solve a problem for which it might not have been designed; for example, bending a coat hanger to retrieve an object in a remote location. Using tools instrumentally, relative to making tools, appears relatively early in human ontogeny (Mounoud, 1996), with skills increasing from infancy through childhood (Connolly & Elliot, 1972).

Most studies of tool use in childhood showing increases in facility with age are drawn almost solely from performance on experimental tasks (Flynn & Whiten, 2008). Developmental descriptions of children's use of objects in children's everyday worlds, encompassing exploration, play, construction, and tool use, are sorely lacking (Power, 2000), thus time budget information is spotty. There is an especial paucity of studies of children's making of tools and innovation in making tools. Three studies, two with university laboratory pre-schoolers and one with African pastoral children, however, provide a relatively consistent picture. First, regarding the university preschool samples, Pellegrini and colleagues (Pellegrini & Gustafson, 2005; Pellegrini & Hou, 2011), observed preschool children's tool use and making in their classrooms. Children spent between 19% (Pellegrini & Hou, 2011) and 23% (Pellegrini & Gustafson, 2005) of their total observed time in tool use. Only in the later study (Pellegrini & Hou, 2011), however, was the sample large enough to calculate a growth curve model, which showed a significant increase in tool use across time. Similarly, in Bock's (2005) pastoral sample of Botswanan preschool-age children, they spent a similar amount of time in object use, 17%, similar to the figures in the Pellegrini studies.

Unlike using tools, tool making is still developing through the early and middle childhood periods, indicative of the relatively complex dexterity and cognition needed (Monound, 1996). Making tools is cognitively complex to the extent that individuals must identify a goal, identify affordances in objects associated with the goal, and consider the means of using tools to meet that goal. Further, the ability to make tools requires a level of behavioural flexibility, such that rather conventional objects, such as pipe cleaners, are redesigned to serve different ends, relative to what they were designed for (Cutting et al., 2011). However, when even very young children (e.g., 30 months of age) observed someone else make a tool, they were able to imitate them (Hayne et al., 2003). However, when they are left on their own, they do not make tools to solve problems successfully until well into middle childhood (Monound, 1996).

The supportive role of adults in children's tool use and tool making suggests that infants' and young children's interest in objects is stimulated when they are interacting with or observing adults using objects. When adults handle objects, for example, children, in turn, become interested in those objects; they may pick up the objects, examine them, and learn about them (Tomasello & Call, 1997). Relatedly, when infants or young children observe adults handling and using objects to solve a problem, such as using a coat hanger to retrieve a toy, they recognize that the hanger can be used to solve the problem and they use it, though not as demonstrated by the model, to solve the problem, something that they might not have discovered on their own (Tomasello & Call, 1997). The ease with which child emulate and imitate adults using tools, relative to their independent performance, is testament to the importance of the social context of learning to use tools. However, when children's tool use is observed in their preschool classrooms, it occurs in both social and solitary contexts and does not attract a significant amount of their peers' attention (Pellegrini & Hou, 2011).

Sex differences in tool use are equivocal, perhaps due to the different ways in which it is defined and contexts in which it is assessed. Specifically, studies of preschool children's tool use are either naturalistic or experimental and in the experimental cases often involve tool making inspired by the Köhler-type (1925) lure retrieval tasks. In some of this work (i.e., tool use tasks) preschool children are presented with an array of objects, some of which are tools that can solve the problem (retrieve the lure). In these tool choice experiments, children as young as 2 years of age chose the optimal objects to retrieve the lure (e.g., Chen & Siegler, 2000); boys seem better at this than girls, though with minimal help, the sex differences are attenuated.

In terms of sex differences in tool use in naturalistic studies, neither of the Pellegrini and colleagues' (2005, 2011) studies nor the Bock (2005) study found significant sex differences in time spent in total tool use. However, sex differences were observed when the specific tools used were disaggregated from total tool use. Among pastoral children studied by Bock (2005), girls spent more time than boys 'play pounding', which involves using mortar-like objects, such as sticks and reeds, to pound grain-like substances. Girls also moved from play pounding to actual tool use, helping adults to pound grain, at an earlier age than boys moved from playful tool use to actual tool use. Boys spent more time than girls in throwing spear-like sticks at targets, and boys were older when they moved from such playful tool use to real hunting. In the case of foraging children, Gosso and colleagues (2005) reported boys more than girls were frequently seen using bows and arrows and slingshots, whereas girls more frequently made tools associated with gathering (for example, making baskets out of palm leaves; indeed, this activity was observed exclusively among girls). So the sex differences observed in some of the experimental studies of children's tool use may be specific to those tasks, rather than a more general sex-related behaviour.

Putative Functions of Object Use

Making inferences about the function of a behavior can be done in a number of ways, including its beneficial consequences and in terms of 'ultimate function', or reproductive fitness (Hinde, 1980). Perhaps the most frequently cited efforts to determine function of object play in the developmental psychological literature involve experimental manipulations where children are 'trained' to play with objects and then they are given similar or different, objects in convergent or divergent problem-solving tasks.

Convergent tasks are often modelled after Köhler's (1925) famous experiments of a chimpanzee using objects to solve problems, such as putting together sticks to reach bananas hung above its head. In the paradigmatic child development experiment in this mould, Sylva and colleagues (1976) presented children with disassembled components of a tool (i.e., sticks and clamps) that had to be assembled in order to retrieve a lure, such as a toy. Children in different conditions were given opportunities to play with the unassembled sticks, observe an adult assemble the sticks, or watch an adult use the clamp non-functionally (a control condition). Play condition children, relative to other conditions, were more systematic in their problem-solving, moving from simple to complex moves and using information from hints and failures more effectively. These findings, however, do not replicate under double-blind conditions (Simon & Smith, 1983).

Using objects in divergent problem-solving situations, or tasks for which there is no one correct answer, is also very common in the child development literature (Sutton-Smith, 1967). Specifically, Dansky and Silverman's (1973, 1975) frequently cited experimental studies examined the effects of 'play' with objects on children's associative fluency, or creative uses for objects. In the first study, Dansky and Silverman (1973) provided children with conventional, but unfamiliar, objects. In one condition they were asked to play with the objects; in others they observed an adult manipulating the objects or were exposed to a control condition. These sessions lasted less than 10 minutes. Children were then asked to list all the uses possible for one of the objects to which they were exposed. For example, creative uses for a matchbox might include using it as a pretend boat. They found that children in the play condition generated the greatest number of creative responses, relative to children in the other conditions.

In the second experiment by Dansky and Silverman (1975), children were assigned to similar conditions to those in the first experiment, but then asked to generate creative uses for objects with which they did *not* interact in their respective treatments. Again, they found that children in the play condition, relative to the other conditions, were the most creative, arguing that effects were due to an induced 'play set,' a temporary, creative orientation to objects presented.

While being widely cited, these studies of associative fluency, like the study by Sylva and colleagues, do not replicate when double-blind procedures are used (Smith & Whitney, 1987). The results in both types of studies, then, were probably due to experimenter bias. Furthermore, one could question the efficacy of an experimental treatment of 10 minutes or so on children's behaviour. An alternative, and perhaps more valid, approach to documenting the role of object play and exploration in tool use would involve documenting the time children spend in different types of object use across a relatively long period of time in their natural ecologies, and then regressing those values onto children's performance in different object use tasks (Pellegrini & Gustafson, 2005). This larger corpus of observations should provide a more valid indicator of children's facility with objects, relative to the relatively short-term studies cited earlier.

Martin and Caro (1985) suggest that if play, or any other form of object use, is to be naturally selected, benefits associated with the construct should outweigh the costs. An important first step in establishing function from this perspective is to document costs and then relate those costs to a beneficial consequence and/or fitness. Time spent in different types of activities with objects during childhood can be framed in this study in terms of behavioural ecology theory advanced by van Schaik (1999) and colleagues where descriptions of the 'costs' associated with an activity serve as an indicator of its importance, or possible function. Costs are typically documented in terms of the resources (time, energy, and survivorship) expended to acquire or learn a skill. Time in an activity is typically expressed as the portion of the total time budget spent in that activity and energy is typically expressed in terms of caloric expenditure in that activity relative to the entire caloric budget (Pellegrini et al., 1998).

The logic of this level of analysis is as follows. Learning and developing specific skills involve different trade-offs between costs and benefits, and individuals tend to adopt the most 'efficient', or optimal, strategies to solve different problems at specific points during ontogeny (Krebs & Davies, 1993). For example, in learning to use tools during childhood, trade-offs are made between different opportunities (e.g., playing with objects vs. learning to use an object through observation or direct instruction) in light of the finite amount of time and calories available. From this view, there should be a correspondence between time budgets and the benefits associated with expenditures in each activity: time spent in different types of activity use should relate positively to using those objects to solve problems.

There are very few time and energy budget studies of children's play, generally (though see Haight & Miller, 1993, for pretend play, and Pellegrini et al., 1998, for locomotor play), and specifically for object use (though see Bock, 2005; Pellegrini & Gustafson, 2005; Pellegrini & Hou, 2011). The problem with documenting costs of object use and object play is compounded with the use of very loose and inconsistent terminology surrounding object use, as discussed above. Consequently, I will use data from the two Pellegrini studies (Pellegrini & Gustafson, 2005; Pellegrini & Hou, 2011) because they used definitions consistent with those presented here and they were put in time budget terms. Pellegrini and Gustafson (2005) observed a modest sample ($N = 35$) of preschool children in their classrooms across one school year. The aim was to use children's object use sampled across the year to predict the use of objects to solve divergent and convergent object-related problems. A subsample ($N = 20$) of children were also asked to participate in three types of object-use tasks (two convergent and one divergent tool task) as well as a spatial IQ task.

The divergent problem-solving task was assessed with an associative fluency task. The first of the two convergent retrieval tasks involved *selecting a tool* (e.g., a plastic toy hoe, a plastic rake head without a handle) with which to retrieve a toy dinosaur that had been placed out of reach of the child. In the second convergent task, children were asked to *make a tool* from Tinkertoy parts and then use it to retrieve a toy. Children were also given a series of seven graded hints if they stalled. The hints were provided in a sequential order but in ways that were appropriate to the phase of the task in which the child was engaged. The hints also provided the child with gradually more specific help in accomplishing the second task. The following dimensions of each child's performance were scored: the total time needed by the child to use one or more of the objects to successfully retrieve the dinosaur, the number of hints provided to the child by the experimenter while completing the task, and the number of swipes (e.g., attempts to use one or more of the objects to retrieve the dinosaur).

There was a paucity of predictive relations between observed object uses and performance on the associative fluency task and on the connected and unconnected lure-retrieval tasks, when spatial IQ was controlled. That exploration was a very low-occurrence behaviour may be partially responsible for these results given the age of the children and the relative familiarity of the objects in the classrooms

Construction and tool use did, however, differentially predict performance on the problem-solving tasks: construction was a significant predictor of associative fluency and performance on the connected tool use retrieval task (time to complete and hints), but it did not predict performance on the making tool (unconnected) task: observed tool use predicted number of hints on the tool-making task. The unconnected task was more difficult than the connected task, as indicated by the differences in time and hints needed to solve each. The time needed to complete the unconnected task was also greater by a factor of four than the connected task, and more than double the number of hints was needed.

Given the paucity of relations between object uses and performance on any of the problem-solving tasks, we might question the often-trumpeted value of play for both convergent and divergent problem-solving tasks with objects, at least as measured in associative fluency and lure retrieval tasks, similar to the argument made by Smith (1988). While this may be true for lack of effects on the lure retrieval tasks, which involve making tools, it is also possible that the task of making tools to retrieve lures is simply too complex for preschool-age children (Mounoud, 1996), even though they are capable of choosing the correct tool at a much younger age. As for the lack of relations for divergent, creativity tasks, it may be, again, that the choice of the task itself is inadequate. Specifically, we might be better served by redefining creative uses of objects in terms of behavioural 'modules' and the social learning implications of others observing novel modules. Modules, as defined by Bruner (1972) and more recently by some evolutionary biologists (e.g., West-Eberhard, 2003), develop as responses to local ecological and material demands. I do not use 'module' to refer to 'innate' brain structures in the same way as some evolutionary psychologists (e.g., Cosmides & Tooby, 1987). Modules, as I use the term, are relatively novel actions constructed by individuals in response to new environments. With experience, these diverse behavioural routines become more focused and relevant to the environments and objects in which individuals are embedded. Speculatively, it may be that play with objects results in the generation of behavioural modules associated with and independent of objects.

Take, for example, a child engaged in object play with pipe cleaners where he connects and bends two separate pipe cleaners into a pretend 'tunnel' for him to drive his toy car through. This specific module of connecting and bending could then be used on similar materials to solve a problem, such as connecting and bending pipe cleaners to be used to retrieve a lure in a restricted physical space. Correspondingly, modules developed in play can be applied to very different types of objects, for example, attaching lengths of rope to make it long enough to pull a wagon.

Further and perhaps more crucially, the social learning implications of novel object use may be the most important function of object play, though it has been virtually ignored, with Bateson (2011) and Pellegrini and Pellegrini (2013) being notable exceptions. They suggested that the behavioural flexibility developed in play may be an evolutionary driver, and at the leading edge of evolutionary change (though see Hewlett & Boyette, 2013, who challenged this as regards hunter-gatherer societies). That is, novel behaviours could be generated in play because of its high intrinsic motivation and its lack of concern for instrumentality. Those novel behaviours that out-compete alternatives will spread through the population and become dominant, in what I label the 'seeding hypothesis' of play. These novel uses should, in turn, attract the attention of peers (Pellegrini & Hou, 2011) and may spread through the population, depending on their usefulness. This hypothesis is consistent with early work with chimpanzees (Chance, 1967), where researchers gauged peer responses to individuals' novel and varied uses of objects by documenting 'attention structure', or the number of chimpanzees looking at chimpanzees as they used objects in different ways.

From this argument, Pellegrini and Hou (2011) observed a children's object use across a year in university nursery school classrooms. Object use was coded as exploration, play, construction, and tool use; each use was also independently scored for novelty and variety. Consistent with claims that object play is a mechanism for generating novel behaviour, they, like Hutt and Bhavnani (1972), found that only object play, not other forms of object use, significantly predicted novelty. As an indicator of the discriminant validity of the claim that play is a novelty generator, exploration, a convergent activity, was negatively and significantly correlated with novelty. That this study found a relation between object play and novel uses of objects may be due to the fact that it sampled novel behaviours more widely than experimental studies, which typically used a single, short-term, contrived task.

Specific to the 'seeding hypothesis', Pellegrini and Hou also found that only novel and creative uses of objects correlated significantly with peer attention structure. Further, novel and creative uses of object play observed during the first quarter of the school year predicted peer attention structure of children using objects creatively in the final quarter of the year, with attention structure for the earlier period statistically controlled. Again, this adds support to the claim that novelty attracts peers' attention, while construction, a convergent activity, was a significant *negative* predictor.

Also consistent with our findings, Wilks and colleagues (2014) found that children copied groups of other children who used objects effectively to solve problems (i.e., the majority bias). It may be that the novelty and effectiveness co-occurred in this experiment, but future research should tease apart the relative attractiveness of children who exhibited either novel or effective object use strategies. While these are results in need of replication, they do suggest that in trying to determine a function of object play researchers may have been off mark on two points. First, they targeted facility in specific tasks, such as associative fluency and lure retrieval tasks, rather than in a more general tendency to use objects in novel and varied ways. Second, and relatedly, researchers in this literature have virtually ignored the social dynamics of such behaviour. It may be that an important function of object play, and perhaps of play more generally, is to provide models to conspecifics of individuals exhibiting these behaviours, in the same way that human (Pellegrini, 2009) and non-human (Chance, 1967) individuals attend to socially dominant members of their group. Paying attention to these individuals may benefit individuals and groups, in turn. Learning to use objects in novel ways via imitation and other forms of social learning is a more effective strategy than having individuals spending time and energy constructing their own modules (Boyd & Richerson, 1985).

While this is possible, researchers must also address the counterclaim that it is not 'economical' for innovative players to share their creations, adding a cost to innovation and thus not likely to be selected (Fagen, 1981). Specifically, there are costs as well as benefits incurred by innovators, while there may be fewer costs and equally high benefits for copiers of innovations. That is, it takes less time and energy to observe an innovation, relative to playing and experimenting with objects, and the innovators are not getting pay-back for their investment if peers can copy, at less cost. This argument is, however, predicated on the assumption that individuals compete with each other for resources and that innovators' benefits will be outweighed by costs when they are copied. This critique also poses a serious threat to the hypothesis that play is a driver in the evolution of innovative object use. Specifically, object play does seem to represent a considerable cost to the extent that it represents between 18% and 30% of children's time budgets in preschool classrooms (McGrew, 1972; Pellegrini & Gustafson, 2005; Pellegrini & Hou, 2011). With this said, the figure is limited to university preschools where the ethos is to stimulate children's play in object-rich environments (Smith, 1988). To get a fuller picture of the actual time budgets of children's object play, they need to be studied in the niches they spend most of their time: home and community.

Even if we assume that object play is costly and that others observe and copy innovative object play, there are indeed costs for 'copiers', as with all social learners. This is because they would have to spend a relatively large amount of time to observe few innovative behaviours, since innovations with objects are typically rare (Fagen, 1981) and, when they occur, are preceded by long periods of experimentation (Huffman & Quiatt, 1986). Further, the innovators may still accrue net benefits from their behaviours being copied if the copiers reciprocate and cooperate with the initiator. Relative costs of innovation will outweigh benefits if 'freeloaders' can use the innovations for their own ends. However, and following the principles of mutualism (Clutton-Brock, 2009), individuals' costly behaviours (e.g., the innovative players) can be attenuated if individuals benefiting from those behaviours (the copiers) reciprocate with beneficial behaviours. This becomes a very plausible hypothesis when we consider that young children are most likely to interact repeatedly with others who share interests in similar activities and that these shared interests are the basis for 'friendship' in childhood. Correspondingly and in the course of these activities, friends are also more likely to be reciprocal and share information with each other (Gottman, 1983). Indeed, children's early altruistic acts are first observed in the context of friends interacting with each other (Kanfer et al., 1981). While these claims are supposition, they are based on sound theory and supporting data, and experimentally testable or testable through theoretical modelling.

Conclusions

In this chapter I have discussed children's uses of objects and presented descriptive data on their uses of objects in exploration, play with objects, construction, and tool use. The distinction among these categories is an important one as, to my knowledge, they have not been frequently differentiated in the child development literature on children's play. First, these categories are distinct, and they should be treated as such, as they have different developmental histories and different implications for using objects to solve problems. Correspondingly, scholars should take care to use labels consistently. With all of this said, much more work is needed, particularly observational work documenting the time spent in different sorts of object use. This advice is in the tradition where science should involve *both* inductive and deductive processes.

This review suggests that children in the industrialized world spend from moderate to substantial portions of their days in different types of object use. With this level of investment, there should be some pay-off for children. There is reasonable agreement among students of play from a wide variety of scholarly disciplines that the pay-off should relate to children's behavioural flexibility. The search for functions of object uses has been elusive, however, in both the experimental and naturalistic literatures. I posit that the behavioural flexibility associated with object play is indeed important, but not for solving contrived problems. Instead, object play and its associated behavioural flexibility probably serves as a model for other children, who, in turn, emulate and imitate these behaviours. By these means, new behavioural strategies can spread through the population.

It should also be apparent from the discussion in this chapter that much more attention needs to be paid to the social context in which children use objects. Future research should attempt to replicate the relation between object play and behavioural flexibility and attention structure. Further, studies using variations on diffusion chains should test this hypothesis experimentally.

References

Amant, R. S., & Horton, T. E. (2008). Revising the definition of animal tool use. *Animal Behaviour, 75,* 1199–1208.

Baldwin, D. A., Markman, E. H., & Melartin, R. L. (1993). Infants' ability to draw inferences about nonobvious object properties: Evidence from exploratory play. *Child Development, 64,* 711–728.

Bateson, P. P. G. (2005). Play and its role in the development of great apes and humans. In A. D. Pellegrini & P. K. Smith (Eds.), *The nature of play: Great apes and humans* (pp. 13–26). New York: Guilford.

Bateson, P. P. G. (2011). Theories of play. In A. D. Pellegrini (Ed.), *Oxford handbook of the development of play* (pp. 41–47). New York: Oxford University Press.

Beck, B. B. (1980). *Animal tool behavior.* New York: Garland.

Beck, S. R., Apperly, I. A., Chappell, Guthrie, C., & Cutting, N. (2011). Making tools isn't children's play. *Cognition, 119,* 301–306.

Belsky, J., & Most, R. (1981). From exploration to play: A cross-sectional study of infant free-play behavior. *Developmental Psychology, 17,* 630–639.

Bjorklund, D. F., & Gardiner, A. K. (2011). Object play and tool use: Developmental and evolutionary perspectives. In A. D. Pellegrini (Ed.), *Oxford handbook of the development of play* (pp. 153–171). New York: Oxford University Press.

Bock, J. (2005). Farming, foraging, and children's play in the Okavango Delta, Botswana. In A. D. Pellegrini & P. K. Smith (Eds.), *The nature of play: Great apes and humans* (pp. 254–284). New York: Guilford.

Boyd, R., & Richerson, P. J. (1985). *Culture and the evolutionary process.* Chicago, IL: University of Chicago Press.

Bruner, J. S. (1972). The nature and uses of immaturity. *American Psychologist, 27,* 687–708.

Bruner, J. S. (1973). Organization of early skilled action. *Child Development, 44,* 1–11.

Burghardt, G. M. (2005). *The genesis of animal play: Testing the limits.* Cambridge, MA: MIT Press.

Chance, M. R. A. (1967). Attention structure as a basis for primate rank order. *Man, 2,* 503–518.

Chen, Z., & Siegler, R. S. (2000). Across the great divide: Bridging the gap between understanding of toddlers' and older children's thinking. *Monographs of the Society for Research in Child Development,* serial no. 261.

Clutton-Brock, T. (2009). Cooperation between non-kin in animal societies. *Nature, 462*(5), 51–56.

Connolly, K., & Elliott, J. (1972). The evolution and ontogeny of hand functions. In N. Blurton Jones (Ed.), *Ethological studies of child behavior* (pp. 329–384). London: Cambridge University Press.

Cosmides, L., & Tooby, J. (1987). From evolution to behavior: Evolutionary psychology as the missing link. In J. Dupre (Ed.), *The latest on the best essays on evolution and optimality* (pp. 277–306). Cambridge, MA: MIT Press.

Cutting, N., Apperly, I. A., & Beck, S. R. (2011). Why do children lack the flexibility to innovate tools? *Journal of Experimental Child Psychology, 109,* 497–511.

Dansky, J., & Silverman, I. W. (1973). Effects of play on associative fluency in preschool-age children. *Developmental Psychology, 9,* 38–43.

Dansky, J., & Silverman, I. W. (1975). Play: A general facilitator of associative fluency. *Developmental Psychology, 11*, 104.

Fagen, R. (1981). *Animal play behavior.* New York: Oxford University Press.

Fein, G. G. (1981). Pretend play in childhood: An integrative review. *Child Development, 52*, 1095–1118.

Flynn, E., & Whiten, A. (2008). Cultural transmission of tool-use in young children: A diffusion chain study. *Social Deveoipment, 17*, 699–718.

Gosso, Y., Otta, E., Morais, M. L. S., Ribeiro, F. J. L., & Bussab, V. S. R. (2005). Play in hunter-gatherer society. In A. D. Pellegrini & P. K. Smith (Eds.), *The nature of play: Play in great apes and humans* (pp. 213–253). New York: Guilford.

Gottman, J. M. (1983). How children become friends. *Monographs of the Society for Research in Child Development, 48* (3), serial no. 201.

Haight, W. L., & Miller, P. J. (1993). *Pretending at home: Early development in a sociocultural context.* Albany: State University of New York Press.

Hallock, M. B., & Worobey, J. (1984). Cognitive development in chimpanzee infants (*Pan troglodytes*). *Journal of Human Evolution, 13*, 441–447.

Hansell, M., & Ruxton, G. D. (2008). Setting tool use within the context of animal construction behavior. *Trends in Ecology and Evolution, 23*, 73–78.

Hayne, H., Herbert, H., & Simcock, G. (2003). Imitation from television by 24- and 30-month-olds. *Developmental Science, 6*, 254–261.

Henderson, B. B. (1984). The effect of context on individual differences in exploratory behavior. *Child Development, 55*, 1247–1245.

Henderson, B. B., & Moore, S. G. (1979). Measuring exploratory behavior in young children: A factor analytical study. *Developmental Psychology, 15*, 113–119.

Hewlett, B., & Boyette, A. H. (2013). Commentary: Play in hunter-gatherers. In D. Narvaez, J. Panksepp, A. N. Schore, & T. R. Gleason (Eds.), *Evolution, early experience and human development* (pp. 388–393). Oxford: Oxford University Press.

Hinde, R. A. (1980). *Ethology.* London: Fontana.

Huffman, M. A., & Quiatt, D. (1986). Stone handling by Japanese macaques (*Macacca fuscata*): Implications for tool use of stone. *Primates, 27*, 413–423.

Hutt, C. (1966). Exploration and play in children. *Symposia of the Zoological Society of London, 18*, 61–81.

Hutt, C., & Bhavnani, R. (1972). Predictions from play. *Nature, 237*, 216–219.

Kanfer, F. H., Stifter, E., & Morris, S. J. (1981). Self-control and altruism: Delay of gratification for another. *Child Development, 52*, 674–682.

Köhler, W. (1925). *The mentality of apes.* New York: Harcourt Brace.

Krebs, J. R., & Davies, N. B. (1993). *An introduction to behavioural ecology.* Oxford: Blackwell.

Lillard, A. S. (2006). Guided participation: How mothers structure and children understand pretend play. In A. Göncü & S. Gaskins (Eds.), *Play and development: Evolutionary, sociocultural and functional perspectives* (pp. 131–154). Mahwah, NJ: Erlbaum.

Martin, P., & Caro, T. (1985). On the function of play and its role in behavioral development. In J. Rosenblatt, C. Beer, M.-C. Bushnel, & P. Slater (Eds.), *Advances in the study of behavior* (vol. 15, pp. 59–103). New York: Academic Press.

McCall, R. B. (1974). Exploratory manipulation and play in the human infant. *Monographs of the Society of Research in Child Development 39*(2), serial no. 155.

McGrew, W. C. (1972). *An ethological study of children's behaviour.* London: Metheun.

Mounoud, P. (1996). A recursive transformation of central cognitive mechanisms: The shift from partial to whole representation. In A. J. Sameroff & M. M. Haith (Eds.), *The five to seven year shift: The age of reason and responsibility* (pp. 85–110). Chicago, IL: University of Chicago Press.

Pellegrini, A. D. (2009). *The role of play in human development.* New York: Oxford University Press.

Pellegrini, A. D., & Gustafson, K. (2005). Boys' and girls' uses of objects for exploration, play, and tools in early childhood. In A. D. Pellegrini & P. K. Smith (Eds.), *The nature of play: Great apes and humans* (pp. 113–138). New York: Guilford.

Pellegrini, A. D., Horvat, M., & Huberty, P. D. (1998). The relative cost of children's physical activity play. *Animal Behaviour, 55*, 1053–1061.

Pellegrini, A. D., & Hou, Y. (2011). The development of preschool children's (*Homo sapiens*) uses of objects and their role in peer group centrality. *Journal of Comparative Psychology, 125*, 239–245.

Pellegrini, A. D., & Pellegrini, A. F. A. (2013). Play, plasticity, and ontogeny in childhood. In D. Narvaez, J. Panksepp, A. Schore, & T. Gleason (Eds.), *Evolution, early experience, and human development* (pp. 339–351). New York: Oxford University Press.

Piaget, J. (1951). *Play, dreams, and imitation in childhood.* London: Routledge & Kegan Paul.

Piaget, J. (1952). *The origins of intelligence in children.* New York: Norton.

Piaget, J. (1967). *The psychology of intelligence.* London: Routleldge & Kegan Paul.

Power, T. G. (2000). *Play and exploration in children and animals.* Mahwah, NJ: Erlbaum.

Rheingold, H. L., & Eckerman, G. O. (1970). The infant separates himself from his mother. *Science, 168*, 78–83.

Ross, H. S., Rheingold, H. L., & Eckerman, C. O. (1972). Approach and exploration of a novel alternative by 12-month-old infants. *Journal of Experimental Child Psychology, 13*, 85–93.

Rubin, K. H., Fein, G., & Vandenberg, B. (1983). Play. In E. M. Hetherington (Ed.), *Handbook of child psychology,* vol. 4: *Socialization, personality and social development* (pp. 693–774). New York: Wiley.

Rubin, K., Maioni, T., & Hornung, M. (1976). Free play in middle and lower class preschoolers: Parten and Piaget revisited. *Child Development, 47*, 414–419.

Rubin, K., Watson, R., & Jambor, T. (1978). Free-play behaviors in preschool and kindergarten children. *Child Development, 49*, 534–546.

Russell, B. (1931/1959). *The scientific outlook.* New York: Norton.

Simon, T., & Smith, P. K. (1983). The study of play and problem solving in preschool children. *British Journal of Developmental Psychology, 1*, 289–297.

Smilansky, S. (1968). *The effects of sociodramatic play on disadvantaged preschool children.* New York: Wiley.

Smith, P. K. (1988). Children's play and its role in early development: A re-evaluation of the "play ethos". In A. D. Pellegrini (Ed.), *Psychological bases for early education* (pp. 207–226). Chichester: Wiley.

Smith, P. K. (2011). Observational methods in studying play. In A. D. Pellegrini (Ed.), *The Oxford handbook of the development of play* (pp. 138–152). New York: Oxford University Press.

Smith, P. K., Takhvar, M., Gore, N., and Volstedt, R. (1986). Play in young children: Problems of definition, categorization, and measurement. In P. K. Smith (Ed.), *Children's play: Research development and practical applications.* (pp. 39–55). London: Gordon and Breach.

Smith, P. K., & Whitney, S. (1987). Play and associative fluency: Experimenter effects may be responsible for previous positive findings. *Developmental Psychology, 23,* 49–53.

Sutton-Smith, B. (1967). The role of play in cognitive development. *Young Children, 22,* 364–369.

Sylva, K., Bruner, J., & Genova, P. (1976). The role of play in the problem-solving of children 3–5 years old. In J. Bruner, A. Jolly, & K. Sylva (Eds.), *Play: Its role in development and evolution* (pp. 244–261). New York: Basic Books.

Tinbergen, N. (1963). On aims and methods of ethology. *Zeitschirift für Tierpsychologie, 20,* 410–413.

Tomasello, M., & Call, J. (1997). *Primate cognition.* New York: Oxford University Press.

van Schaik, C. P., Deaner, R. O., & Merrill, M. Y. (1999). The conditions of tool use in primates: Implications for the evolution of material culture. *Journal of Human Evolution, 36,* 719–741.

West, M. J. (1977). Exploration and play with objects in domestic kittens. *Developmental Psychobiology, 10,* 53–57.

West-Eberhard, M. J. (2003). *Developmental plasticity and evolution.* New York: Oxford University Press.

Wilks, M., Collier-Baker, E., & Nielsen. M. (2014). Preschool children favor copying a successful individual over an unsuccessful group. *Developmental Science, 18,* 1014–1024.

11 Pretend and Social Pretend Play

Complexities, Continuities, and Controversies of a Research Field

Ageliki Nicolopoulou

Social pretend play (sometimes called sociodramatic play) is a subset of the broader category of pretend play, but the boundaries are fluid and ambiguous in both research and practice. The clearest examples of social pretend play involve children, typically from roughly 2–6 years of age, enacting fantasy or everyday scenarios in parallel, semi-parallel, or full cooperation with others – sometimes with adults, but usually with peers. But solo pretend play in which children enact simple or complex scenarios may also be considered social, in that children are reenacting social activities or drawing on culturally available symbolic resources and models. There are also various kinds of interplay between solitary and cooperative symbolic play. And over the years the relative frequencies and emphases of research on pretend play in general (including symbolic play by individual children) and specifically *social* pretend play (symbolic play with others) have shifted in complex ways. This chapter will therefore attempt a comprehensive review of the full range of key research tendencies dealing with symbolic play, alone or with others, and its development.

Pretend or fantasy play is behaviour in a simulative, nonliteral, or "as if" mode (Fein, 1981). It involves various combinations of pretend actions (round hand motion can represent driving), using objects (a block can represent the wheel), and/or verbalizations (a humming noise can represent a moving vehicle). It incorporates deliberate distortions involving what McCune-Nicolich (1981, cited in Kavanaugh 2005) called "double knowledge", that is, knowledge of both the real and imagined properties of objects and situations. Kavanaugh (2005, p. 153) nicely defined pretend play using concepts drawn from Lillard: "[p]retenders project an idea (e.g., serving tea) on to an actual situation (e.g., play partner's empty cup) (Lillard, 2001a) while clearly knowing the difference between the actual state of affairs and the nonactual situations they are enacting (Lillard, 2001b)." Smith (2010, p. 152) notes that this is a stringent definition, ruling out most simulative play by non-human animals and even some initial pretend actions by young children. That is because this definition implies "conscious intention, and an awareness of both the pretend reality and the actual reality, and thus some representational ability". This conception of pretend play as a uniquely human activity also highlights the fact that it is part of a cluster of symbolic activities that include language, self-awareness, and the development of representational abilities.

The Development of Pretend and Social Pretend Play in Children

Many excellent reviews have traced what we know about the development of pretend play (Fein, 1981; Lillard, 2015; Rubin et al., 1983; Smith, 2010), so only a short summary is provided here. Pretend play begins during the second year of life, peaks during the late preschool years, and appears to decline during the early elementary school years. A key impetus for research was Piaget's seminal work on pretend play (1962), based on careful and insightful observations of his three children. Piaget provided a model of (partly) sequentially ordered forms of play from infancy up to 6–7 years of age: practice play, pretence or symbolic play, and play with rules. Furthermore, he asserted that pretend play itself develops through a sequence of increasingly sophisticated phases from a solitary symbolic activity (object play starting during the second year of life) to sociodramatic pretend play (role-play beginning during the latter part of the third year). Even though these forms of play often co-occur and are hard to separate, it is analytically useful to consider their development separately. In fact, Sachet and Mottweiler (2013), drawing partly on Harris (2000), argue that these two forms of play seem to involve different content and thus may offer different benefits for children. With *object substitution*, the child imagines and projects non-social content (pretending that a block is a truck), while with *role-play*, the child imagines and projects social content (pretending to feed the doll, thus enacting the role of caregiver).

The Development of Object Substitution. Object substitutions are the earliest instances of pretend play (Fein, 1981); their beginnings coincide with the onset of language, as part of the emergence of the symbolic function, around the second birthday, and they follow a well-documented progression (Sachet & Mottweiler, 2013). The first object substitutions are simple acts with simple schemes (pretending to drink from an empty cup). A dramatic increase occurs between 15 and 18 months of age (Rubin et al., 1983) and these actions become more complex (pretending to cook food and then eating it). Pretending is in full swing by approximately 24 months of age, with children producing multi-scheme combinations (pretending to make food, putting it onto a plate, and then eating it). Two-year-olds spend 5%–20% of their playtime in such pretend activities, and they can interpret and respond to object substitutions and follow pretend sequences that others perform (Lillard, 2011).

Research following Piaget's lead (e.g., Fenson et al., 1976) also identified three broad developmental trends in the structure of early pretend play: decentration (a shift from self as agent to other as agent), decontextualization (moving away from using realistic objects to less realistic objects), and integration (combining pretend acts to form sequences and narratives). Controlled observational studies, where a child was placed with relevant objects in a laboratory playroom, have confirmed and further delineated these sequences

(Sachet & Mottweiler, 2013). However, these trends are not so clear-cut when children are observed playing in naturalistic settings, such as at home, where siblings and parents may also be present (Dunn, 2004; Haight & Miller, 1993).

The Development of Role-Play and Sociodramatic Play. Social pretend play or sociodramatic play represents inanimate objects from the start and increasingly represents animate characters as well. Thus, children imagine and act out the role of a person or a creature, usually with the help of objects, for brief or longer periods. This type of role-play can occur when children play alone or with an adult partner, but it is most frequent when they play with other children. During the second year, complementary role-play in which children adopt different but related roles – mother and baby, driver and passenger, cooking and feeding – emerges as a key form of play between children, especially friends. This type of play takes years to develop fully; it requires considerable flexibility and sensitivity, as children must learn to cooperate successfully with each other. Thus, while simple forms of role-play can be glimpsed during the second year, it is more frequently observed during the third year. Bursts of sustained sociodramatic pretend play with peers are observed during the fourth year and continue to develop during the next few years (Harris, 2000; Howes & Matheson, 1992; Smith, 2005, 2010).

Harris (2000) delineated three types of role-play that differ depending on the vehicle used for the imagined character/role. The first is having a *personified object*, when the child creates and enacts a role that is projected onto a doll or toy that serves as the vehicle. The second is having a *pretend identity*, when the child acts out or impersonates an imagined character using himself or herself as the vehicle. The third is having an *imaginary companion*, when the child invents an invisible creature or person without the use of any tangible props to serve as the vehicle. This classification covers a wide range of role-playing actions that are not limited to the child's announcing or assigning a given role, with such overt statements emerging as late as 3 or 4 years of age. It also brings out that during role-play children immerse themselves in the part they create and start to act on the world and to talk about it as if they are experiencing it from the point of view of the invented person or creature. In other words, children enter into the make-believe situation they create and adopt the point of view of one of its protagonists. This imaginative immersion into a constructed playworld, which parallels the imaginative immersion into the storyworld when constructing or comprehending stories, is one of the features of pretend play that highlights the close affinities between play and narrative (Nicolopoulou, 2006, 2016), an area that still needs further examination. Research has yet to fully explore the intricacy and complexity of entering into an imaginary world or the complex similarities and differences between play and narrative as forms of symbolic activity.

Furthermore, Harris's classification brings out nicely that the phenomenon of imaginary companions is a form of role-play. While 2- and 3-year-olds' absorption in episodes of most types of role-play is often transient, during the same period some children begin to engage in a form of sustained role-play using imaginary companions. They repeatedly invoke an imaginary person or creature whose identity remains stable over several months and who becomes a kind of companion for the child. By the age of 7, about 63% of children from a sample of American children at some point had had either an invisible imaginary companion or one projected onto an external prop (Taylor, 1999), and a follow-up study confirmed that this form of play continues beyond the preschool years (Taylor et al., 2004).

Distinguishing Fantasy from Reality. Despite children's absorption in pretend play, especially as evidenced in role-play, there is broad consensus that they do not seem to confuse pretence and reality (Bourchier & Davis, 2002; Weisberg, 2013). For example, if a child pretends that a toy pig got dirty and asks his or her play partner to wash it, the other child will tend to respond by pretending to wash the toy pig with something resembling an imaginary sponge and imaginary water. Thus, the children act in the imaginary world as if it were real, but they do not seem to confuse the pretend world and pretend actions with real ones. In fact, these boundaries between pretence and reality seem to be stable, even when children engage in extended pretend play. Even 3-year-olds can generally distinguish real from imaginary situations and understand the use of 'real' versus 'pretend'. Woolley and Wellman (1990) demonstrated that 3-year-old children explicitly use terms like 'real' and 'pretend' in sensible ways, as in 'Let's pretend to play mother.' By 4 years of age, children use pretend in even more sophisticated ways as in 'Pretend I'm not here. I have gone to work.' Even children with well-established imaginary companions, with whom they spend a great deal of time and in whom they invest a good deal of emotional energy, are not confused about the status of their imaginary companions (Taylor et al., 2009).

There are some instances when children may react emotionally to imaginary events or objects as though they were real, such as when children are genuinely afraid of monsters under their bed. In some cases these reactions may indicate that children are frightened of something else, as they know that the monsters are not literally real (Weisberg, 2015). But the issues raised by this occasional blurring of boundaries in children's emotional reactions to imaginary scenarios require further conceptual and empirical exploration.

Is Pretend Play Universal?

Piaget conceptualized the emergence of pretend or symbolic play as part of the development of an individual's cognitive capacities, and thus as a more or less universal phenomenon. He argued that this type of play, emerging around 2 years of age, reflects the appearance and development of the semiotic function, that is, the understanding that one thing (a word or a sign) can stand for something else (an object or an activity in the world). For this reason, Piaget studied the development of pretend play along with the development of other symbolic or representational systems such as language, dreams, and imitation.

Anthropological accounts and cross-cultural studies indicate that pretend play, including role and sociodramatic play, is indeed ubiquitous in human societies, though there seems to be some variability in the amount and types of play (Gaskins, 2013; Lancy, 1996; Smith, 2005, 2010). In both hunter-gatherer and settled agricultural communities, children have been observed using symbolic play to represent aspects of daily life. For example, among the Kalahari San, children use sticks and pebbles to represent village huts and herding cows; among the Hadza of Tanzania, children make dolls out of rags and play at being hunters; among the Parakanã, a South American Indian community, children play with bows and arrows and imitate festivities of their community by singing and dancing as their parents do; and among the Kpelle of Liberia, children imitate adult roles such as being a tailor and reenact routines associated with these roles such as fetching tools, measuring cloth, and so on. Children's play often seems to imitate adult roles and activities in their community, and this play can be seen as a rehearsal of many valued roles in the community that children are expected to learn.

Some anthropological accounts, however, indicate that in certain agricultural communities, especially those with pressing economic subsistence needs, pretend play can be low in frequency (Gaskins, 1999) or greatly "impoverished" (Smilansky, 1968). For example, Gaskins (1999), observing a Mayan village community in the Yucatan in Mexico, saw some fleeting instances of pretend play among children, but these were rare. She argued this was the case not only because play was not encouraged in this community but also because adults placed work demands on the children by asking them to take care of younger siblings, to run small errands, to prepare food, and so on.

Thus, while pretend play by children seems to be present in the full range of cultures and communities around the world, adult beliefs and attitudes as well as the socioeconomic organization of the society with its implications for play resources – objects, time, and space – affect the amount, frequency, and degrees of engagement in children's pretend play. Gaskins et al. (2007) propose that there are at least three different cultural approaches to children's play: cultivation, acceptance, and curtailment. Middle-class American culture provides an extreme example of how play can be culturally cultivated. In their intensive longitudinal study of nine young children from 1 to 4 years of age, Haight and Miller (1993) found that middle-class families provided children with large numbers of toys, specific places for them, and mothers' availability to join in, facilitate, and direct children's pretend play from the early years. They argued that these demonstrate the high value that the adults place on play and help promote children's frequent engagement in pretend activities. In contrast, the Kpelle of Liberia (Lancy, 1996) exemplify a culture in which children's play is accepted but not cultivated. In this culture children's play does occur in large play areas and for long periods of time. In their pretend play, children enact a wide range of scripts with little interference or mediation by adults. Finally, the Yucatec Maya (Gaskins, 1999) provide a good example of a culture that curtails play. Mayan parents give few resources and attention to children's play and allow children to play only when there is no productive activity for children to participate in. When Mayan parents were asked if they liked to see their children play, they responded in the affirmative, but their most common justification was that it showed that their children were not sick. In short, it appears that culturally patterned parental beliefs and attitudes toward pretend play, as well as the ways they mediate and organize children's activities, are important factors in explaining the cultural differences in pretend play we observe in different societies and cultures around the world.

Does Pretend Play Have Important Functions in Development?

The apparent ubiquity of pretend play and the fact that many children spend a considerable amount of time in pretend activities during the preschool years have led generations of developmental and educational psychologists to wonder about the role of pretend play in the larger process of development. It is widely believed that children's play helps promote their development in various ways, and some developmental theorists have forcefully argued that pretend play, in particular, is critical for development. Vygotsky (1967), one of the most prominent of these theorists, argued that pretend play serves a key role in children's cognitive and social development. Vygotsky contended that play helps children begin to achieve symbolic understanding; for example, the pretend objects used in play (a block standing for a car) serve as pivots that gradually help children separate language from objects and actions. Vygotsky also argued that play, as a fundamentally social activity, promotes children's capacities for social understanding and social competence, especially with respect to cooperation and self-regulation (for further explication of this argument, see Nicolopoulou, 1993). The direct and indirect influence of Vygotsky's perspective has informed a great deal of research over the years. Researchers have found beneficial effects not only from spontaneous unstructured free play but also from some efforts to integrate a play element into educational practices for young children (Hirsh-Pasek et al., 2008; Nicolopoulou et al., 2015).

Critical Review by Lillard and Colleagues. There has also been some scepticism regarding these claims, especially in their strongest forms. For example, in several reviews of play research, Smith (2005, 2010) suggested that many researchers and practitioners may have adopted an overly and uncritically positive view of play and its presumed benefits, which he termed "the play ethos".

To examine these issues, Lillard and colleagues (2013) critically reviewed a large body of play research accumulated over the years that had found positive consequences of pretend play for children's development. They organized their ambitious and influential review by the psychological domains of outcomes that researchers have studied: non-social cognitive abilities (creativity, intelligence, problem-solving, reasoning, and conservation), social cognition (theory of mind), social skills, symbolic understanding (early language), narrative, executive function, and emotion regulation. Within each domain, they organized the studies in terms of the methodology used, such as correlational, experimental, or training studies.

Adapting a framework for evaluation suggested by Smith (2005, 2010), Lillard and her colleagues considered three possible relationships that could exist between pretend play and development in each target domain. First, they suggested that "if pretend does crucially *cause* positive developments" (p. 3), then strong positive correlations should be consistently found between pretend play and outcomes in the target domain. Thus, high frequency and quality of performance in pretend play (whether spontaneously occurring or the result of an experimental manipulation or a training program) should consistently correlate with superior performance in the target domain. The second possible relationship is one of *equifinality*; that is, there are valid positive correlations, but the same endpoint could be reached in different ways. In such cases, participation in (or experience with) pretend play is not necessary for the outcome under consideration; other processes or activities could bring about the same outcome. If an equifinal relation holds, then one would expect that variation in pretend play would be associated with an uneven pattern of results. Sometimes a correlation with some alleged benefit might be observed, but sometimes other processes might display a stronger correlation. The third possible type of relationship between pretend play and the development of relevant abilities might be *epiphenomenal*, meaning that both the frequency and quality of play and the positive developmental outcomes result from a third unmeasured factor. In such cases, variations in pretend play would correlate with the outcomes in question only to the extent that pretend play correlated with the factor that was actually responsible for the beneficial outcome.

After considering a large number of studies, Lillard and her colleagues concluded that "existing evidence does not support strong causal claims about the unique importance of pretend play for development" (first type of relation). They acknowledged that what they termed the "causal position" (i.e., the view that play has a unique or essential role in promoting development) might hold for reasoning, language, narrative, and emotion regulation, but that even in these cases more research is needed to provide strong and unequivocal support for this position and to rule out the explanatory influence of other variables (equifinality) or even of a third co-occurring variable (epiphenomenon). Further, they suggested that a verdict of equifinality was supported for the outcome domains of reasoning, theory of mind, and social skills, but again they called for more and better research to rule out epiphenomenalism. In the course of their review, they also discussed common methodological problems that often plague this research, which future research needs to overcome. Overall, they argued that their findings supported Smith's view that researchers have too often uncritically accepted the view that pretend play contributes positively to development, and that this presumption needs to be carefully and critically reexamined.

Lillard et al.'s "review of the evidence" generated useful dialogue along with controversy. Many researchers recognized the value of Lillard et al.'s comprehensive analysis of this large body of literature and of their attempt to systematically assess the strengths and limitations of the reviewed studies. They also saw this review as providing an impetus for future research and a useful model for conducting such research with greater rigor. At the same time, several authors (including Harris & Jalloul, 2013; Nicolopoulou & Ilgaz, 2013) took issue with some of the review's analyses and conclusions on conceptual, methodological, and empirical grounds.

While the evaluative typology offered by Smith (2005, 2010) can serve as a useful heuristic in evaluating research findings, it may need to be applied more carefully and cautiously than was done by Lillard et al. For example, Lillard et al. often characterized the claim that pretend play is *crucial* or *essential* to development as the "causal position" (not a formulation used by Smith). But this formulation is misleading, because both their first position (crucial or essential) and their second (equifinality) entail causal relationships between pretend play and development (Nicolopoulou & Ilgaz, 2013). Showing that there may be more than one way to achieve a desired result does not necessarily rule out the possibility that pretend play may have a causal role in promoting development; it would simply indicate that it is not the *only* causal path to achieve this goal, and therefore not essential or "unique". In this connection, it may be worth noting Smith's earlier assessment (2010, p. 180) that the model of equifinality "is the most supported by the evidence – for pretend play, and indeed for most kinds of play". This would imply that pretend play can indeed promote development, though Smith added that the evidence "is not conclusive".

Harris and Jalloul (2013) criticized the review's evaluative framework from a different angle, arguing that a more careful conceptualization and specification of the variables under consideration is necessary to allow us to conclude that no or low correlation means lack of a causal relation. They caution that the interaction among these variables is often non-linear and dynamic, raising doubt about the expected correlations used as criteria of assessment by Lillard et al.

Nicolopoulou and Ilgaz (2013), after reexamining the research that focused on the relationship between pretend play and narrative development, also questioned what they saw as Lillard et al.'s overly negative assessments of research in this area on empirical and conceptual grounds. They argued that substantial portions of this research were actually stronger and more valuable than Lillard et al. suggested, offering some solid and valuable evidence of beneficial effects of pretend play for narrative development. Furthermore, Nicolopoulou and Ilgaz suggested that Lillard et al., in effect, treated play as a purely individual activity manifesting purely individual abilities or capacities. If the effects of pretend play were found to be influenced "by features of adults with whom children interact, features of the children themselves, and the content with which children pretend" (Lillard et al., 2013, p. 26), then Lillard et al. automatically dismissed these effects as epiphenomenal. However, that approach rests on erroneous premises and may lead to non sequiturs, since social and contextual factors can mediate, specify, and enable play and its consequences without eliminating the causal significance of play. If such factors do play a role in helping enable or promote positive outcomes, that would not necessarily imply that the relationship between play and those outcomes is simply epiphenomenal (see Weisberg et al., 2013, for a partly similar argument).

In short, Lillard and her colleagues did a valuable service to the field with their comprehensive critical review, and they did provide some evidence supporting the argument that a pervasive "play ethos" may at times contribute to overly positive and uncritical assessments of the benefits of pretend play by researchers and practitioners. At the same time, it remains true that researchers also need to guard against taking an excessively dismissive attitude toward the possible benefits of pretend play for children's experience and development. The evidence does not support such an overreaction.

Some Promising Directions

One implication of the preceding discussion is that it is important to bear in mind the analytical distinction between two questions: whether pretend play can promote or contribute to development, and whether it has a necessary, crucial, or unique role in promoting development. Depending on the developmental domains and the specific types of pretend play involved, previous research has produced some encouraging evidence on both counts. But the causal patterns are complex, and Lillard et al. were correct to recommend that "much more and better research is essential" (p. 1) on these subjects.

That raises the question of which approaches to conceptualizing and studying play seem most fruitful, illuminating, and promising. In this final section, rather than attempting to survey the full range of distinct and overlapping tendencies in pretend play research, I will focus on one orienting framework that I consider especially promising for understanding pretend play and its role in children's experience and development.

Play as a Sociocultural Matrix for Development. In my own work (e.g., Nicolopoulou, 1993, 1997a), I have explored and advocated a still-emerging sociocultural and developmental approach to play that draws on my interpretation of Vygotsky's theory of play (1967) and on other sources in psychology and related disciplines. My research has also provided some concrete examples of how this approach might be useful for studying play and its role in children's experience, development, and education (e.g., Nicolopoulou et al., 2010; Nicolopoulou et al., 2015). Such an approach emphasizes that it is misleading to view pretend play as an essentially individual activity that gradually develops into a social-relational one. Rather, we need to view pretend play as a profoundly sociocultural symbolic activity that utilizes children's nascent cognitive, emotional, interpretive, and social-relational abilities in generative social contexts and, in the process, helps these abilities develop further. I continue to believe that this represents a valuable and promising approach that dovetails well with some current tendencies in play research. To elaborate this position, I first need to explicate some key aspects of Vygotsky's theory of play.

A crucial insight behind Vygotsky's theory of play is his insistence on treating it as an essentially social activity, which means not only an interactive activity but also a cultural and imaginative one. For Vygotsky, play is always a *social* symbolic activity. It is most typically a shared activity, but even when a young child plays alone, the themes, roles, and scenarios enacted in play involve the child's appropriation of sociocultural material.

In characterizing play, Vygotsky stresses the presence of two essential and interconnected components: (1) an imaginary situation and (2) the rules inherent in the imaginary situation. In this respect, fantasy or pretend play and games with rules can be seen as two poles of a single continuum: from an explicit imaginary situation with implicit rules (pretend play) to an implicit imaginary situation with explicit rules (games with rules). When a child pretends to be a mother or father, for example, she or he cannot adopt just any behaviour but must try to grasp the implicit rules of maternal or paternal behaviour as perceived and understood by the child or others. An important cognitive effort is involved here. "What passes unnoticed by the child in real life becomes a rule of behavior in play" (Vygotsky, 1967, p. 9). That is even more true for the coordinated activity of social pretend play.

From this perspective, play fuses elements often treated as contradictory: imagination and spontaneity, on the one hand, and rule-governed action, on the other. Play is enjoyable, flexible, and intrinsically voluntary, but it is also an essentially rule-governed activity. Systems of rules (implicit and explicit) are central to constituting the playworld itself, and at the same time these rules derive their force from the child's enjoyment of, and commitment to, the shared activity of the playworld. Indeed, as Vygotsky emphasized, a crucial aspect of the significance of play is that it is one of the first activities in which children self-consciously impose rules on themselves, rather than merely receiving them from others. This is the case, he argues, because the child learns that achieving the satisfactions sought in the imaginary situation requires adhering to the rules implicit in that situation. The rules of play thus become "rules of self-constraint and self-determination" (Vygotsky, 1967, p. 10). In the terminology used by much current research, play requires and promotes *self-regulation*. Furthermore, play is always a *learning* activity because it requires learning and grasping these rules, seeing that they form a system, elaborating on them, and mastering the possibilities of the form of practice that they help constitute. Moreover, inserting elements from the larger culture into the symbolic universe of the playworld forces the child to try to make sense of them, even as they are stylized and transformed. And increasing capacities for self-regulation in thought and in action are closely linked and mutually reinforcing (an idea supported recently by Coolahan et al., 2000; Ursache et al., 2012).

In short, according to Vygotsky, play can serve as a prototype of a form of activity constituted by shared and voluntarily accepted rules, within which children can experience an intrinsic (rather than merely instrumental) motivation to strive for mastery of the possibilities inherent in that practice. In early childhood, play is a crucial matrix for development (Vygotsky, 1967, p. 16). Researchers drawing directly or indirectly on Vygotskian ideas have therefore argued that play activities simultaneously require and help to promote both cognitive abilities and capacities for social competence, such as cooperation and self-regulation (Bodrova & Leong, 2003; Creasey et al., 1998; Diamond et al., 2007).

Pretend Play and Imagination. The sociocultural approach to play as just outlined entails treating pretend play "as one expression of imaginative activity that draws on and reflects back upon the interrelated domains of emotional, intellectual, and social life" (Nicolopoulou, 1993, p. 13). In this respect, it resonates with a number of current directions in play research. For example, Harris (2000) has hypothesized that pretend play plays a critical role in the development of imagination. This is because pretend play involves the capacity to imagine alternative possibilities and to work out their implications while suspending the real world. These capacities, he argues, invade and transform children's developing conceptions of reality itself.

One form or aspect of pretend play that both draws on and enhances imagination and sociocultural understanding is the type of role-play that involves enacting complementary roles (e.g., mother and baby) in recreating some scene or episode. Role-play, for Harris (2000), includes familiar cases where the child adopts a role or identity for the self, such as impersonating a mother or a firefighter. In some cases, the child may use himself or herself to impersonate the role, without necessarily setting their own identity aside; in other cases the child may project the role onto a doll or a toy that serves as a prop. Harris argues that children are flexible in their role-play because they are not acting with a rigid memorized script regarding that specific role, but instead draw on their knowledge of the real world, which they import into the imaginary situation they are creating. Thus, "role play depends on an active process of simulation in which the role player projects him- or herself and the make-believe situation faced by a given protagonist" (Harris, 2000, p. 36). And, in a twist that may seem paradoxical, while the child is well aware of the difference between the real world and the "pretend" context of the playworld, the child draws on and modifies his or her own knowledge-base about the real world to arrive at judgements, plans, and statements that are appropriate for the adopted role. This process highlights the complex and cross-fertilizing interplay between fantasy and reality in children's pretend play. To borrow an illuminating formulation from Vivian Paley (quoted in Nicolopoulou, 1993, p. 17), fantasy play can serve as a "pathway to reality".

Along with a wide range of other researchers (for review, see Lillard, 2015), Harris also argues that pretend play is bound up with, and helps to promote, capacities for social understanding and theory of mind, including the understanding of false beliefs. However, he suggests not every aspect of pretend play may be related equally strongly to theory of mind understanding. Rather, the key type of play in this respect is role-play in which children enact what people may do in a given situation by the process of simulation; that is, they imagine themselves in that same situation and act in accordance with that imaginary situation. It is this type of role-play, Harris argues, that helps children separate the way things are from the way they are represented by another person, which is the hallmark of theory of mind understanding. Thus, role-play is especially important in enhancing children's simulation skills and in turn their mental understanding.

Harris cites some evidence in favour of this hypothesis, suggesting that we should not look for correlations between the frequency of pretend play in general and the development of theory of mind understanding, but instead should focus on relations between theory of mind and specific types of role-play, including imaginative solitary fantasy play and joint play with others (Astington & Jenkins, 1995; Taylor & Carlson, 1997; Youngblade & Dunn, 1995). This hypothesis is still contested (Smith, 2005, 2010). However, I would argue that Harris has provided a usefully suggestive model of how to think about this relationship between pretend play and theory of mind. It may be that we need a better conceptualization and articulation of the reasons why pretend play should support theory of mind development, as well as a careful evaluation and specification of which aspects or types of pretend play should be expected to promote that development.

Another way that pretend play and imagination have been linked to cognitive development is in connection with the development of counterfactual reasoning – which is, of course, an important element of cognitive development. A number of researchers have argued that "pretending and counterfactual reasoning engage the same component cognitive abilities: disengaging with current reality, making inferences about an alternative representation of reality, and keeping this representation separate from reality" (Weisberg & Gopnik, 2013, p. 1368). In both counterfactual reasoning and pretend play, children (and adults) start from premises that they know to be non-factual, suspending their real-world knowledge, and infer (hypothetical) sequences of events, actions, and causal consequences within the context of an imagined

alternative reality. Since "pretending allows children to practice these important cognitive skills" (p. 1368), it seems plausible that participating in pretend
play should help prepare children for the more serious and explicit counterfactual and hypothetical reasoning required for real-world understanding and
analysis. One study cited as offering support for this hypothesis, Dias and
Harris (1990), concluded that pre-schoolers' performance on counterfactual
syllogism tasks improved when the counterfactual premise was couched in
terms of pretence rather than simply stated as part of the problem. A later
study co-authored by Harris (Leevers & Harris, 1999) qualified that conclusion, suggesting that similar effects may be promoted by any instructions that
alert children to the hypothetical nature of the premises. However, the larger
question of whether the frequency and quality of young children's pretend
play helps promote the development of counterfactual reasoning skills
remains open and calls for further research.

In all these respects, pretend play researchers need to carefully identify
and study the elements inherent in pretend play, which is a complex activity,
and study how these may relate to some other psychological capacities and
activities. The challenge is to do this without fragmenting play into its elements in ways that lose an overall understanding of play as a coherent and
distinctive mode of activity. Rather, we should strive for understanding both
the integrity of play in its own terms and the ways it intersects with, draws on,
and influences other cognitive, social, and/or emotional domains. A similar
(though not identical) approach was recently advocated by Weisberg (2015)
for understanding the effects of pretend play on cognitive development. She
argued that pretend play "shares underlying structures with other capacities,
including language, social-cognitive skills like theory of mind, and counterfactual thinking" (p. 1). One implication, noted earlier, is that studying the
parallels, differences, and interplay between pretend play and narrative activity can help shed light on the abilities embodied in and affected by these
activities (Nicolopoulou, 2006, 2016).

Concluding Remarks

For decades, there has been a steady, though never enormous, stream
of valuable research on pretend play in psychology and related disciplines. But
the forms and emphases of play research have fluctuated in accord with
changes in larger research concerns and models. For example, during the
1970s and 1980s the main agendas informing pretend play research in psychology focused on the relationship between play and the development of
cognitive abilities, language, or certain social-relational skills. In the 1990s,
the main emphasis shifted to looking at the relationship between pretend play
(or specific aspects of pretend play) and theory of mind, with other tendencies
focusing on other social skills such as self-regulation. And so on. One side

effect of this variability has been that some promising lines of research have not been followed up as fully or fruitfully as they might have been, and different research tendencies in psychology and related disciplines often need to be integrated more effectively. I have suggested that the sociocultural and developmental approach to pretend play just outlined offers the best prospects for allowing us to understand pretend play in an integrated way while also illuminating its connections and interplay with other dimensions of children's activities, experience, and development.

References

Astington, J. W., & Jenkins, J. (1995). Theory of mind development and social understanding. *Cognition and Emotion*, *9*, 151–165.

Barnett, W. S., Jung, K., Yarosz, D. J., Thomas, J., Hornbeck, A., Stechuk, R., et al. (2008). Educational effects of the Tools of the Mind curriculum: A randomized trial. *Early Childhood Research Quarterly*, *23*, 299–313.

Bodrova, E., & Leong, D. J. (2003). Learning and development of preschool children from the Vygotskian perspective. In A. Kozulin, B. Gindis, V. S. Ageyev, & S. M. Miller (Eds.), *Vygotsky's educational theory in cultural context* (pp. 156–176). New York: Cambridge University Press.

Bourchier, A., & Davis, A. (2002). Children's understanding of the pretence-reality distinction: A review of current theory and evidence. *Developmental Science*, *5*, 397–413.

Coolahan, K. C., Fantuzzo, J., Mendez, J., & McDermott, P. (2000). Preschool peer interactions and readiness to learn: Relationships between classroom peer play and learning behaviors and conduct. *Journal of Educational Psychology*, *92*, 458–465.

Creasey, G. L., Jarvis, P. A., & Berk, L. E. (1998). Play and social competence. In O. N. Saracho & B. Spodek (Eds.), *Multiple perspectives on play in early childhood education* (pp. 116–143). Albany: State University of New York Press.

Diamond, A., Barnett, W. S., Thomas, J., & Munro, S. (2007). Preschool program improves cognitive control. *Science*, *318*, 1387–1388.

Dias, M. G., & Harris, P. L. (1990). The influence of the imagination on reasoning by young children. *British Journal of Developmental Psychology*, *8*, 305–318.

Dunn, J. (2004). *Children's friendships: The beginning of intimacy*. Malden, MA: Blackwell.

Fein, G. (1981). Pretend play in childhood: An integrative review. *Child Development*, *52*, 1095–1118.

Fenson, L., Kagan, J., Kearsley, R. B., & Zelazo, P. (1976). The developmental progression of manipulative play in the first two years. *Child Development*, *47*, 232–236.

Gaskins, S. (1999). Children's daily lives in a Mayan village: A case study of culturally constructed roles and activities. In A. Göncü (Ed.), *Children's engagement in the world* (pp. 25–81). Cambridge: Cambridge University Press.

Gaskins, S. (2013). Pretend play as culturally constructed activity. In M. Taylor (Ed.), *The Oxford handbook of the development of imagination* (pp. 224–247). New York: Oxford University Press.

Gaskins, S., Haight, W. L., & Lancy, D. E. (2007). The cultural construction of play. In A. Göncü & S. Gaskins (Eds.), *Play and development: Evolutionary, sociocultural, and functional perspectives* (pp. 179–202). Mahwah, NJ: Erlbaum.

Haight, W. L., & Miller, P. J. (1993). *Pretending at home*. Albany: State University of New York Press.

Harris, P. L. (2000). *The work of the imagination*. Oxford: Blackwell.

Harris, P. L., & Jalloul, M. (2013). Running on empty? Observing causal relationships between play and development. *American Journal of Play, 6*(1), 29–38.

Hirsh-Pasek, K., Golinkoff, R. M., Berk, L. E., & Singer, D. G. (2008). *A mandate for playful learning in preschool: Presenting the evidence*. New York: Oxford University Press.

Howes, C., & Matheson, C. C. (1992). Sequences in the development of competent play with peers: Social and social pretend play. *Developmental Psychology, 28*, 961–974.

Kavanaugh, R. D. (2005). Pretend play and theory of mind. In L. Balter & C. S. Tamis-LeMonda (Eds.), *Child psychology: A handbook of contemporary issues* (2nd edn.) (pp. 153–166). New York: Psychology Press.

Lancy, D. F. (1996). *Playing on the mother-ground: Cultural routines for children's development*. New York: Guilford Press.

Leevers, H. J., & Harris, P. L. (1999). Persisting effects of instruction on young children's syllogistic reasoning with incongruent and abstract premises. *Thinking and Reasoning, 5*, 145–173.

Lillard, A. S. (2015). The development of play. In L. S. Lieben & U. Mueller (Eds), *Handbook of child psychology and developmental science*, vol. 2: *Cognitive processes* (pp. 425–468). New York: Wiley-Blackwell.

Lillard, A. S., Lerner, M. D., Hopkins, E. J., Dore, R. A., Smith, E. D., & Palmquist, C. M. (2013). The impact of pretend play on children's development: A review of the evidence. *Psychological Bulletin, 139*(1), 1–34.

Lillard, A. S, Pinkham, A. M., & Smith, E. (2011). Pretend play and cognitive development. In U. Goswami (Ed.), *The Wiley-Blackwell handbook of childhood cognitive development* (2nd edn.) (pp. 285–311). Blackwell.

Nicolopoulou, A. (1993). Play, cognitive development, and the social world: Piaget, Vygotsky, and beyond. *Human Development, 36*, 1–23.

Nicolopoulou, A. (1997a). Children and narratives: Toward an interpretive and sociocultural approach. In M. Bamberg (Ed.), *Narrative development: Six approaches* (pp. 179–215). Mahwah, NJ: Erlbaum.

Nicolopoulou, A. (1997b). Worldmaking and identity formation in children's play-acting. In B. D. Cox, & C. Lightfoot (Eds.), *Sociogenetic perspectives on internalization* (pp. 157–187). Mahwah, NJ: Erlbaum.

Nicolopoulou, A. (2006). The interplay of play and narrative in children's development: Theoretical reflections and concrete examples. In A. Göncü & S. Gaskins (Eds.), *Play and development: Evolutionary, sociocultural, and functional perspectives* (pp. 247–274). Mahwah, NJ: Erlbaum.

Nicolopoulou, A. (2016). Young children's pretend play and storytelling as modes of narrative activity: From complementarity to cross-fertilization? In S. Douglas & L. Stirling (Eds.), *Children's play, pretense, and story: Studies in culture, context, and autism spectrum disorder* (pp. 7–28). New York: Routledge.

Nicolopoulou, A., Cortina, K. S., Ilgaz, H., Cates, C. B., & de Sá, A. (2015). Using a narrative- and play-based activity to promote low-income preschoolers' oral language, emergent literacy, and social competence. *Early Childhood Research Quarterly, 31*, 147–162.

Nicolopoulou, A., de Sá, A., Ilgaz, H., & Brockmeyer, C. (2010). Using the transformative power of play to educate hearts and minds: From Vygotsky to Vivian Paley and beyond. *Mind, Culture, and Activity, 17*, 42–58.

Nicolopoulou, A., & Ilgaz, H. (2013). What do we know about pretend play and narrative development? A response to Lillard, Lerner, Hopkins, Dore, Smith, and Palmquist on "The impact of pretend play on children's development: A review of the evidence". *American Journal of Play, 6*(1), 55–80.

Piaget, J. (1962). *Play, dreams, and imitation in childhood.* New York: Norton.

Rubin, K. H., Fein, G. G., & Vandenberg, B. (1983). Play. In P. H. Mussen (Ed.), *Handbook of child psychology,* vol. 4: *Socialization, personality, and social development* (pp. 693–774). New York: Wiley.

Sachet, A. B., & Mottweiler, C. M. (2013). The distinction between role play and object substitution. *The Oxford handbook of the development of imagination* (pp. 175–185). New York: Oxford University Press.

Smilansky, S. (1968). *The effects of sociodramatic play on disadvantaged preschool children.* New York: Wiley.

Smith, P. K. (2005). Social and pretend play in children. In A. D. Pellegrini & P. K. Smith (Eds.), *The nature of play: Great apes and humans* (pp. 173–209). New York: Guilford Press.

Smith, P. K. (2010). *Children and play.* Malden, MA: Wiley-Blackwell.

Taylor, M. (1999). *Imaginary companions and the children who create them.* New York: Oxford University Press.

Taylor, M., & Carlson, S. M. (1997). The relation between individual differences in fantasy and theory of mind. *Child Development, 68*, 436–455.

Taylor, M., Carlson, S. M., Marin, B. L., Gerow, L., & Charley, M. (2004). The characteristics and correlates of fantasy play in school-age children: Imaginary companions, impersonation, and social understanding. *Developmental Psychology, 40*(6), 1173–1187.

Taylor, M., Shawber, A. B., & Mannering, A. M. (2009). Children's imaginary companions: What is it like to have an invisible friend? In K. D. Markman, W. M. P. Klein, & J. A. Suhr (Eds.), *Handbook of imagination and mental simulation* (pp. 211–224). New York: Psychology Press.

Ursache, A., Blair, C., & Raver, C. C. (2012). The promotion of self-regulation as a means of enhancing school readiness and early achievement in children at risk for school failure. *Child Development Perspectives, 6*, 122–128.

Vygotsky, L. S. (1967). Play and its role in the mental development of the child. *Soviet Psychology, 12*, 6–18 (translation of a lecture given in Russian in 1933).

Weisberg, D. S. (2013). Distinguishing imagination from reality. In M. Taylor (Ed.), *The Oxford handbook of the development of imagination* (pp. 75–93). New York: Oxford University Press.

Weisberg, D. S. (2015). Pretend play. *WIREs Cognitive Science.* doi: 10.1002/wcs.1341.

Weisberg, D. S., & Gopnik, A. (2013). Pretense, counterfactuals, and Bayesian causal models: Why what is not real really matters. *Cognitive Science, 37,* 1368–1381.

Weisberg, D. S., Zosh, J. M., Hirsh-Pasek, K., & Golinkoff, R. M. (2013). Talking it up: Play, language development, and the role of adult support. *American Journal of Play, 6*(1), 39–54.

Youngblade, L. M., & Dunn, J. (1995). Individual differences in young children's pretend play with mother and sibling: Links to relationships and understanding of other people's feelings and beliefs. *Child Development, 66,* 1472–1492.

12 Rough Play

Past, Present, and Potential

Jennifer L. Hart and Michelle T. Tannock

Rough play can be defined as a "verbally and physically cooperative play behaviour involving at least two children, where all participants enjoyably and voluntarily engage in reciprocal role-playing that includes aggressive make-believe themes, actions, and words; yet lacks intent to harm either emotionally or physically" (Hart & Tannock, 2013b, p. 108). It includes numerous types of young children's physical and pretend play such as rough-and-tumble, risky play, superhero play, 'bad guy' play, active pretend play, big body play, war play, and imaginative play. It is not exclusive to males (Flanders et al., 2010; Reed et al., 2000; Smith, 2010); however, these play types are predominantly enjoyed by young boys (DiPietro, 1981; Humphreys & Smith, 1987; Jarvis, 2007; Pellegrini, 1989a). They are often considered to be inappropriate by adults because of a general lack of understanding of their playful nature and the misconception that all rough play includes intent to harm (Fletcher et al., 2011; Freeman & Brown, 2004; Hewes & McEwan, 2006; Logue & Detour, 2011; Pellegrini, 1987; Reed et al., 2000). Such perceptions are formed, in part, by the omission of rough play as a beneficial type of play within early childhood curricula and frameworks (Hart & Tannock, 2013b) and the overall context of the play itself (Hart, 2016; Storli & Sandseter, 2015). This chapter offers insight into the origin of rough play, the play in its current form, and its potential within education and care settings.

Past

Young boys are commonly described by adults as being rambunctious, boisterous, and full of energy. Of course, not all boys fit this description, but for those who do the early years are filled with puddles to jump into, logs to jump from, rocks to throw, and sticks to use for prodding. Early childhood is also a time for young boys to chase, pounce, and capture small creatures, including their friends. Several decades ago, *The Lone Ranger* and *The Adventures of Superman* radio shows along with books such as *Treasure Island* and *Peter Pan* influenced young children's play behaviour. In the past, there seemed to be a lack of concern that rough play resided outside the norms of play and child behaviour.

Biological Need

From an evolutionary perspective play is recognized as the foundation for fostering the development of skills necessary for adaptation and survival (Byers & Walker 1995; Pellegrini et al., 2007). Rough-and-tumble play (R&T), or play fighting, which is demonstrated by animals and humans as wrestling one another (Pellis et al., 2015; Pellis & Pellis, 2007), is the most researched and accepted form of rough play. Evolutionary perspectives argue that mammals engage in R&T to practice skills necessary for survival (e.g., social acceptance, catching prey, fleeing from predators) (see Chapters 2 and 4). For example, individuals are faced with the challenge of competing for resources and accessing mates without causing conflict within their social group on which they depend for survival (Flanders et al., 2012). At the forefront of the evolution of play (Sutton-Smith, 1997), Harlow (1962) used the term "rough-and-tumble" to describe the physical behaviour frequently observed among male rhesus monkeys, stating that "real rough-and-tumble play is strictly for the boys" (p. 5), and provided a convincing argument to support a link between genetic factors and young boys' biological desire to engage in rough play. Substantial research dedicated to the study of rats' R&T demonstrates immediate, short-term, and long-term developmental benefits (Pellis & Pellis, 2007). Similarities exist regarding the behavioural effects of play fighting deprivation between monkeys and rats, which provides insight into the correlated consequences of restricting young children's playful behaviour.

Considered to be the foundation for young children's growth and development (Malloy & McMurray-Schwarz, 2004) and the core of early childhood programs, play has gained general world-wide acceptance. Object play, and pretend play especially, is widely considered integral among educators and carers for children's healthy cognitive, affective, social, physical, and language development (Nagel, 2012). However, not all play is alike (Pellis et al., 2015), nor is all play perceived equally by educators, children, and parents (Bauer & Dettore, 1997; Fletcher et al., 2011; Hart, 2016; Logue & Detour, 2011; Logue & Harvey, 2010; Pellegrini, 1989a; Smith & Lewis, 1984; Smith et al., 2004; Tannock, 2008). These differences in perception are probably most troublesome for play types that fall within rough play because many policies and practices arguably negate decades of research that demonstrate its relevance to childhood development.

Rough play is the least studied form of play in humans (Flanders et al., 2012); however, a growing amount of research is dedicated to understanding adults' perceptions about this play (e.g., Bosacki et al., 2014; DiCarlo et al., 2015; Hart, 2016; Storli & Sandseter, 2015). For example, teachers have diverse views of R&T and create 'no-tolerance' policies regardless of the policies of their school (Logue & Harvey, 2010). The creation of such policies is an example of educators' inability to distinguish between rough play and true violence, which may result in teachers incorrectly labelling young boys as seriously aggressive (DiCarlo et al., 2015). Adults' misconceptions, particularly teachers', require more attention by researchers to develop rough play support strategies for educators and children.

Types of Rough Play

Various types of rough play are described in the early childhood literature; many focused on young boys' rough behaviour and sharing contextual characteristics that make individual rough play types difficult to distinctly define. As 'new' types of rough play emerge, it is important for educators to focus on the characteristics and context of the play behaviour rather than its given name.

R&T. Also known as play fighting, rough play, or roughhousing, R&T is a common social play type that encompasses a diverse range of risky physical behaviours that are characterized by wrestling-type movements. It is enjoyed among trusting and caring friends (Fry, 1987; Reed et al., 2000) who chase and flee, tackle, pounce, push, kick, and punch (Blurton Jones, 1972; Humphreys & Smith, 1984). R&T can be considered an aggressive or violent play type – characterized by feigned aggression, sustainability, implicit rules of engagement, reciprocity, and cementing friendships – that is a highly sophisticated, community-building activity enjoyed by skilful players rather than brought to an end by aggressive interactions (Freeman & Brown, 2004). Players take turns being the dominant player and 'follow the rules' that have been established by the group (Pellegrini, 1994; Reed & Brown, 2000) by reading body language, such as the 'play face' (Reed & Brown, 2000), and listening for verbal cues as they progress in their play. Non-friends or 'intruders' who attempt to join in are cause for concern as they have not established a trusting friendship and are likely motivated to cause conflict or inflict harm (Reed & Brown, 2000).

R&T emerges around the age of 3 (when children begin to engage in social play), peaks between 5 and 8 years old (Freeman & Brown, 2004), and develops into games with rules (Humphreys & Smith, 1987; Pellegrini & Purlmutter, 1987) with some characteristics of affection (e.g., punching in the arm) carrying into adulthood.

Big Body Play. Enjoyed by infants, toddlers, and pre-schoolers all over the world, big body play is described as large motor physical activity and includes R&T, rolling, falling, tumbling, horseplay, roughhousing, and play fighting (Carlson, 2011b). Adults, particularly males, facilitate big body play by tossing a child high into the air, catching a child who jumps from a challenging height, and pretending to be overtaken by a pouncing child. This play elicits squeals of delight, ongoing laughter, and the repeated response of "Again!" by the child. Given R&T and big body play have the potential to result in unintended injury, they are considered a form of risky play within educational research.

Risky Play. While focused on young Norwegian children's right to engage in risky play behaviour, Sandseter (2007) identifies specific risky play categories: (1) play with great heights, (2) play with high speed, (3) play with harmful tools,

(4) play near dangerous elements, (5) rough-and-tumble play, and (6) play where the children can "disappear"/get lost. Play fighting, fencing with sticks/branches, and play wrestling are play behaviours that were included within the R&T play category. Sandseter (2007) further describes R&T as high-risk because of the intricacies of identifying play versus real fighting. However, adults perceive some characteristics of R&T play (e.g., wrestling and play fighting) as less risky when compared with other components (e.g., fencing with sticks, hitting, and tripping). Such risk-taking behaviour can be observed in rough play that includes behavioural characteristics beyond those that define R&T. These rough play types may, or may not, include R&T within the realm of the play.

Imaginative Play. War play is defined as a form of imaginary play that includes episodes of pretend fighting and involves acting out roles of violence, aggression, or war witnessed or experienced by children (Malloy & McMurray-Schwarz, 2004). The inclusion of R&T in war play is dependent on the context. Imaginative play includes science fiction themes that take place in space (e.g., Marvel Guardians of the Galaxy), fantasy themes that include magical powers (e.g., Harry Potter), and realistic themes that parallel countries at war (e.g., military forces). Regardless of theme, war play typically involves young children using a variety of toy or imaginary weapons and explosives to 'save the day' by killing the enemy force and destroying their base or killing the evil villain and destroying his secret lair. Children with a parent employed in law enforcement or serving in a military capacity may be observed engaging in a pretend episode of 'killing the bad guys' for the safety of their community or country. Although boys are the prevalent players, a recent shift in the portrayal of female characters in film and television has ignited young girls' interest and acceptance in war play. For example, the resurgence of Wonder Woman and Supergirl – both characters by DC Comics – inspires young girls to use their superhero powers and intellect to fight the forces of evil. Science-fiction heroines, such as Rey and Jyn in recent Star Wars movies, serve as female role models given these characters' courage to engage in battle, tenacity in dire situations, and integrity when making critical decisions. Superhero strength and science-fiction battles are common elements of young children's rough imaginative play. Regardless of the war theme, it is the children's imagination that drives their play behaviour. Thus, there is a close resemblance to other distinct types of rough play that are defined in literature.

Fantasy Play. Peaking during the late preschool years, fantasy play – a component of imaginary play – involves actions, use of objects, non-literal language, and distinct roles (Pellegrini & Smith, 1998). Young girls' fantasy play is more frequent and sophisticated, typically revolving around domestic themes, while play fighting and superhero themes dominate young boys' fantasy play (Pellegrini & Perlmutter, 1987; Pellegrini & Smith, 1998). Although superhero play mimics serious aggression and violence, children are engaged in enjoyable imaginary physical play (Parsons & Howe, 2006). Superhero play is a form of sociodramatic play whereby boys and girls assume the role of a character from a comic book, television show, movie, or book.

Superhero characters have superhuman abilities and signature costumes that sometimes include specific props. For this reason, children enjoy dressing up in capes and costumes accessorized with real or imaginary objects. Boys and girls engaged in fantasy play collaborate to identify a theme, allocate roles, and develop a storyline. Villains and environmental threats tend to be an essential part of superhero play as children shrill with excitement when they overtake an evil threat and save the world. Educators should expect a surge in rough fantasy play during the release of a new movie (e.g., Star Wars Rogue One) or toy (e.g., Nerf Zombie Strike Blaster) and prepare supportive environments that capitalise on young children's play interests (Hart & Tannock, 2013a).

The various terms and definitions that define young children's rough play can exacerbate educators' inability to distinguish it from serious aggression or violence and may be a factor in the elimination of all forms of aggressive behaviour within educational settings. For this reason, it is important to remember that the play context is grounded in pleasure. Simply put, boys and girls enjoy playing, and tend to do so with their friends far more often than with non-friends. This is important to the context of rough play because friendships involve trust, a condition that elicits risk-taking in young children's behaviour such as rough play.

Present

In recent decades, the participation of young children in early childhood education (ECE) and care (ECEC) programs has steadily increased. In the majority of the 34 member countries of the Organisation for Economic Co-operation and Development (OECD), a significant increase in the proportion of children enrolled in ECE programs exists, with 79% of 4-year-olds enrolled in ECE or ECEC programs overall (OECD, 2013). More specifically, between 1970 and 2010 the United States experienced an increase from 20% to 53% in the enrolment rate for 3- to 4-year-old children (NCES, 2012); Australia experienced an increase from 29% in 1987 to 45% in 2002 in the proportion of preschool-age children enrolled; and from 2001 to 2011 the participation rate of European children between 4 years old and the starting age of compulsory education increased by 7% (European Commission et al., 2014). This is particularly relevant because sociodramatic play, including forms of rough play, emerges around 3 years of age (Flanders et al., 2012; Freeman & Brown, 2004).

Today, rough play behaviour is often misunderstood (Hart & Tannock, 2013b; Holland, 2003). A young child who tackles a friend to the ground may be extending an invitation to play, and a child who punches a mate in the arm while walking past is likely expressing affection. Although it is typically within young boys' biological nature to experience the natural world, develop friendships, and express their interests through physical play, it is important to note that not all boys exert such behaviours, while some young girls do. Characteristics of rough play are shown in Table 12.1.

Table 12.1 *Differentiating serious aggression from rough play*

Categories	Types of behaviour	
	Serious	Playful
Motivation	Intent to injure	The target is motivated to avoid the behaviour
	Intentionally damaging play material	Accidental injury
	Child is willing to inflict pain on another	Cooperative
	Does not involve pretence	Voluntary
Duration	Brief	Long
Chase and flee	The child fleeing runs faster, straighter, and rarely looks over shoulder	The child fleeing runs at half-speed and frequently looks over shoulder at chaser
Actions (e.g., hitting)	Physical actions are not restrained	Physical actions are restrained
	Physical assault/snatching toy away	Includes wrestling
	Wresting is uncommon	
Body language	Bodily threat	Relaxed muscle tone
		Smiling and/or laughing
		Play face indicates enjoyment
		Imitation of aggression, fantasy aggression, rough-and-tumble
		Self-handicapping
Emotional	Child lacks empathy, child needs a sense of control, torment is evident	Engage with friends
	Anger is an underlying role in aggression	Prosocial
Expressive	Verbal aggression	High-pitched happy sounds
Role reversal	Roles are not exchanged	Role reversal
Control	Power imbalance, dominance	
Group size	Rarely more than two children involved	Involves two or more children
Climate	Draws a crowd of onlookers	Does not draw a crowd

Source: Adapted from Hart and Tannock (2013b).

Gender Differences

As evidenced across cultures (Fry, 2009; Gosso et al., 2007; Jarvis, 2007; Storli & Sandseter, 2015) rough play is a universal form of play, particularly prevalent in young boys, that is important for the development of males; both human and non-human (Jarvis, 2007). Female teachers view rough play as disruptive behaviour that escalates into noisy, rough, and chaotic play (Bauer & Dettore, 1997) perhaps because most female adults struggle to relate to rough play. For example, in identical environmental situations girls and boys will play and socialize differently; girls tend to be more verbal while boys tend to be more physical (DiPietro, 1981).

Female adults observing young children's rough behaviour, in particular, tend to confound rough play and real aggression and may be biased to interpret their observations according to their personal values (Hellendoorn & Harinck, 1997). As a result, women are more likely to view rough play as serious aggression, while men are likely to perceive it as play (Boyd, 1997; Fletcher et al., 2011; Reed & Brown, 2000), arguably due to intimacy being expressed differently by males and females (Reed et al., 2000). Therefore, females who are observing boys' rough play are often heard saying, 'That's too rough! We don't play like that.' In this common scenario, the female observer is ironically identifying the behaviour as *play*, yet redirecting the children to engage in play that females perceive as more appropriate and safer.

With boys engaging in rough play more often than girls (Smith et al., 2004), literature suggests that the effect of testosterone within young boys is a bio-evolutionary gender difference that contributes to their play behaviours (Jarvis, 2007). For example, Tannock (2011) found that nearly 80% of R&T players were boys, while about 20% were girls. Because teachers lack knowledge regarding developmentally appropriate rough behaviour for young boys (DiCarlo et al., 2015) and misinterpret rough play as being serious aggression (Logue & Detour, 2011; Pellegrini, 1987), young boys are at greater risk for being labelled as seriously aggressive (DiCarlo et al., 2015) and are identified as having problems that concern teachers more often than girls (Molins & Clopton, 2002). Furthermore, as serious aggressive behaviour increases with frequency until approximately 3.5 years of age (Tremblay, 2012), which coincides with the emergence of rough play, it is important for early childhood educators to assess the context and characteristics of young boys' behaviour rather than classifying all verbal and physical forms of aggression as serious with intent to harm.

With a low probability of rough play resulting in injury (Reed & Brown, 2000), young children who engage in rough play are at no greater risk to injury than their peers who play touch rugby or jump rope. For example, in 119 demonstrations of American children engaged in rough play, Reed and Brown (2000) observed one injury that resulted from a child twisting his ankle while running in sand during a time when he was not being chased nor in contact with another player. In other words, the child was injured at a time when he was not engaged in rough play. Additionally, Pellegrini (1989b) found that serious aggression results from rough play in less than 3% of all cases; therefore, the risk for injury is quite low. In cases where rough play escalates into serious aggression, teachers have an opportunity to promote prosocial interaction among young children within a realistic context of conflict just as they have with other forms of social play and learning activities.

Given the biological roots of boys' rough play, it is not typically within a girl's nature to be drawn to a bout of play involving pushing, shoving, pouncing, and tackling without an adult initiating the play (e.g., big body play); therefore, many educators are unable to understand its allure and appropriateness. For example, female teachers perceive rough play as a reason some children are excluded and less liked by peers (Bosaki et al., 2014). In contrast, men typically view boys' physical contact as normal behaviour and perceive boys engaging in rough play as being favoured by peers and likely to perform better academically when compared with boys who do not engage in rough play (Bosaki et al., 2014). As males represent only a small percentage of early childhood educators worldwide (OECD, 2016), it is important that early childhood educators have a thorough understanding of normative development as it relates to rough play behaviour as well as the context for which it occurs.

Benefits and Characteristics

Generations of children have become contributing members of society, for the most part, despite their interest and engagement in rough play. Similar to past play behaviour influenced by the Lone Ranger and *Treasure Island*, current rough play behaviour is often influenced by stories told through books, television shows, and movies. What was once thought to be play is now often considered violence due to a shift in adults' perceptions of rough play in recent decades. The onset of nationalized curricula, school-wide behaviour policies, and fears of litigation likely contribute to educators' and policymakers' negative views of rough play. The promotion of prosocial skills and children's safety and well-being, which leaves risky play types – like rough play – unaccounted for in early childhood settings, may also contribute to these negative views.

Rough play is important for young children's development as it is beneficial to all domains of learning. Of greatest benefit is perhaps the development of young boys' social-emotional skills. There is a general consensus in America that boys exhibit different patterns of play and social interaction when compared with girls, more specifically, reacting physically rather than verbally (DiPietro, 1981; Reed et al., 2000); therefore, a boy may push and shove a peer to communicate his desire to be friends and play. This physical behaviour fosters social competence and self-regulation (Pellis & Pellis, 2007), trust and intimate friendships (Reed et al., 2000), social problem-solving (Pellegrini, 1994), and cooperation (Parsons & Howe, 2006). Rough play provides opportunities for boys to enhance their ability to read peers' facial expressions, monitor verbal exchanges, and infer players' intent (Constabile et al., 1991; Pellegrini, 2003; Smith & Lewis, 1984) as well as explore social boundaries and determine placement within their social group (Logue & Harvey, 2010).

Big body play is an appropriate play that has physical, emotional, cognitive, and social benefits that young children from infancy voluntarily engage in during solitary play, parallel play, or group play (Carlson, 2011b). In early childhood settings, many adults question the appropriateness – much less the developmental necessity – of big body play. However, young boys and girls learn how to compromise, take turns, regulate their body movements, and adapt the intensity of their play as well as experience communication and social benefits, such as understanding verbal and non-verbal cues and the development of empathy and self-regulation (Carlson, 2011b).

In cultures where rough play is common, such as the United States, Canada, the United Kingdom, Australia, and Norway, a universal 'play face' is observed. The play face has been observed in animals as an open-mouthed, teeth-bared expression that looks fierce, yet is playful rather than seriously aggressive (Harlow, 1962). Similarly, researchers have observed the play face in young boys with additional characteristics that include smiles, laughter, and high-pitched happy sounds (see, for example, Fry, 1987, and Tannock, 2008). The play face is probably the most reliable indicator of differentiating rough play from serious aggression for teachers observing children's behaviour from a distance, where verbal communication cannot be heard. This cue is particularly useful in preventing unnecessary interference in young children's physical activity, such as rough play, which is found to elicit better reading and mathematics outcomes for boys when compared with boys who do not play physically (Hirsh-Pasek & Golinkoff, 2008).

Because research exists that concludes types of rough play are not beneficial to child development (see Carlsson-Paige & Levin, 1987; Dunn & Hughes, 2001; Watson & Peng, 1992), parents, educators, and psychologists have differing opinions regarding the potential benefits and harm of war toys in children's play (Hellendoorn & Harinck, 1997). However, it is important to recognize that research supporting the elimination of rough play in early childhood settings is not based on strong scientific evidence. For example, Hellendoorn and Harinck (1997) addressed this issue by investigating Dutch children's imaginative play with war toys such as soldiers, cowboys, GI Joe, Ninja Turtles, pistols, guns, swords, castles, and armed spaceships and concluded that a major influence on all children's behaviours (playful or serious) was formed by the context of their play partners' behaviour and that it is unlikely rough play leads to serious aggression due to their different intention.

Imaginative play is associated with the development of cooperation, conflict resolution, problem-solving, and paying attention to detail (Bauer & Dettore, 1997), skills deemed necessary for young children's first year of compulsory formal schooling. In the United States, imaginative play was found to be significantly relevant to young girls' self-reported positive mood and coping ability when deciding what to do in a situation that requires self-regulation of impulse and aggression (Firoelli & Russ, 2015). Furthermore, imaginative play generally is thought to facilitate cognitive growth including divergent thinking, problem-solving, impulse control, and representational competence (Emfinger, 2009; and Chapter 9).

In support of the decades of research evidencing the importance of rough play, Table 12.2 provides an overview of additional characteristics of rough

Table 12.2 *Benefits of sociodramatic rough play*

	Sociodramatic rough play	
Play type	Characteristics of behaviour	Developmental benefit
Superhero play	Running, jumping, wrestling, and shouting	Social-emotional: develop concepts of right and wrong, good and bad; cooperation
		Aesthetic development: fosters creative expression
		Cognitive development: children engage in higher-level thinking and creativity to sustain a role and cooperatively develop a play theme; practice problem-solving
'Bad guy' play	Superhero play, war, and stealing	Language: opportunities for teachers to foster language development
		Social-emotional: opportunities for teachers to support confidence; children practice negotiation and cooperation skills, share ideas, and are more inclusive with peers.
		Cognitive: opportunities to experience others' perspectives; repetition allows for role-playing changes and experience of different outcomes; develop conflict resolution skills
Active pretend play	Superhero play, play fighting (including wrestling), chase games, and protect/rescue games	Social: explore social boundaries, determine social placement in a group
		Physical: practice and test level of strength, determine agility, develop and practice restraint as they pretend to be aggressive
Play fighting	Voluntary social play	Social: development of typical social behaviour patterns, improved social competence later in life
	Competitive rough-and-tumble play or play fighting	Physical: develops coordination of appropriate body movements
	Playful attack by one partner coupled with playful defence by the other Attack and defence roles alternate	Cognitive: produces experiences with immediate feedback for some brain areas that regulate social behaviour and general cognition
Physically active and imaginative play	Children pretending to be superheroes	Social-emotional: allows children the freedom to explore their world with a sense of empowerment and control; opportunities for perspective-taking; cooperation

Table 12.2 (*cont.*)

| Play type | Sociodramatic rough play | |
	Characteristics of behaviour	Developmental benefit
	Engaged in a pretend adventurous theme such as battling, capture and rescue, attack and flee, submission and defeat	Cognitive: fosters creativity, increases cognitive flexibility; capture and sustain the child's attention throughout the play session; object transformation, role-play
		Language: theme development
	May include physical activity such as running, swinging, wrestling, tumbling, zooming, kicking, hopping, and sliding	Physical: develop more refined gross motor skills; release pent-up energy
Rough and tumble play	An enjoyable play-fighting and chasing activity played among friends	Social: coordination of activities and allocation/alteration of roles
	Contact or mock contact mimicking aggression	Social: practice spontaneous and autonomous competitive and cooperative interactions simultaneously
	Hold/grab/restrain other child, hit and run, hit/kick, wrestle/pin, trip, shoot, boxing, light blow	Language: fosters linguistic responses and creates shared narratives among peers
		Physical and cognitive: spontaneous interactions within the social 'classroom' of the playground; practice controlled and motivated behaviour related to both competition and cooperation; test and recalibrate interaction skills after receiving immediate feedback; improve physical movements

Source: Adapted from Hart & Tannock (2013b).

play and their corresponding developmental benefits to guide the judgements of educators when confronted with rough play.

Sociodramatic Play Interests

Sociodramatic play is a developmentally appropriate and beneficial activity for young children's development (Copple & Bredekamp, 2009) that includes role-play by imitation, make-believe with objects, make-believe with actions and situations, persistence in the role-play, interaction, and verbal communication (Smilansky, 1990). Given the various forms of rough play (e.g., good guys vs. bad guys, Batman, Ninja Turtles), some play may include all characteristics of sociodramatic play, while others do not. For example, each sociodramatic play characteristic is usually demonstrated within young boys' Star Wars play; however, make-believe objects are often absent during wrestling play. Although rough play can be compatible with Smilansky's (1990) description of sociodramatic play and is a pretend play enjoyed among friends, different contexts of young children's rough play are not always perceived as playful (Hart, 2016). For example, 87 of 100 times early childhood educators perceived young boys' behaviour as 'playful' when it involved playing with Nerf foam dart guns, yet play with Nerf foam swords and shields was perceived as being playful only 27 of 100 times (Hart, 2016). Young boys have made it clear that they enjoy physical contact with their friends (DiPietro, 1981; Pellegrini, 1989b; Reed & Brown, 2000) and that the more trusting friendships allow for a greater intensity of physical contact (Reed & Brown, 2000). Yet because early childhood educators are primarily females who relate to feminine demonstrations of friendship, young children's expressions of care and intimacy for one another through physical contact (i.e., pushing, hitting, and shoving) is often misinterpreted as inappropriate behaviour (Reed & Brown, 2000) and left unsupported in early childhood settings.

The Early Childhood Context

Because females make up the vast majority of early childhood and primary educators worldwide (OECD, 2016), early childhood curriculum, environments, and pedagogy are representative of a female perspective with a majority consensus that all rough behaviour, including rough play, is not appropriate in early childhood settings (Hart & Nagel, 2017; Logue & Detour, 2011; Tannock, 2008). At times, preschool teachers perceive rough play to be on the rise (Carlsson-Paige & Levin, 1987, 1995); however, the frequency of rough play is quite low (Boyd, 1997). Research specific to R&T has found (1) that it takes up approximately 10% of young boys' outdoor free play time (Smith et al., 2004), (2) that 5% of all play is R&T (Smith & Lewis, 1984), and (3) that on average, 3.63 incidents of R&T are observed in a 1-hour period (Tannock, 2011). The discrepancy between perceptions and empirical findings may be grounded in gender; however, other contributing factors have an influence. Even among female educators, perceptions of various types of rough play vary significantly (Hart, 2016) and variation in school policies exists (Logue & Harvey, 2010). Within a Norwegian early childhood education and care context, rough play is the most restricted type of play within early childhood indoor and outdoor environments (Storli & Sandseter, 2015).

Adults' Perceptions

Essentially, the elimination of rough play within early childhood settings is largely due to perceptions that conflict with decades of research demonstrating the relevance of rough behaviour within a play context and a general lack of understanding of its developmental purpose. Perhaps teachers' negative perceptions are most influenced by the misplacement of rough play into categories of serious aggression within school behaviour policies alongside the omission of rough play in early childhood frameworks and curriculum. Overall, early childhood educators' negative perceptions and intolerance of rough play are influenced by many factors, which include:

- a lack of understanding of its developmental benefits (Little et al., 2011)
- an inability to manage the behaviour (Reed et al., 2000; Tannock, 2008)
- perceptions that it leads to true anger or violence (Flanders et al., 2010; Pellegrini, 2003; Pellegrini & Perlmutter, 1987; Reed et al., 2000)
- perceptions that it is unsafe (Bauer & Dettore, 1997; Freeman & Brown, 2004; Logue & Harvey, 2010; Reed et al., 2000)
- perceptions that it will cause injury (Little et al., 2011; Sandseter, 2007, 2009)
- an inability to distinguish between rough play and serious aggression (Dunn & Hughes, 2001; Logue & Harvey, 2010; Parsons & Howe, 2006; Pellegrini, 1987)
- the perception that all rough behaviour is serious and is intended to harm (Fletcher et al., 2011; Freeman & Brown, 2004; Hewes & McEwan, 2006; Logue & Detour, 2011; Pellegrini, 1987; Reed et al., 2000)
- the level of training/education of teachers (Dicarlo et al., 2015; Girard et al., 2011)
- the type of rough play in which young children are involved (Hart, 2016; Sandseter, 2009)
- whether toy weapons are included in the play (Carlsson-Paige, 1995; Hart, 2016; Hart & Tannock, 2013a; Parsons & Howe, 2006)
- the players' age (Hart, 2016; Pellegrini, 2003) and gender (DiPietro, 1981; Logue & Detour, 2011)
- whether the play is supervised (Freeman & Brown, 2004; Hart & Tannock, 2013b)

Given that children continue to physically interact during play, despite knowing that it is not acceptable behaviour within their educational setting (Tannock, 2008), educators need to develop a greater understanding of young children's normative development and interest in rough play rather than depriving them of physical sociodramatic play, play that is developmentally appropriate and beneficial for young children's development (Copple & Bredekamp, 2009).

Including research that spans more than three decades, Table 12.2 outlines common behaviours associated with various types of rough play to clarify misconceptions and offer support for teachers. The information may be used to facilitate conversations among adults who are at the forefront of early childhood pedagogy and behaviour policy.

Potential

Because rough play behaviour remains prevalent in early childhood settings despite adults' efforts to suppress it (Logue & Harvey, 2010; Tannock, 2008) children are learning to be secretive and deceitful, playing in locations where their play is more likely to go unnoticed, and lying to concerned adults about their rough behaviour to escape negative consequences for enjoying a bout of play with good friends. As rough play is usually not tolerated in early childhood settings (Carlson, 2011a; DiPietro, 1981; Jarvis, 2007; Logue & Harvey, 2010; Pellegrini, 1987), young boys may be at greater risk for developing antisocial behaviour and serious violent tendencies due to their deprivation of biologically and developmentally normal play, as has been demonstrated in clinical research (see, for example, Brown, 1998).

Supporting Environments

Rough play has the potential to create a positive early learning climate. Children who may capitalize on their interests and have opportunities to release pent-up energy will likely interact with their peers and environment more positively. Guidance for supporting rough play in early childhood settings is available throughout research. Building on decades of knowledge and recommendations by researchers, Table 12.3 offers support strategies for the inclusion of rough play within education settings. It is important to note that all support strategies and guidelines may not apply within every context; therefore, educators may need to make adjustments after consideration for developmentally appropriate, culturally appropriate, and age-appropriate indoor and outdoor play within their settings (Hart, 2016).

Developmental Impact

Given that serious aggressive and disruptive behaviour is one of the most perpetual dysfunctions in children (Lochman et al., 2012), young children who have not developed age-appropriate self-regulation skills are at high risk for chronic serious aggression and antisocial behaviour (Keenan, 2012). Rough play offers opportunities for practicing prosocial skills such as caring,

Table 12.3 *Strategies for supporting rough play*

Categories	Strategy	Support
Designate a play space	Large, soft floor area • A minimum of 25 sq. ft. is suggested	Indoors • Tumble mats • Create a wrestling centre
	Uninterrupted area • Free from non-participating peers • Free from learning activities	Outdoors • Tumble mats • Grassy area
Supervision	3-year-olds	Close proximity. Stand or sit to support and facilitate the play. Avoid engaging in the play.
	4 years and older	Distant proximity. Stand or sit close enough to hear and see. Avoid eye contact. Children may relocate each time they know you are watching. Avoid engaging in the play.
Accessories	Throw pillows, Sqush therapy pillows	Pillow fights
	Foam weapons, toy guns, and small beanbags	Sword fights, blasters, and beanbag bombs
	Capes, masks, costumes, wands, two-way radios, and plastic handcuffs	Superhero or fantasy play: Batman, cops and robbers, Harry Potter, and Star Wars
Group size	3-year-olds	Two children (rotate participants)
	4 years and older	Two or more children Smaller groups express more positive affect: creativity, cooperation, communication
Safety rules	Be safe • No touching or aiming at head and neck • Soft hitting, kicking, punching • Soft pushing, pulling, tackling, wrestling Build trust • Stop the play if friend is not happy • Stop the play if friend is injured • Stop the play if friend is scared • Stop the play if friend is angry Use words • "Stop!" • "I don't like that!" • "It's my turn to be the good guy."	Discuss rules daily Add rules as needed Anticipate conflicts and support resolutions • A participating child is not considered to be a friend of other participants • A participating child often exerts serious aggression elsewhere • Participants are not following the rules • Participants cannot agree on their assigned roles

Source: Adapted from Hart & Tannock (2013b).

turn-taking, perspective-taking, and conflict resolution within a safe and supportive environment. The following list offers short- and long-term benefits that may result with the inclusion of rough play in early childhood settings:

- Children may be more attentive for longer periods of time as pent-up energy is released.
- Children may sustain a positive disposition as their play choices are supported.
- Children's relationships with their teachers may improve as their play interests are respected.
- Children may be honest about their play behaviour when confronted by supervising adults.
- Teachers may spend more time interacting positively with children rather than managing undesired behaviours.
- Schools may experience a decline in behaviour referrals; particularly for boys.
- Children's academic performance may increase due to increase in attention span.
- Peer relationships may improve as rules and play spaces are clearly defined.
- Children's behaviour at home and with their family members may improve due to any combination of the above.

Learning Outcomes

Because play is internationally recognized as a beneficial context for young children's healthy growth and development, it seems appropriate that rough play be acknowledged as a form of play that is beneficial to young children's development within early childhood learning frameworks. For example, America's Developmentally Appropriate Practice (DAP), Australia's Early Years Learning Framework (EYLF), and the United Kingdom's Early Years Foundation Stage (EYFS) are three examples of national initiatives to deliver equitable and quality early learning experiences for young children, yet – apart from R&T briefly mentioned within DAP – neither the various forms of rough play nor their developmental benefits are included (Hart & Nagel, 2017). This is of utmost importance given these mandated documents are intended to guide educators' pedagogy and align their curriculum planning.

The EYLF is a framework of principles, practices, and outcomes that guide early childhood educators' curriculum decision-making to foster young children's learning in areas identified by five broad Learning Outcomes (DEEWR, 2009). Rough play may serve as a facilitator for young children to meet the key learning components within each learning outcome. For example, children who engage in rough play are establishing and maintaining respectful, trusting relationships with other children; evidence of meeting Learning Outcome 1: *Children Have a Strong Sense of Identity*. Similarly, the EYFS outlines seven areas of learning and development that educators must implement to guide their educational programmes in early years settings (DET, 2014). Again, rough play may serve as a facilitator for young children to develop skills in all seven areas and, as evidenced by its developmental benefits, may target the three prime learning areas: (1) communication and language, (2) physical development, and (3) personal, social, and emotional development. Finally, by definition, all forms of rough play meet the criteria of DAP (Copple & Bredekamp, 2009) and provide young children with play opportunities that target the specific domains of learning – physical, social and emotional, cognitive, and language and literacy development – as outlined in the framework.

Summary

Children engage in play with their friends for the pure enjoyment of it. With all forms of play, including rough play, children are voluntary participants who are motivated by its pleasure. Children's enjoyment is evident in their positive body language and verbalizations. A reconceptualisation of rough play is needed by identifying the behaviour as playful and recognising its relevance to early learning and development. As conflict can arise during any type of play, supervising adults can offer guidance and support to foster children's social-emotional development. If any play, not just rough play, demonstrates a pattern of escalating into serious aggression, a change is clearly needed. For example, a child may need to be redirected to another activity due to a low level of friendship with other players, a particular prop/toy may need to be removed or multiples provided, or the play may need to be relocated to a larger area. Educators should support children in their play choices by recognizing that a variety of social play styles are needed to learn prosocial skills (Freeman & Brown, 2004), must analyze the context and identify possible causes of conflict, and make necessary adjustments to support children's behaviour rather than try to eliminate rough play altogether (Hart, 2016; Hart & Tannock, 2013b; Reed et al., 2000).

References

Bauer, K. L., & Dettore, E. (1997). Superhero play: What's a teacher to do? *Early Childhood Education Journal, 25*(1), 17–21.

Blurton Jones, N. G. (1972). Categories of child-child interaction. In N. G. Blurton Jones (Ed.), *Ethological Studies of Child Behaviour* (pp. 97–127). Cambridge: Cambridge University Press.

Bosacki, S., Woods, H., & Coplan, R. (2014). Canadian female and male early childhood educators' perceptions of child aggression and rough-and-tumble play. *Early Child Development and Care, 185*(7), 1134–1147.

Boyd, B. J. (1997). Teacher response to superhero play: To ban or not to ban? *Childhood Education, 74,* 23–28.

Brown, S. L. (1998). Play as an organizing principal: Clinical evidence and personal observations. In M. Bekoff & J. A. Byers (Eds.), *Animal play: Evolutionary, comparative, and ethological* (pp. 243–275). Cambridge: Cambridge University Press.

Byers, J. A., & Walker, C. (1995). Refining the motor training hypothesis for the evolution of play. *American Naturalist, 146*(1), 25–40.

Carlson, F. M. (2011a). Rough play: One of the most challenging behaviors. *Young Children,* 18–25.

Carlson, F. M. (2011b). *Big body play.* Washington, DC: National Association for the Education of Young Children.

Carlsson-Paige, N. & Levin, D. (1987). *The war play dilemma: Balancing needs and values in the early childhood classroom.* New York: Teachers College Press.

Carlsson-Paige, N., & Levin, D. (1995). Can teachers resolve the war-play dilemma? *Young Children, 50*(4), 6–62.

Copple, C., & Bredekamp, S. (2009). *Developmentally appropriate practice in early childhood programs serving children from birth through age 8* (3rd edn.). Washington, DC: NAEYC.

Costabile, A., Smith, P. K., Matheson, L., Aston, J., Hunter, T., & Boulton, M. (1991). Cross-national comparison of how children distinguish serious and playful fighting. *Developmental Psychology, 27*(5), 881–887.

Department of Education (DET) (2014). Statutory Framework for the Early Years Foundation Stage: Setting the standards for learning, development and care for children from birth to five. Runcorn: Department for Education. Available at www.foundationyears.org.uk/eyfs-statutory-framework/.

Department of Education, Employment and Workplace Relations (DEEWR) (2009). *Belonging, being and becoming: The early years learning framework for Australia.* Available at deewr.gov.au/early-years-learning-framework.

DiCarlo, C. F., Baumgartner, J., Ota, C., & Jenkins, C. (2015). Preschool teachers' perceptions of rough and tumble play vs. aggression in preschool-aged boys. *Early Child Development and Care, 185*(5), 779–790.

DiPietro, J. A. (1981). Rough and tumble play: A function of gender. *Developmental Psychology, 17*(1), 50–58.

Dunn, J., & Hughes, C. (2001). "I got some swords and you're dead!": Violent fantasy, antisocial behavior, friendship, and moral sensibility in young children. *Child Development, 72*(2), 491–505.

Emfinger, K. (2009). Numerical conceptions reflected during multiage child-initiated pretend play. *Journal of Instructional Psychology, 36,* 326–334.

European Commission (EC), Education, Audiovisual and Culture Executive Agency (EACEA), Eurydice, & Eurostat. (2014). *Key data on early childhood education and care in Europe.* 2014 Edition. Eurydice and Eurostat Report. Luxembourg: Publications Office of the European Union.

Fiorelli, J. A., & Russ, S. W. (2015). Pretend play, coping, and subjective well-being in children: A follow-up study. *American Journal of Play*, *5*(1), 81–103.

Flanders, J. L., Herman, K. N., & Paquette, D. (2012). Rough-and-tumble play and the cooperation–competition dilemma: Evolutionary and developmental perspectives on the development of social competence. In D. Narvaez, J. Panksepp, A. N. Schore, & R. R. Gleason (Eds.), *Evolution, early experience and human development: From research to practice and policy* (pp. 371–387). Oxford Scholarship Online.

Flanders, J. L., Simard, M., Paquette, D., Parent, S., Vitaro, F., Pihl, R. O., & Séguin, J. R. (2010). Rough-and-tumble play and the development of physical aggression and emotion regulation: A five-year follow-up study. *Journal of Family Violence*, *25*(4), 357–367.

Fletcher, R., May, C., St. George, J., Morgan, P., & Lubans, D. R. (2011). Fathers' perceptions of rough-and-tumble play: Implications for early childhood services. *Australasian Journal of Early Childhood*, *36*(4), 131–138.

Freeman, N. K., & Brown, M. H. (2004). Reconceptualizing rough and tumble play: Ban the banning. *Social Contexts of Early Education, and Reconceptualizing Play (II) Advances in Early Education and Day Care*, *13*, 219–234.

Fry, D. P. (1987). Differences between playfighting and serious fighting among Zapotec children. *Ethology and Sociobiology*, *8*(4), 285–306.

Fry, D. P. (2009). Rough-and-tumble social play in humans. In A. D. Pellegrini (Ed.), *The role of play in human development* (pp. 54–85). New York: Oxford University Press.

Girard, L. C., Girolametto, L., Weitzman, E., & Greenberg, J. (2011). Training early childhood educators to promote peer interactions: Effects on children's aggressive and prosocial behaviors. *Early Education and Development*, *22*(2), 305–323.

Gosso, Y., Morais, M. L. S., & Otta, E. (2007). Pretend play of Brazilian children: A window into different cultural worlds. *Journal of Cross-Cultural Psychology*, *38*(5), 539–558.

Harlow, H. F. (1962). The heterosexual affectional system in monkeys. *American Psychologist*, *17*(1), 1–9.

Hart, J. L. (2016). Early childhood educators' attitudes towards rough play among boys: Exploring the importance of situational context. *Early Childhood Development and Care*, *12*(186), 1983–1993.

Hart, J. L., & Nagel, M. C. (2017). Including rough play in early childhood curriculum and pedagogy. *Australasian Journal of Early Childhood*, *42*(1), 41–48.

Hart, J. L., & Tannock, M. T. (2013a). Young children's play fighting and use of war toys. In R. E. Tremblay, R. B. Barr, R. DeV. Peters, & M. Boivin (Eds.), *Encyclopedia on early childhood development* [online]. Montreal, Quebec: Centre of Excellence for Early Childhood Development and Strategic Knowledge Cluster on Early Child Development. Available at www.childencyclopedia.com/documents/Hart-TannockANGxp1.pdf.

Hart, J. L., & Tannock, M. T. (2013b). Rough play in early childhood settings. *Children Australia*, *38*(3), 106–114.

Hellendoorn, J., & Harinck, F. J. H. (1997). War toy play and aggression in Dutch kindergarten children. *Social Development, 6*(3), 340–354.

Hewes, J., & McEwan, G. (2006). Let the children play: Nature's answer to early learning. In R. E. Tremblay, R. B. Barr, R. DeV. Peters, & M. Boivin (Eds.), *Encyclopedia on early childhood development* [online]. Montreal, Quebec: Centre of Excellence for Early Childhood Development and Strategic Knowledge Cluster on Early Child Development. Available at www.child-encyclopedia.com/sites/default/files/docs/suggestions/let-the-children-play_jane-hewes.pdf.

Hirsh-Pasek, K. & Golinkoff, R. M. (2008). Why play = learning. In R. E. Tremblay, R. B. Barr, R. DeV. Peters, & M. Boivin (Eds.), *Encyclopedia on early childhood development* [online]. Montreal, Quebec: Centre of Excellence for Early Childhood Development and Strategic Knowledge Cluster on Early Child Development. Available at www.child-encyclopedia.com/play/according-experts/why-play-learning.

Holland, P. (2003). *We don't play with guns here: War, weapon, and superhero play in the early years.* Maidenhead: Open University Press.

Humphreys, A. P., & Smith, P. K. (1984). Rough-and-tumble in preschool and playground. In P. K. Smith (Ed.), *Play in animals and humans* (pp. 241–266). Oxford: Blackwell.

Humphreys, A. P., & Smith, P. K. (1987). Rough and tumble, friendship, and dominance in school children: Evidence for continuity and change with age. *Child Development, 58*, 201–212.

Jarvis, P. (2007). Monsters, magic and Mr Psycho: A biocultural approach to rough and tumble play in the early years of primary school. *Early Years: An International Journal of Research and Development, 27*(2), 171–188.

Keenan, K. (2012). Development of physical aggression from early childhood to adulthood. In R. E. Tremblay, R. B. Barr, R. DeV. Peters, & M. Boivin (Eds.), *Encyclopedia on early childhood development* [online]. Montreal, Quebec: Centre for Excellence for Early Childhood Development and Strategic Knowledge Cluster on Early Child Development. Available at www.child-encyclopedia.com/documents/KeenanANGxp1.pdf.

Little, H., Wyver, S., & Gibson, F. (2011). The influence of play context and adult attitudes on young children's physical risk-taking during outdoor play. *European Early Childhood Education Research Journal, 19*(1), 113–131.

Lochman, J. E., Boxmeyer, C., Powell, N., & Jimenez-Camargo, A. (2012). Effective daycare-kindergarten interventions to prevent chronic aggression. In R. E. Tremblay, R. B. Barr, R. DeV. Peters, & M. Boivin (Eds.), *Encyclopedia on Early Childhood Development* [online]. Montreal, Quebec: Centre for Excellence for Early Childhood Development and Strategic Knowledge Cluster on Early Child Development. Available at www.child-encyclopedia.com/documents/Lochman-Boxmeyer-Powell-Jimenez-CamargoANGxp1.pdf.

Logue, M. E., & Detour, A. (2011). "You be the bad guy": A new role for teachers in supporting children's dramatic play. *Early Childhood Research & Practice, 13*(1), 1–16.

Logue, M. E., & Harvey, H. (2010). Preschool teachers' views of active play. *Journal of Research in Childhood Education, 24*(1), 32–49.

Malloy, H. L., & McMurray-Schwarz, P. (2004). War play, aggression and peer culture: A review of the research examining the relationship between war play and aggression. *Social Contexts of Early Education, and Reconceptualizing Play (II): Advances in Early Education and Day Care, 13*, 235–265.

Molins, N. C., & Clopton, J. R. (2002). Teachers' reports of the problem behavior of children in their classrooms. *Psychological Reports, 90*, 157–164.

Nagel, M. C. (2012). *In the beginning: The brain, early development and learning.* Camberwell, Victoria: Australian Council for Educational Research (ACER).

National Center for Education Statistics (NCES). (2012). *The Condition of Education. Report.* Available at https://nces.ed.gov/pubs2012/2012045_2.pdf.

Organisation for Economic Cooperation and Development (OECD). (2013). *How do early childhood education and care (ECEC) policies, systems and quality vary across OECD countries?* Available at www.oecd.org/education/skills-beyond-school/EDIF11.pdf.

Organisation for Economic Co-operation and Development (OECD) (2016). *PF3.2: Enrolment in Childcare and Pre-school.* Social Policy Division, Directorate of Employment, Labour and Social Affairs. Available at www.oecd.org/els/soc/PF3_2_Enrolment_childcare_preschool.pdf.

Parsons, A., & Howe, N. (2006). Superhero toys and boys' physically active and imaginative play. *Journal of Research in Childhood Education, 20*, 802–806.

Pellegrini, A. D. (1987). Rough-and-tumble play: Developmental and educational significance. *Educational Psychologist, 22*(1), 23–43.

Pellegrini, A. D. (1989a). Children's rough-and-tumble play: Issues in categorization and function. *Educational Policy, 3*, 389–400.

Pellegrini, A. D. (1989b). Elementary-school children's rough-and-tumble play. *Early Childhood Quarterly, 4*, 245–260.

Pellegrini, A. D. (1994). The rough play of adolescent boys of differing sociometric status. *International Journal of Behavioural Development, 17*(3), 525–540.

Pellegrini, A. D. (2003). Perceptions and functions of play and real fighting in early adolescence. *Child Development, 74*(5), 1522–1522.

Pellegrini, A. D., Dupuis, D., & Smith, P. K. (2007). Play in evolution and development. *Developmental Review, 27*(2), 261–276.

Pellegrini, A. D., & Perlmutter, J. (1987). A re-examination of the Smilansky–Parten matrix of play behavior. *Journal of Research in Childhood Education, 2*(2), 89–96.

Pellegrini, A. D., & Smith, P. K. (1998). The development of play during childhood: Forms and possible functions. *Child Psychology and Psychiatry Review, 3*(2), 51–57.

Pellis, P. M., Burghardt, G. M., Palagi, E., & Mangel, M. (2015). Modeling play: Distinguishing between origins and current functions. *Adaptive Behavior, 23*(6), 331–339.

Pellis, S. M., & Pellis, V. C. (2007). Rough-and-tumble play and the development of the social brain. *Current Directions in Psychological Science, 16*, 95–98.

Reed, T., & Brown, M. (2000). The expression of care in rough and tumble play of boys. *Journal of Research in Childhood Education, 15*(1), 104–116.

Reed, T. L., Brown, M. H., & Roth, S. A. (2000). Friendship formation and boys' rough and tumble play: Implications for teacher education programs. *Journal of Early Childhood Teacher Education, 21*(3), 331–336.

Sandseter, E. B. H. (2007). Categorising risky play: How can we identify risk-taking in children's play? *European Early Childhood Education Research Journal, 15*(2), 237–252.

Sandseter, E. B. H. (2009). Affordances for risky play in preschool: The importance of features in the play environment. *Early Childhood Education Journal, 36,* 439–446.

Smilansky, S. (1990). Sociodramatic play: Its relevance to behavior and achievement in school. In E. Klugman & S. Smilansky (Eds.), *Children's play and learning: Perspectives and policy implications* (pp. 18–42). New York: Teachers College Press.

Smith, P. K. (2010). *Children and play: Understanding children's worlds.* Chichester: Wiley-Blackwell.

Smith, P. K., & Lewis, K. (1984). Rough-and-tumble play, fighting, and chasing in nursery school children. *Ethology and Sociobiology, 6,* 175–181.

Smith, P., Smees, R., & Pellegrini, A. (2004). Play fighting and real fighting: Using video playback methodology with young children. *Aggressive Behavior, 30,* 164–173.

Storli, R., & Sandseter, E. B. H. (2015). Preschool teachers' perceptions of children's rough-and-tumble play (R&T) in indoor and outdoor environments. *Early Child Development and Care, 185,* 11–12.

Sutton-Smith, B. (1997). *The ambiguity of play.* Cambridge, MA: Harvard University Press.

Tannock, M. T. (2008). Rough and tumble play: An investigation of the perceptions of educators and young children. *Early Childhood Education Journal, 35,* 357–361.

Tannock, M. T. (2011). Observing young children's rough-and-tumble play. *Australasian Journal of Early Childhood, 36*(2), 13–20.

Tremblay, R. E. (2012). The development of physical aggression. In R. E. Tremblay, M. Boivin, & R. DeV. Peters (eds.), *Encyclopedia on Early Childhood Development* [online]. Montreal, Quebec: Centre for Excellence for Early Childhood Development and Strategic Knowledge Cluster on Early Child Development. Available at www.child-encyclopedia.com/documents/TremblayANGxp3.pdf.

Watson, M. W., & Peng, Y. (1992). The relation between toy gun play and children's aggressive behavior. *Early Education and Development, 3,* 370–389.

13 Playing Games with Rules in Early Child Care and Beyond

Ditte Winther-Lindqvist

> We remain deeply contradicted in our cultural attitude toward play. Play is the antithesis of the productive, sensible, and useful. Yet for all its shortcomings, play has always been with us and has always been pervasive, popular, and engaged in with passion.
>
> (Lastowka, 2009, p. 7)

In this chapter, children's playing games with rules is explored with the aim of understanding the social meaning of games and also determining their particular articulation in the developmental age of early care. In Huizinga's famous book, *Homo Ludens: A Study of the Play Element in Culture* (1955), the main point is that not only does play reflect human culture; play is at the core of cultural production, as our creative and competitive impulse to play also is the impulse to create. The recent technological development in digital games has generated a renewed and revitalized discussion about the nature of rules and their function in games and play. However, children's play with rules is still rather unexplored compared with children's pretend playing, and rules *in general* are a poorly understood phenomenon. As the post-structuralist game theorist Tulloch remarks: "There are few concepts as central to the study of gaming as rules: however, there are few concepts so frequently overlooked and under-theorised" (Tulloch, 2014, p. 336). Agreeing with this statement, let us consider children's play with rules and theorize this activity and its personal and social meaning.

The role of rules in children's play is undecided and debated in the literature, and often reflects whether gaming with rules is seen as a version of a universal play phenomenon or considered a play form of its own. Very often the discussion also revolves around whether all playing is considered to be involving rules or whether rules are regarded only as relevant to some forms of play; scholars argue for the former – they think of rules in broader terms, more like a sort of social norms – whereas those who argue that rules are prominent only in games think of formal and explicit rules. Rather than discussing whether or not rules are productive (see Tulloch, 2014, for a recent review) we might ask, what are rules productive for? And what are the rules about in children's playing?

I argue that rules – broadly defined, as well as imagined indeterminacy – is involved in all playing; however, they are unequally dominant in different forms of playing. This claim is theoretically substantiated from within a cultural-historical conception of play as an imaginary and a rule-bound activity. Based on an overview of the discussion around play with rules, and the developmental nature of rules in play, three different forms of rules suggested by Hughes are presented and identified as central to understanding children's gaming in early care settings. Appreciating the focus of childhood sociologists and ethnographers on children's play in everyday-life environments, and outlining the actual practice of children's games with rules, I argue that this practice also reflects their development and that the developmental aspect is important to keep in mind when studying children's play.

For 5-year-olds, a soccer game resembles more a play with soccer than the sporting game of soccer proper. When 12-year-olds play soccer in the schoolyard, their play resembles more the adult version of the sporting game. However, playing not only reflects development, it also entails numerous and varied developmental situations for the children. I argue that playing games with rules, just as in social fantasy play, provides particular exciting contexts for exploring one's own powers of agency in a group, one's social identity as player, and one's relationships with others through the experiences that the play activity produce in a group of peers (Winther-Lindqvist, 2017). In that sense playing is an activity and arena for exploring existential themes in children's lives.

I suggest this underlying motivational structure is a core project when children are performing the game within the constraints of its rules, and when they negotiate interpretations of rules for themselves and others. In that same process, and at the same time, the children are also cultivating their socio-emotional responses to victory, defeat, and frustration in culturally accepted ways, likely to prepare them for participation in the real sporting games of later childhood or in social life in general. In that sense, playing is an activity and way-of-being-together that serves as an excellent point of entry for becoming and developing into a full-grown member of a social community.

Games with Rules: A Tentative Definition

Defining play and differentiating different play forms from one another has kept play scholars and philosophers preoccupied for decades. Lillard (2015) summarizes this issue by distinguishing between various attempts that define play based on either behavioural or experiential categories. The behavioural definitions describe what children do in play and thus focus on play as a particular practice and form of activity. Defining play with reference to its experiential qualities focusses on characteristics regarding the player's attitude, moods, emotional state, and motivations for playing. Most definitions integrate both behavioural and experiential characteristics (see recently Burghardt, 2011). Behavioural definitions tend to lead to discussions of a binary kind, i.e. either an activity is play or it is not play, whereas the experiential definitions seem to lead to a more scalar thinking where an activity/event/interaction can be vested with more or less playfulness (Krasnor & Pepler, 1980).

It has proven impossible to create a satisfactory positive consensual definition of what play is; especially, on the issue of competition and rules vs. imagination scholars differ and dispute and seem to capture the one while losing sight of the other. So, another strategy for capturing the essence of play is to compare it through a contrasting analysis, pointing to similarities and differences between play and other phenomena. Some of the most interesting and widely explored ways forward are analytical comparisons between play vs. work, play vs. ritual, play vs. learning, play vs. drama, play vs. sports, play vs. fighting, play vs. law, play vs. power. Through these contrasting analogies we uncover new aspects or new implications of the variable and fascinating phenomenon of play – yet still without completely capturing it in its entirety. Maybe the Wittgensteinian idea of a family resemblance between essential features of play related to various activities, formats, and experiential qualities is a way to describe the current affairs in respect to the search for a meaningful definition of play (Schousboe & Winther-Lindqvist, 2013, p. 2).

When turning attention to the many different forms of playing, we learn that some play forms we share with other mammals (such as manipulating objects in playful ways, chasing, and rough-and-tumble playing), whereas other playing forms seem more distinctly human (role-play and games with rules). The play forms distinctly human are universal, yet always culturally shaped and historically in change. Games with rules are of this latter category, and especially games played on digital electronic devices serve as an example of how societal and cultural development the form of new technologies changes our world of play and its players.

Different Kinds of Games, Rules, and Moods

Games with rules are a play format creating social communities all over the world, in various cultural variations, relevant to people and communities across the lifespan, an activity ranging from the soccer playing of early childhood to the adult world of highly organized, professional and commercialized sports like Champions League. At some point on this journey, the activity is no longer play; exactly where a game turns into a sport or work is debatable, but nonetheless, there remains a family resemblance between the 5-year-old playing soccer and the professional adult players on TV. This resemblance not only regards the identification on the part of the children, who wish to become like the adults on famous soccer teams, and the obvious fact that those adult players once were kids, just playing soccer in childhood playgrounds. Rather, there are resemblances with regard to the indeterminate outcome of the game, both in each team's performance and on the individual player's part – as well as the assertive efforts put into the mastering of this performance, which comprises deep involvement and sincere emotions.

Without attempting to exhaust the defining characteristics of games, I suggest distinguishing play with regard to different formats (play as activity) and as modes of experiencing (different play moods and attitudes). A preliminary working definition for the play format of games could be: 'Games are competitive with a particular goal in deciding between a winner/loser (individual or team), which is determined through enacting and performing particular roles/tasks within the constraints of explicit rules.' A game is focussed on a particular goal (as opposed to pretend play or rough-and-tumble playing) but no one knows who wins before the game is over. The subjunctive 'What-if' element of indeterminacy is thus central to the game (Bretherton, 1984). Rules are productive because they regulate the social fate and existence of the players, through their restrictive and at the same time transformative function. We need the constraining prohibition (rule as restriction) in order for the game to take the particular form it takes – this becomes strikingly clear in digital games where the game exists only in its legislated version, formed by the possible actions programmed into it (Juul, 2005). However, this also holds true in non-virtual, more freely organized games. The rules are productive because they create the range of action possibilities that define the game itself – so rules are not external or abstract contexts for a game, but internal to the existence of that very game.

Games can be invented and come into being spontaneously through enactment, while rules are also invented along the way. These spontaneous and creative games are common among younger children. However, when we think of games we typically think of culturally recognized and well-known activities like soccer, chess, tennis, and the like. That the rules for these games are explicit and formal does not imply that the players strictly follow them, nor does it mean that the players are not also adhering to more implicit rules in addition to the formal and explicit rules. The actual performing of the tasks in the game can be enacted in a spirit reflecting different play moods, like sociocultural anthropologist Malaby suggests, when he says, "Games relate to a particular mode of experience; a dispositional stance toward the indeterminate" (Malaby, 2009, p. 208). The game can be decided by chance or by mastery, typically in a mix of both, and the gamer's attitude can be more or less vested with imagined scenarios and superstition.

In Caillois's famous classification of games (1961), he builds on and expands Huizinga's competitive element (agon) with that of chance (alea), dramatization (mimicry), and embodied sensation (vertigo), and he lays out their typical psychological attitudes, ranging between ludus and paidia on a continuum (Henricks, 2010). As Caillois suggests, the attitudes of chance and those of mastery are quite different. When being-towards-the-world of chance one lets go of one's fate and places it in higher powers of coincidence, or some higher spiritual order, and hopes to be in luck. Giving in to chance often is accompanied with light-hearted silliness and excitement among children, whereas games relying on mastery (like soccer or chess) entail a being-towards-the-world of alert devotion, due to the challenge and excitement connected to one's performance, playing excellently or badly, winning or losing.

On the difference, the sociologist Henricks writes that regulated competition "celebrates willful assertion whereas games of chance feature willful surrender to external forces" (2010, p. 167). The actual practice of a team game, and thus also a variance in its experiential quality, relies also on the extent to which you are in it to win or mainly in it to join. Again, playing games can result primarily in a strong sense of victory or defeat, pride or shame, or occasionally becoming one with the play through a thrilling sensation of the body-in-action-with-the-ball and a communal sense of fitting into and belonging to the game. I argue that gaming is a distinct play form because performance is more about this committed engagement to mastering the tasks within the rules (and possibly winning) than it is exploring imagined scenarios. However, the informal rules and some of its play moods relevant to the game of soccer among pre-schoolers in early care will be analyzed in this chapter and reveal family resemblances to pretend playing, reflecting the developmental age of the players. Finally, I suggest a more general motivational structure in playing: that of exploring social identities and one's social existence in a community that seems to cut across various play forms as well as across different ages, during childhood and beyond.

Rules: Playing by Them, with Them, and Bending Them

Children's play with rules fascinates scholars from various disciplines and with various objectives. Scholars from the range of humanities engage the theorizing of play, but especially in the last 40 years the study of *children's* play has become a matter of interest to many others than developmental psychologists; childhood sociologists, social anthropologists, and folklorists are all contributing to our understanding of the social and cultural dimensions of children's gaming. Consider the following example of a game of Buck. (Buck is a widespread family game in Denmark, with 52 cards that match each other in pairs, but the card of the buck has no matching card. The players take turns in drawing cards from one another and seeking matching cards. The player who ends up with the card of the buck in his hand loses the game.) The following are from my field notes in a Danish early care environment:

> A group of five-year-old boys are playing inside with 'Buck-cards' before lunch. They lay all the cards front-down at the table and each child turns two cards, first one and then another and looks for pairs. The child turning the card with the Buck loses the game. Ollie shuffles and places the cards on the table. They take turns in turning cards and memorize where cards with

different images are placed: Yeah, I had a match, Andy cries. And the others eagerly have their turn but don't get matches. Two boys start playing with some of the cards and take them up. "They are kissing!!!" the boys giggle... "Stop fooling around – we are playing with all the cards", Ollie says. Another boy, Miles, stands by and watches their playing. He asks if he can join the game, but Ollie says: Nope! Miles then replies: "You are playing it the wrong way. You play it like a game of Memory, but you are supposed to hold up the cards in Buck, like this (he shows how they should keep their cards disclosed on their hand). "We play it our own way", Jamie says, without looking up.

"We play it our own way" could be a motto for how 5-year-old children play games with rules while in early care. The example is of a card game played by the children's own local interpretation of the rules; and its outcome involves both chance and mastery. The example also reflects their community as friends, a community where not all belong (Miles), and the devotion or seriousness ("Stop fooling around") and the urge to be silly (the cards "kissing" one another, and the boys giggling) join forces when the willingness to play and enjoyment of playing by the rules unite them. This, despite the fact that they are playing rules designed for a different game (Memory). Let us take a closer look at the way children's play with rules is conceived in the current debate and use that as an entry point to analyze a particular case study of the same boys we saw playing Buck, when they play another game, that of soccer. In this analysis, I engage the question of what is it that motivates gaming and what are the rules about? This analysis reveals that when pre-schoolers play a game like soccer, they are playing more than gaming. This reflects a developmental feature of their way of being as 5-year-olds. However, they are also playing with their social existence and identities as members of a peer -group and this is the context to the game, which saturates its engagement, just like we find it among older children. This motivational structure also is reflected in the dominant moods and modes of experiencing of the game: that of tension, combined sometimes with euphoria and devotion (Karoff, 2013).

Play Rules in Piaget's Theory

Piaget is perhaps the most cited developmental scholar when it concerns children's play with rules. Although he studied only very few forms of games, he explicitly addressed children's gaming with rules and provided a theoretically consistent explanation for its occurrence and dominance in middle childhood and onwards (Piaget, 1951, 1976). In Piaget's understanding children's play mainly serves them emotionally, and he denies playing any crucial role for intellectual development (Lillard, 2015). Pretence play in young children is rather seen as a manifestation of the concrete operational thinker, when failing to adapt to reality and instead assimilating her or his surroundings to fit her or his needs and desires – hence the emotional function of play (Piaget, 1951). Consistent with this idea, Piagetian thinking suggests that when the mental development of the child reaches the concrete operational stage, the child outgrows pretence play and instead is more motivated by the intellectual challenges provided by games with increasingly complex rules. Piaget's classical studies of children's play with rules thus investigate whether or not the games' rules are followed correctly; how exactly they are articulated and practiced is regarded as mirroring the child's cognitive reasoning and level of understanding.

Piaget recognized that children create their own games and construct their own rules for them. He called these informal games – and he also noted that even though a game always generates a winner, it is the social participation of the game and the joy of challenging oneself through obeying the rules that motivate the players (Baines & Blatchford, 2011). However, as children's activities reflect their mental development, games with rules attracting children reflect a developmental process toward greater and more independent appreciation of abstract, consensual rules that function in a proscriptive and prescriptive way (also in informal, self-made games). The rules in Piagetian terminology are principally unnegotiable, a kind of dogma that is supposed to be followed in the same way, from game to game, and applied to all the participating players, as we expect it to be the case in advanced games and proper sport activities.

Play Rules According to Vygotsky's Theory

Unlike Piaget, who saw games with rules as the third and final category of play in the course of the child's mental development, Vygotsky never devoted any particular attention to children's games or play with rules. Vygotsky solely studied and theorized children's symbolic or pretence play. Seen in this light it may seem odd to draw on a Vygotskian conceptual framework when aiming at theorizing children's games in early care. One of the reasons for engaging Vygotsky's play theory is that it (like Piaget's) is part of a more comprehensive theory of child development, one that is highly sensitive to the institutional, relational, ecological, and emotional aspects of the developing child's participation in the cultural and historically formed everyday life activities. Vygotsky argued persuasively that playing involves both rules and imaginary situations, and this characteristic exactly fits with how pre-schoolers typically play (Vygotsky, 1933). In Vygotsky's view, separate categories for pretence play and games with rules are meaningful only to the extent that they denote different forms of play activities, cultivated also in particular institutional settings and traditions – they are not meaningfully separated because pretence play is free from rules, and games with rules are free from imaginary situations.

A Vygotskian perspective encourages a scalar approach, pinpointing the relative dominance of either pretence or rules in particular play forms

(Vygotsky, 1933; Winther-Lindqvist, 2009). In pretend play, the manifest imaginary situation predominates and the rules by which role enactments are performed are latent and guide behaviours only implicitly. In playing games, we find an opposite situation: the rules are manifest, explicit, and dominate in discussions, negotiations, and performances, and the imaginary situation recedes to a subordinate position (Duncan & Tarulli, 2003).

Another important aspect of Vygotsky's view on play is that it may be best understood with reference to its motive rather than with its fun value or pleasantness. In most experiential accounts, attempting to define play (e.g., its joyfulness, pleasantness, or positive affect) is mentioned as crucial, yet Vygotsky is aware of the wide range of experiences that play can generate and mentions losing a game and performing badly in games as examples. This brings us to the core of the approach suggested in this chapter. Children's gaming is a challenging activity and, in addition to the excitement of the undetermined outcome of the game and each one's mastering of the tasks, the game and playing by the rules is about social existence in a peer group. By analyzing children's real-life playing – in this case games with rules – from a phenomenological-analytic position, we may create a deeper understanding of the motivational structure in playing games with rules and thereby also gain a deeper understanding of its multifaceted role and function in the personal development of the child.

Children's Games with Rules in Real Life

In the 1960s and 1970s, a new sociocultural (anthropological and sociological) tradition within play studies took form (Malaby, 2009). The Opies' (1976) famous studies of children's games in the street and playground was a hallmark in this play-study tradition. Schwartzman's seminal studies of children's playing also illustrates this interest in children as cultural actors, by analyzing the social function and social character of children's real-life play world (Schwartzman, 1976, 1978, 1979). Schwartzman suggested that children's play can be read as text (the actual play episode) within a context (the social reality of the children). She argued that children also play with their social status and interpersonal influence in their play, and thus she seems to have kickstarted a new way of understanding and studying play, not only with respect to the developmental functions, but in its inherent social meaning within a peer group.

This approach reflects a general childhood sociological critique of developmental psychology as studying children as 'unfinished adults' rather than as beings in their own right. The otherwise dominant functional-developmental perspective on children and their play has been called "a progressive rhetoric" (Sutton-Smith, 1997) and a "doctrine of individualism" (Harré, 1986) and is thus criticized for overemphasizing "the tasks of describing the child's developmental process of growing into an adult at the expense of the direct consideration of what the events of everyday life look like in childhood" (Corsaro, 1981, p. 209; 1990, p. 11).

Unlike many developmental theories and studies of children's playing at that time, Schwartzman explored the meaning making that children produce through their play in everyday life, and she described in ethnographic detail the 'rules' they play by. This more sociological and anthropological tradition toward the study of children's play has revealed how children in fact play their games in their natural settings, and stresses negotiation and ambiguity of rules and their implicit character as culturally and socially generative (Hughes, 1991, 1995). This particular take on rules is inspired by scholars who regard all social life and human cultural interaction as governed by and shaped by more or less implicit social rules (Garfinkel, 1967; Geertz, 1976; Goffman, 1969, 1974; Harré, 1977; Mead, 1934).

The notion of rules as meaningful and productive sociocultural practices is consistent with Vygotsky's descriptions of rules as they appear in children's play: there are rules for how to behave as a sister, as a mother, as a prince, etc. Vygotskian rules denote behaviours that are rendered legitimate and meaningful because they are practised within a particular cultural frame of understanding, in accordance with a certain set of expectations, and in that sense Vygotsky's concept of rules resembles more a concept of norms than formal explicit rules. The rules of different play roles and practices and their relevant interconnections function as appropriation of cultural practices and are guiding behaviours, working much more fluidly and unpredictably than from a rational calculus. Rules in this understanding are flexible and negotiable and are not suitable as markers of winners or losers directly.

One of the many advantages of studying children's playing and gaming in real-life contexts is that it serves as a correction to some of the myths regarding children's play, such as that play is unproductive (certainly not socially) or necessarily fun (far from it when you or your team loses or you fall out with a friend over a dispute). In that way, developmental psychologists can learn a lot from the research conducted in the sociological and anthropological play studies; however, taking children's real-life concerns and here-and-now experiences seriously does not necessarily *exclude* a developmental perspective, nor does it necessarily reproduce a doctrine of individualism. In the following I will attempt an analysis that is both developmental and socioculturally sensitive to the qualities and meaning of existence in childhood; this requires operating on a holistic, personal level of analysis, also called a wholeness approach to development (Bang, 2008; Hedegaard, 2008, 2012).

Rules of the Game and Rules for Rules

Within the sociocultural tradition, Hughes (1991) suggests a way of understanding children's games as a framework in which the entire play episode (not the game per se) is the unit of analysis. She finds it necessary to supplement the *rules of the game*, the explicit rules that for instance Piaget took as point of departure, with *rules of the social context* and higher-order gaming rules: *rules for rules*. The explicit rules are those defining the identity of the game, whereas the rules of the social context and rules for rules rather reflect the institutional setting or context for the game and the particular relationships among the players. Hughes argues that the 'rules for rules' denote when and how what rules are to be followed and why in concrete situations. In other words, the meanings on which they rest need to be negotiated on the spot and they mediate between the rules of the game and the social rules. The different forms of rules may be illustrated with an example from my field notes:

> A group of boys are planning their game of soccer and remind themselves that there need to be an equal number of players on each team (explicit rule of the game), but as they start playing another boy turns up and wants to join. He is allowed to play (rule of the social context), because that particular boy is a friend, and therefore the children operate in relation to a more fundamental rule in the children's peer culture, i.e. that you do not exclude a friend from an ongoing play activity (rules for rules) even when, as in this case, an explicit game rule is violated.

There is thus a strong local and contextual feel to how children make use of and practice their games. Hughes argues that we need to take all these kinds of rules into consideration in order to gain greater insight into the meaning and function of gaming among children in their relevant contexts and everyday lives. It is toward these micro-genetic processes of negotiation of rules and identities that we turn next, when analyzing an excerpt from my most comprehensive ethnographic field study of play in Danish early care, conducted in 2006.

Method and Context of Study

In Danish early child care, the children are allowed to play frequently and uninterruptedly during the day. What they play and how much they play reflect to a large extent local tradition and not least ecological-contextual factors. In a recent practice research study that I conducted in seven different day-care centres, there was not a single example of soccer playing among the children. I suspect this reflects, at least partly, that none of the playground facilities and outdoor spaces really afforded this particular game. In contrast, in the early care centre to which we now turn, a group of 5-year-old children not only played soccer frequently, but they played daily, and in the summer most of their time outside was devoted to this game. The material theorized here is based on field observations of these soccer matches among a particular group of boys (and occasionally two girls) playing unsupervised in early child care during 3 months. Fifteen matches were of a minimum length of 15 minutes and of observational quality to be included for further analysis.

The Star Players

Jamie, Ollie, Andy, and Fred are best friends who always want to play on the same team together, but usually cannot because the teams get lopsided and unfair. Jamie and Andy lead in making the teams. Jamie is king of the soccer ground and the boys agree that Jamie is the best player, followed by Fred and Andy. Ollie is the least good at playing among the best players, and he and Andy are the most likely to sometimes play on the other team or act in the role of referee.

The Ordinary Players

Jules, Phillip, Nicky, Noah, and Alex never lead in the making of teams; they are active in debating which rules count, when, and how, but their words never count as the final say. When they are placed alone on the same team, the game usually breaks down quickly, as it is too uneven, so Andy or Ollie always somehow ends up among the ordinary players at some point.

Disenfranchised Players

Cecille and Camille are twin girls who are among the best ball players (in adult opinion), but among the soccer boys they are denied identity as soccer players. They are allowed in only when they get a hold of the ball first, because there is only one ball and one field, so for that reason we sometimes see Jules or Jamie and Cecille racing from lunch in order to be the one to get hand of the ball. If Cecille succeeds, she and Camille can play; otherwise, they are kept off the field by the boys. The girls on the field represent the inappropriate others – they disturb the narrative discursive expectations held by the boys about soccer players and are thus demonstrating the norm by being different from it (Staunæs, 2006). They make visible the norm of masculinity associated with soccer culture in general, and only when an adult participates and decides on rules are the girls included.

Field Notes

It is muddy as the snow is melting. Camille has a hold of the ball and she and Cecille are on the same team – the boys all try to negotiate to join Jamie's other team as none of them wish to be on the same team as the girls. Finally, they settle on teams and Alex is the referee. He starts the game and warns: don't kick it over the fence. Jamie sets out and kicks the ball right over the fence. There is a silent reception in the group as this happens, due to the delay it is about to cause. Jamie looks for a moment embarrassed and frowns. Luckily, some schoolkids are nearby and they return the ball over the fence and the abruption is therefore short. Then they start again and the game is on. Soon the score is 2–2 and the teams fight for the ball. Camille scores (and I clap my hands as customary), but her goal is annulled. It doesn't count!

Jamie, Ollie, and Fred agree immediately. Noah the goal keeper wasn't watching the goal, so it doesn't count. Alex as referee confirms this decision. Camille accepts this and just continues playing the ball and has another shot at the goal and this time Noah saves it and returns it to the field. Alex wants someone else to be referee and tries to convince Ollie and Noah; he looks a bit bored by the fence. Nick is tackled and falls to the ground where he rolls around. No one really takes notice. He blames Alex for not correcting Andy who got at him, and then he leaves the field in anger. Andy and Phillip follow him, in order to encourage him to come back and join the game. He is agitated and demands a free-kick from right in front of the goal. Noah is more concerned with avoiding the ball than preventing the score and Nick scores. He yells in happy excitement and his team celebrates by cheering their victory, roaring and jumping around as they fall around each other's necks in a circle like adult players in professional matches.

Analytical Comments: Flexibility within Stability

Since antiquity, sports of various kinds have been considered crucial to character development in general and intrinsic to masculinity in particular, so games have played a central role in Western history of education; think for instance of the British public school system's cultivation of team sports as character development among pupils (Dishon, 2017). Soccer is an important part of the community in this centre, and clearly the boys identify with this soccer community, its virtues and version of masculinity. Preferred play themes and games often reflect local community values and thus underscore the cultural-historical productivity in children's playing (Fleer, 2013). The two girls in the above example share the passion for soccer, and the skills, but are denied a legitimate belonging to its community, because this social identity is intrinsically connected to being a boy in this community. Even though playing soccer is largely about kicking the ball, tackling, playing together, playing solo, and following rules, the players are not following rules in any conventional way (Lancy, 1984). Rather than following the explicit rules, they seem more occupied with creating rules that fit their world-view and local understandings of the game, themselves, and others.

I suggest (using Hughes's terminology) that children in early care are mostly occupied with rules of the social context and exploring rules for rules, in general, than they are excited about the rules of the game (the explicit formal rules). Maybe this is the case because peer-group life and relationships with peers is still rather new territory with norms, structures, and consequences rather challenging and mystical to 5-year olds. Their disputes around rules for rules (what is fair to this or that person in this situation) reflect and produce their social identities as soccer boys (as opposed to girls) and also reflect and mirror their friendship relations and social status in the group. I have identified the following common rules, which this group plays by (for further analysis of the rules and their negotiation, see Winther-Lindqvist, 2009):

1. The person who finds the ball is always allowed to play and take the lead in deciding who is to be on what team.
2. There are an equal number of players on each team (mostly).
3. If someone is hurt, the player is (mostly) compensated.
4. Red cards are given if an adult kicks a ball in the head of a child. When a child kicks a ball in the head of another child, the sanction (red or yellow card) depends on kicker and victim.
5. A score at the goal gives one point, unless someone has a persuasive argument against it (which is quite often) or if the kick of the ball is so direct/hard and thus perfect, so that the goal-keeper does not have a chance to save it.

The most consistent rule is 'flexibility within stability', i.e., that the same rules do not hold for everyone, in every situation, but that there are patterns of order, a hierarchical system, in which influence, privileges, and sanctions follow concrete persons in relatively predictable ways. The relevant roles of referee, gatekeepers, defender, and forward are negotiated among the boys, but mostly follow a pattern in which James is always in the forwarding role and Andy often ends up countering this position on the other team (and none of them is ever the referee). Central positions are those playing on James's team and Andy's. The rules are far from formulated like prescriptive rules from the beginning; they occur across time and most of them are recognized only as common consensus in action, rather than in verbal presentation. It is striking that fairness and score is a matter of dispute and negotiation, in which the situation at hand is taken into account (if the two teams are uneven in level of competence and prospects of winning, a score can be accepted because a player starts crying). Therefore, a lot of the time on the soccer ground is spent disputing and discussing opinions, rehearsing persuasion techniques, repairing and expressing hurt feelings, and reaching agreement or simply quarrelling. This practice is also evident when they negotiate the making of the teams – who is going to play on which team with whom is often a long, complicated issue and delicate debate, a dispute sometimes leading to fighting among the players. When two parties do not agree, it seems to be the person/player with the strongest alliances and most central position in the game, rather than the person with the best argument or case, who gets his way.

The match is a social event, constituting the 'soccer boys' as an entity, a group, and at the same time each boy is also constituted as a particular player and person, participating from specific positions in the boys' social hierarchy. The girls can play sometimes, but they cannot become part of the group, in this particular constellation. This is part of the ongoing social identity work that children engage in every day among their peers in early care and in the school classroom. Identifications are taken on, refused, disputed, or embraced by the players. They show a different range of influence when it comes to being active in defining the social order and the rules governing their shared play. The explicit rules of the game among these players are so fluid and negotiable that they hardly stand out as different from, or of a different category than, the social rules, or the rules-for-rules in Hughes's terminology. However, the different kinds of rules enable us to understand how playing a game like soccer takes place within a social system of relations in everyday life in ways that become intrinsic to the playing itself. To this age group, in this particular environment, what seems right and wrong, fair or cheating, is completely interwoven with their friendship and immediate concerns with one another. These concerns connect overall to the existential concern of belonging to a particular group (or making clear that some others do not belong) as a recognized member and thus connected to the social identities, relational stories, and status in the peer group among the children.

Play and Gaming as a Culturally Formed Activity with Emotional Value

In a cultural-historical perspective, children's games and playing are interpreted from a holistic understanding of the importance of play for children's development (Fleer, 2013; Hedegaard, 2012). The origin of play is social; it is a learned activity that starts through social encounters in a societal and changing historical context; and it remains an excellent way of developing intersubjectivity (Göncü, 1993). In play, Vygotsky writes, the child is always ahead of his or her normal daily activity. The play creates the zone for proximal development because in play, children can imagine what they cannot yet perform, and they adhere to constraints and regulations that they find too hard/too boring/too challenging to obey in real-life situations. This is the paradox of play according to Vygotsky (1933). Their emotional engagement and involvement in the game ensures that the child also at the same time endures and obeys the rules of the play scenario in challenging ways. To lose a game of soccer without losing face is one such challenge, also cultivated by particular cultural expectations to do with both masculinity and civilization in Western culture (Dishon, 2017). When children play, they engage general desires, like becoming an adult, becoming a star football player, becoming recognized by important others.

The Meaning of Children's Games

In many ways my empirical and theoretical work consists of a combination of classical developmental play theory (Vygotsky's theory) and the more socioanthropological approach to children's real-life games and relationships, inspired by Schwartzman and the work of Hughes and Corsaro. Soccer is about playing together in teams; it is about winning or losing (or at least keeping scores between two competing teams); it is about mastering and performing the tasks of the game well; and it is about being a soccer-BOY among the other boys and belonging to this group (or fighting to become part of it).

However, my contention is that the developmental age and situation of the playing children strongly influence how children appreciate formal prospective rules, and in that sense I agree with Piaget's observation that preschool children are not yet capable nor interested in following prospective formal rules in any systematic manner when playing on their own. In that sense, a team sport like a soccer game among 5-year-olds is in fact more recognizable as playing *with* soccer, and they are *experimenting* with games with rules, rather than actually performing those. A group of 10-year olds obeys the gaming rules more strictly and finds satisfaction in following the rules (rather than playing by their own rules). Annulling a score because someone starts crying in soccer is probably taking it too far for older children, who rather start crying when the explicit game rules are violated.

This reflects a general developmental process, where it follows that rule-governed play more or less replaces symbolic role-playing or pretend playing during middle childhood. A quick look into a schoolyard at middle school confirms this assumption. Hopscotch, hide and seek, various forms of catching and chasing games, soccer, and stickball are much more common in the school playground than in the preschool playgrounds. This may also reflect the particular time-regimes and ecological features for playing in school (in 10- to 15-minute slots in an asphalt jungle). It seems right that rules become an increasingly interesting aspect in these activities (and also the aspect with which the children discuss, negotiate, fall out, and become most agitated).

Undoubtedly, games with rules attract children and grow in significance in children's lives during the school years. But older children also find more or less subtle ways to express sympathies and aggression toward one another during their games, so the rules of rules, and how the rules are sanctioned or bended toward particular players, never cease to be relevant in actual playing. We realize this when we look deeper into what it is that the rules govern. The way rules for rules and rules of the social context are practised and negotiated in the game is about 'sore spots' in the emotional landscape of social inter-action and relational stories between children, which become of paramount importance for the children (Schousboe, 2013). When Nick is tackled and no one pays attention, his feelings are hurt and he is inclined to express his frustration. In a group of friends, he is then taken seriously and persuaded to join the game again – and given a free-kick in front of the goal, testifying to his worth to the group. In that sense he is also maintaining and strengthening his position and relationships during the game as a function of rejoining and taking part in the play.

Taking part in games and play thus is an existential project to children through which the child is exploring and continuing or changing his or her social and relational status in the peer group through the performances and negotiations the play activity provides. This is, I suggest, why games with rules attract and are so popular in peer groups from the minute children are able to perform in these games and onward, through childhood, and into adolescence and beyond.

References

Baines, E., & Blatchford, P. (2011). Children's games and playground activities in school and their role in development. In A. Pellegrini (Ed.), *The Oxford handbook of the development of play* (pp. 260–283). Oxford: Oxford University Press.

Bang, J. (2008). An environmental affordance perspective on the study of development: Artefact, social other, and self. In M. Fleer, M. Hedegaard, & J. Tudge (Eds.), *Childhood studies and the impact of globalization: Policies and practices at global and local levels* (pp. 161–181). New York: Taylor & Francis.

Bretherton, I. (1984). Representing the social world in symbolic play: Reality and fantasy. In I. Bretherton (Ed.), *Symbolic play: The development of social understanding* (pp. 3–41). New York: Academic Press.

Burghardt, G. M. (2011) Defining and recognizing play. In A. Pellegrini (Ed.), *The Oxford handbook of the development of play* (pp. 9–18). Oxford: Oxford University Press.

Caillois, R. (1961). *Man, play and games*, trans. Meyer Barash. New York: Free Press of Glencoe.

Corsaro, W. A. (1981). Friendship in the nursery school: Social organization in a peer environment. In S. R. Asher & J. M. Gottman (Eds.), *The development of children's friendships* (pp. 207–241). Cambridge: Cambridge University Press.

Corsaro, W. A. (1990). The underlife of the nursery school: Young children's social representations of adult rules. In Gerard Duveen and Barbara Lloyd (Eds.), *Social representations and the development of knowledge* (pp. 11–26). Cambridge: Cambridge University Press.

Corsaro, W. A., & Eder, D. (1990). Children's peer cultures. *Annual Review of Sociology*, *16*, 197–220.

Dishon, G. (2017). Games of character: Team sports, games, and character development in Victorian public schools, 1850–1900. *Peadagogica Historica*, *53*(4), 364–380.

Duncan, R. M., & Tarulli, D. (2003). Play as the leading activity of the preschool period: Insights from Vygotsky, Leont'ev, and Bakhtin. *Early Education and Development*, *14*(3), 271–292.

Fleer, M. (2013). *Theorising play in the early years*. Cambridge: Cambridge University Press.

Garfinkel, H. (1967). *Studies in ethnomethodology*. Englewood Cliffs, NJ: Prentice-Hall.

Geertz, C. (1976). Deep play: A description of the Balinese cockfight. In J. Bruner, A. Jolly, & K. Sylva (Eds.), *Play: Its role in development and evolution* (pp. 656–674). New York: Basic Books.

Goffman, E. (1969). *The presentation of self in everyday life.* Allen Lane, UK: Penguin Press.

Göncü, A. (1993). Development of intersubjectivity in the dyadic play of preschoolers. *Early Childhood Research Quarterly, 8,* 99–116.

Harré, R. (1977). Rules in the explanation of social behave. In P. Collett (Ed.), *Social rules and social behaviour* (pp. 28–41). Oxford: Basil Blackwell.

Harré, R. (1986). The step to social constructionism. In M. Richards & P. Light (Eds.), *Children of social worlds: Development in a social context.* (pp. 287–296). Cambridge: Polity Press.

Hedegaard, M. (2008). Developing a dialectic approach to researching children's development. In M. Hedegaard, M. Fleer, J. Bang, & P. Hviid (Eds.), *Studying children: A cultural-historical approach* (pp. 30–45). Maidenhead, UK: Open University Press.

Hedegaard, M. (2012). Analyzing children's learning and development in everyday settings from a cultural-historical wholeness approach. *Mind, Culture, and Activity, 19*(2), 127–138.

Henricks, T. (2010). Caillois' man play and games: An appreciation and evaluation. *American Journal of Play, 3*(2), 157–185.

Hughes, L. (1991). A conceptual framework for the study of children's gaming. *Play & Culture, 4,* 284–301.

Hughes, L. (1995). Children's games and gaming. In B. Sutton-Smith, J. Mechling, T. W. Johnson, & F. R. McMahon (Eds.), *Children's folklore: A source book* (pp. 93–119). New York: Garland.

Huizinga, J. (1955). *Homo ludens: A study of the play-element in culture.* Boston: Beacon Press.

Juul, J. (2005). *Half-real: Video games between real rules and fictional worlds.* Cambridge, MA: MIT Press.

Karoff, H. (2013). Play practices and play moods. *International Journal of Play, 2*(2), 76–86.

Krasnor, L. R., & Pepler, D. J. (1980). The study of children's play: Some suggested future directions. In K. Rubin (Ed.), *Children's play* (pp. 85–95). San Francisco, CA: Jossey Bass.

Lancy, D. F. (1984). Play in anthropological perspective. In P. K. Smith (Ed.), *Play in animals and humans* (pp. 295–303). Oxford: Basil Blackwell.

Lastowka, G. (2009). Rules of play. *Games & Culture, 4*(4), 379–395.

Lillard, A. (2015). The development of play. In R. Lerner (Ed.), *Handbook of child psychology and developmental science*, vol. 2: *Cognitive processes* (7th edn.) (pp. 425–468). New York: Wiley.

Malaby, T. (2009). Anthropology and play: The contours of playful experience. *New Literary History, 40,* 205–218.

Mead, G. H. (1934). *Mind, self, and society: From the standpoint of a social behaviorist.* Chicago, IL: University of Chicago Press.

Opie, P., & Opie, I. (1976). Street games: Counting-out and chasing. In J. S. Bruner, A. Jolly, & K. Sylva (Eds.), *Play: Its role in development and evolution* (pp. 394–412). London: Penguin Books.

Piaget, J. (1951). *Play, dreams and imitation in childhood.* New York: W. W. Norton.

Piaget, J. (1976). Mastery play. In J. S. Bruner, A. Jolly, & K. Sylva (Eds.), *Play: Its role in development and evolution* (pp. 166–172). London: Penguin Books.

Schousboe, I. (2013). Cultural and historical influences on children's play. In I. Schousboe & D. Winther-Lindqvist (Eds.), *Children's play and development: Cultural-historical perspectives* (pp. 215–231). Dordrecht: Springer.

Schousboe, I., & Winther-Lindqvist, D. (2013). Children's play and development. In I. Schousboe & D. Winther-Lindqvist (Eds.), *Children's play and development: Cultural-historical perspectives* (pp. 1–13). Dordrecht; Springer.

Schwartzman, H. (1976). The anthropological study of children's play. *Annual Review of Anthropology, 5*, 289–328.

Schwartzman, H. (1978). *Transformations: The anthropology of children's play.* New York: Plenum Press.

Schwartzman, H. (1979). The sociocultural context of play. In B. Sutton-Smith (Ed.), *Play and learning* (pp. 239–269). New York: Gardner Press.

Staunæs, D. (2006). Mangfoldighedens Zombier og Kloner. *Psyke & Logos, 27*, 681–699.

Sutton-Smith, B. (1997). *The ambiguity of play.* Cambridge, MA: Harvard University Press.

Tulloch, R. (2014). The construction of play rules, restrictions, and the repressive hypothesis. *Games and Culture, 9*(5), 335–350.

Vygotsky, L. S. (1933). *Play and its role in the mental development of the child.* Available at www.marxists.org/archive/vygotsky/works/19333/play.htm.

Winther-Lindqvist, D. (2009). Game playing: Negotiating rules and identities. *American Journal of Play, 2*(1), 60–84.

Winther-Lindqvist, D. (2013). Playing with social identities: Play in the everyday life of a peer-group in day care. In I. Schousboe & D. Winther-Lindqvist (Eds.), *Children's play and development: Cultural-historical perspectives* (pp. 29–55). Dordrecht: Springer.

Winther-Lindqvist, D. (2017). The role of play in Danish child care. In C. Ringsmose & G. Kragh-Müller (Eds.), *Nordic social pedagogical approach to early years* (pp. 95–115). Dordrecht: Springer.

14 Troublesome Binaries

Play and Learning on Screen and Off

Fiona Scott

This chapter explores the relationship between digital technology and the development of play in early childhood. It begins by drawing attention to two points associated with its title. First, 'play' is a contested term, found at the centre of contemporary public discourses about children and childhood. Theorists in diverse disciplines have described play differently, coming to very different conclusions about its nature (Gordon, 2009). A core divide concerns the definition and perceived purposes of play. Developmental psychology traditionally provides rich frameworks for understanding the development of play in humans. Many of our foundational (Western) play theories emerge from the work of psychologists, including Bruner (1983), Erikson (1963), Freud (1917/1956), Piaget (1945), and Vygotsky (1967, 1978). The psychological study of play has provided abundant evidence of the importance of play for children's cognitive, physical, and social development (Gleave & Cole-Hamilton, 2012). Perhaps consequently, emerging studies of children's play with digital media have been dominated by a focus on the educative value of these engagements (Edwards, 2013).

In this chapter, I argue that within the study of early childhood, which I define inclusively as 0–8 years (Farrell et al., 2015), a focus on play should not be limited to a single disciplinary tradition. I argue that the framing of play solely in association with education is not adequate when exploring young children's engagements with digital media. I suggest it is problematic to reduce play only to specific educational functions or to judge its value solely by learning and development. I take a broad approach that values the different ways in which play is understood in a range of disciplinary contexts. Play serves a diverse variety of functions for young children that may or may not fall within the confines of the term 'learning', some examples being identity formation, emotional stimulation and fulfilment, cultural sustenance, and contributing to broader quality of life.

Second, I have intentionally avoided the moniker 'digital play' in the title to draw attention to another tension. Inevitably, research in relation to digital media has tended to focus on the play that occurs in *direct* relation to digital technology. I argue that play with digital media encompasses both play directly *with* a wide range of digital devices and texts and play that draws on digital devices and/or texts as resources (play 'on screen and off'). My rationale for this broader definition is that it is increasingly difficult to separate digital and non-digital (or 'traditional') play in terms of the role they play in young children's lives (Marsh et al., 2016).

In contrast with (and perhaps in reaction to) the binary construction of traditional versus digital play, it is becoming more common to see it argued that digital play *can* serve traditionally educative purposes, if it is explicitly designed with specific learning outcomes in mind (Paraskeva et al., 2010). We must again be aware not to judge the value of all play by its measurable or formally educational functions. Focusing solely on intentionally educative digital technology or media texts or their use in formal learning contexts runs the risk of ignoring or failing to fully value the broader range of important functions that play might fulfil. Accordingly, this chapter adopts a dynamic working definition of the term 'learning', covering playful interactions with digital technologies, digital texts, and the broader range of playful practices and contexts (social, material, and physical) relating to the digital, in a range of home, community, and formally educative contexts.

I begin by reflecting on how traditional developmental theories have been used to understand the development of play in relation to digital technologies. With an awareness of the fluidity in the boundaries between academic fields of study, I then turn to a variety of alternative disciplinary approaches to consider if, and how, they alter or enhance our understanding of children's developing play with digital technologies.

Developmental Perspectives on Play and Digital Devices

The historical relationship between the discipline of developmental psychology and play with digital technology has not always been an easy one. Ever since digital technologies became a part of the human experience, developmental psychologists have attempted to make sense of children's interactions with them. Historically, a large part of this research has fallen into what some have defined as "media effects research" (Bickham et al., 2016, p. 191). This category aims to understand children's relationships with media texts and devices by anticipating (or designing experiments to measure) the so-called effects of their exposure. This approach developed alongside and in the model of influential contemporaneous theories of social learning (Bandura & Huston, 1961), which suggested that children learn social behaviours like aggression through a process of observing, encoding, and repeating the behaviour of others. Taking their cues from this imitative model, the earliest studies characterized children's engagement with television as passive in contrast to the active participation children take in play, thus developing motor and social skills (Riley et al., 1949). From the outset, then, children's assumed passivity distanced digital engagement from traditional conceptions of what it meant to play.

It was not until Piagetian notions of assimilation and accommodation gained traction (Flavell, 1963) that research began to conceptualize the child television audience as more active, although contemporaneous studies still characterized children's engagement with television as "more or less active", depending on the content of the program (Fowles & Voyat, 1974, p. 69). By the 1970s, the ideas of Bronfenbrenner and Vygotsky were beginning to gain authority in the Western psychological community. Bronfenbrenner's ecological model of human development (1979) drew attention to the system of interdependent environments that exert an influence (directly and indirectly) on children's lived experiences. Vygotsky's sociocultural-cognitive theory (1978) conceptualized children's developmental processes in a way that is more useful for understanding children's relationship to television and other digital devices as a form of play, since it acknowledges the importance of social and cultural factors. However, Vygotsky's theory has still not been widely applied to the study of children and the media, especially the concepts of scaffolding and the zone of proximal development (Scheibe, 2007). Wartella et al.'s (2016) review confirms that research has continued to focus on the immediate impact of media use on children's development in areas such as cognition, executive functioning, social-emotional learning, and behaviour.

Van de Voort and Valkenburg's (1994) review highlighted some debates on play and television within the developmental literature. The authors drew multiple, nuanced conclusions. Although they pointed out that one impact of television is a reduction in the total time preschool children spend playing (the displacement hypothesis), they also drew attention to studies that complicate what this oft-cited correlation might mean. These studies contribute to collapsing the unhelpful binary construction of children's digital engagement as somehow other than play, pointing out, first, that time in front of the television can also be time spent in play – i.e., the two are neither binary opposites nor mutually exclusive (Reid & Frazer, 1980) – and, second, that television and other media content is used by children in fantasy play both during and after viewing (James & McCain, 1982). Both points have been more recently demonstrated with regard to a range of digital devices (Scott, 2016).

Arguably, the nuanced debates that Van de Voort and Valkenburg (1994) drew attention to in the 1990s warrant even greater consideration today. Digital devices and media texts are now infinitely more complex in nature than they were 20 years ago. The motion-control user interfaces (e.g., Nintendo Wii) that emerged partially in response to criticisms of the supposedly sedentary nature of digital play are themselves being superseded by moves toward virtual and augmented reality (e.g., Pokémon Go). In 2016, Ofcom reported that 55% of 3- to 4-year-olds and 67% of 5- to 7-year olds in the United Kingdom were using a tablet at home. Such platforms, alongside the increasing prevalence of transmedia texts (Kinder, 1991), blur the boundaries between so-called digital and traditional play further. Despite such developments, both the effects paradigm and the binary construction of digital engagement as somehow oppositional to play are notions that tend to reemerge from time to time in the present day.

Wartella et al. (2016) condemn a focus on the immediate impacts of media use. However, their objections are not to the effects paradigm itself, but rather to the short-term contexts within which psychologists have typically considered this impact. The authors' concluding remarks serve to reaffirm the binary opposition of digital technology and play by constructing only the latter as social and "real-world" experiences (p. 16). Any potential benefits of engagement with television, they suggest, are outweighed by a displacement effect. Many psychological studies are still unlikely to conceptualize children's engagements with digital technologies as explicitly playful. Plenty share the view of children's engagement with media texts and devices as something outside real-world imaginative play and thus both of less value and outside the social processes and practices of bonding with and learning from family. As Stephen and Plowman (2014) point out, much work continues to attend to the issue of how technology may foster or inhibit child development, rather than considering what kind of play digital platforms or texts themselves afford or how they are used socially within the context of the family.

This distancing is at odds with foundational psychological definitions of play. Gray (2009) distils the essence of play down to five characteristics. Play is (1) self-chosen and self-directed, (2) intrinsically motivated, (3) structured by mental rules, (4) imaginative, and (5) produced in an active, alert, but non-stressed frame of mind (p. 480). It is hard to deny that what children *do* with digital texts and devices maps onto many, if not all, of these criteria at different times. Part of the reluctance to conceptualize the digital as a potentially playful context may be that, although play has numerous functions that may or may not be categorized as learning, developmental psychologists have historically tended to value certain functions above others.

The notion of play as an important educational avenue can be traced back to Platonic philosophy (Morris, 1998). While the model of play as learning differs, Sutton-Smith (1997) points out that most play studies in the first half of the century were of the "normative kind" (p. 35) and concerned with assessing the developmental normalcy of children's play against predominantly Piagetian standards. There has arguably existed within much developmental literature a preoccupation with play as a specific *type* of learning. Others are quick to point out that play has a diverse variety of functions, which are each, in their own way, vital to a child's learning and development. Some examples given by Sutton-Smith (1997, pp. 219–220) include play as fate (chance, chaos, and anarchism), play as power (wilfulness, illicit play, cruel play, masks), and play as social context (bonding, intimate play, peer cultures).

Another strong theme of developmental literature relating to play is the role that social others might take in the development of children's play. Again, this interest in the social tends to relate to the notion of play as learning. In play theory, parents have long been viewed as crucial social actors, intervening positively in play to enhance its educative potential. This tradition of parental intervention continues in relation to children's interactions with the digital but is frequently reduced to mediating or limiting children's engagement (e.g., Nevski & Siibal, 2016) rather than positively scaffolding playful learning. Some examples in the latter mould do exist, however. McPake et al. (2013) employ sociocultural theory to explain how children's digital play at home is enhanced through guided interaction from an adult. Scott (2016) illustrates how multiple family members, including grandparents, scaffold children's playful learning in relation to a range of media texts.

Though we have much to learn from careful studies exploring parental interaction in children's playful learning with digital texts and devices, scholars raise warnings about the practices that have resulted from such findings (i.e., play therapy and guided play), some going as far as to say that adult intervention in children's play can contribute to the growing stresses of childhood (Sutton-Smith, 1997). There is a balance to be struck between productive parental engagement with a child's play in relation to certain (normative) learning outcomes and allowing a child the space for play to fulfil its full range of other functions. Bodrova and Leong (2010) revisit Vygotsky to explore role-play in their chapter on play and pedagogy, arguing that, with increasing pressure for formal pedagogies in early childhood classrooms, certain essential forms of play are becoming neglected, particularly solo and peer fantasy play. In this sense, rather than restricting play, digital devices and texts may provide young children with precisely the opportunities for free (uninterrupted) peer fantasy play that are increasingly missing in other realms of their lives.

Scott's (2016) vignette of young boys' role-play offers a brief insight into an ongoing fantasy world co-created by three preschool boys in the same family, based around (but not directly copied from) the TV show *The Powerpuff Girls*. Several psychologically inspired scholars talk about children's solo play with digital devices. Bird and Edwards (2015) use Vygotskian sociocultural theory to demonstrate how young children learn to use technologies as cultural tools, first by exploring the functionality of technologies through epistemic activity, and second by generating new content through ludic (playful) activity. Wartella et al. (2016) also draw on sociocultural theory to suggest that digital media texts or platforms can serve as proxies for (traditionally human) social others, providing children with the affordances necessary to scaffold their learning beyond their theoretical developmental stage. The authors acknowledge something close to playful benefits in the digital, although they avoid the term 'play' and stress that such benefits can occur only in relation to specifically "educational, developmentally appropriate media" (p. 16).

Kinder (1991) returns to Piagetian notions of assimilation and accommodation in her account of the links between television and children's self-directed play with non-specifically educational digital technology. Kinder talks about her own son, Victor, and his continual rewatching of his first favourite film, *The Empire Strikes Back*, demonstrating how Victor's rewatching process can be envisioned as a form of play. Through obsessive rewatching, Victor can bring himself ever closer to understanding via a process of assimilation and accommodation. Victor's repetitious play with *The Empire Strikes Back* is a useful moment to pause in considering children's play with digital texts and devices through a predominantly psychological lens. Kinder's Piagetian analysis of Victor's play neatly ties children's engagement with television into a broader, developmental narrative of play and cognitive development.

Though not always labelled as play, such examples are present within the corpus of psychological work. For example, the National Institute of Mental Health's (1982) review *Television and Behavior* drew on 10 years of research to conclude that children at very early ages are already demonstrating very active strategies for engaging with television, e.g., turning away from dialogue that they do not understand. Such playful interactions with television are strikingly akin to children's repetitious engagement with more traditional texts, as Simcock and DeLoache (2008) show in their study of toddlers engaging with picture books. The authors clearly articulate multiple benefits of repeated engagement with these texts, including increased participation in reading interactions, increased attention to the story, spontaneous labelling, and vocabulary development. Despite the tendency of some developmental discourses to construct play and digital engagement as opposites, children's interactions with television and a range of other digital texts and devices can be (and have been) characterized as playful, even in the most conventionally cognitive-developmental sense of the term.

More than 20 years later, Pedersen and Roswell's (2013) account of another son's Star Wars play provides an opportunity to reflect on the historical continuities and discontinuities in children's play with digital devices and texts, as well as what we mean by play and learning. Initially barred from using the Force Trainer (a Star Wars–themed headset toy relying on emergent 'brain–computer interaction' technology to bring the fictitious proposition of Jedi mind power to life), the first author's son, Blake, is nonetheless irrecoverably drawn to the object. One day, the first author finds Blake wearing the brain headset and running erratically around the garden, scared she will catch him. As the authors argue, understanding such an instance of play necessitates a shift in perspective. I thus turn to a variety of alternative disciplinary approaches to play on and off screen to consider if, and how, they alter or enhance our understanding of children's developing play in relation to digital devices and texts.

Sociological Approaches to Children's Play and Digital Devices

One prominent discourse around children's play is the idea of the child as uncorrupted by society. Dating back to romantic notions of childhood

(Rousseau, Blake), such traditions associate the child's natural disposition with playful engagements with the outdoor environment and continue to exert an influence on societal perceptions of childhood and play (Plowman et al., 2010), not least in relation to the pioneering work of early childhood educators (e.g., Montessori). The model is problematic to the extent that it constructs children's engagements with digital texts and devices as in opposition with natural play, and thus posing a risk to children's play.

Many sociological studies have considered children's engagements with digital texts and devices in terms of socialization, e.g., tracking how television influences children's political (Atkin & Gantz, 1978) or gender role (Signorielli, 1990) socialization. This approach, largely behavioural in its methods, owes much to psychological work such as the Bobo doll study (Bandura et al., 1961), which suggested that children could acquire social behaviours (e.g., aggression) through imitation. Such theories also consider positive societal impacts, perhaps most commonly discussed in relation to *Sesame Street*'s ongoing policy of formative research and prosocial content production (Morrow, 2006). However, the media socialization paradigm again constructs children's engagement with media texts as more passive than playful. Many have criticized the lack of agency afforded to children in their engagement with media texts (Cook, 2010). Additionally, research concerning the digital world and socialization tends to focus on children's ability to become socialized to the world of adult social norms, rather than considering how interchild cultures work (Corsaro, 1979).

By contrast, the new sociology of childhood (James et al., 1998), with its focus on children's rights and an understanding of children as competent and capable agents, provides a useful challenge to discourses that demonize children's engagement with the digital. The acknowledgement that childhood itself is a cultural construct (James & Prout, 2015) reminds us that dominant values and ideas about childhood are contingent on context and are, mostly, created by adults (Hendrick, 1997). A growing body of work offers multiple examples of children's play with, and in relation to, television, video games, and tablet devices, countering the notion that this activity is somehow any less playful or that children are passive recipients of media texts, instead demonstrating their agency. Palmer (1986) details a wide range of activities that occur in relation to television while it is being watched, including performative play. Marsh (2014a) demonstrates how children import and adapt narratives, characters, and themes from computer games in their offline play.

In recent years, scholars have begun to point out some tensions with the new sociology of childhood's analyses of childhood and play, including the fact that such accounts centre explicitly around children, thus privileging human entities over other things (Rautio & Jokinen, 2016). Emergent post-structural (Deleuze & Guattari, 1987), new material (Miller, 2008), sociomaterial (Barad, 2003), and post-human (Braidotti, 2013; Prout, 2004) paradigms all provide alternative frameworks that can be used to understand children instead as part of broader assemblages, within which they are but one constituent part, alongside other bodies and material objects (digital and non-digital). As Carrington and Dowdall (2013) point out, other (non-human) things also have agency and bring with them unique social histories. Some also suggest it is inappropriate to attempt to study children at play as clearly defined entities, since they are always interconnected and defined by this intra-activity (Rautio, 2013). Despite these recent theoretical developments in the study of early childhood, reflecting on the ways in which childhood has been constructed and reconstructed still enables us to think deeply and critically about our assumptions regarding the place of play in the early years and to acknowledge and value the diversity of children's experiences.

Cultural and Media Studies

While some research on children's digital and digital-related play is written from a child-centric perspective, cultural and media scholars centre their thinking around media and culture. Their approaches trace influence, from commercial and public domains, down to the level of the child. Disciplinary boundaries are by no means clearly defined, and this intersection is a strong example of the need for interdisciplinary thinking.

Cultural and media studies provide several theoretical lenses for considering children's play on screen and off. Mass society theory is broadly concerned with critiquing the rise of mass society. The Frankfurt scholars (Adorno, Horkheimer) depict the media as a means of controlling behaviour through constant reinforcement of certain chosen ideological messages, often deemed to be linked to capitalism (Thompson, 1990). Such approaches have been widely criticized for their "supposition that media audiences could be regarded as largely undifferentiated, passive and inert masses" (Gurevitch, 1988, p. 8). The cultural expressions children exhibit in their play (from nursery rhymes to playground games) may indeed "take shape within a broader cultural framework" (Kline, 1998, p. 95). However, many protest the idea that children passively adopt any ideological positions suggested to them by the popular culture they engage with (e.g., Tobin 2000).

Grace and Tobin (1998) illustrate children resisting what they might perceive as the adult or didactic voice in media texts in their use of language, play, and games. Appadurai (1996) counters the dialogue of one-way global domination (e.g., of American culture), pointing out the flows *between* cultures. Marsh (2005) illustrates the notion of cultural hybridity and demonstrates how the mediascapes or globalized narratives of children's popular culture permeate family life; they are not simply adopted by children but are adapted into family practices, becoming significant aspects of family narratives and child identities. Challenging the paradigm of media cultures as ecologies (Bronfenbrenner, 1979; Plowman, 2016), Carrington and Dowdall (2013) propose that we consider the "polycentric landscapes of authority" (p. 213) within which even young children engage with media texts. Similarly, Buckingham and Sefton-Green (1994) suggest popular culture offers a range of symbolic resources, through which young people can make sense of their own lives.

Engaging with the broader study of culture and media allows us to think critically about media platforms and texts themselves, as well as the kinds of contexts or ecologies they provide for play, but to understand children's play within these contexts, we must also study what children *do* with them, as many media scholars have. This work highlights the importance of children's play as a form of power (critical understanding, ideological resistance). Many highlight the need for media literacy to be more embedded in curriculum (Buckingham et al., 2005). The term 'media literacy' must, however, itself be examined. An expanded definition of the term might include not only the skills needed to understand and critically evaluate media texts but also creativity, identity formation, and self-expression.

Digital Literacies and Play in Early Childhood

The study of digital literacies in early childhood is an emerging field and currently in the process of being defined and theorized (Scott & Marsh, forthcoming). An ongoing debate discusses what the terms 'digital literacy' and 'literacy' mean. Historically, literacy has been primarily associated with written language, and some (e.g., Kress, 2003) have argued that since literacy refers specifically to lettered representation, we must find another way to talk about the encoding and decoding practices used in relation to other media. Marsh (2005) characterizes digital literacies as *both* those literacy practices related to digital technologies and a much broader range of communicative practices mediated through new technologies, the latter category paying attention to the fact that young children make meaning using a variety of modes, e.g., gesture and image as well as language.

Prior to the emergence of digital literacies as a field of inquiry, children's play had already been understood as a context for early literacy development. Korat et al. (2002) point to the historic turn from Piagetian to Vygotskian models of learning as a critical moment in the academic study of play's role in literacy development. Though the associated psychological studies did consider social contexts, they also tended focus on school literacy. Many studies explored the relationships between children's use of oral language in play and "school-based literacy events" (Pellegrini & Galda, 1993, p. 168). The origins of early childhood literacy studies lie within the emerging modern discipline of psychology (Gillen & Hall, 2013), although two core developments have distanced the field from mainstream psychological study. First, literacies scholars paid increased attention to wider social contexts of children's literacy learning (families, homes, and communities). Second, they became increasingly interested in paying attention to children's multimodal literacy practices and those outside specifically print-based texts.

Literacies frameworks have tended to consider children's play in terms of skills. Green's (1988) 3D model of literacy has been used to understand its different dimensions. Research is now theorizing and investigating how young children's playful engagement with digital devices and texts fosters literacy and digital literacy development. These studies consider a broader range of social contexts and pay attention to diverse communicative practices. The frameworks used, however, have tended to maintain a focus on skills. Green and Beavis (2012) adapted Green's framework to discuss dimensions of literacy in a digital age: operational, cultural, and critical. Kazakoff (2015) offers an alternative framework for categorizing digital literacy practices in early childhood that is, again, predominantly skills-based.

Kazakoff's (2015) reference to the play afforded by digital tools in early childhood draws attention to a key debate about play. Undoubtedly, digital contexts provide opportunities for the development of children's traditional (print-based) literacy skills (Neumann & Neumann, 2015), but to what extent do digital texts and devices afford unique or *new* forms of play? Digital literacy scholars write compellingly about the specific forms of play afforded by digital games. When people learn to play video games, Gee (2003) attests, they are learning a new *literacy*. Gee affirms that print literacy alone is no longer enough to enable people to communicate effectively in contemporary society – people now need to be literate in a diverse range of semiotic domains. Video games constitute a specific semiotic domain (or group of domains); thus, the play that young children engage with in these domains necessitates a specific form (or forms) of literacy (or literacies). Steinkuehler (2010) describes gaming as a kind of narrative, constructed from the unique "verbs" (p. 61) made available within a game's design. In this sense, the field of digital literacies provides useful frameworks for understanding how certain digital contexts are unique semiotic domains that afford unique and new forms of play.

Conversely, many literacies scholars argue that digital play is not inherently dissimilar from more traditional forms of play. Marsh et al.'s adaptation of Hughes's (2002) play taxonomy illustrates how young children's play with digital devices maps onto the full range of traditional play types (symbolic play, sociodramatic play, social play). Marsh et al. (2016) hypothesize that it is not so much the *types* of play that have changed because of new digital contexts as the *nature* of play: "contemporary play draws on both the digital and non-digital properties of things and in doing so moves fluidly across boundaries of space and time in ways that were not possible in the pre-digital era" (p. 250). Arguably, children have drawn on aspects of popular culture in their play and, in turn, engaged playfully with texts throughout modern history. It is perhaps fair to say that contemporary forms of digital play represent both continuity and discontinuity in relation to the broader history of children's play. Similarly, it is important to recognize that children's digital play might encompass both play directly *with* a wide range of digital devices and texts and play that is tangentially entangled with digital texts or devices (play on screen and off).

Play is implicated in each of the dimensions of digital literacies in different ways. Arguably, criticality is born of playfulness – to produce meaningful critique, one must first understand the domain-specific rules and requirements of a text and, second, transgress them to produce a reading that goes against the author's intention. Kinder (1991) and Marsh (2014b) describe the critical agency demonstrated by very young children at home in their playful curation and reappropriation of existing media texts. Carrington and Dowdal (2013) note that children make their own meanings in their play with physical objects, despite complex commercial back stories. Several digital literacies scholars have begun to discuss the cultural literacy learning that takes place in relation to children's digital play at home (e.g., Davidson, 2009; Dezuanni et al., 2015). At the same time, studying the relationship between play and literacies also opens myriad questions, again drawing attention to the multiple troublesome binaries associated with play, learning, and the digital.

In one sense, literacy is a problematic lens for considering the development of play in children, since it inherently frames what children are doing in terms of skills. On the other, new literacies and digital literacies studies are uniquely valuable in that they help us appreciate aspects or outcomes of play beyond traditional (or 'school') learning. Indeed, these fields were historically predicated on a belief in the importance and value of skills outside school learning. Here, it becomes clear why the debate about the *meaning* of the term 'literacy' is so significant in relation to scholarly narratives of children's play. If literacy is about the development of skills only in the narrowest sense, then it is a poor framework for contemplating the importance of children's play. Though some critics argue against broadening its definition, an expanded definition of literacies helps us to account for the diverse range of functions that play serves (emotional literacy, social literacy).

Play and the Poststructural/Posthuman

The latest reviews of children's media engagement establish continuities and discontinuities in the physical and digital contexts of children's lives. Tablet use continues to rise among the youngest UK children, but at the time of writing 3- to 4-year-olds and 5- to 7-year-olds still spend more time watching television on a TV set than using any other form of media (Ofcom, 2016). Undeniably, developments in the affordances of digital devices and their levels of use is bringing about, and will continue to bring about, changes in some aspects of young children's play at home. Since even very young children now engage with media texts across multiple platforms, including tablets, computers, and smartphones, they can exert control over their viewing to an even greater extent than ever before. Where Kinder's (1991) study saw her son, Victor, play and replay *The Empire Strikes Back* using VCR technology, very young children now play out similar patterns watching, stopping, and repeating short clips via YouTube. The unique affordances of digital platforms, though, enable them to curate (Potter, 2012) and create their own digital texts (Marsh, 2014b). Toys experimenting with brain–computer interaction, meanwhile, rely on electrical activity in the brain to produce some sort of physical response in the external world (Pedersen & Rowsell, 2013). It has been argued that developmental understandings of early childhood are increasingly insufficient in such contexts (Edwards et al., 2009).

This chapter has already touched on post-human and post-structural theory in order to highlight some criticisms of the new sociology of childhood. Broadly speaking, scholars associated with post-humanism take a critical approach to long-established humanist and anthropocentric notions of society, arguing against human beings as stable, clearly defined entities. Instead, many argue, human beings exist in a state of becoming (Haraway, 2003) in relation to, and in association with, other human and non-human entities. Scholars working with notions of post-structuralism, meanwhile, present critiques of structuralism, tending to interrogate and challenge long-established binaries, such as male and female, hero and villain.

These theories offer new frameworks for understanding the roles that digital objects and texts play in children's lives. Developments in the study of the material (Miller, 2008), the post-structural (Deleuze & Guattari, 1987), and the post-human (Prout, 2004) offer perspectives on physical objects and spaces on which a new generation of scholars are beginning to draw in their explorations of children's play. Prout (2004), for example, moves beyond long-standing culture–nature debates, pointing out that digital devices, machines, and technologies are not simply nature or culture alone. They are, instead, networked arrays of natural and social associations. Many draw on Deleuze and Guattari's (1987) use of the term 'assemblage'. Carrington & Dowdall (2013) use the notion of assemblages to consider the complicated contexts within which young children play and make meaning in the modern world. They describe such contexts as "polycentric landscapes of authority" (p. 213).

Drawing on post-human notions, Rautio (2013) suggests that things (including both children and the physical materials of their play) do not exist as clearly defined, separate entities but are in fact constantly in flux. Rautio suggests that they are constantly constituted in connection with, and dependent on, their "intra-actions" (p. 397) with other things. In simple terms, Rautio is suggesting that, in their play, children change the objects they interact with and are, in turn, changed by them. Rooney (2016) finds a similar way to talk about children's relations with the world, describing how children are mutually implicated in constituting the world they exist in, alongside complex arrays of other (human and non-human) things. Marsh (2005) frames post-structuralist ideas in terms of children's identity, drawing on Holland et al.'s (2001) notion of the self-in-practice. Children's behaviour, she suggests, should be viewed as an external indicator not of a constant self, but rather of a self in the process of constructing identities, within particular sociohistorical contexts.

Researchers are currently grappling with children's play in relation to the digital through post-structural and post-human lenses. Pahl (2005) demonstrates how console games offer children the symbolic resources to explore multiple identities in a physically embodied form. Marsh (2005) shows how parents nurture their children's collection of material objects to form part of a narrative web in which that narrative can be experienced (e.g., dolls, comics, cards, or bedding). Echoing Bodrova and Leong's (2010) comments on children's fantasy play, however, Thiel (2015) strikes a note of warning, demonstrating how adult ideologies about how children ought to engage with the physical and symbolic materials of play are internalized, becoming part of the physical assemblages children carry around within their bodies into adulthood. Excessive adult intervention, she is suggesting, may impact on how children engage with both materials and discourses, thus constraining their creativity and risk-taking. Thiel coins the term "muchness" (p. 41) to describe the value of the events and practices that are allowed to happen when children play freely with limited adult intervention. While familiar themes endure, then, it is noticeable that the repertoire of perceived outcomes for children's play is broadening considerably.

Conclusion

Contemporary childhoods take place within complex and shifting global contexts, characterized by both historical continuities and discontinuities. In demonstrating the different things that can be understood about play with digital texts and devices though different lenses, I hope to draw attention to the ongoing need to consider children's play critically and from multiple disciplinary perspectives.

To more fully understand and account for the complex realities of children's play both on and off screen, we must continue to question our fundamental ideas about what play is, what it is for, and how it relates to fluid notions of learning and development. In order that informed knowledge and understanding of young children's play practices on and off screen can be developed, then, it is imperative that a diverse disciplinary range of play research continues to flourish.

References

Appadurai, A. (1996). *Modernity at large: Cultural dimensions of globalization* (vol. 1). Minneapolis: University of Minnesota Press.

Atkin, C. K., & Gantz, W. (1978). Television news and political socialization. *Public Opinion Quarterly*, *42*(2), 183–194.

Bandura, A., & Huston, A. C. (1961). Identification as a process of incidental learning. *Journal of Abnormal and Social Psychology*, *63*(2), 311–318.

Bandura, A., Ross, D., & Ross, S. A. (1961). Transmission of aggression through imitation of aggressive models. *Journal of Abnormal and Social Psychology*, *63*, 575–82.

Barad, K. (2003). Posthumanist performativity: Toward an understanding of how matter come to matter. *Signs: Journal of Women in Culture and Society*, *28*(3), 801–831.

Bickham, D. S., Kavanaugh, J. R., & Rich, M. (2016). Media effects as health research: How pediatricians have changed the study of media and child development. *Journal of Children and Media*, *10*(2), 191–199.

Bird, J., & Edwards, S. (2015). Children learning to use technologies through play: A digital play framework. *British Journal of Educational Technology*, *46*(6), 1149–1160.

Bodrova, E., & Leong, D. (2010). Revisiting Vygotskian perspectives on play and pedagogy. In S. Rogers (Ed.), *Rethinking play and pedagogy in early childhood education: Concepts, contexts and cultures* (pp. 60–73). London: Routledge.

Braidotti, R. (2013). *The posthuman*. Cambridge: Polity Press.

Bronfenbrenner, U. (1979). *The ecology of human development: Experiments by nature and design*. Cambridge, MA: Harvard University Press.

Bruner, J. (1983). Play, thought, and language. *Peabody Journal of Education*, *60*(3), 60–69.

Buckingham, D., with Banaji, S., Carr, D., Cranmer, S., & Willett, R. (2005). The media literacy of children and young people: A review of the research literature on behalf of Ofcom. Available at http://eprints.ioe.ac.uk/145/1/Buckinghammedialiteracy.pdf.

Buckingham, D., & Sefton-Green, J. (1994). *Cultural studies goes to school: Reading and teaching popular culture*. London: Taylor & Francis.

Carrington, V., & Dowdall, C. (2013). 'This is a job for hazmat guy!': Global media cultures and children's everyday lives. In K. Hall, T. Cremin, B. Comber, & L. C. Moll (Eds.) *International handbook of research on children's literacy, learning, and culture* (pp. 96–107). Chichester: Wiley-Blackwell.

Cook, D. T. (2010). Commercial enculturation: Moving beyond consumer socialization. In D. Buckingham & V. Tingstad (Eds.), *Childhood and consumer culture* (pp. 63–79). London: Palgrave Macmillan.

Corsaro, W. A. (1979). We're friends right? Children's use of access rituals in a nursery school. *Language in Society*, *8*, 315–336.

Davidson, C. (2009). Young children's engagement with digital texts and literacies in the home: Pressing matters for the teaching of English in the early years of schooling. *English Teaching: Practice & Critique*, *8*(3), 36–54.

Deleuze, G., & Guattari, F. (1987). *A thousand plateaus: Capitalism and schizophrenia* (trans. Brian Massumi). Minneapolis: University of Minnesota Press.

Dezuanni, M. L., Beavis, C., & O'Mara, J. (2015). 'Redstone is like electricity': Children's performative representations in and around Minecraft. *E-Learning and Digital Media*, *12*(2), 147–163.

Edwards, S. (2013). Digital play in the early years: A contextual response to the problem of integrating technologies and play-based pedagogies in the early childhood curriculum. *European Early Childhood Education Research Journal*, *21*, 199–212.

Edwards, S., Blaise, M., & Hammer, M. (2009). Beyond developmentalism? Early childhood teachers' understandings of multiage grouping in early childhood education and care. *Australasian Journal of Early Childhood*, *34*(4), 55–64.

Erikson, E. H. (1963). *Childhood and society* (2nd edn.) New York: Norton.

Farrell, A., Kagan, S. L., & Tisdall, E. K. M. (2015). Early childhood research: An expanding field. In A. Farrell, S. L. Kage, & K. Tidsall (Eds.), *Sage handbook of early childhood research* (pp. 485–501). London: Sage.

Flavell, J. H. (1963). *The developmental psychology of Jean Piaget*. With a foreword by Jean Piaget. Princeton, NJ: Van Nostrand.

Fowles, B. R., & Voyat, G. (1974). Piaget meets Big Bird: Is TV a passive teacher? *The Urban Review*, *7*(1), 69–80.

Freud, S. (1917/1956). *Delusion and dream*. Boston: Beacon Press.

Gee, J. P. (2003). What video games have to teach us about learning and literacy. *Computers in Entertainment*, *1*(1), 1–4.

Gillen, J., & Hall, N. (2013). The emergence of early childhood literacy. In N. Hall, J. Larson, & J. Marsh (Eds.), *Handbook of early childhood literacy* (pp. 1–12). Thousand Oaks, CA: Sage.

Gleave, J., & Cole-Hamilton, I. (2012). 'A world without play': A literature review on the effects of a lack of play on children's lives. Play England. Available at www.playengland.org.uk/media/371031/a-world-without-play-literature-review-2012.pdf.

Gordon, G. (2009) What is play? In search of a definition. In D. Kushner (Ed.), *From children to Red Hatters: Diverse images and issues of play, play and culture studies* (vol. 8, pp. 1–13). Lanham, MD: University Press of America.

Grace, D., & Tobin, J. 1998. Butt jokes and mean-teacher parodies: Video production in the elementary class-room. In D. Buckingham (Ed.), *Beyond radical pedagogy: Teaching popular culture* (pp. 42–62). London: Routledge.

Gray, P. (2009). Play as a foundation for hunter-gatherer social existence. *American Journal of Play*, *1*(4), 476–522.

Green, B. (1988). Subject-specific literacy and school learning: A focus on writing *Australian Journal of Education*, *32*(2), 156–179.

Green, B., & Beavis, C. A. (2012). *Literacy in 3D: An integrated perspective in theory and practice*. Melbourne: ACER Press.

Gurevitch, M., Bennett, T., Curran, J., & Woollacott, J. (Eds.) (1988). *Culture, society and the media*. London: Routledge.

Haraway, D. (2003). *The companion species manifesto: Dogs, people, and significant otherness*. Chicago, IL: Prickly Paradigm Press.

Hendrick, H. (1997) Constructions and reconstructions of British childhood: An interpretative survey, 1800 to the present. In A. James & A. Prout (Eds.), *Constructing and reconstructing childhood: Contemporary issues in the sociological study of childhood* (pp. 34–62). London: Routledge Falmer.

Holland, D., Lachicotte, W. S. Jr., Skinner, D., & Cain, C. (2001). *Identity and agency in cultural worlds.* Cambridge, MA: Harvard University Press.

Hughes, B. (2002). *A playworker's taxonomy of play types* (2nd edn.) London: PlayLink.

James, A., Jenks, C., & Prout, A. (1998). *Theorizing childhood.* Williston, VT: Teachers College Press.

James, A., & Prout, A. (Eds.) (2015). *Constructing and reconstructing childhood: Contemporary issues in the sociological study of childhood.* Abingdon: Routledge.

James, N. C., & McCain, T. A. (1982). Television games preschool children play: Patterns, themes and uses. *Journal of Broadcasting, 26,* 783–800.

Kazakoff, E. (2015). Technology-based literacies for young children: Digital literacy through learning to code. In K. L. Heider & M. R. Jalongo (Eds.), *Children and families in the information age: Applications of technology in early childhood* (pp. 43–60). New York: Springer.

Kinder, M. (1991). *Playing with power in movies, television, and video games: From Muppet Babies to Teenage Mutant Ninja Turtles.* Berkeley: University of California Press.

Kline, S. (1998) The making of children's culture. In H. Jenkins (Ed.), *The children's culture reader* (pp. 95–109). New York: NYU Press.

Korat, O., Bahar, E., & Snapir, M. (2002). Sociodramatic play as opportunity for literacy development: The teacher's role. *The Reading Teacher, 56*(4), 386–393.

Kress, G. (2003). *Literacy in the new media age.* Abingdon: Routledge.

Marsh, J. (Ed.) (2005). *Popular culture, new media and digital literacy in early childhood.* Abingdon: Routledge.

Marsh, J. (2014a). The relationship between online and offline play: Friendship and exclusion. In A. Burn & C. O. Richards (Eds.), *Children's games in the new media age: Childlore, media and the playground* (pp. 109–132). Surrey: Ashgate.

Marsh, J. (2014b). Purposes for literacy in children's use of the online virtual world Club Penguin. *Journal of Research in Reading, 37*(2), 179–195.

Marsh, J., Plowman, L., Yamada-Rice, D., Bishop, J., & Scott, F. (2016). Digital play: A new classification. *Early Years, 36*(3), 242–253.

McPake, J., Plowman, L., & Stephen, C. (2013). Pre-school children creating and communicating with digital technologies in the home. *British Journal of Educational Technology, 44*(3), 421–431.

Miller, D. (2008). *The comfort of things.* Cambridge: Polity Press.

Morris, S. R. (1998). No learning by coercion: Paidia and paideia in Platonic philosophy. In D. O. Fromberg & D. Bergen (Eds.), *Play from birth to twelve and beyond: Contexts, perspectives, and meanings* (pp. 109–118). New York: Garland,.

Morrow, R. W. (2006). *Sesame Street and the reform of children's television.* Baltimore, MD: Johns Hopkins University Press.

National Institute of Mental Health (1982). *Television and Behavior: Ten Years of Scientific Progress and Implications for the Eighties*, vol. I: *Summary Report*. Available at http://files.eric.ed.gov/fulltext/ED222186.pdf.

Neumann, M. M., & Neumann, D. L. (2015). The use of touch-screen tablets at home and pre-school to foster emergent literacy. *Journal of Early Childhood Literacy*, *17*(2), 203–220.

Nevski, E., & Siibak, A. (2016). The role of parents and parental mediation on 0–3-year olds' digital play with smart devices: Estonian parents' attitudes and practices. *Early Years*, *36*(3), 227–241.

Ofcom (2016). Children and parents: Media use and attitudes report. Available at www.ofcom.org.uk/__data/assets/pdf_file/0034/93976/Children-Parents-Media-Use-Attitudes-Report-2016.pdf.

Pahl, K. (2005). Narrative spaces and multiple identities. In J. Marsh (Ed.), *Popular culture, new media and digital literacy in early childhood* (pp. 126–145). London: Routledge Falmer.

Palmer, P. (1986). *The lively audience: A study of children around the TV set*. Sydney: Allen & Unwin.

Paraskeva, F., Mysirlaki, S., & Papagianni, A. (2010). Multiplayer online games as educational tools: Facing new challenges in learning. *Computers & Education*, *54*(2), 498–505.

Pedersen, I., & Rowsell, J. (2013). May the force be with you: Harnessing the power of brain–computer games. In A. Burke & J. Marsh (Eds.), *Children's virtual play worlds: Culture, learning, and participation* (pp. 118–131). New York: Peter Lang.

Pellegrini, A. D., & Galda, L. (1993). Ten years after: A reexamination of symbolic play and literacy research. *Reading Research Quarterly*, *28*, 163–175.

Piaget, J. (1945). *Play, dreams and imitation in childhood*. London: Heinemann.

Plowman, L. (2016). Rethinking context: Digital technologies and children's everyday lives. *Children's Geographies*, *14*(2), 190–202.

Plowman, L., McPake, J., & Stephen, C. (2010). The technologisation of childhood? Young children and technology in the home. *Children & Society*, *24*(1), 63–74.

Potter, J. (2012). *Digital media and learner identity: The new curatorship*. New York: Palgrave Macmillan.

Prout, A. (2004). *The future of childhood*. London: Routledge.

Rautio, P. (2013). Children who carry stones in their pockets: On autotelic material practices in everyday life. *Children's Geographies*, *11*(4), 394–408.

Rautio, P., & Jokinen, P. (2016). Children's relations to the more-than-human world beyond developmental views. In B. Evans, J. Horton, & T. Skelton (Eds.), *Play and recreation, health and wellbeing* (pp. 35–49). Singapore: Springer.

Reid, L. N., & Frazer, C. F. (1980). Television at play. *Journal of Communication*, *30*(1), 67–73.

Riley, J. W., Cantwell, F. V., & Ruttiger, K. F. (1949). Some observations on the social effects of television. *Public Opinion Quarterly*, *13*(2), 223–234.

Rooney, T. (2016). Weather worlding: Learning with the elements in early childhood. *Environmental Education Research* Online First (pp. 1–12).

Scheibe, C. (2007). Piaget and Power Rangers: What can theories of developmental psychology tell us about children and media? In S. R. Mazzarella (Ed.), *20 questions about youth and the media* (pp. 45–72). New York: Peter Lang.

Scott, F. L. (2016). Young children's digital literacy practices at home: Social, physical and classed. In I. Pereira, A. Ramos, & J. Marsh (Eds.), *The digital literacy and multimodal practices of young children: Engaging with emergent research*, Proceedings of the First Training School of Cost Action IS1410, University of Minho, Braga, Portugal, June 6–8. Available at www.shef.ac.uk/polopoly_fs/1.660127!/file/1st_TrainingSchool.pdf.

Scott, F. L., & Marsh, J. A. (forthcoming). Digital literacies in early childhood. In G. W. Noblit, N. Adams, D. Beach, K. Hytten, F. Khan, Y. Kitamura, J. Lampert, A. Luke, J. Ka Ho Mok, W. T. Pink, P. Groves Price, U. Sharma, & P. Thomson (Eds.), *The Oxford Research Encyclopedia of Education*. Oxford: Oxford University Press.

Signorielli, N. (1990). Children, television, and gender roles: Messages and impact. *Journal of Adolescent Health Care 11*(1), 50–58.

Simcock, G., & DeLoache, J. S. (2008). The effect of repetition on infants' imitation from picture books varying in iconicity. *Infancy, 13*(6), 687–697.

Steinkuehler, C. (2010). Video games and digital literacies. *Journal of Adolescent & Adult Literacy, 54*(1), 61–63.

Stephen, C., & Plowman, L. (2014). Digital play. In L. Brooker, M. Blaise, & S. Edwards (Eds.), *The SAGE handbook of play and learning in early childhood* (pp. 330–341). London: Sage.

Sutton-Smith, B. (1997). *The ambiguity of play*. Cambridge, MA: Harvard University Press.

Thiel, J. J. (2015). 'Bumblebee's in trouble!' Embodied literacies during imaginative superhero play. *Language Arts, 93*(1), 38–49.

Thompson, J. (1990). *Ideology and modern culture: Critical social theory in the era of mass communication*. Cambridge: Polity Press.

Tobin, J. J. (2000). *'Good guys don't wear hats': Children's talk about the media*. New York: Teachers College Press.

Van der Voort, T. H., & Valkenburg, P. M. (1994). Television's impact on fantasy play: A review of research. *Developmental Review, 14*(1), 27–51.

Vygotsky, L. S. (1967). Play and its role in the mental development of the child. *Soviet Psychology, 5*, 6–18.

Vygotsky, L. S. (1978). *Mind in society: The development of higher psychological processes*. Cambridge, MA: Harvard University Press.

Wartella, E., Beaudoin-Ryan, L., Blackwell, C. K., Cingel, D. P., Hurwitz, L. B., & Lauricella, A. R. (2016). What kind of adults will our children become? The impact of growing up in a media-saturated world. *Journal of Children and Media, 10*(1), 13–20.

15 Playing and Imagining across the Life Course

A Sociocultural Perspective

Jennifer A. Vadeboncoeur and Artin Göncü

Drawing on Vygotsky's (1933/1967, 1930/2004) scholarship, as well as current research that exemplifies imaginative play over the life course (Göncü & Perone, 2005; Holzman, 2009), we argue that the motive to play, imagine, and create is present across the life course in everyday activities, yet it is shaped in the relation between individuals and their sociocultural environments. From this perspective, imaginative play emerges through the *social situation of development*: the dialectical relation between an individual, a child or an adult, and his or her historical, social, and cultural environments, including developmental expectations for what individuals do and how they engage in these environments (Vygotsky, 1935/1994). Attending to the relation between individuals and their sociocultural environments moves discussions of imaginative play and playful imagining from universal statements about whether or not a particular form of play exists *in* an individual or *during* a developmental period to investigations into how essential characteristics become visible as individuals participate in, contribute to, and transform the activities afforded and constrained through their environments.

Imaginative play emerges, in part, as individuals attempt to make sense of their lived experiences, to interpret actions and events, and to predict and create their futures. This is the case not only in the lives of young children but also in the lives of older children and adults (S. Brown, 2009; Göncü & Perone, 2005; L'Abate, 2009; Perone & Göncü, 2014). We argue, however, that expectations, norms, and opportunities to participate in playing and imagining are not simply shaped by individual will, but instead are shaped by what we call a *spectrum of agency*, or the opportunities for physical and psychological action that are afforded and constrained by individuals' social situations. A spectrum of agency may vary according to living conditions, including the economic, value, and meaning structures of cultural communities, as well as their traditions of expression (for a review, see Göncü & Vadeboncoeur, 2015). Further, sociocultural expectations and norms regarding activities that make up 'childhood' and 'adulthood' shape opportunities for playing and imagining.

In this chapter, we expand the sociocultural scholarship to describe developmental possibilities that emerge from imaginative play and playful imagining in relation to the kinds of historical, social, and cultural environments that are typical of industrialized countries, including cultural trajectories shaped by participation in schools and workplaces. In the first section, we define imaginative play as a cultural activity drawing on Vygotsky's (1933/1967, 1930/2004) theory and given changing life course expectations. Then, expanding this definition, we elaborate Vygotsky's notion of the *social situation of development* to highlight opportunities for learning and developing through imaginative play and playful imagining across the life course, including social and self-understanding, representing and abstract thinking, word meaning and concept development, and self-consciousness and self-direction (Vadeboncoeur, 2017). The chapter concludes with implications for conceptualizing research on imaginative play and imagining through participation in cultural activities that vary over the course of individuals' lives.

Imaginative Play: Reconceptualizing Cultural Developmental Trajectories

In recent work, we noted the problems with several commonly held assumptions about imaginative play and argued to expand definitional criteria in future research given data and insights emerging from sociocultural research (Göncü & Vadeboncoeur, 2017). Extending our work, we elaborate a sociocultural perspective on imaginative play as grounded in Vygotsky's (1933/1967, 1930/2004) theory – including the characteristics that are essential to situate imaginative play in individuals' social situations of development – and challenge several commonly held assumptions regarding play that derive from positioning childhood and adulthood as dichotomous. Research from this perspective takes into account variations in social and cultural environments co-constructed through the participation of individuals.

Defining Imaginative Play: Challenging Assumptions

Imaginative play builds from an imaginary situation that includes roles with rules for physical and psychological action (Vygotsky, 1933/1967). The triad created by the imaginary situation, roles, and rules provides a flexible narrative structure within which participants can enact and perform a role, in a sense 'becoming' someone or something through the simultaneous creation of a world within which that role is possible (e.g., Holzman, 2009; Lindqvist, 2001, 2003). Children may feed dolls the way they remember being fed or seeing another child being fed. They may play with what 'being fed' as a social practice means, including the roles participants play, the various ways it can be performed, and how it ought or ought not to be done.

Essential to imaginative play is the separation of meaning from objects and/ or actions. Thus, the individual acts 'as if' the object is something that it is not, for example, a broomstick is not a broomstick, but rather a flying dragon. Further, as the individual gallops with the broomstick it is 'as if' he is riding and soaring on the dragon. It is this aspect of imaginative play, the separation of meaning from objects and actions, rather than others such as the desire to engage in an illusory world, that defines the mature form of play (Bodrova et al., 2013). Imposing meaning on an object, not being confined to what the object 'is' and, instead, redefining and repurposing the object as something 'other than' it is, is central for the use and creation of cultural tools and semiotics.

To this descriptive extent, there seems little difference between Vygotsky's and other theorists' view of play. After all, theorists such as Piaget (1962) and Freud (1922/1961) also wrote about imaginative play as a representational activity through which children try to make sense of their experiences. For us, the difference emerges not from the definition of imaginative play but more from the characterization of certain features of imaginative play. For example, scholars have assumed that children engage in play because it is fun and pleasurable (Freud, 1922/1961; Piaget, 1962). A corollary assumption is that it is open-ended and without goals. These are often coupled with a third assumption that play is, or ought to be, freely chosen by the child and unimpeded by adults (for reviews, see Burghardt, 2011; Lillard et al., 2013; Rubin et al., 1983).

Taken together, these theoretical assumptions regarding children's play seem to be buttressed by a cultural dichotomy common in industrialized societies that positions childhood and adulthood as diametrical poles, with childhood as the 'carefree' phase that exists prior to adulthood when responsibilities become the norm. From an *adult-centric* perspective, children's actions are often perceived as frivolous, a sign of immaturity and a phase that children must overcome and leave behind as they develop into adults. The antidote for play, a 'symptom' of childhood, is often to restrict play time and emphasize the engagement of children in tasks to prepare them for adulthood. Influenced by both cultural priorities and psychological theories, *either* the child is learning about reality *or* he is playing with 'flights of fantasy,' often opting for the latter.

A *child-centred* perspective that supports the definition of play as fun, open-ended, and free derives from an attempt to protect children from the imposition of adults who would provide too much structure to a child's day and/or too much responsibility too soon (see Elkind, 2001). This perspective values the importance of play as a childhood activity, indeed, arguing that children have a right to play (United Nations, 1989). In decontextualizing play, however, as one form of activity that children do regardless of their social and cultural context, scholars reify the separation of individuals from their environments, as well as the dichotomy between childhood play and adult work. These dichotomies, and the fragmentation of activities assumed to distinguish childhood from adulthood, are barriers to recognizing the potentially positive implications of attending to imaginative play and playful imagining over the life course and, further, contribute to an ahistorical, asocial, and acultural theorization of play.

In contrast to these characterizations of play, in Vygotsky's (1933/1967) view, while experiencing fun or pleasure in a free, open-ended activity may describe imaginative play during particular moments, it is not essential to the characterization of play. This becomes all the more clear if we remember Vygotsky's conceptualization of the motive for imaginative play: the child's desire to make possible in the illusory world of imaginative play that which is not possible to realize in her socially and culturally shaped 'real world'. That is, if a child pretends to be a doctor in her imaginative play, she does so on recognition that she cannot do so in the non-play world. Fun, pleasure, open-endedness, and freedom do not necessarily characterize this effort. The child's developing ability to create meaning for objects and/or actions does.

Thus, freedom in play emerges from contradiction – the willingness to play by the rules. Indeed, Vygotsky (1933/1967) was explicit in stating that imaginative play is guided by the rules that are embedded in the roles adopted by play participants. The scripts and narratives that co-construct the imaginary situation from moment to moment are always *both* enabling *and* constraining. This dialectic is required for interpreting objects and actions in 'given' and in 'other than given', thus, in 'new' ways. It is the imaginary situation of a magical world with flying dragons, some of whom can be tamed, that enables players to enact and speak from the position afforded by their role. The same narratives that provide the 'rules' about what is and is not consistent for the play scenario are continually renegotiated to include the 'new' in ways that make sense to the players. Imaginative play, as a flexible web of meaning, both enables and constrains; it builds on a given world to create a new world.

From a sociocultural perspective, then, playing and imagining are not flights from reality but methods for *both* establishing, practicing, and testing reality *and* learning to think and act beyond it (see Vadeboncoeur et al., 2016). Imaginative playing and imaging are opportunities to build on the given to create anew. Based on a dialectical relation between reality and imagination, Vygotsky (1930/2004) proposed four specific ways reality and imagination are intertwined, such that "imagination is not just an idle amusement, not merely an activity without consequences in reality, but rather a function essential to life" (p. 13). The *first law*, considered most important, states that imagining builds from material provided by experience, and, thus, creative activity "depends directly on the richness and variety of a person's previous experience" (p. 14). Research on creativity provides direct support for this claim. For example, John-Steiner's (2000) examination of the lives of influential artists and scientists highlighted multiple opportunities for play and creativity provided by their families during their childhoods, as well as the playful approach they took to imagining as adults.

The *second law* emphasizes the extent to which experience itself draws on imagination. Whether reading the news to learn about an event, studying mathematics and history, or listening to a story of a friend's experience, in each case our experience is based on imagining. The strongest support for this claim can be found in Vygotsky's (1933/1967) own discussion of imaginative play serving as a *zone of proximal development* enabling children to use their evolving ideas to experiment with objects and movement, test hypotheses about life, and innovate alternative ways to perform roles and engage in actions that are not currently available to them. For example, when children declare that they are mothers in their play, they use emerging scripts and narratives of 'what mothers do and say' to guide their action and, in the process, explore the role, what it requires, and what is recognized as 'motherly' and 'not motherly' by their play partners. Through these experiences they learn both what is and what is not action that defines the roles of mothers, not universally, but rather in their particular social and cultural environment. This role becomes saturated with new meanings if and when they become parents.

The *third law* emphasizes the affective foundation for the relation between imagining and reality in all experience. In imaginative play, as in the imagination required to extend ourselves into novels, theatre productions, and music, emotions emerge that are felt as deeply and 'really' as emotions in response to 'real life'. Vygotsky's (1930/2004) attention to the unity of affect and cognition is evident in the development of intersubjectivity and attachment through play and the importance of affective attunement between play participants, including children, parents, and teachers (Göncü et al., 2010). More generally, individual differences in responses to life events are, in part, based on the interpretations and meanings that are constructed (see Vadeboncoeur & Collie, 2013). As we discuss in the next part, consideration of such individual differences from a sociocultural perspective enables us to propose a *spectrum of agency* in opportunities for imaginative play that varies over the course of individual's lives.

The *fourth law* highlights the intersection of the imagined and the real in creating, for example, a process, a product, and/or a practice that exists in the world, that is shared and circulated, and that may affect others. Thus, imagining is related to material conditions and has potential material effects. Evidence for this claim can be found both in our quotidian lives in such things as the rapid creation of new technologies and in art and literature that has been in existence for millennia and, indeed, in the production of cultures more generally. Yet Vygotsky (1930/2004) moved beyond the obvious examples of 'crystallized imagination' in the creative arts to advance the idea that creative acts occur "regardless of whether what is created is a physical object or some mental or emotional construct that lives within the person who created it and is known only to him" (p. 7). From this perspective, imagining is a foundational psychological function that is necessary for human and cultural existence, rather than ancillary (see Peleprat & Cole, 2011). Indeed, we learn what is real, in part, by learning what is not; we use pretence to complement and better understand our own lived experiences. The significance of pretence as a method for understanding reality is supported by research that provides evidence for infants' recognition of the difference between reality and pretence (Gopnik & Walker, 2013), as well as children's (Morison & Gardner, 1978).

In summary, in theoretically locating our definition of imaginative play in Vygotsky's (1933/1967) scholarship and establishing as essential characteristics the separation of meaning from object and action, we challenge several assumptions in the literature with three significant implications. First, the separation of meaning from object and/or action characterizes imaginative play; it may not necessarily be fun, open ended, or free. Second, the separation of meaning from object and/or action may also occur in activities that look both similar to and different from play, for example, in activities and exchanges that support the socialization of children and adults (Fink, 2016; Haight et al., 1999; Roopnarine & Davidson, 2015). Third, in parallel to the child holding her teddy to perform the role of 'mommy', an adult engaging in an improv game may hold a banana to his ear to perform the role of someone 'talking on the phone' (Perone, 2011). What is essential in both cases is the separation of meaning from objects and actions that is exemplified as the child acts toward the teddy 'as if' a 'real' baby and the adult utilizes the banana 'as if' a 'real' phone. The dichotomies that have shaped research into playing and imagining – including childhood vs. adulthood, play vs. work, imagination vs. reality – are not suited to the complex process of human development and change over the life course. As Sutton-Smith (1979) famously argued, "the opposite of play ... is not work ... it is depression" (p. 198).

Elaborating Social Situations: Change over the Life Course

Vygotsky (1935/1994) offered the concept of *social situation of development* to describe the relation between an the relation between an individual and her historical, social, and cultural environment given her developmental history. We elaborate this to include cultural perspectives on and expectations of childhood and adulthood that children, youth, and adults grow into, such as preschool settings, K-12 schooling, post-secondary education, and work environments. These social institutions, in turn, vary on the extent to which playing and imagining is valued and/or nurtured. More specifically, cultures have various understandings of appropriate and valued developmental trajectories, as do individuals. In our view, in order to examine imaginative play as an activity over the life course, we need to consider the effects of social relationships, relations, and institutions in social situations of development to begin to see how and under what conditions imaginative play occurs and with what frequency.

Yet acknowledging these effects and the conditions they produce as a method for mapping cultural trajectories in industrial societies is only a beginning. First, while a trajectory may describe a group of individuals in general as they move from one social institution to another, many variations exist within social institutions and in the ways individuals participate in them. Second, individuals neither participate in each of these social institutions, nor do they have the same lived experiences. Lived-through experiences, or *per-ezhivanija*, are the lenses through which meanings are made and potentially, remade over time. Thus, while social institutions, and the relationships and relations that co-constitute them, offer various opportunities to separate meaning from objects and actions, to repurpose an object or an action and act 'as if' the object or action is 'otherwise', experiences are shaped by a *spectrum of agency*: the opportunities for a particular physical and psychological action, in this case imaginative play, that emerge in the relation between an individual and a particular environment. Placing agency on a spectrum highlights the ways in which historical, social, and cultural environments both afford and constrain various possibilities for playing and imagining. For example, in cultures where an oral tradition is dominant, imagination in play may occur through transformations of word meaning (e.g., teasing) in addition to trans-formations in role (e.g., adopting the role of a doctor or teacher) that are commonly seen in cultures where schooling emphasizes reading and writing (Göncü et al., 2007). As the expectations and norms for different periods of life change over time and across cultures, an individual's spectrum of agency, of potential actions, is likely to change as well (for further discussion, see Lancy, 2001).

As an example, consider variations in social relationships and relations created for and with young children (1) when they are cared for by grandpar-ents prior to kindergarten and (2) when children are placed in childcare at 1 year old and then in preschool. In addition to the meaning the child develops over the course of these experiences, these social arrangements reflect cultural variations in the roles played by adults (Roopnarine, 2011), as well as the activities at home and in childcare and the values expressed through these activities. The extent to which imaginative play is seen as a valued activity in these environments, how children engage in play and what it means to them, and how educators, including parents, caregivers, and early childcare educa-tors, link imaginative play and imagining to other activities varies as well (Berk et al., 2006; Bodrova & Leong, 2005). Further, access to social insti-tutions reflects the availability and affordability of day care, as well as national, provincial, and/or corporate parental leave policies and the social arrangements made possible given the work and professional benefits that parents may or may not receive. Social institutions that are accessed vary as do the ways that people will access them given resources, obligations, and expectations in their lives.

Both similarities and differences in an individuals' spectrum of agency continue to exist when children move into formal and variable K-12 school systems. Children and youth might attend public or private schools, schools within schools or alternative programs, or international schools. The experi-ence of schooling may differ if children attend neighbourhood schools or are bussed long distances, if teachers are supported by administrators, if teachers create equitable classrooms with their students, and if class content, size, and composition reflect a teacher's expertise or not. Cultural perspectives on the role of teachers in play, the relation between play and learning in pedagogy, and the time and resources available for play-based approaches to learning will shape opportunities for play (see on various perspectives, Paley, 2004; van Oers, 1996). Unlike learning in early childcare settings, where imaginative play is generally accepted and seen as valuable to some degree, if the particular elementary school the child attends reflects the assumptions of factory model schooling and an emphasis on efficiency, opportunities for play may be reduced over time and replaced with academic instruction and direct exposure to content area knowledge (Bodrova, 2008). This becomes the norm as children move through the grades and transition from elementary to secondary school: opportunities for imaginative play and imagining are reduced. Again, these factors shape individuals' social situations of development and matter specifically for the relative meaning the child makes of his experiences in these contexts in general, and his experiences playing and imagining in particular.

As young adults and adults, opportunities to engage in different forms of post-secondary education – such as community and vocational colleges and universities – sit alongside developmental opportunities that are shaped by professional internships, workplace learning and developing, unemployment, and retirement. For each of these, the degree of consistency between participants' expectations and the expectations and norms of social institutions may afford or constrain opportunities for playing and imagining, as will the meanings participants make of engaging in these contexts, their inclusion and/or exclusion, and the reasons for the above, such as a lack of resources, access to education, or discrimination and/or oppression. Further, cultural assumptions regarding development – for example, that it concludes in adolescence with rational thinking supplanting emotion (Inhelder & Piaget, 1958) – have led to expectations that formal operational thinking can be assumed of all adults and across all domains and that playing and imagining are less important. Research has concluded that this is not the case (e.g., Gardner, 2011; Perkins, 1992); concept development, drawing simultaneously on thinking, feeling, imagining, and creating, is grounded in contexts of use through social practices that form everyday routines (Wells, 2008). In view of this empirical research, it is plausible to expect that adults' degree of involvement in imaginative play and imagining into retirement and older adulthood will vary in relation to expectations, norms, and opportunities made available in their social situations of development.

Indeed, Vygotsky's (1935/1994) theory offers a nuanced account of the process of developing, and one that we extend over the life course. He noted:

> the very fact that the child changes in the process of development, results in a situation where the role and meaning of these environmental factors, which

> seemingly have remained unchanged, in actual fact do undergo a change, and the same environmental factors which may have one meaning and play a certain role during a given age, two years on begin to have a different meaning and to play a different role because the child has changed; in other words, the child's relation to these particular environmental factors has altered.   (Vygotsky, 1935/1994, p. 339)

Thus, a 'general rule' when studying the environments that children and, further, young people, adults, and older adults grow into is to examine the characteristics of the environment not as absolute indicators of developmental effects, but in relation to how an individual has interpreted, lived through, and made meaning of her experiences in that environment.

This perspective challenges the tendency in developmental psychology to assume universal and innate age-related changes (Kaplan, 1986) and offers, instead, a recognition that there is not one single childhood, but different childhoods shaped by cultures (Lancy, 2008; Mead, 1934; Wells, 2009). We would add in parallel that there is not one single adolescence, but adolescences and, further, adulthoods. Universalizing phases over the course of life has essentialized and excluded cultural variation, such that imaginative play may not be visible across cultures and/or may not be visible when defined ethnocentrically (Göncü & Vadeboncoeur, 2015; Göncü et al., 2009). Eschewing an ethnocentric definition of play, research into imaginative play as a cultural activity has offered a remedy to this (Gaskins, 2013; Göncü et al., 1999). Expanding this work, in what follows we begin to address how the essential features of imaginative play – the separation of meaning from objects and/or actions – may be enacted across cultures and over the course of human lives.

Playing and Imagining across the Life Course

Research inquiring into imaginative play as a cultural activity over the life course has begun to address the questions of cultural variations in play, as well as how individuals repurpose objects and enact roles as they imagine their ways into the social practices and institutions that shape their social situations of development (Gaskins, 2013; Göncü et al., 1999; Holzman, 2009). As an individual creates meaning from new experiences, interprets and reinterprets previous experiences, and imagines and anticipates possible futures, imaginative play provides a context for developing several psychological functions, including social and self-understanding, representing and abstract thinking, word meaning and concept development, and self-consciousness and self-direction (Vadeboncoeur, 2017). Our position begins with two assumptions. First, that what is essential to the definition of imaginative play is the separation of meaning from objects and actions as necessary for thinking, feeling, and acting beyond the given to create the new. This separation may be evident in a number of different kinds of activities. Second, that imaginative play, following a number of scholars, may be considered a valuable activity across the life course (Göncü & Perone, 2005; Holzman, 2009; Perone, 2011; Perone & Göncü, 2014).

Social and Self-Understanding

As caregivers introduce infants and young children to worlds around them they are engaged in narration and early forms of 'dialogue' that reflect the caregiver's perspective on both what the infant is attending to and the kinds of objects and actions that the caregiver deems valuable in a particular environment. This forms a basis for social speech, the interpretation of others' perspectives and intentions, and the development of social understanding. In addition, understanding one's self in relation to this environment, in relation to the caregiver, is "done with the help of understanding other people, understanding those around us, understanding social experience" (Vygotsky, 1930–1931/1998, p. 50). Indeed, speech and understanding are inseparable as "manifested identically in both social use of language as a means of communication and in its individual use as a means of thinking" (p. 50). The social speech we use for and with others becomes speech we use for ourselves.

In early life, it is *scripts*, ordered sequences of actions toward a goal (Nelson, 1981), and *narratives*, the recounting of events and experiences (Bruner, 1991), that give shape to life's activities. Often, these scripts and narratives, which are porous webs of meaning, lend themselves to some of the first imaginary situations for imaginative play. During infancy, the first imaginative episodes are based on the decontextualization of activities of self (e.g., pretending to drink from an empty bottle) (Fein, 1981). Later, others are incorporated into pretend sequences (e.g., pretending to feed a doll.) When children reach preschool age, imaginative episodes expand to include both lived experiences of familiar contexts (e.g., going to a doctor's office and purchasing fruit at a market) and cultural narratives, such as fairy tales and stories that explain cultural traditions and rituals.

Given the location of play in childhood and the ways in which play has been characterized as 'childish', play research in development psychology has not emphasized the examination of imaginative play beyond childhood, although adult play and symbolization have been examined in philosophy (Fink, 2016; Spariosu, 1989), anthropology (Goldman, 1998; Turner, 1967), and the performing arts (Spolin, 1963). Notions of play over the life course (L'Abate, 2009) and the importance of play and play histories throughout life (S. Brown, 2009) are shifting cultural perspectives on the potential role of play. In addition, research into whether or not imaginative play exists beyond childhood has been conducted (Perone & Göncü, 2014). In two studies, one using interviews with improv actors and the other using questionnaires with graduate students, the participants were asked to define play and imaginative play to make sure that both the researchers and the participants had shared understandings about the phenomenon. Then, based on insights from previous research and interdisciplinary literature, evidence was gathered regarding the use of pretence and imaginative play to master affectively significant experiences and the extent to which play contributed to social and self-understandings.

Both communities of adults defined play and imaginative play in a way that was consistent with the definitions provided in the developmental literature (Smith & Vollsted, 1985). Participants reported imaginative play through elementary, middle school, high school years, and during adulthood. Indeed, there was exemplary evidence that, at times, imaginative play continued into adulthood with few visible changes in its structure. For example, one improv actor reported that she continued to play with the jewellery box given to her by her mother when she was a little girl, engaging in imaginary conversations representing her experiences. Moreover, both improv actors and graduate students reported that imaginative play helped them to develop understandings about themselves and others. These included recognizing one's responses to events, developing coping skills, and organizing relationships with others. Given both the reliance of imagination on reality (Vygotsky's first law) and the reliance of reality on imagination (Vygotsky's second law), a script for playing house that is useful during early childhood play may continue to be useful during the exploration of relationships as an adult (Perone & Göncü, 2014). Coming to understand new social relationships and one's self in these relationships is a psychological function that continues to develop, thus facilitating our adjustment to and transformation of our surroundings.

Representing and Abstract Thinking

When the meaning of an object is transformed, such as when a child who is feeding a stuffed bear is playing a mommy feeding a child, the child is beginning to think and feel *as if* the meaning is not in the object, but rather that meaning can be created for an object. This is a critical moment in the development of imaginative play: an object, in this case, the bear, becomes what Vygotsky (1933/1967) called a pivot for separating the meaning of a baby from the real baby, thus radically altering the child's "relationship to reality" (p. 12). The stuffed bear is 'baby-like' enough to enable a particular child to relate to it as she imagines she would relate as mother to baby. It should be noted, however, that what makes one object similar enough to be used as another may not be obvious to an adult; the first author witnessed a 13-month-old hold a piece of toast to his ear and say, "Hello!"

Children begin experimenting with more disparate ideas over time, filling the gaps in comfortable scripts and narratives and beginning to stretch meaning with playmates. Puzzle pieces from several different wooden puzzles are thrown in a bowl as vegetables in a soup that needs to cool before eating, stirred with wooden spoons, then loudly slurped (Vadeboncoeur, 2017). Separating meaning from objects and actions becomes a pathway for substituting one object for another, a symbol or gesture for an object, and eventually a word for the same object. The same object can be represented in multiple ways, expanding options for communication and enabling decontextualization; replacing one form of context-bound communication with a form of meditational means that emerges from, but does not rely on, the context enables communicating and thinking beyond the context (Wertsch, 1985). Research provides evidence for the role of imaginative play in supporting the development of literacy (Nicolopoulou, 1997; Nicolopoulou et al., 2006; Paley, 1990, 2004) and numeracy (Ginsburg, 2006).

Our claim is that, when valued, imaginative play potentially continues to serve an expanding role during middle childhood, adolescence, and adulthood, contributing to the ongoing development of representing and abstract thinking in several ways. A similar idea is explored in the work of John-Steiner (2000) with regard to scientific and artistic creativity during adulthood. She described two observations that are relevant to our argument. First, through interviews and examinations of biographies, many notable creative people were raised in home environments that fostered play and exploration. Second, they reported approaching their craft in a playful manner, exploring combinations of possibilities in an effort to reach their goals. While we cannot claim that a playful childhood always leads to playful and creative adulthood, we can claim that imaginative play and a playful approach to exploring the world seems to contribute to abstract thinking, creating, and further development. Indeed, playing and imagining form the basis for core principles in literacy studies (Lemke & van Helden, 2015), innovative education and creative teaching (Sawyer, 1997, 2006, 2012), and K-12 teaching and learning (Goldman & Kabayadondo, 2017), as well as practices in corporate design firms (T. Brown, 2009; Kelley, 2001).

Word Meaning and Concept Development

Participation in and through the scripts and narratives of imaginative play provides flexible patterns of social speech as opportunities to use, practice, and elaborate the meanings of words. Word meaning is the beginning of the development of everyday concepts, or concepts that develop through everyday experience, and academic concepts, or concepts that develop through mediated instruction (Vygotsky, 1934/1987). Everyday concepts emerge through participation in everyday social practices, are deeply felt and concrete, and are often suitable for day-to-day existence from childhood through adulthood (Wells, 2008). Academic concepts emerge through instruction and engagement with verbal and written definitions. They tend not to be readily observable, begin as abstractions, and, ideally, become grounded in concrete experience over time; an example is the concept of 'insulation' (Fleer, 2009). The reverse is the case for everyday concepts, which begin as concrete and become abstracted over time.

Imaginative play supports word meaning and concept development through the development of intersubjectivity regarding meaning and through attending to word play, for example, making words themselves the object of inquiry, repurposing, and pretence. This process is significant as it helps children and adults develop conscious awareness of a concept. Perhaps the best example is Vygotsky's discussion of two sisters who were playing at 'being sisters'; the meaning of 'sisters' was used to shape their roles and the rules of action. Individual variations in the meaning of 'sisters' became visible as the children negotiated how to play together. The rules that define being a 'sister' were enacted, and in doing so, they became part of conscious awareness. Once raised to awareness, the concept of sister, as a social relationship, potentially becomes an object of reflection in terms of both what is general to sisters and what is unique to the participants' experiences as sisters.

In a parallel way, students in a combined grades 4–7 classroom acted out atoms and their attractive or repulsive forces when studying electricity (see Vadeboncoeur, 2017). In order to play the role of a proton and an electron, each student needed to consider his or her own positive or negative charges and whether the student with whom they were paired was positively or negatively charged. Students acted out their parts, discussed whether their actions were an accurate representation of what would happen 'really', and advised each other. The teacher developed this lesson based on the interests of her students, who were labelled with severe learning disabilities and/or attentional difficulties. Concept development was also described by Murray (2011) through the engagement of students aged 11–16 who were diagnosed as having Asperger's syndrome in play, performance, and theatre-making activities. Over the course of the year, they inquired into concepts like affective attunement, trust, playfulness, imagining, and self-belief through their performances and accomplished beyond what was expected.

Learning new concepts over the life course involves imagining oneself into knowledge domains by playing with concepts as psychological objects and/or actions of a discipline with related social practices. Playing with, improvising, and repurposing objects and/or actions – whether material or psychological – is the conceptual play of individuals of all ages: children, adolescents, adults, and older adults alike. Whether university students, writers, bakers, or mechanics, playful imagining is foundational to the conceptual work of day-to-day activities.

Self-Consciousness and Self-Direction

Imaginative play builds from and contributes to intersubjectivity, together defining the imaginary situation as it emerges over time and creating, negotiating, and agreeing to the rules required for the role one wants to play. It is for these reasons that imaginative play further supports the development of self-consciousness and self-direction (Vadeboncoeur, 2017). *Self-consciousness* emerges as the individual seeks to enact the role of a "fictitious 'I' – his role in the games and its rules" (Vygotsky, 1933/1967, p. 14). Doing so requires the development of psychological distance as a participant moves away from her self and into a role by considering how the character might think, feel, and act. *Self-direction*, intentional and creative action, is related to, but not synonymous with, self-regulation (Vadeboncoeur, 2017; see, for self-regulation, Berk et al., 2006; Bodrova et al., 2013). Both self-consciousness and self-direction emerge in two ways: first, in the shifts between being oneself, playing a role, and directing play, and, second, in agreeing to play by the rules that enable engagement in the community created by the players.

A prime example of this is seen in the negotiation of intersubjectivity in imaginative play of children, and children and adults. We know that in order for imaginative play to take place, the players need to negotiate a common agenda for their activities (Göncü, 1993). Research on the play of young children showed that proposals for imaginative play are accepted by partners only if a given proposal is meaningful for all the participants. For example, a proposal to make ratatouille will be followed only if the players think they have some idea of what it is; otherwise, it will be dropped. With agreement to pursue the proposal to make ratatouille, players build from their own ideas to negotiate differences in an effort to 'cook' a French-style vegetable stew. Evidence exists that intersubjectivity is negotiated through the use of turnabouts in which a speaker acknowledges the intention expressed in the turn of the previous speaker, and then she adds a new expectation to the dialogue in her own turn (Göncü & Kessel, 1984). For example, when a child says, "I am the mother," a turnabout following this would be something like, "Oh yes, you are, and I am the neighbour."

Interestingly, such turnabouts are called 'yes, and . . .' statements in the improv world (Perone, 2011). Indeed, an improv partner facilitates the job of her fellow performers by acknowledging their intentions (yes) and then by expanding them (and). From research with children and performers in improv training, an imaginative play episode comes to a halt when the players fail to or choose not to establish relevancy in their dialogue. In order to perform using the principle of 'yes, and . . .', participants need to collaboratively build on what is offered, without negating it, becoming consciously aware of both oneself and the direction of one's actions (see also Holzman, 2009). There exists a fine balance between self-consciousness, self-direction, and consideration for others in the world of imaginative play. However tacit, there are rules established by the roles and play dialogues both enabling and constraining each player in his or her contribution to the ever-evolving imaginary situation.

Conclusion

There is growing interest in and research on play throughout each decade of life and a developing base of literature that examines imaginative play and playful imagining across the life course. Research shows that adults participate in imaginative play; that, for some, it is a meaningful activity across the life course; and that it is shaped by cultural perspectives, expectations, norms, and opportunities to play. While the potential contributions of imaginative play to learning and developing are significant, it must be studied as a cultural activity in relation to cultural priorities and opportunities that shift over the course of individuals' lives. Taking into account cultural perspectives on imaginative play and playful imagining, along with the meanings made of playing and imagining for participants, may help to reduce the effects of cultural dichotomies that separate childhood and adulthood, play and work, and imagination and reality.

In future research, we need to better understand why participants of all ages engage in imaginative play, what participation in play means to participants, how participation shapes their lives, and how playing and playful imagining changes in individuals' social situations across the course of their lives. We need to learn more about the contributions of imaginative play in the four areas mentioned – social and self-understanding, representing and abstract thinking, word meaning and concept development, and self-consciousness and self-direction – and how different social institutions afford and constrain opportunities for imaginative play and playful imagining as valued forms of physical and psychological action. That is, we need to examine to what extent and how imaginative play and playful imagining as cultural activities are valued in different cultures – evidenced in social relationships, relations, and institutions – thus creating a spectrum of agency for participation. Further, with attention to the separation of meaning from object and action as the essential characteristic of imaginative play, it becomes possible to examine the extent to which and how this characteristic emerges in other cultural activities. Although they may vary across cultures, such activities are likely to be linked with the development of imagining and creating.

Building from a sociocultural perspective means examining imaginative play and playful imagining in the changing relations between individuals and environments over time, including both how changes are shaped by cultural variation and how developing psychological functions – in particular, imagining and creating – enable different methods of engaging in and transforming our worlds. For this reason, and with recognition that this is a particular cultural perspective, forthcoming research may contribute to an argument that expands the 'right to play' to include cultural variations of the right to imagine 'other than' and create the world anew.

References

Berk, L. E., Mann, T. D., & Ogan, A. T. (2006). Make-believe play: Wellspring for development of self-regulation. In D. G. Singer, R. M. Golinkoff, &

K. Hirsh-Pasek (Eds.), *Play=learning: How play motivates and enhances children's cognitive and social-emotional growth* (pp. 74–100). Oxford: Oxford University Press.

Bodrova, E. (2008). Make-believe play versus academic skills: A Vygotskian approach to today's dilemma of early childhood education. *European Early Childhood Education Research Journal, 16*(3), 357–369.

Bodrova, E., Gemeroth, C., & Leong, D. J. (2013). Play and self-regulation: Lessons from Vygotsky. *American Journal of Play, 6*(1), 111–123.

Bodrova, E., & Leong, D. J. (2005). High quality preschool programs: What would Vygotsky say? *Early Education and Development, 16*(4), 435–444.

Brown, S., with Vaughan, C. (2009). *Play: How it shapes the brain, opens the imagination, and invigorates the soul.* New York: Penguin Group.

Brown, T. (2009). *Change by design: How design thinking transforms organizations and inspires innovation.* New York: Harper Business.

Bruner, J. (1991). The narrative construction of reality. *Critical Inquiry, 18*, 1–21.

Burghardt, G. M. (2011). Defining and recognizing play. In A. D. Pellegrini (Ed.), *The Oxford handbook of the development of play* (pp. 9–18). Oxford: Oxford University Press.

Elkind, D. (2001). *The hurried child: Growing up too fact too soon* (3rd edn.). Cambridge, MA: Da Capo Press.

Fein, G. G. (1981). Pretend play: An integrative review. *Child Development, 52*, 1095–1118.

Fink, E. (2016). *Play as symbol of the world: And other writings.* Bloomington: Indiana University Press.

Fleer, M. (2009). Understanding the dialectical relations between everyday concepts and scientific concepts within play-based programs. *Research in Science Education, 39*(2), 281–306.

Freud, S. (1922/1961). *Beyond the pleasure principle.* New York: W. W. Norton.

Gardner, H. (2011). *The unschooled mind: How children think and how schools should teach* (2nd edn.). New York: Basic Books.

Gaskins, S. (2013). Pretend play as culturally constructed activity. In M. Taylor (Ed.), *The Oxford handbook of the development of imagination* (pp. 224–247). Oxford: Oxford University Press.

Ginsburg, H. P. (2006). Mathematical play and playful mathematics: A guide for early education. In D. G. Singer, R. M. Golinkoff, & K. Hirsh-Pasek (Eds.), *Play=learning: How play motivates and enhances children's cognitive and social-emotional growth* (pp. 145–165). Oxford: Oxford University Press.

Goldman, L. (1998). *Child's play: Myth, mimesis and make-believe.* Oxford: Berg.

Goldman, S., & Kabayadondo, Z. (2017). *Taking design thinking to school: How the technology of design can transform teachers, learners, and classrooms.* New York: Routledge.

Göncü, A. (1993). Development of intersubjectivity in social pretend play. *Human Development, 36*, 185–198.

Göncü, A., Abel, B., & Boshans, M. (2010). The role of attachment and play in young children's learning and development. In K. Littleton, C. Wood, & J. Small Staarman (Eds.), *International handbook of psychology in education* (pp. 35–72). London: Emerald Group.

Göncü, A., Jain, J., & Tuermer, U. (2007). Children's play as cultural interpretation. In A. Göncü & S. Gaskins (Eds.), *Play and development: Evolutionary, sociocultural, and functional perspectives* (pp. 155–1778). Mahwah, NJ: Erlbaum.

Göncü, A., & Kessel, F. (1984). Children's play: A contextual-functional perspective. *New Directions for Child and Adolescent Development, 25,* 5–22.

Göncü, A., Özer, S., & Ahioglu, N. (2009). Childhood in Turkey: Social class and gender differences in schooling, labor, and play. In M. Fleer, M. Hedegaard, & J. Tudge (Eds.), *The world yearbook of education 2009: Childhood studies and the impact of globalization: Policies and practices at global and local levels* (pp. 68–85). New York: Routledge.

Göncü, A., & Perone, A. (2005). Pretend play as a life-span activity. *Topoi, 24,* 137–147.

Göncü, A., Tuermer, U., Jain, J., & Johnson, D. (1999). Children's play as cultural activity. In A. Göncü (Ed.), *Children's engagement in the world: Sociocultural perspectives* (pp. 148–170). New York: Cambridge University Press.

Göncü, A., & Vadeboncoeur, J. A. (2015). Returning to play: The critical location of play in children's sociocultural lives. In S. Douglas & L. Stirling (Eds.), *Children's play, pretense, and storytelling* (pp. 294–313). New York: Routledge.

Göncü, A., & Vadeboncoeur, J. A. (2017). Expanding the definitional criteria for play: Contributions of sociocultural perspectives. *Learning and Behavior, 45,* 422–431.

Gopnik, A., & Walker, C. M. (2013). Considering counterfactuals: The relationship between causal learning and pretend play. *American Journal of Play, 6*(1), 15–28.

Haight, W. L., Wang, X.-L., Fung, H. H.-T., Williams, K., & Mintz, J. (1999). Universal, developmental, and variable aspects of young children's play: A cross-cultural comparison of pretending at home. *Child Development, 70*(6), 1477–1488.

Holzman, L. (2009). *Vygotsky at work and play.* New York: Routledge.

Inhelder B., & Piaget J. (1958). *The growth of logical thinking from childhood to adolescence* (trans. A. Parsons, S. Milgram). New York: Basic Books (originally published in 1955).

John-Steiner, V. (2000). *Creative collaboration.* Oxford: Oxford University Press.

Kaplan, B. (1986). Value presuppositions in theories of human development. In L. Cirillo & S. Wapner (Eds.), *Value presuppositions in theories of human development* (pp. 89–103). Hillsdale, NJ: Lawrence Erlbaum.

Kelley, T. (2001). *The art of innovation: Lessons in creativity from IDEO, America's leading design firm.* New York: Doubleday.

L'Abate, L. (2009). *The Praeger handbook of play across the life cycle: Fun from infancy to old age.* Westport, CT: Praeger Press.

Lancy, D. (2001). Cultural constraints on children's play. *Play and Culture Studies, 4,* 53–62.

Lancy, D. (2008). *The anthropology of childhood: Cherubs, chattel, changelings.* Cambridge, MA: Cambridge University Press.

Lemke, J., & van Helden, C. (2015). Designing action literacies for fast-changing futures. In J. Rowsell & K. Pahl (Eds.), *The Routledge handbook of literacy studies* (pp. 322–336). New York: Routledge.

Lillard, A. S., Lerner, M. D., Hopkins, E. J., Dore, R. A., Smith, E. D., & Palmquist, C. M. (2013). The impact of pretend play on children's development: A review of the evidence. *Psychological Bulletin*, *139*(1), 1–34.

Lindqvist, G. (2001). When small children play: How adults dramatise and children create meaning. *Early Years: An International Journal of Research and Development*, *21*(1), 7–14.

Lindqvist, G. (2003). Vygotsky's theory of creativity. *Creativity Research Journal*, *15*(2), 245–251.

Mead, G. H. (1934). *Mind, self, and society*. Chicago, IL: University of Chicago Press.

Morison, P., & Gardner, H. (1978). Dragons and dinosaurs: The child's capacity to differentiate fantasy from reality. *Child Development*, *49*(3), 642–648.

Murray, P. (2011). Playing with Asperger's syndrome: 'We're not supposed to be able to do this, are we?' In C. Lobman & B. E. O'Neill (Eds.), *Play and performance* (pp. 155–179). Lanham, MD: University Press of America.

Nelson, K. (1981). Social cognition in a script framework. In J. H. Flavell & L. Ross (Eds.), *Social cognitive development: Frontiers and possible futures* (pp. 97–118). New York: Cambridge University Press.

Nicolopoulou, A. (1997). Children and narratives: Toward an interpretive and sociocultural approach. In M. Bamberg (Ed.), *Narrative development: Six approaches* (pp. 179–215). Mahwah, NJ: Erlbaum.

Nicolopoulou, A., McDowell, J., & Brockmeyer, C. (2006). Narrative play and emergent literacy: Storytelling and story-acting meet journal writing. In D. G. Singer, R. M. Golinkoff, & K. Hirsh-Pasek (Eds.), *Play=learning: How play motivates and enhances children's cognitive and social-emotional growth* (pp. 124–144). Oxford: Oxford University Press.

Paley, V. G. (1990). *The boy who would be a helicopter: The uses of storytelling in the classroom*. Cambridge, MA: Harvard University Press.

Paley, V. G. (2004). *A child's work: The importance of fantasy play*. Chicago, IL: University of Chicago Press.

Peleprat, E., & Cole, M. (2011). 'Minding the gap': Imagination, creativity, and human cognition. *Integrative and Behavioral Science*, *45*, 397–418.

Perkins, D. (1992). *Smart schools: Better thinking and learning for every child*. New York: Free Press.

Perone, A. (2011). Improvising with adult English language learners. In R. K. Sawyer (Ed.), *Structure and improvisation in creative teaching* (pp. 162–183). Cambridge: Cambridge University Press.

Perone, A., & Göncü, A. (2014). Life-span pretend play in two communities. *Mind, Culture, and Activity*, *21*(3), 200–220.

Piaget, J. (1962). *Play, dreams, and imitation in childhood*. New York: W. W. Norton.

Roopnarine, J. L. (2011). Cultural variations in beliefs about play, parent–child play, and children's play: Meaning for childhood development. In A. D. Pellegrini (Ed.), *The Oxford handbook of the development of play* (pp. 19–37). Oxford: Oxford University Press.

Roopnarine, J. L., & Davidson, K. L. (2015). Parent–child play across cultures: Advancing play research. *American Journal of Play*, *7*(2), 228–252.

Rubin, K. H., Fein, G., & Vandenberg, B. (1983). Play. In E. M. Hetherington (Ed.), *Handbook of child psychology*, vol. 4: *Socialization, personality, and social development*. New York: Wiley.

Sawyer, R. K. (1997). *Pretend play as improvisation: Conversation in the preschool*. Mahwah, NJ: Lawrence Erlbaum.

Sawyer, R. K. (2006). Educating for innovation. *Thinking Skills and Creativity, 1*, 41–48.

Sawyer, R. K. (2012). *Explaining creativity: The science of human innovation* (2nd edn.). Oxford: Oxford University Press.

Smith, P. K., & Vollsted, R. (1985). On defining play: An empirical study on the relationship between play and various play criteria. *Child Development, 56*, 1042–1050.

Spariosu, M. (1989). *Dionysus reborn: Play and the aesthetic dimension in modern philosophical and scientific discourse*. Ithaca, NY: Cornell University Press.

Spolin, V. (1963). *Improvisation for the theater*. Evanston, IL: Northwestern University Press.

Sutton-Smith, B. (1979). *Play and learning*. New York: Garden Press.

Sutton-Smith, B. (1994). Does play prepare the future? In J. H. Goldstein (Ed.), *Toys, play, and development* (pp. 130–146). Cambridge: Cambridge University Press.

Turner, V. (1967). *The forest of symbols*. Ithaca, NY: Cornell University Press.

United Nations (1989). *Convention on the Rights of the Child*. Geneva. Available at www.unicef.org/crc.

Vadeboncoeur, J. A. (2017). *Vygotsky and the promise of public education*. New York: Peter Lang.

Vadeboncoeur, J. A., & Collie, R. J. (2013). Locating social and emotional learning in schooled environments: A Vygotskian perspective on learning as unified. *Mind, Culture, and Activity, 20*(3), 201–225.

Vadeboncoeur, J. A., Perone, A., & Panina-Beard, N. (2016). Creativity as a practice of freedom: Imaginative play, moral imagination, and the production of culture. In V. P. Glaveanu (Ed.), *The Palgrave handbook of creativity and culture research* (pp. 285–305). London: Palgrave Macmillan.

van Oers, B. (1996). 'Are you sure?': The promotion of mathematical thinking in the play activities of young children. *European Early Childhood Education Research Journal, 4*(1), 71–87.

Vygotsky, L. S. (1930/2004) Imagination and creativity in childhood. *Journal of Russian and East European Psychology, 42*(1), 7–97.

Vygotsky, L. S. (1930–1931/1998). Pedology of the adolescent. In *The collected works of L. S. Vygotsky*, vol. 5: *Child psychology* (ed. R. W. Rieber) (pp. 3–184). New York: Plenum Press.

Vygotsky, L. S. (1933/1967). Play and its role in the mental development of the child. *Soviet Psychology, 5*(3), 6–18.

Vygotsky, L. S. (1934/1987). Thinking and speech. In R. W. Rieber & A. S. Carton (Eds.), *The collected works of L. S. Vygotsky*, vol. 1: *Problems of general psychology, including the volume Thinking and speech* (pp. 39–285). New York: Plenum Press.

Vygotsky, L. S. (1935/1994). The problem of the environment. In R. van der Veer & J. Valsiner (Eds.), *The Vygotsky reader* (pp. 338–354). Cambridge, MA: Blackwell.

Wells, G. (2008). Learning to use scientific concepts. *Cultural Studies of Science Education, 3,* 329–350.

Wells, K. (2009). *Childhood in global perspective.* Malden, MA: Polity Press.

Wertsch, J. V. (1985). *Vygotsky and the social formation of mind.* Cambridge, MA: Harvard University Press.

PART III

Historical and Anthropological Context

16 Children at Play in Western Europe, 1500–1800

Linda Pollock

The sight and sound of children playing is an ever-present feature of modern societies. Children play even in the direst of situations: enslaved, held in death camps, or living in war zones. Today, play is generally viewed as vital for a child's healthy social and intellectual development and as an essential way of learning. The play ethos perspective holds that play is crucial to a child's overall well-being; aids in the acquisition of cognitive, social, and emotional skills; and is the basis of math and language development (Smith, 2010). The opportunity to investigate, try things out, and imagine stimulates a child's creativity and curiosity and enhances his or her ability to cope with unexpected events or outcomes (Chudacoff, 2007; Clements & Fiorentino, 2004).

Despite the importance placed on play and that the freedom to play has been enshrined as a child's right by the UN Convention on the Rights of the Child in 1989, many current-day experts believe there is a crisis of play deprivation for modern children. Video games, computers, playgrounds, unsafe urban environments, aversion to risk, and early schooling all have contributed to the regulation and restriction of play. Children are outside less frequently, and when they do venture out of the home, are usually to be found in specially designed playgrounds and parks. These play areas may be safer than city streets but they have been criticized for constricting and controlling children, denying them the chance to develop important skills, and limiting the exercise of the imagination (Heath, 2014; Whitebread et al., 2012).

Our lamentation for the loss of spontaneous, unstructured, outdoor play, however, is based on a romantic notion of play in the past: "Children's play throughout history was ... relatively free, intertwined with work, spontaneous, and set in the playgrounds of the wilderness, fields, streams, and barnyards" (Frost, 2010, p. 1). Play is enjoyable and useful for helping children learn about the world, but none of the evidence, not anthropological, evolutionary, nor historical, supports the view that free play is "essential" for appropriate human development (Smith, 2010). Different cultures and historical eras have divergent attitudes to play based on dissimilar social and economic circumstances, gender rules, religious beliefs, and concepts of childhood.

There has never been a time of completely carefree childhood for all: poverty, disease, abuse, work, chores, schooling, rules, and norms have all limited children's playtime (Chudacoff, 2007). In some pre-industrial societies today, play is viewed as being of limited value. Parents expect children to play and regard it as keeping children out of the way until they are old enough to be useful, but they do not encourage it nor generally participate in it. In societies with limited resources, children need to contribute as soon as possible, and play is often seen as incidental to the development of necessary skills (Whitebread et al., 2012). Not all cultural groups are enthusiastic about play as just play, even in technologically developed societies. Low-income parents can be sceptical about the educational benefits of play, whereas middle-class parents are more likely to endorse play as a path to learning (Roopnarine, 2011). Thus, even though much expert opinion stresses the value of unstructured play for children and decries the decreasing opportunities for it, we may be overestimating the amount of time granted this activity in the past and be overwedded to one particular form of children's recreational pursuits. Our idea of what type of play is best for children is based on our view of what a child is or should be – innocent, vulnerable, dependent, playful, and happy – but that is not the only way to define a child.

Early Modern Europe

Western Europe between 1500 and 1800 shared a relatively similar play culture (Willemsen, 2000), although, as scholars have focused on the nineteenth century, remarkably little research has been done on early modern play (Chudacoff, 2007; Corsaro, 2004). The most famous image of ordinary children playing in early modern Europe is *Children's Games*, painted by the Flemish artist Pieter Bruegel the Elder in 1560 (Figure 16.1). A large crowd of boisterous, active children ranging in age from toddlers to adolescents play outside in a town square. Similar images of children's play (Figures 16.2 and 16.3) appeared in two emblem books by Jacob Cats, Dutch poet, politician, and lawyer (Manning, 2002).

Devotional works as the books of hours often included calendars with images of children playing, usually a different game for each month. The games apparently followed a seasonal cycle: sledge riding in winter, butterfly catching in summer, playing with knuckle bones in the butchering months (Willemsen, 2005).

The creators of these images seem to have selected examples from an established repertoire of children games. Around 80 different activities have been identified in the Bruegel painting including: tug of war, blind man's bluff, leapfrog, stilt walking, performing handstands, climbing trees, marching with fife and drum or in imitation bridal and baptismal processions, rolling hoops, whipping tops, and riding barrels, fences, and hobby horses. Girls were usually engaged in different pursuits from boys: twirling their skirts by the river, tending dolls, skipping rope, or playing apothecary (Snow, 1997). These

Figure 16.1 Pieter Bruegel the Elder, *Kinderspiele,* 1560, Kunsthistorische Museum, Vienna.

Figure 16.2 Courtyard of the Dutch abbey of Middelburg in Zeeland, in Jacob Cats, *Silenus Alcibiadis, sive, Proteus vitae humanae ideam, emblemate trifariam variato, oculis subijciens.* Middelburgh: Iohannis Hellenij, 1618. Getty Research Institute, call number 297776.

images of children enjoying themselves seem to capture what we see as the essence of children's play: communal, outside, autonomous, and fun. The illustrations, though, are allegorical, representing the frailties of the world through play. Stilts, for example, symbolize pretension; kites stand for soaring ambition, which can fall; and bubbles portray transient vanity (Manning, 2002). How far do these depictions of children's games capture the actuality of children playing in early modern Europe?

Play was certainly identified with children and 'playfellow' was a frequently used synonym for a child. John Holles, Earl of Clare, for example, hoped that his pregnant sister Arabella would soon have "the cumfort of an other playfellowe

Figure 16.3 In the street near the city hall. Children's Games, by Adriaen Pietersz van de Venne, in Jacob Cats, *Houwelyck, dat is, De gansche gelegentheyt des echten staets.* Middelburgh: J. P. van de Venne, 1625. Getty Research Institute, call number PT5630.

for Will" (Holles, 1627). A child uninterested in playing was thought to be ill. The grandmother of Francis North, aged 5, was anxious because he was "out of order and not so lively nor so good a stomach, and sometimes for 3 or 4 hours in an after noone very dull and will not play" (North, 1890, p. 213). Children required time to play and things to play with. Even Martin Luther conceded "we must give children dolls and hobby horses and other toys" (Marcus, 1978, p. 79). But rather than encouraging children to play, published works usually sought to limit play. Children were warned not to play while eating at table nor while in church (S.T., 1672, images 23, 24). Parents should not "jest and sport" with their children because they would lose their authority and "must expect no more Reverence from them" (Stockton, 1672, p. 136).

Moralists, theologians, and domestic conduct book writers all stressed that children required a great deal of direction and guidance to mature into suitable adults. A German treatise on education stated: "A child is like a wild tree standing alone in a field ... Unless you graft a good nature onto its rude and wild stock it will bear you sour fruit all its life" (Strauss, 1978, p. 97). Children were "wild asses and wild heifers", "wanton and foolish" until they be "broken by education and correction" (Fletcher, 1994, p. 326). From this perspective, play wasted time: "Boys and Girls play away that Time with Drums and Babies, which they might employ to more profitable Uses" (Tryon, 1695, p. 42). Because childhood was "the only proper Season for them to learn the Rudiments of Vertue and Knowledge", parents should not "let their Children throw away that part of their Time" in frivolous pursuits (Tryon, 1695, p. 55). A hundred years later, the same message is reiterated: J. H. Swilden's alphabet book of 1781 admonished children to work hard because: "The hours fly, each in its turn. Remember this, and learn to spend them well: for none of them will ever return" (Baggerman & Dekker, 2006, p. 282). The spectre of the lazy child frittering away a time of life especially suited to the acquisition of skills and knowledge haunted early modern Europe.

All of this meant that education should begin as early as possible: "The sooner a child is put to School, the better it is, both to prevent ill habits, which are got by play and idleness, and to enure him betimes to affect learning and well doing" (Hoole, 1659, p. 2). Thus, as "soon as ever" children "have the use of any reason and speech, they should be taught some better things, and not left till they are five or six years of age to do nothing, but get a custome of wasting all their time in play" (Baxter, 1673, p. 546). And a child should not have long hours of free time. A properly reared boy in sixteenth-century Germany ought to sleep seven hours a night, say his prayers, work hard at school, read incessantly, and memorize a few verses of scriptures every day. He should go directly home without tarrying in the streets after school, using any "time remaining after your chores ... to review and reflect on what you have read at school" (Ozment, 1983, pp. 139, 140).

Even though the moralists frequently complained of parents who thought that childhood was "only a time for fun, joy, and amusement" and thus allowed their offspring to spend their days frolicking in fun (Ozment, 1983, p. 135), many parents took the published strictures to heart. Parents often reflected on their obligations toward their children and how to bring them up properly but rarely commented on the need for or the types of play a child should experience. John Taylor, an eighteenth-century English father, sought to train his children, keep them from sin, not overburden them with work, retain their love and respect, help them learn to read, talk with them, and pray with them but did not apparently strive to play with them nor include amusements in their lives (Taylor, 1820, pp. 118–120). The Taylor siblings probably had some fun but their father did not make playtime a priority. For pious parents, recreation threatened to lead offspring astray. John Banks, born in 1637, stated that with respect to his children:

> I never durst put them forward to Play ... neither could I ever suffer them to go to see or behold any Sport, Game, or Pastime, or Play, that tends to nothing but stirring up of the vain, light mind, and letting loose the wild Nature, and corrupting of Youth. (Banks, 1693, pp. 17–18)

There must have been more children like Walter Pringle, born in 1625, who recollected that he "was much indulged by my parents, and greatly given to playing" (Pollock, 1987, p. 147), but it would have been difficult for children in early modern Europe to spend most of their time at play. Play was associated with young children and was to be put aside as they grew up. Dr Thomas Knipe, master of Westminster School in 1696, was concerned enough that 8-year-old Henry Herbert preferred playing over studying to consider expelling him from school. He complained to Henry's father that:

> he has been so much a child, that when he has been called from his play to his studies, he has stood in the yard crying, and blubbering, and roaring ... because he might not play longer; when other children have gone immediately to their studies, laughing all the way to see him such a child. (Pollock, 1987, p. 148)

Lord Chesterfield wrote to his 8-year-old son Philip in Latin in 1741 telling him that because he would turn 9 the next day, this was "the last letter I shall write to you as to a little boy". Henceforth, Philip must "commence a different course of life ... childish toys and playthings must be thrown aside, and your mind directed to serious objects" (Pollock, 1987, p. 149).

Parents, in harmony with the moralists, wanted children to learn early and deplored indolence. Wealthy parents believed in the value of highly programmed days with long hours of schooling. Anne Halkett, born in 1622, noted approvingly that her mother:

> spared noe expense in educating all her children in the most suitable way to improve them ... [she] paid masters for teaching my sister and mee to write, speake French, play on the lute and virginalls, and dance and kept a gentelwoman to teach us all kinds of needlework, which shows I was not brought up in an idle life. (Halkett, 1875, p. 2)

Ralph Josselin, an English vicar, was delighted that his daughter Anne, born in 1654, went "to learne her book" at 3 years, 10 months; that another daughter Mary, born in 1658, at just over 4 years had a "towardlyness to learn" and at 4 and a half had "an aptness to her booke"; and that his eldest son, Thomas, born 1644, at 5 years, 10 months, was "of a good memory, a good speller, apt to learne, and attaine the hardest words in his bible or accidence in which he reads" (Macfarlane, 1970, p. 91). Conscientious parents ensured that their children worked hard at their lessons or in acquiring the essential skills they would need for adult life.

Play distracted children from studying hard. Balthasar Paumgartner, son of a sixteenth-century Nuremberg merchant, who had a few hours of daily Latin drills by the age of 5, worried his mother. He was an unenthusiastic student and she believed his fondness for playing in the stable was impeding his education (Ozment, 1986, p. 93). Thomas Slingsby, born in 1636 to a minor gentry family, had been taught Latin words for parts of the body and clothes before the age of 4. But then his progress slowed, because, his father thought, he enjoyed playing too much: "I find him duller to learn this year yn ye last . . . I think ye cause to be his too much minding Play, wch takes off his mind from his book" (Slingsby, 1836, pp. 53–54).

Most children in early modern Europe came from poverty-stricken families and, until the advent of compulsory schooling in the late nineteenth century, worked from a young age. In 1532, Christoph Scheurl, a lawyer in Nürnberg, hired 7-year-old Anna Scheurl to watch and rock his 6-month-old baby boy. When she died 3 years later, he employed her 7-year-old sister, Katharina (Ozment, 1999, p. 93). In September 1709, Nicholas Blundell, an English landowner, "went into Town to get some Children to come to pick the Stroke out of Wheat as is for Seed" (Blundell, 1968, p. 229). Thomas Tryon, the son of a tiler and plasterer, born in 1634, was put to work spinning and carding wool at the age of 5. He "grew so expert, that at Eight Years of Age I could Spin Four Pound a day". By the age of 10, he was a shepherd on the weekends and got his own flock to watch about the age of 13 (Tryon, 1695, pp. 8, 10). Dan Taylor, born in 1738, was taught to read by his mother by the age of 3, then worked in coal mines with his father before he turned 5, studying in his evening leisure time (D. Taylor, 1820).

Keeping the needy employed and out of trouble was a perennial goal of European society. Caroline Powys visited a seaport in 1760 with a rope-twisting industry and thought it "charming to see how industrious their poor are – every child of five years being able to earn threepence or a groat [4 pennies] a day" (Powys, 1899, p. 65). It was particularly important to early modern authorities that poor children became accustomed to working from an early age so they would not be a burden on society. Samuel Harmar, in his work on bringing up children "for the good of the land", sought to have "an honest Schoole-master in every Parish" who would "keepe Children out of Idlenesse" instead of "playing in the Streets the better part of the Day" which led "poore children either to become beggers or theeues". In addition, the children should work before and after school. Diligent parents could "enjoune their Children, to get a Penny, before they goe to Schoole and another when they come home." Earning two pennies a day "would be a good helpe towards their maintenance", whereas playing in the street brought "nothing but poverty in the Land, with thousands of curses and oathes, fightings, and other wicked mischiefes" (Harmar, 1642, images 3 and 4). European authorities developed schemes like those of the Salisbury authorities, who in 1626 decreed:

> that all the children of the poor that are not able to relieve them be set to sewing, knitting, bonelace-making, spinning of woollen or linen yarn, pin-making, card-making, spooling, button-making, or some other handiwork as soon as ever they be capable of instruction to learn the same. (Cunningham, 1991, p. 24)

Even noted eighteenth-century philanthropists like Jonas Hanway thought poor children should be put to work, with the caveat that "it should be

Figure 16.4 Cornelius Ketel, *Double Portrait of a Brother and Sister,* circa 1600, inventory nr. MMB.0110 © Museum Mayer van den Bergh, Antwerp.

considered how to make labor as pleasant, or . . . as little irksome as possible, and with a tender regard to the measure of a young person's strength of body or mind" (Cunningham, 1991, p. 31).

Schooling and employment for early modern children undoubtedly restricted time for play; another constraint on playing freely was clothing. Children were not always suitably dressed for physically active games. In portraits of (usually) wealthy children in their best clothes (Figure 16.4), the outfits children wear appear stiff and uncomfortable (Kuus, 2000).

Even the simpler clothes for everyday wear depicted in the Bruegel painting *Children's Games* (Figure 16.1), however, could hinder play. Boys wore long, loose tunics, perhaps with breeches under them. Girls had long dresses with aprons and a cap (Ewing, 1977). Long, cumbersome skirts tangled around legs and discouraged climbing and running. Tight sleeves made it difficult to raise the arms above the shoulders. The corsets worn by young girls were likely to be corded or quilted for stiffness rather than boned but, even so, inhibited bending or turning at the waist and running (Calvert, 1992). Despite complaints about confining clothing from writers like John Locke and Emile Rousseau, children's dress did not become based on comfort and convenience until after 1770 when trousers rather than tight breeches for boys and simple short-sleeved muslin and lawn dresses for girls became the norm (Ewing, 1977).

Nevertheless, notwithstanding such perspectives, restrictions, and admonitions, children managed to carve out space and time to play. In 1505 the Arno river in central Italy froze and children played ball on it (Haas, 1998, p. 150). Roger North, born in 1653, recollected that at the end of the day:

> it was always the custom for the youth of the town, who were men or maid servants, and children, to assemble . . . either upon the green or . . . in a close . . . and there all to play till milking time and supper at night. The men to football, and the maids, with whom we children commonly mixed . . . to stoolball, and such running games as they knew. (North, 1890, vol. 3, pp. 9–10)

Four-year-old Betty Egleton, sick and fretful in 1705, "was often carried to the Window [to watch] some Children at Play in the Street" to take her mind off her pain (Newton, 2010, pp. 469–470). Schoolboys attending Eton in 1766 had fun with "Hopscotch, Headimy, Peg in the Ring, Conquering Lobs (marbles), Trap-ball, Chuck, Steal Baggage, and Puss in the Corner" (Opie & Opie, 1969, p. 4). John Baker, passing the local workhouse in Horsham in 1773, described the children outside as "playing, tumbling about like little puppies" (Blunt, 1909, p. 54). Karl Friedrich Klöden remembered from his childhood in late eighteenth-century Germany enjoying marbles in early spring, ball games at Easter, and kite-flying in the autumn (Heywood, 2001, p. 113). Betsy and Eugenia Wynne, who kept diaries as young girls in late eighteenth-century England, spent hours playing hide and seek or blind man's bluff and throwing snowballs (Wynne, 1935, vol. 1, p. 5).

Children also engaged in fantasy play, reflecting and commenting on the world around them. In sixteenth-century England, Arthur Dee and Mary Herbert, aged 3, "did make as it wer a shew of childish marriage, of calling each other husband and wife" (Pollock, 1983, p. 237). Children staged mock tournaments (Ozment, 2001, 71). Lady Rachel Fane in her early teens in the early seventeenth-century scripted and staged domestic performances, plays, and masques at her home in Apethorpe, Northamptonshire. She used a cast of siblings and servants and composed scripts that focussed on family, work, education, and the household (Chedgzoy, 2007). Molly and Fanny Blundell, aged 8 and 6 in 1712, staged a doll funeral: "with a great deale of Formallity, they had a Garland of Flowers carried before it, and at least twenty of their Playfellows & others that they invited were at the Buriall" (Blundell, 1968, vol. 112, p. 2).

Parents were encouraged to socialize children from an early age by inviting other children to visit, although it was important to expose their offspring only to civilly bred playfellows (Du Moulin, 1673). Wealthier children had scheduled play dates arranged by their parents. George Scheurl, a leading lawyer and diplomat in Nürnberg in the 1530s, brought to his home for his two boys a variety of playmates from artisans to royalty in an attempt to prepare his sons for the world (Ozment, 1983, p. 69). Not all children appreciated these arrangements. Lucy Hutchinson, born in 1620, loved to read but hated needlework and "play among other children". If she was forced to "entertaine such as came to visit me, I tir'd them with more grave instructions then their mothers, and pluckt all their babies to pieces" (Hutchinson, 1810, p. 26).

Children also managed to glean amusement from daily activities. Ralph Verney, born in 1714, was left behind in the country at the age of 6 years and 11 months while his elder brother John went with their parents to London. The rector of Claydon, who was looking after Ralph, assured the little boy's parents he was doing well:

> After Prayers and Dressing, betwixt the Book and the Top and other Diversions, the hours pass smoothly and not unprofitably away . . . He pleases himself with imagination of his Brother's being cooped up in a little house whilst he has the liberty of ranging the garden and the Fields

As he grew up, Ralph enjoyed life on the family estate, ringing the church bells, looking for spiders in undusted bibles, watching men repair brick walls and thatched roofs, helping the carrier unpack, collecting letters from the postman, hiding with the keeper in a tree to watch the deer be driven past, meeting the farm tenants, and going to the local fairs (Verney, 1930, pp. 173, 175).

And children had toys. Although there were few toy shops, toy manufacturers, or amusement books written especially for children before the eighteenth century, early modern paintings and illustrations depict a wide variety of toys, such as rattles, dolls, wheeled horses and wagons, sleds, balls, stilts, miniature gardening tools, marbles, dice, jump ropes, kites, spinning tops, rolling hoops, and hobby horses (Bedeaux et al, 2000; Ozment, 2001). Toys were included in portraits to indicate status and gender: drums, sticks, and hobby horses for boys; dolls for girls (Willemsen, 2000, pp. 62, 64) (Figures 16.5 and 16.6).

Excavated toys confirm that the details in paintings are accurate. Tens of thousands of wooden spinning tops have been dug up in the town centres of the Netherlands, and a ball, knuckle bones, spinning tops, marbles, a gaming piece, and blowpipes were uncovered in the cesspit of the Latin School of Groningen (Willemsen, 2007).

John Locke in his 1693 treatise argued that playthings should not be bought for children; rather, "A smooth Pebel, a piece of Paper, the Mothers bunch of Keys, or any thing they cannot hurt themselves with, serves as much to divert little Children". Children should make their own playthings, and only those beyond their skill, such as "Tops, Gigs, Battledors, and the like" should be paid for (Locke, 1989, pp. 191, 192). Nevertheless, parents and others bought toys for children. Jean Wemyss, Countess of Sutherland, in 1652 recorded in her account book that she bought rattles, a drum, golf balls, and a bow and arrow set for her son James and a doll for her daughter Margaret (Pollock, 1987). Dorothea Herbert in 1777 got an alabaster doll and a miniature house, over which she and her friends had "bloody battles" (Bailey, 2012, p. 89). Alex Burney, aged 2 in 1796, was "exquisitely enchanted with a little penny

Figure 16.5 Isaac van Swanenburg, *Portrait of Catharina van Warmondt,* 1596, The Hague Museum Meermanno, In. No. 16/31.

Figure 16.6 Jakob Seisenegger, *Portrait of a Mother with Her Eight Children,* 1565, Wikimedia Commons.

trumpet". Two years later he received a present of Noah's ark and "as the various animals were produced, looked with a delight that danced in all his features" (Burney, 1854, pp. 79, 152, 154). The Wynne girls had dolls and in 1791 they were given a puppet theatre (Wynne, 1935, p. 53). Children also asked for toys. Six-year-old Balthasar Paumgartner begged in 1591 for a toy horse covered in calfskin (Ozment, 1986, p. 99). Twelve-year-old John Verney in 1723 requested "a pair of battledores and shuttlecocks" (Pollock, 1987, p. 144). The very wealthy could have extravagant toys, but playthings were not just for the well-to-do. It was easy enough for craftsmen to fashion a rag doll or hobby horse for their offspring. In France, children made themselves little flutes or rustic carts, bending branches to form wheels (Heywood, 2001).

The purchasing or making of toys meant that adults conceded that children required some recreation and it was regarded as essential to the maintenance of good health. Exercise, a "vehement, & a voluntarie stirring of ones body, which altereth the breathing", was intended "to maintaine health, and to bring the bodie to a verie good habit" (Mulcaster, 1581, p. 53). William Gouge's domestic conduct book, published in 1622, specifically stated that recreation for "young children especially is needfull for their health" (Gouge, 1622, p. 526). Children who had not been given an adequate amount of exercise would become, in the words of Jonas Hanaway, "pale, languid, emaciated, itchy, hardbellied" (Levene, 2012, p. 125). Thus, "boyes and girles should be playing in the streets", a "lawfull and meet thing, which parents should permit vnto their children" (Gouge, 1622, p. 526). Endymion Porter wanted his young son George to play bareheaded out of doors so he would not get sick (Ewing, 1977). Alice Thornton loved being swung between two adults "by the armes for recreation", a longstanding custom because it was "good to exercize the body of children in growing" (Thornton, 1875, p. 10).

Play also refreshed the mind so that a child could study harder and learn more. Plutarch's advice books for parents, translated throughout the early modern period, pointed out that a child's tender mind could be overwhelmed with too much work. Thus, "some recreation, breathing and refreshing from their continuall labors muste be permytted Children". This would "restaurate and repaire againe their bodyes and mindes to laboure." A lack of recreation, by contrast, would ensure that children would not "long endure in earnest studyes" (Plutarch, 1571 pp. 39, 40). Johannes Sturm reminded his two sons, Philip and Anthony, to take breaks from their studies because physical activity was needed to retain health and refresh a mind wearied from studying: "the minde is most pregnant and fresh when the bodie is in perfite helth, & doth then more quickly apprehende" (Sturm, 1570, p. 9). More than a hundred years later, the same directives applied: "Children must have convenient sport for the health of the body and alacrity of the mind" (Baxter, 1673, p. 546).

Above all else for the wealthier ranks, play in early modern Europe enticed children to attend to their schooling; it is not just the modern world that values the educative aspects of play. Pleasure and delight were the keys to learning: Roger Ascham in his 1570 book on teaching children Latin "counseled parents "bring not vp your children in learning by compulsion and feare, but by playing and pleasure" (Ascham, 1570, p. 10). Desiderius Erasmus suggested that moral precepts could be imparted to children through parables:

> When the little pupil has enjoyed hearing Aesop's fable of the lion being saved in his turn by the good offices of the mouse . . . and he has had a good laugh, then the teacher should spell [the moral] out. (Fudge, 2006, p. 32)

Toys and games could also be employed to teach a child:

> Some have contrived a piece of ivory with twenty four flats or squares, in every one of which was engraven a several letter, and by playing with a childe in throwing this upon a table, and shewing him the letter onely which lay uppermost have in few dayes taught him the whole Alphabet.   (Hoole, 1659, pp. 6–7)

Governesses in eighteenth-century Europe sought to make learning "as much play as possible" using cartographical jigsaw puzzles, educational games such as "A Journey through Europe", and history-based playing cards (Heywood, 2001, p. 93; Shefrin, 2006, p. 197).

Books were published from the seventeenth century on designed to make learning a pleasure for children (Avery, 1995). Abbé Pluche's *Spectacle de la nature* (1732–1751), a nine-volume set of illustrated encyclopaedias for children, was a bestseller throughout Europe. He advocated using children's curiosity to help them to think and reason and claimed that teaching through entertaining methods would lead to real and lasting knowledge. The garden would expose children to surprises in nature like insects. When walking on the beach, adults could draw maps on the sand and devise creative play involving stones, sand, and sticks (Koepp, 2006). Dolls also formed part of a girl's education. Harriot Worthy in 1784 made sure that the childish pastimes of her infant daughter contributed to her improvement: "Her dolls, her playthings, in short, everything which forms a part of puerile amusements, were productive of some instruction" (Bailey, 2012, p. 77). Louisa Hamilton, aged 5, was given a "fine undressed doll" by her mother in 1792 and was told: "You must work very hard for dolly, for poor thing she is quite naked' (Pollock, 1987, p. 144).

Parents often delighted in the playful antics of their offspring but did not analyze what they were doing. Play was just a frivolous, if amusing, activity. For educationalists, however, play had a moral component and they advised parents to watch closely how their children played because this indicated their temperament:

> the nature of children dothe neuer more appeare than in play. If the spiryte and minde of any man be enclined to lie, to noyse, to anger, to violence, to arrogancie, the vice of nature doth shewe it self in play.   (Erasmus, 1560, D1, image 36)

The French author Peter Du Moulin thought that a boy should be able to dispose of some of his toys as he wished "so that his nature be known, whether he be prodigal or sparing, cruel or merciful, that he may be taught to keep the virtuous mean, between the vitious extreams" (Du Moulin, 1673, p. 38). Alexandre-Louis Varet advised parents to have their children "play sometimes before you … because the inclinations of children are more easily discovered in their Play." Children enjoying themselves stand "less upon their guards" and so "their other passions are more free to shew themselves". Thus they reveal, for example, how competitive they are – "the desire they have to overcome others, and the discontent they have for being conquered" – and parents could use that knowledge to manage their children (Varet, 1678, pp. 154–155).

All of the above ensured that some time for recreation was scheduled, and it was permitted when chores, work, and lessons were done. Grisell Baillie, a young girl in early eighteenth-century Scotland, had free time between six and eight in the evening (Pollock, 1987). Otto van Eck, a member of the late eighteenth-century Dutch elite, had scheduled time for play, usually outside, from five to seven p.m. each day (Baggerman & Dekker, 2006). Institutions also allocated some time for play. All schools in the Netherlands had time for fun and socializing. Play was allowed on Tuesdays and Thursdays at a school in Bruges, whereas one near Utrecht had no lessons between noon and two p.m.; instead, "the pupils played in the churchyard under supervision of the headmaster" (Willemsen, 2015, pp. 179, 187).

In the Findel children's home in Nuremberg in the seventeenth century, children spent most of the day in prayers, education, chores, and work but could play outside in the afternoon. Drawings of the children in 1725 show them running about and playing games like hockey in the courtyard (Harrington, 2009). Mary Fletcher established a Methodist home and school for orphans in mid-eighteenth-century England. She assumed that all children would be working for a living, and thus the children got up early and faced busy days of work, chores, and lessons. After five p.m., though, children ate supper and were allowed recreation until bedtime at eight p.m. (Fletcher, 1818). In a London workhouse in Bishopsgate in 1708 children spun wool and flax and had reading and writing lessons from seven a.m. to six p.m., but there was a break from noon to one for dinner and play. Children residing at the parish workhouse of St Andrew Holborn in the early eighteenth century were permitted to play after they had finished their tasks (Levene, 2012). By the end of the eighteenth century, playtime was given a higher priority and apparently more time was allocated for it. Faith Gray, around 1780, set up a boarding school for poor girls: "The children always give over work at six in the evening, whether their tasks be finished or not, and their hours of play are never intruded on" (Gray, 1927, p. 66).

Play was a reward for completing essential activities and was also a means of celebrating. Richard Baxter, as a 10-year-old schoolboy, recalled how the pupils "had leave to play on the day of the king's coronation" (Baxter, 1673, p. 5). Hannah Rathbone noted in 1798: "The children considered this as their father's birthday and played all day" (Rathbone, 1905, p. 74). Christopher Smart's "Hymn for Saturday", written around 1770, begins: "Now's the time for mirth and play / Saturday's an holiday" (Kinnell, 1995, p. 39).

Even when children had the time and opportunity to play, however, they were usually not permitted to play how and when they pleased; rather, "the time, and measure, and kinde of recreation must be well ordered" (Gouge,

1622, p. 526). The question of what was appropriate play for children concerned moralists and parents. Gregory Browne recommended that children "Play not in any thing exceeding modestie and measure" (Browne, 1613, p. 47). "Honest" pastimes included:

> for within dores, lowd speaking, singing, lowd reading, talking, laughing, weaping, holding the breath, daunsing, wrastling, fensing, and scourging the Top. And these for without dores, walking, running, leaping, swimming, riding, hunting, shooting, and playing at the ball.   (Mulcaster, 1581, pp. 53–54)

Because of the association with health and physical activity, playing with a top was vastly preferred over playing with dice or cards (Harmar, 1642). As Richard Baxter put it: "such as well exerciseth their bodies is best, and not such as little stirreth them: Cards and Dice, and such idle spor[ts] are every way most unfit" (Baxter, 1673, p. 546). As today, past parents fretted about suitable pastimes for children. Margaret Woods was deeply concerned about all aspects of her four children's welfare, including playing. She commented in 1799 how difficult it was to know what to permit: "Respecting recreations, it seems very difficult to draw any positive line. Every employment practiced solely for amusement, (even a ride or a walk) may come under that denomination." She finally decided that her children would know they have gone too far down the path of frivolity if they could not return to "serious employment" or had been indulging in activities of which God would not approve (Woods, 1829, p. 171).

Children, of course, could elude supervision and break rules. Schoolboys were notorious for raiding orchards and beehives, breaking hedges and walls, or throwing stones at windows (Harrington, 2009; Thomas, 1976). While he was attending boarding school in Thetford, Roger North recalled "once going down to a sandy place to swim" and being carried downstream to the next town. There, seven miles from the school, the boys got drunk and had to swim home, sobered up by the cold water (North, 1890, vol. 3, p. 11). Hermann von Weinsberg's grandmother criticized his parents in 1524 for being too indulgent and letting 6-year-old Hermann play unsupervised in the streets; after that he was kept more at home. He still managed to find time to play while sent out on errands. On one occasion, he had hung his coat on a tree while playing and it was stolen, for which loss he was spanked on his return (Ozment, 1983, p. 155). Twelve-year-old Otto van Eck in 1793 experienced a similar problem, but with a happier ending. He could not remember where he had left his watch, but going out for fresh air one evening after finishing his lessons, he saw his watch "hanging from a pear tree in the orchard". Then he remembered "how last Saturday, the day I lost it, I climbed a tree for fun and the chain must have caught on a branch and pulled it from my pocket without my feeling it as I was climbing" (Baggerman & Dekker, 2006, pp. 277–278).

Children played unsupervised outside. Coroners' reports have evidence on children drowning in wells or ponds or being burned by fire or scalded with hot water (Hanawalt, 1986, ch. 10). Entries in parental diaries also relate accidents that befell their children while outside playing. In August 1631, Sarah Wallington, aged 34 months, went out "with another littel childe to play as wee had thought but it semes my dafter Sarah left the other child," related her father Nehemiah, who had gone out to look for her. Sarah had wandered quite a way off and was finally brought back home by a woman from the neighbouring village (Wallington, 1899, p. 435). Henry Newcome, aged 10, almost fell off a bridge while playing as a part broke and he had to hold onto the railings until rescued (Newcome, 1862, p. 108). Alice Thornton's 10-year-old daughter Kate, while "plaing with her cozens in Newton barne", fell off the swing and "was taken up dead". Her younger brother, Robin Thornton, aged 8, also fell from a great height: "in his play with his sister Kate and cosen Willy Denton, standing in the window in the hay laith at Newton, which is above four yeards from the earth, he fell down into the laine, neare a great stone" (Thornton, 1875, pp. 164, 170). The siblings recovered.

In towns, street children were ubiquitous because although poor children worked, children under 12 were rarely working full time. Early modern adults usually viewed such children as a nuisance. In seventeenth-century London, a beadle was employed near the Royal Exchange to whip away the "unlucky boys with Toys and Balls" (Opie & Opie, 1969, p. 11). Inhabitants of late seventeenth-century Bristol compared street children to "swarms of locusts in every corner of the street". In 1681, William Cowper of Olney complained that "children of 7 years of age infest the streets every evening with curses and with songs" (Cunningham, 2014, p. 98).

Conclusion

There was no concept of a right to play in early modern Europe but rather an expectation that children would play and that their desire for play would need to be regulated. Adults did not approve of too much play for play's sake; rather, they wanted children to get a head start on the serious business of life, starting schoolwork or acquiring work-related skills early. This meant that play would form only a limited part of a child's life in the past, but it did, nevertheless, have a role. Approved pastimes kept young people healthy, restored the spirits, reinvigorated the mind, and enticed children to study or work. But for children around 6 and older to spend a large portion of their time playing was indulgent, time wasting, and detrimental to their moral and intellectual improvement. Attitudes, however, slowly changed to viewing play in and of itself as something that benefited a child. Portraits made before 1750 rarely depict children in the act of play or in playful poses, while an increasing number of portraits after 1750 do, indicating a new acceptance of play as a desirable part of childhood (Calvert, 1992).

References

Ascham, R. (1570). *The scholemaster or plaine and perfite way of teachyng children, to vnderstand, write, and speake, the Latin tong but specially purposed for the priuate brynging vp of youth in ientlemen and noble mens houses, and commodious also for all such, as haue forgot the Latin tonge ... By Roger Ascham* (STC (2nd edn.)/832). London: Printed by Iohn Daye.

Avery, G. (1995). The beginnings of children's reading to c. 1700. In P. Hunt (Ed.), *Children's literature, an illustrated history* (pp. 1–25). Oxford: Oxford University Press.

Avery, G., & Kinnell, M. (1995). Morality and levity (1780–1820). In P. Hunt (Ed.), *Children's literature, an illustrated history* (pp. 46–76). Oxford: Oxford University Press.

Baggerman, A., & Dekker, R. (2006). Otto's watch. In A. Immel & M. Witmore (Eds.), *Childhood and children's books in early modern Europe 1550–1800* (pp. 277–304). New York: Routledge.

Bailey, J. (2012). *Parenting in England 1760–1830*. Oxford: Oxford University Press.

Banks, J. (1693). *An epistle to Friends shewing the great difference between a convinced estate and a converted estate, and between the profession of the truth, and the possession thereof: with the comfort and sweetness to the soul it affordeth: with a few words of good counsel and wholesome advice both to parents and their children* (STC Wing/B652A). London: Printed by T. Sowle.

Baxter, R. (1673). *A Christian directory, or, A summ of practical theologie and cases of conscience directing Christians how to use their knowledge and faith, how to improve all helps and means, and to perform all duties, how to overcome temptations, and to escape or mortifie every sin: in four parts* (STC Wing/B1219). London: Robert White for Nevill Simmons

Bedaux, J. B., & Ekkart, R. (Eds.) (2000). *Pride and joy: Children's portraits in the Netherlands 1500–1700*. Amsterdam: Ludion Press Ghent.

Blundell, N. (1968). The great diurnall of Nicholas Blundell. *The Record Society of Lancashire and Cheshire, 110,* 112.

Blunt, W. (1909). Extracts from Mr. John Baker's Horsham diary. *Sussex Archaeological Collections Relating to the History and Antiquities of the County, 52,* 38–83.

Browne, G. (1613). *An introduction to pietie and humanitie: containing, first, a short catechisme for vnderstanding the grounds of religion: secondly, certaine briefe and effectuall rules for life and conuersation. Penned specially for the vse of the poore children of Christ's Hospitall in London: but generallie may serue for any other that would be instructed therein* (STC (2nd ed.)/3908.2). London: Printed by E. Allde for E. Weauer.

Burney, F. (1854). *Diary and letters of Madame D'Arblay* (new edn., vol. 6) (ed. C. Barrett). London: Hurst and Blackett.

Calvert, K. (1992). *Children in the house: The material culture of early childhood, 1600–1900*. Boston: Northeastern University Press.

Chedgzoy, K. (2007). Introduction: 'What, are they children?' In K. G. Chedgzoy, S. Greenhalgh, & R. Shaughnessy (Eds.), *Shakespeare and childhood* (pp. 15–31). Cambridge: Cambridge University Press.

Chudacoff, H. P. (2007). *Children at play: An American history*. New York: New York University Press.

Clements, R. L., & Fiorentino, L. (2004). *The child's right to play: A global approach*. Westport, CT: Praeger.

Corsaro, W. A. (2004). Play. In P. S. Fass (Ed.), *Encyclopedia of children and childhood in history and society* (vol. 2, pp. 682–687). New York: Macmillan.

Cunningham, H. (1991). *The children of the poor: Representations of childhood since the seventeenth century*. Oxford: Basil Blackwell.

Cunningham, H. (2014). *Children and children in Western society since 1500* (2nd edn.). Abingdon: Routledge.

Du Moulin, P. (1673). *Directions for the education of a young prince till seven years of age: which will serve for the governing of children of all conditions* (STC Wing/ D2557) (trans. from French). London: Printed for H. Brome.

Erasmus, D. (1560). *The ciuilitie of childehode with the discipline and institucion of children, distributed in small and compe[n]dious chapiters/and translated oute of French into Englysh* (STC (2nd ed.)/10470.3) (ed. T. Paynell). London: Printed by John Tisdale.

Ewing, E. (1977). *History of children's costume*. London: Bibliophile.

Fletcher, A. (1994). Prescription and practice: Protestantism and the upbringing of children 1560–1700. In D. Wood (Ed.), *The church and childhood: Papers read at the 1993 Summer Meeting and the 1994 Winter Meeting of the Ecclesiastical History Society* (pp. 325–346). Oxford: Blackwell.

Fletcher, M. (1818). *Life of Mrs. Mary Fletcher* (ed. H. Moore). London: Thomas Cordeux.

Frost, J. L. (2010). *A history of children's play and play environments: Toward a contemporary child-saving movement*. New York: Routledge.

Fudge, E. (2006). Learning to laugh. In A. Immel & M. Witmore (Eds.), *Childhood and children's books in early modern Europe 1550–1800* (pp. 19–40). New York: Routledge.

Gouge, W. (1622). *Of domesticall duties eight treatises. I. An exposition of that part of Scripture out of which domesticall duties are raised* (STC (2nd edn.)/12119). London: Printed by Iohn Haviland for William Bladen.

Gray, F. (1927). Faith Gray and her diaries. In M. E. Gray (Ed.), *Papers and diaries of a York family 1764–1839* (pp. 171–246). London: Sheldon Press.

Haas, L. (1998). *The Renaissance man and his children: Childbirth and early childhood in Florence, 1300–1600*. New York: St. Martin's Press.

Halkett, A. (1875). The autobiography of Anne, Lady Halkett. *Camden Society*, 13.

Hanawalt, B. A. (1986). *The ties that bound: Peasant families in medieval England*. New York: Oxford University Press.

Harmar, S. (1642). *Vox populi, or, Glostersheres desire: with, the way and means to make a kingdome happy (by Gods help)* (STC Wing (2nd ed.)/H799). London: Printed for Thomas Bates.

Harrington, J. F. (2009). *The unwanted child: The fate of foundlings, orphans, and juvenile criminals in early modern Germany*. Chicago, IL: University of Chicago Press.

Heath, M. B. (2014). Recycled stories: Historicizing play today through the late nineteenth-century Anglo-American play movement. *Journal of the History of Childhood and Youth*, 7(1), 107–133.

Heywood, C. (2001). *A history of childhood*. Cambridge: Polity Press.

Holles, J. (1627). Letter to Thomas Wentworth, Earl of Strafford. Sheffield Central Library, *Wentworth-Woodhouse Muniments* (22, 63).

Hoole, C. (1659). *The petty-schoole Shewing a way to teach little children to read English with delight and profit, (especially) according to the new primar* (STC Wing (2nd ed.)/H2688A). London: Printed by J. T. for Andrew Crook.

Hutchinson, L. (1810). *Memoirs of the life of Colonel John Hutchinson* (3rd edn.) (ed. J. Hutchinson). London: Longman, Hurst, Rees & Orme.

Kinnell, M. (1995). Publishing for children (1700–1780). In P. Hunt (Ed.), *Children's literature, an illustrated history* (pp. 36–45). Oxford: Oxford University Press.

Koepp, C. (2006). Curiosity, science and experiential learning in the eighteenth century. In A. Immel & M. Witmore (Eds.), *Childhood and children's books in early modern Europe 1550–1800* (pp. 153–180). New York: Routledge.

Kuus, S. (2000). Children's costume in the sixteenth and seventeenth centuries. In J. B. Bedaux & R. Ekkart (Eds.), *Pride and joy: Children's portraits in the Netherlands 1500–1700* (pp. 73–84). Amsterdam: Ludion Press Ghent.

Levene, A. (2012). *The childhood of the poor: Welfare in eighteenth-century. London*. Basingstoke: Palgrave Macmillan.

Locke, J. (1989). *Some thoughts concerning education* (ed. J. W. Yolton & J. S. Yolton). Oxford: Clarendon Press.

Macfarlane, A. (1970). *The family life of Ralph Josselin, a seventeenth-century clergyman. An essay in historical anthropology*. Cambridge: Cambridge University Press.

Manning, J. (2002). *The Emblem*. London: Reaktion Books.

Marcus, L. S. (1978). *Childhood and cultural despair: A theme and variations in seventeenth-century literature*. Pittsburgh, PA: University of Pittsburgh Press.

Mulcaster, R. (1581). *Positions vvherin those primitiue circumstances be examined, which are necessarie for the training vp of children, either for skill in their booke, or health in their bodie* (STC (2nd ed.)/18253). London: Thomas Vautrollier for Thomas Chard.

Newcome, H. (1862). *The autobiography of Henry Newcome* (ed. R. Parkinson). Chetham Society Publications, Manchester, vol. 1.

Newton, H. (2010). Children's physic: Medical perceptions and treatment of sick children in early modern England, c. 1580–1720. *Social History of Medicine, 23*(3), 456–474.

North, R. (1890). *The lives of the Norths* (ed. A. Jessop). London: George Bell & Sons.

Opie, I., & Opie, P. (1969). *Children's games in street and playground*. Oxford: Oxford University Press.

Ozment, S. (1983). *When fathers ruled: Family life in Reformation Europe*. Cambridge, MA: Harvard University Press.

Ozment, S. (1986). *Magdalena and Balthasar: An intimate portrait of life in 16th-century Europe revealed in the letters of a Nuremberg husband and wife*. New Haven, CT: Yale University Press.

Ozment, S. (1999). *Flesh and spirit: Private life in early modern Germany*. Harmondsworth, Middlesex: Penguin Books.

Ozment, S. (2001). *Ancestors: The loving family in old Europe*. Cambridge, MA: Harvard University Press.

Plutarch. (1571). *A president for parentes teaching the vertuous training vp of children and holesome information of yongmen* (STC (2nd ed.)/20057.5) (trans. E. Grant). London: Henry Bynneman.

Pollock, L. A. (1983). *Forgotten children: Parent–child relations from 1500 to 1900.* Cambridge: Cambridge University Press.

Pollock, L. A. (1987). *A lasting relationship: Parents and children over three centuries.* Hanover, NH: University Press of New England.

Powys, C. (1899). *Passages from the diaries of Mrs. Philip Lybbe Powys* (ed. E. Climenson). London: Longmans, Green.

Rathbone, H. (1905). *Reynold-Rathbone diaries and letters 1753–1839* (ed. E. Greg). Edinburgh: Privately printed.

Roopnarie, J. (2011). Cultural variations in beliefs about play, parent–child play, and children's play: Meaning for childhood development. In A. D. Pellegrini (Ed.), *The Oxford handbook of the development of play* (pp. 19–37). New York: Oxford University Press.

S.T. (1672). *The childs book and youths book in two parts. : The first teaching an easie and delightful way to read true English . . . : The second containing a method for spelling, a catechism, a confession of faith, a copy book, a perpetual almanack.* London: Printed by E. T. and R. H. for R. Royston.

Shefrin, J. (2006). Governesses to their children. In A. Immel & M. Witmore (Eds.), *Childhood and children's books in early modern Europe 1550–1800* (pp. 181–212). New York: Routledge

Slingsby, H. (1836). *The diary of Sir Henry Slingsby of Scriven, bart* (ed. D. Parsons). London: Longman.

Smith, P. K. (2010). *Children and play.* Chichester: Wiley-Blackwell.

Snow, E. (1997). *Inside Bruegel: The play of images in children's games.* New York: North Point Press.

Stockton, O. (1672). *A treatise of family instruction: wherein it is proved to be the duty of parents and masters of families to train up their children and servants in knowledge of the Scriptures: with directions how this work may be done* (STC Wing/S5701). London: Printed for H. Brome.

Stout, W. (1967). The autobiography of William Stout of Lancaster 1665–1752. *Chetham Society. Remains, Historical and Literary, Connected with the Palatine Counties of Lancaster and Chester*, 3rd ser., v. 14.

Strauss, G. (1978). *Luther's house of learning: Introduction of the young in the German reformation.* Baltimore, MD: Johns Hopkins University Press.

Sturm, J. (1570). *A ritch storehouse or treasurie for nobilitye and gentlemen, which in Latine is called Nobilitas literata* (STC (2nd ed.)/23408) (trans. T. Browne). London: Henrie Denham.

Taylor, D. (1820). *Memoirs of the Rev. Dan Taylor: late pastor of the General Baptist Church, Whitechapel, London, with extracts from his diary, correspondence, and unpublished manuscripts* (ed. A. Taylor). London: Privately printed.

Taylor, J. (1820). *Memoirs of the Rev. John Taylor, late pastor of the General Baptist Church at Queenshead, near Halifax, Yorkshire* (ed. A. Taylor). London: Privately printed.

Thomas, K. (1976). Age and authority in early modern England. *Proceedings of the British Academy, 62,* 205–248.

Thornton, A. (1875). *The autobiography of Mrs Alice Thornton of East Newton, co. York* (ed. C. Jackson).

Tryon, T. (1695). *A new method of educating children, or, Rules and directions for the well ordering and governing them during their younger years shewing that they are capable* (STC Wing/T3190). London: Printed for J. Salusbury and J. Harris.

Varet, A.-L. (1678). *The Christian education of children according to the maxims of the Sacred Scripture, and the instructions of the fathers of the church/written and several times printed in French, and now translated into English* (STC Wing (2nd ed.)/V108). Paris: John Baptist Coignard.

Verney, M. M. (Ed.) (1930). *Verney letters of the eighteenth century from the mss at Claydon House* (vol. 2). London: Ernest Benn.

Wallington, N. (1899). *Historical notices of events in the reign of Charles I*. London: Richard Bentley.

Whitebread, D., Basilio, M., Kuvalja, M., & Verma, M. (2012). *The importance of play: A report on the value of children's play with a series of policy recommendations*. Brussels: Toys Industries for Europe.

Willemsen, A. (2000). Images of toys: The culture of play in the Netherlands around 1600. In J. B. Bedaux & R. Ekkart (Eds.), *Pride and joy: Children's portraits in the Netherlands 1500–1700* (pp. 61–72). Amsterdam: Ludion Press Ghent.

Willemsen, A. (2005). The game of the month: Playful calendars in Ghent-Bruges books of hours. In B. Dekeyzer & J. Van der Stock (Eds.), *Manuscripts in transition: Recycling manuscripts, texts and images. Proceedings of the international congress held in Brussels (3–9 November 2002)* (pp. 419–430). Paris: Uitgeverj Peeters.

Willemsen, A. (2007). The age of play: Children's toys and the medieval life cycle. *Ludica: annalie di storia e civiltá del gioco, 13*(14), 169–182.

Willemsen, A. (2015). 'That the boys come to school half an hour before the girls': Order, gender, and emotion in school, 1300–1600. In S. Broomhall (Ed.), *Gender and emotions in medieval and early modern Europe: Destroying order, structuring disorder* (pp. 175–195). Farnham: Ashgate.

Woods, M. (1829). *Extracts from the journal of Margaret Woods, from the year 1771–1821*. London: John & Arthur Arch.

Wynne, E. (1935–40). *The Wynne Diaries* (vol. 1) (ed. A. Fremantle). London: Oxford University Press.

17 Play in Foraging Societies

Adam Howell Boyette

Research on contemporary foraging, or hunter-gatherer, societies (hereafter, "foragers") is unique in its value for our understanding of human history and diversity. Since the origin of our species somewhere in Eastern or Southern Africa around 200,000 years ago until around 10,000 years ago when some groups began practicing the domestication of plants and animals for subsistence, all human beings lived as foragers. Today, foragers represent a distinct minority of the world's peoples, managing to maintain the oldest way of living on Earth despite constant pressure from neighbouring peoples to give up their autonomy, land, and traditional economic activities (Codding & Kramer, 2016). Understanding how contemporary foragers think, feel, and conduct social and economic life in the world is essential for a full picture of human diversity – and is valuable in its own right. Contemporary foragers are not ancient people in a modern world, but the world's experts at a particularly resilient way of life, whose cultures are as dynamic and responsive to internal and external changes as any on the planet. When it comes to play, research among foragers has taught us much about potential human developmental universals and about how play in forager cultures may underpin the social development of the unique set of cultural traits found only among foragers – traits that are likely at the root of such remarkable resilience.

In this chapter, I will review what we know about play among contemporary foragers. To be clear, I consider "foragers" as those peoples who traditionally lived in small, mobile, politically acephalous groups that subsisted primarily by gathering wild plant foods and hunting wild animals. This definition includes those groups Woodburn (1982) referred to as "immediate-return hunter-gatherers" but not "delayed return hunter-gatherers," as the latter supported larger group sizes, were more sedentary, and, most importantly, had, at least at times, hierarchical social structures (Kelly, 1995). While today few forager groups live primarily on foraged foods and may practice agriculture or wage labour for the natural resource or tourist industries, many self-identify as the first people in their region, who uniquely possess the knowledge to live by wild foods alone (Kidd et al., 2009). It is on the basis of this self-identification and their unique foundational cultural schemas that we can talk about foragers as a group.

As a unifying framework of analysis, I first describe forager foundational cultural schemas – cognitive structures that orient thought and emotion – and the similar ways that foragers change their natural landscapes to support the development of certain social and emotional features of forager culture that are the basis for foundational schemas. I then turn to three overlapping "areas" of play research: play that is in imitation of adults; creative play, including games; and play that reflects and integrates cultural change. Finally, I discuss the view espoused by some that forager childhood, because of its potential evolutionary significance, should be treated as a model for how to organize childhood in modern, Western contexts. According to this perspective, forager play is the ideal that should guide parenting and early childhood education and care policy outside the home. I urge a cautious but hopeful examination of this perspective. In the end, I believe forager play is unique in the ways that forager cultures are unique and that there is a lot we can learn from the careful observation, collaboration, intrinsic motivation, trust, and openness that characterize the forager child group at play.

Defining Play

Play is a notoriously challenging research subject. When asked how to define play, researchers will often say they "know it when they see it" (Smith, 2010) and may be hard pressed in particular instances to say why one thing a child does is or is not play. Making the distinction from some outside, objective viewpoint is much more challenging when children playfully engage in "real" work, as many children in forager societies do (Crittenden, 2016a). Moreover, adults can play as well, and some researchers have claimed that foragers hardly make the distinction between work and play themselves (Lewis, 2016, for the Mbendjele; e.g., see Lye, n.d., for the Batek). In my own view, play seems better seen as a cognitive and emotional state of positive affect and an openness to physical and emotional challenges and learning opportunities rather than any particular set of behaviours (Boyette, 2016b). However, the emergence of economic productivity from "play" for its own sake, even if economically productive, is of interest to those studying the evolution of the human life history and cultural transmission (Bock, 2002; Bock & Johnson, 2004; Boyette, 2016a). With these complexities in mind, I discuss play in a relatively non-reflexive way in much of this chapter. I will use 'play' as the researchers whom I discuss use the term, and will draw from descriptions of children's 'playful', autonomous activities not specifically labelled as play when they are applicable to a full description of the content and contexts of forager 'play' broadly construed. I will also focus on children's play after infancy, when the playgroup becomes the centre of forager children's social world.

Overview of Foragers

Forager Foundational Schemas. Hewlett and colleagues have discussed forager cultures as unified by three foundational schemas: respect for autonomy, sharing, and egalitarianism (Boyette & Hewlett, 2017; Hewlett & Roulette, 2016; Hewlett et al., 2011). Foundational schemas are ways of thinking that organize and motivate behaviour across multiple domains of life (D'Andrade & Strauss, 1992; Shore, 1996). Theoretically, they are internalized during childhood through social and individual learning and are made especially salient by social sanctions against contrary behaviour. These three schemas were derived most directly from our own work among Congo Basin forest foragers, but have been consistently described in part or in whole among all historic and contemporary foragers of whom I am aware – though they are naturally manifest in myriad ways (Lew-Levy et al., 2018).

The respect for autonomy schema means no one can coerce others. Children are generally given as much autonomy as adults and are rarely scolded. Sharing means that resources – including material resources like food, clothes, cigarettes, alcohol, or fire, and immaterial resources such as space and time – are shared as much as possible with all members of the community, and it is expected and acceptable that others will demand shares. Sharing as a foundational schema often manifests as social norms and institutions, and it is worth noting that children's violations of sharing norms may be subject to sanctions – an instructive contradiction with the respect for autonomy schema. Finally, egalitarianism means that all members of the community are equal in their influence and all individuals are given equal respect. As will be described, play behaviour can be seen to both express and reinforce these schemas.

Cultural Niche Construction. Also drawing from our work in the Congo Basin, we (Boyette, 2016b; Boyette & Hewlett, 2017; Hewlett, 2016; Hewlett & Roulette, 2014) have discussed the forager culturally constructed niche as consisting of the features of the physical environment that forager communities have shaped over time in ways that both reflect and reinforce foundational schemas. For example, some tropical or savannah foragers traditionally arrange their small houses in a circle and close in space (Draper, 1973; Turnbull, 1962). Houses are used only for sleeping, and not for privacy (Boyette, 2013; Lee, 2013). Nuclear family homes typically have their own hearth, but there are no spatial boundaries expressed or enforced, and children come and go from anyone's house as they please. This "sharing of space" extends to personal space. In other words, people tend to maintain physical contact with each other when resting or working or when engaged in leisure activities, including play (Draper, 1973; Lewis, 2016; Sugawara, 1984). Moreover, children co-sleep with their parents or others until early adolescence and then continue to co-sleep with same-sex age mates or younger children essentially until they are grown and form their own families (Hewlett & Roulette, 2014).

The openness and intimacy of the living space also means that children are always around other children of different ages, both male and female. These multi-age playgroups become a central feature of the space, with children's groups fusing and fissioning throughout the day, moving from one activity to another. Some forager groups do have 'male spaces', where only men typically gather to chat or eat together (e.g., Lewis, 2015). However, such spaces are gendered only to the sexually mature and children are not bound by any rules of spatial segregation. Thus, the foundational schemas of egalitarianism and autonomy are engendered by the living spaces in which children play.

Among Congo Basin foragers, the domestic space is cognitively separated from the forest (Bahuchet, 1999; Kamei, 2005; Turnbull, 1962), but as noted above, foragers share a strong identity that stems from the self-concept of being people *of* the environment that they must know intimately in order to live – living as part of and in a relationship with the ecosystem as opposed to living in opposition to it, as is a common view among agrarian peoples (Bird-David, 1999; cf. Kenrick, 2002; Lye, 2004). Thus, foragers live intimately with each other and with their natural ecologies.

The advantage of a cultural niche construction perspective is that it connects human actions on the landscape – and the meanings and behavioural patterns they engender – to the intergenerational transmission of culture through children's developmental experiences within cultural spaces (Boyette, 2016b; Hewlett, 2016), and eventually to the evolution of human cultural and biological diversity over time (Odling-Smee et al., 2003). Play within the culturally constructed niche thus becomes a central context for exploring and recreating children's surrounding culture. In the case of foragers, playing in the space contributes to learning the norms governing social relationships within the human community, the traditional knowledge of the environment in which they live, and, as I explain below, the means of production that tie the community to the environment in an economic sense.

Imitative Play

As a result of the openness of forager domestic spaces and the autonomy afforded forager children, nearly all aspects of economic, social, and ritual life are available to children to observe from the day they open their eyes. Thus, it is not surprising that the literature is replete with examples of the precise imitation of adult behaviour observed among forager children. These include what I have called "work-themed pretence" or work-themed play (e.g., the imitation of subsistence and household maintenance activities; Boyette, 2016a, 2016b; Fouts et al., 2016), but also imitation of social and ritual activities.

"Work-Themed Pretence" Play. Based on the available evidence, there seems to be a general increase in the amount of play that is "work-themed pretence" from early childhood through adolescence, and a small female bias after early childhood. Fouts and colleagues (2016) found that an average of 4% of play was "work-themed" among Aka and Bofi 1- to 4-year olds, with a range from 0% to 22%. Gosso and colleagues (2007) observed 21% of girl and 4% of boy Parakanã children's play could be categorized as 'work'. Finally, my observations of Aka children ages 4–16 indicate that "work-themed pretence" constituted 19% of these children's total play, with girls playing significantly more "work-themed pretence" than boys (22.1 vs. 17%; Boyette, 2016a). Similarly, "foraging" constituted approximately 24% of the play activities observed by Kamei (2005) among Baka from 4 to 15 years old.

In each of these studies and others, the types of "work-themed" activities children imitated were as varied as those the children observed around them. 'Gathering' and in-camp activities such as building houses or 'cooking' are very common for boys and girls beginning as young as toddlerhood. Mbuti, Batek, Aka, Baka, and Hadza children build small replicas of the round sapling framed huts they see women build (Boyette, 2013; Crittenden, 2016b; K. M. Endicott & Endicott, 2008; Kamei, 2005; Lewis, 2016; Turnbull, 1962), where they might build a small hearth with a real fire to cook their foraging returns – which may or may not be edible. During my fieldwork, the Aka often used a sardine can as a "cooking pot" should my team have thrown one in our midden pile. Batek children practice using digging sticks in camp, placing any (inedible) roots they might find in a rattan basket (K. M. Endicott & Endicott, 2008). Similarly, digging at the ground or chopping a stump or a house post with a machete was a regular activity among the Aka with whom I worked.

Everyday essential foraging skills such as digging and chopping comprise one of the few domains in which adults have been seen to actively encourage children's learning, and they may start quite early. For example, Hewlett observed a father teach a 1-year old child to dig with a knife (in this case representing a small machete) (Hewlett & Roulette, 2016). The instance, a scene in an hour-long film sample, was remarkable also because it shows a 2-year-old coming to imitate the father's encouragement! Parents in a number of groups have also been seen to encourage foraging skill learning by constructing miniature baskets, bows, and spears, for example, or providing adult versions for practice (Hewlett et al., 2011; MacDonald, 2007). Hadza girls are given their first digging stick at around 3 years old (Crittenden, 2016a)

Proficiency comes quickly from such early teaching and intrinsically motivated practice (Bock, 2002; Bock & Johnson, 2004). For instance, I was taken aback early in my fieldwork when I saw a 7-year-old Aka girl enter a patch of forest beside a garden and, after only a few minutes of chopping were heard, emerge dragging a sapling at least 6 metres long. This same young girl later spent considerable time packing wood into a carrying basket and tying it with a cord, only to abandon the activity without complaint when she failed to bind the firewood properly. Here we see how "work" and "play" are fluid and can be hard to distinguish. This presents a methodological and epistemological challenge for the researcher, one also readily apparent when examining hunting play.

Hunting is obviously a significant element of adult social and economic life among foragers and is a significant theme of children's play, a fact especially noteworthy in light of the argument that the availability of adult work is one major factor motivating imitation. Indeed, most types of actual hunting are done away from the eyes of children, yet this does not stop children from incorporating them into "work pretence." Among Central African net-hunting groups like the Mbuti, Baka, and Aka, groups of children of both sexes enjoy attempting to catch 'game' such as a frog, a child pretending to be an antelope, or a chicken if there happens to be one in camp (Boyette, 2013; Kamei, 2005; Turnbull, 1965). Elsewhere, Batek children pretend to hunt monkeys with blowpipes (K. M. Endicott & Endicott, 2008). Spear or bow hunting play is common among the boys of many groups (Hill & Hurtado, 1996; Kamei, 2005; Thomas, 1959; Turnbull, 1965). Aka boys of middle childhood age (roughly 7–12 years) fashion their own small spears and hunt the small forest rats that come to the periphery of camp. While the rats would often escape, an occurrence that did not seem to deter much from the joy of the hunt, the boys sometimes killed the rats. When a rat was speared, the boys would follow Aka cultural norms and cook and share the meat (Boyette, In Press; also see Kamei, 2005, for the Baka). Thus, we return to our methodological and epistemological challenge: Were the boys playing or was this subsistence labour? Is there a difference?

While it might be hard to describe much of the play engaged in by Western children as 'work' that helps the family economy, forager children's access to the knowledge and means of production blurs the distinction. During my fieldwork, I called the Aka boys' rat hunts 'work' (and, therefore, not 'play') if the boys caught the rat and ate it, using calories produced as my defining criteria. Similarly, if a girl climbed a tree and came down with *Gnetum africanum* leaves to be eaten later, she performed 'work', even if it was in the context of a group of children climbing 'for fun'. I forced such a dichotomization because I was interested in the developmental trade-offs between 'play' and 'work' (Bock, 2002; Bock & Johnson, 2004). Indeed, I found that children worked more and played less as they got older (Boyette, 2016a). However, Crittenden (2016a) makes the reasonable argument that this distinction obscures the essential duality of play and work among forager children. She argues that "children's foraging ... represents a type of 'work play', dually functioning as economic contribution and developmentally significant play" (155). The Hadza children with whom Crittenden works are known for their productivity and have been estimated to bring in as much as 50% of their daily caloric intake, with a great deal of variation between children and within any individual child's daily returns (Blurton Jones et al., 1989; Crittenden & Zes, 2015). For Hadza children, it seems, most hunting and gathering is productive and at the same time playful.

Crittenden's view is consistent with that of Tucker and Young (2005), who found that Mikea children would throw away a great deal of edible tubers during the course of foraging. This observation led them to the conclusion that, for forager children, foraging is an extension of play. I do not see my work nor that of Bock and Johnson as inconsistent with this view. As children get older, their "work-pretence play" comes to resemble more and more the 'work' of the adult members of the community. A major factor that influences the developmental pattern of this trade-off between 'play' and 'work' is the natural ecology in which the children live. For example, the Hadza live in a rocky woodland ecology in which children can easily acquire a great deal of foods independently from early in childhood, whereas Kalahari hunter-gatherers like the !Kung need many more years of experience to successfully navigate their nearly featureless landscape without fear of getting lost or predated upon (Blurton Jones et al., 1989, 1994). To conclude this section, the nature of hunting and gathering lends itself to the fluid integration of developmentally significant pretence or social play throughout childhood. The learning that occurs in such play is profound and greatly facilitated by the autonomy afforded children throughout childhood.

Play and the Adult Social and Ritual World. Children's autonomy and the lack of a separation between adult and child worlds provides more than just the basis for an education in norms and values associated with economic life. As foraging play may help children learn core norms and values such as cooperation, the complementarity between the sexes, and food sharing, children's imitation of adult social and ritual life provides additional opportunities to reckon with foundational schemas.

Turnbull (1978) wrote extensively of children's exploring adult roles in the *bopi*, the children's play space in the Mbuti forest settlement. For example, Mbuti children would collaboratively imitate a recent real conflict between the adults, taking different roles and recreating what was said. Turnbull writes that, should the conflict have ended with bad feelings between the adults, the children would "try and show that they can do better, and if they find they cannot, then they revert to ridicule which they play out until they are all rolling on the ground in near-hysterics" (p. 187). He notes that such collective ridicule is how the most serious conflicts are settled in adult social life. Indeed, "rough joking" is a central means of levelling boastfulness or arrogance among foragers more generally (Hewlett, 1991; Lee, 1969; Wiessner, 2005), making the imitative play of adult conflicts an important means identifying and internalizing the foundational schema of egalitarianism by representing and renegotiating real examples of conflict around social norms and their resolution.

According to Turnbull, within the Mbuti *bopi*, children explore the full range of adult roles and practices. This includes the "bawdy" ridicule of sexual relationships between males and females, which, again, emphasizes – quite playfully – the complementarity of the sexes and expresses the forager values for intimacy, openness, and autonomy. The push and pull of political and spiritual power between the sexes is a constant theme of adult social life among Congo Basin forest foragers, such that children's play serves as important education in sexuality, gender roles, and egalitarian politics (Lewis, 2016; Turnbull, 1978). The Mbuti children also imitate the storyteller role of the elders in their play in the *bopi*. As Turnbull puts it, in embodying the storyteller, children's "intellect and power of reason are being developed in such a way as to reinforce the values learned" (1978, p. 201).

Similarly, others have described children's imitation of traditional dances, which typically have significant associations with critical values around gender, egalitarianism, and sharing (K. M. Endicott & Endicott, 2008; Kamei, 2005; Lewis, 2009). For example, Lewis has written extensively on the role of music in learning among Congo Basin forest foragers (Lewis, 2002, 2015, 2016) and argues that the spirit plays common to foragers of the Congo Basin – *mokondi massana* among the Mbendjele – are a form of community-wide play performance through which individuals learn key skills, knowledge, and values throughout their lives as they take on new roles with each new life situation. For example, while children must learn the basic dance forms, elders must learn the means of feeding everyone who comes to the dance. Among the Mbendjele, *massana* means 'play' (this is also true of the Aka, who live just north of the Mbendjele, although there I found it to be interchangeable with the term *motoko*, which Mbendjele give the more negative connotation of 'unpleasant noise'; Boyette, 2013; Lewis, 2002). The term can be applied widely, from casual infant or child play to the *mokondi massana* dance ceremonies that are the pinnacle of community collaboration. Children's imitation of the larger, community *massana* events is called *Bolu*, which Lewis describes as a "ritual prototype" that contains

> all the basic elements of adult spirit plays, including its own forest spirit and secret area (*njanga*) where the spirit is called from the forest by the initiates who, in this case, are boys aged between 3 and 9 years old. *Bolu*'s secret area creates a space for sharing secrets. It encourages the same-sex solidarity so central to political, economic, and social organization.   (Lewis 2016, 149)

Meanwhile, the girls dance in costume in camp singing *Bolu* songs to entice the spirit to come to camp, just as the adult women do during *mokondi massana*. Lewis draws a parallel between these performances and the complementarity between men and women in hunting game (male) and cooking the meat to feed the community (female). Thus, "*Bolu* launches each Mbendjele's apprenticeship in ritual while implicitly teaching them a range of other skills and cultural models" (Lewis, 2016, p. 150).

It is important to note that a central feature of dance and song among at least the Congo Basin foragers is improvisation (Kisliuk, 1998; Lewis, 2009). Thus, there is a great deal of opportunity for creativity and innovation in the context of *Bolu* and other children's *massana*. In this way, individual autonomy is held up as contrasted with and counterpart to cooperation – between the sexes and with the community – in creating the shared ritual experience.

Finally, while perhaps less dense in its pedagogical value as *Bolu* is for the Mbendjele, it is worth mentioning *lukuchuko*, a gambling game played among the Hadza. Woodburn (1982) originally described the game as played among adult men as an example of a forager sharing institution that functions to separate people from property – a central means of maintaining an egalitarian society. Historically, *lukuchuko* was played with bark disks, and the bargaining was done with arrowheads, bows, or other valuable items. While some skill is involved, luck is a major force in the game. Thus, by playing, men would essentially circulate their valuable possessions among each other and level out variations in material wealth. Hadza boys imitate the men at this game, playing with their own materials (Crittenden, 2016a). While Kenyan shillings are used today instead of materials, the implications of the game for learning the foundational schemas of egalitarianism and sharing remains: what you have must be shared. (See Woodburn's (1966) film *The Hadza* for historic footage of both men's and boys' versions of *lukuchuko*.)

Creative Play and Games

Of course, not all forager play involves the imitation of adult roles and activities. The creative or 'non-imitative' play of forager children also illustrates distinctive forager cultural values. The most distinctive and significant aspects of all forager play as compared with that of children in other types of societies is that forager play is non-competitive and non-aggressive.

The significance of non-competitiveness in forager play cannot be underemphasized. Early cross-cultural comparative studies indicated that foragers do not tend to play strategy games, which require rules and a competitive objective and are associated with political integration and social stratification (Roberts et al., 1959) as well as training for obedience (Roberts & Sutton-Smith, 1962), a value contrary to autonomy. This finding has been substantiated repeatedly by later fieldwork.

According to Endicott and Endicott, among the Batek: "Children's play was strikingly noncompetitive. Games did not have actual rules; children simply created and then repeated activity patterns as they went along. Play was not structured to produce teams of winners and losers" (K. L. Endicott & Endicott, 2014, p. 112). Similarly, Turnbull writes: "The significance of the absence of competitive games is inestimable" (1978, p. 182). For the Mbuti, he goes on, "The only competition encouraged . . . is between the individual and his abilities. To succeed he must conquer his disabilities as best he can, and restrain any excess of ability. To be better or worse than anyone else is to fail ... In a word the goal is equality, through noncompetitiveness" (182). Draper (1976) echoes the marked non-competitiveness of !Kung play but offers a demographic and developmental explanation for its association with equality:

> The limited and heterogeneous assortment of playmates available to a child poses interesting constraints on the kind of games which children can play. Competitiveness in games is almost entirely lacking, and it is interesting to see that in this respect !Kung cultural values against competitiveness and environmental constraint have such a fortunate congruence. To compete in a game or skill one needs one or preferably more children close in age and perhaps sex with whom to compete, but the smallness of group size among !Kung usually ensures that several age-mates are not available. Team sports are similarly unrealistic. Not only can the children not fill out a team; but the players are at such different levels of motor skill, motivation, and cognitive development that it is difficult and unrewarding to play a game involving intense competition, rules, and fairly complex strategy. (pp. 202–203).

In support of Draper's argument, Konnor (1972) noted that during seasonal aggregations of !Kung families, where more same-age, same-sex playmates were available, he observed more physically competitive, rough-and-tumble play. However, I argue that even if it occurs, forager competitive and aggressive play would be a matter of degree less frequent than it is among societies with hierarchical social structures that make competitiveness a value and a useful skill (Boyette, 2016b). Indeed, I show that in comparison to the Aka, children among the neighbouring Ngandu swidden cassava farmers played rough-and-tumble games twice as frequently and rule-based games more than four times as often. Gosso and colleagues also found 'play fighting' to be far less frequent among the Parakanã forager-horticulturalists as compared with urban groups – only 2% of pretence play among boys and absent among the girls (Gosso et al., 2007). Furthermore, when I combined my data with similar systematically collected play data from Baka, Parakanã, and English primary school children, the only significant difference that emerged between groups was the greater proportion of play constituted by competitive games among the Ngandu and English versus the egalitarian groups (Boyette, 2016b).

Among foragers, the only competitive games that have been noted come from outside, non-egalitarian groups. For example, the Aka played football, which they learned from the Ngandu, though score was rarely kept and the teams always seemed quite loose (Boyette, 2016b). Similarly, Kirk Endicott saw Batek children who had been taught football at school change the game so that teams took turns scoring on each other's goals (K. M. Endicott & Endicott, 2008). On the other hand, Crittenden (2016a) observed Hadza girls playing a competitive hand-clapping game that they learned from neighbouring pastoralists. Crittenden (2016a) also describes boys' target practice games as becoming more "playfully competitive" as boys enter puberty, with age-mates trying to best each other. Similarly, the Aka traditional ball game *ndanga* (or *ndaanga*) has a competitive spirit when played by adolescents and young men (Boyette, 2016a). In *ndanga*, there are two teams and the men of each team pass a ball to each other, trying to keep it from the other team. While the play may get very active and some players get competitive with one another, no score is kept, players of all ages come and go, and there is no end goal to the game. The game is over when the fun is over. Additionally, the game integrates hunting and food sharing metaphors. For example, players will announce their intention to pass the ball to a team mate by shouting, "*Dja bima!* " – "Eat food!"

The variety of non-competitive games observed is vast, and they typically support learning essential skills and ethnobiology as well as the values for non-aggression, cooperation, and egalitarianism. As in Turnbull's statement quoted earlier, many authors have noted forager children playing loosely structured games that test individual abilities. Draper's example of this type of play is the !Kung game *zeni*. In this game, a weight with a feather and a leather thong attached is flung into the air, and the object is to send the *zeni* back in the air before it touches the ground by inserting the stick into the thong. Never did she observe the !Kung children count their successes at this game. As noted above for the Hadza, target practice games are quite common, especially among boys. *Ndaanga ya songo* is a spear-throwing game among the Mbendjele (Lewis, 2016), with obvious scaffolding implications for hunting. Turnbull favours the example of the liana swing, a fixture of children's play in the Congo Basin. On the swing, called *djambi* among the Mbendjele (Lewis, 2016) or *ezambi* among the Aka (Boyette, 2016a), children might take turns pushing each other, or older children might test themselves by swinging higher and higher and adding acrobatics (Turnbull, 1962). I have seen older Aka children make multiple *ezambi*s on a large tree out of well-established vines and swing around the trunk simultaneously, which demands trust in the forest and one's playmates to do so safely (Boyette, 2016a).

Aka trust in the forest comes from the substantial amount of time children spend autonomously exploring the forest and interacting with its features. For example, about 18% of Aka children's play was what I called "roaming," or exploring forest trails for the sake of being together in the forest, with no clear destination (Boyette, 2016a). Typically, this involved playful chatting and much interaction with their surrounds. Tree climbing and play on the *ezambi* may be spurred by roaming, as children feel inspired or reach a suitable place to stop. Such interactions with the forest are also noted by Turnbull (1962, 1978) for the Mbuti playing in the *bopi* and by Endicott and Endicott (2014) for the Batek, who find establishing a new camp an exciting opportunity to explore a new environment. Kamei (2005) similarly found "tradition-oriented play" as associated with the forest setting, which Baka children find to be "a mysterious, potentially dangerous but attractive space with creatures for hunting and ample materials for toys" (p. 352).

A remarkable example of the creativity and sophisticated ethnobiological knowledge engendered by forager play – again supported by the autonomy afforded forager children – is the Hadza children's game *rembo* (Crittenden, 2016a). *Rembo* blurs the distinction between 'work' and 'play' like some of the activities mentioned earlier; however, it is a child-only foraging activity never performed by adults. During the short season when weaver birds (*Quelea quelea*) colonies nest in the trees near to Hadza camps, children will coat a stick of less than 1 metre in length with a paste prepared from the sticky pulp of an inedible berry called *rembo*. The children place the stick in a watering hole or other body of water. When fledgling weaver birds fly to the water to drink and land on the stick, they become stuck and are captured by the young foragers waiting nearby. Children of all ages spend hours playing *rembo*, and roasting and eating the birds. As Crittenden notes, children are feeding themselves in the course of this activity, but, "It is clearly also a form of play. During trips to the water's edge to collect their spoils, children run, chase, laugh, shriek, dance, and sing" (p. 168). Hadza adults also harvest the weaver birds, but the children's technique of using *rembo* is their own.

In sum, from the moment they enter the play group, forager children enter a mixed-age, mixed-sex, non-competitive collaborative of fun and exploration. The group, led by older children, scaffolds the values that make the group and its play context – intimately familiar, autonomous, non-aggressive, non-hierarchical, and collaborative – a continuous feature of children's social life, and one that translates smoothly into adulthood.

Play and Culture Change

Naturally, forager peoples and cultures have changed independently and through continuous contact with other groups and other types of societies for thousands of years. It is reasonable to assert that openness to new ideas is forged within children's play, as children explore new materials, ideas, languages, and games. As they mature and enter the wider social and cultural world, some of these are more easily accepted as part of a child's cultural repertoire than others.

The introduction of football and other traditionally competitive games to children's play has been mentioned above. As noted, the rules are typically changed to a non-competitive version to fit the existing foundational schemas of sharing and egalitarianism and the associated norms of conduct (e.g., no boasting for getting more points). Objects from outside cultures are, not surprisingly, incorporated into forager children's play as well. For example, Kamei (2005) notes Baka constructing motor vehicles from available materials. While pretence play with new objects is one thing, more complex pretence play with more elaborate cultural themes from outside forager culture has been observed as well. For example, the Endicotts observed Batek children imitating Indian and Chinese shopkeepers (K. M. Endicott & Endicott, 2008).

Similarly, I will never forget the moment I observed Aka children in a forest camp playing *wali koko*. In the forests of the Central African Republic where I worked, Ngandu villagers, typically women (*wali* in Songo) would bring merchandise out to the forest to trade to the Aka for *Gnetum africanum* leaves (called *koko*). Once acquired en masse, the nutritious leaves are sold by the villagers at markets throughout the region. Throughout my time in the Central African Republic, *koko* commerce had grown substantially, and certain Aka families were more willing than others to specialize in *koko* trade and were therefore bringing in more market goods – and spending more time in the forest with Ngandu villagers. It was in such a camp where I saw a girl of around 7 years old set up upon a stump a small display of 'merchandise' that she was giving to the other children who brought her bundles of '*koko*'. The performance was complete with an imitation of the *koko wali* berating her Aka clients for not bringing enough bundles! In this and other similar camps, Songo was also spoken (instead of BaYaka) more often than in camps with fewer visits from *wali kokos*, even when Ngandu were not present.

More investigation is needed before we can say that such commerce play indicates adoptions of new norms around sharing in the community. However, it is clear that forager children play with such ideas. In some instances, it may be just to make fun of the selfish and loud outsiders (Turnbull, 1962), but with changes in the culturally constructed niche, such as forced or voluntary sedentarization, we can see how such play may be one force leading to culture change. For example, in the Botswanan Kalahari where some San groups have moved to permanent villages with electric wells, boys have incorporated horseback hunting into their play (Imamura, 2016). They build 'horses' and 'spears' out of bush materials and take on the roles of hunter and prey. Imamura attributes this new play to both the children's natural interest in imitating a recently introduced form of hunting performed by adult men and the reduced opportunities for actual small-game hunting, which previously constituted much of the boys' play. Their play, of course, still consists of collaborative and creative exploration of cultural practices, but also reveals a pathway to the loss of traditional foraging skills and knowledge.

Similarly, Pandya (2016) describes the complex changes that have occurred among the Jarawa foragers of the Andaman Islands since the construction of the Andaman Trunk Road (ATR) through their forest. The road has brought the Jarawas in increased contact with the state, poachers, tourists, and other outsiders and has become a new site of play for the youth. Whereas before the road children and adolescents would fuse play and work in the forest, they now 'gather' industrial goods from outsiders at the roadside. They have learned to see themselves through the gazes of the state and of tourists and put on performances emphasizing their 'primitiveness'. By such means, "young Jarawas had, by incorporating into their play the changing matrix of social relations brought about by the ATR, made the roadside a site of gainful work in much the same way as playing with toy bows and arrows that gradually leads to skill in hunting" (p. 196). Pandya notes that this adaptation reflects the evolutionary history of foraging as a flexible and resilient subsistence strategy in the context of changing social and economic environments. Play is a crucial aspect of this strategy, and one by which children can autonomously come to understand forces of cultural change.

Forager Children's Play: A Model for Today?

It has been proposed that, because of our species' long evolutionary history as foragers, the contexts of forager childrearing should be treated as a baseline in terms of what young humans have evolved to expect (Narváez et al., 2012, 2014). A corollary of this premise is that the rise in childhood mental illness in the United States today is a result of the move away from the 'optimal' rearing conditions represented by mobile, immediate return, foraging bands (Narvaez & Gleason, 2012) – those living in what I have referred to here as the forager culturally constructed niche. Thus, proponents of this perspective argue that parents and policymakers can utilize forager childrearing practices as models for 'optimal development'. One proponent of this line of thinking is psychologist Peter Gray, who has put forth a play theory of forager egalitarianism (Gray, 2009, 2012, 2014).

Gray starts from the argument that play across species is fundamentally egalitarian. For example, it requires animals to control aggression (as in play fighting or chasing) so as not to cause real harm and therefore to continue the play. Additionally, adult members of some species play to resolve conflicts and maintain or develop friendships. Thus, during human evolution, play was extended into human adulthood because "it enabled the high degree of cooperation and sharing essential to the hunter-gatherer way of life" (2014, 198). He provides evidence, much as I have here, that the contexts of forager childhood allow for substantial freedom to play (Gray, 2012) and that adult work, religious, and social life is infused with a sense of playfulness (Gray, 2014). Ultimately, he critiques the current mainstream educational system in the United States and elsewhere for emphasizing competition and classroom 'work' over free play and argues that children learn better by following the forager model of learning through play (Gray, 2013).

While the use of foragers as a model of how certain contexts for play may lead to certain social outcomes is reasonable, Gray's theory is problematic. The evidence does not, as he suggests, indicate that play, specifically, leads to egalitarianism. Play among foragers does contribute to the social learning of egalitarianism, as I have reviewed here. However, it also facilitates learning subsistence skills, ethnobotanical knowledge, how to share, and so on.

Additionally, play in other societies contributes to learning inequality and competition (Hewlett & Boyette, 2012). Given that there are no genetic differences between contemporary foragers and other human groups in some complex of genes related to play, we must assume that play universally serves, as it does in other species, as a psychobiological state that opens the body and mind to learning behaviours and cognitive orientations that are of use in the environment in which a child lives. What is unique about foragers is the culturally constructed niche that I have described here, within which children play and learn the values that have made foraging the oldest continuously maintained way of life on Earth.

Now, there are very likely things we can learn from forager play. However, an acknowledgement of contextual differences and caution against romanticism is warranted. For example, many parents and childcare agencies in the West today might object to allowing children to handle sharp knives or raw meat or to play with juvenile wild animals like toys until they die. Yet any forager researcher can attest to each of these being regular occurrences in forager children's daily play. Indeed, they are essential means of learning key skills and knowledge, as I have discussed. Of course, much like non-competitive games, children will not find such things compelling to do if they are not necessarily aspects of observable culture or part of the material basis for their play. Hence, we do not typically let children play with knives and we greatly encourage competition (Lancy, 2008).

It may be reasonable to suggest we take particular aspects of the forager niche and adapt them to the very different contexts of post-industrial life. Indeed, several alternative educational philosophies have done just that, but not because they are part of foraging life. Rather, they meshed with values and cultural models of child development held by their practitioners. For example, you can find such qualities as the value for autonomy, mixed-age groups, non-directive learning, nature exploration, and others at the core of different theories of early childhood education and care, including that of the Sudbury schools studied by Gray (Boyette, 2016c).

Conclusion

I have reviewed the major features of children's play among contemporary foraging societies. Like children all over the world, forager children's play involves imitation of the values, ideas, practices, and material culture they see around them in their cultures, as well as the creation of games unique to their own children's culture, though inspired by what they are learning about adult culture from each other and from adults. Descriptions of forager children's play have shown that what makes their play distinct is the great degree of autonomy afforded children in their play, the non-competitive nature of their own games, and the way they interpret those of other societies with whom they interact. Like children everywhere, forager children are compelled to explore their surroundings, but for foragers these are to a great degree less manicured by human hands than the play contexts of children in other societies, and the autonomy and collaboration afforded by the intimacy of forager communities lends itself to trust and deep interest in the natural world – which yields immense survival value for those children as adult foragers. While children incorporate the new into their play and forager societies face immense challenges in maintaining their autonomy, forager children's play continues to illustrate that forager identity and foundational schemas are central to child development in forager societies and the replication of the most resilient way of life humanity has known.

References

Bahuchet, S. (1999). Aka pygmies. In R. B. Lee & R. Daly (Eds.), *The Cambridge encyclopedia of hunter-gatherers* (pp. 190–194). Cambridge: Cambridge University Press.

Bird-David, N. (1999). 'Animism' revisited: Personhood, environment, and relational epistemology. *Current Anthropology, 40*(S1), S67–S91.

Blurton Jones, N., Hawkes, K., & Draper, P. (1994). Foraging returns of !Kung adults and children: Why didn't !Kung children forage? *Journal of Anthropological Research, 50*(3), 217–246.

Blurton Jones, N., Hawkes, K., & O'Connell, J. F. (1989). Modelling and measuring costs of children in two foraging societies. In V. Standen & R. Foley (Eds.), *Comparative socioecology: The behavioural ecology of humans and other mammals* (pp. 367–390). Oxford: Blackwell Scientific.

Bock, J. (2002). Learning, life history, and productivity: Children's lives in the Okavango Delta, Botswana. *Human Nature, 13*(2), 161–197.

Bock, J., & Johnson, S. E. (2004). Subsistence ecology and play among the Okavango Delta peoples of Botswana. *Human Nature, 15*(1), 63–81.

Boyette, A. H. (2013). Social learning during middle childhood among Aka forest foragers and Ngandu farmers of the Central African Republic. Doctoral dissertation, Washington State University.

Boyette, A. H. (2016a). Children's play and culture learning in an egalitarian foraging society. *Child Development, 87*(3), 759–769.

Boyette, A. H. (2016b). Children's play and the integration of social and individual learning: A cultural niche construction perspective. In H. Terashima & B. S. Hewlett (Eds.), *Social learning and innovation in contemporary hunter-gatherers* (pp. 159–169). Tokyo: Springer Japan.

Boyette, A. H. (2016c). The long view: Evolutionary theories of early childhood education and care. In T. David, K. Goouch, & S. Powell (Eds.), *Routledge handbook of early childhood education and care* (pp. 59–68). London: Routledge.

Boyette, A. H. (In Press). Autonomy and the socialization of cooperation in foragers: Aka children's views of sharing and caring. *Hunter Gatherer Research.*

Boyette, A. H., & Hewlett, B. S. (2017). Teaching in hunter-gatherers. *Review of Philosophy and Psychology*. Available at https://doi.org/10.1007/s13164-017-0347-2.

Codding, B. F., & Kramer, K. (Eds.). (2016). *Why forage? Hunters and gatherers in the twenty-first century*. Albuquerque: University of New Mexico Press Published in Association with School for Advanced Research Press.

Crittenden, A. N. (2016a). Children's foraging and play among the Hadza: The evolutionary significance of 'work play'. In Courtney L. Meehan & Alyssa N. Crittenden, *Childhood: Origins, evolution, and implications* (pp. 155–171). Santa Fe: University of New Mexico Press.

Crittenden, A. N. (2016b). To share or not to share? Social processes of learning to share food among Hadza hunter-gatherer children. In H. Terashima & B. S. Hewlett (Eds.), *Social learning and innovation in contemporary hunter-gatherers* (pp. 61–70). Tokyo: Springer Japan.

Crittenden, A. N., & Zes, D. A. (2015). Food sharing among Hadza hunter-gatherer children. *PLOS ONE, 10*(7), e0131996.

D'Andrade, R. G., & Strauss, C. (Eds.) (1992). *Human motives and cultural models*. Cambridge: Cambridge University Press.

Draper, P. (1973). Crowding among hunter-gatherers: The !Kung Bushmen. *Science, 182*(4109), 301–303.

Draper, P. (1976). Social and economic constraints on child life among the !Kung. In R. B. Lee & I. De Vore (Eds.), *Kalahari hunter-gatherers: Studies of the !Kung San and their neighbors* (pp. 200–217). Cambridge, MA: Harvard University Press.

Endicott, K. L., & Endicott, K. M. (2014). Batek childrearing and morality. In D. Narvaez, K. Valentino, A. Fuentes, J. J. McKenna, & P. Gray (Eds.), *Ancestral landscapes in human evolution* (pp. 108–125). Oxford: Oxford University Press.

Endicott, K. M., & Endicott, K. L. (2008). *The headman was a woman: The gender egalitarian Batek of Malaysia*. Long Grove, IL: Waveland Press.

Fouts, H. N., Bader, L. R., & Neitzel, C. L. (2016). Work-themed play among young children in foraging and farming communities in Central Africa. *Behaviour, 153*(6–7), 663–691.

Gosso, Y., e Morais, M. d. L. S., & Otta, E. (2007). Pretend play of Brazilian children: A window into different cultural worlds. *Journal of Cross-Cultural Psychology, 38*(5), 539–558.

Gray, P. (2009). Play as a foundation for hunter-gatherer social existence. *American Journal of Play, 1*, 476–522.

Gray, P. (2012). The value of a play-filled childhood in development of the hunter-gatherer individual. In D. Narvaez, J. Panksepp, A. N. Schore, & T. R. Gleason (Eds.), *Evolution, early experience and human development* (pp. 352–370). New York: Oxford University Press.

Gray, P. (2013). *Free to learn: Why unleashing the instinct to play will make our children happier, more self-reliant, and better students for life*. Washington, DC: Basic Books.

Gray, P. (2014). Play theory of hunter-gatherer egalitarianism. In D. Narvaez, K. Valentino, A. Fuentes, J. J. McKenna, & P. Gray (Eds.), *Ancestral landscapes in human evolution* (pp. 192–215). Oxford University Press.

Hewlett, B. S. (1991). *Intimate fathers: The nature and context of Aka pygmy paternal infant care*. Ann Arbor: University of Michigan Press.

Hewlett, B. S. (2016). Evolutionary cultural anthropology: Containing ebola outbreaks and explaining hunter-gatherer childhoods. *Current Anthropology*, *57*(S13), S27–S37.

Hewlett, B. S., & Boyette, A. H. (2012). Play in hunter-gatherers (Commentary). In D. Narvaez, J. Panksepp, A. N. Schore, & T. R. Gleason (Eds.), *Evolution, early experience and human development: From research to practice* (pp. 388–396). New York: Oxford University Press.

Hewlett, B. S., Fouts, H. N., Boyette, A. H., & Hewlett, B. L. (2011). Social learning among Congo Basin hunter-gatherers. *Philosophical Transactions of the Royal Society B*, *366*, 1168–1178.

Hewlett, B. S., & Roulette, C. J. (2016). Teaching in hunter-gatherer infancy. *Royal Society Open Science*, *3*(1), 150403.

Hewlett, B. S., & Roulette, J. W. (2014). Cosleeping beyond infancy. *Ancestral landscapes in human evolution: culture, childrearing and social wellbeing*, 129.

Hill, K., & Hurtado, M. (1996). *Ache life history: The ecology and demography of a foraging people*. New York: Aldine de Gruyter.

Imamura, K. (2016). Hunting play among the San children: Imitation, learning, and play. In B. S. Hewlett & H. Terashima (Eds.), *Social learning and innovation in contemporary hunter-gatherers: Evolutionary and ethnographic perspectives* (pp. 179–186). Tokyo: Springer Japan.

Kamei, N. (2005). Play among Baka children in Cameroon. In B. S. Hewlett & M. E. Lamb (Eds.), *Hunter-gatherer childhoods: Evolutionary, developmental, and cultural perspectives* (pp. 343–362). New Brunswick, NJ: Aldine Transaction.

Kelly, R. L. (1995). *The foraging spectrum: Diversity in hunter-gatherer lifeways*. Washington, DC: Smithsonian Institution Press.

Kenrick, J. (2002). Anthropology and anthropocentrism: Images of hunter-gatherers, Westerners and the environment. *Senri Ethnological Studies*, *60*(60), 191–213.

Kidd, C., Kenrick, J., Couillard, V., & Gilbert, J. (2009). *Land rights and the forest peoples of Africa: Historical, legal and anthropological perspectives*. Moreton-in-Marsh, UK: Forest Peoples Programme.

Kisliuk, M. R. (1998). *Seize the dance!: BaAka musical life and the ethnography of performance*. New York: Oxford University Press.

Konner, M. (1972). Aspects of the developmental ethology of a foraging people. In N. Blurton Jones (Ed.), *Ethological studies of child behavior* (pp. 285–304). London: Cambridge University Press.

Lancy, D. F. (2008). *The anthropology of childhood: Cherubs, chattel, changelings*. Cambridge: Cambridge University Press.

Lee, R. B. (1969). Eating Christmas in the Kalahari. *Conformity and conflict: Readings in aultural anthropology*, 27–34.

Lee, R. B. (2013). *The Dobe Jul'hoansi* (4th edn., student edn.). Belmont, CA: Wadsworth Cengage Learning.

Lewis, J. (2002). Forest hunter-gatherers and their world: A study of the Mbendjele Yaka Pygmies of Congo-Brazzaville and their secular and religious activites and representations. Doctoral thesis, London School of Economics and Political Science.

Lewis, J. (2009). As well as words: Congo pygmy hunting, mimicry, and play. In R. Botha & C. Knight (Eds.), *The cradle of language* (pp. 236–256). Oxford: Oxford University Press.

Lewis, J. (2015). Where goods are free but knowledge costs: Hunter-gatherer ritual economics in Western Central Africa. *Hunter Gatherer Research*, *1*(1), 1–27.

Lewis, J. (2016). Play music and taboo in the reproduction of an egalitarian society. In B. S. Hewlett & H. Terashima (Eds.), *Social learning and innovation in contemporary hunter-gatherers: Evolutionary and ethnographic perspectives* (pp. 147–158). Tokyo: Springer Japan.

Lew-Levy, S. R., Lavi, N., Reckin, R., Cristobal-Azkarate, J., & Ellis-Davies, K. (in press). How do hunter-gatherer children learn social and gender norms? A meta-ethnographic review. *Journal of Cross Cultural Research*.

Lye, T.-P. (2004). *Changing pathways: Forest degradation and the Batek of Pahang, Malaysia*. Lanham, MD: Lexington Books.

Lye, T.-P. (n.d.). *Flexible resilience*.

MacDonald, K. (2007). Cross-cultural comparison of learning in human hunting. *Human Nature*, *18*(4), 386–402.

Narvaez, D., & Gleason, T. R. (2012). Developmental optimization. In D. Narvaez, J. Panksepp, A. N. Schore, & T. R. Gleason (Eds.), *Evolution, early experience and human development* (pp. 307–325). Oxford University Press.

Narváez, D., Panksepp, J., Schore, A. N., & Gleason, T. R. (Eds.). (2012). *Evolution, early experience and human development: From research to practice and policy*. Oxford: Oxford University Press.

Narváez, D., Valentino, K., Fuentes, A., McKenna, J. J., & Gray, P. (2014). *Ancestral landscapes in human evolution: Culture, childrearing and social wellbeing*. Oxford: Oxford University Press.

Odling-Smee, F. J., Laland, K. N., & Feldman, M. W. (2003). *Niche construction: The neglected process in evolution*. Princeton, NJ: Princeton University Press.

Pandya, V. (2016). When hunters gather but do not hunt, playing with the state in the forest: Jarawa children's changing world. In B. S. Hewlett & H. Terashima (Eds.), *Social learning and innovation in contemporary hunter-gatherers: Evolutionary and ethnographic perspectives* (pp. 187–199). Tokyo: Springer Japan.

Roberts, J. M., Arth, M. J., & Bush, R. R. (1959). Games in culture. *American Antiquity*, *61*, 597–605.

Roberts, J. M., & Sutton-Smith, B. (1962). Child training and game involvement. *Ethnology*, *1*(2), 166–185.

Shore, B. (1996). *Culture in mind: Cognition, culture, and the problem of meaning*. New York: Oxford University Press.

Smith, P. K. (2010). *Children and play*. Malden, MA: Wiley-Blackwell.

Sugawara, K. (1984). Spatial proximity and bodily contact among the Central Kalahari San. *African Study Monographs*, *3*, 1–43.

Thomas, E. M. (1959). *The harmless people*. New York: Alfred A. Knopf.

Turnbull, C. M. (1962). *The forest people*. New York: Simon & Schuster.

Tucker, B., & Young, A. G. (2005). Growing up Mikea: children's time allocation and tuber foraging in southwestern Madagascar. In B. S. Hewlett & M. E. Lamb

(Eds.), *Hunter-gatherer childhoods: evolutionary, developmental, and cultural perspectives*.

Turnbull, C. M. (1965). *Wayward servants*. Garden City, NY: Natural History Press.

Turnbull, C. M. (1978). The politics of non-aggression (Zaire). In A. Montagu (Ed.), *Learning non-aggression: The experiences of non-literate societies*. Oxford: Oxford University Press.

Wiessner, P. (2005). Norm enforcement among the Ju/'hoansi Bushmen. *Human Nature, 16*(2), 115–145.

Woodburn, J. (1966). *The Hadza*. Film. London: London School of Economics.

Woodburn, J. (1982). Egalitarian societies. *Man, 17*(3), 431–451.

18 Play in South American Indigenous Children

Yumi Gosso, Briseida D. Resende, and
Ana M. A. Carvalho

South America possesses diverse geographical and ecological characteristics: tropical and sub-tropical forests, deserts, prairies, alpine climes, and savannahs, several of these extending across the frontiers of the 13 continental countries. Prior to Columbian contact this diverse continent was to home to a host of distinct indigenous peoples (the same group often names itself differently and/or is quoted with different orthography, e.g., Wapixana/ Wapishana or Karajá/Carajá; our choice was to adopt the most frequently registered name/orthography). A number of them are extinct or nearly extinct, with populations limited to fewer than 100 individuals. Segments of these and other groups live in urban areas, with different levels of intermingling with non- indigenous populations, some of them showing loose ties with pre-Columbian ways of life.

The remaining groups, whose lives emerge principally through anthropological studies, live in indigenous preserves, where they hunt, gather, practice small-scale agriculture and animal husbandry, and generally maintain a way of life within close proximity to nature and largely disconnected from the industrial world. Despite a shared sense of indigenous identity created from the legacy of European conquest and exploitation, each group also considers itself to be unique and possesses a distinct language and cosmology (Guimarães, 2016; Ribeiro, 2012).

This chapter presents the available information on children's play in indigenous groups from different areas in South America. Figure 18.1 depicts the geographic distribution of South American biomes and its 13 countries, and Table 18.1 shows the approximate location of the indigenous groups focused on here.

As shown in Table 18.1, the South American indigenous population is concentrated in the Amazonian region (tropical forest), particularly Brazilian Amazonia. The second largest concentration is in west-central Brazil and eastern Paraguay and Bolivia. Spanish-speaking countries in the continental north share the Amazonian tropical forest biome with Brazil; many Amazonian groups are present both in Brazil and in the neighbouring countries as is also the case with groups living in the Bolivian and Paraguayan *Chaco* and the Brazilian *Pantanal*. Some indigenous groups are still found in the semi-arid northeastern regions of the Brazilian savannah, as well as in the remains of the

Figure 18.1 *Biomes and political divisions. From Begon et al. (2007).*

tropical forest that, up to the sixteenth century, covered most of the Atlantic coast (Atlantic forest) – a region that now comprises the most developed, populous, and urbanized areas of Brazil and where original indigenous groups were extinguished or expelled from the sixteenth century on. The remaining South American indigenous groups are scattered across smaller biomes – e.g.,

Table 18.1 *Location of indigenous groups in the South American territory*

Biomes	Indigenous groups
Tropical forest Amazonian Atlantic	Anambé, Apinayé, Apurinã, Arapaso, Ashaninka, A´uwê-Xavante, Baniwa, Bororo, Caiapó, Deni, Galibi do Oiapoque, Galibi-Maworno, Gavião-Pykopjé, Guajá, Guajajara, Guarani, Ikpeng, Iranxe-Manoki, Kalapalo, Camaiurá, Karajá, Karipuna, Macuxi, Manchineri, Maraguá, Matsés, Mehinaku, Munduruku, Panará, Parakanã, Patamona, Pitaguary, Pykopjé, Cavalcante, Sateré-Mawé, Tapirapé, Taulipang, Tembé, Tikuna, Tiriyó, Trumai, Tukano, Urubu-Kaapor,Wai-Wai, Waimiri-Atroari,Wapixana, Wari, Wayana, Xerente, Xikrin, Yanomami, Yawalapiti, Yawanawá, Yudja
Tropical savannah	Canela, Iranxe, Kaimbé, Paresi, Rikbaktsa
Pampa	Guarani, Pampa
Seasonal tropical forest	Baikari, Kaingang, Guayaki, Kariri-Xocó, Maxacali, Terena, Umutina, Xocó
Desert	Kolla, Mataco, Quichua
Temperate coniferous forest	*Araucanian,*[a] Mapuche
Chaparral	*Patagonian*

[a] Italicized names are those that are used in the relevant literature, even if they do not belong to indigenous idioms.

Patagonian in southern Chile and Argentina (chaparral), *Pampa* in Argentina's pampa, *Quichua* in the Andean montane, and Araucanian in southern montane areas, partly covered by coniferous forest.

The larger number of groups occurring only in Brazil can be due to more than one factor, e.g., the extension of the Brazilian territory and of its less hostile biomes, historical differences in the relationships between native populations and European conquerors, or differences in the amount of available child anthropology research in each country since only the groups on which information about children and play was available were included in this report.

Conceptions of Children, Play, and Education in South American Indigenous Groups

One foundational truism of early education is that conceptions of childhood and child-rearing are as varied as the diverse ways of life and social organization that have emerged in the course of human history (Lordelo &

Carvalho, 2003). Interestingly, however, indigenous societies, perhaps due to the timelessness and relative stability of their way of life, present striking similarities in their conceptions of childhood (Gosso et al., 2005). Parenting in these societies is characterized by intimate and intensive mother–child contact in the first two years of life and is further marked by receptive, cherishing, and tolerant interaction with other relatives and neighbours in the village. These attitudes and relational dynamics persist as the child ages and engages in play with peers and older siblings. Reports on adult attitudes regarding the patient acceptance of children's interference and essayed collaboration in adult activities and on the absence of physical punishment have surprised and sometimes moved foreign observers since the colonial era (Carvalho et al., 2015).

In contrast with the emphasis mainstream contemporary societies place on adult-guided education as the indispensable pathway to successful adulthood, indigenous societies view childhood as a life stage on its own right. Children are not viewed as incomplete human beings who must be led in their pathway to adult life; they are agents in the production and reproduction of their own social dynamics (Nunes, 1999), a perspective that allows tremendous room for free and unsupervised play activities. Playing is a child's right and is indeed the purpose of their existence as children. Thus indigenous parents remain largely unconcerned with formal education, trusting that the knowledge and abilities needed in adult life will be naturally acquired through opportunities to observe and participate in adult activities through open attention (Carvalho et al., 2015). Put another way, children "see everything" in a society where little is forbidden to them (Cohn, 2002a, pp. 138, 122); "they have all the time in the world to learn" and do not need to be evaluated, because "education is everywhere: in the time of the day, of nature, of the sun, of the moon" (Macena, 2016, p. 84).

Indigenous Children at Play

Franco Neto (2010) observes that indigenous children play throughout the day in large and mixed groups (boys and girls), small groups, or as individuals. Many play activities common to different indigenous groups are often practiced under the same or similar name(s), and/or are also practiced by children all around the world, even if occurring in different physical contexts and with different resources. For indigenous groups in closer contact with non-indigenous populations, industrialized toys (e.g., balls, dolls, vehicles) may be available, but locally manufactured toys are also an important aspect of their play cultures. These points are illustrated and elaborated in the next sections.

Nature: The Playground

According to the available literature, indigenous villages do not have man-made playgrounds in their plazas, which are typically surrounded by families' lodgings (Munduruku, 2003). Instead, nature is the playground. Trees are useful for climbing, for hide-and-seek games, and as safe harbours in play chase. Their branches and long external roots also function as slides, swings, and see-saws. These play activities are common to many groups from across South America (Table 18.1, Figure 18.1), e.g., Apinayé (Silva, n.d.), A'uwê-Xavante (Nunes, 1999), Bakairi, Bororo, Tukano, Trumai, Yudja (Grando et al., & Campos, n.d.); Gavião-Pykopjê (Reis & Sousa, 2008), Guarani (Oliveira, 2007), Kaingang, Mehinaku (Gosso et al., 2005), Karipuna (Brito, 2012), Makuxi, Wapixana (Costa, 2013), Maxakali (Alves, 2001), Munduruku (Nascimento & Zoia, 2014), Parakanã (Gosso & Otta, 2003), Rikbaktsa (Grando et al., n.d.), Terena (Brostolin & Oliveira, 2013).

Rivers also serve as favoured play sites. Small children go 'swimming' on the shoulders of older siblings, who are themselves precocious experts in jumping or diving in the water using a fallen tree trunk as a springboard. Older children also swim to reach the opposite bank of the river or allow themselves to pleasantly drift away on the current – e.g., A'uwê-Xavante, Mehinaku (Gosso et al., 2005), Bakairi, Rikbaktsa (Grando et al., n.d.), Galibi Marworno (Codonho, 2007), Kaingang (Amaral, 2011, n.d.), Karipuna (Brito, 2012), Kariri-Xocó (Oliveira, 1999), Maraguá (Yamã, 2013), Maxakali (Alves, 2001), Mehinaku (Ferrari, 2013), Munduruku (Nascimento & Zoia, 2014), Xocó (Bichara, 2003), and Yudja (Grando et al., n.d.). The riverine expertise of indigenous children reflects their intimacy with the river. Parakanã and Xocó boys were observed navigating down the river on tree trunks (Bichara, 2003; Gosso, 2003). Tikuna boys build canoes and use them to fish in the river (Grando et al., n.d.). Munduruku children play flooding the canoe by turning it over and falling in the water only to straighten it, climb aboard, and begin the fun again (Nascimento & Zóia, 2014).

Play fighting in the river was observed among Yawalapiti boys: one boy, standing on his partner's shoulders, tries to toss his similarly mounted rival into the water (Lima, 2008). Play chasing on the river bank is reported among the Kaingang (Amaral, 2011), Kalapalo (Herrero, 2010), Kariri-Xocó (Oliveira, 1999), and Maraguá (Yamã, 2013); and in the river, for Munduruku (Nascimento & Zóia, 2014); Paresi – with the pursuer nicknamed Sucuri, a large snake; and Yudja, where five children on a canoe pursued five other children placed 25 metres away (Grando et al., n.d.). Hide-and-seek in muddy waters is reported for Camaiurá (Gosso et al., 2005). River banks furnish mud to be moulded into animals, houses, and other toys, and/or sand for children to draw in with sticks (A'uwe-Xavante: Nunes, 2002a; Kaingang, Mehinaku: Gosso et al., 2005; Makuxi: Costa, 2013; Manchineri: Calderaro, 2006; Mataco: Montani & Suárez, 2016; Maxakali: Alves, 2001; Costa, 2013; Parakanã: Gosso & Otta, 2003; Xikrin: Cohn, 2002b; Xocó: Bichara, 2003; Yudja: Instituto Socioambiental, 2015).

Awareness of the surrounding nature is also apparent in other play contexts: observing and capturing small animals (Rikbaktsa: Grando et al., n.d.);

fishing, and sometimes cooking and eating the prey (Yawanawá: Grando, 2010); imitating animal behaviour (e.g., pretending that a snake is nearby or using a dead one to playfully menace their peers; A'uwê-Xavante: Carrara, 2002); impersonating a monkey climbing a tree and jumping in the branches (Yudja: Grando et al., n.d.); and playing with live animals such as a small armadillo (Guarani: Jesus, 2010), a small alligator (Tapirapé: Grando, 2014), or domestic creatures like cats, dogs, and ducks (Maxakali: Alves, 2001).

Moonlight and darkness play a role in the choice of play activities. During a full moon, Xikrin children play in the yard but prefer to run, dance, and sing outside under the waning light of a new moon (Cohn, 2002b). Seasonal differences are also linked to different play repertoires. For instance, dry, compact, and smooth soil favours playing marbles (with previously made clay balls or with seeds), whereas in the rainy season the soft wet soil can be used as a canvas for stick carvings or to construct canals, houses, and bridges. Seasonal play differentiation is apparent in riverine activities as well. In the dry season, when the waters are calm and clear, women work on the banks of the river while children play or help them. The water movement is slower and children can observe the trajectory of pebbles thrown in the water. Moderate river conditions also mark the period when young children learn how to swim and when they begin their extensive explorations of the riparian environment. In the rainy season, the deeper and muddy rivers favour more intense physical activities: jumping in the water, being carried by the current, diving to collect thrown objects, play-chase, and hide-and-seek – e.g., among the Arapaso (Pereira, 2013), A'uwê-Xavante (Nunes, 2002a), Kalapalo (Franco-Neto, 2010), and Rikbaktsa (Grando et al., n.d.).

Play Artefacts

Nature is also the source of building material for play artefacts. Diverse play artefacts are mentioned for practically all of the groups on which there is play information. Whether play artefacts are made by adults, by the children themselves, or by both, they are typically constructed from materials in the surrounding environment (wood, straw, leaves, rubber, fibres, clay, stones, shells, etc.) and occasionally from scraps of material brought by visitors (cans, plastic vessels, clothes). Table 18.2 displays frequently mentioned play artefacts and materials used by different groups. These materials are used for weaving, carving, tying, melding, and folding.

Collecting material and manufacturing play artefacts can be in itself a playful activity: girls enjoy weaving small baskets and other objects; boys and girls mould clay into animals, dolls, and utensils even when the artefacts are not meant to be played with. In other cases, artefacts are produced as the first stage of a play activity: for instance, body painting involves first collecting *urucum*, the fruit whose juice is used as a dye, and then extracting the juice and

Table 18.2 *Play artefacts*

Artefacts	Material	Groups (e.g.)
Utensils: fan, small sieve, small broom, basket, tube, drinking vessel, pot	Palm leaves: *babaçu, buriti, tucum, bacaba*; other leaves; straw, calabash shell	Anambé, Apinayé, Apurinã, *Araucanian,*[a] Canela, Kaingang, Tiriyó, Urubu-Kaapor, Wai-wai
Animals: tapir, dog, bird, fish, toad, animal parts	Clay, wood, coconut, straw, wax	Anambé, Apinayé, *Araucanian*, Mehinaku, Munduruku, Tiriyó, Wai-wai, Wayana
Bow and arrow, spear, dart, knife, paddle	Wood, fibres	Anambé, Apinayé, Guajá, Guajajara, Guarani, Karajá, Parakanã, Sateré-Mawé, Urubu-Kaapor, Waimiri-Atroari, Wai-wai, Xikrin, Xocó, Yawalapiti, Yudja
Vehicles (boat, airplane, car)	Wood	Ikpeng, Trumai, Yudja
Dolls	Clay, eye of corn, cloths; leaves (for filling)	*Araucanian*, Ashaninka, Karajá, Makuxi, Trumai
Rattles, buzzers	Deer nails, snail shells, small stone, seed in straw containers	Ashaninka, Mataco, Matsés, Xerente, Wai-Wai, Wayana
Tops	Tucum seeds, small calabash shells; rods, cord	Apinayé, *Araucanian*, Canela, Tiriyó, Waimiri-Atroari, Xerente
Shuttlecock	Corn straw, leaves, cord, feathers	Apinayé, Bororo, Camaiurá, Guarani, Makuxi, Taulipang, Yawalapiti
Ball	Mangaba latex, cloth, leaves	*Araucanian*, Ashaninka, Paresi, Trumai

From Hilger (1957); Oliveira et al. (2015); Silva (2014); Silva (n.d.); Silva & Notzold (2012).
[a] Italicized names are those that are used in the relevant literature, even if they do not belong to indigenous idioms.

using it for painting (Gosso & Otta, 2003); playing with stilts involves first collecting and cleaning forked tree branches to make them (Meirelles, 2012).

Children engage in diverse play activities and games with the objects they construct. As indicated above, in some of these playful activities the goal is the construction itself; in others, the goal is the practice of skills in the use of the artefact (the use of artefacts in more complex games is referred to in the following sections). Boys, individually or in groups, use their bows to practice shooting at targets of varying difficulty: no target (shooting upward), still targets (piece of wood, stone), or small live animals (e.g., Apinayé: Nimuendajú, 1983; Bakairi: Grando et al., n.d.; Guajá, Guajajara, Guarani: IELA, n. d.; Kalapalo, Yawalapiti: Herrero, 2010; Karajá, Parakanã: Gosso & Otta,

2003; Paresi, Tapirapé, Umutina, Xavante: Grando et al., n.d.; Sateré-Mawé: Meirelles, 2012; Urubu-Kaapor: Gosso et al., 2005; Xikrin: Cohn, 2002a, 2002b; Xocó: Bichara, 2003; Yudja: Instituto Socioambiental, 2015). A variant observed in this type of play involves teams of boys trying to target an arc set in motion by an opposing group (Lima, 2008). Other weapons include spears and throwing devices (slingshot, blowgun – a tube through which ammunition is expelled by blowing or pressing a tampon inside the tube, named *macareara angap* or *jawari* in different groups). As with bows, other indigenous missile weapons may be used just for practice or for more elaborate games: ammunition is thrown against a bamboo fence; standing behind it, the targeted boys must deviate from the projectile without moving their feet. These artefacts and their use have been documented among several groups, e.g., Camaiurá (Moisés, 2003), Guayaki (Gosso, 2004), Manchineri (Calderaro, 2006), Parakanã (Gosso & Otta, 2003), Wapixana, Makuxi (Costa, 2013), and Yawalapiti (Lima, 2008).

Tops. These include buzzing tops, tops that turn around a stick or are tied to a cord, and a top that rises upward in a spiral similar to a helicopter helix. The latter is made with large nuts or seeds or bark cut from a tree trunk and filled with seeds. Playing with tops is reported among the Apinayé (Nimuendajú, 1983), Camaiurá (Moisés, 2003), Deni (Ribeiro, 1987), Galibi do Oiapoque (Meirelles, 2012), Taulipang (CTA/ZM, 2009), Yawalapiti (Lima, 2008), and Yudja (Instituto Socioambiental, 2015).

Stilts. After finding two similar forked tree branches and cleaning them to use as stilts, the children practice walking on them; bets are often made on who can walk the longest distance with them (Meirelles, 2012). Stilts are used among several groups in different regions of the continent: temperate coniferous forests, Amazonian forest, pampas in eastern Brazil, and eastern Bolivia (Cooper, 1949): Camaiurá, A'uwê-Xavante (Gosso, 2004), Mehinaku (Ferrari, 2013), and Yawalapiti (Lima, 2008).

Dolls. Manufactured dolls using clay, cloth, and other available materials are reported for several groups, e.g., Caiapó, Canela, Guajajara, Karajá, Tikuna, Yanomami (Gosso, 2004), Maxakali (Alves, 2001), Araucanian, and most of the groups studied by Cooper (1949). A well-known artisanship tradition concerns the Karajá doll, a figure sculpted in clay and embellished with painted or glued/tied ornaments (Ferrari, 2013). Playing with dolls is considered later in the section on make-believe.

Cat's Cradle. Making figures by intertwining a string between the fingers is a widespread favourite (e.g., Camaiurá, Mehinaku: Gosso et al., 2005; Kalapalo: Herrero, 2010; Karajá, Taulipang: CTA/ZM, 2009; Yudja: Instituto Socioambiental, 2015; Wapixana: Costa, 2013). It is usually played by two children who exchange turns, removing the figure from the partner's hands and thus changing its design. Cat's cradle involves the partners' knowledge of the sequence of figures to be built and the motor skills required to make them. The game makes for an interesting example of a play activity whose goal and pleasure is merely to construct something, however transient.

Shuttlecock (an original indigenous creation, *peteca* in Portuguese, from the Tupi word meaning 'strike with the hand'). Constructing a shuttlecock is a complex task that can entertain even small, restless children for hours. Meirelles (2012) reports a group of 4- to 13-year-old Xavante children who spent the whole day engaged in this activity, which involved gathering corn straw in the field to use as filling and also to replace feathers, observing how experienced craftspeople weaved the straw with skilled finger movements, and then imitating them. The denomination of the artefact varies according to group, e.g., *tobdaé* for the Xavante; for the Guarani, *mangá* (or *yó*, a variant that uses corncob as the base of the shuttlecock). Shuttlecocks are also used among many other groups, e.g., Apinayé (Nimuendajú, 1983); A'uwê-Xavante (Grando et al., n.d.); Baniwa (Grando et al., n.d.); Bororo, Camaiurá, Guarani, Yawalapiti (Lima, 2008); Kaigang (Silva, 2014); Kalapalo (Herrero, 2010); Kariri-Xocó (Oliveira, 1999); Makuxi, Taulipang (Cooper, 1949); and Wapixana (Costa, 2013). (A structured game using shuttlecocks is described in the following section.)

A number of other objects are made and used as part of play activities. Yudja girls enjoy making necklaces, bracelets, and other body ornaments with seeds, grains, and other suitable materials (Instituto Socioambiental, 2015). Among Parakanã children, boxes are tied and pulled with cords to transport objects or younger children (Gosso, 2004); balls are made with *mangaba* latex or other materials and used individually or in group games; and masks, drums, and other objects used by adults (scrubbing boards, pans, fishing nets, pestles) are adapted for play activities, often involving make-believe (Bichara, 2003; Gosso, 2004; IELA, n.d.).

Structured Games

The selection of play activities included in this section was based on two criteria: the recognition of a similar deep structure present in different play episodes – e.g., in play fighting, play chasing, and hide-and-seek even if with variable sceneries and conventions (acceptable strokes or 'weapons', who is the next pursuer, safe harbours, or forbidden hiding places) – and Vygotsky's distinction between play activities grounded in pure imagination and those structured play activities governed by rules or an unchanging set of cultural or genre conventions (Vygotsky, 1978).

One aspect that hinders the categorization of some games as play activities in indigenous groups is that the scholarly literature on play often includes children's play and adult games and rituals (Oliveira et al., 2015) in which children may also participate (e.g., in the Toré, a traditional dance present in several groups: Bichara et al., 2012) within the same category. These activities are not spontaneously created or practiced by children and were not included here unless there is evidence that children practice them without adult leadership.

Hide-and-Seek, Play Chase and Play Fight. The deep structure of these games can be recognized in a diversity of play contexts (e.g., hide-and-seek, play fight, and play chase in the river). Multi-age groups of Parakanã and Mehinaku children play hiding, escaping, and being chased by a partner around buildings in their villages (Gosso et al., 2005). In a Maxakali version of hide-and-seek, one child pretends to hurt another child ('jaguar'), who then falls to the ground, while the remaining children run and hide in the woods. The jaguar revives and runs off angrily in search of the prey; the first child to be caught then becomes the next jaguar (Maxakali: Alves, 2001). Another variant of hide-and-seek involves hiding an object: Camaiurá (Moisés, 2003) and Yawalapiti (Lima, 2008) children play Ui'ui, in which a child hides a straw string in the sand and other children try to find it. Variants of play chase include Pira and Cholo. In Pira, one child holds the *pira* (an object carried and exchanged along the game), and pursues other children. The child who is touched takes the *pira* and becomes the pursuer. The game may take place in the river or on land (Arapaso: Pereira, 2013). In Cholo (meaning 'target'), the pursuer 'tags' a partner and calls "*Cholo*", naming that partner as the new pursuer (Araucanian: Hilger, 1957); Xocó children play chase as 'police and thieves' in imitation of television programs available in their village (Bichara, 2003). Children of the Mehinaku and several other indigenous peoples (Cooper, 1949) play the Hawk game, where a 'hawk' (or a 'jaguar') pursues children one by one until they are all caught. Among Mehinaku and Yawalapiti children, the jaguar (*yanomaka*) calls on the services of captured children to aid in their hunt (Lima, 2008).

Other versions of play chase are more elaborate. Kalapalo children play Toloi Kunhügü (Hawk). The leader of the game ('hawk') draws a tree in the sand and the other children ('small birds') choose branches as 'nests'. The hawk approaches the tree, the birds flee and gather around the tree, stomping their feet and singing to challenge the hawk, who jumps to catch them. The birds flee, distract the hawk, and seek shelter in the nests. Those who are caught are 'imprisoned' near the tree trunk. The last to be caught is the next hawk (Herrero, 2010).

In the Tucunaré (large Amazonian fish) game, played by Panará children, rods are placed on the soil to create one square inside a larger square. The inner square represents the deeper part of the river while the outer square, broken by six 'doors', represents the shallows. In the deeper square, four *tucunarés* proceed to chase the 'small fish' (6–10 children standing in the shallows). The small fish tries to escape through the doors since *tucunarés* are too big to follow them through the doors and must return to the depths with their captured prey. Prisoners must stay within the inner square until all the fish are caught (Estelles, 2016).

Umutina children play the Angry Bull game wherein one child is chosen as the 'bull' and others stand together holding hands to create a fence in the manner of the American game Red Rover. The bull moves back some distance and races toward the fence. If the bull crosses the fence, the others run after him and the child who catches him is the next bull. If the bull does not succeed in breaking through the fence, the other children encircle him. The bull asks each child "Which wood is this?"; the children respond at random, and, becoming increasingly 'angry', the bull must break the circle and escape the pursuers until one child catches him and becomes the new bull (Grando et al., n.d.).

Games with play fighting as a core component also involve make-believe, chasing, and/or hiding. In the Kap (Wasp) game, a group of Yawalapiti children find and attack the 'wasp's nest' (a sand pile) where other children (wasps) hum. The attackers try to destroy the nest and are pinched ('stung') and chased by the wasps (Lima, 2008). A'uwê-Xavante children engage in a similar game (Grando et al., n.d.). In the Monkey game, 'monkeys' climb trees and 'hunters' throw sticks to knock them down (Kaingang - Silva, 2014). In the Sugar Cane game (*Suatiya shushuti*), Yawanawá boys and girls collect sugar-cane stalks and cut them into pieces; the boys hold the pieces and the girls try to seize and keep them; the dispute goes on until the children get tired (Grando, 2010).

The Pumpkin Thief game, played among the A'uwê-Xavante, Guarani (Instituto Socioambiental, 2015), and Canela (Gosso et al., 2005), involves an elaborate plot that incorporates make-believe, hide-and-seek, and play fight components alike: children squatting on the ground ('pumpkins') are guarded by 'owners of the field'. Two children ('elders') arrive to buy pumpkins. The owners refuse and the elders pretend to leave at which point the owners leave and elders return to steal the pumpkins. Elders tap pumpkins softly to 'check if they are ripe', and if they are, the elders proceed to hide them. Eventually the owners return and ask the elders about the missing pumpkins, who, in turn, deny all knowledge of recent events. Presently a fight begins between one owner and the elders, while other owners look for the pumpkins and return them, thus restoring the game to its initial state of play.

Other Games. The games presented here resist easy categorization because of their diverse structures and dynamics, from traditional board games to challenge games like jacks, dice, tug-of-war, hopscotch, and others. One commonality they share, however, relates to their status as structured activities that are learned and played in traditional ways.

Camaiurá (Gosso et al., 2005) and Yawalapiti children (Lima, 2008) play Where Is the Fire?, a game where two holes connected by a tunnel are dug in the soil. One child places his/her head down in one of the holes and is covered with sand, with the opposite hole and tunnel serving as a source of oxygen. A playmate asks, "Where is the fire?", and the child must give the correct answer (for instance, the direction of the sun at that moment).

Another 'jaguar' game, Adugo, resembles a traditional board game. The 'board' is drawn in the sand, and seeds or pebbles are moved around on it. A 'pack of hounds' (usually 14 small pebbles) is moved across the board by one player in order to ambush the jaguar (another child who moves a larger pebble, trying to escape and 'eat' the hounds). The jaguar wins if it eats a predetermined number of hounds. If the jaguar is ambushed, the hounds win. The dynamics of the game are similar to those of checkers (Lima, 2008). Adugo is played, with strikingly similar structures and details, among a large and diffuse number of indigenous groups (e.g., Guarani: Meirelles, 2012; Bororo: Moisés, 2003; Yawalapiti: Lima, 2008).

Drawing on the ground forms a key component of other games as well. In the Tipa game, two players take turns 'catapulting' five little stones placed on a wooden spoon so that they fall down inside a circle drawn on the sand (Yawalapiti: Lima, 2008). In another version of a Wasp game, a spiral ('wasp nest') is drawn; younger children try to copy the original drawing with their fingers; if one fails, the others shout and throw sand on him/her (Mehinaku: Gosso et al., 2005).

Guarani children play a form of dice known as the Corn game. Seven corn seeds, painted on one side, are thrown on the floor by each player. Seeds that settle on the ground with the painted side up entitle the player to collect an equal number of seeds from the 'bank', where 21 seeds are kept; the player who ends up with the most seeds wins (Meirelles, 2012). Paresi girls enjoy playing Tidimore, another game related to corn. A corn seed is placed on a stick and *pequi* fruit thrown at it with the intention of knocking the seed from its perch (Grando et al., n.d.).

The structure of Wrestling Manioc (from the Tupi *manyóc*) closely resembles tug-of-war. In this case, the rope is replaced by a queue of tightly embraced children. While the first child in the queue grasps a tree, a puller tries to separate the children by pulling the last child in the queue (A'uwê-Xavante: Instituto Socioambiental, 2015; Camaiurá: Meirelles, 2012) and/or tickling him or her (Guarani: Lima, 2008). Tug-of-war played with a rope has also been documented (e.g., Pitaguary: Galdino, 2007).

In Poï Aru Nhagü (Banana game), two dyads try to prevent each other from throwing down a pile of banana slices while other participants from each team try to hit the opponents with cloth balls (resembling dodgeball) (Tikuna: Abreu, n.d.).

Indigenous children also engage in games common to non-indigenous cultures, including hopscotch (with the playing surface drawn in the sand) (Karipuna: Gosso, 2004), singing and dancing while wheeling hand in hand (e.g., Iranxe-Manoki: PIB, n.d.; Macushi: Pinto, 2010; Yawanawá: Grando, 2010; Yudja: Instituto Socioambiental, 2015); kites (Ferrari, 2013), and marbles (played with balls of dried mud) (Manchineri: Calderaro, 2006). In jacks games, pebbles, seeds, or small sand bags are thrown up and must be collected with the open hand (e.g., Quichua: Bermudez, 2013). Garoz and Iglesias (2006) refer to Palin as an autochthonous game similar to hockey, played by the Mapuche. Meirelles (2012) reports a Xavante game that resembles dodgeball but is played with shuttlecocks (*tobdaés*) instead of balls: two partners, armed with three shuttlecocks each, pursue and try to hit the opponent, who dodges to escape while trying to hit the pursuer; the first to be hit leaves and is replaced by another child.

Some adult games, imported from non-indigenous cultures, are learnt by watching and imitating adults and can be played with adults or by groups of children. Examples are football, volleyball, hockey (e.g., Pampa and Patagonian people: Cooper, 1949; Rikbaktsa, Iranxe, Tikuna, Umutina, Paresi, Bakairi, Ikoeng, Bororo, Yudja: Grando et al., n.d.); tennis played with short wood planks as rackets (Xocó: Bichara, 2003); and bowling, using small bones as balls (Kolla: IBLEL, 2002).

Make-Believe

As mentioned previously, make-believe is an embellishing component of several games and other play activities, where children may pose as predator or prey or interact with a figurative location (e.g., sand pile as wasp nest). That these embellishments are considered secondary relates to the fact that they do not alter the plot or the character of the play activity (e.g., pursue and escape, pursuer and prey). In other cases, where imagination is the principal driver of play (Vygotsky, 1978), make-believe components emerge from the themes: the themes guide the choice of rules, archetypal characters, scenarios, and plots, that can vary in different play episodes with the same theme. For instance, playing house may occur in several different forms that suggest shelters; characters and plots are delimited by the theme (parents and their children, other relatives, visitors; cooking, cleaning, etc.). Playing with dolls delimits other scenes and plots. These delimitations usually reflect the appropriation, by the children, of characteristics of their group's culture – e.g., gender roles (Gosso et al., 2007).

Expanding on this theme, Nunes (2002a) describes the diverse ways in which A'uwê-Xavante girls play house within sheltered places: an empty room, a straw mat shaped like a tent, and in clay houses built by the children complete with internal compartments resembling the style of their actual houses and furnished with objects that represent kitchen utensils or even persons. Pathways can be opened linking several houses where a group of children (girls and boys) play together. Nunes (2002a) points out the core components of these play activities as building and living "in a sheltered world that belongs to the children, either on their own or in groups, [that] at the same time reflects the world around them" (p. 90).

Araucanian girls receive visitors in their 'houses' who arrive riding other children as horses; food and drink are served in the form of leaves and yerba mate drunk from seashells (Hilger 1957). Playing house is also reported among the Kaingang (Amaral, 2011), Xikrin (Cohn, 2002b), Maxakali (Alves, 2001), Munduruku (Nascimento & Zoia, 2014), Terena (Cruz, 2009), and Wapixana and Makuxi children (Costa, 2013).

Playing with industrially produced or locally manufactured dolls has been observed in many groups, e.g., Kaingang (Amaral, 2011), Karajá (Campos, 2002), Kariri-Xocó (Oliveira, 1999), Mataco (Montani & Suárez, 2016), Munduruku (Nascimento & Zoia, 2014), Terena (Zoia & Peripolli, 2010), and Wapixana and Makuxi (Costa, 2013), but is not described in detail by the scholarly literature, perhaps because observers find its notation unnecessary due to its universal occurrence. Nevertheless, variation in the practice among indigenous children is apparent. Xikrin girls were observed cradling a small pumpkin in their arms (Cohn, 2002b), while Yanomami girls cuddled a banana blossom in a sling (Eibl-Eibesfeldt, 1989). One Guarani girl was seen cuddling a small armadillo wrapped in a piece of cloth (Jesus, 2010).

In other instances of make-believe play among indigenous children, playing horse with a branch was observed in Wapixana children (Costa, 2013); Hilger (1957) observed two Araucanian brothers (ages 2 and 5) using a branch as a horse. The boys straddled the bough (which the older boy stripped it of leaves and little twigs) in tandem. Under the guidance of the elder brother, the boys enacted a variety of behaviours and actions associated with riding: whipping the branch with a stick, recreating the jolts of a rider on a galloping horse, and pacing around the yard. In the same village, teenage girls also reported playing horse riding with their sisters when younger and children were observed playing at lassoing (one is the man, the other the horse) and "getting drunk and fighting" (like adult men at fiestas).

Ferrari (2013) reports a peculiar form of make-believe among Mehinaku children, who enacted rituals typical of their group's culture: marriage, death rituals for a lost baby, meeting of tribal chiefs, resorting to a *xamã* (a sorcerer) to attend a 'sick' child. Enacting cultural rituals of their own cultures exemplifies children's awareness and active appropriation of their social environment in their peer cultures (Corsaro, 2005).

Playing with the Body

Scholarly literature on indigenous groups documents a variety of activities in which children use the body in playful ways, in many cases simply "because the body asks for movement" (Nunes, 2002a, p. 88).

Running can be performed in several ways: jumping on one leg or both, backward or sideways, with long or short steps, slowly or quickly, following an imaginary pathway, step by step, with closed eyes, carrying or pushing objects etc. (A'uwê-Xavante: Nunes, 2002b; Camaiurá, Mehinaku: Gosso et al., 2005; Munduruku: Nascimento & Zóia, 2014; Rikbaktsa Umutina: Grando et al., n.d.). Kalapalo boys play Heiné kuputisü, a racing challenge where the racer must run one hundred meters jumping on a single leg, "like a *Saci*"; changing legs is forbidden. (*Saci* is a character present in various indigenous mythologies, depicted as a small, black, one-legged boy using a red hood and smoking a pipe, and whose business is to play tricks and pester animals and human beings.) The runner succeeds if he crosses the finish line; if he fails to finish on only one leg, further training is required (Instituto Socioambiental, 2015). A variant practiced by Matsés children is the Sucuri snake track – a zig-zag track drawn on the sand that the children must go through jumping on one leg (Calderaro, 2006).

Other examples of play activities that involve the body include rope skipping (e.g., Munduruku: Nascimento & Zóia, 2014), whirling, handstands, somersaults (Maxakali: Alves, 2001), swinging on a tree branch, hammocks, improvised swings (Mataco: Montani & Suarez, 2016), human pyramids (Camaiurá: Moisés, 2003; Mehinaku: Ferrari, 2013), jumping from trees, and slipping in the mud (Gosso, 2005; Nunes, 1999, 2002a).

Body painting is typically a female play activity. Xikrin girls paint each other (as older women do in their painting meetings), drawing a variety of designs and motifs with easily removed charcoal. Cohn (2000) emphasizes that Xikrin girls are not merely imitating adult women, who use a more permanent dye and a set of established motifs that signal the painted person's social status, but rather engaging in creative play that may be unassociated with adult rituals. Body painting is also reported for other groups, including the Kaimbé (Queiroz & César, 2014).

Play and Work

Anthropologists point out that indigenous children take active part in adult tasks but also note that they frequently use these as play opportunities (Amaral, 2011; Codonho, 2007; Grando et al., n.d.; Oliveira et al., 2015). Nunes (2002a, p. 73) refers to this sort of activity as "playing at doing real things". A ludic component is apparent when children are washing clothes or dishes in the river, looking after their younger siblings, helping to prepare food, collecting water, and delivering messages. Driving hens out of the house, a task performed by very young children, becomes a play-chasing episode in which the hens are rarely the winners. The river bank also provides a key setting for the confluence of play and work. When girls are helping their mothers with the wash and boys are carrying basins or other utensils needed for the task, they often entertain themselves with bird songs, soap bubbles, filling and emptying vessels they are washing with water or sand, and assessing their respective buoyancies.

Codonho (2007, p. 64) recorded similar scenes among Galibi-Marworno children:

> Children's activities vary according to their age. Girls take their basins to the river bank to wash clothes, help their mother to prepare meals . . . boys also look after younger children, collect fruits, fish, hunt small birds . . . but I cannot

avoid mentioning the ludic character of those activities; as Aracy Lopes da Silva (2002) states [about the A'uwê-Xavante]: "playing – experimenting – working – discovering – learning, in a single experience, a single moment".

Final Remarks

In drawing our discussion to a close, we cannot ignore the fact that anthropological and psychological inquiry is only just beginning to scrape the surface of the play activities of South American indigenous children. Given the dearth of available information, it may be surmised that many of the play activities described herein may be – and likely are – present, but undocumented, within many other indigenous groups.

Even when indigenous children's play is specifically studied, it is often conflated with adult games and rituals, possibly due to the ludic character of these adult activities. Researchers who are used to observing these games may miss the ludic character of children's less structured or unfamiliar play activities and of less conspicuous play artefacts. These challenges continue to inform and obstruct scholarly study of indigenous children's play.

Another potential limitation of the available studies is that many reports on play are based on older persons' recollections of their childhood, rather than on observation of children's activities. These interviews may emphasize differences in comparison with contemporary children play habits (e.g., access to TV, industrialized toys). However, many of the activities reported as enduring traditions are also described in observational studies of other groups (e.g., bows and arrows, races, rope skipping, tops, play fighting, playing house or with dolls, shuttlecocks, and others).

Of critical importance are the educational implications of indigenous children's play. As has already been noted, the view of play and education taken by indigenous cultures and the criteria adopted in this chapter differ markedly from those of the industrialized world. Our choice of children's play activities was based on two premises of a psycho-ethological perspective (Ades, 1986): play as an intrinsically motivated behaviour, performed on children's initiative; and play's possible adaptive value in adult life but also – and equally importantly – in childhood. On these foundations, play activities guided or proposed by adults and the participation of children in adult games were excluded. However, the developmental implications of the children's play activities in terms of the practice of skills and knowledge that will be required in adult life are implicit in their descriptions. Besides the more obvious practice of varied skills and the intimacy with adult activities, Profice and colleagues (2016) suggest that indigenous children's close contact with nature (on a level far exceeding that of most children in the industrialized world) can be the basis of their precocious respect for the natural environment, and not only in terms of its relevance for their adult life, as emphasized by these authors, but, and perhaps even more importantly, for the quality and viability of their childhood when they face the challenges and risks of their physical environment in their free and unsupervised daily play activities.

Changes in societal conditions brought on by contact with non-indigenous populations should always be kept in mind even for indigenous groups living in preserved areas. Preserves in Amazonia are very different from those located on the periphery of urban centres (e.g., Guarani, in São Paulo city). The closer contact with urban life implies changes in habits – including play activities – that may be affected, for instance, by access to TV as exemplified by the already mentioned 'police and thieves' game of Xocó boys (Bichara, 2003) and even, in a few cases, to information technologies (e.g., Makuxi - Pinto, 2010), Terena: Grando et al., n.d.; Wari: Silva, 2011). These changes reinforce the fact that peer cultures mirror and reinterpret their surrounding cultures (Corsaro, 2005) including, in this case, neighbour cultures. In the indigenous groups that constituted this discussion, which still preserve at least partially their way of life, nature pervades culture, hence the universality of its presence in their play activities.

References

Abreu, C. (n.d.) *Brincadeira na aldeia*. Ciência Hoje das Crianças. http://chc.org.br/brincadeira-na-aldeia/.

Ades, C. (1986). Uma perspectiva psicoetológica para o estudo do comportamento animal. *Boletim de Psicologia, 36*, 20–30.

Alves, V. F. N. (2001). O corpo brincante das crianças indígenas Maxakali. Eighth Congress on Physical Education and Sport Sciences of Portuguese-Speaking Countries, Lisbon, Portugal.

Amaral, F. T. (2011). Crianças Kaingang da Borboleta. *Espaços da escola, 21*(69).

Begon, M., Townsend, C., & Harper, J. (2007). *Ecologia: de indivíduos a ecossistemas*. São Paulo: Artmed.

Bermudez, L. (2013, November 17). Los juegos tradicionales en Argentina. Blog. Available at http://lucianabermudez89.blogspot.com.br/search?q=quechua.

Bichara, I. D. (2003). Nas águas do Velho Chico. In A. M. A. Carvalho, C. M. C. Magalhães, F. A. R. Pontes, & I. D. Bichara (Eds.), *Brincadeira e Cultura: viajando pelo Brasil que brinca* (pp. 89–107). São Paulo: Casa do Psicólogo.

Bichara, I. D., Lordelo, E. R., Santos, A. K., & Pontes, F. A. R. (2012). Play and gender issues in rural and urban Brazilian contexts. In A. C. Bastos, K. Urico, & J. Valsiner (Eds.), *Cultural dynamics of women's lives* (pp. 197–208). Charlotte, NC: Information Age Publishing.

Brito, E. M. (2012). A Educação Karipuna do Amapá no Contexto da Educação Escolar Indígena Diferenciada na Aldeia do Espírito Santo. PhD thesis,, São Paulo Catholic University.

Brostolin, M. R., & Oliveira, E. A. C. (2013). Os sentidos do aprender a ser indígena e o viver a infância da criança Terena. *Educação em foco, 16*(22), 143–162.

Available at www.uemg.br/openjournal/index.pgp/educacao emfoco/article/viewfile/329313.

Calderaro, K. C. L. (2006). O Universo Lúdico das Crianças Indígenas. Centro Cultural Povos da Amazônia. Available at www.yumpu.com/pt/document/view/12943469/o-universo-ludico-das-criancas-indigenas-centro-cultural-dos-.

Campos, S. L. (2002). Bonecas Karajá: apenas um brinquedo? *Rev. do Museu de Arqueologia e Etnologia, 72*, 233–248.

Carrara, E. (2002). Um pouco da educação infantil Xavante. In A. L. Silva, A. V. L S. Macedo, & A. Nunes (Eds.), *Crianças indígenas: Ensaios antropológicos* (pp. 236–277). São Paulo: Global.

Carvalho, A. M. A., Moreira, L. V. C., & Gosso, Y. (2015). Fathering in Brazil. In J. L. Roonarine (Ed.), *Fathers across cultures* (pp. 39–62). Santa Barbara, CA: Praeger.

Codonho, C. G. (2007). Apreendendo entre pares: a transmissão horizontal de saberes entre as crianças indígenas Galibi-Marworno (Amapá – Brasil). Master's dissertation, Federal University of Santa Catarina.

Cohn, C. (2000). Crescendo como um Xikrin: uma análise da infância e do desenvolvimento infantil entre os Kayapó-Xikrin do Bacajá. *Revista de Antropologia, 43*(2), 195–222.

Cohn, C. (2002a). A experiência da infância e o aprendizado entre os Xikrin. In A. Lopes da Silva, A. V. L. S. Macedo, & A. M. Nunes (eds.), *Crianças indígenas: Ensaios antropológicos* (pp. 117–149). São Paulo: Global.

Cooper, J. M. (1949). Games and gambling. In J. H. Steward (ed.), *Handbook of South American Indians: The comparative ethnology of South American Indians* (pp. 503–524). Washington, DC: US Government Printing Office.

Corsaro, W. A. (2005). *The sociology of childhood.* Newbury Park, CA: Pine Forge Press.

Costa, E. M. D. (2013). As práticas lúdicas na Comunidade Indígena Tabalascada em Roraima. Master's dissertation, Federal University of Amazonas.

Cruz, S. D. F. (2009). A criança Terena: o diálogo entre a educação indígena e a educação escolar na aldeia Buriti. Master's dissertation, Department of Education, Dom Bosco Catholic University.

CTA/ZM (Centro de Tecnologias Alternativas Zona da Mata) (2009). Reencantando a infância com cantigas brincadeiras e diversão. Projeto construindo o futuro da agricultura familiar. Viçosa. Available at www.mma.gov.br/estruturas/pda/_arquivos/cartilha_reencantando_a_infncia_com_cantigas_51.pdf.

Eibl-Eibesfeldt, I. (1989). *Human ethology.* New York: Aldine de Gruyter.

Estelles, M. (2016) Brinquedos e brincadeiras da (nossa) cultura indígena. Available at https://brasileirinhos.wordpress.com/2016/04/19/brinquedos-e-brincadeiras-da-nossa-cultura-indigena.

Ferrari, A. S. T. (2013). Jogos e brincadeiras: o lúdico no processo de aprendizagem das crianças indígenas. Undergraduate monograph, Federal University of Paraná. www.humanas.ufpr.br/portal/antropologia/files/2013/11/ferrari.brincadeirasindigenas.pdf.

Franco Neto, J. (2010). Quem são, onde estão e em que contexto vivem. In M. Herrero & U. Fernandes (Eds.), *Jogos e brincadeiras na cultura Kalapalo* (pp. 23–41). São Paulo: Edições SESC SP.

Galdino, L. K. A. (2007). Os caminhos da territorialidade da etnia Pitaguary: o caso da aldeia de Monguba no município de Pacatuba no Ceará. Master's dissertation, Federal University of Ceará. Available at www.repositorio.ufc.br/bit stream/riufc/8062/1/2007_dis_lkagaldino.pdf.

Garoz, I., & Iglesias, J. L. L. (2006). Juego, cultura y desarrollo en la infancia: El caso del Palín Mapuche y el Hockey. *Revista Internacional de Ciencias del Deporte*, *2*(20), 33–48.

Gosso, Y. (2004). Pexe oxemoarai: Brincadeiras de crianças Parakanã. PhD thesis, University of São Paulo, Brasil.

Gosso, Y., Morais, M. L. S., & Otta, E. (2007). Pretend play of Brazilian children: A window into different cultural worlds. *Journal of Cross-Cultural Psychology*, *38*(5), 539–558.

Gosso, Y., & Otta, E. (2003). Em uma aldeia Parakanã. In A. M. A. Carvalho, C. M. C. Magalhães, F. A. R. Pontes, & I. D. Bichara (Eds.), *Brincadeira e Cultura: viajando pelo Brasil que brinca* (pp. 33–76). São Paulo: Casa do Psicólogo.

Gosso, Y., Otta, E., Morais, M. L. S., Ribeiro, F. J. L., & Bussab, V. S. R. (2005). Play in hunter-gatherer society. In A. D. Pellegrini & P. K. Smith (Eds.), *The nature of play: Great apes and humans*. New York: Guilford Press.

Grando, B. S. (2010). *Jogos e culturas indígenas: possibilidades para a educação intercultural na escola*. Cuiabá: Editora da Universidade Federal – de Mato Grosso.

Grando, B. S. (2014). Infância, brincadeira e brinquedos em comunidades Indígenas. *RevistAleph*, *9*(22), 97–113.

Grando, B. S., Xavante, S. I., & Campos, N. S. (n.d.). Jogos/brincadeiras indígenas: a memória lúdica de adultos e idosos de dezoito grupos étnicos. Available at http://cev.org.br/arquivo/biblioteca/4024585.pdf.

Guimarães, D. S. (2016). Terms of the dialogue. In D. S. Guimarães (Ed.), *Amerindian pathways: Guiding dialogues with psychology* (pp. 1–6). Charlotte, SC: Information Age.

Herrero, M. (2010). 25 jogos e brincadeiras indígenas do Alto Xingú. In M. Herrero & U. Fernandes (Eds.), *Jogos e brincadeiras na cultura Kalapalo* (pp. 115–181). São Paulo: Edições SESC SP.

Hilger, S. M. I. (1957). *Araucanian child life and its cultural background*. Washington, DC: Smithsonian Institution.

IBLEL (Instituto Boliviano de Lexicografia y otros Estudios Lingüísticos) (2002). *Juegos Infantiles Tradicionales de Bolivia*. La Paz, Bolivia: Instituto de Estudos Bolivianos. Available at http://pt.slideshare.net/Teofilopolicarpo/juegos-infantiles-tradicionales-de-bolivia.

IELA (Instituto de Estudos Latino-Americanos) (n.d.). *Brincadeira das crianças – Aldeia Piraí*. Available at www.iela.ufsc.br/indigena-digital/brincadeira-das-criancas-guarani-pirai.

Instituto Socioambiental (2015) *Povos Indígenas no Brasil Mirim*. São Paulo: Socioambiental Institute.

Jesus, S. C. (2010). Brincadeiras de crianças M'bya Guarani no urbano: reflexões acerca da Antropologia e da Psicologia da Educação. *Educação Santa Maria*, *35*(1), 111–124.

Lima, M. (2008, April 16). Jogos, brinquedos e brincadeiras indígenas. Available at http:// criandocriancas.blogspot.com.br/2008/04/jogos-brinquedos-e-brincadeiras.html.

Lordelo, E. R., & Carvalho, A. M. A. (2003). Educação infantil e Psicologia: para quê brincar? *Psicologia, Ciência e Profissão, 23*(2), 14–21.

Macena, P. L. (2016). O tempo da criança e da natureza na educação diferenciada guarani. In Conselho Regional de Psicologia de São Paulo (São Paulo Regional Psychology Council) (ed.), *Povos indígenas e psicologia: a procura do bem-viver* (pp. 83–88). São Paulo: Conselho Regional de Psicologia.

Meirelles, R. (2012). *Giramundo e outros brinquedos e brincadeiras dos meninos do Brasil*. São Paulo: Terceiro Nome.

Moisés, D. (2003). Expedição conta como brincam os índios: brinquedos, jogos e brincadeiras. *O Estado de São Paulo*, December 8, p. A8.

Montani, R., & Suárez, M. E. (2016). Los juguetes de los wichís del Gran Chaco. *Anthropos: International Review of Anthropology and Linguistics, 111*(1), 127–148.

Munduruku, D. (2003). *Coisas de índio: um guia de pesquisa*. São Paulo: Callis Editora.

Nascimento, R., & Zoia, A. (2014). *Crianças Munduruku: um breve olhar sobre o brincar e sua aprendizagem social e cultural. Tellus, 14*(26), 119–130.

Nimuendajú, C. (1983). *Os Apinayé.* Available at http://etnolinguistica.wdfiles.com/ local_files/biblio%3/nimuendaju_1983_apinaye.pdf.

Nunes, A. (1999). *A sociedade das crianças A'uwê-Xavante: Por uma antropologia da criança*. Lisbon: Ministério da Educação/Instituto Inovação Cultural.

Nunes, A. (2002a). No tempo e no espaço: brincadeiras de crianças A'uwê-Xavante. In A. L. Silva, A. V. L. S. Macedo, & Angela Nunes (Eds.), *Crianças indígenas: Ensaios antropológicos* (pp. 64–69). São Paulo: Global.

Nunes, A, (2002b). O lugar da criança nos textos sobre sociedades indígenas brasileiras. In A. Lopes da Silva, A. V. L. S. Macedo, & A. M. Nunes (Eds.), *Crianças indígenas: Ensaios antropológicos* (pp. 236–277). São Paulo: Global.

Oliveira, A. C., Beltrão, J. F., & Domingues-Lopes, R. D. (2015). O lúdico em questão – Brinquedos e brincadeiras indígenas. *Desidades, 3*(6), 25–39. Available at https://revistas.ufrj.br/index.desidades/article/download/2615/2185.

Oliveira, J. N. (1999). Um pouco de minha infância. *Estudos Avançados, 13*(37), 87–103.

Oliveira, K. (2007). Brincando na aldeia: Brincadeiras de crianças Guarani de uma aldeia Aracruz – ES. Master's dissertation, Federal University of Espírito Santo. Available at http://portais4.ufes.br/posgrad/teses/tese_2195_.pdf.

Pereira, R. F. (2013). Criando gente no alto rio Negro: um olhar Waíkhana. Master's dissertation, Federal University of Amazonas. Available at https://dlc.library .columbia.edu/catalog/ldpd:504892/bytestreams/content/content?filename= Rosilene+Fonseca+Pereira.pdf.

PIB (Povos Indígenas no Brasil) (n.d.). Iranxe Manoki. Available at https://pib .socioambiental.org/pt/povo/iranxe-manoki/2338.

Pinto, B. O. S. (2010). Trajetos institucionais e construção de sentidos subjetivos: história de vida de um índio Makuxi. Master's dissertation, Federal Fluminense University.

Profice, C., Santos, G. M., & dos Anjos, N. A. (2016). Children and nature in Tukum village: Indigenous education and biophilia. *Journal of Child and Adolescent Behavior*, *4*, 320.

Queiroz, C. M., & Cesar, A. L. S. (2014). Infância Recontada em Múltiplas Linguagens relato de uma pesquisa com as crianças indígenas Kaimbé. In *II Seminário Criança/Infância Indígena*. São Carlos. Anais – II Seminário Criança/Infância Indígena. Available at https://infanciaindigena.files.wordpress.com/2014/10/infc3a2ncia-recontada-em-mc3baltiplas-linguagens-carine-m-de-queiroz.pdf.

Reis, R. N., & Sousa, E. L. (2008). A vivência da infância pelas crianças gavião-pykopjê no Maranhão. IX Argentinian Social Anthropology Congress, Humanities and Social Sciences School, National University of Missiones, Posadas. Available at www.aacademica.org/000-080/422.pdf.

Ribeiro, B. G. (1987). *Suma Etnológica Brasileira: etnobiologia*. Petrópolis: Vozes.

Ribeiro, D. (2012). *Confissões*. São Paulo: Companhia das Letras.

Silva, J. C. D. (2014). Bolas, brinquedos e jogos: práticas de lazer e futebol na tradição dos Kaingáng da Terra Indígena Xapecó/SC. Master's dissertation, Federal University of Santa Catarina.

Silva, J. C. D., & Notzold, A. J. V. (2012). Brinquedos e brincadeiras indígenas: relatos de mudanças através dos tempos. In *XI Encontro Nacional de História Oral, 2012, Rio de Janeiro*. *XI Encontro Nacional de História Oral – Anais Eletrônicos*, vol. 1. Rio de Janeiro: ABHO (Brazilian Oral History Organization).

Silva, M. (2011). Os caminhos da arte, cultura e identidade étnica na escola. *Linguagens – Revista de Letras, Artes e Comunicação*, *5*(2), 184–195. Available at http://proxy.furb.br/ojs/index.php/linguagens/article/viewFile/1817/1652.

Silva, M. G. S. (n.d.). *Brinquedos Indígenas na Amazônia*. Belém City. Available at www.museu-goeldi.br/eva/educacao/matdidatico/Brinquedos%20Ind%EDgenas%20na%20Amaz%F4nia.pdf.

Vygotsky, L. (1978). *Mind in society: The development of higher psychological processes*. Cambridge, MA: Harvard University Press.

Yamã, Y. (2013). *Kurumi Guaré no coração da Amazônia*. São Paulo: FTD Educação.

Zoia, A., & Peripolli, O. J. (2010). Infância indígena e outras infâncias. *Espaço Ameríndio*, *4*(2), 9.

19 Play in Societies Influenced by Confucian Values

Eunjoo Jung and Sophia Han

This chapter provides an overview of sociohistorical factors that contribute to the development of children's play in societies influenced by Confucian values. We begin by highlighting core Confucian ideological and cultural values and views about children as a context for understanding children's play, discuss key characteristics of young children's play, provide an overview of contemporary trends in young children's play, and offer considerations for a broader understanding of young children's play in a few Confucian-influenced societies such as Korea, China, Taiwan, and Japan.

Confucian Ideological and Cultural Values

To better understand the play of children in societies influenced by Confucian values, a brief overview of the major tenets of Confucianism is necessary. Confucianism refers to a complex set of ideological principles and behavioural guidelines originally articulated by the Chinese philosopher and educator Confucius (551–479 BCE) (Park & Chesla, 2007). His sayings and ideas have been compiled into a popular book known as the *Analects of Confucius* (Tu, 1998). Several of Confucius' followers adapted and expanded on his original ideas, which have been passed down and spread to surrounding countries over thousands of years. Countries located in the East Asian region of the world, including China, Hong Kong, Japan, Korea, and Taiwan, are classically considered to be societies significantly influenced by Confucian values. It has been estimated that approximately 20% of the world's population – living in these countries and emigrants to other countries – is influenced by Confucianism to varying degrees (Yan & Sorenson, 2006).

Confucianism can be viewed as a basic teaching philosophy for enhancing morality and human relations (Yim et al., 2011). The ultimate ideal is for all individuals to achieve a balanced humanistic perfection through internalizing the core Confucian ideological and cultural values, and subsequently to build a harmonious society (Luo et al., 2013). Having said that, throughout the long history of the Confucian ideal and its application across different contexts, there have been several iterations as to which values best constitute core Confucianism, how many values can sufficiently and adequately represent

Confucianism, and which values should be prioritized over others. We briefly discuss the six most widely and frequently endorsed Confucian ideological and cultural values in the realm of personal development and education: benevolence, righteousness, courteousness, wisdom, filial piety, and self-restraint. Though not directly related to play per se, they have a direct bearing on how children are socialized and the expectations that parents have of them.

Considered the first principle of Confucianism, *Benevolence* (*ren* in Chinese) refers to one's humane actions that express goodness and that reflect love and care of all people. It is the virtue of the virtues, as it is the ultimate guide to all human actions. *Righteousness* (*yi*) refers to one's behaviour and/or belief espousing justice. It is an ability to recognize what is right and wrong and to choose to do the right thing under all circumstances. *Courteousness* (*li*) refers to one's behaviour and/or disposition that is proper, courteous, polite, and respectful to others. It is commonly understood as propriety – a development of social norms and/or a concrete guide to human actions. Along these lines, Confucius' follower Mencius suggested guidelines for five basic human relationships in life (i.e., father and son, king and minister, husband and wife, older sibling and younger sibling, and friend and friend). *Wisdom* (*zhi*) refers to one's knowledge and/or thinking processes. In Confucianism, acquiring wisdom or knowledge is considered to be the first step toward perfection; thus, an expectation is that people should work diligently and persistently to gain new knowledge. *Filial piety* (*xiao*) refers to one's respect, obedience, love, and reverence, especially for parents and ancestors. For young children, it is desired that they respect, obey, and comply with their parents' advice even if they might disagree; for others, it further includes supporting parents or elderly family members and honouring the family name. *Self-restraint* (*yue*) refers to one's behaviour that reflects control of emotions, actions, and thoughts and being in compliance with the society's rules. The focus on harmonious human relationships and putting the group first against personal interest is one of the most characteristic features of collectivist culture, as influenced by Confucian values.

These six values have been influential forces in cultivating human relationships and are still applicable in families, schools, and communities across several Asian societies. For instance, families from Confucian-influenced societies have created a routine practice of using stories and short sayings to teach core Confucian values to their children in family settings and in daily life (Yan & Sorenson, 2006). Until the early 1900s, children began their school day by raising their hands and reciting certain Confucian values from memory as a way of showing respect to Confucius (Rarick, 2007). Early childhood professionals in China believed that it was important to preserve Confucian values to enable children to become well adjusted to society; emphasis on benevolence and courteousness was particularly relevant in this regard (Yim et al., 2013). Similarly, in Taiwan, kindergarten and first-grade teachers have been found to actively promote Confucian philosophy and core values in their everyday teaching practices (Hadley, 2003). Notably, these values are not mutually exclusive in portraying traditional Confucian ideology and culture. While each has a distinct emphasis, they support each other to represent and strengthen Confucianism more holistically (Park & Chesla, 2007).

Traditional Confucian Perspectives Associated with Young Children

In societies where Confucianism plays a role, its influence penetrates all levels of an individual's life – from daily interaction with others, moral values, and thinking styles to standards of society. It guides individual behaviours and disposition, both explicitly and implicitly. Hence, to draw connections between traditional Confucian values and young children's play, we begin by examining broader traditional Confucian perspectives associated with young children.

Adult–Child Relationship. Although Confucius did not directly articulate his views regarding young children, perspectives on young children and their relationship with adults can be gathered from historical documents and classic books published in societies influenced by Confucian values. For instance, Park et al. (2002) explored parents' views regarding children and parent–child relationships in traditional Korean society through analyzing classical books from the Chosun dynasty, when Confucianism was the founding principle of the country. They found that Korean people generally perceived young children as a positive addition to the family, such as a gift from heaven or a motivation for their lives. Parents felt blessed to have a child, so they would willingly express their gratitude to ancestors. Likewise, Takeuchi (1994) reported that Japanese people have historically regarded young children as jewels or objects of adults' love. They believed young children are born with innate abilities and goodness, and, thus, they should not be forced to do unsuitable things in order to develop a good sense of morality and become good citizens.

Turning to adult–child relationships, Confucian values of courteousness and filial piety play a foundational role in human relationships. Traditional Confucianism endorses an 'authority vs. subordinate' social hierarchy among individuals based on various criteria, such as career rank (i.e., king vs. government official; employer vs. employee), gender (i.e., male vs. female; husband vs. wife), and age (i.e., old vs. young; parents vs. children; older sibling vs. younger sibling) (Hwang, 2001). The distinction was strict, such that individuals in subordinate positions (i.e., employee, wife, child) were expected to respect and obey the individuals in authority positions (i.e., employer, husband, parent). In turn, those in authority are afforded greater social resources and opportunities, with an expectation to protect and provide care for their subordinates. This traditional distinction between authorities and subordinates should be understood within the sociohistorical context of Confucianism, developed when such hierarchical systems were a practical necessity to maintain an agrarian social system and to regulate individual behaviour within that system (Feng & Bodde, 1960; Zheng, 1997).

The adult–child relationship is a clear example of this authority–subordinate relationship. Children from a very early age are taught that adults are to be regarded with higher respect than the children themselves or their peer groups. At the family level, children are taught to be obedient to their parents, since authority is solely assigned to parents, a perspective directly affected by the Confucian values of filial piety (Wang, 2014). At the same time, in return for having authority, parents are obliged to manage family assets and provide stability in the lives of their children. Moreover, it was traditionally believed that parental authority was endorsed as part of the courteousness needed to promote order and harmony within family relationships and that cultivation of filial piety is needed to create children who are valued citizens of the larger society (Rosemont & Ames, 2009).

Parenting Practices. In societies influenced by Confucianism, a strict division of gender-based roles and responsibilities between males and females has existed for a very long period of time, encouraged specifically through the Confucian value of courteousness (Luo et al., 2013; Yim et al., 2011). This is rooted in ancient lifestyles in agrarian societies, when female family members were considered the 'family people' who took care of all internal household matters, whereas male members were considered the 'social people' who took care of external household matters (Feng & Bodde, 1960; Zheng, 1997). Accordingly, daily chores related to child-rearing or parenting practices for young children (i.e., nursing, feeding, bathing) were traditionally – and to some degree still continue to be in many countries – perceived as the mother's sole responsibility (Buriel & DeMent, 1997). In many Confucian-influenced societies, from a mother's standpoint, parenting actually began as soon as she was made aware that a child was conceived. This parenting practice, so-called fetal education, was believed to have a significant psychological effect on a child, and therefore, there were suggestions for mothers to abide by certain practices and avoid others when bearing a child (Yoo, 1994). Considering the heavy expectations on mothers with respect to child-bearing, child-rearing, and parenting practices, it was not uncommon for fathers to have a minimal presence during the first few years of a child's life.

In early periods in Confucian societies, fathers and mothers played different roles in raising and parenting their children. Fathers typically performed an authoritarian and disciplinary role, instilling academic and intellectual development along with Confucian values of righteousness and wisdom, and mothers usually performed a softer and caring role by cultivating social-emotional development along with Confucian values of courteousness and self-restraint (Chao & Tseng, 2002). Parenting practices also differed based on the child's gender, because gender-based differentiated expectations and responsibilities were to be transmitted to future generations (Zheng, 1997). For instance, boys were taught to acquire knowledge and skills to become strong leaders and providers for their families, while girls were taught to serve a supporting role within their families. Consequently, formal schooling opportunities to learn academics were more available to boys, while girls usually stayed home to learn how to take care of household tasks from their mothers and/or grandmothers.

Another key feature of parenting practices is the Confucian emphasis on parents' role in the education of their children (Koh et al., 2009; Luo et al., 2013). It was often believed that good parenting is reflected by a child's societal success, which was often based on academic performance. Thus, it was the parent's responsibility to provide the best educational environment possible. It was not uncommon for parents to dedicate or even sacrifice their own life circumstances to better support their children's educational opportunities (Chao & Tseng, 2002). A famous Chinese story tells about Mencius' mother (after her husband passed away) who moved the family home three times in order to send the young son to the best school in the neighbourhood. Mencius, who became one of the best leaders in the country, is a prime example of this type of self-sacrifice.

Education. That Confucianism had a major influence on education is seen in many Asian communities. Confucianism was originally developed and further advocated by the literati, the highly educated class of the society (Tu, 1998). Moreover, wisdom, as one of the core Confucian values, reflects the overall expectations of individuals to pursue continuous education. As a result, interrelated concepts such as wisdom, knowledge, education, and learning have been highly regarded consistently throughout the long history of Confucianism regardless of the specific context.

One primary feature of the Confucian perspectives on education is its emphasis on self-cultivation. This was particularly salient during the early days of Confucianism, when the purpose of education was primarily to gain wisdom and to subsequently elevate one's philosophical understanding of the world (Park & Kim, 1999). In this realm of educational pursuit, the knowledge learned was not necessarily expected to be practical or helpful in one's everyday life, but rather to assist an individual to achieve a higher-level mental and moral state (Cheng, 2016). Educated individuals were expected to be equipped with virtues of wisdom and self-regulation and to realize the virtues of collective good and harmony (Park & Kim, 1999).

Another feature of Confucian perspectives is that education was emphasized as a social ladder that could allow an individual to move toward a higher rank in society (Otsuka & Smith, 2005). Parents regarded their children's school achievements and overall academic success as top priorities and reinforced this belief in their children (Dandy & Nettelbeck, 2002; Jung, 2016; Leung & Shek, 2011; Li, 2004). Not surprisingly, the educational standards were exceptionally rigid. Based on traditional Confucian 'authority vs. subordinate' social hierarchy, teachers held extreme power over students and were perceived to be the holders of wisdom. Teaching usually took a form of lecturing to transmit knowledge to students. Learning was usually evidenced through students' proper sitting posture, quiet listening, and recitation of the materials taught by teachers rather than through any form of play (Eifring, 2015). Children who were able to persevere and follow through were highly touted for their strong will and effort. Such beliefs are easily found in many folktales and children's stories celebrating a person who became a highly honoured leader in society due to his hard work and studies, despite facing many obstacles.

Characteristics of Traditional Young Children's Play

Confucian perspectives have both directly and indirectly influenced many aspects associated with young children, including their play. As noted already, one of the key influences of Confucianism on children's lives is a heavy emphasis on education and learning, mostly defined by hard work and academic success. While appreciating education and academic success is usually considered a positive thing in children, this has created a phenomenon of associating learning with hard work, and discouraging learning through play (Fielding, 1997; Rudowicz & Hui, 1997). This, in turn, contributed to an overall depreciation in the value of children's play, as if it was a distraction from their education and learning. It is not too surprising that not much has been documented or studied regarding young children's play when Confucianism was a prevalent philosophical force across Asian societies. Building on the traditional Confucian perspectives regarding young children, we present three key traditional characteristics of young children's play identified in societies influenced by Confucian values.

Ritual-Based Play. During earlier periods, when the modern concept of children's play was yet to be identified, play originated in traditional events, festivals, or rituals (Yim et al., 2011). Some of these events or rituals were small parts of daily routines within a household, while others were associated with larger celebrations within a community (Kook, 2011). Some smaller ritual-based play activities included observing a family memorial service, making and eating certain types of food, engaging in certain types of activities, and getting to know greeting rituals. By being involved in these events or rituals, Confucian values of courteousness and self-restraint were implicitly reinforced. Children learned to develop respect for adults, honour elders, and be harmonious with peers, families, and neighbours, which eventually led to the behaviours and performances that were expected of children from their families and society.

Ritual-based play activities were typically associated with special festive events, such as the Chinese/Lunar New Year festival, mid-autumn harvest festival, Dragon Boat Festival, and other major holidays (Chang, 2001; Kook, 2011; Yim et al., 2011). These festivals allowed children to play outdoors, play games with traditional toys, and play with adults. For instance, during the New Year period, children accompanied adults when playing with fireworks or '*yut-nori*', as well as enjoying games like jump rope, top spinning, kite flying, playing traditional instruments, and hopscotch with their friends. While there is a variety of ritual-based play that children engaged in, similar types of play activities taking place around seasonal festivals and rituals are observed in other countries influenced by Confucianism. It is worthwhile to note that through these ritual-based play activities, children were invited and allowed to "play" with adults, which is not a common practice under traditional Confucian principles. Moreover, even though there was no play designed for young children, their involvement in rituals and festivals could be seen as an effort to embed and allow them to experience and enjoy playful activities, while fulfilling the larger set of responsibilities associated with rituals.

Group Play. There were more examples of group play than independent play found in traditional Confucian societies, which reflects the Confucian values of self-restraint and group harmony. Furthermore, the Confucian view of ideal children is seen as a significant factor in shaping children's play (Bai, 2005). To be appreciated as good students and good human beings, children were expected to demonstrate certain behavioural features that reflect the ideal image of a child from Confucian perspectives, such as prioritizing group over individual activities and sitting quietly during their educational sessions. Hence, even when children were involved in play, they were expected to follow the prescribed directions to achieve a goal, play harmoniously with their peers, cooperate with others, and not fight with each other. Children were also encouraged to be a good team members by including everyone in play and not discriminating against whom should be included in the play group.

As such, children in traditional Confucian societies were typically less involved in free, independent, or exploratory play. This again can be a reflection of depreciating play, such that adults believed it was not a worthwhile experience to spend time in playful activities unless certain rules and/or goals were guiding children's actions. Even in situations when children were involved in outdoor play activities, they were implicitly expected to be ideal and play harmoniously with others (Nah & Waller, 2015). This can be interpreted as utilizing young children's play as an implicit mechanism to exercise society's preference for a collectivist orientation.

Gendered Play. Confucianism endorses and encourages gender-specific roles and responsibilities through its value of courteousness, and its influences in this domain can be easily found in young children's play (Brooker et al., 2014). Different play activities were permitted for boys and girls, rather than encouraging collaboration across genders (Bai, 2005). For instance, within the ritual-based play previously discussed, there were several play activities that strictly separated boys and girls (Aydt & Corsaro, 2003; Kook, 2011). Usually girls, in contrast to boys, were more likely to be involved in quiet and less active play forms. Some examples of frequently observed activities for girls included reading, being read to, storytelling, listening to stories, drawing, colouring, knitting, beading, playing with pebbles, and working on puzzles (Olds, 1979). Boys tended to play more actively, roughly, and physically by engaging in rough-and-tumble play and ball games. Girls tended to play in a quieter and secluded manner and were more engaged in social and verbal play rather than physical play (Blatchford et al., 2003). Because boys were thought to enjoy more active and physical activities, they joined and played together. They usually dominated playgrounds, spent more time outdoors, and utilized more play resources. Girls would often observe boys' play and be involved in conversations as a form of play, rather than by actually being involved in physical or outdoor activities. Girls were less visible, gathered in small groups, and were frequently involved in solitary play by themselves (Ackerley, 2003). While this gendered play is observed across many other parts of the world, this feature in Confucian-influenced societies was one of the distinct characteristics found in children's play, with boys having more dominant roles and girls having more reflective roles in their everyday lives.

Contemporary Trends in Young Children's Play

As might be expected, children's play characteristics in Confucian-influenced societies have changed over time. While some characteristics of traditional play, like ritual-based play, group play, and gendered play, have been retained, children's play in these societies has become quite similar to those of Western societies (Singer et al., 2009). The recent emergence of pedagogies of play emphasizing the positive role of play in children's development further changed the ways that teachers and families view play as an appropriate developmental experience, rather than as an undesirable use of children's time that hinders their academic success (Synodi, 2010). We discuss a few notable contemporary trends in young children's play that have emerged in societies traditionally influenced by Confucian values.

Reconciling Children's Play with Western Influence. With globalization, which is sometimes subtle and other times evident, changes in parent–child and child–child activities have penetrated contemporary Confucian societies, including in education, family culture, and young children's play (Gupta, 2013; Lee et al., 2011). Traditional Confucian values have been shifting, and focus on the self rather than group harmony, independence rather than interdependence, parallel status rather than hierarchical status, and insubordination rather than obedience are gaining increasing support. Therefore, beliefs and practices regarding the adult–child relationship, parenting, and education, and the subsequent impact on understanding children's play, vacillate between traditional and contemporary values.

There has been an overall shift regarding education from a narrow perspective focused on knowledge and academic success (Lee et al., 2011) to a broader perspective focused more on creativity, imagination, and individualization. This has facilitated bridging the divide in the traditional dichotomy between education and play. For young children, this shift can be evidenced with the introduction of play-based pedagogy in early childhood classrooms in China, Korea, Taiwan, and Japan (Gupta, 2013; Lee et al., 2011). The idea of play-based pedagogy is a relatively new concept that was introduced to Confucian-based societies just over a century ago (Ishigaki, 1992; Shirakawa & Kitano, 2005). Since then, many early childhood teachers in Confucian-influenced societies have received educational training based on the principles of developmentally appropriate practices and play-based pedagogy (Hsieh, 2004). This has influenced societal values and changed educational delivery in classrooms.

This shift also provided context for the changing perceptions of the value of children's play activities. One of the key changes includes the introduction of a new children's play paradigm that encourages more open-ended and individual-oriented perspectives, instead of the traditional group-oriented perspectives (Ahn, 2015). For example, in Japan, teachers believed free play is a helpful experience in children's social-emotional development, and thus were in favour of less control over children's free play time (Whitburn, 2003). Promoting a strong sense of 'self' and independence has become an important endeavour for families and teachers alike (Ahn, 2015; Lin et al., 2016). While free play or play itself has been relatively less valued and neglected in the past, new insights into the pedagogies of play as a vehicle for children's social-emotional and physical development bring a new perspective into the lives of children.

However, recent educational practices involving play and putting children at the centre of practices conflict with traditional views of obedience, harmony, and group-focused perspectives. These not only have led to many conflicting views on early childhood education, parenting practices, and play behaviours (Hsieh, 2004) but also have created the dilemma of giving children mixed messages regarding appropriate behaviours (Ahn, 2015). For instance, preschool teachers who have been educated in Western pedagogies regarding children's play still tend to use more traditional approaches that privilege academic activities over outdoor play, peer play, and pretend play. Children seem to spend less time on outdoor play activities using gross motor skills, peer interactive play, and pretend play (Kwon, 2003). Although taught to be independent, self-respecting, and successful in their competition with others, children exist in a state of transition where they are still required to be harmonious, collaborative, obedient, prioritizing the group over themselves, and respectful to others. Teachers and families too have started to experience conflicts in their views on play in the "globalizing Asian" countries (Gupta, 2013, p. 213). With conflicting messages and clashing views on the role of play in children's lives, various forms of adjustments and reconciliations are surfacing at home, in schools, and in communities across Asian societies (e.g., China, Korea) due to social, political, and economic transformations.

Family Structure and Play Environment. Children's play activities and environments are heavily influenced by changing family structures in contemporary Asian societies, including a growing number of women working as dual earners or single earners. The shift in family structures in Confucian societies has affected how young children spend their time at home, outdoors, and in early childhood education programs. For instance, with the lowered birth rate in Taiwan, children experience difficulties in finding playmates and they tend to join structured recreational activities such as skateboard lessons and dancing classes rather than having time for free play (Chang, 2001). Essentially, this has challenged traditional Confucian-based values of maintaining strong parental authority and taking full charge of raising harmonious and responsible children (Lin et al., 2016). In addition, with more families getting divorced or living singly or separated, the need for early childhood education has taken on greater meaning. Considering these changes, parents and teachers emphasize children's independence and individuality more than ever before.

A feature that seems to persist, however, is that play is still frequently regarded as a reward for the hard work children accomplish. A parent's statement, "You can play when you are finished with your homework" after children return from school (Jung, 2016, p. 75) aptly illustrates a Confucian family value. As another example, in Taiwanese preschool classrooms, although children engage in diverse forms of play and routine play sessions are scheduled, it was still the case that children had to earn or were rewarded with play time for being a good student and working hard to complete classroom tasks (Liang, 2001). It was also reported that most children in early childhood programs are still involved in structured, teacher-led play, rather than child-initiated or free play (Lin et al., 2016).

Parents, especially urban families, have started to raise their children to be more autonomous and independent (Lin et al., 2016). Concurrently, they continue to offer home environments where they still maintain authority, engage in parent-directed play activities, and monitor children's use of play time. For instance, many Korean parents have started their children's educational endeavours as early as 2 years or even younger. Although they may have been exposed to newer perspectives on child-rearing and the importance of play in children's development, they continue to focus on academics, rather than play behaviours (Lin et al., 2016). Accordingly, the play environments that children experience show a mix of traditional perspectives, which value hard work over play, and contemporary perspectives, which emphasize the value of play in children's development.

Recall that children's previous lack of free, exploratory, or individual play time was a concern due to its perceived insignificance to children's development and learning in some Asian cultural communities. In Korea, Japan, and China, for example, physical activity and outdoor play activities have been less valued and less emphasized due to the strong emphasis on academic activities (Nah & Waller, 2015). Even in outdoor play, more academic activities have been honoured and teachers tend to employ more group-focused, rather than individual-focused, activities (Kwon, 2003). Today concerns remain about the lack of free play time for young children, because most early childhood programs are run in extremely structured ways (Lee, 1996).

With the changes in views about the value of play in Asian cultural communities, there are striking similarities in the need for play in children across contemporary Western and Eastern countries. For instance, among 2,400 children across North America, South America, Africa, Europe, and Asia, the major free time activity for children was watching television. Parents who participated in the study mostly agreed that free play and exploratory experiential learning opportunities would be helpful for their children during their childhood (Singer et al., 2009). Nonetheless, parents in traditional Confucian-influenced societies are still debating the merits of play for childhood development. At the same time, many aspects of children's play environments, including the use of toys, games, songs, dances, and play resources appear to be influenced by Western societies (Lee, 1996).

Implications and Considerations

By most accounts, adult–child relationships in Confucian societies are changing. These societies are becoming more practical and less ideological than in past eras. Although Confucian-based societies emphasize respect for elders, obedience, and harmony as the central values to be cultivated, increasingly children are reluctant to remain deferential to their parents (Wang, 2014). As Asian societies continue to move toward Western views of individualism, there is greater appreciation for the role of free play in children's development on the part of parents and teachers. Both want children to develop independence and develop into creative and self-regulated children (Ahn, 2015).

Parenting practices are also shifting. There is less of a gender divide, as well as more autonomy and agency in children (Koh et al., 2009). In the past, the negative effects of over-emphasis on education and academic performance led to a restricted perspective with respect to success and career paths children can aspire toward (Liu et al., 2014). In the changing milieu of Asian societies, the divide between play and academic work is becoming less visible. Children are now using play as a vehicle for resisting and accommodating conflicting views. With the advancement of technology, children are more involved in popular media play, and they have been shown to use this popular media play to resist the Confucian values that they are required to follow to be considered a good student, an ideal child, a good friend, and one who lives harmoniously with others (Hadley & Nenga, 2004). A variety of video games and role-playing games also serve to provide educational components in children's play. With video games and game play, children appear to learn about the conflicts between traditional and contemporary ideologies (Khoo, 2012). Across Confucian-influenced societies, children use certain practices to show their resistance to the Confucian values, while simultaneously maintaining their traditional methods of respecting elders in these play forms (Hadley, 2003). In other words, children's play, games, and toys are now being used as an agentic venue for children to go beyond the "Confucian shadow" (Bai, 2005, p. 9).

With changing societal and family structures in Confucian societies, play forms are changing as well. Play has traditionally focused on educational play, rather than free play, but with Westernization, play is switching to more free and less group-focused play. At the same time, children earn their play time by behaving well and participating in tasks, and hence play is still used as a reward. Some schools are increasing academic time and reducing play time, and there is significant debate regarding the efficacy of such approaches. The debate between direct instruction and play-focused instruction in children's development and academic achievement is, to some extent, another example of what many Confucian societies have been engaged in during these transitional times (Jung & Jin, 2014; Liang, 2001).

In traditional Confucian societies, children's play was relatively less structured by adults or programs. Although the nature of play was based more on rituals and group-based activities, their play was less restricted by certain curriculum requirements. However, with Western influence, children have become more immersed in structured and subject-specific educational play within their programs, with much less free time to be involved in outdoor, collaborative, and group play. In traditional play, there was less effort in linking children's play as a vehicle to succeed in their academic pursuit. However, with modern technology and the introduction of new diverse play resources, play is expected to carry educational currency that is directly related to children's success in contemporary societies.

In current societies, whether they be classical Eastern Asian countries (i.e., China, Hong Kong, Japan, Korea, Taiwan, etc.) that are still highly influenced by Confucian philosophy or Western societies where various pedagogies of play have been introduced and have invited heated debates, the role of play in children's development and growth should continue to be revisited with consideration given to diverse cultures, different ideologies, and changing familial and societal structures. To understand and promote children's play in traditionally Confucian-influenced yet gradually changing societies, children's play needs to be considered through multiple lenses and as an ever-evolving entity in the global context.

References

Ackerley, J. (2003). Gender differences in the folklore play of children in primary school playgrounds. *Play and Folklore, 44*, 2–15.

Ahn, J. (2015). Finding a child's self: Globalization and the hybridized landscape of Korean early childhood education. *Anthropology and Education Quarterly, 46*(3), 224–243.

Aydt, H., & Corsaro, W. A. (2003). Differences in children's construction of gender across culture. *American Behavioral Scientist, 46*, 1306–1325.

Bai, L. (2005). Children at play: A childhood beyond the Confucian shadow. *Childhood, 12*(1), 9–32.

Blatchford, P., Baines, E., & Pellegrini, A. (2003). The social context of school playground games: Sex and ethnic differences, and changes over time. *British Journal of Developmental Psychology, 21*(4), 481–505.

Brooker, L., Blaise, M., & Edwards, S. (Eds.) (2014). *Sage handbook of play and learning in early childhood.* Los Angeles, CA: Sage

Buriel, R., & DeMent, T. (1997). Immigration and sociocultural change in Mexican, Chinese, and Vietnamese American families. In A. Booth, A. C. Crouter, & N. Landale (Eds.), *Immigrant and the family: Research and policy on U.S. immigration* (pp. 165–200). Mahwah, NJ: Lawrence Erlbaum Associates.

Chang, H. -C. (2001). Taiwanese kindergarteners' play and artistic representations: Differences between two classrooms and relationships to parents' and teachers' beliefs about education. Doctoral dissertation, Pennsylvania State University.

Chao, R. K., & Tseng, V. (2002). Parenting of Asians. In M. H. Bornstein (Ed.), *Handbook of parenting: Social conditions and applied parenting* (2nd edn.) (pp. 59–93). Mahwah, NJ: Lawrence Erlbaum Associates.

Cheng, C. (2016). A theory of learning in Confucian perspective. *Educational Philosophy and Theory, 48*(1), 52–63.

Dandy, J., & Nettelbeck, T. (2002). The relationship between IQ, homework, aspirations and academic achievement for Chinese, Vietnamese and Anglo-Celtic Australian school children. *Educational Psychology, 22*, 267–275.

Eifring, H. (Ed.) (2015). *Mediation and culture: The interplay of practice and context.* Chennai: Deanta Global Publishing Services.

Feng, Y., & Bodde, D. (1960). *A short history of Chinese philosophy.* Princeton, NJ: Princeton University Press.

Fielding, R. M. (1997). A socio-cognitive perspective on cross-cultural attitudes and practices in creativity development. *Australian Art Education, 20*(1–2), 27–33.

Gupta, A. (2013). Play: Early childhood pedagogies and policies in a globalizing Asia. In O. F. Lillemyr, S. Dockett, & B. Perry (Eds.), *Varied perspectives on play and learning: Theory and research on early years education* (pp. 213–230). Charlotte, NC: Information Age.

Hadley, K. G. (2003). Children's word play: Resisting and accommodating Confucian values in a Taiwanese kindergarten classroom. *Sociology of Education, 76*(3), 193–208.

Hadley, K. G., & Nenga, S. K. (2004). From Snow White to Digimon: Using popular media to confront Confucian values in Taiwanese peer cultures. *Childhood, 11*(4), 515–536.

Hsieh, M. F. (2004). Teaching practices in Taiwan's education for young children: Complexity and ambiguity of developmentally appropriate practices and/or developmentally inappropriate practices. *Contemporary Issues in Early Childhood*, *5*(3), 309–329.

Hwang, K. K. (2001). The deep structure of Confucianism: A social psychological approach. *Asian Philosophy*, *11*, 179–204.

Ishigaki, E. H. (1992). The preparation of early childhood teachers in Japan. *Early Child Development and Care*, *78*, 111–138.

Jung, E. (2016). Play and Asian American children. In J. L. Roopnarine, M. M. Patte, J. E. Johnson, & D. Kuschner (Eds.), *International perspectives on children's play* (pp. 74–88). New York: McGraw Hill.

Jung, E., & Jin, B. (2014). Future professionals' perceptions of play in early childhood classrooms. *Journal of Research in Childhood Education*, *28*(3), 358–376.

Khoo, A. (2012). Video games as moral educators? *Asia Pacific Journal of Education*, *32*(4), 416–429.

Koh, J. B. K., Shao, Y., & Wang, Q. (2009). Father, mother and me: Parental value orientations and child self-identity in Asian American immigrants. *Sex Roles*, *60*, 600–610.

Kook, S. H. (2011). A study on the change of the children's play. *Journal of Children and Museums*, *2*, 137–165 [in Korean].

Kwon, Y. I. (2003). A comparative analysis of preschool education in Korea and England. *Comparative Education*, *39*(4), 479–491.

Lee, K. S. (1996). Culture and the Korean kindergarten curriculum. Paper presented at the meeting of the American Educational Research Association, San Francisco, CA.

Lee, Y.-J., Lee, J., Han, M., & Schickedanz, J. A. (2011). Comparison of preschoolers' narratives, the classroom book environment, and teacher attitudes toward literacy practices in Korean and the United States. *Early Education and Development*, *22*(2), 234–255.

Leung, J. T. Y., & Shek, D. T. L. (2011). Expecting my child to become 'dragon': Development of the Chinese parental expectation on child's future scale. *International Journal on Disability and Human Development*, *10*, 257–265.

Li, J. (2004). Parental expectations of Chinese immigrants: A folk theory about children's school achievement. *Race, Ethnicity and Education*, *7*, 167–183.

Liang, C. (2001). Play in a working class Taiwanese preschool. Doctoral dissertation, University of Illinois, Urbana-Champaign.

Lin, L., Huang, C., & Wang, Q. (2016). Parenting in contemporary China: The dynamics of interdependence and independence. In N. Guerda, B. Anabel, & L. Debbiesiu (Eds.), *Contemporary parenting: A global perspective* (pp. 59–80). New York: Routledge.

Liu, J., McMahon, M., & Watson, M. (2014). Childhood career development in mainland China: A research and practice agenda. *Career Development Quarterly*, *62*, 268–279.

Luo, R., Tamis-LeMonda, C. S., & Song, L. (2013). Chinese parents' goals and practices in early childhood. *Early Childhood Research Quarterly*, *28*, 843–857.

McLean, M. (1995). *Educational traditions compared*. London: David Fulton.

Nah, K.-O., & Waller, T. (2015). Outdoor play in preschools in England and South Korea: Learning from polyvocal methods. *Early Child Development and Care, 185*(11–12), 2010–2015.

Olds, A. R. (1979). *Designing developmentally optional classrooms for children.* Baltimore, MD: University Park Press.

Otsuka, S., & Smith, I. D. (2005). Educational applications of the expectancy-value model of achievement motivation in the diverse cultural contexts of the west and the east. *Change: Transformations in Education, 8*(1), 91–109.

Park, E., Kim, E., Won, J., Oh, W., Suk, M., & Im, Y. (2002). The parent–child relationship in traditional Korean society described in Korean classic novels. *Child Health Nursing Research, 8*(4), 469–481 [in Korean].

Park, M., & Chesla, C. (2007). Revisiting Confucianism as a conceptual framework for Asian family study. *Journal of Family Study, 13*(3), 293–311.

Park, Y., & Kim, U. (1999). The educational challenge of Korea in the global era: The role of family, school, and government. *Educational Journal, 27*(1), 91–120.

Rarick, C. A. (2007). Confucius on management: Understanding Chinese cultural values and managerial practices. *Journal of International Management Studies, 2*(2), 22–28.

Rosemont, H., & Ames, R. T. (2009). *The Chinese classic of family reverence: A philosophical translation of the Xiaojing.* Honolulu: University of Hawai'i Press.

Rudowicz, E., & Hui, A. (1997). The creative personality: Hong Kong perspective. *Journal of Social Behavior and Personality, 12*, 139–148.

Shirakawa, Y., & Kitano, S. (2005). Research and policy issues in early childhood care and education in Japan. In B. Spodek & O. N. Saracho (Eds.), *International perspectives on research in early childhood* (pp. 137–160). Greenwich, CT: Information Age.

Singer, D. G., Jerome, L., Singer, H. D., & Raeka, D. (2009). Children's pastime and play in sixteen nations: Is free-play declining? *American Journal of Play, 1*, 218–232.

Synodi, E. (2010). Play in the kindergarten: The care of Norway, Sweden, New Zealand and Japan. *International Journal of Early Years Education, 18*(3), 185–200.

Takeuchi, M. (1994). Children's play in Japan. In J. L. Roopnarine, J. E. Johnson, & F. H. Hooper (Eds.), *Children's play in diverse cultures* (pp. 51–72). Albany: State University of New York Press.

Tu, W. (1998). Confucius and Confucianism. In W. H. Slote & G. A. DeVos (Eds.), *Confucianism and the family* (pp. 3–36). Albany: State University of New York Press.

Wang, Y. C. (2014). In search of the Confucian family: Interviews with parents and their middle school children in Guangzhou, China. *Journal of Adolescent Research, 29*(6), 765–782.

Whitburn, J. (2003). Learning to live together: The Japanese model of early years education, *International Journal of Early Years Education, 11*(2), 155–175.

Yan, J., & Sorenson, R. (2006). The effect of Confucian values on succession in family business. *Family Business Review, 19*(3), 235–250.

Yim, H. Y. B., Lee, L. W. M., & Ebbeck, M. (2011). Confucianism and early childhood education: A study of young children's responses to traditional Chinese festival stories. *Early Child Development and Care, 181*(3), 287–303.

Yim, H. Y. B., Lee, L. W. M., & Ebbeck, M. (2013). Preservation of Confucian values in early childhood education: A study of experts' and educators' views. *Asia-Pacific Journal of Research in Early Childhood Education, 7*(1), 51–68.

Yoo, A. (1994). *Traditional child rearing parenting in Korea.* Seoul: Seoul National University Press [in Korean].

Zheng, W. (1997). Maoism, feminism, and the UN conference on women: Women's studies research in contemporary China. *Journal of Women's History, 8*(4), 126–152.

PART IV

Theories of Play and Research Methodology

20 Classic Theories of Play

Thomas S. Henricks

Play studies, like other academic disciplines and interdisciplines, has its classic writings.

Those writings serve several functions for contemporary scholarship. In the fashion of touchstones, the classics are reminders of the issues that preoccupied earlier generations of researchers and of the social and cultural contexts that made those concerns pertinent. More than that, classics are distinguished from other older contributions by the exemplary quality of their execution and expression. Works said to be 'classics' are acknowledged to be the best of their time, conceptions that shaped and energized discourse communities. Although the popularity of those statements rises and falls as researchers move ahead, the very best of them maintain a certain prominence, for they enunciate clearly what it is that scholars wish to know and display an intellectual brilliance that transcends the generations. As Isaac Newton once noted in the case of his own vision, contemporary scholars stand on the shoulders of their great predecessors and continue to address the concerns those earlier writers identified long ago.

This chapter discusses some classic theories of play. For the most part, the theories presented here were created between the mid-nineteenth and mid-twentieth centuries, that is, during a time when the social sciences became established as important, scientifically grounded perspectives for understanding human behaviour and experience. That same period, it should be noted, is associated with the rapid development – and in some views, culmination – of the industrializing, 'modern' world.

Societies of the modern type celebrate the powers and freedoms of individuals, as expanding categories of persons are released from long-standing obligations to kin groups, communities, and guilds. Cultural emphasis shifts from who people have been to who they can become, from significant social connections to private accomplishments. Ideals of personal development, self-realization, and even 'progress' become commonplace and influence many fields of study, including play (Sutton-Smith, 1997, p. 9). As this author has argued elsewhere (Henricks, 2015, p. 6; see also Smith, 2010), this view – which endorses the self-discovered possibilities of all people, but especially children – remains a dominant theme in contemporary play studies.

Another, seemingly opposite, theme of modernity is the rise of new styles of human bonding, commonly called associations or organizations. As in the case of persons, these associations are constructed intentionally and guided by similarly manufactured, formal rules. Nation-states, schools, hospitals, businesses, clubs, and even churches become arrangements that can be modified reflexively, that is, according to the interests and insights of their organizers. One of modernity's great tensions then is between the claims of these interest-based formal organizations and those of the persons who work for them or use their services. As will be shown, some early accounts of play focus on the stresses created by industrialism. And bureaucratic management, which emphasizes the commandments of formal rules and officials, is often seen as the enemy of play.

The classic theories of play described below are attempts to understand the possibilities for personal expression and development in this modern context. In an age that was becoming increasingly secular, scientific, cosmopolitan, and progress-oriented, scholars looked within the person, now conceived universally, to discover the well-springs of possibility. Good persons – and good societies – are thought to result from expressive freedom. Bad societies are those that trap and manage people in the fashion of bureaucracies.

Pointedly, this is not the only way to envision play. As scholars from the historical and anthropological traditions have stressed, and as other contributions to this handbook will describe, play also flourishes in traditional, community-centred societies that look to sacred beings for guidance (see Lancy, 2008; Roopnarine et al., 1994; Spariosu, 1989; Sutton-Smith, 1997). Clearly, play emerges – and functions for society – in various ways.

Theories of Surplus Energy

One of the most important early formulations of play was offered by the German poet and philosopher Friedrich Schiller. It was presented in a series of letters on aesthetic education written for a Danish patron (Schiller, 1795/1965). Schiller was a prominent figure in the emergence of German Romanticism, which expanded the Enlightenment's focus on rationality to include moral and aesthetic themes as well. The earliest of the writings considered in this chapter, its date is important as it coincides roughly with the beginnings of the Industrial Revolution in Northern Europe and the aftershocks of the French Revolution.

Schiller's concern was to reaffirm the importance of the human spirit, and its expressive possibilities, in a fast-changing and newly ideological era. His response (following the philosopher Kant) was to stress a universal dual nature of human beings, both sides of which must be honoured if people are to flourish. One portion of this nature – and a link to our animal kindred – is our sensuality. We are creatures with physical needs and forms of orientation that help us to address these needs through action in the material world. Schiller named this inborn inclination the "sensuous" drive (1965, p. 64).

However, humans differ from other creatures by the extent to which they possess a second, or "formal" drive (pp. 65–66). This is the impulse to impose cognitive or rational form on worldly involvement. People create conceptions of their circumstances and effectively inhabit this patterning of idea and image. This formal drive leads to belief systems of every type and to the exploits of philosophy, science, and art.

However, each of the two impulses is, by itself, deficient. The sensuous drive, if unchecked, produces behaviour that is merely vacillation between urgency and lethargy. The form drive by itself produces ideas that are sterile, because they are untested in the crucible of wider experience. Schiller's gift to play studies then is his positing of a third, or 'play', impulse that mediates the other two commitments (p. 75). When people play, they control their baser emotions by placing these within frameworks of rationally considered rules and restraints. But play also honours the surging demands of life itself, which are to seek out new experiences and explore their physical implications.

For Schiller, then, play is foundational to the pursuit of beauty and other aesthetic commitments. It is the way in which people come to terms with the fullest range of their capacities for living in the world. As he puts it: "Man plays only when he is in the full sense of the word a man and *he is only wholly man when he is playing* " (p. 80, emphasis in original).

When does activity of this sort occur? Schiller's best-remembered theme is his claim that people, like other species, play when they feel themselves satisfied with their standing in the world and thus ready for new adventures. Joyous play (the type he emphasizes) occurs when the "lion is not gnawed by hunger and when no beast of prey is challenging him to battle, his idle energy creates for itself an object; he fills the echoing desert with his high-spirited roaring" (p. 133). In other words, creatures play when they feel themselves in full possession of their powers.

This quality of superabundance, it should be noted, was a more general theme of German Romanticism. The empowered, experiencing subject is prominent in the music of Beethoven and Wagner and in the philosophies of Hegel, Schopenhauer, and Nietzsche. And it is important to the theories of play-based educators like Pestalozzi and Froebel.

Deeper into the industrial age, some of Schiller's ideas were reformulated by British social philosopher Herbert Spencer. Not a trained academic, Spencer was interested in a wide range of topics pertinent to social living. Play was among these topics.

Spencer discusses play within a treatment of aesthetics in his *Principles of Psychology* (1855/1915). There, Spencer recalls but does not reference Schiller's theory directly (p. 627). Like Schiller, he believes that play reflects the ability of higher-level creatures to transcend their basic requirements for living, such as food, shelter, protection from predators, and reproductive opportunities.

Turning from such matters, playful animals are able to focus on two other themes: immediate gratification and increased ability through exercise.

Although Spencer repeats much from Schiller's thesis about surplus energy, he adds that vigour of this sort comes from improved nutrition. And he speculates about the role of the nervous system in playful expression. Essentially, Spencer's theory is that energy collects in nerve centres, which require periodic discharge to maintain proper functioning. Too much build up, as might occur under conditions of restoration and relaxation, makes the creature especially sensitive to external stimulation as well as to internally manufactured "desires" (p. 625). When we play, we impose these desires on the world.

It is worth recalling that Spencer's broader body of work is marked heavily by his interest in evolution, especially after the publication of Darwin's theory of natural section in 1859. Differently from Darwin, Spencer focuses on societal evolution and on the role of individual effort (rather than chance mutation) in such changes. Seen in that light, the play of children features both enculturation (as they play the games designated for them) and opportunities for personal success. Translating cooperation and competition into these game-forms allows participants to have the feelings of triumph apart from activities that are typically more dangerous (p. 631).

Much as play functions for individuals (as a protected opportunity to express and learn), so play marks the development of societies. More complex and advanced societies, as he sees it, shift interaction from selfish, sensory, and sometimes destructive engagements to those that are more sublimated and aesthetic (p. 632). To revisit Schiller's theory once again, play prepares participants to ponder, and actuate, the ideal.

Not surprisingly, the theories of surplus energy have been criticized. People may well play as an expression of physical and psychological exuberance, but they play for other reasons as well. Schiller's postulation of three innate drives (including the urge to play) remains only that; although it is important to note that contemporary neuroscientists continue to seek the deep-brain mechanisms that make play possible (see Panksepp, 1998, 2010). Spencer's ideas about societal evolution and the role of competition in personal and social advancement have been replaced by other accounts of how societies change and of the respective advantages and disadvantages of such changes. Still, the basic issues presented here – play's distinctive integration of sensuality and reason, the connection of play to aesthetic pursuits, the ways in which societies both channel expression and permit creativity, and the implications of the cooperation–competition combination – remain guiding concerns for play studies.

Play as Instinctual Practice, Recreation, and Recapitulation

Other theories, essentially refutations of the surplus energy thesis, were developed. Perhaps the most important of these is Karl Groos's interpretation of play as a practicing of behaviors that in non-playing species are ruled by instinct. A philosopher of aesthetics, Groos argued that the physical play of animals signified an evolutionary advance in behaviour management and was a preparation for later forms of cultural speculation in humans. He presented his theme in two books, *The Play of Animals* (1895) and *The Play of Man* (1898).

Groos's principal objection to the surplus energy thesis is that it does not explain why behaviours take the specific forms they do. Furthermore, he does not believe that imitation, typically observing and copying the practices of older creatures, is sufficient to explain such behaviour (1895/1898, pp. 9–12). That is because animals of the same species, however widely separated or raised, tend to play in much the same way. Another factor, some internal force, must help motivate and organize behaviour.

Although Groos invokes the idea of instinct repeatedly in his book, his interpretation of that concept is flexible. Just as play directives are said to be instinctual, so, it is claimed, is the capacity to imitate, or learn (p. 78). Under such guidance, young creatures practice strategies relevant to food-getting, defence, and courtship, that is, long before these behaviours are actually required for survival. Indeed, he understands youth itself to be a time of preparation for later responsibilities. As he famously declares, *"the very existence of youth is due in part to the necessity for play*, the animal does not play because he is young, he has a period of youth because he must play" (pp. 112–113, emphasis in original).

It might be imagined that Groos's theory applies only to the young, but this is not the case. Playful practice remains relevant throughout life, both to derive satisfaction from successful manoeuvring and to keep skills sharp (p. 81). This general theme, that there are secondary or "psychological" satisfactions – mostly related to personal accomplishment, group bonding, and even the thrill of competitive victory – is developed in the final portions of the book.

Groos concludes with comments about the ways in which play builds a hypothetical or suppositional reality, a world of make-believe characterized by restricted behaviours and consequences. Much as Schiller conceives, this activity is a bridge to the most complicated kinds of aesthetic imagining.

In *The Play of Man*, Groos focuses much more on the role of imitation (1898/1901, p. 2). Still he does not abandon instinct entirely. As he summarizes, "imitation is the connecting link between instinctive and intelligent conduct" (p. 281). What imitation accomplishes then is the progressive release of certain species, and especially humans, from rigid behaviour controls. To that degree, play supports evolution as much as it expresses it.

Much of *The Play of Man* is devoted to analysis of the different kinds of play. To be sure, humans engage in individual play. A very basic form of this is the attempt to control bodily movements and sensations. There is also play with foreign objects, featuring our efforts to move and resist these and to construct and deconstruct things from their elements. Finally, there is the play of the mind, experimentation with memory, attention, and imagination.

However, human play is distinguished by its intensely social nature. We want recognition and response from others, and for such reasons continually join and divide. To be human then is to engage in acts of teasing, shaming, joking, and gossiping, and in public games and contests.

The final section of his book explores the different ways in which play can be studied. Play is sometimes studied "physiologically", that is, as an expression of current physical functioning, including the energy levels emphasized in the previous section. Play may be studied "biologically". For Groos, this means attending to genetic and structural matters as these support individual and species development. There is also the "psychological" viewpoint, which centres on mental awareness and cognitive-emotional functioning. A fourth perspective is the "aesthetic", which explores the meanings of beauty and, more generally, of engagement with natural and cultural form. A fifth is the "sociological", which examines play as a patterning of human relationships. Finally, Groos emphasizes the "pedagogical" perspective, which identifies how play is connected to knowledge-making and personal growth.

Few writers on play have done as much as Groos to identify the range of playful possibilities and to detail so ably the different perspectives for studying play. His effort to connect the physical foundations of animal play with the social and cultural enterprises of humans remains important. His speculations were, of course, based on the animal studies of this time. Later generations of animal behaviour scholars (see Burghardt, 2005; Fagen, 2005), supported by a century of scientific improvements, continue to explore these themes. Finally, Groos's theory of play as practice for later life responsibilities has had its critics, including some of those described later.

Another German philosopher, Moritz Lazarus, offered a quite different theory. Lazarus (1883) was interested in how people are rejuvenated, particularly in social gatherings. In contrast to Schiller's theme of personal exuberance, Lazarus emphasized that play commonly energizes and restores those who entered that setting feeling tired or dispirited.

In that regard, play is to be differentiated from work. Work is dominated by external pressures, habits of seriousness, and long-term goals. Workers experience psychological and physical tensions that have no easy release. Play, on the other hand, is marked by short-term ends, self-direction, and feelings of fun. Players commit themselves to a momentary, carefully partitioned world, literally an "illusion", that buoys their spirits (see Levy, 1978, pp. 88–89).

Lazarus's treatment of the play/work distinction anticipates later analyses of this issue (see Henricks, 2015). More importantly, his emphasis on social settings provides an alternative to the psychological and instrumental approaches that have been dominant in play studies. As a follower of Hegel, Herder, and Herbart, Lazarus wished to understand the foundations of community, both locally and at wider levels. In play, people experience this sense of community and feel empowered by it.

Philosopher George Patrick (1916) offered a twentieth-century reworking of this general approach, though he also returned the discussion to more narrowly psychological ground. Patrick was concerned with the pressures of urban, industrial living, and especially the effects of this on the nervous system. Earlier times, as he saw it, were dominated by the rhythms of agricultural labour that was coupled with festive release. People worked hard for designated periods of time and then gave themselves fully to rest and recreation. In other words, tension was built and expended in clearly anticipated ways.

Twentieth-century people commonly hold jobs that require both continuous attentiveness and restricted physical movement. Factory and office work are prominent examples. Because of this, there is a great need for tension release (pp. 16–17). Although society offers various kinds of escapism, such as drinking, gambling, carousing, and other commodified amusements, Patrick endorsed sports, games, and other outdoor activities as preferable forms of recreation. These allow tension to be developed and released systematically.

Unlike many play scholars, Patrick focuses primarily on adults rather than children. However, in his analysis of children's play, he disagrees with Groos's theory that play is a preparation for later responsibilities. In an industrial society, children's activities – running, jumping, caring for pets, playing marbles, and the like – have little connection to the challenges of adulthood, unless that means adult sport. For that reason, child's play should be seen as both an expression and a cultivation of physical commitments that are deeply engraved in the human constitution. Play of the physical type is taken up naturally (pp. 72–73).

As a traditionalist and moralist, Patrick preferred the older styles of physical play to modern amusements. Children – and adults – need playgrounds. Music and dance are said to be evolutionary commitments. Gender differences in play, as elsewhere, are presented as historic proclivities. When we play, we tread this ancient ground and awaken our capacities.

This thesis – that play is more a looking backward rather than a straining ahead – was given fullest expression by G. Stanley Hall. Hall was a prominent American psychologist who, among many other contributions, championed scientific research in that discipline. Hall's theory of play, like his understanding of human personality more generally, centred on the idea that individuals move through distinct stages of development that reproduce in some fashion the evolutionary development of the species itself.

Hall's approach was inspired by the theories of German biologist Ernst Haeckel, who proclaimed that *ontogeny recapitulates phylogeny*. That is to say, individual creatures in their fetal development display, if only for short periods, traits of species that are their distant ancestors. The best-known example of this in human fetuses is the presence of non-functioning gill arches.

Like Haeckel, Hall believed in invariant stages of development. The traits that contemporary species exhibit are a mix of inherited random mutations (Darwin's theme) and age-old practices that somehow become behavioural proclivities (Spencer's theme). Individuals express and refine these proclivities. In contradistinction to Groos's view about play as practice, Hall (1931, I, p. 202) stresses that "true play never practices what is phyletically new, and this, industrial life often calls for". What play does do is repeat ancient physical exercises, rhythms, and challenges. At least that is what children choose – fighting, singing, dancing, and so forth – when they are allowed to follow their preferences.

What is the proper role for adults in children's play? According to Hall (p. x), the "child revels in savagery". For that reason, more civilized activities should be introduced, at least by age 8. For adolescents in particular, emphasis should be placed on social activities, both cooperative and competitive. This is discovered not only in organized sports and games but also in singing and dancing (p. 212). Pointedly, activities of this sort are not departures from history but rather attempts to align the developing child with the course of civilization itself.

Hall's effort to connect modern play to distinct stages of cultural evolution is no longer fashionable. Neither are his ideas about race and gender differences or about the presumed superiority of 'civilized' peoples. But his commitment to the idea of coherent stages of individual development – and to play's role in this – remains important in psychology. And the view that play is a consultation with age-old physical tendencies as well as an imagining of future possibilities maintains a certain appeal.

Three Psychological Traditions

The dominant perspective in play studies is provided by psychology, both in its strictly academic context and in such applications as psychotherapy and education. Play scholars who concentrate on modern societies – and classic play theorists tend to be examples of this – perpetuate what Sutton-Smith (1997, p. 11) calls the "modern set of rhetorics". These include the ideas that play is an enabler of individual progress, that it focuses on self-exploration, and that it is connected intimately to imagination. These three themes are to be contrasted to the four patterns identified by students of traditional societies: that play is a vehicle for frivolity, that it engages fate, that it explores power relations, and that it articulates community identity. Whether play operates in a traditional or modern context, it constitutes a distinctive pathway for building identity, capability, and experience (Henricks, 2014). And psychology remains a key discipline for illuminating those processes.

In play studies, as in psychology more generally, the Freudian perspective continues to be important. Although Freud did not devote one of his works explicitly to play, he commented on this topic frequently and connected it to other psychological patterns. Pointedly, his view of play fits within his broader view of the psyche as being ever unsettled and conflict ridden. Psychophysical urges (the id), moral claims (the superego), and reason-based evaluations of both internal and external occurrences (the ego) seek dominance. Understandings focused on the future and past as well as on the present preoccupy thought. Only some elements of psychic functioning are recognized consciously. Many concerns operate at deeper levels of awareness, but these too may suddenly rush to consciousness. Seen in that context, Freudian psychology is an analysis of the ways in which deeper and less guarded mental occurrences (primary process thinking) interact with more circumspect, reality-based thinking. In therapy, much is made of verbal slips and errors, jokes, dreams, fantasies, free associations, and compulsions of every sort; for these are all occasions where the mind is trying to evade its own strictures.

Play then is a special sort of activity where people imagine alternative patterns for thought, feeling, and behaviour and then explore the implications of these in behaviour. As Freud (1958, p. 45) puts it, "Perhaps we may say that every child at play behaves like an imaginative writer, in that he creates a world of his own, or more truly, he rearranges the things of his world and orders it in a new way that pleases him better." To that extent, play is an exercise in wish fulfilment or pleasure-seeking. The principal wish, he continues, is to be "grown-up," to have what the child imagines adults to have. Pointedly, play is neither mere fantasy nor daydreaming. It is activity set within a carefully constructed illusory world, which protects the player from the usual repercussions of the words, gestures, and other behaviours that are employed.

In a later work, *Beyond the Pleasure Principle*, Freud (1928/1967) altered his own theory. Observing a small child's game with a wooden reel, he concluded that players do not simply seek satisfaction, or if they do, it is satisfaction of a different sort from what he had previously conceptualized. In the game, the child would throw the reel (which had a string attached) over the edge of his curtained cot. Then, using the string, he would pull the object slowly back into view. The act of throwing the reel seemed to be the most emotionally charged element of the game (pp. 33–34). Because the reel, in Freud's view, symbolized a desired object (perhaps at some level the mother who would leave the boy alone in his cot), the game should be seen as a renunciation of the pleasure principle. There was satisfaction to be sure, as the child waited and then drew the reel back into view. But the game's real pleasure came from the ego's being able to control the psyche's own urges and, more generally, from being able to regulate all the elements of the situation. The therapeutic implications of this approach, especially with regard to children, were developed by Freud's daughter Anna (A. Freud, 1965).

That focus on ego-control was also central to the well-known play theory of Freud's student Erik Erikson. Erikson expanded Freud's ideas about psychic development, describing the pertinence of that concept to the entire life course and catering his analysis on the much more general (or broadly emotional) concerns that preoccupy people at different ages. As Erikson (1963, p. 211) summarizes his approach, play "is a function of the ego, an attempt to synchronize the bodily and social processes with the self". To that extent, play is not simply energetic or creative activity but rather a grappling with pertinent life challenges or issues. When we play we involve ourselves in a range of new roles and circumstances, and experience the latitudes of success and failure that accompany these.

For Erikson, some of these issues include "gravity", "time", "fate", and "causality" (pp. 213–14). There are challenges associated with "social reality" and "bodily drives". As might be imagined, different challenges – and different objects of play – become more or less important as people move through the life course. The most basic, and earliest, forms of play centre on control of bodily movements and sensations. Later play involves the "microsphere", where players try to manage external objects and conditions. The third stage involves operations in the wider "macrosphere", the extended reality represented by other people and relationships to them. Consistently with his broader developmental theory, Erikson stresses the fundamental commitment of people to comprehend the world with an increasingly broad vision, to learn what they can and cannot do in it, and to secure the status of the ego in life operations.

The Freudian tradition has been criticized for its attempt to designate 'universal' life stages, concerns, and meanings based on analyses of a European, urban, middle-class context. Many of Freud's important concepts and themes – ideas about the dynamics of nervous energy, instinctual forces, guilt, sexual repression, female envy of male physicality and status, and so forth – must be interpreted in that light. However, his focus on the ways in which people try to create settings that allow them to work through fundamental emotional challenges remains central to play studies.

A rival theory of play was presented by Jean Piaget. Like Freud, Piaget was committed to the concept of human development, including the identification of distinct stages of comprehension and control. Piaget had studied under another of Freud's followers, Carl Jung, and early in his career wished to become a therapist. However, he shifted his focus to academic psychology and his principal concerns became the cognitive and moral development of children.

In a landmark book, *Play, Dreams, and Imitation in Children*, Piaget presented his theory that play is one of the strategies people adopt to learn what they can do in the world. That learning process, he explained, occurs as an interaction between the biologically (and psychologically) developing child and the challenges presented by the physical (and ultimately symbolically configured) environment. The goal of such interaction is to develop increasingly effective ways of understanding and administering that environment.

There are two poles to this interactive process. At one extreme, interaction takes the form of personal adjustment, or *accommodation*, to environmental challenges. This occurs because the child has not been entirely successful with his or her current strategies or *schemas*. Changes, essentially readjustment of those techniques, need to be made. The opposite pole is the practicing or implementing of those techniques on the environment. Piaget called that pattern of manipulation or exercise *assimilation*.

In Piaget's (1951/1962, p. 89) conception, play is extreme or pure assimilation, when behavioural techniques are repeated "purely for functional pleasure". That is to say, play is an activity that is pleasurable in its own right, when people practice acts of mastery and introduce modest refinements to these. Human *adaptation*, Piaget's broader concern, occurs then as an alternation and mixing of these poles of assimilation and accommodation. Like amateur scientists, players try out their abilities to negotiate otherness, survey their results, adjust their strategies, and try again. Development is equivalent to the establishment of increasingly successful and widely applicable strategies.

As children grow older, they adopt more complex schema and apply these to ever wider circumstances. Certain schemas (perhaps the act of grabbing) are applied to different objects. Particular schemas may be combined (perhaps grabbing and then shaking the object). Acts of self-control expand to include control of objects and then symbolic manipulations. This latter focus – that play involves the manipulation of ideas – is especially important. Playing children learn that what they are doing is a kind of supposition, in which they replace the usual meanings of words and behaviours with self-imposed ones.

Piaget (p. 142) establishes a progression of age-related play forms. Practice play begins in the first months of life. Symbolic play begins in the second year. By age 7, children are preoccupied with social play in games with rules. Indeed, negotiating and administering these rules constitutes a major theme of the experience. Piaget (1932/1966) developed this issue – the role of games in acquisition of morality – in another of his books. As he argued, children learn morality less from adult tutors than from negotiations with peers. Play and games provide these opportunities.

Like Freud's, Piaget's work has been criticized for its presentation of invariant, universal stages on the basis of a European milieu. His view of cognitive and moral development as increasing comprehension and control contrasts with more relational views of these issues. And his theory of play – as assimilation – has been questioned by those who see adjustment or accommodation as an equally important aspect of this behaviour (see Sutton-Smith, 1966). Still, his interactional model of how humans develop – and of play's key role in this process – remains a critically important contribution.

A third tradition stems from the writing of Lev Vygotsky. Vygotsky was familiar with the theories of both Freud and Piaget. He incorporated some elements from each. But his approach is focused much more clearly on action-in-the-world or interaction than on the playful expression of pre-formed ideas and wishes. Said differently, action – and play as a certain type of action – is a process of engagement in which people imaginatively create situations and then respond to the newfound challenges presented there.

Pointedly, Vygotsky (1933/1976, p. 537) rejected both Piaget's cognitive or 'intellectualized' emphasis and Freud's feeling-based or emotional theme. Instead, and in the spirit of Marx, he argued that play is a blending of thought, feeling, and action. More than that, action leads the player to realize new, unanticipated thoughts and feelings. To that degree, play promotes change through a pattern of challenge and response.

Consistently with his broader theory of human development, Vygotsky emphasized how children expand their abilities to conceive and operate within the world. Infants have a "union of affect and perception" (p. 545). They are deeply immersed in the world and react to it in ways they cannot resist. Toddlers begin to realize their separation from this setting; they can move objects about and grant them names. They acknowledge that the external world can influence them, giving them pain as well as pleasure. In that context, they learn to be both subjects and objects, who assume these roles by interacting with otherness.

One of Vygotsky's best-known concepts is the "pivot" (p. 546). Children are aided in their play by physical objects or props, like a long stick that functions as a hobby horse. Such a device is understood by its users to be symbol, not a real horse but an artefact that stands for such. As children grow older, they are able to use increasingly abstract and complicated symbols. But young children rely on physical symbols that approximate the reality represented. Such pivots effectively transport the imagination and facilitate communication with other players.

Vygotsky's approach is distinguished by its clearly social aspects. Adults may present the child with situation-based challenges that cause them to respond and thus change. Peers may do this even more effectively. And the child may also take the role of challenger or questioner. The result is a setting marked by imaginative intersubjectivity, where each person (ideally) takes seriously the invitations of the other.

Vygotsky focused his theory on the symbolic interaction of children. Subsequent researchers have extended this approach to adults as well under the terms of performance theory (see Lobman and O'Neill, 2011). Peer-based, dialogical strategies based on this tradition have also been important in therapy (see Newman & Holzman, 1993; Winnicott, 1971).

Play, Identity, and Social Involvement

Vygotsky's theory emphasizes the ability of participants to create imaginatively – and operate within – new situations and, as part of this process, to inhabit new versions of themselves. However, small-scale social creativity of that sort is only one part of the much broader challenge of living in society. There are also ongoing relationships and matters of social structure, well-established and far-reaching normative and organizational patterns that serve as frameworks for what people can be and do. The character of those frameworks is central to social and cultural theories of play.

In that regard, sociologist George Herbert Mead (1964, pp. 209–228) offered a classic account of the relationship between play and self-development. For Mead, the term 'self' denotes people's ability to think about themselves reflexively, that is, to comprehend and evaluate their dual identities as subjects and objects in social situations and then to direct their actions on the basis of those assessments. Those self-recognitions Mead called the "I" and the "me." Most people believe themselves to possess certain traits, social connections, and life histories. They feel they have certain rights and responsibilities. How do those self-evaluations arise?

Mead argued that role-play and, later, participation in social games is critical to this process. When young children play imaginatively, they "take the role of the other". That is, they attempt to construct in their mind the role – and the associated perspective – of some other person or animal, perhaps a police officer, mother, or shaggy dog. So prepared, they pretend to be that 'other' and, indeed, act out what such a figure would say or do in a specific situation. In solitary play, the child may switch from role to role, sometimes conducting a conversation in first one and then the other voice. This, Mead insisted, is a tremendous cognitive advance, for it requires taking another's viewpoint toward oneself and anticipating what that other will say or do in the moments ahead.

By age 6, children are able to play social games. This involves a much more complicated level of awareness, for it means that the player must comprehend what several different others (each of whom may be playing a different role, as in a baseball game) are expecting at any one time. More than that, these different viewpoints must be assembled into a wider view of what the group as a whole expects of the player and of how it assesses his or her standing and performance.

These two perspectives on personal functioning – what other individuals expect and what groups expect – are extended into even wider understandings of what society expects (what Mead called the "generalized other"). In his view, people seek a broad-based and generally integrated understanding of who they are, but they recognize also that they play different roles in different situations and operate with sometimes conflicting sub-identities. However complicated such self-assessment becomes, play and games serve as foundations for this learning process. For both are exercises in anticipating what others presumably want, in developing coherent responses to these expectations, and then in analyzing the repercussions of those actions.

Another sociologist, Georg Simmel, described this theme of situational expectations even more acutely. In a well-known essay on "sociability", what he called the "play-form" of association, Simmel (1950) stressed the degree to which participants accept the values and norms of the situation at hand. Typically, when one attends a party, soiree, or dance, they know well that the event is to be of a certain character and that there are clear expectations for every person there. Each participant is to support a general spirit of affability and good will, which is in fact the goal of the event. There are expectations for when people should arrive and leave, how they should dress, what they should bring, and (most importantly) how they should behave. Conversationalists should refrain from topics that are too personal (for example, talking about serious difficulties at work or family problems) or too impersonal (for example, general political, religious, and economic matters). If such topics are broached, this should be done in a fanciful or ironic way that implies the ability of people to confront the difficulties that beset them.

Because the guiding theme of the event is to honour all attendees and enhance group morale, participants should continually make and remake social circles. Within these circles, each person should be included in the conversation. When conversations falter, it is the responsibility of the host or hostess to realign the groups. Emphatically, it is not the content of any particular conversation that matters. Rather, the issue is whether all attendees are feeling included and respected. That issue, the conferring of individual – and, by extension, group – respect is the predominant concern. What is being played, at least in this instance, is the complexities of social acceptance and comportment.

Although it is common to think of play events as occasions where people act without reservation, Simmel made clear that this is not the case. When people play, they take on a very specialized role. In other words, they adapt to the requirements of the situation at hand. Many 'personal' concerns and abilities are irrelevant, indeed inappropriate, to that setting. And the experiences of the player – including assessments of fun or pleasure – must be seen as a meshing of in-event satisfactions with the broader self-estimations of the individual.

The play theory of Erving Goffman combines themes from Mead and Simmel. Taken as a whole, Goffman's writing focuses on the ways in which people negotiate identity in social encounters (see Henricks, 2006). Although people continually 'create' social reality in the sense that they reach agreements with one another about the character of the situations they are in, what identities they will hold, and what behaviour they will follow, they do not get to do this just as they would like. That is because there are many external pressures, including wider identities and obligations, that influence the participants and because there are preexisting models directing should happen in that encounter. Said differently, most of the time people rely on prepackaged forms or 'frames' to help them orient, communicate, and pursue joint lines of action (Goffman, 1974).

Play is one of these frames for identity and behaviour. Usually when people prepare themselves for play, they acknowledge that the situation will be of a certain type. In that regard, Goffman (1974, pp. 41–43) identifies seven traits of play. These include the blocking of the ordinary functions and consequences of activity and the exaggeration of some behaviours. There are also "interruptions" of behaviour sequences and "repetitiveness" of those behaviours. Small behaviour patterns are started and stopped, started and stopped. A fifth trait is the event's relative freedom or "voluntarism". Sixth is the practice of "role-switching", especially by alternating positions of dominance and subordination. Seventh and last is separation from "external needs". Once again, these qualities of play tend to be understood by participants or serve as topics for social instruction. In such terms, people learn to play "well" or "fairly".

Goffman emphasized that there are different types of play, such as "make-believe" and "contests". He also stressed that "games" are events of their own sort. Games are activities – or forms for activity – that direct people coherently through a range of interconnected behaviours. Certain situational factors promote the success of games, especially the perception that such an event is "good" or "fun" (Goffman, 1961, pp. 66–79). In that regard, it is helpful to have physical barriers that keep the outside world away. Participants should be positioned at distances that allow them to focus on one another and conduct the activity at hand.

That focus is promoted also by sometimes elaborate cultural devices, such as special costumes, playing implements, rules, and definitions of time and space. Importantly, there should be strategies to ensure "uncertainty of outcome", either through the equalization of sides or by the insertion of chance or luck. Also useful are "sanctioned displays". That is, participants feel more involved when the game explores skills, values, and group identities that have currency in society at large. Focus is also enhanced by the setting of "stakes", specific levels of risk and reward including dares, assaults on character, and money exchanges. Stakes set too high ruin the fun and distract players; stakes set too low may be irrelevant or boring.

Goffman's general theme is that games (and to some extent, all human events) are bounded affairs, with semi-permeable exteriors. The challenge for those involved is to keep both outside pressures (such as calls to "come home") and interior ones (such as hurt feelings) from disrupting what occurs there. It is within such intentionally protected frameworks that players cooperate and compete, gain and lose status, however momentary these experiences may be. Although players can succeed or fail by "making moves", only persons can have "fun". That is because satisfaction is a mixing of broader personal qualities with the requirements of the situation at hand.

In sociological accounts of play, then, the 'inner' world of the play sphere is never entirely separated from 'outer' matters that include the ongoing identities and concerns of the players themselves. Widespread cultural elements – beliefs, values, skills, and artefacts – may be incorporated into the event, either informally or formally by means of rules, playing grounds, implements, and costumes. And organizations – such as schools, communities, and businesses – frequently sponsor play events and understand their own status and interests to be affected by what occurs there.

That patterning of influence can be viewed in a highly critical way. In a classic book, *The Theory of the Leisure Class*, Thorstein Veblen (1899/1934) argued that play was used by the upper class of his time to display status and affirm group solidarity. As he saw it, upper-class sports like shooting and fox-hunting centred on predation, competition, and the desire for bounty (p. 262). To that degree, they were atavistic, attempts to recall an earlier time when the dominant groups held their lands through military prowess rather than economic labour. Whatever the implications of restricted access to leisure and status display, contemporary historians and sociologists have identified many other aspects – beneficial as well as harmful – of the play–society connection (see Henricks, 2006).

Play and Culture

It is important to analyze play in terms of its particular social settings, pertinent identities, and sponsoring groups. But a still greater challenge, at least for classic theory, is to comprehend the relationship of play events to society as a whole. Before the age of colonization and widespread migration, human populations lived in greater isolation than they do now. There were sharp differences in language, religion, custom, and patterns of political and social organization. Although contemporary globalization has blurred further these differences, scholars continue to focus on a key issue: What is variable about human experience and what is the same? Because play is such a basic – indeed, universal – activity, it provides a critical test case for exploring the possibilities of human capability and expression.

A classic analysis of this issue was offered by cultural historian Johan Huizinga. In *Homo Ludens: A Study of the Play-Element in Culture*, Huizinga defined play as a particular pattern of human relating that is shared across cultures and, indeed, precedes their development. His book also advanced a historical thesis. There has been a decline, Huizinga argued, in community-based, peer-oriented public play for adults under the conditions of industrialism. That change corresponds to a more general withering of social vitality and personal exuberance.

Huizinga's famous characterization of play contains five elements. As he (1938/1955, pp. 7–13) describes it, play is a "voluntary activity". It may be bound with ritual and, by that process, acquire an obligatory tone, but in its purer forms it is something people do on their own terms and timing. Second, play is usually differentiated from ordinary affairs. Play behaviours are commonly seen as non-serious, only pretend, and materially "disinterested". Little is gained or lost through participation. A third theme is that play is secluded and limited. This means that play events tend to be cut off from ordinary affairs by the wide variety of boundary-maintaining affairs that were discussed in the earlier section.

Fourth is the quality, seemingly paradoxical, that play "creates order, is order". When people play, they impose artificial constraints on their behaviour (such as agreeing to hop on one leg, sing a designated song, or follow elaborate game rules). Part of play means creating and abiding by such frameworks. But play is creative also in the sense that participants try to assert themselves, in all manner of ways, within this context. That provocative relationship between order and disorder he describes as "tension, poise, balance, contrast, variation, solution, resolution, etc." (p. 10). Fifth, and finally, play tends to surround itself with make-believe. There is commonly a fascination with the arcane and silly, commitments that mark insiders and keep uncomprehending outsiders away.

In Huizinga's view, this pattern of artificially bounded, exuberant creativity is rooted in our species' animal past. As a sort of practicing and exploring, it precedes culture. And it remains important in traditional societies. Especially important, as he sees it, are public play events, occasions when communities gather to reenact their traditions through innovative, zestful expression. Such events are forms of social and self-reconnaissance, when individuals and groups make plain their relationships to one another. They are also times to show what players, as individuals, can do. That setting – what he called the "play-festival-rite" complex (p. 31) – is fundamental to his understanding of how humans have lived in the past – and should live today.

In his book, Huizinga considers a wide range of playful expression – in areas that include law, poetry, war, music, myth, philosophy, and sport. His special interest is the social contest (in Greek, the *agon*), which he sees as generative of new styles of personal achievement and societal refinement. Not the least of these functions is the preservation of the play spirit itself, the feeling that people can engage with one another intimately and creatively, in settings that they themselves control.

The coming of the Industrial Revolution, with its ethic of instrumentalism, endangered this play spirit. The nineteenth century is conceptualized by Huizinga as a grey age dominated by the values of factory and office. A middle-class sensibility, encouraging individuals to be serious, morally upright, and socially aspiring, predominated. Technical excellence – and professionalism – were held to be virtues. People were expected to distinguish themselves from others. In this bureaucratically managed world, communities became less important. Indeed, many public events turned into performances that individuals paid to watch. The very worst examples of this were what Huizinga (p. 205) called "false play", huge parades, festivities, and rallies orchestrated by the governments of his time. *Homo Ludens*, it should be remembered, was written as fascism and communism were rising in Europe. Public life was moving beyond human scale.

Roger Caillois was an admiring critic of Huizinga – and a prominent theorist in his own right. In *Man, Play, and Games*, Caillois (1961) presented his view that play is even more wide-ranging than Huizinga imagined – and more sensitive to societal variation. Caillois's objections to Huizinga's view of play were numerous. Against Huizinga, Caillois claimed that experiences of play are quite different from experiences of the sacred, that gambling and material gain more generally are legitimate themes of play, and that the *agon* (Huizinga's emphasis) is only one pattern of playful engagement. More than that, Caillois stressed that the more rule-bound or game-based forms of play (*ludus*) should be distinguished from play's more spontaneous, free-flowing forms (*paidia*).

Caillois's identification of four major types of play remains important. In addition to the *agon* (social contest), he conceptualizes play as *alea* (explorations of chance), *mimicry* (imaginative disguise and role performance), and *ilinx* (turbulence or vertigo). In his book, he develops these four types, which he considers to be separate expressions of the play impulse.

The latter portion of *Man, Play, and Games* develops his imaginative historical thesis. Earlier, or traditional, societies focus on play as mimicry and as ilinx. That is because the fundamental challenge for people there is to locate themselves in long-standing cultural forms, which themselves express relationships to immanent sacred forces that can never be understood or controlled fully. Play in this setting is a kind of courting, teasing, and propitiating of these powerful elements.

Modernizing societies focus more on social contests – between individuals and groups – and on the role of chance in personal achievement. Play becomes more ludic, or game-like. People find satisfaction in creating social order on their own terms, even as they recognize that many aspects of human affairs cannot be controlled in this fashion. Still, modern play must be understood as a constructive enterprise rather than an immersion into realms of mystery.

Caillois departs radically from Huizinga in the former's valorization of play's darkest and most dangerous modes. Influenced by surrealism, Caillois ponders the possibility of an "instinct for abandonment", a desire to discover dissolution and even death itself (Caillois, 2003, p. 100). Play at that level is a wish to move out of control and consequently to find oneself in realities that stand beyond instrumental rationality.

Partly because of these inclinations, Caillois follows Huizinga in mourning the highly organized play forms of the modern world. There is surely a place for the contemporary emphasis on rational self-regulation. But play in its wider spectrum involves consultation with otherness and its powers. In that light, modern gambling has little to do with older forms of tempting fate. Vertigo has become redefined as amusement park rides and descents into drugs and alcohol. Mimicry has devolved into organized theatre or the commercialized versions of carnival. Largely gone, or so he believes, are the deepest explorations into the collective meanings of being human.

The theories of Huizinga and Caillois, however well expressed, portray only a few dimensions of the play–society relationship. Other views, more scientifically based, have also been important. Cultural anthropologists in particular have shown that play, games, and sports commonly reproduce social characteristics of their sponsoring societies. This is especially so for childhood play, which is commonly seen as socialization for adult responsibilities.

In that light, anthropologist John Roberts and his colleagues demonstrated that societies use play to focus on the central challenges presented to their members, particularly as transmitted by child-raising practices. By the terms of that "conflict-enculturation" approach, games of physical skill are favoured by the economically simplest societies, games featuring cognitive strategy by economically complex societies, and games of chance or fate by societies standing between these extremes (Roberts et al., 1959). In every case, play's function is to give children protected opportunities to explore issues arising from their culture's value systems – and to develop skills set relevant to this activity.

A more empirically textured treatment of this theme was provided by John and Beatrice Whiting and their colleagues. Focusing on six societies – Kenya, India, Mexico, the Philippines, the United States, and Okinawa – the Whitings demonstrated that play activities vary widely and that adults perform quite different roles (see Whiting & Whiting, 1975). Some societies encourage play while others do not; involvement of mothers and fathers differs. More generally, the Whitings placed play into a much wider social context, which includes such as factors as historical occurrences, the natural environment, economic patterns, education, religion, and parental values. This work has been extended and refined by later researchers (see Edwards, 2000).

Current research and theory has questioned the Eurocentric, 'modern' bias that has been prevalent in many studies of traditional and indigenous peoples. As Jaipaul Roopnarine (2011) has summarized, childhood play responds to the particularity of culture and, more precisely, to the complexities of the parent–child relationship. Influential variables include parental warmth, parental belief in the importance of play for development, patterns of encouragement, structuring of opportunities, styles of socialization, and the children's own assessment of the meaning of their activities. Other factors, including ethnicity, education, and social status, also are pertinent. Such findings support the view that modernization is modified, and sometimes resisted, by local traditions and subcultures. People play in many ways and use those activities to address their quite particular circumstances (see Rooparine et al., 2015).

When examined in this broader context, cultural play emerges as a mixture of socialization with activities of self-expression and personal/group achievement. To be sure, play commonly reproduces prevailing values and skills, social hierarchies, and cultural tensions. But it also seems clear, as several analysts have stressed, that play provides alternative, or even anti-structural, responses to those patterns (see Bakhtin, 1981; Geertz, 1973; Turner, 1969).

Some people use play to 'grow up', but others use it to distance themselves from their customary responsibilities and to bond with those they care about. And it is possible that play events are sources of creativity in their own right, in which new themes are explored and subsequently adopted by the sponsoring society.

For such reasons, it is best to see the classic theories as inspirations, or beginnings, of analysis. The quest of the classic theorists, which was to define play's nature and comprehend its general implications, remains very important. But it is also clear that play takes many forms – and possesses many meanings. Societies themselves honour different visions of play. The occupants of those societies are differentiated by age, gender, ethnicity, religion, class, education, and many other factors. Play activities express, and respond to, those differences.

Furthermore, play events vary by their levels of formality, kinds of sponsorship, and fields of endeavour. Those events commonly mix play with the other great life commitments – work, ritual, and communitas – in various ways (Henricks, 2015). Some play activities may indeed be 'progressive' or 'developmental', but others are forms of digression, regression, and resistance (Henricks, 2016; Sutton-Smith, 1997). Some play deals with familiar matters; some forges the new. Expression, creativity, and freedom have many avenues. The challenge for contemporary play studies is to thicken and substantiate such understandings and, on that basis, to reaffirm the possibilities of being human.

References

Bakhtin, M. (1981). *The dialogic imagination*. Austin, University of Texas Press.

Burghardt, G. (2005). *The genesis of animal play: Testing the limits*. Cambridge, MA: MIT Press.

Caillois, R. (1961/2001). *Man, play, and games*. Urbana: University of Illinois Press.

Caillois, R. (2003). *The edge of surrealism: A Roger Caillois reader* (ed. Claudine Frank). Durham, NC: Duke University Press.

Edwards, C. P. (2000). Children's play in cross-cultural perspective: A look at the six cultures study. *Cross-Cultural Research, 34*, 318–338.

Erikson, E. (1963). *Childhood and society* (2nd edn.). New York: W. W. Norton and Company.

Fagen, R. (2005). Play, five evolutionary gates, and paths to art. In F. McMahon, D. Lytle, & B. Sutton-Smith (Eds.), *Play: An interdisciplinary synthesis* (pp. 9–42). Lanham, MD: University Press of America.

Freud, A. (1965). *Normality and pathology in childhood*. New York: International Universities Press.

Freud, S. (1928/1967). *Beyond the pleasure principle* (trans. J. Strachey). New York: Bantam.

Freud, S. (1958). *On creativity and the unconscious* (ed. B. Nelson). New York: Harper and Row.

Geertz, C. (1973). Deep play: Notes on the Balinese cockfight. In C. Geertz, *The interpretation of cultures* (pp. 412–453). New York: Basic Books.

Goffman, E. (1961). *Encounters: Two studies in the sociology of interaction*. Indianapolis, IN: Bobbs-Merrill.

Goffman, E. (1974). *Frame analysis: An essay on the organization of experience*. New York: Harper Colophon.

Groos, K. (1895/1898). *The play of animals* (trans. E. L. Baldwin). New York: D. Appleton.

Groos, K. (1898/1901). *The play of man* (trans. E. L. Baldwin). New York: D. Appleton.

Hall, G. S. (1931). *Adolescence*, 2 vols. New York: Appleton.

Henricks, T. (2006). *Play reconsidered: Sociological perspectives on human expression*. Champaign: University of Illinois Press.

Henricks, T. (2014). Play as self-realization: Toward a general theory of play. *American Journal of Play*, 6(2), 190–213.

Henricks, T. (2015). *Play and the human condition*. Chicago: University of Illinois Press.

Henricks, T. (2016). Playing into the future. In M. Patte & J. Sutterby (Eds.), *Celebrating 40 years of play research: Connecting our past, present, and future* (pp. 169–184). New York: Rowman and Littlefield.

Huizinga, J. (1938/1955). *Homo ludens: A study of the play-element in culture*. Boston: Beacon.

Lancy, D. (2008). *The anthropology of childhood: Cherubs, chattel, changelings*. Cambridge: Cambridge University Press.

Lazarus, M. (1883). *About the attractions of play*. Berlin: F. Dummler.

Levy, J. (1978). *Play behavior*. New York: John Wiley and Sons.

Lobman, C., & O'Neill, B. (Eds.) (2011). *Play and performance*. New York: University Press.

Mead, G. H. (1964). *On social psychology* (ed. A. Strauss). Chicago, IL: University of Chicago Press.

Newman, F., & Holzman, L. (1993). *Lev Vygotsky: Revolutionary scientist*. London: Routledge.

Panksepp, J. (1998). *Affective neuroscience: The foundations of human and animal emotions*. New York: Oxford University Press.

Panksepp, J. (2010). Science of the brain as a gateway to understanding play: An interview with Jaak Panksepp. *American Journal of Play*, 2(3), 245–277.

Patrick, G. (1916). *The psychology of relaxation*. Boston: Houghton Mifflin.

Piaget, J. (1932/1966). *The moral judgment of the child*. New York: Free Press.

Piaget, J. (1951/1962). *Play, dreams, and imitation in childhood*. New York: W. W. Norton.

Roberts, J., Arth, M., & Bush, R. (1959). Games in culture. *American Anthropologist*, 61, 597–605.

Roopnarine, J. (2011). Cultural variations in beliefs about play, parent–child play, and children's play. In A. Pellegrini (Ed.), *Oxford handbook of the development of play* (pp. 19–37). New York: Oxford University Press.

Roopnarine, J., Johnson, J., & Hooper, F. (Eds.) (1994). *Children's play in diverse cultures*. Albany: State University of New York Press.

Roopnarine, J., Patte, M., Johnson, J., & Kuschner, D. (2015). *International perspectives on children's play*. Maidenhead, UK: Open University Press.

Schiller, F. (1965; first published 1795). *On the aesthetic education of man* (trans. R. Snell). New York: Frederick Ungar.

Simmel, G. (1950). Sociability. In K. Wolff (Ed.), *The sociology of Georg Simmel* (pp. 40–57). New York: Free Press.

Smith, P. (2010). *Children and play*. Malden, MA: Wiley-Blackwell.

Spariosu, M. (1989). *Dionysus reborn: Play and the aesthetic dimension in modern philosophical and scientific discourse*. Ithaca, NY: Cornell University Press.

Spencer, H. (1855/1915). *The principles of psychology*, vol. 2. New York: D. Appleton.

Sutton-Smith, B. (1966). Piaget on play: A critique. *Psychological Review*, *73*(1), 104–110.

Sutton-Smith, B. (1997). *The ambiguity of play*. Cambridge, MA: Harvard University Press.

Turner, V. (1969). *The ritual process: Structure and anti-structure*. Chicago, IL: Aldine.

Veblen, T. (1899/1934). *The theory of the leisure class: An economic study of institutions*. New York: Random House.

Vygotsky, L. (1933/1976). Play and its role in the mental development of the child. In J. Bruner, A. Jolly, & K. Silva (Eds.), *Play: Its role in development and evolution* (pp. 537–554). Middlesex, UK: Penguin Books.

Whiting, B., & Whiting, J. (1975). *Children of six cultures*. Cambridge, MA: Harvard University Press.

Winnicott, D. W. (1971). *Playing and reality*. New York: Tavistock.

21 Brian Sutton-Smith's Views on Play

Anna Beresin, Fraser Brown, and Michael M. Patte

For many scholars, Brian Sutton-Smith is regarded as the foremost author on the subject of play. His classic text, *The Ambiguity of Play* (1997), explored seven 'rhetorics' – the prevalent themes among the theories of play. He proposed that play might be seen as 'the potentiation of adaptive variability' (p. 231). In a subsequent interview (Brown & Patte, 2012) he said that to understand play we needed to understand humour. He often described play in terms of its reckless, untamed nature, and he saw children's stories as evidence of that. Sutton-Smith also suggested that "play gives you the freedom to make things up, to do what you like". He sought to identify a link between the role of play and that of dreams in enabling us to understand the events that concern us in daily life. He taught us by his theorizing and his own joyful approach to life that play takes place right across the lifespan. In later life, Sutton-Smith increasingly focused on the concept of play as the source of emotional survival. Indeed, that was to be the theme of his final book, which was published posthumously. This chapter will explore the wide-ranging thoughts of this giant in the field of theorizing about play.

Children's Books

Two more weeks and we shall be
Out of the gates of misery
  (*Smitty Does a Bunk*, p. 12)

Brian Sutton-Smith's unique contribution to the field of play remains rooted in three domains central to his growing up in New Zealand: a keen observation of the dynamics of his own childhood, an awareness of the powerlessness of children, and curiosity about all things cultural. A young athlete with an ear for music, he memorized vocabulary words while playing as goalkeeper for his school's soccer team. He eventually became a teacher, noting with disdain the lack of suitable reading material for his own students. All subsequent writing was filled with sound, with rhyme, and an ear for flatulence and hypocrisy.

His first writings were fiction, written in the vernacular of his youth, tossing him into controversy. As he wanted to capture the complexity of childhood, he based his stories on the adventures of his brother, aka Smitty, and their childhood gang of friends. Some adults were appalled by the law breaking and rule mocking of his prose. Others called him a New Zealand Mark Twain, capturing the culture and language of real life. For Brian, aka Brin, it was an opportunity to entice children to read. For students of play, reading his three novels is an opportunity to see the cultural framing of his own worldview. *Our Street*, *Smitty Does a Bunk*, and *The Cobbers* were initially separate tales – fables, Sutton-Smith called them. Written in the 1940s and later published in book form, they were filled with slang, pranks, bullying, and laughter, and reflect an earnestness in his respect for children to invent, to challenge, and to be loyal to their peers. Concerning the controversy surrounding their publication and whether they would corrupt the morals of young readers, Sutton-Smith wrote:

> Perhaps it would be best simply to let the children read the books (including their own Introduction) as stories to be enjoyed. In the process they will be helped to understand in part their own natures and actions, and thus to resist those impulses (which come to all children) to defy authority, to break rules, and often, to do real damage in bursts of unpremeditated vandalism. (*Our Street*, p. 18)

This theme of trusting children to navigate the strangeness of the adult world, through their wits and through their own culture, runs through his entire career. Sutton-Smith set out to document the extraordinariness of everyday life, the complexity of navigation that is children's folklore. Given that these books are out of print and hard to find, the following includes a set of excerpts, a 'greatest hits' approach to Sutton-Smith's fiction as it relates to children's peer culture.

> Once upon a time there was a middle-sized boy named Brian and he was called "Brin". Now there was nothing unusual in this because very few boys are called by their own name. Sometimes they are called "Snowy", and sometimes they are just called "Stinker", but they are hardly ever called what they really are. So Brin was quite an ordinary sort of boy. (*Our Street*, p. 23)

The story continues with the boys of "our street" deciding what to do that day. Note his use of children's vernacular.

> "I bagz we go to the football," said Smitty.
> "Aw, no," said Gormie.
> "Why not?" asked Brin.
> "Because," said Gormie.
> "Because what?" asked Smitty.
> "Because I bagz we go to the pictures."
> "I bagz we don't," said Brin.
> "I bagz the Zoo," said Horsey.
> "I don't bagz the Zoo," said Smitty.
> "Well, let's see which two we bagz most of the three," said Smitty.

He presented layered portraits of personal dreams within cultural frames, always filled with physical movement.

> After the pictures, they all galloped home.
> Brin thought that he was the chief cowboy and others were Redskins.
> Smitty thought that *he* was the chief cowboy and the others were Redskins.
> Horsey thought that *he* was the chief cowboy and the others were Redskins.
> Gormie thought that *he* was the chief cowboy and the others were Redskins.

> When they arrived at the street the four chief cowboys left each other. Gormie went to his place, Brin and Smitty to their place, and Horsey to his place. They all shut their gates, climbed over them, and went inside, feeling very hungry 'cause they had had only one Eskimo pie each, about six "stickies," and had run all the way home. (*Our Street*, p. 37)

We see seeds of Sutton-Smith's dissertation, a multi-generational play history, as the boys speak to Mr. Barnicoat in *Our Street*:

> Looking at you boys trying to play games here in this poky little street makes me think of when I was at school. In those days we had as many paddocks as we could possibly want to roam in. We had all the hills as far as the eye could see. We had as much bush as we could ever want for hunting birds with our shanghais. Why, at one time I remember we used to get paid a one and six for every hundred eggs or birds heads we took to the council ... That's the money we bought our marbles and tops with. Why, to-day, if you boys fire a shanghai in this street here, you'd knock someone's eye out. I don't know how you kids live.
> ...
> "But we play sports and go to the pictures," defended Horsey.
> "That's just the trouble, my son; it's all organized for you. When you go to the pictures you might be being occupied, but you're not learning much, are you?" (*Our Street*, pp. 68–73)

Our Street concludes:

> Here and there a dog would bark or a tram go by, and nobody would say anything for a long, long time. The grasshoppers would sing in the grass, and the sun would stream down, and Brin and Smitty and Gormie and Horsey would just close their eyes and let the sun seep through their skin.
> It was good.
> And every Saturday it was just the same. (*Our Street*, p. 113)

Although trained as an educator, the twin themes of psychology and cultural history emerge through his ethnographic thick description. In *Smitty Does a Bunk* ('runs away', in local speech) Sutton-Smith plays with this sense of temporal density through repetition:

> And some went this way and some went that, but wherever anybody went, everybody knew that the holidays had come. Two big WHOLE weeks with everyday all full up with holiday, so FULL UP with holiday that there was no room for anything else. So full up with holiday that it seemed to make the air thick. You could smell it. Just as if it were full of fish and chips. And when

they walked and ran and hopped and skipped and just went down the roads from school, everybody was walking and running and hopping and skipping in air that was thick, THICK with all the things that everybody was going to do ... corker big long days, football up at the park, kicks at the goalposts (if they were up), coffeebuns for dinner, flying kites, making hairy-buzzers, tracking each other down in the pines and the Flicks on wet days. You could almost eat all the things to do out of the middle of the thick air. But Smitty went home a bit more quietly than everybody else cause he was thinking about his special idea as usual. He'd thought about it for a long time now. (*Smitty Does a Bunk*, p. 12)

In his novels and his research, there is an ever-present struggle with power, a rooting for the child as underdog.

"Hey! There you boy. What do you think you're doing?" cried the man. Gormie took a frightened look back from the other side of the gate and pelted off down the path without a word. "Nothing," stammered Smitty scrambling to his feet again. "Yes, you were, boy," shouted the man looking at Smitty with a wild screwed up face. One of his cheeks kept jerking up under his left eye just as though it was going to wink. But it didn't. Instead the eye just glared out at them, glared and glared while his face twitched and jumped. "No Sir," muttered Smitty. And then the man pulled a black notebook out of his pocket and took a pencil from the rim of his black hat.

. . .

"What's your name? What's your name?" he jerked out. "Name?" said Smitty, "Name? Ah ah ah ..." "What's your name boy?" "Na-names?" said Smitty. "NAMES!" "All of them?" said Smitty. And the man's eyes grew wilder and wilder and his faced twitched faster and faster. His teeth showed and there was dribble on his lips. Brin moved a little behind Smitty. "Both names?' said Smitty again. "Your NAMES!" said the man. "Honkus," said Smitty suddenly. "WHAT?" "Honkus Piacky. Honkus Spang Piacky." "Spell it." "H-o-n-k-u-s, Spang, Sp-ang, Pi-acky, P-i-acky." The man paused a moment, glared at Smitty, and then rubbing his ink pencil on his tongue he scribbled it all down on this book.

. . .

"And yours?" he hissed turning on Brin his face jerking faster than ever. "Brin, Brin Smith." "THE TRUTH." "It – it – it is the truth," stuttered Brin. "I only want TRUE NAMES," he shouted again. "Yes, ONLY TRUE NAMES WILL BE GOOD ENOUGH, enough, enough enough." "Brin Smith," said Brin again. (*Smitty Does a Bunk*, pp. 63–64)

Children's peer culture became Sutton-Smith's focus, with its paired themes of group stylization and negotiation with adult power. After he met Peter Opie in the United Kingdom, he became even more interested in culture and the history of games, studying and co-publishing with Elliott Avedon in the United States. A prodigious writer, Sutton-Smith exploded with cultural game study in the 1970s:

The Study of Games, with Elliott Avedon (1971)
Childs Play (1971)

The Folkgames of Children (1972)
How to Play with Your Children (And When Not To), with Shirley Sutton-
  Smith (1974)
Games of the Americas (1976)

These books straddled psychology and anthropology, from game analysis (1971, 1972) to the historical cultural (1976) to the tender guide for parent–child play (1972). He was omnivorous as a scholar, curious about the ancient games of traditional cultures (1976) and the invention of culture that begins anew with each child.

His 1953 dissertation on New Zealand games would become *A History of Children's Play* (1981a), and he took great delight in telling its own controversial story. The institution that granted him his degree wanted him to expurgate the unsavoury, rude rhymes from his research, and he initially refused. He wanted to make the case that portraits of children and children's culture need to be unromanticized and that play includes all kinds of ideas, much like art. It is not always going to be pleasant. Eventually, the dissertation was approved with some bits excluded, but to his great delight, the material was made whole again in the eventual published version.

Challenging Piaget

Sutton-Smith first came to the attention of a wider academic audience in the mid-1960s, achieving a certain notoriety when he produced a critique of Jean Piaget's classic work *Play, Dreams and Imitation* (1962). First, he argued against Piaget's view that we stop playing when we develop logical reasoning. Instead, he suggested that we go on playing throughout life; it's only the content of the play that changes. Indeed, there was no greater evidence of this than the way Sutton-Smith lived his own life. When he passed away the numerous obituaries included reflections such as "Brian lived the playfulness he studied", "He played well and deeply and with great heart", and "He was mischievous, funny and playful, yet with a mind as sharp as anyone I had ever met" (Brown et al., 2017).

Second, Piaget had been fairly dismissive of children's play in the formation of intelligence, consigning it to the relatively minor role of "assimilation". In other words, Piaget saw the role of play as that of repetition, practice, and minor variation, largely aimed at confirming the child's understanding of something or reinforcing previously learned abilities. In fact, Piaget (1962, p. 93) described play as the "happy display of known actions". Sutton-Smith challenged this limited view, instead arguing that play also had a major role in "accommodation". He suggested that certain aspects of play, such as humour, pretence, drama, and imagination, give free rein to the mind to go wherever the play frame allows. While the playing mind is exploring and experimenting it is inevitably learning about things. At the same time it is developing the complexity of its learning techniques. In other words, Sutton-Smith argued that play lies at the very heart of human intelligence. The combination of individual children doing this means children consequently develop their own culture.

Children's Culture and Folklore

Perhaps his most famous book on culture and play was the much-cited *Toys as Culture* (1986). Prior to this, toys had been addressed as psychological tools in the Freudian and Eriksonian tradition, and as adult artefacts in anthropology. In *Toys as Culture* he not only faced developmental controversies head-on as cultural topics, particularly regarding gender stereotyping and Barbie, and war play with GI Joe, but examined an essential paradox of toy gifting as a cultural process. He noted that for millennia, children played with each other, rather than objects, and that the rise of toys in the twentieth century was new to the history of childhood. Here he was ahead of his time, as children now play with objects, specifically technological objects, quantitatively and qualitatively differently than in the 1980s. The central paradox of *Toys as Culture* was the concept of isolation: I give you a toy to bond you to me, now go ahead and play by yourself. Perhaps most unusual in the world of academic publishing was the use of the word 'as', meaning that he was uncovering a piece of playful object use, rather than the declarative 'are'.

His interest in paradox was amplified by his respect for the work of anthropologist Gregory Bateson, an early documentary filmmaker and observer of animal play. He wrestled with big thinkers, from Piaget to Huizinga, challenging the cultural assumptions of psychologists and the psychological assumptions of historians. Enamoured with microsociology and conversation analysis, he wrote dozens of essays on games with titles like "Models of Power" and "The Dialectics of Play" and co-authored with Diana Kelly-Byrne *The Masks of Play* (1984). How is a playground like a festival? he would ask. What might post-structuralism offer a theory of play? What might we learn from the new field of video game study?

Sutton-Smith's final academic post was at the University of Pennsylvania where he had a joint position in the Graduate School of Education and in the Department of Folklore and Folklife. At the Graduate School of Education he created a new doctoral program based in the psychology of education called Child Cultures, the first of its kind. There he trained graduate students in the anthropology of childhood, seeing anthropology and its cousin folklore as models in qualitative research methods. Several of his students ended up contributing to his volume *Children's Folklore: A Sourcebook* (1995) as he attempted to bridge his psychological, historical, and folkloric interests. Sutton-Smith was active in the American Psychological Association and in the American Folklore Society, co-creating the Children's Folklore Section. He was instrumental in the founding of the Association for the Study of Play, formerly known as the Association for the Anthropological Study of Play.

Sutton-Smith's career mirrored the trajectory of folklore as a discipline. First, the nationalist portrait of New Zealand games then gave way to genre-based study: games, stories, toys. His anthropological interests made his writings detailed and thick with the unusual focus on the peer group, rather than the individual child. For someone trained and active in developmental psychology, this was most unusual.

Sutton-Smith was clear that his vision of children's folklore was about the culture that children co-create for their own pleasure, rather than folklore for children, although he was fascinated by the lore of fairy tales and legends. With Piagetian training and psychodynamic roots, his focus was on the big group picture of small things. In each of his multidisciplinary writings, in every academic conversation, he would ask us to see within the smallest pieces of play our own cultural assumptions, inviting us to play with the truths we carry about childhood and, for a moment, turn them upside down.

The Seven Rhetorics of Play

That upside-down, inside-out, paradoxical way of approaching the study of play was a reflection of how Sutton-Smith viewed play itself. Since scholars began studying the construct of play, a common working definition on the subject has proven elusive. Sutton-Smith's seminal work, *The Ambiguity of Play* (1997), explores the fluid nature of play and play-like behaviours across various cultures and generations. He examines play through the multiple lenses of education, mathematics, metaphysics, psychology, and sociology. Sutton-Smith argues that play encompasses a wide variety of experiences and meanings, and he advances seven rhetorics as a framework for understanding play. By "rhetoric", Sutton-Smith means "a persuasive discourse or implicit narrative ... adopted by members of a particular group affiliation or discipline to lend validity to their beliefs and interpretations" (p. 8). Sutton-Smith classifies prominent play theories into ancient Western rhetorics (fate, power, identity, frivolity) that are well represented in classical literature and modern Western rhetorics (progress, self, imaginary) that surfaced with recent philosophical and psychological trends over the past 200 years. Each rhetoric is culturally derived and has a certain intrinsic ambiguity that seldom fully encompasses play in its many forms. Each of the seven rhetorics are explored below.

Play as Progress. The rhetoric of play as progress advances the idea that children adapt and develop through play and has dominated twentieth-century Western studies of children's play in the fields of biology, ethology, education, and developmental psychology through the work of Berlyne,

Erikson, Fagen, Piaget, and Vygotsky. Those advancing this rhetoric privilege developmental aspects of play over the enjoyment such activity may engender. Sutton-Smith argues that the progress rhetoric differentiates between the play of children and that of adults and that proponents of this rhetoric view children's play as open and creative, while adult play is closed and uncreative. The belief in play as progress as a credible, scientifically supported notion is highly valued in Western societies, but Sutton-Smith holds that such a belief is more often based on fiction rather than fact. This belief is echoed by Peter K. Smith (2010), who asserts the existence of a "play ethos" or "a strong and unqualified assertion of the functional importance of play, namely that it is essential to adequate human development" (p. 28) in Western societies.

Play as Fate. The oldest and most ancient rhetoric, play as fate, includes gambling and games of chance, and holds that we are played by forces (destiny, gods) greater than ourselves and that one's greatest hope for success lies in luck. This rhetoric steeped in ambiguity stands in stark contrast to the modern rhetorics and their focus on the exercise of free choice. Sutton-Smith argues that play as fate has waned in popularity in the post-modern world among high socioeconomic populations but has a strong foothold within lower socioeconomic groups.

Play as Power. Steeped in the fields of history and sociology and the work of Huizinga and Spariosu, the ancient rhetoric of play as power applies to athletics, contests, and sports. Here, play represents conflict and serves as a means to elevate the standing of those controlling the play. Play as power, along with the other ancient rhetorics, advances collective values of the community at the expense of individual ones. Sutton-Smith refers to this idea as social power and argues that it is foundational in the development of civilization, in mediating social conflicts, in subverting those in positions of power, and in interpreting power relationships within a society. Huizinga endorsed the play as power rhetoric, as evidenced in his "particularly agnostic and machismo view of play history" (Sutton-Smith, 1997, p. 79) and "his definition of play ... that favors the exaltation of combative power" (p. 80). The rhetoric of play as power is ordered, rational, and opposed to the chaos of chance or frivolity. Spariosu disagreed with this assertion and found that play as power from a Western perspective fluctuates between the extremes of order and chaos.

Play as Identity. The ancient rhetoric of play as identity draws on the fields of anthropology and folklore and includes long-standing community celebrations like carnivals, festivals, and rituals. Identity in this context is thought to be cultural in nature and not individual. Here playing to be with others or to identify with a specific group "provides participants with solidarity, identity, and pleasure" (Sutton-Smith, 1997, p. 6). The play as identity rhetoric employs bonding, belonging, and playing as key components in group unification. And although much identity play involves developing cultural identity in a competitive fashion, it can also be cooperative in nature. Sutton-Smith (1997), citing DeKoven, makes this case that "When the game is played only for the good of the larger community that plays it, then it can be well played. If not so subordinated, games may run away with their players and cause friction and conflict" (p. 100). Non-competitive identity play, within specific cultural contexts, breaks down long-standing boundaries and leads to a reintegration within the community at large. Some examples include celebrations such as Christmas, Mardi Gras, and Thanksgiving. Such celebrations dissolve conventional social barriers, incorporate the wider community, and strengthen secondary bonds. Festivals, on the other hand, exhibit a contradictory relationship as they can produce strong feelings of identity and ambiguity among participants at the same time.

Play as Imaginary. Play as imaginary, a modern rhetoric associated with the disciplines of art and literature, posits play as a frame to examine culture or texts to be interpreted through playful improvisations drawing on individual creativity, flexibility, and imagination. Prominent scholars in this literature include Bakhtin, Bateson, and the Singers. Sutton-Smith holds that play as imaginary was born during the Romantic Movement, a time when works of literature like Peter Pan and Winnie the Pooh celebrated childhood imagination and play was afforded the dignity it so rightly deserved. However, Sutton-Smith did not view the imaginary worlds of children through rose-coloured glasses, but rather as a means to deconstruct the realistic society in which they live to suit their emotional responses to it. This rhetoric continues to flourish in modern times due in part to a heightened importance on creativity and innovation as essential twenty-first-century traits.

Play as Self. Play as self is a modern rhetoric associated with the field of psychiatry and advanced by the psychology of flow and peak experience (Csikszentmihalyi, 1991). The rhetoric of self emphasizes freedom, subjectivity, and individualism, all cultural characteristics of the Western world. Personal hobbies and other solitary activities tied to this rhetoric are idealized for the desirable elements provided to the players, including active engagement, fun, freedom, escape, and relaxation. Such activities are thought to be intrinsically motivated. Borrowing from the phenomenological tradition and the work of Gadamer, play as self draws heavily from personal experience, subjectivity, and the relationship between perception and understanding the self.

Play as Frivolity. Sutton-Smith (1997) says that the seventh rhetoric, play as frivolity, "has its own particular place as an opponent to the seriousness of all the other rhetorics, ancient or modern" (p. 201). This ancient rhetoric arose from the practices of the idle and foolish in folklore and literature, which provided alternative ways of experiencing the social order through humour and playful activities. Play as frivolity is immersed in the discipline of pop culture and advanced by the work of Cox (1969), Stewart (1978), and Welsford (1961). Sutton-Smith held that play as frivolity derived from the expansion of urban living, factory work, and an accompanying Protestant work ethic that allotted little time for play and viewed it as frivolous, unpractical, and a waste of time. This view can be found in the early play scholarship of Huizinga (1938), who argued that "no profit can be gained" from play (p. 13). Play as frivolity is oppositional, parodic, and sometimes revolutionary in nature and stands in stark contrast to the work ethic view of play as a worthless activity.

Conclusion to *The Ambiguity of Play*

The *Ambiguity of Play* concludes with the suggestion that what all of these rhetorics may have in common is their relative resonance of adaptive variability. Here Sutton-Smith (1999) cites the work of Gould (1997, 1996a, 1996b), who advances some common links between evolution and play.

> Gould (1997) argues that evolution depends upon the availability of variable responses and that these variable responses, occasioned by the organism's basic flexibility, occur with surprising quirkiness and redundancy. Although he is not talking at all about play, one notices immediately that these characteristics seem to describe play very well. Play is quirky, often being called inversive, paradoxical, fragmentary, disorderly, and nonsensical. Play is redundant, often being called repetitive, stereotypical, compulsive, and ritualistic ... Gould's main argument in favor of the importance of variability is that the greater the repertoire of such variable responses, the less the likelihood that an organism will fail to heir to its own habit-forming, but rigidifying, successes.   (p. 243)

As a final note to the reader, Sutton-Smith presented a concluding paradox. Despite offering a comprehensive critique of the play as progress rhetoric throughout *The Ambiguity of Play*, he had actually created a new form of it as the potentiation of adaptive variability. Just two years later, Sutton-Smith (1999) offered this definition of play:

> Play, as a unique form of adaptive variability, instigates an imagined but equilibrial reality within which disequilibrial exigencies can be paradoxically simulated and give rise to the pleasurable effects of excitement and optimism. The genres of such play are humor, skill, pretence, fantasy, risk, contest, and celebrations, all of which are selective simulations of paradoxical variability.   (p. 253)

Post *Ambiguity*

In *The Ambiguity of Play* (1997) Sutton-Smith sought to show that the majority of attempts to establish a theory of play falter on the fact that so many varied types of play exist. He broadly concluded that, taking all the theorizing together, play might be considered to be a facsimilization of the Darwinian "struggle for survival" (1997: 231). For most animals, that struggle is largely to do with food, territory, and reproduction. For humans the "struggle" is much more complex, encompassing such diverse factors as politics, religion, race, social status, sexuality, and genetic constitution – to name just a few. However, Sutton-Smith subsequently argued that for thousands of years, human conflicts have been represented in different types of game-playing, and this gives us a much more straightforward variety of struggles. Thus:

- **teasing-hazing** is about initiation and gaining membership of social groups
- **games of chance** are about risk-taking and dependency on fate
- **contests** are about competition and succeeding (or not) in physical and mental games
- **festivals** are about celebration of a range of cultural identities
- **imaginative play** is an exploration of our personal originality
- **flow experiences** provide special feelings of all kinds of successful play prowess
- **nonsense** allows us to deviate from orthodoxies of all kinds.

(Sutton-Smith, 2008, p. 139)

Sutton-Smith's post-*Ambiguity* work focused less on the historical and philosophical facets of his "rhetorics" (progress, fate, power, identity, imaginary, self, and frivolity) and more on the biological and psychological aspects of those terms, which he had summarized in the concluding chapter of *The Ambiguity of Play*. For Sutton-Smith (1997) the biological functions were:

- actualizing potential brain connections, which makes more connections possible
- actualizing potential behaviour connections, which makes more connections possible
- modelling a range of neonatal processes, such as unrealistic optimism, egocentricity, etc.
- exemplifying cultural variability
- adaptive potentiation, which enables the transfer of play skills to everyday skills
- modelling exigent processes of adaptation, which enables uncertainties to be tested out first in the virtual world
- reinforcing the feedback of adaptive variability, which stops us becoming rigid in our behaviour patterns.

He summarized the psychological functions as:

- metacommunication
- performance stylization, largely through role-playing
- intensification – remembering Csikszentmihalyi's (1991) concept of flow
- enactive subjunctivity – as if; if I were you; the theory of mind
- structural dialectics, especially focusing on the paradoxical nature of play.

In so doing, he had moved a good distance from his early thinking (which was based on observations in school playgrounds) that play could be viewed as a dialectical experience of order and disorder (Sutton-Smith, 1978). Indeed, he was eventually quite dismissive of the theories of various play theorists who had sought to emphasize the duality of play in some shape or form, for example, Kant's (1800) playful imagination vs. the poison of fanciful play, Schiller's (1965) aesthetic play vs. street play, Spencer's (1855) civilizing play vs. agonistic play, Groos's (1901) preparation for life vs. violent and unruly play, Erikson's (1950) true play vs. pseudo play, and many more, including those of Freud and Piaget.

Sutton-Smith had become very focused on the idea that play represented a kind of metaphorical representation of the human struggle to survive. This idea is explored in great detail in his final work, which he had wanted to be titled 'Play as Emotional Survival'. This was eventually published posthumously in 2016, by the Strong National Museum of Play. The Strong Museum houses the Brian Sutton-Smith Library and Archives of Play; this is a multidisciplinary research repository devoted to the intellectual, social, and cultural history of play. It also houses Sutton-Smith's personal library and papers. His final work is in an edited compilation titled *Play for Life: Play Theory and Play as Emotional Survival*. Here he suggested that humanity has wrongly moved down the path of concentrating on play as a mechanism for educating our youngsters. Especially in modern Western civilizations, play is more often used as a way of enhancing children's literacy and numeracy. It is also used as an excuse for reining in children during recess, or sometimes doing away with recess altogether.

He laid some of the blame at the feet of Freud and Piaget, both of whom present a view of child development where children move from playful irrationality to logical competency. As we have already seen, Sutton-Smith had always challenged the notion that we stop playing when we reach maturity. He also believed children's play had both Dionysian and Apollonian aspects to it and that one of the great hindrances to our consideration of the idea that play concerns the human struggle for survival is the largely modern notion that children are too innocent to be so engaged. On the contrary, Sutton-Smith had spent much of his life conducting research that showed the darker side of children's play, as shown for example in his collections of children's jokes and stories (1981b). Of course he recognized that adults are more complex than children, simply by virtue of having lived longer, but he was clear that they engage in the same forms of play in their attempts to conquer, control, represent, and understand the world.

Sutton-Smith (2016) says that when he came upon *Descartes' Error* (1994), by the neuroscientist Antonio Damasio, he found a link to the play forms discussed previously. Damasio identifies primary and secondary emotions:

- primary emotions: shock, fear, anger, sadness, happiness, and disgust
- secondary emotions: embarrassment, shame, guilt, envy, empathy, and pride

He noticed that the six primary emotions were reflected in the games described by the British folklorists Peter and Iona Opie in their classic text *The Lore and Language of School Children* (1959). That led him to explore whether the primary emotions might be linked to his own "rhetorics", and he found that these were indeed the main emotional drivers therein:

- shock is the dominant emotion in teasing and hazing
- fear is dominant in games of risk
- anger dominates contests
- loneliness (sadness) is the main motivation for festivals
- happiness is the driver for modern consumer play subjectivities known as peak experiences
- disgust is the prevailing emotion in connection with nonsense and profanity.

(Sutton-Smith, 2008)

This discovery led Sutton-Smith to propose that all six play forms have to do with "affect expression and regulation" (p. 141). More than that, however, he suggested that there is always a duality of provocation and rebuttal. Thus:

> hazing involves harassment which is rebutted by player resilience; risks involve dangers rebutted by courage; contests involve attacks rebutted by vigilance; festivals involve loneliness rebutted by inebriation; flow experiences describe narcissisms rebutted by fame; and finally profanities involve deviance rebutted by wit.   (p. 141)

Following on from this, and picking up on his earlier idea that play might be considered to be a facsimilization of the human struggle for survival, he suggested that:

- the shocks of teasing and hazing mimic and mock initiation procedures
- the fears of risk-taking mimic chances with physical and economic fate
- the angers of contests mimic combat, wars and predation
- the loneliness underlying the inebriation of festivals mimics the absence of membership identity
- the happiness of peak experience mimics the central role of individualistic consumer subjectivity in modern life
- the disgust of nonsense and profanity mimics rebellious iconoclasm.

(Sutton-Smith 2008, p. 141)

Sutton-Smith's argument is that without this mimicry and mockery these institutions would overwhelm our lives. He even argued (2016) that the modern fascination with computer games is further evidence of his theory, as these digital play forms now penetrate all areas of modern life, whether as conflict representations of war, business, sports, or many other human functions. While playing participants may not give much thought to the adaptive consequences of what is going on, nevertheless, it is clearly arguable that they are gradually becoming civilized into an acceptance of the legitimacy and significance of these institutions in modern political economic and social life.

This is where the concept of play as emotional survival is at its strongest. Sutton-Smith suggests that one of the major contributions of play in all these circumstances is that participants are able to be successful in expressing and controlling their emotions within the complex kinds of skill that are required during their games. They then take on board a subconscious confidence that they will be able to cope with similar situations in the real world.

Finally, Sutton-Smith went on to explore the significance of Damasio's secondary emotions in this process. It appears, according to Panksepp (2004), that the primary emotions, which are largely expressive, are located in the primitive part of the brain (the amygdala) and the secondary emotions, which are largely regulative, derive from the more recently developed frontal lobes. This distinction is substantially displayed in the largely reflexive behaviour of reptiles, as contrasted with the adaptive behaviour of mammals, which also includes reflective behaviours. Thus, as the ethologist Gordon Burghardt (2005) has shown, mammals play a lot, whereas reptiles generally do not. Sutton-Smith felt this provided support for the idea that mammalian play has to do with the need for protection and stimulation.

However, in these later writings, and especially in *Play for Life: Play Theory and Play as Emotional Survival* (2016), Sutton-Smith also proposed the possibility that the conflict between the reflexive and reflective adaptive systems might in its earliest development have created a dangerous survival issue. Perhaps play appeared millions of years ago as a mutant gene – an alternative to the conflict between these two types of adaptation. Sutton-Smith proposed that play was the mutant gene that enables the integration of the reflexive and reflective aspects of the brain. As such, play, with its six major forms inextricably linked to the six primary emotions, might be thought of not only as a fundamental survival mechanism but also as the major driving force in human evolution.

To summarize, Sutton-Smith suggested four major characteristics of children's play:

- Play is a facsimilization of the struggle for survival. It lets us test ourselves, and master skills we may need in later life.
- Play reinforces human variability in the face of the tendency toward rigidification brought about by successful adaptation. It stops us becoming stuck in our ways when we think we've achieved something or conquered something.
- Play is fundamentally about the potentiation of adaptive variability, which is an evolutionary imperative.
- Play provides a great deal of fun, and in consequence a joy in being alive.

References

Bakhtin, M. M. (1981). *The dialogic imagination*. Austin: University of Texas Press.
Bateson, G. (1972). *Steps to an ecology of mind*. New York: Ballantine.
Berlyne, D. E. (1960). *Conflict, arousal, and curiosity*. New York: McGraw Hill.
Brown, F., & Patte, M. (2012). From the streets of Wellington to the Ivy League: reflecting on a lifetime of play – an interview with Brian Sutton-Smith. *International Journal of Play, 1*(1), 6–15.

Brown, F., Beresin, A., Henricks, T., Meckley, A., & Patte, M. (2017). Brian Sutton-Smith Memorial Panel: A celebration of the life and works of Brian Sutton-Smith. *International Journal of Play*, *6*(1), 96–111.

Burghardt, G. M. (2005). *The genesis of animal play: Testing the limits*. Cambridge, MA: Bradford Books (MIT Press).

Cox, H. (1969). *The feast of fools*. New York: Harper & Row.

Csikszentmihalyi, M. (1991). *Flow: The psychology of optimal experience*. New York: Harper Perennial.

Damasio, A. (1994). *Descartes' error: Emotion, reason, and the human brain*. New York: Putnam.

De Koven, B. (1978). *The well played game*. Garden City, NY: Doubleday, Anchor Books.

Erikson, E. (1950). *Childhood and society*. New York: Norton.

Erikson, E. (1977). *Toys and reasons*. New York: Norton.

Fagen, R. (1981). *Animal play behavior*. New York: Oxford University Press.

Gadamer, H. G. (1960). *Truth and method*. New York: Crossroad.

Geertz, C. (1973). *The interpretation of cultures*. New York: Basic Books.

Gould, S. J. (1996a). *Full house*. New York: Harmony Books.

Gould, S. J. (1996b). Creating the creators. *Discover*, *17*(10), 43–54.

Gould, S. J. (1997). Evolutionary psychology: An exchange. *New York Review of Books*, *45*, 56–57.

Groos, K. (1901). *The play of man*. London: Heinemann.

Huizinga, J. (1955, 1938). *Homo ludens: A study of the play element in culture*. Boston: Beacon Press.

Kant, I. (1800). *Anthropologie in pragmatischer Hinsicht abgefasst*. Konigsberg.

Panksepp, J. (2004). *Affective neuroscience: The foundations of human and animal emotions*. New York: Oxford University Press.

Piaget, J. (1962). *Play, dreams, and imitation in childhood*. New York: Norton.

Schiller, F. (1965). *On the aesthetic education of man*. Translated from the original 1795 text by Reginald Snell. New York: Frederick Ungar.

Smith, P. K. (2010). *Understanding children's worlds: Children and play*. West Sussex, UK: Wiley Blackwell.

Spariosu, M. (1989). *Dionysus reborn*. Ithaca, NY: Cornell University Press.

Spencer, H. (1855). *The principles of psychology*. London: Longman, Brown, Green and Longmans.

Stewart, S. (1978). *Nonsense: Aspects of intertextuality in folklore literature*. Baltimore, MD: Johns Hopkins University Press.

Sutton-Smith, B. (1950). *Our street*. Wellington: A. H. & A. W. Reed.

Sutton-Smith, B. (1961). *Smitty does a bunk*. Wellington: Standard Press.

Sutton-Smith, B. (1976). *The cobbers*. Wellington: Price Milburn.

Sutton-Smith, B. (1978). *Die dialectic des spiels*. Schorndorf, Germany: Verlag Karl Hoffman.

Sutton-Smith, B. (1981a). *A history of children's play*. Philadelphia: University of Pennsylvania Press.

Sutton-Smith, B. (1981b) *The folkstories of children*. Philadelphia: University of Pennsylvania Press.

Sutton-Smith, B. (1986). *Toys as culture*. New York: Gardner Press.

Sutton-Smith, B. (1989). Models of power. In R. Bolton (Ed.), *The content of culture constants and variants: Studies in honor of John M. Roberts*. New Haven, CT: Human Relations Area Files Press.

Sutton-Smith, B. (1997). *The ambiguity of play*. Cambridge, MA: Harvard University Press.

Sutton-Smith, B. (1999). Evolving a consilience of play definitions: Playfully. In S. Reifel (Ed.), *Play contexts revisited: Play and culture studies*, vol. 2 (pp. 239–256). Stamford, CT: Albex.

Sutton-Smith, B. (2008). Beyond ambiguity. In F. Brown & C. Taylor (Eds.), *Foundations of playwork*. Maidenhead: Open University Press

Sutton-Smith, B. (2016). *Play for life: Play theory and play as emotional survival*. Rochester: Strong Museum of Children's Play.

Sutton-Smith, B., & Kelly-Byrne, D. (1984). *The masks of play*. West Point, NY: Leisure Press.

Sutton-Smith, B., & Sutton-Smith, S. (1974). *How to play with your children (and when not to)*. New York: Hawthorne.

Sutton-Smith, B., Mechling, J., Johnson, T., & McMahon, F. (1995). *Children's folklore: A sourcebook*. New York: Garland.

Vygotsky, L. S. (1930). *Mind in society*. Cambridge, MA: Harvard University Press.

Welsford, E. (1961). *The fool*. Garden City, NY: Doubleday, Anchor Books.

22 Methods of Studying Play

James E. Johnson and Pool Ip Dong

Researching play is challenging due to play's diversity, ambiguity, and complexity. Years ago Schlosberg (1947) even declared that play being such a vague concept is scientifically useless, not a researchable phenomenon. Since many different actions, internal states, and even behavioral settings are subsumed under the term 'play', problems of definition, categorization, and measurement of play exist (Smith et al., 1985). The challenge is further compounded by the fact that play occurs over time and may be continuous or intermittent, long duration, short duration, or even fleeting, and may occur in combination with non-play elements. Although play is difficult to define and understand, researchers continue efforts to make progress in their disciplined conceptual and empirical inquiries. This chapter first gestures to the enormity of outlining the conceptual challenge in studying play, followed by a presentation of information about standard quantitative and qualitative methods that are used in researching play; some illustrations are then provided of recent work employing innovative procedures that include ones designed to elicit the player's perspectives. A fall-out from merging researcher-led studies with incorporating the latter is suggested to be results with greater applicative potential.

Grappling with the Concept

Coming up with an adequate conceptual definition or understanding of play has been historically a daunting task across disciplines (Johnson et al., 2015). In Roger Caillois's classic *Man, Play and Games* (1961), we read about the play of vertigo, competition, mimicry, and chance, singly and as admixtures – with our understanding helped along using a bipolar dimension running throughout, with one end the freer *paidia*, and the other end the controlled *ludus*. Play can be free and open-ended but is also rule-bound, fictive, unproductive, and separated from reality. Reading Johan Huizinga's classic *Homo Ludens* (1955), we learn that this author defined play activity as voluntary, not serious but very absorbing, without material gain, rule-bound, conducive to social belongingness, and framed from reality.

Burghardt (2005) has proposed that play behaviour (1) happens when the animal (or human) is relaxed, safe, and not in a high-need state; (2) is *autolectic* (i.e., intentional, spontaneous, voluntary, and often accompanied by positive affect); (3) is frequently seen as repeated behaviour; (4) is not totally without purpose but also not entirely functional as expressed in a given situation; and (5) is typically exaggerated in its manifestation and incomplete because functional elements are dropped off at the end. This definitional scheme is derived from a study of animal play. In the book *Genesis of Animal Play*, a modern-day classic, Burghardt reviews research over the past century indicating that many species' young, especially mammals', observe and explore their environments and also play spontaneously, engaging in many repetitious behaviours.

The consensus among play scholars is that play or playful expressions (playful thoughts and actions) possess certain characteristics. The term 'play' is justified if the expression possesses in a cumulative fashion some or all of these attributes. Generally, play is accompanied by positive affect, is freely chosen, is under the primary control of the player, is motivated from within by the play process, is meaningful primarily as determined by the player, is dynamic and ongoing and often reveals an 'as if' or transformational stance toward ostensive reality, requires relaxed circumstances producing a mental state in players that is not pressured, and is reciprocally related – that is, play actions and play thoughts build on one another (Johnson, 2015). Defining play is very difficult or impossible, and rather than trying to define play better, Burghardt (2005) suggests identifying or illustrating play in some useful way.

Listing various characteristics that point to play when occurring together in a given instance is referred to as the additive model of play. The quest after what play is has also resulted in other noteworthy models, such as play as communication (Sutton-Smith, 1979). According to this model, play is framed from reality, behaviours, and thought that are different from what is serious or in earnest. Player(s) go into and out of the play frame, and communication between co-players is required for them to stay on the same plane. Meta-communications are the required features of any play since subjective states must be shared using signals and cues. Play enactments can be said to happen within the play frame and the negotiations or disputes outside a frame; together, they form a complex, multilayered whole (Bateson, 1956). Bateson considered play paradoxical since both what is and what is not appear to co-exist, as illustrated by dogs' play fighting, with each dog biting the other one knowing that the playful nip connotes a bite, but not what the bite usually entails.

One must acknowledge the dialectic nature and ambiguities that exist in play in order to comprehend it according to Sutton-Smith (1978, 1997). Understanding the dynamics of play requires recognizing the complexities, polarities, and contradictions inherent within observed play. Play contains multiple patterns of meaning over time experienced differently by players participating in the same play episode and by any other person observing the play phenomena (Meckley, 2015).

Another scheme used in grappling with the play concept is to foreground the order and disorder in play that reveals the spirit of play – this entails the play impulse in tension with the player's trying to harness and intentionally use the play (Henricks, 2009). Play can be very disorderly and appear random at one moment, and then morph into something very creative and inspiring. Play that is symmetrical and orderly can turn into something unruly and chaotic. Undoing the order of play can give a player a chance to be methodical and creative in some other way. Indeed, on the one hand, much play seems repetitious, ritualized, and rule-governed, but on the other hand, play is also dynamic and transformative – a combination of pre-frontal cortex (executive function) and amygdala (emotional) forces (Sutton-Smith, 1997).

Moreover, play can be thought of as a dynamic systems process. Similar to any complex system, play is typically open, recursive, non-linear, self-organized, and unpredictable. In play as a system there are phase transitions, and play's initial appearance is important with what follows sensitive to the initial conditions. In systems theory small differences in inputs are held to potentially lead to great output differences with the passage of time (Bergen et al., 2016; Fromberg, 2015). Consider the way in which a player constructs and represents meanings in play, which can begin anywhere. The play then has a life of its own. Play has the ability to go in any direction with starts and stops, twists and turns, and forward and backward movements. Play is a dynamic systemic process with phase transitions (connections across psychological states). Often there are abrupt changes in play – alternating seriousness and whimsy, reality and pretence, sometimes going to a higher level of play. There is always in play the potential for more change. Players are their own change agents, making new opportunities and generating new meanings. Bergen et al. (2016) stated, "Play epitomizes *plasticity* because capacity for change is always present. Thus, play … can be characterized as a nonlinear dynamic system" (p. 17).

The above and other ways of thinking about play are typically very much ahead of our ability to render play empirically manageable. Staying reasonably close to intuitions, insights, and ideas advanced in conceptual work when attempting to operationalize the important constructs for doing empirical work is easier said than done. Brian Sutton-Smith began his graduate seminars on play at University of Pennsylvania by establishing the fact that there are literally hundreds of play forms ranging from mind play, social play, play as performance to festivals, contests, risky play, and deep play (Sutton-Smith, 2011); the multitude of play forms served Sutton-Smith's formulation of his seven meta-narratives of play (i.e., play as progress, contest, chance, etc.) discussed in his classic *The Ambiguities of Play* (1997). He encouraged researchers to retain the spirit of play in the study of it, enjoy the process, and stay always creatively open to its mysteries and ambiguities (Meckley,

2015). The play spirit is integral to research; as Konrad Lorenz (1976) quipped, "All purely material research ... is pure inquisitive behavior ... it is play behavior" (p. 95).

Quantitative Methods

Methods in this camp serve to divide and conquer, with measurement and analysis privileged over synthesis and contextualization. In this form of disciplined inquiry, researchers have categorized types of play. For example, Smith and Pellegrini (2013) suggested locomotor play, social play, parallel play, object play, language play, and pretend play as the main types of play. Fjortuft (2004) used three types of play: functional play, constructive play, and symbolic play. Whitebread (2012) offered five types of play: physical play, play with objects, symbolic play, pretence/sociodramatic play, and games with rules. A variety of play classifications have come from different scholars, theories, or purposes of research.

Quantitative data generation commonly employs questionnaires or direct observations of play behaviours, with results summarized in numerical terms. Quantitative data about play can also come from sociometric techniques and toy inventories (Smith, 2011). Indirect or non-observational means of study of children's play, such as teacher or parent reports using ratings of play of children on hard copies or computer-assisted questionnaires (e.g., Survey-Monkey, Qualtrics), verbal statements during interviews, or written accounts in logs or diaries are quantitative when codified and described with numbers. Quantitative studies use descriptive and often inferential statistics on aggregate data to determine whether variable relations or group differences are non-random.

Researchers commonly borrow or share instruments across borders. The comparability of any written content's meanings across languages needs to be evaluated. Cultural and language validity of questionnaires, interview schedules, and other various instrumentation used in data generation can be checked by translating from the tool's home language into another language and then back again to the home language using independent bilingual experts (for conceptual equivalence) and translators from the countries involved. Back translation is not done in isolation but in the context of collaboration and iteration (Douglas & Craig, 2007).

Aspects of the quantitative genre include (1) sampling and recording play; (2) units of analysis, measurement, and categorization of play behaviour; and (3) analysis and interpretation of results.

Sampling and Recording Play. Here a question is which kinds of behaviours to record (Bakeman & Gottman, 1986). When a broad range of behaviours is of interest, sampling is employed, either *narrative accounts* or *specimen records* of what is happening for a specified period of time. Video records and/or field notes are made to describe the play and the settings. Both general *behavioural states* (e.g., a child is running), and different specific *behavioural events* (e.g., a child is clapping together two toys) can be of importance; usually a few behaviours are of particular interest. Gross (2003) recommends defining events in precise operational terms and to highlight instances of them as they occur in print or digital accounts.

Observational research uses *time sampling* or *rotating time sampling* with predetermined categories sampling a child's manifestation of them over a period of time, estimating the child's propensities to exhibit them in general within a specified place and time frame. Bias is reduced when randomness is built into a predetermined plan concerning who is being observed and when an observation occurs. *Rotating time sample* is operating when a group of children listed in random order are being studied one at a time. A procedural rule might be to skip an unavailable child and go the next child on the list and only return to observe the unavailable child when he or she has returned. Each child must be observed before a second cycle of observations begins. Children are observed in a revolving manner over the number of times or rounds prescribed in the research plan across the time period of the study. Roper and Hinde (1978) suggest a similar method for time sampling that they developed and termed a *multiple-scan sampling* procedure. Avoiding observer bias is the rationale.

Important decisions are faced regarding time frames and segmentation and about how one is to observe and to code the behaviour, either simultaneously or in an alternating manner throughout the period of observation. With videos, making these decisions can be put off since the behaviour revealed in the videos is continuous and one can decide how to segment and code at another time. *Time frames* refer to how much time should be used in sampling the play. *Segmentation* refers to dividing the duration of the time sample into smaller times to accommodate the study's unit of analysis and the categories used in coding and measuring the play behaviours.

The investigator's purposes dictate how lengthy the time sample and temporal segments are within the time sample. Typically, the time frame is from 1 to 30 minutes. Having shorter temporal frames usually means more of them are needed to meet the aims of the investigation. The researcher needs to secure an adequate total sample or volume of play that meets the objectives and is feasible in practice.

Event sampling is used when there is an emphasis on particular events, not players per se. A goal can be to obtain information about the target event over time in relation to an individual and/or group. Descriptive information about play events is gathered in order to make statements about their likely frequency of occurrence in a given place and time frame. Event sampling typically has been used for low-frequency behaviours that are of interest in a given research project, such as sociodramatic play or aggression. A left-to-right slow scanning of the play area (e.g., classroom, playground) is done repeatedly to pick up whether the event of interest is occurring. When the event takes place, the observational record captures information about the event while it lasts. Time limits may be imposed in a study, but usually the observation continues until the event is judged to be completed (Smith, 2011).

Recording techniques include using paper and pencil check sheets and lists, field note forms, and electronic technology. Computers have been used for many years to facilitate data processing and statistical analysis (Bakeman & Gottman, 1986). Data are directly entered into the computer by pressing keys that store information. Audio recording can assist with observations; the researcher orally describes behaviours of interest while observing the players; these data can also be integrated using computers.

Video accounts of play provide for excellent scoring of measurement indices relative to live observations since they can be used in an unhurried manner, and they can be coupled to audio records. Repeatedly viewing and hearing can increase accuracy of coding. Alternative investigative queries can be posed in follow-up study given that video accounts are permanent records. A disadvantage is that one has to code the videos, which is a time-consuming, labour-intensive task. In some studies, the ratio of observation to coding time reaches 1:4. Equipment is often cumbersome and intrusive in the setting of the play observations. Moreover, there are ethical issues (Fletcher et al., 2010). For instance, videographers must not record non-consent players (Lahman, 2008).

Units of Observation, Measurement, and Categorization. Units comprise *play episodes* or *play moments*. Play episodes vary in duration and complexity and can be partitioned as to what is occurring *within* the play episode (i.e., play enactments) and what is occurring *outside* the play frame (i.e., play negotiations and other 'meta-play' behaviours). Also, play researchers can code play moments (Trawick-Smith, 2010) – play or particular play types that are fleeting and/or embedded in other play types or non-play activities. Units of analysis range from longer-duration ones, such as being in a state of parallel play, to brief behavioural events, such as making a social bid to a peer. The units chosen by the investigator are coded with the category system.

The system must be practical in the research setting and able to produce information serving the study's objectives and enabling the investigator to address the research questions. Often selected from those used in past research, it is not uncommon for the coding scheme to be modified to serve specific research aims. Sometimes they are especially devised. Systems entail categories for different play and non-play behaviours of interest and differ with respect to whether systems use linear scales such as the Howes Peer Play Scale (1980) or a matrix like the Parten/Smilansky Play Scale (Johnson et al., 2005). Subcategories can be used to add information about the play. For instance, the investigator may wish to know whether and how a teacher was involved when a child was seen in a particular play state.

A mutually exclusive category system is when every unit is coded by putting it into only one play category. At times, the system is made into a mutually exclusive one by employing *rules of precedence* (Bakeman & Gottman, 1986) that are established and followed by the researcher. Rules of precedence apply to cases when more than one play category seems relevant within a set time frame and the investigator wants to avoid double or triple coding of units because such multiple coding of units makes the observation system non-mutually exclusive, precluding the computation of the kappa statistic.

Coding systems are of two types, either exhaustive or not. Exhaustive ones are when every unit gets coded – all play and non-play exhibited during the observation is accounted for by the coding or classification scheme. It can be useful to add a 'null' or 'garbage can' category (e.g., 'other') to make the system exhaustive and to permit the researcher to compute the kappa statistic (when the system is also using mutually exclusive categories). Operational definitions and classification illustrations including ones for subcategories of play behaviours are needed to prepare observers and to evaluate the quality of their observation coding.

Three indices for units that are aggregated include: (1) frequency, (2) duration, and (3) intensity. Frequency of each coded type or category (and subcategories) of play refers to the number of times the child displayed the particular actions in a given observation session or adding the total frequency across sessions. Duration means the time estimates for each play, either total time or duration for a child doing each type of play over the course of the whole study, or computing the average duration per session or other set time frame useful to consider in a particular study. Intensity of play is the impression of a certain quality of the behaviour, such as the degree of enthusiasm shown. This index is useful, for example, for differentiating rough-and-tumble play from real aggression (Smith, 2011).

Analysis and Interpretation. Descriptive statistics are computed (means and standard deviation scores, etc.) for the variables, and inferential statistical tests are run to estimate whether differences or relations in the aggregate data are non-random. Play can also be examined across time in longitudinal studies. While frequencies are used the most, duration and intensity scores for play variables are sometimes used in analysis. Instead of frequency scores, percentages can be analyzed to avoid loss of information; percentage scores are preferred when there is a need to correct for unequal opportunities or low or zero frequency of occurrence in some play categories.

Play observations are either continuous or non-continuous, and sequential or non-sequential. Continuous data come from observations ongoing without temporal interruption, while non-continuous data mean that there were breaks in the recording. Video records capture continuous streams of play behaviour. Even if the data are not continuous, however, observational procedures could keep track of the certain temporal ordering of the play. Sequential analytic approaches can show the way discrete sequences of behaviour occur, how play unfolds over time. Here it is possible to look for temporal patterns in play behaviour. Transitional probabilities are often calculated for information about how likely certain play states follow others from time 1 to time 2 (Bakeman & Gottman, 1986).

Levels of Analysis. This refers to the use of molar categories and molecular categories or subcategories. Some categories are major ones, such as pretend play. Subcategories provide descriptive detail. For instance, the researcher might wish to keep track of the types of transformations the child displays during pretend play, such as person, object, or situation transformations. Second-order categories can further delineate person transformations into self- or other child transformations. Using dominant and subordinate codes and subcodes results in a hierarchical system. The observer/coder has many 'tags' to stick on the stream of play and must be alert while coding. Data processing entails scrutinizing the categories and subcategories and noting the frequencies (sometimes durations and intensities) of play, deciding on whether to lump some of the minor categories to create new variables.

When interpreting findings, one must evaluate the quality of the methods and procedures employed to generate the data set. The reliability and the validity are always questioned.

Reliability refers to how consistently and correctly units are described and measured. Observations can be split in half and the two parts can be correlated to evaluate split-half reliability, an estimate of the extent to which there is internal consistency in the observations. Here acceptable reliability is usually defined as a correlation of $r = 0.7$ or higher (Smith, 2011).

Investigators may not maintain the alertness demanded for obtaining reliable information. One problem is *behaviour drift* or changing the guidelines or standards for scoring that can adversely affect the reliability in a way that would not be detected by computing split-half reliability coefficients (Smith, 2011). This is because both halves could show the same distortions. Accordingly, *intercoder* or *interobserver* reliability or agreement is typically evaluated.

Training and evaluating observers at the onset is critical. Developing the operational definition of the observational categories is a first priority. Observers are taught and practice recognizing exemplars in group discussions; narrative accounts or video recordings of play are gone over as a training exercise to check how well independent observers are in agreement in their coding. The principal investigator must periodically check for intercoder agreement over the period of time of the study. Addressing behaviour drift or the adverse effects of observer fatigue is important. It is acceptable to evaluate intercoder reliability on about 15%–20% of the total volume of observations interspersed at irregular intervals over the entire observation period.

To assess reliability of this kind, estimates are obtained by computing percentage agreement figures. When A refers to agreement and D refers to disagreement between two independent observers coding the given play units with the same category system, then intercoder agreement (C) = A/(A+D/2). Since agreements can occur by chance, and agreeing that low-frequency behaviours are not happening is too easy, C can be artificially inflated; one must attempt to define 'real' D, or non-random D, for each observer. Investigators usually make category systems that are exhaustive and mutually exclusive so as to calculate the kappa coefficient (Cohen, 1960), which corrects for chance agreements and accounts for low-frequency codes. Also, estimating how reliable play observations are can be done using correlations between the two observers' coding (Smith, 2011).

Validity is another important criterion used in evaluating the methodological quality of the study. Validity can be considered getting it right or correct when interpreting results. Is what the player exhibits correctly taken to be an exemplar of a certain type of play or play preference or competence? Overt play performance may be tapping underlying ability or play style, but it may not. Care is needed in interpreting results. The lack of evidence that a player is capable of playing in a certain way is not evidence of play incompetence. Perhaps the person shows this form of play only under certain circumstances. Questions about what is a valid inference are important, especially with respect to conjectures about play deficits in certain groups or individuals.

A threat to validity often encountered in research is observer effects. It would be imprudent to assume that an observer is only a 'fly on the wall'. The presence of the observer (or video equipment) can suppress or alter play behaviour. Those observed need a chance to acclimate to the observer and instruments; researchers should be as non-obtrusive as possible. Support for the validity of inferences about development or individual differences in play can come from observations in different settings. Teasing apart a play 'trait' (e.g., play ability or style) from a play 'state' exhibited in a particular situation is difficult. For more information about quantitative research methods for investigating play, see Johnson et al. (2014).

Qualitative Methods

Denzin and Lincoln (2000) assert, "Qualitative researchers study things in their natural settings, attempting to make sense of, or to interpret, phenomena in terms of the meanings people bring to them" (p. 3). Researchers using qualitative methods to study play are typically more personally and relationally involved with the participants. They study play often without knowing in advance which are the important variables, having instead an emergent purpose and a willingness to make modifications. The quest here is for meaning aided by induction, subjectivity, and reflexivity (Hatch, 1998).

Qualitative researchers study play over longer durations and in greater depth, using narrative data records and related artefacts, maps, documents, and physical tracings to produce rich descriptions and to construct meaningful interpretations of play in various contexts. Investigators are participant observers or 'participant experiencers'. Qualitative research designs include case studies, ethnographies, co-creating stories, art-based studies, and others.

Graue and Walsh (1998) would see studying play in context as examining and seeking to understand play through being face-to-face with participants, up close over time (proximity and duration), leading to rich narrative descriptions for purposes of theory building (using inductive reasoning). Qualitative researchers embrace the players as persons, not pawns, by entering into a relationship with them (Hatch, 1998). Qualitative study of play often springs from using a sociocultural perspective with play associated with unique combinations of macro- and micro-level influences and consequences, linking play with cultural and community contexts (see Chapters 9 and 17–19 in this volume).

Interpretive work is done on rich, extensive field notes and other data sources, frequently in many kinds of settings (not just classrooms and playgrounds) (Tudge et al., 2011). Many individuals can be included: children, parents, and/or teachers can be observed and interviewed to describe and discuss play; the use of narrative methods is common, such as found in time diaries and logs or repeated in-depth interviews or drawing tasks.

Many guidelines exist to process, analyze, and synthesize qualitative data. For example, constant comparison methods are used to scrutinize texts of transcribed interviews or texts based on field notes to uncover codes that can be used to form categories and uncover themes in the findings. Interpretations and results are typically reported in sample extended quotes, scene and dialogue descriptions, vignettes, anecdotes, and other data representations (e.g., drawings, maps) that document the researcher's insights (Cohen & Uhry, 2007; Eisenhart, 2006).

The term 'validity' is not used in qualitative work because of its association with measurement instruments, and validity concerns relate to the entire qualitative investigation. Instead of being valid or not, qualitative studies are trustworthy, credible, dependable, and transferrable or confirmable when they meet several well-established criteria (Maxwell, 2013).

In qualitative designs (e.g., case studies, case histories, or ethnographies), data are generated with field observations, interviews, focus groups, drawings, video analysis, photography, and verbal or written reflections using multiple sources (interview versus field observation notes) representing the voices of the different participants. Data should be generated over time in close proximity with the participants in the study in order to secure a deep and multidimensional basis for interpretive activity. Being open to negative evidence disconfirming themes or interpretations is another guideline for validity.

The process of combining information from different information and informant sources is called triangulation. Researcher triangulation (and member checking) is employed to improve trustworthiness and refers to having someone who is acquainted with the study but not personally invested to be a sounding board to trade ideas and to talk about what is occurring over the period of the investigation. This person can also be helpful in observing and coding play and evaluating agreement between independent observers/ coders. This person can help in specific decisions and in forming a general understanding about what is going on in the study. For instance, two researchers studying the play of children in an after-school program can work together in mutually observing or interviewing and coding the data, discussing results to reach consensus in making inferences.

The researcher is aided by a member who checks the processing and interpretation of the information, which is typically gathered through interviews or other techniques such as photos or drawings. Research participants are approached by the investigators and asked about the accuracy of interpretations. The participants receive from the researcher transcriptions of the interview to read over and make revisions. For instance, a kindergarten teacher can be requested to evaluate correctness of interview statements from an interview about play values and ideas. Member checking needs to occur soon after the data are generated.

Reliability being linked to measurement is likewise a problem within qualitative research since, like validity, for qualitative researchers reliability pertains to the overall study and not the tools of measurement (Stenbacka, 2001). Qualitative results are unique to the study, and replication is not sought. The producer of the research asks the reader or consumer to evaluate and decide on the merits of each individual study. When a qualitative study is valid, it is assumed to be reliable.

Contemporary Play Research

Many recent studies employ mixed methods and innovative procedures to unravel the complex phenomena of play.

Participatory Photography. Players can be asked to use cameras to construct photo diaries to document play spaces and places. Rose (2001) opines that since taking photographs is usually easy and fun it can be a good way to have participants record and show their perspectives. They are empowered and their photos can yield detailed information suggesting different and various insights; meaningful data can result, showing the reflective lives of participants (p. 317).

Truong and Mahon (2012) examined how children experienced play and place in the Duangkae Centre in Bangkok, Thailand. Researchers initially familiarized themselves with the children and informed them about the research process, which consisted of five sessions: (1) use of visual methods and small group conversation, (2) creation of a visual map of the Centre, (3) photographing favourite play spaces and adding them to the visual map, (4) viewing the photographs, and (5) conversing about changing play spaces. Children shared stories and viewed all the photographs on the computer screen to choose two of their favourites to include in an exhibition, followed by small group discussions of their photographs and stories.

The results indicated variety in what and where the children liked to play: spaces for active play such as tag and ball games, quiet spaces for make-believe play and reading, natural spaces for sand play and climbing trees, and play equipment such as slides and climbers for large muscle movement play. Children's conversations showed four central themes: (1) transforming spaces, (2) experiencing diverse playthings, (3) interacting with playmates, and (4) feeling safe. Children's views led to some modifications at the Centre. More open spaces resulted by clearing or changing the location of equipment; the sand play area was refreshed; a tree house was added; and more naturalistic materials introduced.

Drawings. Concepts of play can be gleaned from drawings (Duncan, 2015). Hence, drawing can be a useful a research tool, revealing a player's definitions and representations of play; such study is done within a social-semiotic framework. Symbolic meanings emerge in a social context and feelings and consciousness about the play state can be revealed.

Like photography, drawings are familiar, easy, and fun, and they can be effective ways for visualizing thoughts (Dyson, 2008) and narrative play (Thompson, 2006). Researching drawings has long been studied for many reasons, including "cognitive, developmental, and socio cultural issues" (Gamradt & Staples, 1994).

In Duncan's (2015) study, researcher asked 4-year-olds, "Will you draw anything you can think of when you hear the word 'play'?" and "Will you draw a person playing?" (p. 54). Data were children's drawings, and also photos, free play scenarios, and conversations with the researcher, and were video recorded and transcribed. Children's concepts of play reflected specific experiences, with whom they played, and significant components of play episodes. The study confirmed that children's drawings can be of service to "facilitate researchers in exploring the broad and transient concept of play, and to explore play from a child's perspective" (p. 70).

Final Remarks

We started by noting the many definitions and characteristics of play in the literature, to convey a sense of the magnitude of the task of studying play using empirical methods. While complex and elusive, play is not scientifically nonsensical. Many have made credible disciplined inquiry using the varied quantitative and qualitative methods reviewed in this chapter. Still, a gulf exists between play in research and in conception. Conceptual evidence about play is abundant, growing, and worthwhile, but it must be joined with new empirical work targeting what we are learning from our constructions.

In an effort to narrow the theoretical-empirical lacuna, more and better studies, especially mixed-method ones, should be conducted using innovative techniques. We have seen this in the two illustrative studies reviewed in this chapter. Recently, scholars have turned more to how players think and feel about play, and not just researchers', teachers', parents', or others' perceptions of the players' experiences. Adding to traditional questionnaires, interviews, and observations used in quantitative, qualitative, and mixed designs that are *researcher led*, newer methods are *player led* where the player is more intricately involved in the play research. Study tools can include an assortment of data generation procedures involving cameras, drawing paper and utensils, audio recorders, and various digital devices to assess and document play and its contexts (Arnott et al., 2016). Researchers elicit from players data to infer their inner states and perspectives; these data can complement data generated from the researchers' points of view. Inferences about play states can also come from brain-wave patterns and other results from neuropsychological research (Bergen et al., 2016).

Innovative techniques to study play have been spawned from the realization that researchers' conceptualizations of the play experience may not match the players' actual experiences (e.g., Rogers & Evans, 2008) and that a more reflexive strategy is required to understand players' views and experiences of play. Researchers need to think about their research practices, adopt a more reflexive approach, and decide carefully when and where they chose to examine play and how they study it. Whether certain naturalistic settings are chosen in studies, or opportunities are arranged and structured for players, the question is: Are players invited to share their take on their own play? (e.g., Glenn et al., 2013). Still, what the player's viewpoint is remains a researcher's inference.

In this vein, research methods and procedures intended to elicit the player's perspective become important in the study of play and play-related phenomena such as players' reflections and representations of their own play. Research conducted to make methodological (as opposed to empirical and theoretical) contributions is needed to learn how to better accomplish the goals of a player-oriented study of play, to do well such 'player action research' or investigations done in collaboration with researchers, studies that are co-constructed by player and researcher. For example, how effective are different ways of establishing rapport with the player, using various verbal (e.g., tone of voice) and nonverbal (e.g., positioning and eye contact) communications? This is particularly relevant when the player is a young child and the researcher wants the child to be comfortable and show authenticity and transparency in response to the study's demand characteristics. Methodological work could include seeing what happens when players are afforded different kinds of opportunities to work with materials and technological gadgets such as robots (e.g., unstructured play) and engage in conversations (e.g., open-ended questions and focus groups). Ways of carefully preparing environments to empower the player to have an authentic voice can be evaluated in such methodological work.

Representations and reflections on play and play itself are different. The former asks for the player's perspective, while the latter rests on the researcher's own interpretations of the observations made of the play activities. Inferences by the researcher are made in each case, researcher-led or player-led studies. Data and perspectives from them together are necessary to achieve a more complete understanding of the play phenomena. Quantitative, qualitative, and mixed methods have a role in investigations that are researcher-led and player-led, making the study of play not just narrowly focused or broadly focused, but also shallow or deep. By including the player's perspective some depth is gained. Researchers can be expected to continue to develop the multiplicity of ways to obtain information not only about play actions but also about players' internal states (feelings and contents of consciousness). Challenging and exciting work lies ahead with ever-developing technology with objects and situations inviting new play forms and making possible new data on players' views about their intentions and actions.

Finally, more holistic outcomes from the study of play can be expected with players' and the researchers' perspectives together included. This contributes to a greater likelihood that results can be applied in practical settings like school classrooms, playgrounds, museums, senior centres, and community centres. Up to now, however, even though researchers, practitioners, and policymakers often share goals, communication problems do exist among them due to a variety of reasons including an overuse of researcher-led studies that are typically laced with technical jargon and are confusing to those who are not professionally trained as researchers; another cause is the differing conceptual frameworks or preexisting beliefs or attitudes among researchers and practitioners. For instance, some parents may prefer more directive interventions with their children when researchers provide results from their studies that point to less directive ones.

Sigel (2006) coined the term "proximity index" in reference to the nearness or remoteness between researchers' and practitioners' views. Holistic study may preempt some of the gaps between research and practice by including the views of players. Practitioners such as teachers and parents may be stimulated to think in different ways about their children. They may be led to rethink ways of teaching or child-rearing. Researchers can conduct studies that enhance the proximity of research for the practitioners. An effort must be made by those doing new research with player-led procedures to understand what kinds of play occur; what play looks like, feels like, and how it is experienced by players; and how play is understood by players and practitioners. This seems now to be a needed complement to efforts by traditional quantitative, qualitative, and mixed-methods researchers; together, researchers can effectively use methods to achieve greater understanding about play with accompanying increased potential for application to practical settings.

References

Arnott, L., Grogan, D., & Duncan, P. (2016). Lessons from using iPads to understand young children's creativity. *Contemporary Issues in Early Childhood, 17*(2), 1–17.

Bakeman, R., & Gottman, J. (1986). *Observing interaction: An introduction to sequential analysis.* New York: Cambridge University Press.

Bateson, G. (1956). The message 'This is play'. In B. Schaffner (Ed.), *Group processes: Transactions of the second conference* (pp. 145–241). New York: Josiah Macy Jr. Foundation.

Bergen, D., Davis, D., & Abbitt, J. (2016). *Technology play and brain development: Infancy to adolescence and future implications.* New York: Routledge.

Burghardt, G. (2005). *The genesis of animal play: Testing the limits.* Cambridge, MA: MIT Press.

Caillois, R. (1961). *Man, play and games.* New York: Free Press (originally published in 1958).

Cohen, J. (1960). A coefficient of agreement for nominal scales. *Educational and Psychological Measurement, 20,* 37–46.

Cohen, L., & Uhry, J. (2007). Young children's discourse strategies during block play: A Baktinian approach. *Journal of Research in Childhood Education, 21*(3), 302–315.

Denzin, N., & Lincoln, Y. (2000). *Handbook of qualitative research* (2nd ed.). Thousand Oaks, CA: Sage.

Douglas, S. P., & Craig, C. S. (2007). Collaborative and iterative translation: An alternative approach to back translation. *Journal of International Marketing, 15*(1), 30–43.

Duncan, P. (2015). Pigs, planes, and Play-Doh: Children's perspectives on play revealed through their drawings. *American Journal of Play, 8*(1), 50–73.

Dyson, A. (2008). Staying in the (curricular) lines: Practice constraints and possibilities in childhood wiring. *Written Communication, 25*(1), 119–159.

Eisenhart, M. (2006). Representing qualitative data. In J. Green, G. Camilli, & P. Elmore (Eds.), *Handbook of complementary methods in education research* (pp. 567–581). Mahwah, NJ: Erlbaum.

Fjørtoft, I. (2004). Landscape as playscape: The effects of natural environments on children's play and motor development. *Children, Youth and Environments, 14*(2), 21–44.

Fletcher, J., Price, B., & Branen, L. (2010). Videotaping children and staff in natural environments: Gathering footage for research and teaching. *Contemporary Issues in Early Childhood, 11*(2), 219–226.

Fromberg, D. (2015). How nonlinear systems inform meaning and early education. In D. Fromberg & D. Bergen (Eds.), *Play from birth to twelve: Contexts, perspectives, and meanings* (pp. 419–434). New York: Routledge.

Gamradt, J., & Staples, C. (1994). My school and me: Children's drawings in postmodern educational research and evaluation. *Visual Arts Research, 20*(1), 36–49.

Glenn, N., Knight, C., Holt, N., & Spence, J. (2013). Meanings of play among children. *Childhood, 20,* 185–199.

Graue, M., & Walsh, D. (1998). *Studying children in context: Theories, methods, and ethics.* Thousand Oaks, CA: Sage Publications.

Gross, D. (2003). An introduction to research in psychology: Learning to observe children at play. In D. Lytle (Ed.), *Play and educational theory and practice* (pp. 33– 41). Westport, CT: Praeger.

Hatch, J. (1998). Qualitative research in early childhood education. In *Issues in early childhood educational research* (pp. 49–75). New York: Teachers College.

Henricks, T. (2009). Orderly and disorderly play: A comparison. *American Journal of Play, 2*(1), 12–40.

Howes, C. (1980). Peer play scale as an index of complexity of peer interaction. *Developmental Psychology, 16*, 371–372.

Huizinga, J. (1955). *Humo ludens: A study of the play-element in civilization.* Boston: Beacon (originally published in 1938).

Johnson, J. (2015). Play development from four to eight years. In D. Fromberg & D. Bergen (Eds.), *Play from birth to twelve: Contexts, perspectives, and meanings* (pp. 21–29). New York: Routledge.

Johnson, J., Al-Mansour, M., & Sevimli-Celik, S. (2014). Researching play in early childhood. In O. Saracho (Ed.), *Handbook of research methods in early childhood education: Review of research methodologies*, vol. II (pp. 473–507). Charlotte, NC: Information Age Publishing.

Johnson, J., Christie, J., & Wardle, F. (2005). *Play, development, and early education.* Boston: Allyn & Bacon.

Johnson, J., Eberle, S., Henricks, T., & Kuschner, D. (2015). *The handbook of the study of play* (2 vols.). Lanham, MD: Rowan & Littlefield.

Lahman, M. (2008). Always othered: Ethical research with children. *Early Childhood Research Journal, 6*(3), 281–300.

Lorenz, K. (1976). Psychology and phylogeny. In J. Bruner, A. Jolly, & K. Sylva (Eds.), *Play: Its role in development and evolution* (pp. 84–95). New York: Basic Books.

Maxwell, J. (2013). *Qualitative research design: An interactive approach.* Thousand Oaks, CA: Sage.

Meckley, A. (2015). A student's guide for understanding play through the theories of Brian Sutton-Smith. In J. Johnson, S. Eberle, T. Henricks, & D. Kuschner (eds.), *The handbook of the study of play* (pp. 393–405). Lanham, MD: Rowan & Littlefield.

Rogers, S., & Evans, J. (2008). *Inside role-play in early childhood education: Researching young children's perspectives.* New York: Routledge.

Roper, R., & Hinde, R. (1978). Social behavior in a play group: Consistency and complexity. *Child Development, 49*, 570–579.

Rose, G. (2001). *Visual methodologies: An introduction to researching with visual materials.* London: Sage.

Schlosberg, H. (1947). The concept of play. *Psychological Review, 54*, 229–231.

Sigel, I. (2006). Research into practice redefined. In A. Renninger & I. Sigel (Eds.), *Handbook of Child Psychology,* vol. 4: *Child Psychology in Practice* (6th ed.) (pp. 1017–1023). New York: Wiley.

Smith, P. K. (2011). Observational methods in studying play. In A. Pellegrini (Ed.), *The Oxford handbook of the development of play* (pp. 138–149). New York: Oxford University Press.

Smith, P. K., & Pellegrini, A. (2013). Learning through play. In *Encyclopedia on Early Childhood Development*. Retrieved from https://pdfs.semanticscholar.org/9ec8/fbe8a1d002c6ca98a1d65f809f105987ed7a.pdf.

Smith, P., Takhvar, M., Gore, N., & Vollstedt, R. (1985). Play in young children: Problems of definition, categorization, and measurement. *Early Child Development and Care, 19*, 25–41.

Stenbacka, C. (2001). Qualitative research requires quality concepts of its own. *Management Decision, 39*(7), 551–556.

Sutton-Smith, B. (1978). *Die dialektik des spiels*. Schorndork, Germany: Verlag Karl Hoffman.

Sutton-Smith, B. (1979). Epilogue: Play as performance. In B. Sutton-Smith (Ed.), *Play and learning* (pp. 295–322). New York: Gardner Press.

Sutton-Smith, B. (1997). *The ambiguity of play*. Cambridge, MA: Harvard University Press.

Sutton-Smith, B. (2011). Play as emotional survival. Interview recorded at the Strong Museum of Play, edited and shown at the 50th anniversary of the International Play Association, Cardiff, Wales.

Thompson, C. (2006). The 'ket aesthetic': Visual culture in childhood. In J. Fineberg (Ed.), *When we were young: New perspectives on the art of the child* (pp. 31–44). Berkeley: University of California Press.

Trawick-Smith, J. (2010). Drawing back the lens on play: A frame analysis of young children's play in Puerto Rico. *Early Education and Development, 21*(4), 536–567.

Truong, S., & Mahon, M. (2012). Through the lens of participatory photography: Engaging Thai children in research about their community play centre. *International Journal of Play, 1*(1), 75–90.

Tudge, J., Brown, J., & Freitas, L. (2011). The cultural ecology of play: Methodological considerations for studying play in its everyday contexts. In A. Pellegrini (Ed.), *The Oxford handbook of the development of play* (pp. 119–137). New York: Oxford University Press.

Whitebread, D. (2012). The importance of play. Toy Industries of Europe (TIE). Retrieved from www.csap.cam.ac.uk/media/uploads/files/1/david-whitebread-importance-of-play-report.pdf.

PART V

Play and Learning

23 Play and Learning in Everyday Family Contexts

Marilyn Fleer

There is long-standing research that examines the relations between culture and play (e.g., Roopnarine et al., 2015), which in contrast to developmental and biologically deterministic views, shows that play is a highly culturally situated activity, often learned in families (Lillard, 2011; Ugaste, 2005). This chapter draws on this perspective to discuss the literature, to theorize the relations between play and learning in family contexts, and to present a case study of family play practices in an Australian community.

Theorizing the Relations between Play and Learning

Van Oers (1999) argued, "From a developmental perspective, play is for Piaget a necessary stage in the development of symbolic activity, *but a state where educational intervention is pointless*" (p. 269; emphasis added). Biology, rather than culture, is foregrounded in this conception of play. Conversely, a cultural-historical reading of play privileges the view that play is an activity that was historically constructed by societies to support a particular family need for children to play. For instance, Elkonin (2005) theorized that as societies changed their technological practices, such as inventing agriculture with the evolution of more advanced tools, children were increasingly unable to participate in food production at an early age. Miniatures were created so that children could practice and develop important skills, such as playing with a spinning top to learn the skill of fire-lighting with a spindle. In this theorization by Elkonin (2005), play emerged as a result of changing societal needs. Therefore, play can only ever be considered as a highly culturally situated activity (e.g., Roopnarine, 2015), and his view helps explain the variations in play and learning practices found in families across communities (e.g., Lancy, 1996; Roopnarine et al., 2015; Scales et al., 1991).

In studying the contemporary play practices in Western technologically developed societies, particularly in the North American context, Sutton-Smith noted an association between toys and achievement (Sutton-Smith, 1986) and a belief in play as progress (Sutton-Smith, 1997) (see also Chapter 21 in this book). Like Elkonin (2005), Sutton-Smith (1997) also examined societal needs and practices in relation to children's play. He theorized that schools as institutions have removed children from work practices, so that valued activities and their associated skills are no longer visible to children, resulting in a need for greater abstraction. Abstraction is necessary because valued practices are learned not in situ, and not for immediate use, but rather for utility much later in life, such as when using accounting software in the workplace or when studying in higher education. Play when conceptualized in the service of education becomes a vehicle for learning.

Consistent with the theorization of play as a cultural practice specific to particular children, families, and communities is a cultural-historical conception of play (see Fleer, 2010, and Chapter 24 in this book). Vygotsky (1966) conceptualized play as the creation of an imaginary situation, where players change the meaning of objects and actions to give them a new sense. To illustrate his conception, he gave the example of a child creating the imaginary situation of riding a horse. The child takes a stick and changes its meaning to that of a horse, and by placing the stick between his or her legs, the child changes his or her actions to be a horse rider. The visual field is given a new sense in the imaginary situation – the stick is now a horse. The child uses the stick as a placeholder for a horse in his or her play. This semiotic activity is akin to abstracted school learning, which van Oers (1999) argues is a cognitive activity because the child selects not just any object as a placeholder, but rather reflects on the relationships between sign and meaning in the imaginary situation. Over time the repertoire of signs increases, and the child begins to rely less on objects and more on language when in the imaginary situation (see Chapter 24 in this book for a more comprehensive discussion). It is argued here that these repertoires of signs, and the meaning systems attributed to them, are highly culturally situated.

Play Is a Learned Cultural Practice in Families

A study by Lillard (2011) investigated how US mothers signal to their infants aged 18 months that they are pretending, showing how play is learned. In two laboratory-based procedures, Lillard asked mothers of 55 infants in one situation to pretend and in another to not pretend. The mothers with infants who were pretending were asked to have a 'real snack' or a 'pretend snack' and in both situations had available objects such as a small pitcher, bowl, and spoon. In the real situation, the bowl had cereal and the pitcher had juice in it. Half of the mothers were asked to pretend to have a snack and then to have a real snack. The order of the procedure was reversed for the other half. Lillard found that mothers used exaggerated actions during pretence, spent longer making pretend motions when compared with real situations, made sound effects during pretence, used twice as many words to refer to their actions, frequently labelled concrete objects, used 'we' more often, talked louder and varied their pitch, engaged in long smiles and more often, and looked at their infants for longer periods during moments of pretence. These structures helped signal to infants that the mother was pretending.

In further studies of how mothers signal pretence to their infants and how infants respond, Lillard (2011) stated, "Slowing the pace of motor actions apparently helps get the point across to younger babies, and as they come to get pretense (perhaps learning to rely on other cues like the placement of smile), then faster movements cue pretense" (p. 293). Lillard (2011) suggested that children appear to be sensitive to pretence at a young age and that "how mothers initially bring children into pretense is an important one, given that the cognitive system would logically be set up to apprehend reality. Mothers behave differently when they pretend than when they do those same things for real, and some of those changes in behaviors might signal to young children that they are pretending" (p. 294). She suggested that these behaviours are akin to social referencing, where mothers engage explicitly in joint attention during pretence through looking at their infants, then engaging in pretence, then smiling at their infants. Lillard found that where mothers engaged in these sequences more often, infants correspondingly displayed smiling back and performing pretence more often. This suggests that children can engage in pretence with their mothers and that this is a learned social practice.

In a more naturalistic setting, Ugaste (2005) studied how pretence was enacted between mothers and children at home in Estonia. She sought to investigate the everyday interactions of five children at home to determine the character of the play and the role of the mother in their child's play world. She used both stimulated interview technique and between 9 and 10 hours of video observations of the children playing at home for each family (a total of 50 hours of video). For the children aged 5 and 6 years, Ugaste noted that most of the mother–child interactions were associated with the development of academic skills. The content of the child-initiated play was in relation to everyday life events, and when in joint play with the mother, the play content involved teaching, such as drawing or introducing letters, or practical skills, such as making dough. These joint activities were found to involve humour and magic and described as fun.

Ugaste also found that toys were generally deemed as boring, unless they afforded the possibility to add something to them and change their function. Toys that had the possibility for instruction were valued by the mothers, which is supportive of their belief in using play for academic learning. Ugaste found that when children played with their mothers, the play lasted longer, and the level of the play was much more complex, with more play scripts, than when children played alone. This has also been reported in previous research in other contexts (see Gaskins et al., 2007), suggesting the role of the adult is critical for the development of play. In the 12 episodes of board games observed by Ugaste, the play was dominated by instruction, such as learning about numbers. The importance of board games for the development of logical thought was evident. Finally, Ugaste found that questioning by mothers was common, and this helped children "to create imaginary situations and to elaborate them" (2005, p. 171).

Both the laboratory-based research of Lillard (2011) and the naturalistic study of Ugaste (2005) suggest that different forms of play are actively taught by mothers. Even though the form and structure of the interactions described in both studies differed (see also Cameron et al., 2011), as would be expected of research with infants and research with pre-schoolers, they both show that play is a learned social practice.

What We Know about Play and Learning in Family Contexts

Research into play and learning in Australian families is not so well understood. In Australia, a culturally diverse country, studies show how Hong Kong immigrant families in Australia scheduled learning and play times at home (e.g., Wong & Fleer, 2012) and used playful family practices for maintaining Chinese heritage language (Li, 2012). Studies also showed play supporting the everyday learning of scientific concepts in some Bangladeshi families living in Singapore and Australia (Sikder, 2015). Because of the diversity of study designs, and the differing cultural backgrounds of the families, the research does not appear to show a pattern, but rather shows a mix of play content and play practices in Australia.

What is known from broader studies that seek to undertake cross-cultural comparisons of play and learning of middle-class families from different cultural backgrounds is that literacy and numeracy concepts appear to dominate family play activities of Western technologically oriented countries. For example, Tamis-LeMonda and colleagues (2013), in a study of mothers from four different cultural backgrounds (African American, Chinese, Dominican, and Mexican) who were asked to engage in block play with their children, found that they mostly taught literacy rather than numeracy concepts with the blocks. Chinese and African Americans were more likely to teach advanced concepts, while Dominican and Mexican mothers taught more basic concepts. Similar findings were reported across many studies, most of which were undertaken in a North American context (see Gaskins et al., 2007). In contrast, some studies reported that parents supported the belief that play enhanced learning, but the play content "was idiosyncratic and individual, and – critically – involved emotional, physical, social and cognitive learning about the family and family life" rather than being solely focused on academic learning (Colliver, 2016, p. 9).

To understand this diversity in content and play practices across cultural communities, some researchers have also studied adult views of their role in children's play. There are studies that report that families state that play is not something that adults participated in, and therefore they do not use play to enhance learning. For example, Gaskins (2015) reported that Yucatec Mayan children participate in a broad range of play activities, but families do not actively resource or mediate play activity. Similarly, Roopnarine (2015) in reviewing the literature and drawing together his own research, found that Caribbean parents do not consider play in the context of academic learning or preparation for schooling. There are many examples of studies across cultural communities that show a variability in beliefs and practices (e.g., Mathur, 2015). Indeed, some cultural communities are dismissive of the play activities of children, valuing work over play (e.g., Chang, 2015). The consistent message from studies is that families do not all value play for supporting learning, and not all families use play in the service of education. Consequently, play practices and the content of the play are not universally the same.

Göncü et al. (2007), taking a cultural stance to the study of children's play, state that "play is only a partially understood activity, the meaning of which varies as a result of the perspective from which it is examined" (p. 155). They argue that play is a cultural expression rather than a universal construct. They suggest that based on research done in middle-class and Western contexts, much of the findings from "previous work have yielded potentially ethnocentric information" (p. 157). In drawing on Sutton-Smith and Brice-Heath (1981), and in line with the arguments of Elkonin (2005), they argue that "cultural differences in pretend play can be connected to varying levels of modernity and technology across culture". In those communities "where schooling is common and therefore functioning on the basis of decontextualized skills (e.g., literacy) is a requirement, pretend play will occur more frequently than in rural cultures where functioning relies on concrete tools of daily life (e.g., features of oral traditions such as storytelling)" (p. 159). They suggest that variations in play activity noted in the literature may be more a function of the responsibilities that children and adult have, rather than their abilities or desire to play or not.

The societal perspective that Göncü et al. (2007) bring to their own research has resulted in new understandings about the play of low-income African American (14 children), European American (15 children), and Turkish children (14 children). Through interviews of caregivers and some children, and through video observations of the children in both home and preschool engaged in free play (aged between 4 and 6 years), they conceptualized the variability in play practices across cultures in new ways. They found, among other things, that studying play for the former two groups was something that the participants agreed was worthwhile. However, the Turkish group were more unsure about this. As with other studies of African American and European American families, they found that play was valued because it contributed to academic learning, preparing them for life and supporting health, growth, and social relations. In addition to the play practices already reported in the literature, the low-income families also identified sound and rhythm play, teasing, and language play. The researchers argued that these new play practices had not been previously reported.

Göncü et al. (2007) suggested that "Adopting a cultural approach enabled us to identify similarities and differences among the three low-income communities included in this study" (p. 175), and importantly they suggested that teasing is a form of symbolic representation and that this and other forms of representation should be carefully considered when undertaking research into play across cultures. By limiting the categories of play to those that have predominantly come from middle-class Western families, many play practices may be overlooked and not captured through the study designs. This is particularly so for laboratory-based studies that create experimental structures (e.g., play activity is set up) and procedures (asking mothers to do specific tasks), which may not give possibilities for identifying other types of play, as might be seen when play is embedded in everyday life of families (e.g., Ugaste, 2005).

Consistent with this view, Cameron et al. (2011) noted, "Observation of play in diverse contexts affords an evaluation of the scope and limits of localised conceptions, and extends appreciation of the rich variations in this phenomenon across cultures" (p. 84). Fasoli (2014) sums up this position by suggesting that "while many advocates emphasize parent–child play to promote certain developmental outcomes, the recognition of alternate models of play provides a position from which to question whether this goal may come at the expense of forms of play that prioritize other values, such as parent–child bonding through joint amusement or learning through peer interaction" (p. 617). This suggestion of alternate models opens up the challenges faced in a monocultural conception of play in study designs, and thus goes to the heart of the methodological problem alluded to by Lilliard in her search for a universal model of play to support children's development (Lillard et al., 2012). She found that "Despite over 40 years of research examining how pretend play might help development there is little evidence that it has a crucial role . . . Because the literature is riddled with weak methods" (p. 27).

If anything, the literature introduced above points to a recognition of the diverse pathways in which play and learning are conceptualized both in families and in research, sometimes in opposition to each other. Consequently, more needs to be known about how families assign meaning to signs in everyday culturally situated activities in the home and community to support play and learning. Like Göncü et al. (2007), by studying at a localized level how children and their families reflect on the relationships between sign and meaning (van Oers, 1999) in everyday practices, it may be possible to gain new insights into the relations between play and learning in some families, for example, in an Australian context.

A Case Study of Family Play Practices in an Australian Community

In this section, an in-depth case study of family members engaged in everyday practices is reported. The overall study of children's development in everyday family practices is described in detail in Hedegaard and Fleer (2013). In this chapter, the play and learning practices of one of the families is analyzed, with a view to understanding the play content, how play is structured by the families, and what the dominant play practices are. In keeping with a cultural-historical conception of play, the focus for this section is on how play and learning is structured.

Participants

The family consist of a mother, father, and four children, Jason (5 years), Alex (4 years), Cam (3 years), and Mandy (16 months), plus Grandmother and Uncle Matthew. Grandmother and Uncle Matthew visit the family home regularly and participate in the family routines, including dressing the children, putting the children to bed, and playing with them.

The family lives in a rural town in south of Melbourne, Australia. The community is made up of primarily low socioeconomic families. The family lives in a rented three-bedroom house, with large back and front yards. There is a small garden shed in the back that contains some toys, the children's bikes, and some general equipment. The adults do not have employment. The family lives close by the children's school. In the carport is an old four-wheel drive. The kitchen and the family room appear to be the two main family living spaces used by the family. Although some dry food can be found in the cupboards, the fridge is relatively sparse. The family is supported by government funds.

Procedure

Two researchers filmed the family, who were engaged in everyday routines (bed time routines, breakfast, play, walking to school), school activities (group time, play time, individual and small group activities), and homework tasks. In line with video ethnography, digital documentation (two cameras following the children) was undertaken for 1–2 hours each time the researchers visited the family home. Longer periods were observed in the school. Observations were made across three observation periods (April, September, and December/January). The family was interviewed in situ and was asked about what was being observed, and if the practices were common for the family. A total of 50 hours of digital video observations were gathered.

Analysis

The study analyzed the data using those constructs from the literature that specifically focused on the structuring of play in families and the content of the play practices observed during the study period. Vygotsky's conception of play was drawn on to identify relevant play episodes for analysis, as well as his concept of *social situation of development* for better understanding the play setting in relation to the children's development. The *social situation of development* concept is discussed later in the results and discussion section. The primary categories used for analysis are shown in Table 23.1.

Table 23.1 *Analytical frame*

Vygotsky's (1966) theoretical conception of play	Structuring of play practices in families	Content of play	Purpose of play
Creation of an imaginary situation	Slowing the pace of motor actions during pretence with infants, and later speeding it up (Lillard, 2011)	Teaching of concepts, such as literacy and numeracy (Tamis-LeMonda et al., 2013)	Play helps academic learning (Ugaste, 2005)
Change the meaning of actions and objects to give them a new sense	Joint attention during pretence through adult looking at the child, engaging in pretence, then smiling at the child (Lillard, 2011)	Elaborating creativity (Gaskins et al., 2007)	Play contributes to academic learning (Gaskins et al., 2007)
Objects or toys as pivots	Toys that allowed for the possibility to add something and change their function (Ugaste, 2005)	Symbolic representation, such as teasing (Göncü et al., 2007)	Play is preparation for life and supports health and social relations (Gaskins et al., 2007)
Games with rules	Instruction of games and fostering social rules (Ugaste, 2005)	Fostered the learning of respect and cooperation (Gaskins et al., 2007); fostering of logical thought through board games with 5- to 6-year-olds (Ugaste, 2005)	Play is preparation for schooling (Sutton-Smith, 1997)
		Role-playing everyday life activities and events (Sutton-Smith, 1997)	Play is used for transmission of sociocultural values (Ugaste, 2005)
		Variability in play practices: sound and rhythm play, teasing, and language play (Göncü et al., 2007)	Some parents are dismissive of play and value work over play (Chang, 2015)

Results and Discussion

Content of the Play

Consistent with the literature on academic learning in families, the results showed that the family used play in the service of education. As with previous studies, the family members taught literacy and numeracy content to their children when in a play context. As expected, the family used a question-and-answer format for teaching academic concepts to their children, such as when playing with a set of marbles and tubes, the father repeatedly quizzed Alex, "What colour is that? (pointing at a marble), What colour is that? (pointing at tube segment)". However, what was unanticipated was how the family embedded academic content in ways that connected with everyday life, such as when Cam picked up a silver pen to show his mother, Grandmother said with great excitement and a slowness of speech to accentuate 'silver' and 'Statesman', "Oh look at this, this is *silver* Mum . . . same colour as Aunty Sam's *Statesman* [car]." In the latter example, Grandmother, in the process of keenly observing the play practices of the children, appeared to amplify educational content in the knowledge of known social contexts, such as the colour of the aunt's car.

In all the observations, except the homework routine, the moments of embedded or explicit teaching of academic content tended to be sprinkled among regular social interactions between adults and children during play, and they were usually personally oriented. For example, when Mandy picked up a plastic letter 'M' from a bucket of shapes and letters, Grandmother said in an amplified manner to her, "M for Mandy." This resulted in Mandy studying the letter more closely. Similarly, when Grandmother discussed the colour of Aunt Sam's Statesman in the context of a silver pen, Mandy, who was standing at the periphery of Cam, Mother, and Grandmother, moved closer to take a look at the pen, suggesting she was paying attention to the colour, possibly because of the amplified nature of Grandmother's social and tonal interactions.

Even though a question-and-answer format was observed in the family, what was more common was how discrete abstracted academic concepts (colour, letters, and numbers) appeared to be ascribed with personal meaning during family play episodes, such as when Grandmother asked Cam to look at the numbers on the phone and to read them with her, and the way in which all the adults associated letters with a representation of particular child (for Mandy, Cam, and Alex) or as representation of a literacy practice (for Jason).

Structuring Collective Imaginary Situations

In line with Vygotsky's conception of play as the introduction of an imaginary situation, where actions and objects are given a new sense, the family regularly initiated imaginary play. In the example that follows, also reported in

Hedegaard and Fleer (2013), Grandmother, Mother, Father, and Uncle Matthew, along with the four children, are playing in the front yard with a football. The activity begins with Father and Uncle Matthew kicking the ball across the yard, while the rest of the family is still inside the house. As the children put on their shoes and join the adults, they are invited into the play by being given an opportunity to return a kicked ball. Mother and Grandmother initially stand near the door following the kicking actions, and later they both join the game.

In the beginning, it is Grandmother who introduces the imaginary situation of a football game by narrating the play. The narration begins by making comments about how the game is being played by the family in the front yard, but as the play continues over 20 minutes, she takes on the language of a football commentator. For instance, an example of the transition from playing at kicking the ball to an imaginary football game with rules and roles is shown below:

> Kicking a football:
> Grandmother says, "It is Jason's turn now. Let him have a go Mandy" [of kicking the ball] ...
> Football game:
> ... Uncle Matthew moves the ball around his body, as though pirouetting it away from Jason to pretend to avoid a tackle. Jason looks on in surprise. Uncle Matthew then passes the football to Jason. Everyone laughs. Jason begins running with the ball and drops it. Mother quickly pounces on the ball, and as she does, she spins Jason around in a gentle tackle.
> The father is in the football game, and calls out in an excited tone, "Quick Jason", to encourage him to keep chasing the ball. Jason holds the ball firmly as his mother pulls him around, while he and the other family members laugh. Grandmother says with umpiring authority, "Free kick to Jason", suggesting that the tackle by Mother went on for too long.

Through Grandmother's commentary and the pretence of Mother in an opposing team and Father as a team member, it is observed that the stationary kicking actions across the yard turn into an imaginary football game. In the football game the kicking of the ball is done on the run in the context of being tackled. In this imaginary situation, the play actions of the children change because of the way the adults have signalled pretence – through the commentary (language) and the exaggerated but gentle tackles (actions). The family is no longer standing in a stationary manner kicking a ball, but rather they are in constant motion chasing the football or tackling each other as part of the rules of the football game. It is now an imaginary play situation as defined by Vygotsky (1966).

Structuring Play to Support Multiple Social Situations of Development in a Family

In a deeper analysis, which goes beyond Hedegaard and Fleer (2013) and what was discussed earlier, it was found that pretence was structured differently for different children in the family. In the example of the football game, it was noted that although the adults change their actions in pretence (language and actions), they do so by structuring their actions in relation to each child based on the social situation of development of each child. This concept was first introduced by Vygotsky (1994) to capture how in a family each child can experience the same environment differently based on his or her social situation of development. This concept is relevant for analysis of the family play practices of this study, because it helps theorize the relationship that exists between the children and their social and material environment (e.g., football play). Vygotsky did not use social situation of development to discuss play, but rather drew on the example of how family speech that surrounds a child can be identical at 6 months, 18 months, and 3 and a half years (number of words heard, characteristics of speech, size of vocabulary, correct usage and grammar, and literary quality and style), but the child's understanding of what is said takes on a different meaning depending on whether the child understands speech or not.

Through drawing on the concept of social situation of development for analyzing how the families structured the play practices, it became possible to see the place of play and learning in the home for the development of Mandy and Jason.

> In relation to Jason:
> Uncle Matthew says, "Here I come", as he runs after Jason, and gently grabs the back of his shoulders. Jason manages to free himself, by shrugging him off, and then quickly and skillfully kicks the ball across the yard. Grandmother calls out "Good kick!"
> In relation to Mandy:
> Uncle Matthew says, "Here I come", as he stamps his feet loudly behind her, in an exaggerated manner, but in very small steps, to signal to her that he is behind her. Mandy continues to hold the ball (rather than kick it) and runs across the yard dropping it as she encounters Jason running toward her.

In following Mandy's perspective, it was found that the family structured the play practices in ways that allowed her to actively participate. Uncle Matthew engages in the same play practices, but modifies his actions so that he sets up the excitement of a potential tackle, both loudly, so she knows he is chasing her, and as small steps so that he cannot catch her. In addition to signalling the pretence of the potential tackle, the adults also support Mandy into entering the play practices, such as was observed regularly in relation to tackling. Overall, the practices show a slowing and a prolonging of the tackling actions. They are gentle and structured within the context of a football game, which is much faster and more forceful for the older siblings.

The imaginary play of the football match gives a dynamic context in which tackling is a key dimension of successful play. Kicking the ball across the yard to another person does not involve tackling. To enter into the play of a game of football, Mandy must be able to successfully tackle. The adults support this transition. Examining the social situation of development of each child makes this transition visible and, through this, gives greater insight into the ways in which the family structured the learning of this valued skill during the pretence of a football game. That is, by studying the relations between each child in the same family environment it was possible to better understand how adults collectively structured play and learning for their children, and through this to understand the meaning of the play practices for the children's learning and development. In sum, being in tune with each child's social situation of development means that the adults can adjust their actions in relation to how each child enters into the imaginary play situation. It also allows for a study of how the adults simultaneously manage the different developmental trajectories of each child so that they each enter into, contribute to, and become a part of the collective play.

How the Family Developed the Children's Play from Object Play to Games with Rules

Previous research involving preschool-aged children by Ugaste (2005) has shown how mothers actively instruct children in the use of board games, as one way of preparing their children for school (problem-solving, academic content, such as numeracy). However, in this study board games were not observed. Rather, in the development of play as conceptualized by Vygotsky, where children move from playing with implicit rules (e.g., role-playing a horse involves implicit rules of how to be a horse) to playing games with rules (e.g., board games or skipping games), the family appeared to structure their play practices in support of a form of collective intersubjectivity for understanding games with rules. For instance, in the collective play of football, the adults used football language to accentuate the rules of play (e.g., free kick, push in the back), including using slogans to collectively bond the family to a particular football club. This was observed after a successful kick by Alex, when Mother engaged him in a 'high five' in support of the kick as she said, "Go Hawkies" (football club).

Other higher forms of play (i.e., games with rules) were also explicitly introduced as part of the collective family play practices, as was observed during the playing of a family game of 'Wearing Dad's Gum Boots' that they had invented. In the example that follows, the explicit signalling of rules is made by the adults but also by the children. In the game, 'turn taking' is an important rule:

Wearing Dad's Gum Boots

The adults and children are all in the kitchen, standing or seated near the kitchen table. Uncle Matthew is at the computer near the kitchen table, while Grandmother and Mother sit at the table. The adults begin talking about a game of putting on boots. Jason leaves the kitchen and collects Father's gum boots from the laundry. As he lifts them, he says, "That's SO big." In the kitchen, the adults talk about the game, with Alex stating, "Mum hasn't had a turn yet of trying them on." As Jason carries the boots into the kitchen, Father asks, "Have you got them on?" Jason laughs in anticipation, as Mother says, "Take your shoes off." Alex is observing closely and says, "I am going to put them on." Father says to Jason, "You try walk'n in them." Jason then places the boots in the middle of the kitchen. He holds onto the table to steady himself, as he slides one leg into left boot, and then slides the other leg into the right boot. Both boots fully cover each leg. Jason walks in a robotic motion across the kitchen while the family members look on and laugh. Cam and Mandy rush up to him, looking into the boots. Cam asks, "Can I try them?" Jason walks back across the kitchen, while Cam and Mandy walk alongside, laughing. All the adults laugh at the spectacle.

After Jason has walked the full length of the kitchen and back, Mother says, "Alex's turn." Jason says, "You can hop!" Mandy rushes across the kitchen, stands in front of Mother, and lifts her leg, signaling she wants Mother to take off her shoe, in anticipation of having a turn. She then sits down in front of her mother, holding her leg up, and pulling at her shoe. Father takes off both shoes, and as he does, Jason says, "It's Mandy's turn." Father lifts Mandy up, and drops her legs into the boots, and walks the boots and Mandy across the kitchen. Everyone laughs.

Although Mandy does not express her wish for a turn in words, she signals her intention through strategically placing herself in front of her mother. It is not just the adults who acknowledge this, but also Jason, who explicitly states, "It's Mandy's turn." A key characteristic of playing games is following the rules, and this play practice appeared to be learned by the children during the process of playing the games. In sum, rules were embedded in the practice of 'collectively playing the game' – 'Wearing Dad's Gum Boots' play. Specific language was introduced, policed by the adults, and re-presented by the children during the practice of play, through saying, "My turn" or through the physical positioning to have a turn. Adults also participated in the game and were expected to follow the rules of the play. Although the play practices observed were not 'board games' (Ugaste, 2005), the structuring of the playful actions in the family during the game builds the foundations for higher forms of play, such as games with rules (Vygotsky, 1966).

Conclusion

In this naturalistic study, it was found that although using play for scholastic achievement was evident in the family, in the traditional sense of numeracy and literacy, what was more common was the semiotic activity of creating a collective imaginary situation. It was found that the adults regularly engaged their children in the process of changing the meaning of objects and actions to give them a new sense (e.g., football game, gum boot game, Aunt Sam's silver Statesman). In line with van Oers (1999), this finding draws attention to how families cognitively support their children at home through creating and maintaining collective imaginary situations for, and with, their children.

Additionally, even though literacy and numeracy content was introduced through a question-and-answer format, learning academic content was primarily embedded in family play, and concepts were amplified by adults to help children pay attention to them (silver, like Aunt Sam's Statesman). This finding contributes to the growing and variable body of research that seeks to understand how families structure learning in play.

Importantly, the study found that the adults and siblings appeared to be in tune with each other's development when in play. The differing social situations of development that were brought to the process of collectively playing were managed by all the adults by giving time and space for participation in relation to the social situation of development of each individual child (e.g., tackling 'threat' by Uncle Matthew was loud and with small steps). Regardless of the type of imaginary play observed over the 12 months, the play was always in motion, sometimes in slow motion due to the social situation of development of a younger child, and sometimes accelerated based on the competence of an older child. It can be speculated that the adults' close attunement to the children's social situation of development contributed to the maintenance and development of the collective play. This expands previous research into how pretence is structured, research that is primarily drawn from studies of dyads in laboratory-based settings.

Consistent with previous research of Göncü et al. (2007), this study found that play appeared to be a learned social practice that the family seemed to value highly. It was shown that games with rules as a higher form of play were collectively introduced, supported, and narrated, with the discourse of rules being embedded into the practices and language of the play (e.g., "My turn"). That is, the children learned about games with rules by playing with each other and with the adults. It was found that the adults either were embedded in the play as players or were in close proximity to the children's play. Both practices enabled adults to expand the play through their direct or indirect roles inside the play. What was different from previous research was that the adults genuinely played with their children, rather than pretending to be a player or a novice.

The conclusions drawn from this in-depth study, conducted over 12 months, are limited because they draw on the play practices of only one low-income family living in Melbourne, Australia. However, it can be argued that the family's repertoires of signs and the corresponding meaning systems appeared to be culturally situated in valued Australian practices. For instance, in Melbourne, football and many other forms of sport are valued community practices. This family appeared to teach specific play practices to their children so as to understand and engage in sport, as a valued form of cultural practice for the family. How the family assigned meaning to the play practice appeared to be culturally aligned with the community value of playing or supporting sport. Consequently, the findings of this study make a contribution to understanding other forms of cultural expressions of play.

References

Cameron, C. A., Hancock, R., Pinto, G., Gamannossi, B. A., & Tapanya, S. (2011). Domestic play collaborations in diverse family contexts. *Australasian Journal of Early Childhood, 36*(4), 78–85.

Chang, P.-Y. (2015). Understanding Taiwanese children's play via constructing and re-constructing: A prospective vision. In J. L. Roopnarine, M. Patte, J. E. Johnson, & D. Kuschner (Eds.), *International perspective on children's play* (pp. 119–133). London: Open University Press/McGraw Hill.

Colliver, Y. (2016). Mothers' perspectives on learning through play in the home. *Australasian Journal of Early Childhood, 41*(1), 4–12.

Elkonin, D. B. (2005). On the historical origin of role play. *Journal of Russian and East European Psychology, 43*(1), 49–89.

Fasoli, A. D. (2014). To play or not to play: Diverse motives for Latino and Euro-American parent–child play in a museum. *Infant and Child Development, 23* (6), 605–621.

Fleer, M. (2010). *Early learning and development: Cultural-historical concepts in play.* Cambridge: Cambridge University Press.

Gaskins, A., Haight, W., & Lancy, D. F. (2007). The cultural construction of play. In A. Göncü & S. Gaskins (Eds.), *Play and development: Evolutionary, sociocultural and functional perspectives* (pp. 179–202). New York: Lawrence Erlbaum Associates.

Gaskins, S. (2015). Yucatec Mayan children's play. In J. L. Roopnarine, M. Patte, J. E. Johnson, & D. Kuschner (Eds.), *International perspective on children's play* (pp. 11–21). London: Open University Press/McGraw Hill.

Göncü, A., Jain, J., & Tuermer, U. (2007). Children's play as cultural interpretation. In A. Göncü & S. Gaskins (Eds.), *Play and development: Evolutionary, sociocultural and functional perspectives* (pp. 155–178). New York: Lawrence Erlbaum Associates.

Haight, W. L., & Miller, P. J. (1993). *Pretending at home.* Albany: State University of New York Press.

Hedegaard, M., & Fleer, M. (2013). *Play, learning and children's development: Everyday life in families and transition to school.* New York: Cambridge University Press.

Lancy, D. F. (1996). *Playing on the mother-ground: Cultural routines for children's development.* New York: Guilford Press.

Li, L. (2012). How do immigrant parents support preschoolers' bilingual heritage language development in a role-play context? *Australian Journal of Early Childhood, 37*(1), 142–151.

Lillard, A. S. (2007). Guided participation: How mothers structure and children understand pretend play. In A. Göncü & S. Gaskins (Eds.), *Play and development: Evolutionary, sociocultural and functional perspectives* (pp. 131–154). New York: Lawrence Erlbaum Associates.

Lillard, A. S. (2011). Mother–child fantasy play. In A. D. Pellegrini (Ed.), *The Oxford handbook of the development of play* (pp. 284–295). Oxford: Oxford University Press.

Lillard, A. S., Lerner, M. D., Hopkins, E. J., Dore, R. A., Smith, E. D., & Palmquist, C. M. (2012). The impact of pretend play on children's development: A review of the evidence. *Psychological Bulletin, 139*(1), 1–34.

Mathur, S. (2015). The ecology of play among young children of Mexican origin and seasonal farmworkers. In J. L. Roopnarine, M. Patte, J. E. Johnson, & D. Kuschner (Eds.), *International perspective on children's play* (pp. 49–61). London: Open University Press/McGraw Hill.

Roopnarine, J. L. (2011). Cultural variations in beliefs about play, parents–child play, and children's play: Meaning for childhood development. In A. D. Pellegrini (Ed.), *The Oxford handbook of the development of play* (pp. 19–37). Oxford: Oxford University Press.

Roopnarine, J. L. (2015). Play as culturally situated: Diverse perspectives on its meaning and significance. In J. L. Roopnarine, M. Patte, J. E. Johnson, & D. Kuschner (Eds.), *International perspective on children's play* (pp. 1–7). London: Open University Press/McGraw Hill.

Roopnarine, J. L., Patte, M. M., Johnson, J. E., & Kuschner, D. (Eds.) (2015). *International perspective on children's play*, London: Open University Press/McGraw Hill.

Scales, B., Almy, M., Nicolopoulou, A., & Ervin-Trip, S. (Eds.) (1991). *Play and the social context of development in early care and education.* New York: Columbia University, Teachers College.

Sikder, S. (2015). Social situation of development: Parents' perspectives on infants-toddlers' concept formation in science. *Early Child Development and Care, 185*(10), 1658–1677.

Sutton-Smith, B. (1986). *Toys as culture.* New York: Gardener Press.

Sutton-Smith, B. (1997). *The ambiguity of play.* Cambridge, MA: Harvard University Press.

Sutton-Smith, B., & Brice-Heath, S. (1981). Paradigms of pretense. *Quarterly Newsletter of the Laboratory of Comparative Human Cognition, 3*(3), 41–45.

Tamis-LeMonda, C. S., Nga-Lam Sze, I., Ng, F. F.-Y., Kahana-Kalman, R., & Yoshikawa, H. (2013). Maternal teaching during play with four-year-olds: Variation by ethnicity and family resources. *Merrill-Palmer Quarterly, 59*(3), 361–398.

Ugaste, A. (2005). The child's play world at home and the mother's role in the play. PhD thesis, University of Jyväskylä.

van Oers, B. (1999). Teaching opportunities in play. In M. Hedegaard & J. Lompscher (Eds.), *Learning activity and development* (pp. 268–289). Aarhus, Denmark: Aarhus University Press.

Vygotsky, L. S. (1966). Play and its role in the mental development of the child. *Voprosy Psikhologii, 12,* 62–76.

Vygotsky, L. S. (1994). The problem of the environment. In R. van der Veer & J. Valsiner (Eds.), *The Vygotsky reader* (pp. 338–354). Cambridge: Blackwell.

Wong, P. L., & Fleer, M. (2012). A cultural-historical study of how children from Hong Kong immigrant families develop a learning motive within everyday family practices in Australia. *Mind Culture and Activity*, *19*(2), 107–126.

24 Leading Children in Their "Leading Activity"

A Vygotskian Approach to Play

Elena Bodrova, Deborah J. Leong, Carrie Germeroth, and Crystal Day-Hess

In the presence of increasing academic demands for early childhood classrooms, fewer hours are devoted to play. Make-believe play is a critical element of childhood and a means for children to communicate, learn, and develop new skills. Theoretical accounts of play have placed emphasis on the importance of play to achieving social and academic competencies; however, there is little known about the levels of play that are required to deliver its benefits. In this chapter we examine the basic principles of Vygotskian and post-Vygotskian theories of play to identify the characteristics that differentiate between mature and immature make-believe play. First, we briefly introduce the importance of play and the current treatment of play in early childhood classrooms in the United States. Then, we examine the main principles of the Vygotskian/post-Vygotskian approach to play, focusing on the idea of play as a leading activity for children of preschool and kindergarten age. Finally, we introduce several applications of Vygotskian theory, an observational tool we have developed to assess the components of make-believe play as defined by Vygotsky, and an instructional approach to support researchers and practitioners interested in supporting make-believe play.

The Importance of Play

Research consistently supports that play is an important part of children's development and learning. It establishes the foundations of later academic learning in areas such as literacy, science, social studies, and mathematics and promotes executive functioning skills that assist with emotional regulation, planning, and memory (e.g., Bergen, 2002; Bodrova & Leong, 2007; Bruner, 1976; Christie & Roskos, 2006; Diamond et al., 2007; Leslie, 1987; Lyytinen et al., 1999; McCune, 1995; Roskos & Neuman, 1998). In the United States, play is included in nearly all (41) states' early learning standards, typically in the domain of social-emotional development. However, the extent to which it is covered varies in terms of breadth and depth, with only a handful of states (six) devoting an entire domain to the development of play in young children.

Many kinds of play are important in the early childhood classroom. From a Vygotskian point of view, however, make-believe play is the most important due to its cognitive and social-emotional benefits for pre-schoolers (Vygotsky, 1967). Make-believe play is the leading activity for children at this age, meaning that it offers a unique opportunity for all children to operate in ways that push their individual "developmental edge" when practiced at a mature level (Elkonin, 1977, 1978). Although it may seem obvious, a somewhat technical definition of mature make-believe play is called for as we begin this discussion. By mature make-believe play, we mean the kinds of play in which children create imaginary situations, take on explicit roles (using the language and rules of the roles), and use objects symbolically (Bodrova & Leong, 2011; Elkonin, 1978). According to Vygotskians, make-believe play, when it reaches its mature state, fosters self-regulation and provides the basis for other activities or interactions that in turn foster the learning of symbolic and emotional thinking, oral language, and the beginnings of literacy.

Current State of Play in US Preschools

Despite the research on play and its inclusion in state early learning standards, teacher preparation programs continue to vary widely in their breadth of coverage for teaching and reinforcing play. While play is repeatedly referenced as a gold standard for learning and development in young children, its inclusion in teacher preparation program requirements is not always explicit. Furthermore, Vu and colleagues (2015) emphasize a lack of professional development in play – "while early childhood educators have been shown to play an important role in developing play situations that can stimulate learning, there is little professional preparation that specifically addresses this issue" (p. 446). They further suggest teachers are ill-prepared to incorporate play within the classroom. Finally, play is often missing from early childhood classrooms due to increasing demands teachers feel to prepare young learners for academic assessments. In one study, Ranz-Smith (2007) found that common values existed between teachers about play, but the transition into providing opportunities for it in their classrooms was scarce due to concerns about academic achievement as measured by standardized assessments. Thus, while research and state standards that guide teachers support the importance of including play in early childhood, the type of play that is most beneficial is ill-defined and infrequently found in pedagogy.

Vygotsky and Play

The Vygotskian quote that in play, the child is "a head taller than himself" has been known by now for almost half a century and has been used and overused for almost this long. Similar to another overused description of play being "a child's work", Vygotsky's quote is now applied to all kinds of play or playful behaviours children can possibly engage in. However, the definition of play in Vygotsky's and post-Vygotskian tradition is very specific and so is the theory that describes the relationship between play and the development of young children.

Play and Its Role in the Mental Development of the Child: Lev Vygotsky's Views

In his lecture 'Play and Its Role in the Mental Development of the Child' (delivered in 1934 and published more than 30 years later), Vygotsky examined different components of play and the way they affect the young child's emerging mental functions and concluded that play "is not the predominant form of activity, but is, in a certain sense, the leading source of development in preschool years" (1967, p. 6). When analyzing play into its components, Vygotsky limited the scope of play to the dramatic or make-believe play typical of pre-schoolers and children of primary school age. Thus, Vygotsky's definition of play does not include many kinds of other activities such as movement activities, object manipulations, and explorations that were (and still are) referred to as 'play' by most educators and non-educators. Make-believe play, according to Vygotsky, has three components, as children (1) create an imaginary situation, (2) take on and act out roles, and (3) follow a set of rules determined by specific roles.

While imaginary situations and roles are often considered defining features of make-believe play, the very idea that play is not totally spontaneous but is instead contingent on players abiding by a set of rules may sound completely counterintuitive. However,

> whenever there is an imaginary situation in play, there are rules – not rules that are formulated in advance and change during the course of the game, but rules stemming from the imaginary situation ... In play the child is free. But this is an illusory freedom. (Vygotsky, 1967, p. 10)

Vygotsky saw all three components of play – imaginary situation, roles, and rules – as having an important role in the formation of the child's mind, in the development of children's abstract thinking, and in the development of conscious and voluntary behaviours – critical neo-formations of early childhood.

Abstract Thought, Symbolic Representation, and Imagination. In play, children act in accordance with internal ideas rather than with external reality. In other words, play requires the substitution of one object for another, requiring the child to begin to separate the meaning or idea of the object from the object itself (Berk, 1994). When a child uses a block as a phone, for example, the idea of 'phone-ness' becomes separated from the actual phone. If the block is made to act like a phone, then it can stand for that phone. In this way, role-playing in an imaginary situation requires children to carry on two types of actions simultaneously – external and internal. In play, these internal actions – 'operations on the meanings' – are still dependent on the external operations on the objects. However, the very emergence of the internal actions signals the beginning of a child's transition from the earlier forms of thought processes – sensory-motor and visual-representational – to more advanced abstract thought. Thus, make-believe play prepares the foundation for two higher mental functions – symbolic thinking and imagination. Contrary to popular views, Vygotsky saw imagination not as a prerequisite of play but rather as its outgrowth:

> The old adage that children's play is imagination in action can be reversed: we can say that imagination in adolescents and schoolchildren is play without action.   (Vygotsky, 1978, p. 93)

The idea that make-believe play supports cognitive development by virtue of supporting the development of abstract, symbolic thought was first outlined by Vygotsky (1967) and then further developed by his student Daniil Elkonin (1978), who extended it beyond the symbolism of children's use of props and toys to include the symbolic nature of role-playing. According to Elkonin, at the centre of make-believe play is the role that a child acts out. Elkonin proposed that children do not act out the exact behaviours of the role they are acting out, but rather they act out a synopsis of those actions. They, in fact, generate a model of reality or construct their own version – something that requires symbolic generalization. Children do not act out everything they have seen 'mommy' or 'daddy' do at home, but distil the essence of mommy-hood and daddy-hood. Elkonin concludes that in make-believe play, children learn to model reality in two different ways: when they use objects symbolically and when they act out the distilled symbolic representation of the role in the pretend scenario. In both instances, the use of symbols is first supported by toys and props and later is communicated to play partners by the means of words and gestures. Make-believe play reflects the universal path of cognitive development from concrete, object-oriented thinking and action to abstract mental action (Elkonin, 1978).

Intentional, Self-Regulated Behaviour. Another way make-believe play contributes to child development is by promoting intentional behaviour. It becomes possible because of the inherent relationship that exists between roles children play and rules they need to follow when playing these roles. For pre-schoolers, play becomes the first activity where children are driven not by the need for instant gratification, prevalent at this age, but instead by the need to suppress their immediate impulses. In play

> a child experiences subordination to a rule in the renunciation of something he wants, but here subordination to a rule and renunciation of acting on immediate impulse are the means to maximum pleasure.   (Vygotsky, 1967, p. 14)

The role of play in supporting the development of self-regulation was also extended by Elkonin beyond Vygotsky's insight about children voluntarily abiding by the rules when playing. The power of play to support the development of intentional behaviours was attributed by Elkonin to several factors. First, to sustain play, children have to voluntarily follow the rules that dictate which actions are and are not consistent with each specific role. They must act deliberately, inhibiting behaviour that is not part of that specific role. Second, to agree on the details of a play scenario or on the specific use of play props, children need to spend some time prior to play in discussing their future actions – essentially planning their play. This play planning is the precursor to reflective thinking, another aspect of self-regulatory behaviour. Finally, in mature play of older pre-schoolers, the roles children play are mostly the roles of adults (doctors, drivers, chefs, etc.) engaged in socially desirable behaviours. By imitating these behaviours in play, children learn to adjust their actions to conform to the norms associated with the behaviours of these role models, therefore practicing planning, self-monitoring, and reflection essential for intentional behaviour (Elkonin, 1978).

Summarizing multiple ways make-believe play impacts child development, Vygotsky concludes:

> The play–development relationship can be compared with the instruction–development relationship, but play provides a background for changes in needs and in consciousness of a much wider nature. (Vygotsky, 1967, p. 16)

To understand the value Vygotsky assigned to play in child development, it is important to view its place in the broader context of Vygotsky's view of human ontogenesis as characterized by development of higher mental functions – symbolically mediated intentional behaviours (Vygotsky, 1997). Since play provides the optimal context for developing both critical aspects of higher mental functions – mastery of cultural signs and symbols and the development of intentionality – it was considered by Vygotsky to be the leading activity of modern day pre-schoolers.

Make-Believe Play as a "Leading Activity"

Vygotsky and his students found that certain types of activities offered unique opportunities for all children to function at the highest levels of their zone of proximal development (ZPD) (Bodrova & Leong, 2007; Karpov, 2005). These so-called leading activities vary by age and provide *all* children of the specified age the greatest opportunity to grow toward their most important developmental accomplishments (Elkonin, 1977; Leont'ev, 1978). Speaking of play as "not the predominant feature of childhood but [as] a leading factor in development", Vygotsky (1967, p. 6) uses the term "leading activity" more as a metaphor than as a theoretical construct.

Post-Vygotskians Alexei Leont'ev (1981) and Daniil Elkonin (1977) elaborated on this idea of Vygotsky's by specifying the distinct features of the leading activities characteristic of children at different ages. Leont'ev (1978, 1981) used the concept of *leading activity* to specify the types of interactions between the child and the social environment that lead to achievement of the developmental accomplishments (he called these "neo-formations") in one period of life and that will prepare him for the next period.

Elkonin further extended the Vygotskian-based theory of child development by proposing a *theory of stages* determined by the changes in the leading activities in which children engage. Elkonin views childhood as determined by the social-cultural context and by a child's role in it as expressed through the child's engagement in leading activity. Consistent with Vygotsky's principle of effective teaching being the one that aims at a child's ZPD, Elkonin defines the goal of education as promoting developmental accomplishments at each age by supporting the leading activity specific to that age.

According to Elkonin, dramatic (make-believe) play is the leading activity of preschool- and kindergarten-aged children (ages 3–6) raised in modern industrial and post-industrial societies. In Elkonin's theory of periods in child development, play is placed on the continuum of leading activities following the adult-mediated, object-oriented activity of toddlers and followed by the learning activity of primary school–aged children (Elkonin, 1977). While some elements of play emerge in infancy and toddlerhood, there are other kinds of leading activities that drive child development in these periods (Elkonin, 1977; Karpov, 2005). In a thorough analysis of play, Elkonin emphasized the importance of play for children's mastery of social interactions, for their cognitive development, and for the development of self-regulation. He identified the essential characteristics that make make-believe play the leading activity of pre-schoolers as the roles children play, symbolic play actions, interactions with play partners, and the rules that govern the play. Thus, only play with a specific set of features is the kind of make-believe play granted the status of leading activity. Other play-like behaviours (such as building with blocks or exploring materials and objects) are assigned secondary, albeit important, roles (Elkonin, 1978).

Creating a Zone of Proximal Development. Leading activities are the optimal activities for development at any particular age period. Although children can and do learn from other activities within their ZPD, leading activities are the most beneficial. Elkonin's theory of play has deepened Vygotsky's ideas about play creating a child's ZPD by proposing the mechanisms that enable children to function in play "a head taller than themselves". One of the ways Elkonin's students were able to demonstrate the unique role of play in the development of higher mental functions was through a series of experiments that compared children's performance on various tasks in play and non-play situations. For example, Manuilenko (1975) found higher levels of self-regulation of children's physical behaviours in play than in non-play contexts.

In her experiments, when asked to act as a 'lookout', children remained at their posts and did not move for a longer period of time than when the experimenter asked them to stand still in a laboratory condition (a mean 12 minutes vs. 4 minutes). Notably, the gap between play and non-play performance was most dramatic in 5-year-old children who were assumed to be at the peak of mature play. At the same time, this gap was virtually non-existent both for 3-year-old children, who had not yet developed advanced forms of play, and in 7-year-old children, who no longer needed the support of play to regulate their behaviours.

In another study, Istomina (1977) compared the number of words children could deliberately remember during a make-believe play session involving a grocery store with the number of words they could remember in a typical laboratory experiment. In both situations, children were given a list of unrelated words to remember. In the make-believe play situation, the words were presented as the items on a "shopping list" to use in a pretend grocery store. In the laboratory experiment, the instructions were simply to memorize the words. Istomina found that pre-schoolers remembered more items in the make-believe play condition and were functioning at a level that older children could demonstrate in the non-play condition that was similar to a typical school task. This study produced a similar pattern of results for the three age groups as found in Manuilenko's study: no difference between play and non-play situations for 3- and 7-year-olds compared with substantial difference for 5-year-olds.

These findings support Vygotsky's view that play "is the source of development and creates the zone of proximal development" (Vygotsky, 1967, p. 16), further demonstrating that new developmental accomplishments do become apparent in play far earlier than they do in other activities.

Mature Play/Levels of Play

Levels of Make-Believe Play: From Isolated Pretend Episodes to Mature Make-Believe Play

With such an important role attributed to make-believe play in child development, it is important to determine if there is a certain level of play that needs to be reached in order for it to be beneficial. Elaborating on Vygotsky's insights on the nature of play, Elkonin (1978, 2005) introduced the idea of *mature* play, emphasizing that only this kind of play can be a source of development in early childhood. Elkonin defined *mature* (he used such terms as *advanced* or *fully developed*) play as a "unique form of children's activity, the subject of which is the adult – his work and the system of his relationships with others" (Elkonin 2005a, p. 19), thus distinguishing this form of play from other playful activities in which children engage. Although Vygotsky himself never used the terms *mature* or *advanced*, the play vignettes in his writings seem to describe play that is fairly advanced. Based on the work of Vygotsky and Elkonin, as well as the work of their students, it is possible to identify several components of mature play (Bodrova & Leong, 2007).

First, mature play is characterized by the child's use of object-substitutes that may bear very little if any resemblance to the objects they symbolize: they use a pipe cleaner as a stethoscope or a box as a boat – it only matters that these substitutes can perform the same function as the object-prototype. As play continues to advance, these object-substitutes eventually become unnecessary as most of the substitution takes place as the child uses gestures or words to describe imaginary objects.

The second characteristic of mature play is the child's ability to take on and sustain a specific role by consistently engaging in pretend actions, speech, and interactions that fit this particular character. The more mature the play, the richer are the roles and the more complex are the relationships between them. Another sign of mature play is the child's ability to follow the rules associated with the pretend scenario in general (playing restaurant vs. playing school) and with a chosen character in particular (playing a chef vs. playing a teacher).

Yet another characteristic of mature play is a high quality of play scenarios that often integrate many themes and span the time of several days or even weeks. Finally, as play becomes more mature, children progress from rudimentary planning followed by extended acting out to extended planning followed by rudimentary acting out. Elkonin argues that "the more general and abbreviated the actions in play, the more deeply they reflect the meaning, goal, and system of relationships in the adult activity that is being recreated" (2005b, p. 40).

In his seminal monograph, *Psychology of Play* (1978), Elkonin described development of each of the major aspects of play first recognized by Vygotsky: imaginary situation, roles, and rules. He then identified four levels of play – from least mature to the most mature – according to how well these aspects are developed.

Level 1. The main contents of play are *actions with objects* directed at the play partner. For example, these can be the actions of a 'teacher' or a 'mother' directed at 'children' as the children are eating lunch. In playing the role of a 'teacher' or a 'mother', the child focuses on the action of 'serving lunch to someone'. The order in which the lunch is served as well as the particular kind of food served by the 'teacher' or the 'mother' is not important. The actions are stereotypical and consist of repetitive motions, e.g., when playing 'dinner', children follow the same routine as they serve salad, main dish, and dessert. The entire script of 'eating dinner' is limited to the actions of serving and eating with no other actions preceding or following these (e.g., setting the table, washing hands). There seems to be no logical order in how the actions are performed. If one child acts inconsistently with how this script unfolds in real life (e.g., serves dessert first), other children do not object.

The roles exist, but they are determined by the nature of the actions instead of determining the actions. As a rule, children do not name the roles they play, nor do they assign themselves the names of people whose role they are playing.

Level 2. Actions with objects remain the main content of play similar to level 1. However, at this level, it is important for the play actions to accurately reflect the structure and sequence of actions as they unfold in real life. When one of the players does not follow the 'real life' sequence of the actions (e.g., a 'doctor' first puts the 'patient's' arm in a cast and then takes an X-ray), the other players do not accept these actions (for example, they do not imitate the incorrect actions in their own play, and if asked if this is the way doctors do it, they may say no), but they do not argue with the player, neither do they explain what was done wrong.

Children label the roles they play. For a child, to play a role means to perform actions associated with this role; this scope of actions is expanded compared with level 1.

Level 3. The main focus of play is now the role and the actions determined by this role; special actions emerge that signal the relationships between the players. An example of such an action would be when a child addresses another child in a way that is determined by the role this child is playing. For example, a 'customer' would ask the 'waiter' to bring a 'kid's meal' for her baby. The roles are distinct and well defined. Children name the roles they will play before the play starts. The roles determine and direct the children's behaviour.

The nature of actions and their logic are determined by the role the child plays. The actions become more varied: for example, the 'mother' does not just put her baby to bed, but also gives him a bath, reads a bedtime story, etc. A special kind of *role speech* emerges when one player talks to another one, using vocabulary, intonation, and register in accordance with the specific roles both of them are playing. Sometimes, non-role-related speech is used as well that reflects the relationships between children themselves and not the roles they play.

If a child acts in a way inconsistent with the real-life logic of actions, other children object by saying, "You're not supposed to do that." The rules are being defined that govern the players' actions. At this point, children are usually better in monitoring their friends' compliance with the rules than their own. When corrected, children treat their mistakes seriously and try to fix them and to explain why they broke the rule.

Level 4. The main content of play is now carrying out actions associated with the relationships between the roles children play. These actions are distinct from other actions associated with playing a role. For example, the relationship between a 'father' and a 'child' is associated with the 'father' being in charge, which is manifested in the way he addresses the 'child' (e.g., "You have to eat your vegetables or you will get no dessert" or "One more time I see you teasing your sister and you will go to your room"). On the other hand, the relationship between the 'doctor' and the 'nurse' is the one of collaboration.

At this level, the roles are well defined. A child playing a role acts in the manner consistent with this role throughout the entire duration of play. The 'role-related speech' is consistent with the role played by the child who uses it, as well as with the role of the child to whom this speech is addressed. The sequence of actions is also well defined and consistent with the logic of these actions in real life. The actions are varied and accurately represent the variety of actions of the person whose role the child plays. The rules that children follow are well defined, with children using the real-life rules as the reference. The actions directed at different players are well defined and distinct. Children object when someone does not follow the logic of actions or breaks the rule. Children go beyond stating "You're not supposed to do this" but refer to the reason for this rule in real life.

Thus, play according to Elkonin starts with the object-centred role-play of 2- and 3-year-olds (level 1) where object-oriented actions determine their choice of roles, and evolves gradually to become the elaborate relationship-centred play of kindergarten-aged children (level 4) characterized by well-defined roles and children's awareness of the reasons behind the rules they adopt. The ability to follow rules in play rather than submit to one's immediate desires seems to start appearing at level 2 but is not fully developed until level 4. Combined with the changes in the use of play props and in the relationships between play roles and play actions, this evolution of play rules allows us to consider level 4 the level of fully developed or *mature* play. Although there is a relationship between children's age and the level of play, with older children being able to engage in more mature play, not all children reach the highest level of play by the end of their kindergarten year.

Assessing Mature Make-Believe Play

Although classroom-based make-believe play interventions present a promising future direction for play research, extant investigations of make-believe play have been complicated by the difficulty of identifying and evaluating make-believe play behaviours. Thus, development of a reliable, classroom-based measure of make-believe play will benefit both research and practice. First, robust observational instruments will allow us to better measure intervention effects on mature play and the extent to which high-quality play may produce social, self-regulatory, and academic benefits in children. Second, such an assessment can be used to determine how the quality of play might be improved in early childhood classrooms, yielding benefits to classroom practice, where play is increasingly used to meet subject-specific instructional objectives.

In the absence of a tool that can effectively measure make-believe play, and in particular the type of mature make-believe play that may have the greatest developmental impacts, we cannot empirically determine if play does have educational value and, if so, its nature and extent. A review of current play assessments clarifies the weaknesses of the existing measures and illuminates the range of items intended to determine the development of the pretend play elements or domains (Germeroth et al., 2013). None of the measures developed thus far has proven to provide a reliable, valid, and complete picture of development across the spectrum and within all subdomains of pretend play, as defined by the key elements of mature play described by Vygotskian theory. Many play measures are not conducted in an authentic context (e.g., in many measures, the teacher completes measure, child plays alone or with assessor outside the classroom), and no existing measure of pre-schoolers' play takes into consideration both child and teacher dimensions.

Mature Play Observation Tool. To address the need for a measure of mature make-believe play that focuses on make-believe play as defined by Vygotsky and throughout this chapter *and* that focuses on *both* children's behaviour and the role of the teacher in supporting this type of play, the Mature Play Observation Tool (MPOT) was developed (Germeroth et al., 2013). The MPOT is based on Vygotsky's definition of make-believe play and his emphasis on the social context of play, combined with Elkonin's definition and levels of *mature* make-believe play. Importantly, the MPOT contains two dimensions: one capturing child actions and behaviours and one capturing teacher behaviours and supports for make-believe play (Table 24.1). Each dimension includes various components that define mature make-believe play.

Table 24.1 *Mature play observation tool descriptions*

Dimension	Component	Behaviours and characteristics
Child	Child-created props	The extent to which props, real or symbolic, support children's role-play within a specific play scenario
	Child meta-play	Children's ability to plan and/or discuss their play scenario and their role within it
	Play interaction	The level of social interaction between children in the play scenario: alone, parallel, associative, cooperative
	Children's role-playing	The extent to which children purposefully maintain their decided roles during the play scenario
	Child role speech and communication	The language and gestures used in the play scenario that are consistent with children's roles
Teacher	Centre management	Systems for managing centre choice/rotations and child behaviour within the centre as needed
	Planned play time	The amount of uninterrupted time planned, structured pretend play takes place
	Teacher intervention	The ways that teachers interact with children to scaffold the play scenario

The MPOT is designed to be a low-inference, four-point scale anchored with specific instructional behaviours and characteristics.

An evaluation of the MPOT was conducted as part of a larger intervention study examining effects of a math- and play-based intervention, relative to an active control condition (a math-only intervention) and a standard classroom context (the business-as-usual condition). The study was implemented as a three-armed cluster randomized control trial, which included measures of children's self-regulation, math skills, and emergent literacy skills. The MPOT was shown to be a reliable and valid measure of make-believe play. Further, both child and adult dimensions, and the overall MPOT scores, were found to have moderate correlations with various self-regulation, math, and literacy outcome measures.

Importance of Social Context in the Development of Mature Levels of Play

Consistent with the main tenets of the cultural-historical approach, Vygotsky and Elkonin viewed make-believe play not as a spontaneous activity inherent to early childhood but rather as an outgrowth of specific interactions young children have with their older peers and adults. When these interactions are absent or lacking in quality, even older pre-schoolers may not rise to the level of mature play described above, but instead continue to engage in immature play similar to that often observed in toddlers. Summarizing results of multiple studies that had focused on adults' scaffolding of pre-schoolers' make-believe play, Elkonin concluded that "play on the threshold of the preschool years does not develop spontaneously, but forms under the influence of child-rearing" (2005a, p. 18). This is why for play to become a truly "leading activity" that drives child development forward, children need to engage in specific interactions with adults who would lead children in their leading activity.

The evidence has been accumulating that play that exists in many of today's early childhood classrooms across the world does not always fit the definition of mature play (Gudareva, 2005; Levin, 2008). Even 5- and 6-year-old children who, according to Vygotsky and Elkonin, should be at the peak of their play performance often display signs of immature play that is more typical for toddlers and younger pre-schoolers: playing only with realistic props, enacting play scenarios that are stereotypical and primitive, and displaying a repertoire of themes and roles that is rather limited (Miller & Almon, 2009; Smirnova & Gudareva, 2004). Children who come to preschool with some play skills often do not acquire new skills by the end of the year or even regress to less mature play (Farran & Son-Yarbrough, 2001).

With the main elements – imaginary situation, roles, and rules – under-developed, this "immature" play cannot serve as a source of child development or create a zone of proximal development. Evidence for this was demonstrated in a Russian study replicating Manuilenko's experiment (Elkonin, 1978), described earlier. The researchers found that demonstrating superior self-regulation in play, a common characteristic of past generations of preschool children, is no longer the case (Smirnova & Gudareva, 2004). In addition, the ability to follow directions at all ages and in all conditions has generally declined: the 7-year-olds at the beginning of the twenty-first century have self-regulation levels more like those of the preschool children of the mid-twentieth century. The researchers attributed this phenomenon to the decline in both quantity and quality of play in preschool and kindergarten. This conclusion was supported by the fact that only 10% of observed 6-year-olds demonstrated a mature level of play, and 48% of the 5-year-olds demonstrated the lowest ("toddler") level of play (Gudareva, 2005).

Similar findings were obtained in another study in the United States, where the correlations between play and self-regulation were found for children playing at a high level, but not for the ones playing at a low level (Berk et al., 2006). Researchers from other countries agree that make-believe play of today's children is not simply different from the play of the past but has declined in both quality and quantity (for reviews, see Johnson et al., 2005; Karpov, 2005). This decline of play is even more troubling in light of declining self-regulation in young children, which puts them at risk of later cognitive and social-emotional problems (Blair, 2002; Blair & Razza, 2007; Raver & Knitzer, 2002; Rimm-Kaufman et al., 2000).

The decline of make-believe play is associated in play literature with such factors as an increase in adult-directed forms of children's learning and recreation, proliferation of toys and games that limit children's imagination, and safety limits set by parents and teachers on where and how children are allowed to play (Chudacoff, 2007). The most important factor, however, is the decrease in adult mediation of make-believe play (Karpov, 2005), affecting not one but all of its components.

Viewing play as a cultural-historical phenomenon, one can conclude that today's social situation almost guarantees that children may not develop mature play unless adult mediation is restored. The idea that we need to teach young children how to play is not a new one. However, until recently it has been primarily discussed in the context of special education. While children with language delays or emotional disorders were thought to benefit from play interventions, typically developing children were expected to develop play skills on their own. This approach, while valid in the past, can no longer be adopted if we want all young children to develop mature play.

The changes in the social context of young children's development do not mean that make-believe play is destined to disappear for good. These changes also create new opportunities such as the availability of high-quality preschool programs for scaffolding make-believe play, although the mechanisms for play scaffolding need to be designed to fit the new social context. For many children enrolled in centre-based early childhood education programs, their classroom is the only place where they can learn how to play. However, learning how to play in today's early childhood classroom cannot simply emulate learning to play in an informal peer group of yesterday. First of all, in the past, most play existed in multiaged groups where children had an opportunity to learn from older *play mentors*, practice their play skills with the peers of the same age, and then pass their knowledge on to the *play novices*. In today's classrooms, children are almost always grouped by age and have to interact with play partners that are as inexperienced as they are. As a result, many of the play skills that children were able to learn in the past by observing and imitating their older playmates now have to be modelled and taught directly by the teachers. In addition, unlike unstructured play of the past that often lasted for hours and days, play time in today's early childhood classroom is limited and rarely exceeds 1 or 2 hours. This means that to achieve rapid progress in the quality of play, play scaffolding in the classroom needs to be designed to strategically target its most critical components.

Instructional Supports for Make-Believe Play: Lessons from Tools of the Mind

The following suggestions for scaffolding make-believe play draw on a more than 20-year-long history of Tools of the Mind – a Vygotskian-based early childhood curriculum (Bodrova & Leong, 2017). By promoting mature make-believe play and playful learning combined with carefully planned cooperative activities, Tools of the Mind was able to increase children's levels of self-regulation/executive function and to improve their academic performance in preschool and kindergarten students (Barnett et al., 2008; Blair & Raver, 2014; Diamond et al., 2007).

Scaffolding the Use of Toys and Props in a Symbolic Way. Many of today's pre-schoolers grow up using extremely realistic toys and, as a result, have a hard time with the concept of 'pretend'. For these children, teachers model how to use props in a symbolic way, gradually expanding the repertoire of different uses for the same object. Over the period of several months, the teachers introduce more unstructured and multifunctional props while at the same time removing some overly realistic ones such as plastic fried eggs. Older pre-schoolers and kindergartners can start making their own props, while younger pre-schoolers should be shown how to make minimal changes in the existing props to change their purpose. An important part of adult scaffolding is monitoring children's language use, making sure that changes in the prop use are accompanied by the changes in prop labelling.

Scaffolding the Development of Consistent and Extended Play Scenarios. Scaffolding play scenarios has several components. First, children often lack background knowledge to build their scenarios. Even to play 'house' or 'hospital' requires knowledge of the setting, roles, and actions associated with these roles. To build this knowledge, teachers use field trips, guest speakers, books, and videos. The choice of places to take children on a field trip and the choice of books and videos is guided by Elkonin's idea of roles being the core unit of play. In other words, when field trips or books centre on objects or animals, very little of their content gets reenacted in make-believe play. For example, when children go on a traditional October field trip to a pumpkin patch, they may see pumpkins and animals in a petting zoo, but they will not see enough people doing different jobs or interacting with each other.

For a field trip to become the background for make-believe play, the teacher has to explicitly point out and show children what the people say and do and how they interact with each other. For example, on a visit to the local restaurant, the teacher asks the waiter to explain what he says and does, who he interacts with, and what a conversation would be like. As the waiter demonstrates this, the teacher points things out. "See how he asks the customer to be seated. He says, 'Please take a seat here.' Then he hands her a menu and says, 'We have several daily specials, we have pot roast with mashed potatoes and a very nice chicken dish with garden vegetables.'" Then the teacher explains that the customer takes a seat and looks at the menu. One of the interesting things we have found is that just because children go to places with their parents, they are often unaware of what is going on around them. Sometimes they are given things to play with so they will be occupied and won't bother the adults. Instead of seeing things that they can role-play, they are oblivious to the language and play scenarios being demonstrated around them.

Discussing the use of books as a fodder for make-believe play, Elkonin (2005b, p. 41) commented that "only those works that clearly and understandably described people, their activities, and how they interacted caused the children to want to reproduce the content of the story in play." The same is true for the videos and the field trips as well as for guest speakers. The Tools of the Mind curriculum provides teachers with detailed suggestions about the choice of ways to build background knowledge necessary for enacting complex play scenarios.

Scaffolding the Development and Maintenance of Play Roles and Rules. As Elkonin (1978) pointed out, the focus points of mature play are the social roles and relationships between people – something that children cannot learn by simply observing adult behaviours. Therefore, to promote mature play, teachers using the Tools of the Mind curriculum engage children in discussions of the purpose of adult behaviours, their sequence, and the cause and effect relationships between different behaviours.

The rules that hold make-believe play together are not arbitrary but are based on the logic of real-life situations (Elkonin, 1978). Not knowing how these life scripts unfold will keep children from practicing self-regulated behaviours by following these rules. This calls for greater involvement of early childhood teachers in children's play than most teachers are used to. However,

Figure 24.1 *An action prompt card for make-believe play.*

for most children this involvement needs to last for a relatively short time; soon they are able to use models provided by the teachers to build their own roles and rules thus require only occasional support of the adult.

A positive impact of explicit modelling of play scenarios on children's engagement in play was found in several studies that involved demographically varied groups of children (Karpov, 2005). It indicates that in today's context, not only at-risk children but all pre-schoolers benefit from in-classroom scaffolding of pretend scenarios. In Tools of the Mind classrooms, explicit modelling of play scenarios occurs in the context of a specific activity called *make-believe play practice.* During this activity, the teacher assumes a pretend role to walk children through sample scripts and demonstrates sample play actions with the props accompanied by the role speech associated with the chosen character. As children get more familiar with the new scripts, they are encouraged to pretend along with the teacher by using gestures and role speech.

To make sure children remember the scripts modelled during the make-believe play practice session, teachers use special action prompt cards that depict the actions modelled (see Figure 24.1) and role prompt picture cards with the pictures of the people (see Figure 24.2). These cards are first used by the teacher as she models the play actions and are then placed in the areas of the classrooms where play is happening. Later in the year, children start producing their own picture cards as they come up with new pretend scenarios.

Planning for Play. Another way to scaffold roles and rules in make-believe play in Tools of the Mind classrooms is by teaching children to plan ahead. Elkonin (1978) identified planning as one of the features of highly developed play, describing play of older children as consisting mostly of lengthy

Figure 24.2 *A role prompt card for make-believe play.*

Figure 24.3 *Example of a play plan made by a preschool child. The writing says,* I am going to make a castle.

discussions of who is going to do what and how, followed by brief periods of acting out. As with other components of play, role planning can benefit from adult scaffolding. Teachers start with asking children what they want to play or what they want to be, encouraging them to discuss the choice of the roles with their peers. Later in the year, the teachers ask children about more specific details of their future play scenarios including what props they might need or whether they need to assume a different role (see Figure 24.3).

By making planning a necessary step in play, the teacher directs children's attention to the specifics of their roles and to the existence of rules associated with them.

Relevance for Today's Early Childhood Education Context

Today's young children do not seem to reach the same levels of play as their peers in the past. Instead of broadly speaking about play as essential in child development, we need to look closely and specifically at types of play and their potential benefits. From a Vygotskian perspective, we find it evident that to enable child development – in other words, to create the zone of proximal development – play itself must not remain frozen at the same level throughout early childhood years, but instead needs to evolve to reach its most mature level. While the concept of mature and immature play may very well apply to many forms of playful behaviours such as building with blocks, movement games, and board games and computer games, it seems logical to explore first the relationship between levels of play and childhood outcomes in the context of play that Vygotskians declared the leading activity of early childhood: make-believe play.

In this chapter we presented the Vygotskian and post-Vygotskian research on play as well as applications for today's early childhood settings. The major lesson learned from the Vygotskians is that make-believe play should be considered a major, central activity for preschool children that deserves the same kind of teacher support and scaffolding as the effort that is currently spent in teaching discrete academic skills. The Vygotskian approach identifies specific elements of play that must be supported and provides a blueprint for instruction in an early childhood classroom. Make-believe play is an important and unique context providing opportunities to learn not afforded by other classroom activities. It should not be considered something extra that can be cut to accommodate more time for academic skills nor should it be used as a means of adding 'entertainment value' for inherently boring and decontextualized drills. Instead, play should be preserved and nurtured as one of "uniquely preschool"– in the words of Vygotsky's colleague and student Alexander Zaporozhets – activities that provide the most beneficial context for children's development:

> Optimal educational opportunities for a young child to reach his or her potential and to develop in a harmonious fashion are not created by accelerated ultra-early instruction aimed at shortening the childhood period – that would prematurely turn a toddler into a preschooler and a preschooler into a first-grader. What is needed is just the opposite – expansion and enrichment of the content in the activities that are uniquely 'preschool': from play to painting to interactions with peers and adults. (Zaporozhets, 1978, p. 265)

References

Barnett, W. S., Jung, K., Yarosz, D. J., Thomas, J., Hornbeck, A., Stechuk, R., & Burns, S. (2008). Educational effects of the Tools of the Mind curriculum: A randomized trial. *Early Childhood Research Quarterly*, *23*(3), 299–313.

Bergen, D. (2002). The role of pretend play in children's cognitive development. *Early Childhood Research & Practice*, *4*(1), 1–13.

Berk, L. E. (1994). Vygotsky's theory: The importance of make-believe play. *Young Children*, *50*(1), 30–39.

Berk, L. E., Mann, T. D., & Ogan, A. T. (2006). Make-believe play: Wellspring for development of self-regulation. In D. G. Singer, R. M. Golinkoff, & K. Hirsh-Pasek (Eds.), *Play=learning: How play motivates and enhances children's cognitive and social-emotional growth* (pp. 74–100). Oxford: Oxford University Press.

Blair, C. (2002). School readiness: Integrating cognition and emotion in a neurobiological conceptualization of child functioning at school entry. *American Psychologist, 57*, 111–27.

Blair, C., & Raver, C. C. (2014). Closing the achievement gap through modification of neurocognitive and neuroendocrine function: Results from a cluster randomized controlled trial of an innovative approach to the education of children in kindergarten. *PloS One*, *9*(11), e112393.

Blair, C., & Razza, R. P. (2007). Relating effortful control, executive function, and false belief understanding to emerging math and literacy ability in kindergarten. *Child Development*, *78*, 647–663.

Bodrova, E., & Leong, D. (2007). *Tools of the mind: Vygotskian approach to early childhood education* (2nd ed.). Columbus, OH: Merrill/Prentice Hall.

Bodrova, E., & Leong, D. (2011). Revisiting Vygotskian perspectives on play and pedagogy. In S. Rogers (Ed.), *Rethinking play and pedagogy in early childhood education: Concepts, contexts, and cultures* (pp. 60–72). New York: Routledge.

Bodrova, E., & Leong, D. (2017 pp. 1095–1111). Tools of the Mind: A Vygotskian-based early childhood curriculum. In M. Fleer & B. van Oers (Eds.), *International Handbook of Early Childhood Education*. Springer: Netherlands.

Bruner, J. S., Jolly, A., & Sylva, K. (1976). *Play: Its role in development and evolution*. New York: Basic Books.

Christie, J. F., & Roskos, K. (2006). Standards, science, and the role of play in early literacy education. In D. G. Singer, R. M. Golinkoff, & K. Hirsh-Pasek (Eds.), *Play=learning: How play motivates and enhances children's cognitive and social-emotional growth* (pp. 57–73). Oxford: Oxford University Press.

Chudacoff, H. P. (2007). *Children at play: An American history*. New York: New York University Press.

Diamond, A., Barnett, W. S., Thomas, J., & Munro, S. (2007). Preschool program improves cognitive control. *Science*, *318*(5855), 1387–1388.

Elkonin, D. B. (1977). Toward the problem of stages in the mental development of the child. In M. Cole (Ed.), *Soviet developmental psychology* (pp. 538–563). White Plains, NY: M. E. Sharpe.

Elkonin, D. B. (1978). *Psychologija igry* [The psychology of play]. Moscow: Pedagogika.

Elkonin, D. B. (2005a). Preface to 'The psychology of play' [Preface: The biography of this research], trans. Lydia Razran Stone. *Journal of Russian and East European Psychology*, *43*, 11–21.

Elkonin, D. B. (2005b). 'The psychology of play' [Chapter 2: The subject of our research: The developed form of play], trans. Lydia Razran Stone. *Journal of Russian and East European Psychology*, *43*, 22–48.

Farran, D. C., & Son-Yarbrough, W. (2001). Title I funded preschools as a developmental context for children's play and verbal behaviors. *Early Childhood Research Quarterly*, *16*(2), 245–262.

Germeroth, C., Layzer, C., Day-Hess, C., & Bodrova, E. (2013, September). Play it high, play it low: Examining the reliability and validity of a new observation tool to measure children's play. Presentation at the Society for Research in Educational Effectiveness Fall Conference, Washington, DC.

Gudareva, O. (2005). Psikhologicheskie Osobennosti Suzhetno-rolevoy Igry Sovremennykh Doshkol'nikov [Psychological features of make-believe play in today's preschoolers]. PhD dissertation, Moscow City University for Psychology and Education.

Istomina, Z. M. (1977). The development of voluntary memory in preschool-age children. In M. Cole (Ed.), *Soviet developmental psychology* (pp. 100–159). New York: M. E. Sharpe.

Johnson, J. E., Christie, J. F., & Wardle, F. (2005). *Play, development, and early education*. Boston: Pearson/Allyn and Bacon

Karpov, Y. V. (2005). Three-to six-year-olds: Sociodramatic play as the leading activity during the period of early childhood. In *The Neo-Vygotskian approach to child development* (pp. 139–170). New York: Cambridge University Press.

Leont'ev, A. N. (1978). *Activity, consciousness, and personality*. Englewood Cliffs, NJ: Prentice Hall.

Leont'ev, A. N. (1981). *Problemy razvitiya psikhiki* [Problems of psychic development]. Moscow: Moscow State University Publishers.

Leslie, A. M. (1987). Pretense and representation: The origins of 'theory of mind'. *Psychological Review*, *94*(4), 412–426.

Levin, D. E. (2008). Problem solving deficit disorder: The dangers of remote controlled versus creative play. In E. Goodenough (Ed.), *Where do children play?* (pp. 137–140). Detroit, MI: Wayne University Press.

Lyytinen, P., Laakso, M.-L., Poikkeus, A.-M., & Rita, N. (1999). The development and predictive relations of play and language across the second year. *Scandinavian Journal of Psychology*, *40*(3), 177–186.

Manuilenko, Z. V. (1975/2014). The development of voluntary behavior in preschool-age children. *Soviet Psychology*, *13*, 65–116.

McCune, L. (1995). A normative study of representational play in the transition to language. *Developmental Psychology*, *31*(2), 198–206.

Miller, E., & Almon, J. (2009). *Crisis in the kindergarten: Why children need to play in school*. College Park, MD: Alliance for Childhood.

Ranz-Smith, D. J. (2007). Teacher perception of play: In leaving no child behind are teachers leaving childhood behind? *Early Education and Development*, *18*, 271–303.

Raver, C., & Knitzer, J. (2002). What research tells policymakers about strategies to promote social and emotional school readiness among three-and four-year-old children. *National Center for Children in Poverty. Facts in Action.* Available at www.factsinaction.org/brief/braug021.htm.

Rimm-Kaufman, S. E., Pianta, R. C., & Cox, M. J. (2000). Teachers' judgments of problems in the transition to kindergarten. *Early Childhood Research Quarterly, 15,* 147–166.

Roskos, K., & Neuman, S. B. (1998). Play as an opportunity for literacy. In O. N. Saracho & B. Spodek (Eds.), *Multiple perspectives on play in early childhood education* (pp. 100–115). Albany: State University of New York Press.

Singer, D. G., Golinkoff, R. M., & Hirsh-Pasek, K. (2006). *Play=learning: How play motivates and enhances children's cognitive and social-emotional growth.* Oxford: Oxford University Press.

Smirnova, E. O., & Gudareva, O. V. (2004). Igra i proizvol'nost u sovremennykh doshkol'nikov [Play and intentionality in modern preschoolers]. *Voprosy Psychologii, 1,* 91–103.

Vu, J. A., Han, M., & Buell, M. J. (2015). The effects of in-service training on teachers' beliefs and practices in children's play. *European Early Childhood Education Research Journal, 23,* 444–460.

Vygotsky, L. S. (1967). Play and its role in the mental development of the child. *Soviet Psychology, 5*(3), 6–18 (originally published in 1966).

Vygotsky, L. S. (1978). *Mind in society: The development of higher mental processes.* Cambridge, MA: Harvard University Press.

Vygotsky, L. S. (1997). *The history of the development of higher mental functions* (vol. 4) (trans. M. J. Hall). New York: Plenum Press.

Vygotsky, L. S. (1998). *Child psychology* (vol. 5). New York: Plenum Press.

Zaporozhets, A. (1978). The role of early childhood in the formation of child's personality. In L. I. Antsiferova (Ed.) Printsip razvitiya v psichologii [The principle of development in psychology]. Moscow: Nauka, 243–267.

25 The Adult as a Mediator of Development in Children's Play

Pentti Hakkarainen and Milda Bredikyte

This chapter deals with the methodologically complicated relationship between children's play and development. Play is changing in modern society and differs in various cultures. Play is said to be children's first independent activity, but adults indirectly guide it. Adult mediation is a methodological challenge for investigation of the relationship between play and child development. Adult mediation is analyzed on the basis of the cultural-historical approach and is connected to the concept of the zone of proximal development (ZPD) in play. We argue that adult participation in play as a role character also creates the ZPD for adults. Children's play is a dilemma in psychological and educational research. There are hundreds of definitions and contradictory explanations about its basic character. On the one hand, play is defined as children's 'free', independent activity; on the other hand, its importance as a preparatory stage for adult life is underlined. In modern society preparation for adult life is a serious challenge because severe crises threaten the future of the whole world. The key problem is, what could be the developmental potential of children's play, and how can it be realized? In order to answer the problem, better scientific explanations about the developmental potential of play are needed.

A review by Lillard et al. (2013) demonstrated the difficulty of getting reliable research data about causal relationships between children's play and development, using traditional methods and methodology. It was necessary to accept that the available studies supposing a causal relationship between play and development are in many cases methodologically unreliable; many principles of empirical study were violated, and the review revealed considerable methodological confusion in this area of play research. A principal issue arising is how can we use experiments in the study of the 'free play' of children, and what causality models are adequate in the study of relationships between play and child development?

The adult's active role in play is not very often a paradigmatic theme in play theories. We think that it is no exaggeration to say that Piaget did not deal with the adult's role in the development of child play. He wrote about symbolic play: "The 'deliberate illusion' which Lange and Groos see in play is merely the child's refusal to allow the world of adults or of ordinary reality to interfere with play, so as to enjoy a private reality of his own. The two- to four-year-old child does not consider whether his ludic symbols are real or not. He is aware in a sense that they are not so for others, and makes no serious efforts to persuade the adult that they are. But for him it is a question, which does not arise, because symbolic play is direct satisfaction of the ego and has its own kind of belief, which is a subjective reality. Moreover, as the symbol-object is a substitute for the reality it signifies, there develops, during the first stages, a kind of co-operation between the two, analogous to that between the image and the object it represents" (Piaget, 1962, p. 168).

Piaget emphasized in his play theory the development of the child's reasoning, in which the basic mechanism formed the dual system of assimilation and accommodation, striving at developmental equilibrium. In play, assimilation dominates over accommodation. Piaget's stages of play development were based on the observations of his own individual children. Play development proceeds through three main stages of ludic behaviour: practice games, symbolic games, and games with rules. Mediating factors in play development were schemes. Careful and detailed analysis of the development from sporadic to deferred imitation preceded Piaget's analysis of child's play carried out using representational images and symbols.

In spite of a similar orientation to the constructive character of child development, cultural-historical theory as elaborated by Vygotsky proposed a different explanation and research methodology. His approach turned Piaget's developmental trajectory upside-down. Vygotsky claimed that early development proceeds from sociality to increasing individuality and independence and not from egocentrism to sociality. Several theoretical concepts and methodological ideas of cultural-historical theory support this direction.

The adult role in play was limited to being an object of a child's imitation in Piaget's approach, but Vygotsky described the adult as active mediator of surrounding culture. Child development was a unique process, in which the end state existed in the form of an ideal of the culture at birth of each individual child. Vygotsky (1978) defined culture as the source of development and formulated a 'general genetic law' of cultural development.

The adult as a mediator in play development logically has to be eliminated from a classical experimental design, because an adult is a distorting variable between cause and effect. The experimental design investigating classical cause–effect relations is based on linear causality, in which cause always precedes effects. Study of causality often focuses on effective causality only, which limits the investigation of causality to only one type.

Toomela (2014) claims that more than 2,000 years ago Aristotle demanded that four types of causality (material, formal, efficient, and final cause) act simultaneously as a system. Aristotle's four causes are:

- The material cause: "that out of which", e.g., the bronze of a statue
- The formal cause: "the form", "the account of what-it-is-to-be", e.g., the shape of a statue

- The efficient cause: "the primary source of the change or rest", e.g., the artisan, the art of bronze-casting the statue, the man who gives advice, the father of the child
- The final cause: "the end, that for the sake of which a thing is done", e.g., health is the end of exercising, losing weight, taking prescribed drugs. (Falcon, 2015)

From the Aristotelian point of view, Lillard et al.'s (2013) research question of comparing the possible causal relevance of variable forms of play as a source of variable forms of development is incomplete. The review tries to answer the question 'Is play an effective cause in child development or not?' But many original studies violate basic rules of the causal-experimental paradigm, making answering impossible.

This chapter focuses on adult mediation and originates from the cultural-historical paradigm. Causality in this paradigm can be called 'systemic, psychological, circular, or mutual' and the paradigm as 'non-classic or post-non-classic'. Here we make an attempt to sketch what theoretical and practical relevance adult mediation may have in play research and educational practice. The space does not allow us to go deeply into the problem of causality, but we have elaborated an alternative approach to 'experimental play research' based on Vygotsky's non-classical methodology using 'mediating interventions' and adult participation in children's role-play.

This approach has been collaboratively developed with Gunilla Lindqvist (1995) and called *play world methodology* (see also Chapter 28). Adults actively design, organize, and carry out social pretend role-play collaboratively with children. Often a story or a combination of several stories serves as a springboard for playworld construction. Playworld events are a 'natural' continuation for moral values and events of a story, as Zaporozhets's (1986) comparative analysis demonstrated.

For us, playworld construction has offered effective tools of indirect play guidance continuing over several months. We agree with Gottman (1986) about the importance of joint experience in play (at ages 3–7 years) as the precondition of coordinated pretend play of a group of several children. Adults actively mediate and organize necessary joint affective experience to children by introducing carefully selected stories, dramatizing collisions of moral values between role characters, constructing imaginary environments, involving children to take moral positions, and helping characters define and solve dilemmas. This has required a completely new approach to educational work: sensitivity for feeling children's affects and moods, ability to show emotions through adopted role characters, and creativity to construct new challenges for children in new play events.

Active, flexible proceeding in imaginary playworlds, taking into account children's ideas and initiatives and revealing them through emotional-dramatic culmination in the story frame by adults, is used in playworld pedagogy. This makes a difference compared with such earlier research approaches as Howes et al.'s (1992) study on collaborative construction of pretend among toddlers, which observed children's collaborative pretend construction with adults, older siblings, and peers in age groups before 36 months. We argue that construction of pretend is a preliminary step to play activity and child development.

In the next section we sketch some general methodological ideas of Vygotsky's cultural-historical approach. He did not use the concept of *play ethos* (Smith, 2010), but the relation between play and child development was one of the main ideas in his writing about play. Culture as the source of development was his central argument. This idea leads to new criteria and stages of play development and to the zones of proximal development in play, which adult mediation supports. The next section is based on our analysis of the ZPD of pretend play, in which we have separated three levels of mediation tasks.

'Play Ethos' of Cultural-Historical Approach

Vygotsky's play ethos is intertwined with other central problems of investigating psychological development. One of the challenges is how to overcome Cartesian dualism – the division between internal and external in psychological analysis. Vygotsky proposed a stage model, in which qualitatively different periods follow each other. During crisis periods, rapid dramatic changes take place, and during latent periods, slower cumulative changes happen. Vygotsky's proposed crisis periods are at birth, 1 year, 3 years, 7 years, 11 years, and 13 years, but a detailed description is given only for the first three periods. A general mechanism moving development forward in play is described by the ZPD, which is one side of a 'general genetic law' of human development.

A specific understanding of the play ethos explains Vygotsky's emphasis in his lectures on play (Vygotsky, 1977). He concentrated on the stage of sociodramatic play, supposing that play can attain the status of a 'leading activity'; in other words, the impact on development is greatest. But the text suggests that he had in mind the development of personality and consciousness. This brings to the fore also specific psychological causality, about which he says that without understanding the specific needs and motivation of play we cannot analyze it as a leading activity (Vygotsky, 1977).

Play as a type of human activity differs from other activity types. Play is directed toward each playing child. In his article on play, Vygotsky (1977) emphasizes sense-making character of pretend play as the consequence of specific subject–object relation of play. Bruner refers to the same situation: "in play 'narrative truth' is judged by its verisimilitude rather than its verifiability" (Bruner, 1991, p. 13). All other activities are directed to external objects and their motivation usually is object oriented. Leont'ev (1978) stated that play process motivates play activity. In play causality, motivation, sign mediation, and orientation come from the subject and are presented to others. In spite of the fusing together of object and subject, children's play has the status of activity. Two scientists have developed this idea. Rubinstein (1947) formulated the principle of unity of consciousness and activity, and Leont'ev (1978) elaborated his theory claiming a similar structure of external and internal activity.

The emphasis of the play ethos in the cultural-historical approach was on cultural development. Vygotsky was interested in what makes child development specific, not in what characteristics it had in common with animal play. His emphasis on culture as the source of higher mental functions separated the cultural line of development from the instinctive regulative basis of animal play (Vygotsky, 1978). K. Buhler's (1918) study on the motivational changes (emotional anticipation) in children's play has influenced Vygotsky's thinking. Both write about a shift in affect from the end to the beginning of action. Vygotsky's emphasis was on generalized affects, and his analytic unit was defined with the concept of *perezhivanie* (emotional living through, or lived experience). Defining motivation as a central factor presupposes a special psychological causality, and understanding development as self-development. A sociogenetic framework (from interpersonal higher mental functions to intrapersonal ones) presupposes at each transition an organization of new forms of mutual interrelations between the growing personality and the child's social situation of acting. The interaction between adult and child moves development forward. In this model, children's initiatives are the focus of adult help. Adults can invite children to a joint activity, but children make the final decisions about play.

According to Vygotsky, the main contradiction of imaginative sociodramatic play is between visual and sense fields. This relation was also the main criterion of separating other play forms from each other. His rough typology included the following play forms in childhood before school:

- infant: clean field and no play
- early childhood: visual and sense field are fused (serious play)
- pre-schooler: visual and sense field are separated (imaginative play)
- school child: internal sense field is coordinated with external visual field
- adolescent: serious play develops in consciousness. (Vygotsky, 2005)

The specific play ethos of the cultural-historical approach has led to an exceptional periodization of play development, in which the main emphasis is on play as a leading activity. Play forms before that are preparatory stages to leading activity, and after, play is mainly a rule-governed activity, in which conscious rules in different forms dominate. The preparatory stage is essential, because without its products transition to imaginative play would be delayed or impossible. This stage produces self-conscious players who are able to carry out personal play actions. Play as a leading activity (imaginative sociodramatic play) produces symbolic function, enhances imagination, and encourages voluntary control of behaviour.

Play Forms and Adult Mediation of Play Development

The main stages of play in the cultural-historical approach are the preparatory stage, play as a leading activity, and play as a form of activity. Transitions from one stage to another happen through psychological crisis (El'konin, 1978, 2005; Kravtsova, 2014; Mihailenko & Korotkova, 2001, 2002; Polivanova, 2000). Play as a leading activity ('play age') starts from the crisis at 3 years and ends with the crisis at 7 years. Developing play is described with the following stages:

Preparatory Stage

Familiarizing play activity, 0–2 years
Representational play (*otobrozitel'naiya*), 1–2 years

(This is not play in the proper sense; the movements and interactions with objects are exploratory and imitative but not consciously included into a meaningful context of rules, scripts, and imaginary situations).

Play as Leading Activity (2–7 Years)

Imaginative play (transformation of objects, oneself, and situations (Vygotsky's 'imaginary situation')

Substages
Solitary directorial representational play (2–3 years)
Sociodramatic role-play (3–5 years)
Games with rules (5+ years)
Developed and expanded collaborative directorial play (*razvitaiya i razviornutaiya rezhisiorskaiya igra*) (6+ years)

Play as an Activity
Games with rules (5+ years)

Subcategories
Mobile games (*podvizhnyie*)
Table games (*nastol'nyie*)
Verbal play (*slovestnyie*)
Computer games

During preschool age (2–7 years), children master increasingly complex ways of constructing play activities. They start from object-oriented actions, then move to short everyday life episodes; the role is already present because the child acts as someone else (driver, mother) but is not aware of that. Later, children move to role-oriented play when they start taking different roles and naming them. In parallel, children become involved in construction play and simple games with rules. At the end of preschool age, play activity is developed in a group of children through the construction of the plot; roles become secondary, subordinate to it. Children develop complex plots based not only on everyday life experiences but also on favourite tales, stories, TV programs, etc. The difference between play as an activity and as a leading activity is its relation to development. Play as a leading activity mediates and produces changes in development, whereas as an activity some other activity has this role (e.g., learning).

How does the adult mediator role change in play development? We have proposed three stages in the construction of the play ZPD before school age (Hakkarainen & Bredikyte, 2008). But there are common general tasks connected to the universal character of mediation in these stages. Piaget mainly focused on one line of development in child's play – the use of symbols and logic. Vygotsky combined together closely the child's relationship to objects and to adults. His analysis of the child's pointing gesture, which he called 'the first social sign', shows this close relationship.

In play development a critical turning point is at about 3 years. Before that the child is dependent on the present situation. The crisis at 3 years (Polivanova, 2000; Vygotsky, 1998) makes the child conscious of self as an individual subject separate from mother–child dyad. Now the same play actions as before the crisis get a new quality. They are no longer closely connected to the present situation. How do imaginary situations and pretend actions become possible? Piaget explained this with the emergence of symbols (relation between signifier and signified), but Vygotsky claimed that play is the child's practical activity and human relations determine its significance. He wrote about this in connection to object substitution: "The object acquires the function and meaning of a sign only because of a gesture that gives it this meaning. From this it is clear that the meaning lies in the gesture and not in the object" (Vygotsky, 1997, p. 135).

From Vygotsky's argument we can conclude what is the central function of the adult in children's play. Adult mediators have to bring sign mediation to children's play. If we believe in Vygotsky, signification of cultural objects is learned through human relationships. In play, imaginary situations are created (according to Vygotsky) in order to cross the boundaries of present situation. He described another essential function in play: "In play thought becomes separated from a thing, and actions originate from the thought and not from a thing" (Vygotsky, 2004, p. 212). This task is not easy for the child. In the beginning of 'play age', after the independence crisis (at 3 years) the child needs adult guidance in two challenges: How to construct imaginary situations? and How to invent object substitutions?

Empirical Investigation of Adult–Child Play

The adult role as a mediator of toddler play is generally reinforced in industrialized societies, but children's 'free' play with peers is more supported among pre-schoolers. This can partly be explained by the fact that after learning basic play skills, children do not seem to 'need' any adult help. But empirical studies demonstrate that advanced social role-play is disappearing and new types of adult support are needed to promote advanced role-play in the new digital era (Hakkarainen & Bredikyte, 2008). Everyday observations show that parents also spend more time with digital devices, which earlier was used for guiding children.

In the following we give examples of three adult intervention studies made during our play research career. The first describes short-term adult play guidance of toddlers' pretend play in day care centres. Then we move to long-term systematic play development in teacher education in the second example. The third example describes collaborative construction of role relationships and play plots, which is required in advanced imaginative play. The first example focused on structural elements of sociodramatic role-play (*fabula*) and later we focus on the creation of playworlds and developmental trajectories of children in them.

Example I: The Zone of Proximal Development of Beginning Role-Play in Day Care

Our first comparative data were collected in two projects at the same university in the 1990s. Hännikäinen (1995) studied the transition to role-play in kindergarten. Hakkarainen (1990) gathered data from older children's 'small city' play (4–6 years) in day care. Hännikäinen collected video material over four months in three different kinds of play of the same toddlers (shopping play in the beginning, doctor play 2 months after the first play, and rabbit play after 4 months). The kindergarten teacher, Ritva, was playing with three girls: Hanna (3 years, 2 months), Katju (1 year, 11 months), and Mari (2 years, 4 months). The teacher proposed the themes and roles, displayed props, and supported children's play events in roles (see Table 25.1).

The micro-genesis of role-play takes place in a short period of time in the day care setting. There is a clear change of participation structure between play observations. During the first two sessions the adult is acting with one child at time, while others are observing this cooperation; or she gives instructions to two children carrying out operations side by side without an idea of doing something together. Instruction by an adult helps to carry out an elementary common action, but this is not enough for a longer chain of actions. The adult has a decisive role in children's role actions. Children are able to keep their role positions in these plays only for a short time (about

Table 25.1 *Adult guided beginning role-play*

Types of role actions	Shopping	Doctors	Rabbits
Exchange of role actions	+	−	+
In role actions	−	*	+
Differentiation between role/reality	*	*	+
Role talk	−	−	+
Meta-communication about role	−	−	−
Mutual understanding	*	−	+
Fluent turn-taking and reciprocity	−	−	*
Talk about play rules	−	−	−
Acceptance of proposed corrections	−	+	+
Suggestion about script/plot	−	−	*

+ Observable feature, − not observed, * emerging feature.
Source: From Hakkarainen & Hännikäinen (1996).

10 seconds) and the adult has to continuously remind about it. She has to 'throw' children back to roles.

The last observed play (rabbit play) is adult initiated just as the two others are. But active children's participation starts from the beginning. There are two child dyads, which from time to time cooperate with each other. Children are able to take their roles and freely move from play to reality and back. There is a lot of verbal communication. Henna and Katju (the girls in focus) have complementary roles, which they play throughout the whole play period. The plot of the play is simple: rabbits are jumping around, go to sleep, wake up, and jump around. Katju asks for help once during the whole period (her rabbit ears fell down and an adult helped her to fix the problem).

When we compared shopping play in the group of 4- to 6-year-old children (Hakkarainen, 1990) with the material above, the situation was completely different. Children were given permission to start their play and they organized play independently. During the play (continuing for almost an hour) only one adult took the role of a buyer, and she disappeared after 2 minutes. But we have to keep in mind that these children probably started their play career from the same situation as 2- to 3-year-old children in the adult-guided play analyzed above.

Example II: Adults as Mediators and Participants in Collaborative Playworld Construction

In our empirical playworld projects (Bredikyte, 2011; Hakkarainen, 2006, 2009; Hakkarainen et al., 2013; Hakkarainen et al., 2017) a conscious methodological goal has been to enlarge the units of play interventions and assessment. We did not focus on the play of individual children, but constructed joint playworlds of adults and children. Following Vygotsky's methodological advice, we constructed group-level interventions. But interventions are not direct play guidance. Zaporozhets's (1986) analysis of the close kinship between story and pretend play convinced us to use different types of storytelling methods (puppet theatre, oral storytelling, drawing and telling a story, teacher in role, etc.) in interventions.

We elaborated El'konin's (1989) idea that role-play might be the first sign of mediated action in the child's life. If this is correct, the sign (child's role) in its genetically primary form represents the other person. Further, El'konin claims that this is only possible as the result of the child's separation from an adult and the appearance of independent actions, in which the adult becomes an internal image. Later this process is explained as appearance of a 'dual subject' in role-play of each individual child (e.g., Kravtsov & Kravtsova, 2010). The child remains himself, but in his own eyes assigns meaning of an adult to play actions.

These ideas have led to a reinterpretation of children's pretending in advanced role-play. Substituting the meaning of an object with the meaning of another object is secondary. El'konin claims that the primary reason for substituting is the role, which a child assumes. He argues, "In advanced play form of a cube carries the meaning of a car because the child turned into a driver. Separation from an adult transforms him into a model. Every thing tells that a role is sign (the child gives meaning of adult to himself). Play action starts from sign, which has meaning of 'adult'. Ergo – arbitrary action because mediated by sign" (El'konin, 1989, p. 519).

The main part of the intervention research took place on a university campus, where early childhood education students took their play courses or teaching practice in our research environment (play laboratory 'Silmu'). A specific methodology opening the route from classic tales and stories to self-initiated play was constructed. A general assignment of students was to help children to elaborate a joint playworld and involve more children. The students were encouraged to take appropriate pretend roles, which children accept. Multi-age child groups offered an opportunity to participate in different types of play (from object manipulation to advanced make-believe play).

Our play intervention was an organic part of Finnish university-level teacher education. The Master's degree program of early childhood education and care was transformed, and its main part was elaborated to *play-generating narrative curriculum*. Promoting child development through play was the main goal of the curriculum and three (or four) courses on play were included. A new type of university education was developed. Playing with children for long periods, intensive planning and reflection of play practice and child development, theoretical studies of child development, and students' own research projects were integrated.

Play intervention without interrupting children's activities was the duty of students, and their aim was to become master players. These aims cannot be attained in Finnish regular day care centres (play is not a leading activity). Several before-noon play clubs were organized on campus for voluntary children staying at home with their mothers.

Play intervention took several forms and play stimulating work methods were elaborated over 8 years. The following types and forms were used:

I. Organizational interventions
   - Club space and time (approximately 4 hours a day)
   - Seven activity corners tempting play
   - Minimal adult rules (don't run on stairs, accept peer's play proposals)
   - Children's free choice of activity (adults cannot force children)
II. Social interaction
   - Students are encouraged to make children their friends
   - Participation in play of children of all ages
   - Master play interaction (mutuality, improvisation, plot elaboration)
III. Content of intervention
   - Construction of dramatic collisions in social relations between play characters
   - Revealing *perezhivanie* (emotional living through) of role characters
   - Construction of holistic plot structure (e.g., two-stroke structure – children first have to create a dangerous situation in order to create a hero to solve it; El'koninova, 2001)
   - Analysis and reflection of interventions.

For us the main problem in play interventions is the dramatic collision in social relations between role characters, because children nowadays do not often have wide enough common experience about cultural ideals. There is no background that would unite children around a play theme. Emotional *perezhivanie* and joint sense-making is lacking, and children are only able to play alone or with one or two peers having the same experiences. As we know from our empirical work, reading a classic tale or dramatizing it quite often does not yield any result. We have constructed a four-step intervention chain, which according to our experience can lead to child-initiated joint play with adult support. A piece of good advice to students was to consciously diminish adult help and let children elaborate the play theme as independently as possible.

We suppose that the construction of the play ZPD requires intermediate steps and adult help because ideal forms of behaviour may be too complicated. For example our dramatized story on friendship ('Eeyore's Birthday') in our play laboratory called forth extraordinary affective reactions and emotional support for the story characters in children, but no joint play activity was started.

We took the following steps in narrative play interventions toward children's 'free' play in different play world sites:

Stage 1: *Unifying theme (fabula).* Observing children's (play) behaviour and activities reveals their interests. The selection of a theme is based on observations, pedagogical documentation, and educational goal-setting for the whole child group and individual children. General themes introducing some basic human values (safety and danger, helping and friendship, coping with fears, cheating or telling the truth, breaking the rules, fighting for leadership, etc.) are most often planned during the year.

Stage 2: *A classic tale or story* is used as a tool of opening and clarifying the theme. Good stories raise questions and aggravate contradictions. Often the moral message is hidden rather than directly revealed. There are always dramatic collisions in a good story, some exciting events to which children respond. The story works as an *integrating tool*: the story form creates a frame, an 'imaginary world', a context and a background for the play events. A well-chosen story provides emotional involvement, motivation, and a safe environment to explore frightening phenomena.

Vygotsky explains with the following example what can be hidden in a text: "The fable, 'The Dragon-fly and the Ant', as translated by Krylov, can be used to illustrate the difference between the word's meaning and its sense. The word 'dance' with which the fable ends has a definite and constant meaning. This meaning is identical in all contexts. In the context of this fable, however, it acquires a much broader intellectual and affective sense. It simultaneously means 'be merry' and 'die'. This enrichment of the word through the sense it acquires in context is a basic law of the dynamics of meaning. The word absorbs intellectual and affective content from the entire context in which it is intertwined. It begins to mean both more and less than it does when we view it in isolation. It means more because the scope of its meaning is expanded; it acquires several zones that supplement this new content. It means less because the abstract meaning of the word is restricted and narrowed to what the word designates in this single context" (Vygotsky, 1934, p. 275).

Stage 3: *Projects* in different activity centres help to clarify specific aspects of the theme. Children can freely choose between their own ideas and projects in different centres. In projects new materials and tasks connected to the theme are introduced, particular skills are developed, or children's own ideas are supported.

Stage 4: *Child-initiated, free play.* Children develop the theme further and new subthemes may emerge. Child's independent play activity is a space for *self-development*, growth, creativity, and learning. The child's 'problems' are best revealed in independent play. Observing children in free play the teacher can see how children apply the knowledge and skills they were aiming at. Children need to have enough time and space for their independent 'free' play activities.

Example III: Collaborative Construction of Storylines and Play Plots

El'konin ended his scientific diary with the analysis of children's role interaction, describing it with the concept of joint collaborative play action (*sovokupnoe deistvie*). In advanced role-play children are not just playing together as independent individuals, but they are deeply oriented to each other's play identity as if two or more subjects carry out each play action with equal responsibility. El'konin uses a simple example to make his point: "I act in a certain way in order to organize, to prepare the action of another. With one hand I hold the nail, with another I hammer. Two hands – like two humans" (El'konin, 1989, p. 518).

We have analyzed children's play interaction in 'free' play in our play laboratory. The children's play was based on the story of 'Little Red Riding Hood'. An adult told the story orally and dramatized its events using a 'transformer' puppet ('Grandmother' appears under the dress of the 'Red Riding Hood' puppet when turned upside-down, and the 'Wolf' appears when Grandmother is turned 180 degrees back again). After oral storytelling, the puppet visited children's homes, but no instructions were given to mothers as to how children could play at home. In the morning of the day of 'free' play our teacher education students organized children's dramatizations of 'Little Red Riding Hood'. Three target children participated as spectators and actors in two dramatizations. 'Free' play took place just before the closing circle and lasted about 8 minutes.

Three girls, Lotta (6 years, 2 months), Liina (3 years, 10 months), and Noora (3 years, 5 months), started their "free" play on the couch. Lotta has the Red Riding Hood transformer puppet in her hand and Liina has a 'Flower Princess' table theatre puppet, which is beautiful, but has a simple stick instead of feet.

The whole play process had the following periods and turning points:

1. Quarrel about the role of Red Riding Hood
2. Adult intervention behind the camera: two Red Riding Hoods!
3. Lotta proposed starting an imaginary trip in a ship (others did not react)
4. Lotta turned the transformer puppet upside-down and assumed the role of Grandmother, which made possible mutual role relations between different characters
5. Collaborative construction of mutual role relations between characters (Grandmother, Red Riding Hood, and the Bear)
6. The bell ring invited children to end the circle and the play stopped.

The dynamics of role relations were analyzed using Lewin's and his followers' approach to Gestalt therapy focusing on the quality of contact (mutuality of intentions, attention, positions, gaze, point of view of other characters) between role characters (Safarov, 2009). The play started with the quarrel between Lotta and Liina. Both wanted to have the role of Red Riding Hood. They tried to get the main role by appealing to the more attractive appearance of the puppet in their hand, and then to the demand of each one's (imaginary) grandmother. Adult intervention stopped the quarrel and confused children, which brought up a new theme of play (a trip aboard a ship). When others did not accept this proposal, Lotta kept turning the transformed puppet in her hand and suddenly revealed Grandmother's face.

Revealing Grandmother's role character of the transformer puppet made it possible to elaborate the relationship system of three role characters (and girls) through the following steps: (1) see and hear the other in the role, (2) accept the novelty of other roles, and (3) mutually accept and coordinate the sense and meaning of role actions.

The girls reproduced the cultural sense of the story in a modified manner. After the appearance of the grandmother character, Noora took the 'Bear' table theatre puppet (instead of the Wolf) in her hand and started to approach the Grandmother and Red Riding Hood characters, growling loudly. Liina (as Red Riding Hood) and Lotta (as Grandmother) accepted Noora's role character. The hidden rules of their roles are copied from their cultural environment – from fairy tales and personal experience. Grandmother provides care and protection for her grandchild.

The Bear is growling loudly. Liina and Lotta look at Noora.
Liina (*to Noora*):   "What do you growl there? Do not threaten me!"

Liina's puppet goes quickly to Grandmother (Lotta).
Liina (*to Lotta*):   "Hi Grandma, I am afraid because the Bear is coming."

Noora's puppet approaches other role characters growling.
Lotta shakes Grandmother puppet in front of Noora's Bear.
Lotta (*to Noora*):   "Bear, clear off, you cannot threaten my daughter!"
Noora: "Mrrrr mrrrr mrrrr mrrr!"

Liina (*after encouragement from Grandmother (Lotta), shakes her puppet in front of the Bear furiously, shouting*): "Bear clear off from the eyes of my mother – my Grandma!"
Liina (*to Lotta*):   "Come on Grandma here!"

The hidden cultural rules of the role characters are visible also in the spatial setting of the play. When the Bear threatens Red Riding Hood, growling loudly, Grandmother moves to the sofa to be between the Bear and Red Riding Hood, thus demonstrating protection against the 'powerful enemy'.

Conclusions

El'konin's contemplation is closely connected to the problem of need and motivation in pretend play. Developers of psychological cultural-historical theory (e.g., Vygotsky, Rubinstein, Leont'ev, and El'konin) look for explanation from adult mediation between child's play and cultural environments. Sign mediation could be an explanation for qualitative change of motivation in pretend play after the crisis at three years, in which Vygotsky believed (Vygotsky, 1977). El'konin's strong belief in a pretend role as a sign was seen in an emphasis of role as the main component of advanced play instead of Vygotsky's imaginary situation.

In the empirical material above, we wanted to demonstrate the change of adult role as the mediator in pretend role-play. At the first stage the adult (day care provider or mother) guides the child's construction of first pretend roles, and their sustainability depends on the adult. Narrative story logic was used as an adult tool in our second example to introduce playworld *perezhivanie* connected to dramatic collisions. The goal is children's 'free' play based on joint playworld experience. Our third example presents the specific play unit, in which collaborative play actions as the system of role relations are constructed between three children. Adult play intervention is extended in this case over one and half months; it is divided between different adults, and their functions are differentiated. The example shows the starting point of storyline construction. Values are transformed into collaborative play actions and their chains into proceeding storylines.

Adult intervention aiming at enhanced construction of storyline in play was experimented on in Mikhailenko's research project. She invited children to playfully elaborate together with adult stories using Propp's shortened version of fairy tale structure as indirect play intervention. The hypothesis was that child's playful experience of story crafting later enhances plot construction in play. Instruction of the basic structure of a story is avoided, ensuring that child's inventive power is more important. This is why improvisation rules are followed in this intervention method (Mikhailenko & Korotkova, 2001, 2002). Story crafting as an intervention method is based on Zaporochets's (1986) theoretical comparative analysis between fairy tales and sociodramatic play, but empirical evidence on the results is not available.

Adult mediation of child development in play is a highly complicated problem and challenge, in which traditional linear experimental research methods are not feasible. There are no invariable causal factors and relations between players, plays, and development. We have to ask what and how an adult mediates in children's play and develop a system approach, which helps us to analyze phenomena into appropriate units as Vygotsky proposed. There are some preliminary methodological ideas helping to focus central systemic relations. Vygotsky emphasized the specific character of signification in sociodramatic role-play, which he presented in a formula. In his terms, sense-making dominates over meaning-making, and narrative logic is used in play construction instead of realistic logic.

The main tool of adult mediation in play, according to Vygotsky, is the creation of an imaginative situation. We claimed that the first step to play activity is pretend role; the next step is collaborative construction of joint play actions; and the third step is joint plot fabrication. Adult mediation becomes more complicated when meanings are separated from objects and sense-making becomes mainly the child's experimentation. The child cannot be forced to adopt cultural values, ideal forms, practices, and emotional reactions. The mediator invites the child rather than instructs him or her on how to behave and change.

Children's play is an excellent example about the need for 'non-classical' methodology based on nonlinear relations. Our interventions (tales, stories, playworlds, adult roles, emotional expressions) do not directly produce some effects in children's play. Development depends on children's interpretations, experiences, and motivation to become different. Too often adults think they know what is best for the child.

References

Bredikyte, M. (2011). *The zones of proximal development in children's play. Oulu: Universitatis Ouluensis E*, 119.

Bruner, J. (1991). Narrative construction of reality. *Critical Inquiry, 18*(1), 13.

Buhler, K. (1918). *Die geistige Entwicklung des Kindes*. [The mental development of the child]. Jena: Fischer.

El'konin, D. B. (1978). *Psikhologiya igry* [The psychology of play]. Moscow: Pedagogika.

El'konin, D. B. (1989). *Izbrannye psikhologiceskie trudy* [Collected psychological works]. Moscow: Pedagogika.

El'konin, D. B. (2005). Psychology of play I–II. *Journal of Russian and East European Psychology, 43*(1–2), 1–89, 1–91.

El'koninova, L. I. (2001). The object orientation of children's play in the context of understanding imaginary space: Time in play and stories. *Journal of Russian and East European Psychology, 39*(2), 30–51.

Falcon, A. (2015). Aristotle on causality. In E. N. Zalta (Ed.), *The Stanford encyclopedia of philosophy* (spring 2015 edition). Available at https://plato.stanford.edu/archives/spr2015/entries/aristotle-causality/.

Gottman, J. (1986). The world of coordinated play: Same and cross sex friendships in young children. In J. Gottman & J. Parker (Eds.), *Conversations of friends: Speculations on affective development* (pp. 139–191). Cambridge: Cambridge University Press.

Hakkarainen, P. (1990). *Motivaatio, leikki ja toiminnan kohteellisuus* [Motivation, play and object-orientation of activity]. Helsinki: Orienta-Konsultit.

Hakkarainen, P. (2006). Learning and development in play. In J. Einarsdottir & J. Wagner (Eds.), *Nordic childhoods and early education* (pp. 183–222). Greenwich, CT: Information Age Publishing.

Hakkarainen, P. (2008). The challenges and possibilities of a narrative learning approach in the Finnish early childhood education system. *International Journal of Educational Research, 47*, 292–300.

Hakkarainen, P. (2009). Development of motivation in play and narratives. In S. Blenkinsop (Ed.), *The imagination in education: Extending the boundaries of theory and practice* (pp. 64–78). Newcastle upon Tyne: Cambridge Scholars Publishing.

Hakkarainen, P., & Bredikyte, M. (2008). The zone of proximal development in play and learning. *Cultural-Historical Psychology, 4*, 2–11.

Hakkarainen, P., Brédikytè, M., Jakkula, K., & Munter, H. (2013). Adult play guidance and children's play development in a narrative play-world. *European Early Childhood Education Research Journal, 21*(2), 213–225.

Hakkarainen, P., Bredikyte, M., & Safarov, I. (2017). Pretend play and child development. In T. Bruce, P. Hakkarainen, & M. Bredikyte (Eds.), *The Routledge international handbook of early childhood* (pp. 70–84). London: Routledge.

Hakkarainen, P., & Hännikäinen, M. (1996). Developmental transition of children's role-play in Finnish day care centers. In Proceedings of Vygotsky centennial conference in Moscow, pp. 132–135.

Hännikäinen, M. (1995). *Transition to role-play: A Piagetian and an activity-theoretical viewpoint.* Jyväskylä: Institute of Educational Science, University of Jyväskylä.

Howes, C., Unger, O., & Matheson, C. C. (1992). *The collective construction of pretend: Social pretend play functions.* Albany: State University of New York Press.

Kravtsov, G. G., & Kravtsova, E. E. (2010). Play in L. S. Vygotsky's nonclassical psychology. *Journal of Russian and East European Psychology, 48*(4), 25–41.

Kravtsova, E. E. (2014). Play in the non-classical psychology of L. S. Vygotsky. In L. Brooker, M. Blaise, & S. Edwards (Eds.), *The Sage handbook of play and learning in early childhood* (pp. 21–30). London: Sage.

Leont'ev, A. N. (1978). *Activity, consciousness, and personality.* Englewood Cliffs, NJ: Prentice-Hall.

Lillard, A. S., Lerner, M. D., Hopkins, E. J., Dore, R. A., Smith, E. D., & Palmquist, C. M. (2013). The impact of pretend play on children's development: A review of the evidence. *Psychological Bulletin, 139*, 1–34.

Lindqvist, G. (1995). *The aesthetics of play.* Uppsala: Acta Universitatis Uppsaliensis.

Mikhailenko, N., & Korotkova, N. (2001). *Kak igrat s det'mi* [How to play with children]. Moscow: Akademicheskij Project.

Mikhailenko, N., & Korotkova, N. (2002). *Igry s pravilami v doshkolnom vozraste* [Games with rules at preschool age]. Moskva: Akademicheskij Project.

Piaget, J. (1962). *Play, dreams and imitation in childhood.* London: Routledge & Kegan Paul.

Polivanova, K. N. (2000). *Psikhologiya vozrastnyh krizisov* [Psychology of age-related crises]. Moscow: Akademia.

Roopnarine, J. L., & Davidson, K. L. (2014). Parent–child play across cultures: Advancing play research. *American Journal of Play, 7*(2), 228–252.

Rubinstein, S. L. (1947). *Osnovy obtshei psikhologii* [Basics of general psychology]. Moscow: Pedagogika.

Safarov, I. (2009). *Towards modeling of human relationships: Nonlinear dynamical systems.* Oulu: University of Oulu Press.

Smith, P. K. (2010). *Children and play.* Chichester: Wiley.

Toomela, A. (2014). A structural systemic theory of causality and catalysis. In K. Cabell & J. Valsiner (Eds.), *The catalyzing mind: Beyond models of causality* (pp. 271–292). New York: Springer.

Vygotsky, L. S. (1934). Thinking and speech. Available at www.marxists.org/archive/vygotsky/works/words/ch07.htm.

Vygotsky, L. S. (1977). Play and its role in the mental development of the child. In M. Cole (Ed.), *Soviet developmental psychology* (pp. 76–99). White Plains, NY: M. E. Sharpe.

Vygotsky, L. S. (1978). *Mind in society: The development of higher psychological processes.* Cambridge, MA: Harvard University Press.

Vygotsky, L. S. (1984). *Collected works*, vol. 3. Moscow: Pedagogika.

Vygotsky, L. S. (1997). *The collected works of L. S. Vygotsky*, vol 4. New York: Plenum Press.

Vygotsky, L. S. (1998). *The collected works of L. S. Vygotsky*, vol 5. New York: Plenum Press.

Vygotsky, L. S. (2004). Imagination and creativity in childhood. *Journal of Russian and East European Psychology*, *42*(1), 4–84.

Vygotsky, L. S. (2005). Appendix. In D. B. El'konin, Psychology of play. *Journal of Russian and East European Psychology*, *43*(2), 90–97.

Zaporozhets, A. V. (1986). *Izbrannye ppsikhologiceskie Trudy I – II*. Moscow: Pedagogika.

26 Play, Learning, and Teaching in Early Childhood Education

Niklas Pramling, Anne Kultti, and Ingrid Pramling Samuelsson

In this chapter we will analyze and discuss the relationship between play and learning in relation to teaching in the particular institutional arrangements of early childhood education (ECE). We will build on some classic but primarily recent empirical research and theoretical elaboration on play, learning, and teaching in ECE. We will highlight the role of the preschool teacher in these processes. An initial meta-note: while it may appear strange to place teaching after play and learning, we have done so in order to highlight the importance of teaching building on and being responsive to play and what children already have learned. Our discussion will to some extent be prospective; that is, our theoretical discussion will lead us to point out, metaphorically speaking, some white or at least grey areas in collective knowing about the relationships between play, learning, and teaching in ECE. In addition to raising such critical questions for further research, we will discuss some of the implications of our discussion for ECE practice and the role of the teacher.

In the Swedish context from which we write, play and learning are often perceived as polarities, particularly when the latter is conflated with teaching. This is probably not unique to, but perhaps even more evident in, Sweden than in other language contexts for a linguistic reason: the word for 'learn', *lära* (*lärande*, 'learning', etc.), can be used, as in English, in the sense of 'she learns to ...' (*hon lär sig ...*), but it can also, different to in English, be used as in *'jag lär dig hur du gör det'* (which literally translates as 'I learn you how to do it'; clearly the position here taken by the word 'learn' would in English be 'teach' or 'show'). That the word *lära* (learn) can be used in both these ways, we argue, leads to many conflated claims where learning and teaching are collapsed into one and the same. This makes the discussion about play and learning in Sweden particularly tense and polarized. This is evident in different social fora and in more popular scientific publications where there is no need to adhere to the criteria of scientific discourse (with peer-review scrutiny). Some of these fora are widely read and the ideas there presented have a far reach into the field of ECE. However, in our present discussion we will clearly

* This research is funded by the Swedish Institute for Educational Research (Skolfi 2016/112).

distinguish between teaching and learning, necessary for discussing their relationship and their respective relationship to play.

Remetaphorizing Key Concepts

Even the most basic concepts of educational theory and research, such as teaching, learning, and education, may need to be reviewed and reconceptualized to inform our discussion about ECE, since these terms have a strong grounding in the tradition of schooling, which is rather different from the tradition of preschool. What we refer to as 'preschool' in this discussion is the institutional setting for children 0–5 years old in Sweden, with university-educated preschool teachers and a national curriculum. The curriculum has no 'goals to achieve'; that is, there is not something particular that children should learn before their transition to school. However, there is what is referred to as 'goals to strive for'. These point out the direction in terms of fields of knowing and various social and personal skills that children should be given the opportunity and support to start discovering and developing. Hence, there is a clear pedagogical direction governing the practice, but whether children appropriate the forms of knowledge and skills outlined is not to be assessed.

Since terms such as learning and development refer to phenomena and processes that are not there for us to point at and see as such, but rather need to be inferred from empirical observation, we invoke metaphors for their conceptualization (Säljö, 2002). This means, among other things, that the basic concepts of educational theorizing are inherently contested in nature; an important part of theory generation is to reconceptualize, or to align with the premise of their metaphorical nature, to 'remetaphorize' these terms to make them relevant to the context of preschool (Pramling et al., 2017). For example, the concept of 'teaching' has traditionally been understood as the transmission of information from knower (teacher) to novice (child/student). In this way, knowledge is reduced to and collapsed with information. However, there is an important distinction to be made between information (as something that can be transmitted and stored in books and other media), on the one hand, and knowledge (as a matter of human sense-making), on the other (Bruner, 1990). In contemporary sometimes called information societies, learning to transform information into knowledge is precisely one of the key competences needed, and that education needs to support children and pupils in appropriating (Säljö, 2010).

The concept of teaching is fundamentally intertwined with the concept of communication. If conceptualizing teaching as the transmission of information, communication becomes the conduit for that transmission (see Reddy, 1993, for an elaboration and critique of the conduit metaphor for communication). However, a radical reconceptualization of teaching can be provided from an entirely different field of study, zoology. In a thought-provoking article published in 1973 but to a large extent unknown within educational theory (for a rare exception, see Marton & Booth, 1997), Barnett (1973) writes that the species-unique practice of teaching – he refers to man as *Homo docens* (teaching man) – consists of three related principles: (1) to intentionally aim at making something known to someone else, (2) keeping at it until this is achieved, and (3) adjusting one's strategies to the responses of the learner. The third point is particularly worth emphasizing and studying empirically in ECE contexts: how preschool teachers adjust their teaching efforts, that is, how they are responsive to the responses of the learner in order to further their knowing. Conceptualized in this way, teaching becomes a fundamentally dialogic activity rather than a unidirectional transmission. How teachers can respond to the responses of learners in a way that not only confirms what they already know (i.e., create continuity in learning experience) but also, at the same time, provide incentive and support in further developing new insight (i.e., establishing discontinuity, allowing new experiences) is pressing to knowledge-building and outlining developmental contemporary educational preschool practices. Particularly how teaching can be orchestrated in the context of play without transforming play into non-play is critical to empirically study and, on this basis, theoretically elaborate.

Teaching, according to Barnett's (1973) reasoning, has an evolutionary basis and constitutes a unique-to-human practice. There is some controversy over the claim that teaching is unique to humans. Later studies reported what could be conceptualized as teaching in ants (Franks & Richardson, 2006), meerkats (Thornton & McAuliffe, 2006), and chimpanzees (Boesch, 1991). However, a critical difference between humans and other species is our social institutions, such as preschool, for developing the growing generation through cultural transmission. The latter kind of institutions and the practices these embody are not found in other species (Tennie et al., 2009). The larger discussion about whether teaching is unique to humans lies beyond the scope of the present chapter; we discuss its nature and relationship to learning and play in the context of early childhood education.

Teaching not only is present in spontaneous interpersonal encounters, such as between caregiver and child, but is also institutionalized in settings such as preschool and school. However, it should be recognized that the practice of teaching as traditionally found in school, with a lecturing teacher and listening and receiving students (who are, accordingly, expected to later be able to reproduce the message), would not qualify as teaching in Barnett's sense, critically lacking the double responsivity of responding (and outlining the practice) to the learner's response. That teaching has been institutionalized means not only that society has developed institutions for reproducing knowing and learning capacities in the growing generation but also that particular forms of promoting this learning have developed. Consequently, with van Oers and colleagues (2003) we can see teaching as an activity system:

> [W]e do not identify 'teaching activity' with 'a teacher's activity'. We begin with the assumption that teaching is a meta-personal cultural activity system, in which

> a teacher may play a prominent role, but in which she/he is not the only actor. 'Teaching', as we know it today, is a cultural-historical product, built up by many generations of teachers, educators and academics. The enactment of the cultural teaching activity by a teacher at any one moment in a particular classroom is always the joint product of different actors.   (van Oers et al., 2003, p. 111)

The point that (preschool) teachers are not the only ones responsible for and active in teaching is of particular importance in the context of preschool. In the nature of this institution, in Sweden and elsewhere, but not globally, activities are generally, almost exclusively, social and group based. Pedagogy is in this context also theme- and play-based in nature. Hence, organizing for children's development in this setting is fundamentally different from the individual achievement and assessment practices of school.

Barnett's (1973) discussion, through its double responsivity criteria, highlights the critical importance to teaching of establishing some form of intersubjectivity. This concept, as discussed by Rommetveit (1974) and others, indicate that participants in a practice need to come to share some perspective on what they engage in (for empirical illustrations with preschool teachers interacting with the youngest children in preschool, see Pramling & Pramling Samuelsson, 2010). Without such shared perspective, participants will engage in different projects and in effect talk past each other.

Intersubjectivity and Alterity

In his theoretical elaboration of the sociogenesis of higher mental functions, Wertsch (1998) introduces the distinction of "two opposing tendencies that may be seen as characterizing social interaction: 'intersubjectivity' and 'alterity'. In any particular episode of social interaction, the relative importance of these two tendencies may vary, but both are always at work" (p. 111). The first of these concepts Wertsch takes from Rommetveit. According to the latter, intersubjectivity is at best temporary and sufficient; it is never total (Rommetveit, 1974). It is also a matter of communicative negotiation. As Wertsch (1998) comments, "Rommetveit's analysis suggests that intersubjectivity should be viewed as a tendency that characterizes human communication – a tendency that operates in dynamic tension with other, often opposing tendencies" (p. 113). Building on Bakhtin, Wertsch suggests that dynamically integrated with the tendency of intersubjectivity in human communication is what may be referred to as 'alterity' (he also uses 'dialogic function' of language), a concept premising multivoicedness. This concept thus denotes difference, and critically the generation of new meaning:

> In contrast to the univocal function, which tends toward a single, shared, homogenous perspective comprising intersubjectivity, the dialogic function tends toward dynamism, heterogeneity, and conflict among voices. Instead of trying to 'receive' meanings that reside in speakers' utterances as envisioned

by the 'conduit metaphor' (Reddy, 1997 [1993]), the focus is on how an interlocutor might use texts as thinking devices and respond to them in such a way that new meanings are generated.   (Wertsch, 1998, p. 115)

How the tension between unifying and differentiating processes plays out in communication among children and between children and preschool teachers in different activities, play and others, is of considerable interest in order to understand how children's learning and development are supported in early childhood education. Which meanings come to be partly shared in order to carry out mutual projects (e.g., play projects), and which different understandings appear, requiring play partners to negotiate how to go on, with the potential to generate new meaning in and from play?

It is also important to realize that pairing the concepts of intersubjectivity and teaching and alterity and playing constitutes a false dichotomy. As already hinted at, both processes – intersubjectivity, which is at best partial and temporary, and alterity – are at play in all human encounters, whether the kind of activities we call teaching or playing. In order to play a mutual play, some intersubjectivity will have to be assumed and achieved, despite play in nature being open as to where it may lead (alterity). If two (or more) children do not establish a shared perspective on what an object, say, a pine cone, is to represent in the play, it is not possible for them to constitute a mutual play where this object plays a role. However, where the play may take them is still open to negotiation, and the role and part played by the object (the pine cone) may also change during the course of the activity.

Play and Playfulness

Few, if any, concepts in the partly overlapping fields of educational theory, educational psychology, and psychology has proven to be so difficult to define as 'play' (for an informative analysis of various definitions of and discourses on play, see Sutton-Smith, 1997). Rather than attempting to define the concept in a clear-cut manner, the later philosophy of Ludwig Wittgenstein offers an alternative. He argues that some phenomena, instead of being definable in a manner that unites all instances and distinguishes these from adjacent concepts, are better thought of as constituting family resemblances. What he refers to as family resemblances is introduced thus:

> I can think of no better expression to characterize these similarities than 'family resemblances'; for the various resemblances between members of a family: build, features, colour of eyes, gait, temperament, etc. etc. overlap and criss-cross in the same way. – And I shall say: 'games' form a family.   (Wittgenstein, 1953, §67)

Hence, according to this reasoning, there is no particular feature (e.g., eye colour or height) that is shared by all members of a 'family' that at the same time distinguish the 'family' from 'other families'. In analogy with Wittgenstein's example of 'games', we argue (cf. also Cook, 1997; Wallerstedt & Pramling, 2012) that 'play' constitutes a 'family'. Given this reasoning, there will be no criteria shared by all activities denoted play that at the same time are exclusive to these activities vis-à-vis adjacent ones (e.g., games, exploration). However, in the nature of constituting a 'family', we may expect some features to be present in activities perceived as play, albeit not in all and not features that are exclusive to these. One such feature, arguably, is open-endedness (cf. van Oers, 2014), that is, that in the nature of play what the outcome of the activity is, that is, where the play takes the players, is not deterministic. However, and this is critical to our reasoning, also such goal-directed practices as teaching are inevitably open-ended. That is, there is no causal relation – or in more contemporary terms, linearity – between teaching and learning, at least if we concern ourselves with more advanced forms of learning than simple stimulus–response patterns as favoured by the behaviourists in the 1930s.

The reason for the dynamic relation between teaching and learning is a basic feature of our psychological set-up: humans are sense-making in nature (Bruner, 1990). This means that we do not simply receive, register, and store information (cf. our initial comments on the distinction between information and knowledge); instead, we make sense, that is, perceive (see, hear, etc.) something *as* something. What sense we make of instruction is contingent on previous experiences, interests, and how we perceive the situation we find ourselves in (Sommer et al., 2010). Hence, if returning to the question of play, while open-endedness may be a feature of activities we see as play, this feature is not exclusive to such activities. Also, to give an example, exploration is open-ended (and, as we have argued, so is the relationship between teaching and learning); this does not mean that exploration and teaching should be labelled play.

A recurring feature of discussions about play, particularly in the context of (Swedish) preschool is the notion of 'free play'. Historically (see, e.g., Clark et al., 1969), the freedom of play has been understood as children being free from the 'influence' – or the 'interference', to use another common metaphor in this regard – of teachers. Such a stance makes it difficult to conceptualize and provide developmental support in play-based settings, as cogently argued by Fleer (2011) and others. A way out of this conceptual cul-de-sac is offered by van Oers (2014), who makes a distinction between 'freedom from' and 'freedom to'. The latter, freedom to, does not preclude the exclusion of preschool teachers from children's play; rather, this question remains open. According to van Oers's (2014) reasoning about play in terms of freedom to, play is contingent on the freedom to go in novel directions. Rather than a separate kind of activity, this perspective further means that "all activities can be accomplished in playful versions or in more strictly proceduralised versions" (p. 62). If any activity potentially can be formatted in a playful or a more strictly procedural way, we can ask of activities children are introduced to, invent, and are engaged in in preschool: What kinds of activities develop? What kinds of roles (positions) does it open up for children to take – as co-creators, co-narrators, or merely responding to questions the teacher already knows the answer to? These are only a few of the possible questions.

The latter kind of activity, theorized in terms of the initiation-response-evaluation/follow-up (IRE or IRF) sequence, has been shown to be characteristic of schooling in many countries and cultures around the world (e.g., Wells & Arauz, 2006). It is less clear that this is a predominant pattern also in preschool, and it should be noted that what is in Sweden referred to as preschool is much less school-like than in many other countries, denoting a holistic, play- and theme-based pedagogical practice without goals to reach (only to strive for, i.e., to 'plant' the 'seeds', to use a common developmental metaphor, of various forms of knowing and interests and experiences).

Another take on the freedom of play is provided by Vygotsky (1933/1966), who argues that every play situation characterized by imagination will contain some rules:

> [T]here is no such thing as play without rules ... The imaginary situation already contains rules of behavior, although this is not a game with formulated rules laid down in advance. The child imagines herself to be the mother and the doll the child, so she must obey the rules of maternal behavior. (p. 9)

In line with this reasoning, Vygotsky further argues, "In play the child is free. But this is an illusory freedom" (p. 10). However, not only does all play, according to this perspective, contain rules and thus restrictions of degrees of freedom, but play is also contingent on previous experience or, in alternative terms, the appropriation of cultural tools (see Wallerstedt & Pramling, 2012, for an exploration with empirical examples). To use a simple example, to be able to play the role one wants, one needs to know which potential roles can be played. That is, without some experience of roles (e.g., work positions such as nurse or doctor), these roles cannot be played. Hence, free play is not free of knowledge, of previous learning, but rather contingent on it.

A further comment in relation to the importance of appropriating cultural tools for developing a repertoire of play (play forms, roles, positions) is that there is an inherent tension in this relationship. Appropriated tools come to structure – that is, semiotically mediate – our perception: this means, on the one hand, that we learn to see phenomena in new ways and, on the other hand, that this makes it increasingly difficult to see the same phenomena in other ways. That is, there is a tension in appropriation between the empowerment and specification of perception, paradoxically making us see the world simultaneously in richer and in more delimited ways (cf. Luria, 1976).

Precise and Vague Language in Instruction

An important finding from psychological research that has not been properly reconsidered in educational theory and practice concerns the relationship between what may be referred to as precise and vague language, respectively. In their study, Langer and Piper (1987) investigated how subtle differences in the introduction of tasks directed participants' attention toward or away from possible solutions to problems. In their investigation (here somewhat simplified), they showed adult participants a number of objects. For one of the groups, the objects were referred to in terms of 'This *is* an X', while for the other group the objects were referred to as 'This *could* be an X'. The objects were labelled as, for example, rubber band, chewing toy for dog, and accessory to hairdryer. Having introduced the objects to the participants, the experiment leader introduced a problem requiring the use of one of the objects previously introduced, a use, however, not following from how the object had been labelled. For example, the problem faced was that the experiment leader mistakenly had written something on a sheet that needed to be erased. The rubber band as well as the chewing object for dog could serve this function. However, only participants who had been introduced to these objects in the terms that they 'could be an X' were able to solve this problem. While the participants in the study were adults, studying at the university, the principle illustrated is of great interest also to theorizing and outlining early childhood education.

There is an inherent tension in our knowledge in that when we refer to objects or phenomena our perception becomes semiotically mediated (Wertsch, 2007) by these cultural tools (categories and distinctions). We learn to see (hear, taste, i.e., perceive) something *as* something (as a member of a linguistic category). This empowers our perception, constituting an important part of what it means to be knowledgeable (cf. Hasselgren, 1981, in the context of teacher education), and, at the same time, teaches us not to pay attention to other features and aspects of phenomena. We have already briefly mentioned this tension in our knowledge. It is vital to children's development that they learn to perceive objects and phenomena as they are conventionally labelled, in order to make themselves understood and understand others (convention) as well as to be able to see objects and phenomena in new ways (creativity). Clarifying, through empirical research and, on this basis, theoretical elaboration, how children learn to see and not see phenomena and objects in different ways therefore constitutes an important problem to research on play, learning, and teaching in ECE. In the context of this discussion it is important to realize that there is no clear one-to-one correspondence between precise and vague language, on the one hand, and teaching and playing, on the other. Both teaching and play could be orchestrated in absolute/precise and/or in vague terms (cf. Fleer & Pramling, 2015, on the use in teaching of 'is' and 'looks like'). Still, the distinction between these forms of speech may provide an incentive for reconsidering the developmental opportunities offered children and supported in teaching and in playing.

That the proclivity of children playing with reality in the form of engaging in imagination may be severely restricted and/or facilitated through different educational arrangements is discussed in a thought-provoking article by

Diachenko (2011), where she argues that "imagination tends to fade out gradually since its functioning … is associated with uncertain situations. By focusing education on certain knowledge, unambiguous answers and the adoption of ready-made models", reducing the role of imagination, she further argues, this results "in its extinction in many children in the school system" (p. 24). While this is a theoretically feasible form of reasoning, whether it captures an empirical phenomenon – for example, in Russian school, or in Swedish preschool, to use the respective horizon from where Diachenko and we write – remains an open, empirical question, albeit an important one to investigate.

While there is some element of freedom – in the sense of open-endedness or freedom to (van Oers, 2014) – the relationship between play and freedom, and implicitly the relation between play and learning and its facilitation through teaching, highlighting the role of the teacher, is anything but clear-cut. Clearly, perspectives where these processes and activities, for example, play and learning, or play and teaching, are constituted as dichotomous, that is, as mutually exclusive phenomena, lack functionality in conceptualizing the developmental opportunities children are given and supported in in a setting such as preschool. How these processes play out in a concrete fashion in such settings is at the forefront of empirical research and theoretical elaboration in this domain.

How Preschool Teachers Relate to Children's Play

In a study on how what they refer to as 'pedagogues', encompassing preschool teachers but also leisure-time personnel in Norway, Løndal and Greve (2015) provide an empirically grounded typology of roles taken to children's play. These are summarized in Table 26.1. Løndal and Greve (2015) refer to the different ways teachers relate to children's play in terms of different approaches: surveillance, initiating and inspiring, and participating and interacting. The identification of three approaches makes their relation to the four orientations (in Table 26.1) somewhat unclear. However, this typology identifies an important field of further investigation and development: how teachers in play-based settings such as preschool can teach in ways that facilitate children's development.

How this can be done in the more particular context of children's musical play (the word 'play' is here intentionally used in both the sense of 'pretend' and 'perform') is shown empirically by Lagerlöf (2016). In her study she shows how children's musical play and learning develop when the preschool teacher participates in their play as a co-participant, entering into dialogue (verbally and through playing on the instrument) with the children's interests and actions, and that the children welcome, even ask for, her active participation. Through participating as a co-participant (an experienced playmate), the

Table 26.1 *Different ways that 'pedagogues' (preschool teachers and leisure-time personnel) relate to children's play*

	High degree of focus on goal	Low degree of focus on goal
High degree of focus on process	A. Teacher/instructor: The pedagogue has a set goal and organizes and directs the activity toward that goal	B. Process oriented: The pedagogue supports the process but does not direct toward a particular outcome
Low degree of focus on process	C. Environmentally oriented: The pedagogue organizes the environment with the intention to reach a particular goal but does not direct the process	D. Chaotic position: The pedagogue does not intend to direct the outcome or the process but supervises and interferes when needed to uphold security

Source: After Løndal & Greve, 2015.

preschool teacher scaffolds the children in coordinating their play suggestions and offering proto tools for creating, listening to, and understanding music. The children, Lagerlöf (2016) shows, start appropriating these tools in developing their play projects in ways that do not happen when they are exploring the instruments on their own.

Another example of how preschool teachers can facilitate children engaging in new activities is provided by Kultti (2016), who shows how the preschool teacher, through remediating a situation, constitutes a new and mutual activity for toddlers to engage in in their play: that they are 'shipmates' on a boat (a transformed swing). Another study shows how young children when playing take the initiative to involve teachers. They show that they want to be supported in their play and to be recognized, want to make the teacher aware of someone doing something wrong in the play, ask for information from the teacher, and express that they want the teacher to take part in their play (Pramling Samuelsson & Johansson, 2009). This study makes another kind of contribution to the discussion about teachers' participation in children's play (cf. earlier discussion).

Closely related to the topics of our discussion but outlined in the terminology of creativity rather than play is Robson's (2015) study on "the roles of adults in supporting and developing young children's creative thinking" (p. 433). Her study takes place against the common background of the debate between child-initiated versus teacher-initiated activity in preschool (cf. our earlier discussions about 'free play' and later discussions about whether to follow children's interests). The study is rather complex, but we will limit our discussion to some features that have direct bearing on the present chapter. Mirroring our claims about the futility in conceptualizing developmental phenomena in dichotomous terms, Robson argues that children learn from other children: "At the same time, Sylva et al. conclude that 'children's cognitive outcomes appeared to be directly related to the quantity and quality of the teacher/adult planned and initiated focused group work for supporting children's learning' (2010, p. 161)" (p. 434). Further discussing the Effective Provision for Preschool Education study, Robson argues: "The choice of practice is not, of course, one of 'either/or', but of the balance between adult-directed/led and child-initiated activity. Sylva et al. (2010) suggest that the 'excellent' settings in their study 'provided both teacher-initiated group work and freely chosen yet potentially instructive play activities' (2010, p. 161)" (Robson, 2015, p. 435). Hence, according to this reasoning, and in line with our previous discussion on van Oers (2014), free play is not conceptualized as 'free from' adult participation; even free activities are considered "potentially instructive play activities" (Robson, 2015, p. 435).

In her empirical investigation, where children 3–4 years old were followed when engaged in different events, Robson (2015) found that boundaries between child-initiated and adult-initiated and adult-directed activities were hard to uphold analytically; participation patterns tended to shift during the course of activities (or events). In addition, Robson found that "[s]ome aspects of creative thinking behavior occur more frequently than others, in particular 'Trying out ideas', 'Analysing ideas' and 'Involving others'. These may also occur more frequently in child-initiated activities. Other aspects, such as 'Engaging in new activity', are associated more strongly with adult direction and involvement" (p. 438). Note the tentative terms; as pointed out by Robson herself, the data were too few to clarify more firmly the nature of these relationships; also, arguably, the categories being partly overlapping and changing in nature do not permit clear-cut distinctions of this kind. However, what is emphasized in her study is that "[a]n interesting aspect of the data is the impact of adults on children's initial engagement and exploration" (p. 440); while some aspects were associated with child-initiated activity, "Other aspects, such as 'Engaging in new activity', are associated more strongly with adult direction and involvement, and the observations point to the particularly important role of adults in supporting children's initial engagement in activities" (p. 445). This finding highlights the important role of preschool teachers in introducing and engaging children in new activities (for example, in the context of our present discussion, new forms of play; cf. Lagerlöf, 2016, earlier) and not only listening to and following children's interests and initiative. This reasoning is parallel to what was found in Løndal and Greve (2015), who report that the children in their study, particularly the younger children, expressed appreciation when teachers initiated new activities and that these activities often developed into child-managed play.

Another key finding from Robson's (2015) study is that "[a]ll adults [i.e., not only preschool teachers] were skillful in encouraging children to make use of prior knowledge, such as reminding them of how to use resources, or ways of doing things. However, teachers, as a group, were more successful [than adults at large] in supporting children in gaining new knowledge" (p. 441; for similar findings, see Swedish School Inspectorate, 2016). Importantly, this says something vital about the competences of trained professionals; preschool teachers are not any number of adults but a group embodying professional knowledge on how to promote children's development (cf. Hasselgren, 1981). As noted by Vygotsky (1933/1966), initially in children's play they play what they have experienced (e.g., a visit to the supermarket) in a way that closely mirrors that actual experience. However, gradually children tend to play in less imitative ways. This development of play indicates that not only is there development of play but, implicitly, that more experienced co-participants including peers and preschool teachers can provide incentive and tools for this development.

Narrative Frame, Scaffolding, and Social Justice

Hakkarainen and Bredikyte (2015) provide important reasoning about the role and possibilities of the adult in children's play and development:

> Adult guidance and help in play should proceed in two main directions: (1) to develop joint activity of children, and (2) to support individual children participating in the activity. Adult help may be needed to keep children in the play frame (inexperienced children constantly 'fall out' of it), or to highlight children's ideas and use them for play construction. Adults should support the whole structure of play when it is starting to fall apart. In practice this means that they have to help individual children to participate in the activity but they also have to take an active role and move the activity one step forward when it is needed. We believe that the direct impact of the adult on development or learning is a fiction. An adult should create the experience through the activities (not just separate tasks), participation in which would demand the child to act on their highest level, which in turn, sooner or later, will move their development.   (p. 41)

Such joint activities may typically take the form of narratives where an imaginary frame to play within is created, maintained, and potentially developed. How preschool teachers can author such narratives and engage children in them is arguably pivotal to their ability to provide developmental incentive and support for children in play-based settings such as preschool (cf. Kultti & Pramling Samuelsson, 2017). How – or in fact even if – they do so is still not sufficiently illuminated. However, in her work, based on a Vygotskian framework, Lindqvist (2003) suggests that "[w]hen adults play roles and dramatise a chain of events, they open a door to a playworld which the children can enter" (p. 69). In doing so she emphasizes that "[a] child's imagination is not captured by an object itself, but by the narrative which gives the object and the actions their meaning" (p. 69). In her studies, the preschool teachers (in her study referred to as 'pedagogues') took part in children's play. Lindqvist argues, "The adults needed to *dramatise the action* in order to provide play with a meaning. The *characters* played by the pedagogues were of particular importance in bringing the play to life because they created a *dialogue* between the adults and the children which opened the door to the fictitious world. The pedagogues became *mediators* " (pp. 73–74., emphasis in original). Through the enacted narrative, children and preschool teachers came to share a 'playworld'.

Like Lindqvist's (2003) work, Hakkarainen and Bredikyte's (2015) reasoning provides a way of thinking about how preschool teachers can support – or in well-known theoretical terms, scaffold (Wood et al., 1976) – children's learning and development without taking away the open-ended nature of play (the *freedom to* play; van Oers, 2014). This is an important question to contemporary theorizing on scaffolding in play-based settings: What is – or should – be scaffolded: the process and/or the product of an activity? (Cf. different stances taken by the 'pedagogues' in studies by Løndal & Greve, 2015, and Fleer, 2015.) Phrased differently, this is the question of whether one scaffolds the development of play or the development of other skills in play activities. Arguably, different developmental trajectories are supported in the two cases.

Our final point will be to emphasize how play and teaching are critical to social justice and to cater to those children who enter preschool with the fewest cultural resources (at least those experiences that are valued by the institution). One feature of 'free play' that we have not yet discussed but which is frequent in more common-sense reasoning is that this notion refers to children's right to choose whatever they wish to play. This ideal, which at first instance appears appealing, tends to be aligned with the notion of following children's interests more generally. However, following children's interests in the social arena of preschool always means to follow the interest of *some* children, the children with rich cultural capital (Bourdieu, 1997), who have ample 'relevant' experience and can communicate these to others. To give an example: some children want to play Star Wars. But any other children who have not seen these films and therefore do not know which characters are available to play, or what the narrative frame of the story is, cannot participate and are unintentionally excluded (or marginalized into limiting positions where they are told what to do). Analogously, we can argue that there is an inherent problem with basing more pedagogical activities – what we have referred to here as teaching – on what some children are interested in. These children will likely have some resources for making sense of such activities, which other children may not have. This results in inadvertently further accentuating rather than counteracting unequal preconditions for children's development. Being engaged in mutual activities where they are supported in developing new insights into *how to play* new forms of play and *through play* to learn new roles, positions, and knowledge is critical to preschool as a socially just institution.

In this chapter we have discussed the relations between play, learning, and teaching, where the latter is conceptualized as inherently socially responsive to children's experiences and play, and critical to creating a socially just institution for all participating children.

References

Barnett, S. A. (1973). Homo docens. *Journal of Biosocial Science*, 5(3), 393–403.

Boesch, C. (1991). Teaching among chimpanzees. *Animal Behavior*, 41, 530–532.

Bourdieu, P. (1997). The forms of capital. In A. H. Halsey, H. Lauder, P. Brown, & A. Stuart Wells (Eds.), *Education: Culture, economy, and society* (pp. 46–58). Oxford: Oxford University Press.

Bruner, J. S. (1990). *Acts of meaning*. Cambridge, MA: Harvard University Press.

Clark, A. H., Wyon, S. M., & Richards, M. P. M. (1969). Free-play in nursery school children. *Journal of Child Psychology and Psychiatry and Allied Disciplines*, 10(3), 205–216.

Cook, G. (1997). Language play, language learning. *ELT Journal*, 51(3), 224–231.

Diachenko, O. M. (2011). On major developments in preschoolers' imagination. *International Journal of Early Years Education*, 19(1), 19–25.

Fleer, M. (2011). 'Conceptual play': Foregrounding imagination and cognition during concept formation in early years education. *Contemporary Issues in Early Childhood*, 12(3), 224–240.

Fleer, M. (2015). Pedagogical positioning in play – Teachers being inside and outside of children's imaginary play. *Early Child Development and Care*, 185(11–12), 1801–1814.

Fleer, M., & Pramling, N. (2015). *A cultural-historical study of children learning science: Foregrounding affective imagination in play-based settings*. Dordrecht: Springer.

Franks, N. R., & Richardson, T. (2006). Teaching in tandem-running ants. *Nature*, 439, 153.

Hakkarainen, P., & Bredikyte, M. (2015). How play creates the zone of proximal development. In S. Robson & S. Flannery Quinn (Eds.), *The Routledge international handbook of young children's thinking and understanding* (pp. 31–42). London: Routledge.

Hasselgren, B. (1981). *Ways of apprehending children at play*. Göteborg: Acta Universitatis Gothoburgensis.

Kultti, A. (2016). Go Edvin! Pedagogical structuring of activities to support toddler participation in an early childcare programme. *International Research in Early Childhood Education*, 7(3), 2–15.

Kultti, A., & Pramling Samuelsson, I. (2017). Toys and the creation of cultural play scripts. In D. Pike, C. á Beckett, & S. Lynch (Eds.), *Multidisciplinary perspectives on play from early childhood and beyond* (pp. 217–230). Dordrecht: Springer.

Lagerlöf, P. (2016). *Musical play: Children interacting with and around music technology*. Göteborg: Acta Universitatis Gothoburgensis.

Langer, E. J., & Piper, A. I. (1987). The prevention of mindlessness. *Journal of Personality and Social Psychology*, 53(2), 280–287.

Lindqvist, G. (2003). The dramatic and narrative patterns of play. *European Early Childhood Education Research Journal*, 11(1), 69–78.

Løndal, K., & Greve, A. (2015). Didactic approaches to child-managed play: Analyses of teacher's interaction style in kindergartens and after-school programmes in Norway. *International Journal of Early Childhood*, 47, 461–479.

Luria, A. R. (1976). *Cognitive development: Its cultural and social foundations* (trans. M. Lopez-Morillas & L. Solotaroff). Cambridge, MA: Harvard University Press.

Marton, F., & Booth, S. (1997). *Learning and awareness.* Mahwah, NJ: Lawrence Erlbaum.

Pramling, N., Doverborg, E., & Pramling Samuelsson, I. (2017). Re-metaphorizing teaching and learning in early childhood education beyond the instruction–social fostering divide. In C. Ringsmose & G. Kragh-Müller (Eds.), *Nordic social pedagogical approach to early years* (pp. 205–218). Dordrecht: Springer.

Pramling, N., & Pramling Samuelsson, I. (2010). Evolving activities and semiotic mediation in teacher–child interaction around simple objects. *Educational & Child Psychology, 27*(4), 22–30.

Pramling Samuelsson, I., & Johansson, E. (2009). Why do children involve teachers in their play and learning? *European Early Childhood Education Research Journal, 17*(1), 77–94.

Reddy, M. J. (1993). The conduit metaphor: A case of frame conflict in our language about language. In A. Ortony (Ed.), *Metaphor and thought* (2nd edn., pp. 164–201). New York: Cambridge University Press.

Robson, S. (2015). Whose activity is it? The role of child- and adult-initiated activity in young children's creative thinking. In S. Robson & S. Flannery Quinn (Eds.), *The Routledge international handbook of young children's thinking and understanding* (pp. 433–447). London: Routledge.

Rommetveit, R. (1974). *On message structure: A framework for the study of language and communication.* London: Wiley.

Säljö, R. (2002). My brain's running slow today – The preference for 'things ontologies' in research and everyday discourse on human thinking. *Studies in Philosophy and Education, 21*(4–5), 389–405.

Säljö, R. (2010). Digital tools and challenges to institutional traditions of learning: Technologies, social memory and the performative nature of learning. *Journal of Computer Assisted Learning, 26*, 53–64.

Sommer, D., Pramling Samuelsson, I., & Hundeide, K. (2010). *Child perspectives and children's perspectives in theory and practice.* New York: Springer.

Sutton-Smith, B. (1997). *The ambiguity of play.* Cambridge, MA: Harvard University Press.

Swedish School Inspectorate. (2016). *Om säkerheten i förskolan* [On security in preschool]. Stockholm: Swedish School Inspectorate.

Tennie, C., Call, J., & Tomasello, M. (2009). Ratcheting up the ratchet: On the evolution of cumulative culture. *Philosophical Transactions of the Royal Society, 364*, 2405–2415.

Thornton, A., & McAuliffe, K. (2006). Teaching in wild meerkats. *Science, 313*, 227–229.

Tomasello, M. (1999). *The cultural origins of human cognition.* Cambridge, MA: Harvard University Press.

van Oers, B. (2014). Cultural-historical perspectives on play: Central ideas. In L. Brooker, M. Blaise, & S. Edwards (Eds.), *The Sage handbook of play and learning in early childhood* (pp. 56–66). Thousand Oaks, CA: Sage.

van Oers, B., Janssen-Vos, F., Pompert, B., & Schiferli, T. (2003). Teaching as a joint activity. In B. van Oers (Ed.), *Narratives of childhood: Theoretical and practical explorations for the innovation of early childhood education* (pp. 110–126). Amsterdam: VU University Press.

Vygotsky, L. S. (1933/1966). Play and its role in the mental development of the child. *Voprosy Psikhologii, 12*(6), 62–76.

Wallerstedt, C., & Pramling, N. (2012). Learning to play in a goal-directed practice. *Early Years, 32*(1), 5–15.

Wells, G., & Arauz, R. M. (2006). Dialogue in the classroom. *Journal of the Learning Sciences, 15*(3), 379–428.

Wertsch, J. V. (1998). *Mind as action.* New York: Oxford University Press.

Wertsch, J. V. (2007). Mediation. In H. Daniels, M. Cole, & J. V. Wertsch (Eds.), *The Cambridge companion to Vygotsky* (pp. 178–192). New York: Cambridge University Press.

Wittgenstein, L. (1953). *Philosophische untersuchungen/Philosophical investigations* (trans. G. E. M. Anscombe). Oxford: Basil Blackwell.

Wood, D., Bruner, J. S., & Ross, G. (1976). The role of tutoring in problem solving. *Journal of Child Psychology and Psychiatry, 17*(2), 89–100.

27 Toddlers' Play in Early Childhood Education Settings

Maritta Hännikäinen and Hilkka Munter

This chapter deals with the play of younger children in the context of centre-based education. Currently, in early childhood education settings, the younger children, up to the age of 3, are mostly placed in groups of their own, although multi-age groups are becoming increasingly common. That is why all teachers should be well informed about younger children's play and have the relevant knowledge and competence to support it. Moreover, teachers working with older children's groups should be aware of the earlier development of play and of children's play experiences to build their educational activities on this knowledge.

Play has its roots in the first years of life; here the focus is on children during their second and third years of life, often referred to as *toddlers* in the literature. Despite the knowledge that has accumulated on toddlers' playing skills and on the psychology underlying the development of play, research on toddlers' play from the educational and pedagogical viewpoints is limited. Shin (2015) criticizes the term 'infant caregiver', which by referring solely to education as care, neglects the bringing up and teaching of younger children that also take place in early childhood education settings. Therefore, we use the term *teacher*, conceiving teachers' work holistically as a combination of the physical and emotional aspects of care, moral aspects of upbringing, and academic aspects of teaching. When considering play, all these aspects of education are of great importance.

Younger children's conditions for play are not equal. There are differences between and within countries in factors such as legislation and steering documents, adult/child ratios, group size, environmental organization, and the education and experience of teachers (Dalli et al., 2011). High staff turnover, inconsistent care, poor working conditions, and low status are often the reality in early childhood education settings of toddlers (Dalli et al., 2011; OECD, 2010). Research shows marked variation in pedagogical aims and in the organization of early childhood education for younger children in different national and cultural contexts (Elfer & Page, 2015).

---

* The responsibility for this article is equally shared between the authors.

Variation also exists between staff in their beliefs and values about working with younger children. Whereas teachers of toddlers report high respect for play and the importance of play in toddlers' lives, research shows that the position of play is generally weak (Grindheim & Ødegaard, 2013; Lemay et al., 2016; Singer et al., 2014). This also applies to the Nordic countries, where play is deemed to be paramount in the early childhood education of younger children (Alvestad et al., 2014).

Here, we focus our attention on the play of toddlers as such – not its impact on children's development. We first describe our view of younger children, and then discuss the development and characteristics of their play, after which we turn to the ways in which toddlers play with each other. Ultimately, the key issue in this chapter is how to support and enrich the play of toddlers in early childhood education settings.

View of the Child

For adults who live, work, and play with toddlers, the critical issue is how they see toddlers, how they comprehend toddlers' life-worlds, and how they understand and perform their relationships with toddlers. These factors affect each other. In this chapter, we share the idea that young children are active, curious, energetic, and full of life. We also acknowledge how crucial the first years of life are and how decisive this time is for brain development and for the overall well-being of the child. We see young children as both competent and vulnerable, resilient and weak, self-directed and in need of adults. To comprehend and support children's play requires that we find ways of gaining access to children's perspectives and enhance our understanding of their experiences. This is challenging when a considerable proportion of a child's daily life is spent in early childhood education settings, confronting adults with the task of interpreting toddlers' mostly non-verbal, embodied interaction.

Elwick et al. (2014) emphasize that while adults have an ethical responsibility to treat infants and toddlers from the outset as genuinely human beings, they nevertheless have to accept that they cannot know them with any certainty. It is not enough to see and read young children's behaviour through adult experiences, developmental theories, or one's own expectations about how children should behave. Often, only the surface behaviour of children is noticed; however, as Degotardi (2010) shows, if teachers' interpretations of infants' behaviour are more complex, their understanding of infants' viewpoints and their interactions with children are also more sensitive and stimulating. But how can this be achieved?

Johansson and Løkken (2014), who, like many others seeking to understand the life-world of children, draw on the philosophy of Merleau-Ponty, conceive the body as the centre of all our experiences. Adults and children see the world and each other from their individual, although intertwined, embodied positions. The teacher, who wants to understand the child, has to understand that each participant in interaction is seer and seen, hearer and heard, and that all of children are both alike and different.

For children, only experiences that have emotional meaning for them are significant. Vygotsky's concepts of *perezhivanie* and *social situation of development* capture this notion from a broader perspective. *Perezhivanie*, which refers to a lived emotional experience as a multifaceted and dynamic unity of imagination and creativity, emotion and cognition, is inseparably connected to the child's environment and determines what kind of influence this environment will have on the child (Vygotsky, 1998). The *social situation of development* is always a system of changing relations among a child of a given age and his or her environment and social reality. What is meaningful for children emerges in this particular social situation of development. This is the most important factor to recognize when contemplating teachers' possibilities to scaffold young children's play.

We want to see children as fellow human beings in society and as plenipotentiary citizens of the future, growing to citizenship from the very beginning, which means respecting their rights. Of special importance are the rights to participation laid down in the UN Convention on the Rights of the Child (1989). Regarding play as central is the first part of Article 31, according to which "States Parties recognize the right of the child to rest and leisure, to engage in play and recreational activities appropriate to the age of the child and to participate freely in cultural life and the arts."

As Duhn (2015) notes, when we speak about participation and its precondition, agency, we are not usually thinking of younger children. If, however, participation and agency are considered together with play, it also becomes easier to see children as active participants in their lives. Duhn (2015, p. 928) states that "infants and toddlers, perhaps, are less caught up in the illusion of a self that controls and governs than older humans who have learned to see, feel and think the self and the world in particular ways." Therefore, toddlers, with their whole bodies, senses, languages, emotions, and spontaneous intentions, can actively take part in everything in their surroundings that excites their curiosity. By using their power of play, they make their contribution to the shared life in early childhood education communities.

Play as Developmental and Cultural Process

We understand the concept of play, in accordance with Vygotsky (1978), as imaginative play, as an activity that happens in the framework of 'as if'. In imaginative or 'pretend' play (the terms 'make-believe play', 'sociodramatic play', and 'role-play' are also used; see Bodrova & Leong, 2015), children make sense of the world by creating an imaginary situation, acting out roles, and following a set of rules determined by these roles. Vygotsky's definition of play is interpreted to mean so-called mature or 'true' play, which reaches its highest level during the preschool years, between 3 and 6 years of age. This definition does not include other related activities, such as corporeal activities, games, object manipulation, and exploration. However, we are looking at the roots of mature play, knowing that all prerequisites for mature play emerge during the first 3 years through different kinds of toddlers' playful and explorative activities and early pretending.

Following Vygotsky's (1978) idea about the child's cultural development first on the social level, then on a psychological level, imagination also appears first interpersonally, then inside the child. The origin of imagination is the emotional communication and imitation between the adult and the child, through which they co-construct a *zone of proximal development*, an activity where learning and development take place. Likewise, somewhat later, a zone of proximal development is co-created in play among children and adults (Hakkarainen & Brédikytè, 2010; Vygotsky, 1978).

Children have a readiness for social interaction and intersubjectivity from birth onward. This is evident in certain embodied, emotional, perceptual, rhythmic, and musical communicative practices that take place between infants and their caregivers (Stern, 1985; Trevarthen, 2012). In this playful interaction, the child feels safe and confident, and, as Engel (2005a) notes, is therefore free to explore the world ('what is?') and imagine possible worlds ('what if?').

Children move in and out of different frames in everyday life, some of which are to do with play and imagination, others with a variety of practical matters (Engel, 2005b). Their experiences are organized in narrative form from the beginning of their joint activity with adults. As Bruner (1990) states, children are interested from birth in temporal sequences of events and unexpected turns in the chain of events. They begin to make sense of what is going on, and play becomes children's narrative about their own life experiences, thereby creating the sense in play.

Ordinary linear categorizations of play, such as object play, role-play and rule play or solitary play, parallel play and joint play, do not do justice to play as a complex, continuously changing activity. How these aspects relate to each other depends on the child's experiences, intentions, and competences and on the institutional conditions for play (e.g., Hedegaard, 2016). Thus, play should not be considered through successive forms of play, but as a cultural and social activity, which emerges in interaction.

Vygotsky's (1998) concept of social situation of development helps us to perceive the developmental changes, and the meaning of children's own subjective experiences, in play. The concept describes the unique, age-specific, inimitable, and emotional relationship between the child and her or his social environment. A transformation in a given social situation of development happens through the developmental crises, which redefine the psychological content of the situation and provide a new impetus and a new direction for the child's psychological development (Karabanova, 2010). Crises are not categorically age dependent. They emerge from the dynamic, changing relationship of the child to her or his environment. The relationship changes because both parties, the child and the environment, change.

According to Vygotsky (1998), emotional interaction with caregivers resolves the crisis of the newborn baby. The first-year crisis involves the beginning of intentional understanding: the child begins to understand that she or he has intentions and that other people also have them. Emerging independent movement opens up a new world of motion to the child. Understanding intentions and sovereign moving mean that the child exhibits her or his own will and personality more clearly. The child forms new relationships, especially with space and objects and to their social meanings. During the third-year crisis, at the end of the second year, when the child's consciousness of self becomes stronger and verbal language begins to take over from immediate perceptions, the child's relation to her- or himself and to other people as separate subjects changes. Now the child has acquired a good foundation for imaginary play. These developmental changes have consistently been confirmed by later infant and toddler research.

All these changes mould children's initiatives and intentions, experiences, and perspectives in their being-in-the world, making up the period when interacting, imitating, exploring, and inventing 'I' in the social world opens the gates to imagination and creativity. As Parker-Rees (2007, p. 11) aptly puts it, "instead of passively copying what other people do, taking up cultural habits as if they were a uniform, they [children] adapt them, play with them and dress up in them, and, in the process, encourage others to see new possibilities in them." How successfully this happens depends on adults' understanding of the importance of play for children.

Toddlers as Players

When a new toddler enters an early childhood education group on her or his first day, she or he will usually look intensively at the other children, following what they are doing. As soon as the toddler feels safe, she or he will join in an ongoing activity in one way or another, demonstrating the desire to act in company with peers. Later, when toddlers begin to play more and more together, they continue closely observing each other. There seems to exist a social pattern of observation, imitation, and joining in others' actions. It is easy to see that imitation is the primary way in which toddlers create companionship and shared joy, inspiring them to engage further in their interaction (Brownell, 2011; Parker-Rees, 2007; Ridgway et al., 2016; Selby & Bradley, 2003).

Development of Imitation and Pretending

The peak period of toddlers' imitation occurs between 18 and 30 months, thereafter decreasing as children begin more and more verbally to negotiate play. In fact, imitation never stops but continues throughout life. Vygotsky (see Holzman, 2010) stresses that children do not imitate everything in their play. They imitate things that while not developmentally attainable in their real lives are nevertheless present in their environment. Imitative, pretend play among children and between children and adults becomes meaningful because children understand it as shared, complementary activity (Rakoczy, 2008; Striano et al., 2001). As Göncü (1998) points out, this requires the children to share a minimum level of emotional similarity and affective needs.

The accumulated research demonstrates that by 30 months of age children have attained the ability to understand the make-believe sequences of others and become full partners in shared pretend play (e.g., Kavanaugh & Engel, 1998; Rakoczy, 2008; Stambak et al., 1985). Children understand the basic intentional structure of pretending as a non-serious fictional form of action and respond appropriately to the imaginary suggestions of their play partners. This is possible, because around 1 year of age, children began to comprehend that people's actions are guided by plans, goals, desires, and beliefs (Agnetta & Rochat, 2004). Briefly, the first half of the second year of life is mainly a period of intense imitation; the next half-year sees shared, simple, imitative pretence; and the third year coordinated pretending, i.e., shared play in the frame of 'as if'. This indicates changes in children's sense of self, their developing conscious self and understanding of themselves, among other things, as social (Brownell, 2011; Rochat, 2010; Stern, 1985).

When children play together, they might smoothly alternate between complementary, solitary and parallel. As Howes (1985) conveys, these are children's ways of acting in a group, sometimes preferring to play alone, sometimes wanting to experience togetherness by imitating. She noticed that about half of the youngest toddlers, aged from 13 to 15 months, participated in reciprocal, complementary games. The children were familiar to each other, the setting was natural, and the toys invited pretend activities. In addition to these prerequisites, the scaffolding role of adults is essential. In such conditions, toddlers spontaneously form small groups of two or three and usually communicate successfully. They engage in cooperative play not only to achieve a common goal but for the playful act of cooperating per se.

Objects, Spaces, and Playing Together

If the social attraction between children arouses the desire for shared play, the play itself is distinctly characterized by the children's changing relations to objects and spaces and by their developing motor skills. Together these three elements modify toddlers' intrinsic style of playing. The ardent desire of toddlers to seek out novel, stimulating ways to engage with whatever is around them – first crawling, then walking, seizing and scrutinizing – opens up options for them regarding what the environment has to offer and what their possibilities for action are. As Gibson's (1979) theory of affordances states, the constraints of the actor and the constraints of the environment mutually contribute to the possibilities for action and so define the self. In this process, Merleau-Ponty (1962) highlights the emergence of synaesthetic perception, which invests the perceived world with meanings and values that refer essentially to our bodies and lives. The body is not 'in' space but inhabits it. These ideas about the physicality and material existence of the human body in the world, replete with cultural meanings for inventing, becomes evident when we look at toddlers in action.

Small replica objects such as puppets, cars, and bricks and big objects such as cardboard boxes, slides, and stairs invite toddlers to act with them and with each other differently. Before the mental image guides the child's actions, immediate perception takes the lead. Whereas small objects invite toddlers to grasp them, to imitate, and to acquire the same toy as a nearby peer has, big objects invite them to run around these objects together, to crawl in and out, to climb up and down, to hide and seek. As demonstrated by Kultti and Pramling (2015), toys work as triggers of and bases for a mutual focal point when communicating intentions and expectations. With small objects, toddlers practice the basic social rules of playing (you don't grab something from another's hand; you must wait, ask, give, and exchange). When they invent what to do with toys together or with the teacher, they practice their first joint play activities. Big objects and the space around them enable children to feel the joy of moving together in an exultant atmosphere. These activities give rise to affiliation and companionship, the first preconditions of joint play. Løkken (2000) proposes that toddlers may connect the meaning 'this toy is for me to play with' with small objects, whereas the meaning attached to big objects is 'this thing is for us to play with'. The meaning of holistic bodily games may be 'this play is for me and for us and moving together'. Therefore, for toddlers, bodily games may have greater social importance than games with small objects.

Montagner et al. (1993) showed in their longitudinal study that over a period from 9 to 19 months of age, toddlers developed not only their motor skills but also their affiliative and cooperative behaviours in a milieu that allowed moving in space with no limitation. The toddlers shared games that were fun and long-lasting with very little aggressiveness or self-centred behaviours. Young children, if they are not restricted by the social or physical environment, run, jump, trample, twist, bounce, and romp together. They engage in playful 'music-making', and by imitating, repeating, and varying these activities they develop shared routines, using various humorous ways to express their shared enjoyment. They create their own jokes by means of laughter, funny gestures, and facial expressions, playing with language and the sounds of words, and by violating expectations and socially agreed meanings (Hoicka & Martin, 2016; Loizou, 2005; Reddy & Mireault, 2015).

We assume that without shared experiences of togetherness and joyful friendship arising from bodily games, mature play would not emerge. Bodily games also develop cooperation skills, which support the emergence of more challenging coordinated joint play with small objects, which in turn is also a prerequisite for mature play. Playing with small objects and toys begins with exploration and continues alternately: when I know what this object does, I ask what I can do with it (Hutt, 1976). Toddlers are impelled to bang, throw, open, shut, empty, fill, pull, push, pile, break – again and again, alone and together. When they invent cultural meanings for objects, they begin to imitate their cultural uses, and real pretending begins. Pretend acts become coordinated into sequences of behaviour such as telephoning, caregiving, and cooking with realistic and substitute objects, and develop gradually from self-referenced pretence to other-referenced pretence (e.g., Fein, 1981).

First Roles, Shared Imagination

Before 'true play' is possible, children must be able to distinguish between inhabiting or being outside a role so that they can direct their roles (Kravtsov & Kravtsova, 2010). This 'dual-positional' aspect of play allows the player to orient her- or himself to the character represented in the game. The playing toddlers are not only Mary and Mathew, but also Mummy and Daddy. They have moved to the imaginative level of playing, guided by spoken language. This happens usually around 3 years of age. Before that children like to probe distinct roles. They are cats, dogs, bears, moving and vocalizing like animals, imitating each other's representations and varying them. With familiar adults, they like to play at role-change totally on the imaginative level, trying to understand how it feels to be another person.

Before verbal negotiating, toddlers have a broad repertoire of strategies for communicating with each other when inviting peers to play, joining in other children's play and during the enactment of play. Engdahl (2011) showed that the play invitation strategies of toddlers aged 17–24 months were mostly based on forms of non-verbal communication such as movements and gestures, offering a toy, looking into each other's eyes, use of voice, one-word sentences, and imitation. Laughter also seemed to attract other children and served as a signal to start playing together. During play, a typical imitation sequence occurred when one child performed an action that another child noticed and repeated, and then the first child varied the repeated action. The children also negotiated silently, for instance, about the possession of toys, by holding the toy in their hands, through movements and gestures and through intense eye contact, which together often led to a mutually acceptable outcome. Sometimes the children were not successful in inviting peers, and then joint play did not arise.

Shared play arises from shared experiences. Young toddlers, who enter the early childhood education setting, have very little in common at the beginning; however, through their activities they show what is familiar to them. Children bring their individual experiences of, for instance, sleeping, eating, shopping, or activities with toys, from home to the education setting. To enable these individual experiences to grow into shared experiences and motives for play, teachers must know how to make use of them. It is crucial to enrich the daily shared activities in the setting itself. Everything that takes place or is present in the group forms common ground and a common history for the children, thereby offering tools and inspiration for joint intentions and shared play. The teacher's task is to create a rich, emotionally appealing environment for the whole group and for every child.

Teachers in Children's Play

To support children who are curious, live in the moment, experience rapid change in their feelings, and inspire each other requires knowledgeable teachers. Such professionals know that a fundamental in the educational program for young children is play and that guiding it requires creative, respectful, and sensitive interactions between teachers and children. Teachers know that while they cannot plan play beforehand, they can plan and realize the conditions for play. They can take an open, flexible, and playful attitude.

Creating a Zone of Proximal Development in Play

In joint play, children and adults together create a zone of proximal development, where they act in emotionally meaningful ways. Such a zone is unique and personally challenging for each participating child. Children's interests, needs, intentions, and initiatives are the cornerstones in building a zone of proximal development, one that will help them to grow "a head taller than himself" (Vygotsky, 1978, p. 102; see also Holzman, 2010). Zuckerman (2007) emphasizes that the cooperation of children and adults does not automatically generate a zone of proximal development. The prerequisite for this is the encountering of each other's minds and the adult's orientation to what is present in the child precisely at the moment of such an encounter. In the context of early childhood education, this is a demanding responsibility for teachers, especially with toddlers.

To create a zone of proximal development in play, it is imperative that the teacher's presence in the toddlers' play is caring and thoughtful. The teacher must have the ability to recognize and identify the children's play intentions and initiatives, to understand their non-verbal ways of communicating by gestures, such as looking and pointing at an object, offering an object, and moving toward an object or a place. All these actions manifest their wishes and will to play and explore their world, alone or together with others. However, the teacher cannot always respond affirmatively to children's initiatives or carry them out as such. When aiming to enrich children's ideas and promote their play, teachers must seek a balance between the children's and their own initiatives. If the teacher fails in this, she or he may hinder and even prevent the development of their further play, as shown by Shin (2015).

Basis for Play: Sensitive Teachers and Sensitivity in Interactions

Understanding of children's intentions – and children at all – is an important adult quality irrespective of child age. The younger the child, the greater the child's need for caring and loving adults with whom to share everyday life through play. In the early childhood education setting, this role is taken by teachers who are sensitive, responsive, physically and emotionally present (Alcock, 2016; Dalli et al., 2011; Degotardi, 2013; Ebbeck & Yim, 2009; Johansson & Emilson, 2016; Singer et al., 2014), and available for and attentive to the needs of every child (Fugelsnes et al., 2013). The studies by Singer et al. (2014) and White et al. (2015) found a strong connection between close, at best continuous, physical proximity of the teacher and higher levels of toddlers' play engagement.

A sensitive teacher is reflective in observing children both as a group and as individuals (Alcock, 2016) and open to the children's experiences, insights, and needs (e.g., Dalli et al., 2011; Ebbeck & Yim, 2009). The teacher listens to the children, reads their emotional cues, body language, and subtle, constantly changing actions and responds to them in ways beneficial to them (Alcock, 2016; Cheshire, 2007; Johansson & Emilson, 2016). She or he expresses appreciation of and respect for the children's ideas and interests (Thomason & La Paro, 2013), praises their efforts and successes, and generally encourages them. The teacher uses a friendly tone of voice and positive gestures, smiles at the children, and seeks eye contact with them. A sensitive teacher hugs and touches the children gently, holds them close, laughs and makes jokes – and expresses delight at being with them (e.g., Hännikäinen, 2015; Monaco & Pontecorvo, 2010).

The teacher's smile seems to be of great importance to toddlers during their first weeks in the early childhood education setting. Zanolli et al. (1997) found that new children in the group responded affectionately to smiling by a teacher earlier than they responded to the affectionate words or physical contact by the teacher. Smiling aroused reciprocal affection between the teacher and the child and encouraged the newcomer to gain acquaintance with the new environment. As Cheshire (2007, p. 37) reminds us, "For a toddler, a smile may be all that is required to reassure an explorer that an adult is nearby and ready if needed."

A sensitive teacher takes responsibility for the atmosphere in the group. When the atmosphere is characterized by empathy and emotional support, babies can learn more about themselves and others, as observed by Adams (2011). A safe, pleasant, and warm atmosphere created by the teacher appears to encourage children to express their attachment and tenderness toward each other as well as to the teacher (Hännikäinen, 2015). Emotionally secure relationships in turn help children become involved in a higher level of social interaction and participate in shared pretend play (Kim, 2016).

Thus, sensitivity is not only a set of personal traits and specific behaviours on the teacher's part. It also includes the adoption of an ethical attitude by the teacher toward the child and the creation of a reciprocal, dynamic, caring relationship between teacher and child (Elwick et al., 2014; Noddings, 1992; Singer et al., 2014). Such an affective bond denotes intersubjectivity, the participation of the teacher and the child in each other's worlds (cf. Merleau-Ponty, 1962). On the child's part, close relationships invite the child to attend to the teacher, seek close proximity to her or him, initiate and respond to the ongoing interaction, and engage in mutual play and laughter with the teacher, as noted by Brebner et al. (2015). Likewise, Pálmadóttir and Einarsdóttir (2015) observed that if the teacher's reactions to the child's bodily expressions in play showed emotional closeness to the child's world, the child expressed pleasure and happiness.

Teachers Participating in Play

Toddlers need to have a teacher available when they play, but they do not always need direct teacher involvement. It is important that the environment offers them the possibility to be close to the teacher if they feel the need for proximity and to distance themselves when they wish to play independently of the teacher (Singer et al., 2014). This means that the teacher should also respect and value children's autonomous, spontaneous play and participate in it simply by being present and by active, careful observation (Fleer, 2015; Jung, 2013; Shin, 2015).

Through keen observation the teacher can judge when and how to interfere in toddlers' play, directly or more indirectly, for instance, by providing materials for play, making suggestions for actions, or resolving disputes (Fleer, 2015; Jung, 2013). Prudent observation of children's play enables the teacher to notice children's attraction to each other and support them in joining in shared play, for instance, by participating together with a child in the play of another child or a group of children (Kultti, 2015). Children may also invite the observing teacher to participate in their play, for instance, to get help with the play materials and interaction with peers, to gain confirmation of their competence in play, to share experiences and joy (Pálmadóttir & Einarsdóttir, 2015), and to feel closeness and safety.

Participation in toddlers' play generally takes place in dyadic or small group interactions with children. However, it is essential that the teacher also pay attention to all the children when engaged in an activity with an individual child (Singer et al., 2014). When the teacher notices other children displaying curiosity in this joint activity, she or he can encourage them to join in (Kultti, 2015). In both dyadic and group interaction, the teacher can promote joint play, for instance, by directing children's attention to each other's play, linking the play to a common theme, or creating a flexible connection to parallel play, as was found by Fugelsnes et al. (2013).

Teachers have multiple roles when playing with young children. They can be material, emotional, and physical supporters, commentators and interpreters, facilitators and leaders, and play partners (Jung, 2013; Shin, 2015). It is self-evident that teachers are responsible for organizing the play materials and space. Children need to know where they can play and where the toys are. It is possible that the various placing of toys, for instance, some in activity corners, some on shelves, some in boxes, and some arranged according to specific play themes, but all always at hand, inspires toddlers to start playing. Shohet and Klein (2010) found that toys were more interesting for toddlers when arranged in real-life sceneries instead of randomly. Even if play materials have regular places, toddlers should not be expected to remain in these places. When toddlers move around the setting, in group rooms, halls, and corridors, the toys move with them, as reported by Rutanen (2012).

The development of toddlers' play can be directly promoted in various ways, as illustrated in the Playgroup Project, which included early childhood education students and toddlers (Hakkarainen et al., 2013; see also Chapter 25 in this book), and in a number of other studies (Fleer, 2015; Jung, 2013; Lemay et al., 2016). These studies emphasize that to support toddlers' play, adults must be actively involved in it. However, the teacher should also be flexible and step aside from her or his own ideas when the child seems to produce something that is meaningful for that child (Lemay et al., 2016). At the same time, to support the creation of joint play, the teacher should help the child understand the intentions of the other children.

We already drew attention to the power of reciprocal imitation in toddler's play. Importantly, teachers should also imitate toddlers. Agnetta and Rochat (2004) noticed how toddlers showed especial interest by smiling and looking when an adult imitated their play actions or played with the same kind of toy as the children. Other active ways to participate in children's play are parallel play, while maintaining eye contact with the child, and playing a role or multiple roles in pretend play (Fleer, 2015; Hakkarainen et al., 2013; Jung, 2013). Whatever the way of participation is, it is essential that teachers communicate their play actions both non-verbally (cf. Singer et al., 2014), thus displaying emotional involvement in play, and verbally, describing the course of the ongoing play.

Unfortunately, teachers may also hinder and restrict toddler's play. Singer et al. (2014) observed that teachers' walking around in the playroom, coming over to children, asking something, and then leaving again induces restlessness in children. Teachers can also be too commanding, ask irrelevant questions, join in play unexpectedly from the children's perspective, and take over children's initiatives (Hakkarainen et al., 2013). Engdahl (2011) showed how play often terminates when the teacher interferes in play by invoking a rule or daily routine. Likewise, when intruding in conflicts and clashes too quickly without following the play or without adapting to children's play logic, joint play may end, as observed by Singer and Hännikäinen (2002). It should be remembered that toddlers often manage to resolve their clashes by themselves.

Shared Experiences in Play

Toddlers are eager to participate in activities in which shared experiences are constructed. The teacher's responsibility is to offer children these experiences by talking together with them about everyday events and occurrences, reading and telling them stories, and by so doing contributing material to their joint play and shared imagination (see Dalli et al., 2011). However, it is not teachers alone who offer shared experiences; children also do this, often with help from teachers.

As discussed earlier, children's experiences expressed in play form a narrative. Play is children's way to understand their cultural world, and the narrative form is very a practical tool in promoting toddlers' play. Play can be viewed as a micro drama through which children live their experiences. The past two decades have seen much theoretical discussion and practical applications about play and narration (Kavanaugh & Engel, 1998; Lobman & O'Neill, 2011; Paley, 2001; Sawyer, 1997). Most of the theorizing and applications have concerned the play of older children. However, teachers who work and play with toddlers can also make use of the idea of narrative in many ways, and good examples of this are available.

The first task for the teacher is to search for the implicit narrative structure of a toddlers' play sequence and, as Engel (2005b) says, render it visible. The teacher then joins in the child's initiative and tries to follow it. When the teacher narrates the child's pretend gestures, she or he confers structure and meaning on the child's non-verbal actions, highlighting the narrative features implicit in the child's actions. When children begin to use words, adults knowledgeable about children and their everyday experiences can grasp the meaning of a single word, understand the narrative behind it, and help the child to develop it into imaginative play. Children, together with adults, actively participate from a very early age in storytelling through narrative discourses. Interactions of this kind influence children's developing abilities to recount and represent events both as real and 'as if'.

Other approaches to supporting and narratively enriching toddlers' play vary from child-initiated to teacher-initiated simple, and later more intricate, stories, which can be dramatized in many different ways, but always in ways that arise from the children's experiences and affect them emotionally. Toddlers enjoy the simple narratives of poems and songs. They are interested in the rhythms, puns, and nonsense contained in nursery rhymes, because they like, as Chukovsky (1971) states, the absurdity of topsy-turvy situations that break up the established and orderly world. These games are played in a linear narrative framework, first setting up, then increasing excitement, and, finally, ending in a climax. Amusing narratives and rhythmic games allow toddlers and teachers to be involved in creative co-participation, strategies that Mallock and Trevarthen (2009) regard as among the most impressive and effective in seeking to achieve togetherness.

Paley (2001), Lobman (2003), and Lindqvist (2001) used drama and improvisation as means of enriching toddlers' play, placing differing emphases on the source of the story, the adults' role, and children's participation. In Paley's method, young children tell personal stories, using at least one word, in a group, then, guided by the teacher, dramatize them, share them with each other, and live through them together. Individual memories and experiences turn into an embodied story and shared play.

Lobman (2003) uses drama-like working as a form of improvisation in which the players collectively create a scene or a story. The use of improvisation shifts the focus away from what the teacher is doing and toward what the teacher and children are doing together. The teacher notices children's play initiatives, accepts the children's offerings, says 'yes and', and generally does not reject what the children are doing. The teacher listens to the children's suggestions and responds with new offers that help further develop the play. Despite the young age of the children (from 20 months to 3 years) in Lobman's study, play often included the whole group. Sawyer (1997), Lobman's main source, underlines the importance of the improvisational quality of children's sociodramatic play: the outcome is unpredictable, there is moment-to-moment contingency from turn to turn, and play is collaborative.

Lindqvist (2001) emphasizes that stories awaken toddlers' imagination, which gives meaning to the play actions and objects. In her approach, the ideas for stories are taken from children's literature and relived by dramatizing certain chains of events from those stories, with some roles played by adults. The play themes deal with the ability to distinguish between reality and imagination, as well as the ability to distinguish between social rules, such as being obedient and having some degree of personal freedom. The fact that the teachers take roles in play situations is one important reason why these themes capture toddlers' attention.

Roles in stories can also be taken by puppets or stuffed animals. For toddlers animals are more captivating. In the Playgroup Project (Hakkarainen et al., 2013), the main protagonist was a lonely teddy bear, who came to play with the toddlers. With the aid of this figure, a common narrative framework was created, based on the toddlers' everyday activities. The teddy bear found a friend, a puppy dog, the two demonstrating the friendship and companionship between peers. It was important that the bear and the dog were able to create narrative continuity, offer the toddlers rituals of actions, and arouse feelings like joy and empathy. In the beginning, the dramas were constructed from children's everyday world, later from children's books and from the toddlers themselves. When younger and older children took part in activities together, the younger ones were eager to imitate their older companions.

For drama presentations to succeed, teachers have to be sensitive to children's hints and responses. To children, the representation of a story is an invitation to play. Spontaneous, flexible interaction with children during this activity needs a lot of improvisation. The expression of emotion through vocalizations should be accompanied by bodily movements and facial expressions similar in quality dynamic. Children aged 2 and 3 years are very well able to follow the events of a story. As Young and Powers (2008) noticed in their theatre project, although toddlers may not understand the semantic content of a story, they may still enjoy an emotional or rhythmical narrative that takes them through familiar and expected series of sounds and actions and makes sense of significant events in their world.

Collaborating and Reflective Teachers Enabling Engaging Play

The creation and maintenance of an unhurried, respectful, and warm atmosphere across the early childhood education setting is the primary precondition for a playful climate and a playful community for engaging toddlers in play. Together, the staff should form a community of learners with joint pedagogical aims and values based on discussions and shared knowledge. The teachers should also seek possibilities to work together, and thereby establish personal relations with other teachers and children from other groups.

Children's play draws deeply on their daily experiences at home. Therefore, collaboration between the teachers and parents or guardians is necessary. The atmosphere of the setting must allow and encourage confidential, continual, open discussions about children's daily lives at home and in the setting. It is also important to offer parents opportunities to meet each other both informally and in organized meetings.

For several reasons, teachers should play wholeheartedly with children, not merely observe and guide their play indirectly. Play is an ideal context for understanding the perspectives of children, getting to know individual children and the relations between them, sharing and gathering experiences, and feeling togetherness as a group. Play together with children gives the teacher strength, meaningfulness, and pleasure in work and helps in the acquisition of greater self-knowledge. To be aware of their subjective feelings connected to their work with children, teachers need to know themselves. They need to reflect on their ways of working and playing with children, to observe not only children but also themselves, and to learn and develop together with children, thereby forming a community of learners with them. Finally, teachers should develop their own playfulness for both their own and the children's benefit.

References

Adams, E. J. (2011). Teaching children to name their feelings. *Young Children, 66*(3), 66–67.

Agnetta, B., & Rochat, P. (2004). Imitative games by 9-, 14-, and 18-month-old infants. *Infancy, 6*(1), 1–36.

Alcock, S. J. (2016). *Young children playing: Relational approaches to emotional learning in early childhood settings.* Heidelberg: Springer.

Alvestad, T., Bergem, H., Eide, B., Johansson, J. E., Os, E., Pálmadóttir, H., ... & Winger, N. (2014). Challenges and dilemmas expressed by teachers working in toddler groups in the Nordic countries. *Early Child Development and Care, 184*(5), 671–688.

Bodrova, E., & Leong, D. J. (2015). Vygotskian and post-Vygotskian views on children's play. *American Journal of Play, 7*(3), 371–388.

Brebner, C., Hammond, L., Schaumloffel, N., & Lind, C. (2015). Using relationships as a tool: Early childhood educators' perspectives of the child–caregiver relationship in a childcare setting. *Early Child Development and Care, 185*(5), 709–726.

Brownell, C. A. (2011). Early developments in joint action. *Review of Philosophy and Psychology, 2*(2), 193–211.

Bruner, J. (1990). *Acts of meaning.* Cambridge, MA: Harvard University Press.

Cheshire, N. (2007). The 3 R's: Gateway to infant and toddler learning. *Dimensions of Early Childhood, 35*(3), 36–38.

Chukovsky, K. (1971). *From two to five.* Berkeley: University of California Press.

Dalli, C., White, E. J., Rockel, J., Duhn, I., with Buchanan, E., Davidson, S., ... & Wang, B. (2011). *Quality early childhood education for under-two-year-olds: What should it look like? A literature review.* Ministry of Education, New Zealand. Available at www.educationcounts.govt.nz/publications/ECE/Quality_ECE_for_under-two-year-olds/965_QualityECE_Web-22032011.pdf.

Degotardi, S. (2010). High-quality interactions with infants: Relationships with early-childhood practitioners' interpretations and qualification levels in play and routine contexts. *International Journal of Early Years Education, 18*(1), 27–41.

Degotardi, S. (2013). 'I think – I can': Acknowledging and promoting agency during educator–infant play. In O. F. Lillemyr, S. Dockett, & B. Perry (Eds.), *Varied perspectives on play and learning: Theory and research on early years education* (pp. 75–90). Charlotte, NC: Information Age Publishing.

Duhn, I. (2015). Making agency matter: Rethinking infant and toddler agency in educational discourse. *Discourse: Studies in the Cultural Politics of Education, 36*(6), 920–931.

Ebbeck, M., & Yim, H. Y. B. (2009). Rethinking attachment: Fostering positive relationships between infants, toddlers and their primary caregivers. *Early Child Development and Care, 179*(7), 899–909.

Elfer, P., & Page, J. (2015). Pedagogy with babies: Perspectives of eight nursery managers. *Early Child Development and Care, 185*(11–12), 1762–1782.

Elwick, S., Bradley, B., & Sumsion, J. (2014). Infants as others: Uncertainties, difficulties and (im)possibilities in researching infants' lives. *International Journal of Qualitative Studies in Education, 27*(2), 196–213.

Engdahl, I. (2011). Toddler interaction during play in the Swedish preschool. *Early Child Development and Care, 181*(10), 1421–1439.

Engel, S. (2005a). The narrative worlds of *what is* and *what if. Cognitive Development, 20*(4), 514–525.

Engel, S. (2005b). *Real kids: Creating meaning in everyday life.* Cambridge, MA: Harvard University Press.

Fein, G. G. (1981). Pretend play in childhood: An integrative review. *Child Development, 52*(4), 1095–1118.

Fleer, M. (2015). Pedagogical positioning in play – Teachers being inside and outside of children's imaginative play. *Early Child Development and Care, 185* (11–12), 1801–1814.

Fugelsnes, K., Röthle, M., & Johansson, E. (2013). Values at stake in interplay between toddlers and teachers. In O. F. Lillemyr, S. Dockett, & B. Perry (Eds.), *Varied perspectives on play and learning* (pp. 109–112). Charlotte, NC: Information Age Publishing.

Gibson, J. J. (1979). *The ecological approach to visual perception.* Boston: Houghton Mifflin.

Göncü, A. (1998). Development of intersubjectivity in social pretend play. In M. Woodhead, D. Faulkner, & K. Littleton (Eds.), *Cultural worlds of early childhood* (pp. 117–132). London: Routledge.

Grindheim, L. T., & Ødegaard, E. E. (2013). What is the state of play? *International Journal of Play, 2*(1), 4–6.

Hakkarainen, P., & Brédikytè, M. (2010). The zone of proximal development in play and learning. Проблема развития. Available at http://lchc.ucsd.edu/mca/Mail/xmcamail.2010_12.dir/pdf6DAHjotjsS.pdf.

Hakkarainen, P., Brédikytè, M., Jakkula, K., & Munter, H. (2013). Adult play guidance and children's play development in a narrative play-world. *European Early Childhood Education Research Journal, 21*(2), 213–225.

Hännikäinen, M. (2015). The teacher's lap – A site of emotional well-being for the younger children in day-care groups. *Early Child Development and Care, 185* (5), 752–765.

Hedegaard, M. (2016). Imagination and emotion in children's play: A cultural-historical approach. *International Research in Early Childhood Education, 7*(2), 59–74.

Hoicka, E., & Martin, C. (2016). Two-year-olds distinguish pretending and joking. *Child Development, 87*(3), 916–928.

Holzman, L. (2010). Without creating ZPDs there is no creativity. In M. C. Connery, W. P. John-Steiner, & A. Marjanovic-Shane (Eds.), *Vygotsky and creativity: A cultural-historical approach to play, meaning making and the arts* (pp. 27–39). New York: Peter Lang.

Howes, C. (1985). Sharing fantasy: Social pretend play in toddlers. *Child Development, 56*(5), 1253–1258.

Hutt, C. (1976). Exploration and play in children. In J. S. Bruner, A. Jolly, & K. Sylva (Eds.), *Play: Its role in development and evolution* (pp. 202–215). Harmondsworth: Penguin Books.

Johansson, E., & Emilson, A. (2016). Conflicts and resistance: Potentials for democracy learning in preschool. *International Journal of Early Years Education, 24* (1), 19–35.

Johansson, E., & Løkken, G. (2014). Sensory pedagogy: Understanding and encountering children through the senses. *Educational Philosophy and Theory*, *46*(8), 886–897.

Jung, J. (2013). Teachers' roles in infants' play and its changing nature in a dynamic group care context. *Early Childhood Research Quarterly*, *28*(1), 187–198.

Karabanova, O. A. (2010). Social situation of child's development – The key concept in modern developmental psychology. *Psychology in Russia: State of the Art*. Available at http://psychologyinrussia.com/volumes/pdf/2010/05_2010_karabanova.pdf.

Kavanaugh, R. D., & Engel, S. (1998). The development of pretense and narrative in early childhood. In O. N. Saracho & B. Spodek (Eds.), *Multiple perspectives on play in early childhood education* (pp. 80–99). Albany: State University of New York Press.

Kim, Y. (2016). Relationship-based developmentally supportive approach to infant childcare practice. *Early Child Development and Care*, *186*(5), 734–749.

Kravtsov, G. G., & Kravtsova, E. E. (2010). Play in Vygotsky's non-classical psychology. *Journal of Russian and East European Psychology*, *48*(4), 25–41.

Kultti, A. (2015). Adding learning resources: A study of two toddlers' modes and trajectories of participation in early childhood education. *International Journal of Early Years Education*, *23*(2), 209–221.

Kultti, A., & Pramling, N. (2015). Bring your own toy: Socialisation of two-year-olds through tool-mediated activities in an Australian early childhood education context. *Early Childhood Education Journal*, *43*(5), 367–376.

Lemay, L., Bigras, N., & Bouchard, C. (2016). Respecting but not sustaining play: Early childhood educators' and home childcare providers' practices that support children's play. *Early Years*, *36*(4), 383–398.

Lindqvist, G. (2001). When small children play: How adults dramatise and children create meaning. *Early Years*, *21*(1), 7–14.

Lobman, C. L. (2003). What should we create today? Improvisational teaching in play-based classrooms. *Early Years*, *23*(2) 131–142.

Lobman, C. L., & O'Neill, B. E. (Eds.) (2011). *Play and performance: Play and culture studies*. Lanham, MD: University Press of America.

Loizou, E. (2005). Infant humor: The theory of the absurd and the empowerment theory. *International Journal of Early Years Education*, *13*(1), 43–53.

Løkken, G. (2000). Tracing the social style of toddler peers. *Scandinavian Journal of Educational Research*, *44*(2), 163–176.

Malloch, S., & Trevarthen, C. (2009). Musicality: Communicating the vitality and interests of life. In M. Malloch, & C. Trevarthen (Eds.), *Communicative musicality: Exploring the basis of human companionship* (pp. 1–12). Oxford: Oxford University Press.

Merleau-Ponty, M. (1962). *Phenomenology of perception*. London: Routledge & Kegan Paul.

Monaco, C., & Pontecorvo, C. (2010). The interaction between young toddlers: Constructing and organising participation frameworks. *European Early Childhood Education Research Journal*, *18*(3), 341–371.

Montagner, H., Gauffier, G., Epoulet, B., Restoin, A., Goulevitch, R., Taule, M., & Wiaux, B. (1993). Alternative child care in France: Advances in the study of motor, interactive, and social behaviors of young children in settings allowing them to move freely in a group of peers. *Paediatrics, 91*(1), 253–263.

Noddings, N. (1992). *The challenge to care in schools: An alternative approach to education.* New York: Teachers College Press.

OECD (2010). *Starting strong III: A quality toolbox for early childhood education and care.* OECD Publishing. Available at http://dx.doi.org/10.1787/9789264123564-en.

Paley, V. G. (2001). *In Mrs. Tully's room: A childcare portrait.* Cambridge: Harvard University Press.

Pálmadóttir, H., & Einarsdóttir, J. (2015). Young children's views of the role of preschool educators. *Early Child Development and Care, 185*(9), 1480–1494.

Parker-Rees, R. (2007). Liking to be liked: Imitation, familiarity and pedagogy in the first years of life. *Early Years, 27*(1), 3–17.

Rakoczy, H. (2008). Pretence as individual and collective intentionality. *Mind and Language, 23*(5), 499–517.

Reddy, V., & Mireault, G. (2015). Teasing and clowning in infancy. *Current Biology, 25*(1), R20–R23.

Ridgway, A., Li, L., & Quiñones, G. (2016). Transitory moments in infant/toddler play: Agentic imagination. *International Research in Early Childhood Education, 7*(2), 91–110.

Rochat, P. (2010). The innate sense of the body develops to become a public affair by 2–3 years. *Neuropsychologia, 48*(3), 738–745.

Rutanen, N. (2012). Socio-spatial practices in a Finnish daycare group for one- to three-year-olds. *Early Years, 32*(2), 201–214.

Sawyer, R. K. (1997). *Pretend play as improvisation: Conversation in the preschool classroom.* Mahwah, NJ: Lawrence Erlbaum Associates.

Selby, J. M., & Bradley, B. S. (2003). Infants in groups: A paradigm for the study of early social experience. *Human Development, 46*(4), 197–221.

Shin, M. (2015). Enacting caring pedagogy in the infant classroom. *Early Child Development and Care, 185*(3), 496–508.

Shohet, C., & Klein, P. S. (2010). Effects of variations in toy presentation on social behaviour of infants and toddlers in childcare. *Early Child Development and Care, 180*(6), 823–834.

Singer, E., & Hännikäinen, M. (2002). The teacher's role in territorial conflicts of 2- to 3-year-old children. *Journal of Research in Childhood Education, 17*(1), 5–18.

Singer, E., Nederend, M., Penninx, L., Tajik, M., & Boom, J. (2014). The teacher's role in supporting young children's level of play engagement. *Early Child Development and Care, 184*(8), 1233–1249.

Stambak, M., Ballion, M., Breaute, M., & Rayna, S. (1985). Pretend play and interaction in young children. In R. A. Hinde, A. N. Perret-Clermont, & J. S. Hinde (Eds.), *Social relationships and cognitive development* (pp. 131–148). New York: Oxford University Press.

Stern, D. (1985). *The interpersonal world of the infant: A view from psychoanalysis and developmental psychology.* New York: Basic Books.

Striano, T., Tomasello, M., & Rochat, P. (2001). Social and object support for early symbolic play. *Developmental Science, 4*(4), 442–455.

Thomason, A. C., & La Paro, K. (2013). Teacher's commitment to the field and teacher–child interactions in center-based child care for toddlers and three-year-olds. *Early Childhood Education Journal*, *41*(3), 227–234.

Trevarthen, C. (2012). Born for art, and the joyful companionship of fiction. In D. Narvaez, J. Panksepp, A. Schore, & T. Gleason (Eds.), *Evolution, early experience and human development: From research to practice and policy* (pp. 202–219). Oxford: Oxford University Press.

UN Convention on the Rights of the Child (1989). Geneva: Office of the United Nations High Commissioner for Human Rights. Available at www.unicef .org.uk/what-we-do/un-convention-child-rights/.

Vygotsky, L. S. (1978). *Mind in society: The development of higher psychological processes* (ed. and trans. M. Cole, V. John-Steiner, S. Scribner, & E. Souberman). Cambridge: Harvard University Press.

Vygotsky, L. S. (1998). The problem of age. In R. V. Rieber (Ed.), *The Collected Works of L. S. Vygotsky*, vol. 5: *Child Psychology* (pp. 187–205). New York: Plenum Press.

White, E. J., Peter, M., & Redder, B. (2015). Infant and teacher dialogue in education and care: A pedagogical imperative. *Early Childhood Research Quarterly*, *30*, 160–173.

Young, S., & Powers, N. (2008). Starcatchers. Final Report. See theatre, play theatre. National Endowment for Science, Technology and the Arts and the Scottish Arts Council. Available at http://starcatchers.org.uk/downloads/research_ report.pdf.

Zanolli, K. M., Saudargas, R. A., & Twardosz, S. (1997). The development of toddlers' responses to affectionate teacher behavior. *Early Childhood Research Quarterly*, *12*(1), 99–116.

Zuckerman, G. (2007). Child–adult interaction that creates a zone of proximal development. *Journal of Russian & East European Psychology*, *45*(3), 43–69.

28 Adult and Child Learning in Playworlds

Beth Ferholt, Robert Lecusay, and Monica Nilsson

Playworlds are designed to enable adults and children to engage in joint pretence as a means of promoting the emotional, cognitive, and social development of both children and adults. Playworlds can be described as combinations of adult forms of creative imagination, which require extensive experience (e.g., art, science), with children's forms of creative imagination (e.g., play), which require the embodiment of ideas and emotions in the material world. The development of both children and adults in this intergenerational, hybrid form of play has been of central interest to playworld researchers in part because, unlike many intergenerational activities, playworlds allow children as well as adults to take the position of expert: play is an activity in which children, not adults, are often the experts.

We (Ferholt, 2009; Nilsson & Ferholt, 2014) have posited that there is a pre-modern condition in which children's play is sometimes integrated with adult activities and sometimes conducted apart from adults, but is not directed, protected, jointly created, nor exploited by adults (Gaskins, 1999), and a modern condition in which children's play is isolated from adult activities, and then either directed toward adult-determined developmental goals or protected from adult interference. Playworlds can be understood as play in a post-modern condition because in playworlds adults engage in adult–child joint play for the purpose of promoting their own as well as children's development and quality of life. Playworlds are idiocultures in which children's play is not controlled or isolated but, instead, is joined with the arts and sciences to allow children and adults to encounter each other from within a particular type of community.

To understand learning in these encounters between people who are sometimes strangers to each other's ways of thinking, in the sense that they are at very different points in the lifespan, Gert Biesta's (2004) distinction between learning in and through the *rational community* vs. in and through the *community-without-community*, which we will discuss in depth later, proves particularly useful. Understanding learning not as acquisition of "content and logic that make up the/a rational community" but rather as "responding, as a response to a question", "when someone responds to what is unfamiliar, what is different, what challenges, irritates or even disturbs" (2004, p. 320) allows us to think about learning in such a way that the essential aspects of development in playworlds remain within our purview. Biesta (2004) uses the term 'Community of Those Who Have Nothing in Common', and his description of the ways that such a community can be created is an apt description of a playworld:

> We can not make or force our students [child and adult participants, in the case of playwords] to expose themselves to what is other and different and strange. The only thing we can do is to make sure that there are at least opportunities within education to meet and encounter what is different, strange, and other; and also that there are opportunities for our students (and teachers, in playworlds) to really respond, to find their own voice, their own way of speaking.   (Biesta, 2004, p. 321)

In playworlds, adults and child participants find their own ways of speaking within their comfort areas, art or science and play, respectively, but also in activities that allow them to speak in ways that they had not known they were capable of and about topics that they had not known they could express. Children in playworlds often surprise the adult participants with the power of their voices and their unexpected ways of speaking, and adult participants in playworlds often surprise themselves and each other with the power of their own voices and their own unexpected ways of speaking. One teacher who had recently participated in a playworld used these words to describe the experience of finding his own voice in his encounters with children in the playworld:

> [H]ere is an analogy ... I have on my football helmet ... and everyone else is playing basketball. The kids are playing basketball ... and if we want to play, we need to get rid of the helmet.   (Ferholt, 2009, p. 17).

This teacher was using this metaphor to explain that adults in a playworld benefit from playing with children because children encourage adults to play with belief and disbelief at the same time (an important play skill), by refusing to play with adults if these adults do not simultaneously believe and disbelieve. Believing and disbelieving simultaneously made this teacher able to express himself 'without his helmet'.

Biesta's understanding of learning within a Community of Those Who Have Nothing in Common is useful in discussing learning in playworlds because of its emphasis on encounters between strangers and its focus on finding one's own voice, but also because we are wary of many other ways of understanding learning in relation to play. The current pressure to discuss play in relation to learning is problematic in ways that can be counteracted using Biesta's understanding of learning, which challenges the 'rational community' in education. The 'Position paper about the role of play in early childhood education and care' (2017) by the 'Rethinking Play' special interest group of the European Early Childhood Education Research Association states these problems concisely:

> Today there is a trend across Europe towards the application of measured and standardized learning outcomes for children in early childhood education and care (ECEC). Within this context related to neo-liberal views of

education, the value attributed to children's play by policy makers in early schooling is linked to concrete (cognitive) learning outcomes rather than a holistic perspective of children's development, leading to an instrumentalisation and regulation of play and a 'schoolification' of ECEC (Hännikäinen, Singer & van Oers 2013: 165; Moss 2007) ... [T]here are several criticisms we may make about these trends towards a new instrumentalist construction of education and learning and its impact on play. These trends demonstrate a clear change of discourse: from children's wellbeing, creativity and diverse meaningful social actions and interactions to a focus on standardized efficiency, rationalization and quest for defined and prescribed excellence in ECEC. As a result, play is restricted and/or redirected. In contrast to the measurable predetermined outcomes, play is very often defined as a process performed by children, not adults, as an 'intrinsically motivated, with no externally fixed outcome' activity (Burghardt, 2010) and one that leads 'who knows where' (Hughes, 2010). (2017, p. 1)

Biesta's understanding of learning can help us to retain our appreciation of the aspect of playwords in which the play leads "who knows where", but it is important to note that playworlds need not be discussed in terms of any understanding of learning. Playworlds take place in a variety of settings (pre-school and elementary school rooms, afterschool settings, therapeutic settings, refugee camps, etc.), many of which are not schools, and include children at a variety of ages. Furthermore, no matter the setting or the ages of the participants, playworlds are often described by the participants not as places of learning but as exciting places of possibility for growth, where all involved are developing as whole people.

The term *playworld* comes from Gunilla Lindqvist's (1995) *Aesthetics of Play*, where playworlds are an approach to early childhood education and care. However, Lindqvist (1995), working as she was within the Swedish EDUCARE system and creating the first playworlds in the 1980s and 1990s, did not study formal learning in playworlds. Lindqvist (1995) was instead interested in meaning-making in playworlds in preschools.

In this chapter we consider learning in playworlds, but we understand learning not in a narrow cognitive sense. Learning is often understood to mean formal learning, i.e., teacher-led and goal directed, and *cognitively* oriented learning, i.e., school-based. This understanding prioritizes a single-minded focus on learning as the product of teaching – that is, as the product of directed instruction – often to the exclusion of the kinds of learning experienced through activities that are self-initiated and that children spontaneously engage in, such as play. Instead, we understand learning more broadly, as transformations due to different kinds of experiences leading to sustained change (Nilsson et al., 2018a).

We discuss learning of both children and adults not only because playwords are designed to promote development of both children and adults, and are especially suited to such studies, but also because we are actively resisting a deficit model of the child, in which children are first seen in terms of their individual progress toward adulthood. We are engaged in supporting what we perceive to be a shift in the early childhood pedagogical discourse toward an understanding of the child as competent, a contributor and therefore a potential a co-creator *with* adults. As well as understanding learning to be interactional, we expect that learning is often bidirectional.

In what follows we present an overview of adult and child learning in playworlds. We then describe an example of adult–child co-participation in a playworld project that took place in a Swedish preschool. We draw on Biesta's (2004) distinction between learning in and through the *rational community* versus the *community-without-community* and also on Aspelin's (2015) concepts of *attitude in relationships* versus *attitude to relationships* as well as Aspelin and Persson (2011) on *co-existence* versus *co-operation*, all of which we will discuss later. These conceptual distinctions form an interpretive framework for discussion and analysis of learning in this particular playworld. We begin our discussion by reviewing findings on child learning in playworlds and we focus our analysis on adult learning in playworlds.

Playworlds: Theory and Method

Forms of play that fit under the umbrella term of playworlds, although they differ in a variety of ways, have emerged relatively recently in several countries: Sweden, Finland, Serbia, Japan, and the United States (Marjanovic-Shane et al., 2011). Playworlds are grounded in the theories of L. S. Vygotsky (1978, 1987, 2004) and the internationally known work of Gunilla Lindqvist of Sweden (1978, 1987, 2004) and Pentti Hakkarainen of Finland (2008; Hakkarainen et al., 2013; Hakkarainen & Ferholt, 2013; and Chapter 25 in this book), as well as in the work of less internationally known theorists and various local pedagogies. Playworlds have proven to be useful tools for the study of a variety of topics in different fields (for instance, children's narrative and literacy skills, socioemotional development, imagination, creativity, the zone of proximal development, agency, motivation, and *perezhivanie*), as well as for the development of school, preschool, and therapeutic practices.

Lindqvist worked from Vygotsky's theory of play with the expressed purpose of designing, implementing, and studying a pedagogy in which adults assume a creative approach to children's play. Lindqvist (1995, 2001a, 2001b; 2003) interprets Vygotsky's theory of play through his *Psychology of Art* (1971) and through a reading of *Imagination and Creativity in Childhood* (2004) that focuses on Vygotsky's assertion that children's play is a creative cultural manifestation in humans. It is from these foundations that Lindqvist (1995) develops her *Creative Pedagogy of Play*, which promotes the study of play and culture in preschools, the study of the aesthetics of children's play, and the study of play as an activity in which children produce results that draw on, but do not mimic, adult achievements.

In the creative pedagogy of play, interaction between adults and children is structured around a piece of children's literature or another work of art, such as an oral folk tale. The adults and children work together to "bring the literature to life" (1995, p. 72) through drama (or, in some cases, dance, although we will here discuss the dramatic playworlds). The participants assume roles, characters from the literary piece, and "make use of the intrinsic dynamism between world, action and character in drama and play" (1995, p. 72). The children and adults concretely transform their classroom into the imaginary world of the chosen narrative through joint scripted and improvisational acting and through joint production of props and sets. Lindqvist gives rich and concrete examples in her publications of implementations of her creative pedagogy of play (1989, 1992, 1995, 1996, 2000, 2001a, 2001b, 2002).

Lindqvist developed her pedagogy in order to investigate the nature of the connections between play and the aesthetic forms of drama and literature, and, in particular, she was interested in how aesthetic activities can influence children's play. The "common denominator" of play and aesthetic forms, which Lindqvist was trying to find, she called "the aesthetics of play" (Lindqvist, 1995). Lindqvist considered one of the most important conclusions of this investigation to be that the development of adult–child joint play is made possible through the creation of a common fiction, which she calls a "playword" (1995). The playworld is created through the activity of bringing the actions and characters in literary texts to life through drama: it is the interactive space in which both children and adults are creatively engaged (see Figure 28.1). In other words, the common fiction of playworlds becomes a common context for adults and children in which all participants are able to find the potential to "provide our existence with meaning" (p. 203).

Vygotsky (1978) states: "Only theories which maintain that a child does not have to satisfy the basic requirements of life but can live in search of pleasure could possibly suggest that a child's world is a play world" (p. 102). Instead, a child's world is as 'real' as our own. Adults are always a part of children's 'real' lives, and thus a part of children's play, and therefore, designing a play pedagogy involves deciding *on the ways that* adults will join children in play, not whether adults will enter children's play at all. It is Vygotsky's (1978)

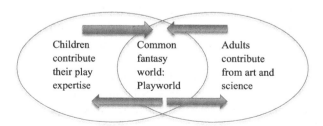

Figure 28.1 *Example of a playworld.*

insistence that a child's world is not a play world, separate from and less real than the adult's world, that supports Lindqvist's conviction that children are never alone in play.

Published Findings from Playworld Studies

Lindqvist's work has had a significant impact outside Sweden, particularly in the United States and Finland. Playworld research in Finland has focused, on the one hand, on the psychological effects of adult–child joint play on children's development and general abilities, such as school readiness (see Bredikyte & Hakkarainen, 2011; Hakkarainen, 2008; Hakkarainen et al., 2009, 2013). On the other hand, Finnish playworld research has also applied a socioculturally oriented critical research tradition to the study of adult–child interaction in playworlds (Rainio, 2010). These studies have focused particularly on the development and manifestations of children's agency and voice in playworld activities (Hofmann & Rainio, 2007; Rainio, 2007, 2008a) and on the challenges occurring in playworld classrooms based on the contradictory relationship between teacher control and management and student agency (Rainio, 2008b, 2010). Playworlds have also been analyzed from a critical gender perspective by Rainio (2009).

In the United States, playworld research has combined quasi-experimental work with deep ethnographic analyses of adult–child participation. For example, in a study conducted more than a decade ago, evidence was gathered showing that participation in a playworld improves children's narrative and literacy skills (Baumer et al., 2005). Data from the same study also showed that playworlds can lead to the mutual socioemotional development of both adults and children (Ferholt, 2009; Ferholt & Lecusay, 2010).

Analysis of US playworlds has also been used to expand Vygotsky's concept of the zone of proximal development (ZPD). Exploration of the ways that adults join children in playworlds shows that playworld activities can create a ZPD that fosters development in both adult and child participants (Ferholt & Lecusay, 2010). Vygotsky primarily described development in the ZPD as vertical improvement across levels, but these findings also allow us to account for horizontal development across borders in the ZPDs.

Work in progress also focuses on the fact that US playworlds have provided unique evidence of the synergy between emotion and cognition, a notoriously difficult process to study, but also one recognized to be of central importance to cognitive and social development. This work includes a study of *perezhivanie* (or intensely emotional lived-through experience) in a US playworld (Ferholt, 2009, 2010, 2015; Ferholt & Nilsson, 2016a, 2016b). *Perezhivanie* is a concept that has been intensely debated recently, in part because it is a concept with the potential to play a key role in connecting psychology with social theory (Blunden, 2016).

Other playworld studies encompass cross-cultural playworld analyses. These include a study of imagination and the use of psychological tools in playworlds that were created in Finland and the United States but were based in the same work of literature (Hakkarainen & Ferholt, 2013). A collaborative analysis of agency and engagement in a US playworld further explores concepts developed in Finish playworlds, such as ambivalence (Ferholt & Rainio, 2016).

Most recently, research examining playworld projects in Swedish preschools have shown how teachers' participation in these projects transforms their relational competence. Observations from this research have also formed the basis for critiques of the dichotomization of play and learning that often shape the pedagogical and policy agendas of early childhood education internationally (Ferholt & Nilsson, 2018a; Nilsson et al., 2018a), the aesthetics of play (Ferholt & Nilsson, 2015, 2016a; Ferholt & Nilsson, 2018b), and creativity in the field of early childhood education (Ferholt et al., 2015, 2016b). Recent playworld research in Sweden has also focused on methodological contributions. A book written by and for researchers and preschool teachers, *Play, Learning and Happiness: Playing and Exploring in Preschool* (Nilsson, Ferholt, Granqvist, Johansson, & Thure, 2018b), describes a framework for future research studies that is called *early childhood education research from within*.

'Early childhood education research from within' is an encounter between theory and preschool. If teachers who believe that children are capable and competent, and who therefore listen closely and respectfully to children, participate in such research, then children are indirectly a part of a research team and their voices can potentially influence early childhood education and scholarship in the field via the academy. Simultaneously, if researchers conducting their research in preschools strive for research that is guided by the interests of teachers and by the teachers' knowledge, then these researchers can act as catalysts, helping preschool activities to change in response to contradictions in these activities. (For a detailed survey of playworld projects and research over the past several decades, see Marjanovic-Shane et al., 2011, and https://quote.ucsd.edu/lchcautobio/polyphonic-autobiography/section-5/chapter-14-adultchild-play-emotion-cognition-and-development-in-playworlds/.)

Interpretive Framework for Discussing Learning in Playworlds

An account of learning in playworlds should acknowledge that, despite the fact that play is an important activity across the lifespan, children have a particular need to play and, simultaneously, that this learning is horizontal as well as vertical. Furthermore, in playworlds the adults and the children often transpose modes of interaction that take place in the playworld to the classroom outside a playworld, and findings in relation to this claim raise the possibility that the creation of a playworld can lead to shared responsibility for directing classroom activities that are not play related (Ferholt, 2009; Ferholt & Lecusay, 2010). These same findings, as well as findings in more recent playworld studies (Nilsson et al., 2018b), show that such sharing can produce emotional-cognitive development, changes in modes of experiencing, and also joy, for adults and children alike.

It is in these deeply experienced, playworld-initiated and playworld-like activities among adults as well as children (in the example below, a discussion among teachers about a playworld in which they are currently participating) that learning in playworlds is made available for analysis in its full, dynamic complexity. In order to understand this learning we turn not only to Biesta's conception of learning but also to his work on finding one's voice, and also to relational pedagogy, to develop an interpretive framework for discussing learning in playworlds. We have found that we are able to further our understandings of this learning by discussing community and co-existence.

Biesta starts us off with an explanation of voice in an alternative to the rational community:

> when we speak with the voice of the rational community, it is not really *me* who is speaking. My voice is simply the interchangeable voice of the rational community. But when I speak to the stranger, when I expose myself to the stranger, when I want to speak in the community of those who have nothing in common, then I have my own voice, then it is *me* who has to speak – and no one else can do this for me. It is, to put it differently, this very way of speaking which constitutes me as a unique individual – as *me*, and no one else. (Biesta, 2004, p. 317)

Lindqvist describes the creation of opportunities on the part of both children and teachers to encounter the strange and to find their own voice in a play-world in these words:

> During the course of the theme, I have seen the teachers become someone in the eyes of the children. They have turned into interesting and exciting people. I have often had the feeling that staff members at a day-care center are perceived as rather anonymous grown-ups. Sometimes, the children will not even notice if a teacher is ill and has been replaced. In a way, assuming roles has liberated the adults – it has enabled them to step out of their 'teacher roles' and leave behind the institutional language which is part of the teacher role in preschools and schools. By virtue of the fictitious role, the teachers have dared to try new attitudes and ways of acting. (Lindqvist, 1995, pp. 210–211)

To constitute oneself as an individual, as a *me*, and no one else, one must become someone in the eyes of the stranger. The teachers become interesting and exciting people to the children, rather than anonymous grown-ups, by leaving institutional (rational discourse) 'teacher roles' behind. Leaving behind the interchangeable voice of teachers, they dare to find the ways of speaking that accompany their playworld attitudes and ways of acting.

The teachers are developing what can be described as their relational competence in such endeavours. Relational competence is considered an important part of teacher professionalism (Aspelin, 2015), and studies indicate that one of the most important aspects of quality in preschool activities are relations between teachers and children featured by responsiveness (*lyhördhet*) and dialogue (Persson, 2015). Aspelin (2015) describes two forms of relational competence: teachers in "attitude *to* relationships" are focused on handling social relations in educational settings and influencing students' relations concerning, for example, teachers, friends, and people in society; in other words, teachers in these relationships are acting 'from outside'; while teachers in "attitude *in* relationships" encounter the student 'from inside' the relationship without preconceptions of what will happen.

We can describe "attitude *to* relationships" as co-operation and "attitude *in* relationships" as co-existence if we apply the following definitions from Aspelin and Persson (2011) to Aspelin's ideas about relational competence:

> Co-existence signifies a personal encounter between two persons. The term has ontological meaning, i.e. human essence is assumed to be realized in this event. Co-existence cannot be defined using conventional behavioral concepts. It stands for an existential meeting in which one person is immediately present vis-à-vis another. In the domain of co-existence, no means are used and no medium stands between persons. Co-existence is characterized by unpredictability and it lacks elements of planning and calculation. Co-existence is a goal in itself; i.e. meaning is inherent in the relationship. (2011, p. 10)

Aspelin and Persson go on to contrast co-operation with co-existence:

> Co-operation represents a process in which individuals coordinate their actions. The process is mediated by social patterns, such as linguistic and paralinguistic rules. Co-operation has an external as well as an internal aspect. On the one hand, it stands for interpersonal communication; on the other, it covers interaction between a subject and his/her surrounding. In the domain of co-operation, people use tools or other means in order to attain different kinds of goals. The activity is defined by some degree of predictability and reticence. Co-operation is created by purposeful action, i.e. it includes goals outside of the relationship. (2011, p. 10)

Lindqvist's observation (cited earlier) – "I have seen the teachers become someone in the eyes of the children" – is closely related to coexistence and attitude *in* relations. "Assuming roles has liberated the adults – it has enabled them to step out of their 'teacher roles' and leave behind the institutional language which is part of the teacher role in preschools and schools" is closely related to Biesta's discussion on "own voices and ways of speaking". The playworld activity appears to enable interactions among "strangers" and thus the creation of a Community of Those Who Have Nothing in Common, in which co-existence and relational competence, understood as "attitude *in* relationships", has a potential to emerge. This is learning through the community without community in playworlds.

It may be that the reason that such learning takes place in playworlds is that teachers encounter each other and the children in ways that go beyond the "rational" and encourage ethical steps toward subjectivity, making them into unique, singular beings with their own voices. Further research on the particular features of playworld activities that promote coexistence, attitude *in* relationships, and Community of Those Who Have Nothing in Common is needed. However, the following discussion illustrates such learning in playworlds.

Learning in Playworlds: An Illustrative Example

The following is an example of adult learning in a playworld. It is drawn from an ethnographic study that took place in three preschools, all of which followed the *pedagogy of listening* and *exploratory learning* approach (Rinaldi, 2006). The study was originally designed to examine if and how the teachers in these preschools adopted, and adapted into their own practices, the playworld activity.

The event that we will present from this study is a discussion that took place among three preschool teachers who participated in the study (we will call them Marie, Elisabeth, and Charlotte). The discussion took place during a teaching reflection and planning meeting. (These meetings took place regularly and were simultaneously documented and attended by two of the chapter authors). This meeting constituted an important turning point in the teacher's incorporation of the playworld activity into their own practice, as it involved the transposition by these teachers of modes of interaction and conflicts, which had taken place in the classroom playworld activity, into the reflection meeting itself.

Chronologically, at the point in the implementation of the research project during which this discussion took place, a picture book had been read to the children several times. The book depicted a story about a princess who awoke to a strange noise. As part of the playworld activity that the teachers had been implementing, Marie had recently appeared outside the preschool window as the princess, sleeping outside and then awakened by the noise. The children, who were 2 and 3 years old, then rushed outside to join the princess on their own initiative. On this first day of role-play, the children joined the princess in all sorts of stories and in 'hearing' many noises, and this joint play continued over the course of many weeks. After just a few weeks Elisabeth joined Marie and the children in the playworld as a 'basement troll'. The basement troll was the source of the noise in the book and was quite scary in the book, and Elisabeth also behaved in scary ways during the joint play. However, although the princess was brave in the book, in the classroom, Marie played a variety of roles in a variety of stories, some of which required more bravery than others.

In brief, the discussion in the teacher's meeting begins with Marie being upset because she feels lonely. She observes that no other teacher wants to play with her when she is in her princess character: the children don't play with her, and neither does Elisabeth, who instead plays with some children on the side. Moreover, Marie finds it difficult to exit the play, as the children are so eager to be with the princess and do not let her take a break.

Elisabeth claims that this is happening because Marie wants to control the situation. This statement upsets Marie, who does not like to be controlling. Marie defends herself, saying that someone has to be in charge, otherwise nothing will happen. Elisabeth says she recognizes herself in Marie, as she (Elisabeth) is twenty years older than Marie. She used to be like Marie, she says.

Marie then accuses Elisabeth of not wanting to play with Marie when in the playworld with the children. Elisabeth admits that this is the case and says that although she does not want to play with Marie, she probably could play with a teacher from a different classroom (Lisa). Marie says: "Yes, but now you have to play with me." The discussion ends with a substitute teacher, who is sitting in, concluding aloud that the teachers in this classroom have difficulty playing together, while this is something they expect young children to be able to manage.

The following is the transcript of the meeting with interpretation and analysis inserted:

> Marie says: "They [the children] want to play with me because I am a princess, but I want to play with them because they are a . . . actually, the same need as they have, I have a need to be with them. It might not be their needs but for me it is easier to play if, I have a need to play with someone that is not Tim [name of a child]. Then I want Tim to be . . . thus, do you understand what I mean? But it might be my needs, it might have nothing to do with the children's needs?"

After discussing the above quote with Marie, we understand her to be expressing the following: Marie is uncomfortable not having co-players. The children are too interested in the princess, which makes Marie feel lonely. She wants the children to be her playmates and enter the playworld in role with her. Marie acknowledges her own feelings and as such she is in an authentic relationship with herself and the children: she is not just a teacher with a 'to attitude', but is instead a person with an 'in attitude'.

> Elisabeth responds: "But I believe you are so obsessed with being, that it should be more theatre. I don't understand how to explain it but I think you are more obsessed because you have demands on yourself, aiming for something. You can't just, don't you have more demands on yourself?"

Here Elisabeth is pointing out two things. She is pointing out that Marie is confusing play with theatre. She is also pointing out that Marie is in need of too much control, something that is a characteristic of the rational community.

Marie: "But you don't play with me [inaudible] . . . Because, that is what I feel. I tried to play with you! And you don't really want to."

Elisabeth (laughter):	"I don't really feel like it. Yes."
Marie:	"When I came there with my princess it was like this, you'd actually rather play with the children."
Elisabeth:	"Yes."
Marie:	"Because when I came into the kitchen and tried like this, then it was like this: "oh yes but" – admit that it was a little bit like that."
Elisabeth:	"Yes, a little bit like that. But I don't feel, I don't know entirely, I don't trust you . . . the play."
Charlotte	(laughing)
Marie:	"No, I felt that!"
Elisabeth:	"Yes, you felt that."
Marie:	"We have to do this again."
Elisabeth:	"Yes, and then I was thinking that whom could I think of playing with? With Charlotte it is probably too hard but I could probably play with Lisa."
Marie:	"But you could not pick her because now it is me."
Charlotte	(laughter)
Elisabeth:	"But then I was thinking like this. This is what it might be like for the children."

The teachers now speak as they might to a friend or to family, about how they feel hurt or vulnerable playing together. They are talking about their working together, as their work includes play. But because they are also meeting each other as people (strangers), not only as teachers (rational) in the playworld play, it is really a discussion about how they are relating to each other's selves that encompasses all areas of their lives. Marie expresses her feeling that the children became a shield, and so something that prevented Elisabeth and Marie from playing together.

The substitute teacher then adds: "Yes, we want the children to be able to play together with everybody and here we can see that that is not so easy all the time."

Elisabeth:	"No!"
Marie:	"No, and we are good at working together but we can't play together."

Soon after this point in the conversation, Marie says to the researchers that they "have never been so honest and open with each other and that is good!"

After this discussion, Marie was eager to write a book to show that they, the teachers, have been part of something "others don't entirely/really understand". We believe that this something is all three teachers bringing to the fore their own voices, that it is this phenomenon that it is rather rare to show and that is difficult to understand. See Nilsson et al. (accepted for publication) for a more detailed description and analysis of this discussion.

The above-described discussion exposed the participating teachers to "what is other and different and strange", and within the discussion they were able to respond in ways that challenged their way of 'speaking' (communicating). This enabled "attitude *in* relations" in the sense of an existential meeting, as in co-existence, in which one person is immediately present vis-à-vis another. Again, co-existence is characterized by unpredictability and lacks elements of planning and calculation, and co-existence is a goal in itself; i.e., meaning is inherent in the relationship.

One of our tentative conclusions from these data is that if the question is how to create a Community of Those Who Have Nothing in Common in the classroom, then we must ask how to do this among teachers, and the way to do this among teachers is to have them encounter the strange and then to find their own voices. This is exactly what seems to happen in all playworlds. One enters into imagining with people (children) who cannot imagine without the material (play), meaning that they always play, and then you (an adult) *must* play, or you have no one to imagine with. Due to this demand, you have the potential to find your own voice. And then you, eventually, become more adept at this 'nothing in common community', such that you are, eventually, able to create such a community with your co-workers as well as with the children.

It is possible that a next step in this learning process is that these adult Communities of Those Who Have Nothing in Common lead to such communities in the classroom with the students, which are outside playworlds. Regardless of whether or not these next steps take place, playworlds are, we claim, an activity for developing relational competence in such terms. And it is in this development that an important aspect of learning in playworlds is readily observable for empirical study.

Concluding Thoughts

Elsewhere (Ferholt & Nilsson, 2018a; Nilsson et al., 2018b; Nilsson et al., 2018a) we have problematized the dichotomization of play and learning. We have argued for a reconceptualization of early childhood education that understands learning and development not as an outcome, primarily, of instruction and teaching but as an outcome of play and exploration. In this work (Nilsson et al., 2018a) we propose a relation between play and learning that we call 'play as learning'.

We argue that one is often confronted with a dichotomy, in which learning is something that happens when teachers teach (engage in direct instruction) and play is something that happens outside the classroom (e.g., during recess), when children are free from adult control and participation (Johansson &

Pramling Samuelsson, 2006). Furthermore, implicit in this pairing is the idea of play understood as a subordinate activity to formal learning. From this perspective, play – viewed as an activity that children inherently enjoy and are therefore attracted to – is seen as something to be leveraged in the service of helping children learn skills and knowledge deemed valuable by someone other than the child, typically a teacher (e.g., "teaching through play"; Bennet et al., 1997). We call this approach play-*for*-learning, where learning is understood specifically as formal learning, i.e., teacher-led and goal directed, and *cognitively* oriented, i.e., school-based learning. And we claim that this approach prioritizes a single-minded focus on learning as the product of teaching – that is, of directed instruction – to the exclusion of the kinds of learning experienced through activities that are self-initiated and that children spontaneously engage in.

In turn, we (Nilsson et al., 2018a) call for a reorientation back to an understanding of play *as* learning, where learning is understood not just in the narrow cognitive sense described above but more broadly as transformations due to different kinds of experiences leading to sustained change. Our claim is that if the field is to further develop its understanding of how learning unfolds in early childhood, then it is play and exploration that should be prioritized as objects of research and pedagogy. Specifically, we propose that rather than focus on play-*for*-learning, research and practice should focus on the organization of preschool activities that provide affordances for play and exploration in ways that promote collaborative adult–child engagement around shared goals, engagement that has the potential to promote not just cognitive development but holistic development.

Playworlds include key areas in which children are the experts and adults are inherently less adept. Therefore, we have found that new understandings of the relationship between play and learning are required if we are to understand learning in playworlds. It is an interest in play-*as*-learning that has led us to discuss learning in playworlds using relevant concepts from the work of Biesta and Aspelin.

References

Aspelin, J. (2015). Lärares relationskompetens. Begreppsdiskussion med stöd i Martin Bubers begrepp 'det sociala' och 'det mellanmänskliga' [Teacher's relational competence. A concept discussion, supported by Martin Buber's concepts of 'the social' and 'the inter-human']. *Utbildning och Demokrati, 24*(3), 49–64.

Aspelin, J., & Persson, S. (2011). Co-existence and co-operation: The two-dimensional conception of education. *Education, 1*(1), 6–11.

Baumer, S., Ferholt, B., & Lecusay, R. (2005). Promoting narrative competence through adult–child joint pretense: Lessons from the Scandinavian educational practice of playworld. *Cognitive Development, 20*, 576–590.

Bennet, N., Wood, E., & Rogers, S. (1997) *Teaching through play*. Buckingham: Open University Press.

Biesta, G. (2004). The community of those who have nothing in common: Education and the language of responsibility. *Interchange, 35*(3), 302–324.

Blunden, A. (2016). Translating *perezhivanie* into English. *Mind, Culture, and Activity, 23*(4), 274–283.

Bredikyte, M., & Hakkarainen, P. (2011). Play intervention and play development. In C. Lobman & B. E. O'Neill (Eds.), *Play and performance* (pp. 59–83). Lanham, MD: University Press of America.

European Early Childhood Education Research Association, the 'Rethinking Play' special interest group. (2017). Position paper about the role of play in early childhood education and care. Available at www.eecera.org/custom/uploads/2017/01/POSITION-PAPER-SIG-RETHINKING-PLAY.pdf.

Ferholt, B. (2009). Adult and child development in adult–child joint play: The development of cognition, emotion, imagination and creativity in playworlds. PhD dissertation, University of California, San Diego.

Ferholt, B. (2010). A multiperspectival analysis of creative imagining: Applying Vygotsky's method of literary analysis to a playworld. In C. Connery, V. John-Steiner, & A. Marjanovic-Shane (Eds.), *Vygotsky and creativity: A cultural historical approach to play, meaning-making and the arts* (pp. 163–180). New York: Peter Lang.

Ferholt, B. (2015). *Perezhivanie* in researching playworlds: Applying the concept of *perezhivanie* in the study of play. In S. Davis, B. Ferholt, H. Grainger-Clemson, S.-M. Jansson, & A. Marjanovic-Shane (Eds.), *Dramatic interactions in education: Vygotskian and socio-cultural approaches to drama, education and research* (pp. 57–75). London: Bloomsbury.

Ferholt, B., & Lecusay, R. (2010). Adult and child development in the zone of proximal development: Socratic dialogue in a playworld. *Mind Culture and Activity, 17*(1), 59–83.

Ferholt, B., & Nilsson, M. (2016a). *Perezhivanija* as a means of creating the aesthetic form of consciousness. *Mind, Culture, and Activity, Symposium on Perezhivanie, 23*, 25–36.

Ferholt, B., & Nilsson, M. (2016b). Early childhood *perezhivanija*. *Mind, Culture, and Activity, Symposium on Perezhivanie, 23*, 25–36.

Ferholt, B., & Nilsson, M. (2018a). Playworlds and the pedagogy of listening. In T. Bruce, M. Bredikyte, & P. Hakkarainen (Eds.), *Handbook of play* (pp. 261–273). London: Routledge.

Ferholt, B., & Nilsson, M. (2018b). Aesthetics of play and joint playworlds. In T. Bruce, M. Bredikyte, & P. Hakkarainen (Eds.), *Handbook of play* (pp. 58–69). London: Routledge.

Ferholt, B., Nilsson, M., Jansson, A., & Alnervik K. (2015). Creativity in education: Play and exploratory learning. In T. Hansson (Ed.), *Contemporary approaches to activity theory* (pp. 264–284). Hershey, PA: IGI Global.

Ferholt, B., Nilsson, M., Jansson, A., & Alnervik K. (2016). Current playworld research in Sweden: Rethinking the role of young children and their teacher in the design and execution of early childhood research. In J. M. Iorio & W. Parnell (Eds.), *Disrupting early childhood education research: Imagining new possibilities* (pp. 117–138). New York: Routledge.

Ferholt, B., & Rainio, A. P. (2016). Teacher support of student engagement in early childhood: Embracing ambivalence through playworlds. *Early Years, 36*(4), 413–425.

Gaskins, S. (1999). Children's daily lives in a Mayan village: A case study of culturally constructed roles and activities. In G. Goncu (Ed.), *Children's engagement in the world: Sociocultural perspectives* (pp. 25–61). New York: Cambridge University Press.

Hakkarainen, P. (2008). The challenges and possibilities of a narrative learning approach in the Finnish early childhood education system. *International Journal of Educational Research, 47*, 292–300.

Hakkarainen, P., Bredikyte, M., Jakkula, K., & Munter, H. (2013). Adult play guidance and children's play development in a narrative play-world. *European Early Childhood Education Research Journal, 21*(2), 213–225.

Hakkarainen, P., & Ferholt, B. (2013). Creative imagination in play-worlds: Wonder-full early childhood education in Finland and the United States. In K. Egan, A. Cant, & G. Judson (Eds.), *Wonder-full education: The centrality of wonder in teaching and learning across the curriculum* (pp. 203–218). New York: Routledge.

Hofmann, R., & Rainio, A. P. (2007). 'It doesn't matter what part you play, it just matters that you're there': Towards shared agency in narrative play activity in school. In R. Alanen & S. Pöyhönen (Eds.), *Language in action: Vygotsky and Leontievian legacy today* (pp. 308–328). Newcastle-upon Tyne: Cambridge Scholars Publishing.

Johansson, E., & Pramling Samuelsson, I. (2006). *Lek och läroplan. Möten mellan barn och lärare i förskolan och skolan* [Play and curriculum. Encounters between children and teachers in preschool and school]. Göteborg: Acta Universitatis Göteburgenis.

Lindqvist, G. (1995). Aesthetics of play: A didactic study of play and culture in preschools. PhD dissertation, University of Karlstad, Research Report 95:12, Social Sciences. SKOBA.

Lindqvist, G. (1989). *Från fakta till fantasi* [From facts to fantasy]. Lund: Studentlitteratur.

Lindqvist, G. (1992). *Ensam i vida världen* [Lonely in the wide world]. Lund: Studentlitteratur.

Lindqvist, G. (1995). Lekens estetik. En didaktisk studie om lek och kultur i förskolan. Forskningsrapport 95: 12, SKOBA, Högskolan i Karlstad. [The aesthetics of play. A didactic study of play and culture in preschools. Acta Universitatis Upsaliensis. Stockholm: Almqvist & Wiksell International.]

Lindqvist, G. (1996). *Lekens möjligheter* [The possibilities of play]. Lund: Studentlitteratur.

Lindqvist, G. (2000). *Historia som tema och gestaltning* [History as theme and gestalt]. Lund: Studentlitteratur.

Lindqvist, G. (2001a). When small children play: How adults dramatize and children create meaning. *Early Years, 21*(1), 7–14.

Lindqvist, G. (2001b). The relationship between play and dance. *Research in Dance Education, 2*(1), 41–53.

Lindqvist, G. (2002). *Lek i skolan* [Play in school]. Lund: Studentlitteratur.

Lindqvist, G. (2003). Vygotsky's theory of creativity. *Creativity Research Journal, 15* (4), 245–251.

Marjanovic-Shane, A., Ferholt, B., Nilsson, M., Rainio, A. P., & Miyazaki, K. (2011). Playworlds: An art of development. In C. Lobman & B. O'Neill (Eds.), *Play and culture studies*, vol. 11 (pp. 3–31). Lanham, MD: University Press of America.

Nilsson, M., & Ferholt, B. (2014). Vygotsky's theories of play, imagination and creativity in current practice: Gunilla Lindqvist's 'creative pedagogy of play' in U.S. kindergartens and Swedish Reggio-Emilia inspired preschools. *Perspectiva, 32*(1), 919–950.

Nilsson, M., Ferholt, B., & Lecusay, R. (2018a). 'The playing-exploring child': Reconceptualizing the relationship between play and learning in early childhood education. *Contemporary Issues in Early Childhood, 19*(3), 1–15.

Nilsson, M., Granqvist, A. K., Johansson, E., Thure, J., & Ferholt, B. (2018b). *Lek, lärande och lycka: lek och utforskande i förskolan* [Play, learning and happiness: Play and exploration in preschool]. Stockholm: Gleerups.

Persson, S. (2015). *Delstudie 4: Pedagogiska relationer i förskolan. Förskola tidig intervention (Pedagogical Relations in Preschool. Preschool Early Intervention). Delrapport från SKOLFORSK-projektet.* Vetenskapsrådet.

Rainio, A. P. (2007). Ghosts, bodyguards and fighting fillies: Manifestations of pupil agency in play pedagogy. *ACTIO: International Journal for Human Activity Theory, 1*, 149–160.

Rainio, A. P. (2008a). From resistance to involvement: Examining agency and control in playworld activity. *Mind, Culture and Activity, 15*(2), 115–140.

Rainio, A. P. (2008b). Developing the classroom as a figured world. *Journal of Educational Change, 9*(4), 357–364.

Rainio, A. P. (2009). Horses, girls, and agency: Gender in play pedagogy. *Outlines – Critical Practice Studies, 1*, 27–44.

Rainio, A. P. (2010). *Lionhearts of the playworld: An ethnographic case study of the development of agency in play pedagogy.* Dissertation, University of Helsinki, Institute of Behavioral Sciences.

Rinaldi, C. (2006). *In dialogue with Reggio Emilia: Listening, researching and learning.* New York: Routledge.

Vygotsky, L. S. (1971). *The psychology of art.* Cambridge, MA: MIT Press.

Vygotsky, L. S. (1978). *Mind in society: The development of higher psychological processes.* Cambridge, MA: Harvard University Press.

Vygotsky, L. S. (1987). Imagination and its development in childhood. In R. W. Rieber & A. S. Carton (Eds.), *The collected works of L. S. Vygotsky*, vol. 1 (pp. 339–350). New York: Plenum Press.

Vygotsky, L. S. (2004). Imagination and creativity in childhood. *Journal of Russian and East European Psychology, 42*(1), 7–97.

29 Play and Literacy

Knowns and Unknowns in a Changing World

Kathleen Roskos

In a world of diminishing mystery, the unknown persists.

– J. Lahiri, *The Lowland*

Some may be familiar with the known/unknowns concept famously summarized by Donald Rumsfeld, a former US Secretary of State:

> There are known knowns. There are things we know that we know. There are known unknowns. That is to say, there are things that we now know we don't know. But there are also unknown unknowns. There are things we do not know we don't know.

At the time the press corps among others derided his statement as utter nonsense. But not so – the concept has a long history in matters of science, which is largely occupied with explicating knowns, investigating known unknowns, and uncovering unknown unknowns (what we don't know yet). And, albeit a tongue-twister statement, the concept applies neatly to the study of relationships between play and literacy that emerged in the twentieth century.

In this chapter I use the concept as a framework for describing play–literacy relationships in the preschool years, particularly in those activity settings where pretend play and early literacy experience intersect in the indoor play environment. Drawing on several decades of play–literacy studies, primarily those in educational settings that serve 3- to 5-year-old children, I discuss the knowns and unknowns pertaining to play–literacy relationships. My twofold goal is to elaborate our understanding of this complex relationship and to spur further research.

Known Knowns

That play and literacy are linked somehow is an intriguing idea, but it is an elusive one scientifically. Play is ubiquitous in early childhood and manifests itself in a variety of forms, both physical and cognitive, which makes it very difficult to define for research purposes and to observe under controlled conditions (Smith, 2010). The definitional issue that dogs much of play research is not lost on efforts to examine play–literacy relationships.

In the world of play research, play–literacy relationships are rooted in pretend play, which emerges at the onset of the preschool years in children aged 3–5. In both Piagetian and Vygtoskian developmental theory, pretend play (symbolic play) has a role in the cognitive development of the child. The theories differ, however, as to its function in the formation of representational thought. From a Piagetian perspective, pretend play is deferred imitation that may occur independent of language, whereas a Vygotskian view credits it as a "leading activity" dependent on language to liberate thought from action (Lucy, 1988). The latter position has deeper implications for literacy development than the former because of its stance on language as a mental tool in play activity, i.e., to represent the real world or a private one.

That said, considerable research has focused on describing the fundamental links between literacy and play in pretend play activity where thought and language converge to create make-believe whether for private or social purposes (see reviews: Roskos & Christie, 2012, 2013; Roskos et al., 2010). The body of work has produced foundational knowledge of the play–literacy nexus that describes what we know, i.e., the known knowns. Much of this foundational knowledge is declarative in nature, as follows.

We know, for instance, that literacy behaviours emerge spontaneously in children's play at home and at school and that these behaviours are more pronounced in supportive literacy environments. Jacob's (1984) pioneering work, for example, revealed Puerto Rican children's use of literacy skills and social behaviours during play; relatedly, Rowe (1998) provides an account of her young son's book-related pretend play. Several descriptive accounts replicate this naturalistic observation at home and school (e.g., Hall, 2000; Roskos, 1987). We learn here that literacy behaviours in the environment do not go unnoticed by young children and appear to be readily incorporated into their spontaneous make-believe activity.

We also know that play environments that are deliberately enriched with literacy materials increase the incidence of emerging literacy behaviours and skills, such as pretending to read, scribbling, reciting the alphabet, recognizing words, etc. Several studies document this finding among preschool children across early childhood settings (Christie & Stone, 1999; Morrow, 1990; Neuman & Roskos, 1992). That the rather simple intervention of increased access to literacy materials in the play environment leads to an increase in literacy behaviours makes a significant contribution to what we know about the play–literacy connection.

Along these same lines there is some evidence that access to literate others in the play environment impacts children's emerging literacy knowledge and skills (Christie & Enz, 1992; Morrow, 1990; Neuman & Roskos, 1993). Vukelich (1994), as a case example, compared literacy-enriched play settings with and without adult intervention. Results showed the added value of teacher guidance that introduces literacy concepts and skills, models literacy behaviours, and extends children's existing literacy knowledge on increasing children's literacy behaviours during sociodramatic play. The knowledge that access to literacy materials plus adult guidance in pretend play activity increases the probability of literacy activity in play is a strong plank in the argument for a play–literacy connection.

We know, too, that pretend play is implicated in the development of narrative skills essential in listening and reading comprehension (Lillard et al., 2013). The research record demonstrates structural parallels between play stories and oral narratives that appear to build an infrastructure for practicing narrative elements (setting, plot, character, resolution) transferable to other contexts, such as oral storytelling, story comprehension, and writing stories (Eckler & Weininger, 1989; Ilgaz & Aksu-Koc, 2005). Descriptive observations also show that when engaged in pretend play children practice role-appropriate behaviour and language that creates and maintains a story-line – exercising skills useful in other decontextualized language contexts, such as storybook comprehension (Cook-Gumperz & Corsaro, 1977; Garvey, 1990; Scarlett & Wolf, 1979).

The thematic-fantasy play (TFP) paradigm (adult-guided story reenact-ment) further suggests the existence of a narrative link between pretend play and literacy. Studies reveal that TFP training improves story comprehension, showing gains in both *specific* story comprehension (understanding the reenacted story) and *generalized* story comprehension (understanding other stories), which implies that the training may improve children's knowledge of narrative story structure (Pellegrini, 1984; Saltz & Johnson, 1974; Silvern et al., 1986). In brief, there is enough evidence to assume an isomorphism between pretend play language and oral narratives that undergirds the oral language processes needed for early literacy.

Finally, we know that guided pretend play in learning centres at preschool may influence critical marker variables of early literacy development, i.e., writing, print knowledge, and oral language abilities (vocabulary, grammar). Learning centres as play-based activity settings afford a broad spectrum of literacy learning opportunities that can help young children learn relevant early literacy skills (e.g., name writing) (Johnson et al., 2005). Quasi-experimental studies show the benefits of guided pretend play for vocabulary learning (Han et al., 2010), for reading and writing words (Vukelich, 1991, 1994), for developing syntactic complexity of spoken language (Vedeler, 1997), and for using metalinguistic verbs in play talk (Galda et al., 1989). Combining game play with storybook reading has also been found to help children learn new vocabulary words (Hassinger-Das et al., 2016; Roskos & Burstein, 2011). Knowing that curriculum-generated pretend play, either child- or adult-led, may influence literacy learning outcomes gives new impetus to the use of play strategies in the early literacy curriculum – a boost urgently needed in an increasingly standards-based approach to literacy edu-cation (Christie & Roskos, 2006).

Known Unknowns

What we know about play–literacy relationships also lays bare what we do not know. And it is in the search for answers to the known unknowns that the knowledge base expands and enlarges our understanding of the play–literacy connection. So, what are the research-driven unknowns that have emerged from the last several decades of play–literacy research? Undoubtedly, there are many unknowns, large and small, but a few are high-priority unknowns in that they have the potential to extend what we know in significant ways, and it is to these high-priority few I turn to next.

High Priority #1: How to implement literacy-rich play environments effectively. A literacy-rich play environment increases the incidence of early literacy behaviours and thereby literacy learning opportunity. This we know. But what makes a literacy-rich play environment work to good effect across diverse settings is less clear.

Much of the research in the play environment domain has focused on examining what happens when specific indoor play centres at school are enriched with literacy resources (materials, adult facilitation). In this respect, the literacy-enriched play centre is an evidence-based intervention in the play environment, although in general it has not been treated in this way. Design features of literacy-enriched play centres vary considerably across studies in terms of intensity, frequency, duration, and conditions, which complicates efforts to identify salient features that might make a difference in learning outcomes. It is unknown, for example, if the amount of time a child spends in literacy-related play centres matters or if the quality of literacy materials has a bearing on learning outcomes. While there is some research that adult facilitation adds value (Neuman & Roskos, 1993), the evidence lacks sufficient detail for consistent implementation of facilitation skills across settings. In sum, the literacy-enriched play centre can potentially help children in educational settings, but its limited specification thwarts testing and the development of evidence-based guidance that can increase the pace and effectiveness of wide-scale implementation.

How do we take what we know and turn it into what we do routinely in early literacy practice? To move in this direction, we need to examine not only what happens in literacy-enriched play centres but also how to make it happen, i.e., the details of implementation. In some arenas, this is referred to as implementation science, which examines the components of change for improved practices in local settings (Fixsen et al., 2005), and in others as improvement science, which iteratively tests implementations to improve practical guidance for evidence-based practice (Bryk, 2015; Rubenstein & Pugh, 2006).

In both approaches to solving problems of practice the goal is to learn how best to use innovation under real-world conditions. This requires collaboration across the boundaries of research and practice so that what matters in each domain remains active in "the kind of context-specific and evidence-informed decision-making that is crucial to making what is possible in theory a reality in practice" (Peters et al., 2013, p. 8). Put plainly, play–literacy researchers cannot plumb the 'how to' of literacy-enriched play environments without including practitioners. Going forward, research attention needs to turn to design thinking that answers questions early educators ask, i.e., What is a 'good' literacy-enriched play environment? What are the essentials? How is it managed and sustained? How should be it be used to meet early literacy curriculum goals? To what extent should literacy-related play be planned and guided?

Einarsdottir's study (2014) in an Icelandic preschool represents this kind of design thinking. In a collaborative action research project between two preschool teachers and university researchers, literacy-enriched play environments that included prop boxes in centres and literacy activities in free play were created in the respective classrooms. Although the relational work between the experts (researchers, practitioners) is not made clear, the report does sketch the teachers' acceptance, adoption, and perceived fit of the play–literacy strategy to their early literacy curriculum goals. As a result of the collaboration, the teachers expressed a deeper conceptual understanding of the play strategy and how to operationalize it in their local settings with better fidelity. But more importantly they described issues of implementation that need to be worked out at the local level for the strategy to work, such as the tension between play and reading readiness instruction. It is these unresolved issues of implementation that often prevent us from using what we know in what we do. And how to overcome these issues effectively and widely for effective implementation remains unknown.

High Priority #2: Priming for literacy through pretend play talk. That pretend play (symbolic play) and literate behaviour share common ground is a pillar of play–literacy research. Both indices of representational competence rely on decontextualized language use to represent ideas and events, including pretend, narrative, and explanatory (meta-play) talk. Correlational evidence shows a positive relationship between language elements used to engage in symbolic play (transforming the here and now, you and me, this and that) and those useful in learning literate language (e.g., syntactic awareness, vocabulary, endophora) (Pellegrini, 1985; Vedeler, 1997; Wasik & Jacobi-Vessels, 2016). At the crux of the relationship is the cognitive demand for linguistically explicit language to communicate meaning, whether between players in pretend play or between authors and readers in storybooks.

What remains uncharted, however, is how the higher-order language processes of pretend play talk (e.g., future-tense markers) and those of literacy intersect to support and advance early literacy development toward the achievement of beginning reading and writing. Pretend play, as Vygtosky argued, belies what it leads to developmentally, and only a "profound analysis" can reveal its evolution and role in representational competencies relevant to literacy, i.e., concept of word or story comprehension. A profound analysis is needed, in short, to explicate the unknowns that now limit our understanding of the shared cognitive and language processes between pretend play activity and early literacy skills.

What constitutes a profound analysis, however, is itself evolving in response to advances in cognitive science. Building on the classic theories of Piaget and Vygotsky, connectionist and dynamic systems theories propose a non-linear view of growth and change that emphasizes behavioural dynamics – the mutual relationship between person and environment – over behavioural stabilities (e.g., developmental stages). Embracing this perspective, dynamic skill theory provides a powerful lens for observing the decontextualized language of pretend play talk and storybook reading across the preschool developmental period (ages 2–5). Using order-analytic techniques (Kuleck & Knight, 1999) and dynamic modelling approaches (Fischer et al., 2007), it offers new analytic possibilities for observing convergence zones where the language skills of pretend play activity are recycled in reading activity to imbue stories and printed words with meaning. Pellegrini (1985) observed, for example, the use of verbs (linguistic, cognitive, temporal) in pretend play talk, hypothesizing that explicit use of this language element is a common factor linking play and literacy. Research evidence, however, has yet to uncover if this specific language use creates a zone of convergence where play skill morphs to early literacy skill. The statistical approaches of dynamic skill theory raise hope for seeing these convergence zones of play talk and early literacy skill by allowing richer analyses of both regularities and diversities in developmental pathways. They permit the observation of small facts on which large inferences depend, namely, the idea that decontextualized language use bridges pretend play and early literacy in the preschool period.

A small-scale analysis from a longitudinal study of parents' decontextualized input in relation to child vocabulary development speaks to this point (Rowe, 2013). Decontextualized utterances in parent–child dyads were recorded with children aged 18, 40, and 42 months and organized into three categories: pretend, explanation, and narrative. In general, decontextualized talk increased child vocabularies over time with explanatory and narrative talk types more influential for vocabulary growth; no association, in fact, was found between pretend utterances and vocabulary growth. However, talking about the past and future in narratives was found to significantly contribute to children's vocabulary development over time. Rowe writes that "by exposing children to narrative discourse, parents can provide their children with experience engaging in conversations about topics removed from the here and now and scaffold their children's ability to produce narrative discourse themselves [e.g. in their play]" (p. 191).

For purposes of examining unknowns in play–literacy research, the nugget here may not be vocabulary, per se, but rather verb tense – the meaning marker of past and future in language exchanges. Temporal verbs are important drivers not only of cohesive narrative accounts between parent and child but also of sociodramatic play between peers. Witness the exchange: "You're gonna be the mom and I'm gonna be the dad. Okay? 'member, Adam, you were the dad before? And then we're gonna go to the beach for a picnic." Studies are replete with exchanges like this that illustrate how players use temporal verbs to organize their complex play episodes and to direct fellow players, thus cultivating a meta-narrative awareness of play episode construction (setting, roles, plot) (Pellegrini, 1985; Roskos, 1987; Scarlett & Wolf, 1979; Silvern et al., 1986). The known-unknown associations between pretend play talk and literate language, therefore, may be more readily observed in an analysis of language syntax, not its semantics. Discoveries, in brief, are hidden in the linguistic details of decontextualized language use to achieve larger narrative purposes, such as creating play stories. The press for literate language in achieving pretend play, it may be argued, builds familiarity with written discourse in oral form and exercises strategies for handling written language in books (e.g., following temporal sequences).

High Priority #3: Testing promising play-based instructional strategies in educational settings. Two lines of play–literacy research have produced play-based instructional strategies that are explicitly linked to essential early reading skills as defined by the National Early Literacy Panel (2008). (See Table 29.1.) Several strategies fall under the umbrella of creative drama and have been shown to influence story comprehension. Others fall into the broad category of educational play and focus largely on increasing word level skills (e.g., name or word writing).

As a classroom technique, creative drama is informal and focuses on the process of dramatic enactment for the sake of the learner, not an audience. Its purpose is not to learn about drama but to learn through drama. Its roots are in pretend play where children transform the here and now, this and that, you and me to create an imaginary world; it blossoms in sociodramatic play where children create make-believe scenarios. Smilansky (1968) first seized on the potential of adult-assisted sociodramatic play for improving children's language skills and paved the way for creative dramatics as a theory-based teaching tool in the language arts curriculum. Among the panoply of creative drama techniques, story reenactment (aka the TFP) is the most promising for developing the language and cognitive abilities associated with early literacy skills, namely, storytelling, story comprehension, and story recall (e.g., Kim, 1999; Marbach & Yawkey, 1980; Pellegrini & Galda, 1982; Saltz & Johnson, 1974; Silvern et al., 1986). While the research evidence is not rock-solid, it does suggest that certain types of pretend play impact certain oral language comprehension skills that are influential in the learn-to-read process (Lillard et al., 2013). Pretend role-play, for example, supports story memory, and toys/props (e.g., puppets) aid story retelling. Social pretend play, common in the preschool play environment, positively influences storytelling abilities.

Table 29.1 *Variables representing early literacy skills*

Variables with medium to large predictive relationships
- Alphabet knowledge: Knowledge of names and sounds associated with printed letters
- Phonological awareness: The ability to detect, manipulate or analyze the auditory aspects of spoken language (including the ability to distinguish or segment words, syllables, or phonemes) independent of meaning
- Rapid automatic naming (RAN): The ability to rapidly name a sequence of random letters or digits.
- RAN of objects or colours: The ability to rapidly name a sequence of repeating random sets of pictures or objects
- Writing or writing name: The ability to write letters in isolation on request or to write one's own name
- Phonological memory: The ability to remember spoken information for a short period of time.

Variables moderately correlated with at least one measure of later literacy achievement
- Concepts about print: Knowledge of print conventions
- Print knowledge: A combination of alphabet knowledge, concepts about print, and early decoding
- Reading readiness: Usually a combination of alphabet knowledge, concepts about print, vocabulary, memory, and phonological awareness
- Oral language: The ability to produce or comprehend spoken language, including vocabulary and grammar
- Visual processing: The ability to match or discriminate visually presented symbols

---

Source: National Early Literacy Panel (2008).

Still, the research evidence does not make a strong case for these play-based strategies as essentials in routine early literacy practice (Lillard et al., 2013; Roskos & Christie, 2013). To build a body of scientific evidence, the research needs are twofold: (1) replicating experimental training studies that show the effects of specific play-based strategies on specific narrative skills (e.g., story comprehension), such as the kindergarten pretend play intervention conducted by Baumer et al. (2005), and (2) identifying and describing implementation strategies (how to) that embed promising or proven play-based techniques routinely in early literacy instruction, such as book-related play as described by Welsch (2008). Limited by a small sample, the Baumer et al. (2005) intervention combines components identified in related research (e.g., the TFP paradigm): reading a story, discussing it, adult modelling of reenactment, and reenactment by children with adult assistance. Replicating the technique with a larger sample and more controls can not only build credibility, but also reveal potential 'fixes' that might strengthen the technique. Relatedly, Welsch's evidence-based book-related play procedure warrants replication with an eye to problems of implementation in real classrooms. Mixed methods designs offer an expeditious approach to these dual needs that in tandem hold promise, but also pose serious challenges to the active role of pretend play intervention in early literacy education.

Turning next to the domain of educational play, which subsumes a variety of play-based activities linked to academic goals (Johnson et al., 2005): investigations of unknowns may benefit from digging into the details. Consider, for example, the Tools of the Mind play-based curriculum (Bodrova & Leong, 2007), which has undergone considerable scrutiny as to its effectiveness on learning outcomes (Farran et al., 2015). Tools of the Mind is a comprehensive, full-day early childhood curriculum with 40–65 Vygotskian-based activities wherein the central activity is sociodramatic play. It focuses on helping children develop learning dispositions (self-regulation) while they are also learning early academic skills (literacy, math). Several longitudinal, large-scale randomized trials of the Tools of the Mind curriculum, however, reveal lacklustre results (SREE, 2012). It simply did not outperform typical or skills-focused pre-K curriculums in diverse classrooms on self-regulation, early literacy, and early mathematics marker variables. Play-based strategies intended to increase self-regulatory, literacy, and mathematics skills did not give children an edge, and in some instances disadvantaged them (e.g., Clements et al., 2012).

But wait – in the Lonigan and Phillips study (2012), comparing skills-focused and self-regulation-focused curricula, sits an intriguing detail relevant to play-based instruction in early literacy learning. The study compared four curricula (see Table 29.2).

Research discoveries await in the details of two Tools of the Mind activities transported to the combination curriculum: play plans and support for plan enactment in play centres. Central to the self-regulation goals of the Tools of the Mind curriculum are written play plans that ask children to make a written plan that describes which centre they are going to play in and what they are going to do there, the role, and the actions (e.g., *play babies and I'm the mom*). Reminiscent of the plan-do-review routine in the HighScope curriculum (www.highscope.org/), the goal is to promote meta-play (the ability to think about play actions) and the ability to create pretend scenarios using language. Play plans advance from drawing and scribbling as representations to scaffolded writing with teacher assistance. Scaffolded writing progresses from making lines for words to spelling attempts for some words to spelling attempts for all words. The salient detail here is the making of lines to "stand for" individual words and attempting to write words on lines to plan for play. The task, in essence, teaches the alphabetic principle, which is a forerunner of word recognition (Ehri, 2014).

During centre play, the teachers help children learn to *enact their written play plan*, which serves as a blueprint to initiate play. Self-regulation is promoted during play itself as children attempt to 'stick to the plan'. Teachers intervene to make sure that children can invent multiple themes, roles, and

Table 29.2 *Language and literacy curricula*

Language/Literacy Curriculum	Key Features
Literacy Express Comprehensive Preschool Curriculum (LECPC) (Lonigan, Clancy- Menchetti, Phillips, McDowell, & Farver, 2005)	• 10 thematic units (each 3–5 weeks long) • Adult-led small group activities in oral language, phonological awareness, print knowledge (10–15 minutes daily)
Tools of the Mind (TOM) (Leong & Hensen, 2005).	• Play plans (written plan that outlines centre play activity and includes drawing and writing) • Self-regulation (enacting the play plan with adult assistance as needed) (40–60 minutes daily)
LECPC + TOM	• Thematic units • Adult-led small group activities • Play plans • Enacting play plans in theme-related centres; sustained make-believe play
Business as usual (BAU)	• Variations of HighScope or Creative Curriculum

pretend scenarios that sustain the play in the same centre for 40–60 minutes at a time. The salient detail here is the cognitive demand *to remember the plan* and *to use explicit language* (endophora) for enactment, both of which are foundational skills of oral language comprehension.

The important point is this: although results of the study did not favour pure Tools of the Mind (nor have any experimental studies thus far), they did show clear and consistent benefits of the combined curriculum for outcomes measuring code-related aspects of reading-related skills (e.g., print knowledge, phonological awareness) across diverse classrooms – on par, in fact, with the strictly skills-focused Literacy Express Comprehensive Preschool Curriculum program. What do we make of this result? It is this, I think: that play and literacy skills intersect in writing play plans and enacting them to the mutual benefit of each domain and that these components are transferrable across early childhood curricula. In other words, these components may work together in any preschool language and literacy curriculum. But we don't know that, and further replication and testing of this 'detail' embedded in strong experimental research is needed across curricula to judge its worth to practice.

Unknown Unknowns

Much remains unknown about the play–literacy relationship, which is understandable given the recency of the idea in the short history of preschool literacy – a mere 30 years or so (Teale & Sulzby, 1986). Certainly, there are plenty of known unknowns to pursue, but the field also faces an abundance of unknown unknowns in a rapidly changing world.

Play is not immune from the digital technologies that pervade everyday life, and indeed grows more complex in play environments that afford online and offline and digital and nondigital play opportunities. The Oxford philosopher Nick Bostrom remarked that one of the greatest unknowns we face (worryingly) is the rise of ever-smarter machines, capable of substituting for and complementing human work. Likewise in the study of play, it is the child's digital habitus – their internalized digital culture – that affords them new ways of seeing, acting, and playing in the world (Zevenbergen, 2007). And it is this uncharted twenty-first-century human–machine interface that forces us to look anew at what play is and what it can do. At the leading edge is an emerging line of research on digital play, which offers pioneering examples of uncovering unknown unknowns that move in this direction. What follows are a few excellent examples.

Exploring Play and Creativity in Preschoolers' Use of Apps, a joint study conducted by a technology and play research group (Marsh et al., 2015) in the United Kingdom, surveyed app access and usage at home, explored how apps foster play and creativity at home and school, and analyzed affordances of the most popular apps, placing a special emphasis on augmented reality apps. Play behaviours were classified using Hughes's taxonomy (2002) adapted to play in a digital environment. The study is descriptive, thus a starting point for probing broadly into what we do not yet grasp about the play–literacy connection in a digital environment. The bottom line is that children's app usage indicated a range of play types and app preferences, but the mechanisms shaping the play experience and related early literacy markers, such as literate language, remain hidden. Apps, after all, are software programs on devices, and devices raise issues of autonomy, automation, and child–device teaming. The study, albeit rich in information, is silent on the ability of apps to support or constrain the tell-tale signs of play-based learning: positive affect, no literality, means-over-ends orientation, and a broad spectrum of learning opportunities (Johnson et al., 2005). It does not venture into more worrying questions, i.e., who's in charge – child or device? Do apps automate play – performing some of the physical and mental work previously done by the child? Can apps improve play by complementing the child's cognitive capabilities? Not meant as criticisms of an important survey of digital play; rather, these are queries for consideration in future research, which seek to uncover unknowns.

Along these lines, The Land of Make Believe is an augmented reality system that directly examines if child-app teaming (complementarity) can improve pretend play abilities. The prototype is designed to encourage autistic children, who characteristically have difficulties with symbolic thinking, to engage in imaginative play (Bai et al., 2015). The interactive system visually conceptualizes the representation of pretence within an open-ended play environment. The child, for example, plays with imaginary props superimposed over those on-screen in a given play scenario (play frame). The app, in brief, makes it easier for autistic children to experience using one thing for another in different play contexts – the augmented reality app *scaffolds* pretence, if you will. Results from an empirical study involving children with autistic spectrum disorders aged 4–7 demonstrated a significant improvement of pretend play in terms of frequency, duration, and relevance using the augmented reality system in comparison to a non-computer-assisted situation. Intriguing in this line of research is the creation of a mixed reality digital play environment where virtual objects are superimposed over real-world images in three dimensions and in real time. While we can observe what children do with these augmented reality apps (see, for example, Marsh & Yamada-Rice, 2016), we as yet cannot see what it means for developing cognitive and language skills linked to literacy, such as representational thinking. How a computer-based app (software) tutors play skills (child) is largely unknown.

One more example involves what we might refer to as 'puppet play 2.0'. Puppet play – a blend of storying and pretending – has a long history in early childhood experience at home and school. Traditional puppet play involves props (glove, sock, finger, rod, marionette) and maybe even a stage where stories well known or newly created are acted out either solo or in collaboration with peers. The critical play–literacy relationship here is embedded in the narrative competencies that puppet play supports (Nicolopoulou et al., 2015). New technologies, however, have transformed puppet play from a manual to a computer-assisted play experience, thus introducing new literacy and play elements into the puppet play experience. Case in point: in a theory-to-practice article, Wohlwend (2015) describes digital puppetry play among pre-schoolers using the PuppetPals app on an iPad. In this app children animate characters using finger-based operating skills (dragging, pinching, swiping) and voice recordings to tell/act out a story. Wohlwend termed this play *collaborative literacy play*, defining it as "coordinated storying, digital literacy learning, multimodal production, and play negotiation" (p. 155). She argues that in a digital world, collaborative puppet play represents a *new* literacy because it demands multimodal meaning-making skills. It integrates traditional literacy skills (e.g., creating/recounting stories) with new forms of media (e.g., visual graphics) in a playful way. As such, the puppet play app supports reading readiness for both traditional and digital reading skills.

Many puppet play skills remain the same in traditional and digital puppet play (e.g., role-taking); however, different skills emerge in the digital play context, and in particular haptic skills that facilitate the coordination of eye, hand, and voice to achieve play goals. Haptic skills involve both tactile perception through the skin and spatial perception commonly referred to as the kinaesthetic sense modality, i.e., location in physical space. A finger swipe on an iPad, for example, is sensed both through the receptors on the skin on our fingers and through the position and movement of our hand and fingers.

Similar skills apply in beginning reading where the skilful handling of eye and hand guide the emerging reader to the print. So, it is tempting to think that the haptic skills of digital puppet play might transfer to those of reading either printed or digital texts. But this hypothesis remains to be proven in any systematic way digitally, although some reading acquisition research, albeit limited, shows that haptic skills support the learn-to-read process. In a multi-sensory training study of the alphabetic principle in kindergarteners, for example, visuo-haptic exploration of print enabled children first to increase performance on letter knowledge and initial phoneme awareness and then allowed better decoding skills of printed words (Bara et al., 2007). Still we are far from unravelling the cross-modal attention processes and skills that digital play recruits and even further from identifying any transfer to emergent print or digital reading.

Before drawing this discussion to a close, there is a final topic of consider-able importance: the rise of robots as play tools in the preschool play environ-ment. Two examples may suffice to illustrate the robot as play tool into the future. One is Keepon, a small yellow creature-like robot designed to conduct non-verbal interactions with young children developed by Heidi Kozima while at the National Institute of Information and Communications Technology in Kyoto, Japan. Keepon is a playful robot engineered with four degrees of freedom (nodding, turning, rocking, bobbing) that displays attentive action, enabling eye contact and joint attention, and emotive action, expressive of a state of mind (e.g., pleasure). Longitudinal field observations with typically developing children and children with developmental disorders, particularly autistic spectrum disorders, interacting with Keepon describe the robot's potential for facilitating social development and interpersonal coordination (Kozima et al., 2009). The designers' research goal is to use the social robot to study, test, and elaborate on psychological models of the development of social intelligence. Particularly relevant to play–literacy research is a focus on interactional synchrony, which involves the temporal coordination of communicative behaviours between interactors to achieve a "goodness of fit" between them (Kozima et al., 2009, p. 13). Interactional synchrony, also termed rhythmic intelligence, is a substrate of pretend play, underlying its tell-tale characteristics of social interaction, co-occurring movements, gestures, talk, body positioning, and coordination, to create a unified, meaningful 'whole'. Playful robots with rhythmic intelligence, such as Keepon, can gener-ate rhythmic patterns (e.g., dance interactions) and also detect rhythmic play in children, so as to maintain engagement and intelligently guide interactions. Robots, in short, can become playmates responsive to a child's social devel-opment and facilitative of social interactions foundational in pretend play. How this play tool might improve pretend play skills that prime literacy learning is open to question.

Another example is a show-and-tell robotic puppet developed by Causo et al. (2015). Still in the design stage, the robotic puppet is composed of hardware, electronics, and software contained in a puppet body, base, and controller. Puppet characters are selected from off-the-shelf hand puppets and fitted over the apparatus. The puppet movement is controlled via a remote control that fits easily in a child's hand. As with other electronic devices, touch, eye contact, and joint attention are fundamental behaviours to maintain puppet–child interactions and to establish interactional synchrony between other puppet players. Preliminary descriptive results indicate some advantage of robotic puppets over traditional play tools (e.g., blocks) in supporting thinking and learning domains of play performance, i.e., constructing knowledge, problem-solving, inquiry, and engagement (Trawick-Smith et al., 2011). Still, whether play with robotic puppets produces an increase in narrative skills in the puppet play process is far from clear.

Concluding Remarks

Speaking to the life course, Jhumpa Lahiri, the author cited at the start, observes how life's mysteries are revealed over time only to make way for new ones. This is no less true in the pursuit of tantalizing questions about the interface of play and language in early childhood that makes way for literacy acquisition. Unknowns as to how this actually works at cognitive, behavioural, and neural levels in literacy development persist, although descriptive, correlational, and experimental evidence is helping to unravel some of the mysteries. It is in pushing at the boundaries of the known that new discoveries of the play–literacy relationship will happen – and from these the leap into the unknown can be made. The play–literacy research field is in dynamic motion and, as the chapter shows, primed for answering practical questions of early literacy pedagogy and also gearing up for addressing new theoretical ones in a changing world.

References

Bai, Z., Blackwell, A. F., & Coulouris, G. (2015, May). Using augmented reality to elicit pretend play for children with autism. *IEEE Transactions on Visualization and Computer Graphics*, *21*(5), 1–14.

Bara, F., Gentaz, E., & Cole, P. (2007). Haptics in learning to read with children from low socio-economic status families. *British Journal of Developmental Psychology*, *25*, 643–663.

Baumer, S., Ferholt, B., & Lecusay, R. (2005). Promoting narrative competence through adult–child joint pretense: Lessons from the Scandinavian educational practice of playworld. *Cognitive Development 20*, 576–590.

Bodrova, E., & Leong, D. (2007). *Tools of the mind*. Upper Saddle River, NJ: Pearson.

Bryk, A. S. (2015). Accelerating how we learn to improve. *Educational Researcher*, *44*(9), 467–477.

Causo, A., Vo, G. T., & Chen, I. (2015). Developing and benchmarking show and tell robotic puppet for preschool education. In 2015 IEEE International Conference on Robotics and Automation (ICRA), Seattle, WA, 26–30 May 2015. doi: 10.1109/ICRA.2015.7140057.

Christie, J. F., & Enz, B. (1992). The effects of literacy play interventions on preschoolers' play patterns and literacy development. *Early Education and Development*, *3*(3), 205–220.

Christie, J., & Roskos, K. (2006). Standards, science, and the role of play in early literacy education. In D. Singer, R. Golinkoff, & K. Hirsh-Pasek (Eds.), *Play=learning: How play motivates and enhances children's cognitive and social-emotional growth* (pp. 57–73). Oxford: Oxford University Press.

Christie, J., & Stone, S. (1999). Collaborative literacy activity in print-enriched play centers: Exploring the 'zone' in same-age and multi-age groupings. *Journal of Literacy Research*, *31*, 109–131.

Clements, D., Sarana, J., Unlu, F., & Layzer, C. (2012, March). The efficacy of an intervention synthesizing scaffolding designed to promote self-regulation with an early mathematics curriculum: Effects on executive function. Paper presented at the Society for Research on Educational Effectiveness annual conference, Washington, DC.

Cook-Gumperz, J., & Corsaro, W. (1977). Socio-ecological constraints on children's communicative strategies. *Sociology*, *11*(3), 411–434.

Eckler, J. A., & Weininger, O. (1989). Structural parallels between pretend play and narrative. *Developmental Psychology*, *25*, 736–743.

Ehri, L. (2014). Orthographic mapping in the acquisition of sight word reading, spelling memory, and vocabulary learning. *Scientific Studies of Reading*, *18*(1), 5–21.

Einarsdottir, J. (2014). Play and literacy: A collaborative action research project. *Scandinavian Journal of Educational Research*, *58*(1) 93–109.

Farran, D. C., Wilson, S. J., Meador, D., Norvell, J., & Nesbitt, K. (2015). Experimental evaluation of the tools of the mind pre-K curriculum: Technical report. Working Paper, Peabody Research Institute, Vanderbilt University.

Fischer, K. W., Rose, L. T., & Rose, S. P. (2007). Growth cycles of mind and brain: Analyzing developmental pathways of learning disorders. In K. W. Fischer, J. H. Bernstein, & M. H. Immordino-Yang (Eds.), *Mind, brain and education in reading disorders* (pp. 101–123). Cambridge: Cambridge University Press.

Fixsen, D. L., Naoom, S. F., Blase, K. A., Friedman, R. M., & Wallace, F. (2005). *Implementation research: A synthesis of the literature*. Tampa, FL: University of South Florida, Louis de la Parte Florida Mental Health Institute, the National Implementation Research Network (FMHI Publication #231).

Galda, L., Pellegrini, A., & Cox, S. (1989). A short-term longitudinal study of preschoolers' emergent literacy. *Research in the Teaching of English*, *23*, 292–309.

Garvey, C. (1990). *Play*. Cambridge, MA: Harvard University Press.

Hall, N. (2000). Literacy, play, and authentic experience. In K. Roskos & J. Christie (Eds.), *Play and literacy in early childhood: Research from multiple perspectives* (pp. 189–204). Mahwah, NJ: Lawrence Erlbaum.

Han, M., Moore, N., Vukelich, C., & Buell, M. (2010). Does play make a difference? How play intervention affects the vocabulary learning of at-risk preschoolers. *American Journal of Play*, *3*(1), 82–105.

Hassinger-Das, B., Ridge, K., Parker, A., Golinkoff, R., Hitsch-Pasek, K., & Dickinson, D. (2016). Building vocabulary knowledge in preschoolers through shared book reading and gameplay. *Mind, Brain and Education*, *10*(2), 71–80.

Hughes, B. (2002). *A playworker's taxonomy of play types* (2nd ed.). London: PlayLink.

Ilgaz, H., & Aksu-Koc, A. (2005). Episodic development in preschool children's play-prompted and direct-elicted narratives. *Cognitive Development*, *20*, 526–544.

Jacob, E. (1984). Learning literacy through play: Puerto Rican kindergarten children. In A. Oberg, H. Goelman, & F. Smith (Eds.), *Awakening to literacy* (pp. 73–83). Portsmouth, NH: Heinemann.

Johnson, J., Christie J., & Wardle, F. (2005). *Play, development and early education*. New York: Pearson.

Kim, S. (1999) The effects of storytelling and pretend play on cognitive processes, short-term and long-term narrative recall. *Child Study Journal*, *29*(3), 175–192.

Kozima, H., Michalowski, M., & Nakagawa, C. (2009). Keepon: A playful robot for research, therapy and entertainment. *International Journal of Social Robotics*, *1*, 3–18.

Kuleck, W. J., & Knight, C. C. (1999). An ordinal sequencing technique for assessing multi-dimensional or hierarchical change models. *Ohio Journal of Science*, *100*, 8–12.

Leong, D. J., & Hensen, R. (2005). *Tools of the mind preschool curriculum research project manual* (2nd ed.). Denver, CO: Center for Improving Early Learning, Metropolitan State College of Denver.

Lillard, A. S., Lerner, M. D., Hopkins, E. J., Dore, R. A., Smith, E. D., & Palmquist, C. M. (2013). The impact of pretend play on children's development: A review of the evidence. *Psychological Bulletin*, *139*, 1–34.

Lonigan, C., & Phillips, B. (2012, March). Comparing Skills-Focused and Self-Regulation Focused Preschool Curricula: Impacts on Academic and Self-Regulatory Skills. Paper presented at the Society for Research on Educational Effectiveness annual conference, Washington, DC.

Lonigan, C. J., Clancy-Menchetti, J., Phillips, B. M., McDowell, K., & Farver, J. M. (2005). *Literacy express: A preschool curriculum*. Tallahassee, FL: Literacy Express.

Lucy, J. A. (1988). The role of language in the development of representation: A comparison of the views of Piaget and Vygotsky. *Quarterly Newsletter of the Laboratory of Comparative Human Cognition*, *10*(4), 99–103.

Marbach, E. S., & Yawkey, T. D. (1980). The effect of imaginative play actions on language development in five-year-old children. *Psychology in the Schools*, *17*, 257–263.

Marsh, J., Plowman, L., Yamada-Rice, D., Bishop, J. C., Lahmar, J., Scott, F., Davenport, A., Davis, S., French, K., Piras, M., Thornhill, S., Robinson, P., & Winter, P. (2015). Exploring play and creativity in pre-schoolers' use of apps: Final project report. Available at www.techandplay.org.

Marsh, J., & Yamida-Rice, D. (2016). Bringing Pudsey to life: Young children's use of augmented reality apps. In N. Kurcikova & G. Falloon (Eds.), *Apps, technology and younger learners* (pp. 207–218). New York: Routledge.

Morrow, L. (1990). Preparing the classroom environment to promote literacy during play. *Early Childhood Research Quarterly, 5,* 537–544.

National Early Literacy Panel (2008). *Developing early literacy: A scientific synthesis of early literacy development and implications for intervention,* pp. 7–8. Available at www.nifl.gov/publications/pdf/NELPReport09.pdf.

Neuman, S., & Roskos, K. (1992). Literacy objects as cultural tools: Effects on children's literacy behaviors in play. *Reading Research Quarterly, 27*(3), 202–235.

Neuman, S., & Roskos, K. (1993). Access to print for children of poverty: Differential effects of adult mediation and literacy-enriched play settings on environmental and functional print tasks. *American Educational Research Journal, 30*(1), 95–122.

Nicolopoulou, A., Cortina, K., Ilgaz, H., Cates, C., & deSa, A. (2015). Using a narrative- and play-based activity to promote low-income preschoolers' oral language, emergent literacy, and social competence. *Early Childhood Research Quarterly, 31*(2), 147–162.

Pellegrini, A. D. (1984). Identifying causal elements in the thematic-fantasy play paradigm. *American Educational Research Journal, 21,* 691–701.

Pellegrini, A. D. (1985). The relations between symbolic play and literate behavior: A review and critique of the empirical literature. *Review of Educational Research, 55,* 207–221.

Pellegrini, A., & Galda, L. (1982). The effects of thematic-fantasy play training on the development of children's story comprehension. *American Educational Research Journal, 19*(3), 443–452.

Peters, D. H., Tran, N. T., & Adam, T. (2013). *Implementation research in health: A practical guide.* Geneva, Switzerland: Alliance for Health Policy and Systems Research, World Health Organization. Available at http://who.int/alliance-hpsr/alliancehpsr_irpguide.pdf.

Roskos, K. (1987). The nature of literacy behavior in pretend play episodes of four and five year old children. Doctoral dissertation, Kent State University.

Roskos, K., & Burstein, K. (2011). Assessment of the design efficacy of a preschool vocabulary instruction technique. *Journal of Research in Early Childhood, 25* (3), 268–287.

Roskos, K., & Christie, J. (2012). The play–literacy nexus and the importance of evidence-based techniques in the classroom. *American Journal of Play, 4*(2), 204–224.

Roskos, K., & Christie, J. (2013). Gaining ground in understanding the play–literacy relationship. *American Journal of Play, 6*(1), 81–94.

Roskos, K., Christie, J., Widman, S., & Holding, A. (2010). Three decades in: Priming for meta analysis in play–literacy research. *Journal of Early Childhood Literacy, 10*(1), 33–54.

Rowe, D. (1998). The literate potentials of book-related dramatic play. *Reading Research Quarterly, 33,* 10–35.

Rowe, M. (2013). Decontextualized language input and preschoolers' vocabulary development. *Seminars in Speech and Language, 34*(4), 260–266.

Rubenstein, L. V., & Pugh, J. (2006). Strategies for promoting organizational and practice change by advancing implementation research. *Journal of General Internal Medicine, 21*(S2), S1–S70.

Saltz, E., & Johnson, J. (1974). Training for thematic-fantasy play in culturally disadvantaged children: Preliminary results. *Journal of Educational Psychology, 66*, 623–630.

Scarlett, G., & Wolf, D. (1979). When it's only make-believe: The construction of a boundary between fantasy and reality in storytelling. *New Directions for Child and Adolescent Development, 6*, 29–40.

Silvern, S., Taylor, J., Williamson, P., Surbeck, E., & Kelley, M. (1986). Young children's story recall as a product of play, story familiarity, and adult intervention. *Merrill-Palmer Quarterly, 32*, 73–86.

Smilansky, S. (1968). *The effects of sociodramatic play on disadvantaged preschool children.* New York: Wiley.

Smith, P. K. (2010). *Children and play.* Chichester: Wiley-Blackwell.

Society for Research on Educational Effectiveness (SREE) (2012). Enhancing executive function and achievement in prekindergarten classrooms: The effectiveness of Tools of the Mind. Paper presented at the Society for Research on Educational Effectiveness annual conference, Washington, DC.

Teale, W. H., & Sulzby, E. (Eds.). (1986). *Emergent literacy: Reading and writing* (pp. 7–25). Norwood, NJ: Ablex Publishing.

There are known knowns [attributed to Donald Rumsfeld]. Wikipedia entry. Available at https://en.wikipedia.org/wiki/There_are_known_knowns.

Trawick-Smith, J., Russell, H., & Swaminthan, S. (2011). Measuring the effects of toys on problem-solving, creative and social behaviours of preschool children. *Early Child Development and Care, 181*(7), 909–927.

Vedeler, L. (1997). Dramatic play: A format for literate language. *British Journal of Educational Psychology, 67*, 153–167.

Vukelich, C. (1991). Learning about the functions of writing: The effects of three play interventions on children's development and knowledge about writing. Paper presented at the meeting of the National Reading Conference, Palm Springs, CA.

Vukelich, C. (1994). Effects of play interventions on young children's reading of environmental print. *Early Childhood Research Quarterly, 9*, 153–170.

Wasik, B. A., & Jacobi-Vessels, J. L. (2016). Word play: Scaffolding language development through child-directed play. *Early Childhood Education Journal, 44*(6).

Welsch, J. G. (2008). Playing within and beyond the story: Encouraging book-related pretend play. *The Reading Teacher, 62*(2), 138–148.

Wohlwend, K. E. (2015). One screen, many fingers: Young children's collaborative literacy play with digital puppetry apps and touchscreen technologies. *Theory into Practice, 54*, 154–162.

Zevenbergen, R. (2007). Digital natives come to preschool: Implications for early childhood practice. *Contemporary Issues in Early Childhood, 8*(1), 19–29.

30 The Problems of Play

Susan Engel

This is how James Thurber explained his approach to writing: "I write humor the way a surgeon operates, because it is a livelihood, because I have a great urge to do it, because many interesting challenges are set up, and because I have the hope it may do some good." After he died, his good friend and colleague E.B. White said, "Thurber did not write the way a surgeon operates, he wrote the way a child skips rope, the way a mouse waltzes." Writing presented Thurber with problems he couldn't resist, and the process, at its best, led him to the kind of intense absorption and delight we often only see when children are at play.

In a similar way, when people would walk past the room in which the psychologists Daniel Kahneman and Amos Tversky worked, they heard a great deal of laughter, a great deal of the time. Yes, they were having fun working out their model of human judgment and decision-making. But they weren't just having fun, and it wasn't just the fact of being together that evoked that intense sense of joy and focus. You can have fun eating cookies, telling jokes, or reminiscing. They experienced profound joy solving complex problems. And like children at play, the process of finding the solution was as satisfying to them as the solution itself. Kahneman's pleasure in thinking was palpable not only to observers but also to himself. The writer Michael Lewis says of Kahneman, "He thought of himself as someone who enjoyed, more than most, changing his mind. 'I get a sense of movement and discovery whenever I find a flaw in my thinking', he said" (p. 131).

Like all intellectual projects, Kahenman and Tversky's started with a problem: What explains the various kinds of flaws people are subject to when making judgments about everyday life? To figure out the answer, Tversky and Kahneman did what serious scientists always do: they gathered data. Then they created a model to explain those data and make predictions about future data.

Thurber, and Kahneman and Tversky, offer exceptional examples of people engaged in sustained intellectual projects. Clearly, few of us have the brilliance, the creativity, or the expertise to pursue ideas that have such an impact on others. But in everyday life people engage in those same processes as they pursue their ideas, however fleeting, small, and imperfect those ideas may be. We take it as a given that by the time people reach early adulthood, most will be capable of pursuing and constructing explanations, predictions, and fresh solutions. But where does the ability to have an idea come from, and how does it begin?

Play Paves the Way for Ideas

An idea is a solution, however temporary, to an intellectual problem. Sometimes the problem requires explaining unexpected or perplexing phenomena (for instance, "Why do people make bad judgments?"). Sometimes the problem requires devising an object or plan that does not yet exist (this might be, as in Thurber's case, a story or essay, but it might also be a new tool such as Facebook, or single payer health insurance). In order to solve intellectual problems people employ two processes: inquiry and invention. Both of these processes begin in early childhood. And though either or both might occur when young children are talking or carrying out various mundane tasks, the best opportunities for children to identify interesting problems and pursue them through exploration and invention is while they are playing. Thus play, I would argue, is the practice ground for building ideas. But for play to foster the pursuit of ideas, it must include three important features.

Commitment

If children pursue ideas in play, it is, in part, because play so often promotes higher-order thinking skills. It is well established by now that play affords opportunities to consider alternative outcomes, imagine things from another perspective, transform objects through language and gesture, negotiate meanings and scripts with other children, and explore the boundary between real and not real, to name some of the most important (Lillard et al., 2013). However, as Lillard has shown in a meta-analysis of play research, it is not clear that play *causes* children to acquire these important social and cognitive skills. It seems more likely that play is one way to acquire and practice processes like problem-solving and counterfactual thinking.

But most of these studies take for granted one essential feature of play that sets it apart from the other contexts in which children acquire higher-order thinking skills: their intellectual investment in the particular kind of play in which they are engaged. Imagine, for a moment, the difference between a child who is answering questions from an adult about what might have happened if Eve had not taken the apple from the tree, for example, and a child who is trying to figure out what might have happened if she had built the walls of her ant house just a little higher. In the first, no matter how momentarily intrigued she might be by the story or the puzzle, it's somebody else's problem. In the second, her counterfactual thinking is in the service of a problem she set out to solve. Nor is this just a matter of motivation or emotional commitment in the activity. Some have argued that when children feel playful, they get more out of the activity because they enjoy it and have some sense of autonomy (Golinkoff et al., 2008). But that is another matter.

In order to pursue an idea, whether it entails gathering information to construct an explanation or putting ideas and objects together to solve a problem in a new way, children must be truly committed to it and stick with it, if only for 20 minutes, but sometimes, as I will show, for days or weeks. The intellectual steps involved in sustained inquiry and invention take time and focus. I propose that certain kinds of intellectual work occur only when they are in the service of an intellectual challenge or puzzle that the individual has identified for him- or herself, the kind that children work toward when they are playing.

There is some evidence supporting the idea that children's personal invest-ment in a proposition or challenge influences their thinking. Nathalie Gjersoe and her colleagues asked 3-year-old children to decide whether various real and toy animals were capable of mental states (Gjersoe et al., 2015). While children consistently thought that real animals could experience various mental states, they were picky about which toys were capable of similar experience. Specifically, children were more likely to attribute mental states to their own favourite toys – in fact, the toys couldn't be of just passing interest to them and were only those toys to which they were strongly attached (e.g., needed in order to go to sleep). It seems that children think differently when they are considering something about which they have strong (and sustained) affect. It's likely, then, that when children play with objects or enact scenarios in which they are strongly invested, they may engage in specific kinds of thinking that are less available to them when they are carrying out tasks that matter less to them.

Goal-Directed

Two well-accepted tenets of play research are that play is intrinsically meaningful and rewarding (rather than being goal directed) and that pretend play is unique. I suggest here that those characterizations need revising, as follows.

Most of the play literature has, understandably, made a distinction between pretend play (enactments of house, good guys and bad guys, Superman, baby animals lost in the storm) and other forms of play (building with blocks, working at the sand table, leaping through an obstacle course). The standard criteria for identifying pretend play include:

- Flexibility transforming objects (for instance, using a hairbrush as a tele-phone or a pillow as a steering wheel)

- Modifying real-world sequences in various ways (killing the bad guy who seconds later jumps up and kills the good guy)
- Expressing positive affect (though children do not always seem cheerful or delighted while playing, they are certainly deeply immersed in the activity for its own sake with little sense of obligation to the demands of others)
- Non-literality (while the child may imitate events from the real world, and often works hard to imitate with great felicity, the behaviors don't have real-world consequences. (Krasnor & Pepler, 1980)

When it comes to understanding how children use play to interpret the world and reenact emotionally significant events, there are good reasons for distinguishing between pretence and other forms of play. However, pretence is not a useful criterion when it comes to the way in which play allows children to practice building ideas. Whether playing a game of mommy and baby bear or figuring out how to make a paper plane that will fly, what matters is that the play is organized to solve a puzzle. In both those examples, for instance, the puzzle is problematic to the child, the solutions to the puzzle are tentative (they don't carry real-life consequences), and therefore in both cases the children may enact the 'solution' several times as they tinker with it and evaluate just how satisfying it is. The point is, often children are pursuing a goal when they play, and that goal is what elicits inquiry and invention. Moreover, the same kinds of flexible problem-solving and transformation are required, whether or not the play involves pretence.

Thinking Backward and Forward

There is one other important feature of play that serves as a precursor to building ideas: the child's actions must have the potential for thought that is free from action. Sometimes when children play they are absorbed and flexible in their actions, but they show little to no evidence that what they are doing is leading to any reflection. Imagine for a moment, the 3-year-old jumping across a mud puddle or roughhousing with a friend. Though she may be having all kinds of thoughts while playing, she is not thinking backward or forward about the preconditions or consequences of her actions. Planning a pretend scenario or envisioning a new kind of paper plane, on the other hand, does elicit and or require such thought. Moreover, there is evidence that children can engage in such abstractions when they are as young as 4; they begin having ideas about the world around them and using various kinds of problem-solving to arrive at those ideas.

Rachel Maggid and her colleagues asked children to decide whether a continuous or a discrete mechanism (visual or auditory) had caused a continuous or discrete effect. Children between the ages of 4 and 6 consistently chose the cause that 'matched' the effect (continuous cause/continuous effect).

Maggid and her colleagues offer this as evidence that in the absence of the chance to collect their own data, prior experience, or testimony from others, children imagine the possible links between causes and effects (Maggid et al., 2015). Prodded to explain perplexing phenomena when they cannot experiment or ask others, children take a stab at having an explanation. In other words, by the time they are 3 or 4 years old, they are not confined to explanations that they can learn from others or from their own actions on the physical world – they can imagine explanations.

Below I present four examples of children between the ages of 3 and 7 at play. In all of the examples, the children are deeply absorbed by specific materials and tasks that they have chosen for themselves. Thus it is not simply that all four children take a playful orientation toward reality, practice flexible thinking, or adopt an as-if stance toward the world, which they might do in other contexts. They are using those skills to solve intellectual problems that they have set for themselves and that matter to them. Identifying the particular problem that frames the child's intellectual processes within their play requires some probing on the part of the observer. The first two examples illustrate the ways in which children use play to collect information and satisfy their curiosity. The second two illustrate the ways in which children use play to plan, tinker, and reorganize information and skills in order to meet a challenge or solve a problem in a new way. In all four examples, I draw on systematic diaries and recordings kept by the parents. In the fourth example I also draw on the materials the children had created and saved. I hope to show that play provides a distinctive if not unique framework within which children engage in the kinds of inquiry and invention that lead to ideas.

When Play Is Guided by Inquiry

The first example involves two brothers, who spent time on an almost daily basis, for nearly 18 months, beginning when they were 3 and 6 years old, playing with a bin of small figures kept in the corner of their shared bedroom. The figures included cowboys, Indians, action figures (Green Lantern, Hulk, Silver Surfer), and various villains (Venom, Dr. Doom). These play episodes ranged from 6 to 48 minutes. Often the play episodes included enacting various scenarios (a fight or a chase). But more than two-thirds of the time in any given play episode, the brothers would sort the figures into a nice guy group and a mean guy group. The younger brother, Ruben, frequently would hold up a figure and say to his older brother, "Quinn, is this a nice guy, or a mean guy?" Quinn would look over at the figure, and answer ("Mean guy. That one's mean. He kills 'em with his fire" or "He's a good guy. He saves all the children"). As they played they kept organizing and reorganizing the piles of mean guys and good guys.

Ruben would often study one of the toys carefully after hearing his brother's designation. Then he'd pick up one from each pile and enact a short action sequence, making sure that each figure exemplified its moral properties. What was Ruben trying to learn more about? I suggest that the best explanation for his questions and actions was that he wanted to know more about what constitutes nice and mean. He used the playtime to explore the figures themselves, probe his brother's knowledge, and try to figure out how one ascertained whether a character was good or not. As with many of us, his long line of questioning about those particular figures was part of a larger intellectual project: What makes someone nice or mean?

The second example concerns a 4-year-old boy, Peter. From the time Peter was about 2 years old, his family had an ant problem in their kitchen. Thus he had plenty of opportunities to watch ants, to try and pick them up, and to hear people talk about them. Peter was also quite interested in other insects, becoming alert and focused whenever he encountered a bug, whether a new variety or a kind with which he was familiar. But during his fourth year he became more absorbed with the ants in particular. And by then the mere sight of them was familiar to him, as was their usual path across the floor under the counter. He also knew, by then, that they headed toward food. As he became more interested in them he also sought out deeper levels of information about them. At least a few times per week, he'd lie on the kitchen floor so that he could see them up close. He'd try to get one to crawl on his finger so that he could inspect it, touch it, and see how it felt as it crawled up his wrist. In one instance he tried unsuccessfully to pick the head off of several ants. At some point that year, he began setting up various obstacle courses using sugar cubes, napkins, and other kitchen items. He seemed fascinated by how circuitous he could make the route, watching them scurry within the boundaries. For a number of weeks he seemed preoccupied by trying to get them to eat various substances (milk, coffee, hard candy, and pieces of meat).

We know that when they are as young as 2 years old, many children began to have specific interests – they look more at trucks than at cars, they become absorbed with a specific class of objects, or they attend to certain kinds of action more than others (DeLoache et al., 2007). Research has also suggested that when children are interested in an object, they are much more likely to explore it with a greater number and type of actions, spend more time focusing on it, and absorb more information about it (Renninger, 1992). Peter's preoccupation with ants exemplifies the importance of interest in prodding children to a wider and more goal-oriented set of behaviours. His activities were not random, nor were they simply aimed at interacting with the ants.

Seen from this perspective, Peter's activities, which ranged from behaviours that were obvious signs of curiosity (watching the ants, pulling their heads off, and putting them back down on the ground) to behaviours that might otherwise have been interpreted as constructive or transformative, for example, his efforts to build little walls that would constrain the ants' path, were actually simply means to find out more about the ants' behaviour and fill in his knowledge gap about them.

Infants and young toddlers exhibit a nearly omnivorous and indiscriminate curiosity about anything and everything that is new. Because curiosity is prompted when someone notices a gap between what they expect and what they encounter, it is understandable that during a phase of life when so little is familiar, and so much is new, they would be curious about many things, much of the time. However, by the time children are 3 years old, much of the everyday world has become familiar, and children turn their attention to the particular events or class of objects that hold special interest for them (which is why, as children get older, though there are individual differences in absolute level of curiosity, children exhibit their highest level of curiosity with some objects more than others).

In Peter's case, fine-grained differences between ants and a need to know more and more about ants seemed to fuel his play. What might have been taken for very different kinds of playful behaviour (building ramps, dismembering ants, arranging food, and setting traps) can all be understood as a somewhat sustained sequence of efforts to satisfy his need to gather information to solve a problem: What are ants like?

When Play Is Guided by Invention

In the third example, three 4-year-old cousins, one girl and two boys, spent the better part of one summer building a cave that became an imaginary home for them. When they were in the fort they enacted various baby animals, a pretend game they had established months before, in which they each took on the role of a certain kind of baby animal (wolf, raccoon, dog). Like the ant play and the mean guy play, this game unfolded over time and emerged gradually, in small steps.

One of the children lived in a house that bordered some woods. Along the woods the children discovered many felled and rotten trees, and any number of rocks and boulders, some of them much taller than the children. One of the boulders was huge. As soon as they saw it, one of the children said, "See it? See it? It's huge. I know what we can do. It can be the cave." During the first weeks of the summer they talked about the work from the perspective of builders ("Let's go work on the cave" or "It's raining. It's gonna break the roof"). The three cousins spent as many as five days of each week together, for stretches of time that lasted between 2 and 5 hours. They would often wander around outside, acting out various scenarios, and periodically climbing among the woods and stones talking about various topics.

Early that summer, they were drawn to the largest boulder on the edge of the woods. Having discovered it, they returned to it several days in a row, climbing between the lower boulders and the highest one, talking a great deal – sometimes about other things (their toys in the house, fragments from a movie they had all seen together recently, and which one of them had longer legs). Then one of them suggested that if they gathered some branches and small tree limbs, they could make a roof between the boulders. Another said, "Yeah, and it could be two caves. A huge one. Two ones. We could live in there. Baby animals." And their project had begun.

As others have documented in children of this age, their narration and the actions it described were in a dynamic relationship to one another – at times the language seemed to precede the action and serve as a plan: "Let's put the strong branches over here. Yeah, that one there. Get it. It can reach from here to your rock." At other times, their talk seemed to accompany their play, often adding a symbolic or transformative element to what might otherwise been a straight-forward construction project: "This is where we sleep. It's over here, where it can't get wet. But just say, you just say, 'Baby Raccoon, I'm cold', and I'll bring you the blanket." And sometimes their language reflected on the project itself. "This isn't working. The sticks are too weak. They're too skinny. We need to make a bridge between the houses. We havta make the bridge strong."

In this example, the children's activity quickly became goal directed. They wanted to build a cave that made the best use of the materials, so that they could pretend to live inside as baby animals. But the goal emerged from their interest in the big rocks, and their sense that they could make something out of the materials at hand. In other words, they were inventing something to solve a problem: How can we make use of these rocks and branches? Their solution was partly physical (collect sticks and smaller rocks to connect the largest boulders) and part representational (imagine this is a cave).

Detailed observations of children inventing things might lead one to think that such invention is quite improvisational, each step or move suggested by the previous one, unfolding in a fairly haphazard way, unguided by an imagined end state. Often children do not seem as if they are systematically trying to solve a problem. And in fact, some studies suggest that children of this age are not able to innovate in order to reach a goal. When adults invite 4-year-old children to manipulate various objects in order to retrieve a small toy from a plastic tube, they are likely to have difficulty. In fact, they can be quite rigid when it comes to devising tools to achieve attractive goals (Beck et al., 2011; German & Defeyeter, 2000). This suggests that at 4 years, children are not capable of invention. Yet in these studies described above, the goal and the means of invention were highly constrained by the adult. It is not that clear 4-year-olds would be equally at a loss were they solving problems that they had claimed for their own and that had fewer parameters.

But innovation does not always involve brand-new actions. Just as often it requires combining familiar elements in new ways. Young children are more adept at such combinations. There is evidence that even when they cannot come up with a novel solution, they can imitate new techniques in order to solve a puzzle. When 4-year-old children watch an adult perform an innovation, they are able to repeat it (Beck et al., 2011). When given the opportunity to put together two different actions that they have seen adults employ separately for specific goals (manipulating pieces of a box in order to move around the pieces within the box and retrieve a sticker), they can combine those actions to achieve their own goal. Subiaul et al. (2015) refer to this as summative imitation. The three cousins engaged in a lot of summative imitation – they mimicked a wide range of building techniques they had seen employed by the father of one of the children. For instance, when they were building their roof, the child whose father was a carpenter insisted that the branches had to fit together tightly so the rain could not get in. And as they added branches, the child kept putting his face very close up from inside their 'cave' to see if light was shining through.

Thus while there is some evidence that children are not capable of innovation on demand, it seems that children can certainly combine elements to solve a new problem.

Nor are children's innovation skills limited to combining learned gestures. In some instances they show more flexible thinking than adults do. In one study, when children watched an adult activate a "blicket box" (a box that lit up and played music when certain blocks were placed on top of an adjacent box) they were more able than adults to figure out that the solution varied. Sometimes one particular individual block activated the Blicket machine, but sometimes only a combination, rather than a block of a certain type, would work (Lucas et al., 2014). Lucas et al. suggest that at 3 years, children still pay attention to the data, but by the time they are 5, like adults, they get stuck on one kind of hypothesis, even in the face of contradicting data. Thus when it comes to shifting one's strategy in response to new data, the younger inventors may have an advantage. Early on the cousins kept affirming to one another that they had to use big branches for the bridge between the two chambers of the cave. But at some point, the girl began laying slender sticks side by side to a second bridge. Upset, one of the others said to her, "You can't. They'll break. We need big ones." She insisted. "No. I'm using this one. I got these. It works, it works. See?" He watched as she lay a heavy rock on the bridge made of small branches. After about a minute, he began adding thin branches to the bridge he was working on.

The small but growing literature on the development of innovation tends to gloss over what may be a crucial step. While 3- and 4-year-olds may be quite rigid at inventing specific novel ways to achieve a goal set by others, they may regularly employ familiar skills (collecting branches, combining materials for height, width, and strength) for novel purposes, like building a cave. By using individual actions that may have been familiar, on materials that may have been novel (broken branches, stones, and leaves) for a new goal (building a cave for baby animals to live in), they were practicing invention.

Another feature worth noting about this example is that it took the cousins weeks to achieve their goal. They discussed it even when they weren't actually building (for instance, two of the children talked about it on the way to visit their cousin, who lived near the cave). In other words, unlike the isolated types of innovation that young children do or do not seem capable of in experimental situations, the inventions they come up with on their own allow them many tries, and motivate them to keep at it.

The fourth and final example describes a game that unfolded over an even longer period of time: two 6-year-old girls, Maude and Sophie, who carpooled to school together, played a game in the car that occurred regularly for 3 years. Maude and Sophie would sit in the trunk seats of Maude's mother's car, facing backward, giving them a feeling of privacy. They had 25 minutes to talk to one another nearly every school day for several years. Their primary activity concerned the construction of an imaginary universe, which they called Bugzeeland. In addition to the records kept by Maude's mother, Sophie kept all the drawings, descriptions, and lists she and Sophie made, and those are reflected in the description below.

The girls agreed early on that Bugzeeland was round, but instead of existing on the surface of the planet, life existed inside the planet. For this reason there was a trap door that one had to go through to get into and out of Bugzeeland.

Characters who lived in Bugzeeland included the Beach Lady (who was very large and sat in her bathing suit on a beach, surrounded by beach umbrellas), the Magician (who guarded a well at the end of the only straight road in Bugzeeland), the P Popcorn Piglets (whom the girls kept referring to as "very normal", saying at times that the Piglets were so normal they were boring), the two "Gods" of Bugzeeland, who sat on the sun's rays at the top of the sphere and watered the planet with watering cans, and some other nameless creatures who stood by the trap door shovelling dust out of the planet, which then turned into stars in outer space. They also periodically named other characters, but did not develop them as fully: the 41sler, the Firegobbler, the Singer Servants, and the Curly Mold Foot Walker. Other places in Bugzeeland included Toe City of Toe, which, they repeatedly affirmed was shaped like a big toe (the nail being a lake), and a neighbourhood shaped like a muffin.

The girls spent months inventing several languages – mostly written – that were used in Bugzeeland. In each case, they wrote in small notebooks, laboriously constructing written systems that were based on the English alphabet, with sounds or letters (or in one case whole words) that corresponded to the letters of the English alphabet, but resulted in languages that contained words not found in the English language. In "O.F." each letter of the alphabet was assigned a different letter (instead of ABCD... it was OFPG...) , similar to a code. In "Zig Zag Manicure" each letter was assigned a symbol. In "And Why" each letter was assigned an entire word (Instead of ABCDEFG... it was And Why All Sky Are Star Dull...). Because all of these languages required memorization in order to be used, the girls created a fifth, more user-friendly language, which they continued to use throughout middle school. They called this Bugzeelish.

As with many children, discussing the details of Bugzeeland's features was not a precondition of their dramatic play but *comprised* the play. There is nothing new in arguing that some children spend the majority of their play activity making up fictional worlds (Engel, 1995, 2005). However, I suggest here that such inventions serve the same psychological function as less fantasy-oriented inventions such as paintings, and musical compositions, as well as the kinds of devices children come up with to serve more pragmatic purposes (building a set of steps to reach the branches of a tree, building a fort to hide from other children, or devising a new kind of paper airplane that will fly longer (Brizuela, 1997; Davies, 1992; Winner, 1985). In all of these examples, children have identified a problem that needs solving. Sometimes they identify the problem quite explicitly, and sometimes it remains implicit.

While the first examples above represent problems that required new information, the second two examples revolve around problems that require putting materials and procedures together in new ways to build things the children have never built before and have not been instructed to build. Take, for instance, the difference between setting the table for the family dinner and constructing a play structure in the woods. In the first, the problem is how to make sure each person has a plate, a cup, silverware, and a napkin, but the solution is simply to carry out a procedure someone has already shown you (put a plate down for each person, then add a cup, a fork, and a napkin). A child who wants to climb on an existing play structure simply begins playing; she doesn't face a problem that needs solving, per se. But the child who decides that she wants a play structure in the woods or wants to figure out what she can do with all the long branches that are lying on the ground has to come up with a new set of procedures. She might borrow elements from other experiences (watching someone else build something, remembering how she used blocks to build an airplane hangar), but she cannot simply carry out someone else's instructions. In that sense, her engagement and joy in making a fort has less in common with certain forms of pretend play and more in common, psychologically, with other kinds of problem-solving that require using old materials and strategies to create new structures, whether those structures are theoretical (Bugzeeland) or physical (a cave).

To sum up so far, in the first two examples children play as a way of gathering information. The problem they are solving is to fill a gap in their knowledge about something in which they have a sustained interest. Curiosity, which is triggered by surprise, explains why, when children have developed an interest in a particular domain (for instance, ants or identifying good and evil), they often play with the same materials again and again, as they satisfy ever-more-subtle or fine-grained levels of surprise within the domain. In the third example, the three cousins invent a new kind of construction to solve a different kind of problem: how to best use the particular materials that attract them. In the fourth example, the problems are subsets of the larger framework of the game. The two girls may have begun their invention simply by enjoying the pleasure of imagining out loud together – constructing a narrative about an alternative universe. Just as writers may begin a new story with no greater plan than to write, and represent in words whatever they are imagining, these girls may have begun with no long-term goal or challenge. However, like many writers, once begun, the activity leads them to interesting problems: Who will live in this universe, what languages will they speak, and what rules will they have? Their inventions solve the problems that their play has led them to.

From Play to Ideas

The play described in these examples remained noticeably 'embodied'. In each case the children acted as if they were gathering information or inventing new solutions. But none of them gave any evidence that they were in fact explicitly exploring an idea. It's reasonable to ask whether children under the age of 7 are capable of considering an idea as an invisible object. And yet there is some evidence that in fact during this very age period (4–7) they become able to do just that. Woolley and Brown (2015) point out that by the age of 4, children understand that some things are real even if you cannot see them, such as sugar dissolved in water, and some things are fantasy even if you can see them, such as Santa Claus. But it is not only objects that might exist without being seen. During this same period, children begin to grasp the wide range of mental phenomena that are real and yet invisible, such as intentions, mental states, and desires (Bartsch & Wellman, 1995). In addition, children of this age begin to understand that an idea is more than just a plan, but a conceptual object.

When my students and I asked 4-year-olds to talk about ideas, they consistently answered by describing their plans to do something (for instance, one child told us her idea was to make a little gadget to keep the window open) or works they had made (children often referred to a drawing or a Lego construction). But by the time they are 6 years old, children have expanded their working definition of 'idea'. When we asked first graders what an idea was, they made it clear they knew it was "something in the mind". For example, one child said, "Um, something that like, that you want to be true kind of, or they couldn't be true, that like you think of them in your mind". But that same child added, "or you can see them, like with your eyes … if I saw a rope ladder, then maybe I would think I could build a tree-house". In other words, their answers suggest that by the time children are 6 they think of ideas as plans, objects (the result of some inventive process), and also as thoughts (explanations, abstractions).

In the four examples I have presented, the children used many of the same elements and processes that people use when constructing an idea. In all four cases, a goal seems to govern all the actions within the sequence and there is plenty of iteration, fact-checking, revising, and shifting along the way. Learning about ants, the moral character of action figures, building a cave, or designing a new universe serve the same function as ideas: to organize information from disparate sources into a specific constellation in order to predict and explain puzzling data or solve a problem in a new way. Play may not be the only route to constructing ideas (Smith, 2010), but it offers one great advantage over other settings (such as didactic practice of each cognitive process, or conversation with adults): when children play, they are solving a problem about which they feel some urgency, however fleeting. They are almost always deeply engaged in the process (it is rare to see a child playing in a perfunctory way, and impossible to oblige a child to play). When children play, they identify problems, consider alternative solutions, learn from their mistakes, judge the efficacy of their solutions, and revise. Play offers one more singular opportunity that mirrors what is required to build an idea: it takes time. During childhood, no play lasts less than a minute. Though adults engage in very brief episodes of play when they use metaphors, irony, or deceit, during childhood, play unfolds in real time. The same might be said of ideas. Though the original kernel or spark of an idea may occur to someone in an instant, for an idea to last the thinker must find a way to represent it symbolically and implement, communicate, defend, or impose it on others. To do these essential things take time.

This brings me to one last way in which the inquiry and invention of play lay the groundwork for more mature idea construction. Children can inquire and invent when playing alone, but they also often inquire and invent with other children while playing. A body of research suggests that children share knowledge with one another (Flynn & Whiten, 2008). At first they seem more likely to share information that they have learned from others. In one test of this Flynn and Whiten taught individual children a novel strategy for using a tool to retrieve a toy from a complex box, and then reintroduced the child and the contraption into the classroom. The first child taught others how to use the tool to retrieve the toy, and those children taught still others, demonstrating the horizontal transmission of knowledge among 4-year-olds. The examples presented in this chapter suggest some of the ways in which children might build ideas collaboratively, first in the form of making categories and plans, and then in a more abstract or verbal mode.

I have argued here that play is primarily comprised of two fundamental intellectual activities: inquiry and invention. Inquiry involves gathering data to explain the unexpected. Invention involves putting things (objects or symbols) together in new ways. Both processes are employed to solve problems. Children only inquire and invent when they are trying to solve a problem that is a problem to them. And this happens most often and most vividly when they are at play. Long after children have outgrown the need to understand ants or invent a new language for another planet, they may be trying to figure out how to explain or predict human behaviour or invent new narrative forms. The problems that inquiry and invention solve in play are a prelude to the kinds of explanations and inventions we call ideas. The line connecting child's play to adults' ideas is not always as indiscernible as one might think. As a young child, living in rural northern England, a little girl invented an imaginary world, which she named Angria. She spent hours and hours, day after day, for almost 5 years, absorbed with inventing the people and events of Angria. When she left childhood behind, she left Angria behind with it, turning her increasingly mature skills toward more adult tasks and concerns. At 31, she wrote *Jane Eyre*.

References

Bartsch, E., & Wellman, K. (1995). *Children talk about the mind*. Oxford: Oxford University Press.

Beck, S., Apperly, I., Chappell, J., Guthrie, C., & Cutting, N. (2011). Making tools isn't child's play. *Cognition, 119*, 301–306.

Brizuela, B. (1997). Inventions and conventions: A story about capital numbers. *For the Learning of Mathematics, 17*, 2–6.

Davies, C. (1992). Listen to my son: A study of songs invented by children aged 5–7 years. *British Journal of Music Education, 9*, 19–48.

DeLoache, J., Simcock, G., & Micari, S. (2007). Planes, trains, automobiles – and tea sets: Extremely intense interests in very young children. *Developmental Psychology, 43*(6), 1579–1586.

Engel, S. (1995) *The stories children tell*. New York: W. H. Freeman.

Engel, S. (2005). The narrative worlds of what is and what if. *Cognitive Development, 20*(4), 514–525.

Flynn, E., & Whiten, A. (2008). Cultural transmission of tool use in young children: A diffusion chain study. *Social Development, 17*(3), 699–718.

German, T., & Defeyter, M. (2000). Immunity to functional fixedness in young children. *Psychonomic Bulletin and Review, 7*(4), 707–712.

Gjersoe, N., Hall, E., & Hood, B. (2015). Children attribute mental lives to toys when they are emotionally attached to them. *Cognitive Development, 34*, 28–38.

Golinkoff, P., Hirsh-Paskek, K., Berk, L., & Singer, D. (2008). *A mandate for playful learning*. Oxford: Oxford University Press.

Krasnor, L. R., & Pepler, D. J. (1980). The study of children's play: Some suggested future directions. In K. H. Rubin (Ed.), *Children's play: New directions for child development* (pp. 85–95). San Francisco, CA: Jossey-Bass.

Lewis, M. (2016) *The undoing project*. New York: W. W. Norton.

Lillard, A. S., Lerner, M. D., Hopkins, E. J., Dore, R. A., Smith, E. D., & Palmquist, C. M. (2013). The impact of pretend play on children's development: A review of the evidence. *Psychological Bulletin, 139*(1), 1–34.

Lucas, C., Bridgers, S., Griffiths, T., & Gopnik, A. (2014). When children are better (or at least more open-minded) learners than adults: Developmental differences in learning the forms of causal relationships. *Cognition, 131*, 284–299.

Maggid, R., Sheskin, M., & Schulz, L. (2015). Imagination and the generation of new ideas. *Cognitive Development, 34*, 99–110.

Nielsen, M., Tomaselli, K., Mushin, I., & Whiten, A. (2014). Exploring tool innovation: A comparison of Western and Bushman children. *Journal of Experimental Child Psychology, 126*, 384–394.

Renninger, K. A. (1992). Individual interest and development: Implications for theory and practice. In A. Renninger, S. Hidi, & A. Krapp (Eds.), *The role of interest in learning and development* (pp. 361–396). Hillsdale, NJ: Erlbaum.

Smith, P. K. (2010). *Children and play*. Chichester: Wiley Blackwell

Subiaul, F., Krajkowsky, E., Price, E., & Etz, E. (2015). Imitation by combination: Preschool age children evidence summative imitation in a novel problem-solving task. *Frontiers in Psychology, 6*, 1410.

White, E. B. (1961). *Writings from the New Yorker 1927–1976*. New York: Harper Collins.

Winner, E. (1985). *Invented worlds*. Cambridge, MA: Harvard University Press.

Woolley, J., & Brown, M. (2015). The development of children's concepts of invisibility. *Cognitive Development, 34*, 63–75.

PART VI

Play with Special Groups

31 Play and Children with Autism

Insights from Research and Implications for Practice

Despina Papoudi and Lila Kossyvaki

Children with autism approach play in a different way to that of their non-autistic peers as evidenced by studies from infancy to childhood. Cognitive theories have been mainly used as a framework to explain play in autism, and socioemotional theories so far have been neglected. This chapter argues that socioemotional theories offer a new framework for explaining the different ways children with autism approach play and the implications that this might have for enhancing their play. This approach is of particular relevance to enhancing play in children with autism and additional intellectual disabilities, and a number of relevant current interventions positioned in the socioemotional framework of understanding childhood and autism are reviewed to identify implications for practice, mainly for school settings.

Nowadays, play is considered an integral part of childhood and the education of children. It is not just a spontaneous activity and occupation, but it also plays a central role in the child's developmental trajectory, as it contributes to cognitive, emotional, social, motor, and language development and the development of literacy, creative arts, and learning (Smith, 2010). The role of play in children's development has been highlighted in the theoretical approaches toward human development and has been generally described as a reflection and a driving force of cognitive, social, and emotional development.

Based on Piaget's cognitive theory (1951), play is approached as a sequence, which starts with the simple handling of objects during the first year of life and continues with functional play from the first until the second year. Symbolic play starts emerging around the second year. According to Vygotsky's sociocultural theory, play is the source of development and is created in the 'zone of proximal development', which is the functional space between what the child can do on his or her own and what the child can do with assistance. Every psychological function, including play, appears "first, between people (interpsychological), and then inside the child (intrapsychological)" (Vygotsky, 1978, p. 57). This approach underscores the predominant role of play in development and the role of interaction in the expression of play. Furthermore, within the

* Many thanks to the mother who provided a narrative of her son's play and to all the children with autism, their parents, teachers, and practitioners who taught us so much about the journey of a child with autism.

theoretical framework of our understanding of the world and our actions as having a communicative and emotional rather than cognitive basis, play emerges in the early communication between infant and mother, which, for the child, constitutes the primary form of social interaction. Trevarthen et al. (1998) argue that infants, before they even begin to curiously explore the world of objects, possess the ability to recognize and engage their attention in an activity with another person, namely, the mother, and, while playing, interact with this person through expressive forms, rhythmical behavioural patterns, and complex emotions. In other words, infant and mother, through the exchange of eye contact, sounds, movements, and facial expressions, jointly participate in play and express their intentions, as well as the mental states they are in, to each other. However, it is widely documented that infants and children with autism have difficulties in engaging in face-to-face interaction and in spontaneous interactive play with their mothers (Mundy et al., 1986, 1987) and their peers (Wolfberg & Schuler, 1993), and therefore the origins of the difficulties children with autism have in play can be associated with the fundamental difficulties in the development of communication, social interaction, and symbolic thinking (Papoudi, 1993, 2015; Trevarthen et al., 1998).

Play and Children with Autism

Autism is a developmental condition presenting wide variation in both the range and the variability of the observed behaviours. Autism as a condition manifests, in its typical form, as 'autism', but also as a wider spectrum, and the term 'autism spectrum' is often used to encompass all the forms of behavioural manifestations of the condition. Kanner (1943) first described autism and noted that children with autism come to the world with an innate inability to form affective contact with other people and that children with autism have normal intellectual functioning. Later, Asperger (1944) described a group of children with high cognitive abilities as having similar behavioural characteristics with the autistic children, and Wing and Gould (1979) used the term 'autism spectrum' to include children with different behavioural characteristics of autism and subsequently different levels of intellectual functioning. However, a high proportion of children with autism are reported to have additional intellectual disabilities. There is no consensus regarding the percentage of individuals with autism and additional intellectual disabilities. One of the first relevant studies gave a 75% comorbidity (Rutter & Lockyer, 1967), while later studies provided considerably lower but variable percentages ranging from 26% (Chakrabarti & Fombonne, 2001) to 40% (Baird et al., 2000). A more recent review of ten empirical studies by Emerson and Baines (2010) gave a very wide range of prevalence rates of intellectual disabilities among children with autism from 15% (Williams, 2008) to 84% (Magnusson, 2001, both cited in Emerson & Baines, 2010). Even fewer studies reported the severity of intellectual disabilities among populations with autism. Fombonne (1999), for example, found that across all the studies he reviewed, 29% of the sample had mild to moderate intellectual disabilities and 42% had severe to profound intellectual disabilities. The IQ of individuals with intellectual disabilities is below 70 (the cut-off for mild intellectual disabilities for Holland, 2011), and as defined by the Department of Health (DoH) in England (2001) these individuals have difficulties in understanding new or complex information and learning new skills. Therefore, the play observed in children with autism is very diverse, and this variability to an extent is related to the range of intellectual disabilities found within this population.

A major developmental milestone of early childhood is the playful, creative, and imaginative interactions between children and their parents, their siblings, and their peers; children with autism may lack this milestone. Over the last 20 years, a series of studies has provided ample evidence toward understanding the sociocommunicative difficulties in children with autism, with a particular emphasis on two major developmental milestones: (1) joint attention, which reflects the difficulty children with autism encounter in sharing attention between adults and objects, and (2) the use of symbols, which refers to the child's difficulty in learning conventional or common meanings for symbols, such as gestures, mimicry, words, and play (Wetherby, 2006). It is well documented in the literature that children with autism encounter serious difficulties in joint attention and in engaging in spontaneous, socially acceptable play, as well as participating in dyadic play and, later, peer play. These difficulties are inseparably connected with the nature of autism, since the main characteristics of the condition include difficulties in social interaction, communication, and symbolic thought.

These difficulties are reflected in the most recent edition of the *Diagnostic and Statistical Manual of Mental Disorders* (DSM-V, 2013) as well as it is previous edition (DSM-IV, 1994). According to the DSM-IV (1994), on the basis of which the majority of published studies have selected their sample, the diagnostic criteria for autism include qualitative significant difficulties in social interaction and in communication; restricted, repetitive, and stereotyped patterns of behaviour, interests, and activities; and delay or significant difficulties in at least one of the following areas, with onset prior to 3 years of age: (1) social interaction, (2) language as used in social communication, and (3) symbolic or imaginative play. Difficulties in social interaction may manifest as absence or limited use of non-verbal behaviours (e.g., eye-to-eye gaze, facial expression, body posture, and gestures to regulate social interaction); failure to develop peer relationships appropriate to developmental level; a lack of spontaneous seeking to share enjoyment, interests, or achievements with other people; and a lack of social or emotional reciprocity. Difficulties in communication may manifest as delays in, or total lack of, the development of spoken language or, in individuals with adequate speech, a marked difficulty in the ability to initiate or sustain a conversation with others, as well as the stereotyped and repetitive use of language or idiosyncratic language and the lack of varied, spontaneous make-believe play or social imitative play appropriate to the child's developmental level. Last, the restricted, repetitive, and stereotyped patterns of behaviour, interests, and activities may manifest as preoccupation with one or more stereotyped and restricted patterns of interest, as inflexible adherence to specific, non-functional routines or rituals, or as stereotyped and repetitive motor mannerisms (e.g., hand or finger flapping or twisting or complex whole-body movements), as well as the persistent preoccupation with parts of objects. In DSM-V (2013) difficulties in social communication and social interaction across multiple contexts remain crucial for the diagnosis of autism, including significant difficulties in developing, maintaining, and understanding relationships, ranging from difficulties in sharing imaginative play or in making friends to absence of interest in peers. The existence of additional intellectual disabilities magnifies the severity of the aforementioned difficulties, as expected.

The following descriptions provided by a mother of a child with autism and intellectual disabilities demonstrate these difficulties in the way children with autism play, and show how difficulties in communication, symbolic thought, and behaviour are entangled in the form of their play.

The Early Years

From an early age he was interested in geometric shape matching puzzles. However, whilst his twin brother would fit the pieces into place using a trial-and-error approach, Johnny would hold each piece in the air, examine it closely, and then fit it into the correct place. He also enjoyed moving his body or watching objects or other children move.

From 2 Years Old

It was not until after Johnny's second birthday that I began to notice obvious differences in the way that he played and interacted with other children. These observations eventually led to his diagnosis. One of my first recollections was that whenever I took him somewhere new, perhaps to visit friends or family, he would walk up and down the fence line of the garden. I also recall his lack of interest in other children of the same age; whilst all the other children played and interacted with each other, Johnny was on his own at the far end of the garden.

Postdiagnosis

Johnny received his diagnosis just before his 3rd birthday. Around this time, some of his earlier playing, such as matching puzzles, seemed to regress. He was finding it increasingly difficult to cope with the environment. He began to engage in safe repetitive activities. For example, watching small sections of DVDs and replaying them. He also enjoyed pushing the discs in and out of the DVD player and putting the discs in and out of their cases.

Instead of appearing ambivalent, he was starting to find having other children to visit our house to be too sensory overloading and stressful. He would often position objects in places in the garden, probably as a coping mechanism. When other children tried to move them he would get very distressed and he would quickly reposition them again.

When he became a little older, I began to observe him wanting to play with other children, but he didn't really know how to play. He would often stand on the edge of a group of children playing, watching excitedly and jumping up and down. At home he started to engage more with his toys. He liked to play with the train set, pushing the trains around the track. However, his play was purely functional and seemed to lack imagination. For instance, if I set up a basic train attached to a carriage, he was unlikely to add other carriages to the train or want to add extra track.

The above narrative of Johnny's case is an illustrative example of how the play of children with autism is described in the existing literature, i.e., that children with autism usually play alone, avoid playing with others, and repeat the same form of play in an inflexible and stereotyped manner. Other characteristics of the play of children with autism include excessive preoccupation with certain toys and an interest in a very limited number of toys. Children with autism are not very likely to develop symbolic play, or they may do so only to a limited extent and after instruction (Kasari et al., 2013). A typical characteristic of their play seems to be that they are fascinated by the appearance of objects, their immediate sensory characteristics, or the opportunities they might offer for simple manipulation, while they remain indifferent to the cultural or symbolic meaning the objects may carry.

Research has shown that children with autism have the ability to explore and use objects functionally but exhibit serious difficulties in acquiring spontaneous symbolic and pretend play during their preschool and school years. The thematic content of the play of children with autism is characterized by a lack of coherence and creativity and by repetitiveness to the point of ritual (Papoudi, 1993). They are usually rejected by their peers, since they have not developed the skills that would allow them to participate as equal playmates (Argyropoulou & Papoudi, 2012; Papoudi, 2008). There is also evidence that in relation to symbolic and pretend play, limitations in creative, playful pretend play among children with autism is related to their restricted interpersonal communication and engagement (Hobson et al., 2013).

Although there is quite extensive literature on play skills of children with autism, there seems to be limited research on how children with autism and additional intellectual disabilities play. It is known mostly from teachers' and parents' accounts that the play of these children is usually solitary, stereotypical, and self-stimulatory (Jordan, 2001). According to these accounts, children with autism and intellectual disabilities tend to play by themselves, engaging in the same play routines, while their usual stimulatory play includes flicking or spinning objects (visual), tapping and clicking (auditory), licking (taste), feeling different textures (tactile), spinning themselves, climbing, and balancing (vestibular), and getting into odd body postures (proprioceptive).

Play in children with autism has been studied in relation to other developmental milestones, such as language development, attachment, and joint attention. It has been found that in children with autism who have developed understanding and production of speech, as well as in children with secure attachment, functional and symbolic play occur more often and at a higher level. There is also evidence that the use of joint attention is connected to the ability for symbolic play in children with autism (Kasari et al., 2011). As regards younger children with autism, what we know so far is that toddlers with autism at 20 months exhibit functional play and pretend play at the same level as infants with developmental delay and their performance in pretend play is at a lower level only compared with that of typical toddlers of the same age (Charman et al., 1997).

Literature has evidenced the supportive role of technology in scaffolding play skills in children with autism. Technology tends to be very popular among individuals with autism because it seems to offer structure, visual supports, control over the environment, and opportunities for repetition. There are a number of relevant studies on the use of video modelling and robots as well as on various technology media to teach pretend play skills in children with autism. However, it has to be noted that despite their significant number, studies focusing on technology-mediated interventions to teach play skills to children with autism are considerably fewer than studies focusing on skills pertaining to the core difficulties seen in autism (e.g., social skills, communication) and academic skills. Video modelling has been widely used for many years to teach children with autism play skills such as toy-related conversational skills (Taylor et al., 1999), social initiation and toy play (Nikopoulos & Keenan, 2004), appropriate verbal and motor play (Paterson & Arco, 2007), play dialogues (Murdock et al., 2013), and verbal compliments given to peers during group play (Macpherson et al., 2015). Furthermore, robots have been extensively used recently in research on teaching play skills in children with autism. For example, they have been used to encourage collaborative play during Lego therapy sessions (Barakova et al., 2015; Huskens et al., 2015) and to improve social behaviours in playing with peers (Wainer et al., 2014). Special attention has been placed on teaching specifically pretend play skills via the use of technology. More specifically, Bai et al. (2013) evaluated an augmented reality system with regard to teaching pretend play, and Hererra et al. (2008) explored the impact of virtual reality on teaching pretend play. The two studies found that pretend play increased in frequency and duration, and there was also some degree of generalization of the learnt skill. In a similar vein, François et al. (2009) found that the use of a robot in a child-led play therapy format could improve the pretend play of children with autism.

The play of children with autism mainly has been been studied within the framework of the cognitive approach in child development (Baron-Cohen, 1987), and research has been carried out in relation to the emergence and the qualitative characteristics of sensorimotor, functional, and symbolic or pretend play. The development of play in infants and young children with autism and, most importantly, the social, interpersonal, and emotional dimensions of play have hardly been studied (Papoudi, 2015).

Play and Social Interaction as a Vehicle of Development and Education in Children with Autism

Children with autism encounter special difficulties in developing play, an activity that is particularly important for children's development and education. With this in mind, studies have been conducted and psychoeducational programs have been designed aimed at teaching and promoting play in children with autism. Studies based on the principles of applied behaviour analysis have shown that children with autism can be taught to achieve basic acts of play through games and their functional use (Kasari et al., 2013). However, an important question is to what extent this indeed constitutes play, given that flexibility, creativity, and fun are not often observed (Kasari et al., 2011; Wolfberg & Schuler, 2006). Any intervention aiming to unfold play should stem from the child's developmental level, the play of the children themselves, and their individual needs, instead of being based on a predesigned program. To this end, interactive play (Seach, 2007) and peer play (Wolfberg & Schuler, 2006) can enable children with autism to fulfil their potential and be included in the school environment. Argyropoulou and Papoudi (2012) applied the principles of intensive interaction and interactive play as an educational approach in a case study of a boy with autism to evaluate its effectiveness in the improvement of his interactions with a pupil in the same nursery. The results showed that there was a significant increase in the social transactions between the boy and his peer and that this approach provided evidence of inclusive practice, contributing to the increase in social transactions between the two peers and to a change in the behaviour of the rest of the children toward the autistic boy, who up until that point had been excluded from his peer group. Research has shown that children with autism are more involved in play activities when an adult or peer participates in the play and when the play corresponds to their developmental level (Kasari et al., 2011). Children with autism, through social interaction, interactive play, and peer play, learn how to play and how to create positive relationships and, as a result, become less isolated, by playing as equal members of a group. It is interaction and connectedness with others that generate developmental benefits in communication, in reciprocity during social transactions, in imagination and thought flexibility, and in the strengthening of the relationship between parents, educators, and children, as well as among the children themselves.

These notions on the role and importance of social interaction in the development of children with autism, and specifically in the development of play, have become the core of psychoeducational models, and their effectiveness has been investigated in relevant research. For example, to encourage interactive play between parents and children, Wieder and Greenspan (2003) suggested the 'floor time' approach, in which the adult follows the child's initiatives and uses words, gestures, and emotional expressions in order to elicit ever-more-complex communicative transactions. In addition, Rogers (2005) and her associates introduced the Denver model as a developmental intervention model that focuses on (1) the development of interpersonal, constructive, and symbolic play; (2) the establishment of relationships characterized by positive affect, reciprocity, and imitation; and (3) the development of speech. In developmental interventions the adults/therapists are expected to follow the child's lead, interpret all of his or her communicative attempts as communicative, and organize the environment in a way to instigate initiations from the child while learning is achieved through strong affect-laden relationships (Ingersoll et al., 2005). Wolfberg (2003), shifting the focus away from the role of adults to that of peers, designed the Integrated Play Groups model to encourage the play of children with autism in social peer groups. In one of her studies (Wolfberg & Schuler, 1993), she describes a multifaceted model for promoting peer play in three children with autism, including a support/instruction system for peer play. In specially designed play areas offering opportunities for construction and sociodramatic role-play, peers functioned as partners in the play of children with autism, based on a series of sessions with opening and closing rituals.

Furthermore, there are a number of studies investigating the impact of interventions based on developmental and behavioural strategies to teach play skills in children with autism. According to behavioural strategies, new skills should be taught in an environment where the antecedent stimuli are clear and systematic reinforcement should follow a correct response (Cooper et al., 2007). For example, Ingersoll and Gergans (2007) explored the impact of Reciprocal Imitation Training on spontaneous imitation skills, employing three mothers and their young children with autism and intellectual disabilities. The goal of the training was to teach children with imitation through play by keeping a balance between modelling actions and following the child's lead (Ingersoll & Schreibman, 2006). Kasari and her associates (2015) explored the effectiveness of a parent-mediated intervention on play skills of children with autism, focusing on joint engagement, joint attention, and play skills, and found an increase in children's play diversity and higher play levels.

Although such practices have been generally shown to have positive results, i.e., improvement in interpersonal communication, play, and language development, they must be applied to a larger number of children with autism and to corresponding control groups in order to confirm their effectiveness and examine these outcomes in relation to learning.

Implications for Educational Practice

The role of play in the education of children with autism, let alone when autism coexists with intellectual disabilities, across the school years has been neglected. There has been a great need to train teachers in teaching play skills to children with autism (Wong & Kasari, 2012). Play is essential in preschool educational settings and is fundamental in the curricula of early childhood education, but it should be supported beyond this, as play can be a vehicle for learning in all ages and across the lifespan. Imray and Hinchcliffe (2014) claim that play should be taught everyday both in and out of the classroom, going far beyond the designated limited play time at school and involving the teaching of literacy and numeracy (Imray & Hadfield, 2017). It is very encouraging that recently there are curricula for children with intellectual disabilities in the United Kingdom that either have play at the heart of any type of learning such as emotional, social, communicative, and cognitive (Fountaindale School, 2015a, 2015b) or target play as a separate area of development (Imray & Hadfield, 2017). The role of schools is crucial, as it is the schools' responsibility to provide breadth of choice and depth of experience in terms of play and to forge strong partnerships with parents and carers (Imray & Hadfield, 2017) to ensure consistency of approaches and generalization of skills.

A recent review of play interventions for children with autism at school by Kossyvaki and Papoudi (2016) showed that a number of studies exploring ways of teaching play skills in children with autism have been conducted at school and have reported effective results, but these studies targeted children up to the age of 12 years old, not looking at play throughout the lifespan. Moreover, only 45% (i.e., 37 of 82) of the pupils recruited in the primary studies had an additional diagnosis of intellectual disabilities. Some studies employed participants with intellectual disabilities, and only two of the 14 total (including 7 children) used purely developmental interventions to teach play, and another three studies (including 29 children) used at least partially developmental methods. Therefore, it seems that developmental approaches are not often used in schools to teach play skills in children with autism and intellectual disabilities.

As this chapter has shown so far, although it is not impossible, teaching basic play skills in individuals with autism and intellectual disabilities can be a challenging task. Children seem to naturally develop play skills, without much effort from their 'guiders' who are often adults or more experienced peers (Imray & Orr, 2015), whereas children with autism and those with intellectual disabilities require different approaches to be taught (Imray & Hinchcliffe, 2014; Jordan, 2001). For example, when taught in a structured developmental way, they might be able to develop even more advanced types of play such as pretend play (Jordan, 2001; Sherratt & Peter, 2002), and therefore the role of adults is crucial in supporting these children to reach their full potential (Sherratt & Peter, 2002).

One element of supporting children with autism and those with autism and intellectual disabilities to develop play skills might be to teach to some extent the mechanics of play (e.g., how to push a car into the garage, dress and undress a doll), but it is even more critical to foster an environment that supports the child's intrinsic pleasure of engaging in play activities, as the existence of fun and excitement is a precondition for play (Sherratt, 1999). Children with autism show a huge diversity in their communication and social interaction skills, and although some children with autism might be desperate to make friends and play, other children may prefer to spend more time on their own. For example, Ross Blackburn (2011), a woman with autism, admits that she used to kick other children when she was at school, as kicking made them go away. She also claims that in the case of individuals with autism who do not like social interactions and who are asked to play with others during break time at school, this demands a lot of effort and that it might not be fair to them, as they end up not getting a break this way.

When teaching play skills, especially in educational settings, the child's current play skills should be assessed and any progress has to be evidenced. There are assessment tools for play that are relevant for children with autism and intellectual disabilities such as the Questionnaire for Play Observation by Beyer and Gammeltoft (1998) and the Social Play Record by White (2010). These can be used as a starting point for professionals and parents, who can then develop their own to better fit their children's needs. Sherratt and Peter (2002) recommend that teachers should be aware of the different developmental stages of play and support the child to move from ritualistic to spontaneous forms of play, from solitary play to social play, and from sensorimotor to functional play. Furthermore, the play environment needs to be organized so distractions are reduced to a minimum and guidance is offered via simple visual cues about the rules, the length of the game, and turn-taking within play activities. Following a simple narrative structure (e.g., favourite fairy tale or video) appropriate to the child's developmental level and involving their interests can also be very effective. The use of technology should be also strongly considered due to its strong presence in educational settings, the popularity of technology among individuals with autism, and the positive research findings on its effectiveness in teaching a broad spectrum of skills, including play skills.

Adults have a very crucial and also complex role to play in the development of play skills in children with autism. Dockett and Fleer (1999, cited in Phillips & Beavan, 2012) argue that adults can have both direct and indirect involvement in children's play and can take on a number of roles, the most important being: (1) the manager (e.g., managing time, space, and resources, doing the assessment and record keeping), (2) the facilitator (e.g., interpreting play), and (3) the player (e.g., engaging in parallel play or modelling how equipment can be used and extending the child's play skills). This role could be enhanced by adopting some of the principles initially developed to promote spontaneous communication in young children with autism and intellectual disabilities (Adult Interactive Style Intervention, Kossyvaki, 2013, 2017). Other relevant interventions such as Interactive Play (Seach, 2007), Intensive Interaction (Hewett et al., 2012), Video Interaction Guidance (Kennedy et al., 2011), and Integrated Play Groups (Wolfberg, 2003) might have similar goals. Therefore, an interactive style with an adult guiding the play of children with autism and intellectual disabilities could include:

- Keeping language simple, describing what the child is doing in order to maintain their attention, and providing some meaningful vocabulary
- Pausing in order to observe the child's play and building on it by responding to the latter's initiatives
- Imitating the child's play, as imitation can be a meaningful way of joining in their play and following their lead; once accepted in their play, trying to teach them something new (e.g., extending the routine)
- Using a range of non-verbal cues (e.g., pointing, symbols) to support understanding
- Creating play opportunities throughout their day to give the child the chance to practice a skill in which they have difficulty
- Creating play opportunities with familiar peers and facilitating peer play.

Conclusions

It is particularly important for children with autism to participate in playful environments, to be encouraged to play, to practice playful activities, and, through interaction with adults and peers, to 'unfold' play itself. It is up to the adults, both educators and parents, to design appropriate environments that will address the individual needs of children with autism in relation to play (Wall, 2010), by incorporating interactive play with themselves and peers (siblings and other children) in their play activity repertoire and by providing guidance that leads to higher levels of play. It is equally important for adults to be very much aware of the extent to which their interactive style facilitates or impedes the development of play skills in children with autism and make adjustments accordingly. Such initiatives are of primary importance when we take into account the research findings that suggest that, ultimately, the difficulties in symbolic play encountered by children with autism are linked not to the *ability for* play, but rather to *performance of* play (Blanc et al., 2005). It is also important to consider that some children with autism prefer to play alone and may find play with other children uncomfortable or even distressing, and this should be respected (Calder et al., 2013) when evaluating and addressing the individual developmental educational needs of a child with autism.

Of great relevance here are also the notions of happiness and well-being, which have not been researched adequately in the field of autism (Vermeulen,

2014). Given that quality of life among adults with autism has been found to correlate with having regular and meaningful recreational activities (Billstedt et al., 2011), more opportunities should be given to access play in all ages especially when autism coexists with intellectual disabilities. In cases like this, play and having fun should not be sacrificed in the name of age appropriateness (Imray & Hadfield, 2017), and the needs of individuals should be considered according to where they are on the developmental ladder as opposed to their chronological age (Hewett et al., 2012). This is in accordance with Theodorou and Nind's (2010) point that 'normative benchmarks' are likely to be challenged when it comes to play and autism. However, more research needs to be done, as the population of children with autism and intellectual disabilities has been largely neglected in the broader autism research (Kasari & Smith, 2013; Pellicano et al., 2014), including play.

Through social interaction and peer play, children develop empathy, social understanding, and tolerance toward different forms of communication and play, while, simultaneously, play itself is enriched by each child's personal and sociocultural experiences (Wolfberg, 2003). By actively participating in a 'play culture', children with autism do not become isolated and acquire access to play and peer play. Lack of access to and support for peer play is most probably the reason behind the image of the socially isolated child with autism, rather than the child's own difficulties in developing peer play (Wolfberg & Schuler, 2006). The existence of a framework – whether in the family, the school, or the community – which enables a 'play culture' and a 'peer culture', can contribute significantly to the improvement of social interaction and communication; the development of creativity, imagination, and symbolic thought; flexibility of thought; and fun and happiness in children with autism.

References

Argyropoulou, Z., & Papoudi, D. (2012). The training of a child with autism in a Greek preschool inclusive class through intensive interaction: A case study. *European Journal of Special Needs Education, 27*(1), 99–114.

Asperger, H. (1944). Die 'autistischen psychopathen' im kindesalter. *European Archives of Psychiatry and Clinical Neuroscience, 117*(1), 76–136.

Bai, Z., Blackwell, A. F., & Coulouris, G. (2013, October). Through the looking glass: Pretend play for children with autism. In *2013 IEEE International Symposium on Mixed and Augmented Reality (ISMAR)* (pp. 49–58). IEEE.

Baird, G., Charman, T., Baron-Cohen, S., Cox, A., Swettenham, J., Wheelwright, S., & Drew, A. (2000). A screening instrument for autism at 18 months of age: A six year follow-up study. *Journal of the American Academy of Child & Adolescent Psychiatry, 39*, 694–702.

Barakova, E. I., Bajracharya, P., Willemsen, M., Lourens, T., & Huskens, B. (2015). Long-term Lego therapy with humanoid robot for children with ASD. *Expert Systems, 32*(6), 698–709.

Baron-Cohen, S. (1987). Autism and symbolic play. *British Journal of Developmental Psychology, 5*(2), 139–148.

Beyer, J., & Gammeltoft, L. (1998). *Autism and play*. London: Jessica Kingsley Publishers.

Billstedt, E., Gillberg, I. C., & Gillberg, C. (2011) Aspects of quality of life in adults diagnosed with autism in childhood: A population-based study. *Autism, 15*(1), 7–20.

Blackburn, R. (2011, September). Logically illogical: The perspective of an adult with autism. Lecture presented at the autism residential weekend, University of Birmingham.

Blanc, R., Adrien, J.-L., Roux, S., & Barthélémy, C. (2005). Dysregulation of pretend play and communication development in children with autism. *Autism, 9*(3), 229–245.

Calder, L., Hill, V., & Pellicano, E. (2013). 'Sometimes I want to play by myself': Understanding what friendship means to children with autism in mainstream primary schools. *Autism, 17*(3), 296–316.

Chakrabarti, S., & Fombonne, E. (2001). Pervasive developmental disorders in pre-school children. *Journal of the American Medical Association, 285*, 3093–3099.

Charman, T., Swettenham, J., Baron-Cohen, S., Cox, A., Baird, G., & Drew, A. (1997). Infants with autism: An investigation of empathy, pretend play, joint attention, and imitation. *Developmental Psychology, 33*(5), 781.

Cooper, J. O., Heron, T. E., & Heward, W. L. (2007). *Applied behavior analysis* (2nd edn.). Upper Saddle River, NJ: Pearson Education.

Department of Health (DoH) (2001). Valuing people: A new strategy for learning disability for the 21st century: A White Paper presented to Parliament by the Secretary of State for Health by Command of Her Majesty March 2001.

DSM-IV (1994). *Diagnostic and statistical manual of mental disorders* (4th edn.). Washington, DC: American Psychiatric Association.

DSM-V (2013). *Diagnostic and statistical manual of mental disorders* (5th edn.). Washington, DC: American Psychiatric Association.

Emerson, E., & Baines, S. (2010). *The estimated prevalence of autism among adults with learning disabilities in England*. Durham: Improving Health and Lives: Learning Disabilities Observatory.

Fombonne, E. (1999). The epidemiology of autism: A review. *Psychological Medicine, 29*, 769–786.

Fountaindale School (2015a). *The pre-formal curriculum*. Available at www.fountaindale.notts.sch.uk/documents.

Fountaindale School (2015b). *The semi-formal curriculum*. Available at www.fountaindale.notts.sch.uk/documents.

François, D., Powell, S., & Dautenhahn, K. (2009). A long-term study of children with autism playing with a robotic pet: Taking inspirations from non-directive play therapy to encourage children's proactivity and initiative-taking. *Interaction Studies, 10*, 324–373.

Herrera, G., Alcantud, F., Jordan, R., Blanquer, A., Labajo, G., & De Pablo, C. (2008). Development of symbolic play through the use of virtual reality tools in children with autistic spectrum disorders: Two case studies. *Autism, 12*(2), 143–157.

Hewett, D., Barber, M., Firth, G., & Harrison T. (Eds.) (2012). *The intensive interaction handbook*. London: Sage Publications.

Hobson, J. A., Hobson, R. P., Malik, S., Bargiota, K., & Caló, S. (2013). The relation between social engagement and pretend play in autism. *British Journal of Developmental Psychology, 31*, 114–127.

Holland, K. (2011). *Factsheet: Learning disabilities*. Birmingham: British institute of learning disabilities.

Huskens, B., Palmen, A., Van der Werff, M., Lourens, T., & Barakova, E. (2015). Improving collaborative play between children with autism spectrum disorders and their siblings: The effectiveness of a robot-mediated intervention based on Lego® therapy. *Journal of Autism and Developmental Disorders, 45*(11), 3746–3755.

Imray, P., & Hadfield, M. (2017). Equals SLD (semi-formal) curriculum schemes of work: My play and leisure. Available at http://equals.co.uk/wp-content/uploads/2016/12/Semi-Formal-SLD-Curriculum-SoW-My-Play-and-Leisure-Preview.pdf.

Imray, P., & Hinchcliffe, V. (2014). *Curricula for teaching children and young people with severe or profound and multiple learning difficulties: Practical strategies for educational professionals*. Abingdon, Oxon: Routledge.

Imray, P., & Orr, R. (2015). Playing to learn or learn to play? Ideas on ensuring that the opportunity to play is continually accessible to learners with SLD/PMLD. In P. Lacey, R. Ashdown, P. Jones, H. Lawson, & M. Pipe (Eds.), *The Routledge companion to severe profound and multiple learning difficulties* (pp. 356–364). London: Routledge.

Ingersoll, B., Dvortcsak, A., Whalen, C., & Sikora, D. (2005). The effects of a developmental, social-pragmatic language intervention on rate of expressive language production in young children with autistic spectrum disorders. *Focus on Autism and Other Developmental Disabilities, 20*(4), 213–222.

Ingersoll, B., & Gergans, S. (2007). The effect of a parent-implemented imitation intervention on spontaneous imitation skills in young children with autism. *Research in Developmental Disabilities, 28*(2), 163–175.

Ingersoll, B., & Schreibman, L. (2006). Teaching reciprocal imitation skills to young children with autism using a naturalistic behavioral approach: Effects on language, pretend play and joint attention. *Journal of Autism and Developmental Disorders, 36*(4), 487–505.

Jordan, R. (2001). *Autism with severe learning difficulties*. London: Souvenir Press (E&A) Ltd.

Kanner, L. (1943). Autistic disturbances of affective contact. *Nervous Child, 2*, 217–220.

Kasari, C., Chang, Y. C., & Patterson, S. (2013). Pretending to play or playing to pretend: The case of autism. *American Journal of Play, 6*(1), 124–135.

Kasari, C., Gulsrud, A., Paparella, T., Hellemann, G., & Berry, K. (2015). Randomized comparative efficacy study of parent-mediated interventions for toddlers with autism. *Journal of Consulting and Clinical Psychology, 83*(3), 554–563.

Kasari, C., Huynh, L., & Gulsrud, A. (2011). Play interventions for children with autism. In S. W. Russ & L. N. Niec (Eds.), *Play in clinical practice: Evidence based approaches* (pp. 201–217). London: Guilford Press.

Kasari, C., & Smith, T. (2013). Interventions in schools for children with autism spectrum disorder: Methods and recommendations. *Autism, 17*(3), 254–267.

Kennedy, H., Landor, M., & Todd, L. (2011). (Eds.) *Video interaction guidance: A relationship-based intervention to promote attunement, empathy and well-being.* London: Jessica Kingsley.

Kossyvaki, L. (2013). Adult interactive style and autism: Reviewing the literature to inform school practice. *Good Autism Practice, 14*(2), 23–32.

Kossyvaki, L. (2017). *Adult interactive style intervention and participatory research designs in autism: Bridging the gap between academic research and practice.* Abingdon, Oxon: Routledge.

Kossyvaki, L., & Papoudi, D. (2016). A review of play interventions for children with autism at school. *International Journal of Disability, Development and Education, 63*(1), 45–63.

Macpherson, K., Charlop, M. H., & Miltenberger, C. A. (2015). Using portable video modeling technology to increase the compliment behaviors of children with autism during athletic group play. *Journal of Autism and Developmental Disorders, 45*(12), 3836–3845.

Mundy, P., Sigman, M., Ungerer, J., & Sherman, T. (1986). Defining the social deficits of autism: The contribution of non-verbal communication measures. *Journal of Child Psychology and Psychiatry, 27*, 657–669.

Mundy, P., Sigman, M., Ungerer, J., & Sherman, T. (1987). Nonverbal communication and play correlates of language development in autistic children. *Journal of Autism and Developmental Disorders, 17*, 349–364.

Murdock, L. C., Ganz, J., & Crittendon, J. (2013). Use of an iPad play story to increase play dialogue of preschoolers with autism spectrum disorders. *Journal of Autism and Developmental Disorders, 43*(9), 2174–2189.

Nikopoulos, C. K., & Keenan, M. (2004). Effects of video modeling on social initiations by children with autism. *Journal of Applied Behavior Analysis, 37*, 93–96.

Papoudi, D. (1993). Interpersonal play and communication between young autistic children and their mothers. PhD thesis, University of Edinburgh.

Papoudi, D. (2008). The inclusion of children with Asperger disorder in the mainstream school. *Hellenic Review of Special Education, 1*, 195–207 [in Greek].

Papoudi, D. (2015). The intersubjective motives of play: The case of autism. In T. Kokkinaki & C. Trevarthen (Eds.), *Intersubjective paths to interpersonal relationships and learning. Elefterna*, Scientific Journal, Department of Psychology, University of Crete, Special Issue, vol. 7 (pp. 202–239). Available at http://elocus.lib.uoc.gr/dlib/8/5/a/metadata-dlib-1329729318-602079-22262.tkl.

Paterson, C. R., & Arco, L. (2007). Using video modeling for generalizing toy play in children with autism. *Behavior Modification, 31*(5), 660–681.

Pellicano, E., Dinsmore, A., & Charman, T. (2014). What should autism research focus upon? Community views and priorities from the United Kingdom. *Autism, 18*(7), 756–770.

Phillips, N., & Beavan, L. (2012). *Teaching play to children with autism: Practical interventions using Identiplay.* London: Sage Publications.

Piaget, J. (1951). *Play, dreams and imitation in childhood*. London: Routledge and Kegan Paul.

Rogers, S. J. (2005). Play interventions for young children with autism spectrum disorders. In L. A. Reddy, T. M. Files-Hall, & C. E. Schaefer (Eds.), *Empirically based play interventions for children* (pp. 215–239). Washington, DC: American Psychological Association.

Rutter, M., & Lockyer, L . (1967). A five to fifteen year follow-up study of infantile psychosis. *British Journal of Psychiatry, 113*, 1169–1182.

Seach, D. (2007). *Interactive play for children with autism*. New York: Routledge.

Sherratt, D. (1999). The importance of play. *Good Autism Practice, 2*, 23–31.

Sherratt, D., & Peter, M. (2002). *Developing play skills and drama in children with autistic spectrum disorders*. London: David Fulton.

Smith, P. K. (2010). *Children and play: Understanding children's worlds*. Chichester: John Wiley & Sons.

Taylor, B. A., Levin, L., & Jasper, S. (1999). Increasing play-related statements in children with autism toward their siblings: Effects of video modeling. *Journal of Developmental and Physical Disabilities, 11*, 253–264.

Theodorou, F., & Nind, M. (2010). Inclusion in play: A case study of a child with autism in an inclusive nursery. *Journal of Research in Special Educational Needs, 10*(2), 99–106.

Trevarthen, C. T., Aitken, K. J., Papoudi, D., & Robarts, J. Z. (1998). *Children with autism: Diagnosis and intervention to meet their needs* (2nd edn.). London: Jessica Kingsley.

Vermeulen, P. (2014). The practice of promoting happiness in autism. In G. Jones & E. Hurley (Eds.), *Autism, happiness and wellbeing* (pp. 8–17). Birmingham: British Institute of Learning Difficulties.

Vygotsky, L. S. (1978). *Mind in society: The development of higher psychological processes*. Cambridge, MA: Harvard University Press.

Wainer, J., Robins, B., Amirabdollahian, F., & Dautenhahn, K. (2014). Using the humanoid robot KASPAR to autonomously play triadic games and facilitate collaborative play among children with autism. *IEEE Transactions on Autonomous Mental Development, 6*(3), 183–199.

Wall, K. (2010). *Autism and early years practice* (2nd edn.). London: Sage Publications.

Wetherby, A. M. (2006). Understanding and measuring social communication in children with autism spectrum disorders. In T. Charman & W. Stone (Eds.), *Social and communication development in autism spectrum disorders: Early identification, diagnosis, and intervention* (pp. 3–34). New York: Guilford Press.

White, C. (2010). *The Social Play Record: A toolkit for assessing and developing social play from infancy to adolescents*. London: Jessica Kingsley.

Wieder, S., & Greenspan, S. I. (2003). Climbing the symbolic ladder in the DIR model through floor time/interactive play. *Autism, 7*(4), 425–435.

Wing, L., & Gould, J. (1979). Severe impairments of social interaction and associated abnormalities in children: Epidemiology and classification. *Journal of Autism and Developmental Disorders, 9*(1), 11–29.

Wolfberg, P. J. (2003). *Peer play and the autism spectrum.* Shawnee Mission, KS: Autism Asperger Publishing.

Wolfberg, P., & Schuler, A. (1993). Integrated play groups: A model for promoting the social and cognitive dimensions of play in children with autism. *Journal of Autism and Developmental Disorders, 23*(3), 467–489.

Wolfberg, P., & Schuler, A. (2006). Promoting social reciprocity and symbolic representation in children with autism spectrum disorders: Designing quality peer play interventions. In T. Charman & W. Stone (Eds.), *Social and communication development in autism spectrum disorders: Early identification, diagnosis, and intervention* (pp. 180–218). New York: Guilford Press.

Wong, C., & Kasari, C. (2012). Play and joint attention of children with autism in the preschool special education classroom. *Journal of Autism and Developmental Disorders, 42*(10), 2152–2161.

32 Play and Children with Sensory Impairments

P. Margaret Brown and Anna Bortoli

Play is an activity emerging in children beginning in the second year of life (Fein, 1981). It has its roots in the earliest routines children experience (e.g., feeding, sleeping, dressing, bathing) and develops through the adoption of characters and roles, the increasingly imaginative use of objects as placeholders, and the invention of objects in the second and third years (Fein, 1981). These routine scripts develop into longer, more complex scripts that incorporate playmates (Westby, 1991). Maintaining a joint play episode toward a satisfactory outcome for all players requires children to have effective communication, the ability to understand the perspective of another, negotiation skills, and awareness that there may be subtle rules not to be violated (Brown et al., 2008). In essence, play with peers requires sophisticated knowledge and social skills. Given this, and the effects of sensory impairments on children's cognitive, linguistic, and social development, the play of children with hearing or vision impairment is important to research. Such knowledge may (1) shed light on the associations between these domains and play, (2) help us to understand the symbiotic nature of these relationships where intervention in any one aspect may promote development in another, and (3) assist early interventionists in direct intervention with children and parents. This chapter reviews research into early play development in these populations of children, how parents support such development, and what is known about the effects of hearing and vision impairment on play with peers.

Children with Sensory Impairments

Infants whose sensory systems are intact come into the world with a preference for the human voice and an interest in gazing at the human face (Owens, 2015). Hearing and vision especially are two primary senses whose development intertwines during the first year of life and become integrated around 9 months of age (Owens, 2015). Being able to discriminate speech sounds and recognize groups of speech sounds as units of meaning while attending to people and objects in the immediate environment creates a condition most conducive to the acquisition of communication skills and language. That is, seeing an object while simultaneously hearing a speaker use the word representing the object (i.e., the 'triangle of reference') is the most powerful condition for early word learning (Webster & Roe, 1998). From about 12 months of age, some children begin to reproduce these early words they have been exposed to (Owens, 2015), and this is often accompanied by the emergence of pretend play (McCune, 1995). Because of the interweaving of vision and hearing abilities, this process will likely be compromised in children with either or both of these sensory impairments.

Both vision impairment (VI) and hearing impairment (HI) vary in type, degree, and aetiology. For those with the most severe conditions, recent advances in technology (such as cochlear implants, the bionic eye currently being developed, and the implementation of early and neonatal screening) have improved children's developmental potential. Importantly, earlier diagnosis brings earlier support for parents from early intervention programmes. Many infants are now diagnosed and their families supported during the first few months, long before the emergence of language and symbolic play. Despite these advancements, there is a dearth of research into these children's play and the precursors of play within this most recent context.

Early Play Development in Toddlers with Sensory Impairments

It is widely accepted that vision supports the development of skills believed to be fundamental to play, such as social interaction; physical, concept, and language development (Bruce & Meggit, 2002; Gray, 2005); shared attention (Roe, 2008); and object permanence (Biggelow, 1990). Despite this, few studies have specifically investigated play development exclusively in toddlers with VI, and the findings are inconclusive. For instance, Chen (1996) found that 20- to 30-month-old children with VI engaged in symbolic play when it was supported by parents. Hughes et al. (1998), however, found that when 40-month-old children with VI played alone at home, more than half their play was exploratory or sensorimotor and symbolic play accounted for a mere 4%. Their play was typical of sighted children of 12–14 months of age. This suggests that children with VI are cognitively capable of producing symbolic play, but when adult support is not available, play regresses to earlier immature forms.

Other studies have included toddlers with VI but as part of a larger cohort (Crocker & Orr, 1996; Troster & Brambring, 1994) or the focus has been predominantly on parental behaviour rather than the child's development (Campbell & Johnston, 2009). It is possible, however, to extract some further findings from Troster and Brambring's (1994) study, which compared questionnaire responses of a cohort of parents of 48-month-olds with VI with those of parents of matched sighted children about their child's types of play and choices of play materials. Similar to Hughes et al.'s (1998) findings, the children in this younger group were more likely to engage in solitary play using noisemakers and less likely to play with complex construction toys than were their sighted counterparts. While this study provided an overview of the early play preferences of toddlers with VI, it was limited to parents' reports, raising questions of validity. No teacher or early intervention practitioners' views were collected. In addition, the play categories were broad and there were no data on frequency, duration, and quality of play. However, Troster and Brambring (1994) raise important questions about possible differences in symbolic aspects of play, especially the use of substitute objects. They suggest that for children with VI, a toy car may not represent a real car since their experiences are coded through sound, touch, and language rather than vision. Further, Troster and Brambring (1994) found that imitation of adult routines was seldom present in children with VI, which form an important basis for later development of symbolic play scripts. Symbolic development in these children may therefore be different rather than delayed and require adaptation of traditional assessment and intervention approaches.

In contrast, more is known about the play of toddlers with HI, although the evidence is mixed. In comparing pretend play in toddlers with and without hearing loss, Gregory and Mogford (1983) found no significant differences in play levels. However, analyses of spontaneous play revealed fewer higher-order play behaviours (such as imaginary play) in the children with HI, and more instances of inappropriate play, suggesting a delay in pretend play in this population. Lyon (1997) found no difference in play levels but a positive association between play and language. Bornstein et al. (1999) also investigated the pretend play of hearing toddlers and those with HI playing with their deaf or hearing mothers and found no significant differences in amount of pretend play, highest level of pretend play, or number of object transformations, despite the hearing status of the children's parents. They found no association between pretend play and language except in the two groups of dyads in which the hearing status of child and mother were mismatched. Similarly, Spencer et al. (1990) compared the play of four Deaf toddlers (i.e., children with HI of parents with HI who used native sign language) and age-matched hearing children. In free play interaction, no significant differences were found for amount of time in pretend play, number of play episodes, level of pretend play, or length of play combinations.

Spencer and Deyo (1993) studied three groups: children with HI with their hearing parents, Deaf children with Deaf parents, and hearing children with hearing parents. Categorizing them by hearing status, no significant differences were found for time spent in sequenced, ordered sequenced, or substitute play, and pretend play overall. Frequency and length of play sequences were also not different. When categorized according to language level, however, differences emerged for time spent in ordered sequences, in substitute play, and for play diversity. These results suggest that language delay is associated with delayed pretend play, not HI.

On a larger sample of children, Spencer (1996) found that toddlers with HI spent more time in pretend play than hearing children, although no difference was found in frequency of pretend play behaviours. She suggested that children with HI may require more time to play given the difficulties they have to overcome. Reanalyzing the data, grouping the children by language level, those with higher language levels produced more abstract behaviours and longer sequences. Low language levels were associated with shorter and fewer ordered sequences. These results suggest specific associations between aspects of pretend play, such as decontextualization (the ability to substitute one object for another) and sequencing, and aspects of language development (e.g., vocabulary size and early combinations).

Brown et al. (2001) compared the play of hearing toddlers and those with HI interacting with their hearing mothers and investigated specific associations with hearing loss. The hearing children produced significantly higher levels of pretend play overall and higher levels for each of the dimensions of pretend play (decentration, decontextualization, sequencing, and planning). Word production was associated with overall pretend play for children with HI. More specifically, word production was associated with sequencing and planning in both groups, with decontextualization in the hearing group, and with decentration for children with HI. More recently, Quittner et al. (2016) found delays in both pretend play and novel noun learning in a large group of children with cochlear implants.

In summary, little is known about the early play of children with VI. Since it is suggested that the play of children with VI may be different from that of sighted children, there is an urgent need for new assessment paradigms to evaluate their symbolic development. Larger cohort studies are required to provide a broader picture of their intervention needs. The case for children with HI is somewhat different. Although there are some inconsistencies in results, findings suggest the play of toddlers with HI from hearing families is delayed, whereas in Deaf dyads play is not affected because of the greater ease of communication. This provides some support for the global pretend play–language link. In addition, Spencer (1996), Brown et al. (2001), and Quittner et al. (2016) suggest specific associations relating to word learning, sequencing and abstract behaviour, respectively. Play should therefore be a strong focus of assessment and early support for families of children with sensory impairments.

The Role of Caregivers in Supporting Toddler Play Development

Studies of pretend play in toddlers have mainly been conducted within the context of parent–child interactions. These early parent–child playful interactions provide a context in which attachment develops, critical to the child's future mental health and well-being (Sroufe, 1996). Moreover, play interactions provide parents with specific opportunities to enhance children's language, cognitive, and social development (Vibbert & Bornstein, 1989). Collectively, the strategies that parents use during these interactions are termed 'scaffolding' (Bliss et al., 1996; Meadows, 1996). How the presence of a sensory impairment will affect parental scaffolding has implications for understanding children's development and for early intervention. Of particular interest is that, in the general population, maternal interactional dominance and directiveness have been found to be detrimental to child learning (Vibbert & Bornstein, 1989), and there is evidence that this is characteristic of the interactive styles of parents of children with sensory impairments (Adenzato et al., 2006; Musselman & Churchill, 1991).

While no research specifically documents the trajectory of pretend play of children with VI during interactions with parents, some evidence shows that the presence of VI in a young child affects the way parent and child interact. For instance, Preisler (1993) found parents described their infant as unresponsive because of the difficulty in establishing eye contact. The lack of vocal and facial responsiveness in children with VI adds further challenge for parents to sustain engagement (Tobin, 1993) and establish joint reference (Roe, 2008). Some evidence shows that mothers of children with VI use more directives (Behl et al., 1996; Perez-Pereira & Conti-Ramsden, 1999), but rather than being counterproductive, this maternal style may be adaptive to the child's attentional needs. In their study of four mother–child dyads, Campbell and Johnston (2009) further found that parents had difficulty responding to their child's informational needs and their language was more likely to centre on what the child was experiencing than on the feelings and intentions of others. They encountered problems using the play activity intentionally to increase their child's understanding. For children with VI, clearly language is the primary means to connect the child with the world outside (Webster & Roe, 1998).

More evidence is available describing the interactions of mothers and children with HI during early play. Lyon (1997) found that maternal modelling was more frequent with younger children with HI who had lower levels of pretend play and language development. In contrast, maternal suggestions and prompts were associated with higher levels of child pretend play. Greater maternal participation in child play was also associated with higher levels of child pretence. Spencer (1996) also investigated two aspects of maternal behaviour: verbal or non-verbal prompts and demonstrations, akin to Lyon's prompts and modelling. Spencer grouped the participants first for hearing status and then for language level. No significant differences between the groups were found for frequency of prompts or demonstration regardless of grouping.

In a subsequent study, Spencer and Meadow-Orlans (1996) investigated simple, sequenced play (SSP), pre-planned pretend play (PPP), language production, and maternal responsiveness in hearing children and those with HI playing with their hearing or deaf mothers. At 12 months of age, only child hearing status predicted time spent in SSP. At 18 months of age, however, language production contributed marginally and maternal responsiveness significantly to the amount of time spent in PPP. This suggests there are some interrelated factors potentially contributing to child pretend play and that these factors contribute differently at different ages.

Blum et al. (1994) found delays of several months in the pretend play of children with HI, particularly the transition from single play behaviours to play combinations. The authors reported high levels of maternal control, a characteristic that has been shown to be associated with lower levels of pretend play in children with typical development (McCune et al., 1994).

Deleau (1993) investigated the ability of hearing mothers and toddlers with HI to maintain pretend play through joint reference. Compared with hearing counterparts, Deleau (1993) found that the HI dyads experienced difficulty in maintaining joint reference, with shorter, less complex play episodes. In a similar study to identify specific maternal behaviours that may hinder shared pretence, Pratt (1991) found that mothers of hearing children were more visually attentive to their child's behaviour and elaborated more often on their child's behaviour, while mothers of children with HI observed their child less and elaborated on their own behaviours. Sequential analyses showed these mothers as more directive when they had their child's attention, suggesting they regarded play interactions as instructional opportunities. Furthermore, increased unrelated behaviours suggested their interactions were less contingent on the child's focus of interest.

Brown and Remine (2004) segmented interactions into four conditions: dyadic play (mother and child using play materials), play commentary (child playing, mother commenting on play), play observation (child playing, mother silently observing), or disengagement (child or mother disengaged). Hearing children produced significantly higher pretence in dyadic play and play commentary situations. For children with HI, only dyadic play was associated with higher levels of child pretence. More frequent modelling of pretence, attempts to gain the child's attention, and reduced levels of abstract commentary characterized the behaviour of the mothers of the children with HI. Mothers with this interactional profile were more likely to be directive, literal, and to produce more play behaviours. It would seem that, although the mothers of the children with HI used some scaffolding techniques found to enhance pretend play in hearing children, problems in maintaining joint engagement with their children may render these interactions less playful and creative.

These early vertical interactions (Hartup, 1989) are considered critical in equipping children with the requisite play skills needed as children move into horizontal relationships with peers. Evidence shows that parents of children with sensory impairments adopt a dominant or directive style of interaction to compensate for their children's sensory impairment. It is possible that this dominance may lead to a dependence on adults in early childhood settings.

Research into Play Interactions with Peers

Most of the research into play with peers in children with VI consists of case studies of single participants (e.g., Celeste, 2006) or small groups (e.g., Celeste & Grum, 2010; Crocker & Orr, 1996; Grum et al., 2014; Pizzo & Bruce, 2010). This is due to the low incidence of this disability, the heterogeneous nature of VI, and the presence of comorbid conditions, making it difficult to isolate the effects of VI.

An early study by Troster and Brambring (1994) found that children with VI engaged in less exploratory, symbolic role-play and play with peers than sighted children. Their play was more solitary and less spontaneous, tending to be repetitive and stereotyped. Play was directed mostly to supportive adults. Rettig (1994) also found less symbolic play. From a social perspective, children with VI have fewer playmates (MacCuspie, 1992) and are rejected more often by peers (Chiba, cited in Celeste & Grum, 2010).

Troster and Brambring's (1994) findings were somewhat contradicted by Crocker and Orr (1996), who found that, although engaging in mostly solitary play, the participants with VI were mainly involved in exploratory and repetitive play. Additionally, although less involved than their sighted peers in the activities, they responded positively when encouraged by an adult to join in. The children with VI were more than twice as likely to be close to an adult and to initiate to the adult. Celeste (2006) found in her study of one girl that, even though she initiated to peers, she did not respond to their overtures nor seek agreement from them. Only a fifth of her play was social, her interactions being brief and normally terminated by the peer. Importantly, Celeste (2006) did note some episodes of imaginative role play. Celeste and Grum (2010), in a follow-up study of another pre-schooler with VI, reported elevated social skills and levels of participation not previously found. They attributed this to the participant's personality, suggesting these results provide evidence for practitioners to design highly individualized interventions.

Grum et al. (2014) subsequently replicated the above methods to investigate play in two 4-year-old Japanese girls with VI. Play was assessed in two settings; either at home and at special school, or at preschool and at special school. One participant was more likely to play in parallel while at school and play in a solitary manner at home, although this child did demonstrate play initiations to peers in school. The other child played in parallel half the time at both preschool and special school, but was equally likely to engage in solitary play at school. At preschool, this child engaged in peer play about 15% of the time. The researchers note that the first participant led her peers, initiated and actively responded, whereas the second child exhibited following behaviours and was less responsive. Possibly these differences also reflect personality traits.

Gaining entry into peer play is an important skill involving clear communication. A study of play entry by Sacks and Wolffe (2006) found that children with VI used language differently in these attempts. Often their language was out of context and related to their personal experiences, which may not have been recognized as an appropriate entry tactic by their peers, leading to rejection. Erin (1990) found that while sighted children used language to extend the social experience, children with VI used language to gain information from the immediate environment or to confirm the physical location of materials and peers. These studies show entering and maintaining play are dependent on effective use of social-pragmatic skills, an area warranting further research and support from teachers.

The peer play of children with HI has been more extensively studied than that of children with VI. Investigations have focused on amount, duration, and type of play; peer interactions; and children's entry skills. Early studies (such as Esposito & Koorland, 1989; Higginbotham & Baker, 1981) found that children with HI spent less time in pretend play, preferring to play alone and generally in constructive activities, while hearing children participated almost equally in dramatic or constructive play. Darbyshire (1977) found that children with HI tended not to play with hearing peers and rarely substituted objects.

Schirmer (1989) found a positive association between the amount of time children with HI spent in pretend play and language development. She found specific associations, such as between multiword combinations and combinations in play, and the coemergence of rule-based utterances with planned pretend play. She concluded that the pretend play and language of children with HI followed typical development, though more slowly. Casby and McCormack (1985) investigated language development and the ability to substitute one object for another in children with HI. Partialling out age, a significant correlation was found between substitute ability and the children's expressive vocabulary.

Brown et al. (1992) investigated pretend play and language use of children with HI playing with hearing peers. Both groups spent similar amounts of time in pretend play, used objects in similar ways, and talked about plans and the meaning of objects, although these utterances were less frequent and abstract for the children with HI. Selmi and Rueda (1998) also found that, with increasing age, the children exhibited a concomitant increase in role, action, and object transformations, although the most abstract transformations were rarely performed.

Antia and Kreimeyer (1997) investigated the effect of social skills training on amount and type of play of children with HI. After intervention they reported a reduction in amount of solitary and parallel play, not apparent in a comparison group with no intervention. Cooperative play increased and was maintained long term. No increase in peer initiations and responses was noted over time for either group. More recently, Bobzein et al. (2013) found that children with HI produced fewer initiations and comments than their hearing peers in one-to-one play, although they took more verbal and play turns. They suggested that this reflected more desire to control the interaction.

In free play, there is evidence that pre-schoolers with and without HI are more likely to select play partners with the same hearing status as themselves (Remine & Brown, 1996) and that this affects subsequent levels of play (Levine & Antia, 1997). For instance, when children with HI played with others with HI, play was more likely to be constructive; with hearing peers dramatic play was more likely.

Entering into peer play runs the risk of rejection for all children (Dodge, 1983). However, observational evidence suggests pre-schoolers with HI have less success than their hearing counterparts and are less persistent (Roberts et al., 1995). Hearing children initiate less to children with HI and are more likely to ignore initiations from them and to overtly reject them (Deluzio & Girolametto, 2011), although this latter trend appears to decrease with age. Certainly, the interactive nature of play in the preschool poses challenges for children with HI (Brown et al., 2008), particularly when children are required to demonstrate reciprocity, empathy, and social problem-solving.

Using a different approach, Wauters and Knoors (2007) analyzed the peer ratings of 18 children with HI and 344 hearing peers in grades 1–5, focusing on peer acceptance, social competence, and friendships. While the groups were similar in peer acceptance and friendship, they differed in their ratings of social competence. The children with HI were rated as more socially withdrawn and lower on prosocial behaviour. Although these findings appear to contradict those found above, these children were slightly older and the data were subjective and not directly observed.

Martin et al. (2011) investigated the entry behaviours of children with cochlear implants. They found that one-to-one interactions led to greater success and more interaction and that, similar to the general population, girls were more successful. Overall, duration of cochlear implant use was associated with increased social competence. More extensive studies of play involving larger groups are required to confirm these findings.

In summary, the evidence suggests that pre-schoolers with sensory impairments spend less time than non-disabled children in cooperative pretend play, particularly in sociodramatic play. Reasons for this may relate to delayed early development of pretence, impoverished peer group entry skills, and delayed social competence. The language delays of children with HI and their heightened reliance on visual awareness of peers rather than the use of their hearing are likely to be contributing factors. In contrast, children with VI lack visual cues, have difficulties in negotiating the play space, and rely heavily on verbal cues to recognize and understand peer interactions. Sighted and hearing peers are likely unaware of these special needs and insufficiently socially and linguistically skilled to include peers with VI or HI unless specifically instructed by teachers.

Particularly important is that the majority of children with HI in the above studies have hearing parents and are acquiring spoken language. A small minority may be Deaf children from Deaf families in which language is signed. Even fewer of these children receive inclusive preschool education where they may be the only child with HI and will be supported by a signing adult. These children should be considered a distinct group of children with HI since little is known about their pretend play skills and interactions with hearing peers.

Play in Children with Sensory Impairments: Benefits and Risks of Inclusive Education

It is held that educating children with sensory impairments in inclusive preschool settings will provide the backdrop for the development, rehearsal, and refinement of social-play interactions in context (Copple & Bredekemp, 2009). However, despite these perceived benefits, inclusion presents challenges for the teacher, child, and non-disabled peers (Brown et al., 2000; Crocker & Orr, 1996; Ely, 2014; Gray, 2005; Jindal-Snape, 2004). Teacher attitudes and confidence are influenced by their perceived levels of their own efficacy and determine the extent to which children with disabilities are accepted as part of the school community (Bunch & Valeo, 2004).

Teachers have raised concerns over the passivity and unresponsiveness of children with disabilities and, in the case of children with VI particularly, their inappropriate use of materials (Tait & Wolfgang, 1984). Celeste and Grum (2010) and Parsons (1986) reported that children with VI tend to mouth and wave objects, preventing potential social play opportunities with sighted peers. They suggest teachers should include experiences for children with VI to learn to use toys and objects appropriately. Moreover, the play environment should be organized to support children's physical and visual needs (Parsons, 1986). Without these interventions, the children may remain solitary, less creative, and more likely to select repetitive activities rather than pretend play (Parsons, 1986). Crocker and Orr (1996) further emphasize the facilitative role of teachers during play for children with VI. For instance, detailed descriptions of the play environment and activities can be given to the child together with demonstrations of appropriate social interactive behaviour. According to Ely (2014) teachers can also provide relevant cues during entry into established activities to ensure the child with VI is aware of who is in the activity and what activity is under way, knows which questions to ask, and is aware of the response within the group. Celeste (2006) suggests it is even more critical for children with VI to be specifically taught social referencing and imitation skills. Skills such as smiling or looking in the direction of the communicative partner are important visual social cues, and these behaviours may be absent for children with vision impairment (Warren, 1984). They will need to be explicitly taught, practiced, and evaluated on a regular basis (Jindal-Snape, 2004; Kekelis & Sacks, 1992).

In terms of children with HI, Bortoli and Brown (2008) suggest teachers adopt a proactive approach in directly instructing behaviours such as turn-taking, initiations, and entry tactics (Brown et al., 2000). Setting up play environments to foster face-to-face interactions and small group play activities would be beneficial given the evidence that children with HI have fewer difficulties interacting in pairs and small groups (Martin et al., 2011).

Research suggests that children choose play companions based on familiarity, age, behaviour, popularity, and appearance (Remine & Brown, 1996). Little is known about how the presence of children with sensory impairments in an inclusive environment is viewed by peers since obtaining such data raises ethical concerns. Simply by asking the views of peers, attention can be drawn to differences that otherwise would not have been noted. However, earlier research showed that sighted children expressed their concerns about vision impairment, resulting in initiations from the child with vision impairment being ignored (Taylor-Hershel & Webster, 1983). In relation to hearing children's ratings of peer acceptance and friendship for children with HI, Wauters and Knoors (2007) found they were rated in a similar manner.

While setting up an intervention study in which peers were the instructors, Hendrickson et al. (1985) observed that after the intervention, children with VI continued to initiate positively and respond to their social partners. Although this suggests the capacity of sighted children should not be dismissed, again ethical questions arise concerning such research practices given that the non-disabled child should also be free to interact by choice.

The familiarity of the environment is a critical factor in enabling play between children (Webster & Roe, 1998). Initially, the family home provides opportunities for social experiences, and as early intervention services are broadened and extend to a preschool program, children find themselves in groups with several children. The social arena and conditions have changed, and for children with VI in particular they are initially foreign. Ely (2014) recommends that transition to preschool is carefully planned by providing prior opportunities to practice play entry skills and the use of communication during play. Use of a controlled environmental set-up may initially be necessary to practice play entry tactics, involving the child with VI being initially partnered with one or two sighted children (Sacks & Wolffe, 2006). This strategy would also be useful for children with HI.

The preschool physical environment must also be taken into account. Sensory overload may contribute to a lack of responsiveness and initiations in children with VI. In addition, background noise needs to be controlled for these children and also for children with HI so that localization and speech discrimination are enhanced (Rettig, 1994; Zanin & Rance, 2016).

Conclusions

In summary, both VI and HI in a child affect the way parents interact with their children with the exception of Deaf children who have Deaf parents.

While parents of children with VI and hearing parents of children with HI are more likely to be directive in their interactions, this would appear to be an adaptation to their child's attentional needs and the need to maintain joint attention. Overall, studies of toddlers with a sensory impairment suggest delayed pretend play, thus they enter formal preschool programmes less well equipped to engage in play. In particular, they are less likely to engage in dramatic play and will experience difficulties in gaining entry and maintaining interactions within the play.

More research is needed on larger groups of children to establish the emergence and development of play in children with sensory impairments. In Deaf children using signed languages we know that their play is commensurate with that of hearing children (Spencer, 1996), but specific studies of the play of Deaf children in inclusive preschools are urgently needed. More research is also needed on the play of children with VI since the evidence is sparse and contradictory. There are several other areas that warrant further investigation: the development of social pragmatic skills, the role of the adult in facilitating peer interaction, and preparation for inclusive environments. In the case of both HI and VI, more research is urgently needed within the context of the current technological advances taking place.

Spencer and Hafer (1998) suggest that play is not only a "window" (p. 132) into a child's development but also a "room" (p. 140) in which development takes place. This being so, it is important that teachers can assess pretend play and create, adapt, and work within play environments conducive to the sensory needs of the child. Play is an important context for parent–child interaction in the toddler years, and our intervention will be most effective if we work with parents and children together as parents are our most important vehicle for intervention. We will need, therefore, to convince parents of the importance of play for development and emotional health and equip them with the skills to play effectively with their child. These include observing the child, knowing when and how to move in without taking over, and scaffolding the child's learning to the next level of development. Careful analysis of play interactions will help identify emerging development and strengths and needs. Maximizing early pretend play may lead to improved opportunities for inclusion. Finally, we should remember that play is fun. It is a creative experience in which children express their unique understandings of their different worlds. Sharing these experiences with others provides opportunities not only to develop self-concept and self-esteem but also to develop relationships and friendships.

References

Adenzato, M., Arditot, R. B., & Izard, E. (2006). Impact of maternal directiveness and overprotectiveness on the personality development of a sample of individuals with acquired blindness. *Social Behavior and Personality*, *34*(1), 17–26.

Antia, S. D., & Kreimeyer, K. H. (1997). The generalization and maintenance of the peer social behaviors of the young children who are deaf or hard of hearing. *Language, Speech, and Hearing Services in Schools, 28*, 59–69.

Behl, D., Akers, J., Boyce, G., & Taylor, M. (1996). Do mothers interact differently with children who are visually impaired? *Journal of Visual Impairment and Blindness, 90*(6), 501–511.

Biggelow, A. E. (1990). Relationship between the development of language and thought in young blind children. *Journal of Visual Impairment and Blindness, 84*, 414–419.

Bliss, J., Askew, M., & Macrae, S. (1996). Effective teaching and learning: Scaffolding revisited. *Oxford Review of Education, 22*(1), 37–61.

Blum, E. J., Fields, B. C., Scharfman, H., & Silber, D. (1994). Development of symbolic play in deaf children aged 1 to 3. In A. Slade & D. P. Wolf (Eds.), *Children at play* (pp. 238–259). New York: Oxford University Press.

Bobzein, J., Richels, C., Raver, S. A., Hester, P., Browning, E., & Morin, L. (2013). An observational study of social communication skills in eight preschoolers with and without hearing loss during cooperative play. *Early Childhood Education Journal, 41*, 339–346.

Bornstein, M. H., Selmi, A. M., Haynes, O. M., Painter, K., & Marx, E. S. (1999). Representational abilities and the hearing status of child/mother dyads. *Child Development, 70*(4), 833–852.

Bortoli, A., & Brown, P.M. (2008). The social attention skills of preschool children with an intellectual disability and children with a hearing loss. *Australian Journal of Early Childhood, 33*(4), 25–33.

Brown, P. M., Bortoli, A., Remine, M. D., & Othman, B. (2008). Social engagement, attention and competence of preschoolers with hearing loss. *Journal of Research into Special Education Needs*, 19–26.

Brown, P. M., & Remine, M. D. (2004). Building pretend play skills in toddlers with and without hearing loss: Maternal scaffolding styles. *Deafness and Education International, 6*(3), 129–153.

Brown, P. M., Remine, M. D., Rickards, F. W., & Prescott, S. J. (2000). Social interactions of preschoolers with and without impaired hearing in integrated kindergarten. *Journal of Early Intervention, 23*(3), 200–211.

Brown, P. M., Rickards, F. W., & Bortoli, A. (2001). Structures underpinning pretend play and word production in young hearing children and children with hearing loss. *Journal of Deaf Studies and Deaf Education, 6*(1), 15–31.

Brown, P. M., Rickards, F. W., & Jeanes, R. C. (1992). The symbolic play of hearing impaired and normally hearing four year olds. *Australian Teacher of the Deaf, 32*, 1–12.

Bruce, T., & Meggit, C. (2002). *Childcare and education* (3rd edn.). London: Hodder & Stoughton.

Bunch, G., & Valeo, A. (2004). Student attitudes toward peers with disabilities in inclusive and special education schools. *Disability and Society, 19*, 61–76

Campbell, J., & Johnston, C. (2009) Emotional availability in parent–child dyads where children are blind. *Parenting Science and Practice, 9*, 216–227.

Casby, M. W., & McCormack, S. M. (1985). Symbolic play and early communication development in hearing impaired children. *Journal of Communication Disorders, 18*, 67–78.

Celeste, M. (2006). Play behaviours and social interactions of a child who is blind: In theory and practice. *Journal of Visual Impairment and Blindness*, *100*(2), 75–90.

Celeste, M., & Grum, D. (2010). Social integration of children with visual impairment: A developmental model. *Elementary Education Online*, *9*(1), 11–22.

Chen, D. (1996). Parent–infant communication: Early intervention for very young children with visual impairment or hearing loss. *Infants and Young Children*, *9*(2), 1–12.

Copple, C., & Bredekamp, S. (2009). *Developmentally appropriate practice in early childhood program serving children from birth through age 8*. Washington, DC: National Association for the Education of Young Children.

Crocker, A. D., & Orr, R. R. (1996). Social behavior of children with visual impairments enrolled in preschool programs. *Exceptional Children*, *62*(5), 451–461.

Darbyshire, J. O. (1977). Play patterns in young children with impaired hearing. *The Volta Review*, *79*, 19–26.

Deleau, M. (1993). Communication and the development of symbolic play: The need for a pragmatic perspective. In J. Nadel & L. Camaioni (Eds.), *New perspectives in early communicative development* (pp. 97–115). London: Routledge.

DeLuzio, J., & Girolametto, L. (2011). Peer interactions of preschool children with and without hearing loss. *Journal of Speech, Language, and Hearing Research*, *54*, 1197–1210.

Dodge, K. A., Schlundt, D. C., Schocken, I., & Delugach, J. D. (1983). Social competence and children's sociometric status: The role of peer group entry strategies. *Merrill-Palmer Quarterly*, *29*, 309–336.

Ely, M. S. (2014). Effective strategies for preschool peer group entry: Considered applications for children with visual impairment. *Journal of Visual Impairment and Blindness*, July/August, 287–296.

Erin, J. (1990). Language samples from visually impaired four- and five-year olds. *Journal of Childhood Communication Disorders*, *13*(2), 181–191.

Esposito, B. G., & Koorland, M. A. (1989). Play behavior of hearing impaired children: Integrated and segregated settings. *Exceptional Children*, *55*(5), 412–419.

Fein, G. G. (1981). Pretend play in childhood: An integrative review. *Child Development*, *52*, 1095–1118.

Gray, C. (2005). Inclusion, impact and need: Young children with a visual impairment. *Child Care and Practice*, *11*(2), 179–190.

Gregory, S., & Mogford, K. (1983). The development of symbolic play in young deaf children. In D. R. Rogers & J. A. Sloboda (Eds.), *The acquisition of symbolic skills* (pp. 221–232). New York: Plenum Press.

Grum, D. K., Kakizawa, Y., & Celeste, M. (2014). Assessment of play behaviours and social interactions of two blind girls: Case studies in Japan. *Anthropological Notebooks*, *20*(2), 61–76.

Hartup, W. W. (1989). Social relationships and their developmental significance. *American Psychologist*, *44*(2), 120–126.

Hendrickson, J. M., Gable, R. A., Hester, P., & Strain, P. S. (1985). Teaching social reciprocity: Social exchange between young handicapped and nonhandicapped children. *The Pointer*, *29*, 17–21.

Higginbotham, D. J., & Baker, B. M. (1981). Social participation and cognitive play differences in hearing impaired and normally hearing preschoolers. *The Volta Review, 83,* 135–149.

Hughes, M., Dote-Kwan, J., & Dolendo, J. (1998). A close look at the cognitive play of preschoolers with visual impairments in the home. *Exceptional Children, 64*(4), 451–462.

Jindal-Snape, D. (2004). Generalisation and maintenance of social skills of children with visual impairments: Self-evaluation and the role of feedback. *Journal of Visual Impairment and Blindness, 98*(8), 1–26.

Kekelis, L. S., & Sacks, S. Z. (1992). The effects of visual impairment on children's social interactions in regular education programs. In S. Z. Sacks, L. Kekelis, & R. J. Gaylord-Ross (Eds.), *The development of social skills by blind and visually impaired students.* New York: American Foundation for the Blind.

Levine, L. M., & Antia, S. D. (1997). The effect of partner hearing status on social and cognitive play. *Journal of Early Intervention, 21*(1), 21–35.

Lyon, M. E. (1997). Symbolic play and language development in young deaf children. *Deafness and Education (JBATOD), 21*(2), 10–20.

MacCuspie, P. A. (1992). The social acceptance and interaction of visually impaired children in integrated settings. In S. Z. Sacks, L. S. Kekelis, & R. J. Gaylord-Ross (Eds.), *The development of social skills by blind and visually impaired students.* New York: American Foundation for the Blind.

Martin, D., Bat-Chava, Y., Lalwani, A., & Waltzman, S. B. (2011). Peer relationships of deaf children with cochlear implants: Predictors of peer entry and peer interaction success. *Journal of Deaf Studies and Deaf Education, 16*(1), 108–120.

McCune, L. (1995). A normative study of representational play at the transition to language. *Developmental Psychology, 31*(2), 198–206.

McCune, L., Dipane, D., Fireoved, R., & Fleck, M. (1994). Play: A context for mutual regulation within mother–child interaction. In A. Slade & D. P. Wolf (Eds.), *Children at play: Clinical and developmental approaches to meaning and representation* (pp. 148–166). Oxford: Oxford University Press.

Meadows, S. (1996). *Parenting behavior and children's cognitive development.* Hove, UK: Psychology Press.

Musselman, C., & Churchill, A. (1991). Conversational control in mother–child dyads: Auditory oral versus total communication. *American Annals of the Deaf, 136*(1), 5–16.

Owens, R. E. (2015). *Language development: An introduction* (9th edn.). Boston: Pearson.

Parsons, S. (1986). Function of play in low vision children. Part 2: Emerging patterns of behavior. *Journal of Visual Impairment and Blindness, 80,* 777–784.

Perez-Pereira, M., & Conti-Ramsden, G. (1999). *Language development and social interaction in blind children.* Hove, UK: Psychology Press.

Pizzo, L., & Bruce, S. M. (2010). Language and play in students with multiple disabilities and visual impairments or deaf-blindness. *Journal of Visual Impairment & Blindness, 104*(5), 287–297.

Pratt, S. R. (1991). Nonverbal play interaction between mothers and young deaf children. *Ear and Hearing, 12*(5), 328–336.

Preisler, G. M. (1993). A descriptive study of blind children in nurseries with sighted children. *Child: Care, Health and Development, 19*, 295–315.

Quittner, A. L., Cejas, I., Wang, N., Niparko, J. K., & Barker, D. H. (2016). Symbolic play and novel noun learning in deaf and hearing children: Longitudinal effects of access to sound on early precursors of language. *PLoS ONE, 11*(5): e0155964.

Remine, M. D., & Brown, P. M. (1996). Playing with peers: Play partner preferences and acceptability into play for preschoolers with and without normal hearing. *Australian Journal of Education of the Deaf, 2*(1), 30–35.

Rettig, M. (1994). The play of young children with visual impairments: Characteristics and interventions. *Journal of Visual Impairment and Blindness, 88*(5), 410–420.

Roberts, S. B., Brown, P. M., & Rickards, F. W. (1995). Social pretend play entry behaviors of preschoolers with and without impaired hearing. *Journal of Early Intervention, 20*, 52–64.

Roe, J. (2008). Social inclusion: Meeting the socio-emotional needs of children with vision needs. *British Journal of Visual Impairment, 26*(2), 147–158.

Sacks, S., & Wolffe, K. (2006). *Teaching social skills to students with visual impairments: From theory to practice.* New York: AFB Press.

Schirmer, B. R. (1989). Relationship between imaginative play and language development in hearing-impaired children. *American Annals of the Deaf, 134*(3), 219–222.

Selmi, A. M., & Rueda, R. S. (1998). A naturalistic study of collaborative play transformations of preschoolers with hearing impairments. *Journal of Early Intervention, 21*(4), 299–307.

Spencer, P. E. (1996). The association between language and symbolic play at two years: Evidence from deaf toddlers. *Child Development, 67*, 867–876.

Spencer, P. E., & Deyo, D. (1993). Cognitive and social aspects of deaf children's play. In M. Marschark & M. D. Clark (Eds.), *Psychological perspectives on deafness* (pp. 65–91). Hillsdale, NJ: Lawrence Erlbaum.

Spencer, P. E., Deyo, D., & Grindstaff, N. (1990). Symbolic play behaviour of deaf and hearing toddlers. In D. F. Moores & K. P. Meadow-Orlans (Eds.), *Educational and developmental aspects of deafness* (pp. 390–406). Washington, DC: Gallaudet University Press.

Spencer, P. E., & Hafer, J. C. (1998). Play as 'window' and 'room': Assessing and supporting the cognitive and linguistic development of deaf infants and young children. In M. Marschark & D. Clark (Eds.), *Psychological perspectives on deafness*, vol. 2 (pp. 131–152). Mahwah, NJ: Lawrence Erlbaum.

Spencer, P. E., & Meadow-Orlans, K. P. (1996) Play, language, and maternal responsiveness: A longitudinal study of deaf and hearing infants. *Child Development, 67*(6), 3176–3191.

Sroufe, L. A. (1996). *Emotional development: The organisation of emotional life in the early years.* Cambridge: Cambridge University Press.

Tait, P., & Wolfgang, C. (1984). Mainstreaming a blind child: Problems perceived in a preschool day care program. *Early Child Development and Care, 13*, 144–167.

Taylor-Hershel, D., & Webster, R. (1983). Mainstreaming: A case in point. *Childhood Education, 59*, 175–179.

Tobin, M. J. (1993). The language of blind children: Communication, words and meanings. In M. C. Beveridge & G. Reddiford (Eds.), *Language, culture and education*. Proceedings of the Colston Research Society, Bristol. Clevedon: Multilingual Matters.

Troster, H., & Brambring, M. (1994). The play behavior and play materials of blind and sighted infants and preschoolers. *Journal of Visual Impairment and Blindness, 88*, 421–432.

Vibbert, M., & Bornstein, M. H. (1989). Specific associations between domains of mother–child interaction and toddler referential language and pretense play. *Infant Behavior and Development, 12*, 163–184.

Warren, D. H. (1984). *Blindness and early childhood development*. New York: American Foundation for the Blind.

Wauters, L. N., & Knoors, H. (2007). Social integration of deaf children in inclusive settings. *Journal of Deaf Studies and Deaf Education, 13*(1), 21–36.

Webster, A., & Roe, J. (1998). *Children with visual impairments: Social interaction, language and learning*. London: Routledge.

Westby, C. E. (1991). A scale for assessing children's pretend play. In C. E. Schaefer, K. Gitlin, & A. Sandgrund (Eds.), *Play diagnosis and assessment* (pp. 131–161). New York: John Wiley & Sons.

Zanin, J., & Rance, G. (2016). Functional hearing in the classroom: Assistive listening devices for students with hearing impairment in a mainstream school setting. *International Journal of Audiology, 55*(12), 723–729.

33 Play and Children with Physical Impairments

Cynthia J. Cress

Play interactions are commonly used to characterize and assess multiple developmental skills in children with and without disabilities. Children's systematic use of play objects for functional or symbolic purposes can represent benchmarks of cognitive development in early childhood, and multiple traditional play scales have been developed to characterize cognitive stages in play (e.g., Belsky & Most, 1981; McCune-Nicolich, 1981). Social behaviours during play can be demonstrations of parent–child or peer interaction skills in children, as well as indicators of social communication concerns using assessments such as the Autism Diagnostic Observation Scale–2 (Lord et al., 2012). The physical control of play objects can be used to demonstrate cognitive as well as fine and gross motor skills of children during independent or facilitated play, reflected in standard developmental assessments such as the Bayley Scales of Infant and Toddler Development–III (Bayley, 2006), Mullen Scales of Early Learning (Mullen, 1995) or Vineland Adaptive Behavior Scales–3 (Sparrow et al., 2016). However, the physical control necessary to demonstrate cognitive, language, or social skills on traditional developmental play assessments limits their applicability to children with physical impairments without specific modifications to account for those physical restrictions (DeVeney et al., 2011).

Children with physical delays and disabilities may be impaired in their ability to demonstrate their motor/adaptive, cognitive, speech/language, and/or social skills through typical play interactions in formal or informal assessments. Primary physical disabilities in children may include congenital conditions such as cerebral palsy that affect motor control and planning, or acquired conditions such as traumatic brain injury that can affect multiple motor and developmental skills. These physical disabilities frequently co-occur with other impairments, such as cognitive, communication, attention, sensory, or social limitations. Other developmental disabilities may also involve physical limitations as a secondary component of the disability. For instance, children with Down syndrome tend to have secondary fine and/or gross motor impairments that affect hand/arm skills, trunk control, speech, and mobility, although the degree of physical involvement can vary widely among children with developmental disabilities. At-risk children such as premature infants may show early physical delays that resolve within typical limits over time, although lingering irregularities in breadth or specificity of physical skills can remain in some children. Children whose physical impairments interfere with their ability to rely fully on natural speech to meet their daily communication needs are considered to have complex communication needs and tend to rely on multiple modalities of communication to express their messages, including gestures, sounds, signs, picture symbols, written words, voice output devices, and computer programs (Beukelman & Mirenda, 2013).

Because of the limitations introduced by a physical impairment, adaptations in assessment of play are necessary to support or bypass children's poor control of the hand–arm skills essential for independent early play actions using objects. Play and adaptive skill assessments such as the Pediatric Evaluation of Disability Inventory (PEDI; Haley et al., 1992) have been developed to take advantage of alternative means for demonstrating cognitive and social skills in play for children with physical impairments. Gesture, speech, and language behaviours produced during structured play samples can be normative indicators of developmental progressions in communication skills with measures such as the Communication and Symbolic Behavior Scales–Developmental Profile (CSBS-DP; Wetherby & Prizant, 2003), and the play temptations for the CSBS have been adapted for use for assessment for infants and toddlers with physical impairments (Cress et al., 2000). Transdisciplinary Play-Based Assessment (Linder, 1993) allows multiple professionals to support the child's interaction and control of play activities to determine independent child play skills and effective methods for parents and professionals to supplement the child's play strategies in intervention.

The impact of physical disabilities on play can vary considerably depending on the types of skills affected. A general delay in play is expected for children with physical impairments regardless of concomitant cognitive impairment, due to difficulty controlling the physical and social tasks involved in play (Cress, 2002). Infants with developmental disabilities showed lower levels of play complexity than developmental age peers at 6, 11, and 15 months, and the duration and frequency of object play was greater for children without disabilities than those with disabilities, even in conditions such as Down syndrome in which physical skills may not be severely restricted (Gowen et al., 1992). However, there is considerable individual variation in type, formality, and diversity of play in children with different degrees of physical impairments (Law et al., 2006). Areas of strength such as interpersonal engagement or task persistence can compensate for physical limitations and result in effective individual and social play strategies. Individuals can have very different preferences for types of play including structured or unstructured interaction, physical or social activities, and solitary or partner-based play. Children may show expected skills at some types of play and fail to meet expectations in tasks for which they have insufficient experience, interest, or control to engage in play activities. The following section discusses high-risk physical skills associated with individual variability in play for children with physical impairments, in particular, control of play objects, coordination of play actions, active engagement in play interactions, and mastery motivation to accomplish play goals.

Issues Affecting Access and Interaction in Play for Children with Physical Impairments

Factors that particularly influence play behaviours in children with physical impairments include the ability to control play objects, ability to coordinate play actions, active engagement in play interactions, and mastery motivation to accomplish play goals.

Control of Play Objects. Most play skill assessments rely on active object control in the environment. There is an interaction between experience or partner support and children's ability to demonstrate control of play objects, even for typically developing children. For instance, infants require repeated experiences at reaching and touching objects to build perceptual-motor mapping and cognitive conceptions of object relationships in their world, particularly during middle infancy (Corbetta et al., 2000; Iverson & Thelen, 1999). Children who do not experience expected amounts and types of physical interactions can show delays in play skills even in early infancy. Late preterm infants showed less active exploration such as mouthing of objects than full-term infants between 5 and 7 months (Soares et al., 2012).

Normative play assessments rely on typical developmental milestones that correspond to specific play behaviours, such as symbolic feeding of dolls, which typically coincides with the development of spoken language in typically developing children, or stacking of blocks, which coincides with cognitive gains in spatial relations and combination. However, for children with physical impairments such milestones may not be appropriately representative of the underlying constructs estimated by the play behaviour. Children who cannot control their hands would not be able to pass 75% of the items on the Mental scale of the Bayley Scales of Infant Development between 9 and 24 months (Cress, 2002), and alternative low-motor versions of developmental or cognitive assessments such as the Bayley Scales are needed to provide a more representative characterization of developmental skills in children with physical impairments (Ruiter et al., 2010).

The accurate representation of underlying skills using play assessment is affected by communication as well as motor and social abilities in children with physical impairment. Motor ability in children with cerebral palsy at 24 months was associated with later social functioning on the Pediatric Evaluation of Disability Inventory (PEDI) at 5 years, but this effect was mediated by early symbolic communication, speech, and play skills as measured by the CSBS-DP assessment (Lipscombe et al., 2016). The PEDI captures the impact of language skills on social interaction and play in 4-year-old children with cerebral palsy, but does not effectively reflect the impact of speech intelligibility on social function in children with cerebral palsy who produce limited speech or speech that is difficult to understand (McFadd & Hustad, 2013). Assessment of play as an estimate of cognition is closely associated with motor scores of children and not necessarily a typical representation of children's cognitive potential for children with physical and/or neurological impairments (Ross & Cress, 2006). Receptive language assessment provides a less physically biased source of information about children's cognitive potential than object-based play for children with physical impairments (DeVeney et al., 2011).

Adapted materials and compensatory strategies are used to support the development and demonstration of play skills in children with physical impairments. Adaptations can be as simple as modifying the grip of the spoon in a doll feeding set to improve physical control or providing a Velcro glove as a strategy to lift objects for children who are unable to grasp toys independently (Beukelman & Mirenda, 2013). Simple movements of any muscle in the body can be used to operate switches that control toys, music, environmental controls such as lights, or communicative messages related to play actions. More elaborate dedicated or computer-based devices can provide integrated control of multiple play actions and messages, sometimes organized around particular play schemes. Picture symbols or topic boards can represent play sequences or messages relevant for different play schemes or topics and can serve as reminders of possible play actions as well as referents for children and their partners to communicate during play interactions. Partner support such as holding up play choices for children to select with gaze or physical behaviours, or demonstrating play actions and messages using accessible strategies for children with physical impairments, can help to compensate for physical limitations faced by children and allow demonstration of effective cognitive, communicative, and social interaction skills in play. For instance, children with developmental delays dramatically increased their appropriate participation in preschool play after intervention using adapted toys customized to their treatment goals and developmental skills (Hsieh, 2008).

Coordination of Play Actions. Children who have impaired voluntary control of hand/arm movements also tend to have poor awareness of the position and motion of their body parts during play. Precise control of play actions such as stacking blocks requires not only range of motion and the ability to grasp and release objects but also dynamic judgment of the position of one's own hand in relationship to the target and ability to adjust that motion in response to sensorimotor feedback throughout the play event. Poor trunk control or independent mobility may restrict potential play positions or locations more than expected for a child's chronological or developmental age. Limitations in coordinating vision with play movements or preservation of primitive reflexes that interfere with intentional movement patterns may cause inconsistent skills at controlling a child's own play actions or imitating play actions of others. Optimal positioning to support the child's own gaze and play actions may not equally support the child's ability to shift attention to play partners and their actions. Children with physical impairments may be relatively more impaired at some aspects of coordinated play actions than others, but limitations in one aspect of a play action tend to have cascading effects on other aspects of play that can be adjusted to compensate for those limitations.

Even simple play actions may be affected by children's poor kinaesthetic sense of their own body movements. Children with a poor sense of body awareness and an excess of uncontrolled movement had difficulty producing actions to express preference that were interpretable by listeners, and benefitted from computer-based recognition of movement patterns and eye gaze to disambiguate their preference behaviours in play (Lesperance et al., 2011). Children with poor kinaesthetic and proprioceptive feedback may have limited awareness of the relationship between their body movements and play actions and have difficulty developing a clear sense of simple relationships such as cause and effect. For instance, a child with cerebral palsy who has involuntary movement of multiple body parts and production of sounds may find it hard to distinguish which of those body movements has caused a play result or which behaviour is the cause of a desired result in a play partner. Increasing children's awareness and control of body movements can have an effect on communication or social elements during play as well. Enhancing motor skills using structured play tasks in children with cerebral palsy also increased the use of intentional communication acts related to those tasks (Jones et al., 1999).

Coordinating gaze with play actions and partners is a natural progression of skill that may be more complex for children with physical impairments, particularly those with complex communication needs. Typically developing children tend to alternate three-point gaze shifts back and forth between a toy and play partner as they are developing symbolic communication and play skills, demonstrating anticipation and association of partner reactions to play events (Wetherby & Prizant, 2003). Children with physical impairments may have difficulty returning their gaze to the original point of origin for a three-point gaze shift (e.g., person–object–person) and instead rely on two-point gaze shifts (e.g., person–object), with limitations on conceptualizing or checking the relationship between partner and play actions because of poor head/trunk control (Arens et al., 2005). Children with cerebral palsy tended to show a wider variety of play strategies if they had effective hand control with better coordinated gaze and attention behaviours (Olswang & Pinder, 1995). Children with complex communication needs who rely on a visual picture symbol or device to communicate during play need to coordinate three separate gaze targets during play (i.e., the play object, partner, and symbol/device) using symbol-infused joint engagement (Adamson et al., 2010), which is a more complex interaction cognitively as well as physically than is required of typically developing children in similar play contexts.

Active Engagement in Play Interactions. Developmental play progressions tend to move from solitary or parallel play to coordinated play events that require active engagement from the child in the play interaction with partners. Some aspects of play engagement may involve watching partner actions with toys, such as infants who learned means–end skills by observing partner play behaviours (Provasi et al., 2001). By the early preschool years, children with typical development were able to problem-solve with tools during goal-directed play more effectively by watching others than by individual exploration manually with those tools (Gardiner et al., 2012). It is expected that typically developing children actively seek out play events, attend to partner behaviours, and generalize skills acquired in one setting to other play interactions.

Children with physical impairments may require more trials of a play activity to learn a cognitive or motor skill than expected in typical development and have more difficulty generalizing newly acquired skills across play contexts, particularly if generalized play contexts require fine-grained adjustment of child play actions in the new context (Magalhaes et al., 2011; Shikako-Thomas et al., 2008). However, if children require physical or procedural support from partners to manage play interactions, they may actually experience fewer play events than in typical development, without the advantage of independent trial-and-error play practice separate from partner-scaffolded play (Cairney et al., 2005; Missiuna & Pollock, 1991). Poor motor control may result in a higher frequency of unsuccessful play actions than in typical development, and fewer successful play actions in physical or social play compared with typically developing peers (Smyth & Anderson, 2000). The high motoric cost of controlling a play action may not be sufficiently offset by the benefit of the play result except in highly motivating circumstances, and children may limit active engagement in play in moderately motivating contexts. This cost/benefit imbalance is a potential contributor to the passive interaction strategies frequently demonstrated by children with physical and neurological impairments (Cress, 2002). For instance, children with Down syndrome, who typically show fine-motor and cognitive impairments, were more likely to show passive behaviour in unstructured play than developmental age-matched peers (Linn et al., 2000).

Typically developing children can demonstrate active engagement in play outside their immediate surroundings as they develop independent mobility through crawling or walking. The onset of locomotion accompanies a wide variety of advancements in children's perceptual, cognitive, social, and emotional development (Campos et al., 2000). The transition to walking is associated with new forms of object play and cognitive or social uses of those objects in typically developing infants around the first year (Karasik et al., 2011; Kretch et al., 2014). Without independent control of the environment, children with physical impairments may have poor active engagement in play and a limited benefit pay-off for initiating play actions given the high cost of the motor actions involved. This potential play and engagement limitation increases the priority for establishing some form of independent mobility for children with physical impairments, even if children will have limited crawling or walking skills. Access to mobility such as wheelchairs is associated with a similar cognitive and play transition at older ages (Tieman et al., 2004).

Mastery Motivation to Accomplish Play Goals. A potential source of overcoming passive play strategies can be through children's mastery motivation. Mastery motivation is the tendency of a person to persist at attempting challenging object- or social-based tasks until success is achieved (Hauser-Cram, 1996). Mastery motivation is a construct presumed to influence children in infancy that expands with experience and continues to affect later learning patterns. Persistence at solving play tasks during infancy predicts toddler cognitive development at 14 months (Banerjee & Tamis-LeMonda, 2007).

Children with physical impairments have been reported to show poor mastery motivation in oriented play such as completing puzzles, as measured by object-based variables such as task persistence (e.g., Hauser-Cram, 1996). However, persistence is an aspect of mastery motivation that was directly correlated with motor skills for children with physical impairments and therefore is restricted by the child's motor limitations (Smidt & Cress, 2004). Social-based aspects of mastery motivation were scored and social play events included in behaviour samples to more completely represent mastery motivation in children with physical impairment. With active partner involvement inherent in social play, the child's limited physical movements can be matched to appropriate types and difficulty of tasks for their abilities. Maternal involvement in interaction and ability to match the task difficulty to their children with cerebral palsy contributed to children's ability to perform and spontaneously master play tasks, in similar ways to children without disabilities (Blasco et al., 1990). All types of object-oriented mastery motivation skills in play were directly influenced by extent of motor impairment in children with developmental and/or physical impairments, but only one social-oriented aspect of mastery in play was affected by motor impairment (Medeiros et al., 2016)

Interaction Strategies for Children with Physical Impairments

Because play involves social interaction with others, play skills in children with physical impairments are not dependent only on individual characteristics of the children themselves. Instead, play is a cooperative event between children and their partners, and the qualities and success of play interactions depend on partner engagement and support as well as child skills. Two primary types of interactants that influence the play of children with physical impairments are parents and peers.

Parent–Child Interactions. Beginning in infancy, parents support child behaviours to play a role in interactions starting with very early involuntary or reflexive behaviours. Even vegetative sounds can be a child turn within play and communicative interaction if parents respond to these behaviours as if they are meaningful. Parent responsivity to early intentional infant behaviours promotes child awareness of the effect of his or her behaviours on the environment and supports the development of more complex intentional behaviours and communication than the infant would demonstrate independently (Yoder & Warren, 2001). Infant play at 12 months was more mature with parent scaffolding of joint attention than during functional play alone (Bigelow et al., 2004). However, this effect may not be seen in children younger than 9 months who do not show differential effects on object processing in conditions of joint attention (Cleveland et al., 2007).

Early prompted and supported experience in infancy has implications for continued development of play and interaction later in life. Infants trained in active reaching at 3 months showed better object exploration and attention focusing skills at 15 months than infants who were not trained (Libertus et al., 2015). Parent labelling and responses to infant initiations with toys were related to later language skills at 14 and 17 months (Newland et al., 2001). Age of single action symbolic play correlates with later symbolic and vocal skills such as frequency of babble, emergence of speech, and multi-object symbolic play (Orr & Geva, 2015). There are bidirectional influences of parent and child characteristics over time that influence the effectiveness of play interactions; infants at 6 months with parents who later had elevated stress showed lower mastery motivation in play than those with less stressed parents, and infants with lower persistence and play competence at 6 months had parents with higher stress at 6 months than infants with better early persistence (Sparks et al., 2012).

Interactions between parent input and play achievements can vary for children with disabilities, including differences in the extent to which parents lower play expectations for children with physical or fine motor impairments. Mothers used fewer strategies for eliciting higher-level play from their children with Down syndrome than expected for parents of premature infants that were mental-age and motor-age matched, related to differences in infant attentional capacity (Landry & Chapieski, 1989). While some research has found lower parent responsiveness or higher parental directiveness in play for children with developmental and/or physical impairments (e.g., Hanzlik, 1990), if parents and children select their own familiar social or toy play strategies there was no higher directiveness in parents of children with physical impairments than expected for typically developing peers (Cress et al., 2008). Interventions to enhance parental responsiveness only affected child play and interaction outcomes if parents were not already demonstrating responsive communication patterns, for children with developmental disabilities (Yoder & Warren, 1998). For parents already responding contingently to child play behaviours, further adjustments in parent response behaviours were not needed to enhance interaction effectiveness.

Children with physical impairments may show subtle or unusual movements not reinforced proportionally in parent social play compared with children with typical development. Communicative behaviours of children with physical impairments were more difficult for parents to reliably observe in play than typically developing children (Yoder, 1987). Although parents of typically developing children tend to focus on conventional hand–arm and vocal behaviours in infancy, parents of children with physical impairments responded contingently more often to non-vocal adult-directed behaviours than vocal adult-directed behaviours (Cress et al., 2013). Early social play routines such as peekaboo and pattycake rely on physical movements and timed reciprocity between parent and child speech in typical development that may be disrupted in the development of children with physical impairments. Alternative assessment and partner training strategies are needed to identify potentially meaningful acts in play by children with developmental and physical disabilities to facilitate responsiveness to these atypical behaviours (e.g., Sigafoos et al., 2000).

Expressive language output about play becomes increasingly important for children once they pass infancy, for children with and without disabilities. For children with complex communication needs, expressive language output is managed by including non-spoken strategies to augment spoken strategies for conveying messages (called augmentative and alternative communication, AAC). Access to communication strategies such as sign or voice output devices can effectively enhance parent–child play without interfering with natural parent interaction strategies for children with physical impairments. When a simple voice output device was added to the interaction to request 'more' of a social or toy play interaction, parents of children with complex communication needs showed as much responsivity to their children as during play interactions without the device (Medeiros & Cress, 2016). There is evidence that access to AAC strategies facilitates rather than interferes with spoken language and play in children with physical impairments, by reducing the cognitive and procedural load of the interaction for the child (Baumann Leech & Cress, 2011; Millar et al., 2006).

Peer Interactions. Although parents of children with physical impairments effectively adjust their interaction patterns to support play in their children, the same type of adjustments are not expected in play with typically developing peers. In a large population study, at least 25% of children with cerebral palsy had significant functional limitations in social interactions, particularly involving peer problems (Parkes et al., 2008). School-aged children with physical disabilities and complex communication needs had fewer communication opportunities with acquaintances and friends than typically developing peers (Raghavendra et al., 2012). Even as early as 18 months, over 70% of children with cerebral palsy were more than one standard deviation poorer than the mean on measures of social development, and a significant relationship between motor ability and social development was maintained at other assessment periods through preschool (Whittingham et al., 2010). However, the impact of motor impairment on social play skills with peers does not equally affect all children with disabilities; no significant relationship between degree of motor impairment and social skills was seen in children with autism once cognitive level was controlled for (Zingerevich et al., 2009). Significant predictors of play in elementary and middle school between children with physical disabilities and their peers were children's physical ability, preference for formal versus informal activities, and family involvement in social and recreational activities (King et al., 2006).

Some of the limitations in peer play for children with physical impairments involve the speed and flexibility of play and communicative behaviours produced. If peers are quicker at producing and adapting play behaviours, then children with physical impairments may take a relatively passive role during interaction. Children with motor coordination impairments spent more time alone or onlooking in play than typically developing peers in elementary school and were less likely to engage in social physical play than peers without disabilities (Smyth & Anderson, 2000). Children with physical impairments who used electronic aided communication systems initiated less and responded more in play interactions with peers in social interaction than non-disabled peers (Clarke & Kirton, 2003). Yet children with effective access to augmented communication systems were better able to manage peer play situations than those without effective communication skills. Children with complex physical and communication needs who relied on aided communication devices to communicate successfully instructed peer partners to build a structure in social play that the partners could not see, although the instructions took longer to convey and had fewer details than those of children with physical impairments who used speech to communicate (Batorowicz et al., 2016). Children who could express their intents through gestural, spoken, or other augmented communication strategies were better able to overcome the social limitations of their motor impairment than children with fewer communication skills.

Play Interventions for Children with Physical Impairments

Play interactions serve as opportunities to apply educational and therapeutic interventions for children with physical impairments, as naturally occurring contexts in which communication, cognitive, physical, and/or social skills are applied for practical purposes in daily activities. Physical, social, communication, and/or cognitive factors affecting play tasks and outcomes account for successful play interventions for children with physical impairments. For instance, providing physical therapy to improve independent sitting skills significantly improved play skills of children with cerebral palsy, particularly children 3–6 years old with relatively severe physical impairments (Ryalls et al., 2016). Both coaching of parent–child interactions and direct neurodevelopmental treatment of children improved playfulness ratings of children with cerebral palsy with developmental ages 3–18 months (Okimoto et al., 2000). Parenting interventions improved the quality and responsivity of interaction during parent–child play for infants who were preterm with physical and/or developmental delays (Evans et al., 2014). Infant physical stimulation combined with home-based parent play interaction coaching resulted in clearer infant play cues and significantly higher scores on infant developmental measures for preterm infants than in families receiving only infant care and safety instruction (White-Traut et al., 2013).

Increasing the amount of physical and procedural support can improve functional and symbolic play outcomes for children with physical impairments, although these partner-supported play actions cannot be scored on formal assessments as independent child skills. Partner management and positioning of play objects elicited effective coordinated gaze shifting in pre-symbolic children with physical impairments who produced few two- and three-point gaze shifts spontaneously (Cress et al., 2007). For older children, multi-step symbolic play is not independently demonstrable in children with physical impairments who cannot control multiple actions or objects. Instead, symbolic play actions are often co-constructed with partners. For instance, instead of independently stirring, scooping, and feeding pretend food to a doll, a child with physical impairments might need a partner to hold up play items to choose the spoon, then ask about possible play locations where the spoon might go and actions to take with the spoon, as a multi-step partner-assisted alternative to independent doll feeding. These play choices can be presented through a variety of object choices, gestures, symbol selections, voice output, words, and signs. Children showed more effective improvement in play when using multiple communication modalities and play schemes than with a single communication modality, such as signs alone (Taylor & Iacono, 2003).

Interventions that focus on naturally occurring daily living and play routines can expand the effectiveness of play interventions beyond the scope of professionals who work with a child only for a limited number of hours. Parents trained in an interactive model during daily play and interactive routines became less directive and more responsive to their children with developmental delays throughout interactions than parents who did not receive those interventions (Tannock et al., 1992). Parents trained to respond to their children with developmental delays within one play context spontaneously generalized strategies to untrained caregiving and play routines (Woods et al., 2004). During play with children who have cerebral palsy, parents and non-disabled siblings were equally responsive to children's interactive behaviours, even for children who were not yet symbolic communicators (Singh et al., 2015).

Active engagement of children with physical impairments in play and communication activities is important for the improvement of appropriate play and social engagement activities. In play with typically developing peers, school-aged children with physical impairments were active contributors to initiating non-serious interaction elements such as shared activity and laughter (Clarke & Wilkinson, 2009). Children with physical impairments and complex communication needs who received communication intervention addressing their production of communicative messages also increased developmentally appropriate motor movements more than children who received interventions focused on understanding others' messages and behaviours (Whitmore et al., 2014). School-aged children with physical and communication impairments with better ability to be independently understood by others participated more often in recreational and social play activities than younger or less communicatively independent children (Clarke et al., 2012). A combination of communication, social, and physical interventions would therefore have a greater likelihood of impact on family and peer interactions for children with physical impairments than any of those interventions in isolation.

Conclusions: Clinical and Educational Implications

Children with physical impairments are at risk for being less active and communicative during family and peer interactions because of the combination of physical, social, communicative, and environmental limitations they experience. However, this risk can be mitigated by effective assessment of communication skills for children as well as skills of their communication partners, and intervention to improve the effectiveness of children's skills within the context of their play environments. Intervention strategies to increase children's independent control of communication, play objects, coordination of play actions, and mastery motivation, as well as provision of frequent, reciprocal and naturally occurring interactive opportunities with families and peers, can ameliorate the limiting effects of a physical disability on effective play skill development.

References

Adamson, L. B., Romski, M. A., Bakeman, R., & Sevcik, R. A. (2010). Augmented language intervention and the emergence of symbol-infused joint engagement. *Journal of Speech, Language, and Hearing Research, 53*, 1769–1773.

Arens, K., Cress, C. J., & Marvin, C. A. (2005). Gaze-shift patterns of young children with developmental disabilities who are at risk for being nonspeaking. *Education and Training in Developmental Disabilities, 40*, 158–170.

Banerjee, P. N., & Tamis-LeMonda, C. S. (2007). Infant's persistence and mothers' teaching as predictors of toddlers' cognitive development. *Infant Behavior and Development, 30*, 479–491.

Batorowicz, B., Stadskleiv, K., von Tetzchner, S., & Missiuna, C. (2016). Children who use communication aids instructing peer and adult partners during play-based activity. *Augmentative and Alternative Communication*, *32*, 105–119.

Baumann Leech, E. R., & Cress, C. J. (2011). Indirect facilitation of speech in a late talking child by prompted production of picture symbols or signs. *Augmentative and Alternative Communication*, *27*, 40–52.

Bayley, N. (2006). *Bayley scales of infant and toddler development* (3rd edn.). San Antonio, TX: Pearson.

Belsky, J., & Most, R. K. (1981). From exploration to play: A cross-sectional study of infant free play behavior. *Developmental Psychology*, *17*, 630–639.

Beukelman, D., & Mirenda, P. (2013). *Augmentative and alternative communication for children and adults* (4th edn.). Baltimore, MD: Brookes.

Bigelow, A. E., MacLean, K., & Proctor, J. (2004). The role of joint attention in the development of infants' play with objects. *Developmental Science*, *7*(5), 518–526.

Blasco, P. M., Hrncir, E. J., & Blasco, P. A. (1990). The contribution of maternal involvement to mastery performance in infants with cerebral palsy. *Journal of Early Intervention*, *14*, 161–174.

Cairney, J., Hay, J. A., Faught, B. E., Wade, T. J., Corna, L., & Flouris, A. (2005). Developmental coordination disorder, generalized self-efficacy toward physical activity, and participation in organized and free play activities. *Journal of Pediatrics*, *147*, 515–520.

Campos, J. J., Anderson, D. I., Barbu-Roth, M. A., Hubbard, E. M., Hertenstein, M. J., & Witherington, D. (2000). Travel broadens the mind. *Infancy*, *1*, 149–219.

Clarke, M., & Kirton, A. (2003). Patterns of interaction between children with physical disabilities using augmentative and alternative communication systems and their peers. *Child Language Teaching and Therapy*, 19, 135–151.

Clarke, M., Newton, C., Petrides, K., Griffiths, T., Lysley, A., & Price, K. (2012). An examination of relations between participation, communication and age in children with complex communication needs. *Augmentative and Alternative Communication*, *28*, 44–51.

Clarke, M., & Wilkinson, R. (2009). The collaborative construction of non-serious episodes of interaction by non-speaking children with cerebral palsy and their peers. *Clinical Linguistics and Phonetics*, *23*, 583–597.

Cleveland, A., Schug, M., & Striano, T. (2007). Joint attention and object learning in 5- and 7-month-old infants. *Infant and Child Development*, *16*, 95–306.

Corbetta, D., Thelen, E., & Johnson, K. (2000). Motor constraints on the development of perception–action matching in infant reaching. *Infant Behavior and Development*, *23*, 351–374.

Cress, C. J. (2002). Expanding children's early augmented behaviors to support symbolic development. In J. Reichle, D. R. Beukelman, & J. C. Light (Eds.), *Exemplary practices for beginning communicators: Implications for AAC* (pp. 219–272). Baltimore, MD: Brookes.

Cress, C. J., Arens, K. B., & Zajicek, A. K. (2007). Comparison of engagement patterns of young children with developmental disabilities between structured and free play. *Education and Training in Developmental Disabilities*, *42*, 152–164.

Cress, C. J., Grabast, J., & Jerke, K. B. (2013). Contingent interactions between parents and young children with severe expressive communication impairments. *Communication Disorders Quarterly, 34*, 81–96.

Cress, C. J., Jara, A., & Bone, S. (2016). A communication 'tools' model for AAC intervention: Case illustrations for two early communicators. *Perspectives in ASHA SIGs, 1*(12), 139–143.

Cress, C. J., Moskal, L., & Hoffmann, A. (2008). Parent directiveness in free play with young children with physical impairments. *Communication Disorders Quarterly, 29*, 99–108.

Cress, C. J., Shapley, K. L., Linke, M., Clark, J., Elliott, J., Bartels, K., Aaron, E. (2000, August). Characteristics of intentional communication in young children with physical impairments. Presentation at the ISAAC International Conference on AAC, Washington, DC.

DeVeney, S. L., Hoffman, L., & Cress, C. J. (2011). Communication-based assessment of developmental age for children with developmental disabilities. *Journal of Speech-Language-Hearing Research, 55*, 695–709.

Evans, T., Whittingham, K., Sanders, M., Colditz, P., & Boyd, R. N. (2014). Are parenting interventions effective in improving the relationship between mothers and their preterm infants? *Infant Behavior and Development, 37*, 131–154.

Gardiner, A. K., Bjorklund, D. F., Greif, M. L., & Gray, S. K. (2012). Choosing and using tools: Prior experience and task difficulty influence preschoolers' tool-use strategies. *Cognitive Development, 27*, 240–254.

Gowen, J. W., Johnson-Martin, N., Goldman, B. D., & Hussey, B. (1992). Object play and exploration in children with and without disabilities: A longitudinal study. *American Journal on Mental Retardation, 97*, 21–38.

Haley, S. M., Coster, W. J., Ludlow, L. H., Haltiwanger, J. T., & Andrellos, P. J. (1992). *Pediatric evaluation of disability inventory*. San Antonio, TX: Pearson.

Hanzlik, J. R. (1990). Nonverbal interaction patterns of mothers and their infants with cerebral palsy. *Education and Training in Mental Retardation, 25*, 333–343.

Hauser-Cram, P. (1996). Mastery motivation in toddlers with developmental disabilities. *Child Development, 67*, 236–248.

Hsieh, H.-C. (2008). Effects of ordinary and adaptive toys on pre-school children with developmental disabilities. *Research in Developmental Disabilities, 29*, 459–466.

Iverson, J. M., & Thelen, E. (1999). Hand, mouth, and brain: The dynamic emergence of speech and gesture. *Journal of Consciousness Studies, 6*, 19–40.

Jones, H. A., Horn, E. M., & Warren, S. F. (1999). The effects of motor skill acquisition on the development of intentional communication. *Journal of Early Intervention, 22*, 25–37.

Karasik, L. B., Tamis-LeMonda, C. S., & Adolph, K. E. (2011). Transition from crawling to walking and infants' actions with objects and people. *Child Development, 82*, 1199–1209.

Kelly-Vance, L., & Ryalls, B. O. (2014). Best practices in play assessment and intervention. In P. Harrison & A. Thomas (Eds.), *Best practices in school psychology VI*. Bethesda, MD: National Association of School Psychologists.

King, G., Law, M., Hanna, S., King, S., Hurley, P., Rosenbaum, P., Kertoy, M., & Petrenchik, T. (2006). Predictors of the leisure and recreation participation of children with physical disabilities: A structural equation modeling analysis. *Children's Health Care*, *35*, 209–234.

Kretch, K. S., Franchak, J. M., & Adolph, K. E. (2014). Crawling and walking infants see the world differently. *Child Development*, *85*, 1503–1518.

Landry, S. H., & Chapieski, M. L. (1989). Joint attention and infant toy exploration: Effects of Down syndrome and prematurity. *Child Development*, *60*, 103–118.

Law, M., King, G., King, S., Kertoy, M., Hurley, P., Rosenbaum, P., Young, N., & Hanna, S. (2006). Patterns of participation in recreational and leisure activities among children with complex physical disabilities. *Developmental Medicine & Child Neurology*, *48*, 337–342.

Lesperance, A., Blain, S., & Chau, T. (2011). An integrated approach to detecting communicative intent amid hyperkinetic movement in children. *Augmentative and Alternative Communication*, *27*, 150–162.

Libertus, K., Joh, A. S., & Needham, A. W. (2015). Motor training at 3 months affects object exploration 12 months later. *Developmental Science*, *19*, 1058–1066.

Linder, T. W. (1993). *Transdisciplinary play-based assessment: A functional approach to working with young children* (2nd edn.). Baltimore, MD: Brookes.

Linn, M. I., Goodman, J. F., & Lender, W. L. (2000). Played out? Passive behavior by children with Down syndrome during unstructured play. *Journal of Early Intervention*, *23*, 264–278.

Lipscombe, B., Boyd, R. N., Coleman, A., Fahey, M., Rawicki, B., & Whittingham, K. (2016). Does early communication mediate the relationship between motor ability and social function in children with cerebral palsy? *Research in Developmental Disabilities*, *53–54*, 279–286.

Lord, C., Rutter, M., DiLavore, P. C., Risi, S., Gotham, K., & Bishop, S. L. (2012). *Autism Diagnostic Observation Schedule* (2nd edn.) Manual (Part I): Modules 1–4. Torrance, CA: Western Psychological Services.

Magalhaes, L. C., Cardoso, A. A., & Missiuna, C. (2011). Activities and participation in children with developmental coordination disorder: A systematic review. *Research in Developmental Disabilities*, *32*, 1309–1316.

McCune-Nicolich, L. (1981). Toward symbolic functioning: Structure of early pretend games and potential parallels with language. *Child Development*, *52*, 785–797.

McFadd, E., & Hustad, K. C. (2013). Assessment of social function in four-year-old children with cerebral palsy. *Developmental Neurorehabilitation*, *16*, 102–112.

Medeiros, K. F., & Cress, C. J. (2016). Differences in caregiver responsive and directive behavior during free play with and without aided AAC. *Augmentative and Alternative Communication*, *32*, 151–161.

Medeiros, K. F., Cress, C. J., & Lambert, M. C. (2016). Mastery motivation in children with developmental disabilities at risk for being nonspeaking: Longitudinal data analysis. *Augmentative and Alternative Communication*, *32*, 208–218.

Millar, D. C., Light, J. C., & Schlosser, R. W. (2006). The impact of augmentative and alternative communication intervention on the speech production of individuals with developmental disabilities: A research review. *Journal of Speech, Language, and Hearing Research*, *49*, 248–264.

Missiuna, C., & Pollock, N. (1991). Play deprivation in children with physical disabilities: The role of the occupational therapist in preventing secondary disability. *American Journal of Occupational Therapy, 45*, 882–888.

Mullen, E. M. (1995). *Mullen scales of early learning.* Circle Pines, MN: American Guidance Service.

Newland, L. A., Roggman, L. A., & Boyce, L. K. (2001). The development of social toy play and language in infancy. *Infant Behavior and Development, 24*, 1–25.

Okimoto, A. M., Bundy, A., & Hanzlik, J. (2000). Playfulness in children with and without disability: Measurement and intervention. *American Journal of Occupational Therapy, 54*, 73–82.

Olswang, L. B., & Pinder, G. L. (1995). Preverbal functional communication and the role of object play in children with cerebral palsy. *Infant-Toddler Intervention, 5*, 277–300.

Orr, E., & Geva, R. (2015). Symbolic play and language development. *Infant Behavior and Development, 38*, 147–161.

Parkes, J., White-Koning, M., Dickinson, H. O., Thyen, U., Arnaud, C., Beckung, E., Fauconnier, J., Marcelli, M., McManus, V., Michelsen, S. I., Parkinson, K., & Colver, A. (2008). Psychological problems in children with cerebral palsy: A cross-sectional European study. *Journal of Child Psychology and Psychiatry, and Allied Disciplines, 49*, 405–413.

Provasi, J., Dubon, C. D., & Bloch, H. (2001). Do 9- and 12-month-old infants learn means-end relations by observing? *Infant Behavior and Development, 24*, 195–213.

Raghavendra, P., Olsson, C., Sampson, J., McInerney, R., & Connell, T. (2012). School participation and social networks of children with complex communication needs, physical disabilities, and typically developing peers. *Augmentative and Alternative Communication, 28*, 33–43.

Ross, B., & Cress, C. J. (2006). Comparison of standardized assessments for cognitive and receptive communication skills in young children with complex communication needs. *Augmentative and Alternative Communication, 22*, 100–111.

Ruiter, S. A. J., Nakken, H., van der Meulen, B. F., & Lunenborg, C. B. (2010). Low motor assessment: A comparative pilot study with young children with and without motor impairment. *Journal of Developmental and Physical Disabilities, 22*, 33–46.

Ryalls, B. O., Harbourne, R., Kelly-Vance, L., Wickstrom, J., Stergiou, N., & Kyvelidou, A. (2016). A perceptual motor intervention improves play behavior in children with moderate to severe cerebral palsy. *Frontiers in Psychology, 7*, 643.

Shikako-Thomas, K., Majnemer, A., Law, M., & Lach, L. (2008). Determinants of participation in leisure activities in children and youth with cerebral palsy: Systematic review. *Journal of Physical and Occupational Therapy in Pediatrics, 28*, 155–169.

Sigafoos, J., Woodyatt, G., Keen, D., Tait, K., Tucker, M., Roberts-Pennell, D., & Pittendreigh, N. (2000). Identifying potential communicative acts in children with developmental and physical disabilities. *Communication Disorders Quarterly, 21*, 77–86.

Singh, S. J., Iacono, T., & Gray, K. M. (2015). Interactions of pre-symbolic children with developmental disabilities with their mothers and siblings. *International Journal of Language and Communication Disorders*, *50*, 202–214.

Smidt, M. L., & Cress, C. T. (2004). Mastery behaviors during social and object play in toddlers with physical impairments. *Education and Training in Developmental Disabilities*, *39*, 141–152.

Smyth, M. M., & Anderson, H. (2000). Coping with clumsiness in the school playground: Social and physical play in children with coordination impairments. *British Journal of Developmental Psychology*, *8*, 389–413.

Soares, D. A., von Hofsten, C., & Tudella, E. (2012). Development of exploratory behavior in late preterm infants. *Infant Behavior and Development*, *35*, 912–915.

Sparks, T. A., Hunter, S. K., Backman, T. L., Morgan, G. A., & Ross, R. G. (2012). Maternal parenting stress and mothers' reports of their infants' mastery motivation. *Infant Behavior and Development*, *35*, 167–173.

Sparrow, S. S., Cicchetti, D. V., & Saulnier, C. A. (2016). *Vineland Adaptive Behavior Scales* (3rd edn.). San Antonio, TX: Pearson.

Tannock, R., Girolametto, L., & Siegel, L. S. (1992). Language intervention in children who have developmental delays: Effects of an interactive approach. *American Journal on Mental Retardation*, *97*, 145–160.

Taylor, R., & Iacono, T. (2003). AAC and scripting activities to facilitate communication and play. *Advances in Speech-Language Pathology*, *5*, 79–93.

Tieman, B., Palisano, R. J., Gracely, E. J., Rosenbaum, P. L., Chiarello, L. A., & O'Neil, M. (2004). Changes in mobility of children with cerebral palsy over time and across environmental settings. *Physical and Occupational Therapy in Pediatrics*, *24*, 109–128.

Wetherby, A. M., & Prizant, B. M. (2003). *Communication and symbolic behavior scales–Developmental profile*. Baltimore, MD: Brookes.

White-Traut, R., Norr, K. F., Fabiyi, C., Rankin, K. M., Li, A., & Liu, L. (2013). Mother–infant interaction improves with a developmental intervention for mother–preterm infant dyads. *Infant Behavior and Development*, *36*, 694–706.

Whitmore, A. S., Romski, M. A., & Sevcik, R. A. (2014). Early augmentative language intervention for children with developmental delays: Potential secondary motor outcomes. *Augmentative and Alternative Communication*, *30*, 200–212.

Whittingham, K., Fahey, M., Rawicki, B., & Boyd, R. (2010). The relationship between motor abilities and early social development in a preschool cohort of children with cerebral palsy. *Research in Developmental Disabilities*, *31*, 1346–1351.

Woods, J., Kashinath, S., & Goldstein, H. (2004). Effects of embedding caregiver-implemented teaching strategies in daily routines on children's communication outcomes. *Journal of Early Intervention*, *26*, 175–193.

Yoder, P. (1987). Relationship between degree of infant handicap and clarity of infant cues. *American Journal of Mental Deficiency*, *91*, 639–641.

Yoder, P. J., & Warren, S. F. (1998). Maternal responsivity predicts the prelinguistic communication intervention that facilitates generalized intentional communication. *Journal of Speech, Language and Hearing Research*, *41*, 1207–1219.

Yoder, P. J., & Warren, S. F. (2001). Intentional communication elicits language facilitating maternal responses in dyads with children who have developmental disabilities. *American Journal on Mental Retardation, 106,* 327–335.

Zingerevich, C., Greiss-Hess, L., Lemons-Chitwood, K., Harris, S. W., Hessl, D., Cook, K., & Hagerman, R. J. (2009). Motor abilities of children diagnosed with fragile X syndrome with and without autism. *Journal of Intellectual Disability Research, 53,* 11–18.

34 A Typology of Play in Medical Settings

Colleen Baish Cameron and Michael M. Patte

In the early part of the twentieth century innovative hospitals for children in North America began introducing play programs. Emma Plank, affectionately known as 'the play lady' and widely accepted as founding mother of the child life movement, instituted the first Child Life and Education program at Cleveland City Hospital in 1955. Her seminal text, *Working with Children in Hospitals* (1962), served as a critical roadmap for health care professionals in addressing the unique developmental needs of children in health care settings. Building on this momentum a group of child life professionals established the Association for the Well-Being of Hospitalized Children and Their Families in 1965. The organization was renamed in 1967 to the Association for the Care of Children in Hospitals and again in 1979 to the Association for the Care of Children's Health (ACCH). A Child Life Study Council was formed within the ACCH with the goal of creating a unique identity, professional practices, and policies, and in 1982 the Child Life Council (CLC) was officially established.

Today, some 400 children's hospitals throughout North America provide child life services to paediatric patients and their families (Child Life Council Directory, 2016). Child life specialists enhance the development and well-being of hospitalized children and their families through psychosocial approaches including normalization, preparation, and therapeutic activities while at the same time minimizing the anxiety and stress of hospitalization and other health-related experiences. Other common health care venues offering child life services include a variety of outpatient clinics, emergency departments, hospice and palliative care programs, camps for children experiencing chronic illness, rehabilitation centres, dental offices, and some funeral homes (Fein et al., 2012; Hicks, 2008). Child life programs like the ones in North America can also be found in the United Kingdom, Japan, Kuwait, the Philippines, South Africa, Serbia, New Zealand, and Australia.

Children explore and decipher the complex world in which they live through play. Play in its many forms enhances cognitive, creative, emotional, physical, and social development (Patte, 2015) and should play a prominent role in all child life programs. As play is a natural modality for children, child life specialists use it to transition children into the medical environment, to help children cope with various stressors, to assess development, to build rapport, to prepare for procedures, to achieve post-procedural mastery, and to ensure children thrive in the hospital setting. While many forms of play are used by child life specialists to assist children and their families to cope effectively with various medical procedures and hospital visits, the three most common types are normative play, medical play, and therapeutic play (Burns-Nader & Hernandez-Reif, 2016). Normative play includes typical activities that all children relish outside the medical setting. Medical play affords children the opportunity to explore basic equipment and supplies (thermometer, oxygen mask, syringe, nebulizer) used by doctors and nurses in common procedures. A third type of play employed by child life specialists that promotes emotional expression and enhances development, psychosocial well-being, and coping skills is therapeutic play.

This chapter explores the purpose and goals for integrating play in medical settings. While play's value in the development of healthy children is well established, the therapeutic power of play for children experiencing illness or disability proves to be even more important. Throughout the chapter we argue for play as a vital component in the care of hospitalized children experiencing a variety of conditions. When children are provided with adequate time and support for play in medical settings, they are able to lessen the impact of their illnesses and reconnect with universal language of childhood known as play.

History of Play Programming in Hospitals: The Emerging Profession of Child Life Specialists

Historically, paediatric health care settings have provided a landscape that requires time and space for play experiences for infants, children, and youth. Stressors associated with medical experiences for infants, children, youth, and families necessitate a continuous examination of the need for play and the benefits of play programming on the psychosocial well-being of paediatric populations. Hospitalization should not mean the interruption of childhood experiences for paediatric patients (Brooks, 1957), and play should be viewed as a humanizing aspect of health care environments for children (Thompson, 1988). The nature of the hospital experience, while therapeutic in the aim to treat and heal the patient, provides residential distress in the development and psychosocial well-being of the paediatric patient. Children in hospitals have been challenged not only with barriers to developmental progression but also with understanding the complex nature of medical care. Specialized planning for play activities that keep in mind the specific difficulties children face in hospitals is required (Plank, 1962). This hardship framework of illness, injury, and trauma includes diagnostic and invasive procedures, medical treatment and intervention, restricted mobility, institutional influences on daily routines, isolation, pain, loss, death, rapidly occurring contact with unfamiliar caregivers, and separation from caregivers and family members (Bowlby et al., 1952; Freud, 1952; Goldberger et al., 2009b; Plank et al., 1959).

In the late 1800s, it became clear that without considering developmental aspects of paediatric medical care, children would not have maximized health outcomes. Floyd Crandall (1897) wrote first about "hospitalism", a term that described the direct impact hospitalization would have on the development of the child, pointing out that children were not designed to quietly lay in a crib from morning to midnight. The hospitalized child would become withdrawn with an emotional tone of sadness and apprehension (Bowlby, 1952). Disruptions in physical, language, perceptual, and motor development influenced by isolation, lack of social contact, and family-based risk factors would result in developmental, physiological, and psychological decline (Brown, 2014; Crandall, 1897; Spitz, 1946).

Play opportunities while hospitalized were becoming vital to a child's emotional well-being, allowing the child to deal with the associated stressors while providing safeguards from fears and anxieties that otherwise became overwhelming (Haller et al., 1967; Jolly, 1968). In the late 1920s, early hospital play programs began to emerge that reflected the larger cultural view -of play and recreation in a child's life (Turner & Grissim, 2014). Advocacy met sceptical viewpoints that opposed play programming, citing fear that more work for hospital staff would ensue and ultimately be disruptive to institutional protocols and procedures, as well as a burden of space, need, and cost (Stone, 1963). By the 1960s, surveys of play programs showed that although there was an overall acceptance of play programming as a standard of care in paediatrics, services and approaches reflected a lack of cohesion across institutions (Grissim & Turner, 2014).

Play programming for children in hospitals allowed for less preoccupation with illness and procedures, providing more opportunity to be interested in play and socialization (Petrillo, 1968). The health care field began to recognize the benefits of developmentally supportive play practices in medical settings. Activity rooms and playrooms were designed to provide space and play materials, creating an inviting space for children to gather, experiment, and create (Tisza & Angoff, 1957). Play programs were being designed to develop a therapeutic community in the hospital, with play being a part of the health care plan (Stone, 1963). While observing children playing can provide valuable insight that can aid in the diagnostic and care plan process, the play area was also recognized as an essential space for educating parents about child development and behaviour (Azarnoff, 1970).

In an attempt to standardize play programming as a means to diminish the negative aspects of illness, injury, and hospitalization, scholar and advocate Emma Plank led the health care field to focus on key goals of programming that would nurture the well-being of the whole child. Plank, influenced by the teachings of Maria Montessori and Anna Freud, advocated for play programming in children's hospitals that would cultivate what was later to become the child life profession (Rubin, 1992). While play can be initiated by any health care team member, the child life profession was establishing itself as the leading discipline for play programming in health care environments. In the 1970s, the field was comprised of service directors with varying academic backgrounds, including child development, education, nursing, psychology, and recreational therapy. Play leaders not only began to meet the developmental needs of paediatric patients through play, but also used play to minimize distress associated with hospitalization.

Repeat observations of hospitalized children demonstrated signs of trauma and developmental adjustment issues, and structured play experiences directly related to the hospitalization were needed (Adams, 1976). While there was an emphasis on interdisciplinary training at the time, it became clear there was a need for a separate, circumscribed role for play professionals in the hospital setting. This was followed by academic and clinical training that focused on play as a developmentally appropriate practice in paediatric health care (Pond-Wojtasik & White, 2009). The term 'play lady' had long described the role of those who were trained in these domain, and would later become formalized in the professional title of 'child life specialist' or 'hospital play specialist'. Hospital play staff would have a command of normative child development and medical terminology, as well as training in play techniques that would address the psychosocial needs of children impacted by illness and hospitalization (Shapiro, 1963; Stone, 1963). The term 'play lady' was later rejected as it reflected societal gender bias that assumed men in nurturing occupations were anomalies (Rubin, 1992). In 1961, Johns Hopkins Medical Center changed the name of the program from Play Activities to Child Life, signifying the broader delivery of services beyond play activities (Wilson, 2014). Child life specialists continued to focus on normative daily experiences, where care goals included mirroring the types of play engagements and materials each individual child would experience at home (Jesse, 1991).

Today, the policy statement of the American Academy of Pediatrics on child life services identifies play as a therapeutic modality that can be adapted to meet the psychosocial and developmental needs of every paediatric age group and should be delivered as part of an integrated model of quality health care (Committee on Hospital Care & Child Life Council, 2006). The creation of play opportunities in medical environments that allow children to discover their emerging developmental abilities, construct meaning of their hospital world, and support their continued growth while hospitalized remains essential (Jesse, 1991; Marchant, 2016). According to Koller (2008), therapeutic play facilitated by child life specialists focuses on the promotion of continuing normalized development that emphasizes the process of play as a mechanism for mastering critical events such as hospitalization and developmental milestones. From meeting the developmental needs of infants in neonatal intensive care units (Brindle, 2006) to decreasing the fear and anxiety levels of paediatric emergency and trauma patients (Goymour et al., 2000), play in paediatric care environments has multiple aspects. Child life specialists continue to use medical play, normative play, and therapeutic play in their work with paediatric patients to support typical development and minimize anxiety associated with medical experiences (Burns-Nader & Hernandez-Reif, 2016). Adaptive play and sensory play have become integral as child life specialists continue to build an inclusive play model for children with and without disabilities, promoting socialization and supportive developmental therapies (Hicks & Davitt, 2009).

Current Play Practices in North American Health Care Settings

In 2013, the CLC set out to document the frequency and range of play policies, practices, and programs in medical settings throughout North America. Surveys were distributed to 464 child life program leaders with 181 responding, producing an average response rate of 39%. The project was funded through a grant from the Walt Disney Corporation titled Advancing the Field of Play for Hospitalized Children. The CLC believes that documenting the range of play programs and services is vital in advancing the crucial role of play in health care settings into the future (CLC, 2014).

Play Spaces

Survey results indicated that a variety of small- and medium-sized play spaces were available to hospitalized children and their families (CLC, 2014). For example, 100% of program directors reported having multiple playrooms with flexible operating hours spanning a variety of developmental stages up to and including adolescents. The majority of playrooms were staffed by child life specialists and volunteers. A smaller percentage were supervised by child life assistants and child life interns. However, some 40% of all playrooms were unstaffed. A much smaller group of programs (44%) provided outdoor play spaces when weather permitted. These areas included traditional playground structures and non-traditional loose parts for the children to explore. Nearly 50% of the outdoor play spaces were staffed.

The Role of the Child Life Specialist

The Association for Child Life Professionals (formerly known as the Child Life Council) reports that child life specialists assist infants, children, youth, and families cope with the uncertainty of illness, trauma, disability, bereavement, and loss. Through developmentally appropriate practice, evidence-based interventions including therapeutic play are at the core of the profession (Association of Child Life Professionals, 2017a, 2017b). By providing play experiences, emotional support to children and families, and psychological preparation for medical events and procedures, child life specialists seek to lessen potential negative impact of health care experiences (Thompson, 1989).

According to McCue (2009), it is critical to examine dynamics that highlight the important nature of the relationship that is developed between the play specialist and the child. The establishment of a *supportive* relationship includes provision of aid or assistance accompanied by interpersonal warmth, trust, positive affect, and respect. In contrast, the establishment of a *therapeutic* relationship indicates a goal of healing to occur as a result of the relationship. This can include the use of play as restoring a child to health, with a pointed goal of having a clear and measurable impact on the child. McCue (2009) also proposed that play support services provided by child life specialists have the potential to be therapeutic, providing opportunities for problem-solving (obstacles in development or psychosocial functioning) and healing. Establishing relationships with children through the process of play facilitates a sense of safety and comfort, allowing the relationship to minimize the child's vulnerability to the effects of trauma and enhance a positive sense of self (Gitlin-Weiner, 1998).

In addition to patient care, child life specialists serve as consultants for environmental design that meets the developmental, social, physical, and emotional needs of children and their families. Ensuring hospital facilities have well-designed areas and multiple play spaces that support the goals of play programming is essential to humanizing health care environments (Association for the Care of Children in Hospitals, 1980). In addition, it is important to know that child life specialists advocate for developmentally supportive care, including the provision of separate play spaces for adolescents, which calls for a specified developmental knowledge of play preferences for hospitalized teens that can often include gaming and socialization activities (Lenhart et al., 2008). Child life specialists also promote caregiver–child interactions through play so that parents can support their child through play experiences that encourage communication and connectedness (Harvey, 1976).

Play Programming

Various types of play were offered to hospitalized children in playrooms, procedure rooms, and the bedside, according to program director respondents. The types of play most frequently offered in hospital playrooms according to survey results included crafts (97%), constructive play and game play (96%), expressive arts (95%), child-centred play (92%), medical play (88%), sensory play (81%), dramatic play (77%), gross motor play (76%), and loose parts play (70%) (CLC, 2014). Of the categories mentioned above, medical play was the most popular play type employed by child life specialists in hospitals (99%). Additional unique opportunities highlighted by program directors that fell into the play programming category included pet therapy, special events (proms, summer camps, teddy bear clinics, gurney journeys, celebrity visits, sports events, carnivals, festivals), and various holiday celebrations (CLC, 2014).

Survey results indicated that certain types of play were favoured within specific hospital departments. For example, distraction play was most prominent in emergency departments, radiology departments, haematology/oncology units, outpatient units, and surgical units, while therapeutic play was favoured in paediatric intensive care units (CLC, 2014).

According to McCue (1988), medical play activities can be divided into four conceptual categories:

1. Role rehearsal/role reversal medical play, where children take on the roles of health care providers and reenact medical procedures on dolls or puppets
2. Medical fantasy play, where children engage in play that utilizes loose parts or standard play materials that are not medical equipment, appealing to those children who may initially avoid medical play materials
3. Indirect medical play, more structured in its presentation, with a goal of exploring, educating, or familiarizing the child with the medical environment through hospital-themed play materials and games
4. Medical art, a process-oriented play experience where children use art materials to express their understandings and emotional responses to their medical experiences.

Medical play continues to be an evidence-based practice utilized as a component of psychological preparation that is designed to reduce distress and pain associated with painful and/or invasive medical procedures (Moore et al., 2015). Medical play that utilizes pretend or real medical equipment offers many benefits, including the alleviation of emotional distress through imaginary play situations, preparation for anticipated medical procedures, provision of catharsis, resolution of internal conflicts, reconciliation of painful or frightening events, and achievement of mastery and coping effectively (Jessee & Gaynard, 2009). Play-based procedural preparation and support interventions that orient a child to the procedure, utilizing unfamiliar or anxiety-producing medical equipment through play, promotes the child's coping during anxiety-producing procedures (Grissom et al., 2016).

Children with acute and chronic illness are not the only population to consider when examining the benefits of play programming in hospitals. As palliative care aims to relieve pain and suffering, addressing psychosocial needs of children and families facing end of life is essential (Himelstein et al., 2004). Play is a critical component in the holistic care framework in paediatric palliative care, as it allows children to reveal their fears and hopes, allowing the supportive adult to interpret the child's journey (Breemen, 2009). The ability of the child to express fears and anxieties in a safe place to play allows him or her the opportunity to escape from the real world into one of their own making, a gift that only play can provide (Boucher et al., 2014).

Play Policies

Directors of child life programs reported having formal written policies on toy cleaning (98%), play (39%), siblings in the playroom (28%), needle play (24%), and screen time (1%). A small number of programs (14%) identified stringent infection control guidelines as a barrier to the play materials/opportunities (loose parts, sand, water, plush toys, sociodramatic play props, group play, etc.) afforded to patients (CLC, 2014). To illustrate the prominent role of play in current child life programs, directors shared that 78% frequently chart play on medical records of patients and that 64% include play as an important ingredient in patient's recovery plans.

Play Training

Survey results indicated that a small percentage (14%) of child life program directors believed that new members of staff had adequate preservice training in play practices and theory. Some 60% of programs discuss specific play interventions for patients monthly or quarterly at staff meetings. Only 25% of programs provided in-service training on play for child life personnel. However, 64% of programs conducted training on the importance/value of play to a variety of hospital staff including administrators, chaplains, doctors, medical residents and technicians, nurses, psychologists, social workers, and volunteers (CLC, 2014). Professional development for child life specialists took place at the annual CLC conference (83%), via webinars (77%), and through college coursework (13%). Only 20% of programs were strongly influenced by prominent play scholars, and Jean Piaget and Erik Erikson were referenced by 69% of the directors. Other prominent play theorists mentioned were Axline, Bowlby, Bronfenbrenner, Csikszentmihalyi, Dewey, Freud, Frobel, Montessori, Parten, and Plank, to name just a few.

Play Innovations

Eighty-four percent of directors touted a variety of play-related innovations in their respective programs. One such innovation focused on offering medical play more frequently, across multiple settings, and with creative, open-ended materials. An additional innovation highlighted the integration of technology play via iPads and other devices across the developmental continuum. A third innovation argued for expanding where, when, and to whom play interventions are offered on a consistent basis (CLC, 2014). Other innovative ideas included creating play experiences based on developmental theory, creating individual play spaces in each patient's room, and using play to facilitate a variety of clinical situations.

Play Barriers

Child life directors were asked in the survey to identify institutional barriers that limited play in their individual programs. The play barriers identified from most to least frequent included inadequate staffing (45%), lack of time, (45%), lack of space (30%), lack of understanding about the value of play (18%), infection control regulations (14%), isolation precautions (14%), and a variety of patient factors including duration of hospital stay and medical fragility (6%) (CLC, 2014).

Associations with Childhood Functioning

Children and families encountering hospitalization can experience a number of stressors that can impact child and family development and how a family functions and copes with some of life's most challenging circumstances. Life-threatening illness, separation from familiar caregivers, unfamiliar environment and routines, altered physical appearance and/or ability to function, lack of privacy and exposure of private body parts, and dealing with the unkind and with loss are examples of situational stressors that occur for children and families in medical settings (Goldberger et al., 2009b). Research has demonstrated the effects of play programming in the reduction of anxiety and stress in children (Burns-Nader et al., 2013; Clatworthy, 1981; Golden, 1983) and hospital-related fears (Rae et al., 1989), and in having more positive feelings about themselves and significant others (Gillis, 1989). Play utilized as a method of preparation for diagnostic procedures has also been found to be effective in reducing the need for anaesthesia for children undergoing radiation therapy as part of their treatment plan (Haeberli et al., 2008). The use of video game play has also been demonstrated as an effective way to minimize pain in children and can be considered a non-pharmacological approach in paediatric pain management (Hoffman et al., 2000; Hoffman et al., 2008; Kaheni et al., 2016; Stoddard et al., 2002).

Suggestions to Improve Play Practices in North American Health Care Settings

Based on data generated from the comprehensive survey conducted by the CLC in 2013, the following are some suggestions to improve the frequency and range of play policies, practices, and programs in medical settings across North America (CLC, 2014):

- creating additional indoor and outdoor play spaces for patients
- improving access to medical play props
- instituting play groups to meet developmental and therapeutic needs of patients

- providing a greater variety of play types to meet the developmental needs of patients
- increasing in-service training on play practices/theories for both staff and volunteers
- developing policies on philosophy of play, digital play/screen time, medical play, sibling play, etc.
- offering further educational opportunities for medical personnel on the value and importance of play
- infusing a wider range of therapeutic play and play materials along with accompanying training for staff on the value of such interventions
- incorporating a variety of loose parts into both indoor and outdoor hospital play spaces due to their developmental benefits
- expanding play programming opportunities in non-traditional areas like waiting rooms
- creating more equity among the types of play offered across child life programs (distraction play, therapeutic play, needle play, recreational play, educational play, post-procedural play)
- improving child life coverage and play interventions in radiology departments
- emphasizing the inclusion of play skills in the evaluation process of child life specialists
- adding specific play techniques and skills to the Child Life Competencies
- including discussions about play and play interventions in staff meetings and in clinical supervision
- creating parent play groups to model developmentally appropriate play practices.

Future Directions

Based on the review of literature on the history and current state of the field of child life and child life programs, we offer the following recommendations for future directions:

1. Initiate a robust research agenda on play in hospitals focusing on how play is related to paediatric health literacy, stress/coping, self- esteem, locus of control, state and trait anxiety, and adjustment.
2. Institute goals and functions of hospital play/play programming across the developmental continuum (infancy to adolescence, children with disabilities).
3. Examine the variety of play behaviours in the hospital environment with a particular focus on cultural considerations.
4. Require academic and clinical training of hospital play workers at both the undergraduate and graduate levels.
5. Examine parent/caregiver engagement in play in medical settings.

6. Explore societal attitudes about play, institutional influences on play, and how it shapes patient experience.

7. Identifying a place for outdoor play and loose parts play within an institutional context.

8. Examine the infection control policies and neutropenic procedures and the impact on play spaces/materials/protocols.

9. Understand the influence of technology on play and child development, specifically as it relates to the experience of the hospitalized child.

10. Explore the current state of play outside the medical setting, and how it is reflected in play programming in children's hospitals.

11. Encourage the use of play as a protective factor in minimizing risks of paediatric medical traumatic stress.

12. Consider hospital design and environments that support, encourage, and facilitate play.

Conclusion

Since its founding in the beginning of the twentieth century, play has served as the cornerstone of the child life profession. Although studies highlighted above document play's vital role in the psychosocial development of children in medical settings, the seminal CLC survey and accompanying report (2014) suggests its implementation in North American hospitals is mixed due in part to three significant obstacles: lack of time, staffing, and space. While the societal and institutional barriers marginalizing play continue to spread, to support the well-being of children, we must remain vigilant advocates for play, as it embodies the very essence of the child life profession.

References

Adams, M. A. (1976). A hospital play program: Helping children with serious illness. *American Journal of Orthopsychiatry, 46*(3), 416–424.

Armstrong, T. S. H., & Aitken, H. L. (2000). The developing role of play preparation in paediatric anaesthesia. *Pediatric Anesthesia, 10*(1), 1–4.

Association for the Care of Children in Hospitals (1980). Statements of policy for the care of children and families in health care settings. *Journal of the Association for the Care of Children in Hospitals, 8*(4), 105–106.

Association of Child Life Professionals (2017a). The case for child life. Association of Child Life Professionals website. Available at www.childlife.org/child-life-profession/the-case-for-child-life.

Association of Child Life Professionals (2017b). Mission, values, vision. Association of Child Life Professionals website. Available at www.childlife.org/child-life-profession/mission-values-vision.

Azarnoff, P. (1970). A play program in a pediatric clinic. *Children, 17*(6), 218.

Azarnoff, P., & Flegal, S. (1975). *A pediatric play program*. Springfield, IL: Charles C. Thomas.

Bolig, R. (2005). Play in healthcare settings. In J. Rollins, R. Bolig, & C. Mahan (Eds.), *Meeting children's psychosocial needs across the health-care setting* (pp. 77–117) Austin, TX: Pro-Ed.

Bowlby, J. (1952). *Maternal care and mental health* (vol. 2). Geneva: World Health Organization.

Bowlby, J., Robertson, J., & Rosenbluth, D. (1952). A two-year-old goes to hospital. *Psychoanalytic Study of the Child*, 7(1), 82–94.

Breemen, C. V. (2009). Using play therapy in paediatric palliative care: Listening to the story and caring for the body. *International Journal of Palliative Nursing*, 15(10), 510–514.

Brindle, L. (2006). The case for play in a neonatal intensive care unit: The work of a hospital play specialist. *Journal of Neonatal Nursing*, 12(1), 14–19.

Brooks, M. (1957). Constructive play experience for the hospitalized child. *Journal of Nursery Education*, 12(2), 7–13.

Brooks, M. M. (1970). Why play in the hospital? *Nursing Clinics of North America*, 5(3), 431–441.

Brown, C. (2014). Play and professionalism: The legacy of Mary McLeod Brooks (1911–2007). In J. Turner & C. Brown (Eds.), *The pips of child life: Early play programs in hospitals*. (pp. 57–64). Dubuque, IA: Kendall Hunt.

Brown, T. (2014). Schools of thought. In J. Turner & C. Brown (Eds.), *The pips of child life: Early play programs in hospitals* (pp. 1–11). Dubuque, IA: Kendall Hunt.

Boucher, S., Downing, J., & Shemilt, R. (2014). The role of play in children's palliative care. *Children*, 1(3), 302–317.

Burns-Nader, S., & Hernandez-Reif, M. (2016). Facilitating play for hospitalized children through child life services. *Children's Health Care*, 45(1), 1–21.

Burns-Nader, S., Hernandez-Reif, M., & Thoma, S. J. (2013). Play and video effects on mood and procedure behaviors in school-aged children visiting the pediatrician. *Clinical Pediatrics*, 52(10), 929–935.

Child Life Council (2014). *Report on findings of play practices and innovations survey: The state of play in North American hospitals*. Rockville, MD: Child Life Council.

Child Life Council (2016). *Directory of child life programs*. Available at http://community.childlife.org.

Clatworthy, S. (1981). Therapeutic play: Effects on hospitalized children. *Children's Health Care: Journal of the Association for the Care of Children's Health*, 9(4), 108–113.

Cooke, R. (1967). Effects of hospitalization upon the child. In J. A. Haller, J. L. Tolbert, & R. H. Dombro (Eds.), *The hospitalized child and his family* (pp. 3–17). Baltimore, MD: Johns Hopkins University Press.

Council, C. L. (2006). Child life services. *Pediatrics*, 118(4), 1757–1763.

Crandall, F. M. (1897). Hospitalism. *Archives of Pediatrics*, 14(6), 448–454.

Fein, J. A., Zempsky, W. T., & Cravero, J. P. (2012). Relief of pain and anxiety in pediatric patients in emergency medical systems. *Pediatrics* 130(5), 1391–1405.

Freud, A. (1952). The role of bodily illness in the mental life of children. *Psychoanalytic Study of the Child*, 7(1), 69–81.

Gillis, A. J. (1989). The effect of play on immobilized children in hospital. *International Journal of Nursing Studies, 26*(3), 261–269.

Gitlin-Weiner, K. (1998). Clinical perspectives on play. In D. P. Fromberg & D. Bergen (Eds.), *Play from birth to twelve and beyond: Contexts, perspectives, and meanings* (pp. 77–93). New York: Routledge.

Goldberger, J., Luebering, M. A., & Thompson, R. H. (2009a). Psychological preparation and coping. In R. H. Thompson (Ed.), *The handbook of child life: A guide for pediatric psychosocial care* (pp. 160–198). Springfield, IL: C. C. Thomas.

Goldberger, J., Mohl, A. L., & Thompson, R. (2009b). Psychological preparation and coping. In R. H. Thompson (Ed.), *The handbook of child life: A guide for pediatric psychosocial care* (pp. 160–198). Springfield, IL: C. C. Thomas.

Golden, D. B. (1983). Play therapy for hospitalized children. In C. Schaefer & K. O'Connor (Eds.), *Handbook of play therapy* (pp. 213–233). New York: Free Press.

Goymour, K. L., Stephenson, C., Goodenough, B., & Boulton, C. (2000). Evaluating the role of play therapy in the paediatric emergency department. *Australian Emergency Nursing Journal, 3*(2), 10–12.

Grissim, L., & Turner, J. (2014). Early play programs in hospitals: 1940s–1970s. In J. Turner & C. Brown (Eds.), *The pips of child life: Early play programs in hospitals* (pp. 25–36). Dubuque, IA: Kendall Hunt.

Grissom, S., Boles, J., Bailey, K., Cantrell, K., Kennedy, A., Sykes, A., & Mandrell, B. N. (2016). Play-based procedural preparation and support intervention for cranial radiation. *Supportive Care in Cancer, 24*(6), 2421–2427.

Haeberli, S., Grotzer, M. A., Niggli, F. K., Landolt, M. A., Linsenmeier, C., Ammann, R. A., & Bodmer, N. (2008). A psychoeducational intervention reduces the need for anesthesia during radiotherapy for young childhood cancer patients. *Radiation Oncology, 3*(1), 17.

Haller, J. A., Talbert, J. L., & Dombro, R. I. (1967). *The hospitalized child and his family*. Baltimore, MD: Johns Hopkins University Press.

Harvey, S. (1976). Report of the expert group on play for children in hospital. *Journal of Advanced Nursing, 1*, 425–428.

Hicks, M. (2008). *Child life beyond the hospital*. Rockville, MD: Child Life Council.

Hicks, M., & Davitt, K. (2009). Chronic illness and rehabilitation. In R. H. Thompson (Ed.), *The handbook of child life: A guide for pediatric psychosocial care* (pp. 257–286). Springfield, IL: C. C. Thomas.

Himelstein, B. P., Hilden, J. M., Boldt, A. M., & Weissman, D. (2004). Pediatric palliative care. *New England Journal of Medicine, 350*(17), 1752–1762.

Hoffman, H. G., Doctor, J. N., Patterson, D. R., Carrougher, G. J., & Furness, T. A. III (2000). Virtual reality as an adjunctive pain control during burn wound care in adolescent patients. *Pain, 85*(1), 305–309.

Hoffman, H. G., Patterson, D. R., Seibel, E., Soltani, M., Jewett-Leahy, L., & Sharar, S. R. (2008). Virtual reality pain control during burn wound debridement in the hydrotank. *Clinical Journal of Pain, 24*(4), 299–304.

Jessee, P. O. (1991). Making hospitals less traumatic: Child life specialists. *Dimensions, 20*(1), 23–24, 37.

Jessee, P. O., & Gaynard, L. (2009). Paradigms of play. In R. H. Thompson (Ed.), *The handbook of child life: A guide for psychosocial care* (pp. 136–159). Springfield, IL: Charles C. Thomas.

Jessee, P., Wilson, H., & Morgan, D. (2000). Medical play for young children. *Childhood Education, 76*(4), 215–218.

Jolly, H. (1968). Play and the sick child: A comparative study of its role in a teaching hospital in London and one in Ghana. *The Lancet, 292*(7581), 1286–1287.

Kaheni, S., Bagheri-Nesami, M., Goudarzian, A. H., & Rezai, M. S. (2016). The effect of video game play technique on pain of venipuncture in children. *International Journal of Pediatrics, 4*(5), 1795–1802.

Koller, D. (2008). Child Life Council evidence-based practice statement. Therapeutic play in pediatric health care: The essence of child life practice. Available at http://citeseerx.ist.psu.edu/viewdoc/download?doi=10.1.1.690.7803&rep=rep1&type=pdf.

Lenhart, A., Kahne, J., Middaugh, E., Macgill, A., Evans, C., & Vitak, J. (2008). Teens, video games, and civics: Teens' gaming experiences are diverse and include significant social interaction and civic engagement. Pew Internet & American Life Project. Available at www.pewinternet.org/2008/09/16/teens-video-games-and-civics/.

Marchant, S. (2016). Child life identity: What's in a name, revisited. In J. Turner & C. Brown (Eds.), *The pips of child life: The middle years of play programs in hospitals* (pp. 17–26). Dubuque, IA: Kendall Hunt.

McCue, K. (1988). Medical play: An expanded perspective. *Children's Health Care, 16*(3), 157–161.

McCue, K. (2009). Therapeutic relationships in child life. In R. H. Thompson (Ed.), *The handbook of child life: A guide for psychosocial care* (pp. 57–77). Springfield, IL: Charles C. Thomas.

Moore, E. R., Bennett, K. L., Dietrich, M. S., & Wells, N. (2015). The effect of directed medical play on young children's pain and distress during burn wound care. *Journal of Pediatric Health Care, 29*(3), 265–273.

Patte, M. M. (2015). The evolution of school recess and corresponding implications for the next generation of children. White Paper for Playworld, Lewisburg, PA.

Pearson, L. (2014). Play as a right: B. J. Seabury (1927–2002). In J. Turner & C. Brown (Eds.), *The pips of child life: Early play programs in hospitals* (pp. 47–56). Dubuque, IA: Kendall Hunt.

Petrillo, M. (1968). Preventing hospital trauma in pediatric patients. *American Journal of Nursing,* 1469–1473.

Plank, E. N. (1962). *Working with children in hospitals: A guide for the professional team.* Cleveland, OH: Western Reserve University.

Plank, E. N., Caughey, P. A., & Lipson, M. J. (1959). A general hospital child care program to counteract hospitalism. *American Journal of Orthopsychiatry, 29*(1), 94–101.

Play Schools Association (1963). *Play in a hospital: Why, how.* New York: Play Schools Association.

Pond-Wojtasik, S., & White, C. (2009). The story of child life. In R. H. Thompson (Ed.), *The handbook of child life: A guide for pediatric psychosocial care* (pp. 3–22). Springfield, IL: C. C. Thomas.

Pressdee, D., May, L., Eastman, E., & Grier, D. (1997). The use of play therapy in the preparation of children undergoing MR imaging. *Clinical Radiology, 52*(12), 945–947.

Rae, W. A., Worchel, F. F., Upchurch, J., Sanner, J. H., & Daniel, C. A. (1989). The psychosocial impact of play on hospitalized children. *Journal of Pediatric Psychology, 14*(4), 617–627.

Rubin, S. (1992). What's in a name? Child life and the play lady legacy. *Children's Health Care, 21*(1), 4–13.

Rutkowski, J. (1978). A survey of child life programs. *Journal of the Association for the Care of Children in Hospitals, 6*(4), 11–16.

Shapiro, S. (1963). Reports on the play program. In Play Schools Association (Ed.), *Play in a hospital: Why, how.* New York: Play Schools Association.

Spitz, R. A. (1945). Hospitalism: An inquiry into the genesis of psychiatric conditions in early childhood. *Psychoanalytic Study of the Child, 1*(1), 53–74.

Spitz, R. A. (1946). Hospitalism: A follow-up report. *Psychoanalytic Study of the Child, 2*, 113–117.

Stoddard, F. J., Sheridan, R. L., Saxe, G. N., King, B. S., King, B. H., Chedekel, D. S., Schnitzer, J. J., & Martyn, J. A. (2002). Treatment of pain in acutely burned children. *Journal of Burn Care & Research, 23*(2), 135–156.

Stone, R. (1963). The administrator of Blythedale Children's Hospital speaks for play. In Play Schools Association (Ed.), *Play in a hospital: Why, how?* New York: Play Schools Association.

Thompson, R. H. (1988). From questions to answers: Approaches to studying play in health care settings. *Children's Health Care, 16*(3), 188–194.

Thompson, R. H. (1989). Child life programs in pediatric settings. *Infants & Young Children, 2*(1), 75–82.

Tisza, V. B., & Angoff, K. (1957). A play program and its function in a pediatric hospital. *Pediatrics, 19*(2), 293–302.

Turner, J., & Grissim, L. (2014). Care and conditions of children in hospitals circa 1930. In J. Turner & C. Brown (Eds.), *The pips of child life: Early play programs in hospitals.* (pp. 13–24). Dubuque, IA: Kendall Hunt.

Wilson, J. (2014). A new era: From play activities to child life at Johns Hopkins. In J. Turner & C. Brown (Eds.), *The pips of child life: Early play programs in hospitals* (pp. 77–88). Dubuque, IA: Kendall Hunt.

35 Play Therapy

An Introduction to Theory and Practice

Elise Cuschieri

> The child stands in front of the doll's house. Slowly he takes the pieces of furniture out, placing them carefully on the cupboard which the house is standing on. Now and then he glances at the adult sitting alongside him. The child continues to take all the furniture out until the house is almost empty, except for some rugs on the floors. He looks around him and surveys the other toys and objects. Silently and purposefully, he reaches for a large blue Playmobil car. He fills it with people and animal figures and then pushes it diagonally into one of the rooms upstairs so the car is sideways with the front half sticking out of the doll's house. He continues to refill the doll's house, placing toy objects such as a dog kennel, a stable, a merry-go-round, swings, slides, some furniture as well as animal and people figures, until each room in the house is filled to bursting point . . .

Writing this chapter has proved to be an unexpected challenge. I thought I would find the task of putting down what play therapy is and what play therapists do to be fairly straightforward. However, once I started writing, I quickly realized that trying to narrow down the complex and multifaceted process that play therapy is into one chapter was more of a challenge than I had anticipated. Just as childhood is about growing and becoming, so too is the process of play therapy, which continues to evolve and change as we learn and understand ever more about what happens in our brains when we play (Kestly, 2014; Panksepp, 2009), as well as the way in which relationships, including the therapeutic alliance, can enhance neuroplasticity (Cozolino, 2014; Siegel, 2012). Play therapy is a creative, exciting, and dynamic way of helping children, but that also means that rather like children themselves, it is hard to do it justice in a few thousand words without the risk of losing some of the insight and subtlety of its practice. This chapter is inevitably a relatively concise overview of play therapy. I refer to theory and principles that I hope many play therapists would recognize and those unfamiliar with play therapy will find accessible and useful, but I acknowledge that it remains my own perspective on play therapy with the inevitable ensuing omissions or insertions of an overview. However, I hope I can convey some of the intricacies and vibrancy of working therapeutically with children and young people that makes play therapy the absorbing and stimulating profession that it is.

Play therapy is a psychotherapeutic approach to working with children, usually between the ages of 3 and 12 years of age, who have experienced emotional and/or behavioural difficulties that are having a significant impact on their typical functioning and development. It forms part of a range of psychotherapies often termed the 'expressive arts' therapies. These modalities, which include art, dance movement, drama, and music, are all sensory-based interventions. Because they all use a specific medium for expression, e.g., play or art, they do not rely on verbal means of communication and are concerned with the regulation of emotion (Stacey, 2008). All of the expressive arts therapies are relational, which means that therapeutic change and healing take place within the therapeutic relationship between client and therapist (Malchiodi, 2015).

'Play' in Play Therapy

> The child stands back, looks at the doll's house and says, "I'm done." For the remainder of his time in the playroom that day, Devon plays with sand, feeling it, commenting on its texture and temperature, letting it trickle through his hands, burying his hands in it, and inviting his play therapist to put her hands in the sandtray too.

A glance at synonyms for the word 'play' include 'enjoy oneself, have fun, relax and occupy oneself' (*Oxford Compact Thesaurus*, 2005, p. 626). The word 'therapy' comes from the Greek word *therapeia*, meaning 'healing'. It is defined as 'the treatment of mental or emotional problems by psychological means' (*Compact Oxford English Dictionary*, 2005, p. 1075). So a somewhat basic definition for play therapy could be presented as 'have fun while healing from mental or emotional problems'. This is, of course, rather simplistic, but healing and resolution from emotional and behavioural difficulties are the desired outcomes in play therapy interventions, and the act of 'having fun' is often a feature in play therapy sessions. However, this is not always the case, and, in the above vignette, Devon plays silently and intently with the doll's house. He is not overtly 'enjoying' himself and it is not until he finishes his doll's house play and moves to the sandtray does he appear to relax and interact with his therapist. So what does play look like in play therapy, how can it contribute to emotional and psychological healing, and what is the role of the play therapist? These and other considerations will be the focus of this chapter.

Before going further, the following principles that are fundamental to play therapy across all models (Landreth, 2002; Ray, 2011; Stewart et al., 2016) should be noted:

1. Play is the child's language.
2. Play can help to regulate emotions.
3. Emotional and psychological healing take place in a relational context.

In this chapter, I will present the core theory that underpins play therapy practice and I will introduce skills necessary to create and maintain a safe therapeutic environment for children where, through play, they are able to express and explore thoughts and feelings that may be related to challenging life events. The role of the play therapist is to facilitate a therapeutic process through which a therapeutic relationship between child and therapist is formed that enables growth and change to take place in the child. The play therapist is trained to understand the metaphors communicated by the child in his play and to observe and recognize patterns and themes that emerge as the child engages with his therapist in a dynamic interaction. I will begin by tracing the historical context and beginnings of play therapy, and the development of play therapy as it is widely understood and practised today, in the United Kingdom and with reference to the United States. I will discuss issues related to practice and will elucidate how healing from past stressors or traumatic experiences can occur within the play therapy process, drawing on clinical material to demonstrate this. The case vignette that runs through the whole of this chapter is based on material drawn from my play therapy practice. Some details have been left out, changed, or altered so as to protect the identity and confidentiality of the child and family, and the name is a pseudonym. In order to facilitate reading and comprehension, I will use the male gender when referring to a child and female for the play therapist; this is not intended to place a bias on either gender.

History of Child Psychotherapy

Using play as a way of helping children to make sense of and resolve difficult life events and experiences has its roots in the pioneering work of child psychotherapists Melanie Klein (b. 1882), Anna Freud (b. 1895), and Margaret Lowenfeld (b. 1890). Their work in the United Kingdom was instrumental in the development of the structure and theory underpinning child psychotherapy as it is known and practised today. All three recognized that through spontaneous play, children can communicate experiences, desires, thoughts, and emotions, both those that are conscious and those that remain on an unconscious level. Klein (1997) and Freud (1974) were heavily influenced by the theories of Sigmund Freud (1949), and it was his work with adults that Klein and Freud drew on to develop the theoretical underpinnings of child psychoanalysis. There were some differences in the way these two pioneers conceptualized their theory and practice. For instance, Klein postulated that spontaneous play in children was akin to the technique of free association in adults. Anna Freud, however, did not agree with this and focused on helping children to acquire conscious understanding of their thoughts, emotions, and behaviour. She also placed emphasis on the importance of the relationship between child and therapist, and of child therapists working with primary carers and school professionals.

Lowenfeld (1991) was also remarkable in her vision and understanding of how to help children, and yet her legacy tends to be less well known compared with that of either Klein or Freud. Lowenfeld recognized that children often find it difficult to verbalize their experiences, and consequently she created techniques that would enable children to communicate their thoughts and feelings without needing to rely on words (Doctor Margaret Lowenfeld Trust [DMLT], 2017). Lowenfeld (1993) developed what is known as the 'Lowenfeld World Technique,' which uses trays filled with sand and collections of miniature toys, representing all aspects of everyday life. The aim of this technique is to enable children to portray their experiences of their lives and inner worlds by playing with the miniatures in the sand. Later, Dora Kalff (see Weinrib, 1983), a Jungian psychotherapist, developed this approach, establishing sandplay therapy that is widely practised today. Lowenfeld also created the 'Lowenfeld Mosaics', which uses coloured tiles of assorted shapes to produce a diagnostic and therapeutic instrument (DMLT, 2017).

Klein, Freud, and Lowenfeld all recognized the important role play held with the children they worked with. Hence, psychoanalytic child therapy offered the first truly organized approach to working psychotherapeutically with children, presenting a theoretical foundation and a clear mode of practice. Today, underpinning all child psychotherapy practice is the notion that play has the capacity to communicate the child's unconscious thoughts, emotions, experiences, and desires. Play therapy has emerged from this tradition, and its practice today places emphasis on the therapeutic relationship and the symbolic nature of play (Landreth, 2002; Ray, 2011).

The Beginnings of Play Therapy

As a response to the methods of psychoanalytic play therapy, a new type of therapy with children emerged in the United States in the 1930s. Proponents of this approach believed that a structured approach to play was necessary for change to take place. Levy (see Landreth, 2002) developed 'release therapy', the aim of which was for the therapist to facilitate trauma-related play with the child, who would experience catharsis as a result of 'playing out' the trauma. Hambridge developed Levy's approach further by actually directing children to 'play out' stressful events from their lives (see Landreth, 2002). Such models of working with children gave rise to the development of therapist-led approaches and techniques that are widely incorporated into therapeutic work with children today.

The Influence of Carl Rogers

In the 1940s, Rogers developed a humanistic approach to working with clients in psychotherapy that he initially termed 'non-directive'. The premise of this approach places trust in the capacity of the client or patient to 'actualize' (Rogers, 2004), which is the innate tendency that Rogers believed all humans have to develop constructive and healthy capacities. In this type of therapy, the therapist is viewed as collaborator rather than expert, and emphasis is placed on the relationship between the therapist and the client, which is based on genuineness, empathy, acceptance, and trust. Furthermore, it places the client in control of the therapeutic process. This was a critical shift in both the attitude and concept of psychotherapy, which up until then had been based largely on the existing diagnostic and prescriptive perspectives of the period, where the therapist was viewed as the 'expert' and the client as 'patient'. Rogers was instrumental in changing concepts about psychotherapy and also terminology. The Rogerian approach became known as client-centred therapy (Rogers, 2003); today this psychotherapeutic approach is widely referred to as person-centred therapy.

Virginia Axline's Contribution to Play Therapy

A theoretically coherent model of play therapy originated from the work of Virginia Axline (1989) in the United States, who developed a way of working therapeutically with children based on the philosophy and principles of Carl Rogers (2003, 2004). Axline, who was a student of Rogers, drew on his client-centred approach to pioneer a developmentally appropriate and sensitive way of working with children. As with Klein, Freud, and Lowenfeld, Axline (1989) recognized that play is the most natural way for children to express themselves and to communicate their emotions, values, thoughts, perceptions, and experiences. She believed that if a child were offered an environment that was accepting and empathic, his innate need to explore, discover, understand, and achieve mastery of his world through play would be satisfied, and he would be able to fulfil his potential. Axline adapted Rogers's 19 propositions of personality development (Rogers, 2003) to form the basis of her theory for work with children who were experiencing emotional and behavioural difficulties and psychological distress.

The role of the therapist, therefore, was to create an atmosphere of permissiveness in the playroom so that the child could experience acceptance and unconditional positive regard, two key relational attitudes that Rogers outlined in his theory about change in person-centred therapy (2007). According to Axline, the play therapist must strive to help the child feel accepted so that he can express his thoughts and feelings in a free way without worrying about getting into trouble, being told what to do, or upsetting his therapist. In her well-known text Dibs, Axline describes how she worked with a young child, observing that "[n]o-one ever knows as much about a human being's inner world as the individual himself. Responsible freedom grows and develops from inside the person" ((1990, p. 67). Axline (1989, pp. 69–70) developed eight basic principles that she considered necessary for the therapeutic relationship in play therapy to develop and for healing to take place:

1. The therapist must develop a warm, friendly relationship with the child, in which good rapport is established as soon as possible.
2. The therapist accepts the child exactly as he is.
3. The therapist establishes a feeling of permissiveness in the relationship so that the child feels free to express his feelings completely.
4. The therapist is alert to recognize the feelings the child is expressing and reflects those feelings back to him in such a manner that he gains insight into his behaviour.
5. The therapist maintains a deep respect for the child's ability to solve his own problems if given an opportunity to do so. The responsibility to make choices and to institute change is the child's.
6. The therapist does not attempt to direct the child's actions or conversation in any manner. The child leads the way; the therapist follows.
7. The therapist does not attempt to hurry the therapy along. It is a gradual process and is recognized as such by the therapist.
8. The therapist establishes only those limitations that are necessary to anchor the therapy to the world of reality and to make the child aware of his responsibility in the relationship.

Adhering to Rogers's approach, Axline (1989) described her way of working with children as non-directive play therapy and emphasized the critical therapist attitudes of congruence, empathy, and unconditional positive regard. Axline's legacy can be seen in the myriad of child therapy approaches that have emerged since her work in the mid-twentieth century. For the past 70 years, play therapy has continued to develop in the United States and, from the 1980s, in the United Kingdom. Practitioners such as Garry Landreth (2002) and Charles Schaefer (2011) in the United States, and Ann Cattanach (1997) and Sue Jennings (1999, 2017) in the United Kingdom have been instrumental in developing play therapy into the sound therapeutic approach that it is today.

Play Therapy Today

Play therapy, as it has developed since Axline, continues to be a developmentally appropriate and sensitive approach to working with children who have experienced challenging life events (Axline, 1989; Landreth, 2002; Ray, 2011). Today there exists a continuum of approaches that integrate elements from allied disciplines and models of adult psychotherapy such as systemic family therapy, narrative therapy, solution-focused therapy, cognitive behavioural therapy, and person-centred therapy. These approaches range from non-directive child-led work, such as child-centred play therapy

(CCPT), which draws on Axline's legacy (Landreth, 2002; Ray, 2011), to more directive therapist-led interventions, for instance, prescriptive play therapy developed by Schaefer (2016). In all approaches, and whatever the theoretical underpinning – person-centred, Gestalt, narrative, cognitive-behavioural – the premise that play is key to growth, development, and healing remains true. Yasenik and Gardner (2004) have developed a decision-making tool for play therapists called the Play Therapy Dimensions Model (PTDM). This model, made up of four 'quadrants', guides play therapists across approaches and theories in identifying the critical elements of the play therapy process in order to make key practice decisions, bearing in mind two main dimensions: the non-directive/directive dimension, which refers to the extent to which the therapist leads the play therapy, and the conscious/unconscious dimension, which is the level of awareness the child has of his play and its relation to his experiences (Yasenik & Gardner, 2004). The PTDM helps therapists to identify which quadrant the child is currently working in and to respond accordingly.

In play therapy, the child can engage in creative thinking and problem-solving. By providing the child with carefully selected play materials and a safe, secure, and containing therapeutic space and relationship, the play therapist offers the child the possibility of exploring and experimenting with a myriad of options without the fear of his play being curtailed or of negative consequence. The child can discharge emotions that elsewhere might lead to reprimands or be kerbed, but which in play therapy can bring feelings of relief and the cathartic release of tension and affect (Landreth, 2002; Schaefer, 2011). The child and play therapist enter into a dynamic process in which the child's life experiences can be expressed symbolically and where his "inner resources are enabled by the therapeutic alliance to bring about growth and change" (British Association of Play Therapists [BAPT], 2013). Play therapy usually takes place in a playroom where the primary medium of communication is considered to be play, while speech is secondary (BAPT, 2013).

The Therapeutic Space

Where and how play therapy takes place are important considerations for play therapists, as these factors can contribute to the degree of efficacy of the process (Landreth, 2002; McMahon, 1992; Ray, 2011). Play therapy can occur in a variety of places, such as a specially equipped playroom or, as is often the case, a room that doubles as something else at other times, e.g., a room in a school or the child's home. While most play therapists are used to working in rooms of varying sizes, Landreth (2002) suggests a room where proximity between child and therapist can be maintained. If a room is very big, the play therapist might feel that she has to follow the child around, and Landreth notes this would "deprive the child of the opportunity to take the lead in approaching the therapist on the child's terms" (2002 , p. 126). On the other hand, if the room is too small, the child might not be able to adequately regulate the distance between himself and his therapist. If play therapy is not taking place in a dedicated playroom, then the physical space needs to be marked out in some way, for instance, by using chairs or table. Ann Cattanach, a dramatherapist who helped to develop play therapy in the United Kingdom, often worked with children in their own homes. She would delineate the play therapy 'safe space' by the use of a blue mat that she laid out at the beginning of the play therapy session and rolled up at the end. She and the child would sit on the mat together so as to share the space as "partners in play" (Cattanach, 2008, p. 62).

However, while the size of the room is important, what is more critical is where the area/room is and what the play therapist does with it to create a therapeutic space. It should be somewhere private, where no one is likely to see, hear, or walk in on what is happening. This helps to ensure that what takes place during play therapy remains private and confidential to the child and therapist. In the United Kingdom, many play therapists explain to children at the beginning of play therapy that what the child plays and talks about in his play therapy session is private but not secret. This is to help the child understand the nature of confidentiality: he is at liberty to talk about what happens within play therapy *if* he wants to. His play therapist maintains confidentiality in a similar manner to a therapist working with adults. However, most play therapists will also meet the parent/caregiver of the child on a regular basis to review the main issues emerging in the child's play. This is to enable a cooperative alliance to develop between therapist and parent/caregiver in which the play therapist can help to convey how the child is making sense of and processing the issues that brought the child to play therapy. In some cases, child-centred play therapists will work directly with parents using filial therapy (Guerney & Ryan, 2013), in which parents become the agents of therapeutic change with their children.

The Materials

With a therapeutic space established, what else is needed? Toys, of course, are a critical component of the play therapy process. Practitioners such as Landreth and Ray offer guidelines for selecting toys and materials that will serve "as a medium for children to express feelings, explore relationships and understand themselves" (Landreth, 2002, p. 132). The rationale that is offered is based on the premise that toys should be carefully selected as opposed to cheerfully accumulated, so it is wise not to assume that any toy will do in play therapy! Landreth (2002, p. 133) suggests the following criteria for evaluating the suitability or otherwise of play materials:

1. Do the toys and materials facilitate a wide range of creative expression?
2. Do they facilitate a wide range of emotional expression?
3. Do they engage children's interests?
4. Do they facilitate expressive and exploratory play?
5. Do they allow exploration and expression without verbalization?
6. Do they allow success without prescribed structure?
7. Do they allow for non-committal play?
8. Do they have sturdy construction for active use?

It can be helpful to think of play materials in terms of categories of toys that will help children to express themselves in different ways and that will also enable the therapist to build a relationship with the child (Ray, 2011). Kottman (2011) suggests five broad areas, which include the following:

1. Family/nurturing: e.g., doll's house, doll family, animal families, baby dolls
2. Scary: e.g., snakes, dinosaurs, dragons, puppets representing scary animals
3. Aggressive: e.g., punch bag, foam swords, toy soldiers
4. Expressive: e.g., paints, markers and crayons, paper, clay, and/or playdough
5. Pretend/fantasy: doctor's kit, masks, magic wands, fabrics

The play therapy space and materials are important because of the type of environment they help to create. The play therapist ensures that every time the child enters the play therapy space, it looks the same and the play materials are stored in the same place. This transmits an important implicit message to the child: the play therapy space is somewhere that is consistent and predictable and which the child can truly 'know'. Together with the therapist's presence, regular contact with the child, and confidentiality, the therapeutic space becomes a safe, containing (Bion, 1984) environment in which the child feels emotionally and psychologically held (Winnicott, 1974).

The Therapeutic Relationship

The following vignette refers to Devon's second visit to the playroom, which pre-dates the previous vignettes in terms of Devon's play therapy process.

Devon stands in the middle of the playroom. He stares ahead, not looking around the room or at his play therapist who is sitting just to his side, ensuring she is in his peripheral vision. His therapist notices that he is twiddling his fingers in what seems to be an anxious response to the situation. In a warm gentle tone, she comments to Devon that he might be finding it strange being in a new room with a new person. She reminds him that he can decide when he wants to look around, just as they had talked about when he came for a first visit with his grandfather the week before. She lets him know there is no hurry. After a few minutes, Devon starts to take cautious glances around the room. His play therapist reminds him that in here he can play with the toys in many different ways. He looks at her fleetingly. The therapist continues to wait patiently until Devon is ready to start exploring the therapeutic space.

Once the room and play materials are set up, the next critical element in play therapy is the role of the play therapist in forming a therapeutic relationship with the child. In CCPT, the therapist does not coax or cajole the child to play but instead facilitates a process in which the child can direct the agenda, focus, and timing of the play therapy. In an initial meeting with the child, the child-centred play therapist may say something like, "This time is just for you. In here you can play in many different ways. If there is something you may not do, I will let you know. We'll be in here together until XXX time." This way of introducing the play therapy time helps the child to start to understand the parameters in which it takes place: it is for a specific amount of time, and although it is a permissive environment, the play therapist will set limits on behaviour that may be harmful to the child or therapist. The child-centred therapist also lets the child know that it is *his* choice whether to tell anyone what he does in play therapy. The play therapist maintains confidentiality unless there is a safeguarding/child protection concern.

The core relational qualities of congruence, empathy, and unconditional positive regard (Rogers, 2007) are considered essential for the development and maintenance of the therapeutic relationship in CCPT, as it is through the dynamic relationship that the child's life experiences can be expressed. It is the juxtaposition of the presence of an emotionally attuned play therapist and the child's innate desire to develop mastery that develops self-esteem and self-efficacy in the child and helps to build the child's capacity to cope, which in turn contributes toward therapeutic growth and change.

The Need for Unconditional Positive Regard

Rogers (2004) postulated that we all need positive regard. However, most of us have grown up with 'conditions of worth' – conditions that we learn as children and believe we must fulfil if we are to gain the love and acceptance of significant others. A child may learn that praise or approval is dependent on him behaving in ways which the parent/caregiver thinks is correct. The child experiences being loved as conditional to conforming to the manner in which his parents wish him to be. In CCPT, the therapist strives to accept the child without condition or demand. The therapist facilitates the development of a permissive environment that will enable the child to feel accepted and under-stood so that he may play out whatever is related to his life experiences that is causing him difficulty. Rogers (2007) termed this "unconditional positive regard". As the child experiences genuine acceptance by the therapist, he feels liberated to try things out in the playroom, to take risks, and to make mistakes.

The child-centred play therapist communicates warmth, respect, and acceptance to the child by consistently and continuously seeking to offer empathy, which is the capacity to understand and to feel the child's emotions. The play therapist enters into the child's world and, as she walks with the child in his world, begins to witness and understand the child's world, which might feel sad, lonely, confusing, or scary. This is often a unique experience for the child, who may have internalized his feelings and become withdrawn like Devon, in the vignette, or might be externalizing his emotions by 'acting out'. The play therapist communicates empathy verbally, through commenting and reflecting on the content of the child's play and the emerging feelings, and non-verbally, by attuning with the child's affective states and communicating understanding and acceptance through facial expression, body posture, tone, etc.

It is well documented that the therapeutic alliance or relationship accounts for around 30% of the difference in outcome studies in psychotherapy, regardless of model or theory (Asay and Lambert, 1999). Recent research in neuroscience has demonstrated that the empathic attunement that develops within the therapeutic relationship creates a prime setting for new neural pathways to develop (Cozolino, 2014). As child and therapist interact within the therapeutic space, engaging emotionally and psychologically, the emotional arousal that ensues creates optimal conditions for the consolidation and integration of these neural pathways (Stewart et al., 2016). Thus what has been known for some time about the importance of the therapeutic relationship (Axline, 1989; Landreth, 2002; Ray, 2011), regardless of approach, is now given further credence from the field of neuroscience.

The play therapist is respectful of and trusts the child's ability to solve his own problems if he is given the opportunity to do so. She believes in the child's inner wisdom and that given an environment with certain conditions, the child will make choices that can lead to positive changes (Axline, 1989). It is through this new way of relating that the child's internal working model (Bowlby, 1988) becomes open to the possibility of change, initially with the child beginning to view himself as worthy of care and nurturance. Later, as this shift takes root, wider change becomes possible.

Children are often recommended for play therapy when their behaviour is deemed by adults around them to be causing problems; for instance, the child may be 'acting out' or may have become quiet and withdrawn. However, the child-centred play therapist does not set out to 'change' the child's behaviour, as this would run contrary to the principle of accepting the child exactly as he is (Axline, 1989). The play therapist recognizes that the child's behaviours are often a response to the chaos and turmoil that the child is experiencing, which in turn is causing the child to feel distressed and overwhelmed. In CCPT, the child is not expected to behave in a particular way; the play therapist accepts him with warmth and positive regard just as he is at that moment in time.

Connecting through Play

Devon stands in front of the sandtray shelves filled with miniature objects and toys (e.g., pebbles, crystals, plastic animals, people, trees, fences, wooden houses, walls, and bridges). He starts to pick out families of animals (e.g., large giraffe and several small giraffes, lion and cubs, etc.) and places them in the sandtray next to the shelves. He uses fences and walls to place the small animals in one section of the sandtray and the large animals on the outside looking in. He continues to do this in silence. Every now and then, his play therapist comments on what he is doing. Devon nods and sometimes looks at his therapist but does not speak until he stops, turns to his play therapist, and says, "I'm done now." His play therapist asks Devon if there is anything he wants to say about his sandtray world. Devon explains that there are lots of babies who need looking after. The big animals watch over the little ones as they play. He says the big ones keep watching so they don't lose any of the babies. The babies are playing and having fun with each other.

Child-centred play therapists track and reflect on the behaviour, feelings, and the content of play while 'staying in the metaphor' in the recognition that symbolic play offers the child the opportunity to play out difficult experiences within the parameters of safe therapeutic distance. Play therapists use reflective listening skills to develop the therapeutic relationship with the child. The therapist uses such skills and techniques in an intentional and consistent manner to convey to the child that she is interested in and wishes to connect with him. Landreth (2002) describes 'be with' attitudes by which the therapist demonstrates to the child "I am here, I hear you, I understand, I care." Through these relational messages, the therapist connects with the child non-verbally and may then go on to use verbal responses to offer comments on the content of the child's play or the feelings being expressed.

In the above vignette, Devon does not talk as he plays and his therapist uses 'tracking' as a way to connect with him and his play, communicating that she is noticing and interested in what is happening. As Devon picks out the animals and placed them in the sandtray, the therapist might say, for example, "I can see you've chosen that figure and you have decided to place it right next to the other one." Until the child names what the objects are, the child-centred therapist avoids 'labelling' the toys, as the child might be using them to represent something that the therapist is as yet unaware of (Landreth, 2002). By verbalizing some of what the child is doing, the therapist expresses to the child that she is fully present and aware, and communicates to him that he is making choices and decisions in his play. Tracking requires sensitive and judicious balancing: too much of it and it can become distracting to the child and might sound like a sports commentary! On the other hand, if the therapist refrains from saying anything, the child might wonder what his therapist is thinking and question whether she is interested in his play. However, it should be noted that silence also has an important role in play therapy, and, in the vignette at the beginning of this chapter, Devon set up the doll's house scene silently and his therapist, recognizing the intensity of the play, respected his silence and communicated her presence and understanding through non-verbal expression, body posture, eye contact, and facial expression.

In play therapy, the child and therapist are frequently involved in co-constructing stories and narratives related to the child's life (Cattanach, 1997). The child may or may not make links between what he is expressing and the experiences to which the play is connected. But it is this process of dynamic co-construction that integrates affect and cognition, which creates self-awareness and change in the child. Panksepp (2009) describes play as one of the major brain sources of joy and says it is one of seven emotional or motivational systems integral to our brains and present when we were born. Panksepp has identified play as having its "own neural circuitry", which means that when children feel safely connected to others, the circuitry of play is naturally activated (cited in Kestly, 2016, p. 15).

The play therapist uses reflection of content and feelings to check whether or not she has understood the child and to communicate this understanding to the child. Reflection is a skill in CCPT that may aid the therapeutic process (Landreth, 2002; Ray, 2011). In reflecting content, the therapist verbalizes what she sees, hears, and feels using the child's language. By mirroring, echoing, and tracking the child's actions and words, the therapist communicates to the child that she is listening to, understanding, and interested in the child's play. The child-centred play therapist does not offer any statement containing value or judgement, and does not compare or criticize the child. Thus a child-centred play therapist will not praise a child in play therapy, as this will communicate that she values one behaviour or emotion over another. However, the therapist will offer statements that increase self-esteem, such as acknowledging the child's capacity to make choices, plan, and execute ideas within the realm of play.

Congruence in Play

The therapist's capacity to be congruent with the child is also an important part of facilitating the child's play. Being congruent with the emotions that are actually present will help the child to connect to his true emotions (Ray, 2011). At times, there may be a discrepancy between the child's emotions and his expression. For instance, a child may play out a big battle in complete silence where emotions are noticeably absent. There may also be a mismatch of emotions when the child smiles or laughs at a scene of destruction and devastation in his play. In such a scenario, the therapist might think about the manner in which the emotions are avoided or disowned, perhaps because it is too painful for the child to connect with the real feelings related to the scene. Emotions may also be denied when, in role-play, the child 'poisons' or kills off his play therapist but then adds, "Just joking." In all these scenarios, it takes skill and careful timing when attempting to be congruent with a child, and the relationship needs to be secure enough that the child does not feel threatened, judged, or admonished.

Play Therapy in Practice

Perhaps this is a good moment to think a bit more about Devon, who has featured throughout this chapter. He was 7 years old when he was referred to play therapy following the sudden death of his father. He and his three siblings went to live with their paternal grandparents, as their mother was unable to provide the care they needed. Not much is known about Devon's early years, but he and his siblings experienced neglect, witnessed violence in their home, and may have experienced physical and emotional abuse. Following an assessment process with his paternal grandparents, I reflected on what I had learnt about Devon's history, life experiences, and the way in which his grandparents talked about him. After meeting Devon for the first time, I reflected further on his presentation and behaviour, his capacity to relate to his grandfather and to me. This time to reflect and formulate ideas about what might help a child best is an important part of the play therapy process. Play therapists will often draw on a range of approaches, such as attachment theory (Bowlby, 1988) and neuroscience, in order to inform their work with a child. In Devon's case, I kept in mind the likelihood that he had not experienced emotional attunement as an infant and had probably developed an insecure attachment with his primary caregiver. I also thought about how infants struggle to develop basic self-regulatory skills (Music, 2014) when they experience such adverse beginnings.

In his early play therapy sessions, Devon was hesitant about exploring the room and appeared very anxious. He spoke little but appeared to listen intently when, for instance, I told him about the playroom and how he might use it. My first priority as his play therapist was to develop a therapeutic space that Devon would experience as being physically, psychologically, and emotionally safe and secure. I was aware that with his father dying so suddenly and with other losses he had already experienced, Devon would be finding it hard to trust that his life could be predictable again. I knew that his sessions needed to be regular (same time, same day, same place) and that I would need to be consistent in the way I interacted with him.

Devon initially played for a number of weeks with the doll's house, rearranging the furniture in the rooms, taking furniture out of the house, and replacing it with objects that seemed out of place and incongruous. The vignette at the beginning of this chapter was from one of his early sessions – the house was overflowing with objects, people, and animals. Devon seemed to be showing me what his life looked like. On a very simple level, it seemed to illustrate what happens when a small house unexpectedly becomes home to four children. On a more unconscious, profound level, Devon seemed to be communicating some of the despair, confusion, and anger he felt when both parents 'disappeared'. At this stage in his play therapy, Devon did not want to talk about what he was creating. He would play intently with the doll's house and I would sit alongside him, paying close attention to what he was doing, sometimes tracking his play, and occasionally reflecting on his feelings when he seemed to become frustrated or upset, saying, for instance, "You were trying to get that in there but it just won't fit; that's frustrating." Devon would often nod in acknowledgement at my reflections and sometimes pause and look at me keenly. He seemed surprised that I could understand him. This emotional attunement helped Devon to feel accepted, understood, valued, and connected in the therapeutic relationship. He started to visibly relax, and as he did so, his capacity for expression increased.

In the vignette earlier in this chapter, Devon used animal families to express his need and desire for safety and nurturance. His experiences of sudden loss, chaotic living conditions, and a new home with his grandparents are complex events for a child of 7 to explain verbally, but play enabled Devon to give expression to them – the doll's house became a chaotic and disordered environment where nothing was where it should be, whereas the families of animals provided care and safety for their young. In a similar way to Lowenfeld's concept of the 'world technique', projective play in play therapy offers children the opportunity to express themselves and explore their ideas, emotions, hopes, and wishes by manipulating small world toys and objects. It helps children in both the expression and mastery of emotional content in a safe and containing way, as it uses symbols and objects to express the inexpressible.

As Devon started to explore the playroom, he found the 'sensory box', containing items such as slime, putty, stretchy creatures, bubbles, cornflour, and washing-up liquid. He was intrigued by the contents and, for a few weeks, used these materials in an exploratory and creative manner – making mixtures, playing with the bubbles, and, for parts of many sessions, placing his hands in water and chasing bubbles. For children like Devon who may have missed out on early interactive experiences with their main caregiver, this type of play helps them to explore both physiological and emotional experiences. It supports emotional regulation, which in turn gives children the opportunity to practise coping strategies and to resolve thoughts and feelings that may have become 'stuck' (Landreth, 2002; Ray, 2011). Devon used this play to soothe and calm himself, try things out, and take manageable risks. He would often return to the sensory box as well as the wet and dry sandtrays after some projective or role-play that was emotionally challenging for him.

For children who are emotionally overwhelmed, anxious, or terrified, we now know that these states trigger "powerful subcortical limbic system activity" (Music, 2014, p. 4), which interferes with self-regulatory and reflective capacities that take place in the higher brain area. Thus the capacity to work with "emotional/bodily regulatory processes" that take place "via the subcortical, evolutionarily earlier brain areas such as the brain stem" (Music, 2014, p. 4) is one of the strengths of play therapy. As Devon experienced the play therapy space as a containing environment and the therapeutic relationship as a secure base (Bowlby, 1988), his affect, behaviour, and development all showed positive signs of progress. He still faced many challenges, but the vignette at the end of this chapter provides a brief view of some of the changes that took place within him during the time he attended play therapy, which was for about a year and a half.

Research and Evidence

So, who might benefit from play therapy? Research in play therapy has shown that children, particularly between the ages of 3 and 12 who experience a range of emotional, behavioural, social, and learning difficulties, can be helped by play therapy. These difficulties may include anxiety disorders, depression, attention deficit hyperactivity, autism spectrum disorders, and oppositional defiant and conduct disorders (Bratton et al., 2017). Research also supports the effectiveness of play therapy in helping children to cope with difficult life events such as chronic illness and hospitalization, loss through divorce or bereavement, abuse, domestic abuse, and natural disasters (Landreth, 2002; Ray, 2011). Since 2000, four meta-analytic reviews have been conducted that have provided evidence that the treatment effect of play therapy for the above life events and difficulties ranges statistically from moderate to high (Bratton et al., 2005; Le Blanc & Ritchie, 2001; Lin & Bratton, 2015; Ray et al., 2015). Meta-analysis is especially useful when there are small sample sizes, which is often the case in play therapy with researchers focusing on treatment for individual studies and small populations. Thus, the four reviews are particularly useful in confirming the effectiveness of play therapy, especially CCPT approaches, across age, gender, and presenting problems (Bratton et al., 2017). Of specific note is that play therapy has been found to have the highest treatment effect when a parent/carer is actively involved in the child's therapy such as in filial therapy (Guerney & Ryan, 2013). This seems to point to a need for greater involvement of parents/carers in their child's play therapy, which could also act as a prevention for further problems developing.

Play therapy in the United States is offered regularly as the treatment of choice in a range of settings, including mental health agencies, residential homes, schools, hospitals, and community organizations (Reddy et al., 2005). Indeed, recently the US government has released endorsement of several play therapy approaches that include CCPT, Child–Parent Relationship Therapy, Filial Family Therapy, Adlerian Play Therapy, and Theraplay. These approaches are now listed as evidence-based mental health interventions that use play therapy as their primary intervention (Ray, 2017). In the United

Kingdom, however, play therapy is still a growing profession. Over the past decade, awareness and understanding of its efficacy has increased, and in the education sector, many schools recognize the benefits that play therapy can offer their student populations. Nevertheless, much still needs to be done in terms of raising awareness and ensuring that adequate funding is available for children who would benefit from accessing non-verbal and age-appropriate psychological support. The importance of ensuring that play therapists are appropriately trained and registered with a professional body is also critical in adequately protecting vulnerable children and young people in our society.

And so the last words go to Devon, a little boy I feel privileged and humbled to have worked with, who showed such determination, courage, and zest for life.

> Devon and I, his play therapist, are walking through a deep dark forest. We are fellow explorers in an unknown land. Devon, the chief explorer, is leading the way. Together we crawl, creep, and jump through trees and bushes. Devon tells me when and how to move. I follow his instructions. Devon shouts out warnings to me, "Now duck!" "Watch out! Pterodactyl overhead." Suddenly, the pterodactyl strikes. It has Devon in its claws and I have to help wrestle the creature off him. A frantic battle ensues and the pterodactyl flies off but Devon collapses on the ground. "My heart is hurt," he croaks. "Quick, now be a doctor and come and help me," Devon stage-whispers to me. I throw off my role of explorer and become a medic, complete with doctor's bag. "Examine my heart," Devon instructs. I follow his instructions, placing a stethoscope on his chest and checking his heart with care and concern. I continually check Devon's non-verbal communications to ensure I am in tune with him, not a step ahead or behind. "Your heart has been hurt by the pterodactyl," I venture. "Yes, ripped up," Devon stage-whispers. He starts to writhe and moan, saying, "Aahh, my heart hurts. The stupid pterodactyl really hurt me." I continue, "Your heart's been badly hurt and it's sounding very weak." "Check if it's going to get better," Devon orders. I continue to verbalize my 'medical findings': "I can hear your heart beating faintly ... it is struggling but it's still pumping ... it's been really badly hurt and it's aching ... but it wants to keep going ... it's not giving up." Devon listens intently, lying still. He urges further examination and I comment on his pain and hurt. Then Devon looks at me directly and says, "My heart's been really bad and it still hurts a lot but it is getting better. One day, it won't hurt anymore."

References

Asay, T. P., & Lambert, M. J. (1999). The empirical case for the common factors in therapy: Quantitative findings. In M. A. Hubble, B. L. Duncan, & S. D. Miller (Eds.), *The heart and soul of change: What works in therapy* (pp. 23–55). Washington, DC: American Psychological Association.

Axline, V. M. (1989). *Play therapy.* New York: Churchill Livingstone.

Axline, V. M. (1990). *Dibs in search of self: Personality development in play therapy* (new ed.). London: Penguin.

Bion, W. R. (1984). *Learning from experience*. London: Maresfield.

Bowlby, J. (1988). *A secure base: Clinical application of attachment theory*. London: Routledge.

Bratton, S., Dafoe, E., Swan, A., Opiola, K., McClintock, D., & Barcenas, G. (2017). *Evidence-based child therapy*. Available at http://evidencebasedchildtherapy.com/research/.

Bratton, S., Ray, D., Rhine, T., & Jones, L. (2005). The efficacy of play therapy with children: A meta-analytic review of treatment outcomes. *Professional Psychology: Research and Practice*, 36(4), 367–390.

British Association of Play Therapists (BAPT) (2013). *History of play therapy*. Available at www.bapt.info/play-therapy/history-play-therapy/.

Cattanach, A. (1997). *Children's stories in play therapy*. London: Jessica Kingsley.

Cattanach, A. (2008). *Play therapy with abused children*. London: Jessica Kingsley.

Compact Oxford English Dictionary (2005). Oxford: Oxford University Press.

Cozolino, L. J. (2014). *The neuroscience of human relationships: Attachment and the developing social brain* (2nd edn.). New York: W. W. Norton.

Doctor Margaret Lowenfeld Trust (DMLT). (2017). About Lowenfeld. Available at http://lowenfeld.org/about-lowenfeld.html.

Freud, A. (1974). *Introduction to psychoanalysis: Lectures for child analysts and teachers, 1922–1935*. London: Hogarth.

Freud, S. (1949). *An outline of psycho-analysis*. London: Hogarth.

Guerney, L., & Ryan, V. (2013). *Group filial therapy: Training parents to conduct special play sessions with their own children*. London: Jessica Kingsley.

Haugh, S., & Paul, S. (Eds.) (2008). *The therapeutic relationship: Perspectives and themes*. Ross-on-Wye: PCSS.

Hubble, M. A., Duncan, B. L., & Miller, S. D. (Eds.) (1999). *The heart and soul of change: What works in therapy*. Washington, DC: American Psychological Association.

Jennings, S. (1999). *Introduction to developmental playtherapy: Playing and health*. London: Jessica Kingsley.

Jennings, S. (2017). Embodiment-Projection-Role (EPR). Available at www.suejennings.com/epr.html.

Kestly, T. A. (2014). *The interpersonal neurobiology of play: Brain-building interventions for emotional well-being*. New York: W. W. Norton.

Kestly, T. A. (2016). Presence and play: Why mindfulness matters. *International Journal of Play Therapy*, 25(1), 14–23.

Klein, M. (1997). *The psycho-analysis of children* (rev. edn.). London: Vintage.

Kottman, T. (2011). *Play therapy: Basics and beyond*. Alexandria, VA: American Counseling Association.

Landreth, G. L. (2002). *Play therapy: The art of the relationship* (2nd edn.). New York: Brunner-Routledge.

Le Blanc, M., & Ritchie, M. (2001). A meta-analysis of play therapy outcomes. *Counselling Psychology Quarterly*, 14, 149–163.

Lin, Y., & Bratton, S. C. (2015). A meta-analytic review of child-centered play therapy approaches. *Journal of Counseling and Development*, 93(1), 45–48.

Lowenfeld, M. (1991). *Play in childhood*. London: Mac Keith.

Lowenfeld, M. (1993). *Understanding children's sandplay: Lowenfeld's World Technique*. Cambridge: Margaret Lowenfeld Trust.

Malchiodi, C. (2015). Neurobiology, creative interventions, and childhood trauma. In C. Malchiodi (Ed.), *Creative interventions with traumatized children* (pp. 3–23). New York: Guilford.

McMahon, L. (1992). *The handbook of play therapy*. London: Routledge.

Music, G. (2014). Top down and bottom up: Trauma, executive functioning, emotional regulation, the brain and child psychotherapy. *Journal of Child Psychotherapy, 40*(1), 3–19.

O'Connor, K. J., Schaefer, C. E., & Braverman, L. D. (Eds.) (2016). *Handbook of play therapy* (2nd edn.). Hoboken, NJ: Wiley.

Oxford Compact Thesaurus (2005). Oxford: Oxford University Press.

Panksepp, J. (2009). Brain emotional systems and qualities of mental life: From animal models of affect to implications for psychotherapeutics. In D. Fosha, D. J. Siegel, & M. F. Solomon (Eds.), *The healing power of emotion: Affective neuroscience, development, and clinical practice* (pp. 1–26). New York: W. W. Norton.

Ray, D. C. (2011). *Advanced play therapy: Essential conditions, knowledge, and skills for child practice*. New York: Taylor & Francis.

Ray, D. C. (2017). Play therapy: An evidence-based practice. *Play Therapy, 12*(2), 10.

Ray, D. C., Armstrong, S. A., Balkin, R. S., & Jayne, K. M. (2015). Child-centered play therapy in the schools: Review and meta-analysis. *Psychology in the Schools, 52*(2), 107–123.

Reddy, L. A., Files-Hall, T. M., & Schaefer, C. E. (2005). *Empirically based play interventions for children*. Washington, DC: APA.

Rogers, C. R. (2003). *Client-centered therapy: Its current practice, implications and theory*. London: Constable.

Rogers, C. R. (2004). *On becoming a person: A therapist's view of psychotherapy*. London: Constable.

Rogers, C. R. (2007). The necessary and sufficient conditions of therapeutic personality change. *Psychotherapy: Theory, Research, Practice, Training. 44*(3), 240–248. (Special section: The necessary and sufficient conditions at the half century mark).

Schaefer, C. E. (2011). *Foundations of play therapy*. Hoboken, NJ: Wiley.

Schaefer, C. E., & Drewes, A. A. (2016). Prescriptive play therapy. In K. J. O'Connor, C. E. Schaefer & L. D. Braverman (Eds.), *Handbook of play therapy* (2nd edn.) (pp. 227–240). Hoboken, NJ: Wiley.

Siegel, D. J. (2012). *The developing mind: How relationships and the brain interact to shape who we are* (2nd edn.). New York: Guilford.

Stacey, Jenny, (2008). The therapeutic relationship in creative arts psychotherapy. In S. Haugh & S. Paul (Eds.), *The therapeutic relationship: Perspectives and themes* (pp. 217–229). Ross-on-Wye: PCCS.

Stewart, A. L., Field, T. A., & Echterling, L. G. (2016). Neuroscience and the magic of play therapy. *International Journal of Play Therapy, 25*(1), 4–13.

Weinrib, E. L. (1983). *Images of the self: The sandplay therapy process*. Boston: Sigo.

Winnicott, D. W. (1974). *Playing and reality*. London: Penguin.

Yasenik, L., & Gardner, K., (2004). *Play therapy dimensions model: A decision-making guide for therapists*. Calgary: Rocky Mountain Play Therapy Institute.

36 Political Violence (War and Terrorism) and Children's Play

Esther Cohen

Play is so important for optimal child development that it has been recognized by the United Nations High Commission for Human Rights as a right of every child (2006). As such, combining 'children's play' with 'war and terrorism' seems incongruous at first sight. Children's play is usually associated with fun and amusement and with the luxury of suspending reality for some time. These mood states appear unsuitable or impossible under collective life-threatening situations. However, an examination of the functions of play reveals a complex relationship between play and coping with the stress of exposure to political violence. In this chapter, I describe how the ability to play and the characteristics of play may be affected by the exposure of children to political violence. I also highlight how play may, nevertheless, serve as an important mechanism for bolstering resilience in the face of adversity, for coping during a traumatic event, and for processing such events in their aftermath. Furthermore, I present ideas relevant to prevention and intervention. The latter focus both on the use of play observation as a diagnostic tool for identifying children suffering from post-traumatic distress and on specific interventions designed to promote healing through play with caregivers and therapists.

One of the first intense and innovative demonstrations of the role of play and imagination in children's experience of war appeared in John Boorman's unique film *Hope and Glory*, released in 1987. This film focuses on a 10-year-old boy who is depicted in a very different way from miserably appearing characters portrayed in other films shortly after the Second World War period. In creating the film, Boorman drew directly from his childhood experiences in London during the Blitz, which he remembers as a great adventure. In the film, the boy lives with his parents and two sisters and has great fun playing with his friends on the city's bomb sites. After their home is destroyed by fire, the family goes to stay with his grandfather, where the boy spends a glorious summer. While the depiction of the air bombardments and family displacement leave out much of the experiences of fear, terror, and loss shared by many exposed to war, it highlights the powers of children's imagination in constructing an alternative reality, which allows for coping in the midst of adversity.

One should also remember that what may have contributed to the boy's ability to use his playful resources was that his family remained intact, without enduring any separation or human losses. The importance of preserving the ties of children with their significant caregivers has long been recognized as important to the emotional security and adaptation of children exposed to war. In their study of children in the same period in London during the German Blitz, Anna Freud and Dorothy Burlingham (1943) observed that children who were separated from their families in the city and sent to safe havens were much more traumatized than children who remained with their families in the bombarded city. They concluded that the disruption of family ties is more traumatic to children than the events of war. The recognition of the importance of human connections in coping with stress, as a protection against later post-traumatic difficulties, has since been documented and widely accepted (Cohen, 2009; Khamis, 2016).

Perroni (2014) points out the revolutionary nature of the exhibition 'No Child's Play', inaugurated in 1997 at the Yad-Vashem Holocaust Museum in Jerusalem, displaying games and toys used by children living in Europe during the Nazi occupation. It contributed to changing earlier conceptions of expected paucity of play under life-threatening conditions. The curator of the exhibition, Yehudit Inbar, explains that in addition to children's need to assume adult roles to help in their family's battle for survival in the ghettos and in the extermination camps, they remained children. Furthermore, she maintains that fantasy, creativity, and play were the manifestations of a basic need for survival (www .yadvashem.org/yv/en/exhibitions/nochildsplay/intro.asp).

Experiences of War and Terrorism and Their Effects on Children's Development and Mental Health

Research interest in how children, and especially young children, are affected by war-related trauma, and how they cope, is relatively new yet has been growing at a fast pace over the last decade. Feldman and Vengrober (2011) explain the continued past neglect of this area by a generally held belief by researchers and clinicians that children lack the cognitive mechanisms to both understand the gravity of such events and keep them in memory. However, new findings point to the increased risk to young children, in comparison to older children and adults, when exposed to different kinds of traumatic events, including those related to political violence. Lieberman (2011) concludes her review of the relevant research by stating compellingly that "children's mental health in the first 5 years of life can be profoundly and lastingly affected by the impact of traumatic stressors, such as domestic violence, child abuse, community violence, and war" (p. 640). The effects of traumatic exposure on young children appear to be widespread and are not limited to post-traumatic symptoms. Such events may negatively affect their biological, emotional, social, and cognitive functioning and manifest in physiological and emotional dysregulation and/or various behaviour problems

(Chemtob et al., 2010; Conway et al., 2013; Lieberman & Van-Horn, 2008; Pat-Horenczyk et al., 2015).

Two recent reviews further strengthen these conclusions. Slone and Mann (2016) reviewed 35 studies that focused on the relationship between political violence and the mental health of children aged 0–6 years. Their review shows that children who were exposed to political violence exhibited increased post-traumatic stress disorder (PTSD) and post-traumatic stress symptoms, behavioural and emotional symptoms, psychosomatic symptoms, sleep problems, and disturbed play. Concurrently, Wolmer et al. (2017) emphasize that since the preschool years are viewed as critical developmental stages, preschool children are more vulnerable to the exposure to disasters and terrorist incidents than older children, and it may have a drastic influence on their health and development.

Moreover, studies suggest that these effects may be more pronounced in young children who are exposed to recurrent or ongoing situations of war and terrorism, in comparison with those who have been exposed to past or single traumatic incidents (Conway et al., 2013; Pat-Horenczyk et al., 2012). Several studies have focused on the effects on children of traumatic events, such as the September 11, 2001, destruction of the World Trade Center towers in New York City. While severe effects on children's well-being have been demonstrated even 10 years later, it appears that such an event is easier to process when the ongoing reality provides a sense of continuous safety. Much of trauma therapy is based on processing a traumatic event, while reminding the child that it happened in the past and is no longer a danger in the present.

Explanations for the added risk under circumstances of continuous terrorism and war underscore the specific characteristics of terror events, such as their unpredictability and indiscriminate nature, which contribute to a continual state of stress and anxiety with no clear endpoint. Children are often exposed in reality, or through the social networks and the media, to gruesome and morbid sights, such as when a bomb explodes in a public place causing death and injury or when exposed to the devastation left by a missile hitting a home. Some terrorist acts such as 'suicide bombing' are hard to grasp. Thus, in political violence, the combination of terrorist attacks and ensuing terrorist threats confound the boundaries between direct and distant trauma (Conway et al., 2013). The cumulative costs of the repeated efforts to adjust to these stressful events may result in increased allostatic load, or even overload, that is, a state in which serious pathophysiology can occur in the brain and in the body (McEwen, 1998). It may thus be expressed in the exacerbation of emotional distress, rather than in habituation to stress or resilience (Pat-Horenczyk et al., 2013).

It appears that children may be affected not only by direct exposure to political violence, but also through the deleterious effects of the traumatic events on their caregivers and communities (Conway et al., 2013; Dyregrov & Regel, 2012; Feldman & Vengrober, 2011; Pat-Horenczyk et al., 2012). Slone and Mann's (2016) review reveals significant correlations between parental and child psychopathology and shows that family environment and parental functioning may serve as moderators of the exposure–outcome association for children. New evidence points to the effects of maternal exposure to political violence on young children even when the exposure preceded the child's birth, and to its continued effects through the pre-adolescent years.

In a recent study, which included observational measures of mothers' emotional availability, Shachar-Dadon et al. (2017) found that retrospective accounts of women's higher exposure to war-related experiences (mostly missile attacks in northern Israel) was related to elevated emotional distress. In turn, mothers' emotional distress was associated with higher levels of maternal separation anxiety, lower emotional availability in parent–child interactions, and lower levels of child adaptive behaviour in 3-year-old children conceived at least a month prior to the exposure.

Halevi et al. (2016) recently went beyond documenting the effects of chronic early trauma on children's mental health to follow risk and resilience trajectories in war-exposed children across the first decade and chart predictors of individual pathways. Their results show that the effects of early stress do not heal naturally and tend to be exacerbated over time with trauma-exposed children. Compared with controls, war-exposed children displayed significantly more Axis I psychopathology and more comorbid disorders. Nearly a third of war-exposed children remained chronically symptomatic, presenting more comorbid, chronic, and externalizing profiles as they grow.

The Functions of Children's Play in Times of War and Terrorism

Given the above findings related to risk and resilience in children exposed to political violence, I will now examine how these effects manifest in children's play. Play is viewed as the child's natural language for the expression of inner experiences and ways of coping, and thus as a behaviour most telling about the child's development and mental health status. Therefore, I believe that we need to examine the functions of play in normal development in order to understand the interplay between play and child adaptation under conditions of stress and political violence.

Play, especially 'pretend play' (also referred to as 'free play', 'imaginative play', and 'symbolic play'), has long been considered of central importance to children's cognitive, social, and emotional development (Ginsburg, 2007; Singer & Singer, 2005; Vygotsky, 1966). In summing up his review of the literature on the benefits of play, Ginsburg (2007) points out that play is important to healthy brain development, as it allows children to use their creativity while developing their imagination, dexterity, and physical, cognitive, and emotional strength. He emphasizes that play allows children to create and explore a world they can master, conquering their fears while practicing adult roles, sometimes in conjunction with other children or adult caregivers. Play helps children develop new competencies that lead to enhanced confidence and the resiliency they will need to face future challenges.

Four main specific functions of play as potential contributors to the child's adaptation to traumatic situations of political violence are discussed next.

First, we should remember that one of the basic functions of play is to produce pleasure, fun, or a sense of engagement and absorption in a satisfying activity in a sphere removed from external reality. Play allows fun and creativity by affording endless possibilities and no attached consequences to fantasized and created content. It therefore is also an arena for experiencing fantasy wish-fulfilment. This function is of particular importance for children in families who live under the recurrent threat of war and terror attacks. Parents under these circumstances often experience high levels of anxiety, depression, and symptoms of PTSD (MacDermid-Wadsworth, 2010). Their ability to engage with the children in fun, creative, and pleasurable activities is greatly reduced. They may even be irritated by their children's engagement in noisy or detached fantasy play. Furthermore, they tend to adopt a "survival mode" (Chemtob, 2005), characterized by hypervigilance, which prohibits any prolonged disengagement from a focus on reality and possible emerging dangers.

Concomitantly, studies with both adults and young children show that positive affect can occur even during periods of distress and has important adaptational significance because it is an important facilitator of adaptive coping with acute and chronic stress and post-traumatic distress (Bonanno et al., 2011; Folkman & Moskowitz, 2000; Fredrickson, 2000). Thus, the potential of play to support the emergence of positive affect is important for children's adaptation.

The second major function of play involves the ability to experience self-efficacy by changing the passive victim role into an active one. Indeed, in play children can experience a sense of agency by becoming "masters of their universe" (Alvarez & Phillips, 1998). This function has already been suggested by Freud in 1920 in "Beyond the Pleasure Principle". He pointed out that a self-initiated game of a year-old child may serve the function of helping the instinctual renunciation of the need for the mother and allowing her to go away without protesting. This is achieved by repeating the experience of separation from a play object and finding it, hence taking on an active role instead of the previous passive position. Thus, this ability to repeat negative experiences in play is helpful in making negative experiences more predictable and facilitating a sense of control. Children exposed to political violence may feel increased agency by repeating and changing in play elements of traumatic experiences they have witnessed or by preplanning for situations that they may fear. These activities may contribute to modulation and regulation of emotions and to controlling anxiety and aggression.

The third important function of play relates to the need for narrative construction in order to process the traumatic event. Events related to political violence are very difficult to comprehend. The perpetrators are usually personally unknown to the victims except perhaps by their group affiliation. Thus, constructing a coherent and empowering narrative appears to be one of the challenges in the aftermath of traumatic events, especially for children. Prichard (2016) argues that through play, trauma memories can be reworked at both a metaphorical and a neurobiological level. Play allows the child to identify and integrate fragmented sensory experiences, reconstruct them to increase comprehension, clarify values, create meaning, and access and express feelings and wishes. Often the narrative helps in establishing a sense of identity and a channel for sublimation and identification. It may also help in developing empathy with others. Singer and Singer (2005) emphasized the contribution of play to narrative awareness and expressive linguistic capacities. Research demonstrates that the ability to construct a coherent trauma narrative is associated with better coping with the events and with post-traumatic growth (Cohen et al., 2010; Hafstad et al., 2010; Wigren, 1994).

The fourth function of play relevant to coping with trauma-related political violence is the opportunities it enables for sharing private subjective experience with others. Halevi et al. (2016) point out the function of social engagement in protecting from developing psychopathology after exposure to political violence. This includes the child's ability for social initiation, sharing and co-constructing play activities with others, and competent use of the environment. In a similar vein, Brom (2014) points out that parallel to early attachment strategies, later attachment strategies are activated when threat is perceived. Attachment has been recognized as a survival mechanism, both during early development and in emergency situations. At times of serious threats, people have a clear tendency to engage in immediate strong bonding with a perceived benevolent authority, as well as with other people they perceive as sharing their fate. This is particularity true for traumatized children, who through play activities with others can counteract feelings of depression, anxiety, and panic, often reported by them (Schonfeld, 2011). Indeed, the analysis of the play patterns of children exposed to terror attacks shows that preschool children who exhibited an ability to create a positive relationship with the play observer also showed a higher level of adaptation (Cohen et al., 2010).

Changes in Children's Play under Conditions of Traumatic Exposure to Political Violence

The sad paradox in the interplay between trauma and play is that while play and playfulness may be helpful in processing traumatic events, exposure to traumatic events may lead to a defensive reduction in children's symbolic play (Drewes, 2001; Feldman et al., 2007). Furthermore, the play, often referred to as 'post-traumatic play', may lose its joyful quality and become repetitious, rigid, serious, or morbid (Cohen et al., 2010; Nader & Pynoos, 1991; Varkas, 1998).

A similar paradox operates with parental support of children's playfulness. Playfulness develops with caregivers who engage with the child playfully, support and enrich his or her play, and use play for affective processing of stressful events (Bronson & Bundy, 2001; Fonagy et al., 2002). However, as mentioned previously, the quality of the parents' caregiving and their emotional availability is often diminished during stressful periods, when their children need them most, due to the parents' depression, anxiety, or post-traumatic distress (Cohen, 2009; Cohen & Shulman, in press).

Post-Traumatic Play

The phenomenon of 'post-traumatic play' has been described in clinical reports as a play pattern observable following traumatic experiences, which is distinctly different from normal play (Wershba-Gershon, 1996). The reports characterize post-traumatic play as driven, serious, lacking in joy, and frequently morbid. Characteristically, such play consists of compulsively repeated themes, which are not resolved (Gil, 1996; Nader & Pynoos, 1991; Varkas, 1998). Additionally, a number of reports point out the defensive reduction in symbolic expression and the concurrent increase in concrete thinking (Drewes, 2001; Feldman et al., 2007). Post-traumatic play is further described as developmentally regressed and involving simple defences, such as identification with the aggressor, identification with the victim, displacement, undoing, and denial (Cohen et al., 2010; Rafman et al., 1996; Terr, 1981).

Feldman and Vengrober (2011) point out that one of the criteria for post-traumatic stress disorder, the reexperiencing domain (criterion B), is typically observed in young children through the expression of trauma reminders in words or gestures during play. They describe compulsive or repetitive play that re-creates elements of the traumatic events, or repeated thoughts, flashbacks, or freezing in response to trauma reminders. Among the symptoms observed in young children diagnosed with PTSD are symptoms of social withdrawal, such as preference for solitary functional play and increased interest in objects combined with decreased interest in people.

One must also keep in mind that opportunities for play are often reduced because of the danger involved in being outdoors, being on the run, in hiding, or living as refugees. In a small study of latency-age refugee children in Australia, MacMillan et al. (2015) found that resettled refugee children, especially girls, demonstrated limited pre-migration play, with higher levels of post-resettlement engagement.

Reports based on clinical observations suggest that engaging in post-traumatic play may be adaptive or maladaptive, curative or harmful (Dripchak, 2007; Nader & Pynoos, 1991; Ryan & Needham, 2001; Terr, 1981;

Webb, 2004). Nader and Pynoos (1991) maintain that the ability of post-traumatic play to alleviate distress depends mainly on the child's perception of control over consequences of his or play activity, his or her ability to cognitively process the trauma and to express forbidden feelings.

In our own study of children exposed to terrorism (Chazan & Cohen, 2010; Cohen, 2006; Cohen et al., 2010), the children showing the best adaptation levels (according to their caregivers) in comparison to those with lowest levels (who exhibited more PTSD symptoms) had a greater tendency to engage in play and displayed more positive affect and engagement in their play. Furthermore, they showed a better ability to plan and play out a coherent, progressive, creative, and satisfying imaginary narrative. Their sense of self-efficacy was evident by displaying their 'awareness of oneself as player' (awareness of being the director as well as the actor in one's play). They also revealed a better capacity for emotion regulation and self-soothing and a greater tendency to engage in relationships with the present adult. All these play characteristics demonstrate the abilities of the better-adjusted children to make use of the beneficial functions of play, which was delineated earlier. The assumption is that the development of these abilities throughout infancy and early childhood may enable children to use them more effectively when trauma strikes, and contribute to their resilience.

In our analysis (Cohen et al., 2010) we identified three patterns of adaptive-defensive strategies employed in play of children exposed to terror events. These were found to be significantly associated with both level of PTSD symptoms and diagnosis. The belief is that the identification of the major pattern employed by an individual child may be helpful both in evaluating his or her level of inner turmoil and in tailoring a supportive or therapeutic play intervention. I therefore describe these patterns and delineate the basic recommended interventions suitable for each pattern.

Reenactment with Soothing. Children rated high on this pattern by the researchers were found to have the best post-trauma adaptation level, based on independent ratings of caregivers. This pattern includes play activity characterized by reenactment or repetition of aspects or themes of the traumatic event. The player freely expresses diverse feelings. As the narrative progresses toward a satisfying ending, the player achieves a sense of relief or satiation resulting in a sense of mastery.

Children who predominantly exhibit this pattern seem to have inner resources allowing them to use play for their own healing. They need opportunities to play and supportive adults and peers who can be attentive as they rework their trauma narratives, regulate their feelings, and continue their normal development. This recommendation is in line with Winnicott (1971), who demonstrated that important psychological transformations could take place via the process of play itself, even without psychodynamic interpretations.

These children are different from the children exhibiting play activity characterized by two different patterns, described later, who were found to show higher levels of post-traumatic symptoms. Therefore, these children exhibiting predominantly 'reenactments without soothing' or feeling 'overwhelmed' need specific therapeutic help in processing the trauma.

Reenactment without Soothing. This pattern is characterized by the repeated reenactment of themes or aspects of the traumatic event. Feelings expressed are often disturbing, both frightening and aggressive. Often, the play activity may be overly rigid and constricted and repeats itself with the same frightening results. Reworking of the traumatic event does not occur, the play does not end with satiation, and the child does not gain relief from terror and fear.

Children who seem 'stuck' in this pattern of rigid repetition, with no resources to see their way out of catastrophe, may need the active intervention of a therapist or a caregiver who is supervised by a therapist. The therapist needs to actively make the child aware that he or she is the director of the play and that in play there are many possibilities one can explore. The therapist may challenge the child to come up with new ideas for protection and winning. He or she may suggest to the child to select one of a number of different ideas. The principle behind this stance is to impart the message that even when the child cannot think of a different or a more positive narrative, the caring adult can see many options for achieving safety. The playful stance accompanying the therapist's choice suggestions is believed to further enhance the sense of security and optimism.

Overwhelming Reexperiencing. This pattern is characterized by the expression of mental states lacking a coherent structure, resulting in overwhelming the child. It is usually manifested by an inability to produce a meaningful narrative and by frozen, disconnected, or tense and hypervigilant behaviour. The impression is that the child refrains from engaging in fantasy to avoid the possible surfacing of frightening memories. Indeed, at times, when the child creates a play narrative, it is about catastrophic events that engulf the child. These enactments characteristically involve a loss of a sense of boundaries, becoming the embodiment of an overwhelming force or, alternatively, of submission. The play activity does not resolve or diminish the child's extreme emotional state; rather, it tends to prolong or intensify it.

For children who seem overwhelmed (due to anxiety, depression, and hypervigilance) and therefore unable to use play to process the trauma, the role of the therapist in play sessions with the child becomes very central. This is in line with Winnicott's (1971) observation that "[p]sychotherapy has to do with two people playing together. The corollary of this is that where playing is not possible then the work done by the therapist is directed towards bringing the patient from a state of not being able to play into a state of being able to play" (p. 38).

Slade (1994) develops this idea further, noting that the literature has emphasized the therapist's role in offering interpretation and deciphering meaning, while neglecting his or her role in the process of creating meaning or make-believe. She argues that for immature children or for children whose capacities for symbolization and abstraction are limited, interpretations of inner feelings and experiences may lead to denial and disorganization. She highlights the importance of the therapist's "simply playing" with the child, and his or her role in leading the child in learning to develop a narrative in play and in gradually integrating affect into it. This co-creation within a growing meaningful relationship helps the development of a reflective self-function. A suggestion is that the same therapeutic needs may be evident in traumatized children, whose previous developmental achievements may have been thwarted by the traumatic experience. Therefore, play with these children often begins on a somewhat lower developmental level than their intellectual level, and thus exerts no pressure on the child. The therapist infuses simple interactions using playfulness and attempts to co-construct a simple imaginative story. The play narrative builds and becomes more complex in a gradual manner, and the child is supported in taking initiatives in broadening the narrative. When the child produces play that is extremely chaotic and incoherent, the therapist may ask the child to slow down and ask his or her help in understanding what is happening and who the characters are. Often, writing down the narrative, which can be retold, pondered, and reread, encourages the child to engage in developing a more advanced, clearer and more coherent narrative.

Conclusions and Practice Implications

In this chapter, I discussed the important potential positive contributions of play to the child's development and resilience. However, it is also demonstrated how forces related to political violence interact to effectively reduce many children's ability to reap the benefits of play. These data have implications for the prevention of mental health problems in children and for necessary intervention.

I join the general recommendations offered by Ginsburg (2007), Macmillan et al. (2015), and Webb (2004) that safe environments be made available to all children in the community and that play be included along with academic and social-enrichment opportunities. This is especially relevant for children chronically exposed to intermittent political violence and for those who have resettled after experiencing such traumatic events. The opportunities for group play with peers are important especially for school-age children as social engagement is associated with better resilience (Halevi et al., 2016).

When it comes to young children our own work strongly supports the suggestion of MacMillan et al. (2015) that fostering parents' participation in play is important for the health of the parent–child dyad. Moreover, often there is a need to build the ability among parents who had limited opportunity to learn and play themselves. Given the paucity of documentation of such programs in the literature, my colleagues and I have designed a program called in Hebrew 'Let's Make Room for Play' (NAMAL) for Israeli mothers and their toddlers who live under the chronic stress of recurrent missile attacks. The major objective of the program was to bolster children's resilience by enhancing their playful interactions with their mothers. The program is a play-based group intervention for eight conjoint dyads of mothers and toddlers who meet once a week for 10 weeks. The theme and activities of each session are organized around a proverb or saying with a relational or developmental message. Reports collected from mothers before and after their participation in the program and analyses of mother–child play observations documented the success of the intervention. They show positive changes in the children and the mothers, as well as in their interactions with each other (Cohen et al., 2014: Cohen & Shulman, in press).

An important part of prevention is the identification of children suffering from post-traumatic distress. Young children have difficulty reporting verbally on their distress. Based on our research (Cohen et al., 2010) and previous research describing post-traumatic play, it appears possible to use play observation to identify young children in need of play therapy treatment. It may be possible to train teachers and school personnel to become sensitive to the indicators of post-traumatic play and pay special attention to the children who may be especially distressed. This is in agreement with Prichard (2016), who points out that timely play therapy intervention for children who have experienced early trauma may prove salient in the prevention of future stress and trauma-related illnesses of the body and mind.

Clinical descriptions and theorizing about the use of play therapy for psychotherapy with children affected by traumatic experiences has a long history (Alvarez & Phillips, 1998). In recent years, the effectiveness of this form of therapy is being empirically documented (Midgley & Kennedy, 2011). Additional models using play as a main vehicle for therapeutic communication have been developed in the last two decades, mostly in order to involve parents in the therapy process of their young children. Among such dyadic therapy models, 'Child–Parent Psychotherapy' is designed to specifically address issues of trauma, albeit mostly trauma related to domestic violence (Lieberman & Van Horn, 2008). The field still needs to develop play-based intervention tailored to the particular needs of children and families affected by war and terrorism. We can only hope that changing the developmental trajectories of such children will contribute to a more peaceful world in the future.

References

Alvarez, A., & Phillips, A. (1998). The importance of play: A child therapist's view. *Child Psychology & Psychiatry Review*, *3*(3), 99–103.

Bonanno, G. A., Westphal, M., & Mancini, A. D. (2011). Resilience to loss and potential trauma. *Annual Review of Psychology*, *7*, 511–535.

Brom, D. (2014). Thoughts about survival mode theory of posttraumatic reactions. In R. Pat-Horenczyk, D. Brom, & J. M. Vogel (Eds.), *Helping children cope with trauma: Individual, family and community perspectives* (pp. 243–248). New York: Routledge.

Bronson, M. R., & Bundy, A. C. (2001). A correlational study of a test of playfulness and a test of environmental supportiveness for play. *Occupational Therapy Journal of Research, 21*(4), 241–259.

Chazan, S., & Cohen, E. (2010). Adaptive and defensive strategies in post-traumatic play of young children exposed to violent attacks. *Journal of Child Psychotherapy, 36*(2), 133–151.

Chemtob, C. M. (2005). Finding the gift in the horror: Toward developing a national psychosocial security policy. *Journal of Aggression, Maltreatment & Trauma, 10*(3–4), 721–727.

Chemtob, C. M., Nomura, Y., Rajendran, K., Yehuda, R., Schwartz, D., & Abramovitz, R. (2010). Impact of maternal posttraumatic stress disorder and depression following exposure to the September 11 attacks on preschool children's behavior. *Child Development, 81*(4), 1129–1141.

Cohen, E. (2006). Parental level of awareness: An organizing scheme of parents' belief systems as a guide in parent therapy. In C. Wachs & L. Jacobs (Eds.), *Parent-focused child therapy: Attachment, identification and reflective functions* (pp. 39–64). Lanham, MD: Rowman & Littlefield.

Cohen, E. (2009). Parenting in the throes of traumatic events: Relational risks and protection processes. In J. Ford, R. Pat-Horenczyk, & D. Brom (Eds.), *Treating traumatized children: Risk, resilience and recovery* (pp. 72–84). Florence, KY: Routledge.

Cohen, E., Chazan, S. E., Lerner, M., & Maimon, E. (2010). Post-traumatic play in young children exposed to terrorism: An empirical study. *Infant Mental Health Journal, 31*(2), 1–23.

Cohen, E., Pat-Horenczyk, R., & Haar-Shamir, D. (2014). Making room for play: An innovative intervention for toddlers and families under rocket fire. *Clinical Social Work Journal, 42*(4), 336–345.

Cohen, E., & Shulman, C. (in press). Mothers and toddlers exposed to political violence: Severity of exposure, emotional availability, parenting stress, and toddlers' behavior problems. *Journal of Child and Adolescent Trauma.*

Conway, A., McDonough, S. C., MacKenzie, M. J., Follett, C., & Sameroff, A. (2013). Stress-related changes in toddlers and their mothers following the attack of September 11. *American Journal of Orthopsychiatry, 83*(4), 536–544.

Drewes, A. A. (2001). Play objects and play spaces. In A. A. Drewes, L. J. Carey, & C. E. Schaefer (Eds.), *School-based play therapy* (pp. 62–80). New York: Wiley.

Dripchak, V. L. (2007). Posttraumatic play: Towards acceptance and resolution. *Clinical Social Work Journal, 35*(2), 125–134.

Dyregrov, A., & Regel, S. (2012). Early interventions following exposure to traumatic events: Implications for practice from recent research. *Journal of Loss and Trauma, 17*(3), 271–291.

Feldman, R., & Vengrober, A. (2011). Posttraumatic stress disorder in infants and young children exposed to war-related trauma. *Journal of the American Academy of Child & Adolescent Psychiatry, 50*(7), 645–658.

Feldman, R., Vengrober, A., & Hallaq, E. (2007). War and the young child: Mother child relationship, child symptoms, and maternal well-being in infants and young children exposed to war, terror, and violence. Paper presented at the European Society for Child and Adolescent Psychiatry 13th International Congress, Florence, Italy.

Folkman, S., & Moskowitz, J. T. (2000). Positive affect and the other side of coping. *American Psychologist*, *55*(6), 647–654.

Fonagy, P. G., Jurist, G., & Target, E. M. (2002) *Affect regulation, mentalization and the development of the self*. New York: Other Press.

Fredrickson, B. L. (2000). Cultivating positive emotions to optimize health and well-being. *Prevention & Treatment*, *3*(1), Article ID 1. Available at http://dx.doi.org.ezprimo1.idc.ac.il/10.1037/1522–3736.3.1.31a.

Freud, A., & Burlingham, D. (1943). *Children and war*. New York: Ernst Willard.

Freud, S. (1971). Beyond the pleasure principle. Part II. Traumatic neurosis and children's play [1920]. In C. L. Rothgeb (Ed.), *Abstracts of the standard edition of the complete psychological works of Sigmund Freud* (pp. 116–125). Rockville, MD: US Department of Health, Education and Welfare.

Gil, E. (1996). *Treating abused adolescents*. New York: Guilford Press.

Ginsburg, K. R. (2007). The importance of play in promoting healthy child development and maintaining strong parent–child bonds. *Pediatrics*, *119*(1), 182–191.

Hafstad, G. S., Gil-Rivas, V., Kilmer, R. P., & Raeder, S. (2010). Parental adjustment, family functioning, and posttraumatic growth among Norwegian children and adolescents following a natural disaster. *American Journal of Orthopsychiatry*, *80*(2), 248–257.

Halevi, G., Djalovski, A., Vengrober, A., & Feldman, R. (2016). Risk and resilience trajectories in war-exposed children across the first decade of life. *Journal of Child Psychology and Psychiatry*, *57*(10), 1183–1193.

Khamis, V. (2016). Does parent's psychological distress mediate the relationship between war trauma and psychosocial adjustment in children? *Journal of Health Psychology*, *21*(7), 1361–1370.

Lieberman, A. F. (2011). Infants remember: War exposure, trauma, and attachment in young children and their mothers. *Journal of the American Academy of Child and Adolescent Psychiatry*, *50*(7), 640–641.

Lieberman, A. F., & Van Horn, P. (2008). *Psychotherapy with infants and young children: Repairing the effects of stress and trauma on early childhood*. New York: Guilford Press.

MacDermid-Wadsworth, S. M. (2010). Family risk and resilience in the context of war and terrorism. *Journal of Marriage and Family*, *72*(3), 537–556.

MacMillan, K. K., Ohan, J., Cherian, S., & Mutch, R. C. (2015). Refugee children's play: Before and after migration to Australia. *Journal of Pediatrics and Child Health*, *51*(8), 771–777.

McEwen, B. S. (1998). Stress, adaptation, and disease: Allostasis and allostatic load. *Annals of New York Academy of Sciences*, *840*, 33–44.

Midgley, N., & Kennedy, E. (2011). Psychodynamic psychotherapy for children and adolescents: A critical review of the evidence base. *Journal of Child Psychotherapy*, *37*(3), 232–260.

Nader, K., & Pynoos, R. S. (1991). Play and drawing as tools for interviewing traumatized children. In C. E. Schaefer, K. Gitlin, & A. Sandgrund (Eds.), *Play, diagnosis and assessment* (pp. 375–389). New York: John Wiley.

Pat-Horenczyk, R., Achituv, M., Kagan Rubenstein, A., Khodabakhsh, A., Brom, D., & Chemtob, C. (2012). Growing up under fire: Building resilience in young children and parents exposed to ongoing missile attacks. *Journal of Child & Adolescent Trauma, 5*(4), 303–314.

Pat-Horenczyk, R., Perry, S., Hamama-Raz, Y., Ziv, Y., Schramm-Yavin, S., & Stemmer, S. M. (2015). Posttraumatic growth in breast cancer survivors: Constructive and illusory aspects. *Journal of Traumatic Stress, 28*(3), 214–222.

Pat-Horenczyk, R., Ziv, Y., Asulin-Peretz, L., Achituv, M., Cohen, S., & Brom, D. (2013). Relational trauma in times of political violence: Continuous versus past traumatic stress. *Peace and Conflict: Journal of Peace Psychology, 19*(2), 125–137.

Perroni, E. (2014). Survival, motherhood and play. In E. Perroni (Ed.), *Play: Psychoanalytic perspectives, survival and human development* (pp. 87–90). New York: Routledge.

Prichard, N. (2016). Stuck in the dollhouse: A brain-based perspective of post-traumatic play. In D. Le Vay & E. Cuschieri (Eds.), *Challenges in the theory and practice of play therapy* (pp. 71–85). New York: Routledge.

Rafman, S., Canfield, J., Barbas, J., & Kaczorowski, J. (1996). Disrupted moral order: A conceptual framework for differentiating reactions to loss and trauma. *International Journal of Behavioral Development, 19*(4), 817–829.

Ryan, V., & Needham, C. (2001). Non-directive play therapy with children experiencing psychic trauma. *Clinical Child Psychology and Psychiatry, 6*(3), 437–453.

Schonfeld, D. J. (2011). Ten years after 9/11: What have we (not yet) learned? *Journal of Developmental & Behavioral Pediatrics, 32*(7), 542–545.

Shachar-Dadon, A., Gueron-Sela, N., Weintraub, Z., Maayan-Metzger, A., & Leshem, M. (2017). Pre-conception war exposure and mother and child adjustment 4 years later. *Journal of Abnormal Child Psychology, 45*(1), 131–142.

Singer, J. L., & Singer, D. G. (2005). Preschoolers' imaginative play as precursor of narrative consciousness. *Imagination, Cognition and Personality, 25*(2), 97–117.

Slade, A. (1994). Making meaning and making believe: Their role in the clinical process. In A. Slade & D. Wolf (Eds.), *Children at play: Clinical and developmental approaches to meaning and representation* (pp. 81–110). New York: Oxford University Press.

Slone, M., & Mann, S. (2016). Effects of war, terrorism and armed conflict on young children: A systematic review. *Child Psychiatry & Human Development, 47*(6), 950–965.

Terr, L. C. (1981). 'Forbidden games': Post-traumatic child's play. *Journal of the American Academy of Child Psychiatry, 20*(4), 741–760.

United Nations High Commission for Human Rights (2006). *A guide to general comment 7: Implementing child rights in early childhood.* The Hague: United

Nations Committee on the Rights of the Child, United Nations Children's Fund and Bernard van Leer Foundation. Available at www.unicef.org/earlychildhood/files/Guide_to_GC7.pdf.

Varkas, T. (1998). Childhood trauma and posttraumatic play: A literature review and case study. *Journal of Analytic Social Work*, 5(3), 29–50.

Vygotsky, L. (1966). Play and its role in the mental development of the child. *Voprosy Psikhologii*, 12(6), 62–76.

Webb, N. B. (Ed.). (2004). *Mass trauma and violence: Helping families and children cope*. New York: Guilford Press.

Wershba-Gershon, P. (1996). Free symbolic play and assessment of the nature of child sexual abuse. *Journal of Child Sexual Abuse*, 5(2), 37–57.

Wigren, J. (1994). Narrative completion in the treatment of trauma. *Psychotherapy: Theory, Research, Practice, Training*, 31(3), 415–423.

Winnicott, D. W. (1971). *Playing and reality*. New York: Basic Books.

Wolmer, L., Hamiel, D., Pardo-Aviv, L., & Laor, N. (2017). Addressing the needs of preschool children in the context of disasters and terrorism: Assessment, prevention, and intervention. *Current Psychiatry Reports*, 19(7), 40–49.

PART VII

Play Spaces and the Rights of Children

37 Play Spaces, Indoors and Out

John A. Sutterby

The 1560 painting by Bruegel the Elder called *Children's Games* serves as introduction to the pastimes of children alive at that time. The painting depicts children playing a number of identifiable games – spin tops, dressing up to play a wedding, and jacks – and engaging in a fair amount of rough and tumble as well. The play space is the public plaza where children together engage in the frivolity of play. It is significant to note that this space for play is out in the open and not separated from daily routines. Until relatively recently there has not been a separation of spaces for play and other pursuits; spaces for play were anywhere and everywhere. Certainly, there have been arenas for public games such as the Olympics, which date back thousands of years. Places for pure play have for most of history been in the public commons and grounds.

The idea of separating off a place for play is a relatively recent idea. The earliest public park space in the United States was the Boston Common, which was first set aside in 1634. Although not strictly a place for play and recreation over its long history, it has evolved to become one of the major attractions of the city of Boston. The development of large urban parks began in the middle of the nineteenth century. A large central area of natural space became a goal of large cities in the United States, starting with Central Park in New York. The design of Central Park by Frederick Law Olmsted and Charles Vaux inspired cities across the United States to reserve or create large green spaces for public recreation (Roper, 1973).

More recently, play has moved out of the public sphere and into the private or commercial space. Playgrounds at schools are frequently kept locked up after hours. Play equipment has found its way into fast food restaurants, which generally requires a commercial contribution in order to play. Many cities have erected beautiful children's museums, which require a cost of admission that is prohibitively expensive for low-income families. Finally, as play has moved online into virtual worlds, players do not have to leave their rooms to interact with players continents away.

Chudacoff (2007) discusses the historical changes to play environments and play materials due to changes in attitudes about children. Play environments have gone over time from being natural to being man-made. The ability of children to move freely has been severely curtailed, as children move from playing in neighbourhoods to playing in shopping malls. He also discusses how the view of the child has changed over time; as adults have used strategies to keep children safe from harm, this has decreased children's opportunities to encounter places for play. The mass production of play materials has also altered the play environment as 'things' for play have become ever more important. Finally, Chudacoff discusses how time for play has changed historically as children enter school at earlier ages and spend more hours and more days in school than ever before.

Places for play for the most part are built and designed by adults for consumption by children. Although play designers may envision a way of interacting with a play space, children rarely confine themselves by choice to those predetermined ideas (Frost et al., 2004). "Over the past century and a half, a special 'children's' area has been singled out in the world culture – toys and games, children's literature, music, theatre, animated films for children" (Smirnova et al., 2016, p. 270). As childhood has become to be defined as more reserved and separated from adulthood, a new space is created by adults for children.

This chapter describes some of the historical development of play spaces, indoors and out. This includes how play has been used as an educational tool through the development of curriculum for play. The chapter also discusses how play materials and space influence the way children interact with the material and with each other. Finally, this chapter explores the spaces for play outdoors as well as the growing area of the virtual world.

Schooling Play Spaces

One of the first places we think of when we consider play spaces is play spaces at school. For more than a century now, play has found its way into the classroom, and images of the traditional preschool or kindergarten of cubbies and blocks and easels comes easily to mind. Play has been seen as beneficial for development at least since the time of Plato (Frost, 2010). More recently, early childhood educators from many places have tried to harness play for education's sake. Some of these educators designed play materials as well as discussing ways of integrating play into the curriculum. Some programs have had a more communal development as many people are responsible for the design and implementation of the program. The emphasis on the design of the play space is an important component of each of these programs. This leads to questions such as, How are the play centres or interest centres arranged in the classroom? How do children move around? What materials are available for play? These are all important questions that differentiate play spaces in schools.

The integration of play into schooling is itself controversial. From the beginning of the kindergarten movement there has been a debate about how much control the teacher should have over the play activities of the children. If play is defined as a freely chosen, intrinsically motivated activity, then the attempts to control the play in the grip of the curriculum often end the play altogether. Children in these situations often subvert the curriculum in order to do what they want for their play activities (Sutterby, 2005). Some have even suggested we should take the word 'play' out of the curriculum completely. Kuschner (2012) writes, "I would argue that once play is put into the service of achieving the academic goals of the curriculum, it is no longer play" (p. 247). The balance between play and work is one that play curriculum designers must consider.

An early play curriculum developer was Frederick Froebel, the father of kindergarten. Froebel was one of the first educators to emphasize the education of young children in schools. He also tried to harness the power of play in his effort. He designed a set of materials and activities called the 'gifts and occupations', which he used to guide children to better understand the natural world around them. The gifts were mostly sets of wooden blocks that children would use for building. This was the introduction of play materials into the curriculum of early childhood. Froebel's idea of the play space was a combination of indoor activities based on his gifts and occupations and outdoor activities such as circle games, hiking, and gardening (Frost et al., 2012).

Brosterman (1997) suggests that the play materials included in kindergarten and the activities that the children engaged in had profound influences on art and architecture. Frank Lloyd Wright, for example, credits the block play he engaged with in kindergarten as influential on his architectural work. Piet Mondrian and Paul Klee also appear to have been influenced by some of these early kindergarten play experiences.

Maria Montessori also developed a well-known curriculum for young children. She developed a set of materials and tasks for children to complete in order to develop their cognitive, practical life, and sensory and motor skills. Although she explicitly denied that her materials led to children playing, the deep engagement and exploration of the materials by the children are often seen as playful (Soundy, 2008). The materials that children interact with in the Montessori classroom are carefully designed to increase in complexity over time and are designed to target specific skills. Montessori emphasized the importance of organization in the classroom and the importance of the children being able to engage in the activities independently. In addition, the development of the child-sized classroom opened many to the redesign of the classroom for the support of play. Montessori controlled the implementation of her curriculum; in the beginning she alone was allowed to train teachers for Montessori schools (Kramer, 1988). Montessori schools have more flexibility now, as they have adapted to changes in culture and values reflected in society today.

John Dewey implemented a play-based curriculum at the University of Chicago Laboratory School. His belief about play was that young children should engage in meaningful activities that reflect the lives of the important adults around them. His ideas for activities for young children were based on their intrinsically motivated desires and the child's free choice of activities

(Frost et al., 2012). Schools that implemented curricula based on Dewey's ideas encouraged children to play adult roles such as storekeeper and cook, roles that they might aspire to do for real as they got older.

The Bank Street Curriculum is closest to what many early educators view as a traditional curriculum for early education using play. Its roots can be found in leaders of the kindergarten movement such as Harriet Johnson, Lucy Sprague Mitchell, and Caroline Pratt. Classrooms based on this model are divided into interest centres such as dramatic play, blocks, and puzzles. The blocks most used in these classrooms are the wooden unit blocks originally designed by Caroline Pratt (1948). Children are free to move around the classroom, selecting activities that are of most interest to them. The teacher acts as a facilitator for play as children have opportunities to play alone and in groups (Biber et al., 1971; Frost et al., 2012). Several new curriculum models such as High Scope and the Creative Curriculum have many similarities to the play environments of Bank Street. These similarities include dividing the classroom into interest centres and having a variety of play materials and activities such as art, puzzles, blocks, and dramatic play props.

Reggio Emilia is a school system located in the city of Reggio Emilia in northern Italy. The preschool program in these schools is based on the work of Loris Malaguzzi. They offer a constructivist play curriculum with an emphasis on aesthetics and creative arts. Children use art techniques taught by an atelierista to explore areas of interest. This program has been influential in schools across the globe as educators attempt to use the outline of the school's curriculum to improve early education. The importance of aesthetics that this program emphasizes is reflected in the beauty of the design of the play space (Fraser, 2007; Rinaldi, 2006).

The development of these play curricula has shaped what is expected in an early childhood classroom. Although some cosmetic differences exist across curricula, there are many commonalities, for example, spaces that recognize that children's bodies require smaller equipment and furniture and that children are more comfortable in nooks rather than playing in wide open spaces. All of these curricula have some sort of material for play, whether it is the didactic material found in a Montessori classroom or the more creative and open-ended material found in art centres in Bank Street and Creative Curriculum classrooms. Finally, there is an emphasis in all of these programs on organization. Materials are organized, the space is planned, and preparations are made for the different types of activities that are going to occur in that space, whether it be messy or quiet or large or small group activities.

Classroom Spaces

Designing classroom spaces depends on the curriculum chosen as well as the theoretical foundation of the program. For example, Vygotskian-based programs such as Bodrova and Leong's Tools of the Mind (2006) are founded on the idea of social constructivism where children learn from each other in the environment. This requires that the child be actively involved with the environment. These programs would emphasize that children are at different levels of development so the classroom space should allow for children to engage in activities at different levels. The classroom play space would also allow for active engagement and would provide opportunities to support children's learning (Ogunnaike, 2015).

Developmentally appropriate practice (DAP) has been a major influence on early childhood play spaces for more than 30 years. The most recent version of DAP and the National Asssociation for the Education of Young Children's position statement again reaffirms play as an important aspect of children's learning and based on that belief recommends that classrooms be set up to support play and that parts of the school day should be devoted to play. The play space needs to have culturally appropriate play materials that are arranged to encourage active learning. They also recognize that play spaces for children should vary depending on age, so play environments for infants, toddlers, pre-schoolers, kindergartens, and school-age children need to be adapted to the specific needs of these age groups (Copple & Bredekamp, 2009).

The theoretical understanding of play and many decades of implementing play in early childhood classrooms has led to some general guidelines for setting up the play environment. Some of the design perspectives across programs that make play more successful are the logical arrangement of the play space, a balance of different types of play materials, and careful organization and display of the play materials. The ambiance of the play space is also important for the facilitation of play.

The age of the child influences how the space is set up, but in general the logical arrangement of space involves dividing the space into recognizable centres for play. They could be block centres or dramatic play centres, sensory centres or writing centres. The arrangement of these centres is based on the play that will take place there. For example, placing noisy centres like blocks and dramatic play together and placing quiet centres like libraries and puzzle centres together helps keep the noisy centres from interrupting the quiet centres. Messy centres like art are usually located near a sink and over a surface that is easily cleaned. There should also be some sort of visual boundary between centres so that children are not distracted by play in other areas. A stimulus shelter is also an important part of the early childhood classroom. Play spaces can be stressful spaces when there is too much stimulation (Bullard, 2010; Frost et al., 2012).

It is important to have a balance of play materials in order to meet the interests and needs of children. This means having open-ended materials like sand and water and closed-ended materials like puzzles. Complex materials with many uses like blocks or sand and simple materials like a book that are meant to be used in only one way both should be part of the classroom inventory. Some realistic materials like toy dolls should be included along with non-realistic, abstract materials like boxes (Frost et al., 2012).

The arrangement and organization of the play materials is also significant. Montessori pioneered the idea of placing materials on low shelves for easy access by children. Today this is a staple across classrooms. Having the materials available helps children be independent, as they do not need to rely on the teacher to access materials. Organization of materials is also important; in an unorganized classroom children will find it difficult to locate the materials they want to play with (Clayton, 2001).

The ambiance in the classroom can be as important as the other factors discussed in encouraging play. The Reggio Emilia schools have especially emphasized that the classroom space needs to be aesthetically pleasing. There is some debate about what makes a pleasing environment. Some classrooms feature bright primary colours, made from plastic and metal, while others prefer natural woods and cotton fabrics. Lighting and classroom displays are also an important aspect of the ambiance of the classroom (Bullard, 2010). Although classrooms vary from place to place, the general design guidelines suggested above are consistently found to have positive benefits for children engaging in play.

Play Materials in the Classroom Space

One of the critical elements of the play space is the play material to be found in that play space. Object play is an important part of children's engagement in play. Although just about any object from rocks to sticks to the honoured cardboard box can be included in play, we also have a large commercial industry that designs, creates, and distributes toys for play. In addition, a subsection of toys has been given the title of 'educational toys' as a way of differentiating them from commercial toys.

Play materials have been categorized based on a variety of characteristics, which are usually determined by what outcomes are expected for them. Play materials might be open ended, such as dramatic play props or sand, which can be used in any way freely chosen by the player. Play materials like puzzles, on the other hand, are seen as closed ended in that the pieces fit together in only one way so there is a predetermined outcome.

The cognitive benefits of play materials are one of the most researched areas of play and schooling. Construction materials such as wooden blocks and boards are associated with gains in spatial knowledge, which can lead to developing the foundations of engineering and architecture (Ness & Farenga, 2016). An opportunity to play with discrete objects like beads or counters has been linked to understanding mathematical concepts such as set development and one-to-one correspondence. Experience in playing with number shapes and geometrical shapes can also lead to the development of mathematical concepts (Reifel, 1984; Sarama & Clements, 2009).

Building with construction materials such as Lego bricks can also help children develop mental imagery important for mathematical concepts. Research suggests that the use of the Lego bricks helped mental imagery in both boys and girls, which is significant in that boys tend to do better at spatial tasks and also are often encouraged in this type of building task (Pirrone & Di Nuovo, 2014). Play materials are also often viewed as significant in interventions with children with disabilities. Early intervention specialists use toys to enhance the home learning environment of children with disabilities to create a more stimulating environment and to encourage play between parents and children (Nwokah et al., 2013; see also Chapters 31 and 33 in this book).

Many play materials have social goals as well. Dramatic play props are often thematic as children are encouraged to engage in play about community helpers, medical play, and domestic play. Engaging with these materials allows children to take on adult roles in order to better understand them. The tools that adults use like phones, car keys, and computers are all of great interest to children as they imitate the actions of the important adults around them. Dramatic play materials also encourage language use as players have to negotiate the roles and activities (Ashiabi, 2007). Play materials that require a great deal of language in order to continue the play, like dramatic play props, can complicate play when children do not share a language, as these materials do not provide enough scaffolding to support communication (Sutterby & Frost, 2002).

Play materials can have therapeutic purposes. Opportunities to play with dolls may encourage children to play out scenarios that are confusing for the child. Board games, small sand toys, and dramatic play materials are frequently recommended for play therapy. Art materials are also often used in therapeutic ways, as free expression is seen as an important way for children to express their emotions. The use of culturally relevant toys and materials also encourages expressive play; in general the play therapy room should reflect the culture of the children being served. This could involve having separate entrances for the centre for a Japanese play therapy room to having bright colours for a centre that serves Mexican American children (Ji et al., 2008; Kranz et al., 2005).

Play materials can also be used to develop academic skills such as number and letter recognition as well as academic skills such as literacy behaviours. Neuman and Roskos (1990) suggested that play environments could be enhanced for young children by emphasizing the placement of literacy material throughout the classroom. They suggested including items such as envelopes, message pads, coupons, and other print items to encourage children to engage in more literacy play. The Roskos and Neuman (2003) play intervention model suggests that children should be engaged in play activities such as sociodramatic play that involves functional uses of print.

Supporters of play would see all toys as educational in some way. However, as noted above, a class of toys has been defined as to be specifically educational. These toys are frequently targeted at middle-class parents who want their children to be engaged in productive pursuits while having fun. John Locke, for example, developed a set of alphabet blocks to teach children the alphabet while encouraging them to stay inside and off the streets (Almqvist, 1994). Dolls and kitchen sets were given to girls so that they could practice the mothering skills that they would be expected to demonstrate as adults.

The early toys that were promoted as educational toys were materials such as plain wooden blocks and chalkboards to promote future educational success, but also were non-directive so as to not interfere with the child's imagination (Almqvist, 1994; Cross, 1997). The idea of educational toys is generally seen as a marketing technique by toy manufacturers who are looking for a sales advantage. Educational toys enjoy a higher status than other toys, which suggests that some toys are not educational. It also suggests that some toys are just for fun, while others have a higher purpose. American Girl Dolls, for example, are designed to promote historical knowledge and literacy development through the combined book and doll lines, as opposed to the more pop culture Barbie, which focuses on fashion and having fun (Cross, 1997).

There are limits to the claims of educational toys and media. A recent example was the recall of Baby Einstein educational DVDs. Research examining the language development of children who spent time watching the DVDs found that children who watched more had fewer words in their vocabulary in comparison to children who did not watch the videos. There is still controversy over the original research. Nonetheless, the media attention to the study forced Disney to recall the DVDs (Bartlett, 2013).

Play materials are a significant part of the play space. The different types of materials elicit different types and forms of play, from active to quiet to interactive to solitary. The appeal of toys comes from what they do for the player. A toy can have functional value in what can be done with it. A toy can also have material value in that it is collectable and worth having just for the sake of it. A toy can have social value in that it is appealing to a group of children, so the play can be shared, and finally a toy can have personal value in that is related to something the child likes to do in real life outside play (Mertala et al., 2016).

Outdoor Play Spaces

Outdoor play is a critical part of children's development. Outdoor play in natural spaces has been linked to many benefits, including reduced anxiety, better fitness, and even better academic attention (Louv, 2012). However, for many years the amount of time spent outdoors for children has been declining. Stranger fear is a leading cause of this decline, as parents are less willing to allow their children to play outdoors unsupervised (Sutterby, 2009). Technology has also been linked to decreases in outdoor play, as children engage in ever-more-immersive gaming experiences.

Smirnova et al. (2016) describe principles of design for children's outdoor playgrounds including considering age, play value, open-endedness, consideration of risk, level of activity, and opportunities to communicate. Play value is enhanced through multifunctional materials like sand and water. The complexity of the landscape also increases play value. Open-endedness allows the child to decide which type of play activity she wishes to pursue. The authors discuss that risk is something that should be taken into consideration as an important function of the play environment. Today's playground in the US context fails in many ways according to these principles. Our focus on risk control has left little freedom to design the high-play-value, open-ended spaces from which children gain the most.

The design of the playground and the types of equipment available there can impact the types of activities in which children engage. A comparison of a typical playground and a nature playground found that they both encouraged risky play; however, the forest playground had few constraints, allowing for greater mobility. This is to be expected as the typical playground had fencing, which the forest playground did not (Sandseter, 2009). An examination of four preschool playgrounds found that large, hard-surfaced areas are more attractive to boys than girls. Playgrounds that have large natural areas attract players to these areas. While playground equipment is popular, it also can encourage a hierarchy of players, from the more coordinated to the less coordinated. Finally, some children seek refuge in soft play areas like sand pits to retreat to when the rest of the playground is hard-paved surface (Dyment & O'Connell, 2013).

The height of equipment and how it is designed can have an impact on how children interact with it as well as what risks they are more likely to take. Children are naturally interested in climbing to a height for various reasons. It could be part of a game, a challenge to overcome, or even an opportunity to observe from a height. But increasing the height of playground equipment does increase the risk of falls, leading to injuries (Frost et al., 2004). Parents generally are more willing to allow older children opportunities to reach heights. Playground equipment that offers children more than two affordances, for example, hand holds and foot holds, is less likely to put children at risk (Wakes & Beukes, 2011).

A growing concern has been the increase in obesity in children. Many communities are trying to increase access to physical activity for children. One study examined what perceived barriers were there for children wanting to engage in physical activity. Lack of space and lack of play facilities were identified by children as being significant barriers. Electronic games were also identified as one of the barriers to physical activity (Pawlowski et al., 2014). Creative, more attractive play spaces can also increase physical activity. Playgrounds are competing against the interest in electronic games. One school program created activity centres to make the playground more interesting and to combine physical activity with academic content (Dotterweich et al., 2013).

Park and Playground Changes over Time

Most playgrounds are designed to meet a few consistent physical play activities: climbing, sliding, swinging, spinning, balancing, and hanging by the hands, arms, or legs. They should also allow for opportunities for children to engage in all types of play from dramatic play to games with rules, and from large group cooperative play to solitary play. How equipment is designed and built changes as new materials for equipment are introduced and as new regulations for the design of equipment are implemented. Playgrounds and playground equipment in the United States have gone through dramatic changes over the last century.

Traditional playgrounds at the turn of the century were designed for physical fitness, with little concern for risk. Injuries and deaths were fairly common and considered one of the hazards of life. Planning for safety did not begin in earnest until after the Second World War. Schools began installing padding under playground equipment or surrounding equipment with material such as sand or pea gravel to make falling less hazardous (Frost, 2007).

Real regulation of playground safety did not come until the Consumer Product Safety Commission published guidelines regulating playground safety in the United States. These regulations cover issues such as surfacing, equipment design, and maintenance of playground equipment. The regulation of what was considered safe on the playground and what was not immediately began to decrease the types of playground events available. European playgrounds are under the regulations of the European Standards for Playground Equipment EN 1176 and EN 1177, which are similar to the US standards.

Currently the International Playground Equipment Manufacturers Association (IPEMA) certifies playground equipment in the United States. Risk of litigation for playground manufacturers encourages them to follow the certification process, which leads to the current crop of cookie-cutter playgrounds, which have few unique elements and designs (Frost et al., 2012). An emphasis on safety can have negative consequences: "the more playground design focuses on safety alone, the more it is seen to negate the very purpose of the playground as a place for children to entertain themselves through physical activity" (Wakes & Beukes, 2011, p. 101).

Another factor in the limitation of what types of playground equipment can be designed is the Final Rule on Accessibility of the Americans with Disabilities Act. This rule required that all new playgrounds and recreation spaces have to be built in such a way as to take into account the accessibility and use of the play space. Playgrounds now are required to have an accessible route to the playground itself, usually a concrete sidewalk. Playgrounds must also have a way of getting from that sidewalk to the equipment, which means the surfacing material around the equipment must be resilient enough to allow a mobility enabling device to pass. Moreover, there needs to be some way for children to access the equipment itself, either by putting facilities at ground level or including ramps or transfer platforms to enable children to access elevated spaces (Thompson et al., 2002).

One major consequence of these two regulatory measures is that the cost of installing a new playground has gone up, especially in comparison to the scrap playgrounds that were built out of wood and used tires that were common in the previous century. Second, the potential creativity has been engineered out of playground equipment, as only 'safe' designs can be approved and built. Third, some types of equipment are favoured by the new regulations and others become less common. Combined deck climbers with events like slides and bridges are more common, as they easily meet the new standards. Swings, by comparison, have been removed from many playgrounds or are not included in playground design. The size of the surfacing required to allow for swings is often too large for small playgrounds. Fixed climbers become more common because they require little maintenance and take up less space. Finally, the new regulations eventually made the common homemade type of playground obsolete as the everyday home carpenter was not aware and had difficulty making the equipment compliant with the regulations (Solomon, 2005).

Democratic Places to Play

The history of parks and playgrounds also is wrapped up in the idea of the public play space as a way to bring people together from all social classes. Central Park was specifically designed to do just that. The park security force hired when the park was opened policed the park and were instructed on how to greet park patrons and to let them know what was expected behaviour in the park. They saw this as a critical part of the park design so that activities such as drinking and gambling would be discouraged in favour of an atmosphere that they felt should be more family focused (Sutterby, 2017).

The child-saving movement grew out of the Progressive Era as a way for children to learn morals and have a healthier happier life in the United States. Playgrounds became part of the child-saving movement. Immigrant children were migrating to the large cities of the country, and there was concern that these children needed outlets other than the streets, movie theatres, and bars. Henry Curtis and Luther Gulick began the Playground Association of America, which set out to bring playgrounds to children across the country. A 'healthy mind in a healthy body' was the impetus for bringing playgrounds to communities. Immigrants were seen as unhealthy, living in substandard conditions; thus, playgrounds would provide them with a healthy outlet. Many of these early playgrounds had play leaders on staff who helped organize games and activities for the children to play (Frost, 2010). John Dewey also saw the importance of outdoor environments for the development and enjoyment of young children. The Industrial Revolution drove workers and their children to large cities. This left children without the experiences of working and playing in safe outdoor environments. Schools then would have to fill that space by creating outdoor environments for play and learning (Rivkin, 1998).

Although the playground movement was successful, especially in major cities, for the most part children were not always able to access playgrounds. Children in impoverished areas, especially rural areas, had no programming for play. They often had great experiences in nature and with peers that required no resources (Frost, 2010). Parks and playgrounds in the South were segregated by law and in the North by custom (Sutterby, 2017). In some cases black and white children would share the same equipment and play spaces, but would not be allowed to be at the park at the same time. When segregation laws were struck down, many in the white community would close pools and other recreational facilities rather than allow them to be integrated (DC Park View, 2013). Today, Latinx children in particular have unequal access to play spaces, which leads to less outdoor play and higher health risks for these children (Arcury et al., 2017).

The next wave of interest in the community play space grew out of an interest to help low-income children access fun and interesting play spaces. The community-built playground movement of the 1970s through the 1990s set out to create play spaces in inner city neighbourhoods. Playground designers such as James Jolley, Paul Friedberg, Tom Jambor, and Jay Beckwith designed and built playgrounds using scrap lumber, ropes, and discarded tires. The emphasis of these playgrounds was unique design, usually with input from the local children and at low cost. Church groups, Rotary Clubs, and parent–teacher associations set out to build playgrounds with the labour of the local community, often in under-resourced areas in urban environments. Although these playgrounds spread quickly across the United States, few of them have survived. Regulations and the fact that the wood and rubber deteriorated over time made them hard to maintain, so parks and schools have generally returned to fixed equipment, as modern equipment needs little maintenance and meets regulations (Frost, 2010; Sutterby, 2017).

Adventure playgrounds, similar to community-built playgrounds, are designed to offer the children a large amount of control over what the playground looks like and what goes on in the playground. Adventure playgrounds were first developed in Europe late in the Second World War in Denmark. These playgrounds were designed as junk playgrounds, where children could construct the playground from building materials under the supervision of a play leader (Frost et al., 2012). Adventure playgrounds are much more common in Europe than in the United States primarily due to lack of financial support and the risk of litigation in the case of an injury, as well as a culture of fear that discourages children from playing in unruly environments. The adventure playgrounds that continue to operate today ideally are open to all children and families, but some charge a fee to cover expenses.

The advantage of adventure playgrounds is that they have play leaders and adult observers on site to check on the materials available and how they are being used (Frost & Klein, 1979; Frost et al., 2012).

Although no one group has taken up the mantle of developing democratic play spaces for bringing all children together, there are a variety of organizations that have begun to work to ensure that children have access to safe play spaces, opportunities to be in nature, and opportunities to go outside (Frost, 2010). Some of these include gardening groups, nature kindergartens and preschools, and groups such as Leave No Child Inside. Solomon (2005) suggests that we turn to architects and novel designers to design play spaces in the future that are unique and engaging. Others have made simpler solutions: street play groups have been developed to encourage outdoor play. Street play groups often use play leaders to guide the play of the participants in a supervised manner close to home (Murray & Devecchi, 2016; Zieff et al., 2016).

Commercial Play Spaces

Pay-to-play has become part of the landscape of play spaces. Unlike public parks and public schools, these pay-to-play spaces are limited to children and families who have the means to pay the price of admission. Requiring financial resources in order to have an opportunity to play in a particular place leaves out children and acts as a de facto method of segregating children by socioeconomic status. Some areas where pay to play is leading to social inequality include fast food restaurants, video arcades, theme parks, sports leagues, and children's museums. Although we place different values on the play that occurs in these venues, they are all limited to those who have the resources.

McDonald's began introducing playgrounds into their restaurants in the 1970s, and this idea has spread to include a number of different restaurant chains. This commercial play space does not charge an admission, but the people playing on the playground are expected to make a purchase. Thus, the idea of play is sold to the costumer as an enhancement of their dining experience. Some have suggested that this combination encourages children to associate food with play, especially unhealthy fast food, which may lead to negative health outcomes.

Video arcades have long been viewed sceptically by parents and leaders in communities. Pool halls and pinball parlours were associated with gambling and have often been made illegal. The heyday of the video arcade came with the invention of video games such as Pong and Space Invaders. The games were designed to separate people from their quarters so that the owner of the arcade could make a profit. The pay-to-play here is obvious in that only people who had the financial resources could play; the rest must watch from the sidelines. Video game arcades reached their pinnacle in the early 1980s and then began a rather rapid decline as home consoles began to mimic and even surpass the games available in arcades. Today video arcades are basically dinosaurs, as only a few survive, but that experience lives on in the memories of the players who were eager to get to the arcade after school and on weekends (June, 2013).

Theme parks are somewhat more accepted by society, but they are also associated with hedonistic experiences. They are also sites of over-the-top commercialism designed to separate people from their money. They are also criticized for offering ticket holders an experience that is presented as antiseptically as possible. The selling of the thrill itself is an important part of the theme park experience, based on g-force–inducing rides and frightening falls that are designed to terrorize the rider (Stanley, 2002). The great expense of attending theme parks again acts as a way of segregating the wealthy from the not so well off, thus depriving them of a shared cultural experience.

Sports leagues are also an area where the cost of participating often leaves out certain children. Children's sports have gone from self-organized activities played in vacant lots with little or no equipment to highly competitive year-round training with highly paid coaches. For the most part, the children who can participate in these leagues are children of means whose families can pay the high entry fees, equipment costs, and travel expenses. Baseball, for example, has very few African American players because of the high costs of 'select' leagues. Soccer is another sport that is not played as a pick-up sport because of the influence of the 'select' leagues. The segregation of players in sports discourages the social development of players and mocks the democratic ideal of sport in society (Ellis & Sharma, 2013).

Children's museums are held in highest regard by society. Local corporations and foundations pay thousands of dollars for naming rights on exhibits to be associated with the local museum. Educational play is promoted in the children's museum as opposed to the crass commercial play that occurs outside. The emphasis on education draws an audience of educated and upper-middle-class patrons who want their children to be engaged in productive activities. Membership costs are often too expensive for low-income families. These museums are aware of this and they often work to have days when the museum is open at no cost. However, the museum also has to cover expenses and so in order to keep their doors open they must raise the funds required to keep everything up and running. So what is often seen as a public good is actually mostly limited to white middle-class families of economic means. The educational benefits go to those who already have great advantages. Although society sees educational play as beneficial, the requirement to charge leaves out a large percentage of the population who do not get to play (Frost & Sutterby, 2017).

Virtual Play Spaces

Virtual reality play spaces continue to grow in number and popularity as they become more interactive and immersive. The desire for advanced technology is often pushed by the need to engage in playful activities. Steven Johnson (2016) suggests that play leads to innovation in many areas of technology. He describes that one of the first uses of the marvel of the computing device was to play games: one of the earliest games was called Tennis for Two. Since then technology has become an integral part of play spaces for both children and adults. With the advent of the internet what was once required for players to be in the same room has now allowed players to interact simultaneously in virtual worlds. There is some debate as to whether participants in virtual worlds are playing a 'game' (Boellstorff, 2008); if we go by the definitions of Caillois (1961) of play, they are at least playing in a sort of dramatic sense.

Game consoles starting with the popular home game device developed by Atari were once required to play computer games. Today any number of electronic devices from cell phones to tablets to laptops are available for people to engage together in play, and they are portable enough for players to take their play opportunities wherever they go.

Participants in virtual reality spaces have many options for deciding how to act (play) in virtual reality spaces, whether they are game spaces like the massively multiplayer online role-playing game World of Warcraft or the more intentionally virtual reality world of Second Life. One important aspect of virtual reality is the selection of an avatar to represent the player. In both games, players spend time deciding on the appearance of the avatar. This could involve changing the clothing of the avatar or even selecting an avatar that is an object or of a different gender (Boellstorff, 2008). Voice is also becoming a significant aspect of virtual worlds as players move from text-based communication to VOIP communication. Players find games with voice activated as a more social experience, which also allows players to free their hands in order to use hand controllers. However, in some situations using voice interfered with interactions, especially in situations where males had taken on female avatars or females had taken on male avatars (Wadley et al., 2015).

Virtual reality spaces can be beneficial for people with mobility impairments. Participants in Second Life, for example, are able to navigate the three-dimensional world, which they have difficulty doing in the real world. The ability to navigate virtual reality spaces has helped children with cerebral palsy to become more playful and creative (Reid, 2004). Virtual reality games have also been used to help children with developmental coordination disorder, as the engagement improves motor learning (Gonsalves et al., 2015). Virtual reality games have also been used for therapeutic purposes for hospitalized children receiving cancer treatments. Playing virtual reality games reduced patients' depressive symptoms (Li et al., 2011).

Boellstorf (2008) discusses how participants in Second Life who have mobility impairments or other health issues are able to have a social life through the game. Virtual reality allows people with mobility impairments to develop their social networks through participating in activities such as attending church services or exploring virtual spaces with others. While players are liberated from their disabilities to a certain extent, at the same time they also can be limited by it, such as in their ability to type or to participate in activities like flying.

Virtual reality most likely will become more prevalent and more immersive. This will continue to draw players away from traditional play activities like outdoor play, with potential health consequences. But it has the potential of replacing other sedentary activities such as television viewing or reading without having an effect on physical activity. The draw of immersive technology and virtual reality allows players to socialize with others and in the near future socialize with artificial intelligence bots within the games themselves. Turkle (2012) suggests we may be moving in the direction of being more attuned to our technology and less attuned to each other, paying attention to our phones and online social media instead of communicating directly with each other.

Summary and Conclusions

Play spaces are constantly changing as new materials, new technologies, and new curricula influence how we visualize what play should look like. Our social goals, values, and culture will determine what choices we make in the design of these play spaces. Will they be open to everyone or will they be limited to a select few? Will they be indoors, outdoors, or in cyberspace? Will the play partners be other children or will they be artificial intelligence robots? The need for play exists for both children and adults, so play spaces and forms of play will continue to be created to meet this need.

References

Almqvist, B. (1994). Educational toys, creative toys. In J. Goldstein (Ed.), *Toys, play and child development*, pp. 46–66. Cambridge: Cambridge University Press.

Arcury, T., Suerken, C., Ip, E., Moore, J., & Quandt, S. (2017). Residential environment for outdoor play among children in Latino farmworker families. *Journal of Immigrant Minority Health*, *19*, 267–274.

Ashiabi, G. (2007). Play in the preschool classroom: Its socioemotional significance and the teacher's role in play. *Early Childhood Education Journal*, *35*(2), 199–207.

Bartlett, T. (2013). Researchers question agenda in 'Baby Einstein' study. *Chronicle of Higher Education*, *60*(3), A11.

Biber, B., Shapiro, E., & Wickens, D. (1971). *Promoting cognitive growth from a developmental interactionist point of view*. Washington, DC: National Association for the Education of Young Children.

Bodrova, E., & Leong, D. (2006). *Tools of the mind: The Vygotskian approach to early childhood education* (2nd edn.). Upper Saddle River, NJ: Pearson.

Boellstorff, T. (2008). *Coming of age in second life: An anthropologist explores the virtually human*. Princeton, NJ: Princeton University Press.

Brosterman, N. (1997). *Inventing kindergarten*. New York: Harry N. Abrams.

Bullard, J. (2010). *Creating environments for learning: Birth to age eight*. Upper Saddle River, NJ: Pearson.

Caillois, R. (1961). *Man, play and games*. Urbana: University of Illinois Press.

Chudacoff, H. (2007). *Children at play: An American history*. New York: New York University Press.

Clayton, M. (2001). *Classroom spaces that work*. Turners Falls, MA: Northeast Foundation for Children.

Copple, C., & Bredekamp, S. (2009). *Developmentally appropriate practice in early childhood programs: Serving children from birth through age 8* (3rd edn.). Washington, DC: National Association for the Education of Young Children.

Cross, D. (1997). *Kids' stuff: Toys and the changing world of American childhood*. Cambridge, MA: Harvard University Press.

DC Park View (2013). Park View playground played interesting role in desegregation of district playgrounds. Available at https://parkviewdc.com/2013/01/03/park-view-playground-played-interesting-role-in-desegregating-district-playgrounds/.

Dotterweich, A., Greene, A., & Blosser, D. (2013). Using innovative playgrounds and cross-curricular activities to increase physical activity. *Journal of Physical Education, Recreation & Dance, 83*(5), 47–55.

Dyment, J., & O'Connell, T. (2013). The impact of playground design on play choices and behaviors of pre-school children. *Children's Geographies, 11*(3), 263–280.

Ellis, J., & Sharma, H. (2013). Can't play here: The decline of pick-up soccer and social capital in the USA. *Soccer and Society, 14*(3), 364–385.

Fraser, S. (2007). Play in other languages. *Theory into Practice, 46*(1), 14–22.

Frost, J. (2007). Genesis and evolution of American play and playgrounds. In D. Sluss & O. Jarrett (Eds.), *Investigating play in the 21st century* (pp. 3–31). Lanham, MD: University Press of America.

Frost, J. (2010). *A history of children's play and play environments: Toward a contemporary child-saving movement*. New York: Routledge.

Frost, J., Brown, P., Sutterby, J., & Thornton, C. (2004). *The developmental benefits of playgrounds*. Olney, MD: Association for Childhood Education International.

Frost, J., & Klein, B. (1979). *Children's play and playgrounds*. Boston: Allyn & Bacon.

Frost, J., & Sutterby, J. (2017). Outdoor play is essential to whole child development. *Young Children, 72*(3), 82–85.

Frost, J., Wortham, S., & Reifel, S. (2012). *Play and child development* (4th edn.). Upper Saddle River, NJ: Pearson.

Gonzalves, L., Campbell, A., Jensen, L., & Straker, L. (2015). Children with developmental coordination disorder play active virtual reality games differently than children with typical development. *Physical Therapy, 95*(3), 360–368.

Ji, Y., Ramirez, S., & Kranz, P. (2008). Physical settings and materials recommended for play therapy with Japanese children. *Journal of Instructional Psychology, 35*(1), 53–61.

Johnson, S. (2016). *Wonderland: How play made the modern world*. New York: Riverhead Books.

June, L. (2013). For amusement only: The life and death of the American arcade. *The Verge*. Available at www.theverge.com/2013/1/16/3740422/the-life-and-death-of-the-american-arcade-for-amusement-only.

Kramer, R. (1988). *Maria Montessori*. Cambridge, MA: De Capo Press.

Kranz, P., Ramirez, S., Flores-Torres, L., Steele, R., & Lund, N. (2005). Physical settings, materials, and related Spanish terminology recommended for play therapy with first generation Mexican-American children. *Education, 126*(1), 93–99.

Kuschner, D. (2012). Play is natural to childhood but school is not: The problem of integrating play into the curriculum. *International Journal of Play, 1*(3), 242–249.

Li, W., Chung, J., & Ho, E. (2011). The effectiveness of therapeutic play, using virtual reality computer games, promoting the psychological well-being of children hospitalized with cancer. *Journal of Clinical Nursing, 20*(2), 2135–2143.

Louv, R. (2012). *The nature principle: Reconnecting with life in a virtual age*. Chapel Hill, NC: Algonquin Books.

Mertala, P., Karikoski, H., Tähtinen, L., & Sarnius, V. (2016). The value of toys: 6–8-year-old children's toy preferences and the functional analysis of popular toys. *International Journal of Play, 5*(1), 11–27.

Murray, J., & Devecchi, C. (2016). The Hantown Street play project. *International Journal of Play, 5*(2), 196–211.

Ness, D., & Farenga, S. (2016). Blocks, bricks, and planks. *American Journal of Play, 8*(2), 201–227.

Neuman, S., & Roskos, K. (1990). Play, print and purpose: Enriching play environments for literacy development. *Reading Teacher, 44*(3), 214–221.

Nwokah, E., Hui-Chin, H., & Gulker, H. (2013). The use of play materials in early intervention. *American Journal of Play, 5*(2), 187–218.

Ogunnaike, Y. (2015). Early childhood education and human factor: Connecting theories and perspectives. *Review of Human Factor Studies, 21*(1), 9–26.

Pawlowski, C., Thomsen, T., Schipperijn, J., & Troelsen, J. (2014). Barriers for recess physical activity: A gender specific qualitative focus group exploration. *BMC Public Health, 14*, 1–10.

Pirrone, C., & Di Nuovo, S. (2014). Can playing and imagining aid in learning mathematics? *Applied Psychology Bulletin, 62*(271), 30–39.

Pratt, C. (1948). *I learn from children*. New York: Simon and Schuster.

Reid, D. (2004). The influence of virtual reality on playfulness in children with cerebral palsy: A pilot study. *Occupational Therapy International, 11*(3), 131–144.

Reifel, S. (1984). Block construction: Children's developmental landmarks in representation of space. *Young Children, 40*, 61–67.

Rinaldi, C. (2006). *In dialogue with Reggio Emilia*. London: Routledge.

Rivkin, M. (1998). 'Happy play in grassy places': The importance of the outdoor environment in Dewey's educational ideal. *Early Childhood Education Journal, 25*(3), 199–202.

Roper, L. (1973). *FLO: A biography of Frederick Law Olmsted*. Baltimore, MD: Johns Hopkins University Press.

Roskos, K., & Neuman, S. (2003). Environment and its influences for early literacy teaching and learning. In S. Neuman & D. Dickenson (Eds.), *Handbook of early literacy*, vol. 1 (pp. 281–294). New York: Guilford Press.

Sandseter, E. (2009). Affordances for risky play in preschool: The importance of features in the play environment. *Early Childhood Education Journal, 36*, 439–446.

Sarama, J., & Clements, D. (2009). *Early childhood mathematics education research: Learning trajectories for young children.* New York: Routledge.

Smirnova, E., Kotliar, I., Sokolova, M., & Sheina, E. (2016). The children's playground in the context of cultural-historical psychology. *Cultural-Historical Psychology, 12*(3), 269–279.

Solomon, S. (2005). *American playgrounds: Revitalizing community space.* Lebanon, NH: University Press of New England.

Soundy, C. (2008). Young children's imaginative play: Is it valued in Montessori classrooms? *Early Childhood Education Journal, 36*, 381–383.

Stanley, N. (2002). Out of this world: Theme parks' contribution to a redefined aesthetics and educational practice. *International Journal of Art and Design Education, 21*(1), 24–35.

Sutterby, J. (2005). 'I wish we could do whatever we want!': Children subverting scaffolding in the preschool classroom. *Journal of Early Childhood Teacher Education, 25*, 349–357.

Sutterby, J. (2009). What kids don't get to do anymore and why. *Childhood Education, 85*(5), 289–292.

Sutterby, J. (2017). From the park to the playground: Building for democracy. In M. Moore & C. Sabo-Risley (Eds.), *Play in American life* (pp. 155–165). Bloomington, IN: Archway.

Sutterby, J. A., & Frost, J. L. (2002). Making playgrounds fit for children and children fit on playgrounds. *Young Children, 57*(3), 36–42.

Thompson, D., Hudson, S., & Bowers, L. (2002). Play areas and the ADA: Providing access and opportunities for all children. *Journal of Physical Education, Recreation & Dance, 73*(2), 37–41.

Turkle, S. (2012). *Alone together: Why we expect more from technology and less from each other.* New York: Basic Books.

Wadley, G., Carter, M., & Gibbs, M. (2015). Voice in virtual worlds: The design, use and influence of voice chat in online play. *Human Computer Interaction, 30*, 336–365.

Wakes, S., & Beukes, A. (2011). Height, fun and safety in the design of children's playground equipment. *International Journal of Injury Control and Safety Promotion, 19*(2), 101–108.

Zieff, S., Chaudhuri, A., & Musselman, E. (2016). Creating neighborhood recreational space for youth and children in the urban environment: Play(ing in the) streets of San Francisco. *Children & Youth Services Review, 70*, 95–101.

38 Recess

Supporting a Culture of Meaningful Play at School

Lauren McNamara

Elementary school recess provides a different kind of setting for play. Historically, schools were designed to focus on teaching and learning, with little attention given to children's need for play during the school day. The buildings, classrooms, scheduling, policies, organizational routines, and practices have been dynamically shaped to focus on educational achievement (Hargreaves, Lieberman, Fullan, & Hopkins, 1996). Non-instructional activities – such as recess – are broadly considered ancillary and are prioritized accordingly with respect to funding and accountability. Playground supervision, equipment, and space is minimized, and this has created a cascading series of consequences: concerns about discipline, safety, and liability. The result is a playground setting that often undermines healthy play for many children. However, contemporary research on play and social relationships has led to a better understanding of the dynamic role of recess on children's health and academic trajectories. This new information has led to more thoughtful approaches to supporting opportunities for play during recess.

Playing at School: The Evolution of Recess

It is generally obvious that children – particularly younger children – cannot be confined to desks and forced attention for very long without becoming restless and distracted. Recess is typically understood as a part of the school day that allows children a break from the confinement and tensions of classroom instruction in order to return to class refreshed and ready to learn. Recess is one of those steadfast traditions that are passed down, unquestionably, from generation to generation. It is rarely the topic of educational reform. Termed 'breaktime' or 'playtime' in the United Kingdom and Ireland and 'fitness break' in parts of Canada, it provides children with an opportunity to interact and engage in play, free from the rigid discipline of a classroom (McNamara et al., 2014).

Or does it?

In the early nineteenth century, S. M. Ellis dared to suggest that schools do away with recess altogether. Ellis was the superintendent of the Rochester, New York, school board and he felt that recess should be abolished because the conditions on school playgrounds were not conducive to play. He argued that recess

> offers unusual opportunities for moral contamination. When four or five hundred boys and girls from all classes and conditions in life – some from homes of drunkenness, misery, abject poverty, and squalor, where profanity and vile epithets form the staple of conversation, and some who, although surrounded by healthier influences, seem by instinct to revel in impurity – are let loose upon the playground, we should naturally expect that words would be spoken and improprieties committed.   (1882, p. 69).

He went on to state that the vast majority of schools in Rochester either had inadequate playgrounds or lacked them entirely. "Out of twenty-seven buildings there are but seven that have suitable playgrounds, while there are ten that have no playgrounds at all . . . It will thus be seen that a large majority of our school children, if they play at all, must play in the streets" (p. 70).

In response, W. T. Harris, at the time the US Commissioner of Education, rose up and argued that classroom discipline called for forced attention, conformity, punctuality, silence, and self-control. He believed that study produced "a great tension of physical and mental powers" (1882, p. 62) and that children must have a chance to relieve the pent-up physical and mental tension through play – lest they become ill. When study is sustained for too long "congestion would be produced, affecting the heart or brain or the digestive function or some local nerve centre" (p. 62). He reminded his audience that preventing this danger was the whole reason that recess was established and that we should seriously question any attempt to abolish it.

Few raised the issue again until the late twentieth century when Dirk Johnson, a journalist for the *New York Times*, noticed that school districts in Atlanta, Chicago, Connecticut, New Jersey, and New York were quietly going about eliminating recess from the school day – with some school boards even going so far as to build new schools without playgrounds (Johnson, 1998). He interviewed educators and found them to be under pressure to boost academic performance and fit all of the curricular requirements into their day. Like most non-curricular activities, they argued that recess is a time that could be better spent on instruction. In his article (1998), Johnson quoted Benjamin Canada, then superintendent of schools in Atlanta, who provided rationale for the decision: "We are intent on improving academic performance. You don't do that by having kids hanging on the monkey bars."

Other journalists took note, as did parents, physicians, child development experts, and advocacy groups – and the debate about recess took root again, this time with a bit more traction. The National Association for Early Childhood Specialists (2001) found that nearly 40% of 16,000 school districts in the United States had modified, discontinued, or considered discontinuing recess. In the United Kingdom, Blatchford and Baines (2006) found the amount of time allocated to recess was gradually being reduced throughout the previous decade, in spite of a longer school day.

The trend continued, and in response, the American Academy of Pediatrics Council on School Health released a policy statement (2013) recommending daily recess. They argued that recess is a necessity for optimal development.

After 130 years, the debate for or against recess was strikingly unchanged. Fortunately, a growing number of researchers are committed to the study of recess. As they investigate the setting more closely, they confirm what many of us instinctively know – the social landscape of recess is not for the faint-hearted. Social conflict, in particular, is consistently documented in the research on recess. Children struggle with exclusion, teasing, hitting, fighting, injuries, altercations, cliques, and bullying (McNamara et al., 2015).

Generally speaking, what the research has found is that limited funding results in minimal supervision, which then has cascading effects on the play-ground climate. Equipment is often restricted because it goes missing and is too costly to replace; in addition, it can be used inappropriately and becomes a liability issue. Children need to be within sightlines of supervisors, which often means they are restricted to a confined space. Rules are often too strict – it is common to have such rules as 'walking and talking only' (i.e. no running or playing), 'no balls', 'no cartwheels', 'no tag'. Little attention is allocated to planning and organization. These limitations have a considerable impact on what happens on the playground – children report boredom and conflict, and administrative reports concern safety, liability, theft, and discipline issues (McNamara et al., 2015). To echo Ellis, these are not settings that are conducive to meaningful interactions and play among the children.

But cutting out recess, it should be obvious, is not the answer. Neither is insisting on it. The answer lies in creating a supportive setting for meaningful play at school. The health benefits of active, healthy play (including risky outdoor play) are undeniable (Barros et al., 2009; Brown, 2009; Brussoni et al., 2015; Ginsburg, 2007; Pellegrini, 2009; Ramstetter et al., 2010). Children are in a school setting for a considerable portion of each day, and therefore it is an important mediator of children's overall health and development – for better or for worse (Stewart et al., 2004). Importantly, the World Health Organization established the Health Promoting Schools initiative (1997) to raise awareness of the influence of the school day on children's overall health trajectories (WHO, 1997). The goal is to encourage schools to look beyond curricular instruction, to consider, carefully, how the social and physical landscapes of the school shape children's feelings of happiness, social connectedness, autonomy, and fulfilment – clear determinants of overall health and academic success. In other words, the benefits of healthy play at school can be realized only if the conditions are supportive.

Research on Recess

Generally speaking, recess is thought to be an unstructured setting for play that should allow children to freely engage with their peers, develop and play their own games, and choose their own levels of physical activity (Barros et al., 2009; Dills et al., 2011; Evans & Pellegrini, 1997). Romina Barros, a paediatrician, and her colleagues (2009) argue that the free and unstructured setting of recess is a necessary time for children to reach important social, emotional, and developmental milestones, and it is generally understood that regularly scheduled breaks of physical activity throughout the school day will contribute to both short- and long-term health benefits. It is well understood that breaks are necessary opportunities to reduce stress, enhance feelings of well-being, stimulate neurological activity, increase energy, and prevent disease (Barros et al., 2009; Centers for Disease Control and Prevention, 2010; Ramstetter et al., 2010). Further, playful interactions mediate cognitive and emotional regulation and facilitate the development of social and emotional competencies such as empathy, problem-solving, emotional regulation, and coping strategies (Bagwell & Schmidt, 2011). These factors support positive physical and psychological health trajectories, which are predictive of both academic success and overall health outcomes (Bagwell & Schmidt, 2011; Blum, 2005; Durlak et al., 2011).

Breaks. Children need breaks in their school day to unwind from the tensions of the classroom. Children are more attentive and alert – and less fidgety – post break. Ramstetter et al. (2010) highlight that students' attention levels begin to wane after about 45 minutes of continuous intense instruction. Therefore, they suggest that regularly scheduled breaks are necessary to help the children regain their focus and consequently maximize cognitive benefits of instruction. Pre and post studies substantiate what most of us intuitively know: that children comprehend class instruction much more efficiently after they have had a break (Barros et al., 2009; Dills et al., 2011; Holmes et al., 2006; Pellegrini & Bjorklund, 1997). This is a particularly important consideration for younger students, high-energy students, and students with attention deficit hyperactivity disorder (Pellegrini & Bjorklund, 1997).

Physical Activity. Recess is recognized as an outlet for physically active play. Engaging in physical activity during recess has both immediate and long-term benefits. Physical activity reduces stress, promotes feelings of well-being, stimulates neurological activity, increases energy, helps maintain a healthy weight, and prevents disease (Barros et al., 2009; Centers for Disease Control and Prevention, 2010; Ramstetter et al., 2010; Sibley & Etnier, 2003). These factors dynamically influence children's physical and psychological health, which is predictive of academic success (Blum, 2005; Durlak et al., 2011).

Social and Emotional Development. Recess is recognized as free time to interact with peers, relatively free from adult intervention (Barros et al., 2009). It provides necessary opportunities for children to engage in meaningful interactions and develop supportive friendships. For some children, especially those in urban, economically challenged areas, these school-based opportunities may be their only chance to connect with their peers (Barros et al., 2009). Peer relationships mediate the development of social and emotional competencies such as empathy, problem-solving, emotional regulation, and coping strategies. In turn, social competence is linked to psychosocial health as children's supportive friendships influence their coping skills. Importantly, children who do not develop effective coping skills are at risk for social, emotional, and/or behavioural problems such as anxiety, depression, or aggression. In turn, these feelings can compromise well-being as well as engagement with school (Fredericks et al., 2004; Pellegrini et al., 2004).

Opportunities for Play. For many children, particularly those in urban areas, school-based playtime may be their only chance in their day to have access to a recreational setting that allows them free time to play (Barros et al., 2009). As noted in this book, unstructured play affords valuable developmental opportunities, and children could benefit from safe spaces and opportunities for unstructured playtime at school.

Disease Prevention. Recess is a social play setting, and we can learn from the work of social neuroscientists. Recent research can now describe how social experiences mediate long-term impacts on health trajectories. Specifically, social experiences initiate a cascading series of physiological responses that trigger activity in the neural, endocrine, metabolic, and lymphatic systems. If these systems are negatively altered, basic and necessary molecular processes are weakened and become vulnerable, ultimately compromising children's overall health (Eisenberger & Cole, 2012).

Challenges on the Playground That Undermine Healthy Play

Arguably, the assumption is that during recess, children will socialize and engage in physically active play. However, the ways that recess is implemented vary considerably from country to country, school board to school board, school to school. A comprehensive study of recess practices around the globe has yet to be completed (see Beresin, 2016). Sometimes the physical play space is divided to separate the younger children from the older children. Conversely, it is not unusual to see 300–500 children outside at the same time, with roughly three lunch monitors supervising. Some schools, usually smaller schools, have equipment and a system for managing the equipment – often the classroom teacher has a basket of equipment the children can use. Some schools have no loose equipment, some have play structures, some have no structures at all, some have stencilled patterns (hopscotch, four-square), some have only pavement. Few schools have natural materials such as hills, logs, trees, grass, and sand. Some schools allow children to bring their personal equipment from home (gloves, baseballs, basketballs); some do not. Some schools have recess buddies or peer leaders. Some schools have organized science clubs or intramural sports practice. Some schools stagger the outdoor time by grade levels, reducing the population that goes outside at any one time. And so on.

Therefore it is difficult to generalize the benefits of recess without a descriptive understanding of what actually happens at recess. My research team (McNamara et al., 2015) reviewed the research from the United States and Canada and we found the following.

Supervision. Teachers take their breaks during recess. Teachers have a set number of hours that are allocated (by unions) for supervisory duty. Therefore, recess is generally staffed by a rotation of teachers. To compensate, schools hire part-time yard duty supervisors to observe the playground during recess (including indoor recess). Importantly, yard duty supervisors have limited experience and training and are not required to have an educational background in child development or education. Job advertisements for yard supervisors in both the United States and Canada required only a high school diploma and local language proficiency.

Minimal Equipment. There is quite a bit of research that suggests equipment availability influences children's engagement and activity levels. However, when playgrounds are minimally supervised – as is the case for many schools – the equipment creates safety concerns and worries about liabilities. Some reports indicate that equipment and/or play structures are broken, rusty, splintered, and/or do not meet safety standards. Principals indicate that equipment is difficult to manage and often disappears; in turn, they are reluctant to purchase replacements because of limited funds. Schools that do provide equipment often report the need to restrict the use of the equipment by enforcing rules, locations, and forms of use – compromising the benefit to the students.

Minimal Activities. While unstructured free play is necessary for children to thrive, the social setting of recess could pose difficulties for some children. An unstructured environment with limited equipment, organization, or support can be very challenging for some children to negotiate (Doll et al., 2003; Knowles et al., 2013; McNamara, 2013; Stanley et al., 2012). Some children do not know how to play certain games and conflict about game rules is common, particularly when time is limited. Students who are not in the 'in crowd' or interested in competitive games may experience rejection and isolation because there is little else to do.

Crowded Spaces. Many school playgrounds are often limited in size and do not provide enough room for children to stretch out and actively play (D'Haese et al., 2013; Huberty et al., 2012; Knowles et al., 2013; Stanley et al., 2012). There are few studies, however, that document the setting space, but the result of crowding is often an increase in frustration, sedentary activity, and social conflict.

Conflict. Children are released from the confines of the classroom and need to burn off their pent-up energy. However, the challenges mentioned earlier, coupled with high energy, can contribute to boredom, discipline issues, disengagement, and sedentary behaviour. This, in turn, can trigger the progression of social conflict – making it more difficult to play and interact in ways that allow children to connect positively with one another. We see this in the research, as aggression, exclusion, and bullying are commonly reported during recess time (Anderson-Butcher et al., 2003; Doll et al., 2003; McNamara, 2013; McNamara et al., 2014; Vaillancourt et al., 2010). For some children, the social atmosphere of recess is one of the most feared times of the school day (Astor et al., 2001; McNamara et al., 2014; Vaillancourt et al., 2010).

Other researchers have documented the playground experiences of children with intellectual and developmental disabilities. This population of children often have fewer opportunities to socialize and play than typically developing peers. They tend to have limited social connections, participate in fewer social activities, and have fewer close relationships than their peers without disabilities (King et al., 2013; Shikako-Thomas et al., 2008). The school playground experiences of children with disabilities are under-researched. Yantzi et al. (2010) found that children with disabilities experience many barriers when accessing school playgrounds, and Woolley et al. (2006) found these children to feel considerably isolated during recess. Furthermore, Yantzi et al. (2010) conducted a "playability" audit of five Canadian school playgrounds, each in a school designated for physically disabled children. There are no Canadian accessibility requirements or guidelines, so they used the accessibility guidelines established by the US Access Board in 2000. Only one of the five met all of the accessibility requirements, and most did not meet the minimum accessibility guidelines.

Creating a Setting for Meaningful Play during Recess

In light of the current research on play, it is clear that there is a very real danger in simply insisting on daily recess. This would only prolong the endless debate. For children, recess means much more than just getting out for a break from academics or freedom from teachers. It is the part of the day that meets their strong social and emotional needs – specifically, their need to connect through play, interaction, and socialization.

As such, the setting of recess needs to be reconceptualized with thoughtful planning and consideration. Children need time during the school day to play and opportunities to connect with their school-based peers in a supportive setting. In my work (McNamara, 2013; McNamara et al., 2014; McNamara et al., 2015) I have come to understand that five things need to be addressed and considered together: (1) the creation of a new position of coordinator, (2) abundance of equipment and activities, (3) redesign of the space, (4) addition of positive, playful role models, and (5) detailed recess policies regarding time, space, supervision, and discipline.

(1) Coordinator, Guide, or Coach. More supervision on the playground is clearly necessary to create an environment that is conducive to healthy, meaningful play. The lack of supervision invites liability issues that pressure educators to be on the safe side. More supervisors are needed to organize, plan, and support students. Moreover, the concept of a 'supervisor' should be reconsidered. The role should be designated for the design and maintenance of an environment that promotes play and supports children – as opposed to reactively intervening when there is a problem. I prefer the terms *coordinator*, *guide*, or *coach*, rather than the traditional term of *supervisor*.

It is clear that large numbers of children and a few distant supervisors cannot promote a safe and meaningful playground environment, but what might an appropriate ratio be? It must be sufficient to have an impact. The educators that I have worked with suggest the same ratio as in the classroom, as it would satisfy needs for support, equipment management, safety, and liability. The Office of the United Nation's High Commissioner for Human Rights (1989) has declared *play* a fundamental right of every child; moreover, children also have the right to *competent supervision, protection, safety, and care* as declared by the United Nations Convention on the Rights of Children (Office of the United Nation's High Commissioner for Human Rights, 1989, Articles 3, 6, and 19, 1989).

Coordinators play an important role in fostering a setting that is conducive to healthy play. First, coordinators can map out the playground, organize play areas, manage equipment, and keep a schedule of rotating activities. Second, they can assist children in developing and maintaining relationships with peers. By taking a proactive position, they can set up favourable circumstances to ensure high levels of compassion, inclusion, and engagement and, in turn, reduce or prevent aggression, anger, and social conflict. Third, coordinators can provide necessary supports to marginalized or vulnerable children who might be experiencing social difficulty on the playground. Fourth, they can train and oversee youth leaders to help assist on the playground. And fifth, they can serve as role models to ensure a culture of play.

(2) Equipment and Activities. Although unstructured free play provides important developmental opportunities, the unstructured, unorganized context of recess at school – large crowds of children of mixed ages, personalities, social skills, and personal circumstances – can be too challenging. In this setting children need options: they need opportunities for structured *and* unstructured play. They need an available continuum of activities that considers the diverse developmental needs, styles, skills, and interests of the children. And they need psychologically safe places to play, where they are protected from the effects of victimization and social rejection.

Along with ample opportunity and spaces for unstructured free play, during recess children can benefit from an array of guided activities. These activities can provide children with opportunities to make friends with peers who share the same interests. I have found that many children benefit from guided, quieter activities such as crafts, drawing with chalk, and book/music clubs because they help mediate connections and friendships, which then pave the way for more engaged, spontaneous, and positive free play.

For the same reason, more active children benefit from occasional guided activities such as dance, yoga, soccer, baseball, and skipping clubs. When children can select an activity based on their personal preference, their social circumstances, and/or their temperament, it allows them to meet and connect with others who are similar. In turn, these meetings are likely to trigger future interactions and playmates, which ultimately leads to feelings of inclusion and belonging (Baumeister & Leary, 1995; McNamara et al., 2014; Walton & Cohen, 2011). On inclement weather days in colder climates, when children are required to stay inside, these guided activities are especially beneficial.

(3) Space. Increasing playground space makes it easier for children to stretch out, play games, use equipment, and engage in all kinds of play. However, more space may not be an option for many schools. It is possible, however, to reduce crowding by staggering and alternating outdoor recess times. It is also possible, and simple, to designate zones for a wide variety of activities, materials, and equipment that include options for free play, active play, guided play, and quieter areas. An effective way to do this is to have a planned, rotating schedule of 'stations' – such as a Frisbee station, skipping station, soccer station, games station, crafts station, and so on.

Additionally, schoolyards are often barren and paved spaces, with little, if any, natural landscape. Children could benefit from grass, trees, hills, rocks, sand, water, logs. The addition of a more natural landscape can improve psychological well-being (Maller et al., 2006), decreasing the amount of social tension on the playground. Furthermore, natural landscapes provide children with more space and opportunity for imaginative and playful interactions (Ginsburg, 2007, 2009). In colder climates children could benefit from indoor areas specially designed for play. These should be roomy enough for all children to utilize during recess.

Many developed nations focus on the health impact of physical and social landscapes in their cities. The Scottish government, for example, has a policy statement on 'Health and Place' that encourages thoughtfulness with respect to designing accessible places that promote community, connection, and playfulness. Their policy includes comprehensive evidence-based guidelines for school playground design and supervision (playscotland.org). There are many organizations that are promoting playful cities and recreational play spaces, and that work should start to cascade into schools. The evidence and desire is there; the challenge lies in the action, which is gaining traction.

The Boston Schoolyard Initiative, for example, pulled together private and public stakeholders to revitalize every school playground in the city of Boston (schoolyards.org). Over 18 years, the project transformed 88 playgrounds from aging, cracked asphalt to colourful, inspiring play spaces. KaBOOM!, a US non-profit organization, encourages city planners to make their cities more playable – for adults and children alike. They raise funds to build in creative playfulness in urban environments – dancing crosswalk lights, painted steps, randomly placed hopscotch stencils, for example (kaboom.org).

Importantly, school spaces need to be universally accessible. Universal design is space designed to meet the needs of the greatest number of people. The Rick Hansen Foundation has created a toolkit for designing accessible playgrounds (rickhansen.com). The toolkit encourages building diversity directly into the design. In other words, the designs promote play spaces that can be used in a variety of ways, by more than one child at a time. Universal design is about creating spaces that foster inclusive communities, and schools are a very important community for children.

(4) Role Models. Positive role models are a very effective mediator of culture change on the playground (McNamara et al., 2014). It is well understood that children observe, imitate, and consolidate the behaviours of others. This is why the role of the coordinators must extend far beyond supervising and officiating – they become an important source of cultural knowledge for children. Children need role models to foster compassion, empathy, and negotiation. The continual presence of supportive role models can mediate and maintain inclusive and accepting behaviours. If recess is a social setting that takes place several times a day throughout childhood, the daily effects are likely to have a cumulative influence on children's beliefs, behaviours, and habits.

Vygotsky (1978) detailed the ways in which culture mediates children's thinking, attitudes, and social behaviours. Culture is the shared beliefs, values, and meanings among members of a particular group or society. These shared understandings play out in the patterns of our social interactions – specifically, in our exchanges, conversations, routines, activities, and behaviours. These exchanges dynamically create a shared understanding of both desirable and undesirable beliefs and attitudes that become internalized and, over time, manifest in actions and behaviours.

Coordinators, then, can arrange for groups of older peers who can serve as 'Junior Recess Leaders'. Junior Recess Leaders can be carefully trained to create and maintain a playful recess climate. Their role is to encourage meaningful play and pro-social behaviours. They learn how to support children as they initiate play, negotiate social groups, sustain positive relationships, and mediate conflict. The consistency, familiarity and daily interactions between the Junior Leaders and the younger children can contribute to a cultural shift in attitudes on the playground.

In our model (McNamara et al., 2014) Junior Leaders are assigned to a station (e.g., skipping station, Frisbee station, yoga station, silly-dance station, chalking station) that is organized by the coordinators to inject playfulness into the setting. The Junior Leaders then are responsible for supporting the children and monitoring the equipment that is associated with that station. They can adopt a more playful and active role with the younger children (rather than strictly supervisory) at the same time offering protective support for vulnerable or marginalized children. Junior Leaders can volunteer for a 10-week rotation of two recesses per week. This prevents burn-out on their part and allows them a chance to enjoy their own recesses. They can elect to do another rotation if they enjoyed their position (most do).

My research teams have found it helpful when the Junior Leaders join the younger children for lunch or snack. They can eat and informally chat. This regular inside/outside interaction encourages positive connections between older and younger students. Over time, too, it allows the Junior Leaders to become familiar role models.

In addition, Playworks (playworks.org) is a national US non-profit organization that has had great success over the last 15 years with their model of 'recess coaches' and 'junior coaches'. Rebecca London and her colleagues (London et al., 2015) explored the impact of Playworks coaches in several schools. Their team found that the additional support on the playground improved overall school climate by providing opportunities for student engagement, conflict resolution, pro-social skill development, and emotional and physical safety.

(5) **Policy.** The increase in research and advocacy on play and health has had an influence on school-based play. A comprehensive review of school-based policies on recess has yet to be done; however, there is evidence of activity. Research in the United States, for example, has found that state laws influence how much time children have for recess (Slater et al., 2013). Whether there should be recess, and how much, is still an active debate. It appears to be the most pressing legislative stance at this time. At the time of writing, for instance, news outlets were highlighting that Florida has voted for a bill that would require a minimum 20 minutes of recess per day. To highlight the contention, another Florida bill, however, may take precedence – in this competing bill recess would be part of physical activity – which could be subsumed by physical education class – would be only for children in grades kindergarten through three, and would not be every day (Associated Press, 2017).

According to the Council of State Governments (2017) only one state, Missouri, currently requires that schools provide a minimum of 20 minutes for recess. Virginia elementary schools are required to have recess, but the amount of time, and how often, is not indicated. Other notable mandates are designed to encourage physical activity and mandate time for physical activity during the school day. None mention recess.

With respect to time, Beresin (2016) laid the foundation for a global survey of recess. She corresponded with colleagues from 30 countries to assess how much time is allotted for recess. On average, Finland, Japan, the Republic of Korea, Turkey, and Israel took the lead at 80–90 minutes per day. At the bottom of the list were China, Bulgaria, Mexico, and Brazil at 0–15 minutes. The United States had an overall average of 0–28 minutes, Canada 15–30 minutes, and the countries in the United Kingdom all had an average of 50 minutes. The poll was informal, and it is very likely that differences exist – day to day, city to city, school to school. In addition, economically challenged urban areas may have limited space, which presents crowding and safety issues. Some of the countries only have half a day of schooling (Bulgaria and Brazil, for example), so decisions about how much time is devoted to recess may reflect the shorter school day.

Where I work, in Ontario, Canada, the last policy update on recess was in 1990. The Ontario Ministry of Education Act states that "there shall be a morning recess and an afternoon recess, each of which shall be not less than ten minutes and not more than fifteen minutes in length, for pupils in the primary and junior divisions" (Revised Regulations of Ontario, 1990, Reg. 298, s. 3 (8)). There is little further detail. More recently, many Ontario school boards have implemented a Balanced School Day schedule, which was conceived and promoted by two principals in Hamilton, Ontario (Peebles & Kirkwood, 2011; Woerhle et al., n.d.). The Balanced School Day schedule removes the entire lunch period and instead provides children with a morning and afternoon break, each consisting of a 20-minute 'nutrition break' and a 20-minute 'fitness break'.

Play England (playengland.org) has identified a lack of play opportunities for children and highlights the importance of play for children. Yet there are relatively little data or policy direction as to children's play in school.

Again, mandating recess time is a start, but much more detail needs to be added. For example, school boards and individual schools have the discretion as to whether or not recess can be withheld for disciplinary reasons. In the context of this volume, this practice may seem rather shocking. But withholding recess is a practice that is used commonly by US teachers for behaviour management (Turner et al., 2013).

Also, the ratio of staff to students needs to be considered, as minimal supervision appears to be a critical influence on the setting (Frazen & Kamps, 2008; McNamara et al., 2015; Schwartz et al., 2012). According to Ontario Principals Council (Ontario Principals Council (OPC), 2007) ratios must fall between 1:8–1:20 for kindergarten students and 1:50–1:100 for elementary school students. In addition, the OPC states that there should be no fewer than two supervisors with continuous and direct sightlines of the students they are supervising. Vaantaja (2016) investigated principals' experiences of recess. She found inconsistencies in supervisor-to-student ratios reported by principals. For the kindergarten students, the reported supervisor-to-student ratio range was 1:12–1:37. For grades 1–8, the ratio ranged from 1:30 to 1:100. In addition, Vaantaja asked the principals to indicate what would help them improve recess. The top three responses, not surprisingly, were: better equipment, more activities, and more supervision.

In my review of recess (McNamara, 2015), a number of studies reported that minimal supervision was a key challenge (Dubroc, 2007; Jarrett & Waite-Stupiansky, 2009; McNamara, 2013; McNamara et al., 2014; Pytel, 2009; Robert Wood Johnson Foundation, 2010; Stanley et al., 2012). The ratios across the studies were inconsistent, ranging from 1:50 to 1:220 students. Importantly, in many schools, teachers take their breaks during recess, so principals need to hire support staff to supervise for the short period of recess – a difficult position to fill.

The situation in the United Kingdom appears to be similar to that in the United States and Canada, in that union regulations require teachers to take their breaks during student break times (Lightfoot, 2007). Many principals that I collaborate with indicate that hired yard staff may be late or not show up at all. It is difficult to find much publicly available policy documentation on this topic. Access to collective agreements is often private, so it is difficult to readily obtain. A review would assist in our understanding of the dynamics that affect supervision on the playground.

Conclusion

Children spend a considerable part of their childhood in the school setting. Playing and socializing with their school-based peers has an important influence on their overall well-being in dynamic ways – for better or for worse. Recess is the main time in their school day that the children have an opportunity to interact with their peers free of classroom constraints. However, dense populations of students, mixed ages and stages, minimal supervision, and uninviting spaces can do more harm than good. But rather than cutting out the time allocated to recess, the setting should be thoughtfully reconsidered and redesigned in order to be a supportive, safe space that invites opportunities for engaging, meaningful, and inclusive play.

In spite of policy, taking action is at the discretion of the school boards, school administrators, and teachers (Hope & Pigford, 2001). Therefore, educators and staff could benefit from an awareness of the value of play in school. Burriss and Burriss (2011) suggest that policy and guidelines for teachers, principals, and school administrators should include examples of play settings and activities, which I have detailed in this chapter.

Further, schools could benefit from collaborating with community groups, governmental organizations, and philanthropic and business partners to assist in carrying out action. Schools are part of the larger fabric of society. The attitudes, beliefs, habits, and behaviours that are acquired in schools follow the children home to influence their overall health and well-being. Undeniably, playfulness, inclusion, creativity, problem-solving, collaboration, and empathy are influenced by what happens on the school playground. Children need these experiences to succeed as adults – but, more importantly, playing with peers in a supportive school setting is a daily, cumulative influence that contributes to their overall happiness. It is a right. It is a need. And that is what really matters to the children.

References

American Academy of Pediatrics Council on School Health (2013). The crucial role of recess in school. *Pediatrics*, *131*(1), 183–188.

Anderson-Butcher, D., Newsome, W. S., & Nay, S. (2003). Social skills intervention during elementary school recess: A visual analysis. *Children and Schools, 25*(3), 135–146.

Associated Press (2017, April 5,). Florida senate approves recess bill for daily school recess. Available at www.local10.com/community/florida-senate-approves-bill-for-daily-school-recess.

Astor, R. A., Meyer, H. M., & Pitner, R. O. (2001). Elementary and middle school students' perceptions of violence-prone school subcontexts. *Elementary School Journal, 101*, 511–528.

Bagwell, C. L., & Schmidt, M. E. (2011). *Friendships in childhood and adolescence.* New York: Guilford Press.

Barros, R. M., Silver, E. J., & Stein, R. E. K. (2009). School recess and group classroom behavior. *Journal of the American Academy of Pediatrics, 123*(2), 431–436.

Baumeister, R. F., & Leary, M. R. (1995). The need to belong: Desire for interpersonal attachments as a fundamental human motivation. *Psychological Bulletin, 117*(3), 497–529.

Beresin, A. (2016). Playing with time: Towards a global survey of recess practices. *International Journal of Play, 5*(2), 159–165.

Blatchford, P., & Baines, E. (2006). A follow up national survey of breaktimes in primary and secondary school. Report to the Nuffield Foundation. Available at www.nuffieldfoundation.org/sites/default/files/Breaktimes_Final%20report_Blatchford.pdf.

Blum, R. (2005). School connectedness: Improving the lives of students. Johns Hopkins Bloomberg School of Public Health, Baltimore, MD. Available at http://cecp.air.org/download/MCMonographFINAL.pdf.

Brown, S. (2009). *Play: How it shapes the brain, opens the imagination, and invigorates the soul.* Toronto: Penguin Group.

Brussoni, M., Gibbons, R., Gray, C., Ishikawa, T., Sandseter, E. B. H., Bienenstock, A., et al. (2015). What is the relationship between risky outdoor play and health in children? A systematic review. *International Journal of Environmental Research in Public Health, 12*, 6423–6454.

Burriss, K., & Burriss, L. (2011). Outdoor play and learning: Policy and practice. *Journal of Education Policy and Leadership, 6*(8), 1–12.

Centers for Disease Control and Prevention. (2010). *State Indicator Report on Physical Activity, 2010.* Atlanta, GA: US Department of Health and Human Services.

Council of State Governments (2017, March). State Policies on Physical Activity in Schools. Research Brief. Available at http://knowledgecenter.csg.org/kc/system/files/CR_activity_school.pdf.

D'Haese, S., Van Dyck, D., De Bourdeaudhuij, I., & Cardon, G. (2013). Effectiveness and feasibility of lowering playground density during recess to promote physical activity and decrease sedentary time at primary school. *BMC Public Health, 13*(1), 1–19.

Dills, A. K., Morgan, H. N., & Rotthoff, K. W. (2011). Recess, physical education, and elementary school student outcomes. *Economics of Education Review, 30*, 889–900.

Doll, B., Murphy, P., & Song, S. Y. (2003). The relationship between children's self-reported recess problems, and peer acceptance and friendships. *Journal of School Psychology, 41*(2), 113–130.

Dubroc, A. M. (2007). Is the elimination of recess in school a violation of a child's basic human rights? Available at http://files.eric.ed.gov/fulltext/ED495814.pdf.

Durlak, J. A., Weissberg, R. P., Dymnicki, A. B., Taylor, R. D., & Schellinger, K. B. (2011). The impact of enhancing students' social and emotional learning: A meta-analysis of school-based universal interventions. *Child Development, 82*(1), 405–432.

Education Commission of the States (2016, April 22). Response to information request, 'Which states have recess policy?' Available at www.ecs.org/ec-con tent/uploads/SIRRecess.pdf.

Eisenberger, N. I., & Cole, S. W. (2012). Social neuroscience and health: Neurophysiological mechanisms linking social ties with physical health. *Nature Neuroscience, 15*(5), 669–774.

Ellis, S. A. (1882). No recess. In *Proceedings from the Department of Superintendents of the National Educational Association* (pp. 66–74). Washington, DC: Government Printing Office. Available at https://books.google.ca/books?id=tXhMA QAAMAAJ&pg=PA338&lpg=PA338&dq=s.a.+ellis+recess&source=bl& ots=PXGgy1Qluv&sig=azkZ2zZ8E2HcQnWLsCC_dYyrSUk&hl=en&sa= X&ved=0ahUKEwjT-YujqOXSAhUE5WMKHb5IDYEQ6AEIH DAA#v=onepage&q=harris&f=false.

Evans, J., & Pellegrini, A. (1997). Surplus energy theory: An enduring but inadequate justification for school break-time. *Educational Review, 49*(3), 229–236.

Frazen, K., & Kamps, D. (2008). The utilization and effects of positive behavior support strategies on an urban school playground. *Journal of Positive Behavior Interventions, 10*(3), 150–161.

Fredericks, J., Blumenfeld, P., & Paris, A. (2004). School engagement: Potential of the concept, state of evidence. *Review of Educational Research, 74*(1), 59–105.

Ginsburg, K. R. (2007). The importance of play in promoting healthy child development and maintaining strong parent–child bonds. *Pediatrics, 119*(1), 182–192.

Gordon, G. (2009). What is play? In search of a definition. In Kuschner, D. (Ed.), *Play and culture studies, from children to red hatters: Diverse images and issues of play* (pp. 1–13). Lanham, MD: University Press of America.

Hargreaves, A., Lieberman, A., Fullan, M. & Hopkins, D. (Eds.) (2010) Second International Handbook of Educational Change. Dordrecht, Springer.

Harris, W. T. (1882). Recess. In *Proceedings from the Department of Superintendents of the National Educational Association* (pp. 59–66). Washington, DC: Government Printing Office. Available at https://books.google.ca/books?id=tXhMA QAAMAAJ&pg=PA338&lpg=PA338&dq=s.a.+ellis+recess&source=bl& ots=PXGgy1Qluv&sig=azkZ2zZ8E2HcQnWLsCC_dYyrSUk&hl=en&sa= X&ved=0ahUKEwjT-YujqOXSAhUE5WMKHb5IDYEQ6AEIH DAA#v=onepage&q=s.a.%20ellis%20recess&f=false.

Holmes, R. M., Pellegrini, A. D., & Schmidt, S. L. (2006). The effects of different recess timing regimens on preschoolers' classroom attention. *Early Child Development and Care, 176*(7), 735–743.

Hope, W. C., & Pigford, A. B. (2001). The principal's role in educational policy implementation. *Contemporary Education, 72*(1), 44–47.

Huberty, J., Dinkel, D., Coleman, J., Beighle, A., & Apenteng, B. (2012). The role of schools in children's physical activity participation: Staff perceptions. *Health Education Research*, *27*(6), 986–995.

Jarrett, O. S., & Waite-Stupiansky, S. (2009). Recess: It's indispensable! *Young Children*, *64*(5), 66–69.

Johnson, D. (1998, April 7). Many schools putting an end to child's play. *New York Times*. Available at www.nytimes.com/1998/04/07/us/many-schools-putting-an-end-to-child-s-play.html.

King, G., Rigby, P., & Batorowicz, B. (2013). Conceptualizing participation in context for children and youth with disabilities: An activity setting perspective. *Disability and Rehabilitation, 35*(18), 1578–1585.

Knowles, Z. R., Parnell, D., Stratton, G., & Ridgers, N. D. (2013). Learning from the experts: Exploring playground experience and activities using a write and draw technique. *Journal of Physical Activity and Health*, *10*(3), 406–415.

Lightfoot, L. (2007). Where's my lunch? Students are not getting enough time to eat, let alone play, as schools chip away at the midday break. *The Guardian*. Available at www.theguardian.com/education/2007/nov/13/schools.uk2.

London, R. A., Westrich, L., Stokes-Guinan, K., & McLaughlin, M. (2015). Playing fair: The contribution of high-functioning recess to overall school climate in low-income elementary schools. *Journal of School Health*, *85*, 53–60.

Maller, C., Townsend, M., Pryor, A., Brown, P., & St Leger, L. (2006). Healthy nature healthy people: 'Contact with nature' as an upstream health promotion intervention for populations. *Health Promotion International*, *21*(1), 45–54.

McNamara, L. (2013). What's getting in the way of play? An analysis of contextual factors that hinder recess in elementary schools. *Canadian Journal of Action Research*, *14*(2), 3–21.

McNamara, L., Colley, P., & Franklin, N. (2015). School recess, social connectedness, and health: A Canadian perspective. *Health Promotion International*, *32*(2), 392–402.

McNamara, L., Vaantaja, E., Dunseith, A., & Franklin, N. (2014). Tales from the playground: Transforming the context of recess through collaborative action research. *International Journal of Play*, *4*(1), 49–68.

Ministry of Ontario Education Act (1990). Revised Regulation of Ontario 1990, Reg. 298, s. 3 (8), Operation of schools. Queen's Printer of Ontario. Available at www.e-laws.gov.on.ca/html/regs/english/elaws_regs_900298_e.html.

National Association of Early Childhood Specialists in State Departments of Education. (2001). Recess and the importance of play: A position statement on young children and recess. Available at http://files.eric.ed.gov/fulltext/ED463047.pdf.

Office of the United Nations High Commissioner on Human Rights (1989). *United Nations Convention on the Rights of the Child*. New York: United Nations.

Ontario Principals Council (OPC) (2007). People for education: Cuts to supervision time. Available at www.principals.ca/Print.aspx?cid=7865.

Peebles, L., & Kirkwood, K. (2011). The views of teachers towards the Balanced Day schedule in five elementary pilot schools in southern Ontario. *Teaching & Learning*, *6*(1), 83–94.

Pellegrini, A. D. (2009). Research and policy on children's play. *Child Development Perspectives, 3,* 131–136.

Pellegrini, A. D., & Bjorklund, D. F. (1997). The role of recess in children's cognitive performance. *Educational Psychologist, 31,* 181–187.

Pellegrini, A. D., & Bohn, C. (2004). The role of recess in children's cognitive performance and school adjustment. *Educational Researcher, 34,* 13–19.

Play England (n.d.). The play return: A review of the wider impact of play initiatives. Available at www.playengland.net/wp-content/uploads/2015/11/The-Play-Return-A-review-of-the-wider-impact-of-play-initiatives.pdf.

Play Scotland (n.d.). Getting it right for play. Available at www.playscotland.org/wp-content/uploads/assets/Power-of-Play.pdf.

Pytel, B. (2009). Pros and cons of recess time in schools: Is recess a mere tradition or a vital piece in education? Available at www.isbe.state.il.us/IRTF/pdf/recess_pros_cons.pdf.

Ramstetter, C. L., Murray, R., & Garner, A. S. (2010). Crucial role of recess in schools. *Journal of School Health, 80*(11), 517–526.

Revised Regulations of Ontario (1990). Available at www.ontario.ca/laws/regulations.

Rick Hansen Foundation (n.d.) Let's Play Toolkit. Available at www.rickhansen.com/Portals/0/WhatWeDo/SchoolProgram/RHSPAdditional/AccessiblePlay/LetsPlayToolkit.pdf.

Robert Wood Johnson Foundation (2010). The state of play: Gallup survey of principals on school recess. Princeton, NJ. Available at www.rjwf.org.

Schwartz, M. B., Henderson, K. E., Falbe, J., Novak, S. A., Wharton, C. M., Long, M. W., & Fiore, S. S. (2012). Strength and comprehensiveness of district school wellness polices predict policy implementation at the school level. *Journal of School Health, 82*(6), 262–267.

Shikako-Thomas, K., Majnemer, A., Law, M., & Lach, L. (2008). Determinants of participation in leisure activities in children and youth with cerebral palsy: Systematic review. *Physical & Occupational Therapy in Pediatrics, 28*(2), 155–169.

Sibley, B. A., & Etnier, J. L. (2003). The relationship between physical activity and cognition in children: A meta-analysis. *Pediatric Exercise Science, 15,* 243–256.

Slater, S. J., Nicholson, L., Chriqui, J., Turner, L., & Chaloupka, F. (2013). The impact of state laws and district policies on physical education and recess practices in a nationally-representative sample of U.S. public elementary schools. *Archives of Pediatric Adolescent Medicine, 166*(4), 311–316.

Stanley, R. M., Boshoff, K., & Dollman, J. (2012). Voices in the playground: A qualitative exploration of the barriers and facilitators of lunchtime play. *Journal of Science and Medicine, 15*(1), 44–51.

Stewart, D. E., Sun, J., Patterson, C., Lemerle, K., & Hardie, M. W. (2004). Promoting and building resilience in primary school communities: Evidence from a comprehensive 'health promoting school' approach. *International Journal of Mental Health Promotion, 6*(3), 26–31.

Turner, L., Chriqui, J., & Chaloupka, F. (2013). Withholding recess from elementary students: Policies matter. *Journal of School Health, 83*(8), 533–541.

Vaantaja, E. (2016). Southern Ontario principals' perspectives on recess in low-income neighbourhoods. MA thesis, Brock University.

Vaillancourt, T., Brittain, H., Bennett, L., Arnocky, S., McDougall, P., Hymel, S., Short, K., Sunderani, S., Scott, C., Mackenzie, M., & Cunningham, L. (2010). Places to avoid: Population-based study of student reports of unsafe and high bullying areas at school. *Canadian Journal of School Psychology*, *25*(1), 40–54.

Vygotsky, L. (1978). *Mind in society: The development of higher psychological processes*. Cambridge, MA: Harvard University Press.

Walton, G. M., & Cohen, G. L. (2011). A brief social-belonging intervention improves academic and health outcomes of minority students. *Science*, *331*, 1447–1451.

Woerhle, T., Fox, S., & Hoskin, B. (n.d.). An examination of the balanced school day schedule. People for Education. Available at www.peopleforeducation.ca/wp-content/uploads/2011/09/An-Examination-of-the-Balanced-School-Day-Schedule.pdf.

Woolley, H., Armitage, M., Bishop, J., Curtis, M., & Ginsborg, J. (2006). Going outside together: Good practice with respect to the inclusion of disabled children in primary school playgrounds. *Children's Geographies*, *4*(3), 303–318.

World Health Organization (1997). Promoting health through schools. Report of a WHO Expert Committee on Comprehensive School Health Education and Promotion. WHO Technical Report Series No. 870. World Health Organization, Geneva, Switzerland.

Yantzi, N. M., Young, N. L., & Mckeever, P. (2010). The suitability of school playgrounds for physically disabled children. *Children's Geographies*, *8*(1), 65–78.

39 Playwork

A Unique Way of Working with Children

Fraser Brown, Alexandra Long, and Mike Wragg

For most adults childhood is seen as a preparation for adulthood. Therefore, adult interventions in children's lives generally seek to facilitate or even speed up the process of maturation. This is substantially true of teachers, social workers, health professionals, and even most parents. Playworkers, on the other hand, see children as autonomous active social agents, who are routinely disadvantaged by imbalanced power relations between themselves and adults. In fact children are arguably the most powerless victims of discrimination of any 'minority' group in society. Playwork seeks to challenge that.

Playworkers recognize that in Western societies the child's freedom to play is becoming increasingly restricted. This is likely to have catastrophic consequences not only for individual child development, but also for the evolution of the human species. The playworker's role is to help children to create environments that enable them to play without unnecessary and intrusive adult intervention. This is what Roger Hart (2008) meant when he said that playworkers work horizontally (collaboratively) with children (rather than from a position of power).

This chapter will review and offer a critique of a number of playwork theories, before focusing on the concept of 'being and becoming' to explore the unique interpersonal relationship between children and their playworkers. Playworkers focus primarily on the child in the present, rather than the adult of the future – the 'being' child, rather than the 'becoming' child. We also refer to the UN Convention on the Rights of the Child to explain and analyze the philosophy and practice of the profession.

The Origins of Playwork in the United Kingdom

While the term 'playwork' is used to describe the profession, as discussed above, it is not a title that has been universally adopted around the world (Cartmel, 2014), albeit it is beginning to be adopted in the United States (Wilson, 2009). Cranwell (2003) provides a useful summary of the advancement of the profession of playwork in the United Kingdom, with its roots in the work of Victorian social reformers. Originating in supervised out of school provision between 1880 and 1940, the services focused on the "social control of children's unregulated time" (p. 33) and the social welfare of working-class families. Cranwell identifies this as laying the foundations for the development of adventure playgrounds, as Lady Allen of Hurtwood harnessed the experiences of 'playleaders' to that point, in the establishment of the first adventure playgrounds in the United Kingdom.

Various authors (Newstead, 2016; Russell, 2013; Voce, 2015; Wilson, 2009) identify the development of the adventure playground movement following the Second World War, as the most significant starting point for the development of playwork as it is understood and practised today. Interestingly Chilton (2018) identifies the leafy suburb of Morden in 1947 as the site of the first adventure playground in the United Kingdom. However, Wilson, speaking about the bomb sites reclaimed by children for their play, describes how "ironically it is out of this devastation that the profession of playwork was born" (2009, p. 275).

During the 1950s and through to the 1970s playwork (or playleadership, as it was originally called) was largely focused on adventure playgrounds and characterized by individuals who were committed to their practice, but who rarely wrote anything down. There were honourable exceptions such as Abernethy (1968), Benjamin (1974), Chilton (1974), and Lambert (1974). However, these publications were more about promoting the cause than developing any substantial theory.

Subsequently, the sector has evolved, and the profession of playwork in the United Kingdom even has its own degree courses. Playwork is now implemented beyond the very special confines of adventure playgrounds. Playworkers can now be found practising across a diverse spectrum of services for children, including hospitals, prisons, children's social care, and schools. Whether this can be attributed to the unprecedented funding for children's play provision from the late 1990s until 2010 (Gill, 2015), is in response to the shrinking of the playwork sector and subsequent need to diversify following the election of the coalition government in 2010 (McKendrick & Martin, 2015), or even is a result of the increased understanding and promotion of the importance of play in the lives of children, is not clear.

So What Is Playwork?

Playwork offers a unique approach to working with children (Play Wales, 2016; PPSG, 2005), though it is often discussed in terms of the space in which it takes place or as an approach to practice (Newstead, 2016). This is perhaps due to the fact that the profession developed within specific spaces and in response to the need for "social control of children's unregulated time and the social welfare of working class families" (Cranwell, 2003, p. 33).

There is much discussion and disagreement, both within the playwork sector and external to it, about what playwork is (Brown, 2008a; Hughes, 2012; Russell, 2012). For example, during an interview, Wilson (2009), a highly experienced playwork practitioner, struggled to articulate what the role of a playworker is, instead choosing to describe the work thus:

> We look at what is around for the children we seek to serve, and for what they are missing. Then we establish an environment that helps compensate for what is missing. Then we watch how children are using the space and share our reflections as a team. Together we make adjustments informed by those observations and reflections. Then we watch some more.   (p. 269)

Echoing the sentiment of Wilson's description, in its most simple terms, and for the purpose of this chapter, playwork is "about creating environments that enable children to generate their own play" (Brown, 2014, p. 10). That said, there are significant complexities inherent in this basic definition. As Brown suggests, it is possible to identify a play to playwork continuum, running from a recognition of play as a "developmental and evolutionary activity", all the way through to playwork as a "compensatory activity" (Brown, 2014, p. 10).

Despite this ambiguity, a national charity for children's play, Play Wales (2015), suggests that there is a need for playworkers to hold a shared understanding of play and the approach taken to interactions with children and the play environment. As such, the Playwork Principles were developed in 2005 by a collective of playwork practitioners from across the United Kingdom, with the ambition of describing the "underpinning philosophy of playwork" (Conway, 2008, p. 119). The Playwork Principles are made up of the eight assertions listed in Table 39.1, and the authors claim that they provide the "professional and ethical framework" for the sector (PPSG, 2005).

Table 39.1 *The Playwork Principles*

1. All children and young people need to play. The impulse to play is innate. Play is a biological, psychological and social necessity, and is fundamental to the healthy development and well-being of individuals and communities.
2. Play is a process that is freely chosen, personally directed and intrinsically motivated. That is, children and young people determine and control the content and intent of their play, by following their own instincts, ideas and interests, in their own way for their own reasons.
3. The prime focus and essence of playwork is to support and facilitate the play process and this should inform the development of play policy, strategy, training and education.
4. For playworkers, the play process takes precedence and playworkers act as advocates for play when engaging with adult led agendas.
5. The role of the playworker is to support all children and young people in the creation of a space in which they can play.
6. The playworker's response to children and young people playing is based on a sound up to date knowledge of the play process, and reflective practice.
7. Playworkers recognize their own impact on the play space and also the impact of children and young people's play on the playworker.
8. Playworkers choose an intervention style that enables children and young people to extend their play. All playworker intervention must balance risk with the developmental benefit and well-being of children.

The Playwork Principles (PPSG, 2005) were developed after a lengthy consultation exercise, and have been officially recognized by SkillsActive (the lead body for education and training in playwork in the UK). Playwork Principles 1 and 2 provide a definition of play and the associated behaviours, and the remaining principles describe the playwork approach to working with children. The Playwork Principles have come in for some criticism, especially in relation to their definition of play. Brown (2008b) says that for a definition to be tenable, it has to apply to all cases of its subject. This, he says, is not true of the definition contained in the Playwork Principles, because it is not always true to say that play is freely chosen, personally directed, and intrinsically motivated. In fact, many forms of play are

- 'chosen', but not 'freely'
- 'directed', but not 'personally'
- 'motivated', but not 'intrinsically'.

He suggests that play takes many forms, not all of which are comfortable for adults to accept. Therefore, as a society we tend instead to idealize play, and in so doing actually understate the value of play. He argues that such a restrictive definition ignores the fact that play has developmental value, even when it is not freely chosen, personally directed, and intrinsically motivated. He expresses disappointment that the playwork profession has fallen into the trap of idealizing its raison d'être, while at the same time claiming special insight into the world of children's play.

Despite this criticism, Brown suggests that it does no harm for playworkers to focus on the particular form of play laid out in the Playwork Principles. In many ways, it is the child-centric, reflective practice that they espouse that offers such a unique approach to working with children. No other workforce associated with children does that. All other such professions have adult agendas somewhere in their priorities. Although he accepts that intervention is sometimes necessary, Brown nevertheless states that "the child's agenda has to be taken as the starting point for the playworkers' interventions" (2008a, p. 10) and that playworkers should adopt the Rogerian humanistic attitude of 'unconditional positive regard' toward the children (Rogers, 1951).

Playwork Principle 6 requires playworkers to ensure that their "responses to children and young people playing are based on a sound up to date knowledge" (PPSG, 2005). As such, some of the key playwork theories will now be discussed.

Early Theory

The first attempts at developing playwork theory began in the 1970s when Hughes (1975) produced his booklet, *Notes for Adventure Playworkers.*

Hughes suggested playworkers needed to focus on four main areas: administration, play associated with the playground, education, and social welfare. This was a fairly simple view of the work, but nevertheless provided a very influential beginning for what was at the time a profession in its infancy. By the 1980s Hughes's thinking had developed into trying to construct a theoretical justification for playwork. In a series of five articles for the magazine *Play Times*, he began to explore the significance of flexibility in children's play – in particular, taking up Bruner's concept of combinatorial flexibility as the starting point for children's creativity during play.

In 1989 Brown took this concept one stage further by formulating the play development concept of compound flexibility, which highlights the interrelationship between the degree of flexibility in the play environment and the degree of flexibility in the developing child. He suggested that playworkers could ensure that this developmental cycle operated effectively by creating an enriched environment for children's play, which offered opportunities for socialization and social interaction, physical activity, intellectual simulation, creativity and problem-solving, and emotional equilibrium (abbreviated as 'SPICE'). However, Brown considers that his concept was often misrepresented, because of the dissociation between the SPICE acronym and the overarching concept of compound flexibility. Instead, the playwork sector more often utilized the SPICE acronym to provide a description of playwork. The acronym has certainly been applied in other areas of work regarding children, particularly in the early years sector (see Harding, 2015, p. 263, for an example of SPICE being used as a "useful reminder of early childhood developmental needs").

Brown's (1989) original intention was to use the SPICE acronym to highlight the critical role that play has for the ideal developmental cycle of a child. His clarification in 2003 focused on the need for a flexible and responsive environment, which offers opportunities for children to make use of that flexibility to develop a wide range of responses to the stimuli within the play space. Brown says that this is not about variety but flexibility, and therefore it is about children having control over their play environment. Subsequently, Brown (2014) has stated that the SPICE acronym does not cover enough of the key factors that make up an enriched play environment. He suggests that when thinking about an enriched play environment playworkers need to think about fun, freedom, flexibility, social interaction, socialization, physical activity, environmental cognitive stimulation, creativity and problem-solving, emotional equilibrium and health, and self-discovery. These things necessarily go hand in hand with the ever-evolving flexible environment that playworkers enable children to create and experience. For a fuller explanation of the compound flexibility concept, see Brown (2014) and Figure 39.1.

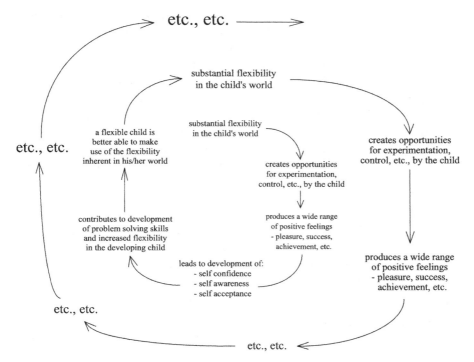

Figure 39.1 *Compound flexibility: a positive spiral.*

Psycholudics

In 1998, the 'Colorado Paper' was presented by Sturrock and Else at the International Play Association conference in the United States. This paper began to explore the playground as a therapeutic space and proposed the theory of 'psycholudics' (the study of the mind at play) (Sturrock, 2003), making claims for the playworker as engaging in therapeutic practice with the playing child. The theory of psycholudics was developed in response to the recognition of the reduction of space for play in the United Kingdom – both physical and psychic (Sturrock & Else, 1998), and the associated negative consequences of this. Sturrock and Else (and later Sturrock, 2003) suggested that if therapeutic interventions focused on "the 're-playing' of neurosis formed in childhood", then playwork happens at "the *precise point* where potential neuroses are formed" (p. 4) and therefore they proposed that playwork has a potentially curative function. In summary, the theory of psycholudics was written by playworkers to describe the process of play from a playwork perspective (Hughes, 2012). As such, Sturrock and Else (1998) made use of Sutton-Smith's (1984) concept of the play cue, and Bateson's (1955) concept of the play frame, to describe the play cycle as follows:

- Prior to the process of play, the child undertakes an internal contemplation. They are stimulated or inspired in some way by the environment, or those within it, to play. They call this the *meta-lude*.
- This is then followed by a *play cue*, which is considered as a communication of the intention to play, given to the environment or another being (human or non-human). This could be something as subtle as a change in body language or as overt as a verbal invitation, which communicates the intention to play. When this cue is responded to either by something in the environment (e.g., an object to jump off) or by another person (e.g., a child responds by assigning a narrative to the play episode or a playworker puts out a crash mat), then this is considered as the *play return*.
- The play is then contained within a *play frame*, which acts as the external or internal symbolic space (for example, the narrative of capturing forts) or physical space (the den, the field, the specific corner of the playground) in which the play occurs. This process of cue and return results in flow, as the play is maintained within the play frame.

There are potentially two ways in which play flow may not be achieved. The first is what Sturrock and Else (1998) call *dysplay*. This occurs when the full play cycle is not experienced because of either the irregular issuing of play cues or the expectation of a particular play return that is not received (as opposed to the lack of a return). As a result, dysfunctional play occurs – hence the term *dysplay*.

The second way in which play flow may not be achieved is as a result of *adulteration*. This is when the child is engaged with another whose play return is more dominant. Hughes (2001, p. 163) defines adulteration as "the hijacking of the child's play agenda by adults with the intention of substituting it with their own." Else (2008) cautions against adult intervention in the play frame. Playworkers should act as observers or, in particular cases, passive participants with the intention only of furthering the play of children. Entering the play frame with any other agenda, Else suggests, would only contaminate the play, resulting in adulteration. Any intervention should be engaged in with the intention of withdrawing from the play frame as soon as possible.

Although it is arguable that all play has a broadly therapeutic value (see Brown, 2018), it has to be said that the majority of children who attend playwork settings are not suffering from any form of mental illness. Therefore, since Sturrock and Else (1998) focus substantially on dysfunction and the development of neuroses, it might be suggested that their paper is more of a justification for specialist playworkers than a complete view of playwork. It is certainly about the rare occasions when it is acceptable for a playworker to intervene in the child's play world.

Intervention in Children's Play

Playworkers take a particular and specific approach to their interventions in children's play, preferring a "high-response, low-intervention" approach (Conway, 2008, p. 122). The Playwork Principles (PPSG, 2005) state that playworkers should "choose an intervention style that enables children and young people to extend their play", and various playwork authors have contributed their thinking in relation to this (Fisher, 2008; Hughes, 2002, 2012; Rennie, 2003; Russell, 2008; Sturrock & Else, 1998). There is a commonly held perception that playworkers stand back and observe children's play, appearing to be 'not doing anything constructive', a perception held by adult participants in a recent research study (Long, 2017). Fisher (2008) suggests that through the application of 'negative capability', a term used to "describe the suspension of all prejudices and preconceptions" (Brown, 2008a, p. 10), playworkers are able to avoid jumping to conclusions and "leaping in to intervene" (Fisher, 2008, p. 178). This unwarranted or uninvited intervention in children's play can result in adulteration, as discussed above, and is therefore to be avoided in a playwork context.

Rennie (2003) suggests that there is a particular skill associated with intervening in children's play, from an entry level, where it is focused on ensuring the safety of playing children, to higher levels of competence, where playworkers extend and enhance children's play through the modification of the environment, and where playworkers are innately able to "recognise play cues" (p. 28). Sturrock and Else (1998) offer what they call an "intervention hierarchy" (pp. 23–25), from *play maintenance*, where there is little contact between the adult and playing child with the only intention of ensuring the maintenance of the play, through to *complex intervention*, where "there is a direct and extended overlap between the playing child and the playworker" (p. 24). For a useful discussion of the practical application of complex intervention, see Sutton (2014).

Hughes (2002) recommends that any intervention in children's play needs to be a "considered and thoughtful process" (p. 9). He identifies eight different intervention 'modes' used to enable playworkers to articulate and assess their "operational style" (p. 12) when intervening in children's play. These modes describe an array of practical playwork techniques, styles, and motivations for intervening in children's play. Hughes's (2012) *intervention guidelines* highlight the occasions where he considers intervention in children's play may be appropriate. He recommends this should be used only in response to an invitation, to support a child to overcome a barrier to play, or to maintain the safety and well-being of the children.

BRAWGS Continuum

The BRAWGS continuum is a model developed by Wendy Russell (2008) and informed by Gordon Sturrock and Arthur Battram. Hence the name is an anagram of those who have influenced the development of the continuum. The model is useful to help identify the diversity of playwork responses to the playing child and is a useful tool to prompt reflective practice (Russell, 2006).

Russell (2008) suggests both an internal and external dimension to the continuum (see Figure 39.2). At one end, Russell identifies the external response of the playworker to be didactic – an approach that values the developmental benefits of play and the need for adult intervention to enable children to realize these benefits. At the opposite end, the external dimension is one of chaos. Russell (2008, p. 86) suggests that "chaotic playwork is unpredictable", where the provision and the practice of the playworkers within it is focused on meeting adult needs, is unreliable and inconsistent, and where the children are left confused. The ideal situation is for the playworker's external responses to the playing child to be ludocentric, or "play centred" (p. 86). This play-centred approach places the emphasis on the intrinsic and personally directed nature of children's play, aligned with the Playwork Principles discussed earlier. This external practice of the playworker is focused on supporting the play process rather than any other adult-led agenda.

The internal dimensions of the model help to identify that often, the practice of a playworker is influenced by internal feelings. These can prompt either a non-ludic, ludic, or para-ludic internal response to the playing child, therefore *potentially* determining the external practice of a playworker. The term *ludic* means to show "spontaneous and undirected playfulness" (Oxford English Dictionary). Therefore non-ludic is not playful, and para-ludic (from the Greek *para*, meaning 'beside') is where playworkers aim for a response that is between the two extremes, supporting children's play and engaging in practice that is reflective of that described by the Playwork Principles.

Where the internal response to the playing child is dominated by strong desires to teach or control children's play, for example, the need to *teach* the child how to build a den or to stop the children running, perhaps due to fears of litigation, then this results in a non-ludic internal response to children's play. Where the personal needs and desires of adults dominate the play, possibly as a consequence of unmet play needs, this leads to a ludic internal response.

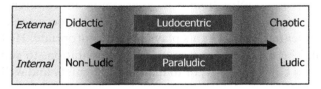

Figure 39.2 *The BRAWGS continuum.*

Russell (2008) suggests that a playworker should aim for an internal response between these two extremes, where "the playworker supports the children's play by joining in if invited, but is aware of their own position of power and authority and does not take over" (p. 88). As such, it is critical to be reflexive when engaging with the playing child, as it is only through a process of self-reflection, in and on practice, that an increased awareness of the internal responses to the playing child can be identified, and therefore an external, ludocentric approach can be assured.

Conflicting Societal Narratives

Playwork is predicated on a number of precepts that contest many socially accepted and taken-for-granted assumptions of childhood, children, and their play. This contestation generates tensions that render a straightforward articulation of the uniqueness of playwork practice challenging, but which can be explicated via the application of the theory of social constructionism. The first of these precepts relates to play itself, the facilitation or enablement of which is cited variously in the literature as the primary purpose of play-work (e.g., Brown, 2008b; Hughes, 2001; Kilvington & Wood, 2010). Whether or not that is particularly helpful in explicating the uniqueness of playwork is subject to conjecture. Nevertheless, playwork tends to adopt a particular conceptualization of play that defies conventional opinion. Play is notoriously difficult to define and a universally accepted definition remains absent from the literature. This is attributed by some to its elusive characteristics (Wood & Attfield, 2005); others argue that because we have all played as children, as adults we regard ourselves as experts and therefore dismissive of further consideration of the subject (Eberle, 2015). Playwork, however, perceives play as an intrinsically motivated bio-psychological drive, the free expression of which is critical to healthy individual and social development (Hughes, 2001; Russ, 2004). Yet despite mounting evidence in support of this interpretation, at least two contrary narratives dominate societal discourse surrounding the subject.

The first of these narratives diminishes play by presenting the behaviour as antithetical to the socially desirable seriousness of work. This work–play dualism, as referred to by Meyer (2010), among others, is attributed by sociologists and cultural historians to the ingrained socializing legacy of the Puritan work ethic that depicted play as a demonic alternative to heavenly salvation (Kane, 2004). Greer (1975, p. 165) observed, "We have been brainwashed into believing there is a split between work and play. Work is productive and good; fun accomplishes nothing and is often evil", and this narrative remains influential in public discourse and policy formulation (Kane, 2004). So, while we may all have played as children and therefore retain a tacit experiential understanding of the process, this becomes overlaid and undermined by a dominant socializing narrative of purposelessness and undesirability.

Salvation in terms of play's social acceptance can be found, in part, in the second dominant narrative. In this discourse the importance of play is acknowledged, but predominantly as an instrument of development or socialization (Powell & Wellard, 2008). Within this narrative play attains acceptability and even desirability providing that it can be designed and implemented by adults to effect a predetermined outcome. This instrumental perspective has predominated research and policy development, as exemplified by the assertion of Liz Truss, at the time Education Minister of the United Kingdom, that play should be "adult-led, planned and purposeful" (Truss, 2013). This perspective is clearly at odds with an intrinsically motivated and personally directed perspective of the behaviour, and diametrically opposes playwork's upheld view, that when the product and purpose of play takes primacy, the behaviour ceases to be play (Brown, 2009).

Yet even within the professional field of playwork, informed by a set of guiding principles that provide a clear definition of play, there remains much discord surrounding the subject. For example, one might well question whether play is always and necessarily freely chosen and personally directed, and indeed whether all intrinsically motivated behaviours can be interpreted as play. These questions in turn evoke the philosophical problem of free will, and whether it is possible for anything we do to be truly freely chosen. The intractability of these deliberations leads one to consider the effectiveness of attempts to articulate the uniqueness of playwork by focussing on it as a practice concerned primarily with the facilitation of play. Rather, one might propose that what could be described as the 'essence' of playwork exists in the particular context and outcome of the relationship between playworker and child.

Interactions between children and adults forge the conceptual space of childhood in which children experience their lived realities (Jenks, 2005). Within this space, perceptions of children's agency interact with aspects of the social policy agenda to further construct and reconstruct children and childhoods (Meyer, 2007; Qvortrup et al., 2009). Social constructionism is defined in this context by Prout and James (1990, p. 1) as the process by which "the immaturity of children is conceived and articulated ... into culturally specific sets of ideas and philosophies, attitudes and practices". A leading construct, referred to by Lee (2001, p. 142) as the "dominant framework", depicts the child as an incompetent, dependent 'proto adult' (James & James, 2004). The future-orientated temporal focus of this construct, which typically informs Western social policy agendas (Fuller, 2007), trivializes and dismisses the everyday, lived experiences of children and emphasizes value in their 'becoming' adult rather than 'being' children. This construct not only implies that competency and value are acquired on the way to becoming an 'adult', but also that these characteristics necessarily (and only) belong to adults, i.e., ones that children cannot possess (James & James, 2004). Influenced by a dominant discourse of 'becoming', policy and practice becomes oriented toward instructing, normalizing, and correcting children (James et al., 1998).

Largely informed by the work of the new sociologists of childhood (e.g., James et al., 1998), playwork adopts a contrary paradigm that, while acknowledging their biological immaturity, conceptualizes children as competent, independent, social actors whose value lies in their 'being' a child as opposed to the adult they will become. The 'being' paradigm, concerned primarily with children's agency, emphasizes the aptitudes and abilities they possess *because* of their biological immaturity (James et al., 1998). While proponents of this paradigm do not necessarily regard children as having equal status to adults, they are considered to be of equal value. Consequently, the views and opinions of children and young people are regarded as being as important as adults', and in some cases more so (Alderson, 2000). Playwork is not alone in adopting this particular conceptualization – the child as 'being' is a prominent rhetorical narrative of many child-focused occupations – but the uniqueness of playwork may be found in its articulation of this construct into practice.

The inescapable reality for child-focused occupations other than playwork, irrespective of the degree to which they may espouse a rhetoric of children's agency, is that they are ultimately responsible to the priorities of government. The outcome of the interactions between practitioners and government policy, which as Fuller (2007) identifies is typically informed by a future-oriented dominant framework, is to reconstruct children and childhood in multiple, coexisting ways, which are often contradictory of one another and tend to diminish children's agency (Qvortrup et al., 2009). For example, interactions with a heavily emphasized child protection agenda in the field of social work reconstruct the child as 'victim' or 'vulnerable and at risk' (Gill, 2007); similarly, a construct of the child as a 'delinquent' or 'threat' may emerge from the interplay between youth work practice and the crime reduction agenda (Muncie, 2015). In both instances the child is reconstructed as subordinate to their adult superior, whose role is to correct the inherent deficiencies of childhood (James et al., 1998).

In working first to the child's agenda, as opposed to that of government, playwork practice is both less susceptible to reproducing these relational power inequalities and actively resistant to doing so. As children's rights academic Roger Hart observes:

> Playworkers work horizontally [collaboratively] with children (rather than from a position of power). I don't know of other professions that do that. Social work, and youth work are generally supposed to do that but they often have this double problem of being the ones that are adjudicating children; they have a power relationship to the Government. (Hart, 2008, p. 1)

The purpose of this explication is not to disparage or imply that playwork is superior to the aforementioned occupations of social work and youth work. The policy and practice objectives of child-focussed interventions across the piece are largely desirable, and meeting them satisfactorily very often necessitates adults being in control. It would also be misleading to suggest that the power distribution in the relationship between playworker and child resides absolutely equally, or that absolute equality is desirable – as stated previously, children are regarded as possessing equal value to adults, not necessarily equal status. As is the case for all child-centred practitioners, playworkers have a mandated legal and moral duty of care to the child under the Children Act 2004 and are the final arbiters of what is considered acceptable in terms of their behaviour and so on. Furthermore, children themselves are desirous of the sense of security that boundaries set by adults provide and the safety they experience from knowing an adult is present and in charge (MacDougall et al., 2009). So, while for playwork a conceptualization of the child as 'being' takes precedence, this is not to the exclusion of the care, guidance, and developmental support one might associate with a paradigm of 'becoming'. Indeed, as Uprichard (2008) observes, looking forward to what a child will 'become' is an important part of 'being' a child.

In this pluralistic conceptual space of childhood, the construct to emerge could be considered as one identified by James et al. (1998) of the child as rights holder. The notion of children as possessing rights is of course not a new one. The children's rights movement mobilized around the same time as other civil rights movements in the mid-nineteenth century. Yet whereas similar such movements were organized by members of the concerned group, children's rights were advanced by adults who believed their moral obligation was to protect a Western ideal of childhood innocence. By 1924, the United Nations adopted the Declaration of Children's Rights, which in 1959 was expanded and retitled the Declaration of the Rights of the Child. Both of these declarations were mainly 'moral' in character and derived from a belief that all children should have the right to a childhood of innocence and protection from the adult world (Stephens, 1995).

In 1989 the United Nations Convention on the Rights of the Child (CRC) replaced the 1959 Declaration. In abandoning the term 'investment' in relation to children, and moving away from the moralizing tone that had characterized previous treaties, the CRC was celebrated by child rights advocates for its apparent rejection of a future-oriented construct of childhood. The CRC also received the unprecedented global support of governments. A major criticism of the Convention, however, is that it is not a legally binding agreement, so it falls incumbent upon individual signatories to ensure children's rights are met through the provision of domestic policy.

So, while child-centred practitioners the world over work to a rights-based discourse that states that the best interests of the child must be the primary concern in all interactions, children and their interests once again become reconceptualized by the introduction of government policy. Consequently, according to Pupavac (2001), most programmes targeting children still emphasize their deviancy and carry a preoccupation with their moral development. As Stephens (1995, p. 32) observes, the CRC's "declaration of universal children's rights gives children the right to be remade in the image of adults. Eschewing subordinating and corrupting conceptualisations of children and childhood, the essence of playwork is located at the heart of the meta-physical space to emerge from a uniquely synergistic relationship between adult and child in which play, the ultimate right of a child to express his or her agency, takes precedence."

In summary then, while the practice of playwork has many commonalities with other sections of the children's workforce, it has many characteristics that set it apart. Playwork is characterized by the following elements:

- A conceptualization of the child that actively resists dominant and subordinating narratives and practices
- A belief that while playing, the 'being' child is far more important than the 'becoming' child
- An adherence to the principle that the vital outcomes of playing are derived by children in inverse proportion to the degree of adult involvement in the process
- A non-judgemental acceptance of the children as they really are, running hand in hand with an attitude, when relating to the children, of 'unconditional positive regard'
- An approach to practice that involves a willingness to relinquish adult power, suspend any preconceptions, and work to the children's agenda
- The provision of environments that are characterized by flexibility, so that the children are able to create (and possibly destroy and re-create) their own play environments according to their own needs
- A general acceptance that risky play can be beneficial and that intervention is not necessary unless a safety or safeguarding issue arises
- A continuous commitment to deep personal reflection that manages the internal relationship between the playworker's present and former child-self, and the effects of that relationship on their current practice.

When taken together, these characteristics have established a thoroughly unique way of working with children.

References

Abernethy, D. (1968). *Playleadership*. London: National Playing Fields Association.

Alderson, P. (2000). *Young children's rights: Exploring beliefs, attitudes, principles and practice*. London: Jessica Kingsley.

Bateson, G. (1955). A theory of play and fantasy. *Psychiatric Research Reports*, 2, 39–51.

Battram, A. (2015). Strategic playwork: A possibility that is neither 'intervention playwork' nor 'environmental playwork'. *International Journal of Play*, *4*(3), 285–290.

Benjamin, J. (1974). *Grounds for play. An extension of 'In search of adventure'*. London: Bedford Square Press of the National Council for Social Service.

Brown, F. (1989). *Working with children: A playwork training pack*. Leeds: Children First.

Brown, F. (2003). Compound flexibility. In F. Brown (Ed.), *Playwork: Theory and practice* (pp. 51–65). Buckingham: Open Unviersity Press.

Brown, F. (2008a). The fundamentals of playwork. In F. Brown & C. Taylor (Eds.), *Foundations of playwork* (pp. 7–13). Maidenhead: Open University Press.

Brown, F. (2008b) The playwork principles: A critique. In F. Brown & C. Taylor (Eds.), *Foundations of playwork* (pp. 123–127). Maidenhead: Open University Press.

Brown, F. (2014). *Play and playwork: 101 stories of children playing*. Maidenhead: Open University Press.

Brown, F. (2018). The therapeutic aspects of play and playwork. In F. Brown & B. Hughes (Eds.), *Aspects of playwork*. Lanham, MD: University Press of America.

Brown, S. (2009). *Play: How it shapes the brain, opens the imagination and invigorates the soul*. London: Penguin Books.

Cartmel, J. (2014) Editorial. *Journal of Playwork Practice*, *1*(1), 3–4.

Children Act 2004 (2004). Chapter 31. London: HMSO.

Chilton, T. (1974). *Playleadership*. London: National Playing Fields Association.

Chilton, T. (2018). Adventure playgrounds: A brief history. In F. Brown & B. Hughes (Eds.), *Aspects of playwork*. Lanham, MD: University Press of America

Conway, M. (2008). The playwork principles. In F. Brown & C. Taylor (Eds.), *Foundations of playwork* (pp. 119–122). Berkshire: Open University Press.

Cranwell, K. (2003). Towards playwork: An historical introduction to children's out-of-school play organisations in London (1860–1940). In Brown, F. (Ed.), *Playwork theory and practice* (pp. 32–47). Buckingham: Open University Press.

Eberle, S. (2015). What's not play? In J. E. Johnson, S. G. Eberle, T. S. Henricks, & D. Kuschner (Eds.), *The handbook of the study of play* (pp. 489–501). New York: Rowman & Littlefield.

Else, P. (2008). Playing: The space between. In F. Brown & C. Taylor (Eds.), *Foundatons of playwork* (pp. 79–83). Maidenhead: Open University Press.

Else, P., & Sturrock, G. (1998, June). The playground as therapeutic space: Playwork as healing. Paper presented at the IPA/USA Triennial National Conference, Play in a Changing Society: Research, Design, Application, June, Longmont, CO.

Fisher, K. (2008). Playwork in the early years. In F. Brown & C. Taylor (Eds.), *Foundations of playwork* (pp. 174–178). Maidenhead: Open University Press.

Fuller, B., with Bridges, M., & Pai, S. (2007). *Standardized childhood: The political and cultural struggle over early education*. Stanford, CA: Stanford University Press.

Gill, T. (2007). *No fear: Growing up in a risk averse society*. London: Calouste-Gulbenkian Foundation.

Gill, T. (2015). Play in the good times: The (English) inside story. *International Journal of Play, 4*(3), 236–240.

Greer, A. (1975). *No grown-ups in heaven: A T-A primer for Christians (and others)*. New York: Hawthorn Books.

Harding, A. (2015). Successful library activities for the early years and ways to promote books effectively. In C. Rankin & A. Brock (Eds.), *Library services from birth to five: Delivering the best start* (pp. 263–274). London: Facet Publishing.

Hart, J. (2006). Saving children: What role for anthropology? *Anthropology Today, 22*(1), 5–8.

Hart, R. (2008). Participation and playwork. *Play for Wales*, issue 24.

Hughes, B. (1975). *Notes for adventure playworkers*. London: Children and Youth Action Group.

Hughes, B. (2001). *Evolutionary playwork and reflective analytic practice*. London: Routledge.

Hughes, B. (2002). *The first claim – Desirable processes: A framework for advanced quality assessment*. Cardiff: Play Wales. Available at www.playwales.org.uk/eng/firstclaim.

Hughes, B. (2012). *Evolutionary playwork* (2nd edn.). London: Routledge.

James, A., & James, A. (2004). *Constructing childhood: Theory, policy and social practice*. Basingstoke: Palgrave McMillan.

James, A., Jenks, C., & Prout, A. (1998). *Theorizing childhood*. Cambridge: Polity Press.

Jenks, C. (2005). *Childhood* (2nd edn.). London: Routledge.

Kane, P. (2004). *The play ethic: A manifesto for a different way of living*. London: Macmillan.

Kilvington, J., & Wood, A. (2010). *Reflective playwork for all who work with children*. London: Continuum.

Lambert, J., & Pearson, J. (1974). *Adventure playgrounds*. Harmondsworth: Penguin.

Lee, N. (Ed.) (2001). *Childhood and society: Growing up in an age of uncertainty*. Buckingham: Open University Press.

Long, A. (2017). It's not just about 'more': A research project exploring satisfaction with opportunities to play, for children in two Welsh neighbouring communities. *International Journal of Play, 6*(1), 24–39.

MacDougal, C., Schiller, W., & Darbyshire, P. (2009). What are our boundaries and where can we play? *Early Childhood Development & Care, 179*(2), 67–75.

McKendrick, J., & Martin, C. (2015). Playwork practitioners' perceptions of the impact on play of austerity in the UK: Comparing experiences in Scotland and SW England. *International Journal of Play, 4*(3), 252–265.

Meyer, A. (2007). The moral rhetoric of childhood. *Childhood, 14*(1), 85–104.

Meyer, P. (2010). *From workplace to playspace: Innovating, learning and changing through dynamic engagement*. San Francisco, CA: Jossey Bass.

Muncie, J. (2015). *Youth and crime: A critical introduction* (4th edn.). London: Sage.

Newstead, S. (2016). JPP Editorial: Why playwork is about much more than 'space'. Available at https://policypress.wordpress.com/2016/01/11/jpp-editorial-why-playwork-is-about-much-more-than-space/.

Play Wales (2015). *The playwork principles: An overview*. Cardiff: Play Wales. Available at www.playwales.org.uk/eng/playworkprinciples.

Play Wales (2016). *Playwork: What's so special*. Cardiff: Play Wales.

Powell, S., & Wellard, I. (2008). *Policies and play: The impact of national policies on children's opportunities to play*. London: Play England/National Children's Bureau.

PPSG (2005). *Playwork Principles* held in trust as honest brokers for the profession by the Playwork Principles Scrutiny Group. Available at www.playwales.org.uk/page.asp?id=50.

Prout. A., & James, A. (1990). A new paradigm for the sociology of childhood? Provenance, promise and problems. In A. James & A. Prout (Eds.), *Constructing and reconstructing childhood: Contemporary issues in the sociological study of childhood* (pp. 7–33). London: RoutledgeFalmer.

Pupavac, V. (2001). Misanthropy without borders: The international children's rights regime. *Disasters, 25*(2), 95–112.

Qvortrup, J., Corsaro, W. A., & Honig, M. S. (Eds.) (2009). *The Palgrave handbook of childhood studies*. Basingstoke: Palgrave Macmillan.

Rennie, S. (2003). Making play work: The fundamental role of play in the development of social skills. In F. Brown (Ed.), *Playwork: Theory and practice* (pp. 18–31). Buckingham: Open University Press.

Rogers, C. R. (1951). *Client-centered therapy: Its current practice, implications and theory*. Boston: Houghton Mifflin.

Russ, S. (2004). *Play in child development and psychotherapy*. Mahwah, NJ: Lawrence Erlbaum.

Russell, W. (2006). *Reframing playwork; reframing challenging behaviour*. Nottingham: Nottingham City Council.

Russell, W. (2008). Modeling playwork: BRAWGs continuum, dialogue and collaborative reflection. In F. Brown (Ed.), *Foundations of playwork* (pp. 84–88). Maidenhead: Open University Press.

Russell, W. (2012). 'I get such a feeling out of . . . those moments': Playwork, passion, politics and space. *International Journal of Play, 1*(1), 51–63.

Russell, W. (2013). The dialectics of playwork: A conceptual and ethnographic study of playwork using cultural history activity theory. PhD thesis, University of Gloucestershire.

Stephens, S. (1995). Introduction: Children and the politics of culture in 'late capitalism'. In S. Stephens (ed.), *Children and the politics of culture* (pp. 3–48). Princeton, NJ: Princeton University Press.

Sturrock, G. (2003). Towards a psycholudic definition of playwork. In F. Brown (Ed.), *Playwork: Theory and practice* (pp. 81–97). Buckingham: Open University Press.

Sturrock, G., & Else, P. (1998). The playground as therapeutic space: Playwork as healing (known as 'The Colorado Paper'). Available as part of the *Therapeutic reader one* (2005). Southampton: Common Threads.

Sutton, L. (2014). Adventure playground and environmental modification: A beginner's guide. *Journal of Playwork Practice, 1*(2), 211–217.

Sutton-Smith, B., & Kelly-Byrne, D. (1984). The idealization of play. In P. K. Smith (Ed.), *Play in animals and humans* (pp. 305–321). Oxford: Blackwell.

Truss, L. (2013). Speech to the Nursery World Conference. Available at www.gov.uk/government/speeches/elizabeth-truss-speaks-about-2-year-olds-policy-and-practice.

Uprichard, E. (2008). Children as 'being and becomings': Children, childhood and temporality. *Children & Society*, *22*(4), 303–313.

Voce, A. (2015). The state of playwork. *International Journal of Play*, *4*(3), 217–223.

Wilson, P. (2009). The cultural origins and play philosophy of playworkers: An interview with Penny Wilson. *American Journal of Play*, *1*(3), 269–282.

Wood, E., & J. Attfield. (2005). *Play, learning and the early childhood curriculum* (2nd edn.). London: Paul Chapman.

40 The Right to Childhood and the Ethos of Play

Lacey E. Peters and Beth Blue Swadener

> Children need to play with a lot of stuff. I love to play 'cuz you can make up stuff in your imagination and can be animals, cats or anything you want! Children would be very tired if all they did was work.
>
> (Chloe Russ, age 7)

In many cases, play is disappearing from childhood and, along with that, opportunities for children to be fully or actively engaged in activities that promote inquiry-based learning, creative expression, risk-taking, problem-solving, social-emotional learning, community building, and social consciousness. Changing early childhood educational policies and practices in the United States and globally have led to more adult-directed teaching and learning, causing alarm among scholars, practitioners, parents, and child advocates, who have called this a "crisis" in early childhood (Almon & Miller, 2009, 2011; Hatch, 2002).

In response to this crisis, people are building on research and literature that speaks to the many benefits of play on children's growth and learning (Gray, 2013; Hirsh-Pasek et al., 2009; Johnson et al., 2005; Linn, 2009; Paley, 2010, 2009). Due to the changing landscape in early childhood, we ask, to what extent should or could play be considered a right or entitlement to young children's educational experiences? Although we do not have a definitive answer to this question, our aim is to argue for adults' responsibilities to take children's rights to play seriously. An often-overlooked opportunity in studies conducted on the benefits of play is the inclusion of children's perspectives through direct consultation as well as observation. Therefore, we situate play ethos in the framework of children's rights and participation (Lester & Russell, 2010) and will provide different ways of looking at play, through the views and life worlds of younger people.

As US-based scholars, our explanations and reflections are bound by our experiences and "pedagogies of place", and we recognize our scope may be limited. Nonetheless, we cannot ignore the traveling discourses of early care and education across transnational contexts, including those of the second author. An underlying tension is that the purposes of childhood are being shaped by globalization and neoliberalism. Children are perceived to be "pre-adult becomings" (Holloway & Valentine, 2000), and decisions are made about their life experiences with the intention that these will lead younger persons to grow into contributing members of society later in life. Acknowledging children and youth as social agents and "citizens in their own right" (Langsted, 1994) is of central importance in combating the issues and tensions we discuss related to children's rights to play, as well as enabling more active participation in their life worlds.

In this chapter, we (re)examine theories and perspectives on the purposes of play. We provide a brief discussion of play advocacy and share some examples of efforts to enact children's right to play in school and community contexts across the globe and in localized spaces, in the broader context of the right to childhood. Then we present research done in collaboration with children, including findings from our research that involved talking to children before and after they entered kindergarten. We conclude with a call to increased action and the use of child's rights-based arguments for participatory practices.

Understandings of Play

> [W]hile universally accepted as an activity of childhood, the processes and mechanisms whereby children's play and playful activities are expressed in different cultural communities and the degree to which governmental bodies, parents, early childhood educators and other caregivers embrace play as a viable means for influencing childhood development are far from uniform.
>
> (Roopnarine, 2015, p. 1)

Johnson et al. (2005) assert that the importance of theorizing play is to help adults better understand their interpretations and responses to play behaviors, in addition to helping individuals explain the benefits of play through multiple lenses. Theories of play generally fall into three categories – classical, modern, and postmodern – and each view is anchored in historical, social, and political contexts (Johnson et al., 2005). Our views are situated in the postmodern realm and we make use of sociocultural and critical understandings of play to examine how current issues and trends in early childhood have caused dramatic shifts in children's play. We also draw from the field of sociology of children and childhood, as well as a children's rights–based framework to offer perspective on the nuances of younger people's life experiences that can either enable or constrain opportunities for play.

Numerous theories have shaped the discourses that explain how play is a vital aspect of people's lived experiences. In the early 1900s Montessori described play as being the "work of children" and espoused the benefits of children's sensorial learning, creative expression, independence, and advanced ways of being. Vygotsky's formative work (1967, 1971) sheds light on the interactions or interrelatedness of biological (pre)dispositions (e.g., brain development) and human interaction. Early on he made the following assertion, which has been used to help others better understand play's benefits on human growth and learning:

> In play a child is always above his average age, above his daily behavior; in play it is as though he were a head taller than himself. As in the focus of a

magnifying glass, play contains all developmental tendencies in a condensed form; in play it is as though the child were trying to jump above the level of his normal behavior. (1967, p. 16)

More contemporary, constructivist theories on play acknowledge children as being active participants in their socialization and seek to explain how their participation within and across social contexts positions them to be valuable and contributing members of society. For example, Rogoff (2003) argues children's play and/or their interactions with others allows them to become familiar with cultural practices, traditions, and localized routines. Scholars in the field of sociology of childhood call constructivist theories into question because of the individualistic nature of human development they espouse, as well as the strong emphasis on preparation for the future rather than respecting children's active participation as younger citizens (Corsaro, 2005). Furthermore, little attention is given to children constructing their own peer cultures and within them rules and routines that can be used to define their agency. As such, Corsaro (2005) imparts the notion of "interpretive reproduction" to acknowledge children as being fully engaged in the process(es) of socialization, with an emphasis on the "innovative and creative aspects of children's participation in society" (p. 18). Play becomes a vital aspect of children's being and becoming so that there is generous opportunity for them to explore, experiment, produce, and reproduce social mores and to engage in collective action with peers and adults.

Although these theories assert the power of play and its influence on human development, social trends have muddled its processes and purposes. Over time, a false dichotomy between work and play has been established and is reflected in many neoliberal early childhood policies emphasizing 'readiness'. Readiness is a challenging construct and is problematized largely because it is defined by a set of fixed goals or outcomes, measured through summative assessments. Cannella and Viruru (2002) deconstruct readiness, arguing it is an "adult privilege", a notion that normalizes children and childhoods and categorizes people in a way that privileges certain skills and abilities over others. Yet readiness is used as a mechanism for early childhood education reform. US policies such as No Child Left Behind and Race to the Top privilege performance-based assessment through the vehicle of high-stakes accountability, which has resulted in a trickle-down effect or "accountability shovedown" (Hatch, 2002), impacting approaches to teaching and learning in early childhood. Furthermore, the introduction and adoption of Common Core State Standards is (re)shaping pedagogy and practices in early childhood settings. In the current context of education reform, mechanisms, like those previously discussed, funnel the myriad of approaches of teaching and learning into a narrow scope or sequence. Rather than play being children's work, it is increasingly viewed as interference or interruption in children's cognitive development and learning. In order to keep play in early childhood classrooms, there is a rebranding of this activity in that adults use phrases such as 'active learning' or 'multimodal learning' to affirm the benefits of engaging in play-based or playful experiences.

Moreover, the disappearance of play can be attributed to adult intentions to decrease the level of disparities across social contexts wherein adults connect the need to 'maximize instructional time' with increases in direct instruction. For instance, scientifically based instructional strategies are privileged as being 'best practice' and adults are encouraged to adopt approaches to teaching that fall in line with structured learning or direct instruction. This is most often seen in domains of language and literacy and mathematics. Cummins (2007) wrote about the shift away from constructivist learning in reading and argued that efforts to employ teacher-directed approaches inappropriately target issues related to student performance and learning in lower-income schools and communities.

Quality rating and improvement systems are having the (perhaps) unintended consequence of narrowing the scope of curricular approaches used in early childhood settings. Dahlberg et al. (1999) describe quality initiatives as prevailing discourses and argue that efforts to achieve or maintain quality are so dominant that definitions of the concept go unquestioned. In a broader, more universalizing scope, quality is usually defined by resource or organizational features of a setting (Dahlberg et al., 1999). The Early Childhood Environmental Rating Scale and other quality measures are used to evaluate the extent to which an early care or education setting meets quality standards that emphasize environmental checklists and often do poorly at evaluating teacher–child interactions, children's engagement with peers (in play), and cultural and linguistic factors and funds of knowledge (Nagasawa et al., 2014). The rating scales are based on notions of child development that are eurocentric and fail to nuance people's life experiences or trajectories influenced by sociocultural factors.

Globalization of assessment of even younger children has also impacted holistic priorities for children, including time for play and the right to childhood. This is evident in a recent initiative of the Organisation for Economic Co-Operation and Development (OECD) to develop and pilot an international comparative assessment of learning outcomes for young children aged 4.5–5.5 years, which has been met by critique and opposition from over 200 early childhood scholars (www.receinterntational.org; Moss et al., 2016; Urban & Swadener, 2016).

Many other social factors have influenced children's access to play, along with the decline of open-ended or unstructured play. Gray (2011) argues that opportunities for children to engage in free play have diminished because adults are seeking greater control over young people's activities. Moreover, he explains that the existential value of play has changed as adult fears and safety concerns have constrained children's autonomy and agency, especially as it relates to outdoor play. Elkind (1981, 2007) raised caution about a "hurried" childhood, and in his later work brought attention to the "power of play" (2007). He points out that certain social issues push children into growing up too fast and that many younger people are engaged in adult-like life experiences too soon. For instance, trends such as children's increasing access to technology and the internet have (re)shaped their engagement and learning and, more specifically, have affected related health issues, led to lack of interaction, and have limited time spent playing outdoors or in unstructured activities. Laidlaw et al. (2015) explain that children's "funds of knowledge" have changed as technology and media have become a larger part of contemporary childhood. They also indicate that children's access to technology helps to increase their participation in their social worlds and that the use of computers and mobile devices can potentially raise social capital. It is important to point out that these concerns pertain largely to people living in Western, mostly Global North settings.

Brian Sutton-Smith (1997) wrote about "sanitizing play" in special education literature since the 1970s and has referenced the "dignity of risk". In many middle-class contexts, children have little or no unsupervised or independent play, and playgrounds offer few opportunities for (reasonable) risk-taking and discovery. There is an array of tensions and contradictions around risk and play. Children in urban settings known for violence often avoid dangerous playgrounds and are warned about being on the street, while middle-class children in more suburban contexts are urged by some parents to get off their devices and take more risks in outdoor play. While play is an instrumental element to the social worlds of all humans, one must also keep in mind the number of factors that have impact over children and their well-being. Structural and systemic pathways or barriers to children's participation in play must also be scrutinized in order to fully understand the construction of their life worlds.

Lareau (2003) examined parenting and child-rearing and explained how socioeconomic status is a mediating factor that has significant influence over people's determination of the purpose of childhood and, correspondingly, shapes opportunities for play experiences. For example, families will expose children to different activities or structure children's life experiences for various reasons, and these reasons largely depend on how they might benefit a child as they grow older or prepare for adulthood. Families may seek out organized sports or have children participate in extracurricular activities rather than allowing them to engage in free or open-ended play. Thus, when adults define play as a form of social capital, whether it is considered be an obligatory or embedded component of childhood or more of a distraction from work or 'productivity', it becomes contrived or less authentic. Children, in turn, are shut out or have limited opportunities to engage in their social worlds through play.

In recent years, a play initiative in Anji County, China – Anji Play – premised in children's right to 'true play' has reignited discussion on risk-taking. Children's rights in this regard are actualized in "sophisticated practices, site-specific environments, unique materials, and integrated technology" to promote love, risk, joy, engagement, and reflection (available at www.anjiplay.com/home/#anjiplay). Adults make a conscious effort to provide children with a chance to make choices about how to play, what to play with, and who they want to play with at any given time. Currently, 14,000 children are involved in Anji Play in China, and leaders of this movement plan for the adoption of Anji Play in programs across the globe. Their aim is to work in communities that are typically underserved or underresourced. This is significant in that similar philosophies that are ideologically democratic or child-embedded, like Reggio Emilia or Reggio-inspired programs, normally tend to serve children from privileged families. In the United States, many play-based programs are accessible to those living in more affluent communities or who have the financial means to pay for tuition-based programming. Education as a practice of freedom (Freire, 1970) then becomes a privilege, and it can be argued that those without access to play-based or playful learning engage in a banking model of schooling.

In the United States, children's rights to protection and provision are typically considered to be the most important to address, as evidenced in illustrations of the shifts happening to children's play, including protecting children from risk and harm. However, their rights to participation are also key to actualizing an ethos to play that captures children's views and voices. As adults aim to make 'right' decisions for children, the assertion that children are not capable of acting in their own best interests because of their young age remains a part of the dominant discourse. Additionally, because all adults were once children themselves, they commonly believe that they can understand what it is like to be young (Mandell, 1988). Consequently, children are often excluded in decision-making about matters that affect their social worlds. More to the point, their views are perceived to be 'inferior' to those of older people. Lahman (2008) advocates for researchers to carry out studies *with* children rather than doing work *for* or *about* them as a means to challenge the likelihood of them becoming 'always othered' in scholarship, policy, or with regard to having influence over their school or life experiences. A number of studies have reflected this ethic by collaborating with children on research, including the work of Laura Lundy and colleagues in Belfast, Northern Ireland, who take a consultative approach with children when beginning any study (e.g., Lundy, 2007; Lundy & McEvoy, 2009; Lundy & Swadener, 2015), and the work of Kylie Smith in Australia, who has led teams consulting with children about their child care, play spaces, and community experiences (e.g., Smith, 2009). Swadener and colleagues (e.g., Swadener et al., 2013) have also consulted with children regarding research design and their daily experiences in child care and kindergarten contexts in the United States and South Korea (e.g., Im & Swadener, 2016).

Children's Right to Play and Freedom of Expression

The 1989 United Nations Convention on the Rights of the Child (UNCRC) made children's rights legally binding in the same way as other human rights. The UNCRC proclaims children's right to enjoy leisure, recreation, and cultural activities; their right to enjoy and to practice their own culture, religion, and language without fear of persecution or discrimination; and their right to privacy, protection, and autonomy. Specifically connected to our work, the UNCRC states that children have, among other rights:

- The right to express their views on all matters affecting them and for their views to be taken seriously (Article 12)
- The right to freedom of expression, including freedom to seek, receive, and impart information and ideas of all kinds through any media they choose (Article 13)
- The right to education that supports the development of the child's personality, talents, and mental and physical abilities to their fullest potential (Article 29)
- The right to play and relax by doing things like sport, music and drama (Article 30).

While many children in the United States are afforded a right to play, we know that adults have authority to determine the types of play that make up a child's life experiences and that these tend to be more structured. In order to reexamine the role of play through the lens of children's rights, adults should ask at a basic level: What different forms of play do children like, and how does this change as they grow older? and How much time are children provided to engage in these different forms of play? To gain more comprehensive understandings of children's views, answers to the question "What do they think about play?" need to be sought. The United Nations Committee's General Comment No. 12, The Child's Right to Be Heard (2009), emphasized children's right to participate in decisions affecting them and to have their views taken seriously. The views expressed by children may add relevant perspectives and experiences and should be considered in decision-making, policy-making, and preparation of laws and/or measures as well as their evaluation (p. 5). What implications does this have for children's right to play? What would change if adults listened to children and used their authentic or "unmediated voices" (Swadener & Polakow, 2010) to actualize children's rights to play? Efforts to listen to children and youth changes people's understandings of childhood in that it allows for people to build greater respect for younger people, but also sheds light on the hardships of children and youth (Mayall, 2000).

Hart (1992) conceptualized a "ladder of participation" that mapped out multiple levels of participation ranging from manipulation to younger people engaging in child-initiated, shared decision-making with adults. He emphasized the importance of children working collaboratively with others, including those who are older or who have more experience. Moreover, he argues that children's participation in community projects is essential to the sustainability and vitality of civic engagement. Others have conceptualized maps to reveal ways children can and do participate in decision-making. For example, Shier (2001) initially drew out "pathways to participation" to illustrate the process of younger people's involvement in decision-making. This pathway also highlights the need for adults to share power and responsibility with children and youth in participation practice. Lundy (2007) connects the notion of children's participation to Article 12 of the UNCRC and identifies four key elements including space, voice, audience, and influence. She argues that voice and children's views can be diluted when adults are not open to dismantling power dynamics that exist because of age or experience. Children should also be provided space or opportunity to grow and develop their voices so they can be listened to and heard in more authentic or unmediated ways. While significant strides have been made with regard to involving children in research, there is room for improvement. Einarsdóttir (2014) sheds light on an ethical tension that exists in conducting research with children in that their voices are often presented as one; thus, a perpetual belief that childhood consists of universalized or similar life experiences remains. In our call to action, we encourage children's advocates to pay close attention to those they invite to participate in research studies. To what extent are the children representative of the diversities of childhoods across social and cultural contexts?

The practical application of children's rights, as well as much of the material written about rights, has been done by adults or youth on behalf of children. Children's rights advocates, and those who see children as "social agents" (James & Prout, 1990) face challenges, in the United States and elsewhere, as views and constructions of children are built on beliefs that they are innocent, less capable, or inexperienced because of their age. The threats to children's play (e.g., fear for their safety, the increase in adult-led, direct instruction in early learning settings) have a stronghold over many adult perceptions on the benefits of free play as well as in early childhood quality rating scales. Moreover, as public funding continues to move into early childhood and as attention to how 'investments' made early can lead to gains later in life, the need to advocate for play becomes even more important. The neoliberal turn in education and the corporatization of schooling also leaves little room for children to engage in open-ended, inquiry-based, and child-embedded learning that has long been a cornerstone of early care and education (Nagasawa et al., 2014). We would welcome a return to earlier prevailing perspectives in the early childhood field that play is children's work and should be taken seriously and given due weight, similar to children's views.

Numerous organizations or institutions are focused on protecting childhood and providing provisions for play or play-based learning, valuing children's rights in this regard. However, acknowledging children's participation in decision-making processes around their lived experiences more broadly has yet to be fully achieved. Northern Ireland–based Play Quest, part of PlayBoard (www.playboard.org/wp-content/uploads/2014/12/playquest.pdf), describes play as a "child size form of citizenship" and is one of many examples of networks and organizations that take seriously articles in the Convention on the Rights of the Child that affirm children's right to play – and have further asserted children's right to childhood.

Advocating Play for and with Children

A number of children's rights–focused organizations and projects emphasize the importance of giving children's views due weight, building capacity for children to express their views or involving them in evaluations of aspects of their community. These organizations also seek to engage people who hold multiple roles in the early childhood community, including researchers, policymakers, public officials, teachers and other professionals, parents, and other family members.

For example, Play Quest provides workshops for children to learn about advocacy and ways of sharing their views with a range of professionals, including city planners, policymakers, police, education leaders, etc. They also educate the public in the loss of physical play space for children and advocate for ways of addressing "play deprivation".

Based on a child's right to play, PlayBoard focuses on promoting, creating, and developing play opportunities that aim to improve the quality of children's lives. It does this through "[t]ackling play deprivation in the community, supporting and encouraging quality play provision, and workforce development" (www.playboard.org). Recommendations coming directly from children have included building playgrounds whenever new houses are built and providing for more opportunities for play in general. "Safe, engaging and appropriate facilities must be designed, taking into account the views and experiences of young people themselves, not just handed down from on high." The Play Quest project aims to help children take control in play. By making their own decisions, they not only become more confident and creative but also gain valuable social skills.

In contrast, the Girl Child Network, based in Kenya, is an alliance of more than 250 children's rights linked organizations that work for the educational and basic right to childhood and well-being of girls and boys in difficult circumstances, including children with disabilities (Musomi & Swadener, 2017; www.girlchildnetwork.org). Countering early marriage of girls as young as 9 or 10, promoting the rights of children with disabilities, and promoting education are some of the many initiatives of this network. The right to play and to childhood itself is also emphasized, but in a different context than many of the play advocacy organizations and networks in the Global North.

In the United States, the Maryland-based international non-profit Alliance for Childhood (www.allianceforchildhood.org) promotes policies and practices that support children's healthy development, love of learning, and joy in living. Its public education and advocacy campaigns focus on restoring play to children's lives, the overuse of computers and other advanced technologies in childhood, the commercialization of childhood, and the impact of high-stakes testing on children and their schools. The Alliance has published reports and position statements. It is a non-profit, tax-exempt organization based in College Park, with partners and affiliates all over the United States and in Europe and South America.

Advocacy for children's play is typically nested in larger critiques and public concerns about prevailing early childhood and broader education policy that have emphasized cognitive development or learning. State legislation has been introduced, even in conservative states such as Arizona, that would require a minimum daily period of recess (e.g., 45 or 50 minutes) in all publicly funded schools. Such public education campaigns bring to light both the promise and the vulnerability of childhood. Quoting the Alliance for Childhood's website, "We act for the sake of the children themselves and for a more just, democratic, and ecologically responsible future." This alliance serves as a clearinghouse for publications and advocate for adventure playgrounds, and provides information on regional and national presentations promoting play and child participation. Recent publications focus on more play and less pressure in early childhood, redefining success to include risk and benefits of risk in play, and an array of topics related to screen time, concerns about early reading, and the case for recess.

Other groups including KaBOOM! (https://kaboom.org/, a movement to save play with emphasis on children in poverty in the United States), Play-Core, and Playworks are among a growing number of organizations promoting play, educating the public, and advocating for more support of play for the balanced and healthy lives of children. The Defending the Early Years Project was founded in 2012 as a mechanism to mobilize the early childhood community to speak out against inappropriate standards, assessments, and inappropriate practices (www.deyproject.org/).

Children's Consultation and Participation in Research

Often missing from the work of advocacy groups, however, is stronger engagement and collaboration with children and youth. While these and many advocacy efforts are critical, the all-too-frequent absence of child and youth voices and initiatives is problematic. From a child participation rights perspective, a first step is involving younger persons in consultation, valuing children's viewsn and giving them due weight (Office of the United Nations High Commissioner on Human Rights, 1989). This section highlights studies that have actively involved children in consultative and direct planning capacities.

Research has demonstrated that young children can tell adults about their lives and experiences and the concerns that they have for people close to them and for their immediate environment (e.g., Alderson, 2008; Diaz Soto & Swadener, 2005; Einarsdóttir, 2014; Im & Swadener, 2016; Lundy & McEvoy, 2009; Lundy & Swadener, 2015; MacNaughton & Smith, 2008; MacNaughton et al., 2007; O'Kane, 2000; Swadener et al., 2013; Waller, 2014). This research supports the argument that young children (1) can construct valid meanings about the world and their place in it, (2) know the world in alternative (not 'inferior') ways to adults, and (3) can provide perspectives and insights that can help adults to understand their experiences better (MacNaughton, et al. 2003, p. 15).

There are numerous ways to elicit children's perspectives on their daily life experiences. For instance, researchers Clark and Moss (2001) developed the mosaic approach, which uses multiple modalities to help adults connect with children and to draw out their thoughts, feelings, and opinions. The mosaic approach encourages children to express themselves through dialogue, art or creative expression, or other mediums or modes of communication so they feel more comfortable and confident about sharing their views. Clark and Moss encourage adult researchers to make use of tools that can help children share their views freely. Adults must also take children seriously and use their meaning-making as a way to build more holistic understandings of our social worlds.

Photo voice or photo-elicitation are visual methods used to help acknowledge children's rights to expression (for instance, Anthamatten et al., 2013; Goodhart et al., 2006; Keat et al., 2009). In a recent study, Izumi-Taylor et al. (2016) asked children to share their views on play, using photo-elicitation as a strategy to draw out their perspectives. Children who agreed to participate were told to take pictures of play and were later asked by the researchers to describe the photographs. Adult researchers interviewed children and posed just one question: "Why does this mean play to you?" Analysis of their responses revealed that children's views on play are related to their interactions with other children, preferred environments, or favourite toys or other materials.

Dockett and Perry (2003) also used photography as a way to draw out children's views on going to school in Australia. In their research, they asked child participants to take photos of things around their school community that mattered to them. As a result, children took pictures of outdoor areas and playgrounds, the classroom and features within it, as well as people. The photos were compiled into books for children to have in classrooms and were used to help people coming into the classrooms learn more about the spaces. Children and adults also added text to the photographs to give them deeper meaning and to convey messages about going to school. Dockett and Perry encourage adults to share resources like these with children and families to help them learn more directly from younger people. This example not only explains how researchers work extensively with children to collect data but shows how to help children see that their views matter. The creation of the children's books is one way adults can be more inclusive of children's voices and perspectives when planning or executing appropriate or responsive programming and practices.

Most studies carried out with children are conducted in Australia and Europe; however, there is a growing body of research in other transnational contexts. Habashi (2017) has done long-term work on political socialization of children, with focus on the unmediated voices of Palestinian youth. Using a journaling project, in which youth regularly met and discussed their journals, poetry, advocacy/activism, and perspectives on realities of life in the West Bank, Habashi's work has long foregrounded voices of youth, who led the project in many ways and have determined its direction. Regardless of where one resides, people of all ages can do more to make cities, neighbourhoods, schools, or streets child-friendly spaces.

While there are methodologies to support researchers to collect ideas from young children, many are adult-centric and fail to recognize that children are competent meaning-makers who have valid and important knowledge that can inform adult knowledge. There is a tendency for researchers to develop methodologies based on what they think children need rather than based on children's experiences. This means that methodologies are still not informed enough by the experiences of children. The methodologies will be far more effective if they are developed in collaboration with children themselves. Furthermore, Mayne and Howitt (2015) found there is a significant gap in early childhood literature between what is considered to be desirable child participatory practices and how research with children is reported. Findings from studies conducted about children are more likely to be shared than those conducted with or by children.

Children's Perspectives on Play and Other Aspects of Their Lives

Peters (2012) worked with a group of researchers who interviewed children to learn more about what it was like to be 4 years old turning 5. This work was part of a large-scale qualitative study that sought family and community perspectives on raising children (Joanou et al., 2012). Prior to conducting the interviews with children, researchers facilitated consultation meetings with children 6–8 years old (Swadener et al., 2013) to gain their insight on what we should be asking their younger peers. This was done in part to take on more of a "least adult role" (Mandell, 1988) in our work with children and also consult directly with children (Lundy & McEvoy, 2011; Lundy & Swadener, 2015). Researchers were also aware that people who were most recently 4 and 5 would have greater expertise on children's life experiences in the early years. During the consultation meetings, children were asked to think of questions we should be asking the child interview participants. Child consultants generated a number of useful ideas, many of which centred on play experiences. Some examples of the questions are: What makes you laugh? and What are your interests? Children also posed questions such as, "What do you do when you have two friends, but one friend only likes you and not the other person?" and "Do you like physical or imaginary things?"

Following the child consultation meetings, children were invited to participate in interviews to talk about what it is like being 4 turning 5 in Arizona. Researchers believed that by listening to children, we could bring attention to the types of activities they are involved in during their first year of formal schooling and that their views would provide adults with a different way of understanding what it is like to be a child in current times.

Child participants were asked to talk about what happened in preschool, or in kindergarten, and some discussed how kindergarten was different from preschool. In response to a question about what happens in preschool, a child said, "You get to do science stuff, and you get to play with friends and you get to do art, and you get to do special projects." When comparing preschool with kindergarten, another child said, "We didn't have to work. All we did was play." Last, in talking about kindergarten, one child said, "First in the morning, in the a.m. class, I always do work, lots of work, and then we go out for recess." In other conversations about kindergarten, children used the word "work" repeatedly to describe what they do, including homework, but also talked about going to "specials," having recess, or engaging in other activities like centre-based learning.

Their talk about kindergarten, and their often happy memories of preschool, reveals how their experiences in school mirror the paradigmatic shifts occurring across the landscape of early childhood as it relates to education reform, readiness, and school success. Bassok et al. (2016) documented the changes that occurred in kindergarten classrooms from 1998 to 2006, specifically related to the 'academicization' of early childhood. They found that adult expectations for children rose dramatically and rapidly during these years and that there was an increase in time spent on subjects connected to testing and high-stakes accountability. According to Bassok and Rorem, instruction in language arts rose by 25%. When asked if they were learning to read in kindergarten, children would make reference to knowing sight words or the acquisition of other discrete skills and knowledge. For example, one child said, "We do numbers all the way to 10. We count. We have sight words kind of. This sight word this week is 'half'." Moreover, they would talk specifically about or allude to their alphabet knowledge (letter and/or sound recognition), phonological awareness, word segmentation, fluidity, and sight word recognition, along with writing and emergent writing. For example, one child mentioned she was "pushing words together" and described her understanding of this process: "The big words, you just break them in half, and like the syllables. Cuz' we do syllables with our names ... like I have three syllables, and she [referring to her sister] has three syllables."

During the interviews, children would also make reference to the guidance and discipline strategies used in their kindergarten classrooms. Behaviourist approaches are common in primary grade classrooms, given large group sizes and the need to encourage prosocial behaviour. As talk emerged about guidance and discipline, children described their thoughts on behaviour tracking systems. One participant explained how a behaviour chart worked in her classroom: "If they be in green, that means they listen. If they be in yellow, you have to try. If they be on blue, they can't get any stamps. If they're on red, they have to call their mom." In another conversation, a child stated, "You go to the principal's when you have no colors and then the principal calls the policeman and then you go to jail."

In schooling practices children are often seen as persons that are socially controlled, and their educational experiences are defined by goals or expectations set by adults. The growing emphasis on adult-directed teaching and classroom management has shifted children's positionality in many learning communities, diluting children's participatory practices in early care and education. Moreover, classroom management becomes behaviour management and children are socialized to follow particular rules that are intended to promote prosocial interactions among children and their peers. The rules influence children's constructions of 'good' and 'bad' and use these labels to make meaning of desirable behaviour or disposition. As children make meaning of classroom rules and guidance and discipline, they are also building perspective on issues related to respect, fairness, community, and individual and collective action, among other things. We also need to point out that many adults are seeking ways to incorporate social emotional learning, positive-behaviour support programs (such as responsive classrooms), and character building activities into curricular frameworks to encourage kindness.

Children's perspectives illustrate how listening to and hearing from children provides a different window into their life experiences. A broader question is, How are their experiences in school connected to their right to play? Children value and benefit from a less academic early years curriculum and opportunities to problem-solve, be creative, and do child-initiated activities. Honouring their views enables older people to make better-informed decisions about policy, programming, and practice, and when children are thought of as being experts on their own lives, their agency has great influence over inclusion and culturally responsive teaching and learning.

Call to Action

Corsaro (2005) argues that children enter culture through their families at birth and subsequently (or simultaneously) interact within different institutional locales (e.g., economic, cultural, educational, and community) as a means to acquire new understandings of their social worlds. As neoliberal forces and other social factors continue to reconstruct play landscapes (e.g., decrease the amount of advocacy for appropriate and responsive pedagogy and practices), the urgency of listening to children and honouring their right to play is evident. Through explicit or sometimes invisible acts, young people demonstrate their adaptability to these changing contexts. Their abilities to navigate vastly different social realms (e.g., schools, home, community), to understand social mores within and across these spaces, and their propensity to build new knowledge across learning domains is often taken for granted. Further, children and young people's resiliency is an embodied skill or quality for which they are not given enough credit.

As research collaborators with a shared interest in elevating children's voices and perspectives in research, policy, and practice, we have been actively seeking ways to advocate for children's rights in the United States. We have looked to other countries and local contexts for examples and guidance in actualizing child's rights-based participatory practices. These examples shed light on the important work happening the world over to include children as valuable members of society – and not just future citizens. Our work weaves together issues related to children's interactions in various social ecologies, as all facets of people's life experiences are inextricably linked. The need to view children and childhood through local and global cultural contexts is essential. Furthermore, variations of child advocacy take shape depending on the extent to which younger people are systematically supported within a community or country. Advocacy and activism can be done on small or large scales, yet simply listening to children and young people can have a tremendous effect on their inclusion in decision-making, as well as opportunities for them to build shared understandings with older peers or adults. Therefore, we encourage readers to engage in ideas about working with children and youth in research, policy, and practice and to think critically about giving their views due weight.

When taking children's participatory practices seriously, it is important to include a diverse range of perspectives. Adults need to be conscious of who is invited to participate or contribute to dialogue and decision-making about the life experiences of young people. All children should have opportunities to engage in participatory practices representing the array of cultural and linguistic backgrounds, socioeconomic echelons, and diverse abilities. Moreover, children of all ages should be considered important contributing members of society. Considering that it is difficult to escape ageist notions of children as less capable or competent, older children and youth (8 years or older) are more likely to be consulted or asked to participate in research or decision-making. Furthermore, participation practices will vary depending on adult views on children and childhood, and it can be hard to dismantle power dynamics or hierarchies between children and adults. Ethical tensions can emerge in obtaining children and young people's consent, facilitating their roles as co-researchers, or disseminating their views (Einarsdóttir, 2007).

As duty bearers to children's rights, we must take children's views seriously and value their life experiences and views. Adults who are mindful of creating "openings, opportunities, and obligations" (Shier, 2001) need to be mindful of the complex nature of child participation practices and prepared to change their views to best meet the needs of young people. As we study many aspects of play across contexts and issues, children have much to teach us about their right to childhood and opportunities to play. Advocating both for and *with* children for these rights honours the ethos of play, respects children as having full human rights, and is urgently needed in these times.

References

Alderson, P. (2008). *Young children's rights: Exploring beliefs*. London: Jessica Kingsley Publishers

Alliance for Childhood (n.d.). Research and advocacy. Available at www.allianceforchildhood.org/.

Almon, J., & Miller, E. (2011). *The crisis in early education: A research-based case for more play and less pressure*. College Park, MD: Alliance for Childhood.

Anthamatten, P., Wee, B. S., & Korris, E. (2013). Exploring children's perceptions of play using visual methodologies. *Health Education Journal, 72*(3), 309–318.

Axline, V. M. (2012). *Play therapy: The groundbreaking book that has become a vital tool in the growth and development of children*. New York: Ballantine Books.

Bartholet, E. (2011). Ratification by the United States of the Convention on the Rights of the Child: Pros and Cons from a Child's Rights Perspective. *Annals of the American Academy of Political and Social Science, 633*, 80.

Bassok, D., Latham, S., & Rorem, A. (2016). Is kindergarten the new first grade? *AERA Open, 2*(1). doi:10.1177/2332858415616358.

Cannella, G. S. (2008). *Deconstructing early childhood education: Social justice and revolution*. New York: Peter Lang.

Cannella, G. S., & Viruru, R. (2002). *Childhood and postcolonization: Power, education and contemporary practice*. New York: Routledge.

Clark, A., & Moss, P. (2001). *Listening to young children: The mosaic approach*. London: National Children's Bureau for the Joseph Rowntree Foundation.

Committee on the Rights of the Child (2009). *General Comment No. 12: The child's right to be heard*. UNCRC/GC/12. Geneva: United Nations.

Corsaro, W. A. (2005). *The sociology of childhood*. Thousand Oaks, CA: Sage Publications.

Cummins, J. (2007). Pedagogies for the poor? Realigning reading instruction for low-income students with scientifically based reading research. *Educational Researcher, 36*(9), 564–572.

Dahlberg, G., Moss, P., & Pence, A. R. (1999). *Beyond quality in early childhood education and care: Postmodern perspectives*. London: Falmer Press.

Dockett, S. & Perry, B. (2002). Who's ready for what? Young children starting school. *Contemporary Issues in Early Childhood, 3*(1), 67–89.

Dockett, S., & Perry, B. (2003). Children's views and children's voices in starting school. *Australian Journal of Early Childhood, 28*(1), 12–18.

Dockett, S., & Perry, B. (2005). 'You need to know how to play safe': Children's experiences of starting school. *Contemporary Issues in Early Childhood, 6*(1), 4–18.

Einarsdóttir, J. (2007). Research with children: Methodological and ethical challenges. *European Early Childhood Education Research Journal, 15*(2), 197–211.

Einarsdóttir, J. (2011). Icelandic children's early education transition experiences. *Early Education and Development, 22*(5), 739–756.

Einarsdóttir, J. (2014). Children's perspectives on play. In *The Sage handbook of play and learning* (pp. 319–329). Thousand Oaks, CA: Sage.

Elkind, D. (2007). *The hurried child: Growing up too fast too soon* (25th anniversary edn.; 3rd edn.). Cambridge, MA: Da Capo Press.

Freire, P. (1970). *Pedagogy of the oppressed*. New York: Continuum.

Frohlich, K. L., Alexander, S. A., & Fusco, C. (2012, 11). All work and no play? The nascent discourse on play in health research. *Social Theory & Health, 11*(1), 1–18.

Goodhart, F. W., Hsu, J., Baek, J. H., Coleman, A. L., Maresca, F. M., & Miller, M. B. (2006). A view through different lens: Photovoice as a tool for student advocacy. *Journal of American College Health, 55*, 53–56.

Gray, P. (2011). The decline of play and the rise of psychopathology in children and adolescents. *American Journal of Play, 3*(4), 443–463.

Gray, P. (2013). *Free to learn: Why unleashing the instinct to play will make our children happier, more self reliant, and better students for life*. New York: Basic Books.

Habashi, J. (2017). *Political socialization of youth: A Palestinian case study*. New York: Springer.

Hall, E. L., & Rudkin, J. K. (2011). *Seen and heard: Children's rights in early childhood education*. London and Ontario: Althouse Press/University of Western Ontario.

Hart, R. (1992). *Children's participation from tokenism to citizenship*. Florence: UNICEF Innocenti Research Centre.

Hatch, J. A. (2002). A special section on personalized instruction accountability shove-down: Resisting the standards movement in early childhood education. *Phi Delta Kappan, 83*(6), 457–462.

Hirsh-Pasek, K., Golinkoff, R. M., Berk, L. E., & Singer, D. (2009). *A mandate for playful learning in preschool: Presenting the evidence*. New York: Oxford University Press.

Holloway, S., & Valentine, G. (2000). Children's geographies and the new social studies of childhood. In S. Halloway & G. Valentine (Eds.), *Children's geographies: Playing, living, learning* (pp. 1–16). London: Routledge.

Im, H. S., & Swadener, B. B. (2016). Children's voice in U.S. and Korean early childhood contexts: Views of preschool and kindergarten experiences. *Australian Journal of Early Childhood, 41*(1), 28–35.

Izumi-Taylor, S., Ito, Y., & Krisell, M. (2016). American and Japanese kindergartners' views of play through the use of photo elicitation interviews (PEIs). *Research in Comparative and International Education, 11*(3), 322–333.

James, A., & Prout, A. (1990). *Constructing and deconstructing childhood*. London: Falmer.

James, A., & Prout, A. (2000). *Constructing and reconstructing childhood: Contemporary issues in the sociological study of childhood*. London: Falmer Press.

Joanou, J. P., Holiday, D., & Swadener, B. B. (2012). Family and community perspectives. In J. Duncan & S. Te One (Eds.), *Comparative early childhood education services: International perspectives* (pp. 101–124). New York: Palgrave Macmillan.

Johnson, J. E., Christie, J. F., & Wardle, F. (2005). *Play, development, and early education*. New York: Pearson Education.

KaBOOM! (n.d.). The state of play. Available at https://kaboom.org/.

Keat, J. B., Strickland, M. J., & Marinak, B. A. (2009). Child voice: How immigrant children enlightened their teachers with a camera. *Early Childhood Education Journal, 37*(1), 13–21.

Lahman, M. K. (2008). Always othered: Ethical research with children. *Journal of Early Childhood Research, 6*(3), 281–300.

Laidlaw, L., O'Mara, J., & Wong, S. (2015). 'Daddy, look at the video I made on my iPad!': Reconceptualizing readiness in the digital age. In J. Iorio & W. Parnell (Eds.), *Rethinking readiness in early childhood education: Implications for policy and practice* (pp. 65–76). New York: Palgrave Macmillan.

Langsted, O. (1994). Looking at quality through the child's perspectives. In P. Moss & A. R. Pence (Eds.), *Valuing quality in early childhood services: New approaches to defining quality* (pp. 28–42). London: Paul Chapman Publishing.

Lareau, A. (2003). *Unequal childhoods: Class, race, and family life*. Berkeley: University of California Press.

Lester, S., & Russell, W. (2010). *Children's right to play: An examination of the importance of play in the lives of children worldwide* (Working Paper No. 57). The Hague: Bernard van Leer Foundation.

Linn, S. (2009). *The case for make believe: Saving play in a commercialized world*. New York: New Press.

Lundy, L. (2007). 'Voice' is not enough: Conceptualising Article 12 of the United Nations Convention on the Rights of the Child. *British Educational Research Journal, 33*(6), 927–942.

Lundy, L., & McEvoy, L. (2009). Developing outcomes for educational services: A children's rights based approach. *Effective Education, 1*(1), 43–60.

Lundy, L., & McEvoy, L. (2011). Children's rights and research processes: Assisting children to (in)formed views. *Childhood, 19*, 129–144.

Lundy, L., & McEvoy, L. (2012). Children's rights and research processes: Assisting children to (in)formed views. *Childhood, 19*(1), 129–144.

Lundy, L., & Swadener, B. B. (2015). Engaging with young children as co-researchers: A child rights-based approach. In O. Saracho (Ed.), *Handbook of research methods in early childhood education: A review of methodologies*, vol. II (pp. 657–676). New York: Information Age Publishing.

MacNaughton, G., & Smith, K. (2008). Children's rights in early childhood. In M. J. Kehily (Ed.), *An introduction to childhood studies* (pp. 161–176). Maidenhead: Open University Press.

MacNaughton, G. M., Smith, K., & Davis, K. (2007). Researching with children: The challenges and possibilities for building 'child friendly' research. In J. A. Hatch (Ed.), *Early childhood qualitative research* (pp. 167–205). New York: Routledge.

MacNaughton, G., Smith, K., & Lawrence, H. (2003). *ACT Children's Strategy: Consulting with children birth to 8 years of age*. Children's Services Branch, ACT. Melbourne: Australia.

Mandell, N. (1988). The least-adult role in studying children. *Journal of Contemporary Ethnography, 16*(4), 433–467.

Mayall, B. (2000). The sociology of childhood and children's rights. *International Journal of Children's Rights, 8*, 243–259.

Mayne, F., & Howitt, C. (2015). How far have we come in respecting young children in our research? A meta-analysis of reported early childhood research practice from 2009 to 2012. *Australasian Journal of Early Childhood, 40*(4), 30–38.

McCooey, R. (n.d.). The revival of free play for children and young people in Northern Ireland. Available at www.qub.ac.uk/sites/childhoodobesityconference/Con ferenceMedia/filestore/Filetoupload,218320,en.pdf.

Miller, E., & Almon, J. (2009). *Crisis in kindergarten: Why children need to play in school*. College Park, MD: Alliance for Childhood.

Moss, P., Dahlberg, G., Grishaber, S., Mantovani, S., May, H., Pence, A., Rayne, S., Swadener, B. B., & Vandenbroeck, M. (2016, August). The OECD's International Early Learning Study: Opening for debate and contestation. *Contemporary Issues in Early Childhood*. Available at https://doi.org/10.1177/1463949116661126.

Musomi, M., & Swadener, B. B. (2017). Enhancing feminism and childhoods in Kenya through stronger education policy, access and action. In K. Smith, K. Alexander, & S. Campbell (Eds.), *Feminism in early childhood*. New York: Springer.

Nagasawa, M., Peters, L., & Swadener, B. B. (2014). The costs of putting quality first: Neoliberalism, (in)equality, (un)affordability, and (in)accessibility? In M. Bloch, B. B. Swadener, & G. Cannella (Eds.), *Reconceptualizing early childhood care and education: Critical questions, new imaginaries and social activism*. New York: Peter Lang.

Office of the United Nations High Commissioner on Human Rights (1989). *United Nations Convention on the Rights of the Child*. New York: United Nations.

O'Kane, C. (2000). The development of participatory techniques facilitating children's views about decisions which affect them. In P. Christensen & A. James (Eds.), *Research with children: Perspectives and practices* (pp. 136–159). London: Falmer Press.

Paley, V. G. (2009). *A child's work: The importance of fantasy play*. Chicago, IL: University of Chicago Press.

Paley, V. G. (2010). *The boy on the beach: Building community through play*. Chicago, IL: University of Chicago Press.

Peters, L. E. (2012). 'When the bell rings we go inside and learn': Children's and parents' understandings of the kindergarten transition. Doctoral dissertation, Arizona State University.

Peters, L., Ortiz, K., & Swadener, B. B. (2015). Something is not right: Deconstructing readiness with parents, teachers, and children. In W. Parnell & J. Iorio (Eds.), *Rethinking readiness in early childhood education: Implications for policy and practice* (pp. 33–48). New York: Peter Lang.

Rogoff, B. (2003). *The cultural nature of human development*. Oxford: Oxford University Press.

Roopnarine, J. L. (2015). Play as culturally situated: Diverse perspectives on its meaning and significance. In J. L. Roopnarine, M. M. Patte, J. E. Johnson, & D. Kuschner (Eds.), *International perspectives on children's play* (pp. 1–7). New York: Open University Press.

Shier, H. (2001). Pathways to participation: Openings, opportunities and obligations. *Children & Society, 15*(2), 107–117.

Smith, K. (2009). Child participation in the early years of education. *Educating Young Children: Learning and Teaching in the Early Childhood Years, 15*(1), 39–41.

Smith, K., Alexander, K., & MacNaughton, G. (2008). *Respecting children as citizens in local government: Participation in policies and services*. Parkville, Vic.: Centre for Equity and Innovation in Early Childhood.

Soto, L. D., & Swadener, B. B. (2005). *Power and voice in research with children*. New York: Peter Lang.

Sutton-Smith, B. (1997). *The ambiguity of play*. Cambridge, MA: Harvard University Press.

Swadener, B. B., Peters, L. J., & Gaches, S. (2013). Taking children's rights and participation seriously: Cross-national perspectives and possibilities. In V. Pacini-Ketchabaw & L. Prochner (Eds.), *Re-situating Canadian early childhood education* (pp. 189–210). New York: Peter Lang.

Swadener, B. B., & Polakow, V. (2010). Children's rights and voices in research: Cross-national perspectives. *Early Education and Development, 21*, 285–286.

Urban, M., & Swadener, B. B. (2016). Democratic accountability and contextualised systemic evaluation: A comment on the OECD initiative to launch an International Early Learning Study (IELS). *International Critical Childhood Policy Studies Journal, 5*(1), 6–18.

Vygotsky, L. S. (1967). Play and its role in the mental development of the child. *Soviet Psychology, 5*(3), 6–18.

Vygotsky, L. S. (1971). *The psychology of art* (trans. Scripta Technica). Cambridge, MA: MIT Press (originally published in 1925).

Walker, N., Brooks, C. M., & Wrightsman, L. S. (1999). *Children's rights in the United States: In search of a national policy*. Thousand Oaks, CA: Sage Publications.

Waller, T. (2014). Voices in the park: Researching the participation of young children in outdoor play in early years settings. *Management in Education*, *28*(4), 161–166.

Index